THE GREAT
CONTEMPORARY
ISSUES

CRIME
AND JUSTICE

THE GREAT
CONTEMPORARY
ISSUES

CRIME
AND JUSTICE

The New York Times
ARNO PRESS
NEW YORK/1974

RAMSEY CLARK
Advisory Editor

Copyright © 1974 by The New York Times Company.
Library of Congress Cataloging in Publication Data.
Main entry under title:

Crime and justice.

(The Great contemporary issues)
Articles from the New York times.
Bibliography: p. 495.
1. Crime and criminals—United States—Addresses,
essays, lectures. 2. Criminal justice, Administration
of—United States—Addresses, essays, lectures.
I. Clark, Ramsey, 1927— ed. II. New York times.
III. Series.
HV6789.C687   364'.973   74-7581
ISBN 0-405-04167-5
Manufactured in the United States of America by Arno Press, Inc.

The editors express special thanks to The Associated Press, United
Press International, and Reuters for permission to include in this
series of books a number of dispatches originally distributed by those
news services.

A HUDSON GROUP BOOK
Produced by Morningside Associates. Edited by Gene Brown.

Contents

Publisher's Note About the Series

It would take even an accomplished speed-reader, moving at full throttle, some three and a half solid hours a day to work his way through all the news The New York Times prints. The sad irony, of course, is that even such indefatigable devotion to life's carnival would scarcely assure a decent understanding of what it was really all about. For even the most dutiful reader might easily overlook an occasional long-range trend of importance, or perhaps some of the fragile, elusive relationships between events that sometimes turn out to be more significant than the events themselves.

This is why "The Great Contemporary Issues" was created—to help make sense out of some of the major forces and counterforces at large in today's world. The philosophical conviction behind the series is a simple one: that the past not only can illuminate the present but must. ("Continuity with the past," declared Oliver Wendell Holmes, "is a necessity, not a duty.") Each book in the series, therefore has as its subject some central issue of our time that needs to be viewed in the context of its antecedents if it is to be fully understood. By showing, through a substantial selection of contemporary accounts from The New York Times, the evolution of a subject and its significance, each book in the series offers a perspective that is available in no other way. For while most books on contemporary affairs specialize, for excellent reasons, in predigested facts and neatly drawn conclusions, the books in this series allow the reader to draw his own conclusions on the basis of the facts as they appeared at virtually the moment of their occurrence. This is not to argue that there is no place for events recollected in tranquility; it is simply to say that when fresh, raw truths are allowed to speak for themselves, some quite distinct values often emerge.

For this reason, most of the articles in "The Great Contemporary Issues" are reprinted in their entirety, even in those cases where portions are not central to a given book's theme. Editing has been done only rarely, and in all such cases it is clearly indicated. (Such an excision occasionally occurs, for example, in the case of a Presidential State of the Union Message, where only brief portions are germane to a particular volume, and in the case of some names, where for legal reasons or reasons of taste it is preferable not to republish specific identifications.) Similarly, typographical errors, where they occur, have been allowed to stand as originally printed.

"The Great Contemporary Issues" inevitably encompasses a substantial amount of history. In order to explore their subjects fully, some of the books go back a century or more. Yet their fundamental theme is not the past but the present. In this series the past is of significance insofar as it suggests how we got where we are today. These books, therefore, do not always treat a subject in a purely chronological way. Rather, their material is arranged to point up trends and interrelationships that the editors believe are more illuminating than a chronological listing would be.

"The Great Contemporary Issues" series will ultimately constitute an encyclopedic library of today's major issues. Long before editorial work on the first volume had even begun, some fifty specific titles had already been either scheduled for definite publication or listed as candidates. Since then, events have prompted the inclusion of a number of additional titles, and the editors are, moreover, alert not only for new issues as they emerge but also for issues whose development may call for the publication of sequel volumes. We will, of course, also welcome readers' suggestions for future topics.

Introduction

Reading this selection of crime stories that have appeared in the Times these past fifty years and more is—what can I say—an experience. Fascinating, amusing, frightening, ironic, sad, absurd, outrageous, incredible, yes—these and more.

Consider some of the articles. On February 15, 1921, it was reported that lax prohibition enforcement was the major cause of crime. "United States Indicted as the Most Lawless Country," read the headline on November 3, 1924. The immigration of European "riff-raff" was featured as a major factor in that lawlessness. Russian immigrants were then 10 per cent of the population of New York City but made up 20 per cent of the defendants arraigned in Magistrates Court. In 1925, nearing the 150th year of our liberty, police announced the abandonment of "tip-over" raids in which saloons were smashed by axe-wielding officers. In April 1929 it was reported that 190 agents had been killed in Prohibition raids in nine years of the Volstead Act—twice as many as all the police killed in the riotous years of the 1960's. In 1931, by summer's end, two-thirds of all federal expenditures for criminal justice went for the enforcement of prohibition. And Al Capone was considered one of the most powerful men in the United States.

James Truslow Adams, in a December 1931 article, analyzed America's glorification of its gangsters. As the Great Depression gripped the country, robbery topped all other crimes. These names appeared often in the pages of the Times and became household words: John Dillinger, Baby Face Nelson, Pretty Boy Floyd, Ma Barker, Bonnie and Clyde.

After World War II, attitudes toward crime shifted from fascination to fear. By April 1949 stories told us "Hoodlums in Park Keep Citizens Out. Fear of Mugging and Robbery After Dark Is Rife Despite Increased City Guard." In June of 1951 we read "Narcotics Menace Held Nationwide—Juvenile Addiction at Epidemic Level in Nine Cities." On March 4, 1960, we are told the "City Plans to Add More Bright Lights to Cut Crime Rate." On March 27, 1964, forty-two years after ten police cars began the nation's first auto patrol to check street crime, the death of Catherine Genovese in Kew Gardens was reported. Thirty-seven people who saw her repeatedly stabbed or heard her screams did not call the police.

Through the election years of 1964, 1966, 1968, 1970 and 1972, "law and order" was a major political issue. The fear of crime was exploited by leaders appealing to raw emotion. Solutions were simple. In October 1970, just before the congressional elections, President Nixon signed a new organized crime bill into law. Addressing Attorney General John N. Mitchell and FBI Director J. Edgar Hoover, the President said, "Gentlemen, I give you the tools. You do the job." The same year Mr. Mitchell ordered the FBI to stop using the names "Mafia" and "Cosa Nostra." On April 25, 1970, David Burnham wrote of police corruption and the name of an honest cop was added to our vocabulary—Frank Serpico.

Times articles on prisons over the years recounted tales of unremitting savagery and despair. In July 1931, the Wickersham Commission, which had been set up to investigate all aspects of crime and punishment in the United States, reached conclusions about our penal stytem that could be reprinted with little change today. The headline read "Prisons of Nation Declared Failure; Outworn, Inhuman." A month later brought the revelation that "New Prison at Attica to be Convicts' Paradise." In 1937 Georgia abolished its chain gangs. During 1939 James V. Bennett, Director of the Federal Bureau of Prisons, announced that 56 per cent of the men released from prison returned. September 1971 brought news of the prison riot and slaughter at Attica. The following month Vice President Agnew assured the nation that the violence and deaths were "caused by the convicts, without question."

Through the years executions were regularly reported. The Caryl Chessman case held our attention for a decade. Headlines announced the Supreme Court decisions striking down the death penalty in June of 1972. Scarcely a year later capital punishment had been revived in nineteen states with others moving swiftly toward it.

As 1974 began we read, "An overwhelming majority of New Yorkers—rich and poor, black and white, conservative and liberal—regard crime as the worst problem they face personally . . ." And so it surely was throughout the nation.

What does it all mean? How can we make sense of madness, learn or understand? Does prior criminal conduct tell us much about the present? Are trends detectable that tell us from whence we come and whither we tend? Does our ignorance so exceed our knowledge that new discoveries of fact are as likely to mislead as lead? Is crime like the weather, affecting us all, but those with poorer shelter and raiment most, everyone complaining, nobody doing anything about it? Does reporting the horribles rivet our attention on events often irrational and inexplicable, creating fear and hatred? Does fear, irrationality and the capricious nature of crime contribute to an aura of incoherence? Does it somehow prevent us from asking why does this happen, how can we prevent it? Can we remember thirty days, or thirty years, and learn from the mistakes of the past?

We are constantly being told that crime is either increasing or declining. Knowing that fact can be the enemy of truth, objective reporting requires a critical analysis of questionable statistics. If we believe most crime is unreported, can we believe crime statistics are reliable? Where statistics are compiled by an interested party—the police or the FBI—can we assume they are reporting "just the facts, ma'am?"

It has often been suggested that crime statistics are a function of the degree to which people in a community have faith in the honesty and efficacy of the police and therefore feel it worthwhile to report a crime. Methods of patrolling a neighborhood may or may not affect crime statistics. How are we to reconcile one story about the effectiveness of high intensity foot patrols and another report of a study showing no effect on the incidence of crime where police presence is multiplied or taken completely away?

The nature of crime must be understood if fear and hatred are to be avoided. Without this understanding the public discussion of crime becomes a bitter struggle between advocates of freedom and the advocates of safety. The two are depicted as mutually exclusive and those who oppose capital punishment, wiretapping, shooting of looters and brutal prisons are called soft on crime. And thus we continue the age-old struggle between savagery and civilization, delaying further the day when government dares to act decently toward its own citizens.

Crime reflects the character of a people. It exposes their capacity to injure one another, to covet and destroy; their inability to control themselves; their cunning, insensitivity and want of love. Crime and society's violent reaction to it are the raw outcroppings of a people's hate, lust, greed, fear, vengefulness, selfishness and sickness. Crime is human conduct.

No single measurement so accurately defines the quality of life among a people as the actual incidence of crime. Crime measures moral worth, character, decency. Society has no greater purpose than to reduce antisocial conduct to the minimum. A people concerned for their character must strive not merely to limit the increase in crime, or even to maintain it at last year's level, letting the poor continue to suffer, holding the line at the central city limits. They must strive, gently and rationally, to eliminate crime, intent on enlarging freedom and safety to the fullest extent nature makes possible.

The solution does not lie in force and segregation. It is not possible, nor acceptable if it were, to find safety by beating down or locking out those who offend. The solution lies in recognizing the sources of crime in ourselves, our values and our environment.

We should begin with the wide open, uninhibited, robust search for truth. What is a crime? Why do we torture ourselves attacking alcohol, addiction, gambling, prostitution, sexual practices of consenting adults, abortion and suicide? Do we really believe it possible to make the world safe for hypocrisy? The pretense of enforcing prohibition in the 1920's undermined the integrity of criminal justice agencies. It corrupted police, prosecutors, judges and jailers, making them too often seem, and sometimes in fact be, the enemy of the people.

To reduce crime significantly and permanently, a society must constantly seek to simplify its definition and increase its understanding of that conduct it would prevent and find effective means for dealing with it. You cannot cure alcoholism with jails, beat heroin out of the bloodstream of addicts with clubs or restore physical or mental health in prisons. These are complex medical and social problems and will continue to cause crime until society deals humanely and rationally with them.

The connection between crime and poverty, poor health, failing systems of education, unemployment and inadequate housing is abundantly clear. Society will not make the extraordinary effort required to solve such enormous problems merely to prevent crime. Indeed it should not. Outrage at the injustice of want in a land of plenty and compassion for the least among us should cause America to redress these grievances.

It may seem easier and too often more appropriate to beat down people who offend. But the sources of crime *are* social injustice and inequality. Plato told us "Poverty is the mother of crime" and Aristotle, "The universal and chief cause of the revolutionary impulse is the desire for equality." When America can consider these ideas without anger, it will begin to realize our common humanity. *Homo sum, humani nihil a me alienum puto* (I am a man. Nothing human is alien to me).

Society must give, generously and gently, to prevent crime. Give the chance for health, homes, knowledge, jobs, self respect. Create, in Earl Warren's phrase, "a political conception of compassion." We must overcome the we-they view of life: good people versus bad people; friends versus enemies. Walt Kelly told us, "We have met the enemy and they is us." There is no enemy. There is only us.

A paramilitary police is the antithesis of a free society. In cities of millions it cannot hope to police out crimes. It becomes the enemy of the people, just as it perceives the people as its enemy. Most crime is never reported to the police in this country. Probably not one serious crime in fifty results in a conviction. No cleverness of system, no refinement of technique, no massive numbers of police can improve that performance even tenfold.

Police, well trained and financed, drawn from the people and integrated into communities, who view themselves and are viewed by the people as social servants, can make a major difference in the quality of life. They are presently among the best early warning systems we have of family break-up, of personality disorder and instability. The police force can be a major system for referring people with problems to the proper social agencies. They can learn methods for minimizing violence even in the midst of ghetto rage and offer some protection to people in their homes and on the streets.

The system of criminal justice is critically important in society. The deterrent capacity of enforcement is insignificant when only a minor fraction of those who commit a crime are proven to have done so, and then only after long delays and manipulated procedure. Harsh penalties, death, torture, imprisonment and the denial of due process of law will not supply the solution. Rather they will make for greater cunning and cruelty. Finally the system itself becomes the enemy.

Our criminal justice system manifests our values. Do we believe in truth? Do we treasure freedom? Will we face problems directly and seek to solve them fairly? Do we want due process for those we abhor even in moments of greatest passion? Do we revere life? Do we intend justice, or seek merely to control by force? Courts speedily processing criminal cases with fairness and dignity would show that we value justice, that reason, truth and principle guide our lives even when we are most emotional.

Segregation of persons charged and convicted of crime into jails and prisons has increased the incidence of antisocial conduct. We have built factories for the manufacture of crime. Both the premise and the practice of penology in America has been false. Our prisons have not protected the public and have failed to rehabilitate the prisoner. Indeed we rarely know what we mean by "rehabilitate," much less how to do it. We hypocritically contend that prisons heal sick souls, when in fact the prisoner is being subjected to a cruel ordeal.

Pretrial detention should be generally abolished as contrary to the principle of presumed innocence and a major deterrent to the offering of speedy trials. Prisons should be abandoned and the great majority of their inmates offered better chances in the community of their choice for health services, education, employment, housing and other needs.

For individuals who are confined, we should provide small community units with maximum opportunity for outservices and visits; there should be a minimum of depersonalization, exposure to instability and alienation. Corrections should avoid confinement wherever possible and seek the quickest possible return to the community. Services should be offered to meet individual need: health care, addiction therapy, detoxification, education, job training, employment, housing, family counseling and legal services.

In the midst of this complex, anxious, mass society, it is difficult to perceive the true causes and effective deterrence of crime. But our survival may depend on it. We have been soft on truth. It will be necessary for us to rededicate ourselves to truth and the vigorous exercise of those three qualities Anatole France tells us caused Lucifer's banishment from heaven—liberty, curiosity and doubt. Under liberty we can seek every fact, however offensive. With curiosity we will be driven to know. And by doubt—constantly questioning—we can avoid error.

Mere chronicling will not suffice. Crime is not a single thread of history that we may slowly unravel. Only rarely will reporting of events give insight into causes, preventions and cures. Just as often it may mislead. We must analyze, test, review—a deliberate, rational effort. We must recall accurately, compare, question and evaluate.

If we will believe in freedom, equality and justice, if we will exhaust ourselves in their pursuits. If we dare to view crime not only as our "worst problem" but as our greatest challenge. If we will look our violence in the face and renounce it as unacceptably inhumane. If we will set the reduction of crime as our highest purpose and translate our anxiety into action. If we will act rationally, compassionately and ardently to prevent crime in every way we can find. If we will strengthen our moral purpose as a people—individuals, organizations, government, schools, churches. Then we will find peace within ourselves and among others and become a gentle people in a just society.

Ramsey Clark

ALPHONSE CAPONE
1899 1947

HE COULD ONLY
HAVE HAPPENED
IN AMERICA

CHAPTER **1**

The Rise of the Gangster

Al Capone's tombstone—as it might have been.
Courtesy The New York Times.

U.S. INDICTED AS THE MOST LAWLESS COUNTRY

Crime Statistics Show 10,000 Murders Yearly
Courts and Gun-Toting Blamed

By EVANS CLARK.

THIS country is suffering under an indictment which proclaims it the most lawless on earth. You will find that the United States must plead guilty to that indictment." Such was the deliberate statement of a Judge of the Court of General Sessions of New York County at the recent induction ceremonies of a fellow Judge. It was not the stricture of the moralist, nor the snap judgment of the professional reformer. It was the well-considered opinion of a man steeped in the actualities of crime as they are unfolded in the greatest criminal court in the world, and yet a man tempered in his judgments by the training and practice of his profession.

"The most lawless nation on earth," Judge Talley charged. That means there is more crime committed in the United States in proportion to the population than in England or France or Italy or any other civilized country in the world. A more serious charge could hardly be brought against a people. Does the evidence in the case sustain the indictment? If we are guilty, what is our defense—what explanation can be given?

Dr. Frederick L. Hoffman, consulting statistician of the Prudential Insurance Company of America, is the first witness. Ever since 1900 Dr. Hoffman has compiled the "homicide rate" for twenty-eight of the leading American cities. Speaking of the figures in his report for 1923, he says:

"This is the most amazing murder record for any civilized country for which data are available. It indicates a state of affairs so startling and of such significance that no Government, Federal or State, can rightfully ignore the situation. The murder rate has practically doubled in twenty-four years. It has shown a persistent upward trend which may be accepted as a definite indication that the moral and legal forces opposed to wrongful death are yielding to the criminal and murderous instincts of a small but suggestive minority of the American people."

Death Toll of Crimes of Violence.

Our next witness is the Special Committee on Law Enforcement of the American Bar Association. Last year this committee made a detailed report on crime in the United States compared with other countries, under the Chairmanship of ex-Governor Charles S. Whitman. The committee estimated that 9,500 persons were killed in crimes of violence in the United States during the year 1921 alone. During the ten years previous, the committee stated no less than 85,000 people were killed. This means that every year more than four times the number of people lose their lives at the hands of criminals in

this country than were killed in the Battle of Gettysburg, one of the bloodiest engagements of the Civil War, and that every five and a half years or so more people are killed in the every-day walks of life in the United States than were killed in the American ranks during the World War.

Property losses suffered by the people of the United States through burglary and robbery are just as striking. On the basis of property losses through thefts that are known for the year 1921 in Baltimore, Boston, Chicago and Washington, it has been estimated that $302,500,000 are lost every year in this way. William J. Burns, formerly head of the Bureau of Investigation of the Department of Justice, estimates that more than $100,000,000 a year in property is stolen from railroad, express and steamship companies and from trucks and piers. Figures published by the American Bankers' Association for the year ended Aug. 31, 1922, show that among their members alone there were 186 hold-ups and 319 burglaries, representing a loss of $1,224,489. That means that every day in the year there is a bank robbery or hold-up of importance, not to mention those committed against banks that are not members of the association.

Comparison With Other Nations.

The evidence so far has proved only that lawlessness in the United States has become a national issue; it does not go to the heart of Judge Talley's indictment. It remains to be shown whether conditions in other countries are better or worse.

Take England and Wales for example. There are more than seventeen times as many desperate criminals among the people of New York—men who would not stop at taking human life—than there are among the people of England and Wales. In the year 1921 there were ninety murders committed in England and Wales, including cities and country districts. During the same year there were 237 murders committed in the single city of New York. England and Wales have a population of 38,000,000. There are less than 6,000,000 in New York. Last year there were twenty-seven murders committed in London, against 262 in New York.

But New York is comparatively free from crimes of violence when some of the Southern cities are considered. The man who walks the streets of Memphis, for example, has 135 times the chance of being shot or beaten or stabbed to death than the man who lives in England and Wales. There were only twice as many homicides in all of England and Wales in 1922 as in that little Tennessee city of 170,000 population.

Take another country—Canada—as closely comparable with the United

States as any. Were it not for an imaginary line on the map Canada might be the United States along a stretch of 4,000 miles of country. Yet there were forty more murders committed in Philadelphia—the City of Brotherly Love—in 1923 than in all of Canada the previous year. Murders were almost forty times as common in Jacksonville, Fla., in 1923 as in Canada the previous year.

It might be imagined that a country like Italy, where the "Latin temperament" is reputed to be hasty of action and slow of thought and where the Black Hand and the vendetta strike in the dark, would far exceed the United States in lawlessness and crime. Dr. Hoffman's statistics show that, as a matter of cold fact, there are twice as many shootings and stabbings to the death in proportion to the population in this country as in Italy. He gives the homicide rate for the United States from 1911 to 1921 as 7.2, while that of Italy for the period of 1910 to 1920 was 3.6.

"With the exception of Italy," says Dr. Hoffman in summarizing the statistics on the comparative criminality of the leading countries of the world based on the homicide rate, "no other country measurably approaches the United States in the murderous tendency of its people"

The Homicide Record.

To prove it he cites the following figures, which show the number of homicides per 100,000 of population as reported in the official records of other countries:

United States	7.2	Norway	0.8
Italy	3.6	England and Wales	0.8
Australia	1.9	Quebec	0.5
South Africa	1.8	Ontario	0.5
New Zealand	0.9	Scotland	0.4
Ireland	0.9	Holland	0.3
Spain	0.9	Switzerland	0.2

Less violent crimes show even more disquieting differences between the United States and other countries. Take robbery, for instance. The New Yorker is thirty-six times as likely to be held up on the street or in his home and forcibly deprived of his valuables as the Londoner; while the risk in Chicago is 100 times as great as in London. In 1921 there were 2,558 robberies reported by the Chicago police—over twelve times the number reported in all of England and Wales. Last year more than six times as many people were robbed in two American cities—New York and Chicago—than in all of Canada.

To pile up figures is unnecessary. Enough evidence is in to establish Judge Talley's indictment on the firm foundation of fact—at least as far as the leading Western nations are concerned. But what can be done about it? Effective action presupposes some clear-cut knowledge of causes. Why is it that America leads the world in crime?

The Chief Justice of the Supreme Court, William Howard Taft, expressed perhaps the most widely held answer to this question in a speech at the Civic Forum in 1908.

"The administration of the criminal law in the United States," he said with dramatic emphasis, "is a disgrace to civilization. The prevalence of crime and fraud is due largely to the failure of the law and its administration to bring criminals to justice. The trial of a criminal seems like a game of chance with all the chances in favor of the criminal, and if he escapes he seems to have the sympathy of a sporting public."

The dictum of Justice Taft has been supported during the past few years by one of the most authoritative groups of experts in the field of law that could possibly be gathered together—the American Bar Association's Committee on Law Enforcement.

"It is our united opinion," the committee reported, "that the means for coping with crime and criminals are neither adequate nor effective."

Court Procedure Called Outworn.

The report compares criminal procedure in the United States with that in England and France and concludes that "our system lacks the three great essentials of law enforcement—celerity, certainty and finality," and recommends a general amendment of the laws concerning practice and procedure. Our procedural laws, the committee states, are "outworn and cumbersome."

Just how outworn and cumbersome our machinery of justice is can be measured by the records of its performance compared with that of justice abroad. The man who plans to commit a burglary in New York knows—if he is anything of a statistician—that he has 13 chances to 1 of escaping the penalty for his crime. But the English crook has only 1-10 of a chance to escape. In 1921 only 7 per cent. of the 6,558 burglaries recorded in New York ended in conviction. Those who committed the remaining 93 per cent. escaped scot free. During the same year only 10 per cent. of those who committed burglary in England and Wales escaped conviction; and in Canada only 20 per cent.

I put the question: "Why do we lead the world in crime?" to District Attorney Joab A. Banton of New York County, who is surely in a position to speak with authority. He answered:

"Our system of criminal procedure was adopted by the Legislature in 1841 and is largely the same now as when it was adopted. It is antiquated. A Judge presiding in one of our criminal courts has very little of the power of an English Judge and none of the power of the French Judge. When we adopted our code of criminal procedure our cities were small and our population largely rural. Conditions have changed since then. I frequently liken the efforts of the District Attorney to bring criminals to the bar of justice to that of a man in an ox cart attempting to overtake one riding in a 1924 model high-priced automobile.

"There are more wasted motions and energy in criminal prosecution than in any other public effort. The Penal Code of New York could be written in such simple language and the judicial machinery could be simplified to such an extent that the penal laws of New York could be enforced at one-quarter the present cost."

Lewis E. Lawes, Warden of Sing Sing Prison, is another man who knows by experience about criminals and their ways. Commenting on the defects of the criminal law in comparison with English procedure, he said:

"Here we have delays; the evils attendant on the pernicious use of the short affidavit; all of the evils connected with our bail methods; the advantages enjoyed by second offenders, who know the ropes, have influential persons to aid them, and who, through their schooling in our methods of criminal procedure, know how to bargain for pleas. The criminals in prison are usually the unsuccessful ones, the failures. Consider the enormous amount of money stolen annually. Yet how seldom we find among those who come to prison the financially successful thief."

Too Much Publicity, Says Banton.

Mr. Banton gave two other reasons for the prevalence of crime: First the inadequacy of the police force and, second, the advertisement of crime in the newspapers.

"We advertise our crime," he said. "I suppose news is something that is unusual. The treatment that our papers give to those accused of crime would rather suggest that the criminal is unusual. What will occupy several columns in our papers is usually told in a 'stick' in a London paper. Too much publicity regarding crime puts the idea of committing crime into the weak mind."

Warden Lawes also commented on this phase of the situation. "This overattention to crime, this overemphasis on all its details, is bad," he said. "The news value is distorted, the public palate is stimulated, until it seems as though nothing but sensationalism is popular. Many young men who have come to prison have told me that they have followed the details of crimes in the newspapers, both as to methods of operation and as to the likelihood of escaping penalties."

Concerning the inadequacy of the police force, District Attorney Banton said: "Our police force is too small and underpaid. As soon as we realize this and increase it to a proportion similar to that maintained in London, we shall have much better results in the detection of crime and the arrest of the criminal."

Richard E. Enright, Police Commissioner, also emphasized this element in the situation. "Our police force," he said, "is the smallest in comparison to the population of any of the great cities." An inquiry for figures on this subject brought from the Commissioner these facts: New Yorkers may feel secure in the knowledge that there are 12,729 members of the Police Department; but few of them know that the actual number of policemen on duty at any given time in the entire city is only 1,526. There are three shifts of

duty, which cuts two-thirds off the force at any one time, and remaining deductions are for details to indoor work, men on sick leave or attending courts and Grand Juries and other necessary work that the police are compelled to perform. Even allowing for the full force, there is only one policeman in New York for every 556 of the population; while in London there is one for every 365; in Paris one for every 276; in Berlin one for every 225, and in Rome one for every 129.

Easy to Buy Pistols.

Commissioner Enright lays the blame for the prevalence of crime in this country largely on the pistol. "Abolition of the pistol would cut down crime one half—that I can positively assert," he says. Officials at Police Headquarters point to the fact that, in spite of the law against carrying firearms in New York State, they are easily obtainable through mail-order houses, and advertisements of them appear in many newspapers and magazines. They point out that in France a robbery committed by a person possessing a pistol is a capital crime.

Chief City Magistrate William McAdoo is equally firm in his conviction that the pistol is one of the chief causes of trouble. "Shootings for gain or plunder, shootings for jealousy, shootings for the pure love of shooting, the revolver pops away by day and night all over the United States like firecrackers on the Fourth of July," said the Chief Magistrate. "We must beget the wholesome disarmament of law-abiding citizens. When the law-abiding people have disarmed we will then know that the only armed people are the crooks and gunmen, and after that we can dispose of them."

"We are a gun-toting nation," said George W. Kirchwey, formerly Dean of Columbia Law School, ex-Warden of Sing Sing Prison, and now head of the Department of Criminology of the New York School for Social Work. "In England no one carries guns," he said. "The man who commits a burglary does not have to, because he knows neither the owner of the house he plans to rob will have one, and neither will the policeman who may apprehend him. The police do not have to carry guns, by the same token, because the criminals do not. In this country every crook has a gun, every policeman has a gun, and a large number of property owners have guns. In a crisis each one, knowing the other is armed, tries to use his first."

Every authority agrees that immigration is a decisive factor in the crime sit-

A TYPICAL CRIMINAL.
Nathan Kaplan, Alias Kid Dropper, Typical Desperate Criminal, Arrested Thirteen Times, Twice for Murder and Twice for Robbing.

uation. That our population is heterogeneous is a truism; but how heterogeneous it is compared with other nations is not so generally known. Take New York for example. Only one person in five that one meets on the streets of New York is a native American of native stock. The 1920 census gives the total population of 5,620,000. An analysis of these five millions and a half on the basis of nationality and birth shows that only 1,160,000 are native-born whites of native parentage. Some 2,300,000 of the whites are of foreign or mixed parentage and 2,000,000 were born in foreign countries. There are 160,000 negroes in addition.

Not less than 38 per cent. of New York's population were actually born abroad. Chicago and Boston have a foreign-born population of 36 per cent. each, Cleveland shows 34 and Detroit 33 per cent. Compare these figures with European cities. New York's Italian-born population is greater than the combined populations of Bologna and Venice. In only three Russian cities—Leningrad, Moscow and Odessa—can a Russian population be found greater than that of New York. Then, too, in London and other foreign cities there are practically no negroes. The color problem does not exist. In the United States the negro population in some cities, like Charleston, S. C., actually exceeds the white.

The Irish-born inhabitants of Boston, the figures show, constitute a little more than 9 per cent. of the population; but they are charged with 15 per cent. of the total arrests. In New York City the Russian born make up 10 per cent. of the population, but make up to 20 per cent. of the arraignments in Magistrates' courts. Negroes are especially prolific of trouble, according to the figures; and these explain, probably, the uniform excess of the homicide rate in Southern cities. In Chicago, for instance, negroes make up 2 per cent. of the population,

but were charged with 13 per cent. of the arrests for felonies.

Scientists and criminologists to whom I put the question of why America leads in crime find deeper causes than faulty procedure, pistols, newspapers and lack of police protection.

Pathology of the Situation.

Dr. Max P. Schlapp, Professor of Neuropathology at the Post Graduate Hospital and Chairman of the Medical Board of the New York Children's Courts, looks upon the prevalence of crime in this country as a symptom—along with increasing feeble-mindedness and insanity—of a basic disturbance in the nation's emotional stability.

"We are headed for a smash in this country," he says, "if we keep on the way we are going. There is a curve in the emotional stability of every people which is an index of their growth and power as a nation. On the up-swing the nation expands and prospers and gains in power with the normal development of emotional life. Then comes a time when emotional instability sets in. When it reaches a certain point there is a collapse. We have almost reached that point. This emotional instability causes crime, feeble-mindedness, insanity. Criminal conduct is a pathological matter, just as is these other disorders.

"Our emotional instability is the product of immigration, automobiles, jazz and the movies. Foreigners who have come to America have left a peaceful, orderly life without any particular emotional shock and have been plunged into a nervous maelstrom. A mere uprooting of their former lives is enough to cause considerable emotional disturbance, but this is heightened by the enormous increase in the nervous stimulation and shock of American life. It is bad enough for Americans, but far worse for those who have not grown used to it. The tremendous growth of pleasure automobiles and moving pictures in this country compared with others and the phenomenal sweep of jazz across the country have drained off far more nervous vitality from our people than those of other countries without putting anything in the way of energy into the reservoir of our national strength.

"Faulty administration of the law, the prevalence of pistols and other so-called 'causes of crime' are not causes. They are themselves common results of a basic instability in our emotional life. If we were stable emotionally, we should have quick and efficient action from our courts, we should not permit a pistol in town—and for the same reason we should also have less crime."

Dr. Bernard Glueck, who has specialized in the psychology of criminals and who was one of the experts who testified for the defense regarding the mental and emotional condition of Leopold and Loeb in the Franks murder case, also sees in the psychology of America's foreign population one of the chief reasons for our excess of criminality.

"A very large proportion of the criminals brought to the bar of justice in this country," he said, "are of the second generation of foreigners who have immigrated to the United States. Children of immigrants almost invariably are imbued with a disrespect for their parents which has broken down the stabilizing influence of the home. Their parents, being old and settled, do not learn English or adjust themselves to American ways as rapidly and as well as their children. This accentuates the natural scorn of youth for age and makes all authority and restraint—even outside the home—seem foreign and ineffectual."

Nation Not Grown Up.

Dr. Kirchwey also looks beneath the surface for the causes of crime. To him it is a matter of a nation that has never grown up. In spite of the fact that outwardly we have the appearance of a civilized community, inwardly we are still in the frontier days. We wear the same clothes as an Englishman and have built cities that rival London; but we think and feel very much as the pioneers of the prairie and the mining camp. Dr. Kirchwey made this comment:

"While the defects of our system of criminal procedure have not been exaggerated by its critics, I believe that it is a mistake to hold them responsible for the deplorable prevalence of crime in this country. These defects are not superficial or merely technical, to be remedied by a new codification of criminal law and procedure, or by any legislative action whatever—even if the desired legislation could be secured. Our slack and slip-shod procedure and the sporting character of our criminal trials are, equally with our criminality, the results of our lack of moral fibre, of an absence of public and social responsibility among us and of a slack and a different attitude toward the criminal.

"The law for the American people is still the law of their own conscience. It was so in the days of the Puritans. This spirit of taking the law into our own hands, so to speak, was carried westward with the pioneers. In the wilderness there was no law except the convictions of the man who was quickest with his gun. Both the legal self-sufficiency of the pioneer and his dependence on firearms are still dominant traits of the American people. We are still, like our frontier forebears, content to live dangerously, to take our chances on getting away with our lives and our property. Our criminal procedure will be reformed when as a people we shall have acquired those qualities which make for law observance and law enforcement, and when that time comes we shall find that our crime rate will have fallen to the lower level of other civilized countries. To put it in a nutshell, we shall be a law-enforcing people when we have become a law-abiding people, and not before."

November 2, 1924

MACHINE GUNS AND GAS ARE EASY TO PURCHASE

No General Laws Prevent the Sale of Devastating War Weapons to Criminals—And They Can Get Industry's Acetylene Torch

By EDWARD H. SMITH.

AMERICA'S criminals have turned the deadliest weapons of modern warfare against society. The other day, near Marion, Ill., one set of liquor gangsters attacked the hangout of a rival "mob" with an airplane, dropping explosive aerial bombs, while the defending bootleggers replied with machine gun fire. A few weeks ago, at Elizabeth, N. J., the murderous gang of the recently slain "Killer" Cunniffe bombarded a mail wagon with machine guns, with deadly effect. And in two bloody outbreaks of Chicago's bootleggers' war machine guns have been employed.

The airplane has been used before by criminal raiders, and other pages have been taken from the Book of war. In repeated instances the marauders, with whom the law seems unable to cope, have made use of poison gas, tear bombs and other forms of war gas. They have long used the gun silencers that were designed for war purposes and they are adopting a variety of other inventions for killing and maiming.

The sinister point is that the dangerous elements are permitted to buy and possess war's most devastating weapons. The menace was great enough when they had nothing more effective than revolvers, automatics and other small arms. What will life in our cities be like if the bandit and gangster are permitted to go on equipping themselves according to their fancy? Machine guns and gas were designed for purposes of war and ought, in all sense, to be available to none but the authorities of the War Department.

Machine Gun Sales.

"Do you mean to tell me," the average citizen asks, "that I can go out and buy a machine gun? That I don't have to have a Government license or something?"

The answer is that outside of New York State any one who has the price can buy a machine gun or a hundred machine guns without hindrance. Dealers are only too glad to have his order, to give him a demonstration and to sell him ammunition by the carload. He is not required to show a certificate of good character or to explain what he wants with such a weapon. In some cases he is asked to leave his name and address for the record. No more.

The excuse for all this indiscriminate selling of a kind of arms for which none but the military ought to or can have legitimate use is that there is no general law against it, and that certain companies and interests may want the guns to protect their property against riots and strikers. One dealer even said that such a weapon might be used by some for hunting geese that were flying high!

What applies to machine guns may be said with greater force as regards poison gas. Any criminal who is chemist enough to know the ingredients of effective gas bombs can purchase them in any drug store and compound them himself. But this is not being done. There is no need of it.

Poison Gas on Market.

There are on the market today a score or more of poison gas devices intended for defensive use against the criminals. Some are cartridges affixed to doors and windows with a mechanism that sets them off if an attempt is made to enter without having first turned back the mechanism with a special key. Others are attached to so-called hold-up alarms, the theory being that they may be set off instantly in case a stick-up is attempted, routing the criminals. Still others are attached to the doors of safes and vaults in minor banks and business houses throughout the country. They discharge their noxious fumes if any attempt is made to attack the strong-box with explosives or with the torch.

There has been a poison gas craze since the war, with the result that some sort of protective gas bomb service against thieves, burglars or bandits has found its way into commercial and domestic equipment. These contraptions are being affixed to the doors of everything from Federal Reserve Bank vaults to hen roosts and the "carnage" among the innocents is extensive. The man who has them installed often forgets about the matter till, some morning, he is prostrated with a puff of chlorine. In several New York instances firemen who were trying to enter locked premises to perform their duty were greeted by such discharges and had to be carried from the building.

The criminal long ago took advantage of the gas fad in two ways. He bought himself a gas mask, which also can be had for the asking by any one who knows where to apply. Thus equipped, he was able to defy the protective devices set up against him. But, far more menacing, he has bought gas bombs right and left. In the Rondout train robbery near Chicago, two years ago, gas bombs were thrown into the mail cars, forcing the clerks to open the doors and admit the robbers. In half a dozen jewelry store hold-ups here and elsewhere the bandits have sprayed tear gas.

Misuse of Gun Silencers.

The same criticism may be leveled at the gun silencer. Some mild attempt is being made to supervise or restrict the sale of that device, yet it is easily obtainable, and crooks are everywhere supplied with it. The Cowboy Tessler gang, recently caught in New York and sent up the river, had no fewer than half a dozen. The notorious Dutch Anderson, mentor and chief to Gerald Chapman, was likewise supplied. Silencers can be picked up in pawnshops, and the police annually dump numbers of them into the bay.

One must ask himself why even one was ever publicly sold. Is there any conceivable use, except criminal concealment and the facilitation of murder, to which such a device can be put outside of the battlefield? The excuse of hunting will not hold. Yet, a few years ago, when Deputy Commissioner Joseph Faurot of the New York Police Department protested against the sale of silencers he was fairly overwhelmed with abuse coming from manufacturers.

In New York State there is the Sullivan law that prohibits the sale or possession of any kind of deadly weapon except by those licensed to own or carry them. Yet it is no secret that the State is choked with firearms. The police of New York City dump hundreds, even thousands, into the bay every year and still they come, to be taken away from thugs, gangsters, bandits, burglars, rum-runners and all the ugly assortment of half-wits and emotional maniacs who make up our criminal population.

Though the Sullivan law is not entirely effective, it has enabled the police on innumerable occasions to send away, at least for short terms, known offenders who were illegally toting pistols and against whom more grave charges could not be proved.

Evasions of Sullivan Law.

But this law has in no practical sense lowered the currency of the deadly pistol. The reasons for this are simple. All one needs to do to circumvent the New York laws and buy a revolver is to take a ferry to New Jersey. There, in every city lining the river, the guns are laid out in interminable assortment. Sporting goods stores, hardware stores and pawnbrokers all sell them.

But all blame is not laid on New Jersey. In scores, perhaps hundreds, of New York City pawnshops pistols are sold without restriction. The writer has seen it done and men who know the ways of the underworld say that there is no trouble about buying pistols in Manhattan.

Even were this not true, the crook in New York would not have to move a foot out of his own room to be supplied with revolvers, automatics and ammunition.

Pick up any mail-order catalogue, any one of the cheaper magazines, many almanacs. You will find the advertisements of pistol concerns on half a score of pages. This one advertises a Colt at $7.85, sent on receipt of the price on five days' free trial. Money back if not pleased. Ammunition extra. It is not a Colt, to be sure, but a Spanish imitation of the American revolver. No matter, it is deadly, and the weapons are being sold.

Another advertisement in the same publication offers a Smith & Wesson (also Spanish) for $8.75, holster and all. Automatic pistols, Krag rifles, Mauser & Luger pistols, Springfield rifles, shotguns and other such weapons are advertised on other pages. One neat little device that attracts attention is a so-called hunting gun with a revolver grip and two barrels, the smaller superimposed on the larger. The latter is a shotgun but the former is a long-barreled revolver capable of high accuracy. This is sold for sporting purposes; but so are they all.

Acetylene Torch and Trick Guns.

There has been some improvement in the advertising situation relevant to small arms. Two or three years ago most of the periodicals carried revolver advertisements. Today these are missing from all but the least conscientious publications—the very ones that reach those who should not have guns.

Several other dangerous instruments are now generally obtainable. The oxy-acetylene torch is one of these. There can be no question of the industrial usefulness of this tool or its need for welding and cutting. Its sale cannot be stopped, yet there eventually must be some supervision, for the torches are falling into the hands of safe and bank burglars and these men are committing more daring and costly crimes with them. It is possible with the torch to burn a hole into any safe or vault not specially designed to resist this special form of attack. The work can be done silently and with astounding rapidity if the torchman knows his business.

Still more dangerous are various shooting instruments, trick guns that, whatever the ideas of their inventors and vendors, can serve none but criminal uses. The other day the writer saw what looked like and was a rather large pocket knife. It had, however, a central chamber and firing pin and a short enclosed barrel terminating in a hole at one end of the knife. This thing held one cartridge capable of firing through a one-inch pine board. At short range this is a deadly weapon and no one will argue that it can have any legitimate reason for being.

Similar devices are enclosed in cigarette cases, match boxes, cane ends, umbrellas, cigar lighters, fountain pens and a variety of other pocket articles. One must ask what earthly good they can do and shudder at the harm latent in them.

Worst of all are the shotgun plugs now being generally sold in sporting goods stores. These are steel and brass cylinders the size and shape of shotgun shells but usually somewhat longer. They are bored in the centre with a rifled barrel of the .32 or .38 calibre, into which regular revolver ammunition is fitted. The firing pin of the shotgun discharges them and they are at least as accurate as revolvers. They are sold as a hunting accessory. The inventor pleads that a man hunting with a shotgun may often come upon a situation where a more deadly solid shot weapon is needed. All he has to do is to insert the plug and the cartridge.

But what about the criminal? In some States possession of a revolver is a misdemeanor. But by putting on a hunting cap and coat and taking a shotgun plugged and loaded with revolver ammunition, one can go forth and kill and probably escape suspicion unless the officer happens to know about this device.

Manufacturers have fought hard against every suggestion of a law forbidding sales of firearms. They say that these laws would be a serious interference with a legitimate industry. They ask what the Government will do in time of war if it closes its gun works and stops the firearms inventor. They scoff at the idea that the criminals can be disarmed by any such measures and point a warning finger at the dismal spectacle of liquor bootlegging. But the machine gun, the gas bomb and the special weapons mentioned do not come under the head of sport weapons. At Geneva thirty-two nations have signed a treaty condemning the use of poison gas even in war.

Meantime, the immediate popular remedy has been to equip the forces of law and order with the same weapons used by the criminals. Thus, in New York today one sees the mail trucks being guarded by United States Marines, armed with machine guns, and the police are equipped with tear bombs for use in mob violence or jail-breaking.

Ex-Police Inspector Cahalane pointed out the other day that the policeman is a peace officer; his main business is to preserve order, life and prosperity. Accordingly, he cannot go about spraying a hail of machine gun bullets in a crowded city in the hope of striking down some bandit or burglar, meantime killing or maiming the inoffensive and intrusive public. Thus he must fight the bloodthirsty bandit and road agent with his old and simple weapons.

One of the points to be considered in connection with the free sale of arms is that not only animals but insane men get and use them. The Harrison Noel case in New Jersey a year ago is in point. Here was a young man of good family, recently escaped from a madhouse. He had no trouble getting a revolver with which he killed an innocent negro chauffeur and a defenseless little girl.

The same kind of lunatic who can buy a revolver would find it only a little more difficult to get a machine gun, take it to the corner of Fifth Avenue and Forty-second Street in an automobile and let fly into the crowd.

CHRONOLOGY OF PROHIBITION

IN 1642 the Colony of Maryland passed the first law punishing drunkards by a fine of 100 pounds of tobacco. In 1648 the Indians in the Valley of the St. Lawrence held a temperance meeting.

The Virginia Assembly in 1664 passed a law prohibiting ministers from giving themselves to excess in drinking. Later Maryland forbade more than one gallon of liquor to be sold to any Indian in one day. About this time the Quakers became disturbed over drunkenness at funerals; but Congress thought it advisable to allow a ration of one-half a pint of spirits and a quart of beer to the navy!

From 1805 until 1919 the battle between the wet and dry elements has been waged vigorously and incessantly, first in townships, second in municipalities, next in the State itself, and finally as a national issue. For a while the temperance movement was confined to church organizations, but in 1833 we find the first record of legislation, when the State of Georgia gave the right of local option to the inferior courts of two counties.

The first Statewide prohibition measure became effective in 1851 in Maine. Other States followed suit.

In 1869 the National Prohibition Party was formed in Chicago.

In 1890 President Corbin of the Reading Railroad ordered the discharge of all employes who frequented drinking places. The next year the Delaware, Lackawanna & Western Railroad discharged employes who signed a petition for saloon keepers for license.

The Anti-Saloon League was founded at Oberlin, Ohio, in 1893.

Between 1893 and 1918 there was a succession of victories for the drys.

In 1917, before we entered the war, 87.8 per cent. of the area of the United States was under no-license and only 12.2 per cent. of the area was under license. At this time 60.7 per cent. of the people were living in dry territory which they themselves had made dry by the referendum vote or by State legislative enactment. Only 39.8 per cent. were living in wet territory.

After the armistice was signed an emergency "wartime" prohibition measure was enacted, Nov. 21, 1918. The Eighteenth Amendment to the Constitution becomes effective Jan. 16.

January 11, 1920

LAYS CRIME WAVE TO LAX DRY ENFORCEMENT

Chicago Commission Reports This as Chief of Ten Causes of Law Breaking.

Special to The New York Times.

CHICAGO, Feb. 14.—In a report made public today by Professor Robert H. Gault, psychologist at Northwestern University and Chairman of the Chicago Crime Commission's Committee on the Origin of Crime, he enumerates ten major causes of crime, and cites improper enforcement of the prohibition amendment as the chief incentive.

The chief permanent underlying causes of crime, Professor Gault declares, may be placed roughly in ten classifications. These are:

Heritage of mental, moral or physical defects from one or both parents.

Unhealthy home environment.

Infective environment as distinct from home environment.

Lack of moral training.

Lack of respect for constituted authority.

Commercialized recreation.

Social or economic injustice.

Immigration of riff-raff from Europe.

Maladministration of justice.

Improper enforcement of prohibition.

Speaking of prohibition under the head of "Lack of Respect for Constitutional Authority," the report says:

"One factor at the present time which is doing much to undermine respect for the law generally is the failure of the prohibition amendment to operate successfully.

"An enormous number of otherwise law-abiding citizens in Chicago and elsewhere are violators of either the letter or the spirit of this law, regarding it as an infringement of their constitutional rights, despite the upholding of its constitutionality in the highest courts of the land.

"A great many citizens violate it wherever and whenever opportunity presents itself. It was estimated recently by one authority that the manufacture of 'home brew' distilled liquor and other alcoholic beverages is going on in two out of every five homes in the country.

Dry Agents Find Big Cities Wide Open; Washington Wants Stricter Enforcement

Special to The New York Times.

WASHINGTON, July 24.—Federal authorities are greatly concerned over the failure of State and city law officers to co-operate with Government prohibition agents. The fact that the anti-liquor laws are being openly flouted in many of the greatest cities of the country causes chagrin and disappointment to the authorities here.

Violations in New York, Chicago, St. Louis, Baltimore and a score of other large communities are reported daily. At the same time local prohibition commissioners report to headquarters that they do not secure proper aid and assistance from police, sheriffs, marshals and other officers sworn by law to enforce the statutes.

So difficult has the situation become that John F. Kramer, the Federal Prohibition Commissioner, has begun consultations with William L. Frierson, Assistant Attorney General in charge of prohibition matters. It will be definitely decided at these conferences just how much responsibility lies with the local authorities and how much may be expected of them. Once that is determined, the Federal officials will almost certainly insist that help must be forthcoming from the city and State officials.

The Prohibition Bureau of the Treasury Department is not as large an organization as some of its division chiefs

desire. Some of them ask for more men, asserting that they are unable to accomplish satisfactory results with the small force at their command. Others wish to start with the organizations they now have, and get these in running shape before building up.

Commissioner Dalrymple of the Chicago Department has been frank and outspoken in his complaint that he is not receiving the aid he should. He has said in authorized statements that Chicago is "wide open."

Vance J. Higgs, Special Attorney General at St. Louis, is another who has issued a statement declaring that he must have more co-operation. These are cited here as typical instances of the failure in many cities to give the looked-for response.

As a desperate step, the Prohibition Commissioner is now considering organizing secret "flying squadrons" in some of the great cities. These "flying squadrons" would be made up of 200 to 300 men, unknown even to other prohibition agents, and working directly under orders from Washington, with perhaps the advice of the local Prohibition Commissioner.

These "flying squadrons" would gather evidence in anticipation of raids, guard the facts carefully, and then, at a designated "zero hour," make simultaneous raids in various parts of a city.

July 25, 1920

Seize Harvard Chemist in Back Bay Dry Raid; "All the Fellows Have Stills," He Explains

Special to The New York Times.

BOSTON, Mass., April 29. — Society circles in the Back Bay have been invaded by prohibition officers in their war upon moonshiners, and as a result Louis Agassiz Shaw, scientist, Harvard professor and member of a socially prominent family, appeared before United States Commissioner Hayes today and was held in $500 bail following arraignment.

One of the finest stills that the prohibition era has brought to official attention was discovered in his home at 6 Marlboro Street, Back Bay, according to the officers, who entered the mansion with a search warrant.

The disclosure of the raid through the Federal Court proceedings today may surprise the city's exclusive realm in which the alleged moonshiner moved, but one of the calm utterances attributed to him by the raiding officers may prove even more of a shock.

Moonshining, according to this quoted statement, is quite a general practice in Boston society.

"All the fellows have stills," he told the officers, according to their assertions.

The still, of 10-gallon capacity, was set up on the top floor of the house, adjoining the ballroom, according to the enforcement agents, and in the room were also found five and one-half gallons of distilled liquor and six gallons of mash.

Professor Shaw, according to the officers, said he had used the product of the still as an ingredient of punch served at dancing parties.

Professor Shaw is a chemist and an assistant in applied physiology at the Harvard Medical School.

He accorded the raiding officers every courtesy, they said, and his butler co-operated in the search. At Professor Shaw's suggestion, the servant procured bags in which to place the seized apparatus and the other alleged contraband. The officers, with their haul, were ushered to the back door, that they might depart with a minimum of display.

April 30, 1921

FINDS FLAW IN DRY LAW.

Official Declares Other Laws Must Be Broken to Enforce It.

Special to The New York Times.

MINNEAPOLIS, Minn., Aug. 3.—The Eighteenth Amendment to the Constitution of the United States cannot be enforced without violating the Fourth and Fifth Amendments guaranteeing citizens against searches without warrants and due process of law, is the statement of Emerson E. Hunt, from June 13 until yesterday supervising Federal prohibition agent for the West, and whose appointment was sponsored by the Anti-Saloon League.

Mr. Hunt's statement was given today as the reason for the failure of Federal authorities to stop flagrant violation of the prohibition laws in Minneapolis, where more than 400 places are selling alcoholic drinks involving a yearly turnover of $12,000,000.

Mr. Hunt is a former minister and an Anti-Saloon League leader. He was relieved of his duties yesterday and ordered to Washington, where he is to receive a roving commission under the National Prohibition Director.

August 4, 1921

Debris From Home Brewing Blocks Sewers in Butte

BUTTE, Mont., Jan. 25.—City sewers on Butte's east side are blocked by large deposits of moonshine mash, including prune seeds, rice, barley, raisins, corn and cherry pits, City Engineer Henry J. Wiegenstein said today.

Home brewers, the engineer concludes, are using sewers for garbage cans to avoid possible detection of their illegal traffic. Six lines of hose, connected to a swirling nozzle, are being used to flush the débris.

January 26, 1922

Jurors Drink Evidence, Disagree and Are Censured

PHILADELPHIA, March 13.—When a jury in Quarter Sessions Court today retired to determine the guilt or innocence of a saloon keeper charged with selling liquor without a license the jurors took with them a half pint of whisky which had been offered in evidence. Nearly four hours later Judge William C. Ferguson ordered them to report. They filed in with the liquor bottle empty and the information that they were unable to agree.

Inquiry from the Court as to what had become of the whisky brought no satisfactory answer, and the jurors were discharged from further service in the court.

Judge Ferguson later announced that he would recommend that the jurors' pay be withheld, and also that he would take steps to have them disbarred from future jury duty.

March 14, 1922

HEARSE HALTED FIVE TIMES.

Bringing Body From Islip Here, It Arouses Drys' Suspicions.

An automobile hearse, driven by Richard Norton for Frank E. Campbell, undertaker, was stopped five times by prohibition agents yesterday on a trip from Islip, Long Island, to this city, he reported on his return here.

Norton was bringing a body here. He reported that he had just left Islip when two men halted him, flashing badges. He convinced them he really was carrying a corpse and proceeded on his way. A little distance further, at Amityville, he was stopped again. At Brentwood more prohibition agents halted him and demanded that he open the hearse. He refused, saying that it was a rule of his establishment that hearses were not to be opened en route. Other detachments of dry agents stopped the hearse at Lynbrook and Long Island City.

Mr. Campbell, it was said last night, would protest against the action of the prohibition agents.

July 24, 1922

SENATE PUTS BAN ON BOOTLEGGERS

Order Calling for Arrests Coincides With Mishap to Waiter Taking Liquor to Member.

JOKE PLAYED ON UPSHAW

Floor Outside His Office Gets Liquor Bath—Haynes Hopeful on Progress of Dry Cause.

Special to The New York Times.

WASHINGTON, Dec. 23.—Taking cognizance of the charges that bootleggers were plying their trade in the Senate and House office buildings, Senator Curtis, Chairman of the Rules Committee, ordered the Sergeant-at-Arms today to instruct the police on the Senate side of the Capitol and in the Senate office building to arrest all bootleggers who entered.

Senator Curtis said:

"I do not know of a single violation personally, and I do not know whether the charges are true, but if they are, we intend to stamp out this traffic at once. My instructions were to make arrests, no matter who was back of the violator or to whom he was making the sale. No amount of political influence will save the man caught violating the prohibition law in the Senate side of the Capitol."

Two hours after the instructions were issued, a man strolled into the Senate wing and was about to enter the restaurant when he slipped on the stone floor, a quart bottle of whisky slid from under his coat and broke on the floor. The fumes spread their aroma throughout the building until some one ordered it to be neutralized with water.

The man who lost his liquor was described as "George," a waiter, and he was reported to be carrying the cheer to a favorite Senator.

On the House side all was quiet except that a large quantity of liquor was discovered on the floor outside the office door of Representative Upshaw, who has been making charges about the illegal traffic. Mr. Upshaw had gone to Georgia and the christening of his portal is supposed to be the joke of a wet.

December 24, 1922

'SCOFFLAW' WINS PRIZE AS STIGMA FOR 'WETS'

Miss Butler of Dorcester, Mass., Gets $200 in Contest With 25,000 Entries.

Special to The New York Times.

BOSTON, Jan. 15.—The prize of $200 in gold offered by Delcevare King of Quincy for the best word to stigmatize those who scoff at the prohibition law and other laws has been won by Miss Kate L. Butler of Dorchester House, Dorchester, Mass. Her word is "scofflaw."

The judges were King, the Rev. H. Talmadge Root, Chairman of the New England Citizenship Conference for Law Enforcement, and A. J. Davis, Regional Superintendent of the Anti-Saloon League. In selecting the winning word from the 25,000 suggested, which came from every State in the Union and several foreign countries, the committee gives five points in its standard:

1. Preferably one of one or two syllables.
2. A word beginning with "S," as "S" words have a sting.
3. A word for the lawless drinker—law, not drink, being the basis.
4. Applying to violations of all laws.
5. A word linked with President Harding's statement, "Lawless drinking is a menace to the Republic itself."

January 16, 1924

15,000 'BLIND PIGS' REPORTED IN DETROIT

Pre-Prohibition Saloons Have Multiplied Tenfold, Police Superintendent Says.

Special to The New York Times.

DETROIT, Mich., Feb. 13.—There are at least 15,000 "blind pigs" and bootlegging joints within the city of Detroit, according to an estimate made tonight by Superintendent of Police William P. Rutledge.

"There were 1,500 saloons in the city when prohibition went into effect, and today there are easily ten times that many places in Detroit selling liquor," the Superintendent said.

"If a policeman goes into an apartment building containing thirty-six apartments he may find five or six bootlegging places, but it would be impossible for him to stand on the sidewalk and estimate how many there were inside. It is just as hard to estimate the number of places in the city, but there are easily 15,000," he said.

The rank and file of the Police Department, as constituted Jan. 1, consists of 1,942 patrolmen and 81 detectives, exclusive of the women's division. If this entire force, working twenty-four hours a day, were assigned solely to the enforcement of the prohibition law there would be, on the basis of Superintendent Rutledge's estimate, 7.41 blind pigs for every policeman.

Superintendent Rutledge explained that the recent order putting an end to "tip-over" raids, in which police entered blind pigs without a warrant and used axes on the furnishings of the place and confiscated the liquor, was issued largely because the method had proved a failure.

February 14, 1925

7

WAR ON BOOTLEGGERS IN BIG WET CITIES IS NEXT ON PROGRAM

New York, Philadelphia and Baltimore Will Be Attacked by Federal Forces.

MOVE ON SMUGGLING FIRST

Strategists Expect Easier Task Here Then—Mellon Anxious to Dry Up Pennsylvania.

END OF RUM ROW HAILED

Aid to Coast Guard Commander Tours Dry-War Front and Finds Only 12 Whisky Ships.

Special to The New York Times.

WASHINGTON, May 16.—The next offensive in the Federal Government's rum war will be directed against the bootlegging sectors. After the Government has conquered the whisky smuggling forces at points on the coasts and along the borders the reorganized prohibition army will concentrate on all other violations.

Secretary Mellon and his chief of staff, Colonel Lincoln C. Andrews, Assistant Secretary of the Treasury, following war methods, intend to move upon the so-called wet cities on the Atlantic seaboard which have received their best supplies of illicit liquor from rum schooners which now, for the most part, have been dispersed.

The Strategy Board of the Treasury is proceeding on the theory that if the main sources of whisky importation are dried up it will be easier to conduct a campaign against the bootlegger in the larger cities. They say that the average patron of the bootlegger will not buy stuff made here out of corn or industrial alcohol converted into synthetic gin, and the closing down on the flow from foreign sources will materially help solve the problem of prohibition enforcement.

The fight against the bootlegger will not be opened until the three Government agencies are well organized and appear capable of successfully contending with smuggling. Then they will tackle the problem of violations in the larger cities, such as New York, Philadelphia and Baltimore, which have depended on the overseas source for their supplies.

Expect General Butler's Help.

General Smedley D. Butler, the "fighting Quaker of the Marines," now Director of Public Safety in Philadelphia, will be brought into the war when the Federal forces sweep down on that city.

Secretary Mellon is very anxious to clean up Pennsylvania, and, since General Butler knows how to combat the bootleggers, he will be asked to cooperate with the Federal contingent which will be rushed to Philadelphia within a reasonable time.

General Butler began a campaign of his own in Philadelphia yesterday, when many policemen were suspended on charges of receiving hush money from breweries operating against the law.

The belief exists here that the Federal authorities, through the State Department, may formally call the attention of foreign Governments to the violation by rum schooners of the navigation law, which requires that ships shall be chartered to go to certain ports, as required by the laws of most countries. Instead of complying with their charters, the rum schooners collect beyond the twelve-mile limit and ply their trade with the smugglers. It is understood that Great Britain is about to take a more vigorous stand against ships carrying liquor as a result of the activities of the American Government.

During the first week of intensive war on rum runners 226 persons were arrested for intoxication in Washington. Twenty-seven alleged bootleggers were arrested during the week. There also were fifty-eight arrests for alleged possession of intoxicants and sixteen for transporting. Much of the liquor being transported probably was intended for the bootleg trade.

The attitude of the Anti-Saloon League on the use of the navy for the suppression of whisky smuggling, which met with the opposition of President Coolidge, is reflected in a statement issued today by Wayne B. Wheeler, counsel for the league.

"The navy should not be used except as a last resort to suppress liquor smuggling," Mr. Wheeler said. "This has always been the position of the Anti-Saloon League. We have not requested the use of the navy. The Coast Guard is doing magnificent work. However, if the organized attack upon the Eighteenth Amendment cannot be stopped by the Coast Guard, an emergency may arise that will justify the use of some of the ships of the navy. The Justice Department ruled in 1923 that no such emergency had yet arisen.

"No specific authorization is given the President to use the ships of the navy in the enforcement of the law except in certain cases, such as execution of court processes—when Federal officers have been obstructed — quarantine laws or neutrality proclamations. These special statutes, however, do not confer authority for the use of the naval vessels to enforce ordinary civil and criminal statutes. In one instance, however, in the suppression of the slave traffic, the military forces were called upon to aid in enforcing criminal laws by express act of Congress.

"Section 5,298 of the Federal Statutes, Annotated, authorizes the President 'to employ such parts of the land and naval forces of the United States as he may deem necessary to enforce the faithful execution of the laws of the United States, or to suppress an insurrection or rebellion in any State or Territory where the laws of the United States are forcibly opposed.'

"Bills have been introduced in Congress to amend the law so as to give the same authority to the President with reference to liquor smuggling. Until that has been done, the President would not be justified in using the navy until an emergency arose which amounted to an attack upon the sovereignty of the nation, or a rebellion from within.

"George Washington, in 1794, used a part of the army to suppress the Whisky Rebellion in Western Pennsylvania. If another whisky rebellion develops which cannot be suppressed by civil authorities, I believe that Uncle Sam has as much red blood in his veins today as he had 131 years ago. I have no reason to believe, however, that the Coast Guard and the civil authorities will fail in their attempt to suppress rum smuggling and bootlegging."

May 17, 1925

JOKES ON PROHIBITION BARRED FROM MOVIES

Even Drinking Scenes Are Banned, Hays Says, if Not Essential 'in Building Up the Plot.'

LOS ANGELES, July 12 (AP).—Will H. Hays, President of the Motion Picture Producers and Distributers of America, Inc., made public today a statement outlining the organization's recently adopted policy that no film produced within its ranks shall in the slightest degree encourage disrespect for any law, especially the prohibition law. The policy was adopted at the annual meeting here some weeks ago of representatives of the association.

Mr. Hays's statement follows:

"Make certain that into no title there be allowed to enter any word, phrase, clause or sentence that directly or indirectly encourages the slightest disregard for law. There might be a tendency to make light of prohibition on the theory that it is a type of humor and might bring the laugh which sometimes follows, but any such treatment of the subject is, of course, a belittling of the statute itself and it is the earnest purpose of the association to make certain that the screen shall never be used in a manner which promotes the slightest disrespect for any law, whatever that law may be.

"Make certain that into no picture there be allowed to enter any shot of drinking scenes, manufacture or sale of liquor or undue effects of liquor which are not a necessary part of the story or an essential element in the building up of the plot. That is, there should be no picturization of liquor, its manufacture, use or effect which can be construed as being brought in unnecessarily as a type of propaganda. It is one thing, of course, if the use of liquor in a picture is a natural element, but quite another thing if it is brought in unnecessarily in any way which can be construed as being for an ulterior purpose or which in any way promotes disrespect for law.

"The motion picture has a definite duty, still more emphasized at the present, of not allowing itself to be misused in any situation. Further it has the continuing duty of positive support of law, order and authority, and the great opportunity which is in pictures measures exactly their great responsibility."

July 13, 1926

SARGENT ASSAILS DRY LAW EVADERS

Attorney General Tells the Missouri Bar Buyers Are Guilty as Sellers.

HITS "PERSONAL LIBERTY"

Protests Excuse for Violations Because Law Conflicts With Convenience or Profit.

KANSAS CITY, Oct. 2.—Attorney General Sargent assailed the plea of "personal liberty" as an excuse for violating the Prohibition law and declared that the buyer of illicit liquor committed as great or greater wrong than the seller, in an address today before the Missouri Bar Association.

The Attorney General urged members of the legal profession to lead the way toward observance of the laws of the country.

"Show those who have not your training and resulting capacity of perception," he said, "that while it is every citizen's right to vote, work, exert all the persuasive influence he has upon molding the law to meet his views, still, whether it does or does not meet them, security for self and country demand personal watchfulness in observance of the law; watchfulness not only to guard against committing offense one's self, but against becoming a party to procuring the committing of offenses by others."

Mr. Sargent said that the proposition that one is justified in violating the law merely because it conflicts with his convenience, desire or profit deserves an instant protest from every citizen who has the safety of society at heart.

Continuing, he said:

February 15, 1921

"From the thought that a law was made for some one else, not for us, is but a step to the notion that it is no matter whether we pay attention to it or not; and from the thought that it does not signify whether or not we obey one law, to disregard of all law, to carelessness about what laws we will regard and what we will ignore; from laxity as to what we will observe and what ignore, to choosing to ignore a part of the law; and finally to arrive at the stage of deliberately flouting a part of the law while strenuously insisting upon the observance and enforcement of another part.

"That in this country the manufacture and sale of intoxicating liquor for beverage purposes shall cease has been solemnly declared by the only final authority we know, the vote of the people. That vote has taken many forms. It was voted as an amendment to the organic law of the nation by the Congress; it was voted as ratification by the States individually; it was again voted as legislation by the Congress; it has been again voted as legislation by all but two of the States.

"Yet, notwithstanding this situation, under the suggestion and stimulation of those who find the traffic profitable, many otherwise law-abiding citizens

continue to so conduct themselves that the violation of the law by others continues and to excuse themselves for such conduct on the ground that the law interferes with their personal desires.

"They say it interferes with personal liberty and that no law which interferes with personal liberty can be valid.

"It is for the purpose of making the matter clear to those who have not taken the time, made the exertion to see to what end this catchword phrase, "interferencee with personal liberty," is used, on what it is founded, to what it tends, that I have undertaken to sift the central idea from the many words.

Laws and Self-Gratification.

"The man (and I am aware there are probably many such in this audience) who, seriously and conscientiously believing the country would be a better place to live in with liquors again freely and lawfully obtainable, advocates a return to that condition has the same right to his opinion, and the same right to express it and give his reasons for it, in speech and print, as has any other man to advocate adherence to the present policy.

"So with the man who argues for a

reversal of this policy because he desires it for his own gratification alone; but I submit to you as lawyers—whether you were for a prohibitory law or against a prohibitory law—that this proposition that one is justified in violating the law because it conflicts with his conveniences, choice, desire, profit, is not to be listened to without instant protest from every citizen who has the safety of society at heart.

"There is no way of determining what policies we will adopt, what our rules of conduct shall be, except by the preponderance of votes of our duly appointed representatives; when a policy is defined, when a rule of conduct is established by that method, it is defined, established, not for the part whose representatives vote for it, but for all, and must be observed by all.

"If those whose ideas do not prevail constitute four-tenths of the whole, is the policy, the rule, any less binding upon them than if they constitute only one-tenth?

"Will it do for any of us, prohibitionist or anti-prohibitionist, Republican or Democrat, protectionist or free-trader, to concede for a moment that it is?

"If it is not the duty, the highest duty of every one, the minority as well as the majority, to comply with the results so ascertained and arrived

at, what is the use, the purpose of voting at all?

"If those whose ideas do not prevail may say, 'Notwithstanding I took part in the decision of this question and should have expected and demanded full acquiescence in the result by all if my party had won, I do not like the decision and shall not observe it,' what remains but that 'all organized government, all liberty, all security are at an end' and 'force alone will prevail?'

"This matter is brought before you with entire confidence that when American citizens see and realize the consequences of their acts they will act correctly; confidence that when any man claiming the status of a law-abiding citizen and contemplating buying a supply of liquor will stop to think that the act he is considering is paying the seller a bribe to violate the law, he will hesitate; when the quality of his action is understood, when the citizen becomes aware that he is choosing between abetting, yes, actually procuring, violation of the Constitution, and yielding, yes, asserting, obedience to it, there will be no question about which way duty lies, and when the choice between inclination and duty is consciously presented, duty wins."

October 3, 1926

190 DEATHS IN RAIDS UNDER PROHIBITION; SEARCH CURB ISSUED

White House Insists Agents Obtain Warrants and Shoot Only in Self-Defense.

AURORA CASE CALLED LOCAL

Federal Government Holds That the De King Killing Is for Illinois to Handle.

LISTS ONLY FEDERAL DEATHS

Lowman Says That Every Officer Involved Was Exonerated at Inquiry or Trial.

Special to the New York Times.
WASHINGTON, April 5.—Official disclosure of the tragedies that Federal prohibition enforcement has

brought was made today in the action of the Treasury Department in giving out reports showing that twenty-five persons had been killed in the past fifteen months. Sixteen of the victims met their deaths in encounters with Federal prohibition agents and Coast Guardsmen, while nine of those killed were in the government's enforcement service. Seven in the latter category were prohibition agents and two were mounted customs officers.

Coast Guardsmen killed five persons in the period covered. No persons were killed by customs officers in that time.

It was disclosed officially also that since the Eighteenth Amendment became effective in 1920, nine years ago, 190 persons have been killed in the enforcement of the prohibition laws. Of these, 135 were citizens killed by prohibition agents and 55 were prohibition agents who met death in the line of duty. The figures for the nine years are:

In 1920, agents 6, citizens 5; 1921, agents 8, citizens 14; 1922, agents 12, citizens 13; 1923, agents 4, citizens 17; 1924, agents 2, citizens 22; 1925, agents 5, citizens 20; 1926, agents 6, citizens 17; 1927, agents 5, citizens 16; 1928, agents 7, citizens 10; 1929, agents none, citizens 1.

Curb on Dry Searches.

Coincident with the Treasury's action in giving out these reports, it became known at the White House that several months ago orders of the most stringent character had been issued to Federal prohibition

officers relative to invasion and search of dwellings and vehicles.

The Federal statutes prohibit such invasion unless the searching officers are armed with warrants issued on sworn statements of knowledge or belief that the prohibition laws are being violated. It was said that it was not known that there had been any violation of these stringent orders.

Incident to this information, it was explained in an official quarter that the Government had ascertained that the killing of a woman by prohibition officers at Aurora, Ill., was entirely a local affair that did not involve the Federal Government in any way.

Evidently the administration is greatly relieved to find that it is not concerned in the Aurora tragedy. Whether right or wrong had been done in the Aurora case, it was said, the investigation now being conducted would not be participated in by the Federal authorities.

Three of the tragedies occurred at sea, the latest of these being the death of a seaman on the Canadian schooner, I'm Alone, in the Gulf of Mexico. Of the other persons who met death in encounters with Federal agents or Coast Guardsmen, two were in California and Wyoming, and one each in Alabama, Arkansas, Kentucky, West Virginia, Missouri, Tennessee, South Carolina, Florida and New York.

Recent Decrease in Deaths.

Seymour Lowman, Assistant Secretary of the Treasurer in charge

of prohibition enforcement, under whose direction the reports were prepared for Under-Secretary of the Treasury Mills, said today that there had been a material decrease in the number of violent deaths incident to prohibition enforcement.

He attributed this to prohibition officers observing a rule issued more than a year ago prohibiting them from using firearms promiscuously. As a result of this rule, he said, prohibition enforcement officers did not resort to the use of firearms except where it was necessary to protect their lives.

The reports made public disclosed that eleven persons were killed in resisting arrest and that four prohibition officers met death during such encounters.

According to Assistant Secretary Lowman, every officer of the government who was not absolved from blame for a prohibition tragedy by a coroner's jury or a grand jury, had been found to have acted in the performance of his duty when cases against them were brought to trial. Several such cases are still before the courts.

Henry H. Curran, president of the Association Against the Prohibition Amendment, made caustic comment on the tragedies recorded in the reports furnished to newspapers by Assistant Secretary Lowman. He said:

"Nobody need be surprised at all this free and easy killing. It always happens when a minority of the people try to ram an unreasonable law down the throats of the majority. There will be more murders than ever when the Jones law gets under way. The Mexicans have nothing on us."

April 6, 1929

NATION'S CRIME BILL PUT ABOVE BILLION

Wickersham Board Staggered by Cost, Is Unable to Estimate the Total.

DRY LAW A GREAT FACTOR

Enforcement Efforts Take Two-thirds of Federal Outlay for Criminal Justice.

Special to The New York Times.

WASHINGTON, Aug. 21. — The American people are paying an annual crime bill running into such figures as to stagger statisticians, according to the twelfth report of the Wickersham Commission, made public at the White House today, in which the law enforcement investigators admitted the total figure of the cost of crime to be beyond its ability to find.

The mere "representative" figures and estimates which the Commission presented to President Hoover to show the nature of expenditures on crime, aggregated a total of more than $1,119,000,000. This figure represented only such items of cost as the Commission's experts could put their hands upon in the comparatively short time in which they had to make the study. The other costs, directly or indirectly attributable to crime, were too numerous and too diverse within themselves to be enumerated and the commission disposed of them either with a discussion of their nature or the further admission that they could not be ascertained.

About the only conclusive figure which the commission presented was that attributable to prohibition. Whatever else the Wickersham body determined or failed to determine about prohibition during its two years of study, it found that virtually two-thirds of all Federal expenditures for criminal justice is now being used in the attempt to enforce the Volstead act.

Cost of Dry Enforcement.

Figures presented in the report, entitled "cost of crime," listed the cost of administering that part of criminal justice related to prohibition at $34,828,550.65, or 66 per cent of a total of $52,786,202.94 expended for all law enforcement activities of the Federal Government during the fiscal year 1929-1930.

The commission found one of the greatest costs incident to crime to be entirely without its power to ascertain. This due to "racketeering" and organized extortion. It was impossible even roughly to estimate the amount to which this might be running annually. These new and modernized crimes constituted such a drain on the resources of the country that a separate and sweeping investigation of this particular branch of criminality was recommended to the President.

The carrying out of an "immediate, comprehensive and scientific nationwide inquiry" into organized crime, the commission said, should make possible the development of an intelligent plan for its control. The commission admitted that the limitation upon time and money made it impossible for it to make it, but said that this more thorough investigation should be carried on by the Federal Government or some other agency with sufficient funds and power.

The report, which is next to the last to be issued by the now extinct commission, said that it should not require the "dramatic effect of some lump sum total figure to emphasize the importance and necessity, from a purely economic standpoint, of dealing adequately with the problem of preventing crime and controlling the criminal."

While the report stressed the enormity of such a task as finding the actual dollar-and-cents cost of crime in the United States, the investigations made on the subject, both by the commission personnel and by two experts, Goldthwaite H. Dorr and Sidney P. Simpson, both members of the law firm of Hines, Rearick, Dorr, Travis & Marshall of New York, demonstrated the "tremendous economic burden imposed by crime upon the community."

The cost of prohibition, in the Federal scheme of criminal justice, was merely cited by the commission in passing, although the expert investigators treated it more at length. But much more than the cost of Federal justice was the cost, both direct and indirect, of crime to other agencies and individuals, said in the report to run into untold figures.

Huge Sums in Police Costs.

The investigators found that a sum much in excess of $247,000,000 is spent annually by the 300 larger cities of the country in dealing with the crime problem; that eleven States pay more than $2,500,000 annually for State police forces; that State penal and correctional institutions, all required because of widespread crime, involve an expenditure of more than $51,000,000 each year.

In addition, large private expenditures are made for protection against criminals. It was mentioned in the report that $3,900,000 annually is paid to companies engaged in providing armored-car service for the transportation of money and valuables. The insured loss due to burglary, robbery, larceny and embezzlement averages more than $47,000,000 annually, according to the commission's findings.

he loss due to extortion and racketeering, the commission said, was altogether impossible of ascertainment, while the Postoffice Department estimated that $68,000,000 was lost each year through organized frauds perpetrated through the mails.

"We believe that this represents only a small portion of the total loss due to criminal frauds," said the report, "and we think it quite probable that the loss due to organized extortion and racketeering is of still greater magnitude."

The report noted that an annual average sum of more than $106,000,000 was paid out for legitimate insurance against criminal acts. Added to whatever total the direct loss of crime might amount to, the commission held that the loss to productive labor of a large criminal population was of major importance. Again, this was impossible of anything like an accurate determination.

However, the loss of productive labor of prisoners and law enforcement officers engaged in apprehending and convicting criminals was placed at about $300,000,000.

Distribution of Costs.

The following table, showing the distribution of the cost of Federal criminal justice during the fiscal year 1929-30 as to various steps, was presented with the report:

Agency.	Cost.	P. C.
Police (criminal):		
Department of Justice	$2,658,156.55	5.0
Other executive departments and establishments	30,245,584.64	57.4
United States marshals	3,020,174.69	5.7
Total police	$35,923,915.88	68.1
Prosecution:		
Department of Justice	198,891.14	.4
United States attorneys	1,758,305.72	3.3
Other agencies	39,780.00	(a)
Total prosecution	1,996,976.86	3.7
Courts:		
District courts	5,615,837.95	10.6
United States commissioners	588,820.91	1.1
Circuit courts of appeals	95,298.95	.2
Supreme Court	31,057.40	.1
Total courts	$6,331,015.21	12.0
Penal institutional treatment:		
Permanent Federal institutions for adults	4,172,204.62	7.9
Federal prison camps	40,582.34	.1
State, county and municipal institutions	3,786,510.00	7.2
National Training Sch. for Boys	207,062.00	.4
General administration	274,171.78	.5
Total penal institutional treatment	$8,480,530.74	16.1
Probation and pardon:		
Probation	21,522.25	(a)
Pardon	32,242.00	(a)
Total probation and pardon	$53,764.25	.1
Aggregate cost	$52,786,202.94	100.0

(a) Less than 0.1 per cent.

There also was included the following table showing to what offenses these costs were chargeable during the fiscal year 1929-30:

Agency.	Prohibition.	Anti-Narcotic.	Motor Vehicle Theft.	Other Criminal.	Total.
Police	$25,644,069.57	$1,648,031.56	$752,553.41	$7,879,261.34	$35,923,915.88
Prosecution	996,720.33	153,364.00	124,104.71	722,787.82	1,996,976.86
Courts	4,308,004.57	373,797.78	273,711.24	1,375,501.62	6,331,015.21
Penal institutional treatment	3,842,416.84	1,377,794.86	925,242.21	2,335,076.83	8,480,530.74
Probation and pardon	37,339.34	2,692.54	2,653.21	11,079.16	53,764.25
Total	$34,828,550.65	$3,555,680.74	$2,078,264.78	$12,323,706.77	$52,786,202.94
Per cent	66.0	6.9	3.9	23.2	100.0

A tabulation showing the distribution of prohibition cost by districts also was included in the report.

Burden Heavy on Cities.

The experts found, however, that the cost of Federal criminal justice, while a growing factor, was rather insignificant in amount to that imposed upon the municipalities throughout the country.

For the same items of expenditures, criminal police, prosecutions, courts, penal correctional activities and parole and pardon, 365 representative cities of more than 25,000 inhabitants in 1930 paid a total of $243,551,915. This averaged $5.47 for every man, woman and child in these municipalities.

The figures were given only as a basis for thought on the subject of "cost of crime" and were intended in no way as a basis for definite estimates. For instance, it was found that in New York City a total of $53,753,865 was spent for criminal justice in 1930, or an average of $7.76 for every inhabitant of the country's greatest city. This expenditure was more than double that of any other city.

The nearest was Chicago, with a total outlay for criminal justice of $22,437,169, or an average of $6.65 per capita. Philadelphia was third with a gross expenditure of $17,069,363, or $8.75 per capita, and Detroit was fourth with a total of $11,434,791, or $7.29 a person.

The biggest aggregate item of expense in administration of municipal criminal justice was found to be the police, being $194,119,511 of the total cost for the 365 cities.

Propose Survey in Every City.

The only recommendation the experts had to make out of their study of the cost of municipal criminal justice was that a survey be made to include as nearly as possible all the incorporated cities of America, so that the people of the country might be impressed with the enormity of the expenditure, particularly in proportion to the costs of their city government.

It was found, for instance, that New York City paid 14.1 per cent of its entire city budget on criminal justice in 1930, while just across the Hudson River in Jersey City, the expenditure for this item was more than 18 per cent of the city's total outlay.

The experts contended that the public expense in administering criminal justice or in protecting the community against the criminal was by no means all of the cost. They estimated that various industries, mercantile establishments and private institutions of varied sorts paid annually about $159,000,000 for watchmen.

They treated it as significant in discussing the cost of crime that an average of more than $4,000,000 had been expended for the past ten years for safes, chests and vaults to protect money and valuables from burglars and robbers. An average of about $10,465,000 annually was said to have been expended for the past ten years for protective services such as burglar alarm devices, police-call service and the like. No estimate could be given of the expenditures for private detective services.

The experts made no attempt to estimate the loss due to crimes against the person, although they said that any full calculation of the "cost of crime" must take in such factors.

Crime Losses Still Greater.

Whatever the cost of administering the criminal law, the commission concluded that the losses inflicted by the criminal upon society were much greater and of far greater importance, "so that it is much more important from an economic standpoint to increase the efficiency of the administration of criminal justice than to decrease its cost."

"True economy in administering the criminal law," said the commission's report, "may well require in many instances the material increase of expenditures for enforcing the law in order to secure efficiency and in order to deal adequately with new types of crime and 'improved' methods of criminals."

The commission had but two major recommendations to make to the President on the subject of "cost of crime," the one for a more thorough and "scientific" investigation of rackets and the other for a revision of the criminal statutes of the State and Federal governments to rid them of obsolete laws and legislation of "doubtful social utility."

"The desirability of confining the criminal law to those fields of social control where its effective operation is of real importance is, we think, entirely clear," the report said, "and the possibility of effecting economies by son confining it appears to be substantial."

The commission's experts admitted, as did the Wickersham body itself, that even an estimate of the loss resulting from criminal acts was impossible to make.

Experts Stress Economic Factor.

"No one can say," Messrs. Dorr and Simpson asserted in their long, separate report, "how many 'rackets' are being operated today in New York or in Chicago or in St. Louis, much less compute the loss to the ultimate consumer resulting therefrom. No more can any one say how many fraudulent bankruptcies, insurance frauds or other fraudulent schemes are perpetrated in the United States annually, much less estimate the amount of loss to the victims of those schemes.

"But this should not blind us to the tremendous economic importance of these forms of criminal acts. We can recognize the immensity of loss due to these forms of crime even if we cannot measure it."

So Messrs. Dorr and Simpson contented themselves with a discussion of cost factors in crime, which they added to a rough calculation of the cost of criminal justice in the Federal organization and representative cities throughout the United States. Figures on Federal criminal justice showed, above all else, the enormous burden placed on the enforcement agencies by a few legislative acts. While prohibition enforcement consumed 66 per cent of the total expenditure, the attempted enforcement of the dry law together with the anti-narcotic and automobile thefts acts required 76.8 per cent of all funds allotted to Federal criminal justice.

The items of cost were listed as police, prosecution, courts, penal institutional treatment, probation and pardon. In all these various items of cost, the part traceable to prohibition enforcement was greater than all the others combined.

They presented certain indicative figures to show the substantial nature of crimes against property, showing that on the basis of experience for the last five years an average $1,800,000 is lost annually due to burglary and robbery of banks; $2,000,000 on account of burglary or robbery of jewelers and $1,100,000 annually due to thefts of freight from the railroads.

In statistics showing bank robberies and burglaries over the ten-year period from 1921 to 1930, the experts showed that the old-time yeggman or safe-cracker had given way in importance, whether because of modern safety devices or the natural evolution of American criminals, to the bolder "stick-up men."

From 1921 the number of burglaries and the amount of losses in such operations showed an almost constant decline, while the number of robberies and their attendant losses were constantly on the ascendency. The following table indicates the trend:

*Year	Burglaries No.	Loss.	Robberies No.	Loss.	Total Loss.
1921	220	$287,745	136	$936,752	$1,224,497
1922	261	249,301	145	905,669	1,154,970
1923	150	176,638	129	459,693	636,331
1924	104	264,528	236	1,074,456	1,338,984
1925	98	244,966	225	1,676,204	1,921,170
1926	54	248,869	203	1,345,235	1,594,104
1927	92	185,560	227	2,010,767	2,196,327
1928	70	156,999	292	1,762,703	1,919,702
1929	52	134,960	327	1,538,616	1,673,576
1930	40	102,694	402	2,003,391	2,106,085
Average	114	$205,226	232	$1,371,349	$1,576,575

*In each case the figures are for the 12-month period beginning on Sept. 1 of the previous calendar year.

Frauds a Large Factor.

The experts' report recalled that an investigation in New York had shown the importance of fraudulent bankruptcies as a factor in the cost of crime. While making no charge in the instance, the experts mentioned that for the five-year period ending June 30, 1929, the average annual excess of total liabilities over total amounts paid creditors in bankruptcy proceedings in the United States amounted to $762,876,688. Securities frauds, credit frauds, confidence games, forgery and counterfeiting, use of mails to defraud, in addition to racketeering, were listed by the experts as crimes with a direct cost factor which it was impossible even to estimate.

Racketeering had become of particular importance since the World War, the experts' report said, and most particularly with the era of prohibition, during which the growth of a link between the racketeer and law-enforcement officers through the payment of "protection" money has become most noticeable.

"The economic aspects of racketeering are of importance in this connection," said the Dorr-Simpson report, "since it is only because of the large profits of organized crime that the funds necessary for wholesale official corruption become available." The experts treated as a significant factor in the cost of crime, the retirement of criminals from productive activity. On the basis of prisoners now in penal institutions, with ample deductions made for their labors while incarcerated, it was estimated that the United States as a community lost annually about $87,000,000 from this factor.

Added to this was the sum of $235,000,000 which the experts estimate

the community has been losing annually by having 170,000 persons employed full time in law enforcement activities.

Recommendations of Experts.

Mr. Dorr and Mr. Simpson presented these, as well as all their other figures, as an argument for the general importance of the economic factor in crime, and not an attempt to establish an aggregate cost of criminal activities in the United States. From their study they had but five short recommendations to make.

"That appropriate steps be taken to develop accurate and annual comparative statistics as to the cost of administration of criminal justice by the Federal Government and by the several States and their municipal subdivisions; that the comparative study of muncipal costs of criminal justice, undertaken and partially completed by us, be finished; that a scientific study of commercialized fraud in all its aspects be made; that a similar study be made of racketeering and organized extortion, and that measures be taken to reduce, so far as practicable, the economic burden now imposed on jurors and witnesses in criminal cases."

"We believe," the report concluded, "that the carrying into effect of these recommendations, in addition to supplying important data as to the economic aspects of crime, will produce results of substantial value in dealing with important problems of law observance and enforcement.

"Of course, such recommendations merely touch the edge of the problem. The heart of it is in the human engineering required in fighting the development of the criminal and in aggressively seeking his rehabilitation."

August 22, 1931

GREAT SOCIAL TEST ENDS WITH REPEAL

Eighteenth Amendment, in Effect for 14 Years, Got Its Real Stimulus From War.

PROTESTED FROM START

Ratified Without People's Vote, It Added to Tax Burdens— Never Fully Enforced.

By RUSSELL B. PORTER.

Repeal of the Eighteenth Amendment means the end of one of the most far-reaching social experiments in the history of the world. It has lasted nearly fourteen years. Never before had there been such an attempt to regulate the habits and customs of a nation of 120,-

000,000 persons of such varied racial strains by sumptuary legislation. It was the first time the power of the Federal Government had been exercised to reach into the private lives and moral conduct of the people of the States on any such extensive scale.

National prohibition followed three-quarters of a century in which the States tried to regulate and control the liquor traffic by State and local option laws. At the time the Eighteenth Amendment went into effect State-wide prohibition was already in effect in thirty-three States, in eighteen of which it had been incorporated in the State Constitutions. Ninety per cent of the townships and rural precincts, 85 per cent of the counties, and 75 per cent of the villages were dry by State legislation. More than two-thirds of the population and 95 per cent of the land area of the United States were under prohibition.

Prohibitionists Not Satisfied.

State and local laws and the temperance campaigns that were conducted for many years in the wet areas did not satisfy the prohibitionists. They argued that tremendous social and economic advantages would follow national prohibition, that crime and insanity would be reduced, jails and insane asylums closed, workmen's pay envelopes diverted to food, clothing and other goods instead of the saloon; industry, trade and commerce stimulated by new buying power.

The Anti-Saloon League raised large campaign funds among members of the evangelical churches, who were devoted to the ideal of national prohibition on moral and social grounds, and among large industrialists and other capitalists who were convinced that it would increase the economic efficiency of the nation and of their own corporations. One of the most effective propaganda campaigns in the history of the country was organized.

The late Wayne B. Wheeler, general counsel for the Anti-Saloon League; the late Andrew J. Volstead, then Representative from Minnesota, and United States Senator Morris Sheppard of Texas were the outstanding leaders of the movement.

Beginning in 1911, when the proposal came before Congress, national prohibition grew in strength as an issue in nearly every year, slowly but surely. It might have taken many years to come to a head had not the World War given it a tremendous impetus through the desire to conserve grain supplies for food instead of alcohol, and to keep liquor from the soldiers. Coming then, when the interest of the nation was concentrated on the war and when millions of men were away in uniform, national prohibition was a sudden surprise and shock to many Americans.

Drafted by Senator Sheppard, the Eighteenth Amendment was submitted to the States by a vote of 65 to 20 in the United States Senate on Aug. 1, 1917, and a vote of 282 to 138 in the House of Representatives on Dec. 17, 1917. The first State to ratify was Mississippi, on Jan. 8, 1918. Nebraska became dry on Jan. 16, 1919, the thirty-sixth State to ratify, completing the three-fourths of the forty-eight States necessary to make ratification effective.

In the end, forty-six of the forty-eight States ratified the amendment, only Rhode Island and Connecticut refusing to do so. Ratification was accomplished by vote of the State Legislatures in the various States, rather than by popular vote in State conventions as specified in the Twenty-first (or repeal) Amendment. The official figures in the forty-eight State Senates were 1,310, or 84.6 per cent, for ratification to 237 against; in the Houses of Representatives, 3,782, or 78.5 per cent, for ratification to 1,035 against.

Meanwhile, on Nov. 21, 1918, ten days after the signing of the Armistice, Congress enacted the Wartime Prohibition Act, which remained in effect until the Eighteenth Amendment became effective, on Jan. 16, 1920, one year after ratification.

The Volstead Act, fixing one-half of 1 per cent by volume as the definition of the alcoholic content of an intoxicating beverage and providing for the enforcement of national prohibition, first as applied to the Wartime Prohibition Act and later the Eighteenth Amendment, was adopted by the Senate and House on Oct. 8 and 10, respectively, in 1919; vetoed by President Wilson on Oct. 27, and passed by Congress over his veto the following day.

The constitutionality of the Eighteenth Amendment and the Volstead Act was challenged, but was sustained in decisions of the United States Supreme Court on June 1 and 7, 1920. The highest court also held that the "concurrent power" granted to the States in the Eighteenth Amendment authorized them only to enforce prohibition, not to thwart or defeat it.

From the very beginning, country-wide protest was engendered by the Eighteenth Amendment and the Volstead Act. Not only were houses divided against each other but also churches, political parties, business organizations, social groups, whole communities. Prohibition became the most controversial issue in the United States since the Civil War.

Dr. Nicholas Murray Butler, president of Columbia University, took the lead among the intellectual, and Former Governor Alfred E. Smith of New York among the political, opponents of the Eighteenth Amendment. Both started early to fight it and carried their opposition consistently to the end, Dr. Butler going so far as to openly advocate revolt against it as utterly contradicting the spirit of the Constitution and the Bill of Rights, if it could not be repealed. Governor Smith split the Democratic party temporarily through his unsuccessful fight for the Presidential nomination in 1924 and his nomination in 1928, when he took a far more advanced stand against prohibition than other wets in his party were willing to take in those days, and when the party platform remained dry.

During the early years of the great experiment the opposition did not gain much headway. Aside from the extremist prohibition leaders, national prohibition had many supporters among such political leaders as Herbert Hoover and Senator William E. Borah, and such industrialists as Henry Ford, who believed that it was entitled to a fair trial in view of the theoretical advantages which would follow if it could be made to work.

No One Deprived of Drink.

With prosperity so great that taxes were not a burden and with bootlegging, rum-running and speakeasies so widespread that no one really was deprived of his favorite beverages, the general public remained more or less apathetic for several years as the prohibitionists pressed the Federal Government to more drastic enforcement activities and as unwholesome social trends developed in American life in consequence of the growing power of the underworld.

Enforcement was most effective in the first two years of prohibition—1920 and 1921—when the country was still under the influence of the wave of dry sentiment that had carried the Eighteenth Amendment into the Constitution. Forty-seven States, Rhode Island being the only exception, adopted State enforcement laws. New York adopted the Mullan-Gage Enforcement Act, but repealed it in 1923, the repealer being signed by Governor Smith despite warnings that it would end his political career.

Throughout the past ten years there has been a progressive disintegration of enforcement.

As the years passed it became apparent that national prohibition, instead of bringing great economic benefits to the country, was diverting billions of dollars from legitimate business channels and from the government's sources of tax revenues to criminal syndicates. Instead of creating a new and better social world, it was obviously bringing the underworld up to a position of such financial and political influence that it could corrupt officeholders and the police on an unprecedentedly broad scale; that it could engage in its private wars, killings, kidnappings, torturings, hijackings and shakedowns, in defiance of constituted authority; that its speakeasies were as bad or worse than the old saloon; that its minor henchmen and hirelings were crowding the courts and jails, and that its openly scandalous conduct was setting a bad example to the youth of the land, not only in excessive drinking, but also in general contempt for law and order.

Enforcement Brings Bloodshed.

Treaties with foreign nations enabling the Coast Guard to search rum runners flying foreign flags within the twelve-mile limit or one-hour run from the American coast, raids on distilleries and breweries, padlocking of speakeasies, seizures of automobiles and trucks loaded with liquor, pitched battles in which both dry agents and rum runners were killed, and thousands of arrests, fines and imprisonments, all figured in the unsuccessful effort to enforce national prohibition.

In 1926 General Lincoln C. Andrews, a retired army officer, appointed as Assistant Secretary of the Treasury to reorganize the enforcement system, asserted that the Volstead Act could not be enforced under existing conditions, that the prohibition agents did not seize more than one-tenth of the illicit stills in operation, and that from 12,000 to 15,000 men would be needed to patrol the borders to stop smuggling of liquor. Emory R. Buckner, then United States Attorney at New York, estimated that "reasonable enforcement" in New York State alone would cost more than $70,000,000 a year, seven times more than the enforcement appropriation for the whole country this year.

In 1929 and 1930 final efforts were made to solve the problem by more drastic enforcement. The Jones "Five-and-Ten" Act, passed by Congress and signed by President Coolidge, provided for five years' imprisonment and $10,000 fine for violations of the prohibition law. The theory was that violators would be frightened into compliance with the law: Greater efficiency in enforcement was expected from transferring the Prohibition Bureau from the Treasury Department to the Department of Justice. Both these efforts failed.

Tax Burden Increases.

As the depression deepened, bringing with it a larger tax burden in terms of a reduced national income, the effects of prohibition in the costs of enforcement and the sacrifice of large potential tax and customs revenues from the liquor industry came to the fore in public discussion in every State. Even in the former dry rural sections the demand became strong to legitimatize the liquor trade so that taxes upon it might relieve the tax burden upon industry, agriculture and the home, and so that a new industry might give impetus to business activity and employment.

At the same time the moral argument against prohibition gained weight with the publication of the Wickersham report in 1931. Of the eleven members of the Wickersham Commission, two favored repeal, seven revision, and only two retention of the Eighteenth Amendment. Moreover, the commission's investigation had confirmed the common knowledge of the failure of the prohibition experiment from the standpoint of social reform.

Last year was the crucial one in the fight against prohibition. The Democratic party put a repeal plank in its national platform and made repeal one of the leading issues of the campaign. John D. Rockefeller Jr. and other former supporters of prohibition among the capitalist and industrial leaders publicly reversed their position. The Association Against the Prohibition Amendment and the Women's Organization for National Prohibition Reform conducted nation-wide propaganda campaigns on almost as extensive a scale as the Anti-Saloon League's campaign for prohibition years ago, whereas last year the Anti-Saloon League made only comparatively feeble attempts to stem the tide.

The result of the election made it clear that the new Congress had a mandate from the people to repeal the Eighteenth Amendment. Even the old lame-duck Congress saw the handwriting on the wall, and voted to submit the repeal amendment to the States. The Senate voted 63 to 23 on Feb. 16, 1933, and the House 289 to 121 on Feb. 20.

Since then the ratification process has gone rapidly. Michigan was the first State to ratify, on April 3. New York voted on May 23. The thirty-third State to vote was Florida, on Oct. 10, which was the last vote before yesterday's repeal elections in six States.

Until yesterday not one State had voted against the repeal amendment, and all the thirty-three States which had voted had given large majorities to repeal except Tennessee, where the majority was about 7,000 out of about 245,000 votes cast.

BEER-RUNNING 'KING' IS SLAIN IN CHICAGO

Dion O'Bannion Is Murdered in His Florist Shop by Three Gunmen, Who Escape.

THEIR AIDS BLOCK TRAFFIC

Six Cars Used to Prevent Pursuit While Slayers' Car Dashes Safely Away.

Special to The New York Times.

CHICAGO, Nov. 10.—Dion O'Bannion, gunman and gang chief, often called "King of the Beer Runners," was shot to death today in his florist's shop at 738 North State Street. His body, pierced by six bullets, lay crumpled on the floor amid the American Beauties and chrysanthemums which he had used as a blanket of respectability to cover his underworld activities.

Two days ago O'Bannion had a new suit made with three special pockets in the trousers—two in front, one behind. Usually each held an automatic. One pocket also held an extra clip, inasmuch as O'Bannion seldom moved without enough ammunition to kill forty-five men if handled with accuracy.

But today he carried only one gun, and it was useless. His right hand, which had been cordially shaking that of one of the three murderers who shot him down, reached vainly for it. From the other hand clattered a pair of shears, for the underworld leader had been following his, daylight calling just before death—snipping stems from chrysanthemums to make funeral wreaths for Armistice Day.

And as the shears rattled to the floor there was a great crash, for O'Bannion's body slumped back into a big plate glass showcase in which reposed the most delicate of roses.

The three men whose guns had snuffed out the life of another of Chicago's gun leaders turned and dashed through the front door. They jumped into a dark colored, nickel trimmed car. At the wheel a fourth man stepped on the accelerator and the already running engine sputtered into a roar. A car behind quickly turned into the centre of the street. Two across State Street did likewise, thus protecting the murder car from traffic. On Superior Street cars from either side of State Street swung up to the corner, blocked other cars and let the killers dash west on Superior and turn south on Dearborn. The six cars which had—by seeming accident—blocked all cars but it, leisurely got back into their proper direction, tooted their horns and drove slowly away.

Tonight special squads of police speeded through the west side searching for the murderers.

"There'll be more murder," said a veteran detective. "More murder, and it will come quick."

Beer and whisky running was the commonly accepted murder background, but politics came in for its share of gossip. O'Bannion stepped out on election day with 200 sluggers, reports go, and helped the Forty-second Ward, normally Democratic, to go Republican by three to one.

William Critchfield, colored, the dead man's porter, is being questioned by the police.

UNDERWORLD POMP AT BURIAL OF CHIEF

1,000 Autos and 26 Truckloads of Flowers Follow O'Banion's $10,000 Coffin in Chicago.

CROOKS PARK THEIR GUNS

Scores of Police Move About Fearing Move for Revenge, but There Is Little Disorder.

Special to The New York Times.

CHICAGO, Nov. 14.—Twenty-six truck loads of flowers, 1,000 automobiles and more than 10,000 persons were at the cemetery today for the funeral of Dion O'Banion, 32-year-old ruler of the Chicago underworld, king of hijackers and, according to the Chief of Police of Chicago, the director of at least twenty-five murders.

Detectives moved on foot through the crowds, mounted policemen trotted among them and uniformed men with guns rode in automobiles, ready for trouble if any one attempted to carry out the threats of revenge which have been made since last Monday when O'Banion was shot down while trimming chrysanthemums in his flower shop, which masked his deals in whisky and lives.

There was reason to be on the alert every minute, for the mortal enemies, as well as the followers of young O'Banion, were at the funeral. Every gang was represented. Hijackers and bootleggers dressed in mourning and rode side by side in the same limousines. It was recognized by gangmen, gunmen, all factions of the liquor traffic and all groups which have trouble with the police as an occasion for forgetting old hates and doing honor to the greatest representative of their general class.

Cathedral Doors Barred.

To the great grief of the family and friends of O'Banion, the doors of the Holy Name Cathedral, where he had served as an altar boy, were closed against the funeral. The services in town were held at an undertaker's chapel which would hold only 100 persons. The $10,000 silver coffin was buried under masses of flowers. The benches seated the widow, the father, other relatives, the close followers of O'Banion and leaders of other gangs.

The master of ceremonies at the funeral was Louis Altiere, O'Banion's pal and lieutenant. Before the room filled up Altiere, in a purple collar and frock coat, a sheaf of lilies of the valley at the lapel, touched his eyes with a handkerchief of dashing pattern and rearranged the flowers in order to give a better effect to the floral tribute of the widow—a pillar seven feet high, made of 2,000 red roses.

"Now play," he whispered, behind a gloved hand, when the pallbearers and other principal mourners had deposited their revolvers with friends and filled the room.

Behind the flowers a stringed orchestra struck up a hymn. The windows of the chapel were thrown up so that the thousands outside could hear the slow and solemn music which was drawn from the stringed instruments by some of the most accomplished jazz artists of Chicago. The crowds in the streets doffed their hats. When the hymn music reached the roof-tops, hundreds of other heads were bared. Such was the demand for space that profiteers charged a dollar a head for the right to see the funeral from the adjacent roofs.

Police Battle to Control Crowd.

Hymn after hymn was played. There was no other service. When the sad music ended the funeral cortege started. The police battled to keep back the crowd which scrambled down from the roofs and rushed for their automobiles.

At the cemetery more than 500 automobiles were parked before the long funeral procession arrived. The services continued quietly until photographers were noticed unlimbering their machines on knolls near the grave. There was a rush for them. Cameras and plates were smashed. Photographers were hustled out of the cemetery.

This outbreak was partly intended as a tribute to O'Banion, for the photographers were looked on as a symbol of the hostile outside world. It was partly selfish on the part of the plate-smashers, as many of them could not afford to have their pictures printed because of the danger that somebody might recognize them.

Thousands of those at the cemetery hate the camera worse than the Bertillon system. When the photographic menace had been ended everything was quiet. From the twenty-six trucks an acre was covered with floral pieces with pious and sentimental inscriptions in violets and forget-me-nots. The biggest of them was a seven-foot wall of carnations bearing in gigantic letters the words: "To our pal—from the gang." Amid sobs from hundreds the splendid coffin was slowly lowered into the grave.

Mayor Dever, incensed by the great publicity given to the challenge of O'Banion's followers to "shoot you out" with the rival gangs which are believed responsible for the murder of O'Banion, directed today that every known gunman in the city be searched for arms.

"It is time," he said, "to determine whether organized outlaws shall continue to shoot and rob with impunity or whether decency and order will prevail."

The police at once began putting the order into effect.

CHICAGO SEEKS HELP TO CHECK CRIME

Gangs Linked With Political Plot to Hush Murder and Bootlegging

By GEORGE P. STONE.

CHICAGO.

ONE muggy night in the Fall of 1919 five obscure Chicago hoodlums "stuck up" a beer truck on a shore road north of Chicago. It was the easiest "job" the five had tackled in their careers as jack-rollers and stick-up men. The truck driver, a flabby rustic from Kenosha, Wis., gave up his load of beer without a squeak of protest and dusted back toward home on the dead run. Prohibition laws were regarded with awe in those days, and the driver did not linger near his beer.

The five hoodlums took the beer to a Chicago saloon keeper. He had none of the stinginess that is second nature to fences, but paid handsomely. Dion O'Banion—who performed sometimes as a singing waiter, sometimes as a safe blower—and his four buddies were set thinking by the unexpected yield of the adventure. Thus it happened that they embraced hijacking as a profession, and a kind of crime, new to Chicago, was born.

That new kind of crime has grown into something like an industry since then. Because of it a reform league, the Better Government Association of Chicago and Cook County, recently petitioned the Senate of the United States for an investigation of law enforcement in Cook County, charging that a conspiracy between crime and politics is shielding murder, robbery and bootlegging. The petition has enlivened local politics and is setting Chicago off on another of those stock-takings that are recurrent in large cities.

Two Classes of Crime.

The stocktaking shows that prohibition has divided crime in Chicago into two major classes. In the one class are the murders, robberies and various misdeeds of bootlegging and beer-running gangs. In the other class are the private crimes, so to speak, of persons not engaged in the industry of breaking the Volstead act.

In detecting, prosecuting and punishing those guilty of crimes in the second class the law enforcement machinery of Cook County shows increasing efficiency. The burglary rate is diminishing. Payroll robberies, street-corner stickups, arson and other once popular crimes are less numerous than in previous years. The Loeb-Leopold case, the current affair of Martin Durkin, and other recent murder prosecu-

tions reflect a zeal that has moved the Chicago Crime Commission to congratulate the Police Department, the State's Attorney's office and the Criminal Court of Cook County.

On the other side of the dividing line law enforcement is strikingly different. Since O'Banion and his four pals did their pioneering more than fifty men have been killed in the war of gangs for control of the several "rackets" of the bootlegging industry in Chicago. Most of the murders are down in the records as "unsolved mysteries." The underworld attributes each killing to one gang or another, but there have been no convictions. Indeed, indictments have not been voted in more than a dozen of the murder cases.

A Street Fight.

Two recent cases that ought perhaps to be counted as exceptions nevertheless show the weakness of the law. One is the case of two men captured in a street fight between four members of the notorious Genna Gang and a detective squad, in which Mike Genna and two policemen were killed. The two captured survivors were indicted and tried. In court they admitted having fired shotguns in the fight, but said they thought the police were rival gangsters. A jury let them off with fourteen years each.

In the other case a wool-witted tough shot a rival gangster to death at a Coroner's inquest into the murder of his brother. Twenty-six years in prison was his sentence.

Highway robbery, burglary and assault by members of bootlegging gangs also have gone unpunished if not unprosecuted. Although the names, habits and crimes of the more eminent gangsters are well known to all Chicago newspaper readers, not one of them has been convicted of anything in the State courts since the bootlegging industry became established. For some reason—public tolerance of bootlegging gangsters' political usefulness, graft or a combination of all three influences—criminals engaged in organized violation of the Volstead act have practical immunity from prosecution, so far as the courts of Cook County are concerned, even when they kill or steal.

Dion O'Banion in his heyday shot a rival in front of a "Loop" theatre, just as the theatre was emptying. He was not arrested for days and never

was prosecuted. The same eminent gangster and a pal who hasn't yet gone the road to the graveyard were caught by a police squad one noon in the act of hijacking a truckload of booze in a downtown street. The case was dropped in a police court.

Terry Druggan and Frank Lake, whose confessed bribery of the Cook County jail staff came to light last Fall, made beer and sold it for two years without arrest, in spite of repeated newspaper "exposés." Not until Federal agents went after them were they molested. They have admitted since to internal revenue agents that they cleared more than $1,000,000 each.

The notorious Genna brothers' activities as wholesalers of alcohol and whisky were described frequently and in detail in Chicago newspapers for months before rivals began to knock off the brothers with shotguns. They were neither arrested nor indicted.

Fund For Corruption.

Charles C. Fitzmorris, who was Superintendent of Police in Chicago during the infancy of the bootlegging industry, declared once that he believed a majority of his men were taking money from beer runners and bootleggers. Morgan A. Collins, the present Chief, said not long ago that he has reason to think that gangsters and promoters back of them were spending $1,000,000 a year on corruption of the police force when he took office.

The Better Government Association's petition to the Senate asserted flatly that important politicians are getting money from protected gangsters. That assertion has many echoes, though substantial proof is lacking. Others, including most politicians in office, hold that only the lower orders of officialdom are getting money.

Another influence that has hindered law enforcement in Chicago is the unwillingness of the gangster to cooperate with police or courts in any way, even against his worst enemies in the underworld. Hoodlums who are shot at do not tell the police about the shooting. They prefer accomplishing their own revenges. They will kill a rival, but won't "squawk" against him.

The police, moreover, find it increasingly difficult to use old fashioned methods of extracting information from criminals. Hoodlums who were down at the heel five years ago now patronize boulevard tailors and speak as casually of "ten grand" as they used to speak of dimes. They command the services of smart criminal lawyers and it is dangerous to use the third degree on a man who has a lawyer ready to "spring" him on a writ of habeas corpus five minutes after the door of the "goldfish room" has swung to.

Prohibition Enforcers Unpopular.

Account must be taken, too, of the attitude of the public toward the Volstead act. Prohibition enforcers are as popular in some parts of Chicago as German tax collectors would be.

If politicians are right in figuring that 75 per cent. of Chicago's vote would be "wet" today, it is inevitable that juries' verdicts, policemen's conduct and office-holders' policies should be affected.

Finally, the gangster is politically useful. When judges of elections are to be intimidated, or "repeating" 's necessary, or ballot boxes must be stolen, there is no device like the old-fashioned hoodlum gang. Laying aside the charges of connivance between political leaders and gang chieftains for the money that is to be got by running beer and booze, the political unity of the gang is enough to make for complaisance on the part of office-holders.

Whatever the cause, the secret wars of the gangs for control of district markets continue. A drive by Mayor Dever against "cheating" breweries in the Fall of 1923 caused a brief interruption. A campaign against alien gunmen is keeping things quiet right now. But such things pass.

The struggle of the gangs began soon after the epochal stick-up by O'Banion and his "mob" on the North Shore back in 1919. It has been unceasing and savage. According to Chief Collins, it is an expression of the hoodlums "tuxedo complex," a post-prohibition acquisition.

"There wern't half as many killers among criminals in the old days," he says. "Toughs used brass knuckles or blackjacks, or just their fists in settling arguments, most of the time. Their quarrels were over women, or personalities, not over opportunities to commit crime.

"But conditions have changed. Hoodlums that used to sleep on benches half the time have suites in lake-front hotels now. They have their hands manicured and dress for dinner. They don't like to fight with their fists any more. If one of them finds somebody in his way, he kills him. 'Aw bump the double asterisk off!' is the watchword nowadays."

Johnny Mahoney, one of O'Banion's partners in the first recorded hijacking, was the first notable to be killed in the gang war. He was found shot to death in a West Side alley one April morning in 1921. O'Banion was credited with the killing. Mahoney, the underworld said, had talked too much.

Avoids Wrath of His Chief.

Six months later Frederick Shope, another of the five men in the original "mob," was shot. He lived nine days, then, in the grip of some unknown fear, killed himself.

By 1923 O'Banion alone was left of the five. Johnny Sheehy had been killed in a café fight; Tom Sweeney, former policeman, had "taken it on the lam" to avoid the wrath of his chief for some unknown offense. With new partners, of whom "Dapper Dan" McCarthy was chief, O'Banion turned from his hijacking to bootlegging and thence to an alliance with John Torrio, head of a syndicate that controlled beer running, vice and gambling in the country towns of Cook County and held a few district monopolies in Chicago.

In defense of one of those monopolies, Torrio and the gangsters in his syndicate fought a memorable "beer war" with the notorious brothers O'Donnell in the Fall of 1923. The O'Donnells, drawing beer from suburban breweries, wanted to cut in on the saloon business "back o' the yards." Four O'Donnell men had been killed, a dozen saloonkeepers had been bombed or slugged, and Mayor Dever's brewery crusade was in full swing before the O'Donnells withdrew.

A year later shotguns told of a break between O'Banion and Torrio. O'Banion, who had become wealthy enough to mask his gang activities behind a smart flower business, was shot to death in one of his shops in

November, 1924. The killing was attributed to Torrio. The actual killer, the underworld said, was one of a family named Genna, of growing influence in the alcohol industry.

Distilleries in "Little Italy."

After the death of O'Banion the Gennas increased in power. A year ago, according to survivors of the crash of their organization, they were operating fifteen basement distilleries in "Little Italy," from which they sold alcohol in truck-load lots.

Then O'Banion's heirs in gangland began striking back. Angelo, one of the Genna brothers, was shot to death from his quarters in a Parkside hotel in a new limousine. A month later, after a street fight with gang enemies, Mike Genna and three retainers collided with a police squad. Mike and two policemen were killed. Before another month had passed, Tony, a third brother, was shot to death.

Since the passing of the Gennas five Italian gangsters have been murdered, mysteriously, in a struggle for control of the brothers' lost monopolies.

But in the meantime Frank McOrlane, a one-time follower, has driven Torrio and his gang out of the South Side. Since last Summer the McOrlane gang has killed six enemies. The O'Donnell crowd, rehabilitated, now stands challengingly in the way again. Another outbreak of gang war threatens there.

Until recently the Chicago public, like most publics, accepted these outbreaks as things apart from politics. A few weeks ago, however, some one unearthed a copy of the "official photograph" of a dinner given by a company of Italian-Americans in October, 1924, in honor of State's Attorney Robert E. Crowe, then a candidate for re-election. In the photograph appear the faces of two of the Genna brothers and two of the putative successors murdered since January of this year. Jim Genna, head of his clan, is seated at the speakers' table. He was one of the principal promoters of the banquet, it has developed. Another face in the photograph is that of John Scalise, one of the two Genna gangsters killed in the fight that was Mike Genna's last stand.

CHICAGO'S RUM RUNNERS TELL NO TALES

They Slay With Impunity, but Give the Police No Clues—Five Strong Bootleg Gangs Are Now Active in and Near the City—A Dozen Lesser "Mobs"

By GEORGE F. STONE.

FOUR gunmen held up two beer runners at midnight on the lonely Sag Road, south of Chicago. Two of the four hustled the captives into an open automobile; the others drove off with the beer. The open car raced in toward Chicago at sixty miles an hour. One of the hijackers sat at the wheel; the other leaned over the back of the driver's seat, holding a sawed-off shotgun under the beer runners' noses.

At a place where the road runs between thickets the man with the shotgun nonchalantly emptied one barrel into a prisoner's chest and neck, then unhurriedly let the other barrel go at the second man. As the bodies slid to the floor of the car the killer climbed over the seat and opened the doors. The driver kept roaring along the black road. Two kicks sent the bodies sprawling into gutter ditches.

One body was lifeless. The other somehow held a spark strong enough to endure a painful crawl over a plowed field to a farmer's door.

"Who did it?" the police asked six weeks later, when the body miraculously had become a man again.

"Nix," said the beer runner. "Don't bother me. I ain't talking."

Knew but Wouldn't Tell.

The police knew who did it. There was circumstantial evidence. But when the survivor refused to talk, indictments based on the circumstantial case were nol prossed.

The six-foot Irish leader of an "outlaw" gang, a gang existing furtively in another "mob's" territory, stood at a south-side business corner, chatting with a newsboy.

"Oh, Spike," some one called from the street. The big fellow looked up into the muzzle of a rifle, thrust through the drawn curtains of a car. He flung the newsboy to the sidewalk and then dropped on top of him as the rat-tat-tat of an automatic rifle sent passersby running for shelter. Bullets fanned his coattails and left a neat horizontal design in the wall of the drug store behind him, but he wasn't hurt.

"Do you know who did it?" a friendly reporter asked him.

"Sure I do," he replied. "I could see Dash and Blank through the curtains. Those double-starred, asterisked hyphens have tried to bump me off twice this week."

Chicago's Happy Hollow Saloon. Capone, the Man at the Left, Is the Reputed Head of a Rum Syndicate.

But when the police questioned him he said, "Beat it! I ain't talking."

It happens again and again. Dead men tell no tales, the outlaws of other days boasted. In Chicago gangland none tell tales, dead or alive. Those who try talking don't talk long. An Indiana man, for instance, made the mistake of identifying a Chicago gangster whom he had seen in the act of murder. The night before the trial he was clubbed to death, almost under the walls of the courthouse in his home town.

Gangs Are Rum Syndicate.

The gangs that maintain this strange unity against the law even while fighting each other are not gangs in the pre-Prohibition sense of the word. They are syndicates selling beer and alcohol at wholesale to bootleggers and cheating saloons. They are made up for the most part of former highwaymen and youngsters who would have been highwaymen if born a decade earlier.

The wars of the gangs are nothing more than ordinary commercial competition, in new terms. Where the salesmen of a business house rely on a good selling talk, the reputation of the firm, and ready smiles, the bootleg gangsters rely on a good selling talk, the reputation of a "mob," and ready guns. Shifts of allegiance aren't uncommon. One gang may hire the star salesman of another. Only a little while ago, according to underworld gossip, the sprightliest killer of a powerful south-side gang was offered "twenty grand" to work temporarily for a north-side gang that was having trouble with over-active competition.

At present there are five strong bootleg gangs in and near Chicago and perhaps a dozen lesser "mobs." The little fellows don't count for much. They are the bootleggers of bootleggery, the "gyps" of this new industry. Now and then one of the "pirates" is bumped off, but most of the fighting is among the "big five."

The five have the Chicago market divided. Each has its territory, its list of customers. Occasionally one encroaches on the field of another. Then the sawed-off shotguns and the automatic rifles settle the dispute. William H. McSwiggin, the assistant State's Attorney whose murder has aroused public feeling in Chicago against this unchecked gang warfare, was the innocent victim of such a "settlement," the police believe. Gangsters he was riding with had intruded upon the market of rivals.

Each Gang a Monopoly.

John Torrio and "Scarface Al" Capone, once divekeepers in the old levee district, are heads of the foremost syndicate. Their field is outside the city limits. Cicero, on the west side, is their stronghold; they operate also in towns on the extreme south side, near the Indiana line.

The most powerful "mob" is entrenched on Chicago's southwest side. Frank McErlane, an ex-convict credited with a dozen murders, and Polack Joe Saltis, another seasoned gunman, are the leaders. Their men-at-heel are the toughest, most ruthless gang in the lot.

Two cousins O'Donnell, Myles and Klondike, are the captains of a gang that controls the "racket" on the west side up to the Cicero line. Willie Druggan, brother of the celebrated Terry, is listed by the underworld as one of the O'Donnells' associates.

In the heterogeneous Maxwell Street district, where the Genna brothers were supreme before rivals' shotguns blew them out of business, the cocks of the walk are Maxie Eisen, Little Hymie Weiss, Dapper Dan McCarthy and other pals of the late Dion O'Banion. They are the buckos who outshot the Gennas last Summer.

The fifth important mob has an ex-convict known as Schemer Drucci and other city friends of Torrio and Capone as leaders. It operates on the north side.

Weird Warning to Sheldon.

The line-ups and territorial claims of the "big five" are common knowledge. The Chicago newspapers contrive to keep informed; the police unhesitatingly pronounce the latest murder "a Torrio job" or "a McErlane bump-off," as the case may be, and sketch the reasons. But except for temporary fade-outs the gangsters go about their business. Their common reticence is a protection. Political alliances help, too. All of the headliners were active in the recent primary campaign.

Of late the Torrio-Capone, O'Donnell and McErlane-Saltis guns have been busiest. The others haven't had trouble, or are lying low.

McErlane and his side-kick, Saltis, are considered responsible for the most ghoulish of the thirty murders committed by gangsters in Cook County since Jan. 1, although the police can't quite verify their suspicions. They have been fighting a crew headed by Ralph Sheldon, an ex-convict, formerly associated with them. A few weeks ago a neighbor asked the police to remove an automobile that had been standing at Sheldon's door for several days. Two traffic policemen called and began writing into their notebooks a description of the machine. They got as far as "contents" and then legged it for the nearest telephone. Inside the car were the bodies of two men subsequently identified as minor deputies of Sheldon. They had been killed, it developed, while delivering alcohol at the saloon of a former McErlane customer. By way of warning their bodies were left at Sheldon's door.

The McErlane gang has disposed of half a dozen other men in less than a year, the police say. The hangouts of the gang are saloons on the southwest side. In raiding one of them a month ago a Detective Bureau squad got six men with long criminal records and a wagon load of shotguns and pistols. From another headquarters, a wagon yard, the police took dynamite, fuses, slug shells for shotguns, steel vests and a great store of beer, one day last Fall.

Live in Style.

The Torrio-Capone syndicate is less crude. When Chicago policemen, deputized for duty outside the city limits, went looking for Capone in connection with the McSwiggin murder they found his Cicero apartment that of a man of means and taste. Hangings and furnishings were really fine, although a bit too florid for most men's liking. In the cellar were good wines, instead of the "needled" beer of the McErlane hangouts.

But when one of the policemen tried to tune in on Capone's expensive-looking radio set he found the common denominator. The panel came off, revealing a short-barreled shotgun, some pistols and accessories for one of the automatic rifles now popular in gangland.

Torrio, Capone's chief, is a New Yorker. The Five Points gang of New York gave him his start. "Big Jim" Colosimo engaged him fifteen years ago as a bodyguard. Torrio was a silent, fearless, capable lad. Colosimo gave him more and more trust. Then Colosimo fell in love with a cabaret singer. The better to do his courting he made Torrio his business agent. By the time "Big Jim" had divorced his wife and married the singer, Torrio had no

one between him and absolute lordship in the levee but the chief himself. They found Colosimo's body in an office back of the famous Colosimo Café. The killer never was identified. Torrio stepped into "Big Jim's" shoes.

Prohibition His Opportunity.

Reform drove Colosimo's successor out of the city after a while. He established himself first as the owner of a string of disreputable roadhouses in the State-line suburbs. Then prohibition made him the most powerful of all the wholesale bootleggers, and he extended his field to include wide-open Cicero.

Except for brief activity on the south side, where he won a savage beer war in 1923, at the cost of a resolute crusade by Mayor Dever against beer running, Torrio has confined himself pretty well to Cicero since then. Vice, gambling and booze "rackets" out there are his and Capone's. Eddie Tancl, ex-prizefighter and saloonkeeper, challenged the Torrio-Capone rule for awhile. He was killed two years ago.

Torrio and Capone have relied on hired killers, most of them from New York, for their sales campaigns. Recently, the police say, they brought a crew of professional gunmen from the east to check the steady invasion of the O'Donnell gang into Cicero territory. All suspicious-looking cars entering Cicero from Chicago at night were stopped by the Torrio gunmen, according to Captain John Stege of the Detective Bureau. Flivvers and other cheap cars weren't molested, but all machines expensive enough to be owned by gangsters were searched. The gang was determined to keep the O'Donnells out of the suburb.

Tragic Salesmanship.

The O'Donnells, on the other hand, were resolved not to let the city limits stop them. They had won over several Torrio customers, it has developed since then, and were after more.

One night the two O'Donnells made flying calls on some of their trade, accompanied by "Jimmy" Doherty and "Red" Duffy, members of their gang, and, for reasons not yet clear, Assistant State's Attorney McSwiggin. Outside the saloon of a man who had switched from Torrio to O'Donnell beer they were waylaid by killers with an automatic rifle. Doherty, Duffy and McSwiggin were killed. The O'Donnells escaped, wounded, and have not been found.

Though convinced that the Torrio-Capone gang did the killing, the police have been unable to uncover a single piece of direct evidence. Torrio and Capone have vanished. The O'Donnells can't be located. And all others picked up for questioning give the same old answer:

"Nix! I ain't talking."

CHICAGO KILLERS HIDDEN FROM POLICE

No Trace Found of Them— Capone Mourns 'Butchery,' Wants War to End.

CHICAGO, Oct. 12 (Æ).—Silence to-night shrouded the identity of the machine gunners who yesterday mowed down five men as the latest deed in the war of extermination between rival gang factions for control of Chicago's liquor traffic.

Every gangster has gone into retirement, leaving the police without a clue to the identity of the men who operated a machine gun last night from an apartment building window opposite Holy Name Cathedral on North State Street, killing "Hymie" Weiss and Paddy Murray, leaders of one gang faction, and wounding W. W. O'Brien, well-known criminal lawyer, and two of Weiss's associates.

It was reported during the day that the police had ferreted out the hiding place of "Scarface" Al Capone, powerful leader of the faction opposing Weiss, and had questioned him. The police, however, would not admit this and Capone was not in custody.

Law enforcement authorities were confident that it was the result of some ramificatio of the two-year-old gang feud, but frankly admitted they were unable to find a trace of the slayers and were likewise powerless to stop a reopening of the machine-gun battle, which they believe imminent.

In a meagerly furnished room Al ("Scarface") Capone, who is reputed to have made millions in beer trans-actions, told his version tonight of gangland feuds in Chicago to a Herald and Examiner reporter.

Capone, whose name has been mentioned in connection with the latest outbreak of gang vengeance, and with others of the past, denounced what he termed the "butchery" and told of repeated attempts at peace, declaring that "there's enough business for all of us without killing each other like animals in the street."

"I've got a boy," Caponi, who is 27 years old, to'd the reporter, showing a photograph of a seven-year-old child. "I love the kid more than anything in the world and next to him I love his mother and then my own mother and my sisters and brothers. I don't want to die. Especially I don't want to die in the street, punctured with machine gun fire.

"That's the reason I've asked for peace. I've begged those fellows to put away their pistols and talk sense home. They've all got families, too. Most of them are kids and haven't got any children of their own, but they've got mothers and sisters.

"What makes them so crazy to end up on a slab in a morgue, with their mothers' hearts broken over the way they died, I don't know. I've tried to find out but I can't. I know I've tried since the first pistol was drawn in this fight to show them that there's enough business for all of us without killing each other like animals in the street, but they don't see it.

"I read in the papers that Hymie Weiss' mother was coming here from New York for his funeral. I know that sweet old lady. She's a wonderful mother. When Hymie was in business with us, many's the night I slept in his house and ate at his table. Why didn't he use some sense and keep out of this shooting stuff?"

Capone, who came here seven years ago from Brooklyn, said that gang shootings started when gunmen, who had come into the beer game at the request of his partners, broke away after they had made a little money, set up for themselves and then started acts of aggression.

October 13, 1926

SCORES INTOLERANCE OF DRY LAW LEADERS

Judge Lindsey Sees in It Menace to the Country—He Favors "Sensible" Modification.

Special Correspondence of THE NEW YORK TIMES.

SALT LAKE CITY, Nov. 19.—Ben Barr Lindsey, quondam Judge of the juvenile court at Denver, has provoked not a little discussion by a statement made in Salt Lake, during a lecture tour, in which he came out flat-footedly as an opponent of the present prohibition system—though he did not offer any very definite substitute. He is still an enemy of the saloon as it was in its palmy days; but he believed "prohibition" as it has worked out is a menace, instead of a blessing.

"I worked for prohibition in season and out of season," the author and lecturer confessed. "I still am against the old-time saloon, and its corrupting influences. But I have been terribly disappointed with prohibition.

"It never has been enforced, and I doubt that it ever will be enforced. As matters stand, we are creating a great deal of lawlessness, because young people know that we are preaching one thing and practicing another. This is having a demoralizing effect upon the youth of the nation, and bringing laws generally into disrespect. Young men and young women are becoming cynical, because they know what hypocrites we are and what conventional lies we are telling them. There is great danger in this situation and it seems to me the time has come for consideration of some sort of sensible modification.

"Among the great dangers with which this country is threatened because of prohibition is the intolerance of certain leaders of the Anti-saloon League and pastors of churches. They say that men who favor modification of the prohibition law are not fit to hold public office. It is bigotry when they oppose in this way men who happen to differ with them in their extreme views about prohibition. Their intolerance is a new stake for the heretics, whom they would burn if they dared."

November 20, 1927

ILLINOIS GANG FIGHTS KEEP CITIZENS AT HOME

Liquor Runners' Warfare Drives Law-Abiding Men Off the Roads at an Early Hour.

MARION, Ill., Oct. 31 (Æ).—A back-to-the-fireside movement has been inaugurated by the law abiding citizens of Williamson, Franklin and Saline Counties as a result of the renewal of warfare between bootleg gangs.

Night driving over Illinois' famous hard roads in this section of the Southern Illinois coal belt is an occupation engaged in almost solely by gang members. The presence of armored cars and armed gangsters has sent many traveling salesmen over nearly forgotten detours.

That citizens have not been convinced of their safety, even after numerous statements from the Birger and Shelton factions that innocent bystanders would not be killed, is evidenced by drawn shades and early retiring.

More townsmen than usual are 'oag along with their wives and children to picture shows at night and returning home with them to tune in on radio programs, or perhaps to pop corn or make candy.

"The men certainly are becoming domesticated," a local theatre manager remarked, after a check-up of a number of men who are seen escorting their families to shows instead of congregating, as usual, in front of the courthouse or on street corners.

Few persons think that bringing State militia back to these counties would mean more than temporary relief unless the troops had orders to clean up every wide-open gambling and bootlegging house and disarm all gangsters.

Unfavorable criticism centres largely against the law enforcement bodies, although the fact that Sheriff George Galligan of Williamson County, has only one deputy has turned the fire away from him.

Galligan further has said that deputizing townsmen is a failure because they have too many excuses for not being able to accompany him on raids.

There is faith in the ability of national guardsmen. No one denies they could handle the situation and the hope commonly expressed is that the State will take a hand in the gang warfare and settle it permanently.

There are those who believe the war is not a serious one, but one that is being carried on with enough boldness to keep the public off the highways and officials in the background to allow undisturbed transportation of liquor.

The policy of more talk and less action between the warring gangsters within the last few days is beginning to restore confidence in many. They feel that the gangster who threatens and bellows is less dangerous than the quiet but more business-like outlaw of former years.

November 1, 1926

CHICAGO GANGSTERS SEIZED IN NEW WAR

One of Three Arrested at Largest Police Station Tries to Shoot Way Out.

MURDER PLOTS REVEALED

Two Killers Wait in Courtroom for "Scarface" Capone, but He Fails to Appear.

CHICAGO, Nov. 21 (Æ).—Rival Chicago gangsters, opening a new war of extermination for gambling supremacy, today carried their feud to the doors of Chicago's largest police station, where it was nipped by the authorities, who for two days have been making a desperate effort to prevent the crack of gangsters' pistols and the roar of their sawed-off shotguns.

A series of raids of machine and shot gun nests by the police last night to frustrate an assassination plot believed directly aimed against Al "Scarface" Capone, notorious gangster, culminated today in the arrest outside the South Park Street Police Station of three armed men, believed to have been Capone's bodyguards, and the unsuccessful attempt of one of them to shoot his way out of the office of William O'Connor, Chief of Detectives.

After questioning the three men, the police said they had obtained information that there had been a plot to kill Capone when he appeared in court today, and that two killers were in the courtroom actually waiting for him. The police said, however, that he did not appear, despite statements of his attorney that he had been there and left.

To night the police with orders to round up all known gangsters were searching the city for them.

"It is very fortunate there has been no murder today in the Detective Bureau of the city's largest police station," said Chief O'Connor. "We won't follow the old plan of letting them fight it out. The next flareup is going to bring police pistols to serve as extinguishers."

Incensed over the brazen effrontery of the gangsters, O'Connor ordered the formation of ten machine-gun squads to drive the gangsters from the streets. He ordered every detective in his department to view the men in custody.

"These are the type of men to hunt for," the Chief said. "When you give chase to gangs like this riding in a car, I hope to go out and find he ton of their car shot off with most of the men in it dead."

All the men in custody, including the three Capone bodyguards, were handcuffed together and Chief O'Connor said he intended to keep them standing all night so his men could view them.

"At least. we'll persecute them if we can't keep them in jail," he added.

The latest feud. the police said. is a result of the efforts of the remnants of the old O'Banion-Weiss-Drucci gang. which turned from liquor running to gain a foothold in the gambling world.

The assassination plot was revealed last week, when an arsenal was found in a rooming house across the street from the home of Antonio Lombardo. head of the Unione Siciliana. the largest Italian fraternal order in Chicago. of which Capone also is a leader. Several arrests were made. and last night. in a downtown hotel. across the street from a cigar store frequented by Capone and Lombardo. police found a second nest of rifles and shotguns trained on the store.

Half a dozen gangsters, mostly Italian. were arrested. and Capone. called to the station to try to identify them. refused to do so. Police booked Capone on a technical charge of disorderly conduct. Sam Martin, alias Samuel Marcus of New York. one of Capone's alleged bodyguard. tried to shoot his way out of the Detective Bureau, where he was being questioned. He was overpowered, however. Another was identified as Tony ("Little New York") Campagni. exconvict and convicted bank robber.

Shortly afterward Andy Aiello and Tony Calafora were arrested outside a Criminal Court room. As the man were arrested an automobile with shotguns protruding from its sides was driven rapidly away from the building. The police said the three Aiello brothers, attempting to supplant Lombardo and Capone in control of the Italian society. have been directing the feud against this faction.

CHICAGO FIRM MAKES GUNMAN A PARTNER

Old Business Concern Takes In Scarface Al Capone as a Protector.

DESPAIRED OF POLICE AID

Gangsters Enlisted as Employes and War in the Cleaning Industry Is Expected.

Special to The New York Times.

CHICAGO, May 27.—Chicago business men are becoming dismayed at the impotency of the city's prosecutive forces and one of them has taken a gangster leader into partnership to guard him. As a result rival underworld gunmen are arraying their forces for war.

Alphonse Capone, the same "Scarface Al" who not long ago was the "king" of the city's bootleggers and vice lords. has been adopted by the cleaners and dyers' business. according to information from the Employers' Association of Chicago. Capone is the invited partner of a leading business man who for years fought the threats. violence and extortions of racketeers.

In consequence there is a possibility of an internecine struggle in the cleaners and dyers' trade, and it is for this, according to G. L. Hostetter. Secretary of the employers' association. that the gangsters are drawn up for battle.

Capone now appears as a principal partner in the Sanitary Cleaning Shops, Inc. The patron of big business introducing Scarface Al is Morris Becker. for forty-two years a leading dyer and cleaner in Chicago.

Gunmen Enlisted as Employes.

Mr. Becker explains. according to Mr. Hostetter. that for some ten years his places have been bombed and burned. his employes slugged and robbed and threatened by lawless competitors. And no one has been punished. Now. says Mr. Becker, that is all over. He has gone into business with Scarface Al Capone. Capone has enlisted his Mafian tribe in the firm.

"I now have no need of the State's Attorney or the Police Department," said Mr. Becker. "I have the best protection in the world."

And since that new partnership became known in the trade, not a threat has come to him, Mr. Becker says. and not even a whisper of a bombing. a beating or a shakedown.

When it was first learned that Becker was opening a new shop and that Scarface Al was a kind of "angel" for it, one Max Krauss, legal adviser for the Master Cleaners and Dyers' Association, which had been the nemesis of Becker, went to Capone's headquarters and asked what it was all about, according to Mr. Hostetter's information.

"Get outa here!" Capone yelled at Krauss, Mr. Hostetter says. "You try to monkey with my business and I'll toss you out of the window."

Walter G. Walker. counsel for the Employers' Association, reported to the association that papers of incorporation were taken out on April 25. 1928. showing as the incorporators of the company Alphonse Capone, John Guzik and Maurice Cowen. Louis Cowen. publisher of the Cicero Tribune and professional bondsman for the Capone tribe. and Joseph Justfeld, town attorney of Cicero. appear as directors.

Capone. according to Mr. Walker, invested $35,000 in the corporation. In addition to Capone and Guzik, formerly a dive keeper, the "protectors" of the firm's prosperity include Philip d'Andrea of the notorious family of feudists, and Frank Rio.

Mr. Becker has informed the Employers' Association that his company intends to slash prices which, he said, had been boosted to profiteering heights by the Master Cleaners and Dyers' Association.

The Master Cleaners and Dyers' Association has recently been charged by Ben Kornick, President of the rival Central Cleaners and Dyers, with responsibility for assaults on the Central drivers and the burning of three of the Central's trucks. Kornick swore out warrants against Albert Doris, an official of the association. and charged that many gunmen were employed to stifle independent competition. For years the Master Cleaners and Dyers' Association has sought to control the entire industry in Chicago.

Now. according to Mr. Walker, the various factions in the industry have all taken to arms and have been scurrying about for good gunmen. Becker landed the big prize in Capone, the lawyer said.

"Becker's company has employed a two-gun gangster and several aids to protect their interests," Mr. Walker asserted. "I am informed that the Central Cleaners and Dyers, after many vain attempts to bring their oppressors to justice, have been negotiating with Abe Schaffner, another notorious gunman.

"'Big Tim' Murphy, who is seldom long without a racket, is trying to muscle his way into the Retail Cleaners and Dyers' Union. All places are being rapidly filled—none but the surest shooting gunmen need apply."

In a formal statement Secretary Hostetter of the Employers' Association said:

"For some years there has been a condition in the cleaning and dyeing business of Chicago having all of the earmarks of a conspiracy by which competition has been strangled and high prices upheld.

"This industry has been shot through with crimes of violence; indictments have been returned only to be stricken off for 'want of prosecution;' independents have been driven from the field."

The statement added that the present situation was the climax of such conditions.

"It means that we are sunk to the savagery of the jungle," said Mr. Hostetter. "Out of this is emerging —has already emerged—a new law so hideous in its potentialities as to make one shudder at the possible consequences."

Until there is a display of violence, State's Attorney Crowe and Commissioner of Police Hughes said today, they had no intention of interfering in the situation created by the entrance of Capone and his cohorts into the factional warfare of the cleaners and dyers.

November 22, 1927

May 28, 1928

7 CHICAGO GANGSTERS SLAIN BY FIRING SQUAD OF RIVALS, SOME IN POLICE UNIFORMS

VICTIMS LINED UP IN ROW

Hands Up Faces to Wall of Garage Rendezvous, They Are Mowed Down

---

ALL TOOK IT FOR A RAID

Four Machine Gun Executioners, Wearing Badges, Made Swift Escape in Automobile.

MORAN'S STAFF WIPED OUT

Liquor Gang Head Missing— Police Chief, Roused by 'Challenge,' Declares 'War.'

Special to The New York Times.

CHICAGO, Feb. 14.—Chicago gangland leaders observed Valentine's Day with machine guns and a stream of bullets and as a result seven members of the George (Bugs) Moran-Dean O'Banion, North Side gang are dead in the most cold-blooded gang massacre in the history of this city's underworld.

The seven gang warriors were trapped in a beer-distributers' rendezvous at 2,122 North Clark Street, lined up against the wall by four men, two of whom were in police uniforms, and executed with the precision of a firing squad.

The killings have stunned the citizenry of Chicago as well as the Police Department, and while tonight there was no solution, the one outstanding cause was illicit liquor traffic.

The dead, as identified by the police, were:

CLARK, JAMES, alias Frank Meyer and Albert Kashellek, convicted robber and burglar; brother-in-law of George Moran, the gang leader.

GUSENBERG, FRANK, who died after the others were killed, but refused to talk.

GUSENBERG, PETER, brother of Frank, a notorious gunman for the O'Banion-Weiss-Drucci-Moran faction.

MAY, JOHN, auto mechanic, thought to be a safeblower before joining Moran gang.

SCHWIMER, REINHART H., a resident of Hotel Parkway, an optometrist, with offices in the Capitol Building, known as a companion of gangsters, but lacking a criminal record.

SNYDER, JOHN, alias Arthur Hayes, Adam Hoyer, Adam Myers; convicted robber and confidence man.

WEINSHANK, ALBERT, henchman of Moran and strongarm agent of Chicago cleaning and dyeing industry.

The dead, the greatest in point of numbers since Chicago gang killings began in 1924 with the assassination of Dean O'Banion, were the remnants of the "mob" organized by O'Banion, later captained by Hymie Weiss and Peter Gusenberg and recently commanded by George (Bugs) Moran.

Capone's Name Is Mentioned.

One name loomed in the police investigation under way this afternoon and tonight. It was that of Alphonse (Scarface) Capone, gang leader extraordinary.

Six of the slain gangsters died in their tracks on the floor of the North Clark Street garage, a block from Lincoln Park and its fine residential neighborhood. A seventh, with twenty or more bullets in his body, died within an hour.

The police found more than 100 empty machine gun shells strewing the floor of the execution room, and there was a report that Moran had been taken out alive by the marauders.

Police Commissioner William F. Russell and his First Deputy Commissioner, John Stege, were bewildered tonight over the fact that the ambush was arranged by two men in police uniforms, wearing police badges, and the fact that the other killers arrived at the scene in an automobile resembling a detective bureau squad car.

Police Declare "War to the Finish."

Tonight an underworld round-up unparalleled in the annals of the Police Department is under way.

"It's a war to the finish," Commissioner Russell said. "I've never known of a challenge like this—the killers posing as policemen—but now the challenge has been made, it's accepted. We're going to make this the knell of gangdom in Chicago."

Reconstructing the massacre as it occurred, police and prosecuting officials were of the opinion that the men were victims of their own cupidity as well as the wrath of their enemies, for they had been stood up against the brick wall of the garage, their backs, rather than their faces, toward the executioners.

This morning about 10 o'clock seven men were sitting about the garage, two in the front, five others behind a wooden partition in the garage proper, according to the investigators' theory.

Four of the men were gathered about an electric stove on which bubbled a pot of coffee. A box of crackers and a half-dozen cups completed the breakfast layout. The men munched away, in between telephone calls.

The fifth man, John May, the mechanic, is believed to have been puttering about the trucks, one of which was loaded with a new wooden beer vat.

There was a noise outside that rose above the clatter of Clark Street traffic, sounding like a police gong. The front door of the garage opened. In marched two men wearing the uniforms of policemen, their stars gleaming against the blue of the cloth. Two men in civilian attire followed them. All were armed, the first two with sub-machine guns, the last two with sawed-off shotguns.

Swift Execution Accomplished.

The two men in the front office threw up their hands, apparently believing a regular police raid was in progress, and marched to the rear. There was a scramble among the men about the improvised breakfast tables as they saw the police uniforms.

One of the men in police uniform probably gave the order to line up, face to the wall, and, sighting May, made him join the others. As the seven stood staring at the whitewashed wall, they were swiftly deprived of their weapons.

Then, it is believed, came the order to "give it to them" and the roar of the shotguns mingled with the rat-a-tat of the machine gun, a clatter like that of a gigantic typewriter.

Evidently May, incredulous that he, an ordinary mechanic, should be included, made a mad leap only to drop within six inches of a man wielding a shotgun.

The machine-gunners probably sprayed the heap of dead on the floor and then the four executioners marched out.

A tailor glanced up from his pressing iron next door, and a woman living near by ran to the street. They saw what appeared to be two men under arrest, their hands in the air, followed by two policemen.

The four climbed into what looked like a police squad car, a fifth man sitting at the wheel, the motor humming. The car roared south in Clark Street, sweeping around the wrong side of a street car, and was lost in the traffic.

When police arrived upon the scene they found six of the men dead. The seventh, Frank Gusenberg, was crawling on the floor toward Police Lieutenant Tom Loftus. Gusenberg died within an hour at the Alexandrian Hospital.

The majority of the victims were dangerous men, with reputations equal to the worst, Deputy Commissioner Stege said.

"Where is 'Bugs' Moran?" Stege asked when his officers discovered the automobile which Moran was supposed to own.

Then came the story that perhaps he was one of the men who walked out of the garage, hands high above his head, followed by the pseudo policemen.

Squads were dispatched to seek Moran. Others were sent after information concerning "Scarface Al" Capone's whereabouts. The latter group came back with word that Capone was at his Winter home in Miami, Fla.

The police recalled that the Aiello brothers' gang of North Side Sicilians had a year or so ago affiliated themselves with the Moran gang, and that the Aiellos and the Capones were deadly enemies. But no Aiellos were found.

Coroner Herman N. Bundesen reached the garage within a half hour after the fusillade. The bodies were photographed and searched.

Cash and Diamond Rings on Bodies.

Lieutenants John L. Sullivan and Otto Erlanson of the Homicide Bureau checked the identifications and kept records of search results.

Peter Gusenberg had a large diamond ring and $447 in cash.

Albert Weinshank proved to be the cousin of a former State representative of the same family name. Weinshank, who recently took an "executive position" with the Central Cleaners and Dyers Company, had only $18 in cash, but he had a fine diamond ring and a bankbook showing an account in the name of A. H. Shanks.

Then a body was identified as that of John Snyder, alias Adam Meyers, alias Adam Hyers, alias Hayes. It was said that Snyder was owner of the Fairview Kennels, a dog track rivaling Capone's Hawthorne course. Chief Egan was told that Snyder was the "brains" of the Moran "mob." Snyder had $1,399.

The body of Mays, the overall-clad mechanic, had only a few dollars in the pockets. He was the father of seven children. A machine gun bullet had penetrated two medals of St. Christopher.

The fifth of the five bodies in the row, flat on their backs with their heads to the south, was recorded as that of Reinhardt H. Schwimmer, an optometrist. Despite his having no police record, it is said that he recently boasted that he was, in the alcohol business and could have any one "taken for a ride."

Closer to the door, face down, with his head to the east, lay John Clark, brother-in-law of Moran, and rated as a killer with many notches in his guns. His clothes contained $681.

Woman's Story Aids Police.

"Bullet marks on the wall," Captain Thomas Condon observed and it was seen that few of the pellets missed their marks, for there were only seven or eight places where the detectives were sure bullets had struck.

Each of the victims had six to ten bullets shot through him. A highpowered electric bulb overhead flooded the execution chamber with a glare of white light. Chained in a corner was a huge police dog, which strained on its fastenings and snarled at the detectives.

The police expressed amazement that the seven gangsters had been induced to face the wall and certain death without a struggle and without resistance.

"That bunch always went well armed," a police captain said.

An explanation was seen in the story of Mrs. Alphonsine Morin, who lives just across the street from the garage. She told of seeing men she thought were policemen coming out after hearing the shooting.

"Two men in uniforms had rifles or shotguns as they came out the door," she said, "and there were two or three men walking ahead of them with their hands up in the air. It looked as though the police were making an arrest and they all got into an automobile and drove away."

"Quite simple," Chief Egan commented. "They would never have got that gang to line up unless they came in police uniforms."

Typical of his life, Frank Gusenberg refused during his last hour to tell the police anything. He was conscious, but he kept defying the police who sought names from him.

Assistant State's Attorney David Stansbury was put in charge of the investigation tonight by State's Attorney John A. Swanson. The police, prosecutor and the Federal authorities were all working together to get trace of the slayers.

Theories about who plotted and carried out the execution were numerous.

"Hi-jackers, no doubt," Chief of Detectives John Egan termed the dead men. Other theories were:

That the victims had been "hoisting" trucks of booze, Canadian beer, alcohol and fine liquors en route from Detroit, and the "Purple Gang" of Detroit had sallied out for vengeance.

That they were involved in the bitter competition of rival organizations of cleaning and dyeing establishments, the Moran gang protecting the North Side concerns and the Capone outfit the Becker system.

That it was a sequel to the sentencing of Alderman Titus Haffa yesterday to two years in Leavenworth Prison for violating the prohibition law. Haffa's ward adjoins the domain which Moran had ruled.

Other detectives said the killing was the work of the Capone "mob."

"It is the answer of the Sicilians

for the killing of Tony Lombardo, and it is a logical sequel to the series of murders starting five years ago with the mowing down on O'Banion," one declared.

Appeal Made to Civic Conscience.

James D. Cunningham, president of the Illinois Manufacturers' Association, representing more than 2,000 industrial concerns centering around Chicago, issued an appeal tonight to "all law-abiding citizens" to assert themselves upon the issue of gang warfare as a result of today's "massacre."

Asserting that the story would be "broadcast internationally as the culminating blot" on the city's name, he concluded:

"Would it not be appropriate for the city and State authorities to call a mass meeting and take steps to instill terror in the hearts of these organized murderers?"

North Side Gang "Dynasty" Falls.

Gang warfare in Chicago began with the slaying of Dion O'Banion in November, 1924. In the fifty months since then, thirty-eight murders, most of them attributed to the enmity between the North Side band founded by O'Banion and the West Side syndicate established by John Torrio and turned over to Al Capone, have been recorded.

Today's massacre marked the end of the proud North Side dynasty which began with O'Banion. O'Banion yielded to Hymie Weiss who was replaced by "Schemer" Drucci, who was succeeded by "Bugs" Moran. And Moran tonight was missing, while seven of his chief aids lay dead.

February 15, 1929

SAYS CHICAGO GANGS HAVE POOLED RACKETS

Newspaper Hears Al Capone Is to Be "Czar" of United Operations.

CHICAGO, Thursday, April 17 (AP).—The Examiner says a peace agreement has been signed to bring an end to war between gangs in Chicago; that the various gangs have pooled their interests and "amalgamated for orderly control of gambling, booze and vice," and that Al Capone has been chosen leader of the united gang.

The newspaper learns that under the terms of the agreement the gang coalition contemplates maintenance of a "community chest" into which are to be poured the earnings of all the gangs' united activities, vice resorts, gambling tables, liquor distribution and the "labor racket."

The principal gangs involved are said to be those of Capone and of George (Bugs) Moran, heretofore competitors in the various underworld activities which so frequently have been the cause of gang murders. William (Klondike) O'Donnel and Ralph Sheldon, also known as gang leaders, are not included in the new organization, the newspaper says.

April 17, 1930

CHICAGO GRAFT ROLL FOUND IN ZUTA BOXES

Canceled Checks, Notes and Accounts Name Judges, Politicians and Police.

COVER 15 YEARS OF CRIME

Papers of Slain Moran-Aiello Leader Unearthed in Investigation of Lingle Murder.

Special to The New York Times.

CHICAGO, Aug. 15.—Records of weekly payments of hundreds of thousands of dollars in protection money from a gangland corruption fund to many public officials, policemen and some individuals making pretensions as reformers were uncovered today by Patrick Roche, chief investigator for State's Attorney Swanson, in two safety deposit boxes used by Jack Zuta.

Zuta, reputed operations chief for the Moran-Aiello North Side gang and alleged instigator of the assassination of Alfred J. Lingle, police reporter for The Chicago Tribune, was shot dead by five gangsters Aug. 1 at Delafield, Wis.

The records were of accounts covering the fifteen years during which Zuta was at first an obscure figure in the vice world and later a leading Chicago racketeer. A methodical man, Zuta is said to have recorded every penny he spent for graft from 1921, when he was a dive keeper, until the day of his murder. His books were a veritable "Who's Who" of Cook County politics and crime.

Canceled checks, notes for large amounts and other evidence from the records in the boxes were made public tonight by Charles F. Rathbun, Assistant State's Attorney, and Mr. Roche.

Prominent Names Revealed.

Officials and others revealed in the evidence as receiving checks from Zuta, or giving notes to him, are:

JUDGE JOSEPH W. SCHULMAN, for more than ten years a judge of the municipal court.

GEORGE VAN LENT, former State Senator and political leader.

EMANUEL ELLER, former judge of the municipal, superior and criminal courts; a son of Morris Eller, boss of the notorious Twentieth Ward.

LOUIS I. FISHER, attorney and brother of Judge Harry M. Fisher of the Circuit Court.

RICHARD J. WILLIAMS, sergeant of police.

Evidence of favors given Zuta by leading politicians and of Zuta's standing in political circle was found.

One item was a canceled check for $500 dated March 27, 1922, on the West Town State Bank, where Zuta maintained an account, payable to the "Regular Republican Club of Cook County." It is signed by Zuta. On the back appears an endorsement in hand-writing "Regular Republican Club of Cook County" and then a rubber stamp endorsement, "Pay to order of Foreman Brothers Banking Company, Charles V. Barrett." Beneath Mr. Barrett's name is written the abbreviation "Treas."

Card From Sheriff Graydon.

Another exhibit preserved by Zuta in his box of souvenirs was a card reading:

County of Cook- Sheriff's Office.
To members of the department:
The bearer, J. Zuta, is extended the courtesies of all departments.
1927, Charles E. Graydon, Sheriff.

The card is one of many hundreds issued by Mr. Graydon during his régime as sheriff, it was stated, the card being generally accepted to give immunity from arrest for traffic and other violations noted by the sheriff's policemen.

Another item was a membership card, 772, to Jack Zuta, in the William Hale Thompson Republican Club, with the printed signature of Homer K. Galpin, chairman.

A financial statement in the records indicated that, in one week, Zuta, as business manager of the underworld syndicate headed by George (Bugs) Moran and the Aiello brothers, paid out $100,000 as "dividends" on the Fairview dog track; the investigators refused to say who received the "dividends." In other weeks, $107,000 was paid from the receipts of four North Side gambling houses.

Only a small part of the evidence was revealed, Mr. Rathburn and Mr. Roche explaining that the items presented seemed to speak for themselves. Other documents revealing many connections between politicians, police officials, public officers and the gangs are in the prosecutor's possession and will be subjected to careful investigation, it was announced.

The prosecutor said it was apparent from the nature of the papers found that Zuta had preserved it deliberately, with the purpose in mind that, should any of the officials involved become "unmanageable" or should he for any other reasons desire to intimidate them, he would display evidence that he had paid them money.

Checks and notes upon which the name of Judge Schulman appears are in the aggregate amount of $5,500. A description of the items follows:

A note for $1,000, dated Dec. 21, 1921, payable three months after date, signed by Joseph Schulman and made payable to himself, endorsed by Schulman in blank.

A canceled check for $500 on the Westtown State Bank, dated Feb. 21, 1922, signed by Zuta, made payable to Schulman and endorsed by Schulman.

A note for $500, dated May 22, 1922, payable four months after date, signed by Joseph Schulman and made payable to himself, endorsed by Schulman in blank.

A canceled check for $1,000, dated Aug. 7, 1922, on the Westtown State Bank, signed by Zuta, made payable to Joseph W. Schulman and endorsed by Schulman.

A note for $1,500 dated Aug. 15, 1922, payable six months after date, signed by Joseph Schulman and made payable to himself, endorsed by Schulman in blank.

A canceled check for $500, dated Nov. 25, 1925, signed by Zuta, made payable to Joseph Schulman and endorsed by Schulman.

A check memorandum of the Westtown State Bank, dated Dec. 29, 1925, stating that a check for $500 signed by Joseph W. Schulman and made payable to Jack Zuta, had been returned by Schulman's bank unpaid.

An effort to reach Judge Schulman was unsuccessful. His home telephone did not answer. Judge Schulman has been on the municipal bench continuously during the period covered by the Zuta papers.

Williams Denies Zuta Dealings.

The name of Richard J. Williams appeared on a note for $600, dated Aug. 2, 1924, payable six months from date, and payable to himself. It was endorsed by Williams in blank.

Sergeant Williams is known as having been a friend of Julius Rosenheim, murdered paid informant of The Chicago Daily News. When Rosenheim, at the suggestion of officials of The Daily News, was placed on the investigating staff of Frank J. Loesch during Mr. Loesch's prosecution of vote fraud as special assistant State's attorney, Rosenheim induced Mr. Loesch also to obtain the services of Sergeant Williams.

Mr. Loesch has since stated that he found both Rosenheim and Williams unreliable. Later Williams appeared on the State's Attorney's roll of police investigators and it was learned that he had been assigned to do work for E. R. Brunker, reformer and had of the Civic Safety Commission. Complaints against the activities of Williams were received by Mr. Roche, when then severed Williams from all connection with the State's Attorney's office.

Williams, interviewed tonight, said he never in his life had any transactions with Zuta.

Two checks of Zuta's appeared to have been cashed by Louis I. Fisher. One was for $500, dated Oct. 4, 1926, on the West Town State Bank, payable to currency and endorsed by Fisher and a scrawled signature which appeared to be "F. G. Bozius." The other was for $100, dated Feb. 11, 1927, on the West Town State Bank, payable to cash and endorsed by Fisher and a scrawled signature which appeared to be "A. C. Kallish."

Louis Fisher has acted at times as counsel for interests promoting dog track ventures. Judge Fisher, his brother, two years ago issued injunctions restraining the police and the State's attorney from interfering with the operation of the Hawthorne and Thornton dog tracks. The Supreme Court, passing on the validity of the injunctions, found that the dog tracks were illegal enterprises.

Checks to Van Lent and Eller.

The checks payable to Van Lent were dated during the time he was a member of the State Senate and a power in west side politics. One is for $500 dated April 4, 1922, and the other for $100, dated Oct. 16, 1926, both on the Westtown State Bank.

Mr. Van Lent could not be located tonight.

A check sined by Zuta for $250, dated April 4, 1922, was made payable to Emanuel Eller. It is endorsed by Mr. Eller and was deposited in the West Side Trust and Savings Bank.

Mr. Eller in 1922 was a candidate for municipal judge and he was elected to that bench in June of that year. He could not be located tonight.

The box also yielded two anonymous letters containing threats against Zuta's life.

To Fight Impounding of Records.

Photostatic copies are being made and State's Attorney Swanson said he would oppose efforts to have the records impounded.

The more important of the two boxes was discovered in the vaults of the Capitol Building here. It was rented under the name of Jack Saleto.

The second box was located in the basement vaults of the American Bond and Mortgage Company Building. There for many months the North Side gang had its business headquarters. It was in the name of Ike Ginsberg, Zuta's first counsin and the executor of his estate.

In the Capitol Building box, besides Zuta's personal records, were twenty-one $2.50 gold pieces, two $5 gold pieces, several diamonds and some other pieces of jewelry.

Mr. Swanson in a statement he issued prior to the making public of part of the records, said:

"A novel result in gangland murders has just been accomplished by the office in charge of Chief Investigator Pat Roche and Assistant State's Attorneys Charles F. Rathburn and James McShane. Due to the leading parts in gangland affairs assigned by the press to the late Jack Zuta, it may be of interest to the public to know that Roche is in possession of the contents of two safety-deposit boxes found in Chicago under an assumed name, but belonging to Zuta.

"Much interest is contained in these boxes pertaining to the connection of Zuta with many persons, but the information so contained therein must be checked, and publicity at this time would hinder the use of such information for investigational purposes."

August 16, 1930

CAPONE ASKS TRUCE IN VAIN IN CHICAGO

Chief Justice Rejects Offer to Quit Racketeering in Exchange for Beer Monopoly.

"COMPROMISE" DENOUNCED

Judge McGoorty Tells New Grand Jury That Choice Is Between "Rule of Law or of Gang."

Special to The New York Times.

CHICAGO, Nov. 3. — Alphonse (Scarface Al) Capone has offered to come to terms with the authorities, it was learned today, and has pledged himself to withdraw his influence from racketeering if he is permitted to continue his leadership in the beer industry without molestation.

Chief Justice John P. McGoorty of the Criminal Court revealed the offer when he read his charge to the November grand jury, which began its duties today. Although he did not name in his charge the maker of the offer, whom he termed "the most widely heralded and most powerful underworld leader in Cook County," the judge later admitted that Capone had made the proposal.

"Such a compromise is unthinkable," the judge told the grand jurors. "That is my answer.

"It is time every citizen manifested his sense of responsibility to his community and his willingness to unite in establishing a rule of law in Cook County."

Then, referring to evidence of "interlocking interests of crime and politics" presented by the previous grand jury and to "those organized criminals known as racketeers, whose deadly blight has alike fallen on business and organized labor," Judge McGoorty continued:

"Labor unions and business, by giving their cooperation to the law-enforcing agencies can be purged of these sinister influences. We must not build a Frankstein monster in our midst that would threaten and perhaps destroy the very fabric of municipal government.

"Yours is a great responsibility and opportunity. I have no doubt you will so accept it.

"The time has come when the public must choose between the rule of the gangster and the rule of the law."

November 4, 1930

WIDE FEDERAL DRIVE ON RACKETEERS; NEW YORK AND OTHER CITIES TO GET AID; $5,000,000 FUND BACKS CHICAGO'S WAR

ALL LAW UNITS 'FORTIFIED'

Attorney General Reveals Concentrated Offensive Against Gangsters.

SKIRMISH WON IN CHICAGO

Special to The New York Times.

WASHINGTON, Nov. 20.—Attorney General Mitchell made known today, that the Federal Government is warring energetically against racketeers and gangsters in the larger cities throughout the United States, and especially in Chicago, headquarters of some of the largest and most extensive gangs with which the authorities have to deal.

The Attorney General announced the "fortifying of all government forces" in Chicago, and indicated that the same policy would follow in other cities requesting Federal assistance.

Mr. Mitchell said that Federal forces in Chicago had been instructed about six months ago to invoke all available statutes for the arrest and prosecution of gangsters. He disclosed that in recent weeks there had been "a gradual strengthening of these forces, putting an increasing pressure upon gangster activities in that particular spot."

The Departments of Justice, Treasury and Labor, through the Secret Service and Bureaus of Prohibition, Narcotics, Internal Revenue and Immigration, have had extra men at work in Chicago all Summer and their activities are to be strengthened, he said.

Ready to Lend More Aid Here.

Mr. Mitchell had not been advised officially of the meeting in New York of forty civic, business and professional leaders, invited by District Attorney Crain to help him fight racketeering, but the same steps he is taking in Chicago will follow in New York City if requested, according to the Department of Justice.

One of the more recent steps toward the campaign in Chicago was the dispatching of Special Assistant Attorney General William J. Froelich to that city to aid the Federal District Attorney there in coordinating the anti-gangster activities of the various Federal agencies.

Federal authorities can cooperate with State and local forces under a number of Federal penal statutes. Among them are the national prohibition law, the Harrison anti-narcotics act, the customs statutes, the Mann white slave law, the Dyer act dealing with interstate transportation of stolen automobiles, the sections of anti-trust laws forbidding interference with interstate commerce and the statutes relating to fraud in payment and reporting of Federal income taxes.

Mr. Mitchell explained that the last two means had been used lately with great success. He cited the conviction in Federal court in Chicago yesterday of Jack Guzik, gambler and Capone aide, on an indictment charging tax evasion.

Guzik is one of the twenty-eight gangsters named by the Chicago crime commission as "publc enemies." The maximum penalty for each three counts on which he was convicted is five years' imprisonment and $10,000 fine. Mr. Mitchell said that the evidence on which Guzik was convicted was gathered by the Department of Justice and the Bureau of Internal Revenue.

Anti-Trust Law Prosecutions.

Prosecutions under the anti-trust laws, it was stated, also have been effective in Chicago, particularly in the case of the Chicago Association of Candy Jobbers, in which a former officer and six members of the association received jail sentences and ten others were fined.

According to the views of the Department of Justice this case developed a method for dealing with racketeers who intimidate business men and destroy their property. Non-members of the Candy Jobbers' Association were assaulted and their places of business bombed. The Federal Government traced the interference to the association, then prosecuted on the ground that an interference with interstate commerce was involved.

The Attorney General said that the Federal activity in Chicago was only one of our numerous efforts" to cope with gangs and rackets. He referred to other cities in general, but it was later stated for him that the Federal Government will take a hand wherever it is requested to do so by the local authorities, but prefers not to take direct action until such a request has been made.

In answer to a question about a complaint from a Chicago grape dealer that racketeers were interfering with his shipments, Mr. Mitchell said he had not heard personally about death threats of gangsters against producers of the new grape wine concentrates if their product was sold in Chicago.

He said he had examined the files of Assistant Attorney General John Lord O'Brian and had found no formal complaint, but that it was possible an oral plea had been made by the grape dealers to Mr. O'Brian, who has been out of the city for several days.

November 21, 1930

INCOME TAX PROSECUTIONS HIT HARD BLOWS AT RACKETEERING

Having Won Success in Chicago, the Federal Forces Have Moved On New York to Conduct Investigations in This City

Associated Press Photo.
Ralph J. Capone.

Fresh from victories won in Chicago, where indictments and convictions have been obtained against racketeers who failed to report their plunder on their income taxes, the Federal authorities have launched a similar campaign in New York. Co-operating with United States Attorneys, investigators from the Internal Revenue Bureau are now looking into the financial operations of a number of New York characters, and the first indictments have been handed down. The following article describes the results of the Chicago campaign which is being repeated in New York.

By FRANK A. SMOTHERS.

CHICAGO.

CHICAGO is beginning to realize that it has a strong weapon against its racketeers and gangsters, who for years have seemed immune from effective attack by the authorities. This weapon is the Federal law, as enforced by George E. Q. Johnson, United States District Attorney for the Northern District of Illinois.

As the years passed, with the city's gang leaders going unpunished, Chicago had grown cynical concerning the ability of State and local officers of the law to cope with them. But for more than a year the city has been acquiring a different impression regarding Federal law and its enforcement, and now that impression is rapidly changing to assurance.

Federal Accomplishments.

The reputation of the Federal weapon rests not upon ballyhoo, but upon facts, among which are these:

A jail sentence for Scarface Al Capone, probably the most powerful gang entrepreneur in America's history, who is designated as Number One in Chicago's list of "public enemies."

A penitentiary sentence for Ralph Capone, his brother, Number Two in the list.

A penitentiary sentence for Frank Nitti, known as "the enforcer," in token of his place as chief of the strong-arm department by which Capone's edicts have been enforced.

A penitentiary sentence for Jake Guzik, also a headliner in the Capone organization, and a Federal indictment against his brother Sam.

Pleas of guilty to Federal charges from Terry Druggan and Frankie Lake, pioneers of the large-scale liquor racket of the Middle West, often designated as the "squires," because they indulge in country estate life.

The Federal arm, in its attack upon outstanding persons, has not confined itself to striking at gangsters. Powerful Chicago politicians have felt it, to their grief. Gene C. Oliver, Assessor of Cook County, and State Representative Lawrence C. O'Brien are under Federal sentence, and a Federal indictment stands against Christian P. Paschen, Building Commissioner in the Cabinet of former Mayor William Hale Thompson.

Income Tax Charges.

In all the foregoing cases excepting that of Scarface Al, the charge has been substantially the same: violation of the income tax laws. Capone's present sentence, a short one, fixed at six months, is for contempt of court. But it is reported that the government is also preparing an income tax case against him, which, if successful, would send him to prison for a considerably longer time.

The attack by the government is a flank attack, as District Attorney Johnson describes it. It has struck, as it were, from the side, a vulnerable side. Gangsters and politicians have found that it is not so easy to cover up income tax violations as certain other matters.

The sentences provided so far, ranging from eighteen months to five years in prison, accompanied by large fines, are sufficiently heavy to have proved uncomfortable to those who received them. To be sure, only Nitti has actually started serving time. Appeals are pending in the other cases in which convictions have been obtained. But little if any hope

is held out for the appeals. Likewise the indictments are taken with great seriousness. Mr. Johnson does not prosecute until he is convinced on the basis of the evidence that he has a case.

Philosophy of the Drive.

What is the philosophy behind the attack, considered in relation to the organized crime problem as a whole? It can be explained best, probably, by the man directing the attack. Without money, Mr. Johnson observes, gang organizations cannot be held together. And so he has asserted:

"The best method of fighting organized crime is to make it impossible to earn this money—that is, wipe out the source from which it comes. The way to do this is to procure evidence and prosecute every violation which may be presented, be it income tax, gun-toting, prohibition, gambling or vice."

Experience shows, however, that punishment of major racketeers on charges of gun-toting, violation of the prohibition laws, gambling, vice or murder is not often forthcoming. And with income tax charges it is forthcoming. Income tax prosecutions work. They send gang chieftains to penitentiary cells; and thus they greatly cripple, when they do not cut off their money-making. Furthermore, the prosecutions are helping to lay the groundwork for civil action looking to the payment of the taxes due from gangsters.

Besides striking at the pocketbooks of the racketeers, the income tax prosecutions and convictions are salutary, in Mr. Johnson's opinion, because they demonstrate that the culprit is not immune to the law. Discussing the convictions of Ralph Capone and Jake Guzik, he has said: "Ralph Capone and Jake Guzik can never again be leaders in organized crime. Their immunity—or gangdom's belief in their immunity—is gone. That was their stock in trade. They will not be able to count on old loyalties when they come out of prison."

In addition to hurting gang morale, this demonstration of the lack of immunity of gang chieftains unquestionably has another important effect: it strengthens public morale. It makes honest citizens feel that there is some use, after all, in taking a stand against organized criminals.

In person Mr. Johnson, the mainspring of the drive, is not the prosecutor standardized in detective stories. A friendly man, with rather soft, wavy hair and a quiet, pleasant manner, he might be thought a cultured minister; and, indeed, he is a church worker of long standing.

In dealing with gangsters, he has shown that his quietness is of a very cool kind. This coolness was well illustrated in a parley which he, with two of his aides, had with Ralph Capone before that self-confident man realized that he was in the income tax toils. Capone had been brought before the prosecutor, so the gangster thought, in connection with prohibition liquor matters, and he was not much concerned over these matters. He was affable; he started out by playing the part of a captain of industry who could afford to be generous with Federal officials. Having asked whether he might smoke, and having been informed that he might, he laid a handful of cigars on the table. A sensitive soul might have been hurt by the fact that nobody took a cigar, but seemingly Ralph was not.

He was a big fellow, and he talked as such. He saw no harm in boasting of his financial prosperity when questions were put to him touching upon it. As the conversation proceeded, he revealed to the quiet, studious District Attorney that he had bank accounts under five different aliases in the Pinkert State Bank of Cicero, Ill., the Chicago suburb which has gained international notoriety for its liquor, gambling and vice activities.

The examination over, Capone was still confident. "You don't have anything on me," he said.

"Only enough to send you to the penitentiary," replied Mr. Johnson.

In the trial, held before a jury in the court of Federal Judge James H. Wilkerson, testimony revealed that between 1924 and 1929 Capone had deposited about $1,871,000 at the Cicero bank. On that basis, it was contended that he had evaded payment of about $300,000 in income taxes, interest and penalties.

Government investigators and prosecutors had done a thorough job of preparing evidence. For example, when defense lawyers attempted to paint Capone as a gambler who had lost heavily in operating a handbook, the prosecution called saloon-keepers to testify that they had paid him $55 a barrel for quantities of beer.

The verdict, given April 26, 1930, was guilty. In June Judge Wilkerson imposed a sentence of three years in the Leavenworth penitentiary and a fine of $10,000.

Thus was brought to a successful issue the first of the income tax fraud cases against major gangsters, and action on the remaining cases followed promptly. In July Assessor Oliver was convicted. His sentence calls for eighteen months at Leavenworth and payment of a $7,500 fine. Special public interest attached to his case during the trial, when evidence was introduced that he had made large sums in "adjusting" taxes. After the conviction, the greatest pressure was exerted in the Federal Building in an attempt to win probation for the politician. But the pressure was futile.

Nitti Pleads Guilty.

Next to fall under Federal conviction was Nitti, the Capone "enforcer," one of the most ruthless gangsters Chicago has known. The best he could do when he found himself enmeshed in trouble with the government was to plead guilty to charges of evading payment of $158,823 in income taxes. Sentenced last December, he is now serving an eighteen-month term in Leavenworth. Also, he was fined $10,000.

Before December was over, Jake Guzik had been sentenced. A jury had found him guilty on charges of evading the income tax laws. According to the prosecution, he had failed to pay a tax amounting to more than $200,000 on a total income estimated at more than $1,000,000 for 1927, 1928 and 1929. Judge Woodward sentenced him to serve five years at Leavenworth and to pay a $17,500 fine.

State Representative O'Brien, having been convicted by a jury in December, was sentenced early in January to serve eighteen months and pay a $6,000 fine. It was shown during the trial that Timothy J. Crowe, when president of the Sanitary District of Chicago in its famous period of "whoopee" and wild spending, was his friend; it happened that O'Brien had a trucking business, and Crowe kept his friend's trucks busy at Sanitary District expense. According to a government agent named Converse, O'Brien had enjoyed a gross income of $436,000 in three years; yet he had not thought it necessary to file tax returns.

Druggan and Lake.

Druggan and Lake, in January, pleaded guilty to the income tax charges against them, but they stipulated that they could change their pleas on certain points in the event the higher court overruled the trial court on similar points in the O'Brien and Ralph Capone cases. Hence, the decisions on the O'Brien and Capone appeals are awaited with special interest. Even in the event of rulings against the government in those cases, however, "the squires," it is understood, will have to serve jail sentences of two years each. And if the government is sustained in the Capone and O'Brien matters, Druggan and Lake will be liable to sentences as high as twenty years or more, and fines of $50,000.

Such has been the progress of the income tax cases to date. There is no question that the Federal drive already has greatly impaired Chicago racketeering business. And the drive is by no means over.

FACED MANY PERILS IN CAPONE ROUND-UP

Squad of Seven Young Dry Agents Credited With Successful Drive on Chicago Gangster.

LEADER ONLY 28 YEARS OLD

Impervious to Threats of Death and Bribes, They Have Been Styled "Untouchables."

CHICAGO, June 17.—The "untouchables" have accomplished their mission.

Now, after writing a number of the voluminous reports that are always so necessary in government business, six prohibition enforcement men, headed by Assistant Chief Special Agent Eliot Ness, will go back to routine tasks—unless their superiors at Washington give them more "special jobs" on the basis of their original Chicago success.

"Go out and actually prove that Al Capone is at the head of this liquor conspiracy," this special group of Federal agents was ordered. So its members, most of them carrying on other regular duties, proceeded quietly to remove the aura of immunity that had been placed upon the dark brow of "Scarface Al" Capone by his gangland followers.

It wasn't long before Chicago's hoodlum world became aware of the persistently annoying activity of the seven men. They began to be known among the gangsters by extremely undignified and unprintable names.

But Agent Ness, now 28 years old—six years removed from his commencement day at the University of Chicago—had studied history during his college days. He also is possessed of a sense of humor. He remembered that the appellations employed to describe his group had been used in the caste history of India to describe the "untouchables."

So "untouchables" it was. And now that word has come to designate the kind of modern government agent, grown up out of prohibition enforcement, who cannot be "touched" by the bribes of gangsters and liquor syndicates.

This little group of men, headed by Ness had been banded together with the ultimate purpose of showing conclusively how a one-time Brooklyn thief had conspired to commit offenses against the peace and dignity of the United States."

Group Comparatively Young.

All of them comparatively youthful, two or three of the "untouchable seven" already had had a good bit of experience in the government service—some having hung up enviable records in the intelligence department of the army, some in the Internal Revenue Bureau and some having been with the prohibition forces almost since the ratification of the Eighteenth Amendment.

But it was in the sweeping raid two and a half years ago on the suburb of Chicago Heights, haven for scores of Capone "alky cookers," that Ness and his men got their first taste of practical investigative work as a unit.

Before that time the chief of the group had capped a year's post-college experience as an insurance investigator by entrance into the prohibition service. He was assigned to the staff of E. C. Yellowley, then administrator for the Chicago district.

Then came George (Hard Boiled) Golding to Chicago, and Ness was assigned to his squad. Fortunately Ness never took part in any of the high-handed forays that made Golding unpopular. Golding was succeeded by Alex Jamie, war-time intelligence operative, who had gone into prohibition work, and Ness became one of Jamie's most trusted subordinates.

Finally came the transfer of the enforcement of prohibition from the Treasury Department to the Department of Justice and W. E. Bennett became chief of the special agents. Ness was made his assistant and in a few months the special Capone assignment was added to his duties.

The famous raid on the Chicago Heights sector, strangely enough, also was the opening wedge into the income-tax investigations that have been pushed by the United States District Attorney, George E. Q. Johnson.

The government for the first time found records in the Heights—records that showed the connection of one Oliver Ellis with the slot-machine syndicate in the suburb. Ellis was soon indicted for violation of the income-tax laws. It was also learned that in Chicago Heights 3,500,000 gallons of alleged alcohol had been produced within a year.

Somewhere behind these disclosures, reasoned District Attorney Johnson, was the influence and maneuvring of Al Capone. The threads were extremely thin, but there were sensitive men on the trail ready to entwine those threads into strands that some day would be strong enough to support an indictment.

Many Bribes Offered

Many have been the bribes that have been offered to the "untouchables" since that fateful day; many have been the efforts at intimidation and the threats of violent death. But the "untouchables" kept pegging away at their task until, with actual documentary evidence, they were able to prove their case.

"We had to weigh our problems," said Ness today, "and find a vulnerable point. We decided on the breweries because their product is bulky and because they have the toughest transport problem. We knew that regularity was necessary in their operation and it wasn't long before we learned of the special hauls on Friday in preparation for Saturday speakeasy business.

"The breweries, too, showed evidences of having the most capital invested, of the most complete organization, the quickest turnover and the greatest income."

And it was the links with the larger breweries of the city that proved Capone's undoing.

What of the offers of bribes and the threats of death that came the way of Eliot Ness and his youthful assistants? Ness is reluctant to talk about them. He calls them side incidents in the larger task of doing a job and doing it well.

There was the time—his fellow agents tell the story—when Ness and Agent A. M. Nabors were calling on witnesses in the Chicago Heights conspiracy case. One hoodlum lieutenant of Capone managed to be at the home of the witnesses, and with him was the usual "gorilla."

After some conversation, the "gorilla" glowered at Ness and then looked inquiringly at his chief.

"Shall I let him have it?" the gang "executioner" almost pleaded.

But Nabors had been busy. He was eyeing the gorilla closely. In his pocket his right hand gripped a revolver. The hoodlum apparently was aware of it.

"No, Joe," he said, "I guess you better not."

A few days later, on a similar visit, Mike Picchi, one of the Chicago Heights gunmen, got in Ness's

He had followed the agent's car to a lonely spot in the suburb. Covered in time, Picchi's car was searched, and in it was found a revolver loaded with dum-dum bullets. The gunman was arrested and taken back to Chicago.

Mingled With Gangs.

During the Chicago Heights investigation it was necessary for the special agents to pose as crooked prohibition men. Often when they went into conference with the hoodlum chieftains, they had no assurance that they would come out alive. For a number of weeks the "untouchables" were on the payroll of the Chicago Heights syndicate at $1,000 a month. Later, in Calumet City, a nearby suburb, they were paid $100 in cash for each still they reported to the "alky cookers." That bribe money later proved to be embarrassing to its givers.

Now the "untouchables" were getting into the "home stretch" of their job and they moved back closer to the city. There followed two successive raids on Capone breweries, one in Cicero and the other on the near South Side. The Federal men crashed in the doors with heavy motor trucks. Instantaneously they spread, before the brewers could make for secret getaways.

For a refreshing change, a raid that had not been tipped off in advance netted some prisoners. It also netted some valuable memoranda that were added to the vast material being marshalled against Capone and his gangsters.

And the time had come to turn the material over to the legal experts, the men who draw up hole-proof indictments. It was done. Ness and his men had completed the task assigned to them.

The "untouchables" are waiting for further orders.

CAPONE SENTENCED TO AN 11-YEAR TERM; JAILED TILL APPEAL

Fine of $50,000 and Payment of Costs Also Ordered— Gang Chief Is Stunned.

SLATED FOR LEAVENWORTH

Judge Wilkerson Sends Him to Cook County Prison Until Tomorrow, Awaiting His Plea.

By MEYER BERGER.
Staff Correspondent of The New York Times.

CHICAGO, Oct. 24.—Federal Judge James H. Wilkerson ended the reign of Scarface Al Capone today.

He sentenced the bulky lord of crime to eleven years' imprisonment, fined him $50,000 and decreed that he pay the cost of his prosecution, which is about $100,000. The fine, the costs and the $137,328 already ascertained as due from Capone for back income taxes, makes his total debt to the government $287,328. Much more in the way of back taxes is expected to be levied before the government is through with Capone.

It was a smashing blow to the massive gang chief. He tried to take it with a smile, but that smile was almost pitiful. His clumsy fingers, tightly locked behind his back, twitched and twisted. He had hoped for a sentence of not more than three years.

Judge Wilkerson, after passing sentence, refused to admit Capone to bail pending appeal. He ordered him at once into the custody of the United States marshal, and for a time it seemed that Capone might start for the United States penitentiary at Leavenworth tonight. Later his attorneys received until Monday to file application for bail with the Circuit Court of Appeals. Capone will spend the week-end in a fifth-tier cell in Cook County Jail.

Dramatic Scene at Sentencing.

The pronouncement of judgment was dramatic. Judge Wilkerson's words, sharply clipped and incisive, rang clear in the hushed court chamber.

When the full import registered on the consciousness of the audience—about 200 persons heard it—a murmur of astonishment broke like surf against the white marble walls. It was the stiffest sentence ever given for income tax evasion.

Capone came in at ten minutes of 10. He looked wide-awake and spruce. A heather-colored, pinch-back suit with a white silk handkerchief in the breast pocket neatly cased his ponderous body. He included reporters and some of the spectators in a wide smile, shook hands with Michael Ahern, one of his lawyers, and sat down at the counsel table.

At 10 o'clock Capone was talking earnestly in a whisper to Ahern, when the door from the judge's chamber opened. The bailiff rapped sharply, every one stood up and Judge Wilkerson, a short, grim-faced man, with iron-gray hair which is almost always slightly tousled, ascended the bench. Capone searched the grim lines of the judge's face as he sat down again.

"The United States versus Capone," the clerk called. "Disposition of motion in arrest of judgment."

A murmur of anticipation swept the chamber. Capone edged forward on his swivel chair, crowding Ahern who sat in front of him. He cupped his hairy right hand over his right ear and his jet-black eyes opened wide under their bushy brows, as if that might help him hear better.

"It was urged here in the argument yesterday," said Judge Wilkerson, "that the counts of the indictment upon which the verdict of guilty in this case was returned are insufficient."

He paused.

"It is my opinion that the averments in these counts are sufficient to comply with the constitutional requirements and the motion in arrest of judgment is denied."

Crystal clear, the words had a biting quality. Capone dropped back in his chair.

Mr. Ahern got up and entered an objection to the court's ruling.

"Let the defendant step to the bar of the court."

Capone got up, planted himself before the bar with his hands behind his back. The marshal came and stood at his side. The room was hushed.

"It is the judgment of the court in this case that on Count 1 of the indictment (a felony count charging income tax evasion for the year 1925) the defendant is sentenced to imprisonment in the penitentiary, in the custody of the Attorney General or his authorized representatives, for a period of five years and to pay a fine of $10,000, and to pay the costs of the prosecution."

Capone tried to smile, but the smile came out a queer twist.

"On Count 5 (a felony count charging tax evasion for 1926) the defendant is sentenced to imprisonment in the penitentiary for a period of five years and to pay a fine of $10,000 and to pay the costs of the prosecution," the judge continued.

Capone jiggled a little and his jaws worked. He licked his lips.

"On Count 9 (a felony count charging evasions for 1927) imprisonment five years and pay a fine of $10,000."

Another murmur broke the silence and died away. Capone's eyes seemed to harden and his fingers locked and unlocked behind his back. He thrust his hands in front of him and squared himself for what was to follow.

"On each of Counts 13 and 18 of said indictment (misdemeanor counts charging failure to file returns for the years 1928 and 1929)," said Judge Wilkerson, "the defendant is sentenced to imprisonment in the county jail in the custody of the Attorney General for a period of one year, and to pay a fine of $10,000, and to pay the cost of the prosecution."

Again the murmur, louder than before. But Judge Wilkerson seemed not to have heard it. He read on:

"The sentence on Counts 1 and 5 is to be served concurrently. The sentence on the other counts are to be consecutive and cumulative, that is to say, the sentences on Counts 1 and 5 are to be followed by the sentences on Counts 9 and 18.

Sentence on Contempt to Run.

"The defendant is under sentence of this court on a charge of contempt (passed last February when Capone failed to appear to plead). He was sentenced to six months imprisonment on that and the case is now pending before the United States Circuit Court of Appeals.

"The sentence on Counts 1 and 5 to be served in the penitentiary may be applied in such a way that he will receive credit by the service of sentence for contempt to the extent of six months. To that extent the contempt sentence is concurrent with the sentence on the felony counts 1 and 5.

"That same thing is applicable to Count 13, but not to 18, but the contempt sentence and Count 13 are not to run concurrently, but consecutively. The felony counts will be concurrent, first to the extent of six months with the contempt sentence and after that to the extent of one year on the misdemeanor counts."

Capone tried to smile again, but the smile was bitter. He licked his fat lips. He jiggled on his feet. His tongue moved in his cheeks. He was trying to be nonchalant, but he looked as he must have felt—ready to give way to an outburst of anger.

"The result is," Judge Wilkerson summed up, "that the aggregate sentence of the defendant is eleven years in the penitentiary and fines aggregating $50,000."

Capone took it like a slap in the face. He understood, then, just what lay before him. His fingers worked savagely.

Felony Count Put First.

Defense counsel then made a plea that Capone be allowed to serve the misdemeanor sentences first in the county jail.

"He will serve the felony count first," the judge answered. "He will serve the felony count before he serves the misdemeanor count. It is ordered that the marshal take custody of the defendant."

He clipped off the words. Capone impulsively stuck out his right hand, caught Albert Fink, of his counsel, by the fingers and then pumped them in a hurried handshake.

"Well, so long," he said swiftly. "Good-bye."

By this time he had worked up a smile and turned as if to go. Ahern passed a blue-backed legal form to the judge and the marshal held Capone back.

"May it please the court, we would like to have a petition for appeal accompanied by an assignment of errors and an order allowing the appeal," Ahern said.

Judge Wilkerson studied the document. He looked up. Capone seemed to be trying to catch his eye.

"I will grant the appeal," he said, "but I shall deny in this case the application for supersedeas."

"Sir?" asked Mr. Fink as if surprised.

"I say I shall deny the application for supersedeas and any other application that is made pending the appeal."

"I might call you Honor's attention to the fact that your Honor has not got the power to deny the application, to deny the supersedeas," argued Mr. Fink.

Plea Is Sharply Denied.

"Motion for supersedeas overruled and the application of the defendant to admit to bail is denied," said

Judge Wilkerson. There was finality in his sharp voice. "The defendant will go in the custody of the marshal."

Capone had turned to listen to his lawyer's appeal for bond, but he wore an air of defeat and hopelessness. He was fidgety—looked as though he wanted to get out of the court room and kick things around.

"Would your Honor accord to this defendant the usual little time which is accorded men who are convicted?" pleaded Mr. Fink.

"I think I shall adhere to my ruling in this case," said Judge Wilkerson. "I have made up my mind that after the motion for new trial or such motion as was made was passed upon this defendant remain in the marshal's custody, certainly until after this D'Andrea matter was disposed of; for that reason, if for no other reason."

He was referring to the case of Philip D'Andrea, Capone's bodyguard, who was arrested a fortnight ago for carrying a loaded revolver in the court room. D'Andrea's case is to come up Tuesday.

"But I think your Honor might instruct the marshal not to take him to Leavenworth until such time as we have a chance to present our matters to the Circuit Court of Appeals," said Mr. Fink.

"I think he probably would not take him to Leavenworth until Monday, in the regular course," said the judge.

"I am ready to go tonight," said Marshal Laubenheimer.

"All right," said the judge; "you may prepare the order."

"Then I understand that my application is denied?" Mr. Fink said.

"Yes."

"But, your Honor," spoke up Ahern, "if we be right on the contention that the appeal operates as a supersedeas, then your specific denial of it is contrary to law."

Review Available, Says Judge.

"You can have it reviewed," said Judge Wilkerson.

"I beg your pardon. Why should I have it reviewed if the law is already settled?"

"I don't understand that to be the law; until I am satisfied that I am in error, the order will stand."

"Your Honor has the authorities in your library. Suppose you look them up?"

"You certainly don't undertake to instruct the court?"

"I don't mean to be impertinent, but I say if you are not familiar with the authorities, there is an opportunity to get familiar, and if my citations be right and that is the law, then your order is inconsistent with the law."

"That is all," said Judge Wilkerson sharply.

The marshal led Capone from the room, deputies falling in on the flanks and rear. Half the spectators in the chamber got up to follow. Flashlights boomed in the hall. Inside, the defense counsel were still pleading for Capone's release on bond.

For an hour or so it seemed that Capone would start for Leavenworth on the 6:20 train out of Chicago, but eventually Judge Wilkerson changed his mind and ordered that he be kept here until Monday to give his attorneys time to file a plea for bail, pending appeal.

As Capone strode into the corridor with his escort of marshals a timid little man stepped up to him.

"Mr. Capone," he said, "I want to serve this."

The bloated face of the gang chief darkened with pent-up anger. He cursed at the little man and drew back his right foot as if to kick him, but changed his mind.

"I have a demand for tax and liens on the property of Alphonse and May Capone," said the little man, a deputy in the internal revenue office. He thrust it at the prisoner.

For ten minutes Capone was held in the marshal's office. When he came out, with his topcoat slung over his left arm and his gray hat jammed on his head, the flashlights opened up again. He walked swiftly to the elevator, but he looked crushed, sort of wilted.

News of the sentence spread around the Loop district like wildfire, and when Capone came down the steps to get into the marshal's car hundreds were waiting to see his departure. The gang chief bowed his head. Arrived at the jail, he was taken down to the basement, while the marshals went through the routine of registering him.

"What do you say, Al?" a reporter asked, as he waited for his cell assignment.

"I haven't anything to say." He smiled a sickly smile, hesitated, and said. "Well, you can say I decided to get through with it."

As the turnkey opened his cell door he hurled his topcoat in ahead of him. The door clanged.

Capone stared at his cellmate, a shabby down-and-outer, detained because he lacked $100 to pay a fine for disorderly conduct. Capone spoke with him a minute or two. He did all the talking, because the down-and-outer seemed awed by his presence.

"I'm gonna help this guy out," said Capone to the newspaper men clustered around the cell. "He needs $100 to pay a fine and I'm gonna help him out."

He pulled a bank note from his pocket and gave it to the frowsy one, who rammed it into a ragged pocket. The reporters left.

"Big News" for Chicagoan.

Out in the streets, Chicagoans could talk of nothing but the Capone sentence. No one seemed to believe that the "Big Shot" was at last on his way to jail; that the man who had controlled the city's warring machine gunners, beer runners, panderers, gamblers and other lawless elements, had finally been tripped up and hog-tied. It was the general idea that "he's too big for that; got too much money and too much influence."

Capone's name is a legend all over the world. Newspapers everywhere have recorded the gang-war killings 1929, in which seven of his enemies of his reign, including the famous St. Valentine's Day massacre in in the Bugs Moran gang were dispatched with machine guns.

Eleven years ago, Capone was brought from Brooklyn by Johnny Torrio, who was then head of the crime syndicate in Chicago, to learn the tricks of the trade. He got $75 a week for the pleasant little jobs hat crop up in the beer, rum and vice rackets. Gradually he worked his way up in the ranks, and six years ago, when Torrio got five slugs from the Moran outfit and decided to retire, Capone stepped into his shoes.

Capone perfected the Torrio organization; enlisted thousands of "alky coolers" in the Italian districts, puting them on regular salaries; exterminated competition and began rolling in wealth. He bought an expensive home in Florida, went in for silk underwear and silk shirts, diamond belt buckles, purchased costly trinkets by the dozen for his friends and even earned a reputation for philanthropy among the unemployed here by setting up soup kitchens.

His followers believed him invulnerable and when the Federal Government set out three years ago to send him to jail for income tax evasion, most people seemed to think it was a joke.

The trial got under way on Oct. 6 and ended eleven days later. Even then it seemed to be the prevailing opinion that Capone would serve no more than five years. Under the sentence passed today, however, he will have to serve at least seven and one-half years with maximum time out for good behavior.

October 25, 1931

CHICAGO GANGSTERS SPLIT INTO 20 GROUPS

No Leader Dares Effort to Succeed Capone's City Rule as Hoodlum Power Wanes.

CHICAGO, May 8 (AP).—Ambitious gang leaders today looked across a field studded with forbidding obstacles toward the throne deserted by Scarface Al Capone.

Disorganization of liquor dealers. a reorganized Chicago police department, concentration of Federal officers in the Chicago district and a changed public attitude toward gangsters were pointed out by authorities as drawbacks toward despotism in gangland.

Chicago gangsters in recent months have reverted to a score or more of poorly organized groups, police said. and not even a Capone could build them into an efficient syndicate of liquor, gambling and vice such as the big leader bossed for years.

Independent liquor dealers outside of the Loop have dared to cut prices in the face of orders to the contrary by the remnant of Capone's organization. Of those anxious to succeed Capone there are many, so many, police say, that none of them would dare a concentrated effort toward city-wide leadership.

Edward (Spike) O'Donnell on the southwest side; Joe Saltis, reputed enemy of O'Donnell and ally of Frank McErlane; George (Red) Barker, alleged labor racketeer: Murray Humphries, specialist in gambling and vice, and Frank Rio, Capone bodyguard, are only a few of the gangsters who have organized their own groups and would oppose violently any attempt at overlordship.

In addition, there is Chief of Police John Allman, whose officers are under orders to harass all known gangsters into obscurity.

Public indignation has resulted in organization of two groups with sufficient resources alone to block widely organized crime. They are the "Secret Six" and the Crime Commission both of which work in close cooperation with Federal authorities.

The drive that started with sending Ralph and Al Capone, Jack Guzik, Terry Druggan, Frank Lake, Frank Nitti and other gang leaders to prison for income tax violations, authorities agreed, has ended with breaking completely the grip of syndicated crime in Chicago.

May 9, 193

The Annals of Scarface Al

By RICHARD R. LINGEMAN

CAPONE. The Life and World of Al Capone. By John Kobler. 409 pages. New York: G. P. Putnam's Sons. $8.95.

There is a trajectory to the fortunes of certain American public figures of the twenties that seems to parallel the decade's: up like a rocket, then swoosh, thud in the thirties. F. Scott Fitzgerald was one; Herbert Hoover another; and, in a less reputable line of work, Alphonse Capone was a third. Now, drawing for the first time on Government files, together with voracious reading in the contemporary sources and interviews with those colleagues lucky enough to have survived, John Kobler has painted a remarkably lifelike, richly detailed portrait of Al Capone and his times. This is a whole and rounded book (and a fascinating one, too) that is indispensable to un-

Andree Abecassis
John Kobler

derstanding the antecedents of organized crime in the United States today. Capone's heyday encompassed organized crime's violent frontier era. He was violent in his own right; nonetheless he was a tireless peacemaker and one of the first to sense —along with his mentor, Johnny Torrio— that crime should be conducted as a business. "There is," he often said, "plenty of business for us all and competition needn't be a matter of murder anyway."

Moral in the Wings

The evolution of big crime in the United States is, of course, not the central theme of Mr. Kobler's book, but it is a moral that is always quietly standing in the wings. The onstage action is the rise and fall of Capone, and it is clear that even though he sought to rationalize the pursuit of crime in a crude way, he was always ready, ruthlessly, to suppress any challenge from a business rival to what he regarded as his own territory.

Dion O'Banion, the smiling choir boy killer who loved flowers and whose own flower shop had the gangster funeral trade all sewed up, was one of many whom Capone had eliminated because they sought to defy him. (Whenever there was a gang murder, O'Banion would automatically order $20,000 or so worth of flowers and set to work making up the $5,000 wreaths that were tributes from "the boys"—including the ones who had caused the killing—to the deceased.) Bugs Moran incurred Al's wrath, the result being the St. Valentine's Day massacre, in which seven men were cut to pieces in a hail of Thompson submachine-gun bullets in a garage (Moran escaped). An estimated total of 400 gangsters were killed in Chi-

cago during the shooting spree of the twenties; only two of the murders were solved. "A real goddam crazy place," said Lucky Luciano, Al's old Brooklyn schoolmate. "Nobody's safe in the streets."

The people of Chicago ducked bullets and went about their business, not really caring so long as it was the hoods slaughtering one another and the beer was good. (Capone seemed to recognize his responsibility to the public; once, when a tourist sustained a severe eye injury from flying glass during a fire fight, Al paid his $10,-000 hospital bill. But that was only one of many acts of charity—or public relations.)

Voters Are Repulsed

Finally the 1928 "pineapple primary," when nearly every possible form of electoral corruption and thuggery was employed by Capone's men, repulsed the voters, and they resoundingly rejected the slate of Mayor William (Big Bill) Thompson ("America first, last and always"), whose administration was in the thralldom of the Capone *apparat*. (Capone estimated his yearly payoffs to the Chicago police department at $30-million; more than half the force was on the payroll.) It remained for the Federal Government to deactivate Capone, however, for tax evasion. And the smarter lawyers could have got him off.

Capone was a blend of striking leadership qualities, generosity, sanctimonious sentiment and implacably cruelty. He worshiped his mother, his little boy, Sonny, and his wife, Mae, as many gangsters worship their families. Yet once, after a big dinner, he had three disloyal satraps tied to chairs and personally beat each of them into a sack of bones with a baseball bat.

Yet there was a part of him that longed for public approval; he thought of himself (how seriously Mr. Kobler doesn't say), as an unjustly maligned man: "Whatever else they may say, my booze has been good and my games have been on the square. Public service is my motto. I've always regarded it as a public benefaction if people were given decent liquor and square games."

When he died in 1947, at the age of 48, of tertiary syphillis, he was a spastic wreck of a man, haunted by dreams of imaginary killers, of processions of, yes, long, black cars bristling with Tommy guns, set to spray his front door with enfilading fire like in the good old days. Ironically, if Capone had submitted to a Wasserman early on—he had a fear of needles, the disease was contracted from a teen-age mistress salvaged from one of his brothels—and a good tax lawyer, he would not have lost six good years in prison, or spent his last years too mentally incapacitated to administer his empire. He would probably have risen high in the Mafia, which he helped organize on a national scale, and lived to a prosperous old age, his money socked away in legitimate business. Instead, he died penniless; Sonny eventually changed his name.

May 21, 1971

ROBBERIES IN LEAD IN NATION'S CRIME

Loss From Rackets Is Also Rising, State Officials Declare in Survey.

KIDNAPPING PROPLEM, TOO

Remedies Urged Include Federal Police and Removal of Politics From Law Enforcement.

CHICAGO, Aug. 20 (AP).—Burglaries and business rackets present the most vexing problems to law enforcement officials and criminologists in a majority of the States, a survey showed today.

Despite the current epidemic of spectacular kidnappings and gang murders, it is the tremendous property loss to thieves and extortionists who prey upon tradesmen that progresses upward without halt, according to officials.

Effective methods of combating these problems, they believe, must include eradication of obsolete laws and legal machinery, divorcement of law enforcement from politics, closer liaison of Federal and State authorities, and swifter justice.

Views of officials follow:

ILLINOIS—Colonel Henry Barret Chamberlin, operating director of the Crime Commission: "No business is safe in Chicago from the racketeer. What we need is secret police."

NEW YORK—Captain Albert B. Moore, inspector of State police: "Racketeering is our greatest crime problem because it involves the public and people who do not want to have anything to do with crime or criminals. Remedy—Take the politics out of law enforcement."

LOUISIANA—R. L. Whitman, Bureau of Criminal Identification: "Burglary of stores is our most pressing evil."

TENNESSEE—Carl Loser of Nashville, assistant prosecutor: "Young men who would not work if they had a chance commit most of the house breaking, highway robberies, larceny and petty theft."

ARKANSAS—State Banking Commissioner Marion Wasson: "Bank robbery causes us the most headaches."

VIRGINIA—Major Rice M. Youell, State prison head: "Seven out of ten of the prison population sent up in the last three years have been incarcerated for forms of stealing."

Whipping Post Praised.

DELAWARE—George Black, Wilmington, Police Superintendent: "Crimes here are largely petty. The effectiveness of our whipping posts and the swift dealing of justice keeps gangsters out."

INDIANA—Al G. Feeney, Director of Public Safety: "Motor law violations are the most vexing crime problem."

PENNSYLVANIA—Major Lynn G. Adams, head of State police: "Paroling and pardoning of hardened criminals and the conduct of jurors who bring in verdicts not in accord with the evidence contribute to the crime problem. The whole machinery of justice needs overhauling."

OHIO—Warden Preston E. Thomas of the State Prison: "The worst problem is kidnapping. Regulation of production and sale of ammunition would help."

GEORGIA—T. O. Sturdivant, Atlanta Police Chief: "The lottery racket is the product of organized crime here. It is a minor offense but it leads to killings."

WISCONSIN—State authorities said they were bothered most by influx of out-of-State gangsters.

MISSOURI—William O. Sawyers, Assistant Attorney General: "State lines and the use of automobiles are great problems. There should be a statute making it a Federal offense for fugitives to cross State lines to avoid arrest."

Kidnapping Leads in Minnesota.

MINNESOTA—Melvin Passolt, head of the State Criminal Apprension Bureau: "Kidnapping is the most troublesome crime."

KANSAS—Roland Boynton, Attorney General: "Bank robberies are the worst crime here. Establishment of State police would go a long way toward putting an end to this."

TEXAS—L. G. Phares, Chief of State Police: "Kidnapping is the present greatest crime. I recommend establishment of a State crime detection bureau."

OKLAHOMA—The outlaw reign was considered the greatest difficulty confronting officials. The Governor advised each county to purchase at least one machine gun.

WYOMING—Gregory Powell, executive secretary of the State Board of Charities Reform: "The most pressing crime problem is stick-ups, burglaries and attacks by penniless unemployed. I suggest the establishment of a Federal police system."

Arizona, Vermont, Connecticut, Kentucky, North Dakota and other States reported no outbreaks other than usual local petty crimes. Montana, however, said cattle-rustling was on the increase, with vigilantes again being utilized.

August 21, 1933

OUTLAW IS HUNTED HERE.

'Pretty Boy' Floyd Wanted for Four Killings in the West.

The police of New York, New Jersey and New England were watching all roads, bridges and ferries yesterday for a Packard automobile believed to contain the Oklahoma outlaw Pretty Boy Floyd and several companions.

A car resembling the one for which an alarm was broadcast from Lansing, Mich., and relayed from Northampton, Mass., on Saturday crossed the Delaware River Bridge going toward Trenton from Morrisville, Pa., yesterday morning. The New Jersey State Police at once broadcast another alarm and police here watched all entrances to the city.

Floyd, an escaped convict, is wanted in connection with four murders in the West. He escaped from his guards while being taken to the Federal prison at Atlanta in November, 1930, to serve a sentence for bank robbery.

January 23, 193

DILLINGER ESCAPES JAIL; USING A WOODEN PISTOL HE LOCKS GUARDS IN CELL

FLEES WITH NEGRO KILLER

Special to THE NEW YORK TIMES.

CROWN POINT, Ind., March 3.—John Dillinger, notorious bank robber and murderer, walked out of the heavily guarded and supposedly escape-proof Lake County jail this morning in a daring escape that rivals the exploits of the heroes of Wild West thrillers.

In the course of his record-making break he locked thirty-three persons in cells or storerooms. From them he forced contributions of $15 for expenses.

He cowed his guards, locking them and thirteen fellow-prisoners in a single cell, after threatening them with a two-ounce piece of wood which he had whittled to resemble a pistol and which he had stained with shoe blacking.

Then, with a Negro murderer, Herbert Youngblood, he helped himself to two of the jail's machine guns and walked to a near-by garage in search of an automobile. There Dillinger and Youngblood overawed half a dozen employes, stole the automobile of Sheriff Lillian Holley and drove away, taking with them Deputy Sheriff Ernest Blunk, the jail's fingerprint expert, and Edward Saagers, a garageman, as hostages.

Hunted by an Army.

About an hour afterward the two felons released Blunk and Saagers at Peotone, Ill., giving them $4 to pay their transportation home.

Having made good his boast that he would escape any jail, Dillinger was being hunted tonight by an army of law officials. One of them was Mrs. Holley, Lake County's Sheriff.

"If I ever see John Dillinger I'll shoot him through the head with my own pistol," the woman Sheriff exclaimed. She had declared Dillinger would never escape from her custody.

The desperado was believed to be somewhere in the Chicago countryside tonight. Police of the city were notified to be on the alert and to shoot to kill if they saw him. The Indiana State Police also were mobilized to scour the countryside for him.

Dillinger had been held here since Jan. 30 for trial March 12 on a charge of shooting and killing Policeman William Patrick O'Malley in the $20,000 hold-up of the First National Bank of East Chicago on Jan. 15. He and three members of his gang, Harry Pierpont, Russell Clark and Charles Makley, had been arrested Jan. 26 at Tucson, Ariz. Seventeen witnesses had identified Dillinger and the State prosecuting authorities were certain that he would be sent to the electric chair.

Guards Saw "Pistol" Made.

In his comparatively brief stay in the Lake County Jail the all-around "bad man" had come to be known among his fellow prisoners as "John the Whittler." His seemingly harmless pastime of playing with a piece of wood and a knife was a matter of amusement to the guards and to the other inmates of the jail. Where he got the knife was not learned.

None suspected that the hobby was part of a cunning plot to effect a jail break. Guffaws greeted Dillinger whenever he boasted to fellow inmates, "I'm going to shoot my way out of this."

The bravado of this latest escape of the resourceful defier of prison bars, once an Indiana farm boy, was typical of his career. He is accused by the police of having robbed more than 100 banks.

He laughed at them and boasted when he was captured after a chase of years that no cell could hold him.

Dillinger's first step in his almost incredible feat came about 8:30 A. M. when Blunk entered the cell occupied by Henry Jellenek and the bank robber to obtain fingerprints of the former, who is held on a murder charge! Blunk was unarmed. Dillinger thrust the blackened toy pistol which looked like the real thing against the deputy sheriff's ribs and commanded him to hurry into a bull pen cell. Meekly, the deputy sheriff obeyed and the cell door clanged behind him.

A minute or two later Warden Louis Baker entered the cell. He, too, was frightened into surrender by the wooden pistol. Hardly had the warden been shoved into the cell beside Blunk when the turnkey, Sam Calhoon, chanced on the scene. In one arm he held a bundle of soap for his charges. In the other hand were the keys of the jail. Also terrified by the bogus weapon, Calhoon yielded the keys to Dillinger and was shoved into captivity with Blunk and Baker.

Turning then to thirteen of his fellow prisoners, Dillinger snapped: "Now, you guys, get in with them."

These convicts, some of them chuckling at what they considered a joke, obeyed. The lock of the bull pen turned on them. Dillinger had accomplished his first step.

Seizes Machine Guns.

Moving carefully for fear of awaking the deputy sheriff, Ernest Baar, who was asleep in a near-by cell with a loaded pistol beside him, Dillinger started downstairs. Baar, who was off duty and who had decided to rest in a place where he would be "ready if there was any trouble," slumbered on.

Dillinger descended to the first floor, and entered the jail office, in which sat an Indiana National Guardsman, Warden Hiles. Hiles, presumably, was helping to keep Dillinger from getting out of the jail.

The Guardsman did not see the bandit slip into the office and take two loaded machine guns, resting on a table in a small booth. Before the Guardsman realized it, he was confronting Dillinger and Dillinger was pointing one of the machine guns at him.

Without further ado, Dillinger forced the militiaman to walk upstairs and enter the bullpen with the other victims.

Then he spoke to Youngblood and Jelinek.

"You two can go with me," he said.

"Yes, sir," said Youngblood.

"I don't want any part of your business," demurred Jelinek. "You go your way. I like it better here."

"O K," answered Dillinger.

He handed one of the machine guns to Youngblood and ordered Blunk to come out of the cell. The deputy obeyed and Dillinger locked the door on the other captives.

Jeers at Captives in Pen.

Then, standing in the corridor, Dillinger surveyed the inmates of the bull pen.

"Ha! Ha! Ha!" he roared. "The joke is on you eggs. I did it with my little wooden pistol."

With the helpless Blunk in the lead, Dillinger and Youngblood went to the jail kitchen, where the matron, Mrs. Lou Linton, was bustling about with her breakfast duties.

"Just be a good girl," said Dillinger. "If you keep quiet, nothing will happen to you."

Mrs. Linton made the promise, and kept it.

With their guns trained on Blunk, the fugitives went through the hall yard into an alley and then to a basement, in which stood two automobiles. Unable to start the motor of either machine, they went through the alley and out of the jail, passing the Lake County Criminal Court Building, in which Dillinger was to have stood trial.

A few moments later, the trio entered the Main Street Garage, about 150 yards from the county jail, entering by a rear door.

In the garage were Saagers, several other employes and Robert Volk, a mail carrier, who carried a pistol. Volk, however, had removed his belt and the weapon was slung over his shoulder. He made no move to shoot, and Dillinger, letting Youngblood do the guarding, turned to Saagers.

"What's the fastest car in the place?" he demanded.

Saagers guessed that the sheriff's machine was the best. It was a Ford V-8, bearing the Indiana license 679-929, and had a red headlight.

Dillinger took it. He shoved Blunk into the driver's seat, ordered Saagers and Youngblood into the rear seat, climbed into the machine and issued orders to Blunk.

"Drive slow and easy. Forty miles an hour is plenty."

The car started away, going north. Avoiding the traveled roads and taking gravel bypaths, the fugitives and their prisoners reached a point about twenty miles east of Peotone, where the machine skidded on the muddy road and toppled into a ditch.

Saagers related later that forty minutes elapsed before one car was pulled back to the road and chains were put on the wheels to prevent further mishaps of such a nature. Dillinger endured the enforced halt patiently.

The car finally righted, the party resumed the flight, driving toward Peotone, which is a few miles from Kanakee. The machine halted about four miles from Peotone.

"You boys have been pretty good," said Dillinger to Blunk and Saagers. "Here's some money to help you back." After tossing them four dollars, he took over the wheel of the machine and sped away. Saagers telephoned from a farmhouse to the authorities, and made his way in company with Blunk into Peotone. There they said that Dillinger seemed to be in high good humor and was especial-

SHERIFF AND HER PRISONER WHO FLED.

Mrs. Lillian Holley.

John Dillinger.

ly pleased with himself for hoodwinking his guards with a wooden pistol.

Saagers said afterward that he had asked Dillinger to give him the toy pistol, but that the man had refused.

"I'm keeping it for a souvenir," he said jauntily. "It's a souvenir of a trial that won't come off on March 12. That trial will never come off."

During the ride Dillinger broke into song, his selection being "The Last Roundup." Blunk said Dillinger kept repeating the line, "Git along little dogy, git along."

Blunk said he had been threatened only once on the ride. He said he tried to swerve into a passing car and cause a wreck that would stop the flight.

"Try that again and you're a dead one," growled Dillinger.

Mrs. Holley, furious at the escape, lost no time in starting pursuit. The moment she learned of the break, she telephoned to the police at nearby Gary, Ind., shouting over the wire:

"Send all the police and guns you've got. Dillinger's loose."

Her chagrin at the escape was in no way lessened by the comment of Governor Paul V. McNutt.

"We offered to take Dillinger to the penitentiary and Sheriff Holley declined," said the Governor. "We have begun our investigation to determine the reasons for the refusal as well as of the other factors in the case."

Governor McNutt ordered a thorough investigation and sent an Assistant Attorney General to Lake County to conduct it.

Early this evening the convicts' automobile was reported seen at Lincoln and Mason City, in Central Illinois. It was headed in the direction of Havana. Those reporting the car stated that two other men were riding with Dillinger and Youngblood and that machine-guns were visible. Havana police reported also that they would investigate a report that the fugitives were hiding in a Summer resort cottage near there.

Although the trail was lost after Blunk and Saagers were released, machine guns were trained on Indiana highways. At the prison at Lima, Ohio, where Dillinger's gangsters are confined, sandbags were thrown up.

The authorities were on the alert as far east as Ohio preparing against the risk of Dillinger striking suddenly anywhere in the region.

Indiana and Illinois highway police were concentrating their efforts in searching near the borderline of the two States, with their headquarters at Bradley, Ill. A report from Midland City, Ill., that Dillinger was speeding toward St. Louis caused the police there to detail five crew cars to be on the lookout at bridges spanning the Mississippi.

In Chicago, police squads were touring the streets in search of the fugitives' car.

Dillinger is 31 years old, about 5 feet 7 inches in height. The police description of him says that he has "yellow slate eyes," chestnut hair, a brown mole between his eyes, a half-inch scar on the back of his left hand and a scar on his upper lip.

The police felt sure that he would disguise himself by dyeing his hair and growing a mustache. They believed he has money cached, pointing out that at the time of his arrest in Tucson he had intended to build up his fortune to $100,000 by bank robberies and then flee to South America.

It was one of Dillinger's boasts that he could "go through a bank" and take all the money out of it in three minutes and forty seconds.

BANDIT'S ESCAPE IN TRADITION

Dillinger Case True to Old Frontier Types

JOHN DILLINGER, the Midwest bad man who broke jail by threatening guards with a wooden pistol, has been called "the country's worst outlaw since Jesse James." His escape technique reminds readers of frontier records chiefly of Black Bart. That stage robber always worked with an unloaded shotgun. He was educated, and believed the "moral effect" of an empty gun at a victim's head was just as good for purposes of brigandage as a loaded gun.

In fact, though the gangsters of prohibition days may have seemed exciting to post-war youth, it is old Wild West stage, train and bankrobbing outlaw that the Dillinger type of public enemy resembles. Black Bart had the Dillinger self-possession. He had left his Illinois home "to collect a living." Between robberies he would swagger round San Francisco, a dandy with a cane and diamond stickpin. Challenges to express drivers, written in rhyme and pinned to a tree, and a lost silk handkerchief that was traced to the laundry, he patronized, led to Black Bart's capture. His real name was Boles.

The James Boys.

Whether Jesse James and his brother killed as many men as legend said, is pure guesswork. Many historians hold that they committed no crime with the intention of taking human life. Jesse was chivalrous. 'Keep your purse, lady; we are the James boys; we don't rob ladies," he would say at a hold-up. Born in Clay County, Mo., in 1847, Jesse James in his 'teens had joined the Southern irregulars of William Quantrell, a noted guerrilla in the Civil War. He was not long in proving himself resourceful and daring.

After the close of the Civil War James and his band of ex-guerrillas were linked to nearly all train and bank robberies occurring in Missouri and Kansas. A reward of $10,000 offered for James, dead or alive, went unclaimed sixteen years. His name became a byword in the Middle West.

James was never caught. He was shot down by two of his own gang. One of them was tried for the killing, sentenced, but later pardoned.

Brockie was a desperado of the wild Boise River country. He would rush toward a victim swearing he would "shoot him as full of holes as a sieve and then cut him into sausage meat." Brockie belonged to one of those plundering bands that beset the trail of pack teams plodding into Western territory with food, ammunition and gold.

Another marauder whose deeds blacken the records of 1861 was Charley Harper. He was about 25, "of erect carriage, clear florid complexion and profuse auburn hair," and preyed upon Pacific gold camps and prospectors.

"Handsome Charley Harper and his band of brigands," records one chronicler, "mounted on strong, fleet horses which they had acquired during the Winter, dashed up the Salmon River Valley, insulting, threatening and robbing. No crime was too atrocious for them to commit, no act of shame or wantonness was uncongenial to their groveling natures."

A Lawless Sheriff.

Milton Sharp specialized in express hold-ups. When Wells Fargo placed a guard with a shotgun next each stage driver, Sharp retaliated by capturing twenty-three such guns before his final defeat at Pizen Switch. Though shackled at the ankles, he broke jail and hid in the desert. The desert starved him, and he surrendered to the law, "taking the rap" for forty years.

Muerilla in California would attend Spanish balls, dance all night, and in the morning hold up his fellow-guests as they drove back to their ranches. But the forerunner of recent prohibition racketeers was Sheriff Plummer of Montana. He always got elected to some regulatory office as a blind for operating a band of horse and cattle thieves—and also in order to possess authority to keep outside desperadoes clear of his territory.

DILLINGER EXCITES INTEREST ABROAD

Hull's Remarks on Wall Street Give London Express Clue to Rise of the Outlaw.

'TIGERS' ENCOURAGE 'WOLF'

Berlin Paper Suggests German Method of Crime Fighting—Sterilization Urged.

LONDON, April 24 (P).—Secretary Hull's trade pronouncements and references to Wall Street in a speech before The Associated Press meeting in New York received prominent position in London newspapers today.

The Telegraph featured a picture of the American Secretary of State, and it gave the most extensive display to his remarks of any speech by a United States leader, outside of President Roosevelt, since the New Deal took effect.

The Express, which long had been critical of the Roosevelt administration and began swinging the other way only a few weeks ago, linked Mr. Hull's remarks editorially with the John Dillinger case.

Saying "you learn about the life of a country by studying its crime sheet," The Express continued:

"Hull said a few words yesterday about Wall Street which will help you understand the atmosphere of the country in which Dillinger works.

"Tigers" of Wall Street.

"When a community lets a pack of man-eating tigers dwell in its midst, it is easy for a lone wolf like Dillinger to slip under the fold gate."

[In his luncheon address Secretary Hull said the government would have been "justly pilloried" had it not exposed and demanded reform of the "outrageous financial manipulations of stock markets and security flotations which stripped millions of individuals of their life savings and left a finance not worthy of public confidence."]

The Express, contrasting the methods of Dillinger and Al Capone, said the change brought about by the Roosevelt administration accounted for Dillinger's "lone wolf" characteristics.

"The Roosevelt revolution, shaking up the whole structure of the American government, has upset organized crime, which fattened on corrupt officialdom," the newspaper declared.

"Lone Raider" Developed.

"Capone had got that business down to a fine art. Nobody has followed him, because conditions have been changed.

"In the present confusion of the economic crisis it is the lone raider type you would expect to flourish. Hence, Dillinger."

There was general approval in high government quarters as well as in the press of Secretary Hull's statement that the Roosevelt administration sought the restoration of world trade on a mutually profitable basis and the preservation of world peace through economic co-operation.

THE EVOLUTION OF A CRIMINAL: THE CASE OF JOHN DILLINGER

A Farm Boy, He Began His First Prison Term After an Amateur Hold-Up in His Home Town; He Emerged a Baffling Desperado

By MILDRED ADAMS.

THE case of John Dillinger has already taken on the qualities of myth and legend. Less than a year has passed since he held up his first bank. Seven months ago his name was unknown outside of his own neighborhood and the files of certain courts and prisons in Indiana. Now, in police annals it is listed among the country's most notorious criminals.

Of all the gangsters who have infested this country in recent years, Dillinger offers the simplest material for laboratory study and the drawing of conclusions which may be useful in some distant and more orderly future. His career is short and its criminal details at least are fairly clear. His public appearances, though greatly magnified in the public mind by rumor, are mostly matters of record. From the moment last Spring when he walked into that little bank in Daleville, Ind., pointed a gun at the girl cashier who was alone there, and took $3,500 away from her, the trail is clear. All the forces that go into the evolution of what the public regards as a major criminal are visible.

Dillinger's Background.

The story of his early youth is far from being either glamourous or exotic. When it is stripped to the bone, one finds in it resentment, idleness, stupidity, cowardice, hysteria and bravado, nothing that is heroic or very unusual. Indeed, the outstanding characteristic in this man's life, up to the moment when the shooting begins, is its extreme ordinariness. Behind the figure of the bandit who has defied the police officers of half a dozen States, and run through the traps laid by Federal authorities, is a person who, so far as early evidence goes, might have been stamped out in gross lots.

Twenty years of commonplace existance in a commonplace family, nine years of confinement in what must have been a very stupid jail, must be balanced against one moment of amateur crime and eleven months of assorted robbery, arrest, jailbreak, shooting affrays. The weight of time, at least, is all on the dull side.

The telling of the story day by day, especially during the last two months when it has gained momentum and fed on the curiosity of the crowd, has a certain element of suspense and excitement. But go back over all its details, and you realize how the legendary quality it has gathered about itself has magnified and distorted it.

Conflicting Stories.

Dates and places differ in different accounts. There are conflict of detail and variety of testimony. There are figures that vary with the imagination of the teller, and hearsay evidence that is more passionate than possible. There are rumors which, subjected to the simple arithmetic of time and space, must some of them be false. There is conflicting evidence, contradictory testimony.

If you can cut through all that and get somewhere near the facts, you find a story that in its essential details might have been duplicated in a thousand families in every State in the nation. John Dillinger was the youngest son of a grocer's clerk who lived in Indianapolis. His mother died when he was only 3, and as his father was busy in the store all day and much of the evening, the responsibility for the grimy little boy fell mostly on the shoulders of an elder sister. Like most older sisters she had troubles of her own, including a beau who finally carried her off and married her while she was very young. He now drives a bakery wagon.

Johnny got through colic and the loss of baby teeth, and his first day at school, and all the rest of the small-boy crises as best he could. About the time he was ready for long pants his father married again, and added a stepmother to the picture. Also he decided to leave the grocery store and buy a farm. It went almost without saying that he was going to need his son to do the chores.

Whether the son objected either to the stepmother or the chores the record does not say. His teacher wanted him to go into high school. He was "a good boy. He never gave me any trouble. He was just ordinary. I rarely had to discipline him. He was never up to any mischief." But he did not care enough about school to make a fight for more of it, and followed his father to Mooresville and the farm.

At this point the record takes on the uncertain flicker of an old film. If John Dillinger did the chores, he spent only a short time at them. He appears in a machine shop, working in a varnish factory, clerking for the Board of Trade in Indianapolis. In that job he shuttled back and forth night and morning on the interurban trolley between the farm and the big city. There he met a girl and fell in love with her. "If my John had ever married that girl, things would be different now. He would be a good boy," his father says. But her people did not like him. He married another girl, and of her his father says, "a nicer woman never lived."

By 1924 the baby of the family, the ordinary small boy who went to school and ran errands and swept out the grocery store, was a married man who seemed to have some difficulty in staying long in a single job. There is no description of him in those days, but it does not take much imagination to picture him. Probably he smoked, probably he drank bootleg liquor. Probably, considering his fondness for feminine society, he was a "nifty dresser." None of these things distinguished him from his fellow-citizens. He was the average man. Not even Mooresville saw anything different in him.

Mooresville, too, was average, the average small town of the older Middle West. It had two main streets where the stores were, and a residence district where houses stood back in shaded lawns. It had a bank and a church or two, a lunch wagon, a park, and a pool hall, where the tough boys gathered in a smoky room to shoot Kelly and tell stories.

Evils of the Pool Hall.

No one who has not lived in a small town knows just how baleful an eminence the pool hall occupies. In New York you may live your whole life unaware of the existence of such an institution, or seeing its second-story signs with an incurious eye. But in a small town the pool hall is the traditional sink of iniquity where Satan finds all the idle hands that he needs. The local minister preaches against it, and the school principal threatens periodically to do something about closing it. Almost always it is controlled by or subservient to the local political boss.

According to the legend—and this is in line with current American small-town belief—the pool hall was Dillinger's first school of crime. There he fell in with the traditional evil influence, which resulted in the attempted hold-up of the local grocer as he came out of the barber's shop one Saturday night in 1924. The crime was amateur to a degree that must make the gunman blush if he ever thinks of it. There was apparently no attempt at disguise, concealment, or flight. Everybody is said to have recognized everybody else. Dillinger hit the old man with a piece of lead pipe, and his accomplice, who turned State's evidence, got two years while Dillinger got from ten to twenty.

If the pool hall was Dillinger's first school of crime, the reformatory was the second. Pentonville Reformatory is said by experts to be clean, reasonably modern, as well run as the average. But it suffers from what seems to be a common complaint among American jails—there are too many people in it—2,340 men and only 1,800 beds. They must sleep in two shifts, or double up, and doubling up is easier for the management. Doubling up made close association with other prisoners possible and the effect of it began to be apparent when Dillinger had been in the reformatory only a short time. He got into trouble almost from the very beginning, kept at it doggedly. Punishment had the apparent effect of making him resentful and intent on getting out. He told the authorities he was a machinist, and was assigned to the molding shop. Almost immediately he "hid out" in an effort to avoid going back to his cell.

Later he sawed through bars over his door and was found wandering about the cell block. He gambled, was disorderly, fought with another inmate, destroyed prison property. In July, 1929, he was transferred to the State Penitentiary at Michigan City, along with his friends whose "rescue" he was later to plan. With him went Harry Pierpont, John Hamilton and other friends of his, older convicts all of them, and apparently his constant associates in the reformatory.

© NANA From Times Wide World.
The Boy Who Went Wrong—
Dillinger at the Age of 17.

Released on Parole.

The lessons he learned in the two prisons were very speedily put into practice when he got out. They were not those of sober and God-fearing industry. In May of 1933 he was released by the parole board on the request of his father, the Mooresville minister and the grocer he had held up. He had been in a reformatory five years and in a penitentiary four.

In July, with another friend of reformatory days who had been released earlier, he walked into a small-town bank and robbed its girl cashier. Two more robberies netted him some $25,000, but when ambition led him into Ohio he was caught. From the Lima jail he was released by his old reformatory friends, who had themselves broken out of the Michigan City penitentiary in a sensational jailbreak whose plans are now credited to Dillinger. They killed a sheriff in the process, and for the first time Dillinger's name appeared in the New York papers.

His career since that time is a matter of common knowledge, but, since the melting of the snow and the freeing of the roads so that he and his gang could operate freely over the whole Mississippi Valley, the facts have come so fast that possibility of analyzing them has been lost. The amount of his stealings has been estimated at about five millions; his acts have been followed by thirteen deaths, six among his own men, six among officers of the law, and one of a bystander.

Questions and an Answer.

Where he learned his skill in crime, how he knew what kind of guns to equip himself with, where to get bullet-proof vests, how to gather together the dregs of the underworld, both male and female, to help him in his swift raids—each of these is a question.

Dillinger's first crime was the most amateur of hold-ups, and there was nothing about it that indicated any special knowledge of anything except the fact that if you hit a man on the head with a piece of lead pipe he will fall to the ground. After nine years in two jails, he proceeded to commit crimes which were organized and effective, which employed all the modern weapons of offense and defense, and which implied various "hide-outs" that could not have been set up spontaneously.

The men he worked with were men he had met and made friends with in those same two jails. The nucleus of his gang—if it is his, and here is disagreement even here—consisted of the ten convicts who broke out of Michigan City penitentiary in September with assistance from the outside which is said to have been planned by Dillinger, though he was himself in another jail at the time of the actual break. Three of them came over a week or so later and got him out.

In other words, the picture presented by the evidence is that of a boy who undergoes in what is called a reformatory an intensive course of training in organized and major crime. His teachers are well-known convicted criminals. His classrooms are the cells and the workshops built by the State to punish and to reform. When he is released it is with special knowledge of existing gang organization. He knew where to go, how to start.

The Public Attitude.

That the State's effort at punishment had not resulted in making him a less dangerous enemy to society than he was when first sent to jail seems clear. Nevertheless, the public attitude toward him, and toward the conditions he represents and the forces which made possible his career, is not yet clear or single-minded.

There is first of all the attitude of the Mooresville people. It is best set forth by a petition circulated this very month and addressed to the Governor of Indiana. In it they asked for a conditional pardon for Dillinger if he surrendered and promised to abide by the State laws.

The attitude of the country at large, as reflected in conversation and in written comment, in questions asked in Congress and in speeches on laws proposed to curb the Dillingers of the future, is divided between indignation and oratory. The one thing which stands out in the whole lamentable picture is the fact that the jails, of which Michigan City penitentiary and Pentonville reformatory are said by experts to be fairly representative examples, do not seem to be doing what the public expects of them.

April 29, 1934

Roosevelt Opens Attack on Crime, Signing Six Bills as 'Challenge'

Extending Federal Jurisdiction to Interstate Gang Offenses, With Death for Some Kidnappers, He Calls on People to Join in War on Underworld.

Special to THE NEW YORK TIMES.

WASHINGTON, May 18.—Romanticizing of crime and tolerating of known criminals were denounced today by President Rooosevelt as he signed six bills designed to break the back of organized crime.

Calling upon the American people to cooperate in curbing underworld activities, he placed himself "squarely behind" the Department of Justice in its task of bringing lawbreakers "to book."

The President's statement was as follows:

"These laws are a renewed challenge on the part of the Federal Government to interstate crime. They are also complementary to the broader program designed to curb the evildoer of whatever class.

"In enacting them, the Congress has provided additional equipment for the Department of Justice to aid local authorities. Lacking these new weapons, the department already has tracked down many major outlaws and its vigilance has spread fear in the underworld. With additional resources I am confident that it will make still greater inroads upon organized crime.

"I regard this action today as an event of the first importance. So far as the Federal Government is concerned, there will be no relenting.

"But there is one thing more. Law enforcement and gangster extermination cannot be made completely effective so long as a substantial part of the public looks with tolerance upon known criminals, permits public officers to be corrupted or intimidated by them or applauds efforts to romanticize crime.

"Federal men are constantly facing machine-gun fire in the pursuit of gangsters. I ask citizens, individually and as organized groups, to recognize the facts and meet them with courage and determination.

"I stand squarely behind the efforts of the Department of Justice to bring to book every law breaker, big and little."

The bills signed make it a Federal offense, punishable with heavy fines or imprisonment, to assault a Federal agent or officer on duty, to rob a Federal bank, to incite or participate in a riot at a Federal prison and to send kidnapping or ransom notes in any form across a State line.

Another bill strengthens the so-called "Lindbergh kidnapping law" by giving a jury power to authorize a death sentence where the victim has not been returned unharmed. It makes it a Federal crime to carry a kidnapped person across a State line and makes a seven-day disappearance presumptive evidence that a kidnapping victim has been so transported.

It is also declared a Federal offense to transport across a State line stolen goods, including bonds and money in excess of $5,000.

A bill making it a Federal crime to cross State lines to escape prosecution or avoid giving testimony was passed by the Senate and House and is now in conference. Another bill regulating the sale of firearms is pending in the Ways and Means Committee.

Twelve crime measures were introduced originally, but four were dropped, partly owing to objections raised in committee by advocates of States' rights who hesitated to grant increased power to the Federal Government.

May 19, 193

BARROW AND WOMAN ARE SLAIN BY POLICE IN LOUISIANA TRAP

Bandit Pair Are Riddled With Bullets as Car Speeds at 85 Miles an Hour.

BOTH HAD GUNS IN HANDS

Ambuscade on the Highway Ends Long Criminal Career of the Pair.

DILLINGER DOCTOR JAILED

Outlaw's Woman Aide Also Convicted — Moley Submits Crime Report.

Barrow's End Is Sudden

Special to THE NEW YORK TIMES

SHREVEPORT, La., May 23.— Clyde Barrow, notorious Texas "bad man" and murderer, and his cigar-smoking, quick-shooting woman accomplice, Bonnie Parker, were ambushed and shot to death today in an encounter with Texas Rangers and Sheriff's deputies.

The 24-year-old desperado, who was accused of twelve murders in the last two years, and his companion whizzed along a little-traveled, paved road near Gibsland, about fifty miles east of here, at eighty-five miles an hour in a high-speed gray automobile, rushing into a carefully-laid death trap.

Before they could use any of the weapons in the small arsenal they had with them, the Rangers and others in the posse riddled them and their car with a deadly hail of bullets.

The onrushing machine, with the dead man at the wheel, careened crazily for an instant and then catapulted into an embankment. While the wheels of the wrecked machine still whirled, the officers, taking no chances with the gunman who had tricked them so often, poured another volley of bullets into the machine.

Both Died Holding Guns.

A moment later the uproar in the otherwise peaceful countryside spot had subsided and the officers swarmed over to the car. They found that Barrow and Bonnie had

TEXAS OUTLAWS SLAIN BY OFFICERS OF LAW.

Times Wide World Photo.

Clyde Barrow and his companion, Bonnie Parker, who were killed in Louisiana by a party that included former Texas Rangers. This photograph was found recently by the police in a hideout from which Barrow had to make a quick get-away.

died with weapons in their hands, prepared to kill at the slightest alarm. The woman was crumpled up on the seat, her head between her knees and a machine gun in her lap. Barrow, a smear of red, wet rags, had been clutching a sawed-off shotgun in one hand as he drove.

The car proved to be a traveling arsenal. In it the officers found three submachine guns, six automatic pistols, one revolver, two sawed-off automatic shotguns and enough ammunition for a siege.

Governor O. K. Allen of Louisiana congratulated Sheriff Anderson Jordan of Bienville Parish, where Barrow and the Parker woman were killed, when he was informed of the details today.

The so-called "Public Enemy No. 1 of the Southwest," a mere hoodlum in Dallas up to 1930, met his end in an ambush that had been planned carefully by Frank Hamer, a former captain in the Texas Rangers, who had clung to Barrow's trail for years.

Hamer, who was recently commissioned as a highway patrolman for the special purpose of getting his man, as well as his gunwoman, trailed Barrow into Bossier Parish, where the criminal was said to have relatives.

It was reported that Hamer had received a tip as to Barrow's whereabouts from the father of a convict who recently escaped from a Texas penitentiary. The father, a resident of Louisiana, whispered

the word to the authorities in the hope of winning clemency for his son.

Several weeks ago Hamer and his fellow officers barely missed the couple at a hide-out at Black Lake. Since then, the Rangers and Sheriff's deputies charted the highways that had been frequented by the pair and then quietly adopted a scheme of watchful waiting.

Once again Hamer picked up a "red-hot" clue to Barrow's trail, this time in Bossier Parish. He anticipated that the outlaw and his woman friend would head west toward Texas. Hamer, a Ranger associate, Sheriff Jordan and his men raced ahead to a point on the highway where they got an unobstructed view of the road. There they hid and waited.

Shortly after 9 A. M. the lookouts recognized the eight-cylinder sedan approaching at terrific speed. Some of the officers coolly walked out into the roadway, motioning and shouting for the driver to halt, while those in the ambuscade trained their weapons on the criminals.

Barrow answered by stepping on the accelerator and reaching for a sawed-off shotgun. In a split second the officers of the law, spurred by the knowledge of Barrow's ruthlessness, opened up their death-dealing barrage.

The first volley appeared to have the effect of a bolt of lightning, and the uncontrolled car shot with its topmost speed into the embankment. The law had settled its score with Barrow and his quick-shooting woman accomplice.

Associated Press Photo.

Frank Hamer, Leader of the Posse That Killed the Bandits.

May 24, 1934

33

BARROW'S KILLINGS DATE FROM PAROLE

2 Brothers Were First Arrested in 1930 for Auto Theft, but Fled From Prison.

ACCUSED OF 12 MURDERS

Biggest Robbery of Their Career Netted $3,500—Woman Aide Had Been a Waitress.

Clyde Barrow was a snake-eyed murderer who killed without giving his victims a chance to draw. He was slight, altogether unheroic in physical appearance.

Bonnie Parker was a fit companion for him. She was a hard-faced, sharp-mouthed woman who gave up a waitress job in a Kansas City restaurant to become the mistress of Ray Hamilton, Texas bank robber. Barrow took her away from Hamilton.

There were two Barrow brothers, Clyde and Marvin Ivan, who bore the nicknames Buck and Ivy. Both, like John Dillinger, were released on parole and from then on ran wild over the Southwest, killing right and left.

The number of deaths attributed to Dillinger and his band after he was paroled totals about thirteen. The Barrows and the Parker woman, when they were turned loose on parole, murdered about twelve persons. The exact number is uncertain. Eight of their victims were policemen or guards.

The Barrows were sons of Harry Barrow, owner of a gasoline station in West Dallas. They began a career of petty crime in San Antonio and Dallas while they were still in their teens, but escaped conviction until 1930. They were "investigated" in a number of motorcar thefts, but managed to squirm out of trouble each time.

First Sentenced in 1930.

Early in January, four years ago, they were picked up in a stolen car in Henrietta, Texas. Marvin was sentenced to four years in Huntsville prison and Clyde, who had confessed not only to the car theft but to two burglaries, pleaded guilty and received a two-year sentence.

On March 8, 1930, Marvin, then a "trusty" or privileged prisoner, walked out of the jail and three days later smuggled saws into Clyde's cell. Clyde cut his way out that night, taking two companions with him.

His freedom was short-lived. He was picked up in Middletown, Ohio, a week later and re-entered Huntsville under a longer sentence. With penalties for the jail break he was supposed to serve fourteen years, but he walked free on Feb. 2, 1932 on a general parole signed by the Governor.

Marvin Barrow, meanwhile, had returned to prison of his own volition. Two days after Christmas, 1931, he surrendered. He had married after his escape, and his wife, Blanche Caldwell, had persuaded him to go back, he said.

A month after Clyde got out on parole he was identified as a member of a band of filling-station looters. That was the limit of his ambition, it seemed. None of his robberies ever netted him and his followers more than $3,500.

His homicidal career started two months after he was paroled. In Hillsboro, Texas, late on the night of April 27, 1932, he awakened John Bucher, a merchant, on the pretense that he wanted to buy guitar strings. Another man was with him. When Bucher turned his back they shot him. Their loot was $40 in cash.

Five months later, at a dance hall in Atoka, Okla., Sheriff C. G. Maxwell and Eugene Moore, undersheriff, saw two young men—strangers in town—drinking out of a bottle. Maxwell told them to put the bottle away.

"We don't permit that here," he said.

"Oh, you don't?"

Out came a revolver. Moore was shot through the heart. Maxwell fell dangerously wounded. The strangers—Clyde Barrow and Ray Hamilton—leaped into their stolen car and got way. They never gave their victims a chance to draw.

At Grand Prairie, Texas, not long afterward, Clyde Barrow's band staged its hold-up masterpiece—a $3,500 raid on the interurban station in the town. They drifted on, in stolen automobiles, while Rangers, highway patrols and town police searched in vain for them on the roads.

They showed up again in the Fall, this time at Sherman, Texas. On Oct. 11 they entered a butcher shop owned by Howard Hall, 70 years old. They poked revolvers at Hall and Homer Glaze, a clerk. Hall tried to push the weapon away. They shot him in the abdomen and left him, dead.

Doyle Johnson, a citizen of Temple, Texas, tried to prevent a young man and a young woman from stealing his car in front of his home, one night in December, 1932. They shot him off the running board of the car as they drove away. That, it turned out later, was the first appearance of Bonnie Parker in the picture.

Clyde Barrow had met her in the Kansas City restaurant. Ray Hamilton, her man, was serving a long sentence for robbery at the time. He had been picked up after the shooting in Atoka. He had quarreled with Barrow over Bonnie and they had gone separate ways.

List of Killings Grows.

Malcolm Davis, a deputy, was shot to death by Barrow at Fort Worth when he approached the murderer's stolen car to inspect the license plates. He got no warning, no chance to draw. A volley of shotgun slugs killed him. That was on Jan. 7, 1933.

Sergeant G. B. Kahler of the State Highway Patrol in Joplin. Mo., and a raiding party located Barrow, the Parker woman, Marvin Barrow and his wife, in a stone house that had living quarters on the upper floor and a garage in the lower floor. It was the morning of April 13.

The garage doors suddenly burst open, a car shot out, its occupants spraying machine gun bullets from both sides. Constable J. W. Harryman and Detective Harry L. McGinnis fell in the road, mortally wounded. When the troopers entered the house they found Marvin Barrow's parole certificate and some cigar stubs marked with the imprint of tiny teeth, Bonnie Parker's signature.

At Alma, Ark., on June 23, Clyde Barrow killed Henry Humphrey, a city marshal who tried to prevent a general-store hold-up, and got away again. Posses roamed the countryside, but the Barrows were elusive. They fled to the woods and lived on canned goods, afraid to venture into a town or village.

In a running fight with a posse outside of Platte City, Mo., the Barrows and Bonnie Parker wounded three policemen and got away. Five days later, on July 24, they were surrounded in a woods near Dexter, Iowa. They fought from behind a barricade formed by a fallen tree.

Marvin Barrow was hit three times in that fight. He and his wife were picked up by the attacking party after Clyde and Bonnie Parker had fled. The fugitives waded a stream, ran through a corn field to a farmhouse, stole the farmer's car and escaped. Marvin Barrow died soon afterward in an Iowa hospital. His wife was sent to the penitentiary under a ten-year sentence.

Another six months passed before Clyde Barrow turned up again, this time at the prison from which he had been paroled. He had hidden three revolvers in a clump of weeds on the prison farm and had sent a letter to Ray Hamilton, describing their location. A short distance from the farm, hidden by trees, he had a fast car, with Bonnie Parker at the wheel.

Hamilton and four other convicts, who knew of the plan, reached the hidden pistols. They killed Major Crowson, one of the guards, and wounded Olan Bozeman, another. Then they headed for the automobile, Barrow covering their retreat with a steady stream of machine gun fire. He and the gun were concealed in a bushy undergrowth. Bonnie Parker kept tooting the horn to guide them. They gained the car and got away.

Gabe Wright, a Negro, captured J. B. French, a "lifer," one of the four who escaped with Hamilton, when French entered his cabin the next day. All the others, including Hamilton, were picked up, one by one, but not before they had done further damage.

At Grapevine, Texas, on the morning of April 2, 1934, State Highway Patrolmen E. B. Wheeler and H. D. Murphy were passing a car parked in the road when, without warning, machine guns mowed them down. Clyde Barrow's fingerprints were found on a whisky bottle at the spot. And there were some cigar butts with tiny tooth marks beside the bottle.

The last murder attributed to Clyde Barrow and Bonnie Parker was committed in Miami, Okla., on April 6. Cal Campbell, a 63-year-old constable, was shot to death and Percy Boyd, police chief, was shot in the face as they approached Barrow's car, which was mired in the mud. The murderers stole a farmer's car to get away.

Clyde Barrow was heard from again when Hamilton went on trial in Texas following his capture in Sherman, in that State. He sent a mocking letter to the authorities in which he scoffed at Hamilton for a published statement that he (Barrow) was the instigator of all the killings. Hamilton was sentenced to 362 years in prison.

That was a month ago. He eluded his pursuers until yesterday.

DILLINGER SLAIN IN CHICAGO; SHOT DEAD BY FEDERAL MEN IN FRONT OF MOVIE THEATRE

REACHED FOR HIS GUN

Outlaw's Move Met by Four Shots, All Finding Their Mark.

HAD LIFTED HIS FACE

Desperado Had Also Treated Finger Tips With Acid to Defeat Prints.

TWO WOMEN WOUNDED

Agents, Tipped Fugitive Was Going to Theatre, Waited While He Saw Show.

Special to THE NEW YORK TIMES.

CHICAGO, July 22.—John Dillinger, America's Public Enemy No. 1 and the most notorious criminal of recent times, was shot and killed at 10:40 o'clock tonight by Federal agents a few seconds after he had left the Biograph Theatre at 2,433 Lincoln Avenue, on Chicago's North Side.

One bullet penetrated the head and another the chest of the desperate outlaw. He died as he was being taken to the Alexian Brothers Hospital. The body was later removed to the county morgue, where the identification of Dillinger was made positive.

According to Melvin H. Purvis, chief of the investigating forces of the Department of Justice in Chicago, and leader of the band of sixteen men who had waited for more than two hours while the desperado viewed his last picture show, Dillinger attempted to put up a fight.

"He saw me give a signal to my men to close in," Chief Purvis said. "He became alarmed and reached into a belt and was drawing the .38-calibre pistol he carried concealed when two of the agents let him have it. Dillinger was lying prone before he was able to get the gun out and I took it from him."

Surgical Disguise Fails.

Dillinger had taken great precautions to prevent his being recognized. His face had been lifted by a surgical process since his last picture was taken and he had dyed his hair a darker shade than its natural light reddish brown.

"It was a good job the surgeons did," Chief Purvis said, "but I knew him the minute I saw him. You couldn't miss if you had studied that face as much as I have."

Two women, passers-by who had no connection with the outlaw, were wounded by stray bullets fired by the Federal agents. They are Mrs. Etta Natalsky, 45 years old, of 2,433 Lincoln Avenue, and Miss Theresa Paulus. Each was struck in the left leg. Their injuries, it was said, were not serious.

Patron of Gangster Film.

Chief Purvis and twelve of his own men, accompanied by Captain Timothy O'Neill and three members of the East Chicago police force, went to the vicinity of the small theatre at about 8:30 P. M.

They had received information during the afternoon that Dillinger would attend the performance of "Manhattan Melodrama," a gang and gun movie featuring Clark Gable and William Powell, in the evening.

The sixteen men were posted strategically, some at all possible exits of the theatre, with groups to the north and south, and one detail on the opposite side of busy Lincoln Avenue. Chief Purvis, seating himself in his automobile a few feet south of the show house, watched.

It was about 8:30 P. M. when Dillinger walked up to the entrance and bought a ticket, or tickets. A Chicago policeman who happened to be at the scene said he was accompanied by two women, one dressed in red, but Chief Purvis said he saw none. Passing into the theatre, Dillinger took a seat.

While he was inside, the agents completed their preparations for his emergence. There were so many of them, and their actions seemed, to the theatre manager and to observers in the neighborhood, to be so suspicious that the police were notified.

Policemen Frank Slattery, Edward Meisterheimer and Michael Garrity, who investigated, were shown Federal badges by the watchers and interfered not at all, although they were not told the object of the agents.

According to Chief Purvis, it was two hours and four minutes before the outlaw walked out of the theatre. He seemed completely at ease. He wore a white silk shirt, a gray tie flecked with black, white canvas shoes and gray flannel trousers. He had on no coat. His hat was a white sailor.

"I was standing in the entrance of the Goetz Country Club, a tavern just south of the theatre, when he walked by," Chief Purvis said.

"He gave us a piercing look. Just after he went by and was midway of the next building, a National Tea Company store, I raised my hand and gave the prearranged signal.

"Dillinger went on, perhaps another dozen feet, and stepped down a curb to the mouth of an alley. My men, at least five or six, were closing in on him suddenly.

"I had thought it possible that he could have a weapon concealed and the plan was to seize him, pinion his arms and make him a prisoner. However, the men were instructed to take no chances.

"Becoming suspicious, Dillinger whirled around toward the men closing in. He was facing, I believe, toward the dark alley when he reached for his pistol. And that was when the shots that killed him were fired. Four altogether were fired. Two took effect. Presumably the two women were hurt by the pair that missed."

Instantly there was a great commotion. The injured women screamed. George Gordon, son-in-law of Mrs. Natalsky and owner of the Goetz Tavern, hearing that she was injured, ran out to the alley. Seeing the body of a man lying wounded in the alley, he cried:

"I think that's my brother-in-law."

The agents, roughly pushing him back, told him to be quiet and not interfere. The victim, they assured him, was not his brother-in-law.

Chief Purvis leaned over the dying outlaw, looked at a gold ring which Dillinger was known to wear as a luck piece at all times, took his pistol from the belt—it was thrust down below the belt—and ordered that he be taken to the nearest hospital.

There was a quick run to the Alexian Brothers Hospital, but the institution would not admit Dillinger as a patient. There was a very good reason for this. He was dead.

The body was laid on the grass in front of the hospital, while four of the agents stood guard over it until the arrival of a deputy coroner. This official gave permission for the removal of the body to the county morgue.

Chief Purvis declined to give out the names of the men who had fired on Dillinger, nor would he elaborate on the manner in which the information leading to the killing had been obtained.

"There were two or three men who fired," he said. "I was not one of them, but they were Federal agents."

Mrs. Pearl Dowss, 924 Montrose Avenue, related that she was only about three feet away from the group of men when she was startled by the shooting. A flying bullet almost struck her, she added. But she was so interested in what had happened that she remained for more than a half hour at the scene.

Some of the observers of the drama declared that the girl in red, who dropped behind Dillinger as he emerged from the theatre, raised her hand, with a handkerchief in it.

It was the opinion of these observers that the girl in red was the "finger" and was cooperating with the agents. At any rate, she disappeared after the shooting and there was no clue to her identity.

Within a few minutes a great throng had gathered about the mouth of the alley. The word had gone forth that John Dillinger, a character known to all as the most determined and wary killer on the continent, had paid his last debt to society.

Also hastening to the scene, and seeking information, were dozens of squads of Chicago policemen, who had been kept in the dark about the presence of Dillinger in the city.

No disclosure was made concerning the length of Dillinger's last stay in Chicago, nor concerning the location of his residence.

The presence of Captain O'Neill and his men from East Chicago, where Dillinger shot and killed Policeman William Patrick O'Malley during a bank hold-up in January, led to reports that they had furnished the clue that brought the kill. This could not be confirmed.

Policemen Slattery and Meisterheimer were in civilian clothes near the scene of the shooting. According to Slattery, one of the Federal agents told him afterward that he was among the luckiest of men.

"When we got the signal you were close to Dillinger," said the agent. "You looked like Dillinger and I was about to shoot you when the other fellows let loose and killed the right man."

J. Edgar Hoover, chief of Bureau of Investigation in Washington, expressed himself as delighted that Federal men had succeeded in ridding the country of its most dangerous criminal.

July 23, 1934

DILLINGER came to his end a few blocks away from the site of the St. Valentine's Day massacre several years ago, but DILLINGER'S type of outlawry is not the one which reached its peak in that famous gangland episode. The difference may perhaps be best summed up by saying that DILLINGER was engaged in direct warfare against society, and that he slew officers of the law and peaceful citizens. It would be more correct to speak of his band than his gang. His followers were strictly in the tradition of the old outlaw bands.

The wars of the real gangs during the golden age before Repeal were waged between rivals. The seven men who were stood up in a Chicago garage on St. Valentine's Day and mowed down by machine-gun fire were not police officers, or bank clerks, or innocent bystanders who were in the way. The victims were rival gangsters and they fell as an incident in the fierce underworld competition for profits. The gangs fed on the general public, but they did not assault or murder quiet citizens. They murdered each other in a struggle for privileges.

Allies of the Underworld. This form of organized crime DILLINGER plainly does not represent. He belongs to the line of JESSE JAMES and not of AL CAPONE and "Dutch" SCHULTZ. He did not prosper on the crime opportunities created by a social phenomenon like prohibition. He was the highway robber as all ages have known the type. Certainly no one has ventured to suggest that DILLINGER in his depredations enjoyed political protection; and that may be said to constitute the hallmark of the post-armistice gangs. The essential feature of organized crime is that it reached into the seats of political power. The underworld can function on a large scale only with the aid of helpers in the upper world.

DILLINGER, in this sense, would not stand for the apogee of the gangster trade. The real peak was reached in AL CAPONE, and the decline began with CAPONE'S departure for Atlanta. The rise of DILLINGER would signalize, in fact, the passing of the old organized underworld, with its large-scale operations and big profits, mainly rooted in prohibition. With the coming of repeal the field of opportunity shrank. The men who fought each other in beer and booze wars, or who would naturally take to such employment, had to turn their hands to bank robbery, kidnapping and other old forms of banditry.

PRETTY BOY FLOYD SLAIN AS HE FLEES BY FEDERAL MEN

CORNERED ON OHIO FARM

Melvin Purvis Leads Officers in Shooting Down Outlaw.

BANDIT FALLS IN FLIGHT

Unable to Use Pistols After Ignoring Purvis's Order to Surrender.

Special to THE NEW YORK TIMES.

EAST LIVERPOOL, Ohio, Oct. 22.—Charles (Pretty Boy) Floyd, one of the most notorious outlaws of the present era, was shot and killed on a farm seven miles from here this afternoon as he fled from Federal agents and East Liverpool police who were closing in on him.

The Chicago Department of Justice head, Melvin H. Purvis, nemesis of the late John Dillinger, was in at the end. Leading four Federal men and four East Liverpool policemen Purvis said he shouted a command to Floyd to halt. The bandit first darted toward a corn crib for cover, then, changing his mind, sprinted toward a wooded ridge. Machine guns and pistols barked and the desperado fell, mortally wounded in the body.

Upon reaching him the agents found he held a .45-calibre automatic in his hand and had a second automatic in a shoulder holster. Neither one had been fired, though the magazines of both were full.

"Who the hell tipped you?" Floyd asked the officers. A moment later he said, "Where is Eddie?" "Eddie," the officers judged, was Adam Richetti, who was captured near Wellsville Saturday, when he and Floyd fought a gun battle with police.

The officers carried the desperado into the farmhouse of Mrs. Ellen Conkle, where he had appeared earlier for food.

Purvis bent close to Floyd, questioning him about the machine gun massacre of five men at the Kansas City Union Station in June, 1933.

"I am Floyd," the dying bandit admitted, but to the last he denied complicity in the Kansas City killings. He lived about fifteen minutes after the burst of fire had sent fourteen bullets into his back and one into his side.

Had Meal at Farmhouse.

The body was brought to an undertaking establishment in East Liverpool.

The outlaw's pockets yielded $120 in cash. Little else was found among his personal effects.

The killing climaxed two days of intensive man-hunting in this area by Federal, State and county officers after Floyd escaped in the gun fight with policemen near Wellsville.

This afternoon Floyd appeared at the Conkle farm and asked for something to eat. He received a meal, and after eating it he asked Mrs. Conkle if she could arrange to get him an automobile to take him to Youngstown. She replied that she would have to wait until the men returned from the fields.

Floyd had been sighted on the farm by Arthur Conkle, brother-in-law of Mrs. Conkle, who notified the officers in East Liverpool.

When Purvis arrived with his Department of Justice agents and the four police officers, including Police Chief Hugh J. McDermott of East Liverpool, Floyd was trying to persuade S. L. Dyke, farm hand and brother of Mrs Conkle, to take him to Youngstown.

Leaping out of their cars, the officers closed in on the gunman. Floyd started to run, but the officers' markmanship prevented him from reaching the shelter of the woods.

Richetti Not Told of Death.

Held in jail at Wellsville while Missouri and Ohio authorities quarreled over his custody, Richetti was not immediately told of his chief's death. Richetti had denied that his companion in the Saturday gun fight was Floyd, but the majority of the officers held that the Oklahoma desperado was there.

The first clue of the bandits, both of whom had been sought as the trigger men in the Kansas City massacre, was provided when a native, Alonzo Israel, became suspicious of them when he saw them camping near the outskirts of Wellsville.

Chief of Police John H. Fultz of Wellsville, accompanied by two citizens, went to the place and commanded the two men to surrender. The suspects opened fire, wounding the chief in the ankle. The police fired back and a moment later Richetti surrendered, unhurt.

Richetti's companion, believed to have been Floyd, fled during the confusion, commandeered a passing car and escaped. When the engine of that machine failed, he stopped another automobile and continued. Near Liston he encountered another posse, so he left the car and fled into the woods.

Though Chief Fultz said he was confident that he had wounded the man, whom he positively identified as Floyd, the stories related later by the owners of the automobiles the fugitive had commandeered were to the effect that he could not have been seriously wounded.

Floyd a Will-o'-the-Wisp.

For a time it was believed that Floyd had made another of the spectacular escapes that have studded his notorious career. A posse of more than 100 Federal and local authorities hunted him through woods and thickets in this section, while officers in surrounding States were on the lookout for him, but the trail grew colder, with no material clews being unearthed until the search suddenly ended in success this afternoon.

It ended one of the most sensational criminal chases in the history of the country, for Floyd had slipped through numerous Oklahoma man hunts in the early stages of his banditry and more recently had eluded nation-wide searches with almost a will-o'-the-wisp ease.

The latest charge of murder was laid against Floyd today. He and Richetti were charged in warrants issued in Columbia, Mo., with murdering Sheriff Roger Wilson and Sergeant Ben Booth of the Missouri State Highway patrol a few days before the Kansas City massacre.

He and Richetti were also the objects of an intensive investigation in Kansas City today by a Federal grand jury which delved into the Union Station slayings. It was believed the jury had planned a speedy indictment of the two outlaws for transportation of a stolen car out of the State so that they could be brought into the jurisdiction of Missouri for trial.

Despite the pleadings of both Federal and Missouri officers, Chief of Police Fultz for hours today steadfastly refused to give up the prisoner who had shot him in the ankle. Even when Sheriff Thomas B. Bash of Kansas City and Federal Agent S. P. Cowley went to Wellsville by plane with a murder warrant for Richetti they were greeted with the same defiance. But tonight Chief Fultz relented and said he would surrender Richetti tomorrow.

Richetti, however, was arraigned here on charges of shooting to kill Chief Fultz and carrying concealed weapons. He was then bound over to the local grand jury.

"Richetti tried to take my life," Chief Fultz said while he still was resisting the prisoner's removal. "He shot one of my citizens and he nicked me, therefore I feel that we have a right to take care of our case. I think I should keep him here where I can keep an eye on him until he comes to trial. We'll see that he doesn't get away."

FLOYD A RUTHLESS KILLER.

Starting as Auto Thief, He Ran Gamut of Violent Crime.

Charles Arthur (Pretty Boy) Floyd wore the mantle which slipped from John Dillinger's shoulders when he fell, bullet-riddled, outside a Chicago movie theatre. Floyd, who had already become known as a twentieth century edition of Jesse James, was called the "most dangerous man alive."

The stories have it that he was born on a farm near Sallisaw, Okla., in the middle of the Poteau mountain country—steeped in the tradition of outlawry. His youth was no different from that of any of the others; his name first got into the records when, barely 20, he married a 16-year-old girl who later left him.

Drifting to Kansas City, he committed the first crime for which the law sought him out. It caught him, too, and he was sentenced to the Missouri penitentiary for stealing an automobile. He was released in 1929 and paired up with Red Lovett, whom he had met in jail and who had been freed a year before. His name became linked with shootings, and some one dubbed him "Pretty Boy" about the same time. He was tall and heavy-set; handsome, perhaps, but in a rugged, scowling sort of way.

Raided Banks in Ohio.

Growing more and more skillful in the art of successfully holding up small-town banks, Floyd transferred his attention to Akron, Ohio. With three companions, he rented a bungalow and began to prey upon banks in the surrounding area. One Winter day the quartet passed a red light in Akron and Patrolman Harland F. Manes blew his whistle. There was a burst of flame from the car and Manes fell dead. The speeding murderers were captured and one of them, Tom Bradley, was sentenced to the electric chair. Another got life imprisonment; but Floyd managed to "beat the murder rap." Nevertheless, he was identified as having taken part in a hold-up at Sylvania, Ohio, and sentenced to fifteen years.

It was his escape from guards on the train taking him to jail—he plunged through a window and down an embankment—that established Floyd as an arch-criminal. His reputation grew steadily; he became a myth, as well as a man. He was likened more and more to the lawless "heroes" of the old West.

On March 25, 1931, the bodies of Wally and Bill Ash, with whom Floyd had become acquainted in Kansas City, were found in a burning car near there. Ballistic tests established that the bullets which had killed them came from Floyd's gun. It was reasoned that the brothers had been rash enough to attempt to double-cross the Pretty Boy.

His name figured from then on in almost every unsolved crime in the Southwest. But there apparently was no doubt about his part in the killing of former Sheriff Irv Kelly of McIntosh County, Okla., in April, 1932. Kelly had warned Floyd he was coming to run him in; Floyd was waiting for him. Kelly was killed, and Floyd escaped again.

Named in Many Crimes.

Early in November, 1932, he raided his home county, seizing $2,530 from the Sallisaw State Bank. A posse pursued his band, but lost the trail in the rough country near the Arkansas border. Six months later, a detective wounded in a Rensselaer (N. Y.) bank hold-up, tentatively identified his picture as that of one of the gunmen.

In June, 1933, he kidnapped Sheriff Jack Killingsworth of Bolivar, Mo., freeing him unharmed the next day. The following month the Department of Justice got on his trail in connection with the Kansas City machine-gun killing of four officers and their prisoner, Frank Nash, on June 17. A note purported to be from Floyd was received shortly after, informing officials he had nothing to do with the crime.

His name was mentioned in the Urschel kidnapping; in a plot to abduct a well-known motion-picture actress at Malibu Beach; in various other sensational crimes and reported crime attempts.

Despite the mailed denial of Floyd's complicity in the Kansas City multiple killing, Federal agents relentlessly pursued him. On Oct. 11 he was trapped by two Iowa officers in a farmhouse near the Minnesota border. There was a running gun battle, but he escaped. Mrs. Ruby Floyd, the wife who deserted and disowned him, supported herself and their son, Jackie, by lecturing on "Crime Does Not Pay." Back near Tulsa, a scrawny-faced, tight-lipped woman predicted that her son would come home in a coffin.

Pretty Boy's mother was right.

October 23, 1934

By The Associated Press.

WASHINGTON, Oct. 22.—The name of George (Baby Face) Nelson tonight was underscored by the Justice Department as the new "No. 1 public enemy."

Only this morning he was "No. 2." But he was elevated when Charles (Pretty Boy) Floyd fell this afternoon under a hail of Federal gunfire.

Nelson, a member of the late John Dillinger's gang, is charged with slaying Carter Baum, Federal agent, at a resort near Mercer, Wis., in April.

And John Hamilton, also a member of Dillinger's broken following, is "Public Enemy No. 2," or close enough to tie with any other contestant for that dubious honor.

October 23, 1934

OUTLAW NELSON FOUND DEAD FROM SLAIN OFFICERS' SHOTS

17 BULLETS HIT NELSON

Dillinger Gangster's Body Abandoned by His Companions.

ASKED UNDERTAKER'S AID

Special to THE NEW YORK TIMES.

CHICAGO, Nov. 28.—The body of George (Baby Face) Nelson was found today, pierced by bullets from the guns of the two Federal agents, Herman E. Hollis and Inspector Samuel P. Cowley, whom he fatally wounded yesterday in a machine-gun battle in Barrington, a suburb of this city.

The end of Nelson's spectacular career of crime, in which he accounted for three of the agents of the Department of Justice, leaves only one member of the old Dillinger gang at large, John Hamilton. The rest were shot down by Federal pursuers or are in prison.

Disrobed and wrapped in a blanket, Nelson's body, which had been abandoned by the man and woman who fled with him in the agents' car after the sanguinary encounter at Barrington, was discovered lying in a roadside ditch at Niles Center, a suburb fifteen miles north of here.

Cowley Succumbs to Wounds.

A few hours earlier Inspector Cowley had succumbed to his wounds in an Elgin hospital.

Nelson, whose real name was Lester M. Gillis, apparently died as he was being driven from Barrington by his companions who abandoned the government automobile after removing the desperado's body, which had been stripped of clothing. The car was found in the western outskirts of Winnetka, another suburb.

The automobile was found first, early this morning. Later a package of blood-stained clothing was discovered in Howard Street in the village of Niles. Suburban police and Inspector H. H. Clegg of the Division of Investigation of the Department of Justice, who flew here from Washington last night, then began a search of Niles Centre.

Meantime, Philip Sadowski, an undertaker, notified the Niles Centre police of a mysterious telephone call received at 7:25 o'clock this morning. The caller, a man said:

"Hello, is this you Phil?"

Sadowski answered in the affirmative.

Undertaker Gets Clue.

"Phil, I want you to go out to Harms Road near Lincoln Avenue," said the caller. "You'll find a body there on the parkway. It's a friend of mine. His name is Gillis and he's been hurt bad."

"Well, I've got to call the coroner then," replied the undertaker.

"No, don't do that," pleaded the caller. "Just go out and get the body. You'll find him covered up with a blanket."

Sergeant Stenson informed Chief A. C. Stolberg, who, when he learned that the call had referred to Gillis, telephoned the Depart-

Associated Press Photo.

George "Baby Face" Nelson.

ment of Justice and awaited the arrival of agents.

At 9:30 o'clock Sadowski reported another call. This time the mysterious person told him the body would be found at Long and Niles Avenues. Following these directions, local police and Federal agents came upon the body at a corner of the highway and St. Paul's Cemetery. A blanket bearing the label Pratt Lane Hotel covered it. A strip of white cloth was bound around the abdomen where there was a wide bullet wound.

An examination disclosed that the skin on the tips of three fingers of the left hand had been filed, as if to change their texture, and the little finger of the right hand appeared to have been treated with acid, probably for the same purpose. Nelson had also grown a small golden-colored mustache.

Nevertheless, certain identification was speedily made by fingerprint records.

Mrs. Juliette Fitzsimmons, Nelson's elder sister, appeared with her husband, Robert, a respectable South Side citizen, at the Cook County Morgue late in the afternoon and further identified the body by scars and the set of teeth.

Mrs. Fitzsimmons admitted telephoning Sadowski this afternoon and asking him to take care of her brother's body. The undertaker had told Coroner Walsh of a "mysterious woman" who called. The sister said she did this after learning over the radio of Nelson's death. Both Mrs. Fitzsimmons and her husband said they knew nothing of the two calls made to Sadowski in the morning. They also at first said they had not seen Nelson "for many years." Later the husband told Coroner Walsh they had seen him last May.

One Bullet Caused Death.

Dr. J. G. Frost, coroner's physician, said that a slug which entered the left side of the abdomen and went out the right side caused death by internal hemorrhage. Rigor mortis indicated that death occurred at about 6:25 A. M., Dr. Frost said.

Inspector Clegg said that a comparison of the slugs imbedded in Nelson's body with the sub-machine gun used by Cowley and the shotgun fired by Hollis established definitely that the two government men had killed the outlaw.

The clothing found prior to the discovery of the body was undoubtedly Nelson's, said Inspector Clegg. Holes in the cloth corresponded with the bullet wounds in the body. A zipper belt on the trousers, probably used as a money container, had been cut open and its contents removed.

One rumor was that Nelson's companion in the Barrington battle was Willie Connors, alias Duffy, who several years ago killed a policeman on the South Side. It was also rumored that Nelson had been told by an informer supposed to be working for the government that the agents were closing in on him.

Hunt Fugitive Companions.

Another theory as to the identity of Nelson's confederate is that he was Alvin Karpis, St. Paul gangster who is alleged to have been involved in the kidnapping of Edward G. Bremer, a St. Paul banker. Karpis is believed to have joined the Dillinger gang after the kidnapping.

Early today government agents searched the Lake Bluff (Ill.) home of Jack Durand, who once served a prison sentence for robbery, and the home of Mrs. Scott Durand, his foster-mother, in the hunt for Nelson's companions. They also raided the roadhouse operated by Mrs. Marie Cernocky, widow of Louis Cernocky, in Fox River Grove, and questioned her two sons, Edward, a law student, and Louis, who owns a liquor store. There were reports that Nelson had hidden for a time in the Cernocky resort.

Several arrests were made, including those of Clarence Leeder, owner of a garage for whom Nelson once worked as a chauffeur, and of Lester Van Huston, a saloon keeper.

The story of the battle at Barrington was told in detail at two inquests today, one over the body of Hollis in an undertaking establishment here and the other over that of Cowley in Elgin.

Both verdicts were that the agents came to their deaths at the hands of unknown persons, the government refusing to reveal its information and the inquests being completed before the body of Nelson was found.

November 29, 1934

NELSON ARRESTED AS THIEF WHEN 13

Neighborhood Leader in Chicago as a Boy, He Was Sent to Penal School.

WAS BANK ROBBER IN 1931

Attracted Public Attention When He Joined in Depredations of Dillinger Gang.

Special to THE NEW YORK TIMES.

CHICAGO, Nov. 28.—For exactly 128 days, George (Baby Face) Nelson bore the title of Public Enemy No. 1 of the nation. He had reached this "peak" after spending half of his twenty-six years in outlawry.

Lester N. Gillis, the name to which Nelson was born, had been branded as "most desperate criminal" because he was a merciless killer, a quick trigger man with an intense hatred of "coppers and G. men." He stepped to front rank in crime when John Dillinger was slain last July 22.

Lester Gillis was the son of a tanner. He was born on Dec. 6, 1908, in a small house at 944 California Street. His parents were of Belgian blood. His father died several years ago but his mother and one of his elder sisters now live at 5,516 South Marshfield Avenue.

He lived the life of a normal city boy. His friends say he was active, daring and an intelligent child. He was a leader in his neighborhood. He attended grammar school and played the usual games. He was frequently in fights and was known as handy with his fists.

His first contact with the law came in 1922, when he was 13 years old. He stole automobile accessories, was detected in the theft and convicted in the Juvenile Court. He was sent to the St. Charles School for Boys. With this conviction the circumstances of his life lost all touch with "usual affairs."

In the school he was intelligent enough to see that he was punished less when he was obedient. He became a model boy, but the penal records show that he had some part in an unsuccessful attempt by a group of boys to escape in 1923. The following year he was paroled.

He broke the parole several months later, was returned to the school and again paroled in July, 1925. He was returned in October of that year and again paroled in 1926.

Here he dropped out of sight for several years. It is possible that he lived as an ordinary citizen, but the police doubt this since, when next he turned up, he was engaged in bank robbery. And it was about this time that he became known as Baby Face. He still used the name Gillis, however.

In February, 1931, he was arrested and charged with several bank robberies, jewel stick-ups and burglaries. He was still a criminal "unknown," however, for in the newspaper clippings of the times a single paragraph is devoted to the arrest.

Convicted of Bank Robbery.

In July, 1931, Gillis was tried for robbery of the Hillside State Bank in Hillside and convicted. He was sentenced to Joliet penitentiary for a term of one year to life, but he did not go to prison, being held for a trial at Wheaton on a charge of also robbing the Itasca State Bank. Again he was convicted and received the second sentence of one year to life in Joliet.

After the double trial he was placed in the custody of a prison guard and started on his way to Joliet. He and his warden rode a train to that city and then boarded a taxicab. On the ride to the prison Nelson, who was handcuffed to the guard, suddenly drew a revolver, which police later reasoned had been given him by his friends on the train.

He forced the guard to release him, drove both the taxi chauffeur and the guard to a lonely cemetery, where he ordered them out of the cab and fled.

From that time he became known as Nelson, although he took several other names as well. Soon after his escape he made contact with the gang led by Dillinger and became an active member of the band. That move made him a "big shot."

Nelson for a time was armorer for the gang, purchasing the machine guns which were their favorite weapons. Then he accompanied them in several bank robberies. He was with them in the Little Bohemia resort in upper Wisconsin at the time last April when Federal agents attempted to capture the entire band.

Escapes in Wisconsin Woods.

In fleeing, after the Federal trap had been sprung too soon, Nelson shot and killed Agent W. Carter Baum and focused attention upon himself thereby. For weeks Nelson hid in the north woods, eventually being able to escape from the posses of trained woodsmen who scoured the territory for him.

Nelson did not rejoin Dillinger when the gang leader came to Chicago and eventually to his death. He was seen in Wisconsin and in Ohio. Immediately after Dillinger was killed the search for Nelson became intensive and he was publicly designated as the Number One desperado.

Nelson married Helen Wawzynak, then working as sales girl in a department store here, in 1928, when he was 20 years old. The couple had two children, a son and a daughter.

November 29, 1934

SLAIN IN BATTLE WITH FEDERAL AGENTS.

Fred Barker.

Times Wide World Photos.

Kate Barker.

FRED BARKER AND 'MA' DIE

Shoot to the Last When Trapped by Federal Agents in Florida.

MACHINE GUN IN HER HAND

Weapons Blaze for Six Hours in Oklawaha as Prostrate Villagers Look On.

MEMBERS OF KARPIS GANG

Mother Credited With Being Brains of Bremer Kidnapping and Bank Robberies.

(Copyright, 1935, by The Associated Press).

OKLAWAHA, Fla., Jan. 16.—Federal agents trailed "Ma" Barker and her son, Fred, long sought as members of the gang that kidnapped Edward G. Bremer, St. Paul banker, to their Florida hiding place today and killed them both after a machine gun battle lasting six hours.

Mrs. Kate (Ma) Barker who has been called the brains of the Barker-Karpis gang held responsible for the kidnapping of Mr. Bremer, died with a machine gun in her hand. Residents of this little village described the scene as "like a war." Barker was 32 and his mother 55.

The battle began soon after daylight this morning when Department of Justice agents, led by E. J. Connelley of Cincinnati, surrounded the house occupied by the Barkers on a shore of Lake Weir. Connelley approached and called to the occupants to surrender.

Machine-gun fire was the answer. The government agents replied in kind, also using tear gas. When the shooting ceased from the house around 11 o'clock, the agents sent a Negro cook, who had been working there, into the building. He returned saying "They are all dead."

"Ma" Barker fell holding a machine gun in her hand. A portion of the drum of ammunition had been exhausted. One shot had killed her. Her son's body was sprawled on the floor with eleven machine-gun bullets in one shoulder and three in the head.

None of Agents Wounded.

The dozen or more government agents escaped injury.

A rumor prevalent was that the mother, seeing her son fall and recognizing that capture was inevitable, ended her own life. She had been credited with having directed the Barker-Karpis gang in a number of bank robberies throughout the Middle West.

After their victory the agents began a systematic search of the bullet-pierced house, hoping to find some of the $200,000 ransom money paid for the return of Bremer. Floor boards were torn up and the garage and the yard searched under flashlights after nightfall.

Four $1,000 bills were found in the clothing of Fred Barker.

The day was an exciting one for the residents of Oklawaha. The village contains only a few scattered houses and stores. It lies about twenty miles southeast of Ocala, the county seat, and 100 miles southwest of Jacksonville.

The Barkers had been here about two months, renting the Summer house under the name of T. E. Blackburn from Carson Bradford, president of the Biscayne Kennel Club of Miami. Neighbors knew little about the "Blackburns" except that they had a great deal of company, mostly late at night. A few days ago a couple called "Mr. and Mrs. Summer" departed after an extended stay.

Many of the neighbors, warned by the agents of impending danger, deserted their homes before the battle started. There still were about 200 cars parked around the lake and streets, however, and most of the residents saw the firing from safe vantage points. Many lay flat on the ground.

Rifles and machine guns would crack for fifteen minutes, then there would be a lull, followed by a renewal of firing from both sides. Most of the shooting from the besieged house came from upstairs, witnesses said. The white home was pock-marked by bullets. The agents said they had fired 1,500 rounds of ammunition.

News of the battle traveled rapidly and several hundred outsiders flocked to the village. Newspaper men and camera men from the surrounding cities sped to the scene. The village has only one telephone and a line was soon formed by those anxious to report the story.

Mrs. A. F. Westberry, whose home is opposite the house occupied by the Barkers, and her daughter fled from their home in a hail of bullets.

"It was like war," Mrs. Westberry related in describing her experience.

"I was suddenly awakened by guns firing. I got out of bed, and as I stood up some bullets came through the closed door between my bedroom and the dining room and hit the head of my bed. I opened the door a crack and more bullets came through the window and hit the face of the door above my head.

"I looked out a window and saw the yard was full of men. From Mr. Bradford's house across the road there was a lot of shooting. I could see streaks of fire from the guns.

"I could see the blazes from the men's guns on the outside. There was a lot of rapid firing like machine guns. My daughter was in bed. I broke open the back window of our room and told her we had to get out. About that time some more bullets came smacking through the dining room window and hit the wall.

"My daughter and I climbed through the window and got down on the ground. We were going to run to my neighbor's house, about fifty yards back of our house. The house from which the bullets were coming was only about a hundred feet in front of my house.

"As we lay down on the ground for a moment we heard the firing coming louder. We got up and started to run to Mrs. Rex's house. As we ran some men yelled at us to stop. We did not stop.

"They began shooting at us. I learned later it was the Federal men. We kept on running and they kept on yelling and shooting. They must have shot at us two dozen times. They didn't know who we were. It was still a little dark. Finally we got to Mrs. Rex's house.

"There appeared to be fifteen or twenty Federal agents. The shooting kept on all morning. Just before noon it stopped. We saw all of the Federal men go into the house. Some of them came out in a few minutes. It was all over.

"My daughter and I went back to our house and inspected the damage. There were three holes in my bed just above where my head had been. There were two holes in the door facing. In the window were two holes looking as if ten or twelve bullets had come through at the same time."

Having already disposed of most of the Dillinger and "Pretty Boy" Floyd gangs, Federal agents had been hunting the Barkers for some time on clues indicating they had come to Florida.

The Barker-Karpis gang has been described as the last of the outlaw bands at large.

At the time of the kidnapping of Mr. Bremer, Department of Justice men named Arthur (Doc) Barker and Karpis as those responsible for the crime.

Officials of the Department of Justice at Washington said inquiries would be made as to whether the Barker gang had been responsible for the kidnapping of William Hamm, also of St. Paul. Ransom of $100,000 was paid for his release.

KARPIS CAPTURED IN NEW ORLEANS BY HOOVER HIMSELF

Another Man and Woman Are Also Seized by 15 Agents Under Federal Chief.

DESPERADO PUT ON PLANE

Destination Is Unannounced, but Ship Pauses at St. Louis —Reported Chicago-Bound.

ALL TAKEN WITHOUT A SHOT

Just Leaving Apartment, They Give Up When Surrounded by Shotgun Squad.

By The Associated Press.

NEW ORLEANS, May 1.—Alvin Karpis, No. 1 bad man of the United States, was captured tonight without resistance by officers led by J. Edgar Hoover, chief of the Federal Bureau of Investigation.

A few hours later the man who succeeded John Dillinger as the country's most-wanted criminal, heavily guarded and manacled, was put aboard an airplane and taken from the city with the destination unannounced.

Without a shot being fired, though Karpis was armed, he was taken into custody along with Fred Hunter, 37 years old, a suspect in the $34,000 Garretsville, Ohio, mail robbery, and a woman known only as "Ruth" as they emerged from an apartment building about half a mile from the center of the business district.

Mr. Hoover made the announcement of the capture with the simple statement:

"We've captured Alvin Karpis, generally known as Public Enemy No. 1—but not to us."

Then he added:

"They were taken without the firing of a shot. Karpis never had a chance. There were too many guns on him."

Indicted in Kidnappings

Karpis is under indictment for the $100,000 kidnapping of William A. Hamm Jr., St. Paul brewer, on June 15, 1933, and the $200,000 kidnapping of Edward G. Bremer, St. Paul banker, on Jan. 17, 1934.

He also is wanted on a charge of murder in connection with the slaying of Sheriff C. R. Kelley at West Plains, Mo., on Dec. 19, 1931.

The three-year hunt from coast to coast and beyond for Karpis was as extensive as that for his predecessor as public enemy No. 1, Dillinger, who was shot in Chicago.

He was the last of the original Karpis-Barker gang. Seven of that band of bank robbers and kidnappers are now dead and the rest have been captured.

Within the past two weeks the Department of Justice had put a $5,000 price upon Karpis's head and added a $2,500 price for information leading to the capture of his pal, Harry Campbell.

Four days ago the postal inspection service followed the department's lead and added a $2,000 reward for Karpis, bringing his price to $7,000, and $2,000 more for Campbell. But Campbell escaped the raid today.

Hoover on Job Several Days

Mr. Hoover said the Bureau of Investigation had known that Karpis had been in and out of New Orleans for the last several months. He, himself, had come here several days ago to direct the manhunt.

Smiling slightly, the chief Federal agent made his announcement of the capture in the Bureau office in the Postoffice Building here about an hour after the raid, which occurred at 5:30 P. M., saying, "I've got something interesting to tell you."

Mr. Hoover did not say how many men took part in the capture but there were reported to have been between fifteen and twenty. Speaking of the three arrested, he said:

"They were in an apartment on the first floor of the building and were leaving the house to enter an automobile when the agents surrounded them.

"The agents called upon them to surrender and they were taken without the firing of a shot."

Shackles were placed on the hands and feet of Karpis and the shackles were then bound together. He and the others were taken to the Postoffice building. Karpis and Hunter, likewise bound, had to be carried by agents.

Karpis had been living at the apartment with the woman, who was about 21 years old, pretty, red-haired and dressed in white. Hunter visited them nightly, neighbors said.

The capture was effected so smoothly and quietly that only persons near by were aware of the Federal agents' latest success.

Witnesses said that when the three left the house agents armed with sawed-off shotguns and other weapons stepped to the sidewalk, and crisply commanded them to surrender. When the desperadoes made no move they were seized and rushed from the scene.

Addison Cole, 17-year-old high school student who lives in the apartment where Karpis lived, said that when he got off a street car late this afternoon he saw a man (later identified as Hunter) walking across the sidewalk.

"A woman was walking behind him," Cole added. "One man was walking on each side of him and another man accompanied the woman. At the same time a third prisoner (Karpis) was being put into an automobile by a couple of government men. He seemed to be resisting to some extent.

"The G-men left with the three prisoners and six more government men remained hidden behind a hedge, one with a sawed-off shotgun, one with an automatic rifle and the rest with pistols.

"I saw one man kicking at a side door. Some others were hustling the crowds away. Finally, one of the men sent for the janitor to open the side door. I went to enter the back door and a man stopped me and searched a bundle I had under my arm. Then he let me go in. I went inside and there was another man in the janitor's room."

Federal agents were posted in the apartment house tonight.

Edward Hoffman, who lives in the house behind the apartment building, said he had rented parking space in his yard to Karpis.

"He seemed all right," Hoffman remarked.

John Campbell, janitor of the apartment building, said he knew Karpis as a mild, pleasant man with a slight impediment in his speech, and only as "Mr. O'Hara."

Campbell declared that "O'Hara" and the woman, who posed as his wife, were the only two of the arrested persons living in the apartment house. The third person "came over every night and talked with them," he said.

Topics of The Times

The last of the kidnappers is in the hands of the Department of Justice's able G-men. The Federal slate of public enemies has been wiped clean. Within the space of ten days Washington has announced the capture of three big outlaws, beginning with ALVIN KARPIS, our distinguished No. 1. The timing has been so dramatic that one might almost suspect a touch of stage direction, as if J. EDGAR HOOVER had all three of his quarry in hand and chose to release them one by one. The effect has been not unlike the knitting women at the guillotine in "A Tale of Two Cities." The American people has been counting gangster heads as they dropped into the basket.

CRIME AND THE POPULAR IMAGINATION

Chicago Forbids All Films Showing Criminals in Action

CHICAGO, Jan. 4.—Motion pictures portraying criminals at work have been barred in Chicago. Chief of Police Fitzmorris announced today that three weeks ago he had given orders to movie censors not to issue permits for any screen drama that showed a crime committed, even though the end of the picture might show the criminal in a prison cell.

"It will make no difference whether the criminal shown is a hero or a villain," said the chief. "Even the showing of a policeman disguised as a burglar is taboo."

The order became public when three youthful robbers, who were sentenced to the State Reformatory at Pontiac, said their crimes had been inspired by a "crook" moving picture.

January 25, 1921

Chicago Boys Make Heroes Of Bootleggers and Bandits

Special to The New York Times.

CHICAGO, March 9.—The heroes of the Chicago boys of today are more likely to be Terry Druggan or Mike Genna than George Washington or Abraham Lincoln, according to a report just made by Charles H. English, Supervisor of Recreation of the Chicago Board of Education.

Where the youth of yesteryear played "Indian and cowboy," the youth of today, Mr. English says, goes in for "bootlegger and hijacker." The Chicago boys' idea is still to learn how to shoot, but he does it by imitating the gunman and the baby bandit.

The girls, Mr. English finds, imitate the dress and manners of the screen "vamp."

March 10, 1926

Two Thugs.

THE PUBLIC ENEMY, based on a story by Kubec Glasmon and John Bright. Directed by William A. Wellman. Produced by Warner Brothers. At the Strand.

Matt	Edward Woods
Tom	James Cagney
Mike	Donald Cook
Mamie	Joan Blondell
Gwen Allen	Jean Harlow
Tom's mother	Beryl Mercer
Bugs Moran	Ben Hendricks Jr.
Paddy Ryan	Robert Emmett O'Connor
Nails Nathan	Leslie Fenton
Bess	Louise Brooks
Putty Nose	Murray Kinnell
Kitty	Mae Clark

It is just another gangster film at the Strand, weaker than most in its story, stronger than most in its acting, and like most maintaining a certain level of interest through the last burst of machine-gun fire. That was not the intention of the Warners, whose laudable motive it was to have "The Public Enemy" say the very last word on the subject of gang pictures. There is a prologue apprising the audience that the hoodlums and terrorists of the underworld must be exposed and the glamour ripped from them. There is an epilogue pointing the moral that civilization is on her knees and inquiring loudly as to what is to be done. And before the prologue there is a brief stage tableau, with sinuous green lighting, which shows a puppet gangster shooting another puppet gangster in the back.

"The Public Enemy" does not, as its title so eloquently suggests, present a picture of the war between the underworld and the upperworld. Instead the war is one of gangsters among themselves; of sensational and sometimes sensationally incoherent murders. The motivation is lost in the general slaughter at the end, when Matt and Tom, the hoodlums with whose career of outlawry the picture is concerned, die violently.

Edward Woods and James Cagney, as Matt and Tom respectively, give remarkably lifelike portraits of young hoodlums. The story follows their careers from boyhood, through the war period and into the early days of prohibition, when the public thirst made their peculiar talents profitable. Slugging disloyal bartenders, shooting down rival beermen, slapping their women crudely across the face, strutting with a vast self-satisfaction through their little world, they contribute a hard and true picture of the unheroic gangster.

The audiences yesterday laughed frequently and with gusto as the swaggering Matt and Tom went through their paces, and this rather took the edge off the brutal picture the producers appeared to be trying to serve up. The laughter was loudest and most deserved when the two put a horse "on the spot," the reason being that the animal had had the temerity to throw Nails Nathan, the gang leader.

There is a reminder of newspaper headlines toward the close when Tom, lying wounded in a hospital, is kidnapped and murdered. The acting throughout is interesting, with the exception of Jean Harlow, who essays the rôle of a gangster's mistress. Beryl Mercer as Tom's mother, Robert Emmett O'Connor as a gang chief, and Donald Cook as Tom's brother, do splendidly.

A. D. S.

April 24, 1931

NEW GANG FILM AT STRAND.

"Little Caesar" Notable for Acting of Edward G. Robinson.

LITTLE CAESAR, with Edward G. Robinson, Douglas Fairbanks Jr., Glenda Farrell, Sidney Blackmer, Thomas Jackson, Ralph Ince, William Collier Jr., Maurice Black, Stanley Fields and George E. Stone; from the novel by W. R. Burnett, directed by Mervyn LeRoy; newsreel and Vitaphone short features. At the Strand.

"Little Caesar," based on W. R. Burnett's novel of Chicago gangdom, was welcomed to the Strand yesterday by unusual crowds. The story deals with the career of Cesare Bandello, alias Rico, alias Little Caesar, a disagreeable lad who started by robbing gasoline stations and soared to startling heights in his "profession" by reason of his belief in his high destiny.

The production is ordinary and would rank as just one more gangster film but for two things. One is the excellence of Mr. Burnett's credible and compact story. The other is Edward G. Robinson's wonderfully effective performance. Little Caesar becomes at Mr. Robinson's hands a figure out of Greek epic tragedy, a cold, ignorant, merciless killer, driven on and on by an insatiable lust for power, the plaything of a force that is greater than himself.

Douglas Fairbanks Jr. as Rico's pal, who brings about his friend's downfall by trying to live a decent life away from his old haunts, is miscast, and in addition suffers by comparison with the reality of Mr. Robinson's portrayal. At times Mr. Fairbanks talks and acts like the cheap Italian thug he is supposed to represent, but more often he is the pleasant, sincere youth who has been seen to so much better advantage elsewhere.

Little Caesar comes to the big town and joins Sam Vettori's gang, one of the two principal "mobs" in that city. Both gangs are under the supervision of Pete Montana, who in turn owes his allegiance to a mysterious "Big Boy," the king of the underworld. Early in his career Little Caesar plans and executes a raid on a cabaret protected by the rival gang, and in so doing kills a crime commissioner. Thereafter, step by step, he ousts Vettori, Pete Montana and the rival gang leader, and soon only "Big Boy" bars his way to complete mastery of the city's underworld.

His pal, Joe Massara, is threatened with the fatal "spot" because he knows too much, and that young man's sweetheart turns State's evidence. The "mob" is broken and scattered, and Little Caesar is cornered and killed by a crafty detective's appeal to the gangster's vanity. Glenda Farrell is excellently authentic as Massara's "moll," and William Collier Jr. contributes a moving performance in a minor rôle. Thomas Jackson as the detective is also noteworthy.

January 10, 1931

CAPONE MORALIZES ON EVE OF SENTENCE

Saying He Has Refused Book and Film Offers, He Scores Effect of 'Gang Stuff' on Boys.

CALLS HIMSELF AN 'ISSUE'

Facing at Least a 2½-Year Term Today, Gangster Chief Points to Drinkers of Beer He Sold.

Special to The New York Times.

CHICAGO, July 29. — Alphonse (Scarface Al) Capone, facing sentence in Federal court tomorrow on charges of violating the income tax and prohibition laws, to which he has pleaded guilty, chatted cheerfully today with friends and advisers and in interviews told of flattering offers from publishers and Hollywood producers, denounced gangland pictures as injurious to American youth and discussed himself as "an issue."

His huge frame clad in pajamas of black silk banded with white, the gang chieftain sat behind a desk in his hotel suite.

Deplores Bad Influences on Youth.

"I've been offered $2,000,000 to write a book, but I won't do it," he said. "I've had lots of offers from moving picture producers, but I feel about that as I do about books.

"You know, these gang pictures—that's terrible kid stuff. Why, they ought to take all of them and throw them into the lake. They're doing nothing but harm to the younger element of this country. I don't blame the censors for trying to bar them.

"Now, you take all these youngsters who go to the movies. You remember reading dime novels, maybe, when you were a kid. Well, you know how it made you want to get out and kill pirates or look for buried treasure—you know. Well, these gang movies are making a lot of kids want to be tough guys, and they don't serve any useful purpose."

Suggests Worse Crimes Than His.

Discussing his going to Leavenworth penitentiary, Capone said:

"I've been made an issue, I guess, and I'm not complaining. But why

41

don't they go after all these bankers who took the savings of thousands of poor people and lost them in bank failures? How about that?

"Isn't it lots worse to take the last few dollars some small family has saved—perhaps to live on while the head of a family is out of a job—than to sell a little beer, a little alky?

"Believe me. I can't see where the fellow who sells it is any worse off than the fellow who buys it and drinks it."

Capone refused to discuss the reason why he was capitulating at the height of his career without a struggle, when, as local Federal officials admit, he could have stalled off imprisonment for at least two years.

"General" Sharing Fate of "Staff."

Various theories have been offered by observers familiar with the ways of gangsters. The one advanced most generally is this:

Capone, the generalissimo of an army of gangsters, is a soldier at heart and expects for himself no more than he expects for his men. One of his trusted lieutenants, Frank Nitti, is already at Leavenworth. His brother, Ralph Capone, Jake Guzik and Jack McGurn are under sentence and see no hope of evading prison.

If he gains his liberty while his men are behind prison walls, he will lose his hold on his army. He will cease to be an idol to his men.

Those who hold Capone in less regard, however, voice a different opinion. Capone, they say, has made his fortune, and wishes to retire, but cannot do so so long as he has his freedom. They insist that the only way he can get out is to be taken out by the government.

Law-enforcement officials contend that Capone sees prison as an easy way out of his hazardous calling,

with a peaceful life as his reward after he has served his term. They expect him to take his family to Italy, or perhaps to a far corner of the United States, to live in obscurity.

2½-Year Term Expected.

Though liable to a maximum imprisonment of thirty-two years in the penitentiary at Leavenworth and a maximum fine of $80,000 for violation of the income tax and national prohibition laws, Capone is not expected to receive a sentence of more than two and a half years, with a fine of about $10,000, when Judge James H. Wilkerson disposes of the case tomorrow.

Over a period from 1925 to 1929, Capone is charged with having attempted to evade a tax of $215,000 on an income slightly in excess of

$1,000,000. The indictment includes six felony counts and two misdemeanors.

The government is expected to occupy most of the day in putting on witnesses, after which George E. Q. Johnson, United States District Attorney, will make a closing statement.

If Judge Wilkerson imposes sentence immediately, Capone will be remanded to the custody of United States Marshal D. C. W. Laubenheimer, who said today that he would place the gangster in the Cook County jail for safekeeping during the night and the next morning would send him to Leavenworth.

It is likely, Mr. Laubenheimer said, that Capone would exercise his privilege of being transported in style. It is only necessary for him to pay his own expenses and those of a deputy marshal and an extra guard to travel in a private car, if he so wishes.

July 30, 1931

WHY WE GLORIFY OUR GANGSTERS

An Analysis of the Influences Which Have Molded the American National Character   and Led Us   To Sympathize With the Criminal While Showing Slight Admiration for the Police

By JAMES TRUSLOW ADAMS

PRESIDENT HOOVER, in his message to the recent convention of the International Police Chiefs Association, after speaking of the "sentimentalism in some people which makes popular heroes out of criminals," asserted that "instead of the glorification of cowardly gangsters, we need the glorification of policemen who do their duty and who give their lives in public protection." The most carping critic of the President could not deny the truth of that assertion, nor deny that, as a nation, we do show very slight admiration for our police and do glorify the criminal. Why?

A double-headed statement may well call for comment on both heads. If we Americans have none of that admiration for our municipal police that a Londoner has for his, there are reasons. Mr. Hoover did not note them but glanced obliquely at some of their causes. "If," he wrote, "the police had the vigilant, universal backing of public opinion in their communities; if they had the implacable support of the prosecuting authorities and the courts; if our criminal laws" did not permit clever criminal lawyers to find loopholes for their clients, and so on, the police would stamp out some of the disgrace of our great cities.

This reminds one of the old saying, "If my aunt had been a man she would have been my uncle." If it were not for the points suggested by the President, and others quite as important, the police might

stand before us as the efficient and incorruptible guardians of our public honesty and welfare. As it is—well, they do not.

But it is with the second head of the President's statement that we are here chiefly concerned. Why do we glorify criminals? I was about to say: Why do we, who on the whole are certainly decent, law-abiding citizens, glorify them? That way of putting it, however, before it was half on paper, brought a sharp twinge of doubt. We are, on the whole, decent. We are kindly, helpful, friendly, hospitable and possess many other decent and admirable qualities; but law-abiding? No, we are not that, for there can assuredly be few of us Americans out of the cradle who are not breaking one or another of our innumerable absurd or wise and often unknown statutes.

With the problem of our lawlessness, and the causes of it, I dealt in an earlier article in THE TIMES and need speak of them here merely to suggest that with us, as contrasted with the English, much of the sharp edges of the terms "lawbreaker" and "criminal" are blunted because we are all, in varying degrees, in the same boat. But if the mere breaking of law does not seem anything very heinous to us, there are limits beyond which most of us would assuredly not venture; and persons who dodge duties on return from Europe, or give themselves the benefit of the doubt on income taxes, or exceed speed limits, or buy a drink, would never

dream of following in the footsteps of criminals like Al Capone. Why then do the people who would never imitate them exhibit the sentimentalism with regard to them that Mr. Hoover properly condemns?

TO find the answer entails probing into our national character and the influences which have molded it. I have just spoken of the English, and if I have done so here, as frequently elsewhere, in comparison with us Americans, it is not with any intention of praising them and dispraising ourselves. It is merely because they are the best yardstick we have for measuring many of our own divergences.

We were also English in our beginning and we did not show any very wide divergence from them, until the middle of the eighteenth century. In tracing our character and ways of looking at life beyond that point, if we find ourselves differing from the English of England but not from the English of the new "dominions," we may look for influences in the environment of a new country, the influences of what we have come to term "the frontier." If, however, we find ourselves diverging both from the English of the old and the new lands, then we have to look for influences other than those of the frontier.

Since Professor Turner, to whom all historians are indebted for the introduction of the idea of frontier influence into the writing of history, first suggested it, it has been immensely fruitful. But it has to be analyzed with more discrimination than some of his followers showed;

and because too much was claimed for it, there seems to be a tendency, about to develop toward denying it altogther. As a historian, I believe that the frontier has been of enormous importance in forming our mind and character, but also that we must be careful in what we attribute to it. There are other factors in the problem. Wherever the English race has been subjected to frontier influence in the United States, Canada, New Zealand, Australia and elsewhere, it has made for democracy and a certain type of self-government everywhere. Titles of hereditary nobility, for example, are as much disliked, and I believe as il legal, in all the British dominions as in the United States. But the frontier has not made out of French or Spanish communities what it has out of English. There are, therefore, other factors in the final resultant.

• • •

ON the frontier, however, there is a certain shift in personal values. Many of the qualities which help a man to success in old cities may be of less than no use on the frontier. Family connections, education, good manners, culture and subtlety of mind are of less value than physical strength, reckless courage, a quick finger on a trigger, complete self-reliance and others of a list that could easily be made up. Now, not all but a good many, and those among the most popular, of the qualities of our gangsters are those which were genuinely valuable and admirable or the frontier. Our frontiersmen ranged all the way down the scale from a man like Daniel Boone to a complete ruffian like Simon Girty, but in the primitive tumult of our later nineteenth-century West it was not always easy to draw the line between a first-class frontiersman and a first-class criminal.

It was somewhat a matter of chance and of accidents which might make one man fit into society while another was declared an outlaw. Jim Bowie, for example, who invented the Bowie knife and could amuse himself by roping and riding alligators, somehow managed to stay on the right side and died a hero in the Mexican attack on the Alamo; whereas Billy the Kid got on the wrong side, became outlawed and was finally shot down by Sheriff Pat Garrett. Billy had twenty-one murders to his credit and ended ingloriously. On the other hand, Wild Bill Hickok, who was said to have killed more white men than any other Western desperado, ended magnificently as a marshal, bringing law and order to Abilene, Kan. So effective was his handling of his "irons" known to be that he had to kill only two men in the course of duty, compared with the thirty-three he had slain before he settled down.

All of these men, on whichever side of the social fence they lived or ended, and countless like them, had certain qualities in common—their fearlessness, recklessness, self-reliance, coolness, disregard of law and life—which appealed even to their enemies. They became more or less national figures and their lives are now, one by one, appearing in the scholarly volumes of the Dictionary of National Biography as these come from the hands of our twenty learned societies. They provided gorgeous, if often sordid, splashes of color in the otherwise all too drab life of America in the last century.

• • •

IT would be easy to draw the immediate conclusion that our present sentimentality over gangsters, stemming as in part it does from the gaping wonder at these desperadoes of earlier generations, was a direct inheritance from the frontier and could be derived from "frontier influence." Here, however, we strike a snag.

As we have noted, wherever parts of the English race have gone out to new lands, they have all changed alike in some respects, and these changes being common to all of them may be attributed to the one common influence of the frontier. But when we come to lawlessness and admiration for criminals, we find a difference. We have developed these traits, but the Australians, New Zealanders, and even the Canadians, dwelling on the other side of a mere imaginary line from ourselves on the same continent,

"Prohibition and the Movies Have Both Emphasized the Public's Interest in the Gangster."

"There Can Be Few Americans Not Breaking One or Another of Our Innumerable Statutes."

have not. In this case, therefore, it is not sufficient just to point to the frontier. There must have been other factors at work among ourselves. What were they? We cannot affirm positively what they were, and if I suggest some as possible they are no more certain than most explorations in new country.

We may note only briefly why these other offshoots of the English did not become lawless as we did, as that is but part of the background of our attitude toward the gangsters. In other articles I have tried to show that although our disrespect for law as law has been increased by the many foolish and unenforceable laws passed by our many Legislatures and Federal Government, notably the fugitive slave act and the prohibition amendment, to name the two greatest examples, it has not derived solely from any one of these but had its roots deep in our Colonial past. For one thing, for a hundred and fifty years we resisted or picked and chose among laws passed by a Parliament overseas ignorant of our local conditions and working under the theory of the old Colonial system. Our later frontier conditions in this respect merely emphasized a disrespect for law which had already influenced deeply our national way of looking at things. Another element in our situation was the colossal scramble for quick wealth which our unlimited resources and our unparalleled rapid increase in population afforded in the nineteenth century.

These factors, as well as others,

have not been operative upon the British dominions as contrasted with the United States. Old as French Canada is, the real development of the British dominions did not begin until after our Revolution had taught the British Government useful lessons in administration and they did not have our long training in disobeying unwise imperial legislation. Nor, rich as the dominions are in natural resources, have their inhabitants been subjected to any such moral strain as we have been by the combination of untold wealth with incredibly swift population growth and consequent temptations for lawless exploitation. Canada, the largest, with an area as great as our own, has even as yet a total population equal only to that of the metropolitan district of New York City. For this and other reasons we pass into an entirely different world with respect to attitude toward law and order the moment we cross the Canadian frontier. While we developed vigilance committees and lynchings Canada developed the Northwest Mounted Police. Our view of law and lawbreaking has become different—and, it must be confessed, much inferior—from that of the English at home or in their new lands.

When we come to our glorification of the gangster, what differences in influencing factors can we find, as compared with the English in contact with frontier influences elsewhere? This is the real key to the problem, and it is not easy to find. We may make, perhaps, three tentative suggestions.

There is, first, a difference between us and the dominions which, in its psychological results, is far from unimportant. We broke away from England in 1783, whereas they are still part of the British Empire. We have developed as an independent nation to an extent that we never would have done as a dependent part of empire, but the dissolution of bonds involved a complete break with the past. Although technically we may be said to be an offshoot of English history, we cut ourselves off from it and left ourselves without a past that we could think of as our own. The dominions still have that English past as theirs. The whole colorful pageant of a thousand years is their own. Not only have they the great tradition of warriors—the heroes of a people—Marlborough, Wellington, Nelson and the rest—but they have all the lighter figures of myth or imagination—the Robin Hoods, the Falstaffs and others. Suddenly cut adrift, for a century or more we looked almost exclusively over our own contemporary scene.

Humanity craves for heroes, legends, color, drama. We had to make our own, unconsciously, from the materials about us, and we found them on the frontier in the West. Our most popular show became Buffalo Bill. The literature designed more especially for the masses, the penny dreadfuls and the dime novels, dealt with the heroes and the bad men of the Buffalo Bill scene, and the reader was not sure but that he admired Bill Hickok more as a murderer than as a peaceful marshal. Of course it was wrong, but one developed a sneaking admiration for Billy the Kid when one read that at 12 years of age he stabbed a man who he said had insulted his mother. And as one followed his saga, to find him dancing with his girl with sangfroid while he knew his life was in danger, escaping from jail by killing two guards when one thought he was done for at last, and trapped at the end because of a love affair, crime took on a certain attractiveness and compelling interest that the life of Washington did not provide. These bad men of the frontier became the folk heroes of the people, the one great people in the world which had lost their past and were unconsciously forming myths and heroes for themselves afresh out of the scanty contemporary material at hand.

* * *

WE may note, again, another point in which we differ from the dominions. They are homogeneous in race. We, on the other hand, are now composite in our mass at large of all the races in Europe. Several of these, forming important elements in our people, have entirely different attitudes toward crimes of passion or of politics from the Anglo-Saxons. How great even a slight difference in stock may make can be seen in New Zealand and Australia, the former settled largely by men of what we may call the "public school class" in England and the latter by those to a great extent of a lower class socially. New Zealand is one of the most conservative parts of the empire, while Australia is one of the most radical.

I do not believe that either our crime or lawlessness is due to the foreign races which have come to us; the conditions in which both have arisen we built up ourselves. But the attitude of the general reading and movie public reflects to some extent that of peoples who, in political vendettas, family feuds and crimes of love, see what the Englishman calls a criminal in a different light. This racial influence probably has merely emphasized the first point I mentioned, our creation of a sort of folk-lore out of our bad men.

* * *

THERE is another way in which our type of immigration has deeply affected us, not only in this respect but in our general attitude toward men and peoples. In this also we differ from the dominions. From the beginning almost every one who has come to the United States has come to escape—escape from religious persecution, economic distress or political repression. Speaking only of some of the larger groups, there have been the Puritans in New England, the Roman Catholics in Maryland, the Irish (Celtic and Scotch), the Germans, the Jews. This background has bred in us as a nation what I have elsewhere called the "under-dog complex," an intense sympathy with any one whom we consider to be oppressed, who is trying to escape from authority, or who is asserting his individuality against whatever powers there be, except the opinion of our own group. Our politicians well understand this and know that public sentiment can be quickly aroused in favor of any people—Indian, Irish, Hungarian, Greek or what not—if they can be made to appear the victims of superior power, or even in favor of a politician if he is hammered too hard by his opponents.

Extremely sentimental as we are, this under-dog complex of ours readily makes a hero of a criminal trying to escape the clutches of the law. It brings about a curious cross between the sporting spirit of the English, which insists upon even the hunted fox or stag's having his chance, and the resentment against the acts of those in power which is the heritage of huge numbers of our citizens.

* * *

PROHIBITION and the movies have both emphasized the public's interest in the gangster, but neither would account for the public's glorification of him unless there had been deeper and more historical causes. Mr. Hoover is right in pointing to the extreme seriousness of the wrong direction in which the public's sentimentality is expended, but there is no easy cure. There are some honest policemen and many who would like to be honest, but as long as the public thinks, not unjustifiably, that police departments are honeycombed with graft, it is not likely to wax sentimental over a policeman.

The fault is not that of the individual patrolman. He is caught in the "system." The big business man wants a political boss who is permanent and understanding, and not a shifting Board of Aldermen to deal with. A street railway magnate may scorn to think of himself as connected with the police levy on a streetwalker, but a boss who gets his and can "deliver the goods" to business men, can build his position only on every one below him in the municipal hierarchy getting his. And so we get the police alliance with crime, and all the dirty business which disgusts the patrolman who wants to feel he is a decent man as much as it does any parlor reformer.

But the system as yet is so strongly entrenched in our life, graft of one sort or another goes so much from the bottom to the very top, even into the highest places of the National Government, that the public is not likely to think of gangsters as cowardly and policemen (and the other forces of law and order) as glorified, but as one crook against another.

Mr. Hoover said to the police convention: "I look forward confidently to the day when the moral forces of every community will rally to your support in the fight against crime everywhere." When that day comes, which God speed, there will be a terrifying rattling of skeletons in highly respectable closets; and as it can come only as the result of a moral regeneration in our entire life, the gangsters may then be thrown in the discard of popular interest.

I suspect, however, that as things unhappily are, the tabloids will fatten for long yet on gangster-folk-hero lore and that the public with its under-dog complex and desire for melodrama, will be more interested in the gangster who shoots up a town than in the policeman who, unjustly perhaps in individual cases, it believes will graft for a ten-dollar bill. For two such bills, at most, a "criminal" once told me he could buy any patrolman in his city. If as a nation we do not take crime seriously no matter who commits it, we can scarcely take the tabloid readers and movie-fans to task for liking their criminal heroes served up to them picturesque and hot.

Ban on Dillinger Escape As Film Thriller Theme

The interest of motion picture studios in the escape of John Dillinger from prison was discouraged yesterday by an announcement from Will H. Hays, president of the Motion Picture Producers and Distributers of America, declaring that the board of directors would not countenance a film based on the Dillinger episode.

"No motion picture based on the life or exploits of John Dillinger will be produced, distributed or exhibited by any company member," Mr. Hays's statement said. "This embraces all the major companies in the motion-picture industry. This decision is based on the belief that such a picture would be detrimental to the best public interest."

DILLINGER FAMILY MAKES STAGE BOW

Farmer, Son, Daughter and Her Husband, in Indianapolis Debut, Talk of Outlaw.

SINCERITY GETS SYMPATHY

'It Was My Son,' Father Says, and Sobs as He Adds: 'I Wish to the Lord It Wasn't.'

Special to THE NEW YORK TIMES.

INDIANAPOLIS, Ind., July 30.— John Dillinger Sr., who buried his outlaw son Wednesday, went on the stage of the Lyric Theatre here yesterday in an effort to recoup the depleted family coffers and pay the desperado's funeral expenses.

He played a "good" house yesterday afternoon and a better one today. The audience, evincing amazement and curiosity, leaned forward to hear what the farmer would say about his son who had been shot down after a nation-wide hunt by State and Federal agencies.

The audience seemed divided in sentiment, some feeling sorry for the Dillinger family in their bereavement and others resenting the stage appearance so soon after the funeral.

With Mr. Dillinger on the stage are Hubert Dillinger, his son, a half-brother of the outlaw; Mrs. Audrey Hancock, his daughter, and Emmett Hancock, her husband. W. C. Gilbert, a professional entertainer, interviews them and expatiates on their lines.

The scene opens with a clarification of the pronunciation of the family name. The farm father says it is "Dill-ing-er," pronounced with the "dill" as in dill-pickle, the "ing" as in wing and the "er" as in the second syllable of ever. He rules out the hard "g" which many have put into the name.

The act reiterated Mr. Dillinger's statement regarding identity of the boy that he brought from Chicago to Mooresville.

"I know it's my son," he said, and at one performance broke into a sob as he added: "I wish to the Lord Almighty it wasn't."

The visit of the hunted man to the farm home of his father on April 8 in company with Evelyn Frechette, the Indian half-breed now in prison for harboring him, was told by different members of the family.

"I certainly was glad to see him," said the father, explaining that he could recall no particular conversation he had had with his son. "I didn't know he was coming; he just dropped in."

Hubert Dillinger said that he did not know of his half-brother's presence at the farm until his father took him aside and told him there was a surprise. Then, Hubert said, John stepped from behind a door and said, "Boo!"

"He acted just like he always did," Hubert commented.

Mrs. Hancock said that her brother did not seem concerned at all by the fact that the farm near Mooresville was under almost constant watch. When she arrived at the home, she said, John was lying on the davenport reading a paper.

"I was so happy," she said. "I never knew whether I would see him alive again or not. I'll never forget that day."

The Dillingers are taking earnestly to their new rôles, but are emphatically not stage people. The father is a simple farmer, kind and gentle and sincere, who never had spoken to an audience larger than a sparse church group before his theatrical engagement.

Mrs. Hancock is a thin woman, who gets most of her sympathetic response when she tells of mothering John when he was left motherless at 3 years of age. The audience remembers her and her husband, however, as the couple who hired guards to break newspaper cameras at the funeral of John and who denounced crowds in general. The crowds happened to contain many lyric patrons who still are cool toward the Hancocks.

Hubert Dillinger's appearance is not greatly unlike his notorious brother's, save that he is much thinner. He has the same slanting mouth that marked John and speaks only from a corner of it. He gets sympathy from the audience by a mention of the repeated questionings he had from officers of the law.

From first to last the Dillinger family's act is of the "ham" variety, but most of it is sincere and the community respects especially the words spoken by the father.

Any one who saw the scramble of the crowds here during John Dillinger's funeral and burial will not doubt that there are enough curious persons over the country to give the act success in many cities.

July 31, 1934

THE SCREEN

James Cagney as the Scourge of the Underworld in 'G Men,' the New Photoplay at the Strand.

G MEN, based on a story by Gregory Rogers; screen play by Seton I. Miller; directed by William Keighley; a Warner Brothers production. At the Strand.

Brick Davis	James Cagney
Kay McCord	Margaret Lindsay
Jean Morgan	Ann Dvorak
Jeff McCord	Robert Armstrong
Collins	Barton MacLane
Hugh Farrell	Lloyd Nolan
McKay	William Harrigan
Gerard	Russell Hopton
Leggett	Edward Pawley
Durfee	Noel Madison
Bill	Monte Blue
Eddie	Regis Toomey
Venke	Harold Huber
Gregory	Addison Richards
Man	Raymond Hatton

By ANDRE SENNWALD.

Mr. Cagney, the unregenerate outlaw of the gangster film, joins the Department of Justice and becomes the scourge of the underworld in the blazing melodrama which opened at the Strand Theatre yesterday. "G Men"—the G standing for government—is a composite fiction which draws its inspiration from the recent war of extermination upon the now defunct public enemies of the Middle West. The photoplay contains several episodes (easily identified with actual occurrences in the war on crime) which have scarcely been equaled for excitement and dramatic vigor since "The Public Enemy" and "Little Caesar." "G Men" is not altogether admirable. At ninety minutes it seems overlong and it is handicapped by the tiresome Cagney formula which makes it inevitable that the star must (1) engage in a snarling feud with his superior, and (2) impose his charm on a chill young woman who resents him up to the fadeout. But "G Men," despite its flaws, is a superior melodrama, and you hardly will find yourself suffering from ennui during its detonating assault upon the assassins of the underworld.

The most spectacular episode is a reproduction of the government's raid on Dillinger's hideout in a Wisconsin lodge. With all their great talent for violence, the Warners convert this bit of current history into a minor war in which the bandits die like rats under the machine guns of the G men. Then there is the thrilling scene, based upon the Union Station massacre, in which the insolent gunmen free their chieftain from the Department of Justice agents as he is being taken from a train.

Mr. Cagney, the first-class acting man, is Brick Davis, a guttersnipe who has been financed through college by a kindly bootlegger. He is stagnating as a respectable lawyer when his old college chum, a G man, is ruthlessly slaughtered while trying to arrest a desperado. Brick joins the Department of Justice in order to avenge his slain pal. When the department sets out to trap the bandits who are terrorizing the Midwest, Brick's knowledge of the underworld and of the tell-tale eccentricities of its leading citizens makes him a valuable man to have around.

Mr. Cagney's performance is the most effective he has given in a long time, and his work is improved by the circumstance that he has abandoned some of the less-attractive mannerisms which have been getting in the way of his army and navy portrayals recently. He has the best of help from a number of good players, particularly Robert Armstrong as the G man with whom Brick carries on the inevitable feud, William Harrigan as the lad's benefactor, Ed Pawley as Public Enemy No. 1 and Barton MacLane as the bad man who escapes from the government's trap. Ann Dvorak plays a gunman's moll pleasantly, but the charming Margaret Lindsay is wasted rather brutally as Mr. Cagney's romantic foil. All in all, you can put "G Men" down as the headiest dose of gunplay that Hollywood has unloosed in recent months.

May 2, 1935

TOPICS

Doubtful G-Men Lesson

If the bad national firearms tradition is ever to be eradicated, it is highly doubtful whether any good purpose is served by the present tremendous vogue of J. Edgar Hoover's G-men. On the surface the vast enthusiasm of young America for Mr. Hoover's trigger agents is an endorsement of law and order. But it is greatly to be feared that the youngsters love in the G-men stories and films the gunplay and not the law and order.

Offhand one would say there is a higher ratio of violent death in the present G-men movies than in the old gangster plays; if, indeed, one can tell where the gangster play stops and the law-and-order play begins. The effect on young nerves must be very much the same whether gunmen put each other on the spot or shoot it out with government agents. The number of pistols being waved in Central Park on fine mornings by young G-men averaging 4 years of age seems to be growing steadily.

October 29, 1937

THE SCREEN: REVIEWS AND NEWS

The Warners Look Back on 'The Roaring Twenties' at the Strand

THE ROARING TWENTIES, adapted by Jerry Wald, Richard Macaulay and Robert Rossen from an original story by Mark Hellinger; directed by Raoul Walsh for Warner Brothers. At the Strand.

Eddie Bartlett	James Cagney
Jean Sherman	Priscilla Lane
George Hally	Humphrey Bogart
Panama Smith	Gladys George
Lloyd Hart	Jeffrey Lynn
Danny Green	Frank McHugh
Nick Brown	Paul Kelly
Mrs. Sherman	Elizabeth Risdon
Mrs. Gray	Vera Lewis
Henderson	Ed Keane
The Sergeant	Joe Sawyer
Michaels	Joseph Crehan
Masters	George Meeker
Judge	John Hamilton
First Detective	Robert Elliott
Second Detective	Eddie Chandler
Lefty	Max Wagner

By FRANK S. NUGENT

As though it were not already the most thoroughly cinematized decade of our history, the Warners are presenting "The Roaring Twenties" (at the Strand) with the self-conscious air of an antiquarian preparing to translate a cuneiform record of a lost civilization. With a grandiloquent and egregiously sentimental foreword by Mark Hellinger, with employment of newsreel shots to lend documentary flavor, with a commentator's voice interpolating ultra-dramatic commonplaces as the film unreels, their melodrama has taken on an annoying pretentiousness which neither the theme nor its treatment can justify. The dirty decade has served too many quickie quatrains to rate an epic handling now.

Stripped of its false whiskers, including that part of the Hellinger preface which goes: "This film is a memory, and I am grateful for it," the picture merely marks the Warners' return to the profitable and visually exciting field where once sprouted such horrendous nosegays as "Public Enemy" and "Little Caesar." For here again we find the fighters of 1918-19 back from the war, discovering they have lost their glory with the armistice, turning to bootlegging and hijacking and murder during the delirium of the speakeasy era, taking a licking in the stock market crash of '29, penning their farewell letters to the world in blood spilling from bullet wounds.

If it sounds familiar, Mr. Hellinger will remind you that it all really happened, as he so gratefully remembers. If it also seems to be good entertainment of its kind (and it is, barring the false dignity the Warners have attached to it), credit it to James Cagney in another of his assured portrayals of a criminal career man; to Gladys George, who has breathed poignance into the stock role of the night club hostess who calls her customers "chump"; to Raoul Walsh, who has kept his story of the hectic years spinning and has staged a dramatic final scene with a punch-line that is the perfect epitaph for the public hoodlum: "He used to be a big shot!"

James Cagney

November 11, 1939

News

Guns Still Bark

"Al" Capone has left his stamp on the nation's popular literary taste; with one reservation. The vogue of the underworld is stronger in the films and the newspaper cartoons, and on the radio than it is in the new books. But radio and the movies draw heavily on the older books, in which the Capone way of life figured so prominently.

As for our so-called comic strips, the stranger from foreign lands or our own historians of the distant future may well wonder how a supposedly humorous people like the Americans came to regard pistols, hand grenades and tommy-guns as comic; they play such an overwhelming part in the so-called comic strip. It is true that most of these lethal weapons are now employed for the discomfiture of international spies and enemies of democracy and for the ultimate triumph of the FBI. But beneath these latter-day forms it is the old gangster passion that manifests itself.

Murder Draws Crowds

More than a dozen years after the repeal of Prohibition and the resultant sharp drop in the wars of the Capones the gangster tradition is vividly alive, though in somewhat disguised form. In the nation's popular amusements the thrillers are often synonymous with the killers. People are still taken for rides and put on the spot. The advent of history's super-gangsters of the Nazi and fascist type has not superseded the old-style non-ideological gunman, just as the dreadful harvest of the war seemingly has not exhausted the possibilities of murder as a theme for popular fiction. On the radio the wars between the hard-bitten law enforcers and the underworld continue to rage.

January 30, 1947

MOVIE MAKERS BAR GLORIFYING CRIME

Film Men Also Move to Guard Against Other Material Offensive to Good Taste

Reacting to criticism from the clergy and other sources both within and outside the trade, the Motion Picture Association of America announced yesterday new and stronger regulations to prevent the glorification of crime and criminals on the screen and to guard against the presentation of other subject material that might be regarded as offensive to good taste.

Eric Johnston, president, recommended to the board of directors at a meeting in the MPA headquarters, 28 West Forty-fourth

Street, changes in existing regulations of the Production Code and the Advertising Code to implement the renewed campaign against crime and indecency.

The board unanimously approved Mr. Johnston's objectives and at the same time struck from the MPA title registration list the titles of more than twenty-five pictures, some currently in release and others contemplated for filming, which are considered to be "objectionable and unsuitable."

New Amendment to Code

A new amendment to the Production Code, the thirteenth to be added during the last several years, specifies that: "No picture shall be approved dealing with the life of a notorious criminal of current or recent times which uses the name, nickname or alias of such notorious criminal in the film, nor shall a picture be approved if based upon the life of such a notorious criminal unless the characters shown in the film be punished for crimes shown in the film as committed by him."

This ruling is regarded in trade circles as aimed directly against the production of several contemplated pictures, chief among which is the life of Al Capone. The projected filming of the ex-gang lord's life, based on a story by Westbrook Pegler, drew considerable adverse criticism. Joseph I. Breen, administrator of the Production Code in Hollywood, rejected the proposed scenario as unsuitable for the screen on Nov. 13. This was the fourth Capone scenario rejected by the Code administration in the last five years.

In a further drastic action the MPA has in effect banned from the screen fourteen pictures, made between 1928 and 1947, by including their titles among those now declared "unsuitable for re-release or re-issue." Among the pictures thus listed are "Dillinger," 1945; "Roger Touhy, Gangster," 1944; "The Racket Man," 1944; "This Gun for Hire," 1943; "The Murder Ring," 1942; "The Killers," 1946; "They Made Me a Killer," 1946; "Born to Kill," 1947; "Shoot to Kill," 1947; "The Last Gangster," 1937; "Me Gangster," 1928; "Gang War," 1928; "Ladies of the Mob," 1928, and "The Racketeer," 1930.

Not Barred Per Se

While the MPA announcement did not specify that the pictures per se were barred from further showing, a spokesman said the action could be interpreted thus because the showing of a picture under a revised title constitutes a violation of Federal Trade Commission practices.

In addition, thirteen titles registered between 1934 and 1947 also were stricken from the MPA's Title Registration Bureau, including three titles submitted last month. The latter are "The Capone Story," "How We Trapped Capone" and "Gun Moll," and, registered earlier this year, were "Al Capone" and "Undercover Man, He Trapped Capone." Still other proscribed titles are "Killer for Hire," "Assassin for Hire," "Killers All," "Baby Faced Killer," "The Gangster's Moll," "Gangster's Glory," "Professional Killer" and "The Killer."

Section XI of the Production Code, stipulating that "salacious, indecent or obscene titles shall not be used," has been revised for the first time since 1930. The new section XI now reads "The following shall not be used: 1. Titles which are salacious, indecent, obscene, profane or vulgar. 2. Titles which suggest or are currently associated in the public mind with material, characters or occupations unsuitable for the screen. 3. Titles which are otherwise objectionable."

This regulation is expected to prevent a recurrence of the unfavorable position in which the industry found itself in regard to the Twentieth Century-Fox production of Kathleen Winsor's novel, "Forever Amber."

The MPA also adopted a new section thirteen for the Advertising Code. The amended version states, "Titles of source materials or occupations or names of characters on which motion pictures may be based should not be exploited in advertising or upon the screen if such titles or such names are in conflict with the provisions of the Production Code affecting titles."

BOGART BALKS AT BOGEY

By HUMPHREY BOGART

HOLLYWOOD.

IT is becoming the fashion to say in Hollywood that the "take-that-you-rat" school of drama is going out, and if I am not as sanguine about this as some of the practitioners of a gentler mode of drama, it is not merely because I earn my living in this department of the workaday world. As the husband of Miss Betty Bacall, the cinema actress and heroine, and a soon-to-become-father, I could be said to have the more than casual interest in the matter possessed by any family head.

But, by virtue of producing my own films, in one of which, "Knock On Any Door" (just completed at Columbia), we have as handsome a bit of screen killing as you will find on any police blotter, I am also financially and artistically interested in the reverse side of the picture. It occurs to me then that, better than most, I am in a position to arbitrate the matter for the film people, for the writers of this sort of goose-pimple literature, and for the public, which has the wit to know what it likes, but not always, there are those who say to like what is good for it.

Personal Note

It happens that the genesis of this fascination with what happens to a gangster in a film was firmly outlined in my own early experience on the screen. Cast in "The Petrified Forest," with Leslie Howard and Bette Davis, I soon found people, who saw the picture, approaching me on the street as if I were the star of the piece. This puzzled me at first, because, naturally, I wasn't.

And then the reason occurred to me. In the picture, for most of the time I was in it, I sat on the floor of a roadside inn with a machine-gun in my lap and spoke exactly ten sides. That machine-gun was at the bottom of it all. We don't use machine-guns in committing murder today on the screen, because it has become legally unfashionable.

You may be just as dead when you are killed by a slug, knife, maul, brass knuckle, belaying pin, poison, billie, shotgun or plain bow and arrow, but you give the impression that, like the nations which go down under cannon instead of poison gas, you have been done in somewhat more humanely, and strictly according to the code.

Pivotal Character

But to get back to that first picture. I really can't blame people for thinking I starred in it—and I say that without pride. No one felt sure just when the gun in my hand would go off, and every one found himself, willy-nilly, wanting to know who would be hit when it did, because if he looked away for a split second it might not be possible to follow the trend of the story from then on in.

That may be—and I think it is—the incidental side of the fascination for a gangster film; but there is a psychologically even more sound reason for genuine interest in this sort of film, especially among Americans. Gangsters are a more or less non-gregarious fringe of the social community who work alone and play alone (except for their molls), and rob and kill when the odds are in their favor. Up to this point they get a merely frightened acceptance of their ability to do more damage than most individuals in a given situation.

Underdog

But, the act committed, you really get down to the reason for the gangster's popularity. We don't hunt him singly, or on equal terms. We call out a horde of squad cars, the National Guard, or the entire FBI, and, after hunting him down like a rabbit, fill him so full of lead even his own mother wouldn't recognize him. Or, if we don't, for the average American the rest of the story stops moving until the gangster has, by some good fortune or some charming device on the writer's part, got away. And who in the audience, at this point, is going to say to himself, "I like those policemen?"

The young gangster, running out into the street, or up some alley, spraying the world he hates with bullets, may not be as morally acceptable as the young Crazy Horse, outwitting an American Army on the march, but, as a dramatic device, he will catch the same amount of sympathy—killer though he is.

Is there not, conversely, some merit in Samuel Grafton's argument that no first-rate novelist has ever yet written a novel about a Republican?

My friend, Louis Bromfield—who, by the bye, is a Republican, lest I be accused of taking sides here, which heaven forbid—has been a deep student of these matters for some time. He tells me that it is the man in struggle, and not the man arrived, who holds the interest of the creative novelist. It is at least worth arguing that there is a modicum of the creative novelist in all of us, and that this absorption with how men get out of difficulties, single-handed and alone if possible, but in any event get out of them, is the stuff of which we weave the warp and woof of our own better dramatic imaginings.

Cure

The cure for the gangster film then, in the light of these matters,

48

seems eminently simple to me. In "The Maltese Falcon" we sent a single individual out against a lot of gangsters, and the result was a whole series of pictures with the lone hero against the gangsters instead of vice versa. We called him Sam Spade, but you could call him Calvin Coolidge and still get the same effect if you held to the rule. I am not in the business of pointing up morals, but even a half-hearted search might uncover one here.

Of course, I don't claim we're changing basic values. You have the cavalry for your winning money instead of the Indians; but you are going to get some killings in any event, and a lot of people are going to be very dead because of misdeeds. Personally, I'll play Sam Spade or Duke Mantee with about the same regard for the two roles. Anyone interested can call the shots.

Screen: 'Bonnie and Clyde' Arrives

Careers of Murderers Pictured as Farce

By BOSLEY CROWTHER

A RAW and unmitigated campaign of sheer press-agentry has been trying to put across the notion that Warner Brothers' "Bonnie and Clyde" is a faithful representation of the desperado careers of Clyde Barrow and Bonnie Parker, a notorious team of bank robbers and killers who roamed Texas and Oklahoma in the post-Depression years.

It is nothing of the sort. It is a cheap piece of bald-faced slapstick comedy that treats the hideous depredations of that sleazy, moronic pair as though they were as full of fun and frolic as the jazz-age cut-ups in "Thoroughly Modern Millie." And it puts forth Warren Beatty and Faye Dunaway in the leading roles, and Michael J. Pollard as their sidekick, a simpering, nose-picking rube, as though they were striving mightily to be the Beverly Hillbillies of next year.

It has Mr. Beatty clowning broadly as the killer who fondles various types of guns with as much nonchalance and dispassion as he airily twirls a big cigar, and it has Miss Dunaway squirming grossly as his thrill-seeking, sex-starved moll. It is loaded with farcical hold-ups, screaming chases in stolen getaway cars that have the antique appearance and speeded-up movement of the clumsy vehicles of the Keystone Cops, and indications of the impotence of Barrow, until Bonnie writes a poem about him to extol his prowess, that are as ludicrous as they are crude.

Such ridiculous, camp-tinctured travesties of the kind of people these desperados were and of the way people lived in the dusty Southwest back in those barren years might be passed off as candidly commercial movie comedy, nothing more, if the film weren't reddened with blotches of violence of the most grisly sort.

Arthur Penn, the aggressive director, has evidently gone out of his way to splash the comedy holdups with smears of vivid blood as astonished people are machine-gunned. And he has staged the terminal scene of the ambuscading and killing of Barrow and Bonnie by a posse of policemen with as much noise and gore as is in the climax of "The St. Valentine's Day Massacre."

This blending of farce with brutal killings is as pointless as it is lacking in taste, since it makes no valid commentary upon the already travestied truth. And it leaves an astonished critic wondering just what purpose Mr. Penn and Mr. Beatty think they serve with this strangely antique, sentimental claptrap, which opened yesterday at the Forum and the Murray Hill.

This is the film that opened the Montreal International Festival!

The Cast

BONNIE AND CLYDE; written by David Newman and Robert Benton; directed by Arthur Penn and produced by Warren Beatty; a Tatira-Hiller Production presented by Warner Bros.-Seven Arts. At the Forum Theater, Broadway at 47th Street, and the Murray Hill Theater, 34th Street east of Lexington Avenue. Running time: 111 minutes.

Clyde Barrow	Warren Beatty
Bonnie Parker	Faye Dunaway
C. W. Moss	Michael J. Pollard
Buck Barrow	Gene Hackman
Blanche	Estelle Parsons
Frank Hamer	Denver Pyle
Ivan Moss	Dub Taylor
Velma Davis	Evans Evans
Eugene Grizzard	Gene Wilder

Warren Beatty in role of Clyde and Faye Dunaway as Bonnie

CHAPTER 2

Organized Crime

Meyer Lansky—alleged financial mastermind of the Mafia.

Courtesy The New York Times.

35 Years Ago—

Arnold Rothstein was mysteriously murdered and left a rackets empire up for grabs.

By SHERWIN D. SMITH

AMERICAN organized crime, which has been receiving so much attention through Joseph Valachi's televised testimony before a Senate subcommittee, would not be what it is today if Arnold Rothstein had not kept an appointment one November Sunday night 35 years ago in Room 349 of the old Park Central Hotel. There, somebody shot him in the groin. Two days later, on Nov. 6, 1928—Herbert Hoover's election day—he died in Polyclinic Hospital. The murder is still carried on the books of the New York Police Department as unsolved. It left a racketeering empire up for grabs —with results that still go on.

Who was Rothstein? To the men who sidled up to his table at Lindy's he was simply "A.R.," the man who had connections everywhere, who could arrange anything—provided there was enough in it for him.

Scott Fitzgerald fictionalized him in "The Great Gatsby" as Meyer Wolfsheim, "a gambler . . . the man who fixed the World Series back in 1919." That wasn't quite accurate. Rothstein was a gambler—big enough and crooked enough to have been approached by the men who conceived the idea of bribing the Chicago White Sox players. But he was also smart enough to let others put in the fix while he sat back and, placing his bets carefully, made a killing.

A Broadway tinhorn, interviewed by The Times after Rothstein's murder, said: "He lived only for money. . . . He wasn't right even with himself. For every friend, he had a thousand enemies." That was closer to the truth, but Rothstein did have friends.

One friend was Damon Runyon. He romanticized Rothstein. Eventually, in the musical "Guys and Dolls," based on Runyon's short stories, Rothstein was transformed into Nathan Detroit, operator of the "oldest established, permanent floating crap game in New York."

ROTHSTEIN ran just such a floating crap game in his early years. Often he would not know until the last minute where it would meet, but a regular could depend on him to materialize from the shadows to answer the question: "Where's the action?" Recalling those nights, William J. Fallon, the criminal lawyer whom Gene Fowler called "The Great Mouthpiece" and whom Rothstein kept on retainer for years, said: "Rothstein is a man who dwells in doorways. A mouse standing in a doorway, waiting for his cheese."

"Mouse" may have been too mild an epithet. But there was cheese aplenty. Rothstein's estate was publicly appraised at $1,757,572. Nobody knows what the hidden assets amounted to.

ARNOLD ROTHSTEIN was born in 1882 in a comfortable brownstone on 47th Street, just west of Lexington Avenue. His father was a self-made textile merchant, so universally trusted that in 1919 he was able to settle a garment-industry labor dispute singlehanded. For that he was honored with a testimonial dinner at which Gov. Alfred E. Smith and Supreme Court Justice Louis D. Brandeis delivered the principal speeches.

Young Arnold was an all-around disappointment. Except for arithmetic—he could see the practical uses of that— he had no interest in school, and after two years at Boy's High he quit at 16. He was already an accomplished pool shark; he perfected his skill at the parlor run by John McGraw, who was also manager of the New York Giants.

In no time at all, he discovered that loan-sharking could be even more profitable than pool-sharking.

Usury is a service of a sort, and providing services—for a fee—became Rothstein's specialty. He set up a clearing house for bookmakers; through Rothstein, a bookie who felt himself dangerously over-extended could lay off his bets with other bookmakers in cities across the country. He branched out into labor racketeering, providing goons for either side. He was believed (it was never proved) to be the fence who disposed of $5,000,000 worth of Liberty Bonds stolen in a series of Wall Street holdups at the end of World War I. Between 1921 and 1924, he provided bail of $14,000,000 in liquor prosecutions alone. All for a fee, of course.

IN Rothstein's business, one thing always led to another. He acquired a Norwegian freighter to bring in whisky from Scotland in 20,000-case lots, and since there was space left over he began to smuggle dope. To cover his operations he bought an export-import firm, and found himself with a thriving sideline business as an art dealer.

He owned an insurance agency, which got the business of those who sought his favors; one afternoon, for example, he wrote nearly $700,-000 worth of policies for the union men of the A.F.L. Building Trades Council. He bought into such legitimate businesses as the Longchamps restaurants and Wallachs clothing stores, and made them rent space in the buildings he owned. He ran a gambling casino on Long Island, decided Queens had a future and launched a giant housing project called Middle Village. In brief, he set the pattern for the modern racketeer.

But he was also an old-fashioned, compulsive gambler. "I always gambled," he once said. "I can't remember when

"A. R."—He set the pattern for today's racketeer, dealing in dope, whisky, insurance, anything that would turn a profit.

I didn't. Maybe I gambled just to show my father he couldn't tell me what to do [psychiatry was becoming popular about that time], but I don't think so. I think I gambled because I loved the excitement."

In the summer of 1928, Rothstein fell into a poker game arranged by a small-timer named George McManus, who happened to have a covey of action-hungry out-of-towners in tow. The game went on for two nights and a day, and Rothstein lost $322,000—all in markers, or I.O.U.'s. At the end, he tore up the slips of paper and gave the winners his word to pay. No one dared to complain. But weeks went by, and Rothstein, with his capital frozen in his varied "investments," did not pay off.

AS organizer of the game, McManus was held by the gamblers' code to be responsible for all debts. He sent a thug to collect. "Beat it," said Rothstein, and the gunman ran. McManus took to drink.

That was the situation on Nov. 4, 1928, when Rothstein received a telephone call at Lindy's restaurant summoning him to Room 349 at the Park Central. He placed the last bet of his life—$60,000 that Hoover would be elected—and left for the hotel. Half an hour

later, at 10:53 P.M., the house detective found him at the foot of the service stairs, fatally wounded.

The gun had been thrown from the window of Room 349; it bounced off a parked taxi and was recovered. The room had been rented by one "George Richards," and the chambermaid identified him from photographs as McManus. An overcoat with McManus's name in the lining was still in the room.

McManus spent the next 24 days in an apartment on Mosholu Parkway in the Bronx while the newspapers screamed and the police insisted they were looking for him. He finally surrendered, by appointment, in a barbershop at Broadway and 242d Street. He was duly tried; the judge directed a verdict of acquittal (on the ground of insufficient evidence, he said), and the clerk of the court returned his overcoat.

It seemed to many New Yorkers that police and politicians were less interested in finding Rothstein's murderer than in losing the records he had kept. "There are more than 40,000 papers [in Rothstein's office files]," said District Attorney Joab H. Banton, "but we believe some might be missing." Indeed, for a time it was officially reported that they were all missing. Those

ABSOLVED—George McManus, who was tried for Rothstein's murder and acquitted on a directed verdict.

that reappeared—with the explanation that they had been mislaid—held nothing embarrassing to any public figure. But they did provide Federal agents with leads for a series of raids that netted an estimated $8,000,000 worth of narcotics.

THAT should have been the end of the Rothstein story, but it wasn't quite. He left two wills, and his wife and mistress had a lengthy court fight over which was valid. By the time a compromise was reached, the estate had been declared insolvent. Even the land for the Middle Village

housing development was seized by the city for $250,000 in back taxes (the city promptly found that it contained a deposit of peat moss worth exactly $250,000).

And what happened to Rothstein's empire of crime? There seems little doubt that it was quickly divided among the leaders of what is now called Cosa Nostra. It is a nice coincidence that the Park Sheraton (as the Park Central is now named) was the hotel where Albert Anastasia was shot to death in a barber chair in 1957. That unsolved murder is still a lively topic among Valachi's questioners.

October 27, 1963

"TAKEN FOR RIDE" GUNMAN EPITAPH

Gangland's Newest Method of Settling Its Feuds By Murder in a Fast Car Has Exact Technique And Is Hard to Stop—Recent Examples

By F. L. YORDAN.

ASHORT time ago Frankie Marlow, notorious gunman, gambler and racketeer, left a mid-town restaurant in response to a telephone call. His friends saw him drive off in a dark sedan with two men. That night his body, riddled with bullets, was picked up beside a lonely country road. Another

gangster, in underworld parlance, had been "taken for a ride"—a facetious expression to designate what has lately become the favorite lethal method of gangdom.

This form of murder, which since Marlow's violent end has repeatedly cropped up in one guise or another, is not old. Its current popularity, in fact, dates back no more than two

or three years, although police authorities trace its beginning to the time when automobiles first came into universal use. In a few years its technique has been refined and its application considerably widened.

Police assign several cogent reasons for gangland's decided preference for this method. They are all summed up in the modern fast automobile. The closed motor car—and cars of this type are almost always employed—offers a convenient torture chamber. Caught in a swiftly moving trap of glass and steel, the victim has scarcely a chance to escape. Cries are not heard; shots are easily mistaken for exhaust explosions. And the automobile provides a quick getaway.

Reasons for "Rides."

The motives for the "ride" are

rooted in the same soil that breeds all gang feuds—"poaching," "shakedowns," internal jealousies and personal revenge. Marlow, for example, according to the police, was slain at the instance of other racketeers who found him an unwelcome competitor in their illicit business—in this case, beer running. And Edwin Jorge, killed last year by a gang of dope peddlers and bootleggers, was killed presumably because he had extorted "blood money" while posing as a Federal agent.

Police annals count few methods more nefarious than the "ride." There are two major variations of this practice. One is to lure the intended victim into the gang's car and kill him there; the other, to surprise the prey as he drives in another car. Still another method frequently included in the same category, but which savors more of kidnapping, employs a car merely to convey the enemy to a spot where the gang may safely "operate" on him.

The differences in technique may be illustrated from actual evidence of some recent outstanding cases. While none of them has been solved in so far as apprehension of the assassins is concerned, in each instance the police have been able to reconstruct the crime to a degree that throws light on the process employed.

The Jerge Murder.

On a drowsy Sunday afternoon in June, Edwin Jerge, or Carter, Chicago bank robber and suspected New York bootlegger and drug peddler, was driving down Broadway in a closed car he had borrowed from a woman friend. A girl sat beside him in the front seat. He drove along leisurely, little suspecting that four men in another car were following him, watching his every move. On reaching Thirty-sixth Street the traffic light turned to red; he halted his car and waited. A car slid alongside. As Jerge turned his eyes automatically in its direction, one of its occupants suddenly whipped out a revolver and fired point-blank. Jerge crumpled in his seat. The murder car swerved round the corner and was quickly lost in a cloud of oil-smoke.

Jerge's companion, uninjured save for a few minor cuts by splintered glass, coolly stepped out and vanished. The police theory was that the girl had been used as a decoy, the murderer and his three confederates waiting near by and then trailing the car.

Frankie Yale's Finis.

Frankie Yale's murder followed Jerge's by less than two weeks, and in like manner. Yale, or Uale, was the Beau Brummel, of the Brooklyn underworld. Thirty-five, smartly attired and with large diamonds sparkling on his fingers, he was driving along a quiet residential section of that borough in his shining

new sedan, when destiny overtook him—destiny in the form of another automobile filled with gangsters. They began to shoot through the rear window of Yale's sedan, and continued to shoot, with pistols as well as sub-machine guns, until their victim dropped.

In reconstructing the crime the police concluded that the assailants were Chicago men, not only because of the machine gun used, but because Yale had figured prominently in the doings of Chicago gangdom in the last decade. They ascribed the murder to a gangsters' feud.

Another case recently come to light disclosed a different aspect of the "ride." No attempt was made to attack the victim in the automobile—that came later. It happened in New Jersey in June. Thomas Bartone, youthful alleged gangster, was doomed to death by a gang with which he had fallen into disfavor. It was decided to kidnap him, take him to the outskirts of a village and there, far from all possibility of intrusion, kill him.

The plan was carried out, with the exception that Bartone lived to tell the tale. Either through fear, or in an unwonted surge of mercy, the gang's delegate assigned to the task merely wounded him in the legs. He has since been caught and sentenced.

What makes Bartone's case atypical was the manner of his capture by the gang. They accosted him late one night, forcing him to enter their automobile at the point of a pistol. Such crudity of technique would have surely failed with a gangster of more desperate character or greater experience.

Gangs go about executing their decrees in a thorough, businesslike fashion. Obtaining the car to be used in the murder is a routine matter. Some gangs keep a number of automobiles registered under false names or equipped with license plates stripped from other cars. Others find it equally convenient to steal one for the occasion.

The latest system is to hire gunmen

from other cities to do a local "job." This is not done because of lack of home talent, but, in the majority of cases, to avoid arousing the suspicion of their prey, and to throw the police off the scent after the murder. The hirelings are carefully selected for their qualifications for the task. Known as "yellow gorillas" by the police, they come from the lowest stratum of the underworld. They shoot to kill, preferably from behind; they never take a chance and never give anybody a chance. Their work commands high prices, and sometimes brings added rewards when neatly executed.

As the day approaches, these men are provided by the gang with all the necessary paraphernalia—automobiles, pistols, shotguns and, in some cases, machine guns. The route is mapped out and studied, the spot where the body is to be discarded is carefully gone over. The getaway is also prearranged. Generally, unless something unforeseen turns up, the plans are carried out as scheduled. But before the "mob" is ready to proceed to the final act, it knows its man, knows his temperament and habits, the places he frequents and the friends he can count upon. These things are important when it comes to taking him on his death ride.

The question often arises how men of the type of Marlow, Jerge and Yale—men who live in the maelstrom of criminal activity, generally fearful of their rivals and often distrustful of their own confederates—ever fall into the trap.

The fact is that many doomed men have eluded it. Al Capone, for instance, is said to have foiled such attempts on more than one occasion. And gangsters with reason to believe they are "wanted" by their enemies make a point of never riding in an unfamiliar automobile or with unfamiliar persons. It is the conviction of a member of the old Homicide Squad that the "ride" does not succeed more than once in a dozen attempts.

'RIDE' VICTIM WAKES ON STATEN ISLAND

Charles Luciania Revives on Beach Where Gangster Foes Dumped Him.

BEATEN, CUT AND GAGED

Declines to Reveal Assailants—Held in $25,000 on Grand Larceny Charge.

Charles (Lucky) Luciania, associate of the late Arnold Rothstein, the notorious Diamond brothers and the late Thomas (Paddy) Walsh, awoke at 2 A. M. yesterday on Huguenot Beach, Staten Island, and thought he was dreaming. He had been "taken on a ride" the night before and was alive to tell about it.

His lips were sealed with adhesive tape, his head was aching from fist and gun butt blows and there was a knife wound on his chin. Luciania tore off the tape and staggered almost a mile before he reached the police booth at Prince's Bay Avenue, where he was intercepted by Patrolman Blanke of the Tottenville Precinct.

"Get me a taxi," Luciania pleaded. "I'll give you fifty bucks if you do and let me go my way."

Blanke ignored the offer; instead he took Luciania to the Richmond Memorial Hospital and telephoned to Detective Charles Schley of the Tottenville Precinct. To Schley the battered man told the story of his ride. Luciania said he was standing on Fiftieth Street at Sixth Avenue on Wednesday at 6 P. M., when a limousine, with curtains drawn, rolled up beside him. Three men leaped from the tonneau, prodded Luciania in the back with gun muzzles, forced him into the machine, and the ride began.

The adhesive tape was applied, then came the kicks and punches and knife wound. Luciania became unconscious and hours later woke up on the beach, staring unbelievingly at the waves rolling in from lower New York Bay.

When the detective began to ask questions, Luciania suddenly became mute.

"Don't you cops lose any sleep over it," he finally burst out, impatiently. "I'll attend to this thing myself, later." He refused to say any more, denied that he had recognized the men who had taken him for the ride and wearily insisted that he had no enemies.

When he was taken before Magistrate Croak later in the day, after a line-up at Police Headquarters, Manhattan, he was held in $25,000 for examination tomorrow on a technical charge of grand larceny.

The detectives were inclined to the theory that Broadway racketeers had thrown Luciana on the beach in the belief that he was dead. He has been arrested many times, but has been convicted only once, according to his fingerprint record. In 1916 he was sentenced to the penitentiary for possessing drugs.

SAYS CRIME IS RUN ON A BUSINESS BASIS

Martin Conboy Holds Ease of Hiding in Big Cities Gives Gangs 85% Immunity.

ASKS CONCERTED ACTION

Attempts to Curb Crime Must Fail Unless All States Join in Them, He Writes in Law Quarterly.

The concentration of wealth in large cities, combined with naturally resulting facilities for concealment, has created the setting which has made possible the development of crime organized on a business basis, says Martin Conboy in an article in the New York University Law Quarterly Review, which will be issued tomorrow.

Seventy per cent of all crime is chargeable to the organizations, or gangs, he says, which enjoy possibly 15 per cent immunity from prosecution. This condition he ascribes to changed conditions which have outdated legal systems based on older forms of society.

The break-up of communal life, Mr. Conboy writes, has made it possible that "the master criminal, if there were such a person, might live for years together within one of those vast cubes which we call apartment houses without his nearest neighbors knowing of his existence, to say nothing of his occupation."

The public has two alternatives under the present situation, he continues. One is to accept it, "allowing the surety companies to distribute the money losses as the losses from fire are distributed, or planning, 'with the long hand,' a campaign for the obliteration of this enemy within our gates."

For this, Mr. Conboy writes, what would seem to be first needed is an authority competent to set in motion, under a single direction, agencies for the detection of potential criminals, for the apprehension of those who commit crime, for the making and keeping of records from and after the first arrest of a criminal, for depriving the gangs of their recruits and their revenues, for the harmonization of prosecution agencies, for the correction of bail abuses, for cleansing the services of corrupt officials and for seeing that punishment is not evaded.

"If the competent authority, the leadership, is found in one State, it will have to be sought for in the others also, for a criminal, if not interfered with, can cross a civic or State boundary as easily as he would a meridian."

NEW YORK RACKETS AT GRIPS WITH LAW

The Practices Revealed in the Poultry Trade Resemble Those in Many Lines

By R. L. DUFFUS.

THAT favorite figure of modern fiction and film drama, the racketeer, again enjoys the spotlight as three material witnesses against New York City's kosher poultry gang insist on sleeping in jail for their own protection in spite of efforts to bail them out which both themselves and their jailers describe as mysterious and sinister.

The live-poultry racket, dramatized for the moment by the efforts of District Attorney Foley and his assistants to drive it out of the Bronx, preserves the classical form painstakingly elaborated during the past fifteen or twenty years in New York and other cities by a long line of gangdom's leaders.

As described by District Attorney Foley, it is an arrangement by which the gangster furnishes protection from his own depredations at a cost as heavy as the traffic will bear, and it is enforced by destruction of property, assault and battery and terrorization. The supposed "big shot" in the racket usually keeps so modestly out of sight that the police cannot find him when they want him, and so clear of direct connection with the activities of his agents and "gorillas" or "strong-arm men" that he can be brought into court only on a conspiracy charge or on a Federal indictment for omitting to make a truthful income tax return.

An Illegal Sales Tax.

Finally, the live-poultry racket resembles many other rackets in that it is the exploitation of a certain race or section of the community by its own members. The Jewish racketeer in the present case preys upon the law-abiding members of his own race, taking advantage of a religious ordinance which goes back to the days of Moses. The artichoke "kings," of whom one or two have been notorious in Greater New York, were Italians, taking advantage of their countrymen's fondness for that delicate form of thistle.

Rackets in grapes, in women's dressmaking establishments, in furs, in the millinery trade, in the laundries and in the cleaning and dyeing business—to take a few which are or have been notorious in New York—have followed somewhat the same pattern. They are a kind of illegal sales tax, largely imposed upon those who are helpless to resist and least able to pay.

The acts alleged in connection with the live-poultry racket, like similar acts perpetrated in connection with other rackets, show the gangster in a most unromantic light—a parasite, a bully and a sneak, never giving his victims a fair chance, courageous only in the sense that his greed sometimes leads him to "muscle in" on the territory of a rival gangster and so run the risk of being "bumped off" by his rival's hired butchers.

Many Elements in Picture.

But if this were all that could be said, the problems of District Attorney Foley in the Bronx and the other prosecuting officials of Greater New York, who sometimes proceed against the gangsters for felony or on conspiracy charges; of the State's Attorney General, who acts against them as illegal combinations; or of the Federal Government, which has an insatiable curiosity as to their incomes, would be simpler. The fact is, however, as even a cursory study of racketeering in New York will show, that other elements enter into the picture.

One element is the enormous amounts of money which racketeers can command when they are successful. We may dismiss as mere guesses the assertions that in Chicago racketeers collect dollar for dollar as much as the city's governing bodies collect in taxes, or that in New York they take in from $200,000,000 to $600,000,000 a year. Those who know most about racketeering are most reluctant to make such guesses. But the sums are admittedly large.

For example, one organization which was nipped in the bud after an inquiry by the Attorney General of New York State had set out to collect $750,000 a year from the 2,500 retail tailor shops in Greater New York. Another tried to collect an initiation fee of $25 and $5 a month from all the neckwear manufacturers. The thousand kosher butchers in the Bronx were to have been assessed an initiation fee of $13 and $5 a month. The syrup racket, operating in Brooklyn, Manhattan and the Bronx, "sold stock" on a basis of $100 down and $6 a week.

Slot-Machine Profits.

The slot-machine racket is estimated to bring in $2,000,000 a month in Greater New York. Racketeers who tried to organize the Italian bakers in the Bronx, of whom there are about 300, charged $10 a month for "protection"—an income of $3,000 a month if they had been successful. Joe Rao, who dipped into one racket too many and received a penitentiary sentence last year, is believed by the Bronx officials who prosecuted him to have had an income of about $4,000 a month. Joseph Weiner, alleged head of the poultry racket, is rumored to have taken in $800,000 a year.

When rackets run into "big money" they are in a position to corrupt any public servant who is corruptible. By means of their affiliations they are also in a position to bring political pressure to bear. The allegations made concerning the political pressure exerted by the racketeers are of the vaguest character, and the casual inquirer hears no mention of specified officials in connection with it. Nevertheless, a corruption fund undoubtedly exists, and it is a huge fund.

An even more dangerous situation is created when rackets, starting in a small way with the usual accompaniments of terrorism and extortion, become large and "respectable," and when, as is sometimes the case, they enable those who submit to them to extort from the public more than they are compelled to pay as dues. The racket then becomes a combination in restraint of trade, able to hire attorneys who have the ability to keep them within the formal limits of the law without greatly hampering their activities and who can defend their agents or principals with some chance of success if and when they are called into court. Some New York City rackets have reached this stage.

Multiply what is known about the profits of individual rackets and racketeers by the number of possible rackets in New York City, weigh the total with the influences just mentioned, and the staggering cost of the system can be appreciated.

"Every car of material which reaches New York by rail," declared Judge Seabury last year, in summing up some of the results of his investigation into the city's affairs, "every cargo that enters its port must pay in some form for the privilege of unloading. Fruits, groceries, vegetables, milk—everything we eat or drink; sand, brick, stone, cement—everything which goes into the buildings over our heads—must pay its toll to the politician-protected racketeer."

How does a racketeer work? Let us return to the case of Joseph Rao, since it happens to be a matter of public record. In February, 1931, a certain Louis R. Engel went into the business of jobbing soda water in the Bronx and upper Manhattan. One day Mr. Engel received a card inviting him to go to an address in Manhattan. After some delay he went, finding three men in an automobile in front of a speakeasy, who demanded that he turn over to them 20 per cent of his gross receipts. One of them told him, he testified, "that they were running the business down in Harlem and people were going to do as they said." Engel gave in to the extent of agreeing to pay 10 per cent.

More Tribute Demanded.

This amount turned out to be unsatisfactory, and Engel, some time later, was "pushed into a car" and taken into the august presence of Joe Rao himself. "He told me," Engel testified, "I was giving his boys pin money. I told him that was the best I could do. He demanded $5,000 or I would have to go out of business. * * * He said he would put me out of business and break my head, have me put on the spot."

Engel finally took his case to the District Attorney's office in the Bronx and Assistant District Attorney William H. Jackson, racketeer specialist in the District Attorney's office, obtained a conviction—one of twenty-one consecutive racketeering convictions which Mr. Jackson has to his credit.

Methods of coercion and intimidation, as actually practiced in Greater New York, have a wide range of severity. The syrup racketeers, broken up not long ago by prosecutions in Kings County, tried to bring rebellious distributers to terms by sending out "dead wagons" ahead of the distributers' trucks. These wagons carried goods which were sold to retailers at ruinous prices or even given away.

The Window-Breaking Step.

The next step in racketeering is window-breaking or the throwing of stink bombs. The latter method has become very popular during the past year or two. A typical stink bomb is about the size and shape of an electric-light bulb. Thrown into a truck, it will ruin clothing or food products. Thrown into a clothing establishment it will spoil everything in the place. It produces an aroma, amounting almost to a flavor, whose nauseating effects linger for many days.

Stink bombs have been in recent use against butcher shops, trucks, fur establishments, millinery shops and cleaning and dyeing establishments. The "organizers" in the latter trade adopted an even more ingenious device. They placed chemicals in clothing sent to be cleaned, with the result that at least one explosion took place in the cleaning apparatus of a large establishment, completely ruining two or three hundred articles of clothing.

The amount of violence used depends on the personality of the "big shot" and the amount of opposition he encounters. Perhaps property loss and a bad beating up are about all that the average inconspicuous victim has to fear.

But a victim who dares appeal to the public authorities for aid is, as the Bronx cases show, in danger of his life.

Even more precarious is the situation of any gangster who incriminates his rivals or associates or who attempts to take business from an aggressive competitor. But this latter menace does not seriously worry the forces of law and order. Few tears were shed at Police Headquarters over the taking off of the late Legs Diamond, and still fewer when Baby-Killer Vincent Coll, as some persisted in believing him to be despite his acquittal on a murder charge, abruptly departed this life.

Can the hold of the racketeer be broken? Can a system which has been said to follow the average New Yorker from birth to death, and to include everything from babies' cribs to coffins, from liquor-running to panhandling, be eliminated?

Not easily, perhaps, and not without constant vigilance. Racketeers are still firmly entrenched in many fields. They are able to hire lawyers who are gifted if not scrupulous. They issue perfectly legal documents which contain such passages as this: "You are therefore urged to apply for membership immediately in one of the above retail organizations in your immediate locality, in order that there may be no confusion with respect to your work on and after July 5, 1932."

What does "confusion" mean? The victim, sucker or prospective member, however he may be described, may guess what it means, but he can prove nothing in advance. Even if laws are broken it is not always easy to prove the connection between an "organizer" and the "agents," "operators" or "strong-arm men" who enforce his decrees.

Yet some progress has been made. Assistant District Attorney Jackson's twenty-one successful prosecutions in the Bronx, carried on despite threats against his life, and supported both by District Attorney Foley and by his predecessor, District Attorney McLaughlin, have certainly made racketeering difficult in that borough. The "big shots" have shown a tendency to keep their precious persons out of the Bronx, though operating through agents. Joe Rao never went there; neither, it is believed, did Joseph Weiner, the alleged higher-up in the live-poultry organization. Slot machines, according to Bronx County officials, have been completely eliminated from their bailiwick.

The State government, under present and past Attorneys General, has accumulated a vast amount of information about racketeering in Greater New York as well as in other parts of the State. Assistant Attorney General Edmund C. Collins, who has charge of this work, under Attorney General John J. Bennett Jr.'s direction, has received and acted on hundreds of complaints and in cooperation with the municipal police has broken up some promising rackets.

The Victim Needs Courage.

If the word of police officers and prosecutors is to be taken, the primary requisite in putting the racketeer out of business is courage on the part of his victim. "Our main difficulty," declared Police Commissioner Bolan last week, "lies with the people from whom money is extorted. If they will come forward and tell us about the conditions, we will guarantee them all the protection at our command." Commissioner Bolan's complaint is general among public officials, and any number of instances to illustrate it can be found.

In the last analysis the racketeer's victim must choose between the protection to which he is entitled as a citizen and the "protection" which the gangster sells at so much down and so much a month. Being an average man with only an average man's share of heroism, he will probably continue to make whatever terms seem to him to promise the greatest safety at the least cost. If public officials are themselves courageous and energetic, he may be emboldened to defy the gangster and appeal to the law.

April 30, 19

DUTCH SCHULTZ TRIAL CAPS A VIVID CAREER

Bronx Boy Who Started Early in the Ways of Gangs Shown to Have Amassed a Great Fortune

By MEYER BERGER.

SYRACUSE, April 26.—When the genial young members of the Bergen Social Club went to dances in the Hub district of the Bronx about fifteen years ago they packed lengths of rubber hose or iron pipe in their trousers to sock neighborhood lads who did not belong to the fraternity.

Arthur (Dutch Schultz) Flegenheimer was a member in good standing, though his prowess with the iron pipe was not exceptional. Benny Sager had a meaner stroke and so did a dozen other Bergen clubbers, but Dutch had a keener mind, and when prohibition came and beer could be transmuted into gold he grew rich and powerful, while the strong-arm boys worked under him as salaried men-at-arms.

As a boy Dutch was an omnivorous reader. He devoured Horatio Alger stuff along with an assortment of other literature when he was a pupil in elementary school in Yorkville, and it is reasonable to believe that if he had not made his fortune in beer, policy and a dozen branches of the racketeering industry, he might have risen to great heights in some other field of endeavor, not necessarily criminal.

Full-Dress Interview.

Reporters who had expected to meet a loutish, unkempt boor went away rather impressed after Dutch gave his first formal interview in his hotel suite here the day before the trial. Instead of the usual "dese" and "dems" type of mugg, they found a broad-shouldered, well-groomed man with a pleasant manner. He was uneasy, but only because he was suspicious. Newspaper men had never been kind to

International New

Dutch Schultz, whose strong-a methods brought in millions

56

him. His voice was deep and rumbling but soft on the ear, and his remarks were high-lighted with humor.

The give-away, if you watched closely for it, was in the gray-brown eyes. Most men of Dutch's stripe who can conceal their true nature in every respect are revealed by their eyes. It was true of Vincent Coll, who looked like a Harvard sophomore—all except the killer eyes. It was true of Jack Diamond.

Another thing that betrayed Dutch's early training, even when he was gravely (but rather shakily) discussing Stefan Zweig, Dickens and Horatio Alger, was the habit of talking out of the side of his mouth. That characteristic is a trick of men who have served long prison terms. Owen Madden has it, and it was noticeable in Waxey Gordon too. It is acquired by men who pass whispers down the line in the jail yard, where speech is forbidden.

"Public Benefactor."

When he spoke of himself as a public benefactor at his first group interview, he was in earnest, though the remark was generally accepted as another bit of Flegenheimer wisecracking. He was probably referring to the fact that he has provided for the widows and families of the twenty or more martyrs who gave their all for the Schultz beer interests in the bloody Coll-Schultz feud that threatened his racket domain in 1931 and 1932.

He probably had in mind, at the same time, his general reputation for generosity to any one who could reach him with a sob story; but this same trait could be found in Capone, in Owen Madden, in the late Larry Fay and in most of the men who acquired great wealth in the prohibition era. Whether he also had in mind his reported philanthropies to policemen and powerful politicians is a matter of conjecture.

Dutch is the son of German Jewish parents. His father was a glazier at one time, worked in a bakery for a while and later set himself up in the livery stable business. The father died when Dutch was only 8 years old, to hear him tell the story, but the policemen who maintain they knew insist that Pater Flegenheimer deserted his family, leaving Mrs. Emma Neu Flegenheimer to support Dutch and his sister Helen.

Early Years.

You get another flash of the Flegenheimer sensitiveness when you ask him about his early schooling. He admits that he got only to the seventh grade, because he had to get out and sell newspapers to add to the family income, but he won't name the dear old school, for sentimental reasons.

He grew up, a stocky, tousled-haired kid, with some reputation as a tough, but he was no tougher—nor as tough—as fifty others in his neighborhood. It was not until he was 17—he's 33 now—that he began to attract the attention of the police. He was arrested in November, 1919, for unlawful entry, but the charge was dismissed. Picked up on that charge a second time, a month later, he was sent to Welfare Island on an indeterminate sentence.

He was shipped from the island to Westhampton Farms, near Goshen, N. Y. He escaped, but was caught not far away, and thirty days were added to his sentence.

Detectives say that when he came out he continued to practice petty thievery—holding up laundry wagons and stealing some of the bundles; grabbing packages from department store wagons (the same apprenticeship as served by the late Jack Diamond, whom he greatly admired, both for his bullet-absorbing qualities and for command of a good vocabulary), and remaining fairly small potatoes until prohibition came in.

He cut his real start around 1928, when he entered into partnership with the late Joe Noe, when he was 26 years old. They ran the Hub Social Club, a beery-smelling dive at 3,468 Third Avenue, then acquired other speakeasies throughout the Bronx and went into the distributing end. His rise, from that point on, was brought out at the trial. He had accounts in eighteen different banks and his ledgers showed beer income of over $2,000,000 a year.

Tracing His Fortune.

The startling sums turned up by the Federal agents in their hunt for Schultz's income were only a drop in the bucket. The government did not lay hands on the deposits accruing from Dutch's control of the highly profitable policy racket. Dutch had driven out fifteen Negro bankers who had controlled the game in Harlem, and disposed of white competitors

That meant more millions. He went into the taxicab racket and made money out of that. He organized the window cleaners of the Bronx and added another source of income. Window washers who wouldn't join suffered fatal accidents; their safety belts gave way.

But Dutch wasn't enjoying all his wealth in any degree of comfort. Three rebellious men-at-arms, the brothers Coll and Charlie (Fats) McCarthy suddenly decided that they would like some of the Schultz fortune for their own. Dutch heard about their ingratitude. Pete Coll was killed on Decoration Day in 1930 and his brother Vince went on the rampage.

Schultz drivers, gun carriers, collectors and even Schultz well-wishers were strewn in disorderly poses all over the Bronx by "The Mick" and his straight-shooting playmate "Fats." One night they raided a Schultz garage on Randall Avenue and forced loyal Flegenheimer fugelmen to smash their own boss's valuable beer trucks and slot machines with Schultz-owned sledge hammers. It didn't end until "The Mick" was machine-gunned to death in a telephone booth and "Fats" went to his reward fighting it out with a detective.

After Joe Noe was killed in November, 1928, while leaving a Schultz business conference in an office over the Château Madrid in Fifty-fourth Street, west of Broadway, Dutch took in as partner Henry Margolis, who went under the name of "Sailor Stevens."

When the Federal grand jury indicted the three partners in 1933 for income-tax evasions, Dutch and his partners fled. Government agents chased them through Canada to California, down to Cuba and Bermuda, and even sought them in the gay capitals of Europe. While they remained fugitives, Dutch sent lawyers to the Treasury Department in Washington offering $100,-000, even more, to drop the criminal charges; but there was no compromise.

Finally he gave up, but with the aid of his attorneys had the case moved to the Northern District, where he was not so well known. He insisted on an "intelligent" jury and helped to pick the men who were to sit in judgment on him. "You can't read faces," he said, "but you can tell an intelligent man when you see one."

Some one suggested that his attorneys might point out that Andrew Mellon, accused of dodging income-tax payment much higher than his, was not being tried on criminal charges.

"Nothing doing," said Dutch. "Why should I drag another guy into my troubles?"

All through, Dutch thought the jury might give him "a break." He was convinced that they would see that the government was persecuting him; that he was just a hard-working beer man who had supplied a thirsty community with something it wanted, and not a cheap tax evader.

DEWEY TAKES HELM IN RACKET INQUIRY; WILL ASK $500,000

Assured of Free Hand and an Adequate Fund to Carry On Wide Investigation.

DODGE PLEDGES FULL AID

New Deputy Seeks Staff of 20 Lawyers—Intends to Set Up Separate Offices.

HIS TASK IS TWO-FOLD

Will War on Public Enemies and Expose Any Politico-Criminal Alliance.

Assured of a "free hand" and an "adequate appropriation," Thomas E. Dewey, a former United States Attorney, accepted an appointment yesterday from District Attorney William C. Dodge to conduct an investigation of vice and racketeering as a special deputy assistant before an extraordinary grand jury.

Mr. Dewey, who is 33 years old, will have the twofold assignment of putting New York's public enemies behind prison bars and exposing the politico-criminal alliance —if such a thing exists—which has made it possible for them to escape punishment thus far.

To accomplish this, Mr. Dewey has told friends privately, may require as much as two years of his undivided time and about $500,000 of public funds. It is his intention, it was said, to establish offices independent of those occupied by Mr. Dodge and to appoint a large staff of lawyers, investigators, accountants and stenographers of his own selection.

Inquiry Starts July 29.

Sometime between now and July 29, the date set by Governor Lehman for the convening of the extraordinary grand jury over which Supreme Court Justice Philip J. McCook has been chosen to preside, Mr. Dewey will make known his requirements to Mr. Dodge, who is

expected to make formal request for the appropriation of the required sum by the Board of Estimate.

The board is not expected to place any serious financial obstacles in the way of the investigation Governor Lehman has ordered. The Fusion administration, which favors the inquiry, controls nine of the sixteen votes on the board and the Tammany members probably will fall in line behind the Governor.

Just before he left for Washington yesterday, Mayor F. H. La Guardia was asked if the city would supply ample funds for the proposed investigation. He replied cryptically that the matter had been "taken up with the Governor," but declined to amplify his remark. Even before Mr. Dewey announced his formal acceptance of the appointment Police Commissioner Lewis J. Valentine pledged "cooperation to the fullest extent of myself and the department together with all the data we have and all the men the investigation needs."

Bar Urged Selection.

Mr. Dewey's appointment as Special Deputy Assistant District Attorney was urged upon Mr. Dodge by Governor Lehman after four Republican leaders of the bar originally proposed by Mr. Lehman had declined to serve and unanimously joined the Association of the Bar of the City of New York in recommending the former United States Attorney for the post. These four were Charles H. Tuttle, George Z. Medalie, Charles Evans Hughes Jr. and Thomas D. Thacher.

Upon reaching his office in the morning Mr. Dodge closeted himself in his private office, refusing to see reporters or even to admit that he had received Governor Lehman's letter directing him to appoint Mr. Dewey to continue the inquiry into vice and racketeering, begun by the runaway March grand jury, which upon its discharge requested the Governor's intervention. Governor Lehman's letter left Mr. Dodge the choice between appointing Mr. Dewey or being superseded as District Attorney of New York County.

At 12:15 Mr. Dodge sent a message to waiting newspaper men announcing that he had forwarded a letter by a messenger to Mr. Dewey's office at 120 Broadway. The District Attorney remained aloof from reporters and would not disclose the contents of the letter.

A little after 1 P. M. Mr. Dewey announced that Mr. Dodge had offered him the appointment as special prosecutor in the investigation into racketeering. Mr. Dewey hastened at once to the Criminal

Courts Building to confer with Mr. Dodge after which he issued the following statement:

"The District Attorney has offered me an appointment as special prosecutor pursuant to the letter of Governor Lehman. I have accepted the appointment upon the understanding that I will have an absolutely free hand, with no interference by the District Attorney and with his full cooperation.

"It is understood that I will accept appointment with the technical title of Deputy Assistant District Attorney, and that all of the members of my staff, who are to be named by me, will receive similar designations. It is my understanding also that adequate appropriation will be made to carry on the work.

"The investigation will follow the broad lines laid down in the Governor's announcement."

In the meantime Mr. Dodge was being interviewed in his office.

"I suppose you all want to know the big news," he said, as reporters filed into his office. "Well, Mr. Dewey has accepted the offer to become special prosecutor in the crime investigation. He will be a special Deputy Assistant District Attorney."

Some one interrupted to ask whether Mr. Dewey's compensation had been agreed upon and Mr. Dodge said that would be settled later. Then he continued:

"Mr. Dewey will make his recommendations to me between now and July 29, when the special term of Supreme Court convenes, by order of Governor Lehman, under Justice Philip J. McCook. Mr. Dewey will recommend the appointment of a staff of assistants as well as the salary requirements for himself and his staff. I must then go before the Board of Estimate and ask a special appropriation to cover the cost of this investigation."

"Did Mr. Dewey ask for a free hand?" the District Attorney was asked.

"He didn't have to ask," replied Mr. Dodge with acid in his voice. "I told him he would have a free hand. He will get 100 per cent cooperation from the District Attorney's office in every sense of the word."

From friends of Mr. Dewey it was learned that he regards the task before him as a more difficult one than that which faced Samuel Seabury as counsel to the Hofstadter Committee. They pointed out that where Mr. Seabury had merely to present a prima facie case of inefficiency and corruption in public office, Mr. Dewey must develop cases which will stand the test of cross-examination before juries.

For the task ahead of him, Mr. Dewey's friends revealed, he wishes to surround himself at the outset with about twenty lawyers, "young enough to be free of entanglements but old enough to have acquired the requisite experience." He has told friends that there will be no volun-

teer workers on his staff, but for those who are chosen it will be "a twenty-four-hour job." He has received applications already from more than forty aspirants for appointment.

Mr. Dewey has indicated privately that his investigation will be along the broadest possible lines, including every form of racketeering as well as organized vice, the policy and bail bond rackets and the simpler methods of levying tribute upon markets and retail merchants.

The newly appointed special prosecutor brings to his task a broad knowledge of racketeering methods and personalities, together with a wide experience in their prosecution. While in Federal office he sent Irving Wexler, alias Waxy Gordon, to the Federal penitentiary for income-tax evasion, obtained the indictment against Arthur Flegentheimer, alias Dutch Schultz, on a similar charge, and tried and convicted James J. Quinlivan, a vice squad policeman implicated in Mr. Seabury's investigation of magistrates' courts.

Mr. Dewey also tried and convicted James J. McCormick, deputy city clerk, who Mr. Seabury showed was accepting gratuities from bridal couples he married in the City Chapel. He prosecuted Patrick J. Commerford for corrupt practices in labor union affairs, and obtained a plea of guilty from Henry Brunder, a policy banker, after an investigation.

Members of the Bronx building racket gang and Joseph Castaldo, head of the artichoke racket, both pleaded guilty to indictments obtained by Mr. Dewey while in the United States Attorney's office. Mr. Dewey also conducted the investigation which resulted in the disbarment of David Paris, lawyer and member of the Legislature, for submitting forged affidavits. It was he whose investigation into the bail-bond racket in the Federal courts brought about a revision of the bail-bond rules.

Upon his retirement from public office Dec. 27, 1933, he was appointed counsel to the Bar Association serving without compensation for an investigation and prosecution of charges against Harold L. Kunsler, former justice of the Municipal Court, who resigned on the last day of his trial before a referee.

He is chairman of the committee on criminal courts law and procedure of the Association of the Bar, chairman of the committee on penal law and criminal procedure, New York State Bar Association, a member of the admissions committee of the City Bar Association and member of the standing committee of the Alumni Association of Columbia University Law School. He is married, has one son, aged and lives at 1,148 Fifth Avenue.

Friends of Mr. Dewey said yesterday it would take him about a month to prepare for the actual opening of the investigation. In the meantime he will have to meet obligations to clients, prepare for the handling of his practice in the two years he expects to devote to the inquiry, and select his staff assistants.

July 2, 193

SCHULTZ DIES OF WOUNDS WITHOUT NAMING SLAYERS; 3 AIDES DEAD, ONE DYING

SHOT IN ABDOMEN FATAL

Gang Chief Protests to Last He Does Not Know Attackers.

BECAME CATHOLIC AT END

Third Henchman Shot Down in Newark Succumbs—One Felled on Broadway Sinking.

GANGSTER HERE IS HUNTED

Schultz, in 'Come Back' Attempt After Tax Inquiries, Had Been Warned of Fate.

Arthur (Dutch Schultz) Flegenheimer, New York's most notorious underworld denizen, and three of his henchmen are dead and another is near death from bullet wounds received in the new outbreak of gang warfare for control of the usury, policy and other rackets which has flared up in Manhattan, Brooklyn and Newark, N. J., in the last forty-eight hours.

Schultz died in the Newark City Hospital at 8:35 o'clock last night. He had been shot through the abdomen by one of two gunmen who attacked him and three of his followers about 10:30 o'clock Wednesday night in the back room of a Newark tavern, around the corner from the Robert Treat Hotel, where Schultz had been living for several weeks.

Yesterday afternoon, knowing that he was about to die, Schultz sent for a priest, who received him into the Roman Catholic Church and administered the last rites of the church. Later he became delirious and sank rapidly until he died. A blood transfusion failed to save him.

Shot Down With Schultz.

In the same hospital Bernard Rosenkrantz, Schultz's chauffeur and chief bodyguard, died early today.

Otto Biederman, alias Otto Berman, and Abraham Landau, alias Leo Frank, died in the hospital yesterday morning. These three were shot down with Schultz in the Newark tavern.

Rosenkrantz had twelve wounds in the abdomen, left foot, left elbow and right wrist. He underwent an operation and had a blood transfusion, but succumbed at 3:20 A. M.

Biederman was riddled with bullets in the abdomen, chest and face, and died a few hours after the shooting. It was first believed that Landau, shot only once, was not seriously wounded, but the bullet severed an artery, causing his death soon after Biederman's.

In Polyclinic Hospital in this city, Martin Krompier, Schultz's chief lieutenant in charge of his Manhattan activities, was also reported to be in a critical condition. He and Samuel Gold, a Broadway handbook maker, were shot by gunmen in a barber shop at Broadway and Forty-seventh Street about an hour and one-half after the Newark shooting.

Fail to Get Clues.

The police were unable to learn from Schultz or his fellow-racketeers who had shot them, or why. Schultz said that he did not know. Biederman shortly before he died tried to tell the police something, but unintelligible sounds came from his lips.

Mrs. Frances Flegenheimer, Schultz's wife, was held without bail last night as a material witness pending investigation of her story, which the Newark police said contained several "discrepancies." They said they had learned that she visited Schultz in the back room of the tavern where he was wounded, an hour before the shooting. She was locked up in Newark Police Headquarters.

She said she had been staying with her husband at the Robert Treat Hotel in Newark until last Sunday, when she went to New York. She returned to Newark the night of the shooting.

An unidentified man telephoned the police to investigate a man and a woman, whom he named, in the killing. He said both had criminal records and were well known to the Bronx police.

Despite the veil of secrecy with which the underworld tries to conceal the motives and methods of its executions and avengements, the New York police received information which led them to believe that both Schultz and Louis (Pretty) Amberg, a racket chief hacked to death and left in a burning automobile near the navy yard in Brooklyn on Tuesday night, were killed by the order of a rival gang leader.

As a result of this information detectives were ordered to look for Charles Luciana, alleged head of the Unione Siciliano in New York, and take him to police headquarters for questioning. Luciana is called "Lucky" Luciana because he is one of the few persons who ever came back alive after being "taken for a ride" by gangland enemies. He was left for dead at the end of an automobile ride in Staten Island but recovered and is said to be a power in New York's underworld circles today, besides owning a string of night clubs and cabarets.

Luciana was formerly associated with the late Arnold Rothstein and Jack Diamond. He is said to have succeeded to the leadership of the Unione Siciliano after the killing of Giuseppe Masseria, known as "Joe the Boss," in Coney Island in 1931. This is the secret organization which Al Capone was said to have headed in Chicago during his heyday in the dry era. Frank Yale, allegedly killed by Capone's henchmen in Brooklyn, was head of the society in New York at one time.

Before Schultz went into hiding over a year ago, as a result of the Federal Government's investigation of his income tax, he worked in harmony with other organized gangs in New York. During his absence, however, rival gang leaders began to intrude upon Schultz's rackets and wean away members of his gang.

Dissension in Ranks Noted.

The police said they have known that Schultz's "number was up" since the time of his surrender in Albany on the income tax charge a year ago. It was observed at his court appearance, when Schultz was tried and acquitted, that there was dissension among his henchmen who appeared as witnesses. That was the reason, it was explained, for the heavy guard thrown around Schultz whenever he appeared in public during the trial.

After Schultz was acquitted, according to the police, he reorganized his gang and attempted to take his former place as head of all the rackets in New York, although he had to keep out of the city because of Mayor La Guardia's warning that he would be arrested if he returned here. He is said to have sent "Bo" Weinberg, then his chief lieutenant, to notify other gang leaders of his intentions. These leaders are said to have organized a powerful combination covering New York, Brooklyn and Newark, and to have sent back word to Schultz to "keep out," as they intended to run all the rackets themselves thereafter.

Weinberg and Krompier were sent back by Schultz to negotiate anew with the rival gang leaders, who this time were said to have made more emphatic threats, warning Schultz that he would be "bumped off" if he tried to get back control of the rackets. Shortly after that, Weinberg disappeared, and the police began to hear reports from underworld sources that he had been killed, and that his body had been sunk in a barrel of cement in the Hudson River. Weinberg has not reappeared, nor has his body been found.

Racial Division Seen.

The police said that the Schultz and Amberg gangs, who remained associated despite Schultz's break with other gang leaders, were known in the underworld as largely "Jewish gangs," whereas the rivals with whom Schultz broke were regarded in the same circles as heads of socalled "Italian gangs."

Police Commissioner Lewis J. Valentine announced at police headquarters that the Schultz-Amberg murders looked to him "like a racial war of extermination, because there isn't an Italian victim, and a fight over spoils."

Asked if he knew anything about Weinberg, Commissioner Valentine said:

"I wish I knew. The streets are full of rumors about his demise."

He said he believed the same gunmen who killed Schultz and his henchman in Newark then separated and came to New York City singly, rejoined and shot Krompier and Gold in the Broadway barber shop.

The commissioner said that as soon as he heard of the Schultz shooting he had ordered detectives to watch all entrances from New Jersey for the gunmen but that this was in vain.

Dewey Gives Leads.

It was also learned that the investigation of New York rackets by Thomas E. Dewey, special prosecutor, had disclosed information which may throw light on the reason other gang leaders did not want Schultz to come back as head of the rackets here. They have begun to make so much money out of the revived usury racket, as well as the policy, horse pool room, alcohol, labor trouble and other forms of underworld activity, it was said, that they were afraid that the return of such a highly publicized figure as Schultz would attract too much public attention to them.

Biederman's connection with Schultz was not known. When taken to the hospital he gave his address as the Hotel President, New York City, but Jean S. Suits, manager of that hotel, said he had not lived there for two or three years. He was known on Broadway as an official race-track handicapper for race tracks in which "Big Bill" Dwyer was interested. He had just returned from a meeting at the Coney Island track at Cincinnati. Gold, another race-track man, denied that he had any connection with the Schultz gang, and said he was merely a friend of Krompier.

The cause of Schultz's death was officially stated as a gunshot wound which pierced the liver and resulted in internal hemorrhages. The bullet passed through his body.

Physicians at the hospital despaired from the beginning of saving his life. He did not realize how serious was his wound until 8 o'clock yesterday morning, when he had a sinking spell. After that his attendants heard him say frequently that he knew he was going to die. "This is the journey's end," he said over and over. "It's death for me."

He had alternate spells of delirium and calm during the day. His wife, his mother, Mrs. Emma Flegenheimer, and his sister, Mrs. Helen Ursprung, were with him at times.

At 8 o'clock last night he had another sinking spell. He lapsed into a coma then and sank steadily until he died. With him at the end were three physicians and a nurse. In a hallway outside the room were his mother and sister. His wife had left the hospital. When a physician told his mother that he was dead she collapsed. A relative drove her from the hospital to her home in the Bronx.

The Rev. Cornelius J. McInerney of Livingston, the Catholic priest who baptized Schultz and administered the sacrament of extreme unction to him during the afternoon, was with him until a few minutes before he died.

When Schultz was registered at the hospital, he described himself as of the Jewish faith. After he realized he was dying, he asked the Rev. Thomas Mulvaney, Catholic chaplain at the hospital, to send for Father McInerney, who is pastor of St. Philomena's Roman Catholic Church at Livingston, a few miles from Newark. He told Father McInerney that his wife was a Catholic and that he wanted to die a Catholic.

During his delirious moments, according to hospital attendants, Schultz talked continuously about the proceedings in the Federal Court in Newark, in which he was fighting removal to New York in his new income tax case. Most of his statements were incoherent or indistinct, but at times he could be understood as giving instructions to his lawyers to "beat the case."

Lucky Charm Recalled.

A telegram from Syracuse, N. Y., with a cryptic message for Schultz arrived at the hospital yesterday morning. It read: "Keep the white elephant busy. We are all with you." The signature was "Ethel." Police investigation revealed that the sender was a woman friend, who had given Schultz a toy white elephant as a lucky charm, and was encouraging him.

Another telegram, from Harlem, read: "Don't be yellow. As ye sow, so shall ye reap." It was signed, Madame Sinclair, Policy Queen. The police were unable to learn its meaning.

In Newark, Deputy Police Chief John Haller, in charge of detectives, said that his information indicated that the killers might have come from any one of three groups —from what he called the "Luciano gang," from the Amberg "mob" in case it believed Schultz responsible for the death of its leader, or even

from disgruntled members of the Schultz crowd itself.

On the table in the back room of the Palace Chop House and Tavern, 12 East Park Street, where Schultz was shot, a sheaf of his business papers were found, according to the Newark police. They said that they appeared to be records of policy, race track and other gambling ventures, and of personal loans. With them, the police added, was a piece of adding machine tape with the figures, 827,253. This was believed to represent dollars and to indicate the magnitude of Schultz's racket operations, according to the police.

Deputy Chief Haller said that the papers were turned over to two Federal agents who went to Newark yesterday afternoon from New York. The agents declined to identify themselves, but were believed to be Treasury Department agents investigating Schultz's income tax.

Slayers' Car Found.

Yesterday morning the Newark police found an abandoned automobile in front of a church about one-quarter of a mile from the scene of the shooting. It was a black sedan, as was the car in which the killers escaped, and contained an empty sawed-off 12-gauge shotgun. Shotgun bullets of the same gauge, as well as .32, .38 and .45 calibre pistol bullets, and two .45-calibre pistols were found on the floor of the tavern. The police said they were certain this was the murder car.

The car was stolen from Mrs. Marie Ford Weiss in Newark on Oct. 14. She identified a pair of white gloves found in the car as her property. License plates on the car had been stolen from another car.

The place where the car was abandoned indicated that the killers had left Newark by way of the Hudson tube to New York.

The police learned that Schultz and his associates had occupied a three-room suite at the Robert Treat Hotel for three weeks, booked as "Mr. Rosenkrantz and party." A .45-caliber revolver was found in the suite.

A revised version of the shooting revealed that Schultz was returning to the back room from a washroom when the shooting began. He had the door open, but closed it quickly.

Then one of the gunmen pushed the door open and shot him. The bullet, which passed through his body, was found on the washroom floor. Other bullets found indicated that more than twenty-five shots were fired by the attackers, and several shots by Schultz's bodyguards. Schultz telephoned to police headquarters for an ambulance after the shooting.

Agents of the New Jersey Alcohol Control Commission informed the police that Schultz had had the run of the tavern where he was killed for some time before the shooting. Twice a day, at noon and in the evening, they said, all other customers were cleared out of the back room, and it was placed at Schultz's disposal as a private dining room and "conference" hall. Usually, they said, Schultz and one of his henchmen ate and conferred there alone, with the door leading into the tavern proper closed. Two armed bodyguards usually sat in chairs in front of the closed doors, they added.

Three Held as Witnesses.

Jack Freeman, bartender and partner in the tavern; Benjamin Bergenfeld, a waiter who attended to Schultz's wants, and King Lou, a Chinese cook, were held without bail as material witnesses. Schultz was said to have been liberal with tips to the bartender and the waiter.

The Alcohol Beverage Control Commission began an investigation to determine whether the license of the tavern should be revoked under the law against rendezvous for underworld characters.

Newark police said that they believed the killers were professional gunmen imported from New York or other cities. Six hats, all with the names of New York stores in them, were found in the back room. Two were believed to have belonged to the killers. The others were accounted for as the property of Schultz and his companions.

Descriptions of one of the gunmen given by the bartender and waiter did not fit with that of Al Stern or Stein, a 21-year-old New York gunman charged by the police with the murder of seven of his former underworld associates, including "Pretty" Amberg, within the last two months. The New York police said that Stern answered somewhat the description of one of the gunmen who shot Krompier, but denied a report that at-

tendants at the barber shop had positively identified his picture.

Besides their main theory that a new gang warfare for control of the rackets was behind the slaying of Schultz, his henchmen and Amberg, the police were also considering the possibility that Schultz may have been killed at the behest of Newark gangsters, who resented possible attempts on his part to "muscle in" on their territory.

Another theory was that Stern might be associated with some smaller gang which might have reason to avenge itself on both Schultz and Amberg for cutting in on their operations, for double-crossing them in some deal, or for failure to help them out with financial aid for some of their members who had been arrested.

Newark police headquarters issued orders, following the shooting, for the organization of a "racket squad" to drive all racketeers and gangsters out of town, break up all criminal gangs and put an end to the rackets in that city.

SLAIN IN GANG WAR.

Associated Press Photo.

Dutch Schultz.

USURY RACKET STIRRED GANG WAR

Collection by Strong-Arm Method Said to Have Been a Stake in Schultz Feud.

KROMPIER A MONEY LENDER

'Enforcers' Slug Victims Slow to Pay on 1,040% 'Book' Which Has 20,000 Borrowers.

The ancient racket of usury, refurbished with the strong-arm methods of modern gangsters, was said yesterday to have been an important contributing factor in the underworld feud which brought about the shooting of Arthur (Dutch Schultz) Flegenheimer.

Martin Krompier, an aide of Schultz, who was shot down in a barber shop at Seventh Avenue and Forty-seventh Street a short time after Schultz was shot in Newark, was said by the police to have been one of Schultz's henchmen in the money-lending game.

Krompier, who has a record of many arrests and discharges, was, it was learned, under investigation along with many others, including Schultz himself, in the usury and other rackets. This inquiry was being conducted by Thomas E. Dewey and his assistants in the course of their special investigation of vice and racketeering.

Usury is an ancient practice, but it was found to have grown prodigiously in New York within the past year. It had reached a point where it would readily form a revenue incentive for a gang murder.

Usury Racket Was Coveted.

A police official declared that within recent weeks Charles (Lucky) Luciano, Louis (Lepke) Buckhouse, or Buchalter, and Jacob (Gurrah Jake) Shapiro, all underworld powers, have been seen in each others' company; a fact which he said was significant and may have indicated a possible combination for the extension of interests, particularly into the usury field in midtown and upper Manhattan, supposedly controlled by Schultz.

The name which the underworld has given to its usury practices stems from Shakespeare. It is called "Shylock racket." It is worked on a system similar to the policy racket or other methods of collecting small sums from numerous persons.

Within a given district some location is picked in which a "book" is kept. There are lenders, also called collectors, who dole out sums of $5, $10 or more, to persons who want to borrow. A growing volume of complaints from large business concerns, extending from the financial district to the other end of Manhattan, has been received at police headquarters, indicating the rapid growth of the racket. These firms complain that their employes, particularly those in the lower salary brackets, are being victimized.

After a person with a job has once gone on "the book," he has little chance of getting off. He is required to pay $1 per week, usually, for each $5 borrowed. The lenders do not wait for him to come in. They wait, instead, at the doors to his place of employment. If a borrower eludes them for a week collectors have been known to go into the offices and demand payment.

When a collector fails to exact the interest a pair of sluggers, called "enforcers," are sent. The failure of borrowers to pay, or their inability to pay, has, it was said, already resulted in a large number of assaults. Cases have been found where as much as three times the original amount was repaid as "interest" although the collectors insist that the original sum remains unpaid.

The "Shylock racket" received a considerable impetus about two months ago when a large number of WPA workers went unpaid for six or seven weeks. These persons, whose incomes were $90 a month, or less, borrowed sums of $5 and $10 because they had to have it for food. They have remained, many of them, in the hands of the sharks since.

Aside from the assaults credited to the failure of borrowers to pay, police also ascribe a number of other crimes of robbery, purse-snatching and petty attempts at extortion to the fear of borrowers, who will go to any lengths to get their instalment interest payments rather than face the ire of the sluggers sent to collect.

It was learned that Dominic Tossone, 19 years old, of 319 East 112th Street, who was the first person to be indicted in the Dewey investigation for attempting to extort money from a real estate agent after breaking windows in a building at 313 East 112th Street, explained that he had been driven to attempt the crime because the "shylockers had him." This explanation was not brought out at the time of his conviction.

There were no conclusive estimates of the value, to the operators, of the Shylock racket. One estimate was that at least 20,000 persons throughout the whole city were paying $1 per week or more to racket collectors. Other estimates put the number much higher than that. The figure of 20,000 represented a minimum "take" for the racketeers of $100,000 per month, with the possibility that it might run as high as $200,000. No sum less than $5 is lent, and no interest payment of less than $1 per week is taken. The racket is based upon a return of 1040 per cent per year.

October 25, 1935

---

7 GANGSTERS SEIZE SCHULTZ RACKETS; FOURTH AIDE DIES

Johnny Torrio, Former Chicago Thug, Reported New Ruler of 'Big Six' Outlaws Here.

POLICE 'UNABLE' TO ACT

Wife of Slain Leader, Trapped in Lie, Is Held — Bernard Rosenkrantz Succumbs.

With Arthur (Dutch Schultz) Flegenheimer and Louis (Pretty) Amberg killed and their gangs demoralized, a new group of outlaw leaders took over control of all the major rackets in New York, Brooklyn and Newark, N. J., yesterday in complete defiance of police efforts to solve the week's gang murders and break up the new combination.

Police officials indicated that they knew the new line-up of underworld powers who are believed to have wanted Schultz and Amberg out of the way, but tacitly admitted that they were unable to get the necessary evidence to do anything about it at present.

According to information in official circles, the power behind the scenes is now Johnny Torrio, an old-time New York and Chicago gang leader, who stepped down from his underworld throne in Chicago early in the prohibition era and was succeeded by Al Capone as head of the chief beer and alcohol rackets during prohibition.

Six Gangs in Group.

The new combination, according to the police, consists of gangs headed by six notorious racketeers: Charles (Lucky) Luciana, Charles (Buck) Siegel, Meyer Lansky, Louis (Lefty) Buckhouse, Jacob (Gurrah) Schapiro and Abe (Longy) Zwillman, the last one of Newark.

Torrio and his six associates are said to wield considerable political influence through connections with district and ward leaders in Manhattan, Brooklyn and Newark. Detectives were "unable" to find any leading racketeers for questioning in the Schultz and Amberg murders yesterday, although Police Commissioner Lewis J. Valentine caused orders to be issued for a round-up of all known gangsters and racketeers who might be able to throw light on the killings. Similar orders were issued in Newark Thursday night, but produced no results.

Although the Newark police said they saw no significance in any of the rambling statements by Schultz, which a police stenographer took down in the Newark City Hospital on Thursday afternoon shortly before the gangster died, Federal agents here who have investigated Schultz and other racketeers saw two possible links to the new combination of racket leaders.

Luciana Known as "Boss."

The Federal agents pointed out that Luciana, as New York head of the Unione Siciliano, a secret organization of Italians, was known in the underworld by the title of "the boss," in connection with Schultz's dying statement that the man who shot him was "the boss himself." They also indicated that the "John" referred to by Schultz might have been Torrio.

If the police theory of the Schultz-Amberg killings is correct, some one connected with the new combination engaged professional gunmen, probably hired assassins from some other city, to come here and to Newark to put these leaders out of the way and break up their gangs in order to prevent any interference with the plans of "the Big Six" for a monopoly of the profitable new usury racket, and the policy, racing handbook, labor trouble and other rackets of the metropolitan area.

There was no doubt that the once powerful Schultz gang was broken up beyond any effort of his henchmen to repair it. The death of Bernard Rosenkrantz, Schultz's chauffeur and chief bodyguard, in the Newark City Hospital yesterday, was the fourth fatality as the result of the shooting of Schultz and his three companions in the back room of a Newark tavern on Wednesday night.

Besides the three henchmen killed with Schultz, who were among his closest associates, another, Martin Krompier, who was shot the same night in a barber shop at Broadway and Forty-seventh Street, this city, was reported to be dying in the Polyclinic Hospital last night. Krompier was Schultz's first lieutenant since the disappearance several weeks ago of Abe (Bo) Weinberg, and with Schultz, Weinberg, Krompier and the bodyguards gone, only underlings are left in the gang.

.61

The police received information yesterday that Weinberg had deserted Schultz and gone over to the new combination shortly before he disappeared. Whether he went into hiding to escape Schultz's wrath, or whether Schultz took vengence on him, is not known. There have been reports that he was killed, and his body, encased in a barrel of cement, thrown into the Hudson River. At first it was believed that enemies of the Schultz gang had done away with him, but yesterday's information threw a new light on his disappearance.

According to the new information, Weinberg seized the opportunity presented by Schultz's flight from New York more than a year ago, in an effort to escape Federal income tax prosecution, to put himself at the head of the Schultz gang. When Schultz was acquitted at his income tax trial in Malone, N. Y., it was said he demanded an accounting of Weinberg for his stewardship of the Schultz interests. At this point, it was said, Weinberg made his alliance with the new underworld powers, and joined them in warning Schultz that it would not be "healthy" for him to try to stage a come-back in the New York racket field.

Schultz's Wife Held.

Mrs. Frances Flegenheimer, a 21-year-old former chorus girl, wife of the murdered gang leader, knows more about the shooting of her husband and his aides than she has told, according to Deputy Police Chief John Haller, in charge of Newark detectives. Because she lied to Haller about her movements the night of the murder, Mrs. Flegenheimer was held in $10,000 bail as a material witness in the First Criminal Court in Newark yesterday.

Haller told reporters that when he first questioned Mrs. Flegenheimer she denied that she had visited the Palace Chop House and Tavern, 12 East Park Street, where Schultz was shot, at any time on Wednesday night, the night of the shooting. It was only after she had been confronted with an employe of the tavern, who identified her as the young woman who called on Schultz

about two hours before he was shot, that she admitted she had been there that night.

Mrs. Flegenheimer then said that she called at the tavern to see her husband about 8:30 o'clock on Wednesday night, on her return from a three-day trip to New York. She added that when she reached the tavern the door of the back room was closed, with a man in a "pea-green suit" guarding it.

New Figure Introduced.

This introduced a new figure into the case, as none of Schultz's bodyguards at the time of the shooting was dressed in a pea-green suit. Mrs. Flegenheimer insisted that she did not know the man's name and that she had never seen him before. Employes of the tavern said they did not know him and did not know when he left the tavern, or whether he was present at the time of the shooting. The police were ordered to look for him, but had no more success in finding him than they had in finding racketeers in Newark.

Mrs. Flegenheimer said that she spent half an hour in the back room with Schultz and one of his bodyguards, with the door closed. Although she said she did not know the bodyguard's name, she identified Rosenkrantz as the man from his picture.

Mrs. Flegenheimer denied that she had taken any of the papers and records to her husband that were found on the table in the back room after the shooting. She said that she stayed about half an hour and went to the Terminal moving picture theatre about 9 o'clock.

Leaving the theatre about 11 o'clock, she said, she walked past the tavern on her way to the tube station for New York and saw a crowd gathered out in front. She insisted that she did not have any idea that anything might have happened to her husband, but thought that the crowd indicated that there had been a "saloon raid."

Consequently, she explained, she walked right on without stopping or asking any questions. She did not stop at the apartment she had occupied with her husband at the Robert Treat Hotel in Newark, but took a tube train for New York.

Saw Shooting in Paper.

She said that she learned about the shooting for the first time when

she bought a newspaper after arriving in New York, about midnight. Even then she did not think it necessary to return to Newark or to telephone to the hospital or to any of her husband's friends in Newark, she told Haller. She said she went straight to her home at 37-45 Eighty-eighth Street, Jackson Heights, Queens, and went to bed without making any inquiries about her husband's condition.

On Thursday morning, after a night's sleep, she said, she telephoned to Schultz's mother, Mrs. Emma Flegenheimer, in the Bronx. This was the first time she had ever spoken to her husband's mother, she added. Later she met her mother-in-law and Schultz's sister, Mrs. Henry Ursprung, and went to the hospital in Newark with them.

Schultz's mother told the police that she did not know until after the shooting that her son was married. His wife admitted that no civil or religious ceremony had ever been performed, but said that they had been married under a "legal contract." She added that she was the mother of two children by Schultz—a 3-year-old girl and a 3-month-old boy. Both were in the custody of her mother, whose whereabouts she did not know, the wife said.

In Schultz's three-room suite at the Robert Treat Hotel, besides a .45-calibre pistol, were found a packet of affectionate letters addressed to "Poppy" and signed "Mommy." With these letters were a picture of a woman with two children and a picture of a child. Schultz's wife said that the letters were not written by her and that the pictures did not portray her or her children.

She told the police that she had stayed with Schultz at the Robert Treat during his "exile" in Newark until last Monday, when she came back to New York. She refused to tell where she stayed, what she did or whom she saw in this city between then and her return to Newark the night of the shooting.

Police Critical of Statements.

"Her answers generally are far from satisfactory and her movements before the shooting need to be checked," said Haller in explaining the demand that she be held in heavy bail. "We will want

to question her in Newark again, and do not want to let her free, except under heavy bail, lest she refuse to return to the jurisdiction."

When arraigned, Mrs. Flegenheimer, a short, slender woman in black velvet dress, wearing heavy glasses, seemed morose and worried. She displayed flashes of temper mixed with evidences of hysteria.

Refuses Lower Bail.

Her attorney, Hyman Halpern, of the Newark law office of Harry H. Weinberger, one of the numerous lawyers who appeared for Schultz in the Federal court in New York in his effort to fight removal to New York for trial on an income tax case, protested against heavy bail. He argued that the woman had come to Newark of her own free will, had answered questions voluntarily, and knew nothing of the shooting. Acting Judge Thomas Guthrie rejected the plea and set bail in the amount asked for by the prosecution.

Judge Guthrie held three employes of the tavern as material witnesses in $1,000 each. These were a bartender, a waiter and a Chinese cook. The bartender is the only witness who saw one of the gunmen, and has given a description of him. Bail was supplied for the woman and the three men and they gained their freedom.

The same judge issued warrants charging murder against three men identified by the police only as "John Doe, Richard Roe and Joseph Roe." Although only two gunmen entered the tavern, the police believe that a third man remained outside as a lookout or at the wheel of the automobile in which the killers escaped.

Federal agents took the business records found in the tavern after the shooting to New York yesterday. The Newark police said these records, which Schultz had been studying shortly before he was shot, appeared to deal with transactions in the policy racket and other rackets involving hundreds of thousands of dollars, but that the government men had asked them to keep all details along this line a close secret until they have time to study the papers thoroughly with a view to leads they may give to other racketeers.

PORTRAIT OF A RACKETEER (STREAMLINED)

He Sits at His Desk, Pushes Buttons, Has a Fling at Culture, and Never Goes Out to the Firing Line

By MEYER BERGER

IN obscure corners of the town you can find a few old-time gangsters of the hob-nail and raw-knuckles period mumbling their scorn of current racketeer bosses who sit at mahogany desks and push electric buttons instead of getting out on the firing line with their hoodlums as orthodox leaders did twenty years ago.

It may be, though, that the old 'uns are just a little envious. There they sit, drooling in their beer unnoticed and forgotten, babbling stale gangster legends while the very lads who worked with them in eye-gouging and pate-thumping campaigns years ago are still in the game and riding high.

The current underworld leaders are, for the most part, men of 50 or thereabout, a rather aged group as racketeers go. Very few of the Volstead period opportunists got any distance past 40. Dutch Schultz, last of the breed, managed to linger on until he was 34, which amounted to cheating the undertaker.

Heading the present list of the city's boss racketeers are the magna cum laude men of the old East Side crime school—Jacob (Gurrah Jake) Shapiro, Louis (Lepke) Buchalter, Charles (Lucky) Luciano, John Torrio and Charles (Bugs) Siegel, dormitory mates of other Turkish bath key men such as the late Monk Eastman, Jack Zelig, and the Four Gunmen of the Becker-Rosenthal case.

It took the bright boys now in control of the racket syndicates a long time to reach the top, but from all indications they won a clear field after the late Arthur Flegenheimer passed from the scene in Newark, murmuring lines that sounded like the mad scene from King Lear.

With "The Dutchman" gone, there remained not a single major underworld princeling of the many that rose when the golden beer and booze flood inundated the city. Owney Madden and the Irish mob that ruled the Golconda midtown at the height of prosperity have silently folded their bullet-proof vests and have left the night clubs and wine-shops to the arrogant Luciano and his Latin retainers.

Waxey Gordon's far-flung beer and rum legions were scattered when the pudgy chief (a former pickpocket who won his letter on East Side battlegrounds with Lepke and Gurrah Jake) was sent to Lewisburg Penitentiary in

shackles a few years ago by Thomas E. Dewey, the little David of the New York Federal District.

The lesser figures of the rum and racket brotherhood of the prohibition dynasty—the slug-collecting Jack (Legs) Diamond, blustery Vannie Higgins, the homicidal maniac Vincent Coll and broad-mouthed Larry Fay—have all stumbled on to the gang chief's Valhalla, property nicked for identification at Charon's Slip.

* * *

THE new leaders are anxious to have the world think of them not as racketeers but as real business men. Mention anything in their presence about the dear old East Side crime school and they wince. They bitterly resent the term "gangster" and never refer to their strong-arm workers as a "gang." They use, instead, the ambiguous term "organization." It sounds more dignified.

Almost all of them maintain well-equipped business offices, with clerical forces hard at work all day. Some have ventured into the strange field of legal enterprise to cloak their lucrative racket interests. The muscle men who are used to intimidate racket victims or to perform the murders incidental to business are not allowed to clutter up the premises, because it wouldn't look nice.

And most of the racket bosses have social ambitions in one form or another. They leave their work for frequent sea voyages. On the most expensive liners in the world they don dinner jackets, discuss current literature and economic trends with more respectable tycoons and merchant princes from Big Bend, and have developed easy table manners. A few even know how to pick the proper wines for each dish.

The literary trend among gang leaders is something comparatively new. The late Dutch Schultz was the first to boast publicly about his reading; as a matter of fact, he sometimes became a bit boring on the subject. He would go into raptures over "The Forty Days of Musa Dagh," particularly the part

that deals with wholesale massacre. Just before his death he was deep in Schopenhauer's "Studies in Pessimism."

Ciro Terranova, the high lord of the Harlem rackets, loves a canter in the park or among the lovely hills of Westchester, because you meet such interesting people on the bridle path. Dutch Schultz liked a good horse, too. He rode in Fairfield, Conn. He inherited his fondness for horseflesh from his father, who ran a livery stable in the Bronx at one time.

* * *

THE East Side crime-school graduates, once devoted to pinochle and stuss, have taken up bridge as part of their program of social improvement, and discuss end-plays and squeezes with as much zest as they used to discuss a particularly neat skull fracture or eye displacement in the early rough-and-tumble gang fights before they acquired culture.

They play a lot of golf, too. The mighty Lepke, Gurrah Jake and Salvatore Spitale may be seen on fine mornings (when there is no police alarm out for them in connection with some fresh gang killing) heading for the greens in Westchester with their own caddies. They favor a certain well-known course in the vicinity of Bronxville.

They're fussy in their choice of caddies, because they require them to be handy with an automatic as well as to have a good eye for lost golf balls. Even the less polished Waxey Gordon liked his putters and irons. When he was on trial for income-tax evasion he whiled away the recess periods with modest accounts of how he once broke 180 out at Dyker Heights. It took his mind off the dull testimony about bootlegging and murders.

Every one of the reigning group of New York racketeers was born in poverty, but you'd never know it from the princely way they live today. When Winter comes they hie southward to the warm Florida coast, where a few own expensive

villas. Al Capone set that fashion, more or less, in order to have a hiding place far from the turmoil of Chicago when things got too hot.

Johnny Torrio and Lucky Luciano turned up in Miami a fortnight ago, just after the murder of Dutch Schultz and three of his followers in Newark, and expressed astonishment upon learning that the New York police were anxious to ask them a few questions about the shooting. They didn't bother to hurry back, though, what with social engagements and all that.

When they are in New York, Mr. Torrio and Mr. Luciano move about with a certain amount of freedom and recklessness that would have excited the envy of the prohibition period racketeers. The competition was so keen and so dangerous for men like Madden, Schultz and their contemporaries that they had to take most of their pleasure indoors. Any venture into the open was apt to be noisy and possibly fatal.

Things seem to have changed a bit now. Mr. Torrio openly participated in a victory celebration in a Democratic clubhouse after the recent primary election in which his man had won despite the bitter denunciation of the opposition charging that the Torrio representative was allied with a murderous group, seeking racket control of the city.

* * *

MR. LUCIANO is a popular figure on Broadway. He may be seen at night clubs owned by himself and a syndicate of wealthy Italians of Manhattan and Brooklyn or he may be found in one of the best seats at Madison Square Garden at important bouts with all his sporting friends around him. Sometimes, though, nostalgia overtakes him, and he goes slumming in the East Side Italian coffee shops in the vicinity of police headquarters, just to show his old friends that success has not made a snob of him.

Most gang leaders, since they have become big business men, are rather fussy about their apparel. They go to the best tailors in town, though they still favor one man who does an especially neat job at fitting armpit holsters into a dinner jacket or sack suit without causing an awkward bulge. The late Dutch Schultz was somewhat less fastidious, but he was an exception.

Dutch was a little tight anyway, and spent freely only when he thought the investment might warrant it. Before his trials in Syracuse and Malone, for example, he dazzled the local citizens by his free-handed spending.

That his spending was merely done for propaganda purposes was proved when the Schultz papers were scrutinized by the police in Newark after the recent shooting. There the account books showed that Schultz, far from being a free spender, kept an accurate account of every penny that went out, including "12 cents for newspapers," "25 cents for bondsman's carfare," "15 cents for cigarettes for bondsman." He is supposed to have passed $1,000 to a hospital attendant, though, just before he died. "Take this," he said, "before the cops get their hands on it."

BORN in cold flats on the East Side and accustomed to taking their night's ease on pool tables when the skull-fracturing and nose-busting wasn't paying dividends back in the early days of the East Side crime school, the present big-shot bosses are making up for it in the most luxurious penthouses in the city. Ciro Terranova had a terraced penthouse overlooking Central Park where he and his retinue often gamboled until daybreak.

Dutch Schultz had a Central Park apartment, too, and Salvatore Spitale, Lepke and Gurrah maintain royal quarters in the vicinity of the city's biggest green spot. Some people cannot understand how renting agents in aristocratic neighborhoods can lease their best apartments to gangster and racketeer bosses. There is the question of proper references for example.

It's fairly simple, though, when you get the set-up. The bankers who handle the racket bosses' accounts, conservative as any other bankers, don't mind giving their names for reference, and a banker's word still carries a lot of weight in the town. In addition, the racketeer boss can always persuade some garment manufacturer to sign as reference, too, just as a business courtesy, and usually a banker and a manufacturer are sufficient.

MOST people still fall into the common error of thinking of gangsters and racketeers as loafers with turtle-neck sweaters, cauliflower ears and protruding maxilla who beat their women and punt their offspring around the flat. That type passed out of existence during the liquor gold rush of 1917.

Your modern racket boss, when he isn't in Miami to avoid embarrassing questioning by loutish policemen after a new murder or series of murders, or when he isn't entertaining a few girls from Minsky's or the Follies, is very apt to be a home man. If he does kick mamma around once in a while, for old time's sake, he does it in the privacy of his own home.

You're more likely to find, though, that he is sending Cousin Hymie through dental college or through the College of Physicians and Surgeons and paying all his expenses; that he sends a check every month to the old folks in Galicia or Stropkof; that he has found some place in his more legitimate enterprises for all near and distant relatives and that he can always be counted on for a handsome gift or sizable check when birthdays or weddings occur in the family.

Your new streamlined boss racketeer—most of them are a bit roundish with good living, and not at all the lean, cadaverous types of the average movie—usually hungers for a bit of art, too. In place of the grocer's calendar with the pink cow and red and orange sun-set that used to grace the walls of his boyhood home he surrounds himself with good paintings. He is satisfied, as a rule, with anything that has some life in it and doesn't collect old masters.

The Italian racketeer chief, when there are no decent fights on, enjoys a night at the opera. On the other hand, he has never quite overcome his weakness for gaudy funerals, riotous weddings with torrents of wine and good, bang-up christenings. He has abandoned the brass band for gang burials, but not without reluctance, and still sighs for the sort of thing that was staged when Joe (The Boss) Masseria was borne to the grave to the tune of sad dirges, with a picture of the late lamented in a six-foot floral horseshoe, borne by proud mourners.

ALL in all, the modern racket boss has come a long way from the orthodox, primitive gangster types of the Nineteen Hundreds. What the old-time slugger and shillelah wielder would think of a gang chief who hires underlings to do his fighting would be worth while listening to, even if it wouldn't be fit to print.

Even the few inactive survivors of the same graduating class that produced Lepke, Gurrah Jake and Bugs Siegel—such men as Johnny Sirocco, who has retired to a Coney Island side-street as keeper of an honest if somewhat sad tap room, and Humpty Jackson, last heard of as a pet shop owner in Harlem—merely shake their shaggy old heads at the way things have changed. But they prefer to withhold comment.

The Old-Time Gangster—His Office Was the Street Corner.

He Pushes Buttons at His Desk, Has a Fling at Culture and Never Sees the Firing Line

"The Racketeer Boss Sits at a Mahogany Desk and Pushes Electric Buttons, and Usually He Has Social Ambitions in One Form or Another."

LUCANIA IS CALLED SHALLOW PARASITE

Probation Report Says Only Asset as Leader Is Calmness Under Pressure.

HIS OUTLOOK IS CHILDISH

Boasts He Was Never a 'Crumb,' or Saver, and Craves Clothes, Pleasure and Money.

Charles (Lucky Luciano) Lucania possesses average intelligence but is "a shallow and parasitic individual who is considerably wrapped up in his own feelings," according to an eight-page report made yesterday by Chief Probation Officer Irving W. Halpern of the Court of General Sessions.

"His social outlook is essentially childish, in that it is dominated by recklessness and a craving for action," the report said. "His only asset as a leader consists of his apparent calmness at times of stress. This characteristic, which appears to have been based on his feeling that he could escape involvement, has passed for reserve and strength.

"As a consequence he is accorded a degree of underworld respect. He manifests a peasant-like faith in chance and has developed an attitude of nonchalance. His behavior patterns are essentially instinctive and primitive, his manner easy, copious and ingratiating.

Scorns the Average Citizen

"His freedom from conscience springs from his admitted philosophy: 'I never was a crumb, and if I have to be a crumb I'd rather be dead.' "

The report explained that Lucania defined a "crumb" as a man "who works and saves and lays his money aside" and it pointed out that this definition would fit the average citizen.

"His ideals of life resolved themselves into money to spend, beautiful women to enjoy, silk underclothes and places to go in style," the report asserted.

It contradicted Lucania's testimony that he was born in this city, asserting that he was really named Salvatore Lucania and was brought here from Italy at the age of 9. He was a chronic truant from school, the report said.

"During this phase of his life the defendant was reared in an impoverished environment on the lower East Side, and at an early age he was beyond the control of his parents," the report said. "His behavior patterns and social attitude during this formative period were largely conditioned by the influence of unwholesome associates, with the result that by the time he was 18 years old, he acquired a definitely criminalistic pattern of conduct."

The report pointed out that Lucania has been arrested twenty-five times, that he is reputedly "the head of the Unione Siciliana, an organization of Italian gangsters, and a dominant figure in the sale of narcotics, policy slips, stolen goods, gambling houses, and the intimidation of business men and unions."

"He is also suspected of having a hand in the slaying of Arthur Flegenheimer (Dutch Schultz)," the report said. It declared that the indications were that Lucania was not a citizen of this country in spite of his claim that he was born here.

Pennochio a Dullard

The report described Thomas Pennochio as "an unresponsive, uncooperative individual of rather dull mentality, the product of a broken home." David Betillo was described as never having had a record of legitimate employment and as a former affiliate of Al Capone in Chicago.

James Frederico was "reared in an unwholesome district," the report asserted, and is "a low and despicable character who of late has had no compunctions about living on the earnings of prostitutes."

Abe Wahrman had an excellent school record, the report went on, but he "became rebellious and ungovernable when his parents insisted that he further his education. Twice in Children's Court as an incorrigible child, since getting out of reform school he has been without legitimate employment and in general has been leading a dissolute and anti-social life."

Record Is Made Public

Lucania's record up to the time he was indicted on sixty-two counts of compulsory prostitution last April 2 was made public after the sentences were imposed by Irving W. Halpern, chief of the General Sessions Probation Bureau. It shows that the convicted man had the police aliases Charles Luciano, "Lucky" Luciano, Charles Lane, Charles Reid and Charles Ross.

The record follows:

New York

June 26, 1916—Violation Section 246, narcotic violation; Special Sessions, penitentiary; paroled Dec. 30, 1916.

Jersey City

Dec. 22, 1921—Criminally carrying a weapon; Criminal Court, discharged.

New York

Aug. 28, 1922—Violation corporation ordinance (business code violation); Magistrate's Court, fined $5.

Aug. 5, 1924—Violation corporation ordinance; Magistrate's court, fined $3.

Dec. 9, 1924—Violation corporation ordinance; Magistrate's Court, fined $2.

June 4, 1925—Violation corporation ordinance; Magistrate's Court, fined $2.

Feb. 7, 1926—Violation corporation ordinance; Magistrate's Court, fined $2.

March 1, 1926—Violation Harrison Act; United States District Court, discharged.

July 20, 1926—Driving without license; Magistrate's Court, sentence suspended.

July 27, 1926—Violation Section 1897, Penal Law; Magistrate's Court, discharged.

Oct. 14, 1926—Violation corporation ordinance; Magistrate's Court, fined $2.

Dec. 16, 1926—Violation corporation ordinance; Magistrate's Court, fined $5.

Dec. 29, 1926—Felonious assault; Magistrate's Court, discharged.

July 6, 1927—Disorderly conduct (gambling); Magistrate's Court, discharged.

July 28, 1927—Material witness, Supreme Court; discharged.

Aug. 3, 1927—Violation National Prohibition Act; United States District Court, discharged.

Nov. 23, 1928—Robbery and assault; Magistrate's Court, discharged.

Oct. 29, 1929—Grand larceny; Magistrate's Court, discharged.

Miami, Fla.

March 7, 1930—Operating gambling device; Criminal Court, fined $1,000.

New York

Feb. 4, 1931—Assault first degree, two indictments; General Sessions, Judge Mulqueen, indictments dismissed.

Cleveland

July 4, 1931—Investigation; police court, released.

Chicago

April 21, 1932—Disorderly conduct; Municipal Court, discharged.

New York

July 11, 1932—Violation corporation ordinance; Magistrate's Court, fined $5.

Miami

Dec. 28, 1935—Criminal registration; Miami police, registered.

New York

April 2, 1936—Violation Section 2,460, Penal Law, four indictments; Supreme Court, extraordinary term, pending.

LUCANIA SENTENCED TO 30 TO 50 YEARS; COURT WARNS RING

Retaliation Against Witnesses Will Result in Maximum Terms, McCook Says.

Sternly warning them that any attempt at retaliation against any of the State's witnesses would result in their being forced to serve their maximum sentences, Supreme Court Justice Philip J. McCook imposed long terms in State prison yesterday on the principal figures in the city's $12,000,000 a year vice ring. The courtroom was heavily guarded by detectives and uniformed policemen as he spoke.

Charles (Lucky Luciano) Lucania, overlord of the ring and the man who, according to the police, ordered the murder of Arthur (Dutch Schultz) Flegenheimer last Fall in order to take over his manifold rackets, received the most severe sentence of all. He maintained his gambler's stolidity as Justice McCook imposed sentence of from thirty to fifty years' imprisonment.

Aides Get Heavy Sentences

David Betillo, his chief lieutenant, was sentenced to from twenty-five to forty years, while Thomas Pennochio, treasurer of the ring, and James Frederico, its field manager, received flat sentences of twenty-five years as third offenders, after each had admitted two previous felony convictions.

Abe Wahrman, strong-arm man for the syndicate, was sentenced to from fifteen to thirty years, while Ralph Liguori, whose function was to hold up disorderly houses whose proprietors had refused to enter the combination, received the relatively light sentence of from seven and a half to fifteen years because of his youth, Justice McCook explained.

The sentencing of three other members of the ring, Jesse Jacobs, chief of the division for bailing out arrested prostitutes; Meyer Berkman, his assistant, and Benny Spiller, loan shark for operators of disorderly houses, was postponed until July 1 at the request of Thomas E. Dewey, special rackets' prosecutor. It was understood that Mr. Dewey hoped to get further information from this trio that would aid him in his investigations, already under way, into various industrial and other rackets.

Bookers Get Lighter Terms

Four bookers of women into disorderly houses, who had pleaded guilty, received lesser sentences than the principals. Jack Ellensteir, who originally went on trial with Lucania and his co-defendants, but pleaded guilty after the prosecution had rested, was sentenced to from four to eight years. Balitzer and Al Weiner, who turned State's evidence, received from two to four years, while David Marcus, who likewise testified for the prosecution but was caught in a lie on the stand, was sentenced to from three to six years.

Luciano and six of his co-defendants arrived at the prison gates in taxicabs, after having made the train trip to Ossining in the custody of ten deputy sheriffs, five New York policemen and three New York Central Railroad officers. They were put into solitary confinement at once.

Prison officials explained they believed the trial had bred animosity among the convicted gang and that serious fights might occur if they were allowed access to one another. The seven will be kept in solitary confinement until the authorities feel it is safe to allow them to mingle with other prisoners. The men will get their meals in their cells and will have very limited periods of exercise.

Luciano surrendered $199.40 at the prison office. When asked the routine question as to what prompted his crime, he replied he was innocent of the charge on which he had been sentenced. The other six also maintained innocence. Pennochio had $15 with him, Ellenstein, $3; Liguori, $4.69; Begillo, $2; Frederico, 95 cents, and Wahrman, $32.18.

In recognition of the underworld importance of Lucania the police took extraordinary precautions before and during the arraignments. Deputy Chief Inspector Edward A. Bracken and Inspector Louis Costuma had five sergeants, forty patrolmen and six mounted men outside the building, where they kept all passers-by moving.

Within the court room and in the corridors outside Detective Captain Bernard Dowd had a score of detectives and an extra detail of court attendants was also on hand. Only reporters and other persons having business in the court room were permitted inside, but about a dozen relatives of the men being sentenced gathered in the rotunda in the court house. Betillo's wife, Pennochio's wife and brother, Jacob's wife and mother and Liguori's mother and sister were among them, all showing obvious signs of strain.

Before the sentences were pronounced counsel for the various defendants made numerous motions for a new trial, all of which Justice McCook denied. Lorenzo P. Carlino, counsel for Liguori, said that he had received information that Jurors Stephen Gerard Smith and Norbert G. Gagnon had received communications during the trial, which had resulted in police guards being placed over their homes and business places.

This state of affairs became known to the other jurors, he said, with the result that the jury was influenced in its deliberations. He asked for a postponement of sentence until testimony could be taken and used as the basis for a motion for a new trial. Justice McCook refused his motion, whereupon Mr. Carlino asked him to state for the record that he had ordered a police guard over the homes of the jurors. "The court has nothing to say about that," Justice McCook replied.

George Morton Levy, counsel for Lucania, moved unsuccessfully for a new trial on the ground that the verdict was against the weight of the evidence. He also attacked without success the constitutionality of the statute permitting the joinder of a series of crimes in one indictment. This was enacted at the request of Mr. Dewey last Spring and was used for the first time at this trial.

Lucania Is Outwardly Calm

Lucania, almost surrounded by detectives and court attaches, was called to the bar at 10:50 A. M. He was neatly dressed in a bluish-gray suit, white soft shirt and black tie. His features, always sullen, looked slightly more haggard than before his conviction, but he was outwardly calm.

When the clerk asked him whether he had anything to say before sentence was imposed he leaned over and held a whispered consultation with his lawyer. Then he straightened up and in a clear, low voice said:

"Your Honor, I have nothing to say outside the fact that I want to say again I am innocent."

Before sentencing him, Justice McCook at this point addressed his warning to all the defendants that any attempt at vengeance on the witnesses who had testified against them would be held against them. He said:

"The evidence upon the trial and reliable information since received have convinced the court that these defendants will be responsible for any injury which the people's witnesses might hereafter, by reason of their testimony, suffer. Let the record show that should any witness for the people be injured or harassed, the court will request the parole authorities to retain in prison the defendants against whom such witness testified, for the maximum terms of the sentences now about to be imposed."

Court Denounces Prisoner

Justice McCook then turned directly to Lucania, who was standing with his weight on one foot and one shoulder drooped.

"An intelligent, courageous and discriminating jury has found you guilty of heading a conspiracy or combination to commit these crimes, which operated widely in New York and extended into neighboring counties," he said. "This makes you responsible, in law and morals, for every foul and cruel deed, with accompanying elements of extortion, performed by the band of codefendants whose records and characters will shortly be discussed.

"I am not here to reproach you, but since there appears no excuse for your conduct or hope for your rehabilitation, to extend adequate punishment."

Justice McCook explained that for purposes of sentence he had divided the sixty-two counts on which Lucania was convicted into three groups. The sentences on the counts in each group would run concurrently, he explained, but the three groups of sentences were to run consecutively. Then he read off the long list of counts in each group and he added:

"These sentences make a total of from thirty to fifty years in State's prison."

Term May Mean Life Sentence

As Lucania is now 38 years old, the sentence, even with time off for good behavior, is virtually equivalent to life imprisonment. His droopy eyelids quivered slightly but he regained control of himself almost immediately and he followed his guards out of the court room with a springy tread.

Thomas Pennochio, alias Tommy the Bull, a short, stout man dressed in blue and wearing a red necktie, was next. He admitted that he had been convicted of grand larceny in 1909 and of attempted burglary in 1914. Justice McCook excoriated him as "a seller of drugs, a thief and an habitual criminal" before imposing sentence of twenty-five years.

Betillo, a short man in a light green suit, was described by Justice McCook as Lucania's "chief and most ruthless aid" and as "an unprincipled and aggressive egotist." He pointed out that the probation report on Betillo left four years unaccounted for, corresponding roughly with the time he spent in Chicago, where, Mr. Dewey has charged, Betillo was one of Al Capone's lieutenants.

"This, in addition to other matters, makes it unimportant as to whether you have any previous convictions," Justice McCook said as he imposed sentences totaling from twenty-five to forty years. Betillo took it with a twisted smile on his lips.

His Youth Fails to Save Him

Frederico, a stocky, dark man, chewed gum slowly as Justice McCook observed that he was "the outside agent for the executives" of the ring, and that he was "an incorrigible criminal, and a low and brutal character." Like Pennochio, he admitted he was a third offender and accordingly received a flat sentence of twenty-five years.

Abe Wahrman, a slight, youthful-looking individual who was also chewing gum, was the only one of the principals whose counsel asked for leniency. David P. Siegel told the court that his client was only 22 years old, had no previous convictions against him, and had helped support his family. He asked the court "to put aside all the exhibitionalism which has attended this case from the outset."

After Mr. Dewey had intervened to say that the probation report showed Wahrman had been a criminal since he was 15 years old, Justice McCook observed that his youthful appearance and lack of a record were deceptive. He imposed sentence of from fifteen to thirty years.

Liguori, a pale, short young man, was lashed by Justice McCook as "a silly imitator of the racketeers you admire." It was his rôle, the court went on, to "supply the routine violence required by a ring directed by better brains than yours." Because of these considerations and his youth, he was sentenced to seven and a half to fifteen years.

Some Human Qualities Admitted

The bookers, who had been carefully segregated from the other defendants because of the bitter hatred between the two groups since Weiner, Marcus and Balitzer turned State's evidence, were brought before the court next. Justice McCook said that their place of imprisonment had not yet been decided upon, and consequently they would be taken to the West Side jail until it was.

Ellenstein was described by Justice McCook as a former real estate man whose "flabbiness of body and soul" led him to take over the business of Nick Montana. However, Justice McCook said, he did not seem to be "essentially vicious" and there was some hope that he might reform; consequently he was sentenced to from four to eight years.

In sentencing Peter Balitzer, alias Pete Harris, Justice McCook made some observations on criminals of his particular type.

"The psychology of the booker is peculiar," the justice said. "He lacks what is ordinarily called a moral sense, but he seems to make some distinctions of his own. He does not regard it as essentially wrong to give employment to girls at what he and they call their work."

Justice McCook said that the State's witnesses had agreed that Balitzer was "not entirely devoid of human feeling" and consequently he would be let off with a sentence of from two to four years. He imposed a similar sentence on Weiner, explaining that he was showing "some regard for your dullness."

Marcus testified falsely at the trial that he had never been arrested in Pittsburgh, and the defense promptly disproved this statement. Justice McCook said that while this was not pertinent to the main issue, nevertheless it would affect his sentence, which was from three to six years.

Mr. Levy tried hard to get the court to permit a thirty-day stay of Lucania's sentence to permit the winding up of his affairs here, but Mr. Dewey said that the police had made elaborate arrangements to take him to Sing Sing and that it would be expensive to duplicate them later. Justice McCook denied the motion and left the court.

Mr. Levy told reporters that an appeal would be made and that he believed there were sufficient errors in the record of the trial to result in a reversal.

Heavily guarded, the six principals in the ring were taken to the Tombs prison for three hours while the commitment papers were made out, a clerical task involving considerable work. At 3:57 P. M. they were taken from the Tombs by a force of nine deputy sheriffs and ten detectives, who accompanied them all the way to Sing Sing.

A crowd estimated at more than 1,500 persons had gathered on the Forty-fifth Street side of the Grand Central Terminal, at Vanderbilt Avenue, when the prison van containing the men arrived at 4:10 P. M., with motor cycle policemen preceding it and on either side, and four cars full of detectives and special guards behind.

June 19, 1936

CITY'S RACKET TRIBUTE IS REDUCED BY DEWEY

Special Prosecutor's Dramatic War on Crime Saves Millions for Citizens, But It Is an Endless Task

By RUSSELL OWEN

When Louis Beitcher, the No. 2 man in the restaurant racket, chose to plead guilty last Monday as he went on trial with others before Supreme Court Justice McCook, a slight fuss was made about it by attorneys for the defense. They objected because Thomas E. Dewey, special prosecutor, let Beitcher make his plea before a panel of jurors waiting examination. But Beitcher had decided that he was better off by taking his medicine than by fighting, and it was not the first time that one of Mr. Dewey's witnesses had decided discretion was the better part of valor.

The scrappy young man with the black mustache who has been putting away racketeers regularly since he was appointed to the job by Governor Lehman in July, 1935, has a way of making an airtight case before he starts trial, and he usually knows what his witnesses are going to say and do. His record of convictions is almost 100 per cent perfect. He makes his raids, gets his evidence, sits tight and says nothing, and then finds ways of making people get on the stand and tell a good part of the truth. So it was not so surprising when Beitcher decided to plead guilty; it was merely another of the dramatic incidents in Mr. Dewey's career since he started on an endless task.

Swift and Relentless

When he was prosecuting Charles (Lucky Luciano) Lucania, and spoiling his nickname by convicting him, he began with obtaining pleas of guilty from three defendants. And then Jack Ellenstein, who had listened for three weeks to the testimony of prostitutes who said he had been their booking agent, gave up and pleaded guilty. Ellenstein disappeared from the scene until he came up for sentence, and Lucania and all the other defendants were found guilty. It apparently has a depressing effect on some of Mr. Dewey's prisoners when they actually find themselves in a court room; they had always wriggled out before.

There has been no lack of the dramatic in the cases Mr. Dewey has prosecuted. He works swiftly and relentlessly. So far he has successfully attacked the policy, vice and fur rackets, and he is now in court in an effort to break the restaurant racket. The bakers' racket is ready for action, and he has begun on the $10,000,000 electrical job racket and the $3,000,000 brick racket.

The total is beginning to run up into a record which is a worthy commentary on the efforts of one and a half years on the part of Dewey and his tight-mouthed assistants and detectives. It has cost nearly $300,000 a year, but the results may in the end save New York perhaps $100,000,000, paid out by business concerns and victims of policy and vice to the big shots who obtain revenue by terrorism. Mr. Dewey's appropriation for 1935, which was only a half year, was $122,000; for 1936, $280,000, and for 1937, $293,000.

The present case which Mr. Dewey is trying concerns a racket which has taken $2,000,000 a year from restaurants and cafés. Jack Dempsey, who is manager of a café opposite Madison Square Garden, is one of his witnesses. The case centers around the Metropolitan Restaurant and Cafeteria Association, which is named in the indictment, together with fourteen men, including two practicing lawyers. They are accused of having organized under the direction of the late Arthur (Dutch Schultz) Flegenheimer, a racket that put them in control of two unions and a so-called protective association. Many of the picketers of restaurants who have been seen around the city are agents of this association. Murder, as well as embezzlement, are charged to the account of the racketeers.

But the ramifications of Mr. Dewey's investigations, carried out

AT THE START OF A NEW COURT DRAMA

Associated Press.

Thomas E. Dewey (left), now pressing trial of the restaurant racket case. An aide, Milton Schilback, is with him.

from his office in the Woolworth Building, reach far beyond the present case. This particular trial is significant only because it shows again the careful methods which must be adopted in any racket prosecution, and the guilty plea of a defendant is but one of the many dramatic incidents which have marked his movements since he began his work in the Summer of 1935.

The methods have always been based upon secrecy, no talking for publication before action, and then a pounce on all the principals and their chief assistants involved in any racket. Mr. Dewey's first big policy raid was a round-up which resulted in many convictions, and it was followed about a year later by another raid, which only a week ago added eighteen more heads of policy rackets to the score chalked up against them. Mr. Dewey has learned that rackets spring up again when the pressure is removed.

It was this observance of the constant vigilance required to keep down the rackets in New York which led to the formation of a committee of "Civic Vigilantes" under the leadership of Harry F. Guggenheim. When one of the several special grand juries investigating this form of crime was dismissed last August it handed up a presentment to Justice McCook urging a city wide group to investigate criminal courts and the activities of prosecuting officers.

The presentment embodied some of the pet ideas of Mr. Dewey, who in a rare speech or two has criticized the operations of criminal law in conditions which make old-fashioned shibboleths of protection outlawed and dangerous. It is a symptom of the way in which various civic officials have been cooperating under the stimulus of the Dewey prosecutions that the day after the presentment was made Mayor La Guardia named Mr. Guggenheim as chairman of the "Vigilantes," and that a few months later it was made known at the City Hall that a "G-Man" bureau, headed by a veteran prosecutor, would be set up to wage an unceasing war on racketeers.

The difficulties which Mr. Dewey has faced have been so constant that he has been in the position of a general staff waging unremitting war on many fronts. First he had to get his evidence, and when he found witnesses willing to talk he had to protect them, generally by locking them up. Much of the money used for these racket prosecutions has gone into the support and protection of hundreds of witnesses. Dewey promised to protect those who helped him, and he apparently has. Reluctant witnesses have been sent to jail for contempt. When one avenue of approach was blocked, another was sought.

When Lucania was arrested in Arkansas and used every possible technicality to evade extradition, a Federal statute was called into play to return him to New York.

Even then Rangers had to be employed to force a Sheriff to obey a court order. Unusually high bail has been set in order to keep prisoners within jurisdiction. For Lucania, $500,000 was asked and obtained.

The present trial is but one of many yet to come, for apparently the prosecutions will continue through the present year. Mr. Dewey at first estimated that he would not show results for his labors until after nine months had passed. He has been at work now for more than a year and a half and there is no end in sight. How long he can afford to continue in his present investigations is problematical, for he is working for much less than he could earn in private practice, and his assistants get less than an able Assistant District Attorney. But he has proved by his own retracking, supported by the appointment of the "Vigilantes," that the war on rackets must go on for years.

LEPKE A GANG LEADER WHO LIKED HIS PRIVACY

Today's Most-Hunted Public Enemy Chose to Walk Quietly and Wield His Power From Behind the Scenes

By FOSTER HAILEY

Gang lords, like dictators, bank presidents, industrial tycoons and leaders of business and the professions, follow no particular pattern in their rise to eminence. Some talk loudly and carry only a small stick. Some vice versa. Take the case of Louis (Lepke) Buchalter, the object of one of the most intensive international police hunts ever made.

During the lush Twenties and early Thirties, before the voters carried their consciousness of crime as far as the ballot boxes, much was heard of the Dutch Schultzes, Vincent Colls, Jack Diamonds, Al Capones and many much smaller fry of the underworld. But little was heard of "Lepke" Buchalter. In THE NEW YORK TIMES "morgue" the first clipping that mentions his name is dated Oct. 26, 1927, and the whole Lepke file is one of which, because of its brevity, many chorus girls would be ashamed.

Yet, it is now known that from the Nineteen Twenties on Lepke was an important figure in the criminal half-world of New York City and from 1927 to 1936 probably the most influential racketeer in the city. District Attorney Thomas E. Dewey and J. Edgar Hoover, chief of the Federal Bureau of Investigation, in commenting recently on his activities have called him one of the most dangerous criminals in the country. Lepke walked quietly through the underworld and talked softly, but he carried a very large stick indeed.

A $30,000 Fugitive

No other man ever ruled the rackets for so long a time as he. A fugitive for more than two years, with a price of $30,000 on his head, dead or alive, he has been able to command enough money and underworld facilities to outwit the combined activities of the crack detectives of New York's police force and the widespread network of the FBI.

Never a lavish spender on personal luxuries during the "fat" years when he and his big, tough, slow-witted Russian-born partner, Jacob (Gurrah) Shapiro, were taking an estimated $5,000,000 a year out of several of New York City's major industries, he is believed to have put considerable ready cash safely away for future use. But the protection he has received has been more than money alone could buy. Gang leaders in cities outside New York, authorities know, must have aided him, either as a payoff on old obligations or because they still fear the one-time overlord of the big town's industrial rackets.

There has been a reign of terror, too, among his former associates and former victims in the city. The hands which held the guns have been those of hirelings, but the motives, Mr. Dewey said in asking for a raise in the city award from $5,000 to $25,000, are those of Lepke. The District Attorney described it as a "war of extermination."

Born in New York

Lepke was born Louis Buchalter on Feb. 12, 1897, in New York City. His father was a hard-working immigrant who wanted his children to grow up to be good Americans. With possibly one exception the other ten did. Most of them still live in New York, respectable and respected.

The elder Buchalter died in 1911 when Louis was 14 years old. The mother, who is still alive and now spends most of the year with one or another of her children in New York, moved to the West.

Louis was supposed to stay with a sister and finish his schooling but, with his mother gone, he was soon on the streets and on his own resources. Roaming the East Side as a minor terrorist of push-cart peddlers, occasionally stealing packages from the delivery trucks which jam the garment district, he met Shapiro, two years his senior. They became intimates and formed a criminal partnership that was to continue more than twenty years.

Monk Eastman, Kid Dropper and Jacob (Little Augie) Orgen were just becoming prominent then on the East Side and the two young hoodlums became hangers-on of their gangs.

The First Arrest

Lepke was arrested for the first time in 1915, but it was an out-of-town foray which brought his first conviction, a luggage-stealing trip to Bridgeport, Conn., in 1916. Released from Cheshire Reformatory after serving two months of an indeterminate sentence he promptly jumped parole and returned to New York. He was just 19. A lot of kids his age were fighting in France, or getting ready to. Lepke had other ideas.

Like Diamond and so many other gang leaders, he became a loft burglar. The wholesale district was full of furs, costly dresses and other merchandise on which a quick profit could be turned if one didn't bother to buy it. Occasionally an old watchman had to be beaten up or killed, but that was all in the night's work.

Convicted Twice in Three Years

Lepke was only a pimply-faced, hard-eyed kid then, however, without political connections or the money for bondsmen or get-away cars. He was twice arrested and convicted in a span of three years, each time pleading guilty to the charge. The first conviction was in January, 1918, under the name of Louis Buckalter; sentence a year and a half. The second was in January, 1920; sentence two and a half years. This time he gave the name of Louis Cohen. The same judge heard both cases.

When he got out of jail in March, 1922, he apparently had learned both his lesson and his way around. He and Shapiro, and their gang, became important cogs in the organization of "Little Augie" Orgen and moved in more important underworld circles. During the next eleven years he was arrested no less than eleven times—once a year —but no convictions resulted.

Business was good and getting better. Labor unions were strong and getting stronger. Young hoodlums with no morals and a quick trigger finger, who were handy with blackjack and brass knuckles, were in demand both by management and labor. It didn't matter to Little Augie or his henchmen which side they were on. Sometimes they were even on both.

It may have been this dual allegiance which led to the dispute which cost Little Augie his life and put Lepke and Gurrah in the saddle. It was 1927 and the Orgen gang had been playing both sides in a Brooklyn labor dispute.

Little Augie Snuffed Out

Whatever the reason, there was a rupture of gang relations, and Little Augie was mowed down on an East Side street. His bodyguard, Legs Diamond, survived his dose of lead only to die several years later under a similar fusilade in an Albany rooming house. Lepke and Gurrah were picked up and questioned. They said they had been enjoying a movie at the time their leader was killed.

Whoever killed Orgen, Lepke and Gurrah profited by it. With Hymie Holtz, also known as Curley, they took over Little Augie's gang. Hymie apparently got in the way in 1931 and disappeared.

Lepke and Gurrah made a combination which was to become the most feared among small business men in the history of the city. With a close-knit organization of about twenty-five men, and many others who could be called in to do special jobs, they set themselves up in the business of extortion.

Sometimes they went through the formality of organizing a "protec-

"JUDGE LOUIE"

Associated Press

Louis (Lepke) Buchalter, object of an international search.

tive" association to which the unwilling members they forced to join paid "dues." Such were the Protective Fur Dressers Association and the Fur Dressers Factor Corporation, whose activities led to the indictment in 1933 of Lepke, Gurrah and 156 other individuals on charges of "interference with interstate commerce" in violation of the Sherman Anti-Trust Act.

Direct Actionists

More often, though, they didn't bother with any such disguise. They merely made out a list of manufacturers or merchants they wanted money from and sent around a couple of the boys to collect. If the victim didn't pay he would get a stink bomb in his shop. If that didn't work his shop would be invaded and his clothing or furs slashed, or, if he was in the flour business, his bags would be opened and their contents scattered around the warehouse.

If all those methods didn't work, the recalcitrant next got a bottle of acid in his face, his skull cracked with a lead pipe, his family intimidated, his workers beaten.

It seems incredible in these days of militant grand juries and prosecutors, unhampered police and protection for witnesses, that those tactics could bring any great reward. Yet it is estimated that they produced at least $5,000,000 a year for the Lepke-Gurrah mob alone. The only protection the payers got was the certainty that they would not be shaken down by any other gang. Lepke and Gurrah saw to that.

A Life of Luxury

The two former East Side package thieves now were living in a style to which they certainly had not been accustomed, or probably ever dreamed of, a few years before. Lepke lived with his wife and young stepson in a fine apartment with a view of Central Park. He held his conferences with his lieutenants in the town's best hotels. Sometimes he and his cronies went on Winter cruises, plotting new extortion schemes between games of shuffleboard and deck tennis. They attended most of the hockey games and all the big fights, visited Los Angeles and Miami, "took the cure" at Saratoga or abroad.

Lepke was different from most of the rest, however, and certainly not the movie version of a gang leader. He always maintained an aura of respectability. Raleigh Clothes, a manufacturing concern with a factory in Baltimore, listed him as a partner of record and he also was interested in the Coat Front Company and the Garfield Express Company, the latter a trucking concern which specialized in garment hauling between New York and New Jersey.

Even in gang circles he was known as a man who talked little, sitting back and listening while others spoke. This gained for him the underworld nickname of "The Judge" or "Judge Louie."

Like a Business Man

A casual observer seeing him leaving his limousine and going into his Central Park West apartment house would not give him a second glance. He looked like a prosperous young business man. He was, but not in the usual sense.

It was this quietness of behavior and action, the lack of personal ostentation, which is believed to have kept him safe so long from the rival guns which intermittently blazed in the underworld and brought down the more shining targets, the Schultzes, the Colls, the Diamonds and the rest.

Also, Lepke was always generous with his men, rewarding faithful work lavishly. In a division of gang profits he was always ready to take what looked like the wrong end of a financial arrangement, if by so doing he could avoid a troublesome enmity. When the occasion required, however, he could be as ruthless as a Capone.

Some day, like all men, he'll come to judgment, at the hands of authority or of some rival gangster. In the meantime he has proved the truth of one old maxim. He became a major figure in his own hard-boiled set by walking softly.

LEPKE'S PARTNER

Jake (Gurrah) Shapiro.

U. S. GANG NETWORK IS BARED IN INQUIRY

Crime Syndicate Dominated by New York Racketeers Is Pictured to Grand Jury

The investigation of persons suspected of harboring fugitives from New York indictments, undertaken by a Federal grand jury prior to the surrender of Louis (Lepke) Buchalter, and continued since, is gradually turning up a picture of national crime that reaches into most of the cities of America and was dominated by a small group of gangsters in New York, it was learned yesterday.

The evidence has been presented to this grand jury by Assistant United States Attorneys John B.

Doyle and William Young, under United States Attorney John T. Cahill. Testimony will continue today with Benjamin (Bug) Siegel as the principal witness. Siegel, with his partner, Meyer Lansky, were the bosses of a gang known as the "Bug and Meyer mob."

They were connected also with Lepke and his partner, Jacob (Gurrah) Shapiro, Charles (Lucky Luciano) Lucania and Joe Adonis of Brooklyn. Called the "Big Six," they were, after the murder of Arthur (Dutch Schultz) Flegenheimer, the confederated bosses of all important racketeering in New York.

Expansion Began in 1931

As early as 1931 the Bug and Meyer gang began to extend its empire. While Lepke's interests were extended to Baltimore—as the grand jury determined—those of the Bug and Meyer gang were extended to Philadelphia, Pittsburgh and Cleveland.

The bosses themselves also moved on. Siegel and Lansky set themselves up in Los Angeles, where, so far as investigators found, they suffered no diminution of the rich living scale they had enjoyed in New York. Another important member of the ruling set in New York was Harry (Dutch) Goldberg, also known as Louis Shomberg. He has more recently been in Reno,

Hyman (Spunky) Weiss, a former member of the gang, took up in Pittsburgh, while Harry (Nig) Rosen and Harry (Greenie) Greenfield transferred their activities to Philadelphia. The rackets enterprises in these cities have been described as somewhat like those in New York before the advent of Thomas E. Dewey as special prosecutor.

The grand jury action is based on the belief that as one prosecution after another was started, by both State and Federal Governments, and more and more members of the New York gangs became fugitives, they simply moved through this intercity, interlocking empire and continued to work for the same bosses.

where his interest is primarily in legalized gambling.

Ex-Partner of Huey Long

Frankie Costello, who also has been a witness before this grand jury, went to New Orleans when his slot machines were banned here in 1934. He made an arrangement with Huey Long for the operation of his machines there—he had more than 5,000 of them "on location" in New York in 1934. Together they set up the Pelican Novelty Company and the annual net profit from that—in a city one-fourteenth the size of New York—was $800,000.

The grand jury here will not, it was said, attempt to take up the question of what political connections these gangsters managed to make in the various cities to which they expanded. However, for the first time in many years a single grand jury is receiving the accumulated data growing in the files of the Federal Bureau of Investigation for years, and as a result of it leads that may be invaluable to prosecutors in other Federal districts are being piled up in Mr. Cahill's office.

It has been described as one of the most far-reaching criminal investigations of recent times.

September 4, 1939

RELES IS TELLING STORY OF MURDERS DONE BY HIS GANG

Leader, in a Surprise Move to Win Leniency, Gives O'Dwyer Facts on Paid Killers

ALSO NAMING 'EMPLOYERS'

Two More Slayings Are Solved as Drive on Syndicate Takes On Added Momentum

Abe Reles, a flashy, blustery little gang boss of Brooklyn's Brownsville section who sold the services

of himself and his retainers to more important crime bosses for jobs of murder, yesterday began to spin out an account of his life and works for District Attorney William O'Dwyer of Kings.

This new and unexpected turn in the ramified investigation of the Brownsville mercenaries involved a deal by which Reles hoped to mitigate his possible punishment—he already was under indictment for first-degree murder in a gang killing—in exchange for the whole truth. His fate hung upon the condition that his story would have to be thoroughly checked and found correct.

At the same time it opened new possibilities in the inquiry that Mr. O'Dwyer and his staff are pursuing and that already has led into Sullivan County and the Bronx, with indictments and arrests piling up rapidly and the locations of the bodies of men long missing being described to officials.

Political Links Possible

All these developments were based upon the stories of Abraham (Pretty) Levene and Anthony (The

Duke) Maffetore, two minor hirelings who killed on orders of Reles and received sometimes as little as $10 to $20 for a job. What Reles knows and what he can tell about are the men who paid for the murders, perhaps something of the reasons that caused them to buy sudden death for their enemies and possibly of politicians and policemen who aided them.

Neither Mr. O'Dwyer nor any member of his staff would say anything about the last possibility, but something of the acceleration that the Reles confession may give to the inquiry was shown late yesterday when Mr. O'Dwyer ordered the arrest of two men—both pals of Reles—for a five-year-old unsolved murder; informed the State police at Sidney, N. Y., where they could find the body of a man named Yoell Miller, long missing, near a Sullivan County swimming pool, and, finally, named as a murder victim Solomon Goldstein, onetime participant in the Fulton Fish Market racket, who disappeared in Sullivan County on Aug. 25, 1936, and whose body has not been found.

This last case was described by Assistant District Attorney Burton B. Turkus as a "contract killing for an overlord of crime in another county." Until he was convicted in Federal court for fish-market racketeering, Joseph (Socks) Lanza was the Fulton Market boss.

Wife Went to Office

The Reles confession, which may lead the inquiry into uncharted fields, was due at least in part to an unborn child. Reles's wife expects, within a few months, to give birth to their second child. At a few minutes after 5 P. M. on Friday she went to the District Attorney's office and asked to see Mr. O'Dwyer, and though she had to wait about an hour because of his absence, she finally talked to him.

She told him that out of consideration for their child, and the expected one, and because she did not want her offspring's father to die in the electric chair, Reles had decided to exchange information for a recommendation of clemency by the District Attorney. The assumption by Reles that he would be convicted was passed over without comment by the District Attorney.

Mrs. Reles left the office weeping because she was told that her husband would have to signify his intention in writing before he would be taken to Brooklyn.

A few minutes afterward Mr. Turkus went to the Tombs Prison, to which Reles had been transferred from the Brooklyn City Prison more than a week before, and Reles signed a statement which Mr. Turkus took to Supreme Court Justice Philip A. Brennan, who signed an order releasing Reles from the Tombs for questioning by Mr. O'Dwyer.

Their conversations went on at intervals in the Brooklyn District Attorney's office through most of the night. Then he was taken back to the Tombs for a few hours and later in the day returned again to Brooklyn for further talk.

It was in the late afternoon, after about half a day more, that things began to happen. First Mr. O'Dwyer authorized Mr. Turkus to give out the information he had forwarded to the State police at Sidney in relation to the two cases involving Sullivan County—bringing to four the number of murders in that county solved since Levene and Maffetore began talking about a week ago—and then he ordered the arrest of Max Golob, best known among his companions as Max the Jerk, and Frank Abbadando for a five-year-old Brooklyn murder.

The victim of this old crime was John (Spider) Murtha, cut down by bullets at the corner of Atlantic and Van Sinderen Avenues on a Sunday morning while strolling with a girl, Miss Florence Nestfield, 28, of 31 Halsey Street, Brooklyn. Golob had been in the District Attorney's office under questioning most of the day after having been brought in during the morning, and Abbadando was already under arrest, charged jointly with Harry (Happy) Maione and Harry (Pittsburgh Phil) Strauss with the theft of an automobile.

Murtha's murder was on March, 1935. He had a long record and was known to the police as the "toughest guy in Brooklyn," having been wounded in pistol battles several times before he was killed. He appeared not so much a gangster of such enterprises as slot machines, narcotics or beer, as one who extorted money from proprietors of speakeasies and houses of prostitution on threats of violence.

Beginning about 1930 and continuing through all the succeeding years, virtually every time Reles was arrested he was in the company of Martin (Buggsy) Goldstein, Maione, Strauss and Abbadando. He and Goldstein currently are jointly charged with the murder of Alex (Red) Alpert, a small-time Brooklyn hoodlum.

The order for a murder charge to be made against Golob and Abbadando left only Maione of the old quintet as yet unnamed in a specific murder case. Strauss has been indicted in Sullivan County in two murders, those of Irving Ashkenas, Brooklyn taxicab driver, and Walter Sage, one-time trigger man for the gang.

Miss Nestfield confronted the pair and identified them both. She said that on the morning when her companion was killed the two men stopped them, told her to stand aside, and then fired on Murtha. What the shooting was about, Mr. O'Dwyer did not say, and the questioning of Golob continued in his office last night. Golob is 29 years old and lives at 598 New Lots Avenue, Brooklyn. He was booked on a charge of homicide at 10:30 o'clock last night, after having been twice at Brooklyn police headquarters during the evening. His first visit there at 7 o'clock was ended before he could be booked when he was recalled to the District Attorney's office for further, unexplained questioning.

Concerning Yoell Miller, Mr. Turkus said: "The District Attorney has communicated with Inspector Maynard of the State police at Sidney, N. Y., and told him that the body of Yoell Miller will be found buried near a drain to the new swimming pool at the Rosemont Inn, one and a half miles from Loch Sheldrake. He was taken out of the Evans House, near Loch Sheldrake, several years ago and slain and his body hidden."

There was no suggestion as to the connections that Miller had or the reason for his murder.

When Levene and Maffetore toured Sullivan County last Tuesday they told District Attorney William Deckelman of Monticello that they had witnessed the murder of a man they knew only as Jack, who was connected with the fish market racket and whose body had been dropped in Loch Sheldrake with enough weight tied on to keep it down.

Sullivan County authorities had suspected that this was Sol Goldstein, who had answered a telephone call at the boarding house at which he was staying in Glen Wild on Aug. 25, 1936, and dropped from

District Attorney William O'Dwyer
Times Wide World, 1939

Abe Reles
Times Wide World, 1937

sight. Mr. O'Dwyer's second message to Inspector Maynard confirmed this. The man as yet unrecovered from Loch Sheldrake, he said, was Solomon Goldstein, 34 years old, a one-time painter who formerly lived at 379 Rodney Street, Brooklyn. He was kidnapped and murdered, the District Attorney said, and the crime was a "contract killing for an overlord of crime in another county."

And thus the murder list grew.

Held Only a Beginning

Thus far, since the frightened hirelings of the Reles gang—Levene and Maffetore—began to unfold their tale of killings, solutions have been provided for four Sullivan County cases, one in the Bronx and two in Brooklyn. But the list, it was made plain in Mr. O'Dwyer's office, has been only begun. He once estimated that Levene and Maffetore had provided information on at least thirty gang killings, and how much this list would be extended by the information that Reles may supply could not be guessed.

The Bronx case was that involving Irving Penn, a music publishing firm executive, who was killed by mistake. He lived in the same neighborhood and vaguely resembled Philip Orlofsky, a man who had had intimate and many connections with Louis (Lepke) Buchalter in garment industry racketeering, and had twice been taken to the office of District Attorney Thomas E. Dewey for examination though he was not a Dewey witness.

Through the information furnished by Levene and Maffetore, and conveyed to District Attorney Samuel J. Foley of the Bronx, the arrest of one Lazarus Black as the man who had put the weapons in the murder car from which the killers took Penn's life was brought about. After an attorney for Black made an unsuccessful effort to obtain his release on habeas corpus, which was denied by Supreme Court Justice Ernest E. L. Hammer, Mr. Foley announced that the identity of the killers had become known, and that they were in jail in Brooklyn. He did not name them.

RELES DESCRIBED AS VICIOUS THUG

Worse Than Dillinger, but He Lacked Latter's Courage, Court Asserted

LED GANGS FOR 17 YEARS

He Offered to Shoot It Out With Any Policeman—Preyed on Small Shops

Abe Reles, a notorious hoodlum in the Brownsville and East New York sections of Brooklyn for the last seventeen years and a leader of gangs of thugs at various periods of his criminal career, was once described by a Kings County Judge as "a real bad man," a fellow "more vicious than Dillinger" but lacking Dillinger's courage. The police concur in the verdict.

A short, coarse-featured man, given to swaggering and bullying, he is known familiarly to the Brownsville residents who manage to get along without doing an honest day's work as Little Abe. He prefers to be called Kid Twist, after the Lower East Side hoodlum of an earlier day who terrorized immigrants and small shopkeepers. Reles may have patterned his activities after the Kid's.

With flashy clothes setting off his heavy jowls, cheap jewelry attracting the eye to his pudgy fingers and an air of importance that changes chameleonlike to bewilderment when rivals or the police press him into a corner, Reles likes to round out the picture of himself by frequent display of bills of large denomination, preferably $1,000, wrapped around a roll that may or may not consist entirely of bona fide United States currency.

Stabbed Car-Washer

The queasy side of Reles's character was illustrated in recent arrests. He was sentenced to a three-year term in the penitentiary in 1934 for stabbing and killing a Negro car washer in a 110th Street garage who had not moved about fast enough to please his fancy. He managed to get acquitted of the murder of another car washer in the same garage, for lack of evidence that he and a companion had beaten the man to death for the same reason.

The incident, according to the court, showed Reles up as the vicious coward he was. But when Kings County Judge Martin, in dismissing the charge, warned that Reles was "one of the most vicious characters we have had in Brooklyn in many years" and declared his belief that the man would wind up either with a life term in prison or by being "put out of the way" by "some good detective with a couple of bullets," the Brooklyn racketeer boasted through his lawyer:

"'Tell that judge that I'll take on any cop with pistols or anything else. A cop counts fifteen when he puts his finger on the trigger before he shoots .'"

Judge Martin replied in kind. "This fellow is brave enough to stab in the back, or shoot a defenseless person, and, with a gang supporting him, might punch or kick an invalid or a near invalid," he said. "He'd never stand up to a square man-to-man fight. He hasn't that kind of courage."

The court's opinion was borne out by a sheaf of complaints, some of them yellowed, by shopkeepers and other small business men to the police of Brownsville and East New York. Reles was regularly engaged in usury, bookmaking, prostitution and similar traditional rackets at various times, but the one activity to which he devoted himself with consistency, ever since he was in his 'teens, was petty extortion by means of vandalism and, often, by the more vicious sorts of violence. Reles is reputed to have crippled many a shopkeeper who dared to refuse a demand for "protection."

Began Crime Career Early

Reles says he is now 34, and so he must have been about 13 years old when he first came to police notice. Then he was charged with felonious assault on his first recorded arrest on May 6, 1923. The charge is one with which many of the hoodlums who have lengthy dossiers at police headquarters started their criminal careers. The younger hangers-on of the street gangs seek to win the notice and the approval of the gangsters they look up to by doing a "strong-arm" job for them. Reles was convicted of the assault but received a suspended sentence.

A few months later he resorted to petty thievery. Again he was convicted, but by the inexplicable processes of the Brooklyn courts the earlier conviction and suspended sentence were forgotten. Sentence was again suspended. Two years later he was sent away for his first jail term when a charge of felonious assault resulted in conviction.

By 1927 he had gained maturity as a figure in Brownsville's lawless fringe. That was back in the days of prohibition, when the more important gangsters of Brooklyn were engaged in the lucrative pursuits of beer-running and speakeasy operations and the mortality among them was as high as the rate of profit. The year marked Reles's first arrest as a gunman; he was accused of a hold-up. Witnesses in court were unconvincing and he was acquitted.

The following year, after he had beaten charges of assault and robbery and grand larceny and had served a six months' term in the city prison on a burglary charge that, somehow, was reduced to disorderly conduct, he was returned at last to the reformatory. When he came out he had not been at liberty long before he was charged with a slaying, the first of five homicide charges he was to face. He obtained the discharge of or was dismissed on all but the last.

During the last decade, according to the police complaints, Reles's activities have been varied. He became an important distributor of slot machines, placing them in candy stores and poolrooms without much difficulty by beating up recalcitrant proprietors. Until the end of prohibition he and associates did some beer trade, pushing the brand of which they represented themselves as salesmen by beating at least one beer garden proprietor on the head with a chair. Between times he answered charges of robbery, assault and, on one occasion, possession of narcotics.

During the last four years, as his activities became more widely known and troublesome to the Brooklyn police, he has had to answer occasional charges of vagrancy. He once threatened to add a personal bail bondsman to his entourage to end the annoyance. These arrests bothered him more than the others. He took to increasing the size of the roll of bills he carried. Formerly when the police or the courts asked his occupation he would reply disdainfully, "Sodajerker"; lately he has acquired an interest in a small restaurant and describes himself as a "luncheonette proprietor."

At various times he has had to defend his position in Brooklyn gangland. Back in 1930, when his interest in slot machines was at stake, rival gangsters shot him twice in the back. Martin (Buggsy) Goldstein, now held with him, was shot in the nose. One man was killed, two others wounded. The following year his feud with the Meyer Schapiro gang came to a climax with Schapiro's assassination. Several times since he has had to meet the challenges of rivals.

ABE RELES KILLED TRYING TO ESCAPE

Sheet Rope Fails After He Lowers Himself From 6th to 5th Floor of Hotel

MOTIVE PUZZLES POLICE

Informer Against Murder Ring Lived in Dread of Bullets of Former Confederates

Sometime after daylight yesterday Abe Reles, squat, bulgy-jawed informer against the Brooklyn murder ring, climbed out on a window ledge on the sixth floor of the Half Moon Hotel on Coney Island boardwalk, fully dressed but hatless. Strong wind from the gray sea tugged at his long, crisp black hair and tore at his gray suit.

Behind him, in the room, lights still burned. Behind him the little radio that had played all night, still blared and babbled. The informer, looking southward, could see surf break against the jetties. He could hear the dolorous clanging of the buoy as it rocked in the tide. He could see far down the deserted boardwalk. It was shrouded in morning mist.

Reles let two knotted bedsheets down the hotel's east wall, two windows north of the hotel's Boardwalk front. Around one end of the upper bedsheet he had twisted several turns of a four-foot length of radio lead-in wire. He had wound the free end of the wire on a radio valve under the window.

He let himself down, on the sheets, to the fifth floor. One hand desperately clung to the sheet. With the other Reles tugged at the screen and at the windows of the vacant fifth-floor room. He worked them up six inches. He tugged again with his full 160-pound weight.

Tries to Save Himself

The strain was too much for the amateur wire knot on the valve. Little by little it came undone.

Reles tried to save himself. He kicked toward the fifth-floor window ledge with his left foot, but merely bruised the shoe leather from toe to heel. He plunged to the hotel's concrete kitchen roof, a two-story extension, forty-two feet below.

He landed on his back, breaking his spine.

Detectives assigned to the hotel guard insisted Reles was asleep when they looked into his room at 6:45 A. M. and again at 7:10 A. M. The three other gangster informers were asleep at that hour, too. There was only one exit from the suite and that was under the eye of one of the policemen. He heard no sound in the room, except the radio, but Reles, the detectives said, played the radio all night, if it suited his fancy—and it often did.

At 7:45 A. M. William Nicholson, chairman of the Coney Island Draft Board, got to his second-floor office in the hotel. He had some recruits going out. Something white outside the window caught his eye. It was the bedsheet, stirred by the sea wind. Nicholson called the hotel's night manager and the manager telephoned to the detectives assigned to guard Reles and three other gangster witnesses in the sixth floor five-room suite.

Detective Victor Robbins, one of the five men in the gangster's guard, climbed out on the roof and knelt by Reles. The informer was dead. He lay on his back, his 5 feet 4 inches sprawled full length, swart features distorted. He was dressed for escape. He had left his topcoat in the room, but he wore the gray suit, a white shirt, blue-gray sweater, green belt, white socks and black shoes. In his left-hand coat pocket the detective found a checkered cap, folded the long way.

The detectives were not sorry to see Reles dead. They made no bones about this. He had been arrogant, surly, unclean in his habits. An internal condition accompanied by frequent hemmorhage, which he took no trouble to conceal, heightened their distaste for the man. He had boasted from the witness stand that in his ten years as an executive in the murder ring he had killed or helped to kill ten men, yet he seemed delighted when his testimony sent five former companions-in-arms to the death house.

But the detectives were puzzled. They could not understand why Reles should have tried to escape.

For almost twenty months, from the moment he turned informer and came under protective custody, he had shown fear if detectives moved out of earshot. When he was taken to Los Angeles to testify against West Coast members of the murder combination he would not enter a room or even an airplane unless a policeman covered him front and back. He was afraid one of the murder ring troopers—a term he invented—would bob up and kill him.

Reles had everything to lose by escape, the detectives reasoned. There was no place he could go without going down before the guns and knives of the men who were in the ring and who are still free. He was particularly in horror of Albert Anastasia, master killer for the ring, who is still a fugitive.

The report that Reles had tried to escape to avoid appearing as a witness against Louis (Lepke) Buchalter, one of the ring's head men who is now on trial in Kings County Court, does not seem to make sense. Reles had talked freely and at great length of Buchalter's operations and of his supervision of combination murders.

A third theory was advanced. There were rumors that Charles (Buggsy) Siegel, West Coast head man for the combination, had persuaded Mrs. Reles that if her husband could get away from the police, the West Coast group would give her $50,000 and help Reles get out of the jurisdiction. Some of the detectives were inclined to shrug this theory off.

A few, but not many, of the detectives were inclined to think that Reles's break for freedom might have been prompted by a quirk of the mind. This group maintained he was mentally erratic and that under pressure of cumulative fears he might suddenly have decided to get away through the window. Reles, these theorists held, got out of Harbor Hospital in Brooklyn only last Sunday after treatment for his internal condition. He came back snarling, quarreling and more petulant than he had previously been.

If Mrs. Reles threw any light on a possible motive for her husband's attempt to escape, the officials withheld it. She was in the hotel room with him until 11 o'clock Tuesday night. They were alone and what they talked about, unless she disclosed it, was secret. Mrs.

Reles, mother of two children by the gangster, seemed to take the news of her husband's death calmly when she was told about it in the District Attorney's office late yesterday afternoon.

She said, "I don't think he should have done anything like that. You boys were always nice to him."

Reles was 35 years old. He was arrested forty-four times during his criminal career, the first time when he was only 13, but already a tough and bully in the Brownsville district of Brooklyn, where he was bred. He was arrested for homicide six times, but never convicted for this, or for any of his other many major crimes. The worst he ever got was an indefinite penitentiary sentence for assault, or a sentence for disorderly conduct.

The men he sent to the death house grew up with him. These included Harry (Happy) Maione and Frank (The Dasher) Abbandano, the first two members of the murder ring brought to trial by District Attorney William O'Dwyer. These men reviled him from the courtroom floor. They are still in the death house, pending appeal. The second pair sent to the death house, chiefly through Reles's testimony, were Harry (Pittsburgh Phil) Strauss and Martin (Buggsy) Goldstein, who had loafed on the same Brownsville corners with Reles. They died in the electric chair a few months ago.

The fifth man was Irving (The Plug) Nitzberg, like the others a friend of Reles's for many years.

Reles—he was Kid Twist to his fellows—openly boasted from the witness stand that he had worked with all these men in a variety of rackets from bookmaking to professional murder. He testified, without reserve, how he had helped them do away with murder ring members who had fallen from grace, or had double-crossed their chiefs. He described in gruesome detail the different techniques they used—the torch, the knife, the icepick and the pistol—and estimated the combination had committed altogether some seventy-five to eighty homicides.

In Reles's home at 3102 Avenue A, Brooklyn, last night, detectives barred neighbors and newspaper men from the door. A few close friends were admitted. Reles's wife and their two children kept indoors.

The body was still in the morgue last night but is to be taken to a chapel today for burial.

LEPKE CONVICTED WITH TWO AIDES; ALL FACE DEATH

Former Gang Chief, Weiss and Capone Found Guilty After Jury Ponders 4½ Hours

TO BE SENTENCED TUESDAY

Prisoners Calm as Verdict Is Returned—Families Barred From Court After Charge

Louis (Lepke) Buchalter, one of the most powerful racketeers in the country's criminal annals, and his two henchmen, Emanuel (Mendy) Weiss and Louis Capone, were convicted in Kings County Court at 2:45 A. M. today of charges of first degree murder, carrying a mandatory penalty of death in the electric chair.

Announcement of the verdict, reached after four and one-half hours of deliberation by a blue-ribbon jury, was made in a court room barely filled with stragglers and detectives. Members of the defendants' families had been ordered out of the court building when the case was given to the jury at 10:15 P. M. by Judge Franklin Taylor. They waited in automobiles across the street, and after hearing the verdict they drove away in a silence broken only by the racing motors and meshing gears along the dark, unlighted side street.

No Display of Emotion

None of the defendants made any display of feeling on hearing the jury's findings, although all three blanched somewhat in the glare of the court's bright electric lights. They shuffled to the clerk's bench, answered questions about their pedigrees in low voices and shuffled off in the company of detectives and Federal Marshals. Heavily manacled, they were taken to their prison cells to await sentence on Tuesday.

As the verdict was delivered by the jury foreman, Lepke wiped his face with a soiled white handkerchief as he heard the end of a drama in which he rose from package thievery and strong-arming of peddlers on the teeming Lower East Side to become leader of an underworld army of 250 thugs and killers with a front office on Fifth Avenue.

For twelve weeks the erstwhile racket chief had sat in the same courtroom surrounded by city detectives and Federal marshals, listening as a procession of his former underlings and close friends, whose lives he once manipulated with the impersonality of a chess player, took the witness stand and revealed the innermost secrets of the criminal organization that had taken an estimated $5,000,000 a year out of several major industries.

Lepke in appearance was a far cry from the sleek well-dressed racketeer police once arrested in a Central Park West penthouse, lounging with several henchmen in silk pajamas and with expensive clothing strewn about the rooms, golf clubs hanging in the closet and brochures for sea voyages on luxury liners brightening up the dressing tables.

Death Verdict Asked

Yesterday his baggy clothes, his drawn face, his damp scalp glistening through his thinning dark hair, gave him a seedy look as he stared sternly while Burton B. Turkus, Assistant District Attorney, urged the jury to find the defendants guilty of first-degree murder in the slaying of Joseph Rosen, former garment trucker, on Sept. 13, 1936, in his candy store at 725 Sutter Avenue, Brooklyn.
nue, Brooklyn.

Thirty-two witnesses and fifty-seven exhibits had been presented by the prosecution to support its contention that seventeen bullets were pumped into Rosen's body on Lepke's orders ccause Lepke feared Rosen would talk about him before investigating authorities. Weiss was named as one of the actual killers and Capone was implicated in the getaway.

"Here for the first time we have the boss, the king pin, on trial for the murder he ordered," Mr. Turkus declared. "We'd love to put on trial every man whose fingers were dipped in Rosen's blood. But you have to break this kind of case from the inside. You must use the finger man and the chauffeur to get the boss. But that's the one that counts.

"The defense has criticized the witnesses we have presented as criminals. Did they think we'd bring witnesses from the halls of Harvard or choir boys? We brought the people they associated with. These defendants selected their own witnesses because these are the people they lived and worked with."

Stares at O'Dwyer

Several times Lepke turned and stared at District Attorney William O'Dwyer of Brooklyn, sitting in a spectator's row five feet away. It was Mr. O'Dwyer who reached out into a cell in the Federal Prison at Leavenworth, Kan., and set in motion the legal machinery that brought Lepke to trial on charges of taking the life of a man under the ruthless precept handed down from the pirates that sailed the Spanish Main—"Dead men tell no tales."

That the racket leader measured the strength of his outlaw world by this precept was illustrated during the trial when a witness declared that Lepke, discussing the refusal of a witness in the Rosen case to hide out, had asserted menacingly in the presence of a lawyer, "All I know is that where there's no witness there's no case."

Principal witnesses against Lepke were Max Rubin, school teacher turned labor racketeer and a star collector of tribute for Lepke, who said that he heard Lepke threaten to stop Rosen from talking and that later he heard Lepke and Weiss discuss the shooting of Rosen. Rubin himself was shot in the head from ambush on a city street after appearing before a grand jury investigating Lepke's activities. But he recovered and later testified against his former boss in three trials.

Members of Rosen's family testified that he had told them that Lepke had driven him out of his trucking business. Underworld figures described events leading up to the crime. Among these were Sholem Bernstein, who drove the death car, and Paul Berger, who said he had "fingered" Rosen for the killers on the eve of the slaying.

The racketeer's defense, in which he called only six witnesses, was that Rosen's business was a financial failure and consequently unattractive to Lepke and that he

had no fear of Rosen's talking. Weiss put in an alibi that at the time of the slaying he was home in bed after a birthday celebration for a younger brother. Capone offered no defense.

Throughout the summing up by Turkus, two extra guards sat close to Weiss, a powerful man reported to have a hair-trigger temper and described by police as "a deadly gunman." Weiss occasionally turned and sneered at Mr. O'Dwyer. Capone was calm throughout.

Exposed by Dewey and Amen

Lepke, who was known as "Judge Louie" to the underworld, a title gained as a man who sat back, talking little while others spoke and yet making all final decisions, came into the public consciousness when District Attorney Thomas E. Dewey denounced him as the outstanding public enemy and indicted him for his industrial rackets.

He had first been prosecuted by Special Prosecutor John Harlan Amen, then a Federal attorney, in the $10,000,000 rabbit fur racket. A jury convicted him after thirty-three hours' deliberation, but the conviction later was reversed.

The Federal Government then named Lepke in a $10,000,000 narcotics ring and Mr. Dewey indicted him in the flour trucking and garment industries. Lepke became a fugitive for two years, with a $30,000 price on his head. He was accused by Mr. Dewey of conducting a "war of extermination" against witnesses, several of whom

were shot down in the street.

The country was blanketed with 1,000,000 police circulars and the Federal Bureau of Investigation spread its network for the fugitive. Lepke was reported hiding in countries all over the world; one report had him carrying out a kidnapping on the Polish-Russian border.

His sources of revenue cut off by systematic prosecution, Lepke finally surrendered, revealing that he had hidden away in New York all the time. He was convicted by the Federal Government in the narcotics case and given fourteen years in Leavenworth, which he currently is serving. He was convicted in Mr. Dewey's cases and given thirty years to serve later.

Then Mr. O'Dwyer uncovered the Brooklyn murder ring, the tightly knit organization of professional killers headed by Abe Reles that sold underworld slayings to crime bosses such as Lepke. Informers told of the Rosen slaying, and Mr. O'Dwyer and his aides began to prepare the case.

So Lepke's downfall came through the prosecutions of Mr. Dewey and Mr. O'Dwyer, both of whom became prominent political personalities on the basis of their work. In less than five years Lepke's criminal empire, carved out with pistol, fists and stench bombs, collapsed in the court rooms that for years had never recorded his presence because of his ability to move in the background, a shadowy figure wielding great power and extorting vast wealth under threat of death.

LUCIANO TAKEN ON SHIP

Secluded by Guards as He Awaits Deportation to Italy Today

Flanked by two agents of the United States Immigration Service, Charles (Lucky Luciano) Lucania was taken aboard the 7,000-ton freighter Laura Keene yesterday for deportation to Italy. The guards will stay with him until the ship sails this morning from Bush Terminal, Brooklyn.

Secluding himself aboard the vessel, Luciano, recently pardoned by Governor Dewey after serving nine years of a thirty to fifty year term for pandering, declined to talk to newspapermen, remarking: "I've seen the press enough." The ex-convict had two visitors but immigration officials would not reveal their names.

November 30, 1941

November 10, 1946

PRISONER'S STORY 'BREAKS' 4 MURDERS BY BROOKLYN RING

Bench Warrants Issued for 6 Unione Silicione Members Accused by 'The Hawk'

ONE REPORTED AMG AIDE

Suspect Said to Have Been an Interpreter With Allies in Italy Recently

For nine years Ernest Rupolo, eagle-beaked and one-eyed self-confessed assassin-for-hire known as "The Hawk," served time in Sing Sing Prison for the shooting of Willie Gallo, a bodyguard of big-shot thugs.

Deserted by his confederates, who failed to provide a lawyer and "advised" him to plead guilty, Rupolo languished in jail. He got out, in January, 1943, after serving the minimum of a nine-to-twenty-year term. In June of this year Rupolo was in court, again pleading guilty to a shooting charge. He admitted he was hired for a $500 fee to take Carl Sparacini, 66 years old, of 13 Wallaston Street, Brooklyn, for a "ride" and

that he had shot him in the face three times, not fatally. But he would not say who had hired him.

By threatening him with a sentence of from forty to eighty years as a second offender, Kings County Judge Samuel S. Leibowitz made Rupolo change his mind.

Reticence Gives Way

Judge Leibowitz delayed the imposition of sentence and Rupolo's reticence began to give way. His disclosures, after more than two months of questioning, checking and trailing of suspects, began to trickle Monday night, and yesterday, despite official attempts at maintaining secrecy, the trickle had developed into a sizable leak.

Information sufficient to "break" at least four murder cases was supplied to police and the Kings County prosecutor's office by Rupolo. He revealed that the perpetrators were members of the Unione Siciliano, self-appointed successors to the old Maffia, or Black Hand Society transplanted here from Palermo, Sicily, in 1899 by an Italian murderer named Ignazio Saietta, sometimes called Ignazio Lupo, meaning The Wolf.

It was the first time in twenty years that the Unione had been mentioned in a murder here. At that time Tony Perino, called the Clutching Hand — his right hand was an iron hook—had taken over as successor to Lupo, but he was later found sprawled in the gutter on Sackett Street, Brooklyn, his brief reign at an end.

Warrants Issued for Six

Rupolo's specific information on the murder of Ferdinand (the

Shadow) Boccia, who was slain on Sept. 19, 1934, only a few hours before the non-fatal shooting of his bodyguard, Gallo, resulted in the issuance of bench warrants on Monday night for six members of the Unione band. Boccia was shot in his uncle's cafe, the Circolo Christofolo Club, at 533 Metropolitan Avenue, Brooklyn, for demanding his promised $35,000 share in a combination rigged card game and fake money-making machine swindle. A few hours later the gang decided to kill Gallo and it was for this job, bunglingly executed, that Rupolo was hired.

The six named in the warrants are Vito Genovese, 43 years old; Michael Mirandi, 49; Peter De Feo, 43; Gus Frasca, 36; George Smurra, 35, and one known as Sally, a diminutive of the Italian name Salvatore, who was listed as John Doe.

The whereabouts of all six were said to be unknown but an interesting sidelight on Genovese was that he was reported recently to have been in Italy acting as an interpreter for the Allied Military Government there. Genovese — 1930 was one of eight named in an indictment in connection with the operation of a counterfeiting plant in the Bath Beach section of Brooklyn, in which nearly $1,000,000 in spurious currency was found.

In this, Genovese followed blunderingly in the footsteps of Lupo, whose downfall was caused by counterfeiting. Sentenced in 1910 to a term of thirty years in Federal prison for counterfeiting, Lupo received a commutation, conditional on good behavior, from President Harding, ten years later. The Wolf established a sphere of influence in the Brooklyn underworld with highly prosperous rackets in

the bakery business, the wholesale grape trade and the Italian lottery. In 1936 he was sent back to serve out the remaining twenty years of his sentence.

Smurra, known variously as "Blah Blah" and "Blackie," was a protégé of Tony Bonasera, onetime "chief" of the Bensonhurst and Bath Beach underworld. When he was arrested in May, 1934, with Rupolo on a charge of consorting with criminals, his record already showed eighteen previous arrests and one conviction for burglary.

When Rupolo "squealed' in defiance of the inviolate rule of "omerta," or loyal secrecy of the original Mafia, he gave the names of three erstwhile cronies who could corroborate his disclosures. These thugs, all serving time in Sing Sing, have been doing their "singing" in the old Bronx County jail at 161st Street and Third Avenue, where many jailbirds were brought for questioning during the Dewey investigations and Brooklyn murder ring inquiry.

Police Commissioner Lewis J. Valentine conferred with Acting Kings County District Attorney Thomas C. Hughes yesterday and it was learned the police head had assumed active leadership of the hunt for the six named in the warrants.

Mr. Hughes said only: "There is nothing that I can properly disclose in this investigation. It has been a secret investigation and I am sorry that any phase has leaked out."

The first tangible result of Rupolo's disclosures was the recent arrest of three men for holding up a card game last year. All were charged with robbery and the case is now pending.

Rupolo, who is 29, started out as a petty thief when he was 14. By the time he was 19 he had a record of six arrests and had served two terms in the penitentiary. He had his eye shot out by a fellow gangster, Harry Green, during a scrape years ago on the West Side of Manhattan. Green had accused him of "squealing."

August 9, 1944

COSTELLO DENIES UNDERWORLD LINKS

Gambler Calls a Press Parley to Express His Outrage at Mafia, Narcotics Stories

Those stories that Frank Costello is connected with the narcotic traffic, that he is boss of the east Harlem racketeers, or leader of a modern Mafia are "the worst type of lies and made out of whole cloth," on the authority of Mr. Cos-

tello himself. In fact, the big-time gambler and slot machine operator whom Fiorello H. La Guardia, when Mayor, delighted to term "bum," called a press conference yesterday to issue a formal statement and to answer questions.

This was the first time probably that a man with a reputation as a gangster and racketeer has used the technique made familiar by governmental bureau chiefs. The unusual conference, attended by a score of reporters and photographers was held in the office of George Wolf, 30 Broad Street, Costello's attorney.

Following the customary pattern, Costello's attorney and his aides distributed the statement, and then Costello sat back to an-

swer questions. He explained that his indignati... over statements published in a morning newspaper and attributed to Col. Garland H. Williams, New York supervisor for the Federal Bureau of Narcotics, led him to call the conference.

Called "Concoction of Lies"

"I cannot allow a charge as horrible as this to go uchallenged," Costello's statement read and added: "I have requested my attorney to allow me personally to repudiate this miserable concoction of lies."

He is a plain business man engaged in a real estate business as president of the 79 Wall Street Corporation, and his other income

is from holdings as a stockholder in a company—the Louisiana Mint Company—that furnishes vending machines in the State of Louisiana, Costello explained.

"Slot machines?" a reporter asked.

"Any machine you insert a coin in is a slot machine," Costello rejoined.

He explained at some length that these machines were "for amusement only," and when questioners persisted that the machines returned slugs that could be cashed, he said:

"Whatever the storekeeper does is not my business. My company buys the machines and puts them in different locations just like weighing machines."

Asked about his income from "vending" machines, Costello replied:

"Well, I wouldn't want to say. All I know is my income is properly reported to the income tax people.".

Newspaper clippings show that Costello was arrested for income tax evasion in 1939 on an indictment returned in New Orleans that charged slot machines had grossed more than a million dollars a year.

Costello, speaking in a husky voice, discussed slot machines in New York that were outlawed in 1934. He said he had operated previously by reason of a permanent injunction that prohibited police interference.

His attorney who was maintaining close watch over the questions and answers, interjected:

"You didn't get that injunction, did you Frank. It was the manufacturer."

"When you operated in New York were you the biggest operator?" the reporters asked, recalling Costello's reputation as the slot-machine king.

"Well, I wouldn't say. No, I don't think so."

"How large was the business?" he was asked.

"Well, I wouldn't care to answer that," Costello replied. No, he had not had any trouble about placing machines he explained in answer to further questions. There have been reports that storekeepers who used rival machines received persuasive visits.

The discussion turned to various Tammany political leaders with whom Costello is reputed to have strong influence and to underworld characters with whom he is said to be associated.

"Well, yes, I know him," he admitted in most cases but denied any influence or close association.

"You have been identified as the power behind Tammany Hall, Mr. Costello. How about that?" the reporters asked.

"Well, they call me everything. That's ridiculous," he replied. He said he knew "lots of Tammany leaders because I was born in New York and I'm a friendly fellow."

"Were you associated with Charley (Lucky) Lucania (convicted panderer who was deported after serving his prison term) and did you see him off?"

Lucania Association Denied

After a brief pause Costello said:

"I was never associated with him."

"But did you see him off?"

"Well, I wouldn't care to answer that question," he said.

Costello's statement said:

"I detest the narcotic racket and anyone connected with it. To my mind there is no one lower than a person dealing in it. It is low and filthy—trading on human misery. Anyone who knows me knows my opinion of narcotics and the low opinion I have of the people dealing in it or with it."

He added that it has become popular to link his name with any type of story to fit any investigation.

"As a result of these baseless stories I wish once and for all to categorically deny any connection with narcotics, Mafia, and East Harlem racketeers."

Asked directly about the Mafia, Costello said:

"I wouldn't know the definition."

He said he had asked District Attorney Frank S. Hogan to permit him to appear before the grand jury in the current narcotics investigation under waiver of immunity.

Mr. Hogan said he had not received Costello's letter, but added that "when the time comes and if I think it necessary, I'll accept Mr. Costello's offer."

December 21, 1946

WEST FEARS GANG INVASION

Evidence That Many Criminals Are Migrating From the East Disturbs California

Special to THE NEW YORK TIMES.

SAN FRANCISCO, Sept. 6— California is taking intensive note of a new type of migrant, not the Okie and Arkie of the Dust Bowl era but the organized gangster. When Gov. Earl Warren announced the other day that he would call a "general crime conference" this fall to cope with a westward trek of "Eastern underworld characters," he had in mind a situation that had been of concern to state and Federal authorities for months.

Among the killings recorded in California since early spring, two in particular convinced law enforcement officers that racketeering in its most vicious sense was seeking roots here. The San Francisco murder of Nick DeJohn, former Chicago gangster, followed by the "erasure" of Benjamin (Bugsy) Siegel, former New York underworld character, in Beverly Hills provided a double warning to Californians that their state was being regarded as fertile soil for cultivation of matters other than agrarian.

For some reason, Senator Sheridan Downey disturbed some law enforcement officials with a statement in Washington on Aug. 24 that "gamblers, racketeers and blackmailers" were streaming toward California and that the state faced a "bloody gang war" unless state officials jumped to "combat this menace."

The first reaction of Attorney General Fred N. Howser, Republican, to this assertion was that Senator Downey, a Democrat, was "popping off" in an effort to slur Governor Warren, Republican. But Governor Warren quickly agreed that gangsters were moving in.

Regardless of the political nuances, it has been revealed that the Attorney General has a long, if incomplete, list of Eastern gangsters who have moved into the state or are on their way.

The California Legislature in the spring took cognizance of the crime situation by authorizing the appointment of five special commissions to make a study of crime conditions in the State.

September 7, 1947

THE SOUTHEAST

Gangsters From Big Cities Unwelcome in Florida

By HARRIS G. SIMS
Special to THE NEW YORK TIMES.

MIAMI, Oct. 4—Floridians, especially those in the Miami area, are much concerned over published reports that gangsters from New York, Chicago and Detroit are converging on Miami and Miami Beach for a big take during the forthcoming winter season.

For many seasons Florida has been embarrassed by the operations of big and little racketeers who have gathered on the lower east coast to mingle with millionaires and prey on them in sundry ways. Each year the racketeers have become bolder, and on several occasions an outcry from the law-abiding citizens has brought intervention by the Governor.

It is less likely that there will have to be an outcry this year. City officials and law-enforcement officers in the threatened area have received as a challenge the forecast of a gangster influx. On both sides of Biscayne Bay a general preparation for greater vigilance is in progress. For one thing, more than 100 patrolmen are being added.

There is one special reason why the visiting racketeers will find the going tougher. Now holding the position of City Manager of Miami is Richard Danner, a former FBI agent who was for several years in charge of the Florida district.

No Kid Gloves

"We're not going to become the dumping spot for any other section," he has promised, "and we won't handle these gangsters with kid gloves, either."

From Police Chief Frank Mitchell of Miami Beach have come similar assurances.

Gambling operations have been one of the chief sources of trouble ever since underworld characters began to follow the wealthy into the Miami area each season.

Last season there was an increase in the more violent operations. During February, Miami had sixty armed robberies, 227 cases of breaking and entering, 307 cases of petty and grand larceny and sixty-one auto thefts.

News Note: An appeal for Federal financial aid for Florida's hurricane-swept area has been made by representatives of fourteen southeast Florida cities, counties and taxing districts.

October 5, 1947

Cities Bid Attorney General Curb Crime Syndicates' Political Aims

Municipal Association and Chicago Crime Commission Urge Inquiry, Asserting Operations Are on National Scale

Special to THE NEW YORK TIMES.

CHICAGO, Sept. 21—Major American cities have asked Attorney General J. Howard McGrath and his Department of Justice to help them stop country-wide crime syndicates from seizing control of their local political machines.

Through the American Municipal Association, representing 9,500 cities, they told the Attorney General that "the matter is too big to be handled by local officials alone; the organized criminal element operates across state boundaries on a national scale."

They then asked that local agencies be informed about the operations of crime syndicates and that "leaders of criminal syndicates be investigated with respect to local political contributions, evasion of income taxes, immigration and citizen status and any other activities."

Chicago's participation in the request was through the Crime Commission, actively headed by Virgil W. Peterson, formerly of the Federal Bureau of Investigation, who is its operating director; through Guy Reed, a banker, chairman of the Crime Commission board, and Austin Wyman, a lawyer, its president.

Mr. Peterson in a recent public statement said that "handbook operators in Chicago today boast that they can produce a minimum of 200,000 votes and unlimited financial support toward election of candidates favorable to them."

The American Municipal Associatio acted through Carl H. Chatters, its executive director, who said, concerning his letter to Mr. McGrath:

"The modern syndicate racketeer is a smooth operator. He is almost the direct opposite of the late Capone in appearance and most of his methods. The 1949 big-time gangster has a high intelligence, and that together with his silence makes him a much greater mob menace to the people and to local government.

"The big shot and his henchmen cultivate all the symbols of respectability. They wear the clothes of impeccable bankers and contribute heavily to worthy causes. They avoid overt connection with the underworld and enhance their protective coloration through holdings in the realms of respected business."

Mr. Peterson said that veritable proof of the fact that crime and gambling syndicates operated on a country-wide basis, rather than locally, had been seen in the activities of Frank Costello, overlord of slot machines, numbers games, policy racketeering, crime and vice in New York City during a number of recent years.

"Costello had a hookup with the late Huey Long, czar of Louisiana's corrupt democracy," Mr. Peterson asserted. "In furtherance of his imperious dictatorship, Long imported Costello from New York to take over slot machines in New Orleans.

"When the late Mayor La Guardia drove Costello out of New York he moved his headquarters to New Orleans at the request of Huey Long. These facts were brought out in a Federal indictment which charges two New Yorkers and four New Orleans men with income tax evasion. A sworn statement was offered by the Government to show that Huey Long himself brought the slots to New Orleans.

"It has been published that 'Costello, czar of slots, told a grand jury that Huey picked him as "the lucky one" to install the machines and run them.'

"Now Huey's brother is Governor of Louisiana and Huey's son is United States Senator from Louisiana and I have been reliably informed that the gangsters, operating through Costello's henchman, Philip (Dandy Phil) Kastel, are planning to grab control of the city elections coming up in October, November and December primaries, and oust Delesseps Morrison, cleanest Mayor New Orleans has had in years, because they can't do business with him."

A spokesman for the American Municipal Association said reports from Mayor Fletcher Bowron of Los Angeles, and Mr. Morrison himself, at a recent Chicago meeting, corroborated Mr. Peterson.

September 22, 1949

Senate Approves Inquiry Into Crime; Barkley Vote Ends Tie on Procedure

By HAROLD B. HINTON
Special to THE NEW YORK TIMES.

WASHINGTON, May 3 — The Senate approved today, 69 to 1, an inquiry into interstate crime, as Administration leaders pushed through their resolution to set up a special committee to conduct the investigation. The latter vote was 36 to 35, with Vice President Alben W. Barkley casting his ballot to break a tie.

The question of a national crime investigation, to include "the development of corrupting influences" by the underworld, has caused increasingly sharp partisan debate in recent weeks. Republican and Democratic Senators have been quick to read possible political repercussions into such an inquiry in an election year.

The tie vote that Mr. Barkley resolved in favor of the Democratic leaders came on the question of adopting a substitute resolution to create a special committee of five to conduct the investigation, instead of the Senate Judiciary Committee, as had been originally proposed. The decision to create a special unit was made by the Democratic Policy Committee several weeks ago.

Senator Estes Kefauver, Democrat of Tennessee, introduced a resolution last January, calling for the inquiry to be made by the Judiciary Committee, of which he is a member. However, J. Howard McGrath, the Attorney General, requested introduction of bills to prohibit the interstate transmission of gambling information and the shipment of slot machines.

These proposals were referred to the Interstate Commerce Committee, and a subcommittee headed by Senator Ernest W. McFarland, Democrat of Arizona, began hearings. This subcommittee last week began delving into the ramifications of bookmaking and interstate gambling, but Senator Scott W. Lucas of Illinois, the majority leader, decided that two parallel inquiries—one by the Commerce Committee and the other by the Judiciary Committee — would be largely duplicating.

A compromise solution was worked out with the chairmen of the two committees, Senator Edwin C. Johnson, Democrat of Colorado, and Senator Pat McCarran, Democrat of Nevada, respectively. It was that a special five-man committee to be appointed by Vice President Barkley would make a single investigation.

Taft Proposal Defeated

The Republicans objected because the Vice President, if he followed custom and named the ranking minority members of the Interstate Commerce and Judiciary Committees, would exclude two Republicans who came to the Senate with high reputations for crime investigation. They are Senators Homer Ferguson of Michigan and Forrest C. Donnell of Missouri. Senator Robert A. Taft sought to rectify this alleged defect today by offering an amendment to require Mr. Barkley to name to the special committee two minority members nominated by Senator Kenneth S. Wherry of Nebraska, the minority leader. This proposal was beaten by a strict party division of thirty-nine Democrats to thirty-one Republicans.

On the next roll-call, however, on the substitution of the special committee, four Democrats—Senators Harry F. Byrd and A. Willis Robertson, both of Virginia; James O. Eastland of Mississippi and John L. McClellan of Arkansas—joined the Republicans to tie the vote. When Mr. Barkley acted to break the deadlock it was the first time in the present session that he had cast his vote under his Constitutional right to decide ties.

After the Senate had decided on the special committee, the final passage of the crime inquiry resolution was a foregone conclusion. Senator Donnell cast the one vote against it.

Mr. Kefauver, who is expected to be chairman of the special committee, has extensive plans, including hearings in large cities where there are reputed to be organized crime syndicates with national connections. He has said that if he were selected, the inquiry would be conducted without bias and on a purely factual basis.

Senator Lucas said today that Democratic leaders wanted the investigation to be no "fishing expedition."

"I want an honest-to-God investigation with no politics," he asserted. "Let the chips fall where they may."

As the resolution was finally adopted, the special committee will have $150,000 to spend and will be required to report not later than Feb. 28. Mr. Kefauver will seek special authority to employ counsel and associate counsel at $17,500 a year each. The House must concur in this, since the salaries exceed existing ceilings for such work.

Press Services Oppose Bill

The. Commerce subcommittee, meanwhile today, continued with its hearings on gambling. It heard cautious protests from representatives of The Associated Press, The United Press, The International News Service and Transradio Press that pending proposals to prohibit or delay the transmission of certain kinds of racing news would approach violation of the freedom of the press guaranteed by the Constitution.

Frank Starzel, general manager of The Associated Press, testified that "in principle, it would be dangerous legislation." He said that odds and prices paid, as recorded on pari-mutuel betting machines in many states, were legal news in those states, and that it would be wrong to prohibit the transmission of such news across state lines.

Earl J. Johnson, vice president and general manager of The United Press Association, was unable to appear in person, and the following telegram was put in the record on his behalf:

"The United Press never takes a position on pending legislation of any kind. The basic responsibility of The United Press to its world-wide clientele is to report the news without bias or prejudice.

"It does seem to me, however. that the original bill and the alternate measure which your committee is examining might be construed as a restraint on The United Press in the performance of its main function—namely, reporting the news.

"If sports can be embargoed from interstate commerce on the grounds that it is used for gambling, then other categories of news, such as stock market quotations and even election returns, conceivably could be embargoed on the same grounds."

William D. Goode, general business manager of The International News Service, and Herbert Moore, chairman of the board of The Transradio Press Service, supported the other press witnesses in warning of possible detriment to the free press if the legislation should be enacted.

Elmer Davis, appearing for the Radio Correspondents Association of Washington, recalled that he testified thirty years ago before another Senate committee against a bill aimed at barring from the mails newspapers that carried racing news, and nothing came of that proposal.

The pending bill hits "not at the objectionable act but at the man who reports the act," Mr. Davis said, adding:

"I do not know whether the Supreme Court has ever defined the extent to which freedom of news transmission by other media than the newspaper is guaranteed by the First Amendment. For obvious reasons. certain governmental regulation of radio broadcasting is necessary; and nobody can prove that, if radio and television and motion pictures had existed at the time the Bill of Rights was adopted, the statesmen of those days would have insisted that its protection be extended to the transmission of news to the public by any means."

J. P. Taylor, Attorney General, of Missouri, told the subcommittee that he believed there was a national crime syndicate, and that it had connections with the racing news services, through control of which it could control the bookmakers.

May 4, 1950

SENATORS REVEAL GREAT CRIME RING

Narcotics Bureau Turns Up List of 800 Persons in Nation-Wide Network

By PAUL P. KENNEDY
Special to The New York Times.

WASHINGTON, June 6—A highly organized combine that is directing a nation-wide narcotics ring with inter-related interests in gambling, counterfeiting, white slavery and extortion, was described today to the Senate Crime Investigating Committee.

Officials of the Bureau of Narcotics during two hours of questioning, turned over a list of 800 persons as members of the criminal network.

Senator Charles W. Tobey, Republican of New Hampshire, speaking for the committee, said that, of the 800 names submitted, fifty were persons convicted of major crimes and about 300 persons convicted of narcotic sales. The remainder, he said, were involved in narcotics, but were also identified with other crimes, including murder.

The list will remain secret, but many persons named in it will be brought before the committee for public questioning, according to Senator Tobey.

Witnesses at Hearing

Witnesses at today's hearing were H. J. Anslinger, Commissioner of the Bureau of Narcotics; M. L. Harvey, Deputy Commissioner, and B. T. Mitchell, Bureau General Counsel.

The narcotics combine is concentrated principally in New York, Florida and California, but Senator Tobey described it as "interlaced and sprawled across the nation."

He said that names the committee had encountered in its investigation of the gambling phases of the combine recurred today in the narcotics investigation. The only name revealed, however, was that of Charles Luciano, deported vice king. The connection in which Luciano's name arose was not revealed.

The international aspects of narcotics traffic were not discussed at the hearing. However, Senator Estes Kefauver, Democrat of Tennessee, chairman of the Committee, said it was expected that the committee would eventually question a representative of the Peruvian Government who has visited this country many times in connection with traffic in cocaine between North and South America.

Few Now Under Arrest

Only a portion of the persons named on the secret list of 800 are now under arrest, Senator Tobey said. Asked why the remainder had not been arrested, the speaker answered:

"We are going to come to that. We feel that a very great weakness in this respect lies in the fact that when a conviction is obtained the sentence meted out is not in proportion to the crime."

He mentioned a bill pending in the House to increase penalties for first, second and third time narcotics violations.

Senator Tobey described the combine as a "notorious breed," well integrated, under "powerful leadership" and with "far-reaching influence." He said the possibility of politics entering the narcotics traffic had not been discussed at the hearing.

An aspect of narcotics violations to be investigated, Senator Tobey declared is the apparent inadequacy of the Narcotics Bureau's budget and man power. He said the bureau was operating with the same budget it had twenty years ago and as a consequence its man power had been impaired. He said there were only 175 Federal narcotics agents in the bureau now.

The committee has not as yet received reports on the amount of narcotics traffic in this country, according to Senator Tobey. It expects to have something definite, however before beginning its questioning of persons on the list.

Senator Kefauver said the committee planned to hold hearings soon in various cities over the country.

June 7, 1950

AFTER THAT $2 BET IS LAID—WHERE THE MONEY GOES

Bookmaker Takes a Good Bite and His Many Helpers Also Get a Cut

By CHARLES GRUTZNER

The horse player who hands $2 to some fellow in his office building, the housewife who places her wager with a neighborhood runner, and the bigger bettor who phones his play directly to the "bookie" are getting a clearer insight these days into what happens to their money.

The average player is beginning to understand how part of every dollar he bets pays the runner's commission, part goes to buy police protection or to bribe other officials, part pays the bookmaker's huge telephone and telegraph costs and still another part stays in the bookmaker's pocket.

Much light has been shed on the mechanics of the gambling racket by the recent investigations on the part of local district attorneys and grand juries and by a Senate group in Washington. A great deal more will be shed during the trial, scheduled to start tomorrow, of Frank Erickson, pudgy central figure in many gambling ventures. He is accused of conspiracy and bookmaking.

A Giant Business

Illegal gambling is one of the biggest businesses in this country of giant enterprises. It has been estimated that $8 billion is wagered each year with bookmakers on the outcome of horse races. This dwarfs the $1.6 billion that is bet legally at the nation's tracks through pari-mutuel machines, which yield $100,000,000 tax revenue to states and localities.

The numbers game does an illegal business of at least $3 billion a year, slot machines take another $1 billion, and $1 billion is bet on baseball, prizefights and other sporting events, according to the American Academy of Political and Social Science. This does not include the "take" of roulette, dice and other games in commercial gambling houses.

The big illegal profit in booking horse races is made possible, strange as it may seem, by the "bite" that the pari-mutuel machines take legally out of wagers made at the track. At the local tracks, the state and the track operators split 10 per cent of the betting pool and the city gets another 5 per cent. This means that for every dollar bet at the track only 85 cents is divvied up among the holders of tickets on horses "in the money."

No Bookmaker Taxes

The bookmaker, who is outside the law, does not contribute to the state or city coffers or the track's upkeep. He pays off his customers at the published pari-mutuel prices, which means that the 15 per cent "bite" is his pudding. On this basis, at least $1 billion is taken out of the game by bookmakers each year.

The bookmaker gets, or takes, still another advantage by setting a limit, usually 50-20-10, on his pay-offs.

This means that he will pay no more than 50 to 1 on a win bet, 20 to 1 on a place bet and 10 to 1 for show, regardless of the official price. Thus, if a long shot romps home and pays $136.50 for a $2 win ticket, $68.70 for place and $32 show to track bettors, the bookie's customers will collect only $102 for win, $42 place and $22 show.

Making book is so profitable that the racketeers offer inducements to promote business. The agent or runner who picks up bets in offices and shops or operates from a candy store or tavern gets 5 per cent for all bets he delivers, "hot or cold"; that is, he gets his commission whether the bet wins or loses.

Partnership Arrangement

Some bookmakers offer their runners partnerships. The picker-up of bets is allowed to retain half on all losing bets. On winning bets 50 per cent is marked against his account, and he draws no commission until he brings in enough losing bets to wipe out his debit. The junior partner is never expected to dig into his own pocket. It is axiomatic that no matter how hard a book is hit occasionally, it is bound to show a profit over a period of time.

The ingenuity that bookies exercise to get new business was highlighted in records seized by Missouri state police who raided "a horse parlor" in a St. Louis suburb two weeks ago. It was established that a gambling syndicate had offered managers of Western Union telegraph offices in many parts of the country a 25 per cent cut on all losing bets they wired to the bookmakers.

Business Tie-In

Printed instructions from the syndicate as to how the Western Union employes should handle the bets were taken by the police, along with copies of messages of thanks to the bookies by the telegraph managers for their rake-off. The St. Louis raid was made on the basis of information obtained by New Jersey police in a raid on the Western Union office at Bridgeton, and indicates how organized gambling gets its tentacles around legitimate business.

The $2 business is usually handled, without going further, by the bookmaker to whom the runner brings it. Heavy betting on one horse in a race sometimes unbalances a book so that the bookmaker risks a big loss if the horse should win. In that case, he lays off some of the wagers to another bookmaker, whose clients may favor another horse. The bookmaker's aim is to balance the wagers so that he takes a profit no matter which horse wins.

Laying off of bets is usually done as a courtesy among bookmakers of similar status and involves neither commission nor service charge. When, as sometimes happens with a widely circulated tip, all the neighborhood books are heavy on the same horse the bookmakers lay off to the syndicate or to one or two top bookmakers in town.

The "bookies' bookies" operate on reverse commission and charge the smaller books 5 per cent for taking risky business off their hands. The big bookmaker, in turn, often pours his excess play into the pari-mutuel machines. He can lay off until almost post time at the track, where he has an underling waiting with a roll of banknotes. At local tracks, which have no public telephones, the money man gets his signal from an agent outside the gate.

Significance of Records

A truckload of records was seized by New York District Attorney Frank S. Hogan's men in a raid on Frank Erickson's Park Avenue office a few days after the big shot had told a Washington hearing that he took bets in violation of the law to the tune of $20,000 to $40,000 a day and conducted that racket entirely by telephone.

The records go far beyond Erickson's profit from the ponies. They give a glimpse into the interlocking directorates of the country's underworld activities, which will assuredly be explored more fully during the Erickson trial.

Of more than surface interest in the Erickson records is the repeated listing of "charity" disbursements, which always come to a proportionate share of each partner's receipts from the gambling venture. It is believed "charity" was the euphemism for bribery of public officials. District Attorney Miles F. McDonald of Brooklyn asserts that notations of "ice" payments found in gambling raids in that borough represent protection money paid to police.

Police Implicated

It was Mr. McDonald who started the current interest in the gambling racket and its possible tie-in with the police last December. With a special anti-gambling squad, to which he appointed rookie cops unknown to the regular members of the force, he has surprised members of one detective division at the premises when his men raided an alleged policy bank and has uncovered "loans" by gamblers to police officers. The trial of a detective lieutenant for perjury alleged in connection with such a loan has been set for June 26 and other cases are pending.

Between the Manhattan and Brooklyn trials, the public may see the specific workings of a general situation that has been pretty well portrayed by witnesses at the Washington hearings.

FRANK COSTELLO'S STORY: FROM RUM TO RICHES

Three Decades in the Life of the Man Who Rose to the Top of Underworld

By WARREN MOSCOW

Frank Costello, the man who hid his face from the television camera, and who walked out on the Senate Committee on Crime, was a young tough, and has been an associate and boss of racketeers for the greater part of his life. He is now 60 years of age, and was first arrested at age 17 for assault and robbery. For the past three or four years he has been attempting to achieve, belatedly, the respectability that sometimes goes with the acquisition of wealth.

In between he was a small-time gunman, bootlegger, slot-machine operator, owner of gambling houses and friend and sponsor of various political figures in New York. There are numerous indications that he inherited, either as trustee or legatee, the powerful background of influence once possessed by Charles (Lucky Luciano) Lucania, though there is nothing to indicate that he was involved in the dope racket for which "Lucky" went to jail, prior to deportation.

There is one difference between Costello and others of his species, like Luciano, Capone, Johnny Torrio, or "Bugsy" Siegel, Costello, once he hit the "big money", preferred "legitimate" operations, which meant avoiding the use of force. He also shunned the spotlight, though he might brag quietly of how he could put things over.

Costello, born in Italy on Jan. 26, 1891, was brought to America by his family at age 4. His steamship ticket listed him as Francisco Castaglia, of which Frank Costello would be a rough Americanization. His mother's name was Marie Severio Aloisa, and when he was sent to jail, in 1915, for carrying a gun—the only time he ever spent in a cell—it was as Frank Severio.

Judge Edward Swann, of General Sessions, read a probation officer's report showing he had been arrested in 1908 for assault and robbery, and again in 1912, for the same offense. Judge Swann said his reputation was bad, that he was known to his neighbors in Greenwich Village as a gunman.

Jail did not reform him. His career since then can best be told in the terms of three decades—the Twenties, the Thirties and the Forties.

THE TWENTIES

After a brief swing at the punchboard business, Costello became a bootlegger soon after that activity became popular. He was indicted, along with "Big Bill" Dwyer and a host of others, for having imported whisky with the help of corrupted Coast Guardsmen. Dwyer was convicted, but Costello, in no sense a big shot at the time, got off with a "hung jury" and a dismissal of the indictment after Prohibition was repealed. He admitted to the Senate committee last week that he had been a bootlegger, who arranged for the importation of liquor from Canada into the United States for illegal resale here.

During this period he became associated with the big shots—"Joe the Boss" Masseria, Arnold Rothstein the gambler — but he stayed out of the limelight. He became an American citizen in 1925, failing to disclose on his application that he had ever been convicted of a crime, and also giving his business as real estate, instead of rum-running.

THE THIRTIES

Prohibition lasted only into the early Nineteen Thirties, and the underworld characters who had quenched America's thirst at their own risk, but also to their gain, sought other fields to employ their talents and their capital. Some of them took over legal breweries. Costello admitted talking to Johnny Torrio, fugitive from the Capone regime, about buying Prendergast Davies, a legitimate liquor house.

"Lucky" Luciano, whose lieutenant Costello seems to have been, made his entry into New York politics. His men, at the point of guns, installed Al Marinelli as a Tammany district leader in lower Manhattan. Joe Adonis, in Brooklyn, influenced the "selection" of another leader around the same period. It was a new era, in which the underworld no longer bought political protection, but furnished its own candidates to provide it. Luciano's men stole enough votes in the close 1933 election to elect a Tammany District Attorney and Borough President, though the latter office was one they had less interest in.

But neither Luciano, nor Costello could control Fiorello H. La Guardia, who knew his underworld, had even dealt with it in his earlier years. Costello by this time had carved out slot machines as his special concession. La Guardia had the police junk the machines, dump them at sea, and Costello stopped "operating" in New York.

But New York remained his headquarters, his sphere of influence. It was in New York, in 1936, that the late Huey Long discussed with Costello the legalization of the slot machines Costello was then operating in Louisiana. In 1938, he was "cut in" on the distribution of two leading brands of Scotch whisky in America. He told the Senate committee that the deal fell through, but he was pictured, five years later, as bragging, as he poured political guests a drink, that they were drinking "his" liquor.

And Costello's political guests increased during this period, for as Tammany went broker and broker during the LaGuardia regime, the underworld was able to sponsor more and more of its "friends" as district leaders. It furnished political manpower, helped to intimidate other contenders, and probably made financial contributions as well.

THE FORTIES

In 1942, when Tammany Hall leader Christy Sullivan was ousted, Luciano was in jail, and Costello was the representative of the underworld that dabbled in politics. Michael J. Kennedy Jr., who possessed only one-seventh of a full vote in the Tammany executive committee out of twenty-five full votes, was one of several candidates for the leadership. Kennedy met Costello, and secured his support. Kennedy was elected leader of Tammany Hall, and Costello's political backing became obviously important.

Since then every leader of Tammany Hall—and there have been five of them—has been chosen with at least the assent of district leaders who took advice from Costello. It showed up spectacularly in the Aurelio case, in 1943, when the then Magistrate Thomas A. Aurelio called up Costello and thanked him effusively for having obtained for him the Democratic nomination for the Supreme Court. The Republican nomination had been previously guaranteed, sight unseen, via a bi-partisan deal. Costello's wire was tapped then by District Attorney Hogan, and readings from those taps at the Senate committee hearings this week showed Costello was then participating in slot-machine sales in Louisiana, was comforting Willie Moretti, New Jersey gambler, in his California resting place and discussing the problems of harness racing with George Morton Levy, operator of the Roosevelt Raceway.

He was a partner of "Dandy Phil" Kastel in the Beverly Club, Louisiana gambling house, and had other gambling interests as well which do not show on the official record.

Private testimony given to the Senate committee and which had not figured in the public hearings at the end of their first five days here showed that Costello met with William O'Dwyer, then a Brigadier General in the Army, at Costello's penthouse suite in 1942. Additional private testimony understood to have been given by Costello himself to committee investigators was that he had frequently "put in a good word for a friend" in political dealings, though he denied issuing orders.

By the late Forties Costello had put surplus funds in real estate, oil leases and other legal activities. He was a man of wealth, and he wanted respectability. But every time Tammany got into trouble, Costello's name would figure in the headlines. Even when he threw a benefit party, at the Copacabana, for the Salvation Army he was disgusted when the newspapers made much of the fact that a host of judges and political figures had found it tactful to attend.

He got so annoyed with the publicity that he arranged for the ouster of Hugo E. Rogers as leader of Tammany Hall, and for the selection of Carmine G. DeSapio as his successor. He hoped that DeSapio would make a good, respectable leader, that the public would forget about Costello, while Costello enjoyed his golf and his friends in respectable retirement, free from politics and racket connections.

But the Senate committee last week insisted on raking up Costello's past, even after his plea, at the start of the hearings, that "I am only asking you to respect fundamental rights and principles, I am begging you to treat me as a human being."

March 18, 1951

COSTELLO INSISTS HE ISN'T IN POLITICS

Lists 14 Tammany Leaders as Mere Social Friends Since He Was 'Burned' in 1943

By RICHARD H. PARKE

Frank Costello admitted at the Kefauver committee hearing yesterday that he knew fourteen Tammany district leaders but he insisted gravely that he had not participated actively in politics since he "burned" his fingers in the Aurelio case in 1943.

As in his previous day's testimony, he sought to convince the committee that he put much too high a value on the social amenities in his frequent meetings with the leaders to discuss politics.

"Doesn't the talk invariably go to politics?" he was asked by Rudolph Halley, the committee's chief counsel.

"Well, if they do," the reputed underworld leader replied, "I don't pay no attention to them."

Costello, who is facing contempt charges, continued his refusal to disclose his "present financial worth" on the ground that to do so would be an invasion of his constitutional rights. The committee agreed to consider a legal brief on the subject by George Wolf, Costello's counsel.

Except for former Mayor William O'Dwyer, the slot machine king and Edward Corsi, State Industrial Commissioner, were the only witnesses at the afternoon session. Mr. Corsi, defeated Republican candidate for Mayor last year, repeated allegations he had made during the campaign that both his opponents—Mayor Impellitteri and former Supreme Court Justice Ferdinand Pecora—were supported in the contest by underworld elements.

Mr. Corsi charged that Thomas Luchese Brown, known as "Three Finger Brown," had been active in Democratic circles at the time. He said he had been informed by Bert Stand, former secretary of Tammany Hall, that Brown had urged the nomination of Mayor Impellitteri as a candidate for City Council President in 1945.

Costello was on the stand for nearly an hour and frequently appealed to Mr. Halley to "refreshen" his memory on the dates and places of his various meetings with political leaders. The names of the leaders with whom he admitted acquaintanceship or friendship were Carmine DeSapio, present leader of Tammany Hall; Harry R. Bell, Vincent Viggiano, Harry Brickman, Louis Di Salvio, Michael Klein, Sidney Moses, William J. Connolly, John J. Merli, Angelo Simonetti, Samuel Kantor, Edward J. McClair, Francis X. Mancuso and Frank Rossetti.

At one point in the questioning, Costello informed Mr. Halley somewhat heatedly that he was "not ashamed of nothing," and added: "I know there are a lot of technicalities here. Mr. Halley, I am going to cross my t's and, as I said before to Senator Tobey, dot my i's."

The witness drew a roar of laughter from the audience in the hearing room when he explained that a meeting between himself, Mr. DeSapio, Mr. Mancuso, Louis Valente and the late Generoso Pope, former publisher, was only to discuss a charity drive.

He agreed that the drive eventually was not staged, but he said he had been asked to use his good offices in getting the use of Madison Square Garden or the Polo Grounds.

"It was a big affair," he commented.

Disagrees With O'Dwyer

He took issue with previous testimony by former Mayor William O'Dwyer that Costello had supported the candidacy of Mr. Valente for Surrogate in 1948.

"I don't think—I didn't agree with Mr. O'Dwyer," Costello told Mr. Halley. "I don't think he made that statement. He could never have made that statement."

"Well, he made it," Mr. Halley retorted.

"Well, I can't help what statement he makes," Costello persisted. "I am making one now."

Costello, in admitting his friendship with political leaders, made it clear that on most occasions his meetings with them were purely social—a luncheon, a dinner or drink or two.

"I divorced myself from any part in politics," he explained, "but if I meet with them I'll eat with them and drink with them and if they do talk politics, I would pay no attention to them."

Costello denied that he ever had had business with Irving Sherman, a friend of Mayor O'Dwyer, or ever had talked politics with him, particularly during the 1945 mayoralty campaign.

"I knew he was for O'Dwyer," he said, "but I did not go into details what he was doing."

Mr. Halley pressed Costello on whether he had continued, in recent years, to "associate with a great many people in politics." Costello replied: "I don't know if you would call it associate—if I meet them I will talk to them and they will talk to me. And we will have a drink, or something."

The reference to former Magistrate Thomas A. Aurelio, for whom Costello is said to have obtained the Democratic nomination for the Supreme Court in 1943, came when Mr. Halley was asking Costello about his interest in the Valente candidacy.

"No," said Costello, "since the Aurelio case I burned my fingers once and I never participated in any candidates."

Mr. Corsi, in his testimony, emphasized that he did not charge that either Mr. Pecora or Mr. Impellitteri had any "direct knowledge" of meetings involving alleged criminals who discussed the candidacies of the two men.

The committee ordered the witness to supply the names of three "investigators" after he had said he had "no direct knowledge" of the charges except through information supplied by his "investigators."

IN HUDDLE AT YESTERDAY'S CRIME INQUIRY

Frank Costello, left, confers with his attorney, George Wolf

March 21, 1951

STORY OF MURDER, INC.: BIG BUSINESS IN CRIME

The activities of an underworld organization widely known as Murder Incorporated are again commanding public interest, this time as the result of hearings held here by the Kefauver crime-investigating committee. What follows is a reconstruction of the story of Murder Incorporated—its activity, its methods, its membership—based on what has been learned since its peak activity in the Nineteen Thirties.

By EMANUEL PERLMUTTER

Murder Incorporated was a gang of racketeers, with a sizable number of professional murderers on its staff, which operated in the Nineteen Thirties in Brooklyn. Its own members did not refer to it by that indelicate name: To the underworld it was the Brooklyn chapter of "The Combination," an informally organized but strong confederation of criminals who staked out claims to various areas of the United States. The late Benjamin "Bugsy" Siegel ruled on the West Coast, the Purple Gang in Detroit, the remnants of the Capone gang in Chicago and Charles "Lucky" Luciano and subsequently Louis "Lepke" Buchalter in New York.

Despite the name, murder was not the Brooklyn organization's principal trade. Its income was derived from a multitude of rackets — liquor distribution through dummy corporations; gambling; syndicated prostitution; muscling in on legitimate businesses; control of labor unions; ownership of nightclubs and roadhouses, and shake-down extortion in many forms—some crude, some refined. Murder was only a means toward an end. It was used to discipline the gang's personnel, to eliminate "competition" and to dispose of "troublemakers" — that is, law-abiding citizens who got in the way.

63 Men Murdered

Altogether, Murder Incorporated and its Manhattan affiliates are known to have executed sixty-three men in and around New York between 1931 and 1940. About as many were probably wiped out in other parts of the country. This may look like a sanguinary record, but there is a paradox behind it. Flourishing as it did in the years immediately following the repeal of prohibition, Murder Incorporated decided it would be wise policy, in view of the danger of public outrage and police crackdowns, to exercise strict control over gang killings. Murder was performed purely for business reasons, not for personal hatred or revenge.

The leaders of Murder Incorporated were Joseph Doto, better known as Joe Adonis; Abe "Kid Twist" Reles, and Albert Anastasia.

These three top men took for themselves different spheres of enterprise. Adonis had the gambling concession and the political connections, and he fronted for the organization. Anastasia was chief of Murder Incorporated's own secret police, the man who controlled the execution of balky underlings or squealers as well as the murder of persons outside the gang who interfered with its activities. (Usually death sentences were handed down by "kangaroo courts" or top individuals in "The Combination," and word of the "contract" was sent to Anastasia. No murder was permitted without his direct authorization. It was he who assigned the men to do the chore.) Reles was the field commander who directed the operations of the killers, the revenue-collectors, the beat-up artists and other rank-and-file members, sometimes participating personally in the important or "special" jobs.

Function of the "Troops"

Below these three men in the table of organization were the "troops," who performed murder for recompense. Their activities were not restricted to murder. They also served as collectors. They were paid regular salaries, from $150 to $250 a week, but they also received little domains of their own—a slot-machine concession here, a string of brothels there, or the privilege of shaking down a limited number of bookies and legitimate business men for "protection."

In the lower echelons were the $50-a-week "punks," the generic rank given to young car thieves, toughs, hoodlums, strong-arm men and killers' apprentices.

Sources of Income

Of all the gang's enterprises, the most profitable was extortion from longshoremen. This was accomplished by acquiring control of six locals of the International Longshoremen's Association, A. F. L., which had jurisdiction on the Brooklyn waterfront. This aspect of the gang's operations was jointly managed by Anastasia and Adonis. By terrorizing the locals' officials, the thugs were able to force longshoremen to fork over a percentage of their daily wages just for the privilege of working.

The gang maintained its hold by the fear it inspired among decent citizens and timid hoodlums alike. Their crimes were often ferocious. Murder victims were garrotted, punctured to death with ice picks, hacked with cleavers, buried alive in sand or lime pits, or burned alive after kerosene was poured on them. One gangster was dumped into the East River with his feet encased in cement. Another was

The New York Times

Albert Anastasia

Associated Press

Joe Adonis

thrown alive into a lake, his body anchored with two slot machines.

The victims were most often members of the gang who had turned informer (or were suspected of squealing), men who wanted to "retire," members who embezzled organization funds or non-member racketeers who were competing for business. But the hoodlums had no hesitation about wiping out law-abiding citizens too. Among these were Peter Panto, a young longshoreman who "made trouble" by trying to lead a revolt against the gang on the docks; and Morris Diamond, a teamsters union official, and Joseph Rosen, a truck owner, both of whom opposed the gangsters in the garment industry. "Lepke" Buchalter was electrocuted in 1941 for the murder of Rosen.

For a long time the Brooklyn mob managed to stay free of the law, except for an occasional pinch on minor charges, through their patronization of lawyers with political connections, usually in neighborhood Democratic clubs.

It was "Kid Twist" Reles whose defection led to the undoing of the gang. In 1940, at a hearing of one of the gang's kangaroo courts, he pleaded the case of "Pretty" Levine, a punk who wanted out.

Leniency Promised

Levine was permitted to live. He was one of the first of the gang to turn state's evidence when taken into custody by William O'Dwyer, then District Attorney in Brooklyn. Reles, realizing that he could be sent to the electric chair by Levine's testimony, made a bargain with Mr. O'Dwyer. He was promised leniency in return for informing on the rest of the gang.

On the basis of Reles' infor-

Associated Press

Abe "Kid Twist" Reles

mation Mr. O'Dwyer and his assistant, Burton Turkus, began rounding up the gang. One by one the small fry—including Levine, "Duke" Maffetore, "Blue Jaw" Magoon, Allie Tannenbaum—turned state's evidence and helped convict the professional killers.

Among those executed in the electric chair at Sing Sing were "Pittsburgh Phil" Strauss, "Happy" Maione, "The Dasher" Abbandando and "Bugsy" Goldstein. Altogether, eight men were executed and more than fifty others were sentenced to long prison terms.

Unsolved Mystery

Reles himself was killed Nov. 12, 1941, when he plunged from the window of a hotel where he was being held in protective custody as a material witness. His death holds, perhaps, the key to a major mystery about "The Combination" that remains unsolved: Why haven't Anastasia and Adonis been convicted? Their connection with the gang was never a secret to the police or to District Attorneys. In his testimony before the Kefauver committee, Mr. O'Dwyer said Reles was the one witness whose testimony could have convicted Anastasia of the murder of Morris Diamond. As Mr. O'Dwyer put it, the state's case against Anastasia went out the window with Reles. The Brooklyn District Attorney's office has since been unable to find any other witnesses whose testimony could be used successfully against Anastasia. Nor has it been able to convict Adonis, who has been indicted at various times on charges of kidnaping, extortion and assault.

Anastasia and Adonis are still alive, active and affluent. Anastasia, now 47 years old, was excused because of illness from testi-

fying at public hearings of the Kefauver committee. But in an appearance before a closed hearing in February, he denied all the crimes attributed to him and said he was a respectable business man, with a dress factory at Hazleton, Pa.

Adonis, now 52, has been cited for contempt of the Senate for his refusal to answer questions asked by the Kefauver committee. There is also pending against him a New Jersey indictment, charging him with operation of gambling establishments. Like Anastasia, he says he is a legitimate business man, his major enterprise being the hauling of new automobiles in the New York area.

Puzzle of Reles' Death

The death of Reles himself adds a corollary, final touch of mystery to the activities of Murder Incorporated. Mr. O'Dwyer told the Kefauver committee he believed Reles fell as he was trying to es-

cape. The police say he died in an attempt to play a practical joke. They say he tied some sheets together and let himself out the window, intending to enter a window on the floor below. Then, so this explanation goes, he planned to return upstairs, walk through the door of his room and surprise his six-man police guard.

But Senator Charles W. Tobey, Republican of New Hampshire, refused to believe the story of what he called the "peek-a-boo" gag. He offered the theory that Reles may have been thrown from that window to destroy the state's murder case against Anastasia. And last week Edward S. Silver, chief assistant to District Attorney Miles F. McDonald of Kings County, announced he had acquired some new information about Reles' death, which he refused to divulge. Police Commissioner Thomas F. Murphy already has begun an investigation into the circumstances of Reles' death.

Martin "Bugsy" Goldstein

April 1, 1951

O'DWYER ACCUSED IN KEFAUVER REPORT OF CONTRIBUTING TO RISE IN CRIME HERE

CRIME HERE SCORED

City Called Major Center —Hogan and McDonald Praised for Fight

NO CONCLUSIONS ON CRANE

Committee Says Luciano Parole Must Be Justified on Basis Other Than Aid in War

Special to THE NEW YORK TIMES.

WASHINGTON, May 1—The report of the Senate Crime Investigating Committee, made public today, identified New York City as "one of the major centers of organized crime," headquarters of the Frank Costello-Joe Adonis-Meyer Lansky "crime syndicate." At the same time the committee cited the city as one that stood out, in favorable contrast to

others, because of the fight being waged against organized crime by District Attorneys Frank S. Hogan and Miles McDonald.

The committee made Costello and former Mayor William O'Dwyer the bullseyes of its New York target shooting, declaring that all that came out about the city could best be told by constant references to the testimony of the two men, racketeer and public official.

Accuses Costello of Perjury

In the case of Mr. O'Dwyer, the committee declared that a single pattern of conduct dominated his official activities, that "no matter what the motivation of his choice, action or inaction, it often seemed to result favorably for men suspected of being high up in the rackets."

The committee accused Costello of consistent perjury. It found, despite his denials, that he had been a continuing force in city politics long after the 1943 date that he set for his own retirement from politics; that he was not the business man today that he pretended to be, but still seemed to be engaged in various illegal activities,

which the committee found hard to trace.

About Mr. O'Dwyer, the committee found the following:

1. That while Mr. O'Dwyer, as Brooklyn prosecutor, had broken up Murder, Inc., he never touched, by indictment or prosecution, the six men he himself had told a grand jury in 1945 were the big bosses of the crime combination, Adonis, Benjamin (Buggsy) Siegel, Lansky, Abner (Longie) Zwillman, William (Willie) Moretti, and Charles (Lucky Luciano) Lucania, all of whom, the committee said, were friends of Costello.

2. That Mr. O'Dwyer found various reasons for not prosecuting Albert Anastasia, waterfront racketeer, until after the principal witness against Anastasia, Abe Reles, was killed by an unexplained fall from a window while in protective custody of the police.

3. That John Harlan Amen's investigation of the Brooklyn waterfront rackets in 1940 was superseded by an O'Dwyer investigation, and that after he got the books and papers Mr. Amen had had to go to court to get, Mr. O'Dwyer suspended the investigation to the point of complete discontinuance.

4. That Mr. O'Dwyer, as Mayor, made various gestures in the direction of suppressing illegal

bookmaking, through Frank C. Bals and later Investigation Commissioner John M. Murtagh, now Chief City Magistrate, but nothing ever came of them.

5. That Mr. O'Dwyer constantly denounced Tammany Hall and Costello, but never told the public he had gone to Costello "for aid in war contracts frauds," and had met Michael J. Kennedy Jr., then leader of Tammany Hall, at Costello's apartment on that occasion. He appointed Costello's friends to public office after he had denounced the underworld leader, the committee noted, and admitted close friendship with Irving Sherman, identified by the committee as a friend of Costello and Adonis.

No Conclusion on Crane Story

The committee refused to draw a conclusion from the conflicting testimony of John P. Crane, president of the Uniformed Firemen's Association, that he had given Mr. O'Dwyer $10,000 in cash on the porch of Gracie Mansion, and Mr. O'Dwyer's flat denial that this was so. The committee said:

"It is hoped that the continued investigation by the District Attorney of New York County will produce concrete evidence to establish the truth."

The committee questioned the

NAMED CRIME LEADER

Frank Costello before the investigating group last March.
The New York Times

udgment of Governor Dewey in aroling Luciano. It declared that hile Mr. Dewey, as District Attorney, had sent Luciano to prison, he latter managed to maintain his contacts with the mob" while in ing Sing and that Lansky worked o get Luciano out, which happened in 1946. Noting that information had been given out that uciano had been paroled because f valuable services in the war, the ommittee found no basis for that onclusion, and added:

"It now appears that the parole ust be justified on some basis ther than that of Luciano's con-ribution to the war effort."

The report told of Lansky and ostello going to Ellis Island to ay good-by to "Lucky," spending t least a half hour alone with him nd of a party held for him the ight before he sailed. The com-ittee pictured the immigration uards remaining at a discreet dis-ance, while husky longshoremen rotected the guests from visitors nd newspapermen.

In dealing with Costello's im-ortance in this city, the commit-ee declared that the single point at Mr. O'Dwyer made a personal all on Costello in 1942 for the vowed purpose of cleaning up po-ntial war frauds at Wright Field, hio, was evidence of the gam-er's status.

The record is complete "with vidence of persons in high polit-al positions going to Costello's ome at Costello's call," the com-ittee held.

It took up Costello's contention

that he was a legitimate business man and found that business took little of his time. He did own a parcel of real estate, but it was handled by a management company; he invested in a company making infra-red ray broilers, but knew little about the product; he invested in oil, but didn't know anything about the oil business.

"The character he gave himself as being a legitimate business man simply cannot be sustained," the committee declared.

On the illegal side, it reported that Costello had admitted a 20 per cent interest in the Beverly Club, elaborate gambling casino in Louisiana; that he once had a share of the Piping Rock Casino in Saratoga, which the committee said other evidence showed was a 30 per cent interest, and that while Costello had told the Senate Committee on Interstate and Foreign Commerce a year ago that he had nothing to do with bookmaking for fifteen years previously, other testimony had made it difficult for the committee to believe this.

The members cited the fact that Mr. O'Dwyer said he knew Costello by reputation as a bookmaker in 1942, when he sought him out; and that starting in 1946, according to the testimony of George Morton Levy, Costello was paid $15,000 a year for four years just to keep bookmaking out of the Roosevelt Raceway on Long Island.

The committee found that it could pay little attention to Costello's testimony under oath, saying, "he admits as much as he has to and does not hesitate to change his story to suit the occasion."

It found that while the New York office of the Bureau of Naturalization and Immigration had at least once urged Costello's denaturalization, on the grounds of fraud perpetrated when he became a citizen, it was probable that he could not be deported as matters now stand.

But if he were convicted for perjury before the Senate committee and for his illegal gambling activities in Louisiana, he probably would be subject to deportation, the committee declared. It urged "careful study and aggressive action" along this line.

In dealing with Costello's political connections here, it noted that he had complete domination over Tammany Hall in 1942, when Mr. Kennedy was leader, and that his influence did not end when Mr. Kennedy went out. Hugo Rogers was a close friend of Costello's and the four men on the Tammany steering committee during Mr. Rogers' leadership, Francis X. Mancuso, Harry Brickman, Sidney Moses and Carmine G. DeSapio, were all "very good friends" of Costello's, the committee said.

It cited as proof of Costello's continued influence the fact that in 1949 Charles Lipsky got Irving Sherman to take him to see Costello to get support for Mr. Lipsky's candidate for Mayor in the event that Mr. O'Dwyer did not run for re-election.

"It is apparent to the committee that despite Costello's protesta-

STUDYING CRIME INQUIRY REPORT

Senators Estes Kefauver, right, and Herbert R. O'Conor discussing a passage in the findings of the committee. Mr. O'Conor will succeed Mr. Kefauver as chairman when the group resumes its hearings.
The New York Times (by Bruce Hoertel)

tions, his sinister influence is still strong in the councils of the Democratic party organization of New York County."

The committee found no Costello influence in Brooklyn apart from that of his friend, Adonis, whom the committee pictured as a man of such importance that leading politicians came to eat at his speakeasy, later restaurant, even though it was in an out-of-the-way, run-down neighborhood.

In dealing with Mr. O'Dwyer's failure to prosecute Anastasia and free the waterfront from its rackets, the committee noted that it did not have time at its public hearings to detail the results of its own investigation, but that it found that:

"The racketeers are firmly entrenched along New York City's waterfront with the resulting extortions, shakedowns, kickbacks from wages, payroll padding, gangster infiltration of unions and large scale gambling.

"Most significant to the committee is that the gangster who still appears to be the key to waterfront racketeering in New York is the same Albert Anastasia."

The report dealt with bookmaking and betting in New Jersey in connection with the New York situation. It found that the gamblers moved to Jersey during the admin-

istration of Fiorello H. La Guardia and most of them kept their headquarters there during the O'Dwyer regime, despite increased freedom of activity in New York.

The committee said that the gamblers operated with impunity in New Jersey, particularly in Bergen County, and that later they began running gambling houses there, depending on New York City clientele brought across the river in private cars. The players received the best to eat and drink, free of charge.

The report identified as New Jersey gamblers Adonis, Salvatore Moretti, Anthony Guarino, James Lynch, James Rutkin, Arthur Longano and Jerry Catena. It said all had close associations with notorious racketeers and several were friends of Costello.

While the Bergen gambling houses reported maximum profits of $250,000 a year for income tax purposes, the committee held it obvious, on the basis of $1,000,000 a month in checks that were banked in New York City alone, that the profits must have run to millions of dollars a year. The committee voiced the suspicion that the men on record as partners in the enterprises in New Jersey were merely dummies for the top members of the eastern crime syndicate.

May 2, 1951

Text of Conclusions and Excerpts From Recommendations of Senate Crime Inquiry Report

WASHINGTON, May 1 (AP)—Following are the text of the general conclusions and a partial text of the recommendations reached by the Senate Crime Investigating Committee in its report filed with the Senate today:

General Conclusions

[1]

Organized criminal gangs operating in interstate commerce are firmly entrenched in our large cities in the operation of many different gambling enterprises such as bookmaking, policy, slot machines, as well as in other rackets such as the sale and distribution of narcotics and commercialized prostitution. They are the survivors of the murderous underworld wars of the prohibition era.

After the repeal of the prohibition laws, these groups and syndicates shifted their major criminal activities to gambling. However, many of the crime syndicates continued to take an interest in other rackets such as narcotics, prostitution, labor and business racketeering, black marketing, etc.

[2]

Criminal syndicates in this country make tremendous profits and are due primarily to the ability of such gangs and syndicates to secure monopolies in the illegal operations in which they are engaged. These monopolies are secured by persuasion, intimidation, violence, and murder.

The committee found in some cities that law-enforcement officials aided and protected gangsters and racketeers to maintain their monopolistic position in particular rackets. Mobsters who attempted to compete with these entrenched criminal groups found that they and their followers were being subjected to arrest and prosecution while protected gang operations were left untouched.

[3]

Crime is on a syndicated basis to a substantial extent in many cities. The two major crime syndicates in this country are the Accardo - Guzik - Fischetti syndicate, whose headquarters are Chicago; and the Costello-Adonis-Lansky syndicate based in New York.

Evidence of the operations of the Accardo-Guzik-Fischetti syndicate was found by the committee in such places as Chicago, Kansas City, Dallas, Miami, Las Vegas, Nev., and the West Coast.

Evidence of the Costello-Adonis-Lansky operations was found in New York City, Saratoga, Bergen County, N. J., New Orleans, Miami, Las Vegas, the West Coast, and Havana, Cuba.

These syndicates, as well as other criminal gangs throughout the country, enter profitable relationships with each other. There is a close personal, financial, and social relationship between top-level mobsters in different areas of the country.

[4]

There is a sinister criminal organization known as the Mafia operating throughout the country, with ties in other nations, in the opinion of the committee. The Mafia is the direct descendant of a criminal organization of the same name originating in the Island of Sicily. In this country, the Mafia has also been known as the Black Hand and the Unione Siciliano.

The membership of the Mafia today is not confined to persons of Sicilian origin. The Mafia is a loose-knit organization specializing in the sale and distribution of narcotics, the conduct of various gambling enterprises, prostitution, and other rackets based on extortion and violence.

The Mafia is the binder which ties together the two major criminal syndicates as well as numerous other criminal groups throughout the country. The power of the Mafia is based on a ruthless enforcement of its edicts and its own law of vengeance, to which have been creditably attributed literally hundreds of murders throughout the country.

[5]

Despite known arrests records and well - documented criminal reputations, the leading hoodlums in the country remain, for the most part, immune from prosecution and punishment, although underlings of their gang may, on occasion, be prosecuted and punished.

This quasi-immunity of top-level mobsters can be ascribed to what is popularly known as the "fix." The fix is not always the direct payment of money to law-enforcement officials, although the committee has run across considerable evidence of such bribery.

The fix may also come about through the acquisition of political power by contributions to political organizations or otherwise, by creating economic ties with apparently respectable and reputable business men and lawyers, and by buying public g...i-will through charitable contributions and press relations.

[6]

Gambling profits are the principal support of big-time racketeering and gangsterism. These profits provide the financial resources whereby ordinary criminals are converted into big-time racketeers, political bosses, pseudo business men, and alleged philanthropists.

Thus, the $2 horse bettor and the 5-cent numbers player are not only suckers because they are gambling against hopeless odds, but they also provide the moneys which enable underworld characters to undermine our institutions.

The legalization of gambling would not terminate the widespread predatory activities of criminal gangs and syndicates. The history of legalized gambling in Nevada and in other parts of the country gives no assurance that mobsters and racketeers can be converted into responsible business men through the simple process of obtaining state and local licenses for their gambling enterprises. Gambling, moreover, historically has been associated with cheating and corruption.

The committee has not seen any workable proposal for controlled gambling which would eliminate the gangsters or the corruption.

[7]

Rapid transmission of racing information and gambling information about other sporting events is indispensable to big-time bookmaking operations. This information is presently being provided by a monopoly operated by the Continental Press Service. The Continental Press Service, at critical times and in crucial places where monopoly of bookmaking is at stake, yields to the domination and control of the Accardo - Guzik - Fischetti crime syndicate, to which it is beholden for its own monopoly in the wire-service field.

The wire service is so vital to large bookmakers that they are compelled to pay what the traffic will bear to the Continental Press Service. This makes it possible for the Accardo - Guzik - Fischetti crime syndicate to participate in the profits of bookmaking operations throughout the country.

[8]

The backbone of the wire service which provides gambling information to bookmakers is the leased wires of the Western Union Telegraph Company. This company, in many parts of the country has not been fully cooperative with law-enforcement officials who have been trying to suppress organized criminal rackets which make use of telegraph facilities.

By permitting its facilities to be used by bookmakers, Western Union has given aid and comfort to those engaged in violation of gambling laws. In some cases, Western Union officials and employes actually participated in bookmaking conspiracies by accepting bets and transmitting them to bookmakers.

It should be noted that during the latter months of the committee's investigation, Western Union has taken steps to prevent this practice and has been more cooperative with the committee.

In many areas, of which New York is a notable example, the telephone companies have cooperated fully with law-enforcement officials. However, in still other areas, telephone companies have been much less cooperative.

Local legislation is apparently necessary in many states to require telephone company officials to refuse facilities and remove existing facilities of suspected bookmakers and to call to the attention of local law-enforcement officials the use of telephone facilities by bookmakers.

[9]

Crime is largely a local problem. It must be attacked primarily at the local level, with supplementary aid, where appropriate, from state and Federal authorities. The conduct of various forms of gambling enterprises, houses of prostitution, the distribution of narcotics, the use of intimidation, violence, and murder to achieve gang objectives are all violations of state laws.

The public must insist upon local and state law-enforcement agencies meeting this challenge and must not be deceived by the aura of romanticism and respectability, deliberately cultivated by the communities' top mobsters.

[10]

The Federal Government has the basic responsibility of helping the states and local governments in eliminating the interstate activities and interstate aspects of organized crime, and in facilitating exchange of information with appropriate safeguard between the Federal Government and local and state law-enforcement agencies as well as between law-enforcement agencies in the various states.

The task of dealing with organized crime is so great that the public must insist upon the fullest measure of cooperation between law-enforcement agencies at all levels of government without buck-passing. The committee feels that it has fully demonstrated the need for such cooperation. The time for action has arrived.

[11]

Wide-open gambling operations and racketeering conditions are supported by out-and-out corruption in many places. The wide open conditions which were found in these localities can easily be cleaned up by vigorous law enforcement.

This has been demonstrated in the past in many different communities and has received added demonstration during the life of our committee. The outstanding example is Saratoga, N. Y., which ran wide open through the racing season of 1949 but was closed down tight in 1950.

[12]

Venal public officials have had the effrontery to testify before the committee that they were elected on "liberal" platforms calling for wide-open towns. The committee believes that these officials were put in office by gamblers and with gamble money, and that in the few cases where the public was convinced that gambling is good for business, this myth was deliberately propagated by the paid publicists of the gambling interests.

In many wide-open communities, so-called political leaders and law-enforcement officials have sabotaged efforts of civic-minded citizens to combat such wide-open conditions and the crime and corruption that they entailed.

[13]

The Treasury of the United States has been defrauded of huge sums of money in tax revenues by racketeers and gangsters engaged in organized criminal activities. Huge sums in cash handled by racketeers and gangsters are not reflected in their income tax returns.

Income tax returns filed with the Federal Government have been inadequate since, as a rule, they contained no listing of the sources of income nor any itemization of the expenses. Gangsters and racketeers, moreover, do not keep books and records from which it might be possible to check tax returns.

[14]

Mobsters and racketeers have been assisted by some tax accoutants and tax lawyers in defrauding the Government. These accountants and lawyers have prepared and defended income tax returns which they knew to be inadequate. At the very least, those who are guilty of such practices could be convicted of a misdemeanor and sent to jail for a year for every year in which they have failed to comply with the law.

The Bureau of Internal Revenue states that it has, to the best of its ability, considering its limited manpower, been investigating these returns. It states further that when it pursues the case of one of these individuals, it prefers to set up against him a case of criminal tax evasion which is a felony, rather than the lesser offense of failing to keep proper books and records, which is a misdemeanor.

Despite this, the committee believes that the Bureau of Internal Revenue could, and should, make more frequent use of the sanctions provided for failure to keep proper books and records than it has heretofore. In any event, the Bureau of Internal Revenue should insist on adequate returns and proper books.

While the great majority of agents of the Bureau of Internal Revenue are honest and efficient, there have been relatively few instances in different parts of the country of lack of vigorous and effective action to collect income taxes from gangsters and racketeers.

[15]

A major question of legal ethics has arisen in that there are a number of lawyers in different parts of the country whose relations to organized criminal gangs and individual mobsters pass the line of reasonable representation. Such lawyers become true "mouthpieces" for the mob. In individual cases, they have become integral parts of the criminal conspiracy of their clients.

[16]

Evidence of the infiltration by

THE SENATE CRIME COMMITTEE MAKING ITS REPORT

Investigators giving details to reporters in Washington yesterday. At the table, left to right, are Senators Lester C. Hunt, Alexander Wiley, Estes Kefauver, Charles W. Tobey and Herbert R. O'Conor.
The New York Times (Washington Bureau)

organized criminals into legitimate business has been found, particularly in connection with the sale and distribution of liquor, real-estate operations, night clubs, hotels, automobile agencies, restaurants, taverns, cigarette-vending companies, juke-box concerns, laundries, the manufacture of clothing, and the transmission of racing and sport news.

In some areas of legitimate activity, the committee has found evidence of the use by gangsters of the same methods of intimidation and violence as are used to secure monopolies in criminal enterprise.

Gangster infiltration into business also aggravates the possibility of black markets during a period of national emergency such as we are now experiencing. Racketeers also have used labor unions as fronts to enable them to exploit legitimate business men.

[17]

In some instances legitimate business men have aided the interests of the underworld by awarding lucrative contracts to gangsters and mobsters in return for help in handling employes, defeating attempts at organization, and in breaking strikes. And the committee has had testimony showing that unions are used in the aid of racketeers and gangsters, particularly on the New York waterfront.

Recommendations

The committee has received many recommendations for controlling organized crime and improving the enforcement of the criminal law and the administra-

tion of criminal justice. Those recommendations have been received from a variety of sources: from public officials, experts on law enforcement, lawyers, accountants, and interested laymen. They all have been given careful attention.

The committee is convinced that there is no single panacea for the widespread social, economic, and political evils that have been uncovered in the many cities in which it has made investigations and held hearings. The committee feels, nevertheless, that while organized crime cannot be completely eliminated from our society, this is no reason for defeatism, for vigorous law enforcement can control organized crime to the point where it is no longer a menace to our institutions.

Any program for controlling organized crime must take into account the fundamental nature of our governmental system. The enforcement of the criminal law is primarily a state and local responsibility. While channels of interstate communication and interstate commerce may be used by organized criminal gangs and syndicates, their activities are in large measure violations of local criminal statutes.

When criminal gangs and syndicates engage in bookmaking operations, operate gambling casinos or slot machines, engage in policy operations, peddle narcotics, operate houses of prostitution, use intimidation or violence to secure monopoly in any area of commercial activity, commit assaults and murder to eliminate competition, they are guilty of violating state laws and it is upon state and local prosecuting agencies, police and courts, that

the major responsibility for the detection, apprehension, prosecution and punishment of offenders rests.

The crisis of law enforcement which has been uncovered by the committee is basically a state and a local crisis. * * *

While the Federal police and prosecuting agencies cannot be substituted for state and local law enforcement in dealing with organized crime, the Federal Government still has a major and vital responsibility in this field. The Federal Government must provide leadership and guidance in the struggle against organized crime, for the criminal gangs and syndicates have nation-wide ramifications. It should establish additional techniques to provide maximum coordination in law-enforcement agencies to insure complete efficiency. * * *

It is with the aforementioned goals in mind that the following recommendations are formulated:

[1]

The Congress, through a continuation of this committee, should for a further limited period continue to check on organized crime in interstate commerce. The basic function of the committee should be to scrutinize the efforts made by the Federal agencies to suppress interstate criminal operations, and particularly the racket squads described in the second recommendation. It will also follow up the legislative recommendations made in this report.

The committee should receive periodic reports from the racket squads recommended to be established in the Justice and Treasury Departments. It should continuously scrutinize the effectiveness of these squads. It should also take steps to facilitate greater cooperation between Federal and state law enforcement agencies. The committee should use its subpoena power to hold hearings from time to time concerning crime situations in which there is a great public interest, or which should be called to the attention of the public.

[2]

A racket squad should be organized in the Justice Department.

The function of this racket squad, which might appropriately be placed in the Criminal Division of the department, must be to clean the country of racketeers, gangsters, and organized criminal gangs by utilizing any lawful means available, including:

(A) Prosecution for Federal crimes;

(B) On-the-spot racket grand jury investigations and inquiries; these, as suggested by the Attorney General, should be held in each judicial district at least once each year;

(C) Gathering and correlating information about gangsters and criminals from all sources, both Federal, state and local;

(D) Stimulating local prosecutions by turning information concerning local criminal situations over to state and local authorities for action. Of course, in such cases proper caution must be exercised to avoid turning information over to corrupt officials or to officials who would use it for political advantages;

(E) Turning information on criminals and gang activities over to specific Federal agencies such as Immigration and Naturalization, Customs and the tax-collecting authorities, for action thereon;

(F) Reporting to this Senate committee and its successor, as well as other appropriate committees.

[3]

Appropriate legislation should be set up an independent Federal crime commission in the Executive Branch of the Government.

This commission should be appointed by the President on the advice and consent of the Senate. It should be composed of three members all of whom are prominent citizens and not otherwise members or employes of the Federal Government. It should be organized promptly and be ready to function on Sept. 1, 1951, the date set for the expiration of authority of this committee * * *.

The functions of the Federal crime commission should be:

1. The continuing study and surveillance of operations of interstate criminal organizations throughout the country.

2. Reports on such criminal activities at periodic intervals to the Interstate and Foreign Commerce Committee of the United States Senate.

3. To make recommendations for hearings to the Interstate and Foreign Commerce Committee of the United States Senate or any other appropriate committee in cases in which the interstate and foreign commerce committee may not be the most appropriate, for more intensive investigation requiring the testimony of witnesses under oath.

4. The maintenance of liaison between Federal investigative and law-enforcement agencies and crime commissions at the state and locals levels with the dissemination to the latter of information respecting criminal operations as may be required in the public interest.

5. Suggestion and encouragement of legislation designed to expedite, facilitate, and encourage better and more intensive law enforcement at all levels of government.

6. The initiation and development of appropriate social study relating to crime, its punishment, and law enforcement.

7. The maintenance of files and records as a national clearing house of information respecting criminal activities in interstate commerce to be made available to properly authorized individuals and groups, subject to suitable security measures, but not to conflict with the interests of any presently established Federal, state, or local law enforcement agency.

Recommendation III is concurred in by all members of the committee except Senator Alexander Wiley who, while appreciating some of the advantages which might be achieved under a Federal crime commission, believes that the possible abuses of such a new agency require his opposition to the proposal. * * *

Senator Wiley believes that voluntary cooperation among Federal investigation agencies can achieve most of the objectives which the committee majority believes can only be obtained by a Federal crime commission. * * *

[4]

The establishment of the Special Fraud Squad by the Bureau of Internal Revenue of the Treasury Department is one of the most effective and useful steps taken to collect taxes from the criminal element. The committee applauds the department for this act and recommends that it be supported with necessary appropriation and that it work in close cooperation with the special racket squad, if set up by the Department of Justice as is recommended by the committee. The Bureau of Internal Revenue should maintain on a current and continuing basis a list of known gangsters, racketeers, gamblers, and criminals whose income-tax returns should receive special attention by a squad of trained experts. Procedures leading to prosecution should be streamlined and speeded up. * * *

This [criminal] list should be supplemented by names furnished by all Federal law-enforcement agencies, by the racket squads of the Justice and Treasury Departments, and by names solicited from the leading state and local law enforcement agencies throughout the country. * * *

It is obvious to anyone familiar with income-tax prosecutions that the procedures presently employed by the Department of Justice and the Bureau of Internal Revenue are entirely too laborious and time consuming. Many complex steps are necessary before an income-tax prosecution is finally decided upon. The committee urges the Bureau of Internal Revenue to make a study with a view to simplifying its procedures in connection with the processing of prosecutions for income-tax frauds. Swift prosecution and punishment are deterrents to crime in the tax field as much as anywhere else.

[5]

The Bureau of Internal Revenue should enforce the regulations which require taxpayers to keep adequate books and records of income and expenses, against the gamblers, gangsters, and racketeers who are continually flouting them. Violation should be made a felony.

The committee has been continually hampered in the course of its inquiry into the activities of known criminals and their political and official allies, by the failure of these individuals to keep and maintain books and records of their income and expenses. * * * Income-tax returns in most instances merely give gross figures of income and expenses without explanation of the nature of these items.

While honest business men comply with this regulation, hoodlums, venal officials, some politicians with underworld affiliations, do not. * * * The committee feels that the obligation to keep adequate books and records of account should bind not only honest business men but also those who profit from crime. Willful failure to comply with this obligation should subject the offender to prosecution and punishment. At present such failure is a misdemeanor. The law should be amended to make it a felony. * * *

[6]

Gambling casinos should be required to maintain daily records of money won and lost to be filed with the Bureau of Internal Revenue. They also should be required to maintain such additional records as shall be prescribed by the bureau. Officials of the Bureau of Internal Revenue should have access to the premises of gambling casinos and to their books and records at all times. Where the casino is operating illegally, in addition to the aforementioned obligations, the operators of the casino should be required to keep records of all bets and wagers.

The cash returns from gambling casinos are fantastic in amount. There is also, at the present time, no way in which the tax returns filed with the Bureau of Internal Revenue by the proprietors of these casinos can be adequately checked. The committee feels that one way of placing gambling casinos under control is to require them to keep daily returns to be filed with the Bureau of Internal Revenue and maintain prescribed books and records. * * *

In order to maintain even a closer check upon the operations of the illegal gambling casinos, the committee recommends that such casinos be compelled to keep a record of all wagering and betting transactions which take place within its walls. * * *

The committee is well aware that these provisions may well put illegal gambling casinos out of business.

[7]

The law and the regulations of the Bureau of Internal Revenue should be amended so that no wagering losses, expenses, or disbursements of any kind, including salaries, rent, protection money, etc., incurred in or as a result of illegal gambling shall be deductible for income-tax purposes.

Under present income-tax law and regulations, criminals and racketeers in computing their incomes for tax purposes are permitted to deduct from their gross incomes the operating expenses and wagering losses of their illegitimate gambling enterprises.

In the opinion of the committee, this is not only incongruous but highly undesirable.

If organized professional gambling is to be stopped by any Federal enactment, this recommendation is best calculated to do so. * * *

[8]

The transmission of gambling information across state lines by telegraph, telephone, radio, television, or other means of communication or communication facility should be regulated so as to outlaw any service devoted to a substantial extent to providing information used in illegal gambling.

Information is vital to large-scale bookmaking operations. The elimination of wire service to bookmakers is therefore of such importance that a practical law must be devised to effect this end. The need is all the more essential because such wire service to bookmakers is now in the hands of Continental Press Service, which enjoys an almost complete monopoly of this activity in so far as it exists on a nationwide scale.

The committee is now working on a specific bill for the purpose of accomplishing these ends, and at the same time, minimizing disadvantages which may incidentally accrue to those who are engaged in the wholly lawful dissemination of news. To the extent that they may unavoidably cause incidental inconveniences to such persons engaged in wholly lawful operations, the committee desires to suggest and urge that these disadvantages be accepted as inevitable and necessary in order to accomplish a very important public purpose. It is believed that the specific legislation will hold any such disadvantages to an absolute minimum.

In general, the committee has in mind a proposal which would require all persons engaged in the dissemination of any information concerning horse-racing or dog-racing events or betting information on any other sporting event by means of interstate or foreign communication to receive a license solely for these purposes from the Federal Communications Commission.

It is proposed that such licenses shall be freely granted to any applicant unless the commission establishes that the granting of such application would not be in the public interest, that the applicant is not of good moral character, or that the information will intentionally be disseminated directly or indirectly to any substantial number of persons who would utilize it primarily to facilitate gambling activities or other activities in violation of the laws of the various states.

No one seeking a license shall be able to evade responsibility for the ultimate use of the information provided by him merely because the ultimate user or any number of intermediate subscribers are independent legal entities.

The committee has given consideration to proposals that all dissemination of betting information in interstate commerce be declared illegal, but has rejected this proposal at least for the present in the hope that the elimination of racing-wire service primarily for gambling will effect the desired result, with the minimum disruption of legitimate news dissemination activities. * * *

The committee intends to propose in the legislation to be submitted that the operation of such a wire service without the requisite license suggested shall be made a felony.

[9]

The internal revenue laws and regulations should be amended so as to require any person who has been engaged in an illegitimate business netting in excess of $2,500 a year for any of five years previously, to file a net-worth statement of all his assets, along with his income-tax returns. * * *

In order to facilitate a check upon the income-tax returns of known criminals and racketeers, the committee recommends that they be required to file net-worth statements so that this essential beginning point for investigation will be available to the Government.

[10]

The transmission of bets or wagers, or the transmission of moneys in payment of bets or wagers, across state lines by telegraph, telephone, or any other facilities of interstate communication, or the United States mails, should be prohibited.

Large bookmaking operations cannot be carried on without using facilities of interstate commerce and interstate communication. * * *

The Federal Government should not permit interstate communication facilities or the mails to carry on bookmaking and gambling operations. It may be argued that the prohibition of all use of interstate communication facilities or the mails to place bets or send money for wagers will throw an unreasonable burden on Federal law-enforcement agencies. Thousands of small bets are made over the telephone to bookmakers. However, the Federal Government should leave the elimination of these transactions to state and local officials. It should concern itself only with the larger bookmaking operations, where the link to organized crime is more clearly apparent.

[11]

The prohibition against the transportation of slot machines in interstate commerce should be extended to include other gambling devices which are susceptible of gangster or racketeer control, such as punchboards, roulette wheels, etc. * * *

The lowly punchboard has attained the proportions of a major racketeering enterprise in many sections of the country. The committee has had before it evidence that the sale and distribution of punchboards are pushed by methods similar to those used in connection with slot machines. Since this is so, then, just as slot machines are barred from interstate commerce, so punchboards should likewise be barred. Other gambling devices, such as roulette wheels, might similarly be barred.

[12]

The penalties against the illegal sale, distribution, and smuggling of narcotic drugs should be substantially increased.

We have seen that there has been a serious increase in the narcotics traffic, particularly among teen-agers. One of the ways to curb that traffic is through the imposition of severe penalties. * * *

Mandatory penalties of imprisonment of at least five years should be provided for second offenders. * * *

[13]

The immigration laws should be amended to facilitate deportation of criminal and other undesirable aliens. To this end, the committee recommends the adoption of the legislative proposal heretofore recommended by the Commissioner of Immigration and contained in Section 241 of S. 716 (82d Cong.), now pending before the Senate Judiciary Committee.

Some of the criminals who occupy key positions in criminal gangs and syndicates in this country are alien-born. Some came into this country illegally. Some have never been naturalized. Others obtained naturalization certificates by concealing their criminal activities.

[14]

The Immigration Act of Feb. 5, 1917, should be amended to provide punishment for smuggling, concealing, or harboring aliens not entitled by law to enter or reside in the United States.

Legislation to this effect has been proposed by the Department of Justice and is endorsed by the committee. * * *

[15]

The Attorney General should be authorized to revoke suspensions of deportation and to make such revocation ground for the cancellation of certificates of naturalization granted aliens who have succeeded in getting their immigration status recognized but who are later found to be ineligible for such relief.

A bill to make this proposal effective is also pending with the House Committee on the Judiciary * * * and is endorsed by the committee and recommended for passage.

[16]

The personnel of Federal law-enforcement agencies should be materially increased. Consideration should be given to eliminating inequities in the salaries of law-enforcement officers, many of whom are woefully underpaid for the duties they perform and the risks they undertake.

In its interim report, the committee drew attention to the fact that Federal law-enforcement agencies were seriously undermanned, and recommended that increased appropriations be granted to such agencies. This action becomes particularly necessary because of the new duties which are thrust upon these agencies in connection with the struggle against organized crime. * * *

Under these circumstances the committee therefore recommends that investigative and enforcement staffs of the Government's law-enforcement agencies should be materially increased. This is particularly vital in connection with the Bureau of Narcotics. Consideration should also be given by the appropriate committees of Congress to increasing the pay of Federal law-enforcement agents to a point which will be commensurate with their responsibilities.

It should be borne in mind that higher salaries for persons engaged in law enforcement will not necessarily result in a drain on the Treasury. Better law enforcement will bring increased revenues to the Government through collection of taxes which are undoubtedly now being avoided by the underworld. * * *

[17]

The existing Federal law with respect to perjury should be tightened; the committee endorses H. R. 2260 (82d Cong.) and recommends its passage.

Under existing Federal law, a person may not be convicted of perjury for making contradictory statements under oath unless the indictment charges and the prosecution proves which of the statements is false. Under the rules of proof in perjury cases, for a conviction to be had, the falsity of the statement made under oath must be established by the testimony of two independent witnesses or by one witness and corroborating circumstances.

The committee favors a revision of the law to provide that perjury shall consist of giving under oath or affirmation, within a period of three years, willful contradictory statements on a material matter, either in proceedings before a grand jury or during the trial of a cases; and such perjury could be established by proof of the willful giving or making of such contradictory statements without proving which one is false. The Attorney General has vigorously recommended this bill.

[18]

The Attorney General of the United States should be given authority to grant immunity from prosecution to witnesses whose testimony may be essential to an inquiry conducted by a grand jury, or in the course of a trial or of a Congressional investigation.

It is clear that the granting of immunity from prosecution would present a means of obtaining needed testimony from one who might otherwise hide behind the Constitutional protection against self-incrimination. * * * This power should, of course, be exercised only with the greatest caution, and only upon the written permission of the Attorney General after he has cleared the granting of immunity with other Federal agencies which might have an interest in the matter.

[19]

The committee favors the passage of legislation providing for constructive service by publication or otherwise upon a witness whose testimony is desired who evades personal service upon him.

Because of its experience with recalcitrant witnesses who evaded service of subpoenas willfully and with obvious intent to hinder and delay the committee's investigation, the committee believes that legislation is necessary to compel the presence of evasive witnesses; hence the foregoing recommendation. * * *

[20]

The committee favors passage of the legislation recommended by the Alcohol Tax Unit of the Treasury Department to prevent racketeering elements from entering the liquor industry and to eliminate any now in it. The committee also favors passage of legislation which will extend the same Federal protection to local option states as is now extended to the wholly dry states against the illicit transportation of liquor into the dry areas.

With respect to the question of racketeering elements in the distribution of liquor there are now pending in the Congress bills * * * which were introduced by Senator McCarran [Pat McCarran, Democrat of Nevada] and Congressman King [Representative Cecil R. King, Democrat of California] and which heretofore have in previous sessions been sponsored by them and other members of Congress. The bills as they now stand require the annual renewal of basic permits to the liquor industry. The committee is of the opinion that annual renewal may impose too much of a burden upon the industry and the Alcohol Tax Unit, and the committee recommends that the proposed requirement be relaxed to the extent of requiring renewal biannually. * * *

In recommending to the committee the passage of this bill, the Alcohol Tax Unit, through its representatives, has pointed out that many of the racketeering elements now in the industry are blanketed under the original post-repeal legislation with the result that the only effective means of eliminating them would be such new legislation.

The committee does believe that the licenses of some individuals might be revoked on a positive determination that they are not persons of good moral character, who would hold licenses against the public's interest. However, the committee is aware of the practical problem involved and therefore feel that the Alcohol Tax Unit must receive the support of the Congress if it is to perform its functions effectively. The committee takes no position on features of this legislation other than the ones specified above. * * *

[21]

The committee recommends that present Federal regulation and application forms which require a listing of individual owners, partners, and holders of Alcohol Tax Unit permits, be amended, so that, in addition to the present requirements, the names of all beneficial owners will be stated; also that the application forms require the disclosure of all previous arrests and convictions. A report should be filed with the Alcohol Tax Unit of every change in such interests or in management as such occurs.

On Nov. 8, 1950, the committee called an advisory meeting of the liquor and beverage industry, representatives of the Alcohol Tax Unit and others interested to meet with the committee. * * * The industry and the Alcohol Tax Unit agreed that the foregoing recommendation would be one beneficial in preventing infiltration by racketeers into the industry, particularly at the wholesale level. They joined in this recommendation and it is highly recommended by the committee.

[22]

The committee recommends that

the Interstate Commerce Commission be required by law to consider the moral fitness of applications for certificates of necessity and convenience as one of the standards in acting upon applications for such certificates or transfers of certificates.

The transportation industry, including interstate transit systems, is especially vital to the economy and security of the nation. The committee does not by this recommendation imply that there has been a substantial infiltration by racketeers into the industry. There have, however, been some incursions, and in view of the fact that the economy of the country depends upon a competitive and completely gangster-free management of this vital segment of business, the committee feels that every means should be used to weed out the criminals and prevent them from obtaining a further foothold. * * *

The committee is giving further consideration to and expects in a later report to deal with the problem of revocation of existing permits where it has been shown to the Interstate Commerce Commission that the holders of such permits do not have the requisite moral fitness.

Where the foregoing recommendations call for new legislation, it will be drafted and submitted to the Senate by members of the committee at the earliest possible time.

JOE ADONIS' LUCK FINALLY RUNS OUT

Jail Sentence Will Cap The Climax of a Long And Shady Career

By JAMES P. McCAFFREY

A medium-sized, good-looking man, in his early thirties, was standing behind the bar of a neighborhood saloon at 260 Fourth Avenue, Brooklyn, on a warm afternoon in August, 1934. Two strangers walked in and ordered a round of drinks.

The strangers had a second round. Then one asked the bartender: "Is Joe Adonis around?"

The medium-sized, good-looking man, in his early thirties, explained that Mr. Adonis was not around. But could he help them?

The two strangers were newspaper reporters. One explained they were checking on a report that Joe Adonis was using his political influence to elect his own candidate Kings County Democratic leader in the fall primaries.

The man behind the bar said he did not know how much influence his boss, Joe Adonis, had in politics, but he invited the two strangers to have another drink on the house. In fact, before the afternoon was over the two reporters had nearly a dozen drinks—all at the expense of the bartender.

A few nights later Joe Adonis met a sports reporter, an old friend, at a Madison Square Garden affair. He related the details of the visit of the two newspaper reporters to the barroom.

Adonis in Person

"You know," Adonis said, "the regular bartender was sick that afternoon and I took over in my own joint. I sent those two reporters out on their ears and they still don't know who Joe Adonis is."

The story, a real one, is typical of Joe Adonis for the last twenty-five years. He has been sending reporters, police, lawyers, judges and prosecutors out on their ears. None of them knows him.

Described as one of the top racketeers of the country by the Kefauver Crime Investigating Committee, Joe Adonis is now awaiting his first trip to prison as a result of his "no defense" plea last Monday to charges of violations of the New Jersey gambling laws.

To his friends, Joe Adonis is considered one of the shrewdest business men in the United States today. To his enemies, mostly prosecutors, he is considered one of the most dangerous criminals now at large in the country.

Still a medium-sized, good-looking man, even though he is 49 years old (and a little paunchy),

Adonis looks like a well-to-do business man or a Wall Street broker. He dresses very conservatively—in tailor-made suits. He speaks just above a whisper in conversation. Now and then he affects a mannerism: he whispers through the corner of his mouth.

The accusations against Adonis have run the gamut—from disorderly conduct to homicide. But he has spent in his lifetime only a few hours in a jail cell, and then only to wait until his bondsman arrived with the necessary bail—it was $75,000 on one occasion. He has paid a total of only $625 in fines for minor brushes with the law.

Life of Luck

Adonis stresses the matter of luck for his success in life. He will gamble on anything. He is very much at home at a dice table, a prizefight or a race track.

But with all these varied activities, Adonis has found plenty of time to invest the money he earned as a bootlegger during the prohibition era in various legitimate enterprises. The Internal Revenue Bureau recently announced that it was checking on his income in the hope of discovering hidden earnings. But Adonis has always been known as a ready taxpayer since the repeal of prohibition in 1933.

A native of a slum area (the Gowanus Canal section of Brooklyn), Adonis was enrolled in a neighborhood elementary school as Joseph Anthony Doto. He got the alias, Adonis, from a slip of the tongue of a friendly partner in a neighborhood crap game.

But Adonis admitted that he was allergic to text books and elementary education. He never got as far as high school. He tried a dozen jobs along the near-by Brooklyn waterfront before he was introduced to Frankie Yale, Brooklyn's ranking bootlegger, in the early days of prohibition.

It was on the night of Feb. 26, 1926, that Adonis had his first brush with criminal law. He was arrested on the Brooklyn waterfront for sitting in a stolen car. In the automobile several pistols also were found. But the charges of automobile larceny and possession of pistols were dismissed a few days later. His rum-running boss, Frankie Yale, was in the courtroom.

Adonis was arrested twice again for violations of the Volstead Act. But these offenses drew only fines. Then Adonis turned to something more secure for his livelihood. He opened a speakeasy known as "Joe's Italian Kitchen" at 260 Fourth Avenue, Brooklyn, just a few blocks from his own home. You could always get an alcoholic drink in the place, but the good food also brought many patrons.

Associated Press

Joe Adonis.

Attracted to Politics

Eventually, "Joe's Italian Kitchen" attracted politicians, public officials and stage celebrities. Adonis, the host, played no political favorites; the speakeasy became the hangout for prominent Republicans as well as Democrats. Adonis began to take an active part in the political conversations.

Over the years he had watched the Irish politicians push his fellow Italians around except on Election Day. Adonis decided to do something about it. He had a wide neighborhood following because of his ready contributions to charitable causes.

"The Democrats haven't recognized the Italians," Adonis confided to a friend in 1933. "There is no reason for the Italians to support anybody but LaGuardia. The Jews have played ball with the Democrats and they haven't got much out of it. They know it now. They will vote for LaGuardia. So will the Italians."

Adonis made no secret of his financial support of Fiorello H. LaGuardia for Mayor in 1933. He contributed a large sum of money for the Republican-Fusion candidate who was opposing John P. O'Brien, Democrat, and Joseph V. McKee, the Recovery party candidate. Adonis still has a receipt for his contribution to the La-Guardia cause. But in the same municipal campaign, the speakeasy owner worked for the local Democratic candidates, many of whom frequented his emporium.

And though the politicians and high members of the Police Department gave an air of respectability to "Joe's Italian Kitchen," there was a group of hoodlums, many of them associates of Adonis in the bootlegging days, who frequented the Fourth Avenue speakeasy. They were the crew who continued at illegal enterprises—the sale of narcotics, the operation of floating crap games, the protection of waterfront hijacking, the use of racket unions and the control of loan sharks.

Gangland Arbiter

Adonis knew them all. He acted as their arbitrator in gang disputes. He used his influence with law-enforcement officials when they had trouble with the police. He was the unofficial underworld spokesman not only in Brooklyn but in many other cities, because of his bootlegging contacts.

Adonis had become a wealthy man during the prohibition era. His wealth continued to grow because of his underworld influence. But if the respectable clientele who frequent his speakeasy knew it, they had little to say about it publicly.

By 1935 Adonis was becoming a powerful figure in politics. His fellow Italians, some of them seeking public office, turned to him for political and financial advice. With his brother, Tony, Adonis decided to move out of the old neighborhood and he set up a high-class restaurant at 71 Pineapple Street, in the quiet Brooklyn Heights section. The new place continued to attract the politicians, but not many of the hoodlums felt at home there.

Adonis decided to branch out into other legitimate enterprises. Known as "J. A." to his intimates, the former speakeasy proprietor became the owner of three automobile agencies in Brooklyn. He also became the power behind an automobile-conveying service delivering new Fords into the metropolitan district from the assembly plant in Edgewater, N. J. Some of his old cronies at rum-running once had helped the management in a labor dispute in Detroit.

Heights of Influence

The former rum-runner was climbing the ladder to real respectability. The politicians turned to him for advice on how his fellow-Italians would vote in the next campaign.

So many went to Adonis for advice or money that he began to forget about the food in his restaurant. He had become the spokesman for a large bloc of Italian-Americans not only in Brooklyn but in other parts of the metropolitan area.

Then came the 1937 mayoralty campaign. Mayor La Guardia had not helped him or hurt him during his first term at City Hall. On the advice of some of his wealthy restaurant patrons, Adonis decided to support United States Senator Royal S. Copeland, who was running in the Republican and Democratic primaries for the Mayoralty nomination. The Senator was opposing Mayor La Guardia and Jeremiah T. Mahoney, the Democratic designee.

Someone told Mayor La Guardia. That was the beginning of the end for Adonis politically and socially in Brooklyn. In frequent Brooklyn speeches, Mr. La Guardia called Adonis "a gangster and the leader of the underworld."

Other prosecutors took up the cry for "good government." Adonis was booked by the New York police on a charge of hijacking a truck loaded with crude rubber. He was arraigned in Brooklyn Felony Court. The complainant said he never saw Adonis before in his life.

But Adonis lost the three automobile agencies because Mayor La Guardia demanded that his agency licenses be revoked. By 1938, Adonis sold his interest in the restaurant on Pineapple Street.

O'Dwyer on the Trail

William O'Dwyer became the District Attorney in 1940. In breaking up the Brooklyn murder rings, the Mayor-to-be predicted he would put Adonis in the electric chair if the necessary evidence was forthcoming. Adonis was considered an intimate friend of Albert Anastasia, the top waterfront racketeer, but Mr. O'Dwyer never even got around to indicting Anastasia.

John Harlan Amen, who was looking into official corruption through an appointment by Gov. Herbert H. Lehman, had Adonis indicted for kidnapping and extortion in 1940, but Adonis was never tried after a co-defendant (at a separate trial) had been acquitted by a jury.

The easy-going Adonis got tired of it all. He slipped into obscurity. His friends said he was operating gambling joints in New Jersey and in Florida. Finally, in 1944, he sold his elaborate home in the Bay Ridge part of Brooklyn and moved to New Jersey with his wife and four children. It is reported that his home in Fort Lee, N. J., is worth $100,000.

In addition to the New Jersey charge that he conspired to violate the state's gambling laws, Adonis has been cited for contempt by the Senate Crime Investigating Committee. He is also under indictment in Manhattan for violation of the gambling laws.

Luciano Rules U.S. Narcotics From Sicily, Senators Hear

By HAROLD B. HINTON
Special to The New York Times.

WASHINGTON, June 27—The Senate Crime Investigating Committee was told today that Charles (Lucky) Luciano, deported New York gangster, still ruled the narcotics traffic in the United States, operating from Sicily.

This testimony was given by Charles Siragusa, an agent of the Treasury Department's Bureau of Narcotics, who recently returned from a trip to Italy, Greece and Turkey inspecting possible sources of heroin exports to the United States.

He read to the committee from an affidavit Luciano recently submitted to Italian authorities on his sources of income. Luciano told them he had taken $22,500 with him to Italy when he was deported, and that friends in the United States had subsequently sent him gifts amounting to "a few thousand dollars."

According to the affidavit, the only commercial venture Luciano has attempted in Italy has been a pastry shop in Palermo, Sicily, and this has been a failure, after operating two years and a half.

Mr. Siragusa and George M. Belk, another agent of the Bureau of Narcotics, were not photographed or shown on the television proceedings, in line with Treasury policy to keep such agents as little known to the public as possible.

According to Mr. Siragusa's interpretation of what he found in Italy, after collaboration with the Italian police, Luciano and Nicolo Gentile, an intimate friend and notorious New York racketeer, were the only known members of the Mafia of United States origin or residence who participated in the meetings of the "grand councils," or policy gatherings, in Sicily. The Mafia is a Sicilian underworld organization.

In recognition of this distinction, the agent said, each is called "Don," a title of respect that indicates high rank in the Mafia.

Mr. Siragusa is of Sicilian descent and speaks Italian fluently, he told the committee. He said he believed the Mafia's principal source of revenue in the United States came from smuggling heroin and other narcotics into the country and distributing them.

The top leaders of the organization in the United States live in New York, he declared.

"If Luciano is not the kingpin," he said, "he is one of the royal family."

Mr. Siragusa named one Gaetano Chiofalo, known as Charlie Young, and Ralph Liguori, two other deportees, as members of the Sicilian branch of the Mafia, along with Joe Pici, who, he said, had been deported from the United States after a conviction of organized prostitution and was now Luciano's chief lieutenant in the narcotics trade in Italy.

Pici, he said, is reputed to have re-entered the United States clandestinely at least once since his deportation. Then, the agent said, he believed Pici had taken fifteen kilograms of heroin to the Mafia mob in Kansas City. The heroin sells for $1,500 a kilogram in Italy and for as much as $10,000 in Chicago, allowing handsome profits to the successful smuggler.

Last April a member of what the agent called "the 107th Street Mob" named Frank Calace was sent to Italy to pick up some heroin. On arrival he immediately made contact with Pici and bought three kilograms, the witness testified.

The Rome police got a tip on the transaction, Mr. Siragusa reported, and arrested Calace on an airplane bound for Palermo. His uncle, who has the same name and was a partner in the deal, was caught later, he said.

He criticized the State Department for issuing passports to known racketeers against the advice of his office. He told the committee that the narcotics traffic was an international business and the ability of the big dealers to travel abroad was of great help to them.

Luciano, he said he discovered in Italy, had made a trip to Germany in 1950 to organize some rackets in the Western zone. When Mr. Siragusa protested to the Italian authorities, Luciano's passport was taken away from him and it was found to contain visas for several countries bordering on Italy, indicating the deported gangster had extensive ideas for regaining his fortunes.

The committe examined Gaetano Martino, an unemployed longshoreman from Brooklyn. The witness said he had seen Luciano in Palermo in 1946 and again in 1947, but denied that he had carried any money or gifts to him or had brought anything back to the United States for him.

Mr. Belk gave an involved account of how he had gained the confidence of Robert Kimbell, whom he described as a wholesale dealer in narcotics in San Antonio, and had persuaded him to turn informer. Working under cover as Kimbell's partner, Mr. Belk obtained the evidence that broke up a large gang of narcotics merchants in Detroit and New York. Kimbell was killed last December in San Antonio by his partner in a quarrel over splitting the profits of narcotics deals.

The committee heard another string of narcotics addicts today, reciting their similar stories of starting to smoke marijuana at an early age, then graduating to the use of heroin and cocaine.

Mrs. Violet Hill Whyte, a Baltimore policewoman, described to the committee a "pad," or narcotics party, to which she had gained admittance. She said there were about twenty people, ranging in age from 17 to 25, lounging about the room in various postures, some reclining, others sitting upright, still others "kicking off" (sleeping off the effects).

She read a letter from an addict describing another "pad." Tickets for this one cost $1.50 and bore on their face the following legend:

"Chicken dinner. Come on up. Let's get high, let's laugh, let's cry."

For their tickets each client received two "reefers" (marijuana cigarettes) and a chicken leg on arrival. Music was incessant. There was a bar in the corner, where liquor, heroin and cocaine were sold. The writer of the letter said she had noticed the marijuana smokers took only soft drinks.

Harry J. Anslinger, Federal Commissioner of Narcotics, and George W. Cunningham, his deputy, told the committee they were exercising all the control of the traffic that was possible with the 180 men they had. Mr. Cunningham said he could use the entire force to advantage in New York City alone.

Mr. Anslinger recalled that the House of Representatives had just cut his office's appropriation below this year's level. He said he hoped the Senate would restore the funds.

June 28, 1951

COSTELLO IS SHOT ENTERING HOME; GUNMAN ESCAPES

Gambler Suffers Superficial Scalp Wound — Attacker Flees in Darkened Car

Frank Costello was grazed in the scalp last night by a shot fired by an unknown gunman in the lobby of his apartment building at 115 Central Park West.

The 66-year-old "boss of racketeers" was apparently attacked in old gangland style. A thug was reported to have followed Costello as he entered his apartment building, fired the single shot from six to ten feet away and then fled in a large black limousine with the lights out.

Costello, who has been free on $25,000 bail pending a Supreme Court review of a five-year prison sentence for income-tax evasion, suffered minor injury from the attack. He was taken to Roosevelt Hospital for treatment of a superficial bullet wound.

The shooting occurred about 10:55 P. M. as the former underworld chief and a friend, William Kennedy, operator of a model agency, returned from a restaurant. Costello got out of their taxicab, said good-night to Mr. Kennedy, and entered the lobby of his apartment building.

Eyewitness' Story

The doorman, Norvel Keith, told the police that just at that time he saw a limousine pull up behind the parked cab. He said a man ran out, rushed toward Costello and shot the gambler as he stepped into the lobby.

Costello dropped into a leather couch in the lobby as Mr. Kennedy, hearing the shot, rushed inside. Costello cried: "Somebody tried to get me," Mr. Kennedy said. The thug rushed back into the street, got into the car, where a driver was waiting, and sped away.

The attack was described by the police as "an apparent assassination." Costello told the police he had not seen his attacker nor heard a shot. The gambler reportedly told the police that as he entered the lobby he felt a sting and then a quick flow of flood.

At the hospital the injury was described as a scalp wound starting just behind the right ear and curving around to the nape of the neck. Doctors said the bullet had not penetrated the skull. One doctor said the bullet wound indicated that Costello had turned to face his assailant as he was shot.

Mr. Kennedy took the wounded gambler to the hospital, where he entered an emergency room at 11:08 for treatment. Before going to the hospital, Mr. Kennedy telephoned Mrs. Costello, who was with friends at the Monsignore Restaurant on East Fifty-fifth Street, near Madison Avenue.

The Costellos had just had dinner with Generoso Pope, publisher of the Italian newspaper Il Progresso, and other friends at the restaurant, and Costello had decided to return early to their penthouse apartment. The building is near Seventy-Second Street.

20 Policemen on Hand

Twenty policemen were sent immediately to the hospital, headed by Deputy Inspector Frederick M. Lussen of the Manhattan West Detective Bureau. Detectives of the Homicide Squad and a police laboratory detachment were sent to the Central Park West address for a thorough investigation.

Mrs. Costello left Roosevelt Hospital, accompanied by two policemen, who took her to the West Fifty-fourth Street station house. Five minutes later, at 12:45 o'clock this morning, Costello, showing blood stains on his jacket and shirt and displaying a bandage around his head, emerged from the hospital. He said: "I didn't see no one, I feel all right."

The police took Costello to the same station house for questioning.

Within a short time the police brought in for questioning Mr. Pope, Mr. Kennedy, the doorman and the elevator operator and George Krull, the night captain in the apartment building.

At 2:30 this morning, two detectives escorted a red-haired, fashionably dressed woman about 28 years of age into the station house for questioning. She was not identified.

It was reported that Mr. Kennedy told the police that he had gotten a good look at the assailant.

The doorman was quoted as saying that the thug was a heavy-set man, about six feet tall and wearing a dark suit and a black hat.

The police said this morning that a slug, "approximately .32-caliber," was found on the floor of the lobby.

Costello has been free on $25,000 bail pending a Supreme Court review of a five-year prison sentence that was imposed on him after he was convicted of evading $28,532 in 1948 and 1949 income taxes. He had served eleven months of the sentence.

Three and one-half years ago Costello was released from prison after serving his first jail term. However, over a long period before that he had had many brushes with the law.

Costello, who has said under oath that he is suffering from cancer, also faces denaturalization proceedings. The Government has indicated that it will try to send him back to his native Italy once it has finished prosecuting him on other charges. The denaturalization action stems from the Government's contention that Costello entered this country illegally.

An earlier effort to deport the gambler failed when the Government's case was voided on the ground that evidence obtained by wire tapping was "tainted." The Government is free to reinstitute its suit, however.

An associate and boss of racketeers for the greater part of his life, Costello was also influential in New York political affairs in the Forties.

Costello's activities were spotlighted in February and March of 1951 by the Senate Crime Investigating Subcommittee's inquiry under Senator Estes Kefauver. He was indicated for contempt of the Senate for walking out without permission from the crime hearing. He was convicted after a second trial and was sentenced to fourteen months and fifteen days in the Federal penitentiary in Milan, Mich.

In addition to his apartment at Central Park West, Costello maintains an estate at Sands Point, L. I.

May 3, 1957

The New York Times (by Larry Morris)

LEAVING HOSPITAL: Frank Costello sitting in back seat of car outside Roosevelt Hospital last night. He was treated for bullet wound in scalp inflicted by unknown gunman.

ANASTASIA SLAIN IN A HOTEL HERE; LED MURDER, INC.

TWO FIRE 10 SHOTS

By MEYER BERGER

Death took The Executioner yesterday. Umberto (called Albert) Anastasia, master killer for Murder, Inc., a homicidal gangster troop that plagued the city from 1931 to 1940, was murdered by two gunmen. They approached him from behind at 10:20 A. M. as he sat for a haircut in the Park Sheraton Hotel barber shop at Seventh Avenue and Fifty-fifth Street.

The trigger-men fired ten shots. Five took effect. The first two caught Anastasia's left hand and left wrist. One tore into his right hip. The fourth got him in the back after he had come out of the chair and had stumbled into the mirror he had been facing as the barber worked. The fifth bullet caught him in the back of the head.

Both killers had scarves over the lower part of their faces. They got away.

Two Weapons Are Found

The pistols used in the killing were dropped right after they were used. One was found a few minutes later in a vestibule just outside the barber shop that opens into Fifty-fifth Street. The other was dropped into a trash basket at the Fifty-fifth Street end of the Fifty-seventh Street BMT subway station. A porter who was emptying the bins found it.

Eleven persons besides Anastasia were in the shop when the gunmen entered—five barbers, two other customers, two shoeshine men, a valet and a manicurist. They, and persons just outside the shop, fled screaming and shouting into the street, with the killers among them or right behind them. Where the killers went no one noticed.

The police last night issued a thirteen-state alarm for two men in the murder. One was described as about 40 years old, 5 feet 8 inches tall, weighing 180 pounds, sallow complexion, wearing a gray suit, dark gray fedora with three-inch brim and dark-green aviator-type glasses. The other was said to be about 30, about 5 feet 5 inches, weighing 150 pounds, light complexion, thin black pencil moustache, wearing a dark brown suit, lighter brown fedora with three-inch brim and dark-green glasses.

Although 100 detectives were thrown into the case immediately by Chief of Detectives James B. Leggett, the police had no positive motive for the killing. There was talk that Anastasia was trying to reorganize the remnants of old racket groups in town, and that the younger hoodlums would have none of his leadership.

In addition, countless underworld figures had scores to settle with Anastasia. For 36 of his 55 years he had plotted gang killings, or had seen to them himself. Of Murder, Inc.'s sixty-three assassinations, thirty-one are supposed to have been Anastasia's handiwork.

The police were quick to throw guards around all persons they questioned in the Anastasia murder yesterday—the barber shop crew, a hotel elevator boy, several men and women might have brushed shoulders with the fleeing gunmen as they left; owners of near-by shops that give upon the barber shop.

The dead man's kin were guarded, too, against their wishes, among them Anthony (Tough Tony), Anastasia, 50-year-old brother. He is a vice president of the International Longshoremen's Association and business manager for Local 1814 of that organization. He lives at 8220 Eleventh Avenue, in Brooklyn's Dyker Heights district.

Lived Behind Fence

Umberto Anastasia lived in rather splendid fashion behind a seven-foot barbed-wire fence at 75 Bluff Road, in the Palisade section of Fort Lee, N. J. Great Doberman pinschers roamed his lawns like sleek dark shadows at night. They would give tongue when strangers went by.

Anastasia drove away from the house at 7 o'clock yesterday morning in a blue 1957 Oldsmobile hardtop sedan registered in the name of his current driver and bodyguard. Anthony Coppola. He parked it at the Corvan Garage, 124 West Fifty-fourth Street, at 9:28 A. M.

An hour-and-a-half later, the 29-year-old bodyguard drove it back to his own home at 450 Park Avenue, Fairview, N. J. Later, a friend drove the car to a parking lot on Centre Street—across from the Criminal Courts Building. The police took it from there to the West Fifty-fourth Street police station.

At 6:30 P. M. the last of the many drivers and bodyguards Anastasia had kept close to him walked into police headquarters here and said he was ready for questioning.

Detectives took him at once to West Fifty-fourth Street, where all the other witnesses had been taken. Mike Mirante, another long-time Anastasia associate, had turned up about

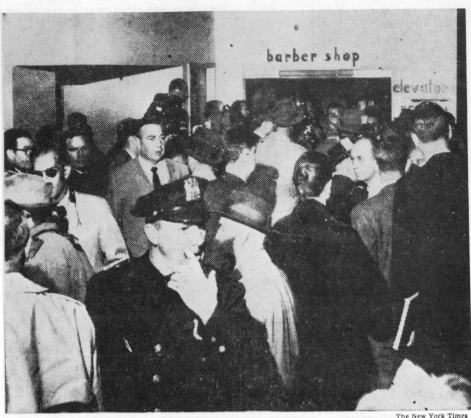

NEWS OF THE MURDER DRAWS THRONGS: Reporters, photographers, policemen and others crowd the lobby of hotel where the notorious gangster was shot by gunmen.

The New York Times

GRIEVES FOR SLAIN BROTHER: Anthony (Tough Tony) Anastasia, left, with police official yesterday.

a half hour before. Detectives took him for questioning too.

The police would not disclose what they had learned from those questioned.

By midnight, the detectives had questioned fifty witnesses, and ten more were waiting their turns. One of the first group was Harry Stasser, 58, of 30 Ocean Parkway, Brooklyn, for ten years Anastasia's partner in the Madison Dress Company. The concern does about a $150,-000 annual gross.

How It Happened

Anastasia strolled into the hotel barber shop at about 10:15 and called greetings to the help. Joseph Bocchino who holds down Chair 4, facing Fifty-fifth Street, gave the chair a few swipes while Anastasia hung up his topcoat and stripped open his white shirt. He was dressed all in brown—brown shoes with rather an amateur polish, brown suit, a rather untidy brown tie.

"Haircut," he said, and he seemed to need one. His hair was thin in front, but thick and lush over-all, especially down the back. He sat upright a broad-chested, broad-shouldered fellow with fleshy nose round but firm chin.

The barber draped a cloth around the gangster's neck swirled the sheet into place and got out the electric clippers for the back of the neck. No one in the shop was jogged out of morning dreaminess.

The room, 35 by 28 feet, was filled with customary hum. The recessed overhead fluorescents lighted the place well, but not with glare. Arthur Grasso, the shop owner, was at the cashier's stand near one of the doors leading from a hotel corridor.

A minute or two later, as Mr. Bocchino plied the clippers from Anastasia's left side, the door opened. The gunmen stepped in. They were middle-sized men, dark and rather broad. Their weapons came out as they crossed the threshold.

One of the two men spoke through his scarf. He told Mr. Grasso: "Keep your mouth shut if you don't want your head blown off." The shopowner's jaw fell. Then his lips compressed. The two trigger-men moved swiftly behind Anas-

Victim's Brothers

Associated Press
Gerardo Anastasio, 45, a Brooklyn pier union agent.

The New York Times
Joseph Anastasio, who died last year at the age of 51.

tasia's chair. If his heavy-lidded eyes had been open—apparently they were not—he might have seen them in the mirror, but he sat, relaxed, with no notion that death was close.

Both men seemed to open fire at once. The shots came in short spurts. One gun roared, and stopped. The other gun roared and stopped. The sound had a weird cadence.

Anastasia leaped forward with the first report. His heavy feet kicked at the foot rest and tore it away. He landed on his feet, weaving. He did not turn around to face the killers. He lunged further forward, still facing the mirror. The second spurt of bullets threw him against the glass shelving in front of the mirror. He grabbed for the shelving and brought a glass of bay rum to the tiles with a shattering crash He took two further shots. Then the last shot—so the police figure it—took him back of the head.

The heavy body turned. Anastasia fell to the floor two chairs away. He fell on his left side. One pudgy hand was outstretched. The fluorescent lights kicked fire from the diamonds in his fat finger ring. He lay still.

The gunmen had said no word after their quiet warning to Mr. Grasso. They did not speak as they strode to the door, guns still in hand. Which way they turned no man seemed to notice. People who had heard the cannonade had dropped to corridor floors, or had fled, some directly ahead of the killers.

Constantine Alexis who runs a hotel flower shop alongside the barber's, watched the crowd

fleeing past his window. He remembered later that there were four or five men in one group heading for a Fifty-fifth Street exit. Someone was hollering: "Somebody's gone crazy in there." The florist dialed frantically for the police.

Police radio cars converged on the barbershop in a matter of minutes. Traffic policemen rushed through the doors. Dr. Robert Cestari came from nearby St. Clare's Hospital and kneeled over Anastasia between the chairs.

He applied a stethescope, looked up and said: "He's dead."

Apparently the bullet at the back of the head had ended Anastasia's life immediately.

Word of Shooting Spreads

Word of the shooting spread swiftly across the city. The radio blared it. Before that, though, a newspaper office had telephoned the story to one of its reporters at Police Headquarters in Brooklyn. He called Anthony Anastasia in the I. L. A. office at 341 Court Street.

The reporter said, "Tony, you know what just happened to Albert?" and Anthony said "No, what happened?" The reporter told him: "Albert was just knocked off over in the Park Sheraton Hotel. Just a couple of minutes ago." The union boss's voice broke. "No," he cried, "no, no." He started to say something more, but his voice failed. He hung up.

Longshoremen sitting in the office sat white-faced at the news. They raced downstairs behind Anthony, one got behind the wheel of his Chevro-

let, and they raced for Manhattan. They made it in almost record time.

When Anthony hurried into the barbershop, a detective held the sheeting aside. The union chief stared at his brother's face as if in disbelief. He spoke no word, but he shook with sobbing.

One of his men touched him on the shoulder. He got up and let them lead him back to the car. He had them drive them to the West Fifty-fourth Street police station. Detectives kept him only a little while. Assistant District Attorney Alexander Herman of the Homicide Division told reporters later, "He was completely cooperative. That's all we can tell you now."

Even before Anthony identified the body, the police had the first of the two murder weapons. It was a .38-caliber Colt revolver, with only one of it's six bullets unfired. The gunman had dropped it in a glassed-in vestibule on his way out to Fifty-fifth Street.

The fact that the second weapon, a .32 with five shots discharged, was found in the subway, seemed fair indication that both killers had run out of the vestibule in the panicky rush that followed the shooting.

The subway entrance in Fifty-fifth Street is only a few steps away. Both weapons, incidentally, were originally sold by dealers out of town; the .32 thirty-seven years ago, the other in 1934. Detectives did not tell in what town they were bought. The guns were turned over to ballistics experts and to fingerprint men.

A few hours later, after an

Hotel Barber Shop Is Scene of Gangster's Slaying

Umberto (Albert) Anastasia was seated in chair in background when two slayers entered shop at Park Sheraton Hotel. As men shot, he got up, then fell near front chair.

autopsy, Umberto Anastasia Jr., son of the dead executioner, came to identify his father. He looked at the figure for only a moment, and turned away. Then he left with Robert Anastasio (Anastasio was the original spelling of the family name and some branches still use it), a nephew of the old gang boss who lives in Brooklyn, original stamping ground of the clan.

Feared By Racketeers

Detectives expressed no sorrow over the passing of Umberto Anastasia. He had been the most notorious hoodlum in New York —probably in the East—for better than twenty years and had managed to cover his tracks every time. It was common knowledge that he fancied himself as The Executioner. Even the fact that he had spent some time in the Sing Sing Prison death house himself thirty-six

Associated Press
GANGSTER MURDERED:
Umberto (Albert) Anastasia. He was 55 years old.

years ago did not seem to lessen his appetite for violence.

Even the underworld "big shots" who moved in The Executioner's private circle stood in deathly fear of him. They included the late Louis (Lepke) Buchalter, chief of rackets in New York City that brought in millions. Frank Costello, Joe Adonis and Augie Pisano, men of might in gambling and night-club operations on both shores of the Hudson, were never easy in his company.

The late Willie Moretti, a mob boss on the New Jersey side, stood in mortal fear of Umberto. He was boxed in, one night in October, 1951, in a dark little inn in Cliffside Park, N. J., and shot to death by four gunmen.

Yet, Anastasia, who managed a peaceful garment factory in Hazelton, Pa., on the side, could seem pleasant, genial and generous.

'Nice to Deal With'

The men in the Park Sheraton barber shop exclaimed over his tips. So did all the other hired hands there. Douglas du Lac, owner of a toy shop in the hotel, had always thought of him as "very much the gentleman, nice to deal with, a man with a real love for kids."

Anastasia seemed to buy toys about twice a month, which was about as often as he came to the barber shop. "Always big

expensive toys, too," Mr. du Lac recalled.

He might have had a spending spree in mind even yesterday, though he never got around to it. When detectives went through his pockets they came up with, roughly, $1,900 in cash, in notes ranging from $1 to $100. He had no weapon on him.

The detectives were not too happy over the murder in one way. They have apparently made no headway into the motives for the attempted murder, last May, of Frank Costello, an associate of Anastasia.

A gunman stepped up to Costello one spring evening in the lobby of his apartment house on Central Park West and cut loose, at fairly close range, with several shots. The gambler got a burning wound, but quickly recovered. He insisted that he knew no reason for the attempt on his life. The police were left baffled.

The Anastasia shooting yesterday was the second of its kind in the hotel in twenty-nine years. Arnold Rothstein, the gambler, who lived there when it was the Park Central Hotel, was shot within its walls on Nov. 4, 1928. He lingered in a hospital a few days after the shooting before dying.

The police acknowledged last night that they were closely guarding not only innocent bystanders in the Anastasia case,

but members of the Anastasia family, too, and the homes of Anastasia associates brought in for questioning.

'Special Attention' Detail

When they threw men around Anthony Anastasia's place in Dyker Heights last night, they termed the move "special attention," a gesture that Anthony has resented on past occasions. Men in radio cars in the neighborhood also had orders to tour by the home once every fifteen minutes.

The District Attorney's office in the Bronx heard of The Executioner's killing with some regret. He was wanted in the Bronx for questioning about the murder of Vincento Macri of 4499 Henry Hudson Parkway, found shot to death and stuffed in a trunk in the spring of 1952. The district attorney thought he might shed some light on the disappearance of Benedetto Macri, Vincenzo's brother, whose blood-stained automobile turned up ten days later on a lonely road in Harrison, N. J. Benedetto's body was never found.

Chief of Detectives Leggett, wearied with work on the Anastasia case last night, finally snapped back a bit bitterly at an innocent who asked: "Why do you think they killed him, Chief?" His answer was: "Maybe somebody didn't like him."

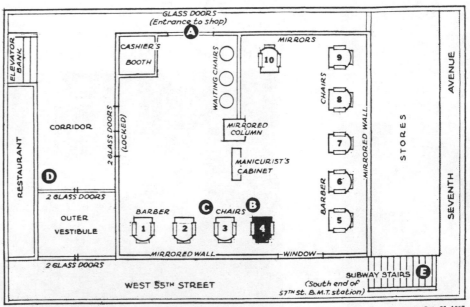

The New York Times   Oct. 26, 1957

Killers entered barber shop through glass doors (A) and took positions at B to fire at victim in chair 4, as barber stood at Anastasia's left. The victim got up, staggered a few paces to right and fell at C. One pistol was found later in corridor (D) of hotel lobby and the other on BMT subway platform (E) at Fifty-fifth Street.

65 Hoodlums Seized in a Raid And Run Out of Upstate Village

Special to The New York Times.

APALACHIN, N. Y., Nov. 14 —State policemen and Federal agents rounded up today sixty-five men whom they described as hoodlums attending a meeting of the "hierarchy of the Eastern Seaboard criminal world."

The men were released because the police said they had "nothing to hold them on." But they were told "to get out of town and stay out of town from now on."

The men, almost all with criminal records of one kind or another, had come from places as far as New Jersey, Ohio, California, Buffalo and Puerto Rico. They drove out of town in a variety of expensive cars, the oldest of which was a 1956 Cadillac.

Among those attending the meeting in this small town of less than 1,000 persons was Vito Genovese, 60 years old, a close associate of Albert Anastasia, the slain boss of Murder Inc. Another was John Anthony De-Marco, 54, of Shaker Heights, Ohio, who has been arrested on charges of murder, bombing and blackmail and dozens of similar charges.

The hoodlums were expensively dressed, some with diamonds in their belt buckles and most with gold watches on their wrists. The police said that the lowest amount of money found on an individual was

$450 and the largest $10,000.

"It looked like a meeting of George Rafts," Sgt. Edgar Croswell, of the Detective Division of the State Police said. "In fact we would have had a harder time getting them if it weren't for the fact they were such city slickers."

Sergeant Croswell was referring to the fact that when the police surrounded the house where the men were meeting, about fifteen of them tried to run away into the woods.

"Those city boys didn't have a chance," he said. "With their fancy shoes and their hats and coats snagging on tree branches, we could grab them easy."

This day started quietly for Apalachin, a hamlet just fifteen miles west of Binghamton, although the State Police had an inkling there would be trouble. This town itself has no police force.

Gangsters had met here before—back in 1956. The host on that occasion had been Joseph Barbara, a man who owns a big house on a hill back in the woods in Apalachin. Barbara has been arrested three times on homicide charges, but never convicted.

The police noted that Barbara was putting out calls to motels in the vicinity of the town making reservations for his guests. He asked for the best and "never mind the price."

Their suspicions that trouble was in the offing were con-

firmed when yesterday the procession of expensive care began to park in front of the motels. By this morning the flow became a flood.

The police even noted that one of those arriving was Lewis Santos, the manager of the Sans Souci nightclub in Havana. Santos arrived at Binghamton by plane.

The police knew that reinforcements were needed and additional State Police were sen to Apalachin so that the force was augmented to fifteen men. Two agents from the Alcohol Tax unit of the Treasury Department also arrived in case any illegal liquor was discovered.

The police noted that at about midday cars began to drive to Barbara's house in Apalachin. The parking area next to the house became jammed.

The police did not have warrants to search the house. But they set up a road block that would prevent the cars from leaving. Then they began to check the license numbers of the cars parked in the lot.

That was enough to panic some of the gangsters. The police said that between twelve and fifteen of them began to make a break for the woods. "They poured out of the doors, windows — everywhere," one policeman said

The policemen were not far behind in hot pursuit. No shots were fired in the race through the forest. But the forest began to wear down the gangsters and in groups of two or three they were picked up by the police.

Back at the house, others gave themselves up—some stripping themselves of all identifying cards before surrendering.

All of them were brought back to the State Police bar-

racks where the police wrung the identities from each. But no one would say what the meeting was all about.

"If we knew why they were meeting," Sergeant Croswell said, "we wouldn't have to let them go. We gave them a rough time in the station house. But we couldn't even make them commit disorderly conduct there."

Sergeant Croswell, 42 years old, is a big man—six feet tall, weighing about 200 pounds—who rarely smiles and makes few friends.

"He'd probably be the only cop in the state who would do it," a friend said, commenting on the sergeant's exploit in Vestal. "He's the antithesis of the kind of cop who would take a free meal on his beat."

He has been in the State Police for eighteen years, the last twelve years in criminal investigation.

There was speculation why the men were meeting, however. The investigation by Senate Select Committee on Improper Activities in Labor or Management into the matter of the garbage hauling racket was one of them. The murder of gang boss Anastasia was another.

Sergeant Croswell, divorced from his wife, lives in police barracks, where he keeps pretty much to himself. Occasionally he visits the homes of friends in the area.

His most striking physical characteristic, apart from his size, is his eyes. They are grey and cold.

In 1947, when the state police were cracking down on lotteries all over the mid-state area, Sergeant Croswell was detailed to pick up a suspect. The man was said to have had $50,000 in cash and to have offered the sergeant a large chunk of it to let him go. Sergeant Croswell turned the man in.

Police List of Hoodlums

APALACHIN, N. Y., Nov. 15 (AP)—The state police released today the names of fifty-eight men who, they said, had attended a meeting at Joseph Barbar.'s home here yesterday.

They said that two others present in the home were employes of Barbara. Their names were not revealed.

The list, as the names and addresses appeared on the State Police records:

BARBARA, Joseph, 51 years old, of McFall Road, Apalachin, the host.

BARBARA, Joseph Jr., same address, his son.

BONANNO, Joseph, 52, of 1726 DeKalb Avenue, Brooklyn, retired.

BONVENTRE, John, 54, of 115 Cleveland Street, Brooklyn, a salesman.

BUFFALINO, Russell, 54, of 304 East Dorrance Street, Kingston, Pa., a drapery and curtain salesman.

CALISI, Roy, 48, of 20 Anderson Place, Buffalo, owner of Club 97.

CANNONE, Ignatius, 32, of 3634 Rath Avenue, Endwell, a restaurant owner.

CASTELLANO, Paul C., 45, of 1737 East Twenty-third Street, Brooklyn, a butcher.

CATENO, Gerardo V., 57, of 21 Overhill Road, South Orange, N. J., owner of a vending sales company.

CHIERI, Charles, 59, of 2 Bridle Way, Palisade, N. J., in transportation work.

CIUELLO, Joseph, 55, of 5311 Denton Drive, Dallas, an importer of food and liquor.

COLLETTI, James, 60, of 1415 Claremont Avenue, Pueblo, Colo.

CUCCHIARA, Frank, 62, of 55-57 Endicott Street, Boston, a cheese manufacturer.

D'AGOSTINO, Domenick, 66, of 2226 Ontario Avenue, Niagara Falls.

DeMARCO, John A., 54, of 3536 Hilldane Street, Shaker Heights, Ohio, a real estate man. He said he had served five years in Ohio State Penitentiary after conviction on a blackmail charge.

DeSIMONE, Frank, 48, of 7838 Adoree Street, Downey, Calif., a lawyer.

EVOLA, Natale J., 50, of 972 Bay Ridge Parkway, Brooklyn, in the garment-delivery business.

FALCONE, Joseph, 55, of 1623 Mohawk Street, Utica, who operates a liquor store.

FALCONE, Salvatore, of 1623 Mohawk Street, Utica.

GAMBINO, Carlo, 55, of 2230 Ocean Parkway, Brooklyn, who works in a labor relations office.

GENOVESE, Michael J., 38, of Gibsonia, Pa., who operates a car wash business.

GENOVESE, Vito, 59, of Atlantic Highlands, N. J.

GUARNIERI, Anthony F. (Guy), 47, of 3619 Royal Road, Endwell, N. Y., who operates a dress factory.

GUCCIA, Bartalo, 66, of 202 Oak Hill Avenue, Endicott, proprietor of a fish store.

IDA, Joseph, of 108 Lincoln Avenue, Highland Park, N. J., owner of a garage.

La RASSO, Louis A., 31, of 115 Donaldson Place, Linden, N. J., a construction labor foreman.

LaDUCA, James V., of Dana Drive, Lewiston, N. Y., a labor union official.

LAGATTUTE, Sam, 58, of 555 Lafayette Street, Buffalo.

LOMBARDIZZI, Carmine, 44, of 114 Strafford Road, Brooklyn, officer in a trading corporation.

MAGADDINO, Antonio, 60, of 1528 Whitney Avenue, Niagara Falls, an undertaker.

MAGLIOCCI, Joseph, 59, of Bay View Avenue, East Islip, L. I.

MAJURI, Frank, 47, of 629 South Broad Street, Elizabeth, N. J., in construction work.

MANCUSO, Rosario, 50, of 926 Arthur Street, Utica, in the concrete business.

MANNARINO, Gabriel (Kelly), 42, of 54 Charles Avenue, New Kensington, Pa., owner of a junkyard.

MIRANDA, Michele A., 61, of 167 Greenway North, Forest Hills, Queens, an auto salesman.

MONACHINO, Sam, 63, of 11 Orchard Street, Auburn, in the beer business.

MONACHINO, Patsy, 50, same address, who operates a beverage company.

MONTANA, John C., 64, of the Central Terminal Building, Buffalo, president of a taxi company.

OLIVETO, Dominick, 50, of 1157 Magnolia Avenue, Camden, N. J.

ORMENTO, John, of 118 Audrey Drive, Lido Beach, L. I.

OSTICCO, James, 44, of 1261½ Elizabeth Street, Pittston, Pa., a transportation manager.

PROFACI, Joseph, 60, of 8863 Fifteenth Avenue, Brooklyn, owner of a distributing firm.

RAO, Vincent, 59, of 192 Dinwoodie Street, Yonkers, a real estate man.

RAVA, Armand, 46, of 1180 Ocean Parkway, Brooklyn, a restaurant owner.

RIELA, Anthony P., 61, of 7 Venvenue, West Orange, N. J., a motel owner.

RICCOBONO, Joseph, 53, of 781 Pelton Avenue, Staten Island.

ROSATO, Joseph, 53, of 34 Thirty-first Street, Jackson Heights, Queens.

SANTOS, Louis, 42, of Havana, Cuba, operator of the San Souci, a Havana night club.

SCALISH, John, 45, of 11-706 East Harrington Avenue, Cleveland, in the cigarette business. He told the police he had served two terms in Ohio State Reformatory after conviction on robbery charges.

SCIANDRA, Angelo, 33, of 108 South Main Street, Pittston, Pa., an orchestra leader.

SCIORTINO, Patsy, 42, of 58 Holly Street, Auburn, who makes bleach for dry cleaners.

SCOZZARI, Simone, 57, of San Gabriel, Calif., an alien who gave his home as Palermo, Sicily.

TORNABE, Salvatore, 61, of 1464 Second Avenue, Manhattan, a beer salesman.

TURRIGIANO, Patsy (Pasquale), 51, of 3015 Watson Boulevard, Endicott, N. Y., a grocery clerk. He said he had been convicted in 1950 for illegal operation of a still.

VALENTI, Frank J., 46, of 1384 Highland Avenue, Rochester, brother of Costenze and his partner in a wholesale produce business.

VALENTI, Costenze P., 31, of 79 Bellvue Drive, Rochester.

ZICARI, Emmanuel, 57, of 103 Squires Avenue, Endicott, a shoe worker.

ZITO, Frank, 64, of Illinois.

Associated Press Wirephotos

Sgt. Edgar Croswell of the State troopers, who set up the raid on Barbara's home.

The Scene of Gangsters' International 'Convention' Near Binghamton

This is the $100,000 home owned by Joseph Barbara, on a hilltop in hamlet of Apalachin, N. Y. State troopers and Federal agents converged on the house Thursday and found 60 men from various states, Puerto Rico, Italy and Cuba.

November 16, 1957

Mafia Involvement Denied

Crime Here Declared to Have No Sicilian Connections

To the Editor of The New York Times:

Regardless of what anyone else may say on the subject, there is no Sicilian Mafia, or simply "Mafia" in the United States. I ought to know.

I have written a number of books on Italians in America. I have met quite a few gangsters, including Al Capone. As editor of the Italian-American Who's Who—sixteen editions—I have visited almost every "Italian" community in the country over and over again. Being Sicilian I have learned a thing or two which the non-Sicilian would not ordinarily learn about so-called "Italian crime" in America.

Now the Mafia was for centuries and what remains of it still is, a strictly Sicilian organization, with noble origins and traditions. During the last 100 years or so it has degenerated into common crime. Mussolini put it out of business but the evil has not been extirpated.

Some members of the Mafia came to this country—chiefly before 1914. Once here they severed for all practical purposes their connections with their "colleagues" across the sea. The distance, the economic and social climate, the motives for the commission of crime, all other "ingredients" were totally different. All that remained was what we might call an "entente cordiale."

Factors in Violence

Of course, there has been, and there still is, crime among Italians in America, just as there has been crime among the Irish, the Germans or other nationalities in America since our earliest days. As America grew richer, as politicians began to grow greedier, as labor began to expand, the nature of crime in the United States began to change, too.

But crime as it exists in America today—regardless of the national origins of its master minds—is strictly in conformity with the American way of life. America was born in violence, has thrived through violence and could not properly go on without violence. Omit violence from the American way of life—specifically, nuclear weapons—and we are sunk.

Actually, crime conditions in America from New York to San Francisco and from Minneapolis to New Orleans were more horrifying than they are today—believe it or not—long before Italian mass immigration began in the Eighteen Eighties.

Getting back to the men who were seized the other day I do not know the reasons which brought them together. But if they were members of a secret organization how is it that, according to the accounts given in the newspapers, none of them was from Chicago, Detroit, St. Louis, Kansas City, New Orleans or San Francisco, to mention only a few of the leading crime centers in America? Let us not be childish or outright ridiculous. What kind of a criminal organization calls a general meeting without any "delegates" from the very cities in which the Mafia is supposed to have taken deep roots?

Products of America

There are in America a number of criminals of Italian extraction, just as we have criminals of other extraction. Those criminals are the product of America, nurtured by America, with a strictly American "modus vivendi" or "modus operandi."

Why then besmirch the good name of the Italians in America—and, incidentally, of our allies across the sea—with an appellative that singles them out from the entire American nation? Why stain the good name of millions of hard-working people, of professional and business men of the highest integrity, of outstanding scholars, scientists and artists, whose contribution to America has not been inferior, by any means, to that of any other group in the country ever since the days of our Declaration of Independence? Why insult the memory of thousands upon thousands of boys who gave their lives for American democracy, including more than a dozen winners of the Congressional Medal of Honor?

If the so-called American way of life is synonymous with fair play, as we usually proclaim, let us have the courage to call our criminal organizations "gang," "band" or "ring," because they are nothing more than simply that.   GIOVANNI SCHIAVO.

New York, Nov. 16, 1957.

November 27, 1957

COUNCIL OF MAFIA MET IN APALACHIN, SAYS A U. S. AIDE

Narcotics on Agenda, State Inquiry Is Told—Mahoney Admits Tie to Delegate

By LEO EGAN
Special to The New York Times.

ALBANY, Jan. 9—The recent underworld convention in rural Apalachin, N. Y., was in reality a session of the Mafia grand council, the legislative watchdog committee was told today.

This description of the meeting, which the police interrupted, was given by John T. Cusack, district supervisor of the Federal Narcotics Bureau.

Mr. Cusack described the Mafia as a well-organized secret fraternal order originating in, and probably still controlled from, the Palermo district of Sicily. He said its members, scattered over the world, dealt in crimes "that prey on human weaknesses."

Mr. Cusack also offered a theory for the recent murder of Albert Anastasia in a hotel barber shop and named two men suspected of responsibility for the 1943 assassination of Carlo Tresca, anti-Fascist editor.

Narcotics Believed Involved

"We are convinced that there was a prominent place on the agenda at Apalachin for the discussion of the manufacture abroad, the importation and distribution of narcotics in the United States," Mr. Cusack told the committee.

At least three narcotic violators of major importance attended the meeting, the witness said. He listed them as Joseph Francis Civillo of Dallas, Tex.; Dominick D'Agostino of Niagara Falls, N. Y., and John Ormento of Lido Beach., L. I. Ormento is known as Big John and was described by the Federal narcotics agent as "one of the most active and important narcotic violators in the United States."

While Mr. Cusack was testifying in one room in the Capitol, Senator Walter J. Mahoney was confirming in another room reports that he had represented a wholesale liquor concern headed by one Apalachin delegate. Mr. Mahoney is the Republican majority leader of the Senate. He practices law in Buffalo.

Stockholders Listed

The Senator insisted that he had never had any direct business contacts with John Montana, the Apalachin delegate in question. Montana is a former Republican Councilman in Buffalo and is active in civic work there. The Senator said he has met him at social gatherings.

Mr. Mahoney emphasized that until the recent disclosure of Montana's attendance at the Apalachin meeting last Nov. 14, he was regarded as a good citizen in Buffalo. As recently as 1956 Montana received a civic award as Buffalo's Man of the Year.

Senator Mahoney said his firm had obtained a corporation charter for the Frontier Liquor Corporation in 1947 at the request of Anthony Naples and Fred Weiss. The charter went unused for lack of financing until 1949, when another law firm, headed by Franklin Brown, a former State Bar Association president, became interested.

In the same year, Senator Mahoney continued, he was asked to represent the corporation in an application for a wholesale liquor license. Montana, he recalled, had a 7 or 9 per cent interest in the concern.

Other stockholders were listed as Wade Stevenson, a former Chamber of Commerce president; Joseph Davis, head of a heating company and chairman of the Niagara Frontier Park Commission, and Frank Ernst, head of an iron works.

The first application, the

Senator recalled, was rejected by the State Liquor Authority because Naples had failed to list an arrest in his record. An amended application was approved.

Since then, Senator Mahoney said, his firm has represented the company on routine matters but he emphasized that he had never made contact personally with anyone in the S. L. A. on its behalf.

He last represented the corporation when its license was renewed in 1956. The S. L. A. is now engaged in an investigation of the license.

Mr. Cusack held the watchdog committee—officially the Joint Legislative Committee on Government Operations—enthralled as he read a 15,000-word report on operations of the Mafia in the United States and the relation to it of various delegates to the Apalachin meeting.

When he finished he was warmly commended by Assemblyman William F. Horan, Republican of Tuckahoe, the committee chairman.

State Aide Testifies

Only two other witnesses were called today. One · was William E. Cashin, director of the Bureau of Criminal Identification of the State Corrections Department. He described the bureau's role as a central identification agency for law enforcement officials of the state. He also gave to the committee the criminal records of those identified as having attended the Apalachin session.

The other witness was Russell Bufalino, a delegate to the gang meeting. He gave the committee his name and address in Kingston, Pa., but invoked his constitutional privilege against self-incrimination in refusing to answer all other questions.

He is under investigation by a Tioga County grand jury, Pennsylvania authorities and a Federal grand jury for the Southern District of New York. He also is being held for possible deportation by the Federal Bureau of Immigration.

Mr. Cusack told the committee that the Apalachin meeting was one of a series that had come to the notice of the Narcotics Bureau.

The first was held in Cleveland in 1928, he said. Others, he added, were held in the Florida Keys in 1952, at a Miami hotel in 1953, in Chicago in 1954 and in Binghamton, N. Y., in 1956.

Some of those at the Apalachin meeting in 1957 were at the Cleveland meeting in 1928, he testified, and listed three.

One of the three was Joseph Profaci of Brooklyn, Mr. Cusack testified. He described him as one of the rulers of the Mafia in the United States. A second was listed as Joseph Magliocco of Brooklyn, who is both a brother-in-law and second cousin of Profaci. A third was named as Joseph Bonanno, who has addresses in both Brooklyn and Tucson, Ariz.

Mafia Activities Described

"The business of the Mafia," the witness went on, "is what we term commercial crimes that prey on man's human weaknesses, such as the illicit narcotics traffic, organized prostitution, counterfeiting, bootlegging, organized gambling, loan sharking and extortion.

"When the opportunity presents itself, the Mafia moves into legitimate business, selecting ventures where their strong-arm tactics and cash resources will bring large profits.

"Our extensive narcotic investigations of various members of the Mafia fraternity during the past eighteen years has repeatedly shown a pattern of either infiltration or complete dominance of several legitimate fields, including organized labor with the follow-up of labor management ventures; the distribution of beer, liquor and soft drinks; the importation and distribution of Italian olive oil, cheese and tomato paste; the control of wholesale fruit and vegetable markets; the baking and distribution of Italian bread and pastries; vending machines of all types and juke boxes; the operation of night clubs, restaurants and bars. Their night clubs are frequently complimented through their interests in model and theatrical booking agencies and in musical recording companies."

Mr. Cusack reported that the organization used intermarriage as a means of promoting solidarity within the organization. He traced the kinship through marriage of several key Mafia figures, including Profaci.

He also cited the guest list at the marriage of Profaci's daughter, Carmella, in 1955 to Anthony Joseph Tocco in Detroit. Those present included such underworld figures as Frank Livorsi, John Odo (Bathbeach Johnny), John Ormento, Alex De Breezi, Angelo Meli, Michael Robino, Anthony Anastasia, Dominick Ferrato, Tommy Dragardi (Johnny Dee), · Mike Miranda, Salvatore Mussaacho (the Shiek), Angelo Polozzi, Peter Liqueral, Vito Genovese and Imnello Ercole (Mr. Tee).

The Mafia is not a monolithic organization controlling all the activities of its members, the witness emphasized. Rather, he explained, it is an association or alliance of many separate groups operating in different fields but bound to give one another such help as they can.

"There is reason to believe," he went on, "that Albert Anastasia's death was caused by a dispute over gambling concessions in an establishment operated by Santo Trafficante in Havana. Trafficante operates the Sans Souci there and was formerly in partnership with Gabriel Mannarino of New Kensington, Pa. Both Santo Trafficante Jr. and Mannarino were among those at the Apalachin meeting."

The witness identified Carmine Galente of Brooklyn as the reputed slayer of Mr. Tresca and reported that Galente was now engaged in a campaign to control narcotics, gambling and other rackets in Brooklyn. These activities are receiving the attention of District Attorney Edward S. Silver. Frank Garafola was listed as the one who had ordered Mr. Tresca's killing.

War Activities Cited

During World War II, the witness said, Mafia members were deeply involved in black market operations and the counterfeiting of both currency and ration stamps. In Italy, he said, several acted as interpreters for official United States groups. While serving as an interpreter, Vito Genovese headed a conspiracy to steal Army trucks and supplies and to sell the supplies on the black market. Mr. Cusack reported. Genovese was arrested and brought back to Brooklyn to stand trial for murder, but he went free when a key witness was found dead.

Much of the narcotics sold in the United States, the witness explained, is manufactured in secret laboratories in France and Italy. The Mafia gets into the picture because it controls distribution, he added.

At the conclusion of Mr. Cusack's testimony, the committee officially recessed until Feb. 6, but it may meet earlier on the call of the chairman.

Russell Bufalino in Albany yesterday. He refused to tell legislative watchdog committee anything about gangland convention he attended in Apalachin, N. Y.

January 10, 1958

U. S. Begins Crime Drive On 100 as Public Enemies

Special to The New York Times.

WASHINGTON, April 10—One hundred public enemies were nominated, but not identified, today for the "highest priority" in the Federal Government's long-range campaign to combat crime throughout the United States.

Attorney General William P. Rogers announced that all the Federal law-enforcement agencies would concentrate their investigative effort on this secret list of hoodlums. Many of them have invaded the legitimate fields of business and labor unions, he said.

Supervising the over-all effort from Washington will be Malcolm Anderson, recently appointed Assistant Attorney General for the Criminal Division.

The Organized Crime and Racketeering Section of the Criminal Division will be strengthened. A special group of former prosecutors is being set up in New York to spearhead the drive.

That group will be headed by Milton Wessel, 34 years old, who was an Assistant United States Attorney in New York in 1953-55.

The Justice Department refused to permit pictures of Mr. Wessel today, inviting the inference that the crime hunters might be going underground, too.

The Federal Bureau of Investigation will investigate the Federal crimes within its jurisdiction. The principal statutes it will be concerned with include those on racketeering, obstruction of justice, extortion, and interstate fraud by wire.

The liaison that the F. B. I. has established with local police through the National Police Academy and the F. B. I. Laboratory is expected to be helpful in this drive.

The Treasury, with its various investigative agencies, will join the campaign. Many offenses committed by racketeers fall within the investigative authority of the Bureau of Narcotics, the Internal Revenue Service and the Secret Service.

Herbert Wiltsee of the Council of State Governments and secretary of the National Association of Attorneys General has expressed interest in the plan and has pledged cooperation.

Information will be gathered from each of the investigating agencies and will be analyzed by lawyers of the Criminal Division.

The special group will first study the pool of information on the 100 top hoodlums now available from all the investigative agencies.

Thereafter the special group will request additional investigation along lines suggested by the examination. They are authorized to request the convening of an investigatory grand jury.

This is not planned to supplant the work now being done by the United States Attorneys, the Justice Department said, but to implement that work.

Congress Action Urged

The Attorney General also noted that the department would urge Congress to act on legislation previously recommended.

Two bills are designed to broaden the Johnson Act, which prohibits the interstate transportation of gambling machines. Two other pending bills prohibit the interstate transmission of gambling information.

The plan to combat crime reflects the thinking of J. Edgar Hoover, director of the F. B. I.; Harry J. Enslinger, Commissioner of Narcotics, and Lieut. Gen. Joseph M. Swing, Commissioner of Immigration and Naturalization.

Officials from the cooperating agencies who took part in the planning included Fred C. Scribner Jr., Under Secretary of the Treasury, and A. Gilmore Flues, Assistant Secretary of the Treasury.

April 11, 1958

Genovese Invokes the Fifth 150 Times in Mafia Study

By JOSEPH A. LOFTUS
Special to The New York Times.

WASHINGTON, July 2—Vito Genovese, reputed "king of the rackets," invoked a Fifth Amendment plea more than 150 times today as a Senate committee accused him of crimes from black marketing to murder.

Three associates of Genovese in the Apalachin, N. Y., hoodlum conclave last November resisted in the same way the questions of the Select Committee on Improper Activities in the Labor or Management Field.

They were Joe Profaci, Brooklyn importer, described as a leader of the Mafia; John Scalish of Cleveland, a vending machine operator, and Michael Miranda of Forest Hills, Queens, whose arrest record includes a notation that he is a narcotics racket suspect.

The Senators are investigating charges that the Mafia, a criminal society with roots in Sicily, is forcing its way into industry and labor unions.

All but Scalish were born in Italy.

Attacks Pardons

Two Republican Senators, Karl E. Mundt of South Dakota, and Carl T. Curtis of Nebraska, retreated somewhat today in their criticism imputing deportation delays to the Justice Department.

Senator Mundt, however, railed against uncompleted sentences by racketeers when it was revealed that Scalish had been pardoned by Gov. George White of Ohio, a Democrat, in 1935 after he had served two years of a ten to twenty-five year sentence for robbery.

"Who does all this pardoning and why?" Senator Mundt demanded. "Was there a pay-off? Financial? Political? I can't understand the situation."

Robert F. Kennedy, chief counsel of the committee, remarked:

"One of the centers of all this is Lucky Luciano. The committee has a good deal of information in New York on his getting out of prison and being deported to Italy."

Sentence Commuted

Charles Luciano's term was commuted when Thomas E. Dewey was Governor. According to testimony yesterday, he is maintaining contact in this country with criminals of Italian extraction.

Mr. Kennedy said that the file was available to committee

Associated Press Wirephoto
BALKS AS WITNESS: Vito Genovese at Senate rackets committee hearing yesterday in Washington. He invoked Fifth Amendment more than 150 times.

members but he did not plan to make it public. He said he did not know whether the file contained material hitherto unrevealed.

Genovese was thoroughly introduced by other witnesses before he took the stand. He peered at the committee through amber lenses and chanted through thin, colorless lips:

"Respectfully decline to answer on grounds my answer may tend to incriminate me."

He made that plea when the committee asked him to identify the preceding witness, Orange C. Dickey, who testified that he had arrested Genovese for black marketing in Italy in 1944 and had brought him back to this country. Genovese was wanted for murder in New York, but the case was dismissed when the prosecution's chief witness died of poison.

Mr. Dickey, now a bakery operator in Altoona, Pa., was a 24-year-old agent of Army intelligence in 1944 when he picked up Genovese as one of the principal figures in an extensive conspiracy to steal Army equipment and supplies and sell them on the black market. He said he had been offered $250,000 to give Genovese a "break." Genovese was then serving the military government as an interpreter.

Mr. Dickey testified that Genovese, in custody, had told him how to fix horse races, the policy racket, and how to provide "muscle men" for either side in a labor-management conflict.

Mr. Kennedy related that in a separation suit in Trenton, Mrs. Genovese had testified that her husband has considerable money secreted in Switzerland, Paris, Monte Carlo, and Italy, and that when she had traveled abroad she carried as much as $100,000.

Yet, Mr. Kennedy said, Genovese reported personal income of less than $7,000 in 1952, and in 1953, and got it up to only $14,000 in 1956.

Profaci, whose legitimate front is olive oil importing, made his plea in barely understandable English.

Mr. Kennedy told him:

"We had a nice talk yesterday. Your English was very good. Your accent has gotten so bad today. You understood very well. What happened to you overnight?"

Mr. Kennedy termed the witness "one of the most powerful underworld figures in the United States."

Senator John L. McClellan, Democrat of Arkansas, committee chairman, said, "I hope the courts will revoke your naturalization and deport you to the land from which you came."

He said he hoped that the courts would do this "with all deliberate speed."

Thomas O'Brien, a staff investigator who has been a New York detective, said cards found on Profaci after the Apalachin meeting indicated relationships with minor officials in the International Brotherhood of Teamsters, the Jewelry Workers Union and the Hotel and Restaurant Workers.

July 3, 1958

Juke Box Dealer Says Hoodlums Beat Him to Gain a Partnership

Brooklyn Man Tells Inquiry He Was Assaulted Until He Agreed to Share Business

By ALLEN DRURY
Special to The New York Times.

WASHINGTON, Feb. 17—A weeping Brooklyn man told Senate racket investigators today that he had been beaten mercilessly, while a juke box drowned his screams, until he agreed to give hoodlums a major part of his interest in a coin-machine business.

The witness, Sidney Saul, identified only as a salesman, told the Select Committee on Improper Activities in the Labor or Management Field that the beating occurred Dec. 19, 1957, at a Brooklyn luncheonette called the Wagon Wheels.

He said the thrashing, administered by three men who had surrounded him at a corner table, "didn't create any excitement at all" on the part of the proprietor, his wife or some customers who were in the place.

Mr. Saul identified his principal assailant as Ernest (Ernie Kippy) Filocomo. He said Filocomo had been accompanied by Charles Panarella and Anthony (Dutch) Tuzio. The three are presently awaiting trial in Brooklyn for the assault.

The witness said Filocomo was "like a wild man" as he beat Mr. Saul's face, leaving his nose "completely out of shape — looking like a horseshoe."

Mr. Saul said that before the beating began, Panarella had slapped him across the jaw and had demanded a partnership in Mr. Saul's business. After that, the witness said, Panarella demanded $500. When he refused, Mr. Saul went on. Tuzio put a coin in the juke box and Filocomo slipped off his coat.

"He [Filocomo] began punching me in the head and face," Mr. Saul told the committee. "When I pleaded for him to stop, they kept saying to each other, 'This fellow's an actor— this fellow's an actor.' It got to the point where I could hardly hold my head up. Then Panarella picked up a metal napkin-dispenser from the table and threatened to bash my head in. Then he asked me for $300. He said that would be cheaper than a new set of teeth."

At that point, Mr. Saul said, he felt he was beginning to lose consciousness, so Panarella ordered coffee for him. After that Panarella raised his demand to $500 again, he testified, and Filocomo started in, "much heavier than before."

Pummeling Ends

Finally, he said, Panarella ordered Filocomo to stop and Filocomo left.

Panarella then renewed his demand for a partnership, the witness continued, and Mr. Saul said he had agreed in order to get away.

Mr. Saul related the beating to repeated demands by Panarella, Filocomo and a man he identified as Larry Gallo that they be given a share of the coin-machine business Mr. Saul began in 1955. He said that at the time he had a route of twenty-two machines.

Mr. Saul testified that he had been under constant police protection since the beating.

Following Mr. Saul's testimony, Larry Gallo, a short, dark, 30-year-old man in a dark business suit, took the stand. He was accompanied by his brother, Joseph, 28, wearing a duck-tail haircut, dark glasses, a black suit and a black sport-shirt buttoned at the neck.

Both Gallos resorted to the protections of the Fifth Amendment against self-incrimination in refusing to testify.

Robert F. Kennedy, the committee's chief counsel, and staff investigators placed in the record information that Larry Gallo had been arrested thirteen times and Joseph seventeen.

Joseph also invoked the amendment when Mr. Kennedy asked if he had not been trying to gain control of the coin-machine business in New York City, West Virginia, Pennsylvania and Ohio.

Mr. Kennedy identified the brothers as key men in Local 19 of the Federated Service Workers Union, a coin-machine union that includes both operators and employes.

Mr. Kennedy also developed, through material placed in the record in conjunction with questioning of other uncooperative witnesses, what he said was a connection between Local 19 and Local 266 of the International Brotherhood of Teamsters.

Local 266 was reportedly formed by coin-machine operators to protect them against labor troubles. These witnesses, all of whom pleaded the Fifth Amendment, included John Amalfitano of Brooklyn, Herbert Jacob of Brooklyn and his brother, Eugene of Levittown, L. I., and Joseph DeGrandis, president of Local 266.

DeGrandis invoked the amendment to this question from Senator John L. McClellan, Democrat of Arkansas and committee chairman:

"This whole thing is designed as a racket to extort. The badge of Local 266 is a badge to extort, is it not?"

Associated Press Wirephoto

Sidney Saul testifies on juke boxes before Senators.

February 18, 1959

GENOVESE GUILTY IN NARCOTICS PLOT

He and 14 Are Convicted as Operators of Heroin Ring After 14-Week Trial

Vito Genovese was found guilty last night of conspiracy to violate Federal narcotics laws. A Federal court jury here also convicted fourteen of fifteen co-defendants.

The panel of six men and six women, which deliberated for twelve hours, returned to the courtroom at 10:05. It acquitted only Louis Fiano, a 48-year-old convict who is serving a Federal term on a narcotics charge.

Those convicted as first-time narcotics offenders must receive a minimum sentence of five years, but they could get up to twenty years. Those convicted as second-time offenders receive a minimum sentence of ten years, but could get up to forty years.

Genovese, a reputed underworld leader, had been accused by the Government of being the head of a multi-million-dollar narcotics ring that imported heroin from Cuba and Europe.

Vincent L. Gigante, 30, of 134 Bleecker Street, also was convicted. He was acquitted a year ago of a murder attempt on Frank Costello, who is believed

by some to be the top man in the shadowy hierarchy of gangland.

The narcotics conspiracy trial ran for fourteen weeks. It was given to the jury at 9:25 P. M. Thursday after a charge by Judge Alexander Bicks that took more than eight hours.

After brief deliberations, the jury retired to a hotel shortly before midnight and resumed its consideration of the case at 10 A. M. yesterday.

When the jury returned to the crowded courtroom last night, many spectators were standing. As the foreman read the verdicts, relatives and friends of the convicted defendants stifled cries in handkerchiefs.

The defendants had been free on bail. Assistant United States Attorney Arthur H. Christy asked that they be remanded to jail. Defense attorneys moved that bail be continued until the sentencing.

Judge Bicks put Genovese, who had been free on $50,000 bail, under $150,000 bail and gave him until Monday to post the extra $100,000. The judge set April 17 for the sentencing. The conviction makes Genovese subject to deportation to Italy, his homeland.

Genovese is reputed to be one of the leaders of the Mafia, an international underworld conspiracy. He was a delegate to the gang convention at Apalachin, N. Y., in November, 1957. He has used the Fifth Amendment 150 times in refusing to tell Senate investigators about his activities.

In his six-hour summing up, which he began on Wednesday, Mr. Christy charged that the accused had operated a vast ring that imported narcotics

from Europe, Cuba, Puerto Rico and Mexico.

The fourteen defense lawyers took a full week to sum up. They pictured Genovese as a legitimate business executive who made $225 a week with a repackaging company.

The defense questioned the timing of the indictment, saying that Genovese and the others were indicted July 8, 1958, by Paul W. Williams, who was then the United States Attorney.

On the following day, Mr. Williams resigned to seek the Republican nomination for Governor. The defense charged specifically that the whole case against Genovese was a scheme to advance Mr. Williams' ambitions.

The Italian-born "king of the rackets," as he has been called, has had many brushes with the law, but he has never been convicted of a crime.

Convicted with Genovese, in addition to Gigante, were:

Alfredo Aviles, 29, of 99 Avenue C, who had been free in $1,000 bail; Charles Barcellona, now serving a term on a previous conviction; Jean Capece, 29, of 22 Spring Street, the only woman defendant; Charles DiPalermo, 35, of 260 Elizabeth Street, who had been free in $15,000 bail.

Joseph DiPalermo, 51, of 246 Elizabeth Street, a brother of Charles, who had been free in $50,000 bail; Natale Evola, 51, of 972 Bay Ridge Parkway, Brooklyn, free in $35,000 bail; Daniel Lessa, 40, of 2885 Sampson Avenue, the Bronx, and his brother, Nicholas Lessa, 36, of 321 Paladino Avenue, both of whom were free in $5,000 bail.

Rocco Mazzia, 48, of 2332 Seymour Avenue, the Bronx, free in $5,000 bail; Carmine Polizzano of 43-54 Forty-Seventh Street, Woodside, Queens, free

in $10,000 bail, and his brother, Ralph Polizzano, 35, who is serving a two-to-four-year sentence in Sing Sing; Benjamin Rodriquez, 29, of 11-33 Sixty sixth Avenue, Queens, free in $20,000 bail, and Salvatore Santora, 45, of 132 Longview Avenue, Leonia, N. J., free in $25,000 bail.

Judge Bicks allowed Mrs. Capace, Evola, Carmine Polizzano, and Gigante to be continued in bail. The rest of the defendants were demanded to jail.

Associated Press

CONVICTED: Vito Genovese, who was found guilty in Federal Court of conspiracy in a narcotics case.

April 4, 1959

NEW YORK NUMBERS RACKET IS BIG BUSINESS

By EMANUEL PERLMUTTER

Representative Adam Clayton Powell Jr. stirred up his Harlem district last week by charging that white racketeers have driven Negroes from control of policy, or numbers, gambling in that area. He accused the police of permitting the white syndicate forces to operate while arresting Negroes.

Police Commissioner Stephen P. Kennedy denied the charge and his men followed up by staging large-scale round-ups in

which they arrested more than 150 persons in Harlem, mainly low-echelon policy employes. The race of those arrested was not disclosed.

The charge made by Representative Powell that more Negroes than white men have been arrested in Harlem is true. But this is explained by the police as follows:

Eighty-two per cent of those arrested on numbers gambling charges in Harlem last year were Negroes. This approxi-

mates the Negro percentage of Harlem's population.

However it is also true that the Negro bankers who once controlled numbers gambling there have either been driven out by the white racketeers or are now working for them.

The policy game is the simplest and most popular form of gambling in New York City. It is the most difficult for the police to control, as well as the one offering the most opportunity for police graft.

100 Million a Year

Betting on the numbers is a poor man's hobby. Wagers are for small amounts—many for as low as a nickel or a dime, although occasionally an affluent player may invest $100 on a number. In the most common form of policy gambling in this city, the player places his bet on any combination of three numbers. He wins if the three numbers he has chosen correspond to three numbers appearing in the same order in a previously designated portion of the day's parimutual betting total at a selected race track.

The police and New York prosecutors estimate that about 1,500,000 persons in the metropolitan area play the numbers each day and that they wager about $100,000,000 a year.

The usual payoff is at 600 to 1 odds. However, the player usually gets only 500 to 1, the remaining 100 being kept as commission by the man who took his bet. In addition, the policy operators lower the odds further on the most popular numbers and those that have won most frequently. Actually, the player should receive 999 to 1 odds, because that represents the number of possible winning combinations.

There is a business hierarchy in the conduct of numbers gambling. Low man in the operation is the "runner," often an elevator operator, a doorman, an orderly in a large hospital, a worker in a factory or office, a housewife or just a plain out-of-work guy who picks up bets from customers on his beat. Players also can make their wagers in candy stores, bars, restaurants and other retail establishments, known as "drops."

Bets made with runners and at drops are picked up by an employe called a collector. He brings the slips with their bets to a controller, who can be

likened to the branch manager of a bank. The controller in turn delivers the slips to the "bank," which is headquarters of the betting ring.

The banker may be a powerful individual operating on his own or the representative of a syndicate. Today most numbers banks in New York are controlled by an Italian syndicate. An average bank does about $15,000 a week business. The large ones average $100,000. Bank locations are changed regularly to avoid police detection.

The runners and drop employes receive a percentage—usually 15 to 20 per cent—of the money bet with them. (They also get a cut of any lucky client's payoff.) They are paid by the controller, out of his 35 per cent of the take. The remaining 65 per cent goes to the banker, who puts up the capital for the operation and takes care of the graft payments. In addition to the field men, the policy-ring personnel includes clerks and bookkeepers who work in the bank tallying the bets and pay-offs. There are also security members of the ring whose main job is to circulate in the vicinity of controllers' branches and the banks on the lookout for the police.

Plainclothes Force

Gambling and vice investigations in New York City are handled solely by plainclothes

The New York Times
Commissioner Kennedy.

The New York Times
Representative Powell.

policemen. There are 457 of the department's 23,897 policemen assigned to this work. Because of the graft temptations to which the plainclothes men are exposed, they are subjected to periodic shake-ups. Such a wholesale housecleaning took place in 1958, when the entire Harlem plainclothes division was transferred as a result of bribery disclosures.

Despite the strict disciplinary regulations imposed by Police Commissioner Kennedy, policy

gambling continues to increase. This is indicated by arrest figures. There were 9,459 policy arrests in 1956; 11,206 in 1957, and 13,252 in 1958. For the first eleven months of 1959, the total was 12,870. A projection indicates that last year's gambling arrests were higher than those in 1958 or any other previous year. These figures are construed by most observers as reflecting increases in gambling rather than improved police work.

January 10, 1960

Gang Strife Linked To Apalachin Edict Against Narcotics

By RICHARD J. H. JOHNSTON

A top Federal narcotics agent said yesterday that the elder statesmen of the underworld decided at the Apalachin gangland meeting in November, 1957, to get out of the illegal narcotics business.

Charles Siragusa, field supervisor of the Treasury Department's Bureau of Narcotics, said the decision was made because the directorate of organized crime had decided the traffic in drugs had become "too risky."

Mr. Siragusa also said the younger elements of organized crime attracted by the enormous profits in the illicit nar-

cotics trade, rebelled against the edict of their elders.

Mr. Siragusa spoke at a symposium on narcotics at Manhattan College. It was the first time a Government official had revealed that a contact had been made between undercover agents and persons privy to the underworld business transacted at the upstate home of the late Joseph Barbara Sr.

Violent Reprisals

The result of the rebellion by the younger mobsters, the Treasury agent said, has been a continuing series of murders, beatings and intimidations within the ranks of gangland, in which the directorate of the underworld still seeks to impose its will.

The Federal agents learned, the speaker said, that reprisals for disobedience "would be by violence" and that this had led to the "subsequent murders of a few top-ranking gangsters who chose to violate the edict

of their criminal bosses."

The symposium on narcotics was under the joint auspices of the Manhattan College Institute for Forensic Research and the Metropolitan Law Enforcement Conference.

More than 300 law enforcement officials from six neighboring states attended the meeting in the college's Smith Auditorium on the campus at Riverdale, the Bronx.

It was recalled at the meeting yesterday that the prosecution in opening the Federal conspiracy case against the gangland figures last year had emphasized that the Government "does not know what went on at the meeting" and that it did not hope to prove what had gone on. Twenty-one of the "guests" at the Barbara home were convicted.

Mr. Siragusa said that the full agenda of the Apalachin meeting of at least sixty top figures in organized crime

would probably never be uncovered.

Another major topic under discussion along with the narcotics matter was "the dispute for power between Vito Genovese and the Frank Costello factions," he declared.

New York could justifiably be described as the illegal narcotics capital of the nation, he asserted.

Mr. Siragusa told the meeting that 45.7 per cent of the nation's 45,391 known drug addicts were in New York State "with almost the entire number coming from the City of New York."

"In the face of such an alarming situation, the State of New York still has not passed adequate narcotics legislation," Mr. Siragusa declared.

He added that the authorities of Mexico were "extremely cooperative" in efforts to suppress drug traffic, but that "the present Cuban regime has contributed little, if anything" to correct conditions that hamper similar cooperation between that country and the United States.

February 28, 1960

20 APALACHIN CONVICTIONS VOIDED BY APPEALS COURT; PROSECUTION IS CRITICIZED

CIVIL RIGHTS CITED

Judges Find Evidence Not Sufficient to Prove Crime

By EDWARD RANZAL

The conspiracy convictions against twenty men who attended the 1957 meeting at Apalachin, N.Y., were reversed yesterday by the United States Court of Appeals.

In a unanimous decision the court held the Government's evidence insufficient to prove that the alleged conspirators had entered into an agreement to lie to investigative bodies about the purpose of their meeting.

It also ordered that the charges be dismissed. All the defendants are free on bail.

The conviction of the men last Jan. 13 had been hailed by Attorney General William P. Rogers as a major blow in the Government's battle against organized crime.

The Court of Appeals noted that the Government had not tried to prove assertions made out of court by some investigators that the conclave was "a meeting of underworld overlords and their vassals, commonly credited with being members of the Mafia, called for various unknown but illegal purposes."

Clark Protests Trial

Yesterday's opinion was written by Chief Judge J. Edward Lumbard. Judges Charles E. Clark and Henry J. Friendly concurred.

Judge Lumbard noted that some of the men had bad reputations and then added: "But bad as many of these alleged conspirators may be, their conviction for a crime which the Government could not prove, on inference no more valid than others equally supported by reason and experience, and on evidence which a jury could not properly assess, cannot be permitted to stand."

Constrained to go farther than his colleagues, Judge Clark in a supporting opinion suggested that the evidence was so doubtful that the case should never have been started.

Right of Privacy Stressed

"For" he said, "in America we still respect the dignity of the individual, and even an unsavory character is not to be imprisoned except on definite proof of specific crime. And nothing in present criminal law administration suggests or justifies sharp relaxation of traditional standards."

Judge Lumbard noted that "there is nothing in the record of the trial to show that any violation of Federal or state law took place or was planned at the gathering."

One of the major holes in the Government's case was that it admittedly did not know what had taken place on Nov. 14, 1957, when at least sixty men, many of whom had long prison records, were guests at the Apalachin estate of the late Joseph F. Barbara Sr.

Holding that no crime was indicated by the mere gathering of the group and that some proof of illegality was necessary for a conviction, Judge Clark wrote:

"* * * otherwise it would seem that a citizen's privacy is subject to invasion at any time on the mere suspicion of any police officer, Federal, state or local, and the presumption of innocence has no potency at the police level."

The meeting at Apalachin broke up after State Police Sgt. Edgar Croswell and two agents of the Alcohol and Tobacco Tax Unit of the Treasury Department had been spotted watching. The guests scattered.

Many were picked up later and questioned. In the main, they insisted that they had come to pay a call on a sick friend—Barbara.

Barbara, who died some months after the meeting, of a heart attack, had been well prepared to entertain a large number of guests on his 130-acre rural estate near Binghamton. He had ordered 242 pounds of choice beef for the occasion.

Special Prosecutor Acted

The meeting became the crime target of a special group set up by the Attorney General to fight racketeers. Its head was Milton R. Wessel. An indictment was returned naming twenty-seven defendants.

It charged that the gathering had been planned in advance and that when those present had become aware that law-enforcement officers had discovered the assemblage they thought there might be an investigation and agreed to give false information to official inquiries.

Of the twenty-seven indicted two won trial severances for illness, four were listed as fugitives and twenty-one actually went to trial. At the end of the Government's case, one was acquitted.

On Jan. 13, after a three-month trial a jury returned guilty verdicts against the remaining twenty. Judge Irving R. Kaufman sentenced fifteen to the maximum five years in prison, four to four years each and the remaining defendants to three years. In addition he fined thirteen of them $10,000 each. He permitted the defendants to go free in bail pending appeal.

In dismissing the charges Judge Lumbard wrote:

"We find that in two essential respects the evidence was insufficient to prove the crime charged. First, we find that the Government failed to introduce sufficient evidence to support a finding that the defendants agreed to lie about the gathering. Second, we hold that the evidence was insufficient to show that the defendants had reason on Nov. 14, 1957, to anticipate that any of them would be called to testify under oath about the events of that day."

No Conspiracy Seen

Judge Lumbard felt that there was no concerted agreement by the Apalachin group to lie about the meeting's purpose. Each, he said, apparently decided on his own to give as little information as possible about the meeting.

Judge Lumbard said that the flimsiness of the evidence against two neighbors of Barbara who were at the gathering "demonstrates the danger of a shotgun conspiracy charge aimed at everyone who gave an explanation inconsistent with the Government's suspicion of the purpose of the gathering."

"The danger of sweeping within the net of such a conspiracy an innocent visitor whose honestly told story may in its omissions have coincided with some falsehood told by others calls for special precautions in this type of case," Judge Lumbard wrote.

He said that perhaps the most curious feature of "this strange case is the fact that after all these years there is not a shred of legal evidence that the Apalachin gathering was illegal or even improper in either purpose or fact."

U. S. Withholds Comment

The Justice Department said it would not comment on the reversal until it had seen and studied the decision.

In addition to concurring in the reversal of the conviction, Judge Clark wrote:

"Chief Judge Lumbard and Judge Friendly authorize me to state that they agree with the writer that the publication by former special prosecutors of accounts and comments regarding this case and the appellants, while this appeal was pending, was improper."

In addition to the conspiracy charge, the indictment also accused three of the defendants, Joseph Magliocco, Joseph Profaci and Pasquale Turrigiano, with perjury. They were said to have lied to a Federal grand jury.

The perjury charges were severed from the conspiracy charge and the perjury case was not presented at the trial. The charges of perjury are outstanding and the three can be tried on this matter only.

Apalachin Zoning Upheld

ALBANY, N.Y., Dec. 1 (AP) —The site of the Apalachin gang meeting will remain a residential area and therefore cannot be commercialized, under terms of a decision today by the Court of Appeals. The court upheld a zoning regulation that bars purchasers of the fifty-eight-acre estate from developing it as a tourist attraction. The 6-to-1 decision was against Larue and Phyllis Quick of Endwell, who bought the estate of the late Joseph Barbara Sr. for $130,000.

December 2, 1960

NUMBERS SYNDICATE IN PENTAGON RAIDED

WASHINGTON, March 15 (AP)—A numbers syndicate operating in the Pentagon was smashed today in a raid by more than a score of Treasury agents.

Federal Attorney Joseph S. Bambacus of Richmond, leader of the raiders, said the racket was grossing a quarter to a half-million dollars a year.

Striking at the lunch hour, the agents arrested thirty-two persons and issued warrants for three others.

"The significance of today's raid is organized crime's ability to make such unbelievable inroads into the nerve center of our nation's defense establishment," Mr. Bambacus said.

Teh prosecutor said the raid had resulted from three months of undercover investigation that gave the agents a good estimate of the amount the ring was taking in.

Six of those arrested were charged with writing numbers and failing to have the required $50 Federal gambling stamp. Warrants were issued for two others on the same charge. The penalty for this crime is one year in prison, a $10,000 fine, or both.

Twenty-six others were charged with participating in a numbers game on Federal property. One other warrant on this charge, carrying a six-month jail term and $500 fine, was outstanding.

March 16, 1961

CRIME CURB IS PASSED

Congress Acts on Measure on Interstate Rackets Travel

WASHINGTON, Sept. 11 (AP) —Congress sent to President Kennedy today a bill making it a Federal crime to travel interstate on underworld business.

The House and Senate in quick succession, and almost without debate, approved a compromise version of the bill they had passed separately. Action was by voice votes.

The measure is one of a series requested by Attorney General Robert F. Kennedy to facilitate action against big criminal organizations. He said that states were hampered by their limited jurisdictions in dealing with such matters.

The bill would provide up to a $10,000 fine and five years imprisonment for interstate travel with the intention of committing a crime or distributing the proceeds of illegal enterprises such as gambling, illicit liquor and prostitution.

September 12, 1961

DEALING IN STOCKS LAID TO CRIMINALS

Attorney General Discloses Moves With Illicit Funds

By United Press International.

WASHINGTON, Jan. 24—The Justice Department is investigating reports that gangsters have been planting illicit profits in the stock market, Attorney General Robert F. Kennedy disclosed today.

In an interview, Mr. Kennedy said there appeared to have been stepped-up efforts by racketeers in recent years to move into legitimate businesses through the stock market.

He said investigators had made "some progress" in the investigation of suspicious purchases of stock in several areas of the nation, reportedly with money from illicit operations.

Mr. Kennedy declined to say where the investigation was centered. But he said there was no evidence to indicate that the major stock exchanges in New York had come under racketeer influence or control.

Other Justice Department sources said investigators had found some instances of manipulation of stock prices by underworld figures.

The sources said this activity took the form of artificially induced buying and selling of a stock, either through an exchange or over the counter, to raise the price.

Other findings have shown that racketeers have gained control of some companies by stock acquisition, the sources said.

An investigation of all stock exchanges by the Securities and Exchange Commission is scheduled for completion later this year under a $750,000 authorization approved by Congress.

Mr. Kennedy also said he hoped for House approval of a bill to require testimony by reluctant witnesses in cases of racketeering in the labor-management field if they were granted immunity from prosecution.

The Attorney General said considerable progress had been made by his department in the last year in dealing with corruption involving labor leaders and employers. But he said inability to get witnesses to testify had hampered enforcement efforts.

Boiler-Room Operation

Government sources believe that some of the boiler-room operations that have been uncovered in recent years have been financed by racketeer elements. A boiler room is an operation in which high-pressure salesmen solicit investors by phone to purchase securities of dubious value.

The growing interest by the underworld in the securities market is said to stem mainly from the public's increasing participation in the market and the obvious gains they can derive therefrom

In June, 1960, Carmine Lombardozzi of Brooklyn, who was a participant in the underworld Apalachin, N. Y., gang conference, was one of forty-seven persons indicted by a Federal grand jury in an alleged $2,000,-000 swindle in the stock of the Atlas Gypsum Corporation, Ltd., of Ontario.

Sold for $3 a Share

The Government charged that the alleged swindlers paid 20 cents a share for stock in the company and then sold it to more than 2,000 persons throughout the country for as much as $3 a share. Lombardozzi agreed to a no-defense plea and received a suspended sentence and five years' probation.

Wall Street sources said there was little opportunity for gangster elements to infiltrate member firms of stock exchanges. They pointed out that stock exchanges have stringent requirements for admission of partners or stockholders of member concerns. Admissions are granted only after a thorough review of the applicant's qualifications and an intensive investigation of his background.

For instance, the New York Stock Exchange requires that its board of governors must approve all full partners and limited partners of exchange firms and voting and nonvoting stockholders of these firms.

The same sources noted that there was nothing to prevent a racketeer from buying stock in a listed or over-the-counter company or from acquiring control of a concern in that fashion.

January 25, 1962

Luciano Dies at 65; Was Facing Arrest

By United Press International.

NAPLES, Italy, Jan. 26 — Lucky Luciano died of an apparent heart attack at Capodichino airport today as United States and Italian authorities prepared to arrest him in a crackdown on an international narcotics ring.

Officials in Naples and Washington announced shortly after the death of the former New York vice lord that he had been under surveillance and was about to be taken into custody.

"We were ready to move against him with the Italian authorities," Henry Giordano, Deputy Commissioner of the United States Narcotics Bureau, announced in Washington.

At the same time, the Naples Revenue Bureau disclosed that one of its agents had been trailing the 65-year-old Luciano when he died. The narcotics ring under investigation was described by United States authorities as having smuggled about $150,000,000 worth of heroin into the United States in the last ten years. It was reported to be one of the biggest uncovered since World War II.

Mr. Giordano said the decision to take Luciano into custody was linked to the arrest of three men in Spain earlier this week. Two of them were fugitives from a narcotics conspiracy indictment in New York City — Frankie Caruso and Vince Mauro. Both were seized in Barcelona, Spain, last Tuesday.

The third man was identified as a Spanish national, Salvatore Maneri, who was arrested in Majorca.

Met Film Producer

NAPLES, Italy, Jan. 26 (AP) —Luciano was stricken after a meeting with Martin Gosch, an American film and television producer, who said later he had flown from Rome to talk about a planned motion picture on Luciano's life.

Long Career in Crime

Charles (Lucky) Luciano, powerful overlord of the New York vice racket in the prewar years, had a longer career than almost any other gang chief.

From 1919 to his conviction in 1936 for compulsory prostitution by Thomas E. Dewey, then a special rackets prosecutor, Luciano was a leading figure on the national crime scene.

He had been arrested twenty-five times in twenty years in connection with crimes ranging from narcotics peddling to assault, from gambling and larceny to bootlegging, selling stolen goods and prostitution.

For all his arrests he went to prison just twice. As a teenager he served a sentence in the penitentiary for unlawful possession of narcotics.

After that sentence he remained free until after Mr. Dewey had presented evidence in General Sessions Court of Luciano's activities as leader of the city's $12,000,000-a-year vice ring. On his conviction Luciano was sent to Sing Sing Prison for thirty to fifty years.

In 1946, when Luciano had served nine and a half years, Mr. Dewey, then Governor, commuted the racketeer's sentence on the condition that he be deported and not attempt to return.

There were reports that Luciano had helped the United States war efforts. But neither Mr. Dewey nor Luciano, who once said he "couldn't talk about those things," ever confirmed the reports. The armed forces formally denied the story.

A Turning Point

It was reputed that Luciano held only one honest job in his life—as a $5-a-week shipping clerk when he was in his teens. He quit the job the day after he won $244 in a floating dice game, deciding then and there that crime paid.

A probation report noted that by the time he was 18, he had acquired "a definitely criminalistic pattern of conduct." The report added:

"His freedom from conscience springs from his admitted philosophy: 'I never was a crumb, and if I have to be a crumb I'd rather be dead.' He explains this by stating that a crumb is a person who works and saves and lays his money aside; who indulges in no extravagance. His description of a crumb would fit the average man."

Most accounts have it that Luciano was born in Lercara Friddi, near Palermo, Sicily, on Nov. 11, 1896. At his vice trial Luciano contended that his place of birth was on the Lower East Side on Nov. 11, 1897.

His parents — his father worked in sulphur mines near Lercara Friddi—migrated to the United States when the boy was 9. He went to Public School 19 on the lower East Side until he was 14 and then got the job as a shipping clerk.

His criminal career spurted when he became an associate of Giuseppe (Joe the Boss) Masseria, who headed the Mafia, the underworld crime cartel that preceded the infamous Unione Siciliano.

When Masseria was shot down in a Coney Island restaurant in 1931, Luciano replaced him. By this time, he also had picked up the gangland name of "Charlie Lucky."

One reason was that two years earlier some associates had taken him for a ride, a routine matter in the criminal vendettas of the period. However, this ride became one of the rare cases in which the victim came back.

He had received a nearly fatal beating that left him with a number of scars. In a day when Hollywood gangland films were the rage, Luciano looked like a movie gangster. He favored expensive clothes—silk underwear and custom-made shirts—and he traveled in fast, sleek cars.

In Loan-Shark Racket

As a director-trustee of the crime syndicate, he moved into the loan-shark racket and was a "protector" of labor unions.

He bought into the slot-machine business, and became a partner of the notorious Louis Lepke Buchalter in Murder, Inc., and was an associate of Arnold Rothstein, later murdered. He fell heir to the management of many of the illegal interests of Al Capone when the Chicago underworld boss went to Federal prison for income tax invasion.

At Luciano's vice trial, a parade of prostitutes, panders, madames and collectors of money from disorderly houses testified how Luciano had profited from the proceeds of compulsory prostitution.

Luciano, whose real name was Salvatore Luciana, complained that he was unhappy living in Italy, even though his home was in a modern seven-room villa and he apparently had unlimited funds.

There was never any clear explanation about where Luciano got his money, but even after his electrical shop went bankrupt last year, he continued to spend heavily.

In 1957, a Senate Crime sub-committee headed by Senator Estes Kefauver charged that Luciano still wielded widespread power in the United States.

Luciano made one public attempt to return here. In 1947 he showed up in Cuba, where he was found living in high style. The resultant publicity and complaint by the United States caused him to be deported back to Italy by the Cuban police.

Throughout his life he was seen frequently with beautiful women. Once asked why he didn't marry, he replied: "I've got enough troubles."

In 1949, however, he did marry a former nightclub dancer, Igea Lissoni. She died in 1958 at the age of 37.

Associated Press
Charles (Lucky) Luciano

Valachi, 'Syndicate' Informant, Began His Crime Career in 1918

Joseph Valachi, the former member of a "crime syndicate" said to be giving information on the criminal organization to Federal authorities, has a criminal record dating back 45 years according to the New York police. Valachi's record showed three aliases — Antony Sorge, Charles Charbano and Joseph Siano.

The information the Government is obtaining from Valachi, according to official sources, is the most detailed it has had on organized crime.

Valachi is a 60-year-old convicted murderer and narcotics dealer. For nearly a year, it was said, he has been telling the Federal Bureau of Investigation about the syndicate.

Once Cellmate of Genovese

The informer was, for a time, a cellmate in the Federal penitentiary in Atlanta of Vito Genovese, a 66-year-old racketeer who was named by Valachi as the top man in the syndicate.

Valachi has told authorities that the syndicate is known as "Cosa Nostra," which means "Our Thing" in Italian.

The Justice Department termed Valachi's disclosures "an extraordinary breakthrough." The department declined to say where Valachi, a Federal prisoner, was now.

Valachi, who is being closely guarded against gangland retribution, is scheduled to testify before the Senate Permanent Subcommittee on Investigations. This panel has been investigating international traffic in narcotics for several years.

According to the New York police, Valachi's record started in 1918 when he was about 15 years old. It shows 18 arrests in a 38-year period prior to his final arrest and imprisonment for dealing in illicit drugs.

Three times previously he was sentenced to prison and once he drew a suspended sentence. Most of the time he walked out of court after winning dismissal of the charges against him.

He was arrested on charges of burglary in 1921 and in 1923. He was accused of grand larceny in 1923, a charge that was later reduced to disorderly conduct. For this he went to jail for 10 days.

Nine days later he was accused of attempted burglary and was sentenced to prison. In 1925 and again in 1929 and 1936 he was accused of robbery. In 1929 he was also accused of extortion, a charge that he faced again in 1934; the charges were dismissed.

He received a suspended sentence for possessing policy slips in 1936. Arrested for the first time on a narcotics charge in 1944, the case was dismissed in Federal court. He was accused again on the same charge in 1948 and in 1955. In both cases no disposition was shown.

August 6, 1963

VALACHI ACCUSES MAFIA'S LEADERS AT SENATE INQUIRY

Calls Genovese the 'Boss of Bosses,' Who Led Gang of 450 in New York

DEATH THREAT CHARGED

Witness Tells of Syndicate Organization—Hopes to 'Destroy' Crime Chiefs

By EMANUEL PERLMUTTER
Special to The New York Times

WASHINGTON, Sept. 27 — Joseph M. Valachi, the underworld killer turned informer, publicly identified today the men he said were the chiefs of organized crime in the United States.

He said he hoped to "destroy" them because they had been "very bad" to their underlings.

Valachi, testifying almost nervelessly under hot television lights in the crowded Senate Caucus Room, presented selections from his previous private disclosures to Federal law-enforcement agencies. Those disclosures have been described as the most detailed and authoritative ever made on the nationwide crime syndicate.

The stocky witness was ushered into the room by a heavy guard of United States marshals. Scores of marshals were scattered throughout the room.

Worked for Genovese

Valachi said that he had been a member of a New York underworld organization run by Vito Genovese, whom he described as the "boss of bosses." The Genovese organization consisted of about 450 men, he said.

Another New York boss, whom he identified as Carlo Gambino, also had about 450 men in his following, he said.

He testified that the third New York boss, whom he had once served, was Thomas (Three Finger Brown) Luchese. Before working for Luchese, he said, he had been a "soldier" for Frank Costello, a power in organized crime.

The witness described the crime organization as consisting of "borgatas," or families, each under the leadership of a "capo," or boss. Each boss had a "caporegima," or lieutenant, who was in charge of the "regime," or "crew," consisting of "soldiers."

Strain to Hear Witness

In his first public appearance before the Senate Permanent Subcommittee on Investigations, Valachi described extortion, murder, assault and other depredations as the stock in trade of what he calls Cosa Nostra, the crime syndicate, which is also known as the Mafia.

Valachi, 60 years old, was alternately jaunty and unctuous. He spoke in a rather hollow, guttural voice that sometimes put his words just beyond the power of his hearers to catch them, even when they strained forward, holding their breath.

Valachi, for whose assassination the syndicate is reported to have offered $100,000, spoke with apparent fearlessness.

He told how Genovese had given him the "kiss of death" in the Federal penitentiary in Atlanta, where both were imprisoned.

Valachi smoked incessantly and occasionally rubbed his palms to wipe off perspiration. He tried repeatedly to avoid the harsh glare of the television lights, with no success.

When Senator John L. McClellan, Democrat of Arkansas, who heads the subcommittee, asked him why he had decided to disclose all to the Justice Department and the Senate, he replied:

"The main reason is simply to destroy the Cosa Nostra bosses and leaders. Through the years they have been very bad to the soldiers [underlings], thinking only of themselves."

"Why didn't you leave the organization?" Senator McClellan asked.

"Once you're in you can't get out. You try, but they hunt you down," Valachi said.

To escape detection by the underworld, he confided to someone at his side before the hearing started, he had dyed his hair red. Normally, his crew-cut is gray.

Valachi said that although he had been a soldier, he had operated his own "businesses," such as policy gambling, slot machines, juke boxes, narcotics and dress manufacturing. He added that he had also owned race horses.

In World War II, he said, he

made his largest windfall, selling ration stamps.

Sheds Light on Bender

"In one year," he said proudly, "I made about $150,000 from ration stamps."

The witness also threw some light on the disappearance of Anthony (Tony Bender) Strollo, who has been missing from his New York haunts. Genovese, he said, told him in the Atlanta penitentiary that Bender had disappeared.

"Did you take that to mean Bender had been killed?" Senator McClellan asked.

Valachi nodded and said, "It meant in our language that he had ordered his death."

"You got it clear?" the witness then asked the Senator.

"Yes, I get it clear," Mr. McClellan replied.

The witness also blamed the organization for the death of Abe Reles, a member of Brooklyn's Murder, Inc., who died on Nov. 12, 1941, when he fell from a window at the Half Moon Hotel in Coney Island.

"How did he fall out?" Valachi was asked.

"They threw him out," the mobster replied.

Valachi said that Genovese was prominent among the Cosa Nostra bosses who ruled the organization through a 12-man commission, but that he had never been able to impose his will on the Brooklyn organizations of the late Joseph Profaci and Joe Bananas.

Questioned About Killing

The witness was asked to estimate Genovese's wealth. He said he didn't know exactly, but that it was considerable and that Genovese had run a lottery, legitimate businesses and gambling casinos in Las Vegas and Havana.

"He's the tightest guy around, he never goes for anything," Valachi said.

Most of the questioning today centered on events leading up to a homicide Valachi was involved in while in the penitentiary. Although he was not questioned about other murders, Valachi said he had "killed for Cosa Nostra on orders."

The witnesses said that after he had been given the "kiss of death" by Genovese, he became suspicious of almost all his fellow prisoners.

Valachi was placed in a cell with Genovese after he was returned to Atlanta in the company of Vito Aguechi, who had been sentenced with him for the same narcotics violation.

The witness said that Genovese, who he said had been best man at his wedding, had invited him to become his cellmate. "How could I say no to him?" he asked the Senators.

Later, Valachi said, Aguechi had asked him to arrange a meeting for him with Genovese, but Genovese refused. From that time on, he declared, his relations with Genovese became

Associated Press Wirephoto

STAR WITNESS: Joseph M. Valachi, former Cosa Nostra member turned informer, prior to testifying at hearing of Senate Permanent Investigations Subcommittee in Washington.

guarded and he soon learned that his former chief had met secretly with Aguechi.

'The Kiss of Death'

"I grew nervous, I couldn't sleep, I didn't know what to do," Valachi said. He said he knew that Genovese intended to kill him.

"He said to me, 'Sometimes when you have a bag of apples, something is touched, has to be removed, or they all get touched,'" Valachi said.

"Then, he grabbed my head and gave me a kiss. I kissed him, too," he went on.

"Is this a ritual?" Senator McClellan asked.

"This is a suspicious kiss," Valachi replied. "I kissed him to let him know I understood."

He said that another prisoner, Robert Wagner, had remarked, "The kiss of death."

Two days later, the witness said, he had himself placed in solitary confinement to avoid assassination. When he emerged five days later, Aguechi shouted "Rat" at him in Italian. Standing nearby, he said, were "Trigger" Mike Coppola and Johnny Dio (Dioguardia), two Cosa Nostra leaders.

Valachi recalled that his uneasiness increased when Dio, a trusty in the shower room,

asked him when he intended to take his next shower.

"I knew what he was going to do," Valachi said. "I didn't take any more showers."

One day, he said, his self-control gave way when he saw a prisoner in the prison yard "who from the rear looked like Joe Beck [Joe DiPalermo], a Cosa Nostra member."

"I picked up an iron pipe and hit him on the head, three times, hard. I knew I had to kill him," Valachi said.

The witness said it was not until he was taken before the assistant warden that he learned he had killed the wrong man.

At one point, Senator McClellan asked Valachi if he thought it might help for Congress to pass a law making it illegal to join such secret organizations as Cosa Nostra.

"If you Senators make such a law, I'd be a happy man," Valachi answered.

Valachi testified for two and a half hours in the morning and for half an hour in the afternoon. He grew progressively weary as the day went on. Finally, Senator McClellan said he would postpone further questioning until Tuesday because "the witness says he is tired."

During the testimony, the

brightly lighted caucus room was crowded with more than 500 persons.

Valachi is currently under three prison sentences. He is serving two narcotics sentences of 15 and 20 years and a life sentence for killing Joe Saupp, the fellow prisoner in Atlanta.

Before he started his testimony today, Valachi posed patiently and willingly for cameramen as he sat in the witness chair. He was dressed in a black suit, white shirt and a silver tie with black squares.

Left School at 15

During brief questioning at the start of the hearing, the witness said he had been born in New York City and had left elementary school at the age of 15. He then worked as a "scow captain" before beginning a life of crime.

After a short career as a member of burglary gangs in East Harlem, he testified, he joined Cosa Nostra in 1930. He had balked at joining the organization at first, he said, because most of its members were of Sicilian descent. Valachi said that he was of Neapolitan parentage and, as such, did not trust the Sicilians.

He explained the origin of Cosa Nostra by saying that it

meant "our thing, our family," in English. He said the members never referred to themselves as the Mafia. This, he said, is a term used by outsiders in referring to the syndicate.

Valachi said that before joining the crime organization he associated with a group of boys. His function, he said, was to drive a getaway car.

"They called us the Minutemen," he said, "because we got away in a minute's time or less. Once I threw a brick into a window on 25th Street West to see how long it would take them [the police] to come."

Valachi said he had been shot twice in his career of crime. Both incidents occurred before joining the Cosa Nostra.

The second time he was shot, the witness said, he was hit in the head. He was looked after by gangland friends.

"They gave me a whole bottle of Scotch while they took the bullet out. A doctor did it. They smuggled me into a hospital. They paid a doctor $2,500 to take out the bullet and treat me for three months."

An Underworld Glossary

WASHINGTON, Sept. 27 (AP)—Here is a glossary, compiled by the Senate Permanent Subcommittee on Investigations, of underworld terms used by Joseph Valachi:

COSA NOSTRA — The name, as used by members (Italians only) of the organized criminal element, to refer to their over-all criminal organization, which he translates as "Our Thing."

FAMILY, BORGATA—The unit or division within Cosa Nostra by which members are subject to authority of one man, called Boss.

BOSS, CAPO—The head or leader of a family.

UNDERBOSS, SOTTO CAPO—Immediately subject to the boss; one who acts in place of the boss in his absence.

CAPOREGIMA, LIEUTENANT—Appointed by the boss to exercise his authority and carry out his orders within the family.

REGIME, CREW—Those members directly under the authority of the caporegima, or lieutenant.

BUTTON MEN, SOLDIERS—The recognized members of a family in Cosa Nostra. It is the initial step of belonging.

PROPAUS, PROPOSAL— Those seeking or being schooled by members for membership in a family.

MADE—Connotes being accepted as a member of a family.

CONSIGLIERI—An individual in each family within Cosa Nostra who acts as an adviser to the boss and family members.

RESPECT—The courtesies required of members for one another and to their superiors in the organization. This attitude must also be shown by superiors to members beneath them, as well as from family to family.

ARGIUAMENDA, A CARPET, A TABLE—Any discussion between members of the Cosa Nostra for the purpose of settling differences.

A MATTRESS — When a war was going on, the families or groups would move into temporary quarters or barracks where the sleeping accommodations would usually be mattresses on the floor.

COMMISSIONE—Group on a national or regional level who hear charges which affect more than just a local family or single regional section.

A FRIEND OF OURS— Form of introduction to indicate a person is a member of Costa Nostra.

A FRIEND OF MINE— Form of introduction used to indicate he is not a member.

VALACHI NAMES 5 AS CRIME CHIEFS IN NEW YORK AREA

Accuses Genovese, Gambino, Bonanno, Magliocco and Luchese as Bosses

CALLS 2 OTHERS KILLERS

Tells Senators of Burning and Bloodletting When He Joined Cosa Nostra

By EMANUEL PERLMUTTER
Special to The New York Times

WASHINGTON, Oct. 1—Joseph M. Valachi calmly recited today the bloody history of a war for control of the Cosa Nostra crime syndicate. From this war, he said, five men emerged as leaders of the New York underworld and administrators of its code.

He identified the leaders of New York's five Cosa Nostra "families" as Vito Genovese, Carlo Gambino, Joseph Magliocco, Joseph Bonanno and Thomas Luchese. Genovese is in prison.

The 60-year-old Valachi, himself a convicted murderer, also gave the Senate Permanent Subcommittee on Investigations the names of two men, still alive, who he said had participated in the still unsolved slayings of four syndicate members in the nineteen-thirties. He testified at the open hearing that he had driven the getaway car in one of the assassinations.

Describes Initiation

The committee and an overflow crowd of more than 500 spectators listened intently as Valachi described his secret initiation into Cosa Nostra in 1930.

The witness told of his induction by ritual oath, bloodletting and the ceremonial burning of paper in his cupped hands to illustrate how he would burn if he betrayed the organization.

Valachi's testimony was often rambling. It often left questions unanswered. It was told in a guttural, illiterate diction that sometimes left his hearers con-

fused. But the sinister story held his listeners in its grip.

The men named by Valachi as killers who are still alive were Girolamo Santuccio, alias Bobby Doyle, and Salvatore Shillitani, also known as Solly Shields.

He said Santuccio—whose alias, "Doyle," he pronounced in Brooklynese as "Derl"—was the slayer of Joseph Pinzolo, a syndicate chief who was found dead of gunshot wounds on Sept. 9, 1930, in Pinzolo's fruit-importing office at 1487 Broadway. The suite had been leased in the name of Luchese.

Valachi testified also that Santuccio and two other men, one known to him only as "Buster from Chicago" and the other called Nick Capuzzi, had killed Alfred Mineo and Steve Ferrigno in an apartment on Pelham Parkway in the Bronx on Nov. 5, 1930.

Valachi said the last information he had had on Santuccio was in 1960, when the latter was living in Stamford, Conn., the owner of a restaurant and mixed up in numbers and book-making."

Valachi said Buster, whom he characterized as a "collegiate type," had been brought by the mob from Chicago, where he had fled from Al Capone.

"He looked like a college boy," the witness said of Buster. "He was 23 years old, about 6 feet tall, weighed 200 pounds. He always carried a violin case."

"What did he carry in the violin case?" asked Jerome S. Adlerman, the subcommittee's general counsel.

"A machine gun," Valachi replied.

"Buster later got killed in an argument at a crap game," Valachi said. "This was in peacetime." He added that Capuzzi had subsequently died of natural causes.

The witness said Shillitani, together with Buster and Capuzzi, had fatally shot Joseph Catania, alias Joseph Baker, outside an apartment house at 647 Crescent Avenue, the Bronx, on Feb. 3, 1931.

Shillitani is now out on parole, Valachi said.

However, the police in New York said Shillitani was still in prison.

Valachi testified that he had driven the getaway car in the Catania murder, and that he had been involved in two unsuccessful attempts to kill Mineo and Ferrigno before they were finally slain without his knowledge and while he was away from the scene of the shootings.

First Slaying 'Contract'

Valachi said his involvement in the Catania murder had been the first "contract" he performed for the syndicate after his initiation into it. During the Mineo-Ferrigno incidents, he explained, he was only on trial.

"Did you get paid for this contract?" asked Senator Edmund S. Muskie, Democrat of Maine.

"No," Valachi replied. "If the organization finds out that any member gets paid for murder for the organization he's in trouble."

"Did you have to take this contract?" Senator Muskie continued.

Valachi shrugged. "We were in a war, Senator," he replied patiently. "We were working like a team, like an army would."

"You mean killing for the organization was like breathing for you?" the Senator asked.

"It was like breathing," the witness replied.

'Moonlighting' Gangster

When Senator Henry M. Jackson, Democrat of Washington, asked Valachi whether he and the other soldiers had received any pay from the organization in this period, the witness responded "about $25 a week."

"I went out on a couple of burglaries so that I could have some money for myself," Valachi added.

"Something like moonlighting, wasn't it?" Senator Jackson commented.

"Well, $25 wasn't a lot of money," the witness said.

The story that Valachi told of the underworld war that has flared intermittently since 1930 was complicated, with gang members and leaders frequently changing sides.

In essence it added up to the following:

Peter Morello, alias "The Clutching Hand," was the "boss of bosses" of Cosa Nostra until his assassination on Aug. 15, 1930, at his office, 362 East 116th Street. Valachi testified that Buster had shot Morello.

After Morello's death, a war for dominance developed between one faction headed by Giuseppe (Joe the Boss) Masseria and another led by Salvatore Maranzano. Masseria had as an ally the "family" headed by Mineo and Ferrigno. Maranzano had a group headed by Gaetana Reina as his ally. Most of the Masseria forces were of Neopolitan origin. The Maranzano "soldiers" or underlings came mainly from Sicily, especially the area of Castel del Mar.

Gang Short of Men

On Feb. 26, 1930, Reina was killed by an unidentified member of the Masseria mob. Masseria installed Pinzolo as Reina's successor, but Reina's old followers then had Pinzolo murdered. Gaetano Gagliano, one of Reina's underbosses, then took over the combine. It was at this juncture that the Gagliano group, in need of manpower, recruited Valachi.

In this war for dominance, Masseria had the support of Al Capone and of Arthur Flegenheimer (Dutch Schultz), the leader of a non-Italian gang, according to Valachi.

After the murder of Mineo and Ferrigno, the strife flared into the open, with Masseria and his followers declaring "death to all Castellamarese" (those from Castel del Mar) throughout the United States, Valachi testified.

The tide of battle soon swung to Maranzano and his allies. At

GIVES MOB HISTORY: Joseph M. Valachi, right, testifies at his second appearance before the Senate crime committee. At left, Laverne Duffy, a committee staff member, stands ready to explain a chart that traces gang evolution in New York area since 1930.

Associated Press

this point, Valachi said, the Maranzano forces numbered 600 men, while Masseria had only a few.

Masseria was assassinated on April 20, 1931, in a Coney Island restaurant. Valachi said Charles (Lucky) Luciano and Vito Genovese, Masseria's deputies, had lured Masseria to his death.

Although Valachi's testimony today did not go beyond this point in the struggle, he said the war had ended with Masseria's murder and Maranzano's ascension to top leadership.

A chart of the warfare, introduced by the subcommittee, showed that Maranzano was killed on Sept. 11, 1931, and that four families then took over, one headed by Luciano, one by Philip and Vincent Mangano, another by Joseph Profaci and the fourth by Gagliano. Ultimately, the control passed to the five leaders named by Valachi today.

Valachi's story of his induction into Cosa Nostra in 1930 had the quality of a movie melodrama. He said he and three others had driven to a private house "90 miles upstate." There were about 40 men in the place, he said; Maranzano, the leader, was among them.

"The purpose was to make us new members and to meet the others for the first time," he said.

Valachi said he had been taken into a large room, where 30 or 35 men were sitting at a long table.

"There was a gun and a knife on the table," Valachi testified. "I sat at the edge. They sat me down next to Maranzano. I repeated some words in Sicilian after him."

"What did the words mean?" asked Senator John J. McClellan, Democrat of Arkansas, the subcommittee chairman.

"You live by the gun and knife, and die by the gun and knife," Valachi said.

The witness said Maranzano had then given him a piece of paper that was set afire in his hand.

"I repeated in Sicilian, 'This is the way I burn if I betray the organization'," he continued.

Valachi said the men at the table then "threw out a number," with each man holding up any number of fingers from one to five. The total was taken. Starting with Maranzano, the sum was then counted off around the table. The man on whom the final number fell was designated as Valachi's "godfather" in the family. Valachi said the lot had fallen to Bonanno.

The witness said that he had then had his finger pricked by a needle held by Bonanno to show he was united to Bonanno by blood. Afterward, Valachi continued, all those present joined hands in a bond to the organization.

Valachi said he was given two rules in Cosa Nostra that night — one concerning allegiance to it and another a promise not to possess another member's wife, sister or daughter.

For the first time, the witness grew grim. "This is the worst thing I can do, to tell about the ceremony," he said. "This is my doom, telling it to you and the press."

The witness started his day's testimony by telling of his life as a member of burglary gangs in East Harlem before he became involved with Cosa Nostra.

He said he had first been a member of a neighborhood burglary gang consisting mainly of Italians, who broke store windows to commit thefts. After a while, he said, he broke with the Italian group and joined a burglary combine known as "the Irish gang," although it was composed of young men of mixed nationalities.

Valachi said rivalry had erupted between the two gangs and that Vincent Rao, still a Harlem underworld figure, had asked him to double-cross the Irish gang. That was in 1924.

"I turned it down," Valachi said. "I told Rao, 'you guys gave me only a contract a dog would do, to double-cross your own friends.' "

"I was thinking of my own principles," he explained to the committee.

Valachi testified that he was sent to Sing Sing in 1925 for a burglary and served 44 months. On his return, he said, he learned that Frank La Puma, one of the Irish gang, had been murdered and that he himself was marked for death.

The witness said he was told that a thug named "Bum" Rogers got "$100 from Ciro Terranova to do the job."

Valachi said that in fear he then had gone to see Frank Livorsi, Terranova's chauffeur and bodyguard, to plead his own case, and that his life had been spared.

Terranova, known as "the artichoke king," was a former henchman of Al Capone, and a long-time power in the underworld.

"Did you feel better after your life was spared?" Senator McClellan asked.

"Well, naturally," the witness replied with a smile.

"Why was Terranova called the artichoke king?" Mr. McClellan continued.

"He had all the artichokes that came into the city tied up," Valachi said. "The artichokes could keep and then he would make his own price."

"Were artichokes so important?" the Senator asked.

"An artichoke is something an Italian must have for dessert," Valachi explained.

At one point in Valachi's testimony, Senator Jacob K. Javits, Republican of New York, asked the witness if Genovese was still in the rackets. Valachi said Genovese had been involved with Meyer Lansky in gambling operations in Havana and Las Vegas, Nev., and that he believed the two were still associated with Las Vegas gambling.

Valachi named Michael Miranda, Thomas Eboli (De Rosa) and Gerardo Catena as the men who were running things for Genovese while Genovese was in Federal prison on a narcotics charge.

Senator Javits asked Valachi if he could elaborate on his statement last Friday that Abe Reles had been thrown out of a window in the Half Moon Hotel, Coney Island, in 1941, while a witness in the Murder Inc., investigation.

Valachi said all he knew was what he had heard in gang circles and that the rumor was that Reles had been killed by his police guards.

Valachi's testimony will reime at 10:30 A. M. tomorrow.

October 2, 1963

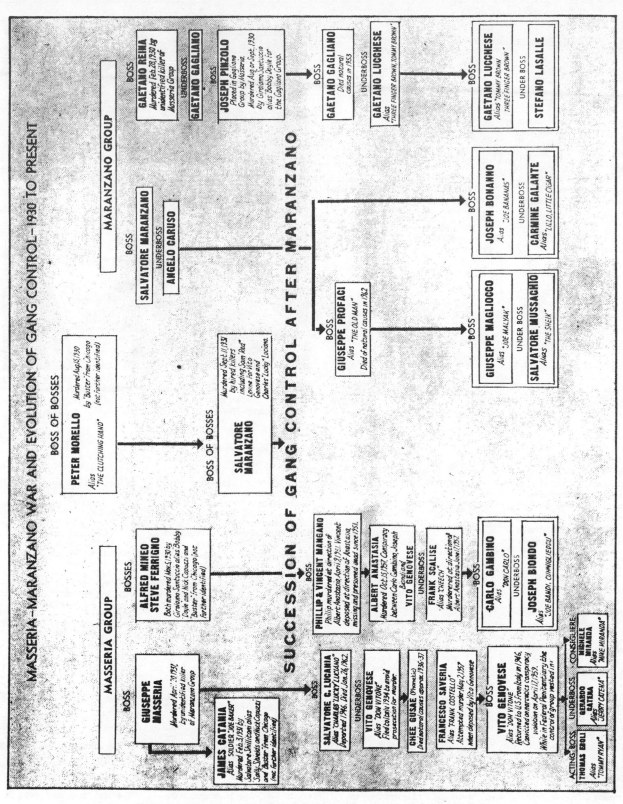

MASSERIA-MARANZANO WAR AND EVOLUTION OF GANG CONTROL—1930 TO PRESENT

MARANZANO GROUP

BOSS
GAETANO REINA
Murdered Feb. 26, 1930 by unidentified killers of Masseria Group

UNDERBOSS
GAETANO GAGLIANO

BOSS
JOSEPH PINZOLO
Placed in Gagliano Group by Masseria. Murdered Aug. or Sept. 1930 by Girolamo Santuccio alias Bobby Doyle for the Gagliano Group.

BOSS
GAETANO GAGLIANO
Died natural causes in 1953

UNDERBOSS
GAETANO LUCCHESE
Alias "THREE FINGER BROWN, TOMMY BROWN."

BOSS
GAETANO LUCCHESE
Alias "TOMMY BROWN, THREE FINGER BROWN."

UNDER BOSS
STEFANO LASALLE

BOSS
SALVATORE MARANZANO

UNDERBOSS
ANGELO CARUSO

MARANZANO GROUP

BOSS
SALVATORE MARANZANO

BOSS OF BOSSES
PETER MORELLO
Alias "THE CLUTCHING HAND"
Murdered Aug 15, 1930 by "Buster" from Chicago (not further identified)

BOSS OF BOSSES
SALVATORE MARANZANO
Murdered Sept. 11, 1931 by hired killers including Sam Red Levine for Vito Genovese and Charles "Lucky" Luciano.

SUCCESSION OF GANG CONTROL AFTER MARANZANO

BOSS
GIUSEPPE PROFACI
Alias "THE OLD MAN"
Died of natural causes in 1962

BOSS
GIUSEPPE MAGLIOCCO
Alias "JOE MALYAK"

UNDER BOSS
SALVATORE MUSSACHIO
Alias "THE SHEIK"

BOSS
JOSEPH BONANNO
Alias "JOE BANANAS"

UNDERBOSS
CARMINE GALANTE
Alias "LILLO, LITTLE CIGAR"

MASSERIA GROUP

BOSSES
ALFRED MINEO STEVE FERRIGNO
Both murdered Nov. 5, 1930 by Girolamo Santuccio alias Bobby Doyle and Nick Capuzzi and Buster from Chicago (not further identified)

BOSS
PHILLIP & VINCENT MANGANO
Phillip murdered at direction of Albert Anastasia April 19, 1951. Vincent deposed at direction of Anastasia, missing and presumed dead since 1951.

BOSS
ALBERT ANASTASIA
Murdered Oct. 15, 1957. Conspiracy between Carlo Gambino, Joseph Bonanno and Vito Genovese

UNDERBOSS
VITO GENOVESE

UNDERBOSS
FRANK SCALISE
Alias "CHEECH"
Murdered at direction of Albert Anastasia June 17, 1957.

BOSS
CARLO GAMBINO
Alias "DON CARLO"

UNDERBOSS
JOSEPH BIONDO
Alias "JOE BANDI, CUNNIGLIEDDU"

MASSERIA GROUP

BOSS
GIUSEPPE MASSERIA
Murdered Apr. 15, 1931, by unidentified killer of Maranzano Group

BOSSES
JAMES CATANIA
Alias SOLDIER "JOE BAKER"
Murdered Feb. 3, 1931 by Salvatore Shillitani alias Sally Streets and Nick Capuzzi and Buster from Chicago (not further identified)

BOSS
SALVATORE C. LUCANIA
Alias "CHARLES LUCKY LUCIANO". Deported 1946. Died Jan. 26, 1962.

UNDERBOSS
VITO GENOVESE
Alias "DON VITONE".
Fled to Italy 1934 to avoid prosecution for murder.

UNDERBOSS
CHEE GUSAE (Phonetic)
Died at direction approx. 1936-37

BOSS
FRANCESCO SAVERIA
Alias FRANK COSTELLO"
Attempted murder Nov. 2, 1957 when deposed by Vito Genovese

BOSS
VITO GENOVESE
Alias "DON VITONE"
Returned to U.S. from Italy in 1946. Convicted on narcotics conspiracy violation on April 17, 1959. While in Federal Penitentiary the control of group rested in:

ACTING BOSS
THOMAS EBOLI
Alias "TOMMY RYAN"

UNDERBOSS
GERARDO CATENA
Alias "JERRY CATENA"

CONSIGLIERE
MICHELE MIRANDA
Alias "MIKE MIRANDA"

Oct. 2, 1963
The New York Times

UNDERWORLD IN PERSPECTIVE: Chart, based on one introduced in yesterday's hearing of Senate Permanent Subcommittee on Investigations, showing the tangled details of the battle for control of gangs in New York area. Control ultimately found its way into hands of five chiefs.

Informer Tells More

By EMANUEL PERLMUTTER
Special to The New York Times

WASHINGTON, Oct. 2 — The Cosa Nostra stopped accepting new members in 1958, Joseph M. Valachi told Senate investigators today.

Adding more chapters to his account of the working of the crime syndicate, he said its "books" were closed in 1931, then reopened in 1954.

"They were kept open until 1958 and then closed because of what Albert Anastasia and Frank Scalise were doing," he testified at the open hearing of the Senate Permanent Subcommittee on Investigations.

The organization, which tried to keep its membership limited except when it was engaged in an underworld "war," he explained, was flooded with recruits by Anastasia and Scalise.

"They charged as much as $40,000 to join and brought in a few hundred men," he said. "That's one of the charges against them."

Anastasia and Scalise, listed by Valachi as "underbosses" in the syndicate, were murdered in 1957.

The 60-year-old reformed thug, a former member of Cosa Nostra, or Mafia, did not testify as to whether the membership rolls had since been reopened.

In the crowded hearing room he gave details of more murders, changes in syndicate leadership and reforms in the organization's inner policies dating to 1931.

Some of the information, he admitted, is based on hearsay. To experienced observers it seemed far-fetched. It reinforced the feeling that much of what he had said was not reliable.

However, law-enforcement officials present indicated they considered much of the testimony creditable.

The Justice Department hopes Valachi's testimony will give impetus to legislation permitting Federal law-enforcement authorities to tap wires and use the information they obtain in courts.

Valachi is scheduled to take the stand again when the hearings resume next Tuesday. He is expected to testify for two days.

Senator Carl T. Curtis, Republican of Nebraska, tried fruitlessly to get information from Valachi about organized crime in his area. The witness said he lacked knowledge of geography.

"Do you know of any Cosa Nostra groups in Omaha?" Mr. Curtis asked.

"I never heard of Omaha," Valachi replied.

"How about Des Moines?"

"Where is that?" Valachi asked. "I never heard of the place."

"Were you anywhere in the Midwest," Mr. Curtis persisted.

"Yeah, in Arkansas."

"You were in Arkansas?" interjected Senator John L. McClellan, Democrat of that state, who is subcommittee chairman.

"I was there for the baths, the 21-day baths," Valachi explained. He was alluding to Hot Springs, a health resort and horse-racing center.

Valachi credited Charles (Lucky) Luciano with having brought law and order to the organization in New York in 1931, after a "14-month war."

He said that Luciano became the acknowledged leader of the syndicate following the murder of Salvatore Maranzano on Sept. 11, 1931. Maranzano had served briefly as "Boss of Bosses" after the slaying of Joe (The Boss) Masseria in a Coney Island restaurant on April 20 that year.

Luciano was prosecuted in 1936 by Thomas E. Dewey, then New York District Attorney, and sentenced to Sing Sing as a white-slaver.

He was subsequently deported to Italy, where he died last year in his native Naples. He was involved there in the illegal narcotics trade, according to Federal authorities.

Valachi testified at length about the Masseria and Maranzano murders. He said that Luciano, Vito Genovese (now in jail) and Ciro Terranova, Maseria's aides, had lured their chief to the restaurant, where they killed him.

Terranova, once a feared figure, did not behave well immediately after the slaying, according to Valachi.

Terranova was supposed to drive the getaway car, Valachi said, but he "was so shaking in putting the key in the ignition, they had to remove him."

"After that, he got 'the buckwheats' [loss of prestige] and his power was taken away from him," Valachi continued. "He died of a broken heart."

After Masseria's death, Valachi went on, Maranzano informed him that he planned to

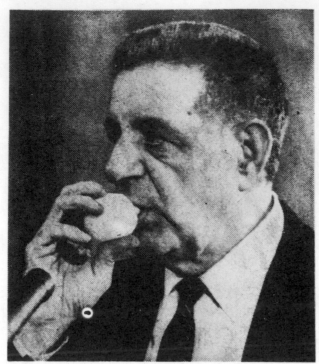

United Press International Telephoto

HOARSE WITNESS: Joseph M. Valachi takes lemon juice to ease the irritation in his throat at appearance before the Senate Permanent Subcommittee on Investigations.

murder a dozen of his late rival's supporters in a new war.

Maranzano listed Luciano, Genovese, Frank Costello, Dutch Schultz and Al Capone (then in Chicago) among his intended victims, the witness said.

Invited Pair to Office

Maranzano invited Luciano and Genovese to his office at Park Avenue and 46th Street, where he planned to have them killed by Vincent (Mad Dog) Coll, according to Valachi.

The assassination, he said, did not occur because "four Jews who posed as cops got there first and killed Maranzano."

He identified the four as gunmen who had worked for Meyer Lansky, a racketeer and gangster. Among them, Valachi said, was Samuel (Red) Levine, who is still alive.

Six years later, he said, Levine told him of his participation in the murder. Levine has a record of 22 arrests, dating to 1921.

As Coll entered the building where Maranzano was killed, Valachi said, the four assassins told him to flee because there

had been a shooting and the police were expected.

Coll, involved in many gangland murders during the Prohibition era, was shot to death Feb. 8, 1932, in the phone booth of a drug store at 314 West 23d Street, near Eighth Avenue. He was 23 years old.

On the day his chief was killed, Valachi told the Senators, "four or five" others were slain. He did not explain why. He identified one as a Jimmy Marino and referred to a "couple more in New Jersey."

The meeting, he said, was followed by a dinner that lasted five nights (with time off for sleeping). About $115,000 was collected from organization leaders and members. The money was for Maranzano and his soldiers who were broke as a result of the war, Valachi said.

"We soldiers never got nothing from him," he added.

The war cost Masseria 40 to 60 men, Valachi said, and "we only lost one."

He did not say who complained.

U.S. Gangsters Who Fled Cuba Said to 'Take Over' in Florida

By EMANUEL PERLMUTTER
Special to The New York Times

WASHINGTON, Oct. 15 — Senate investigators were told today that Florida was a lucrative base for America Mafia gangster refugees from Cuba.

They also heard that New England was a profitable habitat for the Mafia, or Cosa Nostra, crime syndicate.

Testimony on Mafia activities was given by police chiefs from those regions before the Senate Permanent Subcommittee on Investigations. The committee is holding public hearings on organized crime.

Chief Neil G. Brown of Tampa said that Santo Trafficante, a Mafia boss, controlled illegal gambling "throughout the state of Florida.

Police Commissioner Edmund L. McNamara of Boston and Col. Walter E. Stone of the Rhode Island State Police identified Raymond L. Patriarca of Providence as the Mafia boss who controlled organized crime in their areas.

Joseph M. Valachi, the syndicate member who turned informer, identified Trafficante and Patriarca as Cosa Nostra leaders when he testified last week.

A native of Tampa, Trafficante owned and operated the Sans Souci and other Havana clubs and gambling places under the regime of Fulgencio Batista. The gangster and his aides were expelled from the island after Fidel Castro's revolution.

Trafficante, 49 years old, was a delegate to the 1957 Mafia convention at Apalachin, N.Y. He had been questioned earlier that year by the New York City police in the murder of Albert Anastasia, another Mafia leader.

Chief Brown described Trafficante as a business associate of such notorious criminals as Meyer Lansky, Joseph Bonanno, Sam Giancana, Joseph Riccobone and leaders of the crime syndicate throughout the country.

He said that Trafficante maintained residences in Tampa and Miami, but that he carried on his activities from the central Florida area around Tampa, where the Mafia had its strongest organization.

He listed 23 gang killings in the Tampa area since 1928, but said a conviction had been obtained in only one. Fear of reprisals by the syndicate made it difficult to obtain witnesses in the cases, he said.

Another official, Sgt. William Branch of the Orlando Police Department, said the scope of the Trafficante gambling operations was disclosed a few months ago when a raid on one of his places in Sanford, Fla., showed it had a gross revenue of $250,-000 a week.

He said the Mafia gambling operations in Florida consisted mainly of a numbers game known as bolita or Cuba.

The bettor chooses a number from 1 to 100, he explained, and the winning number is drawn weekly. It is the last two digits in the five-digit Cuban national lottery number, which is broadcast every Saturday afternoon over a Havana radio station.

In the testimony dealing with the New England area, Colonel Stone said of Patriarca:

"He has the controlling interest on lotteries, bookmaking, dice games and the provision of wire service in this area. He settles any disputes within the organization."

The police record of the 56-year-old racketeer dates to 1926, he said, and includes several arrests and convictions for hijacking, escaping jail, violations of gambling laws, safecracking, armed robbery, adultery, carrying firearms, auto theft, and suspicion of murder.

The subcommittee's hearings end tomorrow, when police officials from the Buffalo and the northern New York area testify about Mafia operations there.

Senator John L. McClellan, Arkansas Democrat who heads the subcommittee, said that pending hearings on the narcotics traffic had been postponed because of a narcotics conspiracy trial scheduled to start in New York.

October 16, 1963

Las Vegas: Casinos' Hoodlums Face a Cleanup

By WALLACE TURNER

The Nevada Gaming Control Board shows signs of getting tougher with the casino operators.

The three-man control board is charged with enforcing the state laws under which the casinos operate. The most recent demonstration of strength from the board was the case in which it forced Frank Sinatra to dispose of his $3.5 million worth of casino interest in Las Vegas and Lake Tahoe on charges of associating with Sam Giancana, a Chicago hoodlum.

One of the problems that the board faces is that licensed gambling in Nevada has drawn together a greater collection of

State Starting to Act Against Shady Figures Who Run or Patronize Gambling

skilled law violators than exists anywhere else in the country.

This is not to say that everyone connected with gambling in Nevada is a crook. Some casino operators try to run their gambling houses on the same set of principles that they would use in running any other business.

The men who are professional gamblers generally learned their business in an area where casino gambling is illegal, as it is in every state except Nevada.

This gives them an ethical outlook different from that of the ordinary businessman. Thus the nation's economic structure has begun to feel the impact of well-financed but often unethical moves by gamblers into other businesses.

For many years public authorities have been on notice that some casino operators had roots and associations with notorious underworld figures.

They have come out of the underworlds of Detroit, Cleveland, Chicago and other cities of the North, South and both coasts. They have had associations with members of Murder, Inc., and with the international criminal organization.

It was 13 years ago that the Kefauver Committee brought out some of the background and associations of the Nevada gamblers in a one-day hearing in Las Vegas. Nevertheless, some of the figures described unflatteringly that day are still licensed.

In other hearings around the nation, the Kefauver Committee also heard continually of ties of these scattered underworld organizations with the Las Vegas gamblers.

Clifford A. Jones, a Las Vegas lawyer with an interest then in the Golden Nugget, the Thunderbird and the Pioneer Club casinos, described the situation in these words at that time:

"People who came here when the state started to grow, to gamble in the gambling business, they weren't particularly

Sunday school teachers or preachers. They were gamblers. They came here to gamble."

Mr. Jones's law firm represented the estate of the then recently murdered Benjamin (Bugsy) Siegal. One of Mr. Jones's partners in a casino was a part owner in one of the gambling ships that flourished off the California coast, thwarting antigambling laws for a time.

At the time he made those remarks, Mr. Jones also was the Lieutenant Governor of Nevada. Later he ran a casino in Havana and was the central figure in the state Gaming Control Board's attempt about eight years ago to prove that his interest in the Thunderbird Hotel was really a concealed interest of Meyer Lansky, the gambler.

Initially, the board won, but on appeal Mr. Jones was the victor. He no longer is a partner of record in the Thunderbird casino.

More recently Mr. Jones was involved in the controversy that followed the resignation of Robbert G. Baker as secretary to the Senate Democratic majority. It was made known two weeks ago that Mr. Baker arranged a series of meetings last summer for Mr. Jones and two other Nevada gamblers with John Gates, the president of Intercontinental Hotels, Inc., a Pan American World Airways subsidiary.

The meetings were to permit the three gamblers to discuss with Mr. Gates the hope they had of becoming the casino operators in hotels operated by Pan American in Curacao and the Dominican Republic.

With Mr. Jones at the meetings were his partner, Jacob Kozloff, and Edward Levinson, the manager and largest stockholder in the Fremont Hotel in Las Vegas. Mr. Jones and Mr. Kozloff now operate four small casinos in Latin America.

Another figure before the Kefauver Committee was William J. Moore, a member of the Nevada State Tax Commission, which in those days was the licensing body for gambling casinos. Mr. Moore owned a one-twelfth interest in one, the Last Frontier Hotel. The man who watched over the gambling in the Last Frontier casino was a partner in a California gambling ship.

Moore's Viewpoint

Mr. Moore told the Senators that as the only casino owner on the Tax Commission, it was his job to handle the investigations of new applicants and license renewals of gamblers already in business. He said he had recommended a license in Reno for William Graham and James McKay. These two men had been convicted of altering and passing Government bonds stolen from the Bank of Manhattan. Mr. Moore defended the issuance of licenses to men with criminal records.

Some of the infamous names of the American underworld of that period march through those few pages of the record of the hearing in Las Vegas. Mickey Cohen is there, to explain that he once had a piece of a place in Las Vegas, and to say that he knew Lou Rothkopf, a Cleveland underworld figure who was an associate of the group that started the Desert Inn. Meyer and Jack Lansky are discussed repeatedly. The ghost of Bugsy Siegal was invoked with almost every witness.

The theory today is that the law is more stern, that regulation is more strict, and that the gamblers are more attentive. But some still revert to the practices of their youth.

A few weeks ago a Federal judge in Los Angeles gave a probationary sentence of two years and meted out a $1,000 fine to Harold W. Goldbaum, who pleaded nolo contendre to a charge of transmitting horse race bets by interstate wire. The 65-year-old Goldbaum was an executive of the Stardust, one of two Strip casinos operated by a band of former bootleggers and gamblers from Cleveland.

The old-time gamblers on the Strip belong to what someone once called the "gambling fraternity." They know the same people, help each other and follow more or less the same moral and ethical codes.

This sort of conduct is far different from that usually associated with the business world, and when it is imported from the Strip to a business deal, chaos sometimes results.

Las Vegas and the casinos on the Strip have provided a haven for these men. Here they are operating legally for once in the business they know, gambling. They have status within the law, and take the time to plan and work out means of moving into businesses that are legal everywhere.

But when they make these moves into legality, observers have pointed out, they tend to take with them the same business practices they learned in the barred back rooms in New York, Chicago, Miami and Los Angeles. The "fix," the hard shove, the fast fleecing of the unwary all are a part of the training of an apprentice gambler.

Some of them show no indication of going into business, beyond the gambling they conduct on the Strip. A. F. Winter, the surviving member of the group that opened the Sahara Club in the early nineteen-fifties, has retreated to Portland, Ore., where he lives most of the time. He and two other men own the gambling casinos in the Sahara as well as the Mint Club, a downtown Las Vegas place, state records show.

Winter has a background somewhat unusual, even for a

GAVE UP INTERESTS: Frank Sinatra, who relinquished his casino holdings under pressure from the Gaming Control Board.

Nevada gambler. Those who have followed his career remember that his father was a circuit judge in Portland. Winter is a graduate of law school and a member of the Oregon Bar, although he has never maintained a law office.

During the nineteen-forties, Winter and his associates sat at the peak of as efficient a bookmaking and gambling operation as ever flourished on the Pacific Coast. They had a finger in horsebooks in Oregon and Southwestern Washington, and also operated an almost wide-open gambling house in the center of downtown Portland.

Reform Ousts Him

A reform administration was elected in Portland in 1948 and Winter and his associates went to Las Vegas, where they founded the Sahara Club and began to make more money than they knew existed before.

Now Winter dabbles in local politics in Portland, and the money continues to roll in from Las Vegas.

The Del E. Webb Corporation, a publicly owned company headed by the well known construction man, has acquired the physical properties of the Sahara, the most imposing building on the Strip, and the Mint, and is building a hotel to complement the Mint.

Known all over Las Vegas is Wilbur Clark, a small-time gambler who in the mid-nineteen-forties had a dream about building a casino, hotel and a golf course lined with expensive homes on 160 acres of desert along the Los Angeles highway outside Las Vegas.

When Clark went before the Kefauver Committee, he rambled through a confusing story of his trouble with finances. He began construction in May, 1947, and spent all his money, plus all that of his friends. The first $250,000 disappeared as if down a rat-hole.

"...And then these fellows from Cleveland came in." he said suddenly. He explained:

"They are in Reno on vacation and of course they knew, like everybody in the United States knew, that I was trying to get money. I had sat there from 1947 to 1949, was sitting there not finished."

Clark was asked to name his partners, and he answered:

"One of them is named Sam Tucker, Moe Dalitz, Morris Kleinman, and Thomas McGinty. And then there is two or three small ones that I don't know whether they have money in it or not. I know they are in the organization."

Clark got 25 per cent of the stock, some of which he distributed among his supporters, and the Cleveland group, which put up $1.3 million to finish the hotel and casino for its opening in April, 1950, got 74 per cent.

The remaining 1 per cent went to Hank Greenspun, who had been associated with Clark, Mr. Greenspun, now the publisher of The Las Vegas Sun, no longer has stock in the Desert Inn. He said in a recent interview that he has disassociated himself from the Desert Inn over dislike of the Cleveland group.

The partners had two gambling bosses. Clark said that they were "Cornelius Jones, and he represents those fellows and Williams represents my group, Alton Williams." Clark said that he was president, Kleinman vice president, and Dalitz treasurer.

Clark got his training as a gambler working as a craps dealer at Saratoga, Reno and Hollywood, and on the gambling boats Joanne A. Smith and Tango off the California shore. Then he put $25,000 into a down payment on El Rancho Vegas, and made a profit, which he sank into the Desert Inn.

He had been a small-timer until he had his big dream and tied in with "these fellows from Cleveland."

Later on Alvin Sutton, Director of Public Safety in Cleveland, drew this Prohibition-era picture of Dalitz and his associates:

"At the top of Cleveland's bootleggers were Morris Kleinman, Lou Rothkopf, Moe Dalitz, Sam Tucker and Maxie Diamond. They were at the helm of the board of directors. They had the suppliers of Canadian whisky, and their salesmen and thugs to distribute contraband and to reap the harvest of money.... Ruthless beatings, unsolved murders and shakedowns, threats and bribery came to this community as a result of the gangsters' rise to power."

These were also capable businessmen, trained in the rackets' hard school of business. Dalitz has also always operated laundries; during World War II he even did business for the Army. Moreover, Dalitz was once highly successful in helping an acquaintance gain control of two companies that were merged as Detroit Steel Corporation.

Some of his associates were with Dalitz in this transaction, and this may have given the Cleveland organization a taste for the profits to be had from successful deals in corporate finance, and other non-gambling business ventures.

The group made a foray into the stock market in the mid nineteen-fifties, with disastrous results. Today it has branches in hospital construction and operation, golf course construction, apartment development, building management and home development.

The Desert Inn group moved into Havana when Fulgencio Batista, who was running Cuba at the time, opened the city to gambling casinos. The men stayed until April, 1958, when Nevada authorities ordered the state's licensed gamblers to get out of Havana.

They left a lot of their money in Havana. Those from the Desert Inn who had to rid themselves of interest in the Hotel Nacional de Cuba Casino in Havana included M. B. Dalitz, Thomas Jefferson McGinty, Morris Kleinman and Wilbur Clark. Other Nevada gamblers were in other Havana casinos and had to leave.

In the history of control of gambling by the state of Nevada, there have been landmarks demonstrating a toughening attitude from the state in the difficult job of imposing standards on the gamblers.

One of these was the order to get out of Havana. Another came this fall when Mr. Sinatra, the entertainer, abandoned his gambling interests at Cal-Neva Lodge at Lake Tahoe and the Sands on the Strip.

Mr. Sinatra is a man with many friends and an unusual number live in Nevada. He has influence in the state. Yet, when the Gaming Control Board

pushed a complaint against him, he threw in the towel.

This case has importance beyond its surface implications. It has the effect of reiterating the state's right to control who is permitted to visit a licensed gambling place.

In 1960 the Gaming Control Board circulated a "black book," which had 11 sheets of paper bound in a cheap, limp cardboard cover. Each sheet was devoted to a short rundown on a widely known underworld figure. The licensees were told orally to keep those men out of their casinos.

Two of the names were Marshall Caifano and Sam Giancana, both of Chicago.

Caifano, who uses the alias "Johnny Marshall," went to the Strip soon after the book was issued. At first, the licensees, who had been warned after his appearance, refused to order him out of their place. The Gaming Control Board's agents then began to gather up dice and cards and test them and generally to disrupt the gambling operations.

The word was passed and when Caifano went to the Desert Inn, he was hustled out. He has filed suit against many of those who dealt with him that night, charging deprivation of his civil rights. The decision on his complaint could have considerable effect on the claimed right of the Gaming Control Board to control the premises of license holders.

It was Sam Giancana who got Mr. Sinatra into trouble. Giancana, fresh from a court victory in Chicago where he won limitations on the right of the Federal Bureau of Investigation to follow him, swept into the Lake Tahoe area and set up housekeeping in chalet No. 50 at Cal-Neva Lodge, the Sinatra enterprises. He was there to visit his friend, Phyllis McGuire, who was singing at Cal-Neva, Mr. Sinatra's friends have explained.

On Sept. 11, Edward A. Olsen, chairman of the Gaming Control Board, signed a complaint, which said this entertainment of Giancana "reflects discredit upon the States of Nevada and the gaming industry." He also asserted that Mr. Sina-

tra associated with and spoke to Giancana without asking him to leave Cal-Neva Lodge.

"Frank Sinatra has for a number of years maintained and continued social association with said Sam Giancana well knowing his unsavory and notorious reputation, and has openly stated that he intends to continue such association," Mr. Olsen asserted.

Mr. Sinatra also was accused in the complaint of phoning Mr. Olsen with the attempt to intimidate him with "vile, intemperate, obscene and indecent language." An employe of the Cal-Neva Lodge, Paul (Skinny) d'Amato, was accused of trying to force a bribe upon an employe of the Gaming Control Board. Another employe, Edward H. King, a Palm Springs (Calif.) lieutenant of Mr. Sinatra's, was accused of avoiding a subpoena.

The board absolved Mr. Sinatra's partners of any part in all these actions, but it demanded that he surrender his 50 per cent ownership in Cal-Neva Lodge gambling and his 9 per cent interest in the license at the Sands, one of the top places on the Las Vegas Strip. One estimate placed the value of Mr. Sinatra's holdings at $3.5 million.

After questioning the Gaming Control Board members in closed sessions, Mr. Sinatra's counsel issued a statement saying the singer would get out of gambling, rather than fight the charge against him.

Two Martins There

Mr. Sinatra's departure from Nevada gambling leaves the entertainment world represented by the 2 per cent of the Riviera Hotel held by Tony Martin, and the 1 per cent of the Sands held by Dean Martin.

Other change is coming gradually to the Strip, with more and more emphasis on the morally unmarked personalities brought in as top management.

An example of this is at the Desert Inn where a respected San Diego lawyer, J. A. Donnelley, has been appointed executive vice president. This job was formerly held by Allard

Associated Press

PERSONA NON GRATA: Sam Giancana, a hoodlum listed in "black book." He was guest of Frank Sinatra at lodge in Lake Tahoe.

Roen, one of those who was convicted in the United Dye & Chemical stock fraud case. That case was a part of the stock market foray that put the entire Desert Inn organization into great jeopardy.

Mr. Donnelly has practiced law in San Diego for about 30 years and has a reputation for honor and integrity. For about the last 15 years the Desert Inn has been one of his clients.

Now he moves in as successor to Roen, and also to Dalitz, who at age 63 shows indication of spending more time on the golf course and less in the casino.

Mr. Donnelley's assumption of authority certainly will be subject to Dalitz's wishes. But as the shift in control comes, it will weaken those bonds that bind the Desert Inn to those older figures in the underworld who share with Dalitz the memories of the rum-runners on the Great Lakes and the wide-open gambling houses of Covington and Newport, Ky.

Roots of the Gallo-Profaci War: Youth vs. Age, Need vs. Plenty

By EMANUEL PERLMUTTER

Youth against middle age. Need against plenty. Truculence versus contentment. Obscurity versus status.

These contrasts are believed by the police to be the causes of the underworld war between the Gallo and Profaci gangs that led yesterday to indictments against the Gallos on charges of trying to kill off their rivals.

The head of the Profaci gang is Joseph Magliocco, a heavy-set, benign-looking man of 65 who lives in East Islip, L. I., in a baronial type of mansion protected by a stockade fence.

Magliocco rides horses and grows tomatoes on his estate. His expensively dressed visitors are usually other middle-aged or elderly men whom he entertains on his 39-foot yacht or at the private steam bath that he maintains in another dwelling.

Magliocco, who was born in Sicily, speaks broken English and he affects meekness and mental lethargy in his confrontations with law-enforcement authorities.

When he was brought in for questioning last August by the Suffolk County District Attorney in connection with the murder of a member of the Gallo gang, he clutched his heart, wolfed down pills and acted bewildered. He hardly acted the part of the head of a gang involved in murder, gambling and other forms of law-breaking.

In contract, the members of the Gallo gang are not affluent. They are young men. They are American-born. And they are not meek.

During a police interrogation, Joe Gallo, who is now in jail, heard a detective say "Frank Costello owns New Orleans," implying that Costello ran the rackets in that city.

"Who gave him New Orleans?" asked the hoodlum known as Crazy Joe. "Eisenhower? If you're strong enough to take it, it's yours."

Most of the Gallo members live in South Brooklyn tenements or in low-rent apartments. They have to scrounge for weekly subsistence. They are on the constant lookout for Profaci gunmen pledged to assassinate them.

The Profaci Mafia family is an old one, with national status in the underworld. Its long-time leader was Joseph Profaci, who died last year of cancer. He was related by family and marriage to Mafia chiefs in other cities.

The Profaci organization, now run by Magliocco, the late leader's brother-in-law, is more than 30 years old. It was started by Profaci after the assassination in 1931 f Salvatore Maranzano, who headed a Mafia branch whose members all had Sicilian backgrounds.

Although Profaci had been a gunman for Maranzano, he was able to make his peace with Maranzano's enemies, mostly of Neapolitan origin. These enemies consisted of such future underworld chiefs as Vito Genovese, Frank Costello, Charles "Lucky" Luciano and Albert Anastasia.

Profaci ruled his family with an iron hand and he became a ranking member of the Mafia national ruling commission. He and Magliocco developed considerable legitimate business as well as racket interests. They led quit, church-going lives in their communities.

The Gallo members, starting as "soldiers" or underlings in the Profaci organization, never had a chance to advance in their trade. They were restricted to payments for individual jobs and rarely were given racket enterprises for themselves.

Since they were young and in need of funds for liquor and girl friends, they resorted to robberies, hijacking of trucks and other forms of law-breaking. They were frequently involved in barroom brawls and encounters with the police. These fights served to estrange them further from their Mafia bosses, who sought to avoid police attention by leading exemplary private lives.

Police officials have tended to regard the Gallo gangsters as a throwback to the freewheeling mobs of the Prohibition era. But they could never achieve the status of these underworld predecessors.

December 11, 1963

U.S. Fight on Organized Crime Brings Wide Rise in Convictions

Special to The New York Times

WASHINGTON, Jan. 11— The Justice Department's fight against organized crime is beginning to show substantial results in terms of actual cases.

Figures released by the White House this week disclosed a sharp rise in the number of persons indicted and convicted in the special organized crime campaign.

The intensified campaign was started by Attorney General Robert F. Kennedy when he took office in 1961. Its key has been the pooling of information on key suspects by various Federal agencies, which often had been at odds or ignorant of each other's material before.

The Federal Bureau of Investigation, which had not been deeply involved in the crime problem, has become much more so. Working with it have been, among others, two Treasury agencies—the Bureau of Narcotics and the Internal Revenue Service.

The organized crime section of the Justice Department's Criminal Division has been pooling the information gathered by these intelligence units. And it has been putting together cases against those it believes are major figures in the national underworld.

In 1963 the Justice Department obtained 288 convictions of racketeers and others in the organized crime category. That compares with 45 in 1960, the last year before the coordinated drive; 73 in 1961 and 138 in 1962.

Indictments rose even more sharply, with 49 individuals indicted in 1960, 121 in 1961, 35 in 1962 and 615 last year.

Violations of various laws are involved in these cases. Racketeers have been prosecuted under antigambling, tax, narcotics, extortion and other laws.

President Johnson, in releasing the figures, paid a particular tribute to Mr. Kennedy. He said "it should be recognized that the intensified Federal effort against organized crime stems in large part from the deep interest and leadership of the Attorney General. His efforts deserve our appreciation

January 12, 19

Mafia Steps Up Infiltration And Looting of Businesses

By CHARLES GRUTZNER

The Senate Permanent Investigations Subcommittee, which is drafting a report on organized crime, has found that underworld penetration of business and industry has reached a degree undreamed of a generation ago.

The subcommittee, headed by Senator John L. McClellan, will submit later this month its recommendations for new laws to cope with the situation.

The national crime organization, known variously as the Mafia, Cosa Nostra and the Syndicate, lurks in the mainstream of American life like a crocodile, taking an annual toll that runs into billions of dollars, a New York Times survey has found.

Only its snout—gambling, usury, murder, narcotics and other flagrantly criminal enterprises—is discernible to the average citizen.

The bulk of the body, submerged from view, is recognizable only by experts, most of whom are law-enforcement officers or government investigators.

This part of the syndicate is reported to have taken over bowling alleys, real estate holdings, food packaging concerns, industrial plants, Wall Street brokerage houses and trucking companies, and to be eating its way into banks, union welfare funds, the construction industry and other components of the national economy.

Information on these activities is being developed for grand juries, and tomorrow a classic case of a business takeover will be climaxed with the sentencing here of three notorious members of the Mafia.

Estimates of the amounts drained from the public by organized crime are at best educated guesses because of the surreptitious nature of the rackets. Investigating bodies have been told that organized gambling involves $7 billion a year in the United States, that loan sharks take $1 billion and that the narcotics trade comes to $350 million.

No one has attempted to estimate the Mafia's take from its infiltration of legitimate business. Investigators—who have only scratched the surface—say the yield is enormous and may become the chief source of underworld income.

Government officials have disclosed that at least two grand juries are investigating the take-over of commercial banks by Mafia elements. Most of the banks involved are said to be in the East and Middle West.

The investigations staff of Senator McClellan is reported to be preparing for hearings to determine whether gangsters were involved in a number of recent bank failures. A report about the questions these failures raise appears on page 1 of the financial pages, Section 3.

"If the black flag of the underworld were to unfurl atop one of the tallest skyscrapers in New York it would be a fit symbol of how the Mafia has gained control of that building and many other real estate holdings," a Federal investigation said.

United States Attorney Robert M. Morgenthau, who has three grand juries delving into the mysteries of the Mafia, has found that real estate is a favored field of the gangs because the use of dummy fronts has long been accepted even in legitimate realty transactions.

Using dummy fronts, the real owners of a business, the men who put up the money, never have to list themselves as owners or partners or as even being involved in any way in the business.

Such dummy fronts are useful in other than the realty business as well. Gangsters operating behind dummies who have no criminal records can corrupt honest businesses before their connection is detected.

In such set-ups it is difficult for the Government to prove even that a gangster is involved in a legitimate business much less prove that he has broken the law in any way.

But the Mafia is not proceeding unhindered. Federal and local law enforcers have inflicted more punishment on its members in the last 12 months than in any other year.

1,500 Identified Here

Since Joseph M. Valachi, convicted narcotics trader and murderer, turned against the Mafia and helped to identify 317 members in late 1963, the authorities have identified 1,500 members of the five New York gangs—or families—of the organization.

The secret organization is believed to have at least 5,000 members throughout the United States, and they have been subjected to increasing pressure.

An indication of this is in the figures cited by Nicholas deB. Katzenbach, United States Attorney General, on Federal convictions for gambling, narcotics, bootlegging, prostitution, public corruption, syndicate-operated frauds and labor-management and other racket crimes. There were 45 such convictions in 1960 and more than 500 last year.

Also, the Senate investigating subcommittee has been at work. Part of its forthcoming report will be based on information developed since Valachi broke the underworld code and appeared before the committee in open session in 1963.

In The Times's survey dozens of Federal and local investigators were interviewed and police files were searched in New York, Washington and elsewhere.

Detective Sgt. Ralph Salerno, an expert on the Mafia in the Police Department's central investigation bureau, said in one interview that it had taken a long time for the public and for many law officials to accept the fact that crime was organized on a national basis.

Authorities Moved Slowly

"For too many years," he declared, "we were called cloak-and-dagger detectives for insisting there was a criminal organization with ties across the country. I'm not talking only of an apathetic public but about policemen and enforcement officials who would not or could not accept the evidence."

Sergeant Salerno, olive skinned and broad shouldered, declared the modern Mafia is engaged in almost a cradle-to-the-grave scheme to mulct the national economy of billions.

"They're in nearly everything from kiddie ride parks to pension funds," the sergeant said. "You can't overestimate the areas they're moving into. They don't usually come in with guns, but with money, lots and lots of money from gambling and narcotics to take over legitimate business.

"Why, they put such heavy money into one bank that one of their guys was made a director. So what did he do? He lent large sums of bank money to one of their fronts at 6 per cent, and within 24 hours that money was in the Shylock racket bringing the mob over 100 per cent."

"Call it Mafia, Cosa Nostra or what you will," Sergeant Salerno said, "but organized crime has become one of the biggest businesses in the United States and is trying to act like big business.

"Hoods like Dutch Schultz never went without two bodyguards. Today's bosses of organized crime have a lawyer and accountant instead. There are fewer murders, usually limited to suspected informers, except for an intrafamily power struggle, like when the Gallo boys in Brooklyn rebelled against Joe Profaci."

A classic exposition of how the Mafia seized and raided a legitimate business, drained it of $745,000 in three months and bankrupted it was developed in a six-weeks trial in Federal Court here that ended with the conviction last Dec. 30 of six men and a Brooklyn wholesale meat and poultry concern.

The individuals, to be sentenced tomorrow, face up to five years in prison and $5,000 on each of eight counts. The company faces a $10,000 fine.

It took nearly four years to bring the looters to book.

They are: Peter Castellana, a member of the Gambino Mafia family and a second cousin of its leader, Carlo Gambino; Joseph Pagano, a member of the Vito Genovese Mafia family, twice convicted in narcotics cases, and named in the Valachi testimony as one of the three killers in the unsolved 1952 murder of Eugene Giannini, whom the Mafia suspected of being an informer for the Bureau of Narcotics; and Gondolfo Sciandria, an uncle of Castellana.

Also Joseph Weinberg, his son Stanley Weinberg, and David Newman, former officers of what had been the legitimate Murray Packing Company, Inc., in the Bronx.

Also in the cast of characters, but not a defendant in the Federal bankruptcy case, was Carmine Lombardozzi, one of the most versatile of the Gambino Mafiosi, whose loan-shark talents were a factor in this case.

Up to Dec. 1, 1960, the Weinbergs and Newman were operating Murray Packing as a legitimate supplier of meat, poultry and eggs to meat wholesale houses and markets. Among their customers was the Pride Wholesale Meat and Poultry Corporation, whose president was Castellana.

Pride was one of several meat businesses run by members of the Gambino gang. Castellana also owned or had interests in 10 retail supermarkets.

In December, Murray Packing found itself short of money and became ripe for the loan-shark action. Pagano was then a $150-a-week salesman for a Murray subsidiary, the Mercury Hotel Supply Company. He told the elder Weinberg and Newman he could get them the money.

The trail of intrigue and looting, as developed for a jury by Albert J. Gaynor, executive assistant to Mr. Morgenthau, led from Pagano to Castellana, who was half-owner with Lombardozzi of the Jo-Ran Trading Corporation.

A Jo-Ran check for $8,500, bearing Lombardozzi's signature, was given to the Murray Packing owners, who agreed to pay 1 per cent interest a week. A series of weekly checks for $85 was put in evidence of interest payments without reducing the $8,500-indebtedness.

In January, the Weinbergs and Newman were forced to sell one-third interest in their concern to Pagano and to make him president so he could "protect the investment."

Pagano now was running the show at Murray Packing. His signature was required on every check, along with one other principal.

The Pride company, which had been buying about $1,000 a month worth of products from Murray, now began a wild spree of buying. Its purchases in January, 1961, came to $241,-000. In February they were $298,000, and in March they zoomed to $922,000. Oddly, the billings were at prices below Murray's own costs. This was a strange windfall for Castellana's company.

In eight days, beginning March 20, the Pride company paid $750,000 to Murray Packing. This was a lot of money even in a Mafia operation, and Castellana had to borrow $150,-000 from a legitimate factor to round it out.

Castellana had an account in the Commercial Bank of North America. Pagano got Murray Packing to transfer its account to the same bank. This is where Sciandria entered the picture.

Sciandria, who had been put into a food-distributing business and had himself bought $200,000 worth of poultry from Murray Packing that month, became Castellana's messenger in the money transfers.

Sciandria was taking Castellana's checks, payable to Murray Packing, to the bank, where he would meet Pagano. Pagano would present the checks and a deposit slip to a teller to whom he also handed a Murray Packing check made out to himself in the same amount. In this way Murray was milked of as much as $125,000 in a single day and $745,000 in about a week with the connivance of its original legitimate owners.

The processors across the nation who had supplied Murray Packing had not been paid. During the bankruptcy proceedings it developed that the conspirators had transferred $112,-000 more of Murray assets to defraud the creditors.

The whereabouts of the $745,-000 in cash drawn by Pagano remains a mystery. During the bankruptcy hearings before the trial Pagano was sentenced to prison for contempt for refusing to tell. He has remained there for 19 months without telling.

What of the Future?

The Mafia family heads, who amassed in outright rackets and criminal enterprises the fortunes now being invested in so-called legitimate businesses, are now mostly in their 60's and 70's. Of interest to sociologists and criminologists is whether the nature of their operations will change after the old Dons vanish from the scene.

Their sons, many college trained, have a yearning for respectability. They want to move in polite society. They don't want their wives and children pointed out as part of the underworld. They could, if they chose, live comfortably on returns from legitimate investment.

But will they follow the mores of their college and legitimate business associates or will family traditions keep them in the racket ruts?

Arnold Sagalyn, director of the Treasury Department's office of law enforcement coordination, and this country's representative in Interpol, the international police organization, said that in organizations like the Mafia and the Triad societies of China crime had become a way of life.

"The law is your enemy in everything," Mr. Sagalyn said. "If you have trouble, you settle it yourself. You believe your own code is the only law."

The Mafia code is not inviolate among those who profess it. Mafiosi have in many instances broken its rules, betrayed and murdered fellow members. The sons of the old Dons may wear Brooks charcoal grays and carry Abercrombie attaché cases, they may even content themselves with legitimate increment of their fathers' criminal fortunes, but observers of the Mafia believe there will be a continuing stream of young punks ambitious to start new fortunes outside the law and that they will use the trappings and traditions of the old Mafia.

Membership in this hard-core criminal brotherhood, sealed in a rite that involves pricking a finger to draw blood and burning a piece of paper sometimes cut in the shape of a saint, is limited to men of Italian birth of descent.

Although the rite is the same as in the centuries-old Sicilian Mafia, the modern American Mafia is neither a branch nor a counterpart of the secret society that gained renewed strength in Sicily after the Allied Military Government put into local offices Mafiosi whom Mussolini had imprisoned.

The strength of the Mafia does not mean that Italians have a monopoly on organized crime. It seems to indicate only that the Italian criminals had a greater talent for organization than the Irish, Jewish and German gangs they fought for control of bootleg liquor and other rackets in the streets of New York and other cities during Prohibition.

"The organization has a working relationship with other criminal organizations made up of people of varying ethnic and religious backgrounds," according to William G. Hundley, chief of the Organized Crime and Racketeering section of the Department of Justice in Washington.

It has been estimated that

as many as 750,000 nonmembers are employed in Mafia enterprises or associated in joint ventures. This includes collectors, runners and other cogs in bookmaking and numbers rackets, narcotics pushers, hired thugs, agents for the loan sharks and the fronts in countless business manipulations.

The Mafia leaders have on occasion utilized killers from other ethnic groups to carry out executions. In their lighter moments the Mafiosi refer to their Jewish hirelings or associates as the Kosher Nostra.

3 Juries at Work

Since last February three Federal grand juries in New York have devoted themselves to the war against the Mafia.

One has been concentrating on the affairs of the section, or family, headed by Thomas (Three Finger Brown) Luchese, who has long directed gambling, loan shark, labor racketeering and vending machine operations in addition to owning several garment and fabric companies here and in eastern Pennsylvania.

Five lieutenants have been given immunity from prosecution but have gone to jail for contempt rather than talk. Several other members of the gang have been fugitives since the investigation began, but the grand jury has gleaned from other witnesses information on which it hopes to hand up indictments soon.

Luchese is reputed to be the local Mafia's political liaison man. He has been particularly strong in Tammany Hall and has wielded influence in mayoral campaigns and leadership contests. His son attended West Point on a Congressman's recommendation.

A second grand jury is ferreting out the affairs of the Mafia family headed by Joseph (Joe Bananas) Bonanno. The night before his scheduled appearance before that jury, Bonanno was, according to his lawyer, kidnapped at gunpoint. Federal officials believe the kidnapping may have been a hoax to enable Bonanno, who is still missing, to avoid going before the jury.

A third grand jury is studying the over-all Mafia picture and the inter-relations of its different families. Eventually grand juries will give individual attention to the three other New York-based families.

One of these has as its titular leader Vito Genovese, who is serving a 15-year term in Federal prison for narcotics offenses. Thomas (Tommy Ryan) Eboli, listed by the F.B.I. as involved in gambling, juke boxes and extortion, is understood to be acting boss of the Genovese family with Gerardo (Jerry) Catena, underboss in charge of New Jersey.

The second due for individual attention is the gang still known as the Profaci family, although its millionaire head,

Joseph (The Old Man) Profaci died in 1962 of cancer.

Profaci's brother-in-law Joseph (The Fat Man) Magliocco ruled briefly and weakly from an East Islip, L. I., mansion behind a wire fence. The Fat Man's death from natural cause in December, 1963, led to rivalry among several underlings for his warped crown.

The principal contenders were these notorious hoodlums: John (Sonny) Franzese, listed by the F.B.I. in half a dozen different crime categories and reputed boss of Mafia-controlled bars and nightspots in this city and on Long Island; Nicholas (Jiggs) Forlano, a graduate of Sing Sing with a long police record, and Charles (The Sidge) LoCicero, who was running a major gambling racket while operating a furniture distributing company.

The heads of the other Mafia families here, shying away from the publicity some of the more bizarre Mafiosi were attracting, decided Magliocco's successor should be a member with an almost clean record.

They thumbed down the principal rivals and agreed on a comparative unknown. The new boss of the old Profaci family was identified at a recent public hearing of the State Investigation Commission as Joseph Colombo, a Brooklyn real estate salesman.

Mr. Colombo is a salesman for the Cantalupo Realty Company. He lives in a $47,000 home just off Dyker Beach Park. He is listed by the F.B.I. as a gambling operator. His police record shows only a 1956 arrest for disorderly conduct and two 1958 arrests for vagrancy, all of which resulted in acquittal or dismissal.

The third gang to be investigated is that headed by Carlo Gambino. A chart prepared for the McClellan committee's hearings in 1963 identified 81 present or recent members of the Gambino group. The number of identifications has now been brought to 200 and it is believed there may be 500 members in this large family.

Gambino is a specialist in labor racketeering and loan sharking, but members of this group are active in almost every racket from narcotics and gambling to disposing of stolen goods, extortion and murder.

While Mr. Morgenthau and his grand juries are directing new blows at the Mafia from their base in the Federal Court House at Foley Square, investigations that may bring additional indictments are being pressed across the two rivers that flank Manhattan.

United States Attorney Joseph P. Hoey, whose jurisdiction includes Brooklyn, Queens, Richmond, Nassau and Suffolk, has a staff of experts analyzing the accelerated movement of Mafia men and money into Long Island industries and rackets.

In Newark, United States

Attorney David M. Satz Jr. is directing assaults throughout New Jersey against the Mafia, which is strong in the northern area near New York City and also has a branch in the area near Philadelphia.

Local Inquiries Pressed

Because of the interstate spread of many Mafia operations, many of the major cases have been developed by Federal agencies. But the District Attorneys in all the metropolitan area counties are coordinating their work with that of the Federal men and are bringing Mafiosi to book for violations of state laws.

New York District Attorney Frank S. Hogan's rackets bureau under Chief Assistant Alfred J. Scotti, is keeping tabs on Mafia activities here. In Brooklyn, District Attorney Aaron E. Koota has a special squad of eight detectives under Assistant District Attorney Albert V. DeMeo concentrating on the Mafia.

In New Jersey, Essex County Prosecutor Brendan T. Byrne has a special grand jury looking into the Mafia, including its alleged pipelines into some police departments. A reporter who had made inquiries in Newark police circles about the Mafia was astounded when he later made a Mafia contact and learned that the underworld knew that he had talked with the police.

160,000 on File

In New York, the F.B.I. has excellent liaison with the Police Department's Central Investigation Bureau, an outgrowth of the Italian squad set up in 1904 to stamp out the extortion racket run here by the Unione Siciliane, also known as the Black Hand.

There are 160,000 index cards in the C.I.B. files in a downtown office building where the listing "C.I.B., Inc.," on the lobby board thinly masks the fact that a police unit occupies an entire floor.

The index cards refer to records of all sorts of crimes and rackets and to dossiers on thousands of individuals. They include, besides known criminals and their suspected racket associates, information about presumably innocent businessmen in whose enterprises Mafia money has been invested.

Assistant Chief Inspector John F. Shanley, former C.I.B. head, worked with the F.B.I. and the McClellan committee staff in drawing up the charts that delineated the ramifications of the Mafia. Chief Inspector Shanley, now commanding officer of the Police Commissioner's confidential investigating unit, has been succeeded in the C.I.B. by Deputy Inspector Arthur Grubert, an officer with a distinguished record of detective work.

One of their most difficult jobs has been keeping up with the criminal infiltration of business and industry.

Moving In on Business

Bookmakers, loan sharks and dishonest fronts work in concert to enmesh businessmen in situations that result in takeover of their businesses. The owner of a business who is in debt for gambling is steered to a loan shark who lends him enough to pay off his bookmaker so that he may resume gambling.

With interest compounded at 1 per cent a week (in some cases 2 per cent) the businessman is soon so deep in hock that the Mafia puts in one of its members as a partner. It may continue the partnership; it may eventually crowd out the original owner; or it may siphon off capital and bankrupt the business.

Sometimes the organized underworld chisels its way into a legitimate business by lending money at exorbitant interest to a garment manufacturer or a housing developer or contractor who cannot get a bank loan because the risk is too great.

At other times the infiltration has begun with the legitimate purchase of stock or other investment in an honest business of some of the Mafia profits from gambling, narcotics and other rackets.

One Wall Street brokerage house refuses to recommend any real estate investment to its customers because it is so difficult to trace Mafia infiltration in real estate. While most real estate firms are run honestly, the companies where Mafia control is known or suspected include some of the very large owners of offices buildings and developers of land.

The State Investigation Commission developed testimony at its recent hearings that the investing public had already been swindled of millions of dollars through brokerage houses of which racketeers connected with the Mafia had gained control.

Gangsters had taken over the investment houses after making loans at exorbitant interest to their owners, who were unable to keep up their payments. The Mafia then used these brokerage houses to promote the stock of fraudulent companies, one of which resulted in losses by the public of $1.25 million; another of $1 million.

An independent survey of Government officials and market experts pointed to more than a score of companies whose stock is traded on the New York or the American Stock Exchanges or over-the-counter as having Mafia fronts in key positions.

Prosecution Difficult

In at least one large city the vending machines in public buildings, including the courthouse, are owned by the Mafia. There are hundreds of other cases in the metropolitan area where Mafia ownership of or partnership in important legitimate business is known to government investigators. But assembling evidence to warrant an indictment for criminal conspiracy—the most likely charge—is a slow and difficult task.

In another business area, the State Liquor Authority is aware of tight Mafia control over many bars and night clubs in Greenwich Village, in midtown, on the fashionable East Side and out on Long Island.

Most of the bars that cater to male and female homosexuals are Mafia operations and some are bases for blackmail of deviates from wealthy families.

Ten Mafiosi whose connection with the criminal organization did not become known until they were arrested at Apalachin, N. Y., when Mafia leaders met there in 1957, had their liquor licenses canceled in 1958, but since then the S.L.A. has been unable to prove Mafia ownership.

The S.L.A. has canceled more than 125 licenses on the ground of hidden ownership. About 75 per cent of the licenses were canceled in New York and its suburbs and others in Buffalo, Utica, Rochester, Syracuse, Albany, Troy, Elmira and Schenectady.

Investigators Needed

Donald S. Hostetter, a former F.B.I. man who is chairman of the liquor agency, said that with 45 investigators to handle all types of liquor-law violations throughout the state it was difficult enough to prove the existence of a false front but impossible to get behind it. That, he said, would require "an army of investigators and accountants."

"It's impossible to open a joint in the Village and stay in business without a Mafia partner," said one operator. He hinted that a few crooked policemen cooperated with the gang and issued summonses for violations, real or fancied, against places without Mafia protection.

Since the disappearance of Anthony (Tony Bender) Strollo, who is believed to have been murdered for reaching for too much power, Thomas (Tommy Ryan) Eboli is understood to be overseer of the bar and night club racket in this city for the Genovese family.

The Mafia also has been tied to corruption of the courts here.

Anthony (Tony Ducks) Corallo, a member of the Mafia family of Thomas Luchese, was the go-between in the bribery of Supreme Court Justice Vincent Keogh and former Assistant United States Attorney Elliott Kahaner. The three were convicted in 1963 and sentenced to two years in prison in a case involving an attempt to influence a Federal judge in a bankruptcy fraud case.

On the national level statesmen of the underworld make up a commission whose membership is usually from 9 to 12 or 13 heads of families from the areas of greatest strength.

The Men In Control

The present commission, according to the best information available to the Department of Justice, includes four members from the New York-New Jersey metropolitan area; Gambino, Luchese, Catena representing the imprisoned Genovese, and John (Johnny Burns) Morales representing the Bonanno family.

The other members are believed to be as follows:

Stefano (Steve) Magaddino of Buffalo, 73-year-old boss of organized crime from western New York to the Ohio Valley, is believed to be chairman of the commission.

Sam (Momo) Giancana, 57, boss of all rackets in the Chicago area, who came to New York recently to discuss with local Mafia bosses a reorganization of the missing Bonanno's clan.

Joseph Zerilli of Grosse Point, Mich., whose group controls illegal activities in the Detroit-Windsor (Canada) area and in Toledo and Youngstown, Ohio. A Zerilli son is married to a daughter of Joseph Profaci, late head of one of the New York Mafia mobs.

John Scalish of Cleveland, who got a 10-to-25-year prison sentence for robbery in 1933 but was pardoned only two years later. He attended the Apalachin meeting and is believed to be part owner of a Las Vegas Hotel.

Angelo Bruno, boss of the Philadelphia rackets, who also has Mafia associates in southern New Jersey and in Florida. Joseph Ida, former commission member from Philadelphia, has returned to Italy.

Sebastian (Big John) La Rocca, 63, of Pittsburgh, whose record of arrests began in 1922 and who has been convicted on a gun charge and for lottery and larceny. He managed a pardon of his lottery and larceny offenses.

Raymond Patriarca, 60, of Providence, R. I., boss of the Boston mob and of rackets throughout New England. He has been arrested more than 20 times since 1926 on a variety of charges.

13 Seized in Queens In 'Little Apalachin'

The police broke up what was apparently a meeting of top Mafia leaders from all over the country in the basement of an Italian restaurant in Queens yesterday afternoon, and seized 13 underworld figures.

Chief Inspector Sanford D. Garelik called the meeting "a little Apalachin," and said the raid was part of the Police Department's campaign "to rid the city of top hoodlums."

The police said the 13 would be charged with "consorting with criminals."

Among the 13 seized were Thomas (Tommy Ryan) Eboli, reputedly the acting head of the Vito Genovese Cosa Nostra "family" in Brooklyn; Carlos Marcello of New Orleans, La., sometimes described as the Mafia boss in the South, and Michele (Mike) Miranda of Queens, reported to be a top lieutenant of the Genovese family.

Miranda attended the 1957 conference of 63 underworld chieftains in Apalachin, N. Y., which was broken up by the state police.

Queens District Attorney Nat H. Hentel announced that all 13 men would be subpoenaed to appear before a special grand jury he plans to call.

Detectives of the 112th Precinct made the seizures yesterday afternoon in a basement dining room of La Stella Restaurant, at 102-11 Queens Boulevard, in the Forest Hills section. The police said no weapons had been found.

The police burst in as the 13 men were in the middle of a meal, at about 2:30 P.M. None offered resistance, or even stood up in surprise, according to a detective who took part in the raid.

"They acted like gentlemen, just like your grandfather," the detective said.

The police did not put handcuffs on them and transported the 13 diners—who neglected to pay their check—in police cars.

The men were questioned at the Maspeth station house, a process that the police said was complicated by the men's "uncertainty" of their names, ages and addresses.

At the station house, before each was questioned, the 13 were read a statement advising them of their constitutional rights. They were ushered into a station house waiting room, and called out one at a time for questioning. Several lawyers appeared, in order to advise their clients on what to say.

W. L. Davis, lawyer for Eboli, complained that his client had been "held without being charged for many hours, stripped of his clothes, searched, and interrogated." He said these were "violations of the civil rights of all these men."

Mr. Hentel was at the station house, last night, along with Mr. Garelik and agents of the Federal Bureau of Investigation and the Treasury Department.

Mr. Garelik said the arrested men were "all in $300 suits, and they are all well-fed."

"All of the men had large amounts of cash on them," he said. "The least amount anyone was carrying was $600, most of it in $50 and $100 bills."

The police would not permit newsmen into the station house for a time. They clustered around outside with curious neighbors and television crews. The building, at 53-37 72d Street, is in a quiet residential section.

The questioning was still going on at 2:30 this morning.

In a similar raid last October on a restaurant in downtown Manhattan, seven Cosa Nostra figures were seized, including three of the men picked up yesterday: Eboli, Miranda, and Anthony (Tony the Sheik) Carillo.

All seven were charged with consorting with known criminals. They were acquitted within a week, after being released in their own recognizance.

In addition to the local Mafia figures at the Queens meeting yesterday, the police said, underworld figures from New Jersey, Florida, Texas, California, Louisiana and Arizona were present.

Anthony Corillo, 42, of New Orleans (not Tony the Sheik) was another picked up. The police said they thought he was a lieutenant in the Genovese family, and active in Louisiana.

Others were identified as Joe Colombo, 45, of Brooklyn; Domenck Alongi, 39, from Teaneck, N. J.; Joseph N. Gallo, 54, of Astoria, Queens; Joseph Marcello, Carlos's brother, 56, of New Orleans; Frank Gagliano, 36, of New Orleans; Carlo Gambino, 59, of Brooklyn; and Aniello Della Croce, 52, of Manhattan.

Also seized were two owners of La Stella, Joseph and Jack Taliercio, of Queens.

Mr. Garelik called the raid, which was planned by the department's Central Investigation Bureau, "the biggest since Apalachin."

The Apalachin raid, on Nov. 14, 1957, at the estate of Joseph Barbara Sr., broke up what the state police termed a "crime convention." Those attending were questioned and released.

Two years later 21 of them were tried on charges of conspiracy to obstruct justice by concealing the purpose of their meeting. Twenty were found guilty, but the United States Court of Appeals overturned their convictions.

There was no indication last night what the meeting was about, or how the police had learned of it.

Among the 13 hoodlums seized yesterday was Santo Traficante, active with the Mafia in Cuba before the Castro takeover, and now said to be the boss of the underworld organization's Florida operations.

'These raids are good because we can see who is boss," one detective said, "not because they tell us, but because of the way they act toward one another. We can judge a Mafia boss's importance by the respect or deference the other men show him."

The police said that the charge of consorting with criminals was a collective one and that each of the men would have to be questioned before any charges could be filed.

September 23, 196

State Joins Boston Offensive In Gang War Costing 42 Lives

By HOMER BIGART
Special to The New York Times

BOSTON, Feb. 9—Attorney General Elliot Lee Richardson summoned all district attorneys of eastern Massachusetts to the State House today to plan strategy against Boston's gangland war.

In what has become known as "the second Boston Massacre," 42 men have been slain in three years of fighting between underworld factions for control of Greater Boston's million-dollar-a-week loan shark racket. None of the murders has been solved.

Mr. Richardson noted in an interview that so many unsolved homicides had made "blatantly evident" the operations of a "second government"—the underworld.

Strangely, law enforcement officials have been under no strong public pressure to stop the mayhem. Proper Bostonians were said to feel that the local hoodlums were saving the Commonwealth money by rubbing —the favored local term is "squashing"—each other out.

"The animals are shooting the animals" was the way Police Commissioner Edmund L. McNamara put it recently.

The cycle of murders seems to have started with a macabre discovery of a mutilated corpse on May 4, 1964.

Morris Cohen, of Brighton, was summoned by the police to recover his stolen car. Stuffed into the compartment was a headless cadaver, subsequently identified from fingerprints as Francis R. Benjamin, a small-time felon who had been released on two weeks earlier from state prison.

Benjamin's slaying was followed by other gruesome discoveries. Usually the victims were found in trunk compartments. In staid Wellesley, the trunk of an abandoned car revealed a decapitated body from which the hands were also severed, frustrating attempts at identity.

But sometimes the victims were thrown into the harbor or into suburban streams. And as the war intensified, methods of operation improved. In at least two instances, hoodlums overtook their victims in fast-moving cars and dispatched them with armor piercing bullets.

Few Bystanders Killed

In all the gunplay only two innocent bystanders were killed, one of them deliberately because he had just witnessed a gangland slaying in the Mickey Mouse Cafe in Revere. The other was emerging from a christening party in Roxbury was apparently a victim of mistaken identity.

What caused the falling-out among the loan sharks? Local

observers say it began at a picnic of hoods on Salisbury Beach in 1960.

The guests included all the leaders of the mob of the late Edward J. (Punchy) McLaughlin, a gang of loan sharkers and gamblers from Charlestown and their women. There was also another element, a somewhat lesser school of loan sharks led by the late James J. (Buddy) McLean.

It seems that George Mc-Laughlin, a short, jowly brother of Punchy insulted the wife of a friend of Buddy McLean. He spat in her face and called her a whore. Whereupon Buddy, whose smooth, fair countenance sometimes made people think of a grown-up choir boy, beat up George McLaughlin.

The resulting McLaughlin-McLean feud continued until both gangs were virtually extinct.

Bernie McLaughlin, another of Punchy's brothers, was shot down at high noon on Halloween, 1960, in Charlestown's noisy, grimy City Square, where he had a walking loan shark operation that preyed mainly on longshoremen. Six shots were blasted into Bernie's head and although the square was teeming, nobody saw a thing.

McLean was held as the key suspect but a grand jury failed to indict him. Punchy himself was shot dead Oct. 20, 1965 as he stood at a West Roxbury bus stop. He had been wounded in two previous attempts on his life: first he was shot several times in the face in Brookline, so badly that his jaw had to be wired for several months; then he was ambushed in Westwood and doctors had to amputate his bullet-shattered right hand.

Nine days after the slaying of Punchy, Buddy McLean, emerging from a Somerville cafe, was killed by shotgun blasts at point-blank range.

That took care of the leadership. McLean was dead and so were all the McLaughlins except George, who has been sentenced to the electric chair for murder.

The extinction of gang leadership did not, however, stop the slaughter. Impressed by the fact that murders could be committed with apparent impunity in Greater Boston, hoodlums continued the struggle for power.

3 Factions Apparent

Attorney General Richardson said today that there seemed to be at least three tightly knit factions — one operating in the North End under the apparent leadership of Gennaro Anguillo, the reputed Cosa Nostra leader in Boston; another, based in East Boston and Revere, led by Joseph (Barboza) Baron, who is now under $100,000 bail on a gun-carrying charge, and a third, operating in Somerville under Howie Winter, a former lieutenant of Buddy McLean.

Baron's bail problem resulted in a double slaying last Nov. 15. Two of his friends, Arthur C. Bratsos, a 32-year-old loan shark of Medford, and Thomas J. DePrisco, 24, of Roslindale, an "enforcer," were on a bail-raising foray into the North End.

They were slain in the Nite-Lite Cafe and then driven in Bratsos's Cadillac to South Boston. There the car was abandoned with the bodies in the back seat. Bratsos had collected more than $50,000 from hoodlums—much of it in $1,000 bills, according to the police.

Yesterday Ralph Lamattina was described by the prosecution as an "underworld kingpin."

Last Saturday the 42d victim of the gang war was found in the trunk of his car. He was Andrew Von Etter, 27, who was awaiting trial for embezzlement. He had been garroted with a rope before his skull was fractured with a tire iron.

After a one-hour meeting with nine district attorneys, Attorney General Richardson said there was general agreement that the lack of immunity legislation was the chief obstacle to getting evidence against the gangsters. Mr. Richardson said he would press for a bill that would enable any district attorney to grant immunity to key witnesses.

New York has an immunity law that eased police efforts to break up Murder, Inc., by enabling Abe Reles to turn state's evidence.

February 10, 1967

FEDERAL AGENCIES OPEN UNITED DRIVE TO COMBAT MAFIA

Organized Campaign Begun to Attack Infiltration of Business by Crime

By MAURICE CARROLL
Special to The New York Times

WASHINGTON, Feb. 21—The Mafia's infiltration of legitimate business has come under a coordinated attack by a variety of law enforcement agencies.

Henry E. Petersen, head of the Justice Department's organized crime section, told today how he had set up such an operation in New Jersey. Eventually, he indicated, the new approach will be tried against Mafia groups in big cities across the nation.

"Many of these legitimate businesses serve as a cover for tax frauds, a depository for illegally obtained funds," he said.

In the six years that the organized crime section has been working, he said, it has put together a file of 300,000 businesses and businessmen thought to have Mafia ties. The files list 3,115 "so-called principals," he said.

President Urged Drive

The drive was signalled last May when President Johnson, at a White House meeting, called for a renewed attack on organized crime, Mr. Petersen said.

In New Jersey, where he said the program "has really shaped up," he and a couple of assistants met with local representatives from various agencies—the Federal Bureau of Investigation, the Internal Revenue Service, the Bureau of Narcotics, the Labor Department—and asked for a detailed plan of attack on Mafia operations.

The plan was submitted in a month and modified a bit at the Justice Department. Then Mr. Petersen based a full-time representative in New Jersey and had another commute between there and Washington as a liaison.

Several Cities Included

He has set up similar operations in Philadelphia, Miami and Boston and will do the same soon in Kansas City and Chicago, he said. Eventually he will get to New York, but the priority of that visit was low, Mr. Petersen indicated, since Robert Morgenthau, the United States Attorney there, already has a 10-member staff working on organized crime.

Mr. Petersen said the five Mafia "families" in New York were headed by Joseph Colombo, Vito Genovese, Gaspar DiGregorio, Carlo Gambino and Gaetano Luchese. In Northern New Jersey, he said, the chiefs were the Catena brothers, Gerardo and Gene.

He said he was satisfied so far with progress of the new drive, but that he did not believe that there was any one answer to the problem of organized crime. The theory of the present drive, he said, was "to refine, to systemize, to program" the anticrime campaign. "The best answer," he said, "is continuity."

February 22, 1967

125

Success of Cosa Nostra Is Linked To Use of Big Business Methods

Special to The New York Times

CHICAGO, March 7—Law agencies have failed utterly to penetrate the ruling councils of organized crime because of the Cosa Nostra's successful adaptation of big business methods to their operations, 750 crime-fighting experts were told here today.

The crime syndicate clearly understands and uses modern methods of screening, recruit-ment, training, organization and promotion, said Ralph Salerno, retiring sergeant supervisor of New York detectives.

"Any allusion to, or illusion of, the penetration of organized crime constitutes an exercise in semantics," Mr. Salerno told the first national symposium on law enforcement, science and technology.

The three-day meeting began today at the Illinois Institute of Technology Research Center. It was called to study the structure of organized crime and the technical gadgetry, such as improved fingerprint classification, telecommunications, and voice analysis by computer, that has been developed to combat it.

Mr. Salerno likened organized crime to large corporations and government in its establishment of a flexible personnel policy designed to work despite losses through death, convictions and deportation.

He and Henry Peterson, chief of the Justice Department's Organized Crime Section, agreed in a panel discussion that penetrating the crime syndicate was far more difficult than getting inside information on "pseudo-public" groups like the Communist party and the Ku Klux Klan.

Mr. Peterson said the Cosa Nostra, or Mafia, was so well organized that he wouldn't be surprised to learn that it had a representative at the symposium.

Co-sponsors of the symposium are the Justice Department's Office of Law Enforcement Assistance and the Illinois Institute of Technology Research Institute's Law Enforcement Science and Technology Center.

March 8, 1967

U.S. AIDE CHARGES LABOR-CRIME LINK

Justice Official Ties I.L.A. and Teamsters to Mafia— Fitzsimmons in Denial

By FRED P. GRAHAM
Special to The New York Times

WASHINGTON, March 29—The chief of the Federal Government's organized crime unit charged today that the teamsters' union and the East Coast longshoremen's union were linked with each other and the Cosa Nostra.

Henry E. Petersen, chief of the Justice Department's Organized Crime Section, which co-ordinates the Government's interagency fight on crime, made the statement during a discussion session at a conference of law enforcement leaders here.

Frank E. Fitzsimmons, general vice president of the International Brotherhood of Teamsters, in a telegram of protest to Mr. Petersen this evening, called the statement "slanderous." Spokesmen for the longshoremen were unavailable for comment.

Mr. Petersen, who apparently did not know that the informal seminar was open to reporters, refused later to elaborate on his statements.

He has rarely spoken on the record to newsmen in the past and is not widely known outside of law enforcement circles.

His statement came as he delivered a casual, 10-minute explanation of the Government's program to combat organized crime. The statement was made this morning to a group of about 80 panelists, during the second day of the Justice Department's two-day National Conference on Crime Control.

Mr. Petersen said that four or five years ago, Senator John L. McClellan's Senate rackets committee was very much concerned about reports of a possible merger between the Teamsters and the International Longshoremen's Association.

No formal merger took place, but Mr. Petersen said, "I know for a moral certainty that this amalgamation exists."

Furthermore, he said, "In the upper echelons they have more than an effective liaison between the I.L.A., the Cosa Nostra and the Teamsters."

He said that the Government had identified about 5,000 persons across the nation who are members of the Cosa Nostra, the nationwide crime syndicate that was formerly known as the Mafia.

Shortly after Mr. Petersen spoke, Chief Justice Earl Warren said in a prepared speech to the delegates that "so long as businessmen in the name of private enterprise associate with hoodlums, accept their business, and peddle their influence, communities are bound to be unhealthy."

Chief Justice Warren's speech stressed the unhealthy impact of organized crime, as compared with street crime, and he said that "corruption is the basis of organized crime."

He specified corruption among policemen, prosecutors, courts, city councils and businessmen, but he did not mention unions.

"Organized crime can be stopped because it is a direct assault upon the community in which it thrives, and no crime syndicate can openly defy the law in any of its money-making activities if the community is determined that it shall not exist," he said.

Speaking to a group that includes a large delegation of police officers and prosecutors —some of whom have attributed rising crime to court decisions —the Chief Justice suggested looking at the beam in one's own eye "rather than at the mote in our neighbor's."

In an unusual move for a Chief Justice Mr. Warren had strong praise for President Johnson's anticrime efforts. He declared that the President's program afforded "the greatest opportunity the nation has ever had to rid itself of organized crime and at the same time destroy the conditions which inevitably breed degradation and crime of every description."

One panel session this morning produced a rare admission from a high official of the Federal Bureau of Investigation that wiretapping and eavesdropping were useful investigative tools.

The statement, from James H. Gale, the assistant director in charge of the bureau's efforts against organized crime, came during an exchange with Eliot H. Lumbard, special assistant counsel for law enforcement in New York.

Mr. Lumbard said wiretapping and eavesdropping "had been intensely useful" in the state's anticrime efforts, and expressed concern that law enforcement would suffer a serious blow if police eavesdropping was abolished.

President Johnson has asked Congress to outlaw all police eavesdropping except in national security cases, and the Supreme Court has agreed to consider the constitutionality of the New York law that permits court-supervised bugging by the police.

Mr. Lumbard said state officers in New York, using wiretapping, had jailed several important racketeers, while Federal officials in New York had been able to convict only minor figures.

Mr. Gale responded from the audience with statistics on successful F.B.I. prosecutions.

Asked by Mr. Lumbard if eavesdropping had proved useful, Mr. Gale said, "Yes. It was useful."

Mr. Lumbard asked how this could be squared with recent assertions by Attorney General Ramsey Clark that Police eavesdropping was an inefficient law enforcement device. Mr. Gale declared that he would stand on his earlier statements on the subject.

March 30, 1967

U. S. CRIME STUDY SEES COSA NOSTRA AS GROWING PERIL

Report Finds Syndicate Is Increasingly Penetrating Legitimate Businesses

CORRUPTION IS FEARED

New York Is Headquarters of Broad Organization— Sample City Surveyed

By FRED P. GRAHAM
Special to The New York Times

WASHINGTON, May 14— A report for the national crime commission warned today that the growing penetration of legitimate business by the Cosa Nostra crime syndicate threatened increased corruption of public officials at all levels.

The special report on organized crime, made by a study group, said that the "syndicate," using business techniques and college-trained people, is diversifying its activities to the point that it must "involve local officials at every level of local government."

"All available data indicate that organized crime flourishes only where it has corrupted local officials," the report said.

As an illustration the report carried a detailed study of corruption in a city given the fictional name of "Wincanton," which reliable sources outside the commission identified as Reading, Pa.

It concluded that, with the exception of the Congressman and the City Treasurer, every level of government had been tainted by systematic or "free lance" corruption.

The report noted, however, that a reform movement was now under way.

The corruption included payoffs by gamblers, prostitutes and moonshiners to police officials, state legislators, city councilmen and other officials.

A survey showed that most citizens knew about the bribery but not that the amounts were so high, and that the local people saw no need to restrict the illegal activities, which they enjoyed.

The report said that city officials had tolerated prostitution so long as the prostitutes kept up their protection payments. One madam, the report said, gave officials $500 each week for not arresting any of her girls.

One city official, according to the report, was given $5,000 for agencies." However, Mr. Vorenberg said, the commission had decided that it would be unfair to "name names and places," so few details were made public.

Among the disclosures were:

¶The wealthiest and most influential Cosa Nostra elements operate in eight states: New York, New Jersey, Illinois, Florida, Louisiana, Nevada, Michigan and Rhode Island.

¶Other groups operate in Arizona, California, Colorado, Delaware, Massachusetts, Missouri, Ohio, Pennsylvania, Texas and Wisconsin.

The report said that this is not an exclusive list of crime syndicate activities. For instance, Cosa Nostra leaders operate a variety of illegal activities throughout New England from their base in Rhode Island.

¶The 24 Cosa Nostra "families" are ruled by a "commission" representing nine top families, five of which are in New York City, which is considered the crime syndicate's national headquarters. The national crime syndicate has about 5,000 members, all of Italian descent, but it employs many other persons, without regard to race, color or creed.

¶Racketeers have moved in on legitimate businesses ranging from accounting and stock brokerage to yeast manufacturing. They control companies with nationally known brand names, and one "family" alone owns $300-million in real estate.

The syndicate usually gets its foot in the door of a business by investing its revenues from crime, foreclosing usurious debts, accepting business interests in payment of gambling debts or by extortion.

Once in control, it uses the business as a respectable front in order to perpetrate bankruptcy frauds or to peddle bogus securities, the report said.

In another special research paper published with the report, Donald R. Cressey, dean of the College of Letters and Science at the University of California, Santa Barbara, said that this business activity was prompting members of the crime syndicate to send their children to college.

Professor Cressey, a sociologist, found that most of the sons study accounting and business administration in anticipation of joining the crime "family" later. One unnamed college has an over-representation of these future Cosa Nostra members in its student body, he said.

He found a decline in the use of "muscle" in maintaining internal discipline and concluded that the increasing complexity of the syndicate's organization and activities would make it more difficult to combat the syndicate.

However, he predicted that a rebellion could break out within the ranks of the syndicate within the next decade as uneducated gangsters were pushed aside by the new executive-suite types in the criminal hierarchy.

The report to the commission found that New York and Chicago had the worst problems in organized crime and also made the most effective law enforcement efforts against organized crime. Among the states, it found, only California and New York have maintained antiracketeering programs that consistently produced convictions of major figures in the syndicate.

One of its major recommendations is that each state, district attorney and city police force in areas that have organized crime have a specialized unit to fight it.

The report said that only 12 of the 19 cities that acknowledged having organized crime had special antiracketeering units.

The report also recommended that at least one investigative grand jury be empaneled each year in localities that have organized crime. General laws on witness immunity should be passed by Congress and the states, the report said, so that minor gangsters can be given immunity from prosecution and compelled to testify against major ones.

Other recommendations were for tougher jail terms for lawbreakers involved in organized criminal activity, the creation of a permanent joint Congressional committee on organized crime and the assignment by every major newspaper of a full-time reporter to investigate organized crime.

The report repeated the ambiguous position on evesdropping by the police that the commission, known formally as The President's Commission on Law Enforcement and Administration of Justice, took in its report to the President last February.

Today's report of the Task Force on Organized Crime repeated the statement that a majority of the commission favored laws to permit wiretapping and "bugging" by the police under rigid judicial controls.

New Laws Urged

However, since the commission was divided on the issue and the Supreme Court is expected to rule soon on the constitutionality of a New York law that permits court-supervised bugging by the police, the commission's formal recommendation was merely that Congress should pass new legislation on eavesdropping.

One of the special studies appended to today's report was a detailed analysis by Prof. Robert G. Blakey of Notre Dame Law School of laws governing the gathering of evidence by anti-racketering officials.

Profesor Blakey concluded that rigidly controlled eavesdropping by the police would shield citizens' privacy better than the present statutes and judge-made rules, which are often ignored. He urged the enactment of laws to permit eavesdropping by the police against known racketeers under strict conditions.

Judges, under his plan, could authorize electronic surveillance for a limited time only, and every jurisdiction would have an absolute limit on the number of surveillances that could be in operation at any time, according to its population.

For instance, Mr. Blakey suggested that New York State, with a population of 16.8 million persons, could have no more than 80 in effect at any time.

He also recommended that an inventory of the bugs be published each year, so that those who had been subjected to surveillance would know about it.

To prevent any erosion of the privacy of the professions, his law would forbid electronic surveillance of licensed clergymen, physicians or lawyers, whether or not they were Cosa Nostra figures.

Associated Press

James Vorenberg, executive director of National Crime Commission, outlined study conducted on organized crime by John A. Gardiner of University of Wisconsin.

May 15, 1967

Crime in Westchester

The Roots of Organized Racketeering Run Deep in Suburban Life and Stress

By CHARLES GRUTZNER

To New Yorkers accustomed to thinking of the suburbs in terms of tranquil, green-carpeted homes occupied by executives and their well-groomed wives and advantaged children, recent disclosures of deep underworld penetration in Westchester County come as an image-wrenching surprise. How could organized crime gain such a foothold in an area supposed to be free of the ills of the cities? The fact is that many of these ills—blight, congestion, poverty, ghettos and corruption—have moved to the suburbs on the crest of the vast waves of migrants who fled the cities in the last two decades.

News Analysis

Organized crime has moved with them. The transplanted horse player looked for a new bookie; the newly arrived numbers player sought out the nearest store to drop his bet. Bookies, numbers operators, narcotics peddlers and loansharks all florished in the service of their new clients, and as the illegal take and the suburbs both swelled, big-time racketeers began moving into the areas outside the city and its highly organized law enforcement system.

Once the gamblers, narcotics sellers and loansharks gain a place in a community, the course of organized crime is set: It moves to take over, wholly or in partnership, by investment, muscle or overt terror, whatever illegitimate businesses it can reach. Then it reaches for legitimate businesses.

An Industry Take-Over

This was illustrated recently when Federal investigators disclosed that 90 per cent of the private garbage and trade waste disposal in Westchester was in the grip of members of the powerful Genovese and Gambino families of the Mafia.

The capture of the waste carting industry in Westchester by Mafia forces was no overnight phenomenon. It was a process that had gone on for 15 years and was accompanied by such acts of terrorism as the burning of trucks and the dumping of varnish into the gas tanks of trucks owned by those who resisted. Today, there are only about a half-dozen truly independent cartage companies left in Westchester.

To a lesser degree than in the waste disposal industry, Mafia gangsters have muscled their way into established bars, restaurants and nightclubs and have drained their profits.

There is nothing unusual in the way that organized crime has taken root in Westchester. The same kind of operations has been and still is, carried on in Nassau and Suffolk Counties, in Northern New Jersey, and in a few of the urbanized areas of Connecticut—directed in many cases by the same Mafia families who are involved in Westchester crime.

An Important Outcry

In some suburbs, however, the racket operations are neither as open nor as blatant as in parts of Westchester, largely because local law enforcement has been more vigorous and effective in some communities than in others.

Attention was first focused in Westchester principally because an important outcry against criminal influence in the suburbs was made in the Westchester city of Mount Vernon.

The outcry took the form of a dramatic gesture by Prof. Bert E. Swanson, a Sarah Lawrence College political sociologist, who had been meeting every two weeks for more than two years with residents interested in finding remedies for some of the county's community problems. On June 19, Professor Swanson called off further meetings and charged that projects for the betterment of that city had been torpedoed by the forces of organized crime.

Asked about Professor Swanson's charges, United States Attorney Robert M. Morgenthau, whose area of responsibility for investigating and prosecuting violations of Federal law includes Westchester, said that the county was "one of the major problem areas" for effective law enforcement.

Reactions Are Mixed

At the same time, The Department of Justice let it be known that it was investigating organized crime in the suburbs of metropolitan areas across the nation and had been doing so for some time.

In Westchester, there were mixed reactions to the disclosures of organized crime. Some local officials, who had been complacent about the open gambling, were critical of Professor Swanson, Mr. Morgenthau and the press for their public disclosures. A chain of Westchester newspapers and a New Rochelle radio station launched attacks upon the sources of information.

Said Edwin G. Michaelian, the County Executive:

"I think we have a clean county. If there is any evidence of organized crime Mr. Morgenthau should present it to the proper law enforcement officials."

Westchester District Attorney Leonard Rubenfeld conceded that bookmaking and policy gambling were problems in the county, "but no more so than anywhere else."

A short time later, however, Mr. Rubenfeld's investigators arrested an officer of a Mamaroneck and New Rochelle garbage collection company on charges of threatening and intimidating a competitor. They also seized five men on charges of running a million-dollar-a-year gambling operation out of a Mount Vernon gasoline station.

Mr. Rubenfeld said the garbage company official was a member of a family with high underworld connections and described the men arrested in the gambling raid as having strong Mafia ties.

Baby-Carriage Sleuthing

Although some community leaders resented the disclosures of crime in Westchester, two ministers—one in Mount Vernon and another in New Rochelle—applauded. Members of their flocks—including housewives who said they had snapped photographs of gambling transactions with cameras hidden under the bonnets of their baby carriages—provided Mr. Morgenthau with evidence of crime in their area.

The hostility of some officials toward the disclosures of criminal influence and the apathy by many more provide a significant clue to the success of the underworld in the suburbs.

Many public officials prefer to close their eyes to any disturbing problem that might "rock the boat" of suburban life. And many suburbanites prefer to ignore such problems as long as they do not intrude on their own comfortable neighborhoods.

"They don't care how much gambling goes on around Mount Vernon's Third Street as long as their own street is kept free of muggers, drunks and housebreakers," said one churchman.

Apathy Is Scored

A similar view was expressed strongly by Jacob Grumet, a member of the State Investigation Commission. The commission, after a long investigation of local law enforcement in Westchester, reported in 1964 that gambling was wide open and that laxity and police corruption occurred in many of the 39 separate police forces in the county.

Publication of the commission's report forced the ouster of some policemen and led to the defeat of a few administrations in local elections. But some of the suspected police officers have since been promoted, some repudiated politicians have since been returned to office, gambling is as wide open as before and inroads have been made in other areas of criminal activity.

"If the public keeps electing the same kind of corrupt officials it can't expect good law enforcement," Mr. Grumet declared.

The principal recommendation of the commission's 1964 report was for the creation of a county police department. Nothing came of it. Westchester still has 39 separate police forces, most free of corruption and some alert to the menace of organized racketeering.

Some law enforcement experts still believe, however, that a county police department, which need not eliminate local police forces, is needed to combat deeply entrenched organized crime.

MAFIA IS GIVING UP HEROIN MONOPOLY

Spanish-Speaking Mobsters Reported Taking Over Most of Smuggling Activities

By CHARLES GRUTZNER

The Mafia, which has long had almost a monopoly in the smuggling of heroin into the United States, is letting Cuban and South American racketeers here take over a large part of the import business.

Federal investigators and some local prosecutors report lessened Mafia activity in narcotics and a substantial increase in direct dealings by Spanish-speaking racketeers with the French-Corsican heroin manufacturers and their Canadian agents. Their findings are based on recent seizures and on some cases still under investigation, but they are unwilling at this time to predict how far the trend may go.

At present the Mafia still has substantial interests in narcotics, and its members control interstate distribution.

Solid Contacts Established

With New York the main distribution point for the rest of the nation, almost all heroin imports for many years were arranged by the five major Mafia families in the metropolitan area. They have the large cash reserves, amassed from gambling and other ventures, needed to buy heroin abroad in lots of from 2 to 95 kilograms, at $20,000 or more per kilogram (2.2 pounds).

The local Mafia bosses have also had the European connections necessary for a trans-Atlantic flow. Their solid contacts with the French-Corsican ring had been established in many cases through the American Mafiosi's blood brothers in Italy, who bring the basic opium from the Near East to the European refiners.

The Mafia families in New York and New Jersey still have cash reserves much bigger than they can reinvest in gambling and loan sharking, but they reportedly have decided that it is safer to put their surpluses into so-called legitimate businesses, where they have already invested millions and corrupted some of those businesses, than to gamble for the big and quick returns from narcotics with the risk of long prison terms.

A second factor in the lessening of Mafia activity in heroin smuggling, according to some Federal officials, may be a breach in the goodwill between the American and French-Corsican principals.

Underworld talk persists that relations have been taut, perhaps to the breaking point, for about a year as a result of the seizure by Federal agents of 95 kilos (209 pounds) of heroin. The seizure, the largest ever made in this country, had a wholesale price tag of $2.8-million and would have retailed at $100-million after being diluted and packaged here.

The Mafia's importers have refused to pay the bill because the heroin was confiscated before they took possession. The French have insisted on some reimbursement for their loss.

William L. Tendy, the assistant United States attorney who prosecuted the case that brought long prison terms to five of the conspirators in the abortive deal, was asked about the reported strain in international criminal relations.

"All I can say is that someone lost a lot of money, and that's more likely to lead to disenchantment than to happiness," was Mr. Tendy's guarded reply.

Frank Dioguardi, a mobster in the Mafia family of the late Thomas (Three Finger Brown) Luchese and the operator of a Miami Beach nightclub, was sentenced to 15 years, and his brother-in-law, Anthony Sutera, got 10 years. Samuel Desist, a retired Army major who had arranged the $2.8-million deal while a resident in France, got 18 years, and two members of the French syndicate got 20 years each.

The sentences were imposed in Federal Court here on Aug. 30, 1966, less than nine months after the arrests were made here and in France. So far as is known, there have not been any major seizures since then in which members of the Mafia have been the direct importers of heroin.

Large Sums of Ready Cash

There have, however, been several recent cases of heroin importation from abroad by Cuban and South American nationals who have had the large sums of ready cash needed for such operations. Spanish-speaking racketeers have long been narcotics traffickers, either as distributors and retailers of heroin for the Mafia importers or as importers of cocaine from South America and marijuana from Mexico. But they have until now lacked the European connections essential to bring in heroin.

Practically all heroin, regardless of where the basic opium originates, is imported from Europe, directly or by way of Canada, Cuba or Puerto Rico. Cocaine comes from South America, where the coca bean grows. Marijuana comes in by truckload from Mexico and is also grown widely in the United States, especially in the Southwest.

Norman R. Matuozzi, the regional enforcement chief of the Bureau of Narcotics, and James W. Randolph, the chief of the Bronx District Attorney's narcotics bureau, are interested in the changes that are taking place.

"The Mafia once had practically a monopoly of the narcotics traffic here," said Mr. Matuozzi. "They dominated the heroin imports. Now we are finding some disjointed groups, not affiliated with the Mafia, who have developed their own connections abroad and are bringing in substantial amounts of heroin."

Mr. Matuozzi said that the Mafia bosses here appeared to be tolerating the gradual entry of the non-Mafia enterprisers into heroin smuggling. The Mafia, usually quick to strike down or ruin intruders in any of their rackets, has not moved against the new smugglers.

Large amounts of cash are required of the newcomers to get deliveries from the non-trusting French heroin manufacturers. Some of this money was amassed by its owners in working for the Mafia as pushers; some came from numbers-game profits, and some has been brought in by Cuban refugees. Mr. Randolph said that at least one narcotics dealer, convicted in the Bronx this year, was an undercover agent of Fidel Castro.

In another Bronx case, two Cuban nationals and a Puerto Rican are awaiting trial as members of an alleged ring handling $300-million a year in narcotics.

Highest Grade of Heroin

Detectives who raided the Grand Concourse apartment of Luis Sotomayer and his wife, Olga, on July 1 found 15 pounds of 90.2 per cent pure heroin, which Chief Assistant District Attorney Burton B. Roberts called the highest grade of heroin ever seized in this country. When bail was set for the Sotomayers and for Angelo Damian, Mr. Damian's wife, Consuelo, emptied $120,-

Associated Press

Frank Dioguardi, who was a Mafia heroin operator.

500 in cash from a shopping bag and pledged the bondsman to bring $79,000 more as bail collateral.

But after the defendants were indicted, State Supreme Court Justice Joseph A. Brust increased the bail to a total of $850,000, which even they could not meet. They are in jail awaiting trial.

In setting the high bail, Justice Brust remarked that he had noticed, from hearings in other narcotics cases, that "there does seem to be a pattern of narcotics coming from Cuba."

In still another non-Mafia heroin smuggling case this year, George Varsa was arrested on March 23 in his managerial office at the Foreign Trade Import Company, at 90 West Street, where Federal agents found 12 pounds of heroin concealed in the same number of French-manufactured oscilloscopes — devices used to measure television wave lengths.

Almost simultaneously, the French police seized another 12 pounds of heroin and more oscilloscopes in Paris, where they arrested four associates in an electronics firm and a tailor. Investigations are continuing here and in France into the intended ultimate destination of that flow of heroin.

The present apparent Mafia retreat is not the first time that the order to get out of narcotics has gone out from high in the criminal organization's hierarchy, but never before have the local Mafiosi had such good reasons for obeying.

With Frank Dioguardi having only one year of his 15-year prison term behind him, John (Big John) Ormonto, a fellow member of the Luchese family, has rounded out five years of his 40-year sentence for narcotics smuggling. The

Mafia group retains the name Luchese because no successor has been chosen yet to Three Finger Brown.

Carmine Galante, underboss in the Joseph (Joe Bananas) Bonanno family, who was convicted with Ormonto, is serving a 20-year term.

Vito Genovese, head of the largest Mafia family, is behind the bars of Leavenworth, doing a 15-year stretch as the mastermind of an operation which imported heroin and other narcotics from Europe, Puerto Rico, Cuba and Mexico with distribution throughout the United States. Twenty - seven members of that ring went to prison.

The Federal Bureau of Narcotics has an imposing list of other convicted narcotics traders in those three families and in the families headed by Joseph Colombo and Carlo Gambino.

As far back as 1948, Frank Costello, then "boss of bosses" of the Mafia in the East, issued an order to get out of narcotics. Another such order, with the threat of death for disobedience, came out of the national Mafia conference at Apalachin in 1957. There was a similar edict in 1960.

Each time there was a partial and temporary withdrawal, but each time the lure of enormous profits to be quickly gained resulted in a full-scale resumption. Several lesser dealers were murdered on orders from above for not heeding the threat.

Eventually even the family leaders who had attended the Apalachin meeting put some of their surplus funds back into narcotics. The big bosses thought they were safe because they had insulated themselves from the actual operation.

But the conviction of Genovese and the effectiveness of the new Federal conspiracy law, beginning about 1959, led to such a wide retreat after the 1960 order that eventually there was a shortage of heroin here.

The shortage caused prices to soar so high that a few retired smugglers came back for "one shot" deals.

"They'd get a bankroll, bring in one lot from abroad and sell it to the retailers and then get out," said a Federal agent. "It was like taking one roll of the dice for high stakes. The risk was great, but the profit was fantastic."

Things got back to normal once more, with the Mafia at the top, until the current influx of Spanish-speaking heroin importers.

"Maybe it won't be the same old story of backsliding," said one Federal agent. "The odds are really against them. A narcotics trafficker can get up to 20 years on each count, and we usually get a two-or three-count indictment against them. That's the first time out. A second offender can get up to 40 years on each count."

September 2, 1967

Mafia Increasing Investments in Business on L. I.

By CHARLES GRUTZNER

The directors of organized crime on Long Island, whose gambling operations have been crimped by crackdowns on two huge bookmaking rings in the last year, are increasing their investments in several legitimate businesses.

Organizational changes are in the making also in the Mafia groups on Long Island because of the recent death of Thomas (Three-Finger Brown) Luchese of Lido Beach, the abdication of Gaspare DiGregorio of Smithtown from leadership of another Mafia group, and the expected imprisonment of John (Sonny) Franzese of Herricks, boss of several rackets in Nassau and Suffolk controlled by the Joseph Colombo gang.

A team of New York Times reporters has surveyed the extent of organized crime on Long Island. Their findings, based on observations and on interviews with law enforcement investigators, elected officials, businessmen, clergymen and others, show how the criminal network crosses city and suburban boundaries.

A Brooklyn-based Mafia family reaps profits from loan sharking in Nassau. An ex-convict in Manhattan had been handling labor relations for a Long Island builder until his Mafia tie-in became public knowledge. Gangsters who had a stranglehold on private garbage removal in Nassau until their local domination was broken several years ago are now in a similar racket in Westchester and New Jersey.

Federal agents are now quietly looking into what may be a rebirth in Suffolk of the waste removal racket, with a possible return of the racket operations in Nassau.

In a Suffolk sequel to the bloody revolt in Brooklyn by the Gallo Brothers against leaders of the Profaci Mafia family (which has since become the Colombo family), two Profaci gunmen murdered Louis Marriani, a Gallo hoodlum, in Port Jefferson. They are serving life terms in prison.

District Attorney William Cahn of Nassau said recently that his rackets bureau was investigating suspected criminal control in several industries. He declined to discuss details except to say, by way of illustrating the difficulty of obtaining evidence:

"We know of gangster control in some areas of the food business but we haven't got the witnesses to prove it in court. We called in the managers of several markets and asked them about suppliers we knew were victimizing them, but they wouldn't give evidence.

"They insisted everything was all right although they knew that we knew it was all wrong. They were scared."

From other sources it was learned that profits from loan-sharking, gambling, extortion and other illegal ventures were being put into certain bakeries, motels, night clubs, trucking companies, laundries, service stations, jukebox and vending machine businesses, meat wholesaling and other supposedly legitimate enterprises on Long Island as elsewhere in the metropolitan area.

Nassau County is the home of more of the top directors of organized crime than any other suburban area in the nation. More than 100 bosses who direct rackets throughout and beyond the metropolitan area are either summer or year-round Nassau residents.

Most of them do not flaunt their rackets in their home communities. There they play the role of solid citizen and are insulated from the day-to-day operations.

Until the death in July of Luchese, who lived in a $100,-000 ranch home at 74 Royat Street in Lido Beach, the census of Mafia hoodlums in Nassau included the heads of three of the five major groups who control most of the organized crime within 100 miles of New York City.

Mafia bosses living in Nassau include Carlo Gambino, whose expensive waterfront home is at 34 Club Drive, Massapequa, and Joseph (Joe Bananas) Bonanno, who alternates between Tucson, Ariz., and the home of his eldest son Salvatore (Bill) at 1555 Tyler Avenue, East Meadow.

John Ignazio (Johnny Dio) Dioguardia, of Point Lookout is said by Federal and local investigators to be a candidate for Luchese's vacant throne. Dioguardia, at 54 a convicted extortionist with a long record of arrests for labor racketeering and assaults is free on bail, awaiting trial for bankruptcy fraud. He and Paul Vario Sr. of Island Park face competition for the leadership from several Luchese henchmen in other parts of the metropolitan region.

Five Dio henchmen who tried

130

to cut into the carwash industry on Long Island were sent to prison in 1961 for extortion.

Franzese Makes Investments

According to law-enforcement officials, Franzese has never let neighborhood niceties keep him from forcibly pushing his criminal interests in his home county. A bigtime loan shark, he has invested his gains in a variety of legitimate businesses in Nassau and some in Suffolk.

Franzese is reported to have a concealed stake in several bars, motels and cocktail lounges, including places patronized by homosexuals. A sideline in the operation of such spots is the blackmailing of wealthy or prominent patrons.

Not content with those sources of income, Franzese has directed bank robberies. He is free on $150,000 bail pending a decision on his appeal from a 50-year Federal prison sentence for masterminding a series of bank robberies. His gang, which got $16,600 in a holdup of a Long Island savings and loan association two years ago, also robbed banks in Queens and Salt Lake City.

Franzese is to go on trial Oct. 16 in Queens on first degree murder charges in the gangland execution of Ernest (The Hawk) Rupolo. The Mafia had suspected Rupolo of informing against Vito Genovese, head of a Jersey-based family, who is now serving a 15-year term for narcotics smuggling. Rupolo's slashed body, with one eye shot out, was found in Jamaica Bay on Aug. 24, 1964, hands bound and concrete blocks tied to his legs.

The consensus in the underworld is that Franzese will be out of action for a long time.

If the underworld is right and the prison gates clang behind Franzese, his lucrative rackets will become a lure for other gangsters. A Federal investigator who has concentrated on the doings of the Colombo organization said: "There may be some bloodletting in the scramble for Sonny's rackets."

Colombo Gets Prize

Joseph Profaci (The Olive Oil King), a former Mafia boss, had favored the black-haired, steely - eyed Franzese and helped him climb above some of his seniors. After Profaci's death from cancer in 1962, the leadership went to his brother-in-law Joseph (Fat Man) Magliocco, who lived fearfully in a mansion behind a chain-link fence on a waterfront estate in East Islip, Suffolk County. His fear rose from the revolt of the Gallo brothers—Albert, Larry and Joseph (Crazy Joe)—against the elders of the Profaci family. The fued's casual-

ties were more than a dozen murder victims in two years.

Upon Magliocco's death from a heart attack in December 1963, the chief contenders for the leadership were Franzese, then only 42, and Charles (The Sidge) LoCicero, a 61-year-old illiterate who was later to mark an "X" as his signature when he pleaded guilty to income tax evasion. LoCicero appeared to have an advantage because he had just negotiated a truce with the Gallos.

As things turned out, however, neither Franzese nor LoCicero got the approval of the heads of other Mafia families whose opinions carried weight in underworld councils. They unexpectedly came up with Joseph Colombo, who was known chiefly as a salesman for a big real estate company in Brooklyn. Colombo has only one conviction on his record, and that was for gambling.

While he avoided open conflict with Colombo, Franzese's exploits brought more unwelcome notoriety upon the clan.

Colombo and other Mafia bosses are resentful of Franzese's high-handed ways, but according to high police sources, any attempt to oust him may lead to desperate resistance from some of the hoodlums closest to Franzese.

Most of Long Island resident directors of organized crime are not as rambunctious on the home grounds as Franzese has been.

"The county has been referred to as the bedroom of organized crime," said Mr. Cahn, "because so many of the leaders have homes here. But most of the important ones do not operate locally. They try to keep their underworld identity from their neighbors."

Mr. Cahn and Suffolk District Attorney George J. Aspland keep files on all resident members of organized crime. The prosecutors harass them from time to time, even when they have no grounds for arrests. This treatment has been responsible for the departure of several racketeers to less hostile surroundings.

'We're Watching Them'

"Every once in a while we let them know that we know they're here and that we're watching them," Mr. Cahn said.

The District Attorney said he has invited the hoodlums to visit him and chuckled at the recollection of two such visits from Lorenzo (Chappie) Brescia, who is listed by the F.B.I. as a member of the Genovese family.

Brescia said he was working for a meat company the first time he came in, but was unable to answer questions about beef prices. He volunteered that

turkeys were fetching 40 cents a pound.

"Is that dressed?" asked Mr. Cahn.

"Naw, that's ready for cooking," replied the self-described meat salesman.

Some time later, called in again, Brescia entered smiling and said: "Hello, Mr. District Attorney."

"Still in the meat business?" asked Mr. Cahn.

Brescia's smile broadened into a grin as he took a sheet of paper from a pocket and answered, "Yes, and this time I brought a price list."

The F.B.I. chart describes Brescia as a gambling operator and a specialist in extortion.

The meat industry is under continuing investigation because of its infiltration on Long Island by members of three Mafia families. Besides the Genovese family, members of the Luchese and Gambino gangs are in it.

Racketeer Makes Mattresses

Directly behind Carlo Gambino's baronial mansion in Massapequa is the smaller home, befitting a loyal vassal of Ettore Zappi, who is described in the official records of the Senate investigations subcommittee as a labor racketeer and loan shark.

Mr. Cahn's files list Zappi as president of the Convertible Mattress Corporation of Brooklyn.

Gambino, who heads a criminal organization of more than 200 members, has a share in almost every type of racket. One of his roles has been that of labor racketeer.

He was for many years the central partner in S.G.S. Associates, a labor relations firm whose clients included big manufacturing, real estate and development companies, among them William J. Levitt, builder of the housing communities on Long Island and elsewhere.

S.G.S. was dissolved two years ago after Gambino's role in it was exposed, but Gambino, 65 years old and suffering from a heart ailment, is still a formidable power in organized crime throughout the metropolitan area and beyond.

There is a belief, however, that Gambino may be about to yield management of the family rackets. He has already entrusted his nephew Paul Castellano with increased responsibility.

Castellano lives in Brooklyn, and Aniello Della Croce, the family's nominal underboss, lives in New York's "Little Italy" on Mulberry Street, close to police headquarters. Although the succession of either one to full leadership would remove the seat of the Gambino family's power from Nassau, it would not curtail any of the organized crime there, but

United Press International

Carlo Gambino, a boss in Mafia, lives in Massapequa, L. I., on the waterfront.

Johnny Dio is candidate for Mafia head on Long Island.

would merely change the location of its leadership.

Gambino, who entered this country illegally in 1921, has been under deportation proceedings since 1957 following his detention by the state police in the raid of the Apalachin meeting of Mafia bosses from across the nation.

The void that will follow Gambino's retirement, deportation or death is expected to be filled peaceably with the advice and consent of the elders of other Mafia families.

After Joseph Bonanno was kidnapped in October, 1964, by Mafia enforcers and downgraded because he reportedly had sought to have Luchese and Gambino murdered, Gaspare DiGregorio was chosen as boss of the Bonanno rackets at a high council meeting held at the Villa Capra in Cedarhurst, L. I.

DiGregorio, who lived then in the Long Island community of North Babylon and had a garment factory in Brooklyn, had in his favor that he was sponsored by Stephen Magaddino, powerful upstate boss in the Mafia, and the fact that he had never been convicted of a crime.

But, in a return from exile that is rare in the Mafia, Bonanno and his son Salvatore have wrested control from DiGregorio.

The Genovese family, which is reported to control many of the bars and nightclubs in Greenwich Village and on Manhattan's fashionable East Side catering to sex deviates, has extended its operations to Long Island. A member of the family, Edward (Eddie Toy) DeCurtis, is to go on trial this fall in Nassau County Court with Danny Fatico and John (Vicious Vivian) Vignini on charges of keeping a disorderly house and conspiracy to violate the alcoholic beverage control law.

The charges resulted from a raid two years ago at the Magic Touch, an Island Park nightclub described by Mr. Cahn as "a cesspool of depravity," DeCurtis has been named by the police as the concealed owner of the Magic Touch.

Enforcement activities against organized crime are more vigorous and better coordinated in Nassau and Suffolk than in many other suburban areas. They have the only two county police departments in the entire metropolitan region.

The Nassau County Police Department, created in 1925 as one of the first in the United States, is 2,600 strong. These policemen have full jurisdiction in 70 per cent of the area in Nassau, the remaining parts being patrolled by 24 village departments that range in size from four policemen in Mill Neck to a 73-man force in Long Beach. Even where there is a village police force, however, the county police have jurisdiction in homicide and racket investigations.

The Suffolk County Police Department, set up seven years ago, is patterned after that in Nassau. It has jurisdiction in the county's five most populous towns, with the five sparsely populated towns in the eastern portion patrolled by local departments.

This contrasts with the situation in Westchester, where local rivalries often prevent cooperation among the 40 separate municipal and town police forces, some of which are effective and honest while others are inefficient with evidences of corruption.

Corruption in several of the local police forces in Westchester was disclosed in an investigation by the State Investigation Commission, whose 1964 report urged creation of a Westchester county police department. Similar laxity and official corruption has been observed, more recently by other investigators.

There have been no police scandals in Nassau or Suffolk such as those that have arisen from time to time in Westchester or in several New Jersey communities.

Mr. Cahn, in a recent interview, discussed the organized crime enterprises that were under investigation in Nassau. He said:

"There is no question that organized crime has tried to take over here and continues to try to infiltrate such fertile ground. The population explosion in the suburbs holds the lure of riches wherever the racketeers can get a foothold. It's our job to keep them from making that foothold secure."

Special rackets bureaus, in the offices of the Nassau and Suffolk prosecutors, have broken up several rackets on Long Island in recent years. The operation in Nassau of a $50-million-a-year garbage disposal racket, which flourished also in New York City, Westchester and New Jersey, was crippled with the conviction in 1959 n Nassau County Court of Vincent (Jimmy Jerome) Squillante of New Hyde Park.

Although the State Court of Appeals later reversed the extortion conviction of Squillante, his brother Nunzio, and Bernard Adelstein, business manager of Teamsters Local 813, the backbone of the Nassau operation was broken.

As a result, many of the Nassau towns and villages created municipal garbage systems and set up strict regulation of private carters of industrial and business waste.

An alleged city-suburban crime link, uncovered by the Suffolk County police, led to the arrest a few months ago of two members of the Luchese gang in simultaneous raids on their expensive homes.

The two men, Joseph Laratro and Aniello Migliore are said to have run a huge bookmaking operation in Queens by day and to have commuted to seeming respectability in their Suffolk homes.

In Migliore's home in Huntington, the police found records that they said listed $70,000 in bets for the previous weeks. Police said the pair ran a $20-million-a-year bookmaking operation employing 65 runners, out of a scrap metal yard owned by Laratro in Corona, Queens. Laratro is waiting trial for possession of the eavesdropping equipment, Migliore for possession of bookmaking records.

The faucets in Laratro's $150,000 home in fashionable Lloyd Harbor are gold-plated and the bathroom scale recedes automatically into a wall. There, the police seized eavesdropping equipment, possession of which is a felony for someone with a criminal record, which Laratro has. Laratro, who keeps a boat moored in the harbor, exclaimed to the arresting police: "What will the neighbors think? I'll have to move!"

Associated Press
John (Sonny) Franzese is under a prison sentence.

October 8, 1967

If you are willing to put up your body for collateral—

Just Call 'the Doctor' for a Loan

By FRED J. COOK

THEY call him "the Doctor." You will meet him, if such is your misfortune, in the swankiest nightclubs, his curvaceous young bride dangling on his arm. "Meet my friend, the Doctor," the maître d' will say, performing the introductions. "The Doctor" is always most charming. A man in his fifties, he dresses like the owner of a million-dollar wardrobe. It is hard to imagine that he is in reality a hybrid—a species of spider-vulture who spins a web in which to enmesh his victim so he can pick clean the bones.

Though names cannot be used in this portrait, the Doctor (a nickname of unknown derivation) is no figment

The Mafia boss doesn't keep written records. It's smarter to file the facts in your head.

of the imagination. He exists. He is, authorities say, one of the largest and most vicious loan sharks operating in New York, just a step down the ladder from Carlo Gambino, probably the most powerful of the reigning chieftains of the city's five Mafia families. Detectives who get up with the Doctor in the morning and follow him through his daily routine until they put him to bed at night know the pattern of his days by heart—and are completely frustrated because he operates the safest and most remunerative racket in the underworld.

He has no visible means of support, but he has put up his new bride in an expensively furnished mansion in one of the finer residential sections of the city. He never "works," as other humans know the term, but when he has been stopped and questioned by police, he has never had less than $7,000 in sweet cash upon his person — and sometimes he has had as much as $15,000. "You can never charge him with vagrancy," one prosecutor says, with a sour smile. Unlike a master bookie, he has no fixed headquarters, no elaborate telephone setup, no army

of runners. He simply circulates. And in the best and most expensive places. And among the "best" people.

The far reach of such an operator was brought home to New Yorkers recently when former Water Commissioner James L. Marcus was indicted on charges of participating in a $40,000 kickback scheme on a city contract. According to investigators, Marcus was in deep financial trouble on several fronts, not the least of which was a reported $50,000 loan-shark debt to Mafia mobster Antonio (Tony Ducks) Corallo. Corallo was arrested with Marcus as his alleged partner in the kickback scheme. Later, two men were charged with taking part in a plot to murder a Government witness in the Marcus case. The episode, as reported, is similar to innumerable less publicized events in at least two ways: (1) The shark's victim was an intelligent, experienced person — professional people and substantial businessmen are the loan shark's favorite targets; (2) the victim found that when he was over a barrel with a loan shark, he was over a barrel with the Mafia — and that is being over a nasty barrel indeed.

THE popular conception of the loan shark as a two-bit hoodlum lending $5 on Monday and collecting $6 the next —the typical "six for five" operative — is an anachronism bearing virtually no relation to current reality. As Sgt. Ralph Salerno, the now-retired racket expert of the city's Bureau of Criminal Investigation (B.C.I.), told the New York State Commission of Investigation in its loan shark probe three years ago: "No self-respecting loan shark . . . would ever want to admit, even to his best friend, that he has loaned less than $100."

At the same hearings, then Assistant District Attorney Frank Rogers, of New York County, testified: "A loan shark that we know lent a million dollars in the morning and a million dollars in the afternoon." Loan-sharking is so remunerative, he said, that one mob boss had pyramided $500,000 into $7.5-million in about five years — and there were, in New York County

alone, "at least 10 men who are comparable to him."

The conclusion of all the expert witnesses was that loan-sharking is, on a national scale, a multi-billion-dollar resource of the underworld and that, while its gross take is less than gambling, it is preferred to gambling because it is so safe it almost defies prosecution.

This safety factor (which breaks down only when the shark is caught using violence to enforce collection or committing some other overt crime, as is charged in the Marcus case) is probably the reason that top mob bosses have been more openly connected with loan-sharking than with more risky enterprises, such as gambling and narcotics. Vito Genovese, the onetime boss of bosses, now in Federal prison, had nakedly obvious ties to loan-sharking, and the same is true of one of his principal deputies, Thomas (Tommy Ryan) Eboli. B.C.I. Deputy Inspector Arthur C. Grubert testified before the Commission of Investigation that his bureau had identified 121 master sharks in the five Mafia families of New York. He broke the figure down this way: 51 in the Genovese family; 37 in the Gambino family; 18 in the Profaci family of Brooklyn, now run by Joseph Colombo; 12 in the Luchese family; three in the family of Joseph (Joe Bananas) Bonanno.

Grubert made it clear that he was talking about only the two top echelons of the loan-sharking pyramid. There are, all investigators agree, four operating levels. On the top level is the family boss. Just under him are his trusted principal lieutenants. The lieutenants have their own subordinates to whom they funnel money for investment, and these third-echelon underlings, besides lending out much of it themselves, split up the rest of the money and pass it down to the fourth and lowest level, the working bookie and street-corner hoodlum. Sergeant Salerno gave a graphic description of the way it all works. He said:

"A big racket boss could have a Christmas party in his home, to which he invites 10 trusted lieutenants. He doesn't have to write their names down. He knows their names. They are friends of his. . . . He can take one million dollars, which is not an inconceivable amount of cash, and distribute that, $100,000 per man to these 10 men. All he has to tell them is, 'I want 1 per cent a week. I don't care what you get for it. But I want 1 per cent a week.'

"He does not have to record their names. He does not have to record the amount. They are easy enough to remember. And if you stop to think that, 365 days later, at the next year's Christmas party, the only problem this gang leader has is where he is going to find five more men to hand out half a million dollars that he earned in the last year on the same terms. . . ."

This usurious interest (the gang chieftain's 1 per cent a week becomes 52 per cent a year) is known in the trade as vigorish—or "the vig." (There is a theory that the term derives from the word "vicarage" and refers to the contributions given the vicar by his parishioners.) Naturally, the rate goes up as the money is filtered through the various echelons, and each takes its cut. On the second level, where the principal lieutenants dwell, the vigorish may amount to 1.5 or 2 per cent a week, and on the lowest operating level, where most ordinary loans are made, it will be 5 per cent a week—260 per cent a year. And the underworld, ruthless and insatiable, has a whole arsenal of neat devices by which even this horrendous figure can be hiked.

THE Doctor is one of those top-level lieutenants who would be invited to the big chief's Christmas party. Only in his case, he would probably not be given a piddling $100,-000 to put to work, but something more like a million. "He is a big, big money mover," says one detective. "They trust him. He has hundreds of thousands of dollars working at any one time."

Rarely, if ever, does the Doctor participate in the direct lending of his hoard of cash. He works through his subalterns, parceling out his share of the underworld treasury among as many as 30 underlings on the third echelon of the pyramid; they make the actual loans and collections and, in turn, put some of the money to work through street-corner bookies and hoods. Under such circumstances, life for the Doctor becomes one unvarying round of seemingly innocent social contacts.

Since he is a late-night man-about-town, the Doctor hardly ever rises much before noon. He may then have a late brunch with his bride, daughter of a Mafia chieftain, and then he will get into his Cadillac and begin his rounds. His first stop is almost invariably at the home of his former, divorced wife with whom he apparently maintains amicable relations. Detectives theorize that the former wife's home is probably a contact point at which he picks up messages or cash that may have been left for him. After a short stay here, the Doctor drives on to a small business office that he maintains as an ostensibly legitimate front. Detectives have been unable to discern any real business being conducted here, and they deduce that the office serves as another contact point.

After the office stop, the Doctor's routine may vary slightly, depending upon the day of the week. Monday is especially busy in the loan-shark racket. It is the day when new loans are being laid out, when collections are made, when the misdeeds of defaulters must be weighed and penalties assessed. The Doctor regularly visits his favorite Italian social club, where he sits around chatting with old cronies; but it is noticeable that, on this one day of the week, his stay is always more protracted and his talk longer and more earnest.

After the business at the club has been transacted, it's off to the plushier bistros of Manhattan, where the Doctor circulates, much like the lord of the manor, with maître d's bowing and scraping and bartenders bobbing their heads in welcome and subservience. They all know they had better. Many are so deeply in hock to the Doctor themselves that they will probably never again be able to call themselves free men, and in some instances the pit has been dug so deep that the Doctor is in fact the secret owner of the business. A favorite rendezvous in the past, a plush restaurant just off Park Avenue in the midtown section, was forced to close eventually because his silent partnership became too loud and the State Liquor Authority revoked the liquor license.

"You can watch all this activity, and it's most frustrating," says a dectective who has camped on the Doctor's trail. "He goes into a place, has a drink, chats with the bartender who is a 'steerer' of his [sending along loan customers]. Perhaps he picks up a message or some cash that has been left. How can you tell? It's all very casual, very hard to detect. Perhaps he wanders off to the men's room, and, just by chance, one of his lieutenants follows, and a word is dropped or money changes hands. There is little you can do about it."

It all adds up to a pretty gay way of life for the Doctor.

"He's a real swinger," a detective says, "and he's very vain. He goes to a health club regularly for exercise. And he's always been young-chick-crazy. Until he married his young wife, you'd see him almost every night with a different babe, all stacked. Now he makes the rounds with her."

The Doctor has one other noticeable trait. He is famous for his nasty temper. "He has a very short fuse," the detective says, "and he'll get into a fight at the drop of a hat. This generates fear, and it's a failing that is really very valuable to him in his business. All he has to do is to show up at a restaurant where some guy owes him money, and the guy begins to quake."

There is one other angle to the Doctor's business, and this, too, is highly remunerative. Underworld informants picture him as the secret proprietor of floating crap games. A free spender who likes to gamble is put in touch by a steerer; a fancy limousine picks him up at his apartment or hotel and whirls him away to the spot selected for the evening's pleasure. The game, being an underworld enterprise, is apt to be rigged to the eyeteeth; but even if it is not, the law of averages can generally be counted upon to leave the eager roller with a flat wallet. Then comes the pièce de résistance. The fever is still upon the sucker; having lost all, he wants to gamble more "to get even." And would you believe it? There at his elbow, just waiting to be of service, is one of the Doctor's sharks. Need another $500, buddy? Gladly, gladly, says the shark, turning it over.

The shark, of course, knows his customer; he's already checked his credit rating; he knows he can't lose. If the gambler's luck changes, he pays back the shark on the spot—$600 for the $500 he has just borrowed. If, as is more likely, he blows the extra $500, too, he must pay up $600 within 24 hours. "This is one of the neatest rackets going," a detective says. "They aren't interested in the profits of the game so much as they are in the loan-sharking at the game. That's where the real money is. It's easy to run $10,000 into $15,000 in a single night loan-sharking."

INEVITABLY, with a business as intricate as the Doctor's, it becomes necessary, as it is not in a more streamlined operation, to keep some detailed records. It is fairly simple for the family boss who has parceled out $1-million in chunks of $100,000 to each of 10 principal lieutenants to keep his accounts in his head; but when you split up hundreds of thousands of dollars into hundreds of chunks, the transactions become too complicated. Even an agile brain cannot retain the details without the help of a written record. Authorities have been successful in obtaining one such account sheet of the Doctor's. It contains a long column of figures that look as if they were taken from a bank's daily ledger. Scanning the column at random, one notices amounts ranging from $13,000 to $43,000, each representing a loan. Some of the loans are identified only by nickname or initial; others have names spelled out beside them — including names of subsidiary Mafia figures to whom the Doctor apparently had funneled some of his money.

"We're sure this sheet represents loan-sharking busi-

Drawing by Arno Sternglass.

IT'S A GRIM BUSINESS — The loan shark lends money at exorbitant interest, often to respectable clients; if they default, he squeezes them dry—backed by all the power of the Mafia—until they are destitute, or dead.

ness," the prosecutor who has it says, "but when we questioned the Doctor about it, his alibi was that this was just an ancient record, representing transactions from years and years ago when he was in the bookmaking business."

Even when authorities get an indubitably current record, it is extremely difficult to make much sense, still less a legal case, out of the mysterious chicken scratches. One investigative unit recently came into possession of a red-covered, loose-leaf pocket notebook containing the rec-

ord of transactions of a bookie-shark on the lowest level of the Doctor's ring. The flyleaf carries an unexplained notation: $15,000.

"This apparently was the money entrusted to him to lend out," a detective says.

The $15,000 item is followed by these other unexplained entries: $7,300, $3,900, $700. Out at the side of the page, the last sum is broken down into three other amounts: $250, $350, $100—apparently representing three smaller loans that made up the $700. Who got the money? There is no way of telling.

"The guy who had this book carried it in his head," the detective says. "He knows who got the $7,300, who got the $3,900; he doesn't have to put down names."

Some of the inside pages of the notebook do contain more information. In transactions involving week-by-week payments over periods of several months, the shark had to keep a careful record. But even here the entries tell little. There are designations like "Brother," "Billy," "Fred." Just who they are is anybody's guess. One of these accountings shows that $500

was lent to be paid back at a rate of $50 a week for 12 weeks—a mere $600 for $500. Regular payments were made, except for one week. However, the borrower paid $100 the next week, was never delinquent again and the account was marked closed at the end of the 12 weeks.

Not all borrowers were so lucky. One account in this book deals with a loan that started out at $11,600. The borrower — whose name appeared beside the figures— made regular payments at the start, but then the burden obviously became too heavy. His

135

payments lapsed for weeks. Penalties were assessed. These and the accumulations of vigorish boosted the indebtedness, despite what had been paid, to $16,898. There the account ends—permanently. The man who borrowed but could not pay was found murdered in a city alleyway, and investigators trying to solve the case are operating on the theory that he paid with his life for having had the bad judgment to cost the syndicate money.

SUCH gory episodes point up a fact of life: the borrower is always at the mercy of the shark, and the shark, backed by all the awesome, terroristic power of the Mafia, is utterly ruthless. Coupled with his ruthlessness is a devilish cunning that is always devising new ways of getting people in his power—and then driving them right through a wall.

Take the case of the prosperous bar owner who tried to do his daily good deed, found himself caught in the middle and was almost devoured by a shark. The bar owner had a good, free-spending customer whom he had known for quite some time. One day the customer confided that he was in a financial bind and needed to borrow some fancy cash. So the bar owner, trying to do a favor for a patron, passed him on to his favorite loan shark. The customer and the shark made their deal, and for a time everybody was happy. But then the customer, evidently unable to pay, skipped the city — and the sharp ivories of the loan shark closed on the bar owner who was informed *he* was responsible for and had to make good the loan.

"If you introduce someone to a loan shark," says one investigator, "you make yourself responsible for the payments. If the friend you've recommended takes off for Florida or Samoa, leaving the debt unpaid, they come to you to collect. It is just like co-signing a note in legitimate business. This is one way many bartenders and bar owners find themselves suddenly in deep, deep trouble."

The trouble gets just as deep as the loan shark in his generosity chooses to make it, for the shark makes up the

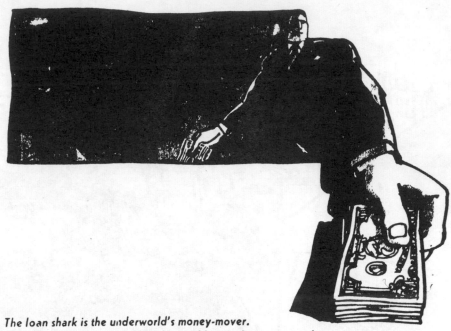

The loan shark is the underworld's money-mover.
He takes "black" money from the gambling and narcotics rackets
and turns it "white" by funneling it into legitimate trade.

rules of the game as he goes along, and the other player, the borrower, hasn't a thing in the world to say about it. If a borrower defaults for a couple of weeks or a month, the shark can assess any penalty that comes into his usurious mind—and the borrower has to pay or flee the country or risk being dumped in some dank gutter.

Frank Rogers, in his testimony before the Commission of Investigation, cited a case that began with a $6,000 loan to a businessman. The borrower made three payments, then missed two. For this heinous offense, the loan shark decided that the $6,000 would now be converted into $12,000, with the accompanying double vigorish. When the hapless borrower could not begin to pay this suddenly doubled load, the shark upped the principal to $17,000, then $25,000. "Just by simple mandate from the loan shark," Rogers testified, "you are in an irreversible situation. He says, 'This is the loan,' and that is it."

Once a victim has been driven completely through the wall by such devices, the shark sometimes grins his suddenly friendly smile and says, "O. K., I'm now your partner. I own half your business."

This doesn't mean he's

really forgiving anything; he's simply stopped piling it on. But he still expects his vigorish on the old loan—and half his new "partner's" profits besides. The situation then rapidly deteriorates to the point of utter hopelessness, which is what the shark wants. Then he may say magnanimously, "Look, we will swap even. We will forget the loan, you forget the business. It is now all mine." The entire process, Rogers said, sometimes takes less than six months.

Such takeovers, Rogers told the investigation commission, run the gamut "from nightclubs to optical stores to brick companies." And, as testimony before the commission showed, to Wall Street brokerage houses and banks.

THE loan shark, then, is the indispensable "money-mover" of the underworld. He takes "black" money tainted by its derivation from the gambling or narcotics rackets and turns it "white" by funneling it into channels of legitimate trade. In so doing, he exacts usurious interest that doubles the black-white money in no time; and, by his special decrees, by his imposition of impossible penalties, he greases the way for the underworld takeover of entire businesses. Perhaps

the best single illustration of how it all works was put on the record by the Commission of Investigation in its probe of the First National Service and Discount Corporation.

This was an underworld loan-sharking operation that was actually incorporated as an ostensibly legitimate business. It had a suite of offices at 475 Fifth Avenue, and its front man was an operator known as Julio Gazia, alias Julie Peters. He described himself frankly as "a Shylock, a five-percenter." Some of the largest names in the underworld and its affiliated loan-sharking ventures weave in and out of the story of First National.

The original loan of $21,600 was supplied by Thomas (Tommy Ryan) Eboli, strong man of the Vito Genovese syndicate, and by Charles (Ruby) Stein. Stein, with his partner, Nicholas (Jiggs) Forlano, is known as one of the largest loan sharks in the city, with direct ties to the highest echelons of the Mafia. When additional money was needed for loans, it was obtained from Mike Genovese, brother of Vito, and Joseph (Joe Ross) De Nigris, known as a reliable "old soldier" of the Genovese family and a close aide of Eboli. Money from these underworld sources was lent to Julio Gazia and First National at 1.5 and 2 per cent a week —and was put out by Gazia at a minimum of 5 per cent a week. With money turned over and over from paid-up loans, First National lent approximately $400,000 in 25 months and reaped a gross profit of at least $150,000, probably much more.

Borrowers testified before the commission that they lived in abject terror of what would happen to them or their families if they did not pay. The wife of one borrower, subjected to a blitz campaign of threatening and obscene telephone calls, collapsed and had to be hospitalized. The others had good reason for their fear, the commission reported, for Gazia employed two hoodlum-enforcers—Anthony Scala, who liked to be known as "the leg breaker," and Anthony (Junior) De Franco.

An attorney who had become a partner of Gazia in the First National caper gave the commission an inside view of some of the goings-on. On one occasion, Gazia lent $22,000 to the proprietor of an optical company, who agreed to pay $1,100 a week "vig" on the loan. Later another $6,500 was lent. This raised the "vig" to $1,425 a week, and the optical company executive found eventually that he simply couldn't pay it. Though he had paid Gazia and First National $25,000 in interest, he still owed the entire principal of the loans, $28,500—and the $1,425-a-week "vig" went on and on, endlessly. He tried frantically to borrow from friends and failed.

At this point, the underworld called a "sit-down"—a meeting presided over by an underworld baron of acknowledged stature. Presiding as a justice in a kangaroo court, the underworld chieftain hears the evidence and decrees what shall be done—what lump sum the loan and accumulated vigorish can be settled for (this is never less than three or four times the original principal) or, in lieu of that, what retribution shall be exacted from the defaulter. In the case of the optical company owner, Eboli himself presided at the sit-down, held in a Greenwich Village restaurant, and he decreed that an aide, Dominick Ferraro, should take over the

optical company and go to West Virginia to operate its plant there. In the course of a few months, the new "management" looted the concern of every dime in the till and drove it into bankruptcy.

Why do supposedly sensible men get themselves into such binds? The optical firm owner who lost all gave the commission a succinct answer: "I needed the money."

It is a refrain that is heard again and again. Certain kinds of businesses are especially vulnerable. In the garment business, an uncertain and cyclical industry, the owner of a dress factory often finds himself caught in a sudden squeeze; either money is tight or he does not have the kind of credit he needs at a bank —so he goes to a loan shark. Many a tavern owner begins business after spending years as a cook or bartender. He does not have much capital. By the time he has rented and furnished his place, he is running short of funds with which to lay in the costly supply of varied liquors that he needs to woo a well-paying clientele— so he goes to the loan shark. In the construction industry, capital can be tied up in long-term projects; when the crush for cash for a new venture becomes acute, a sum like $1-million may be needed the day after tomorrow—and so the construction company executive, too, goes to the loan shark.

THERE are an infinite number of entrapment techniques. Take a typical case. The steerer at a bar introduced the resident loan shark to the son of a wealthy businessman. The son had junior executive status in his father's business, was a bit of a playboy and was drawn by the shark's sinister character and reputation. It did something for his ego just to be seen in the company of such an eminent Prince of Darkness.

The shark and Junior began to bet together. It started on the $10 level. Then Junior wanted to move up to the $100 class, but he didn't have that kind of money. Kindly Shark, slapping him on the back, reassured him: "O.K., old buddy, don't worry about a thing. I'll back you." The betting grew apace. Soon Junior was gam-

bling $1,000 a clip with the bookie to whom Kindly Shark had introduced him.

Before he met K.S., Junior had been betting $10 a week on Saturday football games. That was his speed. Within 90 days after meeting K.S., Junior was betting $4,000 each Saturday. The inevitable happened quickly. Came a series of disastrous weekends when all Junior's teams could do was

The contractor began to list his collateral for a loan, but the shark wasn't interested. "Your body," said the shark, "is your collateral."

lose—and he had, of course, no money with which to pay the thousands he owed. Now Kindly Shark's teeth showed. It was no longer: "Don't worry about a thing, old buddy." It was: "Pay up, old buddy—and damn quick." In desperation, Junior embezzled a large sum of money from his father's firm with which to square himself with the underworld.

Worldly-wise individuals are also caught in this trap and forced into paths of crookedness. Sergeant Salerno told the investigation commission of the case of "a nationally known broadcaster, a sports broadcaster, who became involved with the Shylocks. This man was party to a sit-down, and the conversation that took place at that sit-down—you would think that this man was a chattel, a piece of baggage; they were going to buy or sell him. . . ."

Two loan sharks among his

creditors, Sergeant Salerno said, bought up all his indebtedness for "a very low percentage on the dollar." Then they used his services to recoup their investment. "He ended up steering affluent people, who knew his reputation, knew who he was, to a crooked dice game in order to earn a percentage of what they would be fleeced of, to be applied against his indebtedness."

SUCH is the unsavory picture. What can be done about it?

There must certainly be increased public understanding of the problem. Prosecuting officials have shouted themselves hoarse in the past, but the public still seems to think of the loan shark as an accommodating fellow who is offering a valuable service. The Commission of Investigation was told of one contractor who borrowed $1-million from a second-echelon loan shark for a construction project. The contractor began to list for the loan shark all the collateral he could put up to guarantee the loan.

The shark wasn't interested. "Your body is your collateral," he told the contractor, and with these words, for the first time, the contractor understood the kind of a deal he was entering.

The public *must* be made to understand, officials say, that when a man borrows from a loan shark, his body is, indeed, his collateral. There is a lien on his life. "Anyone who borrows from a loan shark is leaving himself open to strong-arm methods," one prosecutor said. "People should borrow only from legitimate sources; otherwise, they are borrowing, not just money, but a sackful of trouble."

Public understanding—and cooperation—is needed to make the laws work. Before the State Commission of Investigation's probe in 1964-65, there was no legal limit on the amount of interest that might be charged a corporation and no limit on what could be charged an individual on loans over $800. The loan shark was not only safe, he was legal—as long as he did not beat up someone to enforce collection or become directly involved in some form of embezzlement.

As a result of the investigation commission's exposure of the loan-sharking racket, new and more stringent laws were passed. Now it is illegal to charge a corporation an annual interest of more than 25 per cent, and it is illegal to charge an individual, no matter what the size of the loan, more than 6 per cent. But prosecution is still difficult: it takes a witness to make a case, and the witness who is willing to testify against a loan shark, with the terrifying shadow of the Mafia looming behind him, is a rare species and exceedingly difficult to find.

IT sometimes happens, but all too seldom, that a victim is driven to such a degree of desperation that he flees into the arms of the law. One such rarity occurred in late November, 1967, when Berthold Kahn, of Spring Valley, N.Y., became so hopelessly entangled with loan sharks and their vigorish that he could see no way out. Threatened, in fear of his life,

A Mafia family chieftain calls his top aides together. He gives each man $100,000 to lend out. "I don't care what you get for it," he says. "I want 1 per cent a week."

he sought out the Federal Bureau of Investigation in New York.

F.B.I. agents listened to his story, but they had no jurisdiction. Since the loan sharks involved came from Brooklyn, the agents suggested to Kahn that he see District Attorney Aaron E. Koota, of Kings County. Koota and his assistant, Irving P. Seidman, in charge of the Rackets Bureau, have been waging a long and vigorous campaign against loan sharks and the underworld's infiltration into legitimate businesses. But, like other investigative agencies, they have had their problems in getting essential witnesses to talk.

Kahn arrived at Koota's office virtually quaking with fear about 4:30 P.M. on Friday, Nov. 24. He wanted to telephone his wife, he said; and, when he did, what she told him only increased his terror. In his absence, she had received a telephone call from some tough-talking characters. They informed her that her husband had not kept an appointment he had made with them, and they declared they

were going to come out to his house that night to teach him a lesson.

This incautious announcement of intent was all the authorities needed. Seidman got in touch with New York State Police, and Brooklyn detectives and State Police staked themselves out in Kahn's home. They waited until 3:30 A.M. when, true to their promise, three **hoods** came pounding on the door, shouting to Kahn to open up and asking him if he wanted his arms and legs broken. Having heard all they needed, the detectives moved in and arrested the trio on extortion charges.

With the arrest, Kahn and his family breathed a huge sigh of relief. They had cleared at least the first, terrifying hurdle, but it will be many days and weeks before they feel entirely safe. They can never be certain that some of the arrested hoods' friends won't come calling—though actually, authorities say, this rarely happens after an arrest has been made. Once the law has interested itself in a particular case, the loan

sharks tend to stay away. After all, why risk bothering with a man on whom the police are probably keeping a protective eye? Why risk the danger of an assault rap or even a murder rap, when you can go out tomorrow and keep turning over 5 per cent a week—260 per cent a year? The loan shark does not readily give up his vigorish, but he is, after all, a businessman, and there are occasions when it is better to take the smaller loss in pursuit of the greater profit. That greater profit will not be threatened unless there are many, many more cases like the one in Spring Valley.

"This case just goes to show what can be done, how law enforcement authorities are prepared to cooperate and act any time we can get the help of the public," District Attorney Koota says. "But we have to have that cooperation. It is the only way we can ever stop this racket. If we had that, we could put these racketeers out of business tomorrow; and if we don't get it, this will continue and get worse." ■

Mafia Leaders Settle 'Banana War'

By CHARLES GRUTZNER

The "Banana War," marked by at least six murders here and several other shootings and bombings in Arizona, has come to a halt in a negotiated peace based on redistribution of rackets in the New York metropolitan area long controlled by Joseph (Joe Bananas) Bonanno.

Under terms of the treaty, some details of which are still before an underworld board of arbitration, Bonanno and his son Salvatore (Bill) retain interests in rich enterprises in other parts of the nation but recognize Paul Sciacca, choice of the Mafia's national commission, as boss over their former fiefs in the East.

The war for control of the Bonanno operations here had its origins in the kidnapping of Joseph Bonanno on Park Avenue on Oct. 21, 1964, by two agents of the Mafia hierarchy, which had condemned him to death for having allegedly plotted against the leaders of two powerful Mafia families based in New York.

Bonanno talked himself out of that death warrant, according to Federal investigators, by agreeing to give up all of his activities here.

The shooting in the "Banana War" did not begin, however, until Jan. 28, 1966, when followers of Gaspare DiGregorio, chosen by the national commission to take over the Bonanno underworld family, fired more than 20 shots and chased Salvatore Bonanno over a backyard fence in Brooklyn. He was not wounded.

The shoot-out in Brooklyn was a warning to Salvatore to stop rallying some of those still loyal to his father to challenge DiGregorio's leadership. A few months later, on May 17, 1966, Joseph Bonanno returned here after hiding out for 19 months following his forced abdication.

Shootings with deadlier accuracy began claiming victims in both factions. The war continued when Sciacca, with the approval of the national commission, supplanted

This wedding in Brooklyn was followed by a reception at the Woodbury Country Club on Long Island at which followers of Bonanno and Sciacca factions of the Mafia met in convivial harmony, despite earlier feuding. The principals in the marriage at Regina Paces Votive Shrine were Anthony Sciacca, whose father, Paul, stands to right of the bride, and Florence Rando, a niece of Frank Mari. Mari had been wounded during the feuding.

DiGregorio, who had proved himself an inept leader.

Sciacca, whose only arrest, on a burglary charge in Brooklyn in 1930, resulted in dismissal, operates a dress factory in Brooklyn. He is 59 years old and lives in Massapequa, L. I.

Agents of the Federal Bureau of Investigation, the New York City Police Department's Central Investigation Bureau, and law enforcement officers and investigators here and in other cities have maintained physical and electronic surveillance of some of the principals and have obtained information from underworld informers.

Some Events Listed

This, together with the halt in shootings, brings into focus the following circumstances an events:

¶Joseph Bonanno, 63 years old and suffering with a chronic heart ailment, has become a recluse in his home in Tucson, Ariz. Lieutenants in charge of his far-flung enterprises, who formerly reported directly to him, now must deal through Salvatore.

¶A series of explosions damaged homes and businesses in Tucson owned or frequented by Bonnanno associates. Police-

men who investigated what sounded like a shot at Bonanno's home last July 4 were told by a bodyguard that what neighbors had heard was only a rock thrown against a plate glass window. The bombings and other harassments have now stopped.

¶Salvatore Bonanno has sold his Cape Cod type home in East Meadow, L. I., from which he had directed much of the strategy against Sciacca, and has moved to San Jose, Calif., where he has taken residence in a modest $20,000 house at 1419 Lamore Drive. Law enforcement agents say he is staking out business interests of his own in the California area whose reputed Mafia boss, Joseph Cerrito, is an old-time friend of the elder Bonanno. Salvatore travels regularly between San Jose and Tucson.

¶Air travel time between New York and the West Coast is five hours, but it took Salvatore Bonanno seven weeks to cover that distance, stopping en route in major cities for conferences with local Mafia bosses.

¶Bonanno loyalists and Sciacca henchmen, who a short time before would not have sought one another's company without guns in their hands,

disported together convivially at a wedding reception last Sept. 14 at the Woodbury Country Club on Long Island.

Deserted Bonanno

The reception celebrated the marriage of Paul Sciacca's son, Anthony, to Florence Rando, a niece of Frank Mari, a former Bonanno lieutenant who had been shot, but not fatally, on July 13, 1966, because he had deserted Bonanno and joined the Sciacca camp.

The party, attended by more than 200 guests, followed a religious ceremony performed at the Regina Paces Votive Shrine in a Brooklyn parish to which the Mafia has long been partial.

Joseph Profaci, the late "Olive Oil King" who headed one of the most powerful Mafia families until his death in 1962 and whose niece Rosalie is married to Salvatore Bonanno, was credited by the police in 1952 with having brought about the return to the shrine, at 65th Street and 12th Avenue, of altar gems worth $100,000 stolen eight days earlier.

The gems, two golden crowns studded with 500 diamonds and other jewels and blessed by Pope Pius XII, had been taken by a thief from an altar painting in the shrine. Msgr. Angelo R. Cioffi, pastor of the shrine and of its nearby mother church, St. Rosalia's Church, to whom a special delivery postman delivered the stolen treasure, later told applauding parishioners that the recovery of the crowns was a miracle.

Profaci Role Assumed

Although the theft remains an official mystery, policemen who worked on the case said they believed that Profaci, a parishioner and generous contributor, had sent word through the underworld that the thief's life would be forfeit unless he returned the crowns to the church.

Federal and local police agents, some of whom followed the festive wedding parade from Brooklyn to the Long Island country club where other agents and Nassau County detectives had already placed the premises under watch, compiled nine pages of car license plate numbers.

Among the guests they spotted were Philip (Rusty) Rastelli, Anthony Lisi and several others identified by the Mafia experts of the Central Investigation Bureau as Bonanno aides who had remained loyal to their embattled chief during the months that bullets were flying. But on Sept. 14 the gregarious back-slappers felt no shoulder holster under any former foe's tuxedo jacket and the only bulges under cummerbunds came from well-fed stomachs, not weapons.

Police officials have put as much stock in these signs as in other evidences of peace, or at least truce, because in the Mafia important decisions, treaties, business deals and sometimes executions are often sealed at weddings, christenings, funerals and other traditional gatherings of a clan.

3 Loyalists Sought

Investigators close to the developments predicted yesterday that one result of the cessation of gunfire would be early surrender of three Bonanno loyalists sought since April by the Bronx District Attorney's office as witnesses in a grand jury inquiry into the attempted murder of William Gonzalez. Bronx District Attorney Burton B. Roberts has said that the three, for whom subpoenas have been issued, are friends of Mr. Gonzalez' and are not suspects.

With peace declared in the quarrel within the Mafia, the police reason that the missing witnesses no longer fear that they, too, may be marked for death. Mr. Gonzalez, an employe of Sam Perrone, a Bonanno bodyguard, was shot outside his Bronx home three weeks after Perrone had been shot dead in front of his Brooklyn warehouse.

The police believe both shoot-

ings were in reprisal by Sciacca's men for the shootings of Bonanno deserters who had joined Sciacca.

When the missing witnesses return, clearing themselves of fugitive status, they will be asked by the grand jury what they know about the enemies of Mr. Gonzalez, but no one expects them to violate the Mafia's code of omerta (silence). The missing wtinesses are Vito DeFilippo, his son Pasquale, and William Riviello.

Journey to Canada

Mr. Riviello had been employed in Perrone's warehouse. The DeFilippos, father and son, had been among six members of a Bonanno expeditionary force led by Salvatore Bonanno who were arrested in Montreal in November, 1966, along with Louis Greco, identified by Canadian authorities as head of the Montreal Mafia.

The six from the United States were deported from Canada after being given two-day jail sentences, which were suspended, for illegal possession of loaded guns found in their two cars.

According to one Federal official, the Bonanno faction will lose lucrative interests in eastern Canada under the peace treaty.

Sciacca, underworld sources say, has been magnanimous about letting Bonanno satraps, who had held out against him until recently, retain their own gambling, loan-sharking and other illegal enterprises in return for recognizing him as the new boss in the East.

A few of Joseph Bonanno's oldest cronies, who have been with him since he took the first steps more than 40 years ago in the Ridgewood district of Brooklyn on his crooked path to a nationwide rackets empire with international connections, have quit the local scene and settled near him in Tucson or elsewhere in the West.

Carlo Simari, the elder Bonanno's bodyguard, has not been seen since last April. There is speculation that he may have been a target of the same executioners who gunned down Sam Perrone, Salvatore's bodyguard.

The only threat to the newfound peace, investigators believe, is the complaint by some of the lower-echelon Bonanno loyalists that they have lost out in the rearrangement. This is being arbitrated by the bosses and *consiglieri* of the other Mafia families here.

The elder Bonanno, a native of Castellamare del Golfo in Sicily, entered this country illegally from Havana in 1924. After leaving this country briefly in 1938 he made a legal re-entry from Canada. He became a naturalized citizen in 1945.

The New York Times
Salvatore (Bill) **Bonanno** assists his father, Joseph.

Associated Press
Joseph (Joe Bananas) Bonanno, ill, went to Tucson.

Although he has been arrested on many charges, including running machine guns for the Al Capone gang in Chicago, the only conviction on his record is for violation of the Federal Wages and Hours Law.

He is now under indictment on charges of obstruction of justice, stemming from his disappearance and long exile while under subpoena to testify before a Federal grand jury that was investigating organized crime here. His trial has been delayed by repeated heart attacks.

The casualty list of the "Banana War" includes the following:

¶Frank Mari, the Bonanno deserter, wounded by gunfire in the Bay Ridge section of Brooklyn on July 13, 1966.

¶Three Sciacca henchmen—Frank Telleri and the D'Angelo brothers, Thomas and James—machine-gunned to death by a lone executioner on Nov. 10, 1967, as they sat at a table in the Cypress Gardens restaurant in Queens.

¶Peter Crociata, a Sciacca gangster, shot last March in Brooklyn's Ridgewood neighborhood. He survived.

¶Sam Perrone, Salvatore Bonanno's bodyguard, killed last March 11.

¶Michael Consolo, 64-year-old former narcotics smuggler, shot dead last April 1 near his home in Middle Village, Queens. The police believed at first that he was killed for having deserted Bonanno for Sciacca. But subsequent under-

world information was that he had switched back to Bonanno. It is now believed he was executed for the second defection.

¶William Gonzalez, one of Perrone's employes, shot near his Bronx home last April 5. Mr. Gonzalez has since testified before a Bronx grand jury.

¶Franciso Crociata, 72-year-old kin of Peter Crociata and like him a deserter from Bonanno to Sciacca, shot, but not fatally, last April 16.

¶Charles (The Sidge) LoCicero, an old-time gambling boss and a loan shark high in the former Profaci family of the Mafia (now reputedly headed by Joseph Colombo), shot dead last April 19 by a masked gunman in a Brooklyn luncheonette. His murder was not ascribed at first to the Bonanno-Sciacca war, but has been reassessed on the basis of later information from the underworld.

According to talk among Mafia members, Joseph Bonanno was infuriated by the murder of Perrone, a close friend. Bonanno, who reportedly believed, probably with good reason, that the campaign to wipe out him and his coterie had the permission of the heads of the other local Mafia families, is said to have threatened: "The next time they hit one of my men, they lose one of their *capos* (captains), first in one family, then in another."

Law enforcement investigators believe the threat of escalating a fight within one Mafia family into a general war among organized crime gangs led the top men in the Mafia to bring pressure on the Bonanno and Sciacca factions to make peace. There have been no murders here in that feud since LoCicero's.

November 24, 1968

U.S. Anticrime Force in Brooklyn Strikes Again

By SYLVAN FOX

The arrest of eight persons in Brooklyn yesterday brought to about 90 the total seized there by a new Federal anticrime "strike force" since it was organized in April.

The new arrests involved persons—some with known links to the Mafia—suspected of having received stolen goods. But tracking down and recovering stolen property is only one facet of the strike force's work in Brooklyn and of similar forces around the country.

Their main target is nothing less than the entire range of organized crime in the United States.

"I think this is now the best weapon we have against organized crime," Joseph P. Hoey, United States Attorney for the Eastern District of New York, said of the Brooklyn unit.

About two weeks ago the House Republican Task Force on Crime told President-elect Richard M. Nixon that the strike forces in Brooklyn and in several other cities over the country should not only be retained by the new Administration but should also be expanded.

Other Cities Added

The first strike force was

8 New Arrests Bring Total to 90 in Drive Against Organized Criminals

organized in Buffalo in 1966 on an experimental basis by Attorney General Ramsey Clark and Henry Petersen, head of the Justice Department's section on organized crime and racketeering.

The plan proved so effective that it has now been extended in addition to Brooklyn, to Detroit, Philadelphia, Miami and Chicago, and the Justice Department expects to establish similar units soon in Kansas City, New Orleans and St. Louis.

The Brooklyn force is a typical example of how the units are organized.

It consists of six Justice Department lawyers plus supervisory agents from the Bureau of Customs, the Immigration and Naturalization Service, the Internal Revenue Service, the Labor Department, the Federal Bureau of Narcotics and Dangerous Drugs, the Secret Service, and the Royal Canadian Mounted Police.

The Brooklyn strike force is headed by Daniel P. Hollman, a 38-year-old Fordham Law School graduate who is a former assistant United States attorney and a former special assistant attorney general of New York State.

The Federal Bureau of Investigation is not represented. Law enforcement sources say that the bureau, while cooperative on a case-by-case basis, is cool to the idea of joining in a project that cuts so completely across agency lines.

The basic value of the strike force, Mr. Hollman said, is that it systematically permits virtually all crime-fighting agencies in the Federal Government to work together and pool information on a daily basis.

"I can get a complete exchange of information," Mr. Hollman said. "If I need income-tax returns, I can cut all kinds of red tape."

Mr. Hollman and his force operate from a suite of tightly guarded offices on the ground floor of the Federal Building in downtown Brooklyn. A visitor can penetrate the security only by approaching a locked door, picking up a red wall telephone, informing a secretary of his business and being admitted by buzzer.

The strike forces also, for the first time, concentrate sub-

stantial investigative and legal manpower on the specific problem of organized crime.

"It's a question of having all these resources and making use of them and concentrating just on one area," Mr. Hollman said.

In the short life of the Brooklyn unit, it has racked up a total of 30 indictments naming 66 defendants, almost all of them known or suspected Mafiosi. The force now has about 25 active investigations under way.

Among those indicted as a result of the force's efforts are Carmine Lombardozzi, Thomas Mancuso, Anthony (Tony the Gawk) Augello and Salvatore Passalacqua, all reputed to be prominent figures in the organized crime syndicate.

A special Federal grand jury was empaneled in May to handle cases brought by the Brooklyn strike force.

Manpower Shortage

Mr. Hoey, under whose general supervision the force operates, explained that his office, like those of many United States attorneys around the country, lacks the manpower to concentrate on organized crime.

"This force can devote six attorneys and eight supervising agents working full time on this problem," he said. "This is a greater concentration of manpower than has ever been placed on this work in this district—or anywhere else, for that matter."

December 20, 1968

The Underworld and How It Succeeds

By SIDNEY E. ZION
Special to The New York Times

TRENTON, Dec. 27—In a curious way, Mafia investigations, such as the one about to begin next week in New Jersey, have tended to obscure the real nature of organized crime, the underlying reasons for its success and its natural dependence on official "cooperation." The sensational nature of the testimony, made zestier by the childish but strange nicknames of the Mafiosi, such as "Three - Finger Brown" and "Joe Bananas," seems to confirm the mystery and romance of the mob as depicted by Warner Brothers films of the nineteen-thirties.

News Analysis

Inquiries on Mafia Tend to Hide Its Nature

As a result, organized crime, in reality a rather prosaic industry with bureaucratic rules cut to its own peculiar need, is transformed into a literal "underworld," existing entirely outside the confines of society.

And yet, as virtually all law enforcement officials and crime commissions have pointed out, the Mafia is first and foremost a huge gambling enterprise, protected by public servants

and supported by the general public. Indeed, its huge profits, its sophisticated organization, its "legitimate" enterprises were in a vital sense created and made necessary by the very criminal law that seeks to destroy it.

Monopoly Profit

Thus, by outlawing nearly all forms of gambling, the country has structured, in Prof. Herbert L. Packer's phrase, a "crime tariff," which, like the protective tariffs for industry, has served to secure a kind of monopoly profit for the underworld.

Law enforcement officials estimate that up to $50-billion a year is illegally wagered, in one form or another, in the nation,

turning a profit of approximately one-third of the gross intake.

This profit represents "our most generous subsidy to organized crime," Mr. Packer, a professor at Stanford University Law School and a recognized authority on crime, wrote in his newly published book, "The Limits of the Criminal Sanction."

Law enforcement experts agree that gambling profits provide the revenues for the more nefarious activities such as loansharking and narcotics, although in recent years the Mafia has greatly decreased its traffic in drugs.

On the other hand, there is said to have been a great increase in the mob's infiltration and investment in legitimate businesses. This appears to enrage the public more than any Mafia activity save narcotics.

141

yet ironically it can be traced directly to the criminal law.

For it was not until the Federal Government in 1932 convicted Al Capone of income tax violations that the mob felt a need for legitimate "fronts" to justify their standard of living. Capone's conviction was based on the theory that his proven expenditures showed that he had a larger income than he reported for tax purposes.

To get around this, law enforcement agents say, underworld figures have gone into legitimate business so they will have legal income to report.

As to why crime is organized, the need for organization was always logical but apparently did not become clear to the underworld until the latter days of prohibition when the gang wars proved too self-destructive.

As a result, crime reports say, a nationwide division of spoils, which included working agreements with Jewish, Irish and other gangs not permitted into the Mafia, was set up by top underworld figures.

While Federal and local law-enforcement men say they know a good deal about the organization of crime, they have not been able to convict many of the men they name as Mafia leaders.

One reason why this is true, they say, is that it is one thing for them to know that Joseph (Joe Bayonne) Zicarelli runs gambling in Jersey City and another thing to prove it. The "top guys" do not sell policy slips house to house or take telephone bets on Giant games. Also because of the sophisticated organization of crime, the bookmaker who does take the bets may not even know the identity of the person to whom he phones in his bets.

The law enforcement establishment, with the notable exception of Attorney General Ramsey Clark, has long asserted that if it could use information collected through wiretaps many of the major figures would now be in jail.

However, Mr. Clark has pointed out that wiretapping was legal until 1934 and admissible in Federal Courts until 1937—a period that encompassed the "golden era of crime in America." Furthermore, wiretapping has been legalized in New York by statute for 30 years. Before then it could be used because there was no Federal prohibition. Although some top New York mob figures were said to have been apprehended through taps, most were not.

Last June, court-ordered wiretapping and bugging were made legal by Congress and perhaps during the next year their efficacy will be better judged.

The New Jersey Legislature will probably, in the view of most politicians here, pass a wiretap bill this session as a result of the impending hearings and investigations.

In any event, prosecution of Mafia leaders would be difficult because, as the President's crime commission has said, "Organized crime flourishes only where it has corrupted local officials."

While crime investigators say that it is common for the Mafia to try to buy policemen and local officials who can have a direct effect on their operations it is unusual for them to try to infiltrate state legislatures.

Some of them appear to be puzzled by the current investigation in Jersey as to whether six legislators have links to the Mafia. The investigators say that the Mafia generally does not try to influence statewide legislation.

However, they say that Mafia leaders are happy to have as friends anyone in any position of power anywhere and that some legislators, in addition to operating on the state level, have considerable influence in their home counties.

December 28, 1968

Genovese Dies in Prison at 71; 'Boss of Bosses' of Mafia Here

By United Press International

SPRINGFIELD, Mo., Feb. 14 —Vito Genovese, chieftain of the underworld in New York, died of a heart ailment today at the Medical Center for Federal Prisoners. He was 71 years old.

Ruled 'Family' of 450

By CHARLES GRUTZNER

Vito Genovese's throne, from which he ruled as "Boss of All Bosses" of the Mafia in the New York area, rested on the coffins of several predecessors —in whose murders he is believed to have conspired.

Genovese reportedly issued orders from prison to a "family" of 450 racketeers and infiltrators of business and politics in New York and New Jersey.

In the Atlanta Penitentiary, where the stocky, pallid boss began serving a 15-year sentence for narcotics smuggling, he was able to choose his cellmates and, according to law enforcement officials, send orders to his underbosses beyond the walls. After being transferred to Leavenworth, he continued to awe and to rule fellow prisoners and Mafiosi working in his varied outside enterprises.

Genovese insisted in a conversation with a fellow inmate at Leavenworth last June that he had been framed on the narcotics charge.

"They gave me a bum rap in the narcotics case," he said. "I wouldn't have minded if they got me on income tax evasion because that would be fair."

It was Genovese's highhanded exercise of authority in Atlanta, according to the Department of Justice, that led to the first public exposure of the organizational set-up of the Mafia, sometimes called the Cosa Nostra.

Genovese allegedly ordered the execution within the Federal prison of one of his "soldiers," Joseph Valachi, who shared his cell. Valachi, in a frenzy of fear, killed another prisoner— whom he said he mistook for his appointed executioner—and later became the star witness before a Senate committee in 1963 on the operations of the major national crime syndicate.

Born Near Naples

Genovese was born in Rosiglino, near Naples, Italy, on Nov. 27, 1897. He was 15 when he arrived here and settled with his family in Mulberry Street, then the heart of New York's "Little Italy."

Starting with thefts from pushcarts, he advanced to errand boy for the mustached Mafia dons and graduated to being a collector for the Italian lottery and to crimes of violence. The first of his many arrests came when he was 19. That brought him a short prison term for carrying a pistol.

By cunning and by a power to dominate lesser criminals, Genovese advanced to a Mafia echelon that won him the title of Don Vitone. In 1931 he and another ambitious second-

Associated Press, 1958
Vito Genovese

stringer — Salvatore Lucania, better known as Charles (Lucky) Luciano — started a skein of intrigue that eventually put Luciano, and later Genovese, on top of the metropolitan Mafia.

The pair, underlings of Giuseppe (The Boss) Masseria, are said to have sold out their leader to Salvatore Maranzano, who aspired to the title of Boss of All Bosses.

Wined, Dined and Killed

Genovese and Luciano lured Masseria to a Coney Island restaurant, where he was wined and dined and shot dead. His killer has never been identified. But Maranzano's dream of empire was short-lived. He was murdered less than six months after Masseria, and those who arranged that liquidation, according to Valachi, were Luciano and Genovese.

The year 1931 was a turning point also in Genovese's domestic affairs. The funeral of his first wife, who died of tuberculosis, had in its large cortege some of the most powerful chieftains of the underworld—a sign of Don Vitone's status.

Genovese, soon after his wife's funeral, let it be known that he wanted to take as wife Anna Petillo, who already had a husband.

The body of Mr. Petillo, dead by strangulation, was found shortly afterward on a roof. Don Vito and the widow Petillo were united in marriage 12 days later. The ill-starred union was stormy for 20 years before ending in a legal separation.

Genovese, who was as laconic as he was cold in his dealings with his associates, was moved by the break-up of his second marriage to an emotional uncertainty.

"What she step on my heart for?" he was said to have asked his mother-in-law after Anna had left him.

In court hearings on support money, the second Mrs. Genovese branded her husband as a racketeer with a huge income from nightclubs, gambling and other enterprises.

Cruel and Greedy

Meanwhile, Maranzano's murder had left Luciano—who had no aspirations to be Boss of All Bosses — as head of the largest of the five major "families" here, with Genovese as his underboss.

Don Vito, who had gone into the quick-profits but dangerous narcotics trade, was a cruel and greedy underboss. He is reputed to have had several of his "soldiers" killed when they held out on his share, bungled an operation or came under suspicion, justly or unjustly, of treachery.

One such murder, that of Ferdinand (the Shadow) Boccia in 1934, backfired against Genovese and forced him to flee to Italy, with $750,000 in cash.

He became close to Mussolini, gave $250,000 to the Fascists and received the highest decorations from Il Duce. After Mussolini's fall, Genovese wormed his way into the confidence of American Army Occupation authorities, became a major black marketeer of American gasoline and other supplies and was riding high until a captain in the Criminal Investigation Division identified him as the Mafioso wanted for murder.

Obstacle Is Removed

Genovese was returned to Brooklyn for trial, and again murder appeared to remove an obstacle from his path. The state's chief corroborative witness, Peter La Tempa, was fatally poisoned in Raymond Street Jail, where he was in protective custody.

During Don Vitone's long exile in Italy, Luciano had been sent to prison in 1936 for 30 to 50 years for compulsory prostitution, and Frank Costello (Francesco Saveria) succeeded him as boss of the underworld family.

Genovese's return home did not bring his automatic restoration to the family throne. He began, according to law enforcement forces, a whispering campaign to undercut Costello.

Suspecting Albert Anastasia, head of one of the other Mafia families, of an alliance with Costello, Genovese allegedly engineered Anastasia's murder in the Park-Sheraton Hotel barber shop on Oct. 25, 1957. This was five months after a gunman had creased Costello's skull in an assassination attempt.

Costello got the double message and eased himself out of the scene and Don Vito realized his dream of heading the biggest Mafia family in the United States.

Met at Apalachin

His ascension to power was approved by Mafia leaders from across the country at a convocation, shortly after Anastasia's assassination, in Apalachin, N. Y., which was raided by state troopers before all the business was settled.

One of the items on the agenda, according to the police, was an order from the Mafia's 12-man national commission — of which Genovese was a member — to get out of the narcotics business because it exposed too many Mafiosi, including weak "brothers" who might turn Government witnesses, to the possibility of arrest.

But Genovese's greed proved his undoing. He bankrolled a big narcotics smuggling operation, but Federal agents learned of it. The result was that Genovese and 14 co-defendants got prison terms. Genovese would have been eligible for parole in March 1970.

Genovese, who wore expensive clothes and spent much of his time in nightclubs he controlled before he fled to Italy, lived in the year before his imprisonment in a modest five-room white clapboard cottage in Atlantic Highlands, N. J.

Blended Into Neighborhood

He had lived with his second wife in a pretentious mansion in the same town until their separation. He sold the mansion and its ornate furnishings during her lawsuit.

Whether in mansion or cottage, the dark-haired Genovese blended unspectacularly into the neighborhood. His hair began graying and thinning before he went to prison. He wore dark glasses in the city, but seldom on the streets of Atlantic Highlands. To some of his neighbors he appeared a conservative businessman instead of one of the nation's top racketeers.

And he was, in his way, a businessman. Realizing as early as 1925 that a "legitimate" business could be a cover for illegal operations as well as a source of income, he set up the Genovese Trading Company, handling waste paper and rags. Gradually, he expanded his legitimate businesses along with his rackets.

With Genovese's death, an underworld "caretaker" government takes over the gangs' affairs until a permanent successor is chosen. The caretakers are the same three persons who have been running things on orders that Genovese reportedly sent from prison. They are Gerardo (Jerry) Catena of South Orange, N. J.; Michele (Mike) Miranda of Forest Hills, Queens, and Thomas (Tommy Ryan) Eboli of Englewood Cliffs, N. J.

Law enforcement agents, who have been watching developments in the Mafia through informers, had divided opinions yesterday on the permanent successor.

"Nothing will be settled until there is a sitdown among the leaders of the other Mafia families in the metropolitan area, and their choice is approved by the national commission," said a police expert on organized crime. He added:

"That won't be until some time after the funeral, out of respect. And they might even come up with a dark horse."

The funeral will be held next week from the Anderson Funeral Home in Red Bank, N. J. The day has not yet been decided.

Genovese's daughter, son and brother were at his bedside when he died. He had been transferred to the medical center from the Federal prison at Leavenworth on Jan. 30.

Transcripts of F.B.I. Bugging Disclose the Methods and Intrigues of the Mafia

Following are excerpts from transcripts of electronic recordings made by the Federal Bureau of Investigation from 1961 to 1965. They were made at places frequented by Simone Rizzo (Sam the Plumber), DeCavalcante and two co-defendants, Gaetana Dominick (Corky) Vastola and Daniel Annunziata, in a conspiracy-extortion case awaiting trial. The transcripts were filed in Federal Court in Newark. They consist of direct transcriptions of recorded conversations and F. B. I. summaries of such conversations.

Murders and Executions

Following is an F.B.I. summary of a conversation in which one unidentified man discusses a murder he helped to carry out in New Jersey:

Tony related that he had to do a job once and he did it all by himself 30 years ago. He repeatedly mentioned the name Fillipo and he said that he and possibly two others put Fillipo on a truck and tied him up. They drove him to a park but the location was not satisfactory so then they put him in a car and drove him to a farm. Tony related that Fillipo was in the car and one of the others with him had turned up the car radio so that Fillipo's screams could not be heard. One of the subjects with Tony kept a gun to Fillipo's head. They took Fillipo to a farm and inside the garage on the farm cut Fillipo's throat. Tony described the conditions of the weather at this time as cold and he said that Fillipo's body was buried somewhere close to the farm. For some unrelated reason, they decided to move Fillipo's body from the grave site and so they went to dig him up. At this point Tony stated that he saw a sight that he had never seen before after they dug up the body and he was scared. "We dug him up after he died, and his hair was still growing, the dead man was hairy, never saw this before."

An F.B.I. informant (NK 2461-C] tells of a Mafia discussion of machines that will dispose of bodies:

NK 2461-C advised that subject and two unknown males on 9/3/64 discussed the various types of machines suitable for disposing of a body. One machine was mentioned as being capable of turning a body into a "meatball."

One unknown male said the best machine was that which smashed up automobiles. Subject, however, said he was looking for the type of machine which pulverizes garbage. The unknown male stated the only type "we" know of that will pulverize garbage is the machine Louis [Larasso] told the unknown males about the other day, and added, "They're working on it now."

Informant said no specific use for the machine was mentioned. It appears that subject wants the machine on hand in event he needs it.

Two Mafiosi discuss the best way of disposing of someone. (The F.B.I. identifies "R" as Angelo (Gyp) De-Carlo and "T" as Anthony (Tony Boy) as Boiardo.

De Carlo further suggested that the best way to dispose of someone is to give the individual a fatal shot of dope and put him behind the wheel of his automobile where he will be found.

R: That's what they should have done with Willie [Moretti].

T: Oh yeah.

R: You got five guys there, you talk to the guy. Tell him this is the lie detector stuff. You tell him, "You say you didn't say this—"

T: How many guys are you going to con?

R: Well if you don't con him then tell him. Now like you got four or five guys in the room. You know they're going to kill you. They say, "Tony Boy wants to shoot you in the head and leave you in the street or would you rather take this, we put you behind your wheel, we don't have to embarrass your family or nothing." That's what they should have done to Willie—

T: How about the time we hit the Little Jew—

R: As little as they are they struggle.

T: The Boot hit him with a hammer. The guy goes down and he comes up. So I got a crow bar this big, Ray. Eight shots in the head. What do you think he finally did to me? He spit at me and said you (obscenity).

R: They're fighting for their life.

S. Ray, you told me years ago about the guy where you said let me hit you clean.

R: That's right. So the guy went for it. There was me, Zip and Johnny Russell. So we took the guy out in the woods and I said, "Now listen." Zip had the——on him. I said, "Leave him alone Zip." I said, "Look"—Itchie was the kid's name. I said, "You gotta go, why not let me hit you right in the heart and you won't feel a thing?" He said, "I'm innocent, Ray, but if you've got to do it . . . ." So I hit him in the heart and it went right through him.

S: The guy we were supposed to (inaudible). They were spitting all over me, you know.

R: Oh well, I would have left them on the street.

S: They didn't want them on the street. They didn't want the rest of the mob to know that permission——

R: But I mean a guy like Willie. "We like you and all but you gotta go. You know it's an order. You gave enough orders."

T: I don't think Willie would have went for it.

R: I think he would. He would have tried to talk his way out of it but he would have went for it.

T: It would have been better.

R: Sure, that man never should have been disgraced like that.

S: It leaves a bad taste. We're out to protect people.

A conversation between De Cavalcante and two men:

SAM: Jack, what happened to Pickles [Angelo Piccolella] two weeks after he broke away from me?

JACK: He got killed.

MARTY: The guy in Elizabeth, huh?

SAM: Yeah, he was away two weeks. I told him that was what was going to happen to him. So when people don't want to listen.

MARTY: He tried to be a big man?

SAM: Well.

Marty departed at this point.

Corruption of Labor

In the following conversation, Joseph (Whitey) Danzo and Gaetano (Corky) Vastola describe to DeCavalcante their plans for setting up a dummy labor union at a factory in New York:

SAM: I like to talk [about money] first so there's no misunderstanding. What end do you feel Joe should get?

CORKY: Twenty-five per cent for here. Because there's two guys and myself over there. That's three of us. (To Joe.) So you're the fourth guy.

SAM: Do you think that's right—to forget me?

CORKY: Forget you?

SAM: Yeah.

CORKY: Well—that's what I told Mike, but—Yeah!—let's make it five! I'll take 20 per cent.

JOE: Me, too.

SAM: All right. Joe, you're satisfied with 20 per cent?

JOE: Yeah, I'm satisfied.

SAM: Now, how about the dues there? Where do the dues come in now?

JOE: I use the dues for his books, stationery, and to set him all up.

CORKY: What are the dues a month?

JOE: Well, you can make yours five dollars, but I only have four here.

CORKY: And what is the initiation fee? Ah—but I'm gonna waive the fee to set up the shop.

JOE: Right. Then you could charge 25, 50 or 75 dollars—whatever you want. Why not 10 now and anybody that comes in after—25?

Corky: All right.

SAM: Well, how are you gonna make a score if you're cheap?

CORKY: Well, I'm gonna make the score this way. When I sit down with the the the boss [management], I tell him how much it's gonna cost him in welfare, hospitalization, and all that. Say a plant with 200 people will cost him $4,000 a month—just for hospitalization. So, altogether I make a package out of it. [I'll say] it's gonna cost $100,000 a year. Let's cut it in half and forget about it." And walk away. I show him first what it's gonna cost—then how much I'm gonna save by walking away.

SAM: Well, you have to organize the plant so nobody else walks in there—then you wind up with the dues every month. That's $300 a month. You could do that?

JOE: Sure. He could give a solid contract for three years—where he won't get hurt.

SAM: Then you get a pay every year.

Discussion of Arson

Following is a conversation between DeCavalcante and Bobby Basile about burning a restaurant and an F.B.I. summary of "a possible arson at the Stagecoach Restaurant in Easton, Pa."

BOBBY: Mr. Maglie wants to burn down his joint—and I got the guy.

SAM: Who's the guy?

BOB: Russ.... As far as Pussy's [Anthony Russo] concerned—he says O.K. It's up to you now.

SAM: What's he want to pay for it?

BOB: He's gonna pay 5,000. That's all—I'll give him a break. He's got 90,000 insurance on it.

SAM: I don't even know nothing.

BOB: O.K. Done—O.K.?

SAM: How's he gonna pay you—when he collects the money or what?

BOB: He's gonna give . . . I let the kid make the arrangements. I didn't step in. I just introduced them. So—he's gonna give the kid a thousand—to get the stuff, you know.

SAM: I don't want to know nothing about it.

BOB: You don't want to know. . . . all right? So I told Pussy, and he said, "Well, I don't care." I said, "Look, then I didn't tell you nothing? You want to leave it that way?" "Yeah," he said, "I don't care."

SAM: Forget about it.

BOB: O.K. I didn't tell Pussy I spoke to you or nothing—so, it's forgotten.

On 6/3/65, NK 2461-C advised that subject was contacted by his cousin, Robert (Bobby) Basile. They discussed Joe Maglie (Joseph Miglianna), an Easton, Pa., gambling figure who has owed a long-standing debt to DeCavalcante. Basile has been actively attempting to collect what is owed and, on this occasion, he reported to DeCavalcante that Joe Maglie wanted to burn his restaurant.

Basile said he had suggested that Russ (last name unknown) would be the one who could carry out Joe's plan and to this end had discussed the matter with Pussy (Anthony Russo), since Russ is "Pussy's man." Russ had no objections so Basile would merely introduce Russ to Joe, providing DeCavalcante gave his approval.

In response to DeCavalcante's question, Basile told him that Joe had his place insured for $90,000 and had agreed to pay $5,000 to have it destroyed. He also said that Russ would need $1,000 in advance in order to buy the materials. DeCavalcante gave Basile his approval.

On 7/4/65, by teletype, Philadelphia advised that a radio news broadcast reported that the Stagecoach Restaurant, Easton, Pa., was gutted" by fire early on 7/4/65, and that local investigators were attempting to determine the cause of the fire.

On 7/6/65, NK 2461-C reported that at approximately noon that date, Basile contacted DeCavalcante and immediately told him that "Joe from Easton had an accident with his place." Basile said he had called Joe's home and had left word for Joe to call him back. DeCavalcante remarked, "That's terrible," whereupon Basile responded with laughter.

It is suggested that Philadelphia, through an established source, advise authorities, either police or civil, that the Stagecoach fire may have been deliberately set.

Manners and Morals

Corky comes to DeCavalcante's office to complain about having been arrested.

CORKY: I got pinched. I'm out on $10,000 bail. I just got out yesterday. Oh, you didn't know nothing about it?

SAM: No.

CORKY: I sent word.
SAM: Who you send word with?

CORKY: With Rudy—I was supposed to go with them upstate, and I got pinched Monday. I'm out on $10,000 bail.

SAM: On what?

CORKY: Burglary, grand larceny and coercion — and they [the New York City police] know everything. They have all the tapes — with Rocky, Mikey Dee, Frank, everybody. They let me listen to tapes for two hours. All I did was give them my name and address.

SAM: I want to put this on record with you. I don't know if this is a trap or not.

They said, "Look, Corky, being that you're giving your name and addddress to us, you're not afraid of us. Be afraid of your friends. I said, "What do you mean?" They said, "When Mikey Dee called—we'll let you listen to the first part of the tape, but we can't let you listen to all of it." Mikey Dee called Rocky in Chicago—er, in Hot Springs, and he said, "Hey, my God, that guy's getting unbearable. I can't stand it no more." (To Sam) This is when I was asking for my money. So Rocky says to him, "Don't worry, that jerk —we'll take care of him in our own way." Understand? Now, I just want to put this thing on record with you because if I see one phony move with these guys, Sam —you see. I got to tell you these things—right?

SAM: Right.

CORKY: Now besides, I didn't get my money! I've got to pay the bail bondsman $460. I ain't got a quarter to give to the lawyer.

SAM: How come they didn't pick up Mikey Dee? Do they have him under suspicion?

CORKY: They got everybody. They showed me everybody's pictures. Get word to Frankie [Cocchiarol] they're going to try to kidnap him out of Long Branch. They said, "We know Frankie's in Long Branch—we're gonna kidnap him."

I said "pass"—I kept saying "pass." They said, "What do you men by 'pass'?" I said, "I've given you my name and address. Now I say 'pass,' that makes it easy." They said they would give me a week to go out and brik that stuff back, but I told I wasn't no messenger boy. So they said I was a wise guy and booked me.

SAM: Let me tell you something. They're [Rocky and Mikey Dee] not going to touch you or they'll have their heads blown off. They talk tough to try to impress one another. Rocky had bet-

ter mind his own business—he's hanging from a limb himself. So don't get too impressed with them.

CORKY: Sam, believe me, I'm not impressed at all. I just wanted to put it on record with you because if I see a bad move. I'm going to knock them right down—I'm not going to wait.

SAM: No—now let things cool off. Those guys have a lot to answer for themselves. Because Bobby and I had a long conversation this week. I understand your responsibilities—and Frank too. You know I work one way—and that's the right one. Saying a thing and doing it are two different things.

CORKY: like the way you work.

Another gang leader, Joseph Arthur Zicarelli, complains to DeCavalcante:

JOE: Let me ask you a question—you're no dummy and neither am I. I've been around a long time. I've been stealing and knocking around since I was 12. Twelve years old! And I know one thing. I never brought my troubles to anybody! If the guy wasn't involved or I wasn't cutting no money with him. Now here's a guy—I let him in on different things to see that he makes a buck. I let him in! And on top of it—he's going the other way! These guys that he's cutting the money with. Where the hell are they? Why come to me? Not that he's come to me for money. I'd send him money —don't bother me! Don't come near me. I'm hot enough as it is. They were gonna give me a million years! I know what's going on with me. I'm on the razor's edge and I'm just lucky enough that I stay clean enough and I'm getting by. Most of the time I'm doing nothing. I take a ride, where do you think I go? I see my old man, I go see my wife, I go see my kids—I don't go no place. I stay away from people!

I see you more than I see anybody in this whole thing. And when I go any place—I'm so careful! If anything turns up I wouldn't come. But these guys! Two agents were parked around the corner with New York plates one day. [I said], "Hey, do you know you brought the agents here?" [They said], "So what? We ain't doing nothing." [I said], "Are you out of your mind? How do you know what I'm doing?"

SAM: That's right. How do they know what you're doing?

JOE: They don't think the way we think. You ought to make a request to have me with you . . . under no captain. Just with you. What the hell, I'm from Jersey. . . . I guarantee I'd share everything with you.

SAM: Listen, to hell with the money. I'd want to be with you if we were the brokest guys in the world.

A conversation between De Cavalcante and his cousin, Bobby Basile.

SAM: Before I forget—who would you suggest to send down there?

BOB: Send down where, Sam? Newburgh?

SAM: Newburgh. Somebodys needs to be shown a lesson . . .

BOB: We were discussing this last night.

SAM: With who?

BOB: With Frank [Cocchiaro].

SAM: It's the guy that—his name is Gus.

BOB: Is he with Frank Casino [Francesco Cucola] this guy?

SAM: No, he's an outsider.

BOB: Well, why can't John La Mala handle it himself?

SAM: John is known over there. He hasn't got no boys to send.

BOB: Well, how about those tough sons he's got?

SAM: They know the guy!

BOB: All right. Then we'll send two guys up there. Two guys enough?

SAM: You may need three. This guy's a big guy.

BOB: All right. I'll send four.

SAM: Send three guys. You only need one guy to look the situation over. Then meet with Joe [last name unknown] tonight at the club to make the appointment.

BOB: Well, see now. You don't give me enough time. 'Cause I can't reach these kids now. These kids work at night.

SAM: Well, tell Frank— then get these kids.

BOB: All right.

SAM: And you have to see Joe anyhow—Miranda.

BOB: That's taken care of —next?

SAM: What else is new?

Attempted Briberies

Following is an F.B.I. summary of a conversation concerning the Staten Island police:

Corky continues to tell Sam about a Joe Columbo and the opening of a crap game in Staten Island. Joe asked Corky to see a certain Lt. in S.I.P.D. and it was finally agreed on to pay the P.D. $2,850 a month. The only agreement was that no cars were to come from N.Y. but that the people in S.I. were to go in cars and pick up people in N.Y. and bring them to game.

The F.B.I. made this transcript of a conversation concerning the bribery of the police. The bureau identifies "R" as DeCarlo, "S" as DeCavalcante, and "T" as Boiardo.

S: You know, Tony, 30 or 35 years ago if a —— was even seen talking to a cop they looked to hit him the next day. They figured he must be doing business with the cop.

R: Today if you don't meet them and pay them you can't operate.

T: The only guy I handle is Dick ——. Gino (Farina) and them guys handle the rest of the law. About seven or eight years [ago] I used to handle them all.

S: Did you ever see the way Ham operates on 14th Street?

R: For $5,000 Ham and Tony (Bananas) thought they bought a license.

S: This was before the $5,000.

R: They walk into precincts and everything. You can't have a man and be seen with him. He's no good to you then.

S: And how long do you think it will take the Federal men to find out?

R: The Federal men, they know everything that's happening.

Dissension in the Mafia

A conversation early in 1965 with DeCavalcante and an individual the F.B.I. tentatively identified as Joseph LaSelva of Connecticut, described as DeCavalcante's underboss:

SAM: You know over there, I told you, there's Bonanno [Joseph Bonanno] and his whole outfit—a committee of nine guys.

JOE: Well, you said five.

SAM: Yeah—it was five originally. Well they got everybody — Johnny Burns [John Morales], Billy [Salvatore Bonanno], the Bonanno kid, Bonanno, and a couple other guys.

JOE: How about that Joey . . .

SAM: Bayonne [Joseph Zicarelli]?

JOE: No, not Bayonne.

SAM: Notaro [Joseph Notaro]?

JOE: Yeah.

SAM: Well, I straightened him out a couple of weeks ago, but there seems to be a little hard feelings. He stuck with Bonanno. In fact we were supposed to hit some people over there but we straightened that out—

Carlo [Gambino] and I straightened out. We're gonna take them in—and everybody comes under the rules. The men are all supposed to forget the old sores.

JOE: How about the kid Sally [Bonanno], the son.

SAM: We don't trust him.

JOE: He's got two sons What about the other kid?

SAM: Well, Joey — he's nothing. He'll be all right. . . . Well, they haven't decided yet what to do with the father. . . . This guy robbed his own mother. We figure we'll take him to Florida.

JOE: Who, Joe [Bonanno Sr.]?

SAM: Yeah. The guy ruined himself. See, Gasparino [Gaspar De Gregorio] looks like the favorite to be the boss. He's got the commission behind him.

The F.B.I. interrupts the conversation at this point with the following summary: "Joe expressed pity for Joe Bonanno who had enjoyed great respect and prestige. Joe felt he must be getting senile."

SAM: He put [Joseph] Magliocco up to a lot of things. . . . like to kill Carl.

JOE: Well, Magliocco that was his son's father-in-law.

SAM: He put him up to hit Carl and Tommy Brown [Thomas Lucchese].

JOE: Well that must have had something to do with [Joseph] Profaci's outfit?

SAM: Yeah. Now they feel that he poisoned Magliocco. Magliocco didn't die a natural death. Because the only one who could accuse him [of plotting against Gambino and Lucchese] was Magliocco. See Magliocco confessed to it. But this Joe didn't know how far he went. Understand? So they suspect he used a pill on him—that he's noted for it. So he knows the truth of all the damage he done. But they feel he don't know how much the other people know. He'd come in and deny everything but he knows he coudn't deny he made people when the books were closed.

JOE: Out on the coast there was some friction, wasn't there?

SAM: Well, he tried to take California over when they were having trouble. He sent the kid out there with 40 guys. The commission stopped him and that's where the trouble started. If he'd have listened to me that time I went to talk to him this thing would have been all straightened out. They would have just bawled him out.

JOE: It's a shame. What was he, 58-59 years old, and the prestige he had! What was he looking for anyway? It's really bad for the morale of Our Thing, you know? When they make the rules and then break them themselves. He's been in 20 years.

SAM: Thirty-three years he's been in.

A conversation between DeCavalcante and Frank Majuri, his underboss, on Oct. 16, 1964, was critical of the Mafia's national commission for giving Joseph Colombo of Brooklyn the seat on the commission from which Bonanno had been ousted. It continued:

SAM: First of all—you see —the commission is all out of order. They told me, "Please, Sam, don't mix in. You're sincere but you don't know how they'll take it. What you mean is right." (A reference to DeCavalcante's efforts to mediate the dispute between Bonanno and several other bosses.) Every five years they're all supposed to retire and all the bosses make guys on the commission. Understand what I mean? Now where's a guy like Chicago [Sam Giancana] . . . where does he fit on the commission? You hear this guy talk and he's a nice guy. You can enjoy his company. But he's a jokester. "Hit him! Hit him!" [kill him]. That's all you hear from this guy.

FRANK: They don't analyze those things—they're cut and dried.

SAM: Do you know what the commission is? They are all . . . born [possibly Italian born].

FRANK: That's right. I don't think this Joe Zerilli (Detroit boss) is such a hot tomato.

SAM: Hey, wait, Joe's a nice guy!

FRANK: Yeah, but I'm saying, he's not like, you know. . . .

SAM: He's an old-timer and an old hand at certain things. Understand what I mean? He can do—the thing. So it's not nine individual minds [There were then nine members of the commission]. There's three! These three are yesmen, they let him take over the command. You may call them ignorant, but they do it. He's got that sewed up. He says, "After all I'm old. Things are this way, that way, blah, blah. . . ."

FRANK: These guys they got. . . .

SAM: You know, I've heard all these guys talking —my father makes more sense than all of them . . . [conversation whispered, out of range] . . . Us, we're not even a little crumb in the basket.

Participants in Recorded Mafia Conversations

Following are descriptions of some of the participants in the recorded conversations and others they mention:

DANIEL ANNUNZIATA—One of the three defendants in a Federal conspiracy-extortion case for which the electronic recordings were presented as evidence.

ROBERT BASILE—A young man, identified by the police as having Mafia connections and a cousin of Simone DeCavalcante, Mafia leader.

ANTHONY (TONY BOY) BOIARDO—The principal figure in the Valentine Electric Company in Newark, and son of Ruggerio Boiardo, who is said to be a Mafia leader in New Jersey.

JOSEPH (JOE BANANAS) BONANNO—The head of a Mafia family who was deposed in the early nineteen-sixties.

SALVATORE BONANNO—Son of Joseph Bonanno and husband of Rosalie Profaci, niece of the late Joseph Profaci. He is said to be a high-level overseer of mob interests on the West Coast.

FRANK (BIG FRANK) COCCHIARO—A former New York City bookmaker, burglar and forger who moved his base of operations to Long Branch, N. J., about three years ago.

ANGELO (GYP) DeCARLO—Said to be a capo, or leader, in the camp headed by Simone Rizzo DeCavalcante.

SIMONE RIZZO (SAM THE PLUMBER) DeCAVALCANTE—The central figure in the recorded conversations, one of the three defendants in the case and, reputedly, the boss of the sixth largest Mafia family in the metropolitan region.

CARLO (DON CARLO) GAMBINO—Successor to the Mafia family that had been led by Albert Anastasia until he was murdered in 1957.

JOSEPH LaSELVA—Said to be DeCavalcante's principal representative in Connecticut, running illegal operations in Bridgeport and Waterbury.

THOMAS (THREE FINGER BROWN) LUCHESE—Successor to Frank Costello as head of one of the principal Mafia families. Luchese died two years ago.

JOSEPH MAGLIOCCO—The head, until his death in 1964, of the Mafia family now headed by Joseph Colombo. The transcript raises doubt about whether his death, attributed at the time to a heart attack, was natural.

JOHN JOSEPH MORALES—Said to have been a captain in the Bonanno Mafia family.

ANTHONY (LITTLE PUSSY) RUSSO—Allegedly the head, until recently, of the DeCavalcante's operations in Monmouth County, N. J.

GAETANO DOMINICK (CORKY) VASTOLA—The third defendant in the conspiracy-extortion case.

JOSEPH (BAYONNE JOE) ZICARELLI—Identified by investigators as the Mafia chieftain for Hudson County, N. J.

United Press International

Carlo Gambino

Associated Press

Joseph Bonanno

Anthony (Little Pussy) Russo

Associated Press

Thomas Luchese

June 13, 1969

NEW TAPES BY F.B.I. LINK POLITICIANS TO JERSEY MAFIA

Lacey Releases Transcripts as De Carlo Faces Court on Extortion Charge

PAYOFFS ARE INDICATED

Kenny, Carey and Wilentz Among Leading Names Used on Recordings

By CHARLES GRUTZNER
Special to The New York Times

NEWARK, Jan. 6—Boasts by members of the Mafia of dealings with major political figures and law enforcement officials were disclosed today in the conspiracy-extortion trial in Federal Court here of Angelo (Gyp) De Carlo and three other defendants.

Twelve hundred pages of transcripts and logs made by the Federal Bureau of Investigation of conversations among De Carlo, a reputed captain in the Mafia family of Gerardo (Gerry) Catena, and his associates were ordered made public by Federal Judge Robert Shaw. Defense lawyers who had asked to examine the transcripts privately protested making them public.

The transcripts are unsworn documents and do not constitute evidence. Most of those named in the transcriptions could not be reached for comment immediately.

Overheard Electronically

The conversations, eavesdropped electronically from 1961 to 1965, covered alleged situations that included the following:

¶The willingness of John V. Kenny, Hudson County Democratic leader, to put himself under obligation to the Mafia by asking De Carlo to intercede with Newark Mayor Hugh J. Addonizio to appoint a Kenny supporter as administrator of Martland Medical Center.

¶The raising of cash contributions by De Carlo and his criminal associates to elect Mr. Addonizio, then a Congressman, as Mayor in 1962, and De Carlo's boast: "He'll give us, the city."

¶De Carlo's complaint that Catena "must have gave over half a million" dollars to Carmine G. De Sapio, former New York County Democratic leader and that De Sapio "probably stuck a couple of hundred thousand right in his pocket." De Sapio was found guilty in Federal Court, New York, last month of conspiracy in a contract kickback scandal.

¶De Carlo's complaint that Dennis F. Carey, powerful Democratic chairman of Essex County in the early nineteen sixty's, "double-crossed" the mob after "taking plenty of money."

¶Underworld influence over Dominick R. Capello, then the Superintendent of State Police, and Dominick A. Spina, Newark Director of Police, who were referred to familiarly as "Cappy" and "Dick" in talks about past and future favors.

¶Pay-offs by gamblers to police in Middlesex County, which brought protests from De Carlo on the ground that the racketeers were protected by the county's most powerful politician, David T. Wilentz, Democratic National committeeman from New Jersey.

¶At the time of the tapings, Mr. Carey, Mr. Kenny and Mr. Wilentz were generally considered the three most powerful Democratic chairmen in the state.

Mayor Addonizio and 14 co-defendants pleaded not guilty last month to a Federal indictment accusing them of conspiracy in collecting kickbacks from city contractors. Among the defendants were 10 present or former Newark city officials.

Mayoral Race Discussed

In a discussion of the role the underworld associates would play in this city's 1962 mayoral campaign, De Carlo gave his views on getting money to elect Mr. Addonizio, then a Congressman, over the incumbent Mayor, Leo Carlin, and several other aspirants. De Carlo said that he would arrange to have five donors contribute to the campaign.

Plans were discussed for buying off another candidate who might hurt Mr. Addonizio's chances in the nonpartisan municipal election.

Mayor Addonizio last night referred calls to his lawyer, who was not immediately available. Repeated attempts to reach him were unsuccessful.

Mr. Capello's wife answered his home phone in Hackensack and said she thought he would be back late in the evening, but repeated attempts in the night to reach him were to no avail.

Mr. Kenny was reported to be in Florida and could not be reached.

Calls to Mr Wilentz's telephone was answered by a message that it had been temporarily disconnected at his request.

Asked to comment on the transcripts, Mr. Dolan said: "It's ridiculous, absolutely ridiculous."

The tapes, which reflect also discussions about loansharking operations, a scheme to get Frank Sinatra, the singer, to put up money for purchase of a Jamaica hotel and its possible development into a gambling resort, are regarded in law enforcement circles as important as the 2,000 pages of "DeCavalcante papers" made public last June by David M. Satz, then the United States Attorney for New Jersey. Mr. Satz's successor, Frederick B. Lacey, physically released the transcripts today.

The DeCavalcante transcripts, also made by the F.B.I. between 1961 and 1965, were of conversations among Simone Rizzo (Sam the Plumber) De-Cavalcante, boss of a Jersey-based Mafia group, and business and underworld associates. The transcripts were made public by Mr. Satz in response to a request by DeCavalcante's lawyer in an extortion case—which has not yet been tried—for disclosure by the Government of any electronic surveillance.

DeCavalcante's lawyer had not asked that the disclosure be made only to the defense, and was surprised by the public disclosure. Defense lawyers in the De Carlo trial had tried to limit disclosure to the lawyers, with the conversations not made public. They were overruled by Judge Shaw.

In the current case, as in the DeCavalcante papers, the Government has contended that the eavesdropping, which was illegal at the time it was done, was not the source of information that led to the indictments. Mr. Lacey had offered the transcripts to the court in November and Judge Shaw had reserved decision until today on making them public.

Both the DeCavalcante and De Carlo buggings shed light on the day-by-day workings of the Mafia, its humorous sides as well as its illegal operations, in depth and detail that surpassed the disclosures made in 1963 before a Senate committee by Joseph M. Valachi, the deserter from the Mafia.

Harold (Kayo) Konigsberg, reputed king of the loansharks and a convicted extortionist, was overheard asking De Carlo: "Will you tell me why everybody loves you so much?"

"Well, because I'm a hoodlum," replied the white-haired, portly underworld character. "I don't want to be a legitimate guy. All those other racket guys who get a few bucks want to become legitimate."

In the same conversation, Konigsberg, who is serving a 10-year term in Federal prison for possession of stolen merchandise, explained to De Carlo how a master loanshark operates. He said:

"If I loan a guy $5,000, we get $250 a week [interest]."

Evidently surprised by the high margin of profit, De Carlo was heard to say: "$250 a week? We get $100 a week for $5,000."

"You're scabs!" exclaimed Konigsberg in obvious indignation. "You'll have to organize, you guys."

The transcript of a conversation between De Carlo and a man the F.B.I. said was believed to be James Del Mauro, an attorney, on Jan. 15, 1963, was preceded by a Government notation which said: "De Carlo and his visitor discussed the political situation, chiefly the influence of John V. Kenny with Joseph P. Kennedy Sr. and the folly of Attorney General Robert Kennedy. He noted that there is a squad of 26 men investigating matters in Las Vegas."

The recorded conversation then went like this:

DE CARLO: I'd like to find out what happened to him and De Sapio—I never asked Kenny. I think De Sapio must have stuck that money he gave him right in his pocket.

DEL MAURO: That's what happened.

There followed DeCarlo's remark about Catena "must have gave him over half a million."

The De Carlo talks were rife with allusions to alleged payoffs to politicians and law enforcement officials for protection of gambling. In a discussion of open gambling in Middlesex County, De Carlo told Irving Berlin, a bookmaker:

"We just got a deal for the main guy—$500 a month, I'm waiting for an answer."

Berlin asked: "Is it Dolan you mean—with Dolan?" The F.B.I. eavesdropper inserted the identification "[Middlesex Prosecutor Edward J. Dolan]."

De Carlo answered "yeh," but Berlin then said: "Dolan ain't even included, he told me."

In the same conversation De Carlo complained: "Every one of them's gotta be paid. We know. We had that county before. We paid every one of them. Any one of them can dump the applecart: We know. We had Wilentz; we paid Wilentz."

The F.B.I.'s bracketed identification was "[David T. Wilentz, Middlesex County Democratic leader]."

Mr. Kenny, the Hudson County Democratic leader, was named repeatedly in the transcripts. De Carlo called Mr. Kenny on Aug. 8, and was overheard by an F.B.I. agent, who reported:

"From De Carlo's portion of the conversation, the informant determined that Kenny requested De Carlo to contact Newark Mayor Hugh Addonizio in an effort to have Kenny's man appointed as hospital administrator of Martland Medical Center."

"De Carlo replied: 'What will I do with my man, make him call Tom? [Jersey City Mayor Tom Gangemi]."

The People v. the Mob; Or, Who Rules New Jersey?

By FRED J. COOK

NEWARK.

THE headline-making trial begins. U. S. Attorney Frederick B. Lacey—a commanding 6 feet 4 and 225 pounds, a man who walks at a trot—rises and asks Judge Robert Shaw: "Your Honor, may I use the lectern? I have so many notes." The judge nods and Lacey wheels the lectern to a spot front and center, before the jury box.

The jurors are brought in. They settle themselves with the usual self-conscious bustle and look up at Lacey and the judge, the sober citizens composing themselves with an air of appropriate seriousness as they prepare to listen to a fantastic story of gangland intrigue and brutality.

The Federal prosecutor goes into his opening address, and it quickly becomes apparent that the business with the lectern was just a bit of expert stage-managing. Frederick Lacey does not need such a prop for his notes; his case is in his head. He speaks in a deep, resonant voice, clearly and distinctly, leaning casually across the lectern toward the jury. When he reaches an especially dramatic point, he rests his right elbow on a corner of the lectern, his lower arm and pointed finger stabbing at the jury. He captures and holds all eyes.

The tale that he unfolds is one that, varying only in details, is to be repeated again and again in the Federal Courthouse in Newark during the next two years. In a series of trials just beginning, jury after jury will be asked to decide cases which, in their cumulative effect, are expected to provide the most graphic study in American criminal annals of the complete subversion of a city —and, indeed, of much of a state— by the money and muscle of the underworld.

The case Lacey outlines to the Newark jury on this particular day deals with the international financial machinations of a shady Newark insurance broker, Louis Saperstein, who departed this world in late November, 1968, mysteriously loaded

with "enough arsenic to kill a mule." It is a tale that involves literally hundreds of thousands of dollars in an international stock scheme. The money for this gambit in high finance —all cash—had been obtained, Lacey says, from Angelo DeCarlo, variously known as "Ray" and "the Gyp," who is identified as a capo in the Jersey Mafia family formerly headed by the late Vito Genovese. DeCarlo's favorite racket over the years has been loansharking, and he and three associates are on trial for having tried to collect thousands of dollars a week in "vigorish" (the loan shark's term for usurious interest) from Saperstein, allegedly beating him in the process "until his face turned purple and his tongue bulged out."

As Lacey speaks, there reposes in the courtroom behind the prosecution table what can only be described as a time bomb. It is an aluminum file cart, much like the kind used in supermarkets, and it is piled high with some 1,200 pages of white printed transcripts, the product of four years of industrious Federal Bureau of Investigation wiretapping and bugging of the phone and premises of Angelo DeCarlo. The transcripts are records of conversations in which DeCarlo and his associates brag about having a stranglehold on the city of Newark and much of New Jersey. Before the day is out, Judge Shaw will make the transcript public.

Throughout the drama of Lacey's speech, Angelo DeCarlo sits impassively, to all appearances the most unflappable man in the courtroom. He resembles nothing so much as a simple Italian *paisano*—67 years old, silver-haired, short and stocky, with an impressive paunch. He is wearing a shapeless gray suit with a light brown sweater under the coat to guard against the winter's chill. He has a heavy face, a long, sharp nose and a shelving chin; and when he waddles out into the corridor among his waiting henchmen, his lips curve around a big cigar in an almost cherubic smile. But there is nothing cherubic about him now. He swivels around in his chair at the defense table, turning his back on Lacey with a kind of bored indifference, his tight lips twisted in a hard travesty of a smile while the cold remote eyes, devoid of any trace of humor, stare out at the courtroom spectators with never a blink.

SUCH is the scenario. It is one that will be repeated almost endlessly in the coming months as U. S. Attorney Lacey and his young assistants wade through a mushrooming pile of indictments that, on their face, outline the most complete network of crime and official corruption that has yet to be brought to trial in an American courtroom. There has been nothing remotely comparable to this since the Murder, Inc., trials of 1940; and by comparison even Murder, Inc., was pallid stuff.

The late William O'Dwyer, who rode to glory on that exposé, contented himself with sending to the electric chair the expendable strong arms of gangdom; he never touched their bosses, Joe Adonis and the late Albert Anastasia. Nor did he disturb the political superstructure without whose complaisance the organized underworld could not exist. In this perspective, the current Jersey investigation harbors a far more explosive potential.

The potential began building almost half a century ago — from that time to this, to put it bluntly, Newark has been dominated by the mob—and it is a remarkable and notable fact of life in Newark that no underworld mogul of the first rank has ever suffered much more than a gentle slap on the wrist from the forces of the law. When a big-time mobster gets in deep trouble, something almost invariably happens.

THE story goes back to Prohibition days, to the nineteen-twenties. Newark, New Jersey's largest city and only a short truck haul from the thirsting fleshpots of Manhattan, became virtually the bootleg capital of the Eastern seaboard. In the gangland wars of the era, a czar of czars emerged. He was Abner (Longie) Zwillman, a Newark Jew who came to rule one of the toughest mobs in gangland history. Zwillman's underworld rivals seemed to meet their Maker in the most gory fashion, but the mob ruler himself was always leagues removed from the awful deed.

His free use of muscle and a native organizational genius made Zwillman the most important bootlegger on the East Coast. In Port Newark, then far more isolated from the central city

than it is today, his rum-running fleets operated on almost a regular ferry schedule; and all up and down the inlet - dented New Jersey shoreline, especially in Monmouth and Ocean Counties, Longie's men ran a gantlet of unseeing Coast Guardsmen until they could reach haven in the arms of local policemen and sheriffs. The magnitude of the Zwillman operation may be gleaned from official estimates that his mob reaped a $50-million bonanza from bootlegging between 1926 and 1931, and that at the peak of its operation it was importing about 40 per cent of the bootleg liquor flowing across the nation's borders.

Such rapidly accumulated millions catapulted Zwillman into a position of enormous (and not too secret) political power. He became known as the Democratic boss of Newark's old Third Ward and his money helped to finance many a state gubernatorial campaign. The scuttlebutt of the times was that Longie Zwillman requested just one little favor from gubernatorial candidates who benefited from his largesse — the right to name, or at least to approve, the new Attorney General. There was never any proof of such a deal, but events frequently lent credence to the rumors. Mobsters were rarely inconvenienced in New Jersey, and the state became increasingly a haven for gangsters.

The path of an underworld chieftain is never smooth, however, and so it was with Longie. As he rose in power, so did a rival, Ruggiero (Richie the Boot) Boiardo. Just as Zwillman became the political power of the Third Ward, Boiardo achieved dominance in the First. And there was no love lost between them.

They were oddly contrasting types. Boiardo was the flashy Prohibition mobster, complete with a $5,000 diamond-studded belt buckle. Zwillman was the suave businessman of crime, a strangely dual personality. He had married into society; he knew how to conduct himself like a gentleman, and his heart bled all over his public sleeve for the poor. In the blackest pit of the Depression, he reached into his bootleg millions and paid the cost of running a soup kitchen for the impoverished in Newark's Military Park. He later established a similar soup kitchen at a Catholic church. There was, however, nothing benevolent about him when the issue was a test of underworld power; and this fact Richie the Boot Boiardo was to learn at great expense.

THE bloodletting was preceded, as is so often the case in the treacherous

quicksands of the underworld, by a great show of fraternity. Longie and Richie the Boot announced in 1930 that they had composed their differences, and just to show how much they loved each other, they threw a bash that was to become the talk of Newark. The party roared into its second sunset and terminated then only because The Newark News had begun to show some interest in the merriment. It spoke much about the political climate in Newark that gangsters and politicians mingled indiscriminately; among the politicians present were a former U.S. Commissioner, a candidate for the State Assembly and—most unfortunately—Paul Moore, a Democrat who was running for Congress. Moore committed the indiscretion of having his picture taken with the Boot and his belt buckle. Moore's rival, the late Representative Fred Hartley, had thousands of copies of the picture distributed in the Eighth Congressional District, and Moore later lamented that the photograph had played a large role in his defeat.

If Richie the Boot thought that the two-day wassail had made Longie Zwillman his bosom pal, he was soon to be disabused of the notion. Shortly after the party the Boot stepped out into the daylight at 242 Broad Street and encountered a hail of bullets sprayed from a sniper's nest across the street. Sixteen slugs perforated Boiardo's anatomy, and his life was probably saved by his $5,000 diamond belt buckle. "The shot that almost certainly would have killed him, ripping through his intestines, hit that belt buckle and ricocheted away," says a man who remembers the incident.

When Richie recovered, he was

sent to prison for 2½ years because he had been carrying a gun himself when he was put upon on Broad Street. But prison was not the tough ordeal for the Boot that it is for most. He was packed off to Trenton State Prison in March, 1931. However — though regulations provided that prisoners must serve at least one-third of their sentences before they could be considered for less rigorous confinement—Richie the Boot was whisked away to the minimum - security Bordentown Prison Farm after only four months. And rumors soon began circulating that witnesses had seen the Boot, as big as life, circulating in his old Newark haunts, especially at night and on weekends.

The police investigated—but, of course, found no proof.

Freed after 16 months at Bordentown, the Boot returned to his old racket leadership in the First Ward, and he and Longie evidently agreed to divide Newark between them; the law remained a bystander.

Just how ineffectual the law was during this period was illustrated in 1939, when Richie got into difficulties with the State Alcoholic Beverage Control office. The A.B.C. seemed to have the irrational notion that the Boot, as a convicted gangster, had no business operating a tavern called the Vittoria Castle. In the subsequent hearings, some high police officials testified to Boiardo's estimable character. Acting Capt. Joseph Cocozza of the Essex County Prosecutor's staff testified that he and his wife often dined with the Boot and the latter's wife, and he added: "We have never connected him with any gang in our work." The deputy police chief in Newark and the sergeant in charge of the morals squad added their voices to the chorus, testifying that Richie was simply "trying to earn an honest living."

Reality, of course, bore no resemblance to these official pronouncements. Last summer the Government released transcripts produced in four years of surveillance of Simone Rizzo (Sam the Plumber) DeCavalcante, who, says the F.B.I., is a Mafioso of the first water. In the DeCavalcante tapes, the real story of Richie the Boot, still active at 80, began to emerge. The revelation came when some of the boys got together in Sam's office to talk over the finer points of murder. Participants in the conversation, according to the F.B.I., were Sam the Plumber, Ray the Gyp DeCarlo and Anthony (Tony Boy) Boiardo, Richie's son and heir. It went like this:

TONY BOY: How about the time we hit the little Jew . . .

RAY: As little as they are, they struggle.

TONY BOY: The Boot hit him with a hammer. The guy goes down and comes up. So I got a crowbar this big, Ray. Eight shots in the head. What do you think he finally did to

ADVERSARY: U. S. Attorney Frederick B. Lacey, right, who is leading the campaign against the mob in New Jersey, talks to newsmen. "If our system is to survive," he says, "there must be people who are willing to fight corruption."

me? He spit at me and said, "You ——."

THE tapes released at De-Carlo's trial Jan. 6 add another startling dimension to the picture. Richie the Boot's private citadel is a great stone mansion (built in part with slabs his wrecking company crews had torn from the old Newark Post Office when it was demolished) that sits upon a wooded plot of several acres in Livingston, N. J. The mansion is approached by a drive at least two city blocks long, and at one turn the startled visitor comes upon a monument to megalomania. There, life-size and in full color on a life-size white horse, sits a stone Richie in all his splendor, while around and below him, mounted on stone pedestals, are some nine busts—also in full, glorious color—of members of his family. The Boiardo castle, isolated behind a thick screen of trees at the end of the drive, is an errie place; and, according to the F.B.I.'s transcripts, some shudderingly sinister things have happened there.

On Jan. 7, 1963, according to the F.B.I. tapes, DeCarlo and Anthony (Little Pussy) Russo—a mobster who once bragged that he had Long Branch in his hip pocket—discussed some of the macabre events that had taken place on the Boiardo estate. Russo warned DeCarlo never to go near the place alone if Boiardo tried to lure him there. According to Russo and DeCarlo, there was an incinerator for human bodies at the rear of the estate, up behind the Boiardo greenhouse. ". . . Ray, I seen too many," said Little Pussy. "You know how many guys we hit that way up there?"

DeCarlo: What about the big furnace he's got back there?

Russo: That's what I'm trying to tell you! Before you go up there . . .

DeCarlo: The big iron grate.

Russo: He used to put them on there and burn them.

Little Pussy and Ray the Gyp agreed that Richie the Boot was "a nut" because he disposed of not only the bodies that resulted from his own business endeavors, but also

those that any other mob chief chose to pass on. According to Russo, the late Thomas (Three-Finger Brown) Luchese, for years the ruler of one of New York's five Mafia families, used to turn over the bodies of his victims to Boiardo for burning. ". . . He'd give them to me and we'd take them up," Russo told DeCarlo.

The picture that emerges from the transcripts contradicts the bland contentions of Newark policemen that Richie the Boot was an estimable character trying to earn an honest living. Of course, back in 1939 the police did not have F.B.I. tapes to apprise them of the facts of life, but still there were events that seemed to speak for themselves. In the election of November, 1932, for example, the 11th District of Longie Zwillman's Third Ward gave all the Republican candidates except Herbert Hoover just eight votes; Hoover got nine. And the Democrats, almost to a man, registered 587. The suspiciously stuffed ballot boxes were impounded but somehow managed to flit

151

past bemused guards and out of the City Hall basement as if they had been carried on a witch's broomstick. Few people in Newark had any doubt that the witch who had performed this magical deed was Longie Zwillman, and there was a terrific hullabaloo that included a number of indictments. Then, of course, nothing happened. Nobody was convicted.

This "no conviction" refrain became familiar in Newark as scandal after scandal whimpered to a silent and forgotten end. More than 20 indictments have been returned against public officials over the years; officials have been criticized and censured; business firms and contractors doing business with the city have been indicted. But seldom has anyone had the misfortune to be convicted.

Perhaps it is just a coincidence, but during these decades when the law and the courts seemed unable to fight their way out of a paper bag, the buddy-buddy relationship of the underworld with Newark's politicians remained one of the world's worst-kept secrets. The love affair probably never received greater public exposure than at the wedding of Tony Boy Boiardo in 1950. More than 2,000 guests turned out, and among them were Mayor Ralph Villani, now president of the City Council; Hugh J. Addonizio, then a Congressman, now the indicted Mayor of Newark, and Rep. Peter W. Rodino, still a Democratic Congressman from the 10th District.

SUCH is the background of Newark. After decades of scandals, after the sputtering of innumerable exposés that have fizzled like pieces of punk in a cloudburst, Newark has once more been propelled into the spotlight as a graphic study in mob rule and political corruption.

The reasons go back to the Newark riot of 1967. On July 12 of that year the predominantly Negro Central Ward exploded in one of the worst race riots in the nation's history. The outburst lasted for days, left 26 persons dead and inflicted property damage estimated at $10.4-million. Even today, large sections of the Central Ward stand in

HOW IT ALL BEGAN—Captured rum runners' boats, 1925. Newark, just a short haul from a thirsty Manhattan, became the bootleg capital of the East during Prohibition, and the czar of bootleggers was Longie Zwillman, whose quick fortune allowed him to begin the mob dominance of the city.

blackened, boarded-up ruins, resembling nothing so much as the gaping chasms left in a city destroyed by war.

In an effort to determine the causes of the Newark outbreak, Gov. Richard J. Hughes appointed a commission headed by Robert D. Lilley, executive vice president of American Telephone and Telegraph. The Lilley commission's report in February, 1968, was a shocker. It found that an important underlying cause of the 1967 riot was "a pervasive feeling of corruption" in Newark, and declared: "A former state official, a former city official and an incumbent city official all used the same phrase: 'There is a price on everything at City Hall.'"

Though the commission did not go into specifics, its blast at Newark touched off widespread reaction. Essex County Prosecutor Joseph P. Lordi began an 18-month grand jury investigation, and state legislative hearings were held. Prof. Henry S. Ruth, who had been deputy staff director of the President's Commission on Law Enforcement and the Administration of Justice, touched sensitive political nerves when he declared that, in his opinion, "Official corruption in New Jersey is so bad that organized crime can get almost anything it desires." Another expert witness assured flabbergasted officials that Professor Ruth was ab-

solutely right. And, capping all, William J. Brennan 3d (the son of the Supreme Court Justice) remarked in a speech in December, 1968, that a number of legislators were entirely "too comfortable" with organized crime.

Brennan's remark almost prostrated the New Jersey Legislature, but events were to vindicate the young prosecutor. The Nixon Administration came to office on the cry of law and order and a pledge to fight crime. A new U. S. Attorney for New Jersey was to be appointed, and Senator Clifford Case, for years the best Republican vote-getter in the state, recommended Frederick Lacey.

AT 48, Lacey was a partner in the law firm of Shanley and Fisher. His roots go deep in Newark. His grandfather was at one time a Republican Freeholder in Essex County; his father was Newark police chief for eight years; his mother still lives in the Vailsburg section of Newark, where he was born and went to school. A Phi Beta Kappa graduate of Rutgers University and a graduate of the Cornell Law School (where he was editor of the Law Review), a lieutenant commander in the Navy, a former city councilman in Glen Ridge, Lacey had moved at a furious pace to the top of his profession and was considered an

expert on cases involving aerial and medical law. He specialized in trial work, was generally considered brilliant at it and represented some of the largest corporations in the nation in especially difficult cases.

When the bid came from Washington, he went down to the capital to discuss the proposition with Attorney General John N. Mitchell. "I was making big money, really big money at the time," he says, and he didn't see how he could take the $29,000-a-year U. S. Attorney's post. He was about to reject the offer when he received a call from William Sutherland, a 73-year-old lawyer.

"When you're my age," Lacey says Sutherland told him, "and you look back on your life, your pride will not be the size of the estate you are going to leave, but what you have accomplished. I know that you have an extremely lucrative law practice but when you get to this point the money you didn't make won't seem to matter so much. What you might have accomplished in a few years as U. S. Attorney could well be the one thing in your life you would be proud of."

This conversation with Sutherland, Lacey says, "pried my thinking and had a lot to do with changing my mind."

There was another consideration. Lacey, as a young

lawyer, had had one direct and shocking confrontation with big-league New Jersey crime. Throughout the nineteen-forties and into the fifties —until the Kefauver investigation threw a wrench into the machinery — the Mafia families of New York and New Jersey had run a veritable capital of crime in Duke's Restaurant, opposite the Palisade Amusement Park. Here a working crime council held daily conclave. It consisted of Joe Adonis, Frank Costello's partner, as chairman of the board; Albert Anastasia, the enforcer; the Moretti brothers, Willie and Solly, and Anthony (Tony Bender) Strollo, the right arm of Vito Genovese. On Tuesdays, the council met with some of the top czars of the national syndicate. Longie Zwillman might come up from Newark; Frank Costello from New York; Meyer Lansky from Florida. When Zwillman wasn't present, his proxy was voted by Gerardo (Jerry) Catena. After Zwillman committed suicide in 1959, Catena rose in power and is now reputed to be the ruler of the Jersey wing of the Genovese family. New York detectives, Internal Revenue agents and Federal Bureau of Narcotics agents were aware of the pivotal importance of Duke's Restaurant, but when they tried to go over to New Jersey for a little sleuthing, they were often chased out of town by local policemen.

When the lid finally blew off, under the threat of a Federal investigation, it caused a scandal that rocked the New Jersey State House. The charge was that the Adonis-Moretti combine had paid Harold John Adonis, a clerk in Gov. Alfred E. Driscoll's office and no relation to gangdom's Joe, $228,000 over a period of 19 months for protection at the state level. Frederick Lacey, a young assistant U. S. Attorney, inherited the chore of prosecuting both Harold Adonis and Albert Anastasia, and he got convictions against both.

"In that case," Lacey says now, "I found conditions shocking—and I hadn't considered myself at all naive. But I had never encountered the broad evidence of corruption of public bodies, business and labor unions. It became

my fixed and firm conviction that organized crime was taking us over. And everything that I have seen so far in this office reinforces that conviction."

WHEN he decided to accept the U.S. Attorney's post, Lacey says, he had a firm understanding with Attorney General Mitchell. First, he explains, there is one theory that a U. S. Attorney should simply prosecute the cases handed to him by Federal investigative agencies; Lacey thinks a U. S. Attorney should be aggressive and actively develop cases if the situation seems to warrant it. The Attorney General agreed. "Next," Lacey continues, "I was assured I would have a free hand in selecting my staff and in the direction we would go. Wherever our leads take us, that's where we will go."

Lacey believes that the public, so long apathetic about syndicated crime, must be shocked and aroused, must be made to understand that when it places a $2 bet with a bookie or plays the numbers it is feeding the treasury of the underworld — and paying for the corruption of its own officials. In a speech to a bar association gathering at Seton Hall University in South Orange on Nov. 29, some three weeks before his investigation exploded in a rash of indictments, Lacey told his audience: "I want to challenge you—indeed, to goad you— to accept obligations, to assume responsibilities . . . unless you, as leaders, arouse an apathetic public to stem the tide of crime in this nation, our society as we know it is doomed."

He added: "Organized crime is, in the vernacular, taking us over. First, it corrupts law enforcement and office holders. Second, it corrupts unions and makes a mockery of the collective - bargaining concept. Third, it corrupts the businessman. Organized crime . . . cannot operate without corrupting law-enforcement personnel. I flatly state that it will not even go into a muncipality unless and until it has bought its protection against raids and arrests."

THIS was the reasoning that led Lacey to commit his most

controversial act so far, his advocacy of the release of the DeCarlo tapes. Though he stood mute in open court as the DeCarlo defense fought public disclosure, he is known to have strongly favored full publicity. Governor Hughes, who left office Jan. 20, and many legal experts and concerned citizens have been aroused by this action, appalled at the damage that may be done to innocent persons through the publication of the chitchat of gangsters. Lacey, however, feels that the public good outweighs any possibility of individual harm. He takes the attitude that the only way the public can be made acutely aware of the reality of the criminal menace is by publication of the recorded words of the mobsters themselves.

The man who takes these attitudes remains something of a conundrum to many. "I don't think they know what they're letting themselves in for, he's a dynamo," said one of his law partners when Lacey was appointed. The prosecutor is the kind of man who does his push-ups every morning to keep in shape. He has worked for years on a 60-hour-a-week schedule. He likes to drop remote classical allusions into routine press conferences, perhaps quoting Alexander Pope or some other favorite authority. One day baffled newsmen had difficulty getting the point, and one of them said: "Oh, don't mind him. He's a Phi Beta Kappa and he has to show off his learning." This leads some people to think Lacey a bit pompous, but he tells the anecdote himself, chuckling about it in high good humor.

As for the future, he says flatly: "I do not entertain any political ambitions. When I took this job, I gave a commitment to Senator Case and Attorney General Mitchell that I would stay as long as I could afford to do so financially, or until I felt I had the office organized and matters well in hand. Then all I want to do is to return to my private trial practice in New York and New Jersey."

Law enforcement, Lacey feels, is primarily the responsibility of the localities and the states; it is not a job for

Federal authority alone. Federal prosecutors, he believes, can set standards, can goad and stimulate, but in the final analysis the bulk of the burden must be borne by local and state agencies. And so he has proposed a series of remedial laws for New Jersey.

One proposal that goes to the roots of the gangland structure would impose a stiff jail sentence upon anyone convicted in connection with organized gambling—the bookie or the numbers runner, for instance. In the past, all too many judges have considered such offenders to be small fry of little consequence and have imposed only minor fines; but Lacey argues that their activities are basic to the system that pours an estimated $50-billion into the coffers of the crime syndicate each year.

Lacey's other proposals include the adoption of a state antitrust law modeled after the Federal Sherman Antitrust Act; it would give the state the power to act in cases in which gangland money has infiltrated legitimate business and then, by extortion and threat, driven out all competition. Another cardinal Lacey proposal calls for the creation of an organized crime unit in the State Attorney General's office. The unit would be under the direction of a Deputy Attorney General and would have the authority to investigate anywhere in the state—a provision that should make it more difficult for the underworld to establish its customary fixes on the local and county levels.

ALL of this, however, will represent no final solution, Lacey feels, unless the public can be aroused from apathy. In a recent interview, he explained his philosophy.

"In our schools and colleges," he said, "we teach political science in terms of defining the powers of various offices and officeholders, the requirements to vote and so forth—and all of this is largely irrelevant. Relevant instruction in political science today is going to have to be aimed at getting at the roots, at showing and explaining the decaying moral fiber of those who are elected to office, those who are in law enforcement.

"If the younger generation and the university groups finally come to the terminal point in their thinking — that any government that is so corrupted isn't worthy of survival—then we who have done nothing to stop this, we who have consented to the existence of such a system by our inaction, will have only ourselves to blame. This is the evil of organized crime. It corrupts and it destroys. It destroys the officeholder, and therefore destroys the confidence of the public in its government and representatives.

"This is what I think is happening in our society today."

So the vital question raised by the current Newark probe is this: Will the public be stirred from its decades-long apathy by the flood of indictments and the inside-the-mob revelations?

The answer is mixed. There is indignation in Newark, and there is also indifference. A two-month public-opinion poll in which a group known as Focus on Newark questioned 4,000 persons indicated that if Mayor Addonizio had been running for re-election in November or December he would have been favored, 2 to 1, over his nearest rival. Newsmen interviewing Newark residents came up with some who expressed shock and indignation, but others were like the man who shrugged his shoulders and said: "This has been going on for a long time. Frankly, I don't care. I don't really care."

If the impact of the more damaging DeCarlo tapes or the upcoming trial of Mayor Addonizio (who's been indicted in an alleged kickback scheme involving mob-dominated businesses) should change this attitude, the New-

WITNESS: Abner (Longie) Zwillman, once the pre-eminent Newark mobster, testifies befor a Senate committee in 1951, eight years before he committed suicide. He and Ruggiero (Richie th Boot) Boiardo, originally violent enemies, later apparently agreed to divide Newark between them

ark municipal election this year will probably resolve itself along racial lines. In that event, City Councilman Anthony Imperiale, the karate instructor and white militant in the heavily Italian North Ward, is seen as the probable white candidate against Kenneth A. Gibson, the Negro former city engineer. Though this shabby industrial city of some 407,000 is estimated to be more than 60 per cent Negro and Spanish-speaking, there are many who feel that Imperiale just might win in such a contest—a result that would certainly intensify the racial polarization of Newark.

EVEN Lacey concedes that the reaction to his probe falls short of the universal cry of outrage he might have wished. On the one hand, he has been highly praised by responsible citizens, and an encouraging number of tips have come from the public. "We have received many letters and telephone calls offering information," he says. "Most of these are anonymous, but in cases where people are willing to identify themselves we keep their identity absolutely confidential, of course. Some of the tips obviously come from crackpots, but there have been, nevertheless, what I would regard as a startling number of good leads."

This is encouraging. Far less so is the old bromide that Lacey hears time and again: "You are always going to have crime and corruption." The implicit corollary to that is, of course, "So why are you getting so excited about it?"

The prosecutor shakes his head in vexation and retorts:

"To that, I say, 'Yes, but you are always going to have to have people who are willing to fight it. It is true that there always have been and always will be people who have frailties and who yield to temptation, but that is only part of the story. If our system is to survive, there must also be people who are willing to fight, willing to oppose, this kind of corruption.'" ■

The Mafia in Jersey: Nervous and 'No Longer Above the Law'

By RONALD SULLIVAN
Special to The New York Times

TRENTON, March 15—Last winter the New Jersey Mafia was riding high, with many of its most important figures basking under the tropical Miami sun or standing with other high rollers in the gambling casinos of Puerto Rico and Nevada. But this winter has been something else. Many of the most important Mafia leaders are now working in jail laundries and kitchens, others are either in or on their way to Federal prisons, and at least one has simply disappeared. All the rest are reported very nervous, to say the least. The Mafia apparently fell from riches to rags in a little more than one year; it was a little more than a year ago that Federal and state law enforcement authorities in New Jersey opened a new drive against organized crime and corruption in a state that has been castigated as one of the most corrupt in the nation.

News Analysis

And if the indictment, conviction and jailing of Mafia members is to be the yardstick by which the drive against organized crime can be measured, officials here say New Jersey has apparently scored a resounding success.

Several top law enforcement officials report that the arrests are having a dramatic impact throughout virtually every Mafia organization in the state.

Officials Optimistic

According to the administration of Gov. William T. Cahill, the jailings also are having an impact upon the public. "The guy on the corner is now being shown that Mr. Mafia is no longer above the law," one official remarked. "He is being shown results, and that's no small success in a state like New Jersey."

William F. Hyland, chairman of the State Commission of Investigation, said tonight that the coordinated Federal and state drives were "obviously having a very upsetting impact upon organized crime." He and other officials are now optimistic about achieving what Thomas E. Dewey did in New York more than 30 years ago in driving out racketeers.

"But in this sense," Mr. Hyland said "we simply don't want to drive them someplace else—like New York—we want to accomplish the job here."

An indication of the Mafia's troubles on both sides of the Hudson—and its plans for recouping its position—was seen over the weekend when law-enforcement agents reported that a new "boss of bosses" had been named for Mafia operations in the New York-New Jersey area.

He was identified as Carlo Gambino of New York, who, the agents said, has the job of acting as arbitrator for the six Mafia families in the area.

On the surface, at least, the Mafia's ruling hierarchy in New Jersey has been virtually neutralized. For example, Gerado (Jerry) Catena, the reputed successor to the late Vito Genovese as the top Mafia figure in Jersey, was jailed here yesterday for the first time since 1934.

Catena, who still sported his Florida tan in the Mercer County courthouse, was jailed indefinitely on civil contempt charges after refusing to testify before the State Commission of Investigation. He joined another reputed Mafioso, Joseph (Joe Bayonne) Zicarelli in the jail laundry where both began washing the clothing of their fellow inmates until both were transferred to the nearby state reformatory at Yardville.

Catena's lawyers attempted to get him freed last week on a writ of habeas corpus, but Federal Judge George H. Barlow rejected their request for bail and their argument that the commission had violated his constitutional rights.

A third reputed Mafioso, Anthony (Little Pussy) Russo, who has been under medical treatment also has been sent back to jail. Russo, said to be involved in Monmouth County rackets, is scheduled to do K.P. Like Catena, Zicarelli and Russo were also jailed for refusing to talk to the investigation commission.

Zicarelli also faces trial on a murder conspiracy indictment handed down by the new statewide grand jury, and Russo faces up to five years imprisonment on a perjury conviction.

Other Mafia members are having their troubles, too.

Angelo (Gyp) De Carlo, a reputed lieutenant in the Catena Mafia family whose conversations recorded by the Federal Bureau of Investigation made national headlines in January, is in the Federal Penitentiary in Danbury, Conn.

He was sentenced this week to 12 years on a Federal extortion charge.

As the 68-year-old De Carlo was taken away, he told a bystander, "I've got to die some time, and I might as well go this way."

In Newark, Ruggiero (Richie the Boot) Boiardo, reputedly another important member of the Catena organization, was sentenced to two to three years in prison last year on a numbers-racket conviction in Essex County Court. And his supposed successor in that organization, his son, Anthony (Tony Boy) Boiardo, was indicted in December on Federal bribery and extortion charges along with Mayor Hugh J. Addonizio and a number of other Newark city officials.

Still other leading Mafia figures are in trouble with the law. Simone Rizzo (Sam the Plumber) DeCavalcante, the reputed Mafia leader whose bugged conversations created a furor over organized crime here last June, was indicted by a Federal grand jury in Newark on charges of running an interstate gambling ring.

DeCavalcante also faces another trial this spring on a Federal indictment involving a gun and extortion charge.

Russo's reputed successor in Monmouth County, Frank (Big Frank Condi) Cocchiaro, has been missing since last summer, after fleeing a Commission of Investigation hearing here.

Catena Tops All

But in the opinion of a number of high law enforcement officials, the most dramatic score against the Mob was achieved here this week with the jailing of Catena. Not since Genovese was imprisoned in 1959 on a Federal narcotics conviction has such an important Mafia member been put behind bars, they say.

In fact, with Genovese's death last year, law enforcement authorities reported that Catena succeeded Genovese on the Mafia's nine-member ruling national commission.

One high law enforcement official reported that many police authorities "were hearing that the Mob is confused and disorganized on all fronts." He said that strongarm methods and such blatantly illegal activities as gambling, loansharking and numbers betting were being curtailed in some areas. However, he said there was no way to measure the impact upon the legitimate enterprises controlled by the Mob.

Politically, many officials here believe that the apparent success achieved thus far against organized crime will enhance the image of Governor Cahill and of the Nixon Administration. But most observers here still point out that it is crime in the street, and not the Mafia, that—along with the cost of living—dominates political concern in New Jersey.

Crooked Deals in Swiss Accounts Aided by Inaction of Banks

BROKERS DECLINE TO QUERY CLIENTS

Secrecy Foils Attempts to Study Tax Evasion, Stock Fraud and Crime Loot

By NEIL SHEEHAN

Special to The New York Times

WASHINGTON, Nov. 30 — Last spring the senior partner in a New York brokerage house was told by the vice president of a Swiss bank with whom he regularly did business: "A fellow will come to your office in the next few days with $100,-000 in cash. Take it. The money's for us."

Several days later a man appeared with $100,000 in cash in an envelope. The broker accepted it without demur and put the money in a safe. Other men came and went on the same errand a number of times in the next few weeks until the broker had accumulated $840,-000 in cash.

The Swiss bank official flew to New York on one of his frequent trips to the United States to solicit business and to pick up this and other deposits.

Both he and the broker were summoned to the Manhattan office of Robert M. Morgenthau, United States Attorney for the Southern District of New York.

"Do you know what you've been doing?" they were asked.

"No," the men replied in puzzlement.

"You've been taking payoffs for heroin."

The eyes of banker and broker rounded in shocked surprise. "We didn't know that," they said.

'Didn't Think About It'

"What did you think you were doing," an assistant United States attorney asked.

"I didn't really think about it," the broker said.

"I thought it was something a bit illegal, maybe diamond smuggling," said the Swiss banker, a stout, well-scrubbed, neatly tailored man. "But I didn't know it was narcotics. If I had, I would never have accepted the money."

Mr. Morgenthau and other law enforcement authorities have found this close-your-eyes-and-pass-the-money attitude to be common to much of the Swiss and American banking and brokerage community.

Coupled with Swiss bank secrecy, the attitude has repeatedly frustrated the lawmen's efforts to restrict the use of Swiss banks, not only for massive tax evasion and securities frauds by supposedly respectable Americans, but also as the principal haven for illicit money from organized crime.

The late Louis Schrager, a principal figure in the Meyer Lansky organized crime syndicate who ran the numbers racket on Manhattan's West Side and in the garment district and part of Brooklyn until his death in 1967, negotiated one of many profitable arrangements for himself through a Swiss bank and an old line New York private bank and brokerage firm, Laidlaw & Company.

Bonds Were Collateral

In April of 1964, Schrager wanted to transform about $400,000 worth of 3 to 4 per cent interest, municipal bearer bonds, a negotiable type that does not carry the purchaser's name, into a better investment. He had the bonds turned over to the Nassau, Bahamas, subsidiary of a Geneva bank. Bahamian civil law protects bank secrecy there.

Using the bonds as collateral, a vice president of the Swiss bank negotiated a $375,000 loan from Laidlaw to the Bahamas subsidiary. The $375,000 became a time deposit for Schrager at the Bahamas subsidiary and paid 5 per cent interest. Laidlaw charged 5 per cent interest for the loan and the Swiss bank in turn got $375,000 to lend elsewhere at higher interest rates.

To prove it could negotiate the bonds, the Swiss bank gave Laidlaw the original of a letter of transmittal from the purported owner. The letter was signed, "I.S.I.S. Ltd., Gene Bernard." No address was given. Laidlaw's attorneys looked over the documents and approved the transaction as legally sound. No one asked what I.S.I.S. did or who Gene Bernard was.

Gene Bernard is an alias of a corrupt Miami accountant and I.S.I.S. Ltd., was a dummy corporation administered by him and a crooked lawyer-accountant team in Cleveland.

Letter Transferred

In the summer of 1965, Schrager and his financial managers discovered that the Swiss bank had given Laidlaw the I.S.I.S. letter. They had assumed the Swiss bank would say it owned the bonds itself, and demanded that the bank retrieve the letter so that no link to themselves would exist in Laidlaw's files, where it could be subpoenaed.

The Swiss bank explained to Laidlaw in a series of complicated negotiations that its client, I.S.I.S. Ltd., did not want its name appearing in the loan file. Laidlaw protected itself financially by having the parent Swiss bank guarantee the loan to the subsidiary and returned the original I.S.I.S. letter. Again, Laidlaw did not inquire into I.S.I.S. and Gene Bernard. It did, however, keep a copy of the letter, which was subsequently subpoenaed by a New York grand jury.

The two-and-a-half-year loan was finally terminated in October of 1966. By that time, Laidlaw's interest charge had risen to 6¾ per cent.

American brokerage firms likewise restrain their inquisitiveness when buying or selling stock for a Swiss bank, although brokers readily concede their awareness that the Swiss are probably trading for a third party.

Only a Service

When questioned about this attitude by law enforcement officials, bankers and brokers usually say they are merely performing a professional service and that questions about the real participants would be inappropriate.

Swiss bankers elaborate this opinion more carefully. In a speech to a shareholders' meeting in 1967, F. W. Schulthess, chairman of the Swiss Credit Bank, one of the three largest, denounced "scurrilous publicity" alleging that Swiss bankers "were covering up crooks, that we were guarding the fortunes of corrupt dictators and international gangsters."

The question is: what is criminal? The answer seems to be, depending on which legal system you favor, that crime in the United States is legitimate profit in Switzerland.

Mr. Schulthess's bank was one of the six that allegedly helped Alfred M. Lerner, president of the First Hanover Corp., an ostensibly respectable Wall Street brokerage firm, reap $400,000 to $500,000 from stock frauds last year. The Swiss Credit Bank handles accounts for men who would be considered "crooks" in most Western societies—members of the Lansky syndicate, like Edward Levinson of Las Vegas casino renown, Bernard Bercuson and other purported hoteliers.

No Cooperation

"In the two major areas where Americans are breaking the law, tax and securities violations, the Swiss will not cooperate with us," Mr. Morgenthau says.

Swiss bank secrecy can be broken and a banker forced to give information on order from a Swiss court. Swiss courts will issue such orders, however, only for offenses recognized as crimes in Switzerland, and tax and securities violations are not considered criminal there.

Millions of dollars of Mafia "black money" flows into Swiss accounts each year and is, so the joke goes, "washed clean in the snows of the Alps."

Minimum Balance

Schrager ran a good deal of his numbers racket winnings through a Geneva account labeled "Winn's Trust." He kept a minimum balance of $400,000.

Schrager used the Mafia device of false mortgages and loans to launder the dollars into "white money" to purchase motels and other real estate in Florida.

In this manner Swiss bank secrecy is fostering the growth of a phenomenon that law enforcement officials consider highly corrosive to the social fabric — partnerships between supposedly legitimate businessmen and organized criminals for mutual gain. The line between entrepreneur and crook blurs in this gray world.

One bank in Switzerland, owned by a cluster of American businessmen and organized criminals, functioned principally as just such a laundry shop for "black money" from illicit operations.

It was called the Exchange and Investment Bank and had well appointed Geneva offices. The major owners were Garson Reiner and Benjamin Wheeler, two New York brassiere manufacturers who helped start the peek-a-boo tre. d in women's fashion when their company, Exquisite Form Industries, Inc., introduced the see-through bra in 1964.

Other owners included Levinson, the Las Vegas casino operator for the Lansky syndicate; Benjamin Siegelbaum, a Lansky associate with like duties, and Lou Poller, a friend of the imprisoned teamster union leader, James R. Hoffa, and former president of the Miami National Bank.

From 1963 through 1967, millions of dollars in shady money flowed in and out of this Geneva bank each year through the Miami National Bank and various Bahamian and New York banks.

One incident in November of 1966 illustrates the nature of the Geneva bank's operations.

A man telephoned the National Bank of North America in New York and said he was rushing in from the airport with a large cash transfer from Geneva. Would officials please hold the bank open past the 3 P.M. closing time?

They obliged. He arrived with a sack hefty with $221,800 in cash for the Exchange and Investment Bank. Investigators later found he had left his name off the transfer form and the New York bank employes had never asked his identity.

Samuel Cohen, a New York and Miami Beach multimillionaire who owns a share in the Flamingo Hotel in Las Vegas, allegedly "cleansed" in the neighborhood of $2-million in "skim," untaxed gambling profits, and earnings from other enterprises through the Exchange and Investment Bank and another Geneva bank in the mid-1960's. He controls the Miami National Bank.

Besides its Las Vegas interests, Mr. Cohen's family firm owns a major share of the Eden Roc, Deauville and four other posh Miami Beach hotels and about 70 apartment buildings in New York City.

He repatriated the money from Switzerland as purported loans from the banks to meet his mortgage payments and deducted the interest on the loans in his tax returns.

Offered $15-Million

An estimate of how profitable the Exchange and Investment Bank's laundering work was can be ascertained from a proposal that Mr. Wheeler, who served as its vice president, is said to have made in 1964 to the Geneva representative of a leading Wall Street brokerage house. He offered the broker $15-million with which to trade stocks in the bank's name on New York exchanges.

In early 1967, one group of hoodlums attempted to defraud the Chase Manhattan Bank of nearly $12-million through this Geneva bank. The fraud was detected before the money could be transferred with a forged bank order and the Exchange and Investment Bank was named as a co-conspirator in the New York Federal grand jury indictment.

This abortive theft, and an intensive investigation by Mr. Morgenthau's office, compromised the Geneva bank's usefulness to the underworld. Messrs. Reiner, Wheeler and the other owners sold the bank's Swiss license to a French bank last March.

The bank records were reportedly destroyed before the sale.

Own Money Manager

The Lansky organization keeps its own resident money manager in Switzerland. He is John Pullman, an old bootlegging compatriot of Lansky. Russian born, naturalized as an American citizen, then denaturalized in 1954 and renaturalized as a Canadian, Pullman lists his occupation as "retired." He lives in Lausanne when he is not busy in Geneva, Zurich, London or Toronto conferring with members of the Lansky apparatus, making investments for a commission and picking up cash deposits for the Swiss Credit Bank and other institutions.

When American officials argue that the Swiss should help them prosecute organized criminals for tax, securities or mail fraud, the Swiss answer that the United States should convict these men of some internationally recognized crime such as kidnapping or murder. But this is a difficult prospect, with the strict rules of court evidence and stringent limitations on wiretapping in the United States.

In their determination to carry on discreet business with American clients, the Swiss banks have also found powerful allies within the United States financial community.

The major American banks have been acting in concert to fight off any intrusion in the Swiss area. They, in turn, have rallied support at times from the State Department and the Treasury.

Seek Good Relations

The Treasury wants Swiss cooperation in maintaining the international balance of payments and monetary stability. The State Department is intent on preserving good relations because the Swiss have been helpful in American intelligence gathering activities, while the banks, and their allies, the brokerage houses, have a financial stake in unhampered commerce with the Swiss. They covet the commissions and interest charges on the enormous Swiss business.

Last year, for example, Swiss banks bought and sold $11.3-billion worth of American stocks and bonds, by far the largest foreign traders.

Many big American banks are, in fact, seeking legal precedents that would allow their Swiss branches the same immunity from American courts and authorities that Swiss banks have.

Last summer the Federal grand jury for the Southern District of New York subpoenaed a $200,000 certificate of deposit from the First National City Bank as evidence in a stock fraud. The certificate was purchased from First National City's Geneva branch for an American broker.

In a counter-motion in court First National City attorneys argued that the certificate was in the physical possession of their Geneva branch and therefore could not be surrendered because this action would violate Swiss bank secrecy.

The Justice Department then halted Federal court litigation to pry loose the document and took the diplomatic route of attempting to obtain a surrender order from a Swiss court, a procedure that has rarely yielded results in a securities case.

Mr. Morgenthau and his aides say that First National City and Chase Manhattan also are not microfilming checks and other records to the extent they once did. Experienced Internal Revenue Service agents likewise say that in recent years they have encountered noticeably less cooperation and far quicker destruction of such bank records as deposit slips and teller cash sheets.

Mr. Morgenthau says this change gives the upper-class criminal another measure of protection by depriving law enforcement agencies of vital evidence.

Virtually All' Filmed

The successful prosecution of the brokerage firm of Coggeshall & Hicks last August for violating the credit limitations on stock trading for five years through the Arzi Bank of Zurich originated with the discovery of microfilmed copies of canceled checks to the Swiss bank from American customers of the brokerage house.

A spokesman for First National City said the bank still microfilmed "virtually all checks" except for "a relatively small number" that clear through its central office. Those checks not microfilmed are also confined to accounts "on which there has never been any investigation or inquiry," he said.

A Chase Manhattan official said the bank had not altered its check microfilming procedures in 10 years. The bank does not microfilm all checks that originate and clear within New York, but does keep a record of others.

When the affluent are convicted of Swiss bank crimes, the punishment is often relatively lenient in comparison to sentences imposed on poor people for common crimes. The difference apparently stems from the general attitude of judges and the penalties prescribed by law.

The penalties for most stock and bond trading frauds are a $10,000 fine and two years in prison, or both, for each specific

Meyer Lansky is thought to have deposited millions of dollars in Switzerland.

violation. The prosperous defendant invariably hires prestigious lawyers who litigate exhaustively.

'Great Respect'

Robert S. Keefer Jr., the principal partner in Coggeshall & Hicks, pleaded guilty to an indictment charging $20-million in illegal trading over five years. He was represented by Simon H. Rifkind, a judge for nine years in the United States District Court for the Southern District of New York, where the case was being tried.

"Judge, I might as well say it now, I will say it later anyway, that they have chosen well in having you," Irving Ben Cooper, the presiding judge, said prior to the sentencing. "You know you have the great respect of this court."

Mr. Rifkind compared his client's offense to breaking "a traffic regulation."

In those five years of easy credit with the Arzi Bank, Mr. Keefer's firm had received $225,000 in illegal commissions, besides the profits accumulated by its customers and Mr. Keefer and his associates on their clandestine stock trading. During the grand jury investigation, Mr. Keefer had repeatedly perjured himself.

Judge Cooper gave him a tongue lashing, a $30,000 fine and a suspended sentence.

Stole TV Set

Last August, a week after Mr. Keefer's sentencing, James C. Harris, an unemployed shipping clerk, appeared before Judge Cooper. Harris is a Negro, married, with two children and has a prior record for attempted armed robbery in

1964. He was now charged with stealing a Japanese television set worth less than $100 from an interstate shipment from a bus terminal. He got a year in jail.

This disparity in punishment is not a personal quirk of Judge Cooper's. It is common to his fellow judges on the New York District Court and to others in similar positions elsewhere.

In the view of most students of the problem, any effective measures to mitigate Swiss bank crime will have to be taken unilaterally by the United States.

Mr. Morgenthau believes there must be systematic enforcement of the law through far greater scrutiny of Swiss transactions.

Mr. Morgenthau feels that far more is at stake in Swiss bank crime than simply illegitimate profit. He is convinced that the integrity of the American legal system and the willingness of the average citizen to obey the law are endangered.

"When you talk about the Swiss bank criminal, you are talking about people who hold positions of trust and responsibility, people whom the little man is supposed to look up to and who are now committing crimes," he says.

"Perhaps that's why the poor man gets so cynical about justice, because there are two forms of justice. It's not in what happens after the indictment. The poor have means of defense now. It's that the wealthy man doesn't even come before the bar of justice. He isn't indicted.

"The Warren Court created equality of defense, but not equality of indictment, equality of enforcement. If we're going to expect the poor man in Harlem or Bedford-Stuyvesant to obey the law, then we've got to make the rich man on Wall Street obey it too."

Swiss to Help U.S. Trace Illegal Funds

By THOMAS J. HAMILTON
Special to The New York Times

GENEVA, Aug. 17—Switzerland and the United States have agreed on a draft legal aid treaty under which the Swiss Government will help track down money hidden in Swiss banks by agents of "organized crime."

In such cases, the evidence to be provided by Switzerland will include tax-evasion matters pertaining to organized crime, Swiss officials said today, but the exact conditions were not disclosed. Although final negotiations will not begin until September, United States sources expressed the belief that these would produce only minor changes in the draft treaty.

The draft treaty would not permit the United States to obtain evidence directly. The Swiss Government does not have access to records of Swiss banks and cannot get it without a court order obtained for prosecution of a crime under Swiss law.

Under the tentative arrangement, the Swiss Government would appear in behalf of the United States to request a court order against a person indicted for a crime that also constituted a crime under Swiss law.

For two years, Swiss negotiators have said that Switzerland could not violate the secrecy of Swiss banks, which provide numbered accounts for greater privacy, to help Washington track down tax evaders. This position was reaffirmed today in a Swiss communiqué from Berne announcing the draft treaty.

Not a Swiss Crime

The communiqué said that, while the United States had requested a general strengthening of the cooperation between the two governments in tax matters, Switzerland felt that such questions should be settled in accordance with a United States-Swiss convention ruling out double-taxation.

Tax evasion is not a crime in Switzerland, and the draft treaty would provide for mutual cooperation in punishing offenses that are crimes in both countries.

The current round of negotiations, which began July 13, brought a concession, however, when Switzerland agreed to broaden the definition of common crimes to include "organized crime with international repercussions."

The Swiss delegation, the communiqué declared, recognized that organized crime involved "a particularly dangerous form" of criminal action, and, therefore, agreed that "a departure from the customary methods of legal aid" was justified to suppress it.

The three Swiss negotiators, headed by Pierre A. Nussbaumer, head of the Foreign Ministry's Finance and Economics Section, who announced the agreement today, amplified on this point at a news conference in Berne.

They said that, compared with the "extensive requests" made by the United States, Switzerland had made few concessions, and that the draft treaty constituted virtually no change from Swiss laws on tax evasion and banking secrecy.

But, they added, the Federal Cabinet felt that "exceptional measures" were justified in combating gangs operating on an international scale who used "sophisticated" methods in handling considerable sums of money.

In such cases, they said, "Switzerland would be ready to help suppress offenses involving taxes and banking operations."

Dozens of Crimes

The United States negotiating team, which includes officials of the State, Treasury and Justice Departments, and the Securities and Exchange Commission, has already returned to Washington.

United States sources in Berne said that the 50-page draft treaty provided detailed machinery for defining the cases of "organized crime" for which Switzerland will grant exceptional treatment.

The Swiss reportedly agreed to include evidence on tax evasion in material about a criminal whom the United States was prosecuting for crimes recognized by both countries. But no information was available on the definition of "organized crime with international repercussions."

The agreement reportedly lists dozens of crimes that are punishable under both Swiss and American law. Apart from the tax-evasion problem, the most serious issue was said to be that of definition, since the Swiss criminal code and the American code are different.

Switzerland already has legal aid treaties with France, West Germany and other Western European countries, but, as the communiqué noted, this represents the first such agreement that Switzerland has made with a country with an "Anglo-Saxon" criminal code.

Earlier this month in Washington, the Senate Banking and Currency Committee passed a bill designed to stop the affluent from using the secret Swiss bank accounts to commit tax evasion, stock frauds and other crimes.

The legislation seeks to circumvent the Swiss bank secrecy. It would impose enough record-keeping requirements on banks, other financial institutions and individuals so that the guilty can be apprehended, tried and convicted on evidence existing in the United States.

The bill is now before the Senate. The House had already passed a strong bill.

Mr. Nussbaumer, the head of the Swiss delegation, made it clear, however, that the bank accounts of Americans would remain secret in all cases where evidence by the United States failed to convince the Swiss authorities that the person involved was cooperating in organized crime.

Gambino Is Called Heir to Genovese As 'Boss of Bosses'

By CHARLES GRUTZNER

For the first time in the 10 years since Vito Genovese entered Federal prison, where he died a year ago, there is again a "boss of all bosses" over the six Mafia "families" in the New York-New Jersey metropolitan area.

The new overlord, according to detectives and Federal agents who listen in on conversations in the underworld, is 67-year-old Carlo Gambino, who has homes at 2230 Ocean Parkway, Brooklyn, and at 34 Club Drive, Massapequa, L. I.

Gambino, who was described yesterday by Inspector Robert J. McGowan, head of the Department's Central Investigation Division, as "the most powerful of all the family bosses in the country," is listed by the Department of Justice as a member of the Mafia's national commission.

The national commission, with seven present members and two other seats temporarily vacant, takes a hand in the affairs of the 23 semi-autonomous Mafia families from coast to coast only when their problems and disputes can not be resolved at the local level.

Gambino, according to police officials, functions as overseer of the six locally based families and arbitrator of disputes within and among those groups. The long-vacant post of regional "boss of all bosses" has been reactivated because of trouble and uncertainty of command in several families caused by recent jailings of local leaders,

murderous rivalries and territorial disputes.

Reports of law-enforcement officers who have Gambino under surveillance indicate that he has been receiving a steady flow of visitors from the other families and that Aniello Dellacroce, reputed underboss in Gambino's own family has been sitting as a mediator or underworld judge at hearings—sometimes held in the Ravenite Social Club at 247 Mulberry Street near Police Headquarters —where disputes are argued and awards and penalties meted out.

Gambino has been for the last three years under a deportation order for having entered this country illegally as a stowaway in 1921. This has not, however deterred his peers in the underworld commission from confirming his authority as regional boss. And the Mafia is confident, according to official eavesdroppers, that his deportation will be delayed further, perhaps forever.

Gambino suffers from a cardiac ailment that has served repeatedly to postpone deportation proceedings begun 12 years ago. But his heart condition has not incapacitated him from directing the operations of one of the biggest and richest families, according to law-enforcement sources.

High Court Gets Case

He has at last exhausted all but one of the legal resorts open to him. His lawyer, Edward J. Ennis, petitioned the United States Supreme Court on Friday to review the findings of the other Federal courts. Even if the court refuses to review the case, there is doubt whether Italy would agree to accept Gambino, who left his native land when he was 19.

When and if Gambino should depart or otherwise cease to be a Mafia boss, his successor as head of the family—but not necessarily as boss of bosses— would probably be Dellacroce,

according to knowledgeable sources.

Dellacroce, who is 55 years old, was described at a recent public hearing of the Joint Legislative Committee on Crime by Edward J. McLaughlin, the committee counsel, as a conniver plotting against Gambino. But other official investigators say that Dellacroce is completely loyal to Gambino and that Gambino knows this.

Dissension in Family

The insinuations of disloyalty made against Dellacroce were described by a law-enforcement official as being the legislative committee's way of taunting Dellacroce, who had refused to answer questions, in the hope that he might be angered enough to make a denial, which would open the door to more productive questions and answers.

Despite the deportation threat, affairs within the Gambino family are more stable than in any of the five other local families.

There is dissension in the former Genovese family because Gerardo (Jerry) Catena, who is on the national commission as acting boss of that family, has become too enamored of his affluence and pseudo-respectability to give proper attention to the gambling, loan-sharking, labor racketeering and other areas in which most of the family finds employment.

Before Catena was jailed on March 4 for an indefinite term for refusing to answer questions of the New Jersey Commission of Investigation, a "soldier" in his family was overheard complaining to his captain: "That rich —— Jerry is semiretired. He's playing golf while we're breaking our —— to bring in the money."

Meanwhile, Thomas (Tommy Ryan) Eboli, who with Catena and Michele (Mike) Miranda acted as family caretaker during Genovese's long imprisonment, is reputedly "coming up fast and strong" because of

his success in the family's enterprises.

There are problems in the four other New York and New Jersey families, too, for Gambino. One is the disappearance six months ago, and presumed murder, of Frank Mari and two of his henchman in the family whose titular leader is Paul Sciacca.

Seek to Avert War

Mari reputedly had been receiving favored treatment from Sciacca over Philip (Rusty) Rastelli, a 51-year-old ex-convict who was Sciacca's underboss. The national commission is reported to have appointed Rastelli and two other members of the Sciacca family as temporary administrators to seek, with Gambino's help, to keep the situation from developing into an underworld war.

Simone Rizzo (Sam the Plumber) DeCavalcante, head of a New Jersey family having close relations with Catena, is scheduled for early trial in Newark on a Federal charge of extortion and is also under indictment as an alleged boss of an interstate gambling ring. The selection of an acting boss will have to be resolved if circumstances limit DeCavalcante's opportunities for action.

The leadership of the family of the late Thomas (Three-Finger Brown) Luchese has remained open since July, 1967, as has the place Luchese held in the national commission.

Joseph Colombo, whom the F.B.I. lists as boss of a Brooklyn-based family, was arrested on March 6 on a five-count indictment charging perjury, to which he is to plead in court on March 26.

The Colombo family affairs are also in disarray because the police are investigating whether two Colombo "soldiers" who have vanished were murdered after a kangaroo court trial in a Bensonhurst clubhouse frequented by members of that family.

'Mafia' Loses Its Place In Federal Vocabulary

WASHINGTON, July 23 (UPI)—With President Nixon's concurrence, Attorney General John N. Mitchell has told the Justice Department and the Federal Bureau of Investigation to stop using the terms "Mafia" and "Cosa Nostra" because they offend "decent Italian-Americans."

In a confidential memorandum to all division and agency heads, including the director of the F.B.I., J. Edgar Hoover, Mr. Mitchell said:

"It has become increasingly clear that a good many Americans of Italian descent are offended. They feel that the use of these Italian terms reflects adversely on Italian-Americans generally, and there is no doubt that their concern is genuine and sincere."

A department spokesman said that the order resulted from complains to Mr. Mitchell and was not inspired by recent protest demonstrations against the F.B.I. by Italian-Americans in New York City.

NIXON SIGNS BILL TO COMBAT CRIME

Gives 'Tools' for 'Total War' to Mitchell and Hoover

WASHINGTON, Oct. 15 (UPI) —President Nixon signed his anticrime bill today under unusually tight security precautions in the Justice Department building. He praised the bill as a major tool in the fight against organized crime and terrorism.

The new law, Mr. Nixon said, will give the Federal Government the means "to launch a total war against organized crime, and we will end this war." He added that it "should be a warning to those who engage in these [terrorist] acts that we are not going to tolerate these activities."

Handing the signed bill to Attorney General John N. Mitchell and J. Edgar Hoover, director of the Federal Bureau of Investigation, Mr. Nixon said: "Gentlemen, I give you the tools. You do the job."

The ceremony was conducted on the second floor of the Justice Department building, three-quarters of a mile down Pennsylvania Avenue from the White House.

Invitation a Requirement

The five - story building swarmed with Secret Service men, who blocked normal passage through the halls leading to the second-floor auditorium where the ceremony was held.

Only invited persons were allowed to enter the closed area, and three to four guards at each entrance checked credentials. Secret Service agents with walkie - talkies guarded every entrance to the building that provided access to the auditorium.

Mr. Nixon entered through an inner courtyard, where employes stood behind ropes held by Secret Service men. There was a loud cheer as the President entered the building.

Later the President toured a new communications center at the District of Columbia police headquarters, accompanied by Mr. Mitchell and Police Chief Jerry V. Wilson. Greeting policemen along the way, Mr. Nixon commented to one pa trolman: "Now with the crime bill signed, we ought to take off jet-propelled."

The crime bill, given final Congressional approval Monday, provides the death penalty for anyone convicted of a fatal bombing.

It permits F.B.I. agents to investigate and Federal attorneys to prosecute bombings and arson on college campuses and at every other institution or organization that receives Federal financial help.

Extra Judicial Terms

To fight organized crime, the measure permits judges to impose additional sentences of up to 25 years on certain "dangerous and adult special offenders" who are convicted of crimes that carry lesser penalties.

The legislation also does the following;

¶Makes it a crime to use money from organized crime to establish a legitimate business in interstate commerce.

¶Makes it a Federal crime to participate in a conspiracy to obstruct the enforcement of state or local gambling laws.

¶Establishes Federal control over interstate and foreign commerce in explosives.

¶Creates a national commission to determine if the crime bill or any current laws infringe on individual rights.

The President also signed legislation creating a system of public defenders for persons financially unable to get adequate legal aid in criminal cases. The bill provides for two different types of public defender systems in judicial areas where 200 or more appointments are required every year.

The Federal Public Defender Organization will be manned by salaried Federal employes under the supervision of a Federal public defender. The other system, the Community Defender Organization could be any nonprofit defense counsel service. The Government would pay the costs on a per-hour basis.

The two systems could be used only to supplant, not replace, the appointment of private attorneys.

Colombo: The New Look in the Mafia

By NICHOLAS GAGE

At the $125-a-plate testimonial dinner given for him March 22, Joseph Colombo Sr. posed for a traditional family portrait — the benign patriarch surrounded by his wife, four sons, two daughters-in-law and a 5-year-old daughter.

A portrait of Colombo's other "family," according to law-enforcement officials, would show Colombo in the same central position, but the supporting cast would be different. At his right, the law enforcers say, would be the underboss of Colombo's Mafia family, and on each side of them five capos (captains). Behind this first line of leadership would stand about 200 family members and associates.

Federal, state and local agents who follow the activities of this group say that it represents a new generation in the Mafia. "The Colombo group has a style and character all its own," said an assistant district attorney in Brooklyn.

"Most of its members are American-born, free-wheeling men not so bound to tradition and eager to find new ways to exploit the system," said a Federal agent. "Like Colombo, the family's capos are well-spoken, polished and innovative."

Unlike some older family bosses, Colombo has concentrated on getting him involved in legitimate business. "It is almost a fetish with him," said the Federal agent. "We believe Colombo himself has interests through fronts in about 20 businesses in New York."

Colombo urges members of his family to hold some kind of legitimate job to help justify their expenditures, law enforcement officials said. Colombo has worked as a salesman for Cantalupo Realty Company, 1434 86th Street, Bensonhurst, Brooklyn. Law enforcement officials divide the history of the Mafia in the United States into three periods. Until 1931, it was led by gangsters born and raised in southern Italy. Then a group led by Charles (Lucky) Luciano took over and these men were more attuned to the new country. But they feared public exposure and remained mindful of Mafia traditions.

The Colombo family represents the beginning of a period even more sophisticated than that of Luciano's era, law enforcement officials believe.

Colombo refused to grant an interview to discuss the contention of law enforcement officials that he heads such a group, but he has publicly denied leadership of any organized crime element.

Law enforcement officials, citing information gathered from monitored conversations and from underworld informants, said that they had a clear picture of the structure and membership of the Colombo family.

Youth Takes Over

Unlike the other Mafia families in New York, the law enforcement officials said, the Colombo group is made up of young men. Colombo, 48 years old, is the youngest Mafia leader in the country, they maintain, and most of his capos are in their 30's or early 40's.

The big exception is Salvatore Mineo, the underboss, who is 73. But he is believed to be rather inactive, given the title by Colombo to keep the job from going to one of the ambitious capos, some of whom harbor grudges against their leader.

When Colombo took over the family in 1964, he sidelined most of the old guard then in power and replaced them with younger men pressing for position.

The story of how Colombo came to power is frequently discussed, not only among law officials, but also inside the Mafia. Colombo's rise, for example, was a topic in the taped conversations of reputed New Jersey Mafia leader, Simone Rizzo DeCavalcante, that were released by the Federal Bureau of Investigation on a Federal court order in 1969.

Colombo's break, these conversations indicate, came in 1962 when Joseph Bonanno, leader of a New York family and a member of the Mafia national commission, decided to try to become the dominant force in the Mafia.

Assassin Pulls Switch

Bonanno's reported plan called for the killing of three Mafia leaders, Carlo Gambino and Thomas Luchese, both of New York, and Stephano Magaddino of Buffalo. He gave the contracts for the assassinations to a colleague, Giuseppe Magliocco, who in turn farmed them out to Colombo, a newly appointed capo in the Magliocco family.

Instead of carrying out the contracts, Colombo told Gambino about the planned coup. Bonanno ultimately was forced to surrender leadership of his family. Magliocco repented of his part in the scheme, was fined by the commission and died shortly afterward.

The leadership of Magliocco's family and his seat in the commission went to Joseph Colombo, apparently as a reward for exposing Bonanno's plans. The DeCavalcante tapes indicate that Colombo's booster was Carlo Gambino, who, Federal agents say, is one of the most powerful Mafia bosses in the country.

Until his elevation, Colombo was considered a lightweight by his colleagues, the DeCavalcante tapes make clear. Police officials say Colombo spent most of his time playing up to powerful Mafiosi like Gambino. "He was the Mafia's Sammy Glick," said one officer.

A similar assessment was expressed by DeCavalcante and his underboss, Frank Majuri, in one of the taped conversations released in 1969. Here is part of the exchange:

DeCavalcante: This guy [Colombo] sits like a baby next to Carl [Gambino] all the time. He'd do anything Carl wants him to do . . .

Majuri: I told you, Sam, I was surprised when I heard he was in there [head of the Brooklyn family]. I would never have made that guess.

DeCavalcante: What experience has he got? He was a bustout guy [petty gambler] all his life.

Majuri: How can they make a guy like Joe Colombo sit at the commission?

Colombo inherited his association in the family he ultimately took over from his father, Anthony Colombo, who was garroted in 1938 and found dead in his car next to the body of a woman friend, Christine Oliveri, who had also been strangled. The crime was never solved.

The Mafia family Joseph Colombo came to rule, according to lawmen, differs in several aspects from other families in New York. Its approximate 200 members and associates make it small in size compared, say, to the Carlo Gambino family, which is believed to be four times as big.

The Colombo family rackets are almost exclusively in Brooklyn and Long Island, whereas the interests of several of the other families are spread out all the way from New Haven to the outskirts of Philadelphia.

Law enforcement officials say that the rackets of the Colombo family—about 20 of whose members are under current indictment—include numbers and sports gambling, hijacking, fencing in stolen goods and loan-sharking—the lending of money at usurious interest.

$3-Million in Loans

"Our informants tell us that Colombo's family has at least $3-million in the street," one Federal agent said. He explained that the money has been lent to individuals who could not get credit through legitimate channels at interest ranging from 20 per cent to 250 per cent.

Before going to work for Cantalupo Realty, Colombo was employed for six years as a salesman for Pride Wholesale Meat Company, which was controlled by Peter Castellano and Paul Gambino, brother of Carlo Gambino. Castellano was identified by the Senate Permanent Subcommittee of Investigations in 1965 as a captain in the Gambino family.

For 10 years before joining the meat company, Colombo worked intermittently as a longshoreman, according to information he once volunteered to a credit investigator. And before that, he spent three years in the Coast Guard.

During his service period, he went absent without leave three times, according to his military record. For his last offense, he was sentenced to a year's confinement, but he received a discharge before completing the sentence because he suffered from "psychoneurosis."

A medical report in his record says he was "unable to adapt to the restrictions of military life because of tension and instability . . ." For two years after his discharge in 1945, he received a disability allowance of $11.50 a month as a result of his nervous disorder.

Unemployed, but Loyal

Colombo became a salesman for Cantalupo Realty nine years ago. Anthony A. Cantalupo, president of the company, told the New York State Legislative Committee on Crime last year when it questioned him about his famous salesman that he considered Colombo "a perfect gentleman." He added that Colombo had "the sincerest group of clients—they don't cheat him out of his commissions."

The other prominent figures in the family, according to law enforcement agents, follow Colombo's example in having legitimate jobs, with one notable exception. He is Nick Bianco, who the agents say left the Mafia family of Raymond Patriarca in New England to join the Colombo group.

Bianco has not had a steady job for years, they say, but Colombo indulges him because he values his loyalty.

Colombo puts a high premium on loyalty. Although otherwise an astute leader, according to law enforcement officials, he picks his closest associates not for their intelligence or imagination but for their loyalty to him. "As a result," said one agent, "most of the men nearest him are third-raters."

The official said that Colombo takes such care to surround himself with absolutely loyal men because he fears hostile factions within his own family. The hostility goes back to the early nineteen-sixties when the family, not yet under Colombo's rule, was torn by an internal conflict known as the Profaci-Gallo war.

The family was then led by Joseph Profaci, a powerful Mafioso who owned a 328-acre estate with its own airport in Hightstown, N. J. In 1961, a dissident group in the family, led by Larry, Albert and Joseph Gallo, began kidnaping Profaci lieutenants in a dispute with Profaci over illegal profits. Profaci died of cancer in 1962, but the war continued under his successor, Giuseppe Magliocco.

The conflict finally faded when a close and powerful ally of the Gallos, Tony Bender, suddenly disappeared. Later Joe Gallo was sent to prison for extortion and Larry Gallo died of cancer.

But Joseph Gallo, who is called Crazy Joe, was released last month and, informants have told the police, Colombo is more than a little uneasy at having him back in circulation, although Gallo is on parole for four years and must be cautious.

The man in his family Colombo is said to fear most, however, is Carmine Persico, 37, the tough leader of a pow-

erful faction within the family. Persico, however, is afraid to move against Colombo as long as Colombo has Gambino's support. At the same time, Colombo is loathe to attempt to purge Persico because it may touch off another round of internal warfare.

'Bad Blood' Reported

Police believe that there has been "bad blood" between Persico and Colombo for several reasons. Persico, according to the law officials, was a zealous follower of Profaci and felt that Colombo did not give strong support to the late boss in the war against the Gallos. He was furious when Colombo took a conciliatory position toward the Gallos after he became head of the family.

Persico has always felt that Colombo did not deserve to be given the leadership of the family over more experienced capos, informants have reported, and he has expressed the belief that Colombo has not treated his faction fairly, giving it the most dangerous and least profitable assignments.

The Persico faction is heavily involved in hijacking and loan-sharking, according to the police. Persico was sentenced to 14 years in prison for hijacking in 1969 and is free on bail pending appeal of his case.

While few others in the Colombo family feel the intense hostility of the Persico faction toward their boss, informants have told law enforcement officials that Colombo's unorthodox tactics have caused considerable grumbling among many family members.

They complain that Colombo's well-publicized attacks on the F.B.I. and other law enforcement agencies have made all family members targets of lawmen. "You do Joe a favor these days and you wind up in trouble," said one member of the family to a law enforcement official recently.

F.B.I. agents deny focusing special attention on any particular group of criminals, but they acknowledge greater success on organized crime cases in general. "When you have to walk through a picket line to get to the office, you tend to

work a lot harder," said one agent.

Grumbling about Colombo has been heard also in other Mafia families. The chief criticism, according to informants, is that Colombo has had the Italian-American Civil Rights League, which he founded, stage demonstrations whenever he has been arrested, but he has shown little interest when other Mafia figures faced the same problem.

Testimony Is Recanted

Colombo has said that he started the league last year after his son, Joseph Jr., was arrested by the F.B.I. on charges of conspiracy to melt silver coins into more valuable ingots. The son was acquitted last month after a key Government witness suddenly recanted his testimony.

Colombo and his wife, Lucille, live with their two unmarried sons and daughter in a split-level house at 1161 83d Street, Brooklyn, about a half mile from the Cantalupo Realty Company.

He also own an estate at Blooming Grove, N. Y., near Goshen in Orange County. The estate, which has tennis courts, a handball court and a swimming pool, was assessed five years ago at $86,200.

The Internal Revenue Service has contended that Colombo could not maintain these properties and his comfortable life style on his income as a real estate salesman, which was reported as ranging from $18,000 to $35,000 in the last eight years.

Colombo is under Federal indictment that accuses him of evading $19,169 in Federal income taxes from 1963 to 1967. He is free on bail pending appeal of a conviction March 11 for committing perjury in his application for a real estate broker's license.

He was sentenced to one to two years and a half years in prison for lying about his criminal record, which includes 13 arrests and three convictions—two fines for gambling and a 30-day contempt sentence in 1966.

Colombo has also been impli-

cated in a $75,000 jewel robbery in Nassau County and is under indictment on a charge of contempt of court in Brooklyn.

Confrontation Still Due

Colombo's most dramatic confrontation with the law, however, promises to come out of a Federal indictment accusing him and 30 others of interstate gambling violations. The complaint charges that Colombo directed a gambling operation with a weekly gross of $50,000 to $100,000. Evidence in the case, the complaint says, includes legally monitored conversations at the home of Phyliss Schettini, who is described in the complaint as a "close friend" of Colombo.

Colombo's future in the Mafia, law enforcement agents believe, depends on two factors —how he survives the legal battles now facing him and how long his mentor, Carlo Gambino, 69, stays alive.

If Colombo's legal problems result only in minor jail terms and if Gambino is around for several years to back him, said the law officials, Colombo will emerge as one of the most formidable Mafia leaders in the country.

But, the law officials added, if Colombo has to spend a long time in prison or if Gambino, who reportedly suffers from a chronic cardiac condition, dies soon, Colombo may find the leadership of his own family slipping from his grasp.

United Press International
Joseph Colombo Sr.

Colombo Shot, Gunman Slain At Columbus Circle Rally Site

Killing of Assailant Not Done by Police, Official Says

By WILLIAM E. FARRELL

Before thousands of stunned spectators and amid heavy police security, Joseph A. Colombo Sr., the 48-year-old reputed chief of a Brooklyn Mafia family, was shot in the head and critically wounded at Columbus Circle yesterday less than an hour before a massive Italian-American civil rights rally began.

Colombo's assailant, a 25-year-old black man named Jerome A. Johnson, of 88 Throop Avenue, New Brunswick, N. J., was shot to death at the scene, but it was still not clear last night who had shot him—the police, associates of Colombo or unknown third parties.

The police reported that Johnson was wearing a special Unity Day press pass that he obtained from officials sponsoring the Italian-American Civil Rights League rally.

Two Bullets Removed

After five hours of brain surgery at Roosevelt Hospital, Colombo was reported still in a coma at 3 A.M. today, and his chances of survival were estimated by surgeons to be "less than 50-50." Two bullets were removed, one from the midbrain and the other from the back of the neck.

Chief of Detectives Albert A. Seedman said last evening that the attack on Colombo was planned and that the police were "convinced" that Johnson was killed by an unidentified bodyguard of Colombo and not the police.

Several reputed underworld leaders were picked up for questioning, including the Gallo brothers, Joe and Albert, of Brooklyn, and Carlo Gambino, who have long been reported feuding with Colombo.

The major questions facing the police, Chief Seedman said, were: Who killed Johnson? What was the purpose of the shooting of Colombo? Who else was involved?

The sudden spurt of gunfire took place shortly after 11:45 A.M. within 100 feet of the gaily festooned statue of Christopher Columbus, which was bedecked, as was the surrounding area, with plastic tatters of red, white and green—the colors of the Italian flag.

Pandemonium engulfed the area, sending hysterical spectators, many of them women clutching small children, spilling uptown toward 61st Street.

So sudden was the violent outbreak in the area near the statue of Columbus and close to a large stage set up for the second annual Unity Day celebration of the league that the police — both uniformed and plainclothes men who were in the area—were initially as stunned as the spectators.

Within seconds, however, a phalanx of policeman, abetted by rally captains of the civil rights league, which Colombo founded last year, were cordoning off the scene of the violence.

Band Starts Up

There were shouts of "A colored guy did it!" and cries of "They got Colombo!" as a band struck up some music in an attempt to soothe the throng.

Within minutes, Colombo, who was reported to have received shots in the left jaw and lower parts of the right side of the head, was taken to Roosevelt Hospital, a stream of blood gushing from his neck and mouth.

Soon afterward, the body of Johnson was removed to Roosevelt Hospital as well, leaving an area within 25 feet of the stage stained with two pools of blood. The black horn-rimmed spectacles that Colombo wore were on the ground in the area fenced off with police barricades.

Dr. Evron Hanson, chief of neurosurgery at Roosevelt Hospital, said that Colombo was not breathing when he was placed in the ambulance, but that his breathing had been restored by an artificial respiration unit.

While the band played and shocked bystanders stared at the scene of the shootings, a man, later identified as Anthony Seccafico, who is reported to be a friend of Colombo's brother-in-law, Mike Sevino, picked up a blood-stained imitation-leather valise from the ground.

He was quickly seized by the police. Seccafico said, "I'm looking for Joe Colombo's bag." A pouch in the valise was opened by the police, and it contained a .38-caliber Colt pistol. The main part of the valise contained tricolor lapel pins of the civil rights league.

Seccafico was handcuffed and taken to Police Headquarters for questioning.

Several eyewitnesses gave accounts of the frenzied scene.

Carl Cecora, a 30-year-old rally captain, said: "I was standing by the fence and Joe was talking to everybody. This colored girl came up to him and said, 'Hello, Joe.' And he smiled and said, 'Hi ya.'"

"She was with a guy, a colored guy taking pictures, and they asked Joe to pose and everyone to spread out, and before you know it, the shooting started," Mr. Cecora said.

"Everybody jumped on him [the man with a gun]."

Mr. Cecora said the girl and a companion fled and "were over the barricade before anyone realized. I saw the colored guy lying on the ground and he looked dead to me."

At this point, Mr. Cecora was interrupted by detectives and was taken in for questioning.

At his news conference, Chief Seedman said that several ranking police officers had been near Colombo just prior to the shooting and that Colombo had been checking on the venders authorized to sell refreshments at the unity rally.

One of the policemen near Colombo was Deputy Chief Inspector Thomas Reid, who said he heard "two shots—maybe three," and along with other policemen pounced on "a black man with a gun."

"It was all over in a matter of seconds," Inspector Reid said. "I saw a hand sticking out with a gun and I jumped for the gun."

"A shot went off," Inspector Reid said, "we were holding on to his hand—I don't know who shot the black man."

The confusion at the scene was reflected at the 18th Precinct station on West 54th Street, where detectives were interviewing uniformed policemen who had been among the hundreds assembling for the noon rally.

One captain, muttering in disgust at the comments the detectives were eliciting, was overheard to say: "Damn it. Didn't any one of these guys see or hear anything but a bunch of damn firecrackers going off."

Just east of the shooting scene, looking down on, it was a camera platform used by a freelance television crew retained by the civil rights league to film the proceedings.

A man who identified himself as James Delmonico, a 33-year-old freelance, said he witnessed the shooting.

"I watched Colombo walking," Mr. Delmonico said. "I saw a black man jump out behind the back of his [Colombo's] head. He fired three times with an automatic pistol. Colombo fell.

"There were two more shots, I think. They crowded around the guy with the gun. Colombo had blood all over his head. The black man looked like he got hit three or four times."

Near Colombo on the scene were members of his family, including his son Anthony, a vice president of the Italian-American Civil Rights League.

Minutes after the shooting, Colombo's sister, Loretta, was sobbing on the grandstand. She was soothed by Mrs. Anthony Colombo. Another woman said, "Your mother's going to come out and see you like this, you'll kill her ... don't let your mother see you like this."

Another woman said, "It's only in the arm. I heard he was only shot in the arm."

The group moved toward a yellow school bus and Mrs. Anthony Colombo became hysterical.

A rally captain, noticing she was in danger of fainting, slapped her face. Finally she revived a bit, and the two women were ushered into the school bus and driven off.

Several young women who worked at the civil rights league office at 635 Madison Avenue reported that several threatening calls had been received after the shooting and that "a man called and said he was going to machine gun the whole Colombo family."

Later in the afternoon, Barry Slotnick, the league's attorney, ordered the office closed.

There were no signs during the afternoon of activity at the Colombo house at 1161 83d Street, between 11th and 12th Avenues, in the Bensonhurst section of Brooklyn.

The house is made of brick with a garage and porch facing the street. It has a wrought-iron fence and gate providing access to a side alley that leads to the living quarters.

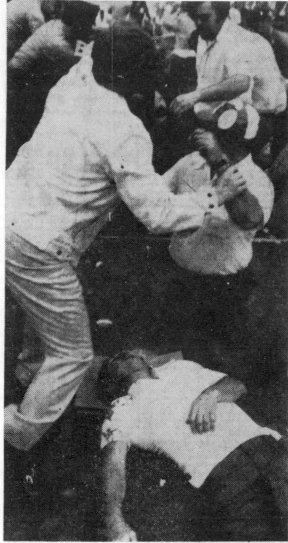

United Press International/Dirck Halstead

Two men who had gone to the aid of Joseph A. Colombo Sr. turn at the sound of gunfire as the attacker is shot.

At his news conference, Chief Seedman said that Johnson had shown some kind of a pass to Unity Day officials and they had issued him their own working press badges embossed with the Italian tricolor. The police, he said, had not found the original card Johnson had used to show the Unity Day officials.

Chief Seedman said that Joseph Gallo had been questioned for about an hour and a half and released.

"He's through for the day," Chief Seedman said when asked if Gallo's release was permanent.

Gambino, Chief Seedman said, was questioned for 40 minutes and "just answered a few questions."

"He told us that Colombo and he were the best of friends and that he was grief-stricken," the chief said, adding that he planned to talk today with "well-known hoodlums." He did not identify them.

The police official said that the two Gallo and Gambino had been sought for questioning because of "stories of friction between the Gambino guys and the guys headed by Colombo." He provided no other details.

Chief Seedman said that four guns had been impounded and were being studied. A police spokesman said that one of the weapons came into the possession of a patrolman at the scene of the shooting when it was lobbed through the air, fell at the policeman's feet and was retrieved by him.

A high-ranking officer at the scene shook his head and said: "Nobody knows what happened. We know there were more guns here than what we have."

One of those who tried to bring normalcy to the scene was Richard Azeez, a rally captain, who said he had tried to shield Colombo's body after he fell.

"It was an hour before my legs stopped shaking," Mr. Azeez said as he manned a post to keep unauthorized persons from flooding the area of the stage.

Officials of the civil rights league repeatedly implored the crowd to remain orderly and exhorted them in the name of Italian unity.

Within 45 minutes after the shooting, the Unity Day program began on schedule, at noon, and soon persons were leaning against the barricades that cordoned off the site of the shooting

Dr. Hanson, the attending neurosurgeon, described Colombo's operation at a news conference. The major wound was caused by a bullet that entered the left back of the head to a depth of three to four inches and lodged near the midline of the cerebellum's hemispheres. Major vascular surfaces were damaged.

The second slug was removed from the back of the neck. A third slug, near the lateral side of the left jaw, was not considered critical and was left in Colombo by surgeons.

"The problem is how much intrinsic damage was done" during the period of heavy bleeding and clotting before the operation, Dr. Hanson said.

Outside the hospital, near the corner of Ninth Avenue and 58th Street, a group of 25 men, four women and two children marched in a slow oval until 10 P.M. reciting prayers, the Hail Mary and The Lord's Prayer.

"St. Jude help Joe Colombo, St. Joseph protect him," they chanted. A breeze kept blowing out religious candles they carried.

June 29, 1971

A Crime Family's 65-Year Journey Into 'Legitimacy'

"You can trust members of your own family first, relatives second, Sicilians third, Italians fourth, and forget about the rest of them." —Giuseppe Lupollo

By FRED FERRETTI

When Giuseppe Lupollo arrived in New York from southern Italy in 1905 he began immediately to create a Mafia family dedicated equal-ly to crime and to legitimate pursuits.

That family, held together with bonds of blood and marriage, has become — in its fourth generation — virtually divorced from crime, according to a two-year research study done by a three-member anthropologist-sociologist team led by Dr. Francis A. J. Ianni of Columbia University. Dr. Ianni calls it a process of "legitimization."

Dr. Ianni, who is director of the Horace Mann-Lincoln Institute of School Experimentation, part of Teachers College, said he had received permission from the family to observe it from within, and that his prime concern was in studying the interrelationships among the four biological families that make it up.

He said he was not interested in "blowing the whistle on anybody—I was interested in how Italian-American society is held together; in the

164

very real and strong concept of kinship."

"Giuseppe Lupollo" is not the real name of the founder of the family, Dr. Ianni said, nor is the family name "Lupollo," but the family is in the New York area, and is one that the Justice Department has called one of the area's crime families.

In his study, which will be published by the Russell Sage Foundation, Dr. Ianni has changed all of the names of family members, giving them the names of Italian and Sicilian towns, "and not from ones that their ancestors came from."

Giuseppe Lupollo came to this country in 1905 with $300 or $400, the study relates, and immediately set up two businesses, one an illegitimate moneylending operation, the other an entirely legal grocery selling imported foods.

In succeeding years and through generations, Giuseppe Lupollo channelled sons, grandsons and relatives into legitimate and illegitimate businesses, making clear distinctions, according to Dr. Ianni, "but always placing more and more emphasis on the legitimate."

Now, after four generations, of the 27 males now in the family, only four are in businesses which are considered illegal — gambling or usury. All the others are professional men or employed in legal businesses.

Among the conclusions that Dr. Ianni and his two colleagues, Dr. Franco Cerase, a University of Rome sociologist, and Elizabeth Reusse, an anthropologist at New York Medical College, came to are the following:

¶A shared kinship-based moral code defines behavior within Italian-American crime families, not fear or coercion; there is a collective amorality toward authority structures that are outside of the family. Secrecy and silence in the face of official inquiry are not conditions of membership, but ingredients of culture that define organized crime, Italian-American style.

¶There is no central "commission" or "board of directors" that runs organized crime; there are no "bosses" or "underbosses" and no secret initiation or membership ceremonies such as those attested to by the late Joseph Valachi.

¶An unwritten, but strictly adhered to, "authority structure" exists in Mafia families, so that "the earlier the generation the higher the rank; within generations, the Lupollo lineage takes pre-

cedence over others; and specialists within groups have higher prestige than nonprofessionals."

Dr. Ianni said that to think of crime organized nationally is "part of the general tendency in the United States to look for conspiracies."

Last month Dr. Ianni was invited to lecture on his study of the Lupollo Mafia family before the National Institute of Law Enforcement, under Justice Department auspices. He said later that he was received "politely" by his audience, and that although some people "agreed with me, most didn't."

He said that American society was "not really familiar with family kinship patterns, so that if people know each other, are related to each other by marriage, and happen to be in the business of crime, then we say they must be associating for ulterior purposes."

"Kinship is infinitely more important than crime. If they stopped being criminals they'd still be tightly knit," he said. Dr. Ianni admits, however, that despite his belief that there is no such thing as a nationwide network of crime called either "Mafia," "La Cosa Nostra," the "Honored Society," or the "Camorra," it is "possible that such a thing might exist."

Yet, he maintains, the kinship model of Italian-American crime families is disappearing. After three genera-

tions "the family is losing its insistence on father-obedience and mother-respect and the authority structure is making alliances with power establishments in the larger society."

Dr. Ianni said the study of the Mafia family was a natural outgrowth of his study of Italian-American culture and of secret societies. He said he met someone who "people said was in the Mafia" in 1965, and through him met other members of the family.

Some Talked, Some Didn't

He said he interviewed many members of the Lupollo family, and people who were not in the family but who knew it. "Some talked freely, some would not speak at all. Being Italian myself helped too."

Dr. Ianni says he found generally that people were quite willing to talk of past generations, "but not about the present." He asserted that he found "antagonism toward outsiders — it was not fear, but a strange conception of honor; protect the family at any cost."

The gravitation of Italian-Americans to crime "is no different from the Jews and Irish who, when they were the dominant minority, went into crime," he declared.

"Organized crime is not something new. Jesse James was leader of a criminal organization. But organized crime cannot exist without at

least the tacit approval of large segments of society. Their services, generally gambling, are services which society thinks are illegal and immoral but which it still wants provided.

"Minority groups discover organized crime is a good way to make money without any particular expertise, so they became organized criminals. What is peculiar to Italians is the southern Italian concept of kinship."

As this kinship weakens, "the families must weaken and they will give way to the next wave of aspiring ethnics, just as the Jews and the Irish did before them."

He said this displacement was already apparent. In New York, blacks, Puerto Ricans and Cubans are displacing Italian-Americans in the policy and numbers rackets. In some cases this is a peaceful transition, with the Italian families leasing numbers concessions for a fee.

Dr. Ianni maintains that the outlook for Italian-American crime families "is not a promising one," because of assimilation, the breaking down of kinship patterns and the emergence of organized crime in other minorities.

His study shows, he said, that "a Mafia does exist, but its character is a compound of a cultural attitude and a web of kinships, which are attributes peculiar to the Italian scene, rather than the big-business pattern, which is a projection of the American imagination."

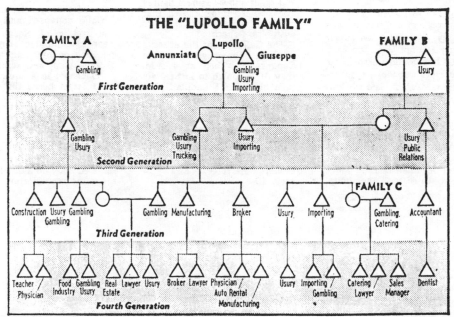

THE "LUPOLLO FAMILY"

May 29, 1971

Joe Gallo Is Shot to Death in Little Italy Restaurant

By ERIC PACE

Joseph Gallo, the Mafia figure known as Crazy Joe, was assassinated early yesterday as he celebrated his 43d birthday in a restaurant on Mulberry Street one block east of Police Headquarters.

The police said they knew neither the identity nor the motive of the middle-aged killer, who also wounded Gallo's bodyguard in a gun battle that spilled out into the narrow streets of the Little Italy section. The killer fled by car.

But Gallo's sister, Mrs. Carmella Fiorello, sobbing over her brother's body, reportedly said, "He changed his image—that's why this happened." She was treated for shock.

"This is a gangland operation," said Chief of Detectives Albert A. Seedman. He added that he had learned yesterday that Gallo planned to reactivivate a civil rights group called Americans of Italian Descent.

The head of the group, former Representative Alfred Santangelo, said Gallo had met with him and volunteered his services.

Another organization, the Italian-American Civil Rights League, was founded by Joseph A. Colombo Sr., whose Mafia family has feuded for years with Gallo's clan.

Well-placed informants said yesterday that the Colombo family had discussed "getting" Gallo ever since Colombo was critically wounded in an assassination attempt last June 28.

But Chief Seedman, speaking to reporters outside the bullet-pocked restaurant, said the killing might also have stemmed from rivalry within the Gallo family, which has long been powerful in Brooklyn. He added that "the speculation is wide open at this time."

Chief Seedman said the police planned to arrest the body-guard, Pete Diapoulas, 42, for illegal possession of a .32-caliber pistol found outside the restaurant, Umberto's Clam House, at 129 Mulberry Street. No other arrests were made yesterday.

Diapoulas was reported in satisfactory condition at Beekman-Downtown Hospital after being shot in the left hip. He was under police guard.

Gallo was pronounced dead in the same hospital after being taken there in a police car. He was shot in the left elbow, 'eft buttock and back. The shot in the back killed him, making him the third gangland murder victim in 24 hours.

A reputed mobster, Bruno Carnevale, was shot to death in Queens on Thursday and another man with organized-crime connections, Thomas Edwards, who sometimes used the surname Ernst, was killed later in the day on Staten Island.

The police found no links between the three killings in the first hours of intensive investigations that followed Gallo's death, at 5:30 A.M.

"Somebody either followed him or was given information about where he was," Chief Seedman said. "Then the assassin walked in with just one thing in his mind — to get Gallo."

With Gallo was his bride of three weeks, the former Sina Essary, whom he had courted after being paroled last March from the Ossining State Correctional Facility, where he had served eight years for extortion. Since then he had been seen with Jerry Orbach, the actor, and other show-business figures and had let it be known that he was writing his memoirs with Mrs. Orbach.

The Gallos spent the evening drinking champagne at the Copacabana. Then at 4 A.M. they drove down to Little Italy in a black 1971 Cadillac plastered with stickers that advertised Americans of Italian Descent.

With them were the burly Diapoulas; his date, Edith Russo of Brooklyn; Mrs. Fiorello, and Mrs. Gallo's daughter by an earlier marriage, Lisa Essary, 10.

The police and hospital authorities gave this account of what happened next:

The black Cadillac cruised slowly through the neighborhood, which Chief Seedman said was "definitely not Gallo territory." Then it parked outside the restaurant, which Gallo had never visited before. It stays open until 6 A.M.

The party sat at two butcher-block tables at the rear, near a side door. Gallo and Diapoulas took chairs facing the wall. They drank soda pop and ate what Robert Daley, the deputy police commissioner in charge of press relations, called "Italian delicacies." Mr. Gallo, jolly and relaxed, had just ordered a second helping when the assassin strode silently in the side door.

He was about 5 feet 8 inches tall, witnesses said, and had black hair, with a bald spot in the front. He wore a light tweed car coat, and a .38-caliber pistol was in his hand.

Women screamed and customers hit the floor as he started shooting. The bodyguard and at least one unknown man who was seated at the bar returned the fire. All told, the police said, four guns were involved and 20 bullets were fired.

Mortally wounded, Gallo staggered out the front door as the killer kept firing after him, shooting out the front-door transom. Then the killer fled out the back door, chased by the unknown man, who also kept on shooting.

The killer hopped into a waiting car, probably with an accomplice at the wheel, and escaped through the darkness.

Gallo collapsed and died in the middle of Hester Street, near his Cadillac, while Diapoulas stood by him and Mrs. Fiorello wept and screamed.

Policemen in a squad car on Mott Street heard the screams, picked up Gallo's body and the bodyguard and sped to the hospital, with the women in the Gallo party following.

There attendants stripped off Gallo's pinstripe suit and placed his slender, lightly muscled body on a device called a cardiac resuscitation cart. In an effort to revive him, they switched on a mechanical plunger that pumped Gallo's heart.

Meanwhile, Diapoulas refused to give any details of the assassination while his wound was being dressed. He told attendants, "I don't want to give you a hard time, but I'm not going to give you information." He declined to say where the shooting took place—or even to give his name.

Mrs. Fiorello wept hysterically and said: "They shot my brother. He was a very good man, a kind man."

She wore an ankle-length jersey dress, as did Miss Russo and Mrs. Gallo. The sleepy child put Gallo's gray fedora on her head.

The police mounted a guard over Gallo's body until it was taken out of the hospital, and detectives swarmed in to question the grieving women. Mrs. Fiorello was put under sedation and sent home later in the morning.

Little Italy was in an uproar. Witnesses reported seeing the gleam of pistols at tenement windows, and the police blocked off Mulberry Street before Chief Seedman arrived on the scene.

Mr. Seedman said his men would question "any people in the Colombo family who've indicated hostility to Gallo."

He said the investigation of the Colombo shooting last summer had been making progress, but he added, "I couldn't rush that investigation just because of this occurrence."

Just after the Colombo shooting, high police officials indicated that arrests would be made soon, but there have been none so far.

With Chief Seedman was Deputy Commissioner Daley. He stood shivering in the icy drizzle and murmured: "He made a mistake, Crazy Joe did. He should have gone to bed last night."

Down Mulberry Street, Sal Lapolla, a liquor store owner, was philosophical about Gallo's death. "These people, it's their choice," he said. "It's their life they lead. It's not our kind of life."

April 8, 1972

A KEY GANG FIGURE SLAIN IN BROOKLYN

Eboli Is Felled by 5 Bullets in 15th Mafia-Style Killing in the Last 13 Months

By EMANUEL PERLMUTTER

Thomas Eboli, also known as Tommy Ryan, a top leader of the Mafia in the New York area, was gunned down in traditional gangland fashion early yesterday on a quiet residential street in the Crown Heights district of Brooklyn.

His body was found at 1 A.M., sprawled face down, on the sidewalk in front of 388 Lefferts Avenue, a block from the Empire Boulevard police station. There were five bullet holes in Eboli's face and neck.

The killing was the latest in a series of underworld shooting that started with the critical wounding of Joseph A. Colombo Sr. in Columbus Circle in June, 1971, and include the slaying of Joseph (Crazy Joe) Gallo in a Little Italy restaurant in Manhattan last April. They are believed tied in with changes in the Mafia high command.

Since the Colombo shooting at least 15 men with alleged Mafia links—including Eboli—have been killed in the continuing gangland war.

The police said they had no witnesses to the Eboli shooting and no suspects.

Fragments of Glass Found

An autopsy performed at the Kings County Hospital Morgue showed that death had been caused when the bullets entered the skull and brain of the 61-year-old underworld chieftain.

Fragments of glass were found in and around the bullet wounds. Similar pieces of glass, believed to be from the windshield or side window of an automobile, were scattered in the street several feet from Eboli's body.

Detectives trying to reconstruct the shooting concluded that Eboli had been shot at close range as he sat in a car parked at the curb near an overhanging tree.

They theorized that Eboli then staggered from the automobile and may have been shot again before he collapsed at the edge of the sidewalk.

The right-hand pocket of Eboli's blue jacket contained $2,077 in cash. The body had a diamond ring on one finger and a gold crucifix around the neck. His snap-brim gray straw hat was also found near him.

Five spent .32-caliber cartridges and one of .22 caliber were near the body.

Passersby and curiosity seekers could still see the blood stains on the sidewalk late yesterday.

A police alarm was broadcast for a 1971 dark Cadillac with New Jersey license plates VFD 334, possibly with a shattered window, which Eboli was known to have been using.

He lived with a common-law wife in an $800-a-month apartment at 4 Horizon Road, in the Horizon House high-rise complex, in Fort Lee, N. J., but was in the process of moving to a new home he had reportedly bought in Paramus, N. J.

Eboli operated mainly in Manhattan, where he was reputed to oversee the West Side docks and bar and night club interests of the Genovese crime family.

Detectives could not say for sure yesterday what Eboli was doing in that part of Brooklyn, which is four blocks from the site of what was once Ebbets Field and also near the Empire Boulevard entrance to Prospect Park.

Deputy Inspector James P. O'Brien, who was in temporary charge of Brooklyn detectives, said at the scene: "I think he was here for a meet and somebody knew about it and got him. Or maybe he was lured here to set him up."

Shortly after the shooting, the police found a small Plymouth with a New Jersey license plate about three blocks from the scene and took it to the Empire Boulevard station. In the rear of the car they found an M-3 machine gun with a silencer attached and 24 .45-caliber bullets, not the caliber used on Eboli.

A yellow truck which had been seen near the scene of the shooting a short time before it occurred was also taken to the station house. It was registered to the Ferrara Fast Freight Company of 49 Downing Street, Manhattan.

The police said the truck had been reported stolen recently from the West Houston Street area of lower Manhattan.

The working class neighborhood where Eboli was found is ethnically mixed, with many Italians, Negroes and Puerto Ricans living in old, small private dwellings. There are a good number of Jews, too, in some apartment buildings of 30-year vintage.

Some residents of the area said they had heard male voices saying, "Let's get out of here" emanating from the cab of the yellow truck before the shooting. There was nobody inside when the police found it, although the motor was running.

Eboli's body was found by Patrolmen Drew Siegal and Nicholas Palmiotto, who were flagged down in their radio car by a pedestrian who said he had heard shots.

Eboli's police record included a half-dozen arrests on minor charges of gambling or disorderly conduct. He had appeared before several public agencies and local grand juries investigating organized crime.

From 1959, when Vito

Associated Press

Thomas Eboli

Genovese began serving a sentence for narcotics violation, until 1969, when Genovese died in a Federal penitentiary, Eboli shared caretaker leadership of the Genovese crime family with Gerardo (Jerry) Catena and Michele (Mike) Miranda, an elder in the underworld.

Eboli had suffered several heart attacks in recent years and, according to the police, had been functioning as underboss to Catena, who is now in prison in New Jersey for refusing to answer crime investigators' questions.

Despite his long involvement in the criminal world, Eboli served only one prison term. That resulted from a 60-day sentence imposed on him in 1952 when he leaped into the ring at Madison Square Garden and assaulted a referee because a boxer he was managing had lost the fight decision. His arrest record dated to 1933.

He was born in Italy and became an American citizen in 1960.

Crime 'Families' Taking Control of Pornography

Law Aides Say They Dominate Movies and Books—Entry in 'Massage' Field Reportedly Marked by Intimidation

The following article was prepared by Ralph Blumenthal and Nicholas Gage.

In less than four years, organized-crime "families" in New York have made pornography their fastest-growing new racket.

While it does not approach such staples as gambling, loan-sharking or narcotics in earnings, according to law-enforcement officials, it has surpassed all the rackets the families have developed in the last decade.

In New York, organized crime dominates the production and distribution of pornographic movies, books and magazines, controls many of the stores that sell these materials and is now moving in on the growing number of "massage parlors," the officials said.

Inquiry Under Way

They said that Mafiosi were believed to have interests in two plush East Side massage parlors and that they were also moving in on a number of West Side parlors, often using intimidation to secure an interest.

The office of District Attorney Frank S. Hogan of Manhattan is investigating a rash of fire bombings, beatings and demands for "protection" payoffs involving so-called massage parlors in midtown over the last seven months.

Often dingy storefronts where patrons pay $10 and up for about a half hour of "massage" and feminine company, the 70 massage parlors in midtown are sometimes also places where patrons can arrange to pay extra for sex acts.

Among the figures who have become active lately in the massage parlor field, investigators told The New York Times, is Martin Hodas, a leading peep-show distributor with about 20 outlets. After Mr. Hodas's arrest on bribery charges Nov. 30, Deputy Police Commissioner William P. McCarthy said Mr. Hodas "deals directly with heads of families" of organized crime.

Commissioner McCarthy declined to elaborate on his statement linking Mr. Hodas with Mafia figures.

Investigations by Federal, state and local agencies have made it possible to assemble a detailed picture of how organized crime penetrated the field of pornography, and siphoned off vast sums by ignoring creditors and dealing in hard-to-trace cash accounts.

What has attracted crime figures to businesses related to pornography is the tremendous profits such enterprises generate.

Two years after Joseph Brocchini, a reputed Mafioso known by the police to have been minimally successful in traditional rackets, went into selling sex books and magazines, he purchased a $200,000 home in Westchester County. Brocchini is listed by the Justice Department as a member of the Mafia family of the late Thomas Lucchese.

Racketeers have also discovered that pornography has a major advantage over traditional rackets. Confusing and sometimes contradictory court decisions make distributing pornographic material a lot safer than making book, selling heroin or loan-sharking.

The investigation of District Attorney Hogan has reportedly not determined precisely to what extent the outbreak of violence in massage parlors is due to rivalries of independent operators or to organized crime's efforts to control the business.

In the first recorded fire bombing on May 10 at 4:47 A.M., flames destroyed the Palace parlor at 410 West 42d Street. It is no longer open.

On July 25 at 5:40 A.M., another massage establishment, the French Studio at 436 West 42d Street was fire-bombed. But it is open again.

In September, according to police sources, a third premises at 54th Street and Eighth Avenue was destroyed by flames. And elsewhere on Eighth Avenue, the sources said, two other places were closed by another operator, Michael Purro, after he was allegedly "pushed around." Mr. Purro could not be reached for comment.

Other operators and managers have reported being approached by hoodlums for "protection" money. One such incident involved Charles Principato, also called Charlie Prince, a manager of several massage parlors, including the French Studio. He confided recently to an undercover city investigator that he had been approached by unidentified men for $1,000 a week in "protection" money. Mr. Principato could not be reached for comment.

Inquiry on Disappearance

One of the most detailed cases of intimidation developed so far—although there are still many questions under investigation because of the flight of the central figure—involves an operator named Nick Valentine.

Among his known establishments were the Palace and the Harem as well as Caesar's Harem, 601 Eighth Avenue, and Ancient Rome, 109 West 42d Street.

Last summer, Mr. Valentine complained to Mr. Hogan's office that he had been beaten. And then, as an investigation began, Mr. Valentine disappeared. Recently, however, The Times learned, he was spotted on two occasions in Sardi's Restaurant—and then dropped out of sight again.

As investigators have pieced the story together, Mr. Valentine—who has no known police record — was abruptly removed as the operator of the Harem about the time of the beating some months ago and replaced by two competitors, Jerry Gomberg and George Kaplan. Among the places Gomberg and Kaplan took over at about that time was the Geisha at 414 West 42d Street.

The Geisha's owner, investigators have learned from a court-authorized seizure of records and hidden tape recordings, was Mr. Hodas.

The connection, if any, between the change of management at the Harem and the fires at the Palace and the French Studio has not been explained.

But sometime before the blaze at the Palace, Mr. Valentine had reportedly instituted a cut-rate policy that offered a 15-minute massage for $7.50 instead of the standard half hour at $10 to $15. His employes reported receiving some threats, presumably from competitors, police sources said.

2 Seized as Suspects

When, weeks after the fire bombings, two suspects were charged with the crimes, one of them, Earl Jones, 42 years old, listed his address as 414 West 42d Street — the Geisha, two doors from the Palace. The other, was identified as Dexter Morton, 29, who listed his address as the Times Square Motor Hotel.

Meanwhile, Mr. Valentine was apparently seething over his removal from the Harem. According to police sources, he went there one night and began punching at the partitions. Mr. Hodas, who was there at the time, called the police and Mr. Valentine was subdued.

The police were somewhat taken aback at being called to the parlor by a man whom they had been investigating.

On another occasion, Mr. Valentine visited Alex DiLorenzo, the real estate executive, to complain about having been locked out of the Harem.

Mr. DiLorenzo's associate, Sol Goldman, who is listed as the principal in the corporation holding the property where the Harem is situated, confirmed that Mr. Valentine had complained to them. Mr. Goldman added: "He was not supposed to show dirty books and dirty pictures there."

About the same time — the sequence has not been clearly established by investigators— Mr. Valentine complained to Mr. Hogan's office of being beaten with a lead pipe in another of his massage parlors, Ancient Rome. Then he disappeared.

But some months later, in early October, Mr. Valentine appeared in Sardi's Restaurant where he fell into a casual conversation at the bar with a stranger. Then, leaving to "go out and check some of my joints," he dropped out of sight. He was seen in Sardi's again two weeks ago.

Bribe Reported

The latest episode involving massage parlors came on Nov. 30 when six persons were arrested on charges of offering to bribe a police sergeant for protection from police raids. The case is still pending.

The six were Gomberg and Kaplan, an associate of theirs named Jerry Limo, Mr. Hodas, and two associates of Mr. Valentine, Charles Principato and Martha Bollerman, also known as Martha Valentine.

The officer, Sgt. Sidney Patrick, who heads a special Times Square cleanup task force, had been wired to record evidence of bribery while he pretended to be accepting payments or offers.

At first, the suspicious operators sought to persuade him to strip for a massage so they could check him for wiring but he dissuaded them. On one occasion, Sergeant Patrick later recalled, Kaplan, a large man, made a move to search him, but the officer escaped by whispering the admonition "Nobody touches me."

According to police records, Gomberg faces charges stemming from the discovery of an allegedly unlicensed pistol in a car of his that was towed away for a parking violation April 21 and routinely searched. He also faces charges for prostitution violations. His record includes five years' imprisonment on burglary charges.

Kaplan, police records show, was arrested on homicide charges four years ago when a man he had allegedly beaten died from injuries. But a grand jury later dismissed the charges.

Decoy Operation

Mr. Hodas was indicted in April on 11 counts of wholesale promotion of obscene material, arising out of the decoy operation of a sex-oriented bookstore by undercover policemen.

Although Commissioner McCarthy has said that Mr. Hodas "deals directly with heads of families" of organized crime, the peep-show entrepreneur has apparently not been immune from the consequences of internecine mob struggle.

During the summer of 1971, the police received reports that a gunman had fired shots at Mr. Hodas in one of his 42d Street offices and that his family in Lawrence, L. I., had been threatened. At that time, police sources said, his peep-show machines were being shoved out on the sidewalk and replaced by machines provided by Brocchini, the reputed Mafioso, who was then operator of the Jo-Mar bookstore at 138 West 42d Street.

Mr. Hodas did not respond to messages left by The Times at his office at 113 West 42d Street and could not be reached for comment.

While the fire bombings and reports of intimidation generally signify mob attempts to muscle in on massage parlors, according to law enforcement sources, the field still has many independents.

Their entry into the field quickly swelled the number of midtown parlors from a dozen last year to about 70 now—after a change in state law opened the massage field to nonprofessionals.

The City Council is currently considering a bill that would require massage parlors to disclose their ownership and financing.

Two men connected with the Mafia family of Joseph A. Co-lombo Sr. are considered the pioneers in bringing organized crime into pornography.

In 1968 John Franzese, a captain in the Colombo family, toured peep shows in the Times Square area and concluded that the independent operators running them were prospering, the police said.

Until he went to prison for bank robbery in 1970, Franzese worked feverishly to take over a number of the peep shows and seize a major part of the market in the vending machines in which the sex films are shown. His efforts were continued by other Colombo family members after Franzese began serving his 50-year term.

Also in 1968, Cosmo Cangiano, reputed to be an associate in the Colombo family, opened up a laboratory in Staten Island to mass produce hard-core pornographic films, according to court records.

At first, he ran into problems with development but solved them by bringing in Michael Zaffarano, a convicted pornographer associated with the Mafia family now led by Natale Evola.

Within a year, Cangiano became the major distributor of pornographic films in the country in what was becoming a booming business.

50,000 Reels Found

When Federal agents raided one of Cangiano's distribution centers in 1969, they found 50,-000 reels of hard-core pornographic films. Further investigation disclosed that the reels, which cost about $3 each to print in color, were being sold in other parts of the country at retail prices ranging from $25 to $65.

Cangiano was convicted in 1969 of violating the Federal statute against transporting pornographic materials across state lines and was sentenced to five years in prison and fined $30,000. He has been free pending appeals of his case. Meanwhile, he was indicted two more times on similar charges.

Cangiano was convicted because his films depicted only sexual acts. Other Mafiosi are known to be investing in films in which the sexual acts are part of some kind of story line. The films are often shown in commercial theaters.

"Once you have any kind of a theme in a sex film, the question of redeeming social value comes up and it is almost impossible to get a conviction," a Federal prosecutor said.

The United States Supreme Court has virtually ruled out pornography convictions on material that may be shown to have possible "redeeming social value."

A picture of how organized-crime elements penetrated and ran the pornography industry here was offered in testimony at public hearings of the State Commission of Investigation in 1970.

Quarters Add Up

Witnesses told of vast and concealed profits — peep-show machines alone of a single operator collected more than $1.5-million in quarters in a single year—of intimidation, mysterious, silent partners, byzantine leasing arrangements and a seemingly insatiable market.

The inquiry focused on the activities of less than a dozen major operators and their links to various families of organized crime.

At one end were the distributors, two of the industry's most active being Star Distributors Ltd. and the CAD-Bark-B & H conglomerate.

Star, according to the testimony, was a failing business until Robert Di Bernardo — who had no experience in publishing and was linked to the New Jersey crime family led by Simone DeCavalcante—joined as a corporate officer. Then Star began prospering and expanding.

The CAD-Bark-B & H group was headed by Brocchini.

One way this operation made money, it was shown, was by ignoring its creditors, the printers of the sex books it sold.

As one expert police witness put it: "If you are not paying anything for a book and you are getting $1.17 for it and if you have printed close to one-half million of these things, then, in effect, you are making somewhere about 500,000 times $1.17."

The creditors, the testimony showed, were afraid to press their claims.

Another method of maximizing profits, the hearings disclosed, was by the so-called "knock-offs"—illegal reproduction of published works.

The other major step in the operation was the outlet — usually the bookstore. These, it was shown, were generally rented from real estate interests that had bought up large blocks of leases from property owners.

Multilayered Operation

This interposed at least one legal structure between the landlord and tenant and had the effect and objective, according to the testimony, of helping to conceal the identity of the operator.

The unusually high rents charged for the storefront premises—an average of $2,000 to $3,000 a month—gave an indication of the enormous profits involved, the State Investigation Commission found. Some leaseholders even insisted on day-to-day agreements—only opening the store for the operators every day if a daily share of the gross was handed over as rent.

Extra Income for Clerks

The only other overhead cost for the operators, the staff salaries, cost them $125 a week for each clerk.

The clerks augmented their salaries by selling hard-core items not on display. Often, the clerk and store operator would split these profits. Under-the-counter sales in a Times Square location, witnesses testified, could earn a clerk as much as $500 a day extra.

The profit potential was shown to be enormous. Operators could purchase playing cards for 27 cents a pack and sell them for $7 or more. Sets of photographs that cost very little to prepare, since they could be printed from discarded film, were sold for whatever the buyer would pay.

As for the profits in peep-show machines that provide viewers with a minute or two of sex film for 25 cents, the testimony showed that Mr. Hodas's East Coast Cinerama Theater, Inc., brought in $1.52-million from peep shows in 1969, which the company divided about 50-50 with the operator of each bookstore location.

The coin, it was testified, was divided by weight. But the coins went to the bank for counting—not deposit. In this way, S.I.C. accountants testified, Mr. Hodas's company made off with $596,075 that did not appear in company books.

The methods racketeers use to gain footholds in the industry were also described in the hearings.

Third Partner Added

In one case outlined, a peep-show distribution company, called Motion Picture Vending Inc., was founded by Robert Genova and Arthur Volgarino.

Then, for no reason that either of the two could explain convincingly to the commission, they suddenly decided to make a third man Lawrence Abbandando, who allegedly lived in Florida and took no part in the operations, a full, one-third partner.

Before that, Abbandando had been observed in the Times Square area, visiting book stores with John Franzese, the Colombo family captain.

Additional information on the organization of the pornography industry here came from a decoy, sex-oriented bookstore operated by undercover policemen early this year.

The unusual investigation resulted in the indictment of 12 men and six corporations on 540 counts of wholesale promotion of obscene material and exposed once again links between pornography operations and the Colombo, Carmine Tramunti and DeCavalcante crime families.

Most of the trials are still pending.

During that undercover operation, an episode never made public indicated one direction the pornography industry was taking here.

As the policemen ordered pornographic materials to learn about the distributors, one of the undercover men recalled, they were approached by two suppliers who tried to persuade them to forget about installing peep shows and "get girls instead."

The suppliers offered to provide the "massage" girls on the basis of a 50-50 income split with the store operators or $500 a week, whichever they preferred. When the policemen rejected the offer, the suppliers grudgingly provided the requested peep show machines.

Black Racketeers Challenging the Mafia

Special to The New York Times

NEWARK, Sept. 3 — The Mafia, entrenched in New Jersey for decades, but confronted with aggressive law enforcement in recent years, is being challenged by another aggressive force—black racketeers.

Law enforcement officials on the Federal, state, county and municipal levels emphasized in a series of interviews that their knowledge of black organized crime was much more limited than their information on white racketeers.

But they said that they had gathered enough information to show the following:

¶In the last decade, blacks have pushed the Mafia out of some slum neighborhoods and reached working relationships with white racketeers in other black neighborhoods under which blacks pay 10 per cent of their gross to whites in return for political and police protection.

¶The blacks have laid off bets with the white organizations, which have far greater financial resources.

¶They have branched out into loan-sharking and sports bookmaking, both traditionally white operations, and are assuming a greater role in narcotics wholesaling.

¶Blacks have risen to managerial positions, such as controllers, in white-operated numbers banks. However, the blacks have failed to reach the decision-making level, or, of course, membership in the Mafia.

"Organized crime is probably more integrated than a great majority of law enforcement agencies in New Jersey," one Federal investigator said.

Explaining why law enforcement officials have more information on whites than on black members of organized crime, one Federal investigator said: "For the longest time our intelligence system was white oriented. To be honest I think most of us thought of black crime as street crime, muggings, robberies and small-time drug peddling."

Because of this, law enforcement agents said, black organized crime has grown for the most part unhampered by the kind of offensive that has since the early nineteen-sixties resulted in the imprisonment of major Mafia figures in New Jersey.

These include Vito Genovese (his convictions for narcotics trafficking led to an opening for blacks because the word went out for whites to stay away from the business); Jerry Catena, who is believed to have succeeded Genovese as the Mafia leader in New Jersey; Simone DeCavalcante, who pleaded guilty to running a $20 million-a-year gambling operation; Ruggiero Boiardo, convicted of operating a $12-million-a-year numbers game in Newark and suburban Essex county; Joseph Zicarelli; Anthony Russo; Angelo DeCarlo, and Angelo Bruno, among others.

According to law enforcement sources, the black gains in organized crime (not necessarily the Mafia) were, except for what may be a black-controlled numbers game in the predominantly white area of Port Newark, strictly limited to black neighborhoods in the increasingly black cities of New Jersey.

"When the day comes that blacks are involved in white neighborhoods then you'll see white politicians and society get all upset over black organized crime," said one black Federal investigator.

"It's just the same with narcotics, as long as it was confined to the ghetto no one — except blacks—were concerned with it, but the minute it spread to the white suburbs everybody launched their war on drugs," the investigator said.

These achievements by the black mobsters were not based on any commitment to civil rights by their white counterparts, but rather were based on practical grounds and on violence.

Law enforcement officials point to the following random incidents in recent years as indicative of a changing racial make-up in organized crime:

¶In 1968 and 1969, numbers runners working for Ruggiero Boiardo in the black lower Vailsburg and North Newark sections of Newark were continually robbed or kidnapped by blacks. Finally, officials believe, an arrangement was made (four blacks were shot to death before the accord was reached) in which a black organization assumed control of the numbers and used the Boiardo organization for laying off bets and for its police and political connections.

¶A major numbers game in Newark's South and Central wards is reported operated by a black family headed by a woman, Mrs. D'Alama Sutton, 49 years old, who was arrested in July on a gambling charge.

¶A white loan shark connected with the Russo organization is reported to have helped finance a small black narcotics operation in Asbury Park. The significance of this, investigators said, was that years ago it was unheard of for white loan sharks to lend money to blacks.

¶Three weeks ago, former State Senator James M. Turner, who is white, was indicted on a charge of trying to fix a parole for Earl Davis, a black man who had been active in Gloucester and Camden Counties and is now serving a state prison term on a bookmaking conviction.

¶In addition to the sporadic violence between white and black underworld figures, there has also been violence between black and black in New Brunswick, Jersey City and Newark.

Black Gains a Spur

Of course, there have been black mobs operating in black neighborhoods well before the civil rights movement. But the drive for greater black equality in legitimate society has also served as a spur for the black racketeers, according to law enforcement officials.

In the nineteen-sixties, the white-controlled lotteries—the traditional form of gambling in black neighborhoods—began to hire black runners, since whites were too conspicuous. However, the blacks began to demand higher positions of authority, along with greater salaries, and the whites slowly and grudgingly yielded to their demands.

"The temper of the times made it more practical for blacks to be on the streets and running things locally than whites," once source said.

"These rackets were just too lucrative to risk over a matter of principle, so the white racketeers became equal-opportunity employers," he said.

The Making of 'The Godfather'— Sort of a Home Movie

By NICHOLAS PILEGGI

As was his custom before the drive home from work with his son, the old man walked across the narrow, tenement-lined street in Manhattan's Little Italy to buy some fresh fruit. The grocer, who had known him for many years, helped the old man sort out some prize oranges and, as a gift, handed him a perfectly ripened, home-grown fig. The old man smiled, accepted the backyard offering with a slight nod and started toward his car. It was then that he spotted two gunmen.

He called out to his son and began to sprint toward the safety of his car with surprising speed for a man of his age, but the gunmen were too quick. As they opened fire, the old man seemed caught in a great leap, suspended momentarily in the air, his arms thrown protectively around his head. Loud shots hammered through the street, bright oranges rolled across the gray pavement and the old man crashed onto the fender of his car and collapsed. The people of Mott Street watched in silence from tenement windows, fire escapes and rooftops as the gunmen slipped away. Then, to spontaneous applause, the grim street tableau came to life, and the old man—the godfather, Marlon Brando—lifted himself slowly from the ground, smiled at the cheering crowd and bowed.

At 11 o'clock on April 12, just as Brando was getting shot on Mott Street, Carlo Gambino, one of New York's real godfathers, sat around the corner in a Grand Street cafe, sipping black coffee from a glass and holding 18th-century Sicilian court in 20th-century New York. He had arrived moments earlier in the company of his brother, Paul, and five bodyguards. It was his custom, as well as his duty as head of a Mafia family, to hear at regular intervals the endless woes of racketeers, dishonored fathers and deportable husbands. They were ushered before him, one at a time, from a waiting area in a restaurant across the street. He was the final judge to people still willing to accept his decisions as law.

BACK on Mott Street, two Mafiosi assigned to observe the movie production were unaware of his arrival. For hours, they had been watching Brando getting shot. They had had innumerable cups of coffee and had adjusted their open-throat, hand-ironed shirts so often that their collars had begun to wilt. Neither of them had been impressed when they heard Brando was to play the godfather, so they watched his performance critically. They volunteered to grips, cameramen and extras that they would have preferred Ernest Borgnine or Anthony Quinn.

"A man of that stature," one of them said, pointing to Brando, "would never wear a hat like that. They never pinched them in the front like that. Italian block, that's the way they wore them, Italian block."

They did not like Brando's wearing his belt below his trouser loops, either.

"He makes the old man look like an iceman. That's not right. A man like that had style. He should have a diamond belt buckle. They all had diamond belt buckles. And a diamond ring and tie clasp. Those old bosses loved diamonds. They all wore them. Brando makes the guy look like an iceman."

In truth, Brando did not look like the traditional double-breasted, wide-lapeled, blue-serge racketeer. He had **accepted the advice of an Italian-American friend, rather than the Mafiosi themselves, and made himself look old and bent. He wore a sack-shaped suit of an undistinguished brown stripe and an outsize overcoat. He wore a cardboard-stiff white shirt with a collar at least two sizes too large and a striped tie so indifferently knotted that its back, label and all, faced front. The make-up man, who was never very far away, had fixed Brando with an elaborate mouth plate that made his jaw heavy and extended his jowls. Brando's complexion was sallow, his eyes were made to droop on the side** and with his graying temples and mustache many people on Mott Street that day did not recognize

him until the filming began.

The two Mafiosi did approve the vintage cars and were amused by the street lamps, pushcarts and prices, circa 1940, tacked up in store windows. But they did not like the way the godfather's assassins fired their guns.

"They hold pieces like flowers," one said.

Shortly before noon a third man came up behind the pair and whispered:

"The old man's around the corner."

The two men were stunned.

"You kidding?" one asked.

"Believe me, he's around the corner."

"Kee-rist!"

"Shooo!"

Without further hesitation—and with the same pitch of excitement most neighborhood people saved for a peek at Brando—the trio left the movie set. They walked quickly toward the intersection and stopped. One of them darted his head around the corner of the building for a quick peek and shot back to his friends: "He's there. He's there. I see his car. I see Paul's guy."

MARIO PUZO'S best seller may have started out to be just another multimillion-dollar movie for Paramount, but it wasn't long before its producers realized that to the Mafiosi themselves the making of "The Godfather' was like the filming of a home movie. Before Puzo's book, cops-and-robbers novels and films about organized crime left the mobsters cold. "The Godfather" was different. When it was published in 1969 word quickly spread across the country's most regularly tapped telephone wires about this different book on the "honored society." It was their "Forsyte Saga." It was filled with bits of underworld gossip, and its characters could be compared to live dons, singers, movie moguls and hit men. It depicted not only their lives, but the lives of their **children, wives, enemies and friends. It emphasized their peculiar code of honor rather than their seedy, greedy little maneuverings. It dealt with** their strong sense of family and their passionate loyalties. It romanticized and exaggerated their political power, wealth and influence in legitimate business. But most important, it humanized rather than condemned them. The godfather himself, for instance, was shot because he refused to deal in the dirty business of narcotics. Sonny Corleone, his impetuous heir, was killed in an ambush because he tried to save his pregnant sister from a brutal husband. Michael Carleone, the godfather's college-educated war-hero son, assumed his father's Mafia mantle not out of greed, but from a sense of responsibility to his father, who, for all his illegal activities, was a far more honorable man than all the crooked cops, venal judges, corrupt politicians and perverted businesmen who peppered the plot.

Though certain Italian-American politicians and organizations condemned Puzo for defaming all Italians, the author heard no such criticism from the society about which he had written. In fact, shortly after his book's publication, Puzo found that some Mafiosi were anxious to meet him. They wanted to compare notes with the author of "The Godfather." They, like other fans, refused to believe that the book was all fiction. In Las Vegas he found that a gambling debt he had run up was somehow marked paid. When Puzo protested he was told, "It's a certain party's pleasure." On other occasions, bottles of champagne would arrive at his table unordered. Multisyllabic names were whispered in his ear by reverential headwaiters, and men with sunglasses and diamond rings waved at him across darkened restaurants.

SIX weeks before the Mott Street shooting of Brando, Albert Ruddy, the film's producer, was uncertain whether he would be able to make the movie at all. Paramount had been deluged with letters describing the project as anti-Italian and threattening demonstrations, boycotts and wildcat strikes by everyone from maintenance men to electricians. Letters had come from Congressmen in New York, New Jersey, Connecticut, Louisiana and Pennsylvania, as well as from dozens of New York State legislators, judges, civic leaders and businessmen.

One of them began: "A book like 'The Godfather' leaves one with the sickening feeling that a great deal of effort and labor to eliminate a false image concerning Americans of Italian descent and also an ethnic connotation to organized crime has been wasted. . . . There are so many careers and biographies that could be made into constructive and intelligent movies, such as the life of Enrico Fermi, the great scientist; Mother Cabrini; Colonel Ceslona, a hero of the Civil War; Garibaldi, the great Italian who unified Italy; William Paca, a signer of the Declaration of Independence; Guglielmo Marconi, and many, many others."

The letter was signed by "the Grand Venerable of the Grand Council of the Grand Lodge of New York State's Sons of Italy." It also informed Paramount that the studio could expect an economic boycott of the film, petitions of protest from all Sons of Italy lodges, regional meetings to plan protests, a complaint filed with the State Human Rights Division and demands that no governmental authorities give the production any cooperation whatever.

And as if this were not enough, there were rumors of union walkouts, work stoppages and boycotts. Ruddy could envision costly delays. He had already run into trouble trying to negotiate with householders in Manhasset, L. I., for a site that looked like a godfather's compound. The entire community and its bureaucrats had ganged up to sabotage his efforts.

"First, they'd complain that we would bring additional cars into the area and take up parking space," Ruddy said. "So we'd promise to bus our people to the locations. Then they'd say they didn't want buses in the area. Some said that if we did use their homes for the mall and the wedding the newspapers couldn't know about it. How could we guarantee that? We were ready to pay, rent, replant, repaint, replace everything in the area for them. We were ready to make all kinds of concessions, but in the end I realized that they just didn't want us. They never flat came out and said no, but it amounted to the same thing.

"For example, the godfather's compound is surrounded by a stone wall, which we had planned to build to our own specifications out of Styrofoam. Well, one day a local official arrives and says we can't build a wall in Manhasset over three feet high that isn't permanent. I tried to explain that sections of the wall had to be removable for special camera angles, to say nothing of the time and expense of building and then tearing down a 12-foot stone wall to run over several people's property. Manhasset was full of that kind of stuff. I began to see the place as a swamp full of quicksand, and before I drowned I decided to start looking for another site and a little help."

Ruddy is a tall, thin, nervously enthusiastic man who sees himself as a shrewd manipulator. At only 36, after all, he had managed to parlay the dubious distinction of producing "Hogan's Heroes" for television and two money-losing films ("Little Fauss and Big Halsy," "Making It") into the job of producing Paramount's biggest potential money maker. Ruddy had always been able to talk his way through obstacles. It was his gift of glibness that got him into the movies in the first place. According to a brief biography put out by Paramount, Ruddy's knowledge and enthusiasm so impressed the Warner Brothers president, Jack L. Warner, at a party that Warner hired Ruddy for an executive post on the spot. At the time of this fortuitous meeting, Ruddy was working for a construction company in Hackensack, N. J.

ON Feb. 25 Al Ruddy went for help. He went in search of a godfather of his own. On that night he was driven to the Park Sheraton Hotel for his first meeting with Joseph Colombo Sr. and about 1,500 delegates of the Italian-American Civil Rights League. Colombo was not only the boss of one of New York's five Mafia families and thereby qualified for godfather status, but also the founder of the League, with which he had established himself as the dominant force in New York's Italian-American community.

In the year since he had founded his group, Colombo had drawn 50,000 people to a rally in Columbus Circle; had forced the Justice Department to order the F.B.I. to stop using the terms "Mafia" and "Cosa Nostra" in its press releases (and had watched the Governors of New York, Connecticut, Alaska, Texas and South Dakota follow suit); had persuaded Frank Sinatra to come to New York to help him raise money at a concert in the Felt Forum, and had been named Man of the Year by The Triboro Post, a New York neighborhood weekly. After 48 years of hiding behind his lapels, Colombo had emerged as a formidable public figure. He posed for pictures, kissed children, signed autographs, talked to Dick Cavett and Walter Cronkite and generally comported himself more like a political candidate than a Mafia boss.

Ruddy approached Colombo confidently that night because he had previously sat in midtown restaurants with Colombo's son, Anthony, and worked out a tentative accord. Ruddy had agreed to delete "Mafia," "Cosa Nostra" and all other Italian words from the script. He had promised to allow the League to review the script and change anything it felt was damaging to the Italian-American image. And finally, he had agreed to turn over the proceeds of the film's New York premiere to the League's hospital fund.

When Ruddy arrived at the Park Sheraton and found 1,500 members of the League seated in the Grand Ballroom looking very dour, he was at first confused. Colombo's son quieted a few of the early boos by telling the delegates about the script deletions Ruddy had agreed to make. He told the crowd about the League's getting the proceeds of the premiere.

"I couldn't care less if they gave us $2-million," the elder Colombo suddenly interjected. "No one can buy the right to defame Italian-Americans."

It was Ruddy's turn then. He said the film would depict individuals and would not defame or stereotype a group. It was really a movie about a corrupt society. A movie about America today. A movie about what happens to poor immigrants faced with prejudice and discrimination. He pointed out that there were many roles in the film, and certainly not all of the bad guys were Italians.

"Look at who's playing the roles," Ruddy said, about to continue with a list of non-Italian villains in the film.

"Who is playing?" Colombo suddenly asked.

"Lots of people," Ruddy said.

"How about a good kid from Bensonhurst?" Colombo asked.

Ruddy smiled. Now he understood. During all his discussions with Anthony Colombo, casting had never been mentioned. Soon, with Colombo pointing to one delegate after another and Ruddy nodding in agreement, the crowd began to cheer as bit players and extras were chosen. At the end of the meeting, Colombo himself inserted in Ruddy's lapel a pin designating him a captain in the League.

Of course not everyone was enchanted with the Ruddy-Colombo agreement. New York State Senator John Marchi felt Colombo would gain a "psychological lift" from such an agreement and that his League would "undoubtedly get more members, because the whole presentation makes it look like the League came home with some prize." When the terms of the agreement appeared on the front pages of newspapers across the country, Charles Bluhdorn, chairman of Gulf and Western, the conglomerate of which Paramount is a part, was outraged. Bluhdorn was reported to have been so angered and embarrassed by Ruddy's arrangement with Colombo—especially when The New York Times published the Page 1, three-column headline: " 'Godfather' Film Won't Mention Mafia"—that he seriously considered firing Ruddy as the producer. However, Bob Evans, Paramount's vice president in charge of production, kept a cooler head. Anyone like Evans, who got his start in the garment center, knows better than to disregard the men in the big hats. Evans knew how much trouble Colombo and his League could make for the film. So Evans prevailed, Bluhdorn's rage was calmed, the furor in the press died down and Ruddy stayed on.

THE moment he reached that agreement with Colombo, Ruddy's troubles were over. There were no more Manhassets. Suddenly, with Colombo's imprimatur, the threats of union woes evaporated. Planned demonstrations and boycotts were called off. A location for the godfather's mall with a garden large enough for the huge wedding sequence was found on Staten Island, and Colombo's men made a house-to-house tour of the neighborhood, smoothing ruffled Italian-American feathers. Somehow, even the protest letters from Italian-American groups stopped once it was understood that an agreement had been reached with the League. When the filming actually began, Ruddy found that with Colombo's men around, instead of being harassed by neighborhood toughs, shaken down by various unions, visited by corrupt cops and generally treated like any other movie company in New York, "The Godfather" troupe was untouchable. The owners of old-fashioned restaurants, funeral parlors and waterfront bars who had been reluctant to rent their facilities to Ruddy changed their minds. One Mulberry Street restaurant whose owner had sworn to his regular customers that no member of "The Godfather" cast would eat in his place had to set up special tables for the actors and crew. "They're O.K.," a League official told the owner. "Let 'em alone." Ruddy even managed to miss being caught in the middle of a war by finishing his location filming in New York just before Colombo was shot and gravely wounded at a League rally at Columbus Circle on June 28.

Before the shooting, Colombo's power could be felt everywhere. During the New York filming, for example, the father of one project member found himself in a hospital recuperating from a minor heart attack. On his second day there, an enormous basket of fresh fruit and flowers arrived bearing red, white and green ribbons and a card signed by Mr. and Mrs. Joseph Colombo Sr. The patient had never met Colombo, had never even seen him, but the presence of that basket changed his hospital life. Doctors began filing into his room to look at it. Smiles materialized on the faces of nurses he had never seen before. The hospital dietitian would arrive in the morning to ask if there was anything he might particularly enjoy that day. His family's visiting hours were suddenly made flexible, and orderlies appeared with the chairs, ice and extra glasses that had been so difficult to find before the Colombo basket arrived.

BESIDES enjoying the benefit of Colombo's help with community relations, the Paramount people found they had uncovered the best of all possible technical advisers. Ruddy and his assistant, Gary Chasen, began to join Colombo associates for drinks at Jilly's and dinners at the Copa. They visited a few of the League's neighborhood offices and eventually were introduced to a couple of the men about whom their movie was being made. Soon such actors as Jimmy Caan, who plays the impetuous Sonny Corleone in the film, joined the socializing.

"They've got incredible moves," Caan said. "I watched them with each other and with their girls and wives. It's incredible how affectionate they are to each other. There's tremendous interplay. They toast each other—'centanni,' 'salute a nostra'—all of this marvelous Old World stuff from guys who were born here and don't even speak Italian.

"I noticed also that they're always touching themselves. Thumbs in the belt. Touching the jaw. Adjusting the shirt. Gripping the crotch. Shirt open. Tie loose. Super dressers. Clean. Very, very neat."

Caan, who prides himself on his mimicry, says he is really indebted to a number of these men for whatever credibility he brings to his part.

"Their moves are easy. You can watch and fake that. But their language, that's something else. They repeat certain words, like 'Where you been, where?' They have a street language all their own. It's not Italian, certainly, and it's not English. One guy, to indicate to another that someone they both knew had been killed, raised his hands in front of him, fixed his fingers like guns and pointed them to the ground. 'Baba da BOOM!' he said, and they all laughed. When we'd go to a bar or somewhere, they were always known. They didn't go where they were not known. They always bought a bottle, too. They didn't buy drinks by the glass. Always a bottle."

Caan, in fact, was seen in the company of Carmine (The Snake) Persico and other federally certified Mafiosi so often and had absorbed so many of their mannerisms that undercover agents thought for a while that he was just another rising young button in the mob.

There was an aura about the production that was unmistakable, just as there is an aura of real and imagined power around the honored society itself. A few of the actors began to think of themselves as Mafia heavies. One supporting player got so confused about who he was that he joined a carload of enforcers on a trip to Jersey to beat up scabs in a labor dispute (as it turned out, they had the wrong address and couldn't find the strikebreakers). And a few Mafiosi began to think of themselves as actors, demonstrating hand gestures and facial expressions over and over for their theatrical pals.

As if assuming the style of their advisers, an extraordinary number of actors and technical people began getting into various degrees of trouble with the police. One actor was arrested for driving with a forged license while another spent a night in jail when a desk officer misread the charge against him as "switchblade" instead of "switched plates." Even the off-duty cops hired as guards on the film got into trouble with their colleagues. They had been instructed by Paramount's public relations office to buy, beg or wrestle cameras away from any photographers who might have taken pictures of Brando in his godfather make-up. Paramount had a deal with Life magazine in which a cover picture of Brando in full make-up would be virtually assured if the movie company could keep other pictures of him from being published. Unfortunately for the moonlighting cops, one of the photographers they roughed up was from The Daily News, and within 20 minutes an inspector, two captains and a deputy police commissioner were on the scene questioning them.

WHEN "The Godfather" opens next spring, Paramount will not only have the distinction of being the first organization in the world to make money on the Mafia, but will also have conned Mafiosi into helping them do it. Now, with the film being edited, Joe Colombo in critical condition, his lieutenants in hiding and Al Ruddy no longer available for their calls, a few mobsters have begun to see that they have been taken. Seated glumly in their Brooklyn cafes or slouching outside their social clubs, they realize that their movie days are over. They no longer go to Jilly's and the Copa with movie stars. There are no more private screenings at the Gulf and Western Building. Today their only contact with Hollywood and the movie they helped to make is through the business section of the trade journals, where they read that their godfather is being turned into a goldmine of by-products. Paramount's merchandising staff is selling the rights for Godfather sweatshirts, Godfather spaghetti and Godfather parlor games. There will be Godfather pizza franchises and Godfather hero shops, bakeries and lemon-ice stands. Books about the filming of "The Godfather" are being commissioned by Paramount, a Godfather television series is planned and another film, called for now "Son of Godfather," is being discussed.

"And when it comes out," one Colombo man active in the first film's production admitted, "it'll cost me three bucks and an hour on line to see." ■

August 15, 1971

Moving and Brutal 'Godfather' Bows

By VINCENT CANBY

Taking a best-selling novel of more drive than genius (Mario Puzo's "The Godfather"), about a subject of something less than common experience (the Mafia), involving an isolated portion of one very particular ethnic group (first-generation and second-generation Italian-Americans), Francis Ford Coppola has made one of the most brutal and moving chronicles of American life ever designed within the limits of popular entertainment.

"The Godfather," which opened at five theaters here yesterday, is a superb Hollywood movie that was photographed mostly in New York (with locations in Las Vegas, Sicily and Hollywood). It's the gangster melodrama come-of-age, truly sorrowful and truly exciting, without the false piety of the films that flourished 40 years ago, scaring the delighted hell out of us while cautioning that crime doesn't (or, at least, shouldn't) pay.

●

It still doesn't, but the punishments suffered by the members of the Corleone Family aren't limited to sudden ambushes on street corners or to the more elaborately choreographed assassinations on thruways. They also include life-long sentences of ostracism in terrible, bourgeois confinement, of money and power but of not much more glory than can be obtained by the ability to purchase expensive bedroom suites, the kind that include everything from the rug on the floor to the pictures on the wall with, perhaps, a horrible satin bedspread thrown in.

Yet "The Godfather" is not quite that simple. It was Mr. Puzo's point, which has been made somehow more ambiguous and more interesting in the film, that the experience of the Corleone Family, as particular as it is, may be the mid-20th-century equivalent of the oil and lumber and railroad barons of 19th-century America. In the course of the 10 years of intra-Mafia gang wars (1945-1955) dramatized by the film, the Corleones are, in fact, inching toward social and financial respectability.

For the Corleones, the land of opportunity is America the Ugly, in which almost everyone who is not Sicilian or, more narrowly, not a Corleone, is a potential enemy. Mr. Coppola captures this feeling of remoteness through the physical look of place and period, and through the narrative's point of view. "The Godfather" seems to take place entirely inside a huge smoky plastic dome, through which the Corleones see our real world only dimly.

Thus, at the crucial meeting of Mafia families, when the decision is made to take over the hard drug market, one old don argues in favor, saying he would keep the trade confined to blacks — "they are animals anyway."

This is all the more terrify-ing because, within their isolation, there is such a sense of love and honor, no matter how bizarre.

The film is affecting for many reasons, including the return of Marlon Brando, who has been away only in spirit, as Don Vito Corleone, the magnificent, shrewd, old Corleone patriarch. It's not a large role, but he is the key to the film, and to the contributions of all of the other performers, so many actors that it is impossible to give everyone his due.

Some, however, must be cited, especially Al Pacino, as the college-educated son who takes over the family business and becomes, in the process, an actor worthy to have Brando as his father; as well as James Caan, Richard Castellano, Robert Duvall, Al Lettieri, Abe Vigoda, Gianni Russo, Al Martino and Morgana King. Mr. Coppola has not denied the charac-ters' Italian heritage (as can be gathered by a quick reading of the cast), and by emphasizing it, he has made a movie that transcends its immediate milieu and genre.

●

"The Godfather" plays havoc with the emotions as the sweet things of life — marriages, baptisms, family feasts — become an inextricable part of the background for explicitly depicted murders by shotgun, garrote, machine gun and booby-trapped automobile. The film is about an empire run from a dark, suburban Tudor palace where people, in siege, eat out of cardboard containers while babies cry and get under foot. It is also more than a little disturbing to realize that characters, who are so moving one minute, are likely, in the next scene, to be blowing out the brains of a competitor over a white tablecloth. It's nothing per-sonal, just their way of doing business as usual.

The Cast

THE GODFATHER, directed by Francis Ford Coppola; screenplay by Mario Puzo and Mr. Coppola, based on the novel by Mr. Puzo; director of photography, Gordon Willis; editors, William Reynolds and Peter Zinner; music composed by Nino Rota; produced by Albert S. Ruddy; distributed by Paramount Pictures. Running time: 175 minutes. At Loew's State I and II, Broadway at 45th Street; Loew's Orpheum and Cine Theaters, Third Avenue and 86th Street; and Loew's Tower East, Third Avenue, near 72d Street. The Motion Picture Association of America's Production Code and Rating Administration classifies this film "R—restricted, persons under 17 not admitted unless accompanied by a parent or adult guardian.")

Don Vito Corleone........Marlon Brando
Michael Corleone..............Al Pacino
Sonny Corleone..............James Caan
Clemenza........Richard Castellano
Tom Hagen..............Robert Duvall
McCluskey..............Sterling Hayden
Jack Woltz..............John Marley
Barzini..............Richard Conte
Kay Adams..............Diane Keaton
Sollozzo..............Al Lettieri
Tessio..............Abe Vigoda
Connie Rizzi..............Talia Shire
Carlo Rizzi..............Gianni Russo
Fredo Corleone..............John Cazale
Cuneo..............Rudy Bond
Johnny Fontane..............Al Martino
Mama Corleone..........Morgana King

March 16, 1972

The Godfather:

A Few Family Murders, But That's Show Biz

The Italian-American Civil Rights League had insisted that the words "Mafia" and "Cosa Nostra" be expunged from the script of "The Godfather." And they were nowhere to be heard last week as the film, starring Marlon Brando as the aging Mafia leader Don Vito Corleone, opened in Manhattan to the sound of critics' cheers and ringing cash registers. Such ethnic epithets as "wop," "dago," "guinea" and "greaser" were liberally peppered throughout the dialogue, but there was not a single offending five-letter word beginning with "M."

Most everyone was content. The financially sagging film industry, and especially Paramount Pictures which produced the show, was jubilant. Bob Evans, head of production at Paramount, predicted that the movie version of Mario Puzo's novel would join the select company of "Gone with the Wind," "The Sound of Music" and "The Graduate" as an all-time top grosser. And the public, already in midstream of a love affair with the Mafia, turned out in droves.

By Friday afternoon, at a time when most New Yorkers might be expected to be wending their way back to the office from a long lunch hour, seats were sold out at most of the five theaters showing the film. By nightfall, in a heavy thunderstrom, long lines of umbrellas stretched for blocks back from the box offices, reminding one observer of "an Italian funeral."

The Mafia is big box office everywhere these days, from book stalls to toy stores, where the Godfather game has been selling briskly for months. The producers of "The Godfather" movie were so confident that the Mafia market would stay hot that they began working on a sequel to "The Godfather" even before they released the original.

Why the fascination with the Mafia? Certainly the mystery behind the organization, with its initiation rites and elaborate code of honor, is a factor. Reading about and viewing men who can seemingly flaunt the law at will but have precise rules of conduct to live by offers vicarious satisfactions to an American public that feels both rootless and powerless. Or perhaps it's just nostalgia for the extended family.

In all the romance with the Mafia, the impact of the organization on the public is somehow forgotten. "The financial cost of organized crime is not limited to the vast illicit profits of gambling or narcotics," wrote the late Robert F. Kennedy. "When the racketeers bore their way into legitimate business the cost is borne by the public. When the infiltration is into labor relations, the racketeer's cut is paid by higher wages and higher prices—in other words by the public. When the racketeer bribes local officials and secures immunity from police action, the price exacted by corrupt law enforcement—incalculable in dollars — is paid, again, by the public."

Such somber thoughts, however, don't seem to trouble those who flock to see The Godfather triumph over his enemies. The resounding success of "The Godfather" in both book and movie form, in fact, has set off a host of imitators. It was reported last week that three other movies on the Mafia were about to begin shooting, including one based on "The Valachi

Papers" by Peter Maas. The film's producer, Dino De Laurentis, added a note of authenticity when he announced that he had received a telephone call warning him to "stop the picture."

The spate of books and films about the underworld has reportedly inspired more than one mobster to think about putting down his gun and picking up a pen. "Crazy Joe" Gallo, scourge of the Mafia establishment during the Profaci-Gallo war in the early 1960's, has already made it official. He has signed up with actor Jerry Orbach, whose wife is writing the mobster's memoirs. Gallo was wed to a dental assistant last week in Mr. Orbach's home. Who will be Boswell to Mr. Big —Carlo Gambino, the most powerful Mafia boss in New York? To what lucky writer will Sam Giancana tell all? Contrary to the prophesies of "Honor Thy Father" author Gay Talese, the Mafia may not fade away but simply go into show business.

Pending future revelations, our best guided tour through the daily life of a Mafia Don is "The Godfather." It reveals that Mafiosi eat pasta, love their wives and children and place a great deal of emphasis on such virtues as honor, respect and family loyalty. By current standards there is very little sex in the film. The only interruptions to the scenes of carnage are scenes of eating and of family festivities.

But the real virtuosity of the film is in its varied and vivid portrayals of murder: by machine gun, bombing, stabbing, but most frequently by a well-placed bullet between, or sometimes in, the eyes. The garrotings are particularly eye-popping.

All the people done away with by the Corleone family are obviously baddies, and unattractive to boot. The members of the Don's family, on the other hand, are good-looking and kind to children. (The old Don dies from a heart attack while playing joyfully in his garden with his grandson.)

An East Side audience last Friday night murmured with satisfaction every time an enemy of the family was dispatched, and the slaughter was choreographed with such precision that one member of the audience was heard to sigh "Beautiful!" at a particularly sanguine execution.

In one scene a rival tells Don Corleone's *consigliere*: "I don't like violence, Tom. I'm a businessman. Blood is expensive."

He might have added that it can also be quite profitable.

—NICHOLAS GAGE

March 19, 1972

Image of the Mafia

The 'families' must keep up with the Joneses—and there's the boredom of hiding out to be contended with.

By GAY TALESE

When the average American citizen thinks about the Mafia, he usually contemplates scenes of action and violence, of dramatic intrigue and million-dollar schemes, of big black limousines screeching around corners with bullets spraying the sidewalk.

This is the Hollywood version and it wildly exaggerates reality, ignoring the dominant mood of Mafia existence: endless waiting, tedium and hiding, excessive smoking, over-eating, lack of physical exercise, reclining in rooms behind drawn shades, being bored to death while trying to stay alive.

With so much time and so little to do with it, the member of the Mafia tends to become self-consumed and self-absorbed, focusing on minutiae and magnifying them, overreacting to each sound, overinterpreting what is said and done, losing perspective of the larger world beyond and his very small place in that world, but nevertheless being aware of the exaggerated image that the world has of him; and he responds to it, believes it, prefers to believe it, for it makes him larger than he is, more powerful, more romantic, more respected and feared.

He can trade on this and profit from it. He can exploit the fact and fantasy of Mafia mythology as effectively as does the F.B.I. director at budget time, the press whenever organized crime is topical, and the movie-makers whenever they can merchandize the myth for a public that invariably wants its characters larger than life — tough-talking, big-spending Little Caesars.

The Mafia man is influenced by the myth and often chooses to live the lie. It feeds his compulsion to lease a Cadillac or Lincoln when he can barely afford payments on a Volkswagen, and to always give the appearance of prosperity, power; although in so doing, the mafioso's life becomes more complex in the larger world where Federal agents are watching him, tapping his phone and bugging his home.

The Mafia man is consequently forced into an almost schizophrenic situation—while he pleads poverty to Internal Revenue, he is also attempting to impress his friends by picking up checks in night clubs and driving big cars.

But he really has no alternative, if he seeks respect in the underworld, or

indeed in the so-called legitimate world of American capitalism, where there exists grudging admiration for dominating "Godfathers," possibly because their style and drive reaffirm American businessmen's belief in individualism and free enterprise.

Thus, it is not difficult to understand why Frank Costello has long been on friendly terms with the Wall Street and merchant princes with whom he takes steambaths at the Biltmore, or why Lucky Luciano was a respected resident at the Waldorf.

The opulence and influence of gang leaders today, however, is highly inflated by Federal law-enforcement authorities, a fact apparent to any reader of the published F.B.I. transcripts of recorded conversations between Mafia members, whose dialogue is characterized by elaborate haggling over remarkably small sums of money.

It is also obvious to anyone who has visited a Mafia leader's home that the residences described as "palatial" are in fact quite small and modest. Many crime reporters seem to have a fixation, too, about building up small Mafia feuds into "wars." A recent war in New York involving the Bonanno "family," which began in 1966 with shootings on Troutman Street in Brooklyn and extended through 1969, accounted for nine deaths; and the Profaci-Gallo rivalry in Brooklyn between 1961 and 1963 accounted for only a dozen murders, which is possibly less than the number of murders each month among married American couples.

If compared with publicized atrocities by allied troops on civilians in Asia, the exploits of the Mafia hardly seem to justify the public attention that it receives; and it would not be receiving it were it not for the mythology factor, the George Raft reality, the fact that the Mafia today, like Communism in the fifties, has become part of a national illusory complex shaped by curved mirrors that give an enlarged and distorted view of everything it reflects, a view that is widely believed because it fills some strange need among average American citizens for grotesque portraits of murderous villains who bear absolutely no resemblance to themselves.

October 5, 1971

Marlon Brando, alias The Godfather

CHAPTER **3**

A Sickness in Society

Youth Delinquency Growing Rapidly Over the Country

Year's Rise Is 20% in City and State, 10% in Nation—Study Attributes Lag in Correctives to Public Attitude

By LUCY FREEMAN

Juvenile delinquency is on the rise in the city, the state and the nation. It increased 20 per cent in New York City last year over 1950, 20 per cent in the state and 10 per cent in the country as a whole.

The upward trend that started three years ago is continuing at a sharp incline, reversing the decrease that began at the end of World War II, according to the latest figures released by authorities for a study of delinquency conducted by THE NEW YORK TIMES.

National authorities are concerned about the rise, as indicated by court statistics, but they are even more concerned about the scarcity of thoughtful, intensive plans for combating delinquency on a steady basis.

The public gets alarmed in sporadic cycles, perhaps first about sex offenders, then narcotic addicts, but lacks convictions about the causes of delinquency, they say. This makes it difficult to set up treatment facilities to help seriously troubled children or to prevent delinquency.

"The lack of treatment facilities represents a serious gap in almost every locality in the nation," says Richard Clendenen, national authority on delinquency. He is consultant on training schools in the Division of Social Services, United States Children's Bureau.

The scarcity of persons who possess both the artistry and skill to help children is another weakness in the nation's effort to curb delinquency.

As youth seems to be committing more serious offenses, like resorting to narcotics and the use of violence, the courts are getting more emotionally disturbed children. This extreme behavior of youth, authorities suggest, may reflect the impact of the Korean war and the psychological effects of national and international insecurity.

Leaders in the field are concerned about the large number of children kept in jails, sometimes alongside hardened criminals. One-tenth of the 1,000,000 children apprehended annually by the police are sent to jails because communities have no other place for them, Mr. Clendenen estimates.

What is delinquency? Ten experts are likely to give ten different answers. However, many authorities agree that "delinquents" are likely to be emotionally disturbed children whose rebellion against law and order reflects deeper revolt against the adult world.

Therefore, they say, to obtain from these children a future respect for the law it is necessary to help them feel secure and happy enough so they have no cause to rebel.

Delinquency usually rises following the start of a war and in times of economic prosperity. Adult crime decreases during prosperity. The reverse occurs during depressions, with adult crime increasing and juvenile delinquency decreasing, the Children's Bureau notes.

Effects of Defense Program

The increase today is attributed, in some part, to the effects of defense mobilization. Families are once again on the move, women are entering the labor market and the number of "latchkey kids" is growing.

"Whenever a nation goes through a period of tension, the children are apt to suffer," Mr. Clendenen says.

He believes that the psychological effect on youth of the general insecurity is important, with boys facing service in the armed forces and girls facing the possibility of husbandless homes if they marry and have children.

"The reasons for children getting into trouble are the same yesterday as forever—revolt, rebellion, the need for self-expression, denied to them, somehow, in a natural way," says John Warren Hill, Chief Justice of the Domestic Relations Court of New York.

"However, the form in which the revolt expresses itself is undoubtedly more serious today than previously, perhaps because of the heightened, more startling pace of life. Those in revolt seem to be revolting more violently."

Many authorities feel that narcotic addiction in youth has been "overly dramatized." It has occurred chiefly in the large coastal cities where there is access to the drug.

"Addiction is a serious symptom of troubled youth, but we feel that the youngsters involved represent only a small portion of those in need of good services," says Mr. Clendenen. "They have drifted into this kind of escape pattern by reason of access to the drug. We feel that if we can control the source of distribution, this symptom of maladjustment may be more easily taken care of than others."

"Many things are happening just as destructive to children in the long run, about which we are far more complacent," he warns. He mentions stealing and truancy, saying these are related to the fundamental problem of conflict with the adult world, and may result in narcotics addiction, other serious offenses or in crime in later years.

Preventives Cut Court Load

One reason that crimes brought to court may appear more serious is that community agencies have been doing a better job in handling the less serious cases and the courts tend to get the difficult children that other agencies have tried to help and failed. A better preventive job is also going on in the community.

Justice Hill observes this in discussing the city's problems. He reports that court cases are still increasing, with more in the first two months of this year than a year ago. He emphasizes, too, that the court is not the only "barometer" of delinquency, because the schools, private agencies and juvenile aid bureau are working to keep children out of the court, to help them before they get into serious trouble.

New York is not keeping abreast of developments in other parts of the country, according to Will Turnbladh, executive director of the National Probation and Parole Association. Justice Hill is the first to recognize this, for he has been battling for better court care for eighteen years.

One handicap in New York is that the head of the Children's Court is lost in the large city administration, authorities explain. In Ohio, for instance, judges have a greater control over their budgets and do not have to go begging to City Hall.

Courts are better staffed in many communities than in New York, offering higher salaries, longer tenure and lower caseloads. Some courts require full professional training, but New York cannot command this because of the low salaries. Probation salaries start at $2,960 here as compared with $3,600 and $4,000 in some other places.

Staff turnover is high because of the low salaries. Justice Hill said that it was 20 per cent last year as compared, for instance, to 10 per cent in Connecticut over a three-year period. In Connecticut the caseload is thirty-five for a probation officer; in New York it is sixty, in addition to fifteen or more investigations a month.

Lack of Mental Care Provision

The Children's Court here is "woefully handicapped" by inadequate psychiatric facilities, both diagnostic and treatment, says Justice Hill. The diagnostic clinic handles 1,800 to 2,000 cases a year, many of which must wait six weeks to two months, and present treatment services provide for only 200 children a year, whereas at least 500 additional children are equally in need.

Institutional facilities are not available for many children who should be committed. For a large group of children under twelve, there is no place and any delinquent child who is "pre-psychotic" and whose parents refuse to commit him, or who is "a borderline mental defective," must be returned home, regardless of the seriousness of his offense.

There are few facilities for "the psychopathic child" who should be segregated, "not sent to an institution which offers a treatment program for the child who knows the difference between right and wrong and who is able to adhere to the right," Justice Hill says.

The appointment of judges as a political reward, rather than on the basis of their understanding of human relations, is another sore spot in the city's attempts to provide better care for its troubled children.

Warning that statistics may be misleading, Justice Hill says: "For instance, our calendars used to be full of children whose offense was jumping over a subway turnstile, hopping on a bus, begging alms or shining shoes without a permit. That is no longer considered delinquency for the court."

There were 5,538 allegedly delinquent children in 1951 compared with 4,805 in 1950. This is the highest number since 1945 when there were 6,008. But there were 6,640 cases in 1943 and 6,975 in 1944, a sharp rise from the 4,904 in 1942.

Of last year's cases, 14.7 per cent were committed to institutions from New York City as compared with 16.7 per cent from the rest of the state. In the city 52.6 per cent were placed on probation as compared to 56.4 per cent in the rest of the state. Of last year's cases, 4,558 were boys and 980 girls. Brooklyn was the borough with the highest number of delinquents, followed by Manhattan.

"The increase, however, is not so important as what we are doing to meet the over-all needs," Justice Hill sums up.

Steps Taken by City Groups

In an attempt to meet the city's needs the New York City Youth Board is approaching the problem of delinquency with a far-reaching program that centers on mobilizing existing resources, working toward better coordination and granting financial aid to expand effective means of treatment.

Early treatment of maladjusted youngsters whose behavior could develop into delinquency, "reaching out" with service to parents who are either unaware of their children's problems or too frightened to seek out resources, and substituting constructive social and athletic programs for anti-social gang activities are also in its approach.

A series of studies, expected to have nation-wide significance, is being conducted by the Citizens Committee on Children of New York City. They show how various agencies can function in a protective and preventive role, starting with the schools, then the police, and finally the courts.

Alfred Kahn, research consultant to the committee, who is on the faculty of the New York School of Social Work, is directing the studies. The last one, "A Court for Children," will be completed this fall. The first, "Children Absent from School," was published in 1949, and the second, "Police and Children," in 1951.

Figures show that while New York City's increase is 20.3 per cent in 1951 over the year before, for the rest of the state the increase was 14.3 per cent over the 1950 total, according to Commissioner Lee Dowling, head of the New York State Youth Commission.

"While a percentile increase of 20 per cent is not considered alarming, the Youth Commission is continuing to watch and look into the situation very closely, as previous studies show that, particularly in metropolitan war industry areas, juvenile delinquency swings upward during a defense preparation period and further upward during a war period," he says.

The Commission plans to continue to examine the situation in any community reflecting an abnormal increase in an effort to identify the causes so the community may deal with the situation, he notes. It will report on conditions so that each locality may mobilize its resources "to counteract these influences and protect its children, for causes vary community by community and no single reason will apply on a state-wide basis."

Probation Services Weak

On the national scene, the Children's Bureau reports that juvenile court delinquency cases in 1950 were 4 per cent higher than 1949, just as the 1949 figure was 4 per cent above 1948.

Reports to the Federal Bureau of Investigation on police arrests of youths under 18 showed the 1950 figure was 5 per cent over 1949. Such arrests during the first six months of 1951 were 9 per cent above those in the 1950 period.

To the juvenile courts over the country come 300,000 children each year. Both the courts and the police who bring in the children are failing to make full use of their ability or that of available community resources to help the children, authorities say.

Too many of these children are separated from their families and sent to institutions because the courts do not have probation officers. Less than half of the counties in the country have a juvenile probation service and many of these are not very strong services.

To the country's training schools are committed 35,000 boys and girls. Some of these schools are extending an understanding hand, but some are still operating on a fifty-year-old philosophy, even beating and starving children as disciplinary measures.

Thousands of adolescents are homeless and without supervision and many of them become delinquent. Large numbers are then committed to training schools and remain there indefinitely. Plans to care for the children after they have left institutions are almost nil. Small group homes for them would help reduce delinquency, authorities say.

The problem of getting trained personnel to work with children is stressed by Dean Kenneth D. Johnson of the New York School of Social Work, a former Juvenile Court judge. He has pioneered in programs to train social workers for this field and to get salaries raised.

Great numbers of courts, and other agencies as well, are handicapped by the complete lack of clinical facilities to treat the severely disturbed child.

Uneven Institutional Care

The country's laws permit injustices to children. For instance, some states still allow the commitment of children to penitentiaries. The lack of uniform state laws prevents cooperation between states in relation to both the control and treatment of children who get into trouble.

The training schools over the nation vary in the type of treatment they give. Some of the publicly operated schools, such as the Illinois State Training School for Boys in St. Charles, the training school in Topeka, Kan, and the schools in New York and New Jersey, are extending to the children an understanding hand.

Of the private residential treatment centers, Hawthorne-Cedar Knolls in Pleasantville, N. Y., maintained by the Jewish Board of Guardians, is internationally known for its progressive program.

The Child Welfare League of America is conducting a nation-wide study of residential treatment centers which will contain a description of both the medical and non-medical. Joseph Reid, assistant executive director, and Helen Hagan, research consultant, are in charge of the study, to be published soon.

Authorities are urging that the crime problem be attacked at its source and that services be improved for the care of delinquents and prevention of delinquency. They maintain that the reason we are still attacking the symptoms and results, rather than causes, is that the public holds the attitude that children who rebel must be "punished" rather than helped to understand themselves more deeply.

There must be a change in this attitude, they contend, that will come only with an understanding that in many instances these are emotionally ill children. Then, they say, delinquency can be materially cut down over the nation. Only when the public is willing to back better care for troubled children will there be progress in such areas as probation, appointment of wise judges, preventive work in schools and more intensive treatment by training schools and community agencies.

Philosophy Now Definitive

More general acceptance of the newer philosophy about delinquency is urged. It is expressed thus:

"If a child is emotionally healthy, his actions will be normal, healthy actions. If he is suffering from emotional turmoil, his behavior and his reactions will show it."

Dr. Robert M. Gluckman, psychiatrist and clinical director of therapy, Illinois State Training School for Boys, says this in an introduction to "Why Children Misbehave," a Better Living Booklet for Parents and Teachers written by Charles W. Leonard, the school's superintendent

One thing that confuses discussion about delinquency is its varying quality. "Juvenile Delinquency and the Schools," a recent report of the assistant superintendents of the Board of Education, New York City, says:

"One of the characteristics of delinquency is its shifting frame of reference. The child who steals and is apprehended is legally a delinquent; the one who steals without being apprehended, is not. The boy who breaks a store window and whose parents refuse, or are unable, to pay for it is a delinquent; the one whose parents pay for it is not.

"The girl involved in sex difficulties in a culturally deprived home frequently is labeled delinquent; the one from a home better able to care for her is not. The child who is emotionally disturbed and commits an anti-social act is a delinquent if his family is unable to obtain psychiatric service for him, while another child with the same problem who received such help is not a delinquent.

"The child in a slum area who becomes a nuisance on the street because of the lack of recreational facilities may be labeled a delinquent, while the child with the same drives and similar behavior in a more privileged area where recreational facilities are available, or where the family can afford special facilities, is not.

"Perhaps these are some of the reasons why underprivileged areas yield so large a proportion of delinquents, compared with privileged areas. Other factors enter, of course."

Juvenile delinquency, in addition to being associated with broken homes, family strife and emotional stress, is also part of broad social and economic problems such as slum housing, low incomes, discrimination against minority groups and lack of employment and educational opportunities, authorities say. They urge communities to attack all problems adversely affecting children, if they are serious about reducing delinquency.

Teen Gangs Spawned by Longing for Friends

How One Street Club Got Sidetracked as a Social Unit

By CHARLES GRUTZNER

There are between eighty and 100 juvenile gangs that fight one another in the streets of New York. Yet, there is no such thing as a typical street gang.

The gangs vary greatly in size, composition, dress, protocol, choice of weapons and degree of criminality. One of the few things they have in common, besides pushing delinquency statistics to new heights and constituting a top civic worry, is that they are all—even the most murderous—founded on friendship.

"The guts of the whole problem is that these are friendship groups of teen-agers," said James E. McCarthy, who directs nineteen field workers of the City Youth Board assigned to twenty-two gangs. These twenty-two were, and some still are, among the worst street gangs in East Harlem and Brooklyn.

"Maybe it sounds funny to put it like this," said Mr. McCarthy. "But practically all these kids who cut, shoot and bop one another joined up for friendship. For every street club that went bad somewhere along the way, there are ten or more that stay out of serious trouble."

Story of One Gang

Here is the story of one gang, how it began as a social club, where and why it got off the track to run wild in the jungle of waywardness, and what is happening to it now:

The Minotaurs are sixty-five boys, between their fifteenth and twentieth birthdays. Thirty-eight have police records; fifteen are known to use narcotics, although less than half of these have reached the stage of addiction to heroin.

There is a "debbie" (debutante) adjunct of about three dozen girls, aged 14 to 17. The sorority, not as tightly organized as the boys' club, has greater fluctuation of membership. The girls are the "steadies" for the gang's "sessions" (house parties and dances). Some carry their boy friends' knives and guns.

The Minotaurs, operating in East Harlem, are Puerto Ricans. In other parts of the city are gangs exclusively or predominantly Italian, Irish or Negro, and many of mixed membership. Somewhere among the street fighters are found members of almost every nationality group of substantial strength in New York's population.

Some youth gang fights are caused by racial friction in communities of shifting population, where such tensions run high among adults, too. Most often, though, the issues have nothing to do with ethnology.

On many occasions gangs of the same race or color fight against one another.

Minotaurs is not the true name of the gang. Similarly, fictitious names will be used for other real gangs. This is necessary to protect their members from notoriety. Public identification would endanger and possibly destroy whatever relationship the Youth Board workers have established with gang members in proving their "regularity" by helping find jobs, outfit teams, arrange dances and aiding some of them clear themselves of trouble.

Avoid Mass Fights

The Minotaurs, like many of the longer-established gangs, avoid "rumbles" (mass fights) if a sneak raid on an enemy will avenge an insult or settle a score. A raid is made by two to six chosen members, using pistols or knives. The Minotaurs prefer these two weapons. If they are mobbed, or forced to use mass strength, they use also lead pipes and baseball bats.

Like some larger entities, the Minotaurs exaggerate their armed strength. They try to give the impression that every other fellow carries a "piece" (firearm). There are maybe half a dozen firearms in the aggregation. Perhaps half the members carry knives.

Why do they fight, if not for fun? They fight—unless mediation, often arranged by the Youth Board workers, results in keeping peace without losing reputation—because a member has been "jumped" by a rival gang. Perhaps the worst insult is when a Minotaur is waylaid and his blue and fuchsia blazer ripped.

Wars start, too, when outsiders try to "crash" a "session" or a rival wins a gang member's girl. Gang fights also start over unpaid loans, minor thefts, or the sort of rhubarb in an athletic contest similar to what, in a National League ball park, would cause nothing more drastic than Leo Durocher's being banished to the showers.

The Minotaurs became involved in at least one quarrel, where bloodshed was narrowly averted, because of the way a Golden Nugget walked down their street. There is a "cool" way of walking that is recognized in Spanish Harlem as a studied insult to bystanders. A Minotaur demonstrated it yesterday — a slow, deliberate, pantherlike light tread, chin high, eyes half closed, and head swaying very slightly from side to side. It was the epitome of aloofness and disdain, once witnessed forever after recognizable.

There was a time when virtually nothing short of physical attack would rouse the Minotaurs to arms. It wasn't that they were "chicken," either. They were a street club then, much bigger than now, but not a street war club.

The East Harlem Minotaurs, in their early and peaceful years, didn't even call themselves Minotaurs. They called themselves the Carib Lords and grew, from about 1945 to 1950, to about 150 members ranging in age from 11 to about 22, and graded as Midgets, Juniors, Intermediates and Seniors, with a Debutante sorority.

The Carib Lords had stickball and other teams. They had their "sessions" and picnics and they made good use of the facilities of a neighborhood settlement house. They were much like the 1,000 or more street clubs that today draw little police attention outside the Police Athletic League.

There was at that time a Minotaur gang, under sinister leadership, on Washington Heights. It was made up of Puerto Rican youths. The leader, a flashy, well-heeled character who called himself El Toro, found life among the Latin colony on Washington Heights too drab. Over in East Harlem, the "Barrio" of New York's Spanish-speaking population, the girls were prettier and there were more of them; the dances livelier; the bars gayer; and night life in general much more colorful.

The original Minotaurs continued their warfare with other upper West Side gangs, but El Toro and his closest cronies spent ever more time in East Harlem. Their escapades there led inevitably to fights with indigenous gangs. The Minotaurs "rumbled" with the High Hats and the Palms. The Carib Lords, not being a war gang, played it neutral at first.

Needed New Allies

El Toro, spreading himself out in East Harlem, needed new allies. But they had to be fighting allies. El Toro began cultivating certain Lords. He spent freely and made a big splash at "sessions" and settlement house functions to which he wangled invitations. He had the money to spend; he was "pushing" narcotics. His police record included also arrests for assault and other crimes.

Some of the younger Lords, seduced by the flamboyant way of life El Toro seemed to hold out for them, became restive within their club's legal channels. They called for joining the wars to "make a rep" for themselves. The situation caused the eventual dissolution of the Carib Lords. The bolder members went over to El Toro, organizing an East Harlem Minotaur gang. The evil influence triumphed, for the time being, over the good.

El Toro, a waif who had been in and out of institutions since early childhood, was now a stocky 5 foot 7, a "shrewdie" who had a boy of 15 or younger carry his knife. Thus, in his several arrests, he managed to avoid the charge of carrying a weapon. The boy was kept, by his age, out of any but Children's Court. El Toro hung about settlement houses and evaluated gang rumors. He picked up the outcasts of other street gangs to recruit his strength.

A restless soul, El Toro grasshoppered over the metropolitan area, building up or taking over local gangs. At one time the Minotaurs had more than twenty loosely federated units in East Harlem, West Harlem, the Bronx, Brooklyn and Newark. Besides pushing narcotics, El Toro dealt in girls and extortion. He is now in jail awaiting trial on one of several charges.

A stickler for formality and written reports, probably as a result of his institutional upbringing, El Toro made the Minotaur meetings more ceremonial than those of most gangs. Minutes were kept and votes taken whether to "burn" (fight) or "talk" (mediate) over an insult, real or fancied. There was balloting, too, on where and when to have a "session," what color trousers to buy (gray flannels were chosen); how to deal with this or that rumor; and what to do about that puzzling character, the "job man."

The "job man," it turned out, was a fellow, a few years older than most Minotaurs, who sometime in 1951 began hanging out in bars, candy stores and other places frequented by the gang. He'd drop nickels in the jukebox, stand treat for beers or Cokes, and openly courted the good graces of the gang members.

Was he "queer"? Was he a cop? What was his game, anyway? For a while he was treated with undisguised hostility, later with suspicious toleration. He got jobs for a few of the fellows. Someone asked what was his racket, and he replied he was a social worker sent by the Youth Board to try to help the fellows.

New Friend to Gang

"You mean you get paid doing this kind of stuff?" asked an amazed Minotaur. The youth worker was eventually accepted as a friend. The Youth Board sent other workers to the gangs with whom the Minotaurs fought.

Soon other gangs began asking why they didn't have a worker assigned to them. This wasn't because they were getting soft; it was a matter of "rep." You just didn't figure as a real tough gang unless the Youth Board sent you a worker.

In this sort of climate, the youth workers make some head-

182

way, lose some ground, but somehow wind up making gains for law and order. The Minotaurs have in the last four years killed one boy in a street fight, shot three others and knifed several, none fatally. Two of their own members were killed, one shot non-fatally and several knifed.

The Minotaurs still meet formally about once a week. They pay 25 cents a week dues. Their blazers, with club name stamped in large letters and the boy's name embroidered small, cost $20, half of which comes from the treasury and half is defrayed by the boy. But if a youngster hasn't the money, a vote is taken and the club meets the full bill. The boys wear garrison belts—thick leather with heavy metal buckle. This is part of the street uniform and is handy in a fight.

The Minotaurs are one of eighteen East Harlem gangs with an aggregate membership of about 750 boys and girls. These gangs, which were or still are social problems, devote only a small fraction of their time to anti-social activities, but the danger of a "rumble" or a "Jap"—as they call their sneak raids—is always there.

The 750 members of the problem gangs are a small but certainly not insignificant fraction of the 21,000 youths between the age of 15 and 19 living in East Harlem. How do the 750 differ from the more than 20,000 others? There's no quick and easy answer, said Mr. McCarthy.

A large percent of the gang members come from broken homes, are chronic truants and can't seem to get along in school. But many of the gang members are bright. They feel a need to "belong," said Mr. McCarthy. The old lure of friendship.

The word "gang" is taboo among the field workers. They call them street clubs. They see their job chiefly as turning the anti-social clubs, as they call the gangs, back to social neighborhood clubs. Ralph W. Whelan, executive secretary of the Youth Board, said yesterday that some of the new funds voted by the Board of Estimate to combat delinquency would be used to assign workers to other gangs, especially in the Bronx.

Vitality of Schools Sapped By Delinquency Rise Here

Survey Shows Educators Bear Brunt of Old Problem That Has Its Roots in Swiftly Changing Social Order

By MILTON BRACKER

New York City's public school system is being harassed and sapped by increasing problems of discipline and delinquency.

But the problems are being projected into the schools by the swiftly changing life of the community—not the other way around.

That central fact—the conclusion of a month's inquiry—is overlooked or misunderstood by thousands of New Yorkers. They are naturally distressed and fearful over recurrent incidents of outrage and crime involving pupils. Some—but not the gravest—of these incidents have taken place in or near schools.

The metropolitan school system comprises 1,000,000 pupils, 40,000 teachers, 800 schools. It is a $407,278,035 item in the 1955-56 budget. That means 23 cents out of every budget dollar.

The situation in the schools is disturbing but not frightful. It is receiving constant attention. The May 8 report by Deputy Mayor Henry Epstein pointed up both the concern of the city administration with delinquency generally and with the schools' varied potential to combat it. A committee of the Board of Education to study means of implementing the report was appointed even before the document was placed before the Board of Estimate.

For by and large the schools tend to curb delinquency, not to foster or spread it. The recent incidents within the schools—the occasional assaults, extortion, fire-setting, theft and vandalism that have made news—should be viewed in perspective.

During unannounced visits to dozens of schools on all levels in all boroughs and in private conversations with principals and teachers after school hours the educators on the committee were asked among other things what was the "worst" single disciplinary or delinquency episode in their experience.

There were some shocking replies. A man who is now an associate superintendent of schools had witnessed the fatal stabbing of a 9-year-old girl by a schoolmate at Public School 119 in West Harlem. He recalled how, when they brought in the 12-year-old offender, she had kept insisting, "I don't want to look at her, I don't want to look at her." Many teachers recalled the fatal shooting of a mathematics instructor at Junior High School 49, Brooklyn, by former pupils who had invaded the schoolyard.

There were other grim recollections. A woman was chased around a gym by an adolescent "yammering obscenities." Another was pursued and threatened by a girl gang as she escorted home the victim of its extortion.

But every one of these incidents occurred more than ten years ago. The stabbing of Margaret Patton, witnessed by John F. Conroy, then a district superintendent, took place on May 9, 1944. The teacher, Irwin Goodman, was killed by zoot-suiters on Oct. 2, 1942. (Two months later, in a letter to Police Commissioner Lewis A. Valentine, the Teachers Guild appealed for protection against further incidents "which vary in gravity from outright murder to mere threat.")

Other Instances 30 Years Ago

The other instances dated from one to three decades ago. The point is, gross and criminal misbehavior in the city schools is not a new phenomenon. Many teachers believe that the "tough" schools of 1955 are nothing in comparison with those to which they were assigned, say, in 1935.

That was the year in which a man arriving at Junior High School 83, in East Harlem, was advised to "wear a bullet-proof vest." The school served Italian and Negro populations. It was the year Mussolini invaded Ethiopia.

But without losing perspective, it is still possible to list certain types of abuses that seem to be increasing. The school system is vast, and the data are often incomplete and invariably qualified. But the following elements emerge:

¶The general level of respect for authority, of classroom dress, discipline and language, has declined. Pupils take "freer" behavior for granted, and they get annoyed quickly when they think it is about to be curtailed.

¶The stress and strain on teachers and principals because of disciplinary matters has increased and tend to vitiate the curricular program. It is much harder to "save the teacher's face" in classroom incidents. The situation is chronically worse in the 105 junior high schools, but acutely worse in the thirty-one vocational high schools where the city's 8,000 continuation school students reluctantly attend classes.

¶Overt delinquency—violence, gang behavior, theft, vandalism—is likely to be more common in schools in deteriorated neighborhoods. But neurotic and even psychotic behavior, and the disruptive influence of the problem child, may play havoc in a "country club" or "silk stocking" school.

New Conventions Accepted

The post-war trend toward less respect of pupil for teacher has been widely noted. (Charles H. Silver, president of the Board of Education, has reminded that the cycle of war, family instability and delinquency, caused the "same problem" after both the Civil War and World War I.) To an extent, the free and easy attitude has been accepted by many teachers, as by many parents. The old schoolroom conventions no longer apply.

The fact that dungarees and an unzipped, star-trimmed windbreaker are often standard attire for boys, and that neckties are rare, is not in itself important. But a fad for garrison belts may be important, if only because they make cruel weapons. Some principals have banned them. More significant is the fact that the careless informality often carried with it a rough, tough cynical attitude that approaches outright hoodlumism as its limit. This harsh informality is noticeable in girls, too, although for timeless reasons they are still likely to be neater.

One trend often cited was that girls share—and in some cases predominate—in the increased use of the oral and written language that ranges from casual vulgarity through arrant profanity and obscenity.

Whether the girls realize that their use of certain phrases would have been considered incredible twenty or thirty years ago is debatable. Some teachers believe the girls simply take lower language standards as part of a way of life.

But a majority of sources agreed that girls' corridor, washroom and even classroom language was unmistakably worsening. The principal of one combined elementary and junior high school in East New York sighed that "we're down to the plaster" in terms of trying to keep the girls' washroom free of scrawls. And the dean of girls in an academic high school in Queens noted that both audible and visible evidence—on walls, in notebooks and in handbags—suggested that the girls were the worst language offenders.

Direct aggressive use of foul imperatives by a pupil to a teacher is more often—but not always—attributed to a boy. At a "tough" Manhattan high school, where a sixth-grade girl had scalded the ears of a substitute teacher on his first day, the mother was summoned. The teacher said later she seemed more annoyed by being called than by her child's offense.

Wear and tear on faculties is severe in the junior high schools, primarily because these schools handle the most robustious teenagers—13 to 15 years old. Confronted with what some called "adolescent tyranny," junior high school principals are not shielded from classroom incidents by deans and department heads, as in the high schools. The principal is likely to be right behind the firing line all day. It tells on him.

Moreover, the junior high school division is expanding more rapidly than any other. As of February, more than 2,000 of its 5,088 teachers were substitutes or elementary school teachers on waivers. In general, the percentage of substitute and inexperienced teachers is greatest in the junior highs. When Deputy Mayor Epstein referred to a "real need for re-evaluation of our teacher rotation policies," the reference applied closely to the situation in this division.

An early teen-ager, often fortified by a gang organization, is quick to sense the vulnerability of a substitute. Two recent cases of teacher-punching by junior high school pupils merely pointed up an old and uneasy relationship.

But inevitably, the problem is most serious in the vocational schools—sometimes unjustly called the "dumping ground" of the system. Here the pupils are usually over 15. Their median I. Q. runs eighteen or twenty points below that in the academic highs and—perhaps most importantly—the school population includes a few hundred boys on a "continuation" basis. These are all 16 and working full time, but are required by law to attend classes four hours a day, one day a week, until their seventeenth birthday.

There are few exceptions to the rule that these part-timers dislike, resent, even hate going to school. Their teachers are fully aware of this reluctance.

The most recent court appearance of a youth charged with assaulting a teacher involved a continuation student at the East New York Vocational School annex. The teacher had refused a request for a pass to leave school early.

Many of the boys regard the continuation system as "senseless." And last year the Superintendent's Committee on Delinquency in the Secondary Schools recommended scrapping the continuation attendance system and substituting a "program of guidance and follow-up of 16-year-olds who may be working."

At one vocational school, proud in general of its classroom relations despite a poor neighborhood and the reputation for being one of the "worst" schools in the system, faculty members openly refer to the part-time students as "almost uncontrollable." One teacher called the continuation school program a "farce."

Manifestations of Hostility

Brooding hostility is common among the part-timers in a school such as this. During the reporter's visit, a continuation group was gathered thinly in an assembly hall for the scheduled showing of a guidance film. For some reason, the film had failed to show up. The class was left to spend the period listening to popular music, which filtered down hoarsely from a loud-speaker over the entrance.

Near the rear sat a sullen boy with tousled dark hair. One arm was draped over the back of his seat. He did nothing. He said nothing. But there was on his face the most naked expression of bitterness. He was bored, distrustful and angry. He was a stark symbol of the problem of the continuation school system, although many of his contemporaries show their feelings in a cocky, pugnacious or destructive way.

Finally, with regard to the incidence of overt delinquency, it is possible to gauge the trouble within a school by the delinquency rate in the surrounding community. Official figures of the New York City Youth Board show the aggravated nature of the problem in certain neighborhoods.

For example, in a strip of Manhattan between West 125th and West 165th Streets, the rate of 5 to 20-year-old offenders has risen steadily since 1951. The strip includes nine public schools. Six of them are in areas in which the rate has nearly doubled.

In these schools, many of the pupils come from homes where both parents work—the child is likely to appear in class with an apartment key around its neck. Or the child may come in sleepy, because its shared bed is in an overcrowded room in which adults stay up late watching television. But the situation is worse when there is only one parent, or where more than one family live together and the marital and parental status of the adults is dubious.

From homes such as these often come the pupils most likely to become truants, to snatch purses, to set fires, to run in gangs, to abuse or attack the teacher. But the picture presented by such homes is still only part of the over-all school delinquency problem.

There are also the humble but respectable homes where, as Mr. Epstein pointed out, the parents, like many down the preceding decades, "have failed their children, not out of malice or indifference but because they did not know the new ways—or were too troubled getting acquainted with a new land and a new way of life."

Moreover, predelinquency also shows up in the "good" schools in the upper middleclass neighborhoods where, according to worn-down teachers in other areas, it must be a joy to teach.

This is not always so. Overt delinquency may be less in such a school, just as the delinquency rate for the neighborhood is lower. But neurotic behavior persists. There are cases of withdrawal, aggression, vandalism and theft. Occasionally a pupil is kept from becoming a court case because its parents can afford to satisfy the demands of a complainant.

In such schools, teachers see the influence of some parents' marital difficulties and social pretensions. In one elementary school on Madison Avenue the question of who is or is not invited to a classmate's home has had classroom ramifications.

The contrast between a "tough" and a "silk stocking" school within a few miles of each other on the same thoroughfare was put, ironically, by one experienced educator. She acknowledged that in some homes that send children to the first school there was often "no father" and there were sometimes "two fathers." But in the other school, she observed, owing to divorce and remarriage, many of the children had "two sets of parents."

"Sometimes I wonder which is worse," she remarked.

The delinquency rate affecting the first school was 60.8 for each thousand as against 7.1 in the second. The educator knew this. But she was making the point that in both cases the influence of an irregular parental situation was likely to show up in school. The child may become a "legal" delinquent in one instance and a fearful or bullying neurotic in the other.

The overburdened school system must cope with both.

May 23, 195☐

Juvenile Delinquency: A Variety of Views

The rise in juvenile delinquency continues to baffle parents and disturb the experts. Here is a sampling of opinion, representing many fields, on what is behind the persistent problem and what may be done about it.

CAUSES

"Nothing is more conducive to child delinquency than a monotonous, day by day existence where the child is never encouraged, or where he is never sure of himself and those around him." —Judge Sarah T. Hughes, Dallas, Texas.

"An element of oversight, carelessness, disinterest or ineptitude in the discharge of parental duties appears in almost every case. In some we find willful fault." —Judge George W. Smyth, Westchester County, N. Y.

"Separated parents contribute their full quota to a child's delinquency. By separated, I mean not only the divorced; I am speaking also of the parents who have broken every pledge * * * yet who still live under the same roof to harass the very life and joy out of their children." —Judge Camille Kelley, Memphis, Tenn.

"Ambitious parents who do not know their children's capabilities and try to fashion them into grooves for which they are unfitted, excessively yielding parents who cannot control their children, and lack of instruction as to how to associate with others—these are but a few of the many important etiologic factors in the situation." —Dr. Eugene

Davidoff and Elinor S. Noetzel, Syracuse, N. Y., Psychopathic Hospital.

"There is a definite relationship between a child's concept of law and order and adult attitudes toward income-tax evasion, traffic ticket fixing and the simple instructions to a child to tell the bill collector mama isn't home, when she is."—*Former Senator Robert C. Hendrickson, N. J.*

"The positive correlation between the rate of delinquency and war and cold war cannot be ignored. It is hard to instill those built-in controls of hostile behavior when children are being reared in a world that reeks of hostility."—*Bertram Beck, Federal Children's Bureau.*

"We recognize no moral law as binding nations, as superior to selfish national interest. Furthermore, a society that practices racial discrimination, resulting in tolerated injustice, can hardly impress its children with a reverence for moral law."—*Rev. Robert W. Searle, Home Advisory Council of New York.*

"The over-all impressions gained by the monitors from the majority of television programs for children is that life is cheap; death, suffering and brutality are subjects of callous indifference; and that judges, lawyers and law officers are dishonest, incompetent and stupid."—*Journal of the American Medical Association.*

"Programs interestingly depicting antisocial conduct, crime, murder, influence children to antisocial attitudes and lead to aggression. * * * Not all children are influenced by such programs. But no child escapes a trauma."—*Judge Jacob Panken, New York, N. Y.*

"Comic books are definitely harmful to impressionable people—and most young people are impressionable. * * * Comics definitely are factors in children's glorification of the wrong attitudes toward sex and violence."—*Dr. Frederic Wertham, New York psychiatrist.*

"Underlying youth's activity in crime is a prevailing disrespect for all law and constituted authority. If they are to be permitted to thumb their noses and scoff at the courts who seek by fatherly advice and gentle treatment to give them their liberty in the hope that they will be good boys, simply because it seems wrong to punish them in their tender years, then we deserve our fate when they grow to menace our future security."—*Judge Thomas J. Courtney, Cook County, Ill.*

"Somehow we must get at the causes, must clean up the conditions which breed criminals. We will find them, I think * * * even in a lack of understanding on the part of some of our correctional institutions."—*Senator Estes Kefauver, Tenn.*

CURES

"Parents should be encouraged to follow their natural inclinations until they find that what they believe in does not produce results. If their efforts are ineffective, they should turn to counseling or family service provided by the community."—*Robert C. Taber, Director of Pupil Personnel and Counseling, Philadelphia, Pa.*

"I believe that if parents were held responsible by law as they are held responsible by Almighty God for their children and their children's conduct * * * If parents were to pay for the damage which their children do during hours of free time * * * then these children and the parents would cooperate better, and would understand the real responsibility that parents and children have to one another and be more mindful of what is mine and what is thine."—*Father Edward J. Flanagan, Director, Boys' Town, Neb.*

"We suggest that arrangements be made with the public school authorities to provide weekly evening sessions of guidance to parents * * * Such weekly sessions would, of course, be open to all parents, but conviction of a parent as contributor to a child's delinquency should be followed by probation conditioned upon the compulsory attendance of such parents at these parent-guidance sessions."—*Dr. Sheldon Glueck, Harvard Law School.*

"Too few homes have parents whose interests go beyond the four walls of the home. * * * Children should live in an atmosphere of great concerns, where parents really care about the deep distresses of people and about ways in which to increase the happiness of others."—*Dr. Harry A. Overstreet, author.*

"The hallmark all along the line seems to be deprivation, both for the youngsters and for their parents. Now deprived people need support. * * * They may need individualized psychotherapeutic support if they are upper income people whose essential problem is profound emotional insecurity. * * * They may need support in the form of a grocery bill being paid, with a few bars of candy thrown in, if poverty is their chief problem."—*Dr. Donald Bloch, psychiatrist, Bethesda, Md.*

"I believe it should be the function of education to provide for these children after school hours. It should give them something in the way of education in citizenship and good morals, and fair opportunities for recreation under wholesome conditions."—*Judge George W. Smyth.*

"Too long, in large cities, we have depended upon what we call philanthropies, where people in privileged circumstances decide what the people in these blighted areas need, and in how large doses. That doesn't work. * * * We have to use * * * the organized effort of the people who live in those areas."—*Clifford Shaw, Illinois Department of Public Welfare.*

"There is probably no better way to encourage children to use television effectively than to set a good example. Parents who view the less desirable programs can hardly expect their children to be more discriminating."—*Prof. Paul W. F. Witt, Teachers College, Columbia.*

"Any undesirable comics would disappear off the newsstands if parents took sufficient interest to look over the comics their children read and to direct their reading."—*Dr. John R. Cavanagh, U. S. N.*

"We must compel respect for law and order. Youth must be made to feel the consequence of his misdeeds."—*Judge Thomas J. Courtney.*

"The juvenile courts that are most successfully meeting the needs of the child are using child guidance or psychiatric clinics as well as trained personnel."—*Prof. T. Earl Sullenger, University of Omaha.*

"Immediate attention needs to be given the critical problem caused by the overcrowding of existing institutions for juveniles."—*The Prison Association of New York.*

Compiled by FRANCES RODMAN

Senate Report on Child Crime Discards Traditional 'Causes'

By BESS FURMAN
Special to The New York Times.

WASHINGTON, May 5—The Senate Subcommittee to Investigate Juvenile Delinquency discarded today many traditional "causes" of child crime.

Lack of organized recreation, poor housing and low economic status were tossed out as real factors in the rise of delinquency.

The group blamed instead weak family life and lack of psychiatrists, social workers, and other therapeutic forces to prevent or cure the personality problems arising from family and social strains at all economic levels.

The subcommittee has been delving into various aspects of delinquency for almost four years, holding hearings in many parts of the country. The 252-page report by the panel summarizes all previous studies and outlines scores of Federal state and local measures to control delinquency.

Repeatedly it urged more research in the social sciences. The report said that many areas of special problems, including vandalism, never had been researched.

Legislative and other plans for dealing with a series of special problems were given. These problems included delinquents in the armed forces, juvenile drug addicts and alcoholics, delinquency along the Mexican border, pornography and vandalism.

If the delinquency rate continues upward at the 1948 through 1955 pace, the report warned, more than 1,000,000 children will appear before the courts in 1965. The estimated figure for children coming before the courts last year is 530,000 and, by 1965, the Bureau of the Census predicts, there will be 50 per cent more boys and girls in the 10 to 17 age group.

However, the subcommittee said that it had not relied completely on a projection of the census and crime statistics in predicting future trends. It expressed the view that an increasing awareness of the problem plus preventive and treatment measures taken by Federal, state and local governments might affect the trend.

Writing its new philosophy for dealing with juvenile delinquency, the group toppled old tenets in part as follows:

RECREATION

"The findings of some research attempt to persuade the public both that delinquency is caused by a lack of healthy organized recreation and that a good program in sports is the solution for prevention and rehabilitation.

"Elaborate and costly programs are based upon these fallacies and receive wide popular support because of the readiness of a sports-loving public to accept so simple an explanation and remedy.

"This was pointed up clearly when the President called together famous sports figures all over the nation in an attempt to determine what could be done about rising delinquency rates. This action indicated the presupposition that recreation was the answer to the problem.

"Careful studies have shown in fact that delinquents are generally more interested and skillful in games and sports than non-delinquents. They have been shown to have more frequent club affiliations, even in alleged character-building agencies and they are more adept at leadership in their group affiliations. In the real sense, the delinquent is on the average considerably more socialized than are his non-delinquent contemporaries. In fact, it is partly through his group interests and activities that he gets into trouble in the first place."

The report further stated: "The inability or failure of the schools—in spite of their advantageous position to serve such a function—to discover and secure aid for disturbed children provide little hope that the playground directors will do so. The difficult boys generally are either excluded, disinterested, or a potential source of infection to the others in the group."

HOUSING

The report states that slums may be cleared and the new housing projects that take their place may provide "a ready-made gang."

"Perhaps this explains why 13½ per cent of the total juvenile delinquency cases came from housing projects in Boston in one year." Also, "there is more to raising a good boy than housing him."

SOCIO-ECONOMIC STATUS

"For almost every case where you can demonstrate socio-economic depression in an area where a delinquent child lives, you can find a comparable child coming from the suburbs of your large cities who commits the same acts, who is surrounded not only by the necessities of child-life but by the luxuries.

"In both rich and poor the impulse to steal and kill is alike. What is called murder in the slums is called a crime of passion or honor in the elite section of the city.

"If poverty is the cause of delinquency, we should be singularly free from it in comparison with other nations. We are not.

"Anti-social attitudes are certainly not class-limited. In fact they may well exist as commonly among people of adequate income who commit more sophisticated and subtle offenses and who are less frequently arrested or convicted for their infractions of the code. * * *

"De-emphasis of materialism would be a great accomplishment in the prevention of illegal behavior not only among adult criminal offenders but in the effect that such materialism has on child rearing. Yet this change seems a highly improbable development in modern society."

The subcommittee also said that "if society is to achieve any really effective curtailment of law violation, it must come largely through the medium of family since it is there that attitudes of conduct are bred, out of which anti-social lives develop. Better children can come only from better parents."

The panel made clear that punitive jailing of parents of delinquents was farthest from its thoughts.

Instead, it said:

"A really constructive approach to the problem comes from an increasingly effective family social work—the goal being to strengthen family life through assisting individuals and family units insofar as possible to improve the circumstances essential to wholesome family living * * * These agencies have come to recognize the significance of personality maladjustments in a family breakdown.

"One of the major needs in facing the problems of delinquents is making adequate provision to assure that the services of psychiatrists, psychologists and social workers are available to youth in and out of school. Many of the children who fail to adjust in school, prior to becoming delinquent, show symptoms indicative of social and emotional problems * * * Exploration of the child's totality of hopes, fears, ambitions, disappointments and the like would form the basis of therapy."

The subcommittee is a division of the Senate Committee on the Judiciary. As constituted, it now consists of Senators Thomas C. Hennings Jr., Democrat of Missouri, chairman; Sam J. Ervin Jr., of North Carolina and Matthew M. Neely of West Virginia, Democrats, and William Langer of North Dakota and Alexander Wiley of Wisconsin, Republicans.

However, the printed report listed the chairman as Senator Estes Kefauver, Democrat of Tennessee, under whom much of the work was done. When he resigned, Mr. Neely came on the subcommittee and Mr. Hennings became chairman.

DELINQUENCY LINKED TO WEALTHY YOUTHS

Special to The New York Times.

WASHINGTON, Aug. 27—The habits and thoughts of Americans were put under scrutiny today at the fifty-second annual meeting of the American Sociological Society.

F. Ivan Nye, professor at Washington State College, said in a paper that delinquent behavior was as prevalent among middle and upper class juveniles as in the lower classes. He reported on a survey made by himself and three faculty associates.

He stressed that it was the poorer youths who got arrested and their court records formed the basis for most of the statistics on the subject.

Arthur Niederhoffer, an instructor in the New York Police Academy, agreed. He reported on a survey of delinquency in New York City. Middle class youths, he declared, "commit crimes so serious and so frequent that never appear on the record that it is amazing that they get away with it."

August 28, 1957

YOUTH CRIME TIED TO NEW MIGRATION

Philadelphia Judge Ascribes Problem to Influx From South and Puerto Rico

By WILLIAM G. WEART

Special to The New York Times.

PHILADELPHIA, July 17—The migration into Philadelphia of about 500,000 persons from the South and from Puerto Rico since 1930 was blamed today for the city's juvenile-delinquency problem.

President Judge Adrian Bonnelly of the Municipal Court, which handles all juvenile cases, thus traced the problem in testimony before the Juvenile Delinquency subcommittee of the United States Senate Judiciary Committee.

The subcommittee, headed by Senator Thomas C. Hennings Jr., Democrat of Missouri, completed two days of public hearings in the Federal Building here. Earlier this year, the group held hearings in New York and Chicago.

Judge Bonnelly said the city was in the midst of the "crisis" he foresaw in 1924, when he told a Congressional committee that if the doors of Ellis Island were closed to European immigrants, the doors would be opened to migration from the South of "technically bonded slaves" into the industrial cities of the North.

Racial Changes Noted

Since 1930, the judge reported, the racial composition of Philadelphia has been changed by integration of new inhabitants from the South and Puerto Rico.

Between 1930 and 1953, he testified, "the number of white children 7 to 15 years residing in Philadelphia increased 2.9 per cent, while the number of non-white children increased 89 per cent."

Judge Bonnelly told the subcommittee "these so-called juvenile delinquents are the offspring of unmarried mothers, putative fathers, unsanitary homes and lack of leadership among their own people."

"The result," he said, "is debauchery."

Victor H. Blanc, District Attorney of Philadelphia, reported an increase in juvenile crime here in the first four months of this year. He said a total of 2,303 boys and girls under 18 were arrested in the first four months of 1959, compared with 2,179 in the corresponding period of last year.

July 18, 1959

Arsenal Of Delinquency

By WILLIAM McINTYRE

THE Europeans who regard America as a contemporary Roman Empire have new affirmation of their appraisal: juvenile delinquents in New Jersey have revived an ancient Roman weapon called the cestus. The pugilists of two thousand years ago reinforced each hand with a heavy circlet of leather—which was often loaded with lead or iron. The N. J. J. D.'s modernized this handy device by adding a bristling row of sharp nails.

The arsenal of delinquency is growing. "Use of dangerous weapons by youths and children under the age of 21 is much greater than indicated by arrests," said a lieutenant of the New York City Police Youth Division. One thousand sixty-seven arrests for possession of dangerous weapons were made last year.

There are almost a hundred fighting, or "bopping," gangs in New York City with an average enrollment of thirty-five or forty members. Half the gang members—by conservative estimates—carry dangerous weapons, or have them readily available. More liberal estimates claim three-quarters of the gang members are armed. No one knows how many local juveniles not associated with gangs possess arms, but there are undoubtedly thousands.

The dangerous weapon has become a status symbol of delinquency. It gives color, glamour and prestige to the Big Man who carries it; and, the more dangerous the weapon, the more "rep," or prestige, it brings.

THE Sullivan Act has made it very difficult for juvenile delinquents to arm themselves with conventional hand guns—a police permit is necessary to buy them. As a result, they have learned to make their own: the famous "zipgun." The barrel of this piece of gutter ordnance is made of a length of automobile-radio antenna, metal tubing whose bore neatly accommodates a .22-caliber bullet. Segments of the tubing are either taped to a wooden frame, or else fixed inside the barrel of a toy pistol.

In the toy pistol, the firing mechanism is powerfully strengthened by heavy rubber bands looped behind the hammer. In the wooden-frame zipgun, an ordinary, sliding-bolt lock used on doors serves as the firing device. Again, rubber bands — or springs — hooked around the stud of the sliding bolt, snap the bolt forward to strike the base of the cartridge. A .22-caliber cartridge needs no firing pin to explode it; a sharp blow on the base is sufficient. In spite of the ingenious design, however, a zipgun is wildly inaccurate—it is almost as dangerous to fire one as to be the target.

The source of supply of zipguns obviously can't be shut off, and furthermore, the police must apprehend an owner with one in his possession in order to prosecute him. Consequently junior gunmen often use girl friends, or "debs," as gunbearers. A female can be searched only by a policewoman, and the toughs know that it's usually difficult for patrolmen to secure the assistance of a policewoman for chance investigations. What is more, young children are often coerced into carrying the weapons.

The police feel that zipguns could be eliminated as a serious problem if the sale of ammunition were controlled by state laws. If a hunting license, a pistol permit, or a membership card in a reputable rifle association were necessary to purchase ammunition, they say, virtually none would get into the hands of zipgunmen.

Legislation to control sale of ammunition passed the

187

state Senate as part of Mayor Wagner's program in the last session at Albany, but subsequently suffered a decisive defeat in the Assembly. Opponents, taking the point of view of hunting clubs and rifle associations, argued that such a restriction would infringe on the constitutional rights of an individual to bear arms.

Next to zipguns, knives are the most dangerous weapons in delinquency land. Until about three years ago, the switch-blade knife was the favorite weapon in this category. This pocket dagger has a folding blade that springs into place when released by a safety-catch. When state legislation specifically outlawed it, the "gravity knife" became the favorite for a brief period. This ingenious design features a hollow handle out of which the blade slides when released by a catch. An amendment to the law banned the gravity knife as well. Now both these weapons play a minor role in the arsenal of juvenile delinquency.

Under state law, a concealed knife whose blade exceeds a four-inch length is illegal, but an unconcealed knife can be any size. Consequently, many cutlery merchants in New York City deal in a colorful assortment of commando daggers, hara-kari knives, machetes, throwing knives, bolos, hunting knives and bayonets. Inevitably, many of these reach the hands of juvenile delinquents.

Knife-like weapons also include beer-can openers, razors and cleavers. The array is so variegated that state laws don't cover them adequately. As a result, local police in booking offenders have had to cite a section of the city's Administrative Code.

This section of the code is so inclusive that it proscribes practically every instrument, of whatever size, capable of penetrating or cutting. Under this sweeping regulation, even a Boy Scout could be held a criminally armed juvenile. The code section is scheduled to come under fire before the Court of Appeals. The American Civil Liberties Union, carrying the attack, contends it violates constitutional rights.

LAWS prohibit the carrying of bludgeons —yet they are carried and used. They include chains (dog, bicycle and tire), sandbags, blackjacks, billy clubs, rubber hose, segments of heavy electrical cable, whip-like automobile radio antennas and, cruelest of all, a variety of small industrial conveyor belt, one side of which is closely set with sharpened metal teeth a quarter-inch long.

When asked why so many young people risk arrest for carrying weapons, a policeman shrugged and laconically conceded they knew how overcrowded the "correctional" facilities are. The small-fry hoods knew they would probably escape punishment, he said, simply because there's no place to put them.

Anyway, it's clear that the people who are attempting to eliminate the arsenal of delinquency in New York are getting no further than the delegates to the disarmament conference in Geneva.

May 1, 1960

Fighting Gangs Vanish From the City's Ghettos

By THOMAS BUCKLEY

No one knows on what garbage-strewn street in Williamsburg or Brownsville or Central Harlem the last rumble took place, or who was killed or hurt and who was arrested.

But it happened four or five years ago. Then suddenly, after a decade of mounting violence, the era of the fighting gangs in New York came to an end.

There have been attempts since then to revive the old gangs with the colorful names —Cobras, Enchanters, Corsair Lords, Social Crowns—or to start new ones, sometimes based, in the case of Negro youths, on a racist doctrine borrowed from the Black Muslims.

Only one of these, so far as the police and social agencies know, has managed to remain in existence more than a couple of months. It is called the Five Percenters and it is composed of perhaps 25 youths who live in or near St. Nicholas Houses, at St. Nicholas Avenue and 127th Street.

The Five Percenters take their name from their contention that only 5 per cent of all Negroes are militant enough to redress their grievances against ill-treatment by whites.

While the Five Percenters, who affect shaved heads, paratrooper boots and a tough swagger, are suspected of occasionally beating up white youths who find themselves near the St. Nicholas project, they can find no gangs to fight, even if they were so inclined.

Capt. Joseph Mulloy, commander of the Police Department's Youth Investigation Unit, which used to keep tabs on 200 or more fighting gangs, said that aside from the Five Percenters he did not know nowadays of a single such gang.

Elsewhere in the East, in Washington, Newark and Philadelphia, the police report that youth gang activity has lessened markedly or disappeared. In Chicago and Los Angeles, however, the gangs number 200 or more and fights are frequent.

But, as New York stands poised at the start of another long and possibly hot summer, neither the police nor any of the social agencies that deal with ghetto youths see any likelihood of a revival of the gangs.

"There could be trouble, of course," said Frank Arricale, executive director of the New York City Youth Board, "but it will come, if it comes at all, as it did in 1964 — from thousands of youths individually, in pairs or threes, suddenly coalescing for a violent purpose."

Why did the fighting gangs disappear? Each organization that has dealt with the problem offers a list of reasons. For the most part they are the same, differing only in emphasis.

Views Described

The police believe that aggressive patrolling by the Youth Division, which has now been disbanded, increased the possibility of arrests to the point where the fear of courts and jail outweighed the desire for combat.

The Youth Board believes that its dedicated young workers, who went into the streets to win over the gangs to peaceful pursuits, tipped the balance.

Agencies such as Mobilization for Youth believe that their work in providing vocational and recreational opportunities for slum youth must not be overlooked.

All these organizations unquestionably played important roles, but they agree there were other causes that led to the disbanding of the fighting gangs.

Prof. Lewis Yablonsky of San Fernando Valley State College in Los Angeles, author of "The Violent Gang," said recently there was a good deal of faddism in the organization of gangs, and that juveniles had passed to other forms of thrill-seeking.

The War Influence

"There was the influence of the World War II and Korea stories of commandos and raids," says Mr. Arricale. "After a while it just stopped seeming important."

"Gang members were deprived youngsters trying to achieve some kind of status, looking for identity, prestige," says Professor Yablonsky. "Their violence was a kind of existential validation — an attempt to prove to themselves that they were alive — and it took wild, weird, almost artistic forms."

The slums have become more and more disorganized in the last 20 years, he went on. Where once the populations and their ethnic make-up were relatively stable, now there is constant movement in and out. Neighborhoods are obliterated by urban-renewal projects.

Mr. Arricale said: "There's no 'turf' left to defend any more, and kids aren't as confined by their own sections of the city. They're apt to go to Coney Island for kicks now."

This view has been substantiated in recent weeks by outbreaks of bottle-throwing and rowdyism at Coney and many experts fear that the outbreaks will become more serious as the summer goes on.

A decade ago, as the size of the gangs increased, so did the viciousness of their encounters. Fifty or more youths on a side, accompanied by auxiliary forces of girls (called debs) and boys as young as 9 or 10 (Tiny Tims), would meet head-on with flailing chains, auto aerials, knives, zip guns that fired a .22-caliber bullet with fair accuracy over short distances, and sometimes with regular pistols.

It was not unusual for one or two boys to be lying dead on the street and for a half-dozen or more to be badly injured by the time the police arrived.

"A lot of the kids told us that they finally got too scared to fight," said Mr. Arricale.

With the end of the gangs came, some observers think, an increased use of heroin. This has now been replaced by stimulant pills — amphetamines and Benzedrine — and marijauna, wine and whisky.

Along with this has come what Mr. Arricale regards as even more disturbing — "the terrible sense of disaffiliation, cynicism and apathy" that seems to grip ghetto youth.

Since the end of the fighting-gang era, the Youth Board has been trying to help such youngsters find a place in society through individual counseling, the finding of jobs and referrals to such antipoverty agencies as Mobilization for Youth and Haryou.

It is a difficult task. "So many of them seem utterly unreachable," Mr. Arricale says. Under the circumstances, he and many others in the field believe the break-up of the gangs was not entirely a blessing.

There is nothing wrong with a gang as such, they say. Boys have always formed gangs. And even the violent ones could be, and were, turned to peaceful, socially acceptable paths

"It was like an Indian tribe when the missioneris arrived," said Connie McCullough, the Youth Board's Central Harlem supervisor. "If the missionary could convert the chief, he could get the whole tribe without any additional effort."

"In the same way," he said, "if we could persuade the gang president and the war councillor to stop bopping," we could turn the whole gang around."

A few days ago a couple of former gang members in Harlem sat in a cafe on Lenox Avenue, talking about the old days. One of them was an apprentice printer, Carl — at their request, last names are withheld — known to his friends as Keno. He was once war councillor of the Crowns, who had their headquarters at 133d Street and Seventh Avenue.

"There got to be other things to do," he was saying. "Jobs and girls and things. Some of our guys got sent to jail, you know, and we just began losing our heart for fighting."

Willie, who did his fighting on 129th Street, summed it up by saying, "We were children then."

June 26, 1966

CHILDREN'S CRIME RISING ACROSS U.S.

Serious Offenses Committed by Youngsters Under 13— Violence Not Uncommon

By WAYNE KING

Crime by children, some of it serious and committed by youngsters not yet in their teens, is arousing growing concern among parents, the police and school authorities across the country.

While it is not new, juvenile authorities generally agree that the problem has grown substantially worse in the last few years, both in the number of offenses and their seriousness. And while there is a lack of national statistics that might back it up, there is a feeling that both the victims and the perpetrators are getting younger.

For the most part, the crimes are "petty" in terms of the money or property involved—shakedowns for lunch money, bicycle thefts, pilfering from school lockers—but some are serious and violence is not uncommon.

Reports from school and law enforcement officials in 13 cities indicate that the trend noted in 1969 by the National Commission on the Causes and Prevention of Violence is continuing. The commission found that in the 10-year period 1958 through 1967, there was a 300 per cent increase in assaults by 10 to 14-year-olds and a 200 per cent increase in robberies by this age group.

"We've had just about everything in schools short of murder," says Harry S. Hodgins Jr., chief security supervisor for the Baltimore city schools, "everything from ordinary shakedowns for lunch money right through armed robbery in the halls at pistol point."

Off the school grounds, the problem is worse. The Baltimore police report that last year there were 12,835 arrests of suspects under 18, up from 10,594 in 1969.

526 Under 10 Arrested

Moreover, in the age group 10 years and under, there were 526 arrests, including one for murder, 22 for robbery, 169 for burglary, six for auto theft, 12 for arson, nine for aggravated assault, 104 for larceny and four for narcotics violations.

In Los Angeles, as in most other cities, bicycle theft has become commonplace, and the police department there is considering creating a 25-man "bike section" to handle the problem.

In the Roslindale section of Boston, a woman complained that "in our neighborhood, I hear you can go up to a kid in front of the local ice cream shop and say you want a 10-speed Peugeot racing bike and he'll ask you what color."

The Best Indicator

Although not considered the most serious child crime problem — shakedowns and "muggings" — are regarded as more dangerous—bicycle thefts are probably the best indicator of the growth of crime committed by children against other children.

The police and other juvenile authorities generally agree that the other categories, particularly shakedowns, are not reported as often because of the threat of reprisal and the generally lower dollar value of the stolen property.

Robert Ehrman, a disciplinary officer in the Sacramento school system, says instances of extortion, backed up by threats, are increasing more noticably than other problems.

"It's usually a two-or-three kids-on-one thing," he said, "extortion or just the sheer delight of scaring the hell of some small kid."

A Common Pattern

The greatest increase and highest incidence is from the fifth or sixth grade through the ninth grade, Mr. Erhman observed, a pattern reported by most other school officials.

Although the problem of petty extortion is not a new one—a Pittsburgh school principal recalls a situation 12 years ago in which one student demanded and got 50 cents from another student each school day for two years — juvenile officials say it has grown serious within the last three to five years in most areas.

The reasons given by police and school officials vary, but those most often cited are "a general breakdown" in family discipline, racial animosities and changing school patterns that place poor children in contact with the more affluent. The general increase in crime by all groups is also cited.

For whatever reasons, juvenile crime rates have been rising far faster than the adult rate. From 1960 through 1970, according to the Federal Bureau of Investigation police arrests for all criminal acts except traffic violations rose 31 per cent, while arrests of those under 18 more than doubled—a pace more than four times the population increase in the 10 to 18 age group.

Adult arrests for violent crime in the same period went up 67 per cent, while for juveniles they increased 167 per cent.

Generally, the police and other officials who deal with juvenile offenders keep no related statistics on the victims of juvenile crime, and there is, thus, no accurate gauge of an increase in children's crime against their peers, although there is general agreement that the problem is getting worse.

Reaction to increased youthful crime has largely taken the form of more policing of schools and surrounding areas, usually with private guards. Dade County schools had a security force of five men in 1968: today it has 98. Most other school systems have bolstered their patrols similarly, but parental concern remains.

"Mothers are frightened these days of what might happen to their daughters at school," said a Miami teacher whose three children attend public schools. She reported that at a Coral Gables Junior High, many girls were afraid to enter lavatories because of shakedowns by other girls, some of whom have brandished razors.

And a Boston father said: "My 14-year-old son got punched in the mouth at a park the other night because he wouldn't yield up a radio when ordered to by a peer who was drunk.

"It was not a traumatic experience," he said. "My kid was a little bit small and thinks that most things can be settled nonviolently."

October 4, 1971

Crime and Violence Rise in City Schools

By LEONARD BUDER

The number of reported acts of crime and violence in and around city schools increased from 333 in 1970 to 580 last year, according to Board of Education figures.

These incidents involved assaults on teachers and students, including rapes, attempted rapes and molestations; robberies and purse snatchings; the setting off of smoke and fire bombs; and telephoned and written threats against school staff members.

Among the "untoward" incidents reported to board headquarters during the 1971 calendar year were 285 assaults on teachers and other school personnel—two fewer than in 1970 but well above the figures for previous years.

Last January and February there were a total of 170 such incidents reported, including 88 assaults on school personnel. If this rate continues, headquarters officials said, the 1972 totals will far exceed those for last year.

197 Arrests in 1971

The headquarters records show a total of 197 reported arrests of youngsters and adults last year in connection with school incidents, compared with 102 in 1970. However, officials' point out that arrests are sometimes made days and weeks after the incident and are often not reported to headquarters.

Parent and student complaints about violence in the schools and attacks on youngsters going to and from school have become a recurring theme at recent public-agenda meetings of the Board of Education. At these sessions, unlike the regular calendar meetings, speakers can bring up any subject they wish.

At last Tuesday night's board meeting, a group of parents and elected officials from the northeast Bronx said that about 350 students had been kept home from Adlai E. Stevenson High School since last September out of fear for their safety. A parent spokesman said that students were being "mugged, robbed, intimidated, harassed and stabbed" by other students, who were members of south Bronx gangs.

Although the board's figures are generally regarded as an imprecise barometer — many school incidents are never reported to headquarters — such groups as the United Federation of Teachers, the High School Principals Association and the Council of Supervisors and Administrators have asserted that school violence was increasing.

Supervisors, teachers and headquarters officials who were interviewed recently also said that while school violence and unrest have been a persistent problem in this city as well as elsewhere for many years, there was a different character to the problem today.

Dr. George Patterson, an assistant superintendent at headquarters, who handles school security matters, said: "A few years ago, there were more group confrontations. Now we largely have pretty vicious individual assaults."

Similarly, George Altomare, the United Federation of Teachers' vice president for academic high schools, said:

"The schools are not the focal point of violence aimed at change. School issues are not involved, as they were some years ago, when students organized protests, peaceful and violent, to bring about change. Now it is student against student."

Although there was sometimes a racial or ethnic element — one Manhattan high school has been torn by conflict between blacks and Dominicans—in many schools, Mr. Altomare said, the problem was "essentially nonracial."

Edward Muir, the U.F.T.'s representative on the school stability team set up last year by the School Chancellor, Harvey B. Scribner, noted that there has been a re-emergence of "fighting gangs" in such areas as the south Bronx and northern Manhattan. These gang conflicts, he said, frequently spill over into the schools.

Handguns Proliferate

"The tragic element that distinguishes this from earlier gang activity is the proliferation of handguns among teen-agers," Mr. Muir said. "The 'Saturday night special' [a cheap, small-caliber gun] has hit the high schools."

He added that he had heard of four shootings in and around schools in recent months.

Dr. Patterson also said he had heard that an increasing number of students were carrying guns.

"Some carry guns out of bravado, some for business—a stickup — and some for self-defense," he said.

Scribner Voices Concern

Chancellor Scribner, who in the past has emphasized that violence in the schools was, to a degree, a reflection of the violence in society, said yesterday that he was very concerned about the problem.

"Every student and teacher has the right to go to school in safety and without fear for his safety," he said.

Dr. Scribner said that he was planning to implement new measures to enable the high schools to cope more effectively with problem youngsters, including those who persistently refused to attend classes but congregated in school buildings and, in some instances, endangered the safety of others. He said these measures would be disclosed soon.

'Untoward Accidents' Listed

The record of school incidents is compiled by a unit of the Office of Educational Information Services at central headquarters. Each school day the office gives Dr. Scribner and other top officials a "Log of Untoward Incidents" reported by the schools. Among the incidents reported recently were the following:

¶ An English teacher at a Brooklyn junior high school was assaulted by two intruders he had encountered in the hall. They hit him on the head with a hammer and knocked him down a flight of steps. The teacher was taken - semiconscious to a hospital.

¶ Students from a Bronx high school were attacked by a group of youths while waiting for buses. Several students were injured.

¶ Two students sitting in the lunchroom of a Manhattan high school were attacked by four unidentified assailants. Both youngsters suffered stab wounds of the back and other injuries.

¶ An 8-year-old boy, on his way back to class from the lavatory, was "accosted by a male intruder who dragged him to the fourth-floor landing leading to the roof and sexually assaulted him."

¶ A Queens principal was robbed at gunpoint in his office by a young man, shortly after the end of the school day.

Occasionally the reports contain assertions from parents that teachers have assaulted their children.

Pupils Express Fear

Many school officials who were interviewed recently said that the daily reports gave only a fragmentary picture of the situation.

One Board of Education official, who did not want to be identified, said that in many schools pupils were afraid to go to the toilet for fear that they would be accosted by other youngsters, who will demand or take their money, or be "molested" by "outsiders."

The official said that pupils and teachers also shunned deserted corridors and stairways during the school day and that principals often advised teachers not to remain alone in their classrooms during free periods or after school.

Deputy chancellor Irving Anker recently issued a directive to principals that women secretaries should not be asked to remain in the school office alone after school hours. The directive, issued in response to complaints from secretaries, said that when secretaries were asked to work after school, adequate protection must be provided for them.

An analysis of school incidents made a year ago by George Lent, who kept the headquarters log until he went on leave last fall, found that 70 per cent of the assaults on school personnel were committed by students, 10 per cent by parents of students and 20 per cent by intruders.

School officials generally re-

School Violence				
Schools	Incidents		Arrests	
	1970	1971	1970	1971
Elementary	97	209	19	33
Intermediate-Junior High	164	230	51	102
Academic	59	124	25	55
Vocational High	13	17	6	7
Totals	333	580	101	197

Source: Board of Education Office of Education Information Service

The New York Times/March 19, 1972

The above table lists the number of violent incidents reported to the Board of Education in 1970 and 1971 and the number of arrests made. Some of the incidents were resolved without being reported to the police and some arrests were not linked to incidents referred to police.

190

port that intruders are a steadily growing problem. Some of the outsiders are adults, often drug addicts seeking something to steal.

But a number of them, Dr. Patterson said, are truants from other schools who prey upon younger pupils or are out to settle an old score. High school students, he noted, sometimes invade junior high schools and junior high school pupils may go to nearby elementary schools.

Mr. Lent also estimated that 30 to 60 per cent of all school incidents are not reported to headquarters.

Albert Shanker, president of the teachers' union, said that many teachers, parents and students do not report incidents to local school officials because they "have no confidence in the school system's procedures for dealing with violence" and fear that a complaint could possibly lead to another assault.

He said that "the question of safety and working without fear" would be a major item in the union's forthcoming contract negotiations with the Board of Education.

Not included in the board's tally of untoward incidents, although mentioned in the log, were bomb threats received by schools — a headquarters aide said that these had become "almost too numerous to count"— and acts of vandalism, fires and thefts occurring during nonschool hours.

During one week earlier this month, 13 city schools were targets of bomb threats, including one Brooklyn elementary school that received five threats in a 55-minute period.

Some schools have also been plagued by fires of suspicious origin. At one Bronx high school recently, there were four false fire alarms one day. The next morning a fire was discovered in a classroom closet, forcing the evacuation of the building. An hour after classes resumed, another fire was discovered, this time in a lavatory, and again the building had to be evacuated.

Youth Gangs' Violence Found Rising in 3 Cities

By DONALD JANSON
Special to The New York Times

PHILADELPHIA, April 15 —A group of black teenagers asked a 15-year-old white boy for a dime on a street on the southwest side here, then stabbed him to death when they didn't get it.

When a 52-year-old white veteran of the Battle of Iwo Jima went to south central Los Angeles to take food to a destitute black friend, a street gang of 15 to 20 black youths waylaid him and beat him to death without provocation.

At New York's newest high school in the Bronx, half of the lavatories are kept locked so security guards can better cope with the rash of assaults and robberies aimed largely at white students by black and Puerto Rican gangs.

In an apparent resurgence of street gang activity, violence by young men from the pre-teens to the early thirties is once again a big problem in some major United States cities.

A nationwide check of 12 cities indicates that the violence is concentrated in the country's four largest cities —New York, Chicago, Los Angeles and Philadelphia. Why the activity is intense now, after a decade of comparative calm, is unclear.

For more than a decade after the rumbles of the nineteen-fifties, the drug scene replaced gang wars as a focal attraction for idle youths in the slums and racially tense neighborhoods of many cities.

Heroin has decreased gang activity in Chicago, the street-gang capital, though 700 gangs retain their identity there, and violent deaths, beatings, robberies and shakedowns continue.

"More brothers gettin' killed," said a former "gang-banger," as warring gang members are known on Chicago's black West Side, "because there are more guns. But gang-bangin' itself is dying off. Now, too many brothers are too busy noddin' on the junk."

The slackening in Chicago is allowing the three other major cities to catch up. New York and Los Angeles are experiencing a strong resurgence in street violence. Philadelphia, with 160 killings attributed to street gangs in the last four years, never lost this virulent form of lawlessness in slum neighborhoods.

Differences in pattern from the early rumbles are marked. Gangs still war on each other, but more often now their victims are not members of gangs, often they are passersby chosen at random on the spur of the moment.

Race Sometimes a Factor

Often race appears to be a factor in selecting victims. And fatalities are more numerous now because "Saturday night specials," the cheap small-caliber handguns that have become readily available to all, have largely replaced homemade zip guns.

The most aggressive gangs have brazenly widened their "turf" by invading school corridors and even neighborhood homes.

Edward Muir of the United Federation of Teachers in New York said:

"The tragic element that distinguishes this from earlier gang activity is the proliferation of handguns among teen-agers. The 'Saturday night special' has hit the high schools."

Not all of today's gangs are prone to violence. Many work for community betterment and seek to rid their neighborhoods of drug abuse.

Youth workers believe that teen-agers join gangs for self-protection and for a sense of belonging to something, a consequence of a lack of home life and jobs in the slums.

Some gang members condone and even participate in violence out of outrage at a "system" they feel has sentenced them to deprivation.

"Each and everyone of us here hates where we live," said a young member of a Bronx gang during a discussion of gang problems held recently by a community group in New York. "We want out."

"They feel we aren't people, you know," a member of the Black Spades said of the authorities.

'Help a Brother'

In Chicago, a Black Disciple put it this way:

"Gangs give folks something to be proud of. My parents couldn't afford to put me in the Boy Scouts. So me and the rest of our guys started getting together. Our main function is to help a brother. It's a thing where guys care about each other."

So they wear the "colors" of the Flaming Skulls, the Golden Guineas and scores of other big and little gangs. Some form federations of gangs such as the Zulu Nation in Philadelphia. Others remain small, even block size. Most are racially segregated — all black, all Puerto Rican, all of Mexican derivation, or all white.

The Crips, a gang growing rather rapidly in the black neighborhoods of Los Angeles, prescribes black gloves for the left hand and gold earrings for the left earlobe and favors a walking stick.

One explanation for the name and the canes is that founders at Washington High School were crippled at the time and used walking sticks.

The Crips and other packs of youths such as those who murdered the Iwo Jima marine veteran, N. J. Orr, have been sweeping through south central Los Angeles and Watts, beating, robbing, raping and occasionally killing, sometimes entering homes to do so.

The terror has instilled widespread fear. William F., a typical retired pensioner, will not leave his apartment after dusk. The mother of a 15-year-old girl who was raped by gang members decided that her daughter would not press charges after two weeks of late-night phone calls threatened fire-bombing and window smashing if she did.

350 Students Stay Home

Attacks on children going to and from school have become a major problem in each of the gang-ridden cities. Parents have kept 350 students home from Stevenson High School in the Bronx since last September. Others have been transferred to private and parochial schools.

In some New York schools, pupils are afraid to go to the toilet for fear of assault or robbery. Some principals have advised teachers not to remain in their classrooms alone.

In Philadelphia, where street gangs contributed to a 34 per cent increase in major crimes last year, Superintendent of Schools Matthew W. Costanzo proposed a $500,000 program to hire nonuniformed guards to line "safety corridors" to and from schools in gang-infested neighborhoods.

The proposal followed an experiment at Bartlett Junior High School on the south side in which the principal, vice principals and nonteaching staff members acted as guards at opening and closing hours after attendance had dropped to 70 per cent of enrollment.

The principal, Anthony Gian Petro, said that previous patrolling inside the building had been unsatisfactory because children got beaten up outside, and patrolling immediately outside helped only until the children got across the street.

Safety Plan Quashed

But the safety corridor plan was quashed when Mayor Frank L. Rizzo said that any patrolling should be a police function. He announced a police crackdown on street gangs, but it has yet to stem the violence.

In mid-February, the day after the son of the late actor Ed Begley was beaten, stomped and stabbed by a gang of 25 black youths in Los Angeles in the third such incident of the afternoon, the Los Angeles City Council also ordered a police crackdown.

Billy G. Mills, council president pro tem, said that the increase in murders, robberies and assaults had imposed a "crisis of intimidation and fear" on parts of Los Angeles "by roving groups of young people ranging in age from 10 to 30."

The age range is the same in the other cities. Gang membership in each of the four cities ranges from 4,000 to 6,000.

After six months of research by a special force on gangs,

Mayor Lindsay of New York announced allocation of $1-million to the city's youth service agency for programs to deal with the resurgence in gangs and gang violence.

The programs will include job training and placement, recreation and remedial education.

"Our goal is not only to break up those gangs already in existence," the Mayor said, "but also to prevent the formation of new ones."

The Chicago police department, which once pursued a hard line, now talks less about breaking up gangs and more about "working with youth organizations and gangs."

Its gang intelligence unit, which once used infiltration, massive raids on living quarters and hundreds of arrests on misdemeanor charges to harass the Black P. Stone Nation (formerly Blackstone Rangers) and other gangs, has been reduced to 60 policemen compared to 220 three years ago.

Chicago Violence Reduced

The softer line, the incapacitating inroads made by heroin and community patrols formed by black adults have all had an effect in reducing gang violence in Chicago.

So have programs that give gangs something productive to do. Chicago's Conservative Vice Lords, for example, now operate a chain of shops with Federal funds and a gift from W. Clement Stone, an insurance executive and leading financial backer of President Nixon in his political campaigns.

In the draft of a report, soon to be completed, on hearings in Philadelphia last year, the United States Commission

on Civil Rights criticized some police methods of dealing with street gangs, for example taking members singly to the "turf" of a rival gang and leaving them there to return home as best they can.

The commission attributed at least one death to this practice, which, it said, appeared to be "designed to exploit the danger of the situation at the expense of the young people rather than to expedite corrective measures."

Not all of the new and continuing gangs are prone to violence. Even most of those that are quick to fight bar hard drugs for members, although a few have become dealers in drugs.

Many gangs have neighborhood improvement goals, such as forceful eviction of pushers, cleanup of streets and back lots, registration of voters and even peace among gangs.

Umoja, a West Philadelphia organization, arranged peace talks in February among several gangs, stressing the senselessness of blacks killing blacks in gang warfare.

Nine East Los Angeles gangs formed the federation of Barrios Unidos to try to end rumbles and turn youthful energies instead toward combating drug abuse, police "harassment" and inequities in education.

United Youth Federation

To seek a truce in their sporadic warfare with whites and blacks, a Puerto Rican gang in Milwaukee had pins made saying "United Youth Federation." The pins showed three clenched fists, one black, one brown and one white.

But even the peacemakers

walk a tight rope in attempts to bring communication into today's street gang subculture. Sometimes the difficulty is that gang presidents, vice presidents and war lords cannot always control hotheads or gun-loving marginal members.

Robert Benjamin Cornell, 25 year-old vice president of the Ghetto Brothers in the Bronx, was beaten and stabbed to death by members of the Seven Immortals and the Black Spades in December when he sought to negotiate peace among several warring gangs.

In January, Eduardo Vincenty of New York's youth services agency was shot in the head while trying to stop a gang fight. He had helped to get endorsements from scores of gangs for a Family Peace Treaty binding them to negotiate before settling disputes by force.

Last month, Anthony Rennie, teen-age member of the Black Assassins in New York, was shot to death while seeking a truce with the Shades of Black.

But while rundown neighborhoods in the largest cities tremble before the depredations of street gangs, smaller cities have had little recurrence of the problem. Some authorities "credit" drugs for this.

"Guys are so busy hustling to get drugs for themselves, or to steal to buy them, that they don't have time to organize gangs," said Al Turner, project manager of the Miami Model Cities Development. "The drug problem has ruled out street gangs here."

In Detroit, where the biggest youth problem also is narcotics, the police department's gang unit changed its name and now handles other matters.

Crime Rate of Women Up Sharply Over Men's

By STEVEN V. ROBERTS
Special to The New York Times

LOS ANGELES, June 12— Women are gaining rapidly in at least one traditional area of male supremacy—crime.

Statistics across the country disclose that the female crime rate for most offenses is rising faster than the male rate. In Los Angeles County, for instance, male arrests went up 10 per cent in 1970 while female arrests rose 23 per cent in the year, an increase that Sheriff Peter Pitchess called "startling."

It is always difficult to compare criminal statistics, and not every city reports the same findings, but the general trend is clear. Federal Bureau of Investigation figures show that from 1960 to 1969, male arrests for major crimes rose 61.3 per cent. For females, the increase was 156.2 per cent.

Thus, women accounted for 16 per cent of the arrests for major crimes in 1969, compared with 10 per cent in 1960. Among juveniles, the increases in arrest were 78.2 per cent for males and 211.8 per cent for females.

The heaviest increases in crimes by women are those against property, such as larceny and embezzlement, and in narcotics violations. But women are also committing more robberies, assaults and crimes involving alcohol.

Most experts in the field agree that the phenomenon has many causes. But the main explanation seems to be that women have more opportunities than they used to have for all kinds of activities, legal and illegal. As Sheriff Pitchess put it:

"As women emerge from their traditional roles as housewife and mother, entering the political and business fields previously dominated by males, there is no reason to believe that women will not also approach equality with men in the criminal activity field."

"Things are different, that's all," added one of the sheriff's aides. "Crime reflects conditions in society as well as anything else."

The F.B.I. arrest figures indicate that the trend toward more crime by women is accelerating. From 1964 to 1965, the female rate rose faster than the male rate in seven of the bureau's 30 categories. From 1968 to 1969, the rise in crime for women was greater in 24 categories.

Individual cities report similar patterns. In Cincinnati, women accounted for 17.5 per cent of all larcenies in 1959. Ten years later they committed 37 per cent of the larcenies.

More Girls in Court

In Boston, Judge Francis G. Poitrast of the Juvenile Court said that he used to see 10 boys in his courtroom for every girl. Now the ratio is 3 to 1.

Ten years ago, the women of Raleigh, N.C., passed 15.5 per cent of the bad checks in town. Today they pass 35 per cent. Their share of the larceny arrests has also risen, from 17 per cent to 27 per cent.

In New York City, crime statistics for women were not immediately available.

However, a spokesman for the Department of Corrections said that with the increased use of drugs in recent years the number of women arrested had increased "dramatically."

He said that many cases involved "mixed pairs," where a woman and her male companion worked together to rob men seeking a pickup.

The woman would lure the man to a darkened hallway or to a hotel room where he might be mugged or bluffed out of his money.

Law enforcement personnel, sociologists, and other students of crime attribute the rise in female arrest rates to three broad causes: the changing attitudes of society, of women themselves, and of the police.

Prof. Gene Kassebaum, a sociologist at the University of Hawaii, noted that men had always been "massively over-represented" in crime.

"Certain kinds of opportunities to commit crimes are more open to the traditional male sex role in society than to the female role," he explained. "Just as there were more job opportunities open to men, even where women were equally qualified, it was also true for criminal opportunities. A perfectly well-qualified girl was discriminated against if she wanted to be a car thief. No one taught her how."

Drug Role Prominent

Thus as society accepts women in a wider variety of roles, their chance to commit crimes also expands. If there are more women in business, say the experts, there will be more women embezzlers.

Some believe the most powerful force affecting female criminality is drugs. "There was a time," said the Los Angeles Sheriff, "that the drug culture and the criminal culture were one and the same. Now drugs have gone over to other strata of society, and they've taken people from those strata and put them in with groups that might tend to be crime prone."

Once involved with drugs, a girl might become an addict and steal to support her habit, or she might be arrested for possessing or dealing narcotics.

The police also blame a "general breakdown of inhibitions" and the fact that in some quarters an arrest is no longer a stigma but a "badge of honor."

This is particularly true in political demonstrations, where women often play as large a role as men; but some women have also absorbed the radical cliche that "crimes against property" are permissible.

"This month," said Jean Standage, a Federal probation officer in San Francisco, "I had something we rarely saw in the past—two women bank robbers. The girls' feelings were totally different from what they might have been 10 years

Total Arrest Trends by Sex, 1960 Compared With 1969

| | ♂ Males | | | | | | ♀ Females | | | | | |
| | Total | | | Under 18 | | | Total | | | Under 18 | | |
Offense charged	1960	1969	% change	1960	1969	% change	1960	1969	% change	1960	1969	% change
Violent crime (Murder, forcible rape, robbery and aggravated assault)	88,499	151,010	+70.6	14,724	35,572	+141.6	10,603	16,671	+57.2	1,051	3,478	+230.9
Property crime (Burglary, larceny $50 and over and auto theft)	326,636	519,620	+59.1	162,756	280,876	+72.6*	37,542	106,940	+184.9	16,261	50,500	+210.6
Other assaults	109,336	164,338	+50.3	10,701	25,411	+137.5	11,843	23,043	+94.6	1,857	6,216	+234.7
Forgery and counterfeiting	17,187	20,766	+20.8	1,161	2,235	+92.5	3,342	6,145	+83.9	348	702	+101.7
Embezzlement and fraud	28,088	36,662	+30.5	642	2,001	+211.7	5,026	12,878	+156.2	145	504	+247.6
Stolen property; buying, receiving, possessing	8,664	31,460	+263.1	2,335	9,638	+312.8	812	2,945	+262.7	168	705	+319.6
Weapons; carrying, possessing, etc.	29,033	62,326	+114.7	6,225	10,460	+68.0	1,703	4,424	+159.8	188	509	+170.7
Prostitution and commercialized vice	7,452	8,512	+14.2	121	261	+115.7	18,181	32,753	+80.1	272	599	+120.2
Narcotic drug laws	26,384	155,035	+487.6	1,421	33,835	+2,281.1	4,520	27,874	+516.7	241	8,519	+3,460.9
Drunkenness	1,110,400	968,746	—12.6	11,210	26,267	+134.3	94,268	71,747	—23.9	1,290	3,954	+206.5

Source: Uniform Crime Report-F.B.I.
Based on comparable reports from 1,832 cities representing 78,027,000 population and 642 counties representing 16,826,000 population.

ago. Banks are the enemy now. One girl did it to get money for drugs for her boy friend. The other girl did it just to get money."

Narcotics is another area where attitudes are changing, and women are likely to be involved. "A lot of people don't think narcotics is a crime," said Lieut. Murle Hess, who processes prisoners at the Sybil Brand Institute, the women's jail here. 'It's one of those things that everybody is doing and they feel they just happened to get caught."

As society changes its attitude toward women, women are changing their views themselves. Prof. Marvin Wolfgang of the Criminology Research Center at the University of Pennsylvania, said:

"As women become more involved in what have traditionally been masculine roles, one might assume that the more protective qualities of the culture which kept them in a feminine, passive role will dissipate, if not disappear. Women could become more aggressive personalities."

Many experts agree with Professor Kassebaum, who said:

"Statistics on criminal behavior are generally a combination of two things. They tell something about what people are doing, and second, they tell something about what the law enforcement agencies are doing."

It is partly a question of which comes first—rising crime or rising interest, but most policemen acknowledge that they are more suspicious of women today. Phil Lewis, a social work consultant to the Dallas police, said:

"We in the criminal justice system are becoming less tolerant of women. They are being apprehended more frequently and not sheltered as in the past, when we tended to overlook the women."

Suspects Not Ignored

Not only are women committing more crimes, they are also more likely to be seized for their indiscretions. "In the past, if there was a robbery in a neighborhood, we'd ignore a suspicious-looking woman," said Sheriff Pitchess. "We didn't think a woman would be involved. But now we'd be

as likely to check a woman as a man."

A second aspect to police behavior is the attitudes and priorities that govern a force. Here in Los Angeles County, the sheriff has placed top priority on enforcing narcotics laws, which often net a high percentage of women. And he has cleaned out the hippie element on Sunset Strip, a drive that also increased female arrest figures.

In Raleigh, N. C., as in many cities, the police and store owners are cracking down on shoplifting, one of the major areas of female crime.

Most experts agree that the female crime rate will continue to rise faster than the male rate. Women will continue to take a larger role in society, and there is no indication they are innately more honest.

In fact, two students at the University of Baltimore recently conducted an experiment in which they carefully wrapped 615 packages and left them in the backs of taxicabs. According to the drivers, the packages were taken by 124 men and 211 women.

U.S. Notes Sharp Rise In Delinquency of Girls

WASHINGTON, April 11 (UPI)—Juvenile delinquency among girls 10 to 17 years old rose twice as fast as crime involving boys of the same age group from 1969 to 1970, a Government crime report said today. The report blamed the "more aggressive, more independent" behavior of girls.

In 1970, the report said, juvenile courts for the first time handled more than a million cases involving boys and girls. But the report, based on a study by the Department of Health, Education and Welfare, said that the rate of increase in delinquency cases slowed for the first time in five years.

The report said that, although delinquency was still primarily a boy's problem, the boy-to-girl ratio of court referrals narrowed from 4 to 1 in the mid-nineteen-sixties to 3 to 1 in 1970.

Of the 1,052,000 juvenile court cases in 1970, based on a national sample, 799,500 involved boys and 252,500 involved girls.

Crimes covered by the statistics included aggravated assault, burglary, larceny and auto theft, the use of drugs and truancy.

June 13, 1971

April 12, 197

NARCOTIC MENACE HELD NATION-WIDE BUT GRAVEST HERE

Juvenile Addiction at Epidemic Level in Nine Cities, Federal Commissioner Declares

VAST CITY TRAFFIC NOTED

$100,000,000 a Year in Street Sales Reported to Legion— Stricter Laws Urged

By ROBERT C. DOTY

Narcotic addiction among juveniles has reached epidemic proportions in nine major cities from coast to coast and is at its worst in New York, Federal narcotics officials here and in Washington said yesterday.

Lack of parental control and the "social disintegration" of the large urban centers were blamed for the phenomenon in statements by Harry J. Anslinger, United States Commissioner of Narcotics, in Washington, and by speakers at the American Legion conference on narcotics here.

The problem is most acute in New York, the Legion meeting was told by Assistant District Attorney Irving Slonim, with street sales of narcotics amounting to at least $100,000,000 annually. Mounting prices of narcotics "shots," he said, had driven many young addicts to crime to obtain funds for supplies, bringing the problem into the open.

Conditions in Other Cities

Mr. Anslinger, according to The United Press, said the wave of youthful addiction had been noted also in Philadelphia, Detroit, Chicago, St. Louis, New Orleans, San Francisco, Washington and Baltimore.

But only in New York, he said, had addiction been reported among teen-age youths still in high school. His bureau, he declared, could put an end to narcotics peddling if adequately equipped with "tools" in the form of laws providing compulsory prison terms of five, ten and twenty years for second and third offenders. Congress now is considering such legislation.

The theme of stiffer penalties for illicit narcotics dealers was stressed by a dozen speakers at the Legion meeting at the Waldorf-Astoria Hotel and by Senator Estes Kefauver, Democrat of Tennessee, in a radio interview.

The former chairman of the Senate Crime Committee described the wave of youthful addiction as a "terrible and awful menace," endorsed proposals for strengthening the Narcotics Bureau and urged parents to bring home to their children "the truth about what happens when they become narcotics addicts."

Dr. Victor H. Vogel, director of the United States Public Health Service narcotics hospital at Lexington, Ky., told the Legion conference that admissions of teen-age youths there had risen from fifty-two in 1948 to a peak of 440 in 1950—more than half of them from this city.

"Judging from news accounts, we are seeing only a small proportion of the teen-age narcotics addicts that exist in the large cities," he said.

However, he and other speakers drew a distinction between persons who had reached the stage of physical dependence on narcotics —the true addicts—and those who had experimented occasionally but had escaped enslavement. Many youthful users of narcotics in the latter class could be saved by prompt countermeasures the conference was told.

Dr. Vogel termed false a prevalent belief that a narcotic addict was required to plead guilty to a felony charge to obtain admission to the Federal hospitals. Addicts volunteering for first cures make up 80 per cent of admissions, he said, and records of their cases are entirely confidential.

Medical and rehabilitation methods at Lexington were praised by Irving Geist, a sponsor of the Four Chaplains Memorial Placement Center, Inc., which seeks establishment of a narcotics hospital and farm here, and by Dr. Morris Hinenburg, medical director of the Federation of Jewish Philanthropies. Both, however, urged new buildings for young addicts to permit their segregation from more sophisticated adult narcotics users.

Attorney General Nathaniel L. Goldstein, whose investigating committee last week focused attention on the youth problem, urged the Legion to direct its efforts toward establishment of more stringent Federal and state laws against narcotics peddlers and toward better educational and rehabilitation work among young people.

Mounting juvenile addiction rates were a sign of "social disintegration—failure to keep up with the problems of urban life," said Austin McCormick, Professor of Criminology at the University of California and formerly New York Commissioner of Corrections. Youth, he said, found itself unable to develop ethical concepts in an atmosphere of poverty, alcoholism and racial prejudice, and sought escape in narcotics. A broader approach than provision of additional treatment facilities was needed, he declared.

Mrs. Sylvia Singer, assistant district attorney and chairman of a subcommittee of the Welfare Council of New York City studying the problem of youthful addiction, outlined a program for immediate action by city and state officials to establish new facilities for treatment of victims.

Mrs. Singer and Raymond M. Hilliard, executive director of the council, in a separate statement issued yesterday, urged opening a reception unit to classify and begin treatment of young addicts, and a long-term treatment unit providing psychotherapy and occupational therapy to readapt patients to community living.

Mr. Anslinger, Police Commissioner Thomas F. Murphy and Superintendent of Schools William Jansen are scheduled to address the Legion group today at final sessions of the three-day conference.

TRUMAN SIGNS BILL FOR NARCOTICS WAR

Stiff Prison Terms Mandatory in Repeat Offenses—Board Set Up to Study Problem

Special to THE NEW YORK TIMES.

WASHINGTON, Nov. 2—President Truman approved today legislation making severe prison sentences mandatory for repeat offenders against Federal narcotic laws. He declared that addiction had reached "serious proportions."

He created by Executive order an Interdepartmental Committee on Narcotics composed of representatives from six Government departments. It will study narcotics law enforcement and such problems as prevention and control of addiction and treatment and rehabilitation of addicts. It will recommend such local and Federal legislation as it deems to be needed.

In signing the bill the President expressed concern over the increased illicit peddling of narcotics, particularly to youth.

"The tragic effects of drug addiction upon the individual, the family and the community as a whole are only too self-evident," he said.

Range of the Penalties

The bill signed today, the last passed by the first session of the eighty-second Congress, provides a prison sentence of two to five years for a first offense, five to ten years for a second, and ten to twenty years for a third. It allows fines of up to $2,000.

One provision of the measure long desired by Federal narcotics officials makes it impossible for hardened violators to avoid serving time in prison. The provision ends the discretionary power of judges to impose suspended sentences on repeat offenders.

In his statement, the President noted that he was aware "some objection" had been raised to the limitations on Federal courts in sentencing offenders.

The committee will have one representative from each of the departments of the Treasury, State, Defense, Justice and Agriculture and from the Federal Security Agency. Its chairman will be named later by the President from among its members or as an additional member.

The national legislative committee of the Veterans of Foreign Wars, in a resolution voted today, urged stronger state narcotics laws, with stiffer penalties for offenders. It heard pleas for the death penalty for persons selling narcotics to teen-agers.

June 18, 1951   November 3, 1951

DEATH DEMANDED FOR HEROIN SALES

Senate Panel Urges U. S. to End 'Murder on Installment Plan'—Addictions Growing

By C. P. TRUSSELL
Special to The New York Times.

WASHINGTON, Jan. 9 — A Senate investigating panel urged Congress today to authorize the death penalty for heroin smugglers and peddlers in extreme cases.

These traffickers in "the most deadly" of narcotic drugs, Senator Price Daniel, the Texas Democrat who headed the country-wide inquiry, told the Senate, were "selling murder, robbery and rape." He pleaded that they be dealt with accordingly under law.

"Their offense is human destruction as surely as that of a murderer," he added. "In truth and in fact, it is 'murder on the installment plan,' leading not only to the final loss of one life but to others who acquire this contagious infection through association with the original victim."

Addicts had testified before the Senate panel that they had spread their habits like cases of mumps.

The Daniel subcommittee, a unit of the Senate Judiciary Committee, made a lengthy list of recommendations for curbing the flow of heroin and other narcotics. It proposed appeals by the American Congress to international organizations to cooperate in controlling production of opium, marijuana and other sources of narcotics.

If Congress fails to act, Senator Daniel said, it will contribute to a problem growing more serious.

Shocked Investigators

The picture presented by Senator Daniel was one that he acknowledged had shocked the investigators. As he repainted it before the Senate, the shock appeared to spread widely among other members.

It was largely a picture of the narcotic situation in the United States. Addiction is now three times as strong as it was at the end of World War II, the report said. Some 60,000 addicts were known to the authorities. Youths, the report showed, entered the narcotic taking field to an alarming rate; about 13 per cent of addicts now were found to be under 21 years old.

As of now, the report emphasized, the United States had more addicts than any other western nation. Further, it held, a discouraging number is still at large.

Federal, state and local law, combined with inadequate enforcement forces, were seen losing the fight against the smuggling and peddling. The top members of the narcotic rings are hard to catch. Furthermore, the report said, narcotic enforcement agents are being hampered in their work.

Other Roadblocks

The panel report pointed out that the agents could not tap telephone wires in their work.

Nor, it was emgphasized, could agents carry arms, search without a warrant or make an arrest forthwith. The report urged that enforcement powers be strengthened and that larger appropriations be made to throw more agents into the field, with power to intercept wire communications under strict court direction.

The proposed death sentence for extreme cases of heroin smuggling and peddling would not, of course, be mandatory. It would be imposed only when the juries hearing the cases recommended it. However, the panel suggested, it would make smugglers and peddlers stop, look and listen.

REPORT QUESTIONS NARCOTICS POLICY

Bar-Medical Unit Suggests U. S. Fosters Addiction

By KENNETT LOVE

The Federal Bureau of Narcotics may unwittingly be encouraging drug addiction and the international traffic that feeds it, according to a report published last week.

The report was made by a joint committee of the American Bar Association and the American Medical Association. It urges a thorough review of Federal policies and suggests that the addict be regarded not as a criminal but as a patient needing medical treatment.

The report is one of the strongest attacks ever made on the Federal agency and the views and policies of its chief, Narcotics Commissioner Harry J. Anslinger. It was published by the Indiana University Press in a 173-page book entitled "Drug Addiction: Crime or Disease?"

A Federal narcotics agent, Edward R. Cass, was said to have questioned officials of the press and the university this month about the financing of the publication and the reasons for it. The book has had an advance sale of more than 1,250 copies.

Ex-Magistrate an Author

One of the authors of the report is Morris Ploscowe, a former New York City magistrate. He wrote:

"The very severity of law enforcement tends to increase the price of drugs on the illicit market and the profits to be made therefrom. The lure of profits and the risks of the traffic simply challenge the ingenuity of the underworld peddlers to find new channels of distribution and new customers."

Rufus King, a Washington lawyer and former counsel to Senate crime investigators, wrote a section of the report dealing with the handling of the narcotics problem by European countries.

He said they approached it from a medical rather than a criminological point of view. The proportion of addicts to the total populations of the countries discussed is a minute fraction of the proportion in the United States, he said.

England's Policies

"It is stated here without hesitation," he wrote, "that England has no significant drug addiction problem, no organized illicit trafficking, and no drug-law enforcement activities that could be regarded as comparable to those which preoccupy our own authorities.

"The key to this difference appears to be that the British medical profession is in full and virtually unchallenged control of the distribution of drugs.

"The controlling fact is that the medical profession accepts and treats addicts as patients so that virtually none are driven to support a black market."

The report asserts that narcotics do not in themselves cause criminal behavior but that the compulsion to obtain drugs, to avoid withdrawal pains, leads addicts to commit property crimes to obtain money for drugs.

The report was completed in 1959 and was given limited circulation. The Federal bureau then published a denial of the charges and a defense of the policies.

The final report was signed by C. Joseph Statler, Dr. R. H. Felix and Dr. Isaac Starr for the medical association and by Mr. King, Judge Edward J. Dimock and Abe Fortas for the bar association.

GOVERNOR SIGNS ADDICTS AID BILL

Offenders in Minor Cases to Be Sent to Hospitals Instead of to Jails

ROCKEFELLER HAILS ACT

Says It Will Save Hundreds From Drug Enslavement— Vote Measures Passed

Special to The New York Times.

ALBANY, March 22—Legislation to permit narcotics addicts who are not hardened criminals to be hospitalized rather than imprisoned after arrest was signed by Governor Rockefeller today.

The Governor predicted that the program would "save hundreds and ultimately thousands of young narcotics addicts from a life of enslavement to drugs."

The new law permits a judge to authorize medical treatment for addicts who have been arrested on relatively minor charges of use or possession of drugs, rather than as wholesalers, "pushers" or other criminals.

Such addicts who are sent to hospitals also would receive a program of after-care to insure their rehabilitation. If the treatment proved successful, the charges against them would ultimately be dropped.

The legislation also sets up a central narcotics office in the Mental Hygiene Department and establishes a state Council on Drug Addiction to advise in formulating state policy on narcotics problems.

In approving the bill, Governor Rockefeller renewed his request that the Federal Government establish a narcotics treatment hospital in the New York City area. The two Federal institutions are in Kentucky and Texas.

In other developments, final approval was given by the Senate to a proposed constitutional amendment that would permit a New York resident who has lived in his election district for thirty days to vote in Presidential elections. Under present law, only voters who have lived in the state a year, the county for four months and in the district for thirty days may participate in national elections.

Voting Plan Passed

The Senate also passed and sent to the Governor a bill that would automatically continue the registration of a person who voted once every three years. The present Permanent Personal Registration Law requires voting once in two years.

The Assembly approved and sent to the Senate a measure to set up a new state agency to borrow money and make loans to rehabilitate substandard housing. The bill will not take effect until 1964 because an enabling constitutional amendment is also required.

A bill to permit televising sessions of the Legislature or its committees with the consent of a majority of the members and any witnesses appearing was approved by the Assembly and sent to the Senate.

Legislation that would have barred contracts for a lifetime series of lessons in dancing, gymnastics or other physical or social activities was defeated by the Senate. Members complained it was too loosely drafted.

DRUG ADDICTION RULED NO CRIME

High Court Voids California Law Penalizing Use

Special to The New York Times.

WASHINGTON, June 25—A California law making it a crime to be a drug addict was struck down by the Supreme Court today as a "cruel and unusual punishment" in violation of the Constitution.

The unusual statute does not require any proof that the defendant used or bought any drugs or had any in his possession. Mere proof that he is "addicted" subjects him to jail for a minimum of ninety days and up to a maximum of a year.

The vote was 6 to 2 on the court to hold the law unconstitutional.

Justice Potter Stewart wrote the majority opinion and was joined by Chief Justice Warren and Justices Hugo L. Black, William O. Douglas and William J. Brennan Jr. Justice Douglas wrote an additional opinion for himself.

Justice John Marshall Harlan found the statute invalid as "arbitrary," not as a cruel and unusual punishment. Separate and strongly worded dissents were filed by Justices Tom C. Clark and Byron R. White.

It is the Eighth Amendment to the Constitution that prohibits "cruel and unusual punishments." The provision is seldom invoked in the courts, and observers had difficulty today remembering any case in which a criminal conviction had been reversed on that ground.

The case involved Lawrence Robinson, who was stopped by the police in Los Angeles one night. They found needle marks on his arm, and they said he had admitted using narcotics occasionally. He denied any such admission.

They were held without bail. No date was set for sentencing.

Each could get up to five years in jail and a $10,000 fine.

At trial the judge instructed the jury that it could convict Mr. Robinson even if it found no proof of actual use of narcotics by him. So long as it found him an addict. He was convicted and given a ninety-day sentence.

To put a man with leprosy or mental illness in jail as a criminal, Justice Stewart said, would universally be regarded as cruel and unusual punishment. He said narcotics addiction was an illness that could even be contracted involuntarily, as by an unborn child from its mother.

"We hold," the opinion concluded, "that a state law which imprisons a person thus afflicted as a criminal, even though he has never touched any narcotic drug within the state or been guilty of any irregular behavior there, inflicts a cruel and unusual punishment.

"To be sure, imprisonment for ninety days is not, in the abstract, a punishment which is either cruel or unusual. But the question cannot be considered in the abstract. Even one day in prison would be a cruel and unusual punishment for the "crime" of having a common cold."

Justice White's dissent drew particular attention today. He said the California statute should be read, to save its constitutionality, as requiring some proof that the defendant had used narcotics in the recent past.

"I deem this application of 'cruel and unusual punishment' so novel," Justice White said, "that I suspect the court was hard put to find a way to ascribe to the framers of the Constitution the result reached today, rather than to its own notions of ordered liberty.

"If this case involved economic regulation, the present court's allergy to substantive due process would surely save the statute and prevent the court from imposing its own philosophical predilections upon state legislatures or Congress.

"I fail to see why the court deems it more appropriate to write into the Constitution its own abstract notions of how best to handle the narcotics problem, for it obviously cannot match either the states or Congress in expert understanding."

The case was argued for Mr. Robinson by S. Carter McMorris of Del Paso Heights, Calif., and for Los Angeles by its deputy city attorney, William E. Doran.

Narcotics Panel Requests Lighter Penalty for Addicts

Study Criticizes Laws

By ROBERT C. TOTH

Special to The New York Times

WASHINGTON, April 4 — A Presidential advisory group called today for lighter Federal penalties against small peddlers and "victims" of narcotics, coupled with a "massive attack" on importers and large distributors of illegal drugs.

Penalties should be made to fit the offense, the group said in an interim report. For narcotics users who do not intend to peddle the drugs, it said, emphasis should be on rehabilitation rather than imprisonment. This is "virtually impossible" under present law, the group declared.

The recommendations were submitted by the President's Advisory Commission on Narcotic and Drug Abuse. The panel urged a coordinated Federal attack on the "skillful, ruthless and well-financed" illicit traffic in both narcotics and the so-called "dangerous drugs" such as the barbiturates, amphetamines (pep pills) and tranquilizers.

Key recommendations by the commission included:

Creation of a specially trained team within the Justice Department to investigate and prosecute importers and wholesalers. Currently, investigations are made by the Treasury Department's Bureau of Narcotics and prosecutions are handled by the Justice Department. However, the commission does not recommend abolishing the Bureau of Narcotics.

Legislation for strict Federal control over the manufacture, sale and distribution of all habit-forming depressant, tranquilizing and stimulant drugs that can result in damage to the individual or society.

A "high priority" master plan for a comprehensive research program looking into all aspects of drug abuse—physical, psychological, social, economic, and legal. Current efforts are fragmented, often undermanned and underfinanced, and generally inadequate, the group said.

The commission also suggested that more border inspectors be hired to cut down smuggling. Only 5 per cent of smuggled narcotics are now intercepted, according to the Treasury Department.

President Kennedy said the report "begins to open the door to understanding about users of narcotics and abusers of the law." He said the recommendations would be "studied carefully" by Federal agencies and promised that the agencies would cooperate fully with the commission requests for advice in preparing its final report, due Nov. 1.

The seven-member commission is headed by E. Barrett Prettyman, former Chief Justice of the United States Court of Appeals for the District of Columbia. It was established on Jan. 15. Its creation followed the first White House Conference on Narcotic and Drug abuse, held last Sept. 27 and 28.

Mr. Kennedy told the White House conference there was "universal agreement" that the two key objectives in this field were eliminating illicit traffic in the drugs and "rehabilitation and restoration to society of the drug addict."

Narcotics include marijuana, cocaine and the opium derivatives, notably heroin. The "dangerous drugs," those that may have detrimental effects upon the individual and on society, produce hypnotic effects, or depress, stimulate, tranquilize, alter perception, or cause hallucinations.

The opiates and barbiturates, and "even certain tranquilizers," the commission said, "can cause physical dependence." The rest usually do not cause addiction.

The commission's report gave considerable attention to Federal laws. It urged that a more clear-cut distinction be made between importers and wholesalers, small peddlers and the victim who possesses the drug with no intention to sell.

The report criticized present narcotics laws for establishing mandatory minimum sentences —two years in jail and $20,000 fine — with probation, parole, and suspended sentences permitted only for first offenders.

These laws, the commission declared, deprive the courts of discretion, increase court case loads, and add to the nation's economic burden because of the cost of imprisoning the offenders.

Most important, "they have made rehabilitation of the convicted narcotics offender virtually impossible, since there is no incentive for rehabilitation where there is no hope for parole," the panel said.

The commission urged the Justice Department to prepare legislation that would ease the law except for the importers and wholesalers. It recommended that small peddlers be subject to a fixed maximum sentence, rather than a mandatory minimum one, and be eligible for parole but not probation.

Persons found in possession of narcotics who do not intend to sell the drugs, should be liable to "indeterminate" prison terms and both probation and parole, the commission said. It urged that any changes in the law also permit review of the cases of persons now in prison.

The Justice Department was also asked to advise the commission whether addicts can be voluntarily committed to Federal treatment centers for a prescribed length of treatment. Addicts often seek treatment at these centers but leave before it is completed. They can be forced to stay only if convicted of a criminal offense.

Civil commitment raises constitutional questions, however. The Commission wanted legal advice on this point before preparing its final report.

The report endorsed a bill now before Congress to require manufacturers of barbiturates and amphetamines to account for all such drugs made, shipped, received, sold or distributed. It suggested extending the bill to cover tranquilizers as well as future drugs that are found dangerous.

It cautioned, however, that the regulations "should not at this time parallel" present narcotics laws because such strict rules would inhibit legitimate medical use of the drugs.

Other members of the commission are Dr. James P. Dixon, president of Antioch College, Yellow Springs, O., James R. Dumpson, Commissioner of Welfare of New York City; Dr. Roger Egeberg, medical director of the Los Angeles County Department of Charities; Harry Mapes Kimball, former chairman of the California Special Study Committee on Narcotics; Austin MacCormick, New York, executive director of the Osborne Foundation; and Dr. Rafael Sanchez-Ubeda, of St. Vincent's Hospital, New York. The executive director of the commission is Dean F. Markham.

Dr. Markham is a social psychologist who was planning director for the White House Conference on Narcotic and Drug Abuse.

April 5, 1963

State Tries New Answer to Riddle:
How to Cure Addiction

By JOHN SIBLEY

Special to The New York Times

ALBANY, April 2—When Governor Rockefeller called on the Legislature to enact his $81-million program to eradicate drug addiction, his special message rang with confidence and promise.

His "war on narcotics addiction," the Governor declared, would remove the pushers from the streets and schoolyards, preventing "these evil carriers from spreading their contagion." And it would "restore the addict to a useful, drug-free life."

The Legislature approved the program this week in the closing hours before its Easter-Passover recess. But even the Senators and Assemblymen who led the floor fight echoed none of Mr. Rockefeller's buoyant optimism.

Speaker after speaker voiced frustration and doubt. Many declared they were supporting the program only because it was "better than nothing at all."

Most of the debate focused on a controversial section under which any addict could be committed against his will for a treatment program lasting up to three years.

Assemblyman Max Turshen spoke more frankly than some of his colleagues when he commented: "We haven't got the medical answer, so we've got to do the next best thing. We've got to keep these people off the streets."

'Concentration Camps'

Albert Blumenthal, one of a group of reform Democrats who fought to delete the compulsory commitment section of the Rockefeller bill, put it more strongly. He said:

"We're deluding the public if we say we're going to cure addicts by locking them up for three years. Perhaps we should tell the public that we're faced with a threat as great as bubonic plague, and until we find a cure we're going to set up a concentration camp in every community."

No matter whose statistics are used, the percentage of addicts treated under existing programs

who stay "clean" is distressingly small. Under the state's Metcalf-Volker Act of 1962, addicts arrested for certain crimes can choose to undergo treatment rather than face trial.

Of 1,500 arrested addicts admitted to the Metcalf-Volker program from Jan. 1, 1964 to June 30, 1965, 80 per cent were rearrested, including 52 per cent of the relatively small number of addicts who completed the program. Of 1,742 in the program in that period, 1,207 "absconded" from treatment.

"Quite frankly, gentlemen, the addict doesn't want to be cured," said Senator Edward J. Speno, who sponsored the Governor's bill in

the Senate. "We have to force him to be cured."

The preamble to the Rockefeller bill asserts:

"Experience has demonstrated that narcotic addicts can be rehabilitated and returned to useful lives only through extended periods of treatment in a controlled environment followed by supervision in an aftercare program."

Opponents argued that with medical science's present understanding of addiction it was futile to speak of cure even with enforced treatment, and that the Rockefeller program was in fact one of incarceration.

"The Governor calls this human

renewal," said Harlem Assemblyman Percy Sutton. "I call it human removal."

The reform Democrats, joined by a handful of colleagues, proposed to substitute for the Rockefeller program one of their own. Theirs would have set in motion a massive research program in quest of a synthetic drug that could be used to withdraw addicts from true narcotics.

Proposals Defeated

Pending such a discovery, they proposed to authorize physicians to administer maintenance doses of narcotic drugs in the course of treating addicts. This, they argued, would take the profit out of illicit drug traffic and help keep others from becoming addicted.

These proposals, introduced in the form of amendments to the Rockefeller program, were defeated by overwhelming votes in both Houses.

The Rockefeller compulsory commitment program is patterned after a California law that has been in effect since 1961, a statute that has survived lawsuits contending it violated addicts' civil liberties.

A number of Democrats have denounced the Rockefeller program as an election-year grandstand play. They point out that the effective date of the legislation is April 1, 1967, and contend that, if he were sincere, the Governor would have set it in motion at once.

The Governor's critics also note that, although the legislation appropriates $6-million for the establishment of a narcotics control commission and $75-million for construction of hospitals and clinics, no such funds are provided in the Rockefeller budget.

The Governor reportedly plans to ask for the $6-million in the supplemental budget to be adopted near the end of the current legislative session. He has said he will ask the Federal Government to provide two-thirds of the $75-million for construction.

The New York Times (by Gertrude Samuels)

THERAPY FOR ADDICTS: Governor Rockefeller's $81-million program to combat drug addiction was adopted by the Legislature last week. Photo shows doctor-patient consultation at the Federal narcotics hospital in Lexington, Ky.

The Drug Scene: Nation's Illegal Traffic Is Valued at Up to $400-Million Annually

NEW YORK CALLED DISTRIBUTION AREA

Most Marijuana Smuggled From Mexico Lands Here, in Chicago or Los Angeles

By MARTIN WALDRON
Special to The New York Times

REYNOSA, Mexico — In a dingy nightclub on Reynosa's main street, where the noise was overpowering and the light dim, an American with a half-dozen empty margherita glasses on his table was negotiating to buy marijuana.

"I have heard that it can be done," said the waiter, who had pocketed a sizable tip. "But I do not know exactly how."

He lingered at the table long enough to pick up the empty glasses. "Perhaps if you will wait," he said.

Fifteen minutes and one drink later, a young Mexican, laughing and showing his teeth in the dim light, sat down at the table with the American.

The Parking Lot

"You are driving?" he asked.

"Yes."

"There is a parking lot in the square behind this building. If you could bring your car there."

"It is already parked there. A yellow Ford with Texas license plates."

The Mexican pondered a moment. "How much did you have in mind?" he asked.

"A half pound," the American said.

"If it could be done, it would be expensive."

"How much?"

"Forty dollars." It was within the price range that had been predicted by a narcotics agent in the United States.

"Half now, half on delivery."

"All now, please."

After a token argument, the Mexican shrugged and agreed to take $20 then. He put the bill in his pocket. "Wait here," he said, standing and buttoning his raincoat.

In 30 minutes, perhaps less, he returned. "Your car is ready to travel," he said, sliding into the seat he had vacated.

"Is it still raining?"

He shook his head, took the other $20 in payment, refused a drink and vanished once again.

An Odor of Hay

Under the front seat of the rented automobile, there was a small package, wrapped in paper, about the size of a pack of king-size cigarettes. The package weighed perhaps a half-pound, at least half of it in paper.

The crumbly vegetable matter inside the wrapper had an odor of old hay. Satisfied that it was indeed marijuana, but not the half-pound he had paid for, the American held it for a moment, and then scattered it in the mud puddles of the parking lot. He rolled the paper wrapper into a ball and skittered it across the top of the automobile parked next to his.

Then he drove to the border, paid a 4-cent toll to cross the dilapidated bridge into the United States, and stopped at the customs station. A United States customs officer, yawning in the post-midnight quiet, asked:

"What country are you a citizen of?"

"The United States of America."

"What did you buy in Mexico?"

"Nothing I brought back."

The customs officer waved the automobile through.

The four ounces or so of marijuana sold by the smiling Mexican to a stout American reporter in a dim nightclub were only an infinitesimal part of the traffic in illegal drugs.

The traffic, the authorities say, is worth $300-million to $400-million a year.

Besides spending $100-million on marijuana each year, Americans spend $225-million on heroin, $25-million on black market amphetamines and barbiturates, and $5-million on cocaine. The amount spent on the hallucinogens such as LSD, STP, peyote and mescaline cannot be guessed with even reasonable accuracy.

The illegal traffic has been so lucrative that dozens of men have been murdered in fights for territory rights. The profit has led police officers to sell protection, diplomats to join smuggling rings, and Negro gangsters in Chicago, Houston and Los Angeles to challenge successfully the Mafia for distribution rights.

The patterns of the illegal traffic vary widely. Where heroin, for example, is smuggled into the United States in lots of three or four pounds, marijuana may be brought in from Mexico by the ton.

Wholesalers seeking loads for New York, Chicago, or Los Angeles have camouflaged marijuana under scrap iron or lumber, and packed it in automobile doors and upholstery. Much has been smuggled in by boat and by airplane.

Periodically, the Mafia is rumored to have moved in on the marijuana traffic, but both state and Federal narcotics agents deny this. For big-time gangsters, the profit in marijuana is too small.

It takes no more ingenuity to smuggle a pound of heroin than it does a pound of marijuana, and a pound of heroin will retail for $50,000, while a pound of marijuana may bring no more than $100.

Grown in Durango

Most Mexican marijuana is believed to be grown in mountain villages in the east and west branches of the Sierra Madre. "It's the real treasure of the Sierra Madres," said a narcotics agent.)

Jack Carpenter, an undercover agent for the Texas Bureau of Narcotics, said that marijuana, although illegal, flourished in parts of Mexico because officials got part of the selling price.

"There is this one little town where the mayor has the marijuana concession," he said. He also guessed that the captain in charge of the Army garrison in the district shared the profit, too.

Mr. Carpenter said that peasants, who planted an acre or two to "sell to the man," grew most Mexican marijuana.

"Most of them don't smoke many of the Mexican peasants, marijuana is something smoked by witches and vampires."

"They grow a lot of marijuana down in the state of Durango," said Walter E. Naylor, a former Texas Ranger who now is chief of the Texas Narcotics Bureau.

Inexplicably, Minnesota has been the biggest marijuana-growing American state. Of 1,630 acres of marijuana destroyed by narcotics agents in the United States in 1964, 1,130 of them were in Minnesota. In 1965, of the 1,925 acres they destroyed, 1,239 were in Minnesota.

Most marijuana smuggled into the United States from Mexico goes to New York, Chicago or Los Angeles. Then it is sold in wholesale quantities and delivered throughout the country by airplane, bus or freight lines.

Much of the traffic is unstructured, loosely involving students, underworld elements and citizens who are members of neither one group nor the other.

A recent graduate of Amherst in Massachusetts, who sold 11 kilograms of marijuana to students last fall, said that he was no longer dealing because a local professional had warned him that his operation was getting too big. The graduate recalled that his first shipment — 2.5 kilograms — had been sent to him by Railway Express from a friend in California.

"He figured he'd be clever and send it to a false name, but he didn't know that in Massachusetts you have to it themselves," he said. "To have identification to pick up the package," he said.

"We kept saying we were picking it up for a friend, but the Railway Express guy kept saying, 'Just identify the contents and we'll open it up and see if it's your package.'

"We kept saying, 'Well, it's personal and we're just doing him a favor.' We had to come back three times with phony stories. It really got dangerous."

The students and other amateurs who smuggle directly from Mexico have learned to avoid another danger—being betrayed to customs by the Mexican sellers.

"Two carloads of them will go to Reynosa or Matamoros," Mr. Carpenter said. "One group will make the buy, having it delivered to their car. Before they return, they will transfer the marijuana to the other car.

Traffic at Border

"One car will come back through Del Rio and the other through Brownsville. If the pusher has sold their tag number to customs, the customs officer won't find anything if they search the car where the marijuana was delivered to."

It is believed that most marijuana enters the United States at the California border, where the steady flow of automobiles and trucks from Mexico, perhaps 25,000 a day, makes frequent checks for contraband virtually impossible.

At San Ysidro, Calif., for example, just north of Tijuana, eight lanes of traffic flow into three check points. Peddlers always have time to hawk plaster statues of Christ and of bulls, birds and frogs to the drivers as they inch their way toward the customs stations.

Still, the customs officials, though pressed to avoid monumental traffic jams, do pull some automobiles aside for an inspection. In the last three years, they have seized more than 25,000 pounds of marijuana, enough to make more than two million cigarettes.

Reynosa is only one of a half-dozen Mexican border cities where much of this marijuana, and amphetamines, too, can be bought with a trifle of patience and a supply of money.

Two weeks before he bought the marijuana, the American had been seated in a nightclub in another border town. He was with Mr. Carpenter, the undercover agent from Texas, and Mr. Carpenter's wife, a former stripper who had worked a nightclub circuit in Mexico.

Mr. Carpenter, posing as a hippie, bought amphetamine tablets from a waiter as easily as he might have bought a drink.

In testifying before a Senate committee in July, 1964, John E. Storer, chief of the California Bureau of Narcotic Enforcement, said:

"Anybody with an automobile can be a narcotics peddler by driving to Mexico and purchasing any quantity he desires.

"There is no need for a complex organization. There is no need for the intricate planning, ingenuity, and know-how that is required for a shipment from the Middle East."

Mr. Storer's statement, however, does not seem to apply to heroin.

Equipped with the names of several notorious distributors—Telesfora Parra Lopez, who is known as Pipas, Juan Hernandez, known as Big Brother, Miguel Barragan, Salomon Sandez Jr. and Urbano Siquieros—an American reporter tried to buy heroin in Tijuana. He was unable to find the distributors.

Onslaughts on Tijuana dives on three occasions brought offers of women, pills, pornographic movies and "unusual entertainment," but not heroin.

Waiters, bartenders, "B" girls and furtive men peddling various items professed to have heard only of Sandez, who had just died in a Mexican prison from an overdose of heroin.

"You need some contacts to buy heroin in Mexico and besides, you look like a police officer," said Joseph H. House, supervising agent in Southern California for the California Narcotics Bureau.

French Heroin Weak

There has been a ready market for the dark brown Mexican heroin (French heroin is white) on the West Coast and in Chicago. A Chicago narcotics officer said the less potent French heroin was sometimes so diluted with milk sugar that it was not even addictive.

Actually, the traffic in French heroin begins in Turkey. Opium farmers there, who are licensed by the government to grow opium poppies for medical and scientific use, regularly overproduce their allotments, and this overproduction is sold to black market brokers.

This is smuggled from Turkey into remote areas of Syria or Lebanon, usually by camel, and then taken to Aleppo in Syria or Beirut in Lebanon, where morphine is extracted from the opium.

The morphine, about one-tenth the volume of the original opium, is then smuggled to illegal laboratories in France, where it is turned into heroin. Most of the smuggling from the Middle East into France is done by seamen, and most of the laboratories are in or near Marseille.

Although diplomats and businessmen have been involved in smuggling heroin into the United States, most routine traffic has been carried out by seamen and airline employes. Inside the United States, the Mafia dominates distribution, particularly in New York.

In 20 years, investigations by the United States Bureau of Narcotics have resulted in the convictions of more than 60 members of the Mafia, including Vito Genovese, who was generally viewed as the top man in the Mafia. He is now serving a 15-year sentence.

Illegal drugs sold outside of New York are often under the control of Negro gangs, and drug traffic has begun to rival prostitution as the major source of income for some Negro criminal organizations.

The Negro Gangsters

"We have some very sophisticated Negro gangsters in Chicago," said Lieut. Thomas E. Kernan, head of the Chicago police narcotics squad.

"It is our opinion that arrangements to get heroin are made through the Mafia," he said, adding that Negro crime syndicates handled the actual distribution.

Throughout the United States, there are more than 50 Negro gangsters known as major narcotics distributors in the United States.

Walter Lee Carlton of Mobile, Ala., several years ago became a wholesale heroin dealer in Los Angeles. He was the West Coast distributor for Louis Fiana of the Vito Genovese family of the Mafia, the narcotics bureau said.

Leroy Jefferson, from Warren, Ark., was one of the top, if not the leading, narcotics figure on the West Coast from 1957 to 1959.

Jefferson sold so much heroin and marijuana "that several New York-Italian groups were actually fighting to get him as a customer," the narcotics bureau said.

The new mobsters appear to have taken lessons from the Mafia. "In the last two years, eight or 10 of our narcotics informers have turned up dead." Lieutenant Kernan said. Rat poison, he said, has been a favorite murder weapon.

Quite aside from the hard narcotics, the peddling of the so-called dangerous drugs—barbiturates and amphetamines—has become so extensive that in 1966 Congress created a new agency to stop it.

The agency, the Bureau of Drug Abuse Control, part of the Food and Drug Administration, has 299 investigators assigned to pill control, and in the last 18 months they have made more than 1,000 arrests.

Underworld Moving In?

Nonetheless, the bureau has not been able to establish a definitive pattern for the black market pill operation.

"We have been getting some indications that organized crime is the source of many of the pills being sold illegally," said Jerry N. Genson, chief of criminal investigations for the bureau.

The bureau estimates that, of 3.9 billion amphetamine pills manufactured in the United States in legal laboratories in 1966, 1.7 billion ended up on the black market. Of 3.1 billion barbiturates, 500 million were sold on the black market.

Mr. Genson said that millions of pills had been stolen by hijackers, who seized them while they were being shipped to wholesale druggists. Others were stolen in the laboratories by employes, some of whom used fictitious orders from legitimate wholesalers to cover up the thefts.

Furthermore, the chemical formulas for the pills are widely known and the ingredients are readily available. Old pill-making machines, discarded by licensed manufacturers, have been salvaged and many are in use in Mexico to make black market pills.

Often, these pills can be identified by their being slightly misshapen, the result of being made by a machine with worn dies.

The pills are sold nearly anywhere—in pool halls, bars, truck stops or on street corners—Mr. Genson said.

Many of the pills, especially the amphetamines, find their way into the hands of high school students.

In California, where the problem is particularly acute, 881 teen-agers were arrested in the first six months of 1967 for violating laws on dangerous drugs. In the same period, 3,116 adults were arrested.

Joseph House of the California narcotics bureau said his agents had seized millions of pills that were sent out by drug manufacturers who did not take the trouble to find out where the pills were going.

He opened a safe in his office and showed a visitor several cardboard drums of amphetamines.

Diverted to Los Angeles

"This drum," he said, opening a lid, "was ordered by a Mexican from the Bates Laboratory in Chicago."

"The Mexican wrote that he owned a drug store in Mexico and needed the pills for it," he said.

"They have to know that no drug store in the world could sell one of these drugs in a lifetime, but they will ship 10 or 12 of them to one store, no questions asked."

The amphetamines being exhibited were seized by California narcotics agents when the Mexican picked them up at a warehouse in San Ysidro, Calif., and took them to Los Angeles instead of Mexico.

On the black market, a drum of pills could be worth as much as $35,000. Sold on prescription, they normally would bring about $7,000.

"We need a new Federal law requiring all dangerous drugs to be shipped in bond to a bonded warehouse," said Mr. House. "This would give us a better check on where these pills are going."

In April of this year, agents of the Bureau of Drug Abuse Control raided four laboratories—in Birmingham, Ala., Englewood, N. J., Jersey City and Seattle—and seized the equivalent of more than 12 million pills from unlicensed manufacturers or from manufacturers without inventory control.

In the same month, the agents seized more than 1 million pills from two Kansas City doctors of osteopathy.

However, the illegal sales by physicians and druggists are believed to be small. From July, 1965, through July, 1966, the latest dates for which figures are available, there were only 51 prosecutions of pharmacists and physicians. There are more than 250,000 physicians in the United States and about 53,000 retail drug stores.

In the last year, eight service station operators and truck drivers have been convicted in Federal court for illegally distributing amphetamines to truck drivers.

Danger to Drivers

"This is a very dangerous practice," a narcotics agent said. "These drivers may be completely exhausted and not know it because of the effects of the pills."

In the last year, agents have been assisting state agencies in trying to stop the manufacture of LSD.

"The LSD situation has calmed down in some parts of the country, but is worse in others than it was before," Mr. Genson said.

On Dec. 21, agents from the bureau arrested Augustus O. Stanley 3d, 32, a proficient chemist, who was once a student at the University of California. They said he had manufactured 10 million doses of LSD in a home laboratory in a San Francisco suburb.

Stanley, who is something of a hero in the hippie world, and two other men and two women were charged with conspiring to manufacture a controlled drug illegally.

Nevertheless, the authorities do not believe there is an organized LSD traffic in the United States. Much of what has been seized, they say, apparently has been manufactured for home consumption.

The Federal and state authorities deny the recurring rumors that the Mafia is involved in the LSD traffic. Whether or not the Mafia moves in on LSD and other drugs will depend, of course, on how great is the American demand for them.

Certainly, The Times survey has found, the use of drugs is growing. Moreover, there is every possibility that it will continue to grow, and that the next generation will be even more drug oriented than this one. Drug use and drug abuse have become a fact of—and a challenge to—American life.

January 12, 1968

Addicts' Victims Turn Vigilante

Violence and vigilante groups are becoming widely accepted by slum residents as the most effective way of ridding their neighborhoods of narcotics addicts.

Attacks by armed gangs have taken place, many of them, apparently unnoticed or ignored by the police, and residents of besieged neighborhoods say they are planning offensives against junkies. They are prompted, they say, by the failure of law-enforcement and other city agencies to reduce or even control the spread of heroin.

"We warn the pushers: In this block you do not push," said the 17-year-old leader of a gang that prowls the Lower East Side. "We tell the dope fiends: Here you do not steal. If they listen to us, fine. They push their poison someplace else. If they do not listen, we get them."

For the poor, as well as for officials who face the problem every day, drug addiction in New York seems to defy solution even as it grows more acute.

The police have not been able to eliminate it or even effectively control it; various therapeutic programs have shown both promise and failure and those in charge often show an inability to cooperate with one another; and hospitals, which have the potential for doing much, have thus far been either unwilling or unable to do anything substantial.

The result is a social crisis of immense cost and complexity that has ravaged communities, disrupted the city, and continues to drain human and financial resources —with no end in sight.

A two-month study of the narcotics problem by The New York Times indicates that in areas infested with addicts, the residents now regard retribution as preferable to promises of protection and plans for therapeutic programs that never seem big enough, prompt enough or workable.

The emerging pattern of violence is evident mostly on the Lower East Side and in Harlem and a few areas in Brooklyn. In other areas, such as the Hunts Point section of the Bronx, the fear of junkies and pushers has led not to counterattack, but to a fearful capitulation of spirit and an acceptance of a Wild West kind of lawlessness.

The addict who used to be tolerated as a nuisance or even embraced as a "sick" friend is now hated as a sneak thief and feared as a mugger; the pusher who used to be disdainfully regarded as a ne'er-do-well or perhaps even admired as a poor boy who had made it big, is now despised as a menace to the children who can easily buy narcotics in the schoolyard.

Among the investigation's findings are these:

¶At least one large, organized group of Puerto Ricans and Negroes have beaten up pushers and addicts on the Lower East Side in the area between Second and 14th Streets and along Avenues C and D. One gang member said he was doing it "because the junkies are destroying my people."

Other groups of teen-agers and young people have formed gangs and say they are planning to do the same thing elsewhere on the Lower East Side and in Harlem.

¶More common than the youth gangs are self-defense groups among adults. There are more than 90 tenant patrols operating in the city's public-housing projects, and the city is paying patrol leaders $2.50 an hour.

¶Tenement-dwellers on the Lower East Side have armed themselves not only with clubs and knives, but also with rifles and handguns, to protect themselves and their buildings. One group on East Seventh Street has even purchased walkie-talkies for patrol use.

¶Although the police deny

any knowledge of the armed self-defense groups, members say that the police have, in fact, encouraged them. One patrolman is credited with teaching tenants how to make clubs of old table legs.

¶Mail theft by heroin users is so frequent that the Post Office is spending $360,000 a year on overtime in the Bronx and in Brooklyn for special protection.

Not a New Approach

Vigilante groups are not new, either here or elsewhere, nor is violence new as a means of dealing with community problems. But the growing preference for applying these tactics to drug pushers and users is viewed by some observers as a portent of widespread acceptance of an oversimplified, punitive solution to a vastly complicated issue.

Animosity toward the addict has reached such a point in some neighborhoods that politicians who have supported progressive approaches to addiction control are under increasing pressure to support any action that will take junkies out of circulation.

An aide to one liberal state legislator, who asked that his name not be used, said: "Don't kid yourself that this 'sweep the streets' business is limited to conservatives. It's probably even more intense in the poorer neighborhoods. The people who are demanding it are the very people who used to provide the impetus for liberal legislation."

The new and intense loathing of the addict is coupled, in the slums, with an ambivalence toward the police. People say they want more police protection, but also say they have lost faith in the police.

Poor families have lost their television sets to addict thieves. The current militancy against addict and pusher is heightened by the fact that families are now losing much more than television sets. They are losing young sons and daughters. For the facts clearly indicate that addicts are getting younger with every passing year.

Dr. Michael Baden, associate medical examiner of New York, says that in 1967 the median age of addicts who died after using heroin was 28. Now the median age is 22.

In 1966, there were 33 teen-agers who died in New York after taking heroin. Last year the number rose to 72. But in three months—June, July and August—71 died this year. Sixty per cent of them were black and 30 per cent were Puerto Rican. Addicts aged 14 are not uncommon these days and slum residents report that 8-year-olds are experimenting with heroin bought in the schoolyard.

Neighborhoods Vary

The state of hostilities that now exists in the most beleaguered neighborhoods is one that nobody wants to talk about. The tenement-dweller is angry but he does not like to speak of retribution; the role of gun-toter is not one he is easy with. He does not like making war on people he knows.

Nor does every neighborhood react to the problem in the same way. Chinatown, for example, has a very small, though growing, problem among its teen-agers, but no defense measures were observed there. A resident of the neighborhood said most parents refused to admit that any problem existed, since the use of heroin carried with it a terrible stigma among the Chinese.

People of Italian extraction on the Lower East Side also have a small but developing addiction problem among their young. But no organized defense groups are evident in Little Italy, either, and junkies are almost never seen there. Addicts with Italian names, however, appear in Puerto Rican blocks on the Lower East Side.

"The Italians will not tolerate dope addicts in their midst," said a resident of Little Italy. Asked how the Italians managed to prevent addicts from swarming over them, he replied: "We do it like we have always done it. If we have a problem in the neighborhood, we settle it in the neighborhood."

The same ethnic groups reacted differently in different places. The Puerto Ricans of the Lower East Side were "turf"-oriented, well aware that they had a problem and predisposed to settle it themselves—an attitude similar to that of the Italians to the west of them, although not so well established.

But in the Hunts Point section of the Bronx the Puerto Ricans seemed more submissive, less sure of themselves, distrustful of both police and pusher.

In Harlem at least three groups advocate dealing very firmly with the addict. Some members of all groups admitted they were armed when they went into the street to search for addicts. Others said they dealt with addicts and pushers only with their fists. The intention among members of all three groups was simply to drive addicts and pushers from their neighborhoods—there was little talk of rehabilitation or hospitalization.

Perhaps the most outspoken proponent of a street offensive against addicts and pushers is the Rev. Oberia Dempsey of the Upper Park Avenue Baptist Church, who believes there are 250,000 heroin users in Harlem alone. He carries a revolver with him because he fears that pushers may attack him for his firm stand on narcotics.

When Mr. Dempsey speaks of the problem his language may seem more reminiscent of what one can hear from the most conservative law-and-order advocate, rather than a Harlem preacher. But the similarities are superficial. Mr. Dempsey talks out of desperation, not ideology.

"We don't advocate taking the law in our own hands," he said, "but the emphasis of the law is placed on protecting the rights of the criminal, not the decent citizen. I think every addict who is on the streets must be removed from Harlem. The government should set up health camps outside the city, in old Army bases upstate. A lot of so-called bleeding-heart liberals could go up and act as counselors."

Another group advocating a militant approach is the Harlem Youth Federation. Its president, Hannibal Ahmed, is currently under indictment, charged with conspiring with five other Harlem Negroes to kill a white policeman every week. They have all pleaded not guilty.

Mr. Ahmed and his colleagues are particularly concerned about the increased use of heroin among children and what they call the inability of the police to do anything about it.

Federation members talk to children whenever and wherever they can, alerting them to the perils of narcotics use. Frequently, when they meet with groups of children, they sing this song, to the tune of "Old Mac-Donald":

Eee-I, Eee-o, drugs must go,
  Dah-dah-dah-dah-dah.
The pushers must be off-off-off,
  Dah-dah-dah-dah-dah.
The people must work both
  day and night,
Time for us to put up a fight.
Eee-I Eee-o drugs must go
  Dah-dah-dah-dah-dah.

Mr. Ahmed says that "some of the older brothers are giving dope to 10-year-olds and there is no place for them to get help."

The Harlem Youth Federation has a mattress in its 125th Street headquarters and its members stand ready 24 hours a day to help any addict who wants to detoxify himself.

This summer 28 of the federation's 60 members asked Harlem residents between 110th and 155th Streets how they thought addicts should be handled in the community.

Violence Advocated

The consensus was summed up by such comments as "Knock their heads in," "They are killing our people" and "They should be killed."

The head of the third group advocating drastic measures against addicts is John Shabazz of the Black Citizens Patrol, an organization claiming 155 members. It was formed about a year and a half ago.

Mr. Shabazz, a former associate of Malcolm X, said he wanted no money and no help from the police—only that, starting this fall, his followers would try to "discourage" those who would sell narcotics in Harlem public schools.

"We have the names and photographs of pushers," he said, "and we will have people inside the schools to turn over the names to the proper authorities. If they don't deal with the problem, we will have to deal with it our own way."

A former Harlem heroin dealer who estimates he made $4,000 to $5,000 a week on sales of about four pounds, was asked how he justified what he did. The dealer, whose name cannot be used, replied:

"I never gave it a thought whether it was right or wrong. It was just a way of making money. I was never in any trouble. You can get into trouble by selling some bad dope. I knew I was getting good dope from the people I was dealing with."

He insisted however, that "I never sold to kids." The dealer was disconcerted recently to learn that his teenage son used heroin.

Mr. Shabazz was invited to lecture to a group of teen-agers in a church basement in Central Harlem. The spirit of the meeting was almost evangelical.

Mr. Shabazz: Only a first-class jackass would stick a needle in his arm and shoot up. What kind of fool would do that?

'You Know What To Do'

Teen-agers (in unison):

203

Somebody who don't have nothing else to do.

Mr. S: What kind of dope is here in Harlem?

Teen-agers (shouting): Cocaine! Heroin! Weight pills! Reefers!

Mr. S: What's the youngest age of an addict that you've heard of? Teen-agers: Eight!

Mr. S: Where do drugs come from in the schools? Teen-agers: Pushers!

Mr. S: Do the pushers go to school? Teen-agers: Yes!

Mr. S: And what school has more drug pushers than any other?

Here the teen-agers were not unanimous, filling the room with shouts of the high schools they knew—George Washington, Louis D. Brandeis, Charles Evans Hughes, Benjamin Franklin.

Mr. Shabazz then told the teen-agers that if anyone came up to them and offered them drugs, "you know what to do—knock the hell out of them." The youngsters applauded.

The Harlem groups are for the most part only threatening violence, but one gang on the Lower East Side has already skirmished with pushers. Gang members say that one of their number was murdered last year; retaliation, they say, from the pushers.

The gang, which has a name but does not want it published, claims more than 100 members. It is armed and is led by a 17-year-old youth who will be called Ramon here.

"We have agents who follow junkies and pushers around," Ramon said. "We know every one of them. We know when pushers get the stuff and we know when particular junkies need a fix. We know exactly what is going on in this neighborhood, which is more than I can say for the police."

But perhaps the most disquieting experience is talking to ordinary people—black and white, poor and not so poor—who are not members of gangs, not especially young, are not violent and do not want to be. People whose only contact with violence has been on television now talk calmly and seriously of violence as necessary for their survival.

A 62-year-old man who had worked as a guard said he never walked in the hall of his lower East Side building unless he carried a loaded revolver in his hand. A professional trumpet player in the same neighborhood who was mugged twice took karate lessons and did battle with a junkie who tried to mug him in the hallway outside his apartment.

A pregnant housewife who lives nearby says she now thinks of simple household implements as potential weapons.

Several other women said they were purchasing small spray cans of chemical irritants and carrying them in their purses; still other women were carrying knives and cans of pepper.

A young woman in the Brownsville section of Brooklyn says she will kill the next addict who tries to steal anything from her apartment; a neighbor said he recently waited behind a door for two hours with a baseball bat for the addict who had unsuccessfully tried to get into his apartment earlier.

"The good Lord took a liking to him," the man said, "because he didn't come back and that's what saved me from killing him."

The superintendent of a tenement near the corner of East Seventh Street and Avenue D carries a gun, as does his wife. "I tell the junkies," he says, "You fool around with me and I'm gonna fool around with you."

Over and over the visitor finds evidence that some neighborhoods have become armed camps, filled with people who believe that the only way to survive in New York in the year 1969 is with guns, knives and chemicals.

Charles Parker, a Bronx resident who was the prime mover recently in forming a coalition of youngsters and adults who patrol the streets and report wrongdoing to the police, says that he and many of his neighbors have bought big television-radio-phonograph consoles because "you can't carry one of those babies down a fire escape."

The trumpet player who took karate lessons is Marc Levin, 27, who lived at 278 East Seventh Street for five years, but has since moved to a relatively quiet part of Greenwich Village.

Although Mr. Levin, a quiet man of average height and weight, is more interested in practicing his horn, he practiced karate four to five hours a day after he was mugged a second time.

Offers Gift Record

He recalls that the second time, he gave the junkie $2.35 (all he had) and offered to give him an auto-graphed copy of a jazz record he had cut called "The Dragon Suite." But some people approached and the junkie ran off—without the record.

The junkie had brandished a knife, and that frightened Mr. Levin, who then began to study self-defense techniques.

The third attack—the one that prompted his flight from the Lower East Side—took place last April 24 shortly before 7 P.M. Mr. Levin was wearing a suit (which made him stand out in his neighborhood) and was walking on Seventh Street near home.

"This tall, skinny kid, I guess he was about 6-foot-2, he had a butcher's knife. I remember looking at the knife pretty closely because it looked like the kind my old man cuts onions with (His father owns a kosher delicatessen in Bayonne).

"He followed me into the building and up on the third floor, when I was getting the key out of my apartment (3-B) he rushed me. I threw my groceries at him, gave a karate yell and tried to kick him in the groin. But my foot didn't connect.

"I yelled, 'hey, rube!' a signal I had prearranged with my neighbor, Tony Rivera in 3A. Tony had a lead pipe and was prepared to come out into the hall if there was ever any trouble. I yelled 'Help! help! help!' The guy was about 20 feet from me. He was deciding if he should take me or run. But people started coming and he ran down the stairs. Then I noticed my wrist was slashed."

In May, Mr. Levin left 278 East Seventh Street.

Tenants Form Patrol

Afterwards, the tenants in Nos. 272, 274 and 278 formed a patrol. It was composed of 20 men, all volunteers, who took turns guarding the building. Every stranger was stopped, then escorted upstairs to his destination. The men were armed with lead pipes and handguns, and one man even used a sword.

Although Deputy Inspector Joseph Fink, commander of the East Fifth Street Police station, said he did not know of the existence of any such group, a member said that a patrolman got out of his squad car one night and "taught us how to make clubs out of table legs—after all, we were doing his work."

The tenants' patrol has become inactive in recent weeks because members grew tired of giving it so much time.

Also, more police now patrol in the area.

Not all tenants' patrols are so informal. Ninety-two of the New York City Housing Authority's 157 projects have "citizens' patrols" that are subsidized by the authority this year at the rate of $50,000 to $75,000.

The money goes to recruiters and patrol supervisors, who are paid $2.50 an hour for a maximum 20-hour week and for coffee and pastries for patrol members, who spend long evening hours guarding the lobbies. The 4,500 project residents who are just members are not paid, they volunteer.

A visitor to the Rutgers House Project on the Lower East Side found that most patrol members were elderly Jews, joined by a sprinkling of Puerto Ricans and Negroes. So far, patrol members have made no arrests.

Jerry Schulman, who until recently was director of the Rutgers Community Center, said that Chinese residents of the project refuse to join the patrol and stick together so closely that they seldom called the police if anything went wrong.

A Chinese resident of the area offered another explanation. The police back home are corrupt he said, and many new arrivals think that the police here must be just as bad.

Mr. Schulman says that Italians and Jews will not hesitate to call the police, but that Italians will not join the patrol. Mr. Schulman attributes this to their "individualistic make-up."

But Mrs. Louis Cammarota, who briefly joined the Rutgers tenant patrol and then quit, said she did so because she thought someone qualified ought to do the patroling, "not a bunch of old people."

Irving Levy, a 68-year-old widower who used to be a house painter before he retired, is one of the most active members of the project's citizens' patrol. Asked why he put in the hours and risked injury, he said "I have nothing else to do. And besides, I used to be in the Marine Corps Reserve, so you can see I'm qualified for this."

But Mr. Levy feels he lacks real authority and complained that recently a couple of teen-agers ripped off the armband he wears. "If I had a uniform," he said, "or a special officer's badge and maybe a club and a pair of handcuffs, then I could do a job."

September 23, 1969

Photographs for The New York Times by BARTON SILVERMAN

On East 125th Street, strong warnings are posted in front of the Rev. Oberia Dempsey's church. He is a stanch advocate of combating narcotics traffic through a street offensive.

Addicts Steal $2.6-Billion

Despite the complexity of the narcotics problem, the arithmetic of it is simple. There are an estimated 100,000 heroin users in New York City. The average habit costs slightly over $30 a day, which most addicts cannot support through ordinary jobs. Therefore, they swindle people out of money if they can and steal if they cannot.

Dr. Michael Baden, associate medical examiner, estimates that the city's heroin users are spending at least $850-million a year with pushers on the street, and may be stealing as much as $2.6-billion a year in property.

The reason for the discrepancy between what is stolen and what is spent is that addicts frequently receive less than two-thirds of the real value of stolen goods.

Most of the stealing goes unreported, Dr. Baden said, because so many of the victims are either relatives and friends who are reluctant to lodge a complaint, or others who feel there is little the police can do.

Rightly or wrongly, many people are blaming addicts for most of the burglaries, robberies and muggings in the city. Although no comprehensive study has been done, Governor Rockefeller has estimated that perhaps half the reported crime in New York is the work of addicts.

George F. McGrath, Commissioner of Corrections, reports that of a total prison population of 13,500, 40 per cent of the men are considered to be addicts, and at least 60 per cent of the women.

September 23, 1969

27 STATES RELAX MARIJUANA LAWS

9 Others Also Expected to Reduce First Possession to Misdemeanor Status

By LINDA CHARLTON

In about two-thirds of the 50 states, drug abuse laws covering the possession of marijuana have been or are in the process of being revised to ease the penalties for first offenders.

Since the trend toward relaxation of generally stringent state laws began about three years ago, at least 27 states have reduced the status of first-time possession from a felony to a misdemeanor and have lessened the penalties accordingly. Similar legislation is under consideration and believed likely to pass in nine others.

According to one source in the Justice Department's Bureau of Narcotics and Dangerous Drugs, the impulse toward revision springs from the nature of the marijuana "problem"—that is, the pervasiveness of marijuana use.

"It's the middle-class family that's being hit now," the source said, "and they're the ones who wield the power,

they're the ones demanding changes in the law."

More than 90 per cent of all drug abuse cases are handled at the state level, where penalties for first offenders have been generally severe. One example is Virginia, where until the law was revised this year, the minimum penalty for possessing more than about a half-teaspoonful of marijuana was 20 years in jail, the same minimum penalty set for first-degree murder.

Similar changes—making a distinction between marijuana and "hard" drugs such as heroin and between the possession of marijuana and its sale, and reducing sharply the first-offense penalties for possession — were recommended at the Federal level by the Nixon Administration last year. They were incorporated in a bill that passed the Senate in January without a dissenting vote and is now in the House.

Not that the argument about marijuana has died down. It continues on both the scientific and political levels. Some researchers contend that it is both potentially harmful in itself and tends to predispose its users to other, more dangerous drugs. Others describe the product of the flowering tops and leaves of the female Indian hemp plant as "relatively harmless intoxicant."

Along the political spectrum, there are views as opposed as those of Vice President Agnew, who described the typical "theatrical radical" of the campus as arriving at college with "his pot . . . secreted in his knapsack," and the American Civil Liberties Union, which has urged the abolition of all criminal punishment for the use or possession of marijuana.

The In-Between View

The present majority view however, seems to be somewhere in between, neither equating marijuana with revolution nor favoring its legalization. The goal of much of the revision seems to be similar to that expressed by Senator Thomas J. Dodd, the Connecticut Democrat who was a sponsor of the Senate bill. "It will duly punish the youngster who experiments with a marijuana cigarette, but it will not ruin him for life," Senator Dodd said of the bill.

A common factor in many of the state-level revisions is the clear distinction between, on the one hand, the possession and use of marijuana and, on the other, its sale. Not infrequently, as in Illinois, the penalties for selling marijuana have been increased. The pending Illinois legislation would raise the present 10 years to life penalty for a first-offense sale to 15-years-to-life.

This would seem to indicate a recognition of the fact that a great many Americans have at one time or another used marijuana for fun, not for profit. The Federal Government recently estimates that there were 600,000 habitual users, 2.4 million "social users" and three million "experimenters" in the United States.

It has also become clear that since there are six million Americans who have at least taken a tentative drag on a "joint," this fact alone cannot categorize them. And this, too, is being acknowledged by persons such as Rear Adm. Arthur B. Engel, the superintendent of the United States Coast Guard Academy, who said of several cadets who were expelled for marijuana use earlier this year: "They weren't bad kids. This is just a sign of the times."

Some Proposals Fail

Attempts to reduce criminal penalties for the use of marijuana to what two New York City district attorney called "a more realistic level" have not always succeeded. In Colorado, such an attempt has failed in the legislature for three years running. In Massachusetts, a number of bills introduced to ease present laws are believed to have only a fair chance of passage because, according to Dennis M. Sullivan, the Assistant Attorney General in charge of legislative affairs, many legislators are wary of involvement with liberalizing measures.

But states as disparates in geography and character as Virginia, Wisconsin, Kansas and Maryland have enacted legislation this year changing the status of possession and personal use of marijuana from a felony to a misdemeanor; similar legislation is pending in a number of other states, including Ohio, Michigan, Hawaii New Jersey, and Florida. A bill that would have provided for probation rather than a jail term for a first offender passed in one house of the Mississippi legislature but was defeated in the other.

One exception to the general liberalizing trend was New Hampshire, where the legislature approved a measure that made the possession of one pound or more of marijuana a felony instead of a misdemeanor.

May 11, 1970

Addict Control: No Solution in Sight

Police View on Control of Drug Addicts: Many Problems but No Solutions

"Why can't the police stop the drug traffic?"

The question is heard all over New York these days, asked with almost as much frequency at Midtown cocktail parties as on the front stoops of Brownsville, Harlem and Hunts Point.

Although Federal and local agents have sleuthed their way to impressive hauls of heroin and have arrested some distributors, the drug is as easy to get in New York as it ever was.

Law-enforcement officials offer several explanations

for the easy access to heroin, chiefly lack of manpower. The 120 Federal narcotics agents working in and around New York record prodigious hours of overtime each week; the narcotics squad of the New York City Police Department has 480 men at full strength, less than 2 per cent of the city's total police manpower.

Yet even the police concede that the solution does not lie just in additional manpower—or even in more arrests and drug seizures.

One precinct commander in the Bronx, who asked to remain anonymous, noted ruefully that during periods when heroin was hard to get on the streets (junkies call these times "panics"), the price went up and confirmed addicts then had to steal even more than they usually do.

As for effectively "sealing" United States borders to heroin grown abroad and smuggled here, no law-enforcement official interviewed during the preparation of this series thought it was remotely feasible.

Deputy Chief John R. McCahey of the Narcotics Squad estimated, for example, that one medium-sized ocean-going freighter has about 35,000 places in which heroin could be hidden. A kilo of heroin, worth $20,000 to $25,000 wholesale in New York, can easily be tucked into the space of a shoe box.

"It is impossible," says Chief McCahey, "to check everything."

Clearly, too many factors overseas, where the poppies are grown from which heroin is made, are outside police control. The domestic control problem is complicated by lapses in communication among local and Federal law-enforcement agencies, which sometimes seem to regard one another as rivals rather than participants in a common cause.

The problem is complicated in the New York area by these factors:

¶Drug addicts accused of crimes are violating parole and bail privileges in discouragingly large numbers and are not showing up in court to face charges. The addicts then presumably continue to steal to buy heroin. A study by the Vera Institute of Justice, a private agency that seeks court reform in New York, showed that in a group of addicts in the Bronx 37 per cent "failed to appear" when their cases were called. The study also said that "it is quite likely that the actual default rate among addicts is higher than this, because a number of crimes with which addicts were commonly associated were not included in the study."

¶Despite the efforts of top police officials, there was no perceptible, uniform policy for attacking the drug problem at the precinct level. One precinct commander said

it made no sense to arrest pushers; another said he pursued pushers but not users. Other police officers said it made little sense to deal with either pusher or addict; and still others said they thought there was merit in applying pressure on both pusher and addict in the street.

¶In slum neighborhoods, suspicion of the relationship between the police and drug pushers is wide spread. Sources within the Police Department said that some of their colleagues were taking bribes and that the department was not doing enough to clean itself up.

High Officers Criticized

"The breakdown in law and order does not start on the street," said one detective, who asked that his name not be used. "It starts at a very high level in the Police Department where top brass protect the department, whether it's right or wrong."

¶An unevenness in police service was observed in some neighborhoods. In several instances the police failed to respond to telephone calls from residents that might have enabled them to apprehend drug addicts in the process of stealing.

¶Stolen property is being purchased from drug addicts in beauty parlors, bars, and slum gambling houses, in poor neighborhoods, in some instances by the very residents who are complaining most about the conduct of the police. Moreover, because they distrust the police and also fear retribution from pushers and addicts, these same people are most reluctant to testify to the crimes they have witnessed in the streets.

In its study of bail-jumping among addicts, the Vera Institute found that almost half the addicts who failed to show up "had not returned to court during the nine months after default." The analysis was based on a four-month study of 339 addict defendants in the Bronx Criminal Court in March of 1968.

The problem of addicts who violate bail or parole worries the police, who feel that most addicts, when free, will continue to steal to support their habits.

Bronx District Attorney Burton B. Roberts feels that suspected addicts should be denied bail and treated in much the same way as a person suspected of being a psychotic. "Both the addict and the psychotic can do great damage both to them-

selves and to society," he said.

Pre-Trial Detention Opposed

The Vera study did not advocate pre-trial detention. It pointed out that while "37 per cent of the addict-defendants jumped, 63 per cent did not. A blanket policy of pre-trial detention would result in confinement of approximately two defendants who would not have jumped for each thwarted jumper."

The addict-defendants who were released in their own recognizance and thus posted no money jumped bail more often than those who had to post bond. The study reported that they failed to reappear at a rate 20 per cent greater than those addicts who had to post bail to get out.

These facts, the study said, suggest that a cash bail "may be a more effective deterrant to flight by a narcotically involved defendant than personal recognizance." But the analysis also emphasized that the posting of money alone cannot be the only factor in considering the problem of bail jumping.

At the present time, if a police officer thinks that the person he has arrested is a drug addict, he fills in a "CR-1" form in which he states that he observed the physical symptoms associated with the use of narcotics —scarred arms, dilated pupils, drowsiness.

But Vera contends that the CR-1 form is not a completely satisfactory way to identify addicts since "the police officer is not a medical expert and physical symptoms observed, or thought to be observed, by him are not clinical proof . . ."

Shortcomings of System

The lack of a precise means of identifying addicts, according to Vera, "hampers the ability of the administrators of justice to give proper consideration at the bail-setting stage to a large percentage of defendants, including both those who are in fact addicts but are not identified as such, and those who are erroneously assumed to be addicts."

Vera says that in the present New York criminal court system, "it is all but certain that many addicts pass through the system unidentified, even though substantial proof of addiction may be available."

The study said that a means must be found to inform judges about the drug use of a defendant he may

consider for bail, and urged consideration of a plan under which suspected addicts would receive physical examinations before they were arraigned. "Obviously," the study said, "a number of serious legal and medical questions would have to be met before a judgment on the feasibility of such a procedure could be made."

District Attorney Roberts, alarmed at the rise in the last few years of serious crimes committed by addicts, feels those questions must be answered soon. In recent weeks he has been advocating a plan that would deny bail to anyone suspected of being an addict. The plan would work this way:

¶If an arresting policeman has "probable cause" to believe someone is a drug addict, the defendant would be taken to Rikers Island penitentiary immediately after arraignment, promptly tested by doctors for heroin in his urine, then re-arraigned in a court facility set up at Rikers Island.

¶If doctors concluded that the defendant was an addict and if the defendant was not a hardened criminal and wished to confirm the doctors' report, he would be considered for a civil commitment to a facility run by the State Narcotic Addiction Control Commission.

¶If the man was accused of a serious crime he would have to be tried within 90 days. If for any reason he was not tried within 90 days, bail would have to be set.

¶If the defendant wished to contest the findings and claim he was not an addict, a hearing would have to be held within four weeks "before a judge who would make a determination if there is probable cause to detain the defendant without bail as an addict."

Mario A. Procaccino, the Democratic candidate for Mayor, issued a narcotics policy statement Tuesday that embraced most of Mr. Roberts's ideas and also proposed a massive, voluntary methadone program. Methadone, a synthetic addictive drug that blocks the desire for heroin in many addicts, would be given to any addict who wanted it under Mr. Procaccino's program.

Objections to Roberts Plan

A New York Supreme Court justice and several lawyers, all of whom asked to remain anonymous, were asked what they thought of Mr. Roberts's plan. They raised these objections:

¶Under the Roberts plan

a policeman would have the discretion to determine who might be an addict. Policemen are not qualified to do this. Moreover, they could interpret "probable cause" to harass suspected criminals who might or might not be either criminals or addicts.

¶The Roberts plan would come into effect only after heroin addicts were caught in the commission of a crime. It says nothing of the tens of thousands who are never caught.

¶The facilities of the State Narcotic Addiction Control Commission have come under criticism recently as being more custodial than rehabilitative.

¶If addicts were to be accorded all the guarantees of law, including the right to choose counsel at arraignment, the problem of getting a private lawyer to Rikers Island in time for arraignment would be serious.

¶Since the court system is woefully overloaded now, it is doubtful that it could really dispose of all addiction hearings within four weeks and trials within 90 days.

Police Disagree on Tactics

Along with the disagreement among legal authorities is the lack of agreement among the police themselves on how to cope with heroin addicts.

In the Brownsville section of Brooklyn Capt. John E. Wilson of the 73d Precinct (an area with probably thousands of addicts) feels that arresting pushers is an ineffective way of dealing with the problem because "somebody takes his place."

But Capt. George S. Cerrone of the 75th Precinct in the East New York section of Brooklyn says he believes in arresting pushers to "dry up the source." Deputy Inspector Anthony J. McNally of the 41st Precinct in the Hunts Point section of the Bronx says he thinks it makes sense to arrest the pusher but not the user.

Other police officers said they felt it was a waste of time to arrest either pushers or users because the real powers in the drug trade went untouched. A few other policemen said they thought it was necessary to keep the pressure on both pushers and addicts so that no neighborhood would become an easy mark for them.

Community Hostility

Some policemen expressed reluctance to make drug and other arrests in slum neighborhoods because of what

they considered a lack of support from the community.

"All I have to do is tell one whore to move on," complained one Bronx patrolman, "and around here, I'd have 50 people yelling police brutality."

Mayor Lindsay recently announced that he wanted the police to intensify their efforts against the drug traffic. He indicated that he felt the problem heretofore was complicated by a lack of funds for narcotics operations and pledged that more money would be provided.

What would be an arrestable offense in some sections of the city goes almost unnoticed in others.

A visitor to the Hunts Point section (called Fort Apache by some of the embattled residents) observed at least three instances in which the police did not respond to calls that might have enabled them to catch addict-burglars at work.

On one occasion in early July a woman saw several young neighborhood heroin users on the roof of a building at the corner of Tiffany Street and Southern Boulevard. They were carrying a portable television set, a toaster and an iron. Although she telephoned the police three times, they never responded. The junkies got away.

On another occasion, when the same woman saw a policeman who appeared to be on the verge of having serious trouble with a small crowd at the same intersection, she called the 41st Precinct, which dispatched a squad car almost instantly.

Deputy Inspector Anthony J. McNally of the 41st Precinct said he believed his men were responding to calls as quickly as possible.

However, a Roman Catholic priest who used to work in Hunts Point thought that local policemen there "regard Hunts Point as a garbage can and they think their only job is to keep the top on it and not let the garbage out."

On the Lower East Side, the leader of a street gang that is confronting addicts and pushers in the street said, "When you talk to kids around here about cops, they just laugh."

Drugs Reported Missing

Members of the gang, some of them former heroin users, said that when the police conducted raids they did not always account for all the cash or all the drugs confiscated.

Harold Rothwax, a lawyer for Mobilization for Youth who has represented some poor defendants accused of possessing narcotics, said that some of his clients have told him that they had more heroin in their possession than they were charged with having. "I see no reason why they would not tell me the truth about that sort of thing," Mr. Rothwax said.

He said there was a feeling in some neighborhoods that the police kept some heroin either to sell themselves or perhaps to plant on a particular suspect they wanted to arrest.

Loyalty and Bribery

Harold Foner, a criminal lawyer who represents the 3,300-member Traffic Squad Benevolent Association, said: "There is an awful lot of bribery. The department, out of a mistaken kind of loyalty, protects these men.

"Policemen who take bribes know they can't be prosecuted. It's practically impossible. That's why they do it. Once you're labeled an addict or a prostitute, even if you tell the truth, nobody will believe you."

A spokesman for the police Department declined to comment on the criticism.

Another internal problem of law enforcement concerns the degree of cooperation among Federal and local officials. And although Federal and city police agencies say they are cooperating, there appear to be some communications gaps between them.

Deputy Chief McCahey pointed out that the New York City Narcotics Squad maintained liaison with Federal narcotics agents. But he also conceded that the liaison did not include the exchange of briefings on specific current cases. The result is that Federal and local agents could be working on the same leads and not know about it. But Chief McCahey added: "I don't know that this has ever happened."

F.B.I. Fears Disclosures

Sources in the Federal Bureau of Investigation said they feared disclosure of information by inept or corrupt local lawmen. Other F.B.I. sources conceded the existence of a continuing rivalry between the F.B.I. and agents of the Federal Bureau of Narcotics and Dangerous Drugs, although it is perhaps diminishing.

A new Federal-city task force was set up in July to

deal with the narcotics problem. It is composed of Federal narcotics agents, customs inspectors and New York police. Among other things, the task force hopes to utilize existing resources more efficiently.

But whatever the internal problems of enforcement may be, it would be inaccurate to blame these alone for the formidable drug problem that exists in so many New York neighborhoods.

Part of the problem lies within the neighborhoods. In Harlem, for example, junkies find it relatively easy to sell stolen merchandise to church-going middle-class residents who deplore the lawlessness that surrounds them.

A Harlem drug addict who estimated that he stole more than $400 worth of goods each week to support his habit said that one of the easiest places to dispose of stolen merchandise was in Harlem beauty salons.

"Let's face it," he said, "people up there aren't exactly the wealthiest people in New York. If some housewife can pick up a brand-new television set for $15, she'd be a damned fool to turn it down so that she could pay $200 in a store."

The head of a Bronx antipoverty unit who is highly critical of police behavior admitted to a reporter that he recently purchased 50 pounds of spareribs that had been stolen by drug addicts from a warehouse.

'Now I'm Sorry'

"I can tell you now I'm sorry I did it," the man said. "But when the spareribs were offered to me at such a low price I rationalized it, saying: 'Well, you may as well buy them. If you don't, somebody else will.'"

The task of keeping heroin out of the country remains much as it has always been: overwhelming.

Turkey is still the major source of illicit heroin. William J. Durkin, regional director of the Federal Bureau of Narcotics, estimated that 80 to 85 per cent of the heroin sold in this country originated in Turkish poppy fields.

The poppies in Turkey are grown ostensibly for the manufacture of morphine, which is used as a pain killer all over the world. Though acreage used for this purpose is regulated by the Turkish Government, Mr. Durkin pointed out that it is relatively easy for a farmer in Turkey or any place else to exceed his quota, and it is extraordinarily difficult for police to catch him. The country is vast; the numbers of policemen checking on farmers are few.

Other current sources of heroin are Communist China, Thailand, Burma, Laos and Mexico. There is no poppy growing in the United States.

Marseilles, France, and Beirut, Lebanon, remain centers of narcotics traffic. In and around both cities, small "factories" exist where the raw opium is transformed first into a morphine base and then into heroin, the preferred form of the drug in the United States.

Markup on Heroin

At present, a kilo of good-quality heroin costs about $4,000 in Marseilles. The same kilo is worth six times

that amount to wholesalers in New York. By the time it reaches the street, passing through many hands, the original kilo, cut (diluted) and recut, sells by the milligram. A $3 bag contains about 7.5 milligrams of heroin. This constitutes an astronomical markup.

Mr. Durkin estimated that 1,500 to 2,500 kilograms of heroin came into the United States in 1968, much of it through New York, the biggest single point in world narcotics traffic, both in terms of consumption and distribution.

Asked why French and Lebanese police do not shut the factories down, Mr. Durkin explained that the factories were both small and mobile and thus hard to find. He said that police abroad

— as here — must have some basis for obtaining warrants to conduct raids, and evidence is hard to get.

Mr. Durkin said that although members of the Mafia with large bankrolls played a major role in the international drug trade, they were by no means alone. A number of Latin Americans are also in the business, probably independent of the Mafia, he said, as well as a major narcotics ring in Australia that has nothing to do with the Mafia.

The Federal Narcotics Bureau maintains bureaus in many cities abroad. These include Paris, where many of the Marseilles heroin runners live; Lima, Peru, now a center for cocaine traffic; Seoul, South Korea, a dis-

tribution point for heroin sold to U.S. servicemen in Asia; Hong Kong, a major relay point for heroin originating in Communist China that is bound for the United States; and Bangkok, Thailand, a relay point for heroin made in Thailand and Laos.

Federal agents are also stationed in Rome, where some deportees from the United States have engaged in drug traffic, Beirut and Marseilles.

In New York, Mr. Durkin's men concentrate on levels higher than the street pusher. He believes that getting pushers off the streets all over the city would require a saturation level of local police. And such a mobilization of manpower to fight the onslaught of heroin at present seems unlikely.

September 25, 1969

Governor Signs His Drug Bills And Assails the Critics Again

By WILLIAM E. FARRELL
Special to The New York Times

ALBANY, May 8 — With panoply and fanfare and some caustic words for his critics, Governor Rockefeller signed into law today the final version of his bills providing harsher penalties for traffickers in dangerous drugs.

At a ceremony in the ornate Red Room of the Capitol — surrounded by legislators, Republican leaders, two early supporters of his plan who work in Harlem and many television cameras — Mr. Rockefeller called his bills "the toughest antidrug program in the nation."

He applauded the Legislature for adopting the bills and for standing firm "against this strange alliance of vested establishment interests, political opportunists and misguided soft-liners who joined forces and tried unsuccessfully to stop this program."

Asked later to elaborate on who composed this "strange alliance," the Governor replied: "Well, the Judicial Conference opposed it, the District Attorney's Association opposed it, there were police officials up here opposing it."

District Attorneys, judges, civil libertarians, the Association of the Bar of the City of New York, Mayor Lindsay and many others have repeatedly

assailed the Governor's drug-pusher plan as one that would thwart police efforts to get small-time pushers to inform on big-time distributors of narcotics and inundate an already-overloaded court system with thousands of new trials.

During the long weeks of negotiations over the final version of his plan, the Governor withstood these complaints and said he would provide whatever court facilities, judges and personnel were needed after his plan went into effect Sept. 1.

Today, at both the beginning and the end of his remarks in the Red Room, Mr. Rockefeller strongly implied that if his plan failed it would be because of those elements in the state's criminal-justice system most critical of it.

At the beginning of his speech, the Governor said: "We are creating the strongest possible tools to protect our law-abiding citizens from drug pushers—providing that the police, the District Attorneys and the courts throughout the state are willing to use these laws vigorously and effectively."

At the end, he said emphatically: "It remains for those who make up our law-enforcement system to use these powers effectively for the people's protection. The police must act aggressively in enforcing these drug laws. The District Attorneys must prosecute forcefully. The judges must act firmly."

The new state laws call for

the imposition of mandatory minimum prison sentences, a limited form of plea-bargaining and a system of "mandatory life sentences" that would permit parole but require lifetime supervision of the person paroled.

They represent modifications of the Governor's orginal plan, put forth in January, in which he had asked for mandatory life sentences for drug traffickers with no opportunity for plea-bargaining and no possibility of parole.

Turns It Around

But the modifications did not assuage the critics, who contended, among other things, that the Governor's limitations on plea-bargaining would cripple police efforts to recruit informers by allowing arrested pushers to plead guilty to lesser offenses.

In his speech, the Governor turned around the argument made by critics that his plan would swamp the courts with additional trials.

Mandatory minimum sentences, he said, "will help eliminate the clogging of the courts caused by 'revolving door' multiple arrests and appearances in court of pushers."

"The program prevents pushers from using plea-bargaining as a blackmailing device to escape sentence and return to the streets," he said. "It elicits the support of citizens in the war on the pushers of drugs by providing $1,000 rewards for information leading to the arrest and conviction of a dangerous drug pusher."

Mr. Rockefeller also announced that he was submitting legislation authorizing him to appoint up to 100 additional

judges "as needed" as well as to create necessary additional courtroom facilities.

Election-Year Plums

Queried later by newsmen, Mr. Rockefeller acknowledged that many of the judges might not be appointed until next year, when he is expected to seek re-election and will be able to dangle judicial plums before tempted legislators.

He declined to say whether the judgeships would be permanent or temporary. Earlier this year he said he wanted authorization to appoint 100 temporary judges.

One of those invited to the signing ceremony was the New York City Council President, Sanford D. Garelik, a former Chief Inspector in the police force, who said the bills represented a "turning around" of the city's drug epidemic.

As the television lights dimmed at the ceremony's end, the Governor congratulated the Republican lawmakers present.

As an official photographer set up his equipment he said to several of them: "Sure I've got time. Shall we take some individual shots first?"

One legislator who was not asked to the ceremony or the picture-taking was Assemblyman Dominick L. DiCarlo, Republican-Conservative of Brooklyn, and the closest thing to a nemesis the Governor had in the G.O.P. ranks on his drug plan.

Mr. DiCarlo, chairman of the Assembly Codes Committee, favored a tough stand on pushers, but said that the Governor's plan would "unbalance the law." He got a bill of his own passed in the Assembly, a testimonial to his hard work on the issue, but it has no chance in the Senate.

May 9, 1973

Magistrate Assails the Term 'Mugging' And Identifying Prisoners by Their Race

Magistrate J. Roland Sala, in Brooklyn Felony Court, assailed yesterday the use of the term "mugging," which he said was a misnomer for old-fashioned robbery and assault, and he said he would "enjoin any newspaper or news agency from identifying a defendant according to race, creed or color, unless the identification is an essential part of the story or of the crime charged."

"I will bar the one responsible for the story from any court room in which I sit," he announced.

The magistrate's remarks were made during the arraignment of John Manzi, 29 years old, of 402 Fifty-sixth Street, and Thomas Feehan, 19, of 450 Sixty-first Street, both of Brooklyn. Manzi and Feehan are white. They were accused by Sergeant James E. Simpson, who is stationed at Fort Hamilton, Brooklyn, of seizing him last Thursday night, forcing him into a cellar at 5907 Fourth Avenue, beating him and robbing him of $160 in cash and a watch.

The defendants waived examination and were held for the grand jury. Defense counsel asked for a reduction of the $10,000 bail which had been set in each case by another magistrate, and Assistant District Attorney Clarence Wilson vigorously opposed the request. In granting it, and fixing bail at $5,000 each, Magistrate Sala said:

"I am going to reduce this bail and I have something to say for the record. Exaggerated severity of punishment serves no useful purpose. It does not stop crime.

"Now as to mugging, that is a misnomer. It is just plain robbery. Robbery is a venerable crime, as old as man."

Councilman Adam Clayton Powell Jr., Fusion-American Labor party representative in the City Council from Harlem, introduced a resolution at the regular meeting of the City Council yesterday demanding that local newspaper publishers omit from all news stories any words that would describe the race of a person connected with a crime. The resolution was referred to the committee on city affairs.

April 14, 1943

BROOKLYN MEETING CALLS ON GOVERNOR TO REMOVE MAYOR

Rally Is Stormy as Patrolman Depicts Crime Conditions and Negro Resents 'Slurs'

LA GUARDIA DEFENDS RULE

Insists Police Are Keeping Order — Valentine Report Still Undisclosed

Soon after Mayor La Guardia, in his weekly radio talk, had defended his administration against charges of laxity in crime prevention, a stormy mass meeting was held yesterday afternoon in Brooklyn's "Little Harlem," the Bedford-Stuyvesant section, at which a resolution was adopted calling upon Governor Dewey to remove the Mayor for "misfeasance."

The meeting, held under the auspices of the Midtown Civic League in the Bedford Branch of the Young Men's Christian Association at Bedford Avenue and Monroe Street, was attended by 500 persons, a score of them Negroes. Its disruption was threatened several times after one of the speakers, a patrolman off duty and in civilian clothes, drew an analogy between crime conditions in the East Bronx,

where he is attached, and the Bedford-Stuyvesant section, and declared that responsibility for them was due to an "influx of sunburned citizens who come up from the deep South mistaking liberty for license."

A Negro probation officer attached to Special Sessions Court in Brooklyn hotly defended his race from these "slurs"; whereupon he was hissed and booed, and more than half of those at the meeting started for the doors. They were brought back by Sumner A. Sirtl, president of the league, who pleaded for a fair hearing, and the resolution urging the Mayor's ouster later was adopted by a voice vote.

Grand Jury Testimony Recalled

The resolution set forth that both the Mayor and Police Commissioner Lewis J. Valentine had admitted under oath to the August Kings County grand jury "that conditions of lawlessness existed in the Bedford-Stuyvesant section" and that both had said they were "powerless to do any more than they have been doing to ameliorate these conditions." Commissioner Valentine, the resolution said, testified that conditions would become progressively worse and certainly would not get better.

"The actions and testimony of Fiorello H. La Guardia as the Mayor of the City of New York," the resolution charged, "clearly indicate misfeasance in office."

It then petitioned Governor Dewey "to cause an investigation to be made into the acts and conduct" of the Mayor and to remove him from office.

Mayor La Guardia, without mentioning the police report on the survey of "Little Harlem" crime conditions, turned over to him by

Commissioner Valentine on Saturday, assured the people of the city that they "have nothing to fear" and that "our Police Department is performing its duty." Law and order, he declared, have been and will continue to be maintained and crime has never "gotten beyond the control of our Police Department and it is not getting beyond the control of the Police Department at this time." Actual figures, number of arrests and convictions, he said, are all "matters of record."

Police Morale Called Low

The speaker who touched off the fireworks at the Brooklyn meeting said he was David Liebman of 297 Wyckoff Avenue, Brooklyn, a patrolman attached to the Simpson Street station in the Bronx.

He told of some "mugging" cases he had worked on, using the phrase "sunburnt elements," and said the cure for conditions was to be found in education and a decent home life.

"If we had more policemen," he declared, "we would be able to do a better job. The Mayor should investigate why the morale of the Police Department is at its lowest ebb in ten years."

Patrolman Liebman told reporters he was a former marine, a graduate of the University of Alabama, and interested in juvenile delinquency and sociology.

He said that after his talk he was approached by a man in civilian clothes who said he was a police lieutenant attached to the Thirteenth Inspection Division. Patrolman Liebman said the man asked him for his identification and told him charges would be preferred against him.

The Negro probation officer identified himself as Henry S. Ashcroft of 758 Putnam Avenue, Brooklyn.

"You have been treated to a fine tirade against the Negro race," he told the hostile audience who booed and hissed him. Continuing after the chairman had restored a semblance of order, Mr. Ashcroft said Negroes in the section had been trying for years to obtain proper housing and additional schools and playgrounds.

"We hear a great deal about police being shackled," he said. "What these speakers seem to want is to have the police use their clubs as they please."

Cries of "no" were heard from the hall.

Mgr. Belford Criticizes Mayor

Among the speakers at the meeting, which lasted for three hours, was Mgr. John L. Belford, pastor of the Roman Catholic Church of the Nativity, Madison Street and Classon Avenue, Brooklyn. He declared that property in the section had been deteriorating for years, bringing in undesirables, until much of it was "unfit for human habitation and should be destroyed."

Telling of efforts to obtain more police protection, Mgr. Belford said: "We went to the captains of the precincts but they told us that the cops were badly needed for strikes and other duties. Out of 100 policemen who were stationed in each precinct, sixty to sixty-five were available for precinct work."

Mgr. Belford told of vain trips to City Hall, saying: "The only way to get to see the Mayor is by some sort of public assault on him."

"The month of November is a hard month—a bad month for flowers, little flowers and big flowers, and especially to a politician who has been put on the spot by the grand jury," he said of the Mayor.

Mayor Praises Valentine

There was no indication from the Mayor when he would release the Valentine report. He left City Hall saying only: "It'll all come out, it'll all come out."

The Mayor declared in his radio

speech that he had confidence in Commissioner Valentine, a "faithful public servant who has served the city for forty years."

"By my appointment," the Mayor said, "he is the responsible head of our Police Department and as long as he is, he shall have my full and complete support, cooperation and confidence."

The Mayor promised equal treatment under the law for all, saying that people in some areas were living under "difficult conditions" but that "poverty is not a crime."

Replying to criticism of a supplemental survey which he ordered Welfare Commissioner Leo Arnstein to make into relief in the section, the Mayor said: "I want to assure the people that no one in want will be deprived of aid, help or relief, because some one happened not to like them, their religion or their color."

He replied, too, to assertions that crime in the area was the result of a lack of recreational, health, educational and other improvements, declaring "no one section has been ignored or neglected and no section will be ignored or neglected."

Only the war, he said, had retarded the "terrific pace" of public improvement activity.

Sala Attacks Presentment

Magistrate J. Roland Sala, in a statement issued at his chambers in the Brooklyn Felony Court, yesterday termed the grand jury presentment "incredibly unfair, totally unfounded and replete with errors."

Saying that he was "casting my political future out the window," the magistrate declared: "I can't be too severe in my criticism of those judges and public officials who by their irresponsible utterances are contributing to the hysteria, chaos and prejudice."

The Rev. Raymond J. Campion, pastor of St. Peter Claver's Roman Catholic Church, 2 Jefferson Avenue, Brooklyn, attributed crimes in the area not to police laxity, but to bad housing, lack of proper employment and racial discrimination. He spoke yesterday morning at the De Porres Interracial Center, 20 Vesey Street, at an interracial meeting of the Catholic Laymen's Union.

The clergyman assailed the greed of landlords, declaring that Negroes had to pay high rents "for awful quarters," and also said that "they pay too much money for food in the store."

An interracial committee representing thirty-five civic, labor, religious and social service groups, issued a statement yesterday following a meeting held on Thursday at the Carlton Avenue Y.M.C.A., 405 Carlton Avenue, Brooklyn, declaring that its members "have not noted any sharp increase in crime in the section, and are at a loss to understand the motivation of the grand jury."

The committee expressed its "concern" over the Mayor's order to review relief cases in the area, and said it expects to hold a community-wide meeting on the results of its study of the situation.

November 22, 1943

HOODLUMS IN PARK KEEP CITIZENS OUT

Fear of Mugging and Robbery After Dark Is Rife Despite Increased City Guard

POLICE MORE OPTIMISTIC

Rise in the Number of Arrests of Thugs This Year Is Cited as Gain on Crime

Fear of mugging, purse snatching and terrorism by youthful gangs is keeping residents in the vicinity of Central Park out of the park after dark despite an increased detail of detectives and plainclothesmen, it was learned yesterday.

Police officials said that the situation is well in hand. They cited the fact that there has been no increase of crime reported from within the park. Their reports showed a greater number of arrests of degenerates since March 1 than in the comparable period a year ago.

Police statistics also showed a greater number of depredations by juveniles for the same period. But on the whole, one police official said, the picture is no worse than in previous years.

E. Ross Winkler, superintendent of the Fifth Avenue Hospital, 106th Street and Fifth Avenue, said that staff doctors and members of the nursing staff had said they "would not go into the park after dark on a bet."

He said there had been several purse snatching cases by juveniles

in the last year from hospital employes walking at night outside the park on Fifth Avenue. He also reported considerable vandalism in the neighborhood with car windows being smashed and accessories stolen.

The hospital's emergency room reported that in the last ten days they treated four persons stabbed in the park who had to be hospitalized.

Officials at Mount Sinai Hospital, 100th Street and Fifth Avenue, said they believed the situation in the park was better now than it has been in a long time. However, many expressed doubts that they would walk in the park after dark.

Attack on Importer Latest

The latest serious incident reported occurred in the park near Eightieth Street at 9:30 P. M. on April 10. John F. Elliott, 45-year-old importer of Mexican fabrics, of 993 Fifth Avenue, said he was walking near the weather station when two frightened boys, about 12 years old, ran up to him. A gang of fifteen youths, between 10 and 15 years old, was on their heels.

The two boys asked Mr. Elliott to escort them out of the park because they were afraid. The trio walked toward Fifth Avenue with the gang trailing. A block from the avenue Mr. Elliott told the boys to go ahead; they had nothing to fear. The boys ran followed by half the gang. The rest of the gang stalked behind Mr. Elliott.

Failing to catch the two boys that part of the gang walked back towards Mr. Elliott. Suddenly he was struck on the shoulder with the limb of a tree, then tackled and thrown to the ground. He fought back and the gang fled after he had received a sharp "punch" in the back.

Mr. Elliott was treated at Fifth Avenue Hospital by Dr. Alphonso A. Lombardi for a stab wound in the chest, a cut lip and two black eyes. The blade of the knife, at least three inches long, pierced the covering around Mr. Elliott's right lung causing a partial collapse. He remained in the hospital for a week.

POLICE SETTING UP NIGHT CRIME DETAIL; NEW ATTACK IN I.R.T.

200 Men in 100 Cars Will Be on Streets in 'Critical Hours' to Curb Muggings, Rapes

PISTOL BATTLE IN SUBWAY

Hide-and-Seek Fight in Tunnel After Assaults on 2 Women in W. 103d St. Station

The police will begin today a stepped-up drive against crime, particularly the muggings and rapes that have been occurring with increasing frequency in the city during the night-time hours.

Announcement of the new policy came just as two more attempted criminal attacks against women were reported. These attacks came at 4 P. M. yesterday in the I. R. T. subway station at Broadway and 103d Street and resulted in an eerie, hide-and-seek pistol battle in the tunnel north of the station, during which the criminal escaped.

At 6:30 P. M. Police Commissioner George P. Monaghan issued a statement saying that special details of detectives riding in unmarked cars would begin to patrol the streets during the "critical hours of the night."

The new tours of duty will be flexible, with the bulk of the men assigned to the most dangerous areas. The Commissioner said that 200 men in 100 cars would be assigned to the job and that the officers supervising the work would participate in the patrols themselves.

Borough Commanders Assembled

Two and one-half hours earlier Chief of Detectives George A. Loures had assembled his borough commanders at Police Headquarters to tell them of the new plan. He ordered them to put as many detectives on the streets as possible, especially in the areas where crimes of violence have been increasing. He did not divulge to the press the particular areas he had in mind.

It was also disclosed at City Hall by Mayor Impellitteri that 400 new men would be added to the police

April 21, 1949

force on Oct. 1. The Mayor said that it was his belief that the number of muggings and rapes in the city would be decreased as new men were put on street patrol. He said that additional patrolmen were being made available for foot duty by Commissioner Monaghan's policy of assigning only one man to each patrol car wherever possible, instead of the customary two men.

The first word of yesterday's attacks in the subway came when a dishevelled woman stepped off a southbound express train at Ninety-sixth Street and Broadway and told Transit Patrolman Theodore Wolff that she had been attacked by a towering, lean Negro.

The woman, who later disappeared after giving the police a false name and address, said that she had fought off her attacker on the 103d Street platform and fled into a train just as its doors closed.

Patrolman Wolff told her to telephone for help and took the next train to 103d Street. Alighting on the northbound platform, he looked across the tracks and saw a second attack being made at the north end of the southbound platform.

He raced across the overpass connecting the two sides of the station. He said later that the attacker was a Negro, about six feet four inches tall, fairly thin, about 30 years old and dressed in a gray suit. The victim was a young woman in a rust-colored suit. She had been forced against the wall when she sighted the policeman.

"Officer, it's a rape," she screamed. The Negro turned and jumped to the tracks. Patrolman Wolff fired a shot at him as he ran up the tracks. The woman disappeared and had not reported to the police last night.

Above ground, a dozen police cars from two precincts and an emergency servi division car converged on the station and the 110th Street station as Patrolman Wolff started the chase up the dimly lit tunnel. He ran all the way to 110th Street and searched the three tracks on a slower return trip without sighting the fugitive.

He started north again along the usually idle center track that is used to feed empty trains toward the origins of the evening and morning rush crowds.

'Knocked Down and Shot At'

Sgt. George A. Hartwell of the West 100th Street precinct started south from the other end of the tunnel at 110th Street. He was walking along the southbound tracks. Both men had drawn revolvers.

As Patrolman Wolff passed a signal post, he related, the fugitive "jumped me and knocked me down and shot at me." Fleeing from the patrolman's fire, which amounted to thirteen shots during the melee, the Negro leaped between the posts separating the center track from the southbound track.

There he saw Sergeant Hartwell approaching from the north. He fired, knocking the sergeant's hat off.

The sergeant said later that he could not see him in the darkness, so he threw himself to the tunnel floor and waited for a second shot, firing at the flash when it came.

A southbound subway train stopped when the first shot was fired at Sergeant Hartwell, the motorman apparently mistaking it for a torpedo on the rails. It resumed operation after the sergeant had returned the second shot, he said, forcing him to look to his own safety.

After that, southbound traffic was stopped, resuming shortly before 5 P. M., Board of Transportation officials said.

There was no trace of the fugitive after the train went through. The police continued to search the tunnel and guard the exits for an hour and a half. They said there were no emergency exits between the two stations and that they believed the man had escaped by jumping aboard a train.

Both Sergeant Hartwell and Patrolman Wolff said there was a good chance they had wounded their quarry. An alarm was sent to hospitals to be on the lookout for a wounded Negro answering the fugitive's description.

All the shooting except Patrolman Wolff's first shot took place deep in the tunnel, away from the platforms. The Negro fired, in all, about four shots at Patrolman Wolff and two at Sergeant Hartwell, a total of twenty from both sides.

Northbound traffic was slowed but not halted during the battle and the subsequent search.

Traffic in the streets above was

The New York Times

AFTER SUBWAY GUN FIGHT: Theodore Wolff, subway patrolman for the Board of Transportation, is covered with grime as he talks with reporter at 103d Street and Broadway.

brought almost to a standstill, however, by the hundreds, perhaps thousands, of persons who swarmed toward the exit kiosks after the alarm had been given by the scattering of persons on the platforms when the incident began.

Indignation was mixed with curiosity in the rumor-trading crowds. Some were heard to criticize juvenile delinquents, the police and the city administration.

On Monday a 30-year-old woman clerk, Florence Luise of 2070 Third Avenue, was stabbed in the arm as she approached her place of business on West Forty-second Street, near the Avenue of the Americas. She said her attacker, a Negro, had been molesting her for a week, after trying to make advances in Bryant Park.

She said that on one occasion, which she reported to the police, the man was waiting when she entered her apartment building elevator. He attempted to choke her, she said.

September 17, 1952

CRIME INCREASING, F.B.I. REPORT SAYS

Hoover Foresees Record High Level This Year if Trend of 6 Months Continues

Special to The New York Times.

WASHINGTON, Sept. 22 — J. Edgar Hoover reported today that crime was on the increase in the United States. If the current trend continues, he said, major crimes will reach an all-time high this year.

The Director of the Federal Bureau of Investigation estimated that 1,136,140 major crimes were committed during the first six months of 1954. This was an increase, he said, of 88,-850, or 8.5 per cent, compared with the first six months of last year.

A major crime is committed, Mr. Hoover said, every 13.8 seconds.

In percentage of increase crime is outstripping the growth in population. Mr. Hoover noted that the increase in population from June, 1953, to June, 1954, was less than 2 per cent, whereas the six months increase in crime this year exceeded 8 per cent.

"Generally, the larger cities report substantially higher crime rates than the smaller communities," Mr. Hoover said in his semi-annual crime report.

The report showed, however, that crime in rural areas rose 11.9 per cent in the first half of 1954 as compared with an increase of 7.2 per cent in urban communities.

Mr. Hoover said that each day during the first six months of this year an average of thirty-five persons were feloniously slain and 252 persons were feloniously assaulted.

Each day forty-eight rapes were committed, 608 cars were stolen and 197 robberies and 1,454 burglaries perpetrated. A crime of murder, manslaughter, rape or assault to kill was committed every 4.3 minutes.

The greatest increase in major crimes was in robbery, which jumped 20.4 per cent. Burglaries rose 13.2 per cent and larceny 9 per cent.

The increase in murder was only 0.9 per cent; rape, auto theft and negligent manslaughter were down 1.2, 2.3 and 3.9 per cent respectively.

September 23, 1954

LEIBOWITZ URGES CUT IN MIGRATION TO COMBAT CRIME

Judge Offers Statistics to Hearing on Delinquency Among Puerto Ricans

VIEWS HOTLY DISPUTED

Javits, Celler and Civic Body Defend the Newcomers—Senate Inquiry Adjourns

By PETER KIHSS

Kings County Judge Samuel Leibowitz called on Mayor Wagner and other officials yesterday to discourage migrants "from all parts of the country and the Caribbean" from coming here until the city had overcome crime-breeding slums.

The often outspoken judge stirred up new controversy when he made public figures that Puerto Ricans, with only 7 per cent of the city's population, were involved in 22.3 per cent of the city's juvenile delinquency cases. Puerto Ricans, the figures also indicated, were involved in 20.8 per cent of the cases of older individuals awaiting trial in one institution.

The figures were contained in a document the judge submitted while appearing before a Senate subcommittee on juvenile delinquency, which is holding hearings here.

Price of Discrimination

The figures also indicated a similar pattern among Negroes, who are estimated to total 11 per cent of the city's population. Negroes were reported to total 46.3 per cent of the citywide cases awaiting trial in the Brooklyn House of Detention.

At the hearing in the United States Court House in Foley Square, Council President Abe Stark declared that "the price we pay for discrimination against minority groups is reflected in the fact that their resentment and frustration cause them to commit almost half of the crimes of violence in the nation, even though they represent little more than 10 per cent of the total population."

Mr. Stark's statement, his assistant, Leonard P. Stavisky, said later, referred to Negroes and Puerto Ricans, and was based on studies by his office of reports by the Bureau of Census, Federal Bureau of Investigation and other sources.

A quick reaction against the figures submitted by Judge Leibowitz came from Joseph Monserrat, chairman of the Puerto Rican Community Self-Help Program. Mr. Monserrat said he was sure they were accurate on what they covered, but "the danger lies in the possibility of misinterpreting them."

Referring to the youthfulness of the Puerto Rican population here, Mr. Monserrat said Puerto Ricans comprised 33 per cent of Manhattan's school children—but less than 30 per cent of Manhattan's juvenile delinquency cases.

He said "The Puerto Rican Study, 1953-57" by the Board of Education—the only one of its kind—"showed that the Puerto Rican children had a lower delinquency rate than the other children in the same neighborhoods."

The study was by Dr. J. Caye Morrison and was made public last April 6. It covered School District 10 in East Harlem and District 11, stretching from West Harlem to the Hudson River. In these districts, the report said, "the Puerto Rican children were offenders at the rate of 12 per 1,000; the non-Puerto Ricans at the rate of 14 per 1,000."

Yesterday's hearings, conducted by Senator Thomas C. Hennings Jr., Democrat of Missouri, chairman of the subcommittee, closed two days' sessions. The subcommittee plans to move on to other cities to study increasing teen-age gang violence around the nation.

Javits Disagrees

At yesterday's sessions, Senator Jacob K. Javits, Republican of New York, as a witness, disputed Judge Leibowitz's plea against migration. "I believe that ultimately, as was true of other waves of migration, we will integrate the migrants," Senator Javits said. He said every citizen was "entitled to freedom to travel and the best we've got."

Representative Emanuel Celler, Democrat of Brooklyn, had testified before Judge Leibowitz spoke. Mr. Celler noted outside the hearing, as had Judge Leibowitz in testifying, that Puerto Ricans had a constitutional right to come here.

"We should not discourage them from coming," Mr. Celler said. "We need them for the hard chores and rough work. If they do not come, most of our hotels, restaurants and laundries would close. We need new-seed immigration."

Answering some of the criticism Judge Leibowitz later said:

"The Puerto Rican Government itself has been trying to divert these people from coming to New York City. All I wanted to do is to get the man in City Hall to open his mouth, to do a little talking not only to Puerto Ricans but others who are going to be jammed into these terrible slums which cause juvenile delinquency."

With this comment he reported he had received a letter from the Puerto Rican Department of Labor, Migration Division, dated Tuesday, that said in part:

"The Puerto Rican Government has done extensive work to make conditions in New York City known to persons thinking about migration. They have been informed of the extremely poor housing, the cold weather, the high cost of living, the probabilities of exploitation, the existence of prejudice and discrimination. Such information has not notably affected the size of the migration."

Judge Leibowitz, who has presided over county grand jury inquiries into relief and housing problems, told the hearing that he had first made his plea on migration to Mayor Wagner after their joint tour of Brooklyn slums last February.

Links Crime to Slums

He said he had noted that migrants from other parts of the mainland and the Caribbean were coming here, "looking for a better life," but crowding "into rat-infested places where they can't have a chance in the world." He said he had asked the Mayor "to get on the radio and tell them to give us a chance to catch up."

Asserting that he wanted to avert delinquency caused by slum-dwelling, the judge charged the city was "pampering and protecting slumlords." The Welfare Department, he said, was paying slum rents in "thousands of cases" for relief recipients.

Although the State Rent Commission may reduce rents to $1 a month when city departments certify buildings as dangerous to life and health, Judge Leibowitz said city agencies had certified only seventeen such cases in Brooklyn last year.

Recalling how the late Mayor Fiorello H. La Guardia had occasionally sat as a magistrate, Judge Leibowitz urged that Mayor Wagner act as a judge some time and personally 'sentence "slumlords" to jail.

Judge Leibowitz also called for a state law to require one year's residence in the state before eligibility for relief here. Only Rhode Island and New York, among all states, he said, have no such residence law.

Mr. Monserrat insisted in his comment later that Puerto Ricans came here for work, not relief, as evidenced by the fact that migration has dropped during mainland recessions.

The Puerto Rican Labor Department's letter to Judge Leibowitz had reported that states with high residence requirements for relief got more migrants than New York. Among these were listed California,

213

Florida, Michigan, Ohio, Arizona and Maryland.

Judge Leibowitz's submission of figures on Puerto Rican delinquency came as a rebuttal to an advertisement in Wednesday's newspapers by Mr. Monserrat's group of 162 organizations representing Puerto Ricans here. The advertisement had said "Puerto Ricans are involved in only some 8 per cent of the city's crime, which is roughly equivalent to our proportion of the population."

Judge Leibowitz said he was offering "the true figures" from Presiding Justice John Warren Hill of the Domestic Relations Court and from other official quarters.

Council President Stark pressed his plan for a $100,000,-000-a-year "emergency program of Federal subsidies" to settlement houses and other agencies against delinquency. He said this could prevent 2,000,000 youngsters from turning to crime at a cost of less than $50 a year, as against the $4,000 annual cost for a youth in a reform school or correctional institution.

Mr. Stark's program would set up a National Youth Co-ordinator, and provide Federal aid in services for children of migrants. Each year, he said, 5,000,000 Americans move across state lines and 5,000,000 across county lines, uprooting 4,000,-000 children and teen-agers. In addition, 1,250,000 aliens enter the country, he said.

Varying appeals for greater Federal action against delinquency threaded the testimony of most of the day's eleven witnesses.

District Attorney John M. Braisted Jr. of Richmond charged that television programs inspired many crimes. He proposed that the Federal Communications Commission "implement an effective code of good practice, or at least set the standards for the same, to supplant the morally bankrupt and apparently ineffective present code of the industry."

Others who testified were District Attorney Edward S. Silver of Kings County; Assistant District Attorney Irving Anolik of the Bronx; Miss Helen M. Harris, executive director of United Neighborhood Houses; Ralph Tefferteller, associate director of Henry Street Settlement, and Jackie Robinson, former baseball star.

Following are figures submitted yesterday by Kings County Judge Samuel S. Leibowitz to the Senate subcommittee on juvenile delinquency. Those for Domestic Relations Court cover juvenile delinquency adjudications. Those for Warwick Training School are from the state Department of Social Welfare and those for the Brooklyn House of Detention come from the city Correction Department.

Domestic Relations Court

A. Delinquency—First eight months of 1959, including School Part:

Borough	All Children	Puerto Ricans	Per Cent Puerto Ricans
Manhattan	2,414	722	29.9
Brooklyn	3,579	745	20.8
Bronx	1,549	516	33.3
Queens	1,266	38	3.0
Richmond	225	2	.9
Total	9,033	2,023	22.3

B. Total population of New York City in 1958.....8,010,000
Total Puerto Ricans in city as of July 1, 1959
  (7.17 per cent of city population)..........575,000
Total population of Manhattan in 1958........1,830,000
Total Puerto Ricans in Manhattan as of July 1,
  1959 (15.3 per cent of population)........280,000
In 1958, 13,245 children were brought to Domestic Relations Courts in all five boroughs as delinquent. Of these, 2,721 were Puerto Ricans—20.5 per cent.

C. Above shows for Puerto Ricans:
  City-wide—22.3 per cent of delinquents, against 7.17 per cent of population.
  Manhattan—29.9 per cent of delinquents, against 15.3 per cent of population.

Brooklyn House of Detention

Extraction or Color	Number	Per Cent
Puerto Rican	185	20.8
Negro	414	46.3
White	294	32.9
Total	893	100.0

Cases by boroughs: Brooklyn, 342; Bronx, 120; Manhattan, 317; Queens, 100; Richmond, 14.

Warwick

Extraction or Color		Ages
Puerto Rican	20 per cent	Warwick receives some 12-13 year-olds, all 14-year-olds, some 15-16-year-olds. Ninety per cent of all boys are from eleven upstate counties; about 400 boys are from New York City.
Negro	54 per cent	
White	26 per cent	

Following are other figures received by Kings County Court from state and city Correction Departments. Sing Sing figures cover 1958 state-wide commitments, about 95 per cent being from metropolitan area; Elmira reports cover 1958 commitments from New York City alone.

Sing Sing Prison

Ages	Whites Total	%	Negroes Total	%	Puerto Ricans Total	%	Others	Total
All	387	27	757	53	268	19	7	1,419
21–29	186	25	387	53	163	22	1	737
30–39	120	25	284	58	83	17	2	489
40–49	52	39	67	50	15	11	1	135
50–up	29	50	19	33	7	12	3	58

Elmira

Extraction or Color	REFORMATORY (Ages 21-25) Number	Per Cent	RECEPTION CENTER (Ages 16-18) Number	Per Cent
Puerto Rican	50	22	139	22
Negro	97	43	291	47
White	79	35	194	31
Total	226	100	624	100

City Plans to Add More Bright Lights To Cut Crime Rate

The city will install $1,100,000 worth of mercury vapor street lamps by June 30 in high crime areas and on heavily traveled thoroughfares.

The Grand Concourse in the Bronx and Northern Boulevard from the Nassau County line to the Queens end of the Queensboro Bridge will be completely illuminated with the 24,500-lumen lamps. For these projects 3,000 lamps will be used.

The lights will also be installed in the Bedford-Stuyvesant area of Brooklyn, on York Avenue from Sixtieth Street to the East River Drive, and in parts of the West Side of Manhattan.

Commissioner Armand D'Angelo of the Department of Water Supply, Gas and Electricity said yesterday that the lamps would provide two and a half times the illumination at 10 per cent less energy cost than that of the incandescent lamps used in most of the city.

They are "color-corrected," he said, "so that they do not have adverse effects on women's make-up and some complexions."

If the city's experience is borne out the lights also will reduce the incidence of murder, assault and rape. In June, 1959, a 49 per cent drop in these crimes was reported in five areas where the lamps had been installed.

March 4, 1960

Police Tell Women How to Avert Crime

New York women were warned yesterday not to take short cuts when walking alone at night and not to put keys under mats, but to double-lock their doors, and to report suspicious behavior by adults near schoolyards and playgrounds.

The admonitions were made in a four-page leaflet published by the Police Department entitled "A Message to Women."

The green-and-white leaflet provides a list of "do's and dont's" for women to protect themselves and their children from loiterers, burglars, muggers and molesters. It stresses the need for remaining calm and for notifying the police quickly in the event of trouble.

Starting today the department will begin distributing 100,000 copies of the public information bulletin to Parent-Teacher Associations and women's organizations here.

The leaflet notes that the police should be informed of a suspect's physical characteristics, dress, distinguishing marks and "any outstanding peculiarities in appearance or actions."

"If there are two or more men," it advises, "concentrate on one. Compare his physical proportions and age with someone you know."

Police Headquarters may be reached by dialing "O" for operator or directly by use of the police telephones on sidewalks.

Here are some of the department's counsels to women:

¶When you leave your home, don't advertise it with notes. During overnight absences from home, cancel newspaper and milk deliveries.

¶If you lose your door key, have locks changed immediately.

¶Lock entrance doors at all times. "Some burglars make a career of finding open doors."

¶Insist that callers identify themselves before you open a door, or, better still, install a peephole.

¶Equip doors with a chain and a bolt as well as a spring lock.

¶If awakened by an intruder, don't try to apprehend him. If threatened by a robber, do as you are told.

¶Don't display large amounts of money in public.

To protect their children, women are further advised to do these things:

¶Teach the child to report to them any suspicious persons or attempts by unknown adults to approach him or become friendly with him.

¶Instruct the child to follow the safest route to and from school.

¶If the child is to arrive home after dark, arrange to meet him.

¶Know the child's playmates and where they congregate.

April 18, 1960

U.S. CRIME AT PEAK; ROSE 12% LAST YEAR

WASHINGTON, Feb. 28 (UPI)—Attorney General Robert F. Kennedy reported today that crime in the United States reached a record in 1960, with a 12 per cent increase over the year before.

Robberies increased by 18 per cent, burglaries by 15 per cent, major larcenies by 11 per cent and auto thefts by 7 per cent. Murders and rapes increased by 4 per cent and aggravated assaults by 3 per cent. None of the major categories of crime showed a decrease.

The crime report was compiled by the Federal Bureau of Investigation from records submitted by the police in cities with a population of more than 25,000.

J. Edgar Hoover, F.B.I. director, said it was a "shocking situation" that the smallest percentage increase, for cities of more than 1,000,000 population, was 9 per cent. Cities with a population of 25,000 to 250,000 showed an increase of 14 per cent. Those with a population of 250,000 to 1,000,000 reported an increase of 11 per cent.

Mr. Hoover also said that juvenile crime had continued to increase.

Large cities had a 7 per cent increase in this category, compared with a 5 per cent rise in rural areas and small cities. There was a 6 per cent increase in juvenile arrests. Adult arrests increased by 2 per cent.

March 1, 1961

INSURANCE COSTS CLIMB WITH CRIME

Premiums Up in City—Some Coverage Hard to Obtain

By SAL R. NUCCIO

New Yorkers, whose town many insurance underwriters would like to forget, are finding it increasingly difficult and expensive to insure their property against criminal losses.

Casualty and inland marine insurance rates on personal and mercantile property generally have increased in recent years, as has the crime rate. Coverage on which premiums have not increased appreciably has become mode difficult to obtain.

A person seeking insurance must first be accepted by the broker, and then by the underwriting company. The broker, assuming he is not a small operator seeking to place any business that comes his way, feels that he must be selective in the placement of lines, so as not to jeopardize his accounts with insurers by showing large losses. The insurers, in turn, feel that they must be selective, so as to keep their loss ratios down.

The primary crime protection sought for personal property is provided by residence theft, or burglary, policies; by inland marine "all-risk floaters" on jewelry and furs, and by automobile physical-damage policies. Major mercantile lines cover hold-up, robbery and plate-glass damage, which is often caused by burglars or vandals.

Brooklyn Is Risky

Undesirable risks under these policies are referred to by insurance men as "K. O." (keep off) risks, and, of the five boroughs, Brooklyn is said to have the greatest number of "K. O." lists. Densely populated low-income areas in the city are high in the "Keep-Off" category, as are the sections on the fringes of these areas.

With reference to one of these areas, Ernest E. Johnson, new president of the United Insurance Brokers Association and a broker for the last seven years, at 271 West 125th Street, said:

"You find underwriters making judgments about an area they know nothing about. Some feel that a riot will break out every twenty-four hours in Harlem, which actually is comparable to any other low-income area."

Mr. Johnson said that it "is not easy" for the average broker in his area to place policies covering criminal losses. In his own business, he attempts to keep "a balanced book," having proportionate amounts of all types of insurance. He observed that if more brokers did that the insurers would not have the argument, in rejecting applications, that there was too much high-risk business—casualty, in this case—being offered.

Brokers, or agents, who have a large volume of business often have doubtful risks accepted by the underwriter as an accommodation. Individuals who might otherwise be considered bad risks are sometimes issued personal policies, if they carry large amounts of insurance on their businesses.

Most underwriters conceded that, "to survive," as one of them put it, they have tightened up their underwriting rules. A representative of a large company doing a sizable business in this city disagreed with this, saying that the concern was not writing less burglary, robbery and related policies than it had been ten or fifteen years ago.

However, he pointed out, the emphasis is not on selling these lines as it was then but on selecting from what came in unsolicited. "We must be selective," he said, "because the people who want to buy this protection usually are the ones who need it most."

One underwriter observed that "we have a different type of thief now who will go for anything." As a result, the list of vulnerable items has grown larger, and this is taken into account when an application is being considered. Aside from jewelry, furs and cash, the growing list includes clothing, radio and television sets, liquor, tobacco, tools and food.

A personal line that has shown a large rate rise is the jewelry policy for residents of any borough but Richmond. It costs $2.25 a year for each $100 of value up to $5,000, and $1.75 a $100 for the next $5,000, against $1.60 and $1.10, respectively, in 1950. As with other types of insurance, the premium for a three-year policy is 2.7 times the annual rate, compared with 2.5 several years ago.

It is understood that a proposal for a 12.5 per cent increase in the jewelry rate has been filed with the State Department of Insurance. The current loss-and-expense ratio for this line was put at 61.84 per cent, which means that 61.84 cents of each premium dollar earned goes toward settlement of claims. The break-even point was said to be a loss ratio of 52 to 53 per cent.

In the mercantile field, certain risks are considered especially hazardous. For a supermarket, burglary insurance costs $30 a year for each $1,000 of protection, and hold-up coverage costs $14.20. Until a few years ago, when the rates were increased, companies were not writing this risk, which was then rated in the less-expensive grocery store category. Current grocery store rates (with one attendant) are $10.50 a $1,000 for hold-up and $21 a $1,000 for burglary insurance.

One device that helps to reduce losses is the deductible clause, which also reduces the premium. This is used extensively in New York on automobile comprehensive policies, which cover losses from fire, lightning, theft and other causes, such as windstorm, water damage, malicious mischief and vandalism. The deductible clause, set at $50, makes the policyholder a self-insurer for amounts up to $50 on all claims but the primary ones of fire and theft; partial thefts—hu   ps, tires, etc.—are not excluded.

A rising rate of crime is not a problem peculiar to New York. Related insurance problems are faced in other cities to a greater or lesser degree. In Los Angeles, for example, a loss ratio of 56.32 per cent on jewelry "all-risk" policies reportedly brought about a request for a 20 per cent increase in rates. They are now $1.60 a year for each $100 of protection up to $5,000, and $1.20 a $100 for the next $5,000—considerably below the prevailing New York rates.

In many cities, however, certain rates are higher than those in New York. It costs $2.40 for each $100 of protection on mink in Chicago, while the rate here is $1 for all furs, including mink.

But whether it be in New York, Chicago, Los Angeles or anywhere else in the country, the time has come for insurance men to brace themselves for their busiest season. For the incidence of crime, as usual, is greatest from now until the end of the year, when "burglars are doing their Christmas shopping."

POLICE DECOY UNIT GOES INTO ACTION

Men Posing as Women Seize 2 in New Drive on Crime

An alleged attacker in Central Park and an alleged money-snatcher in Washington Square met unpleasant surprises last night. Their victims turned out to be young patrolmen disguised as women.

The arrests marked the beginning of Operation Decoy, a drive by the Police Department to reduce crime in areas where attacks have been frequent.

The decoys were chosen from the 200 members of the tactical patrol force, a detail of young patrolmen designed to reinforce precincts that have special crime problems.

Last night in Manhattan, ten decoys, some in women's clothing and some dressed as derelicts, went into action for the first time. Each was accompanied at a distance by a pair of "back-up" men in casual attire.

At 10:30 two of the decoys drew their quarry.

Patrolman Robert Crowley, 25 years old, wearing a skirt and blouse, bobby socks, loafers and a scarf, walked down the stairs into Central Park at 110th Street and Central Park West. Fifty feet behind were his back-up men.

A man stepped from shrubbery behind Mr. Crowley, the police said, reached around him and ripped his blouse. The patrolman identified himself and grappled with the man, who drew a six-inch steak knife, the police reported.

The back-up men went to Patrolman Crowley's aid, and one of them, Louis Eannelli, 29, was scratched on the hand. The suspect fled. Each of the three policemen fired a shot in the air. The man tripped and fell and was captured.

He was identified as Frederick Bailey, 46, of 710 Atlantic Avenue, Brooklyn. He was described by the police as a former mental patient with a long record of arrests. He was charged with felonious assault and violation of the Sullivan Act.

Meanwhile, Patrolman Bruce Brennan, wearing a blue dress, blue sweater, yellow kerchief and high-heeled shoes, was apparently dozing on a bench in the southeast corner of Was ington Square Park. A blue shawl on his lap covered his hands.

A man sat down at the other end of the bench, then moved closer. Patrolman Brennan appeared to doze on.

The man reached into a purse under the decoy's elbow, the police said, and took two one-dollar bills. The decoy and his back-up men subdued him after a fight.

The prisoner, identified as James Stitt, 40, of 160 Bleecker Street, was accused of larceny. He was quoted by the police as saying, "The shawl fooled me."

Patrolman Brennan is a son of Deputy Chief Inspector Jeremiah F. Brennan, commander of the Seventeenth Division in Queens.

St. Louis Is Credited

A Police Department spokesman said Commissioner Michael J. Murphy had borrowed the idea for the decoy operation from St. Louis, where a similar squad has made many arrests in the last fifteen months. The operation was credited with having helped to reduce crime in St. Louis by nearly 12 per cent last year.

The police spokesman here said policewomen often served as decoys here, but were not being used in the present nighttime operation because of the danger. He said a woman attacked as Patrolman Crowley was would have been injured.

37 Who Saw Murder Didn't Call the Police

Apathy at Stabbing of Queens Woman Shocks Inspector

By MARTIN GANSBERG

For more than half an hour 38 respectable, law-abiding citizens in Queens watched a killer stalk and stab a woman in three separate attacks in Kew Gardens.

Twice the sound of their voices and the sudden glow of their bedroom lights interrupted him and frightened him off. Each time he returned, sought her out and stabbed her again. Not one person telephoned the police during the assault; one witness called after the woman was dead.

That was two weeks ago today. But Assistant Chief Inspector Frederick M. Lussen, in charge of the borough's detectives and a veteran of 25 years of homicide investigations, is still shocked.

He can give a matter-of-fact recitation of many murders. But the Kew Gardens slaying baffles him—not because it is a murder, but because the "good people" failed to call the police.

"As we have reconstructed the crime," he said, "the assailant had three chances to kill this woman during a 35-minute period. He returned twice to complete the job. If we had been called when he first attacked, the woman might not be dead now."

This is what the police say happened beginning at 3:20 A.M. in the staid, middle-class, tree-lined Austin Street area:

Twenty-eight-year-old Catherine Genovese, who was called Kitty by almost everyone in the neighborhood, was returning home from her job as manager of a bar in Hollis. She parked her red Fiat in a lot adjacent to the Kew Gardens Long Island Rail Road Station, facing Mowbray Place. Like many residents of the neighborhood, she had parked there day after day since her arrival from Connecticut a year ago, although the railroad frowns on the practice.

She turned off the lights of her car, locked the door and started to walk the 100 feet to the entrance of her apartment

at 82-70 Austin Street, which is in a Tudor building, with stores on the first floor and apartments on the second.

The entrance to the apartment is in the rear of the building because the front is rented to retail stores. At night the quiet neighborhood is shrouded in the slumbering darkness that marks most residential areas.

Miss Genovese noticed a man at the far end of the lot, near a seven-story apartment house at 82-40 Austin Street. She halted. Then, nervously, she headed up Austin Street toward Lefferts Boulevard, where there is a call box to the 102d Police Precinct in nearby Richmond Hill.

'He Stabbed Me!'

She got as far as a street light in front of a bookstore before the man grabbed her. She screamed. Lights went on in the 10-story apartment house at 82-67 Austin Street, which faces the bookstore. Windows slid open and voices punctured the early-morning stillness.

Miss Genovese screamed: "Oh, my God, he stabbed me! Please help me! Please help me!"

From one of the upper windows in the apartment house, a man called down: "Let that girl alone!"

The assailant looked up at him, shrugged and walked down Austin Street toward a white sedan parked a short distance away. Miss Genovese struggled to her feet.

Lights went out. The killer returned to Miss Genovese, now trying to make her way around the side of the building by the parking lot to get to her apartment. The assailant stabbed her again.

"I'm dying!" she shrieked. "I'm dying!"

A City Bus Passed

Windows were opened again, and lights went on in many apartments. The assailant got into his car and drove away. Miss Genovese staggered to her feet. A city bus, Q-10, the Lefferts Boulevard line to Kennedy International Airport, passed. It was 3:35 A.M.

The assailant returned. By then, Miss Genovese had crawled to the back of the building, where the freshly painted brown doors to the apartment house held out hope of safety. The killer tried the first door; she wasn't there. At the second door, 82-62 Austin Street, he saw her slumped on the floor at the foot of the stairs. He stabbed her a third time—fatally.

It was 3:50 by the time the police received their first call,

from a man who was a neighbor of Miss Genovese. In two minutes they were at the scene. The neighbor, a 70-year-old woman and another woman were the only persons on the street. Nobody else came forward.

The man explained that he had called the police after much deliberation. He had phoned a friend in Nassau County for advice and then he had crossed the roof of the building to the apartment of the elderly woman to get her to make the call.

"I didn't want to get involved," he sheepishly told the police.

Suspect Is Arrested

Six days later, the police arrested Winston Moseley, a 29-year-old business-machine operator, and charged him with the homicide. Moseley had no previous record. He is married, has two children and owns a home at 133-19 Sutter Avenue, South Ozone Park, Queens. On Wednesday, a court committed him to Kings County Hospital for psychiatric observation.

When questioned by the police, Moseley also said that he had slain Mrs. Annie May Johnson, 24, of 146-12 133d Avenue, Jamaica, on Feb. 29 and Barbara Kralik, 15, of 174-17 140th Avenue, Springfield Gardens, last July. In the Kralik case, the police are holding Alvin L. Mitchell, who is said to have confessed that slaying.

The police stressed how simple it would have been to have gotten in touch with them. "A phone call," said one of the detectives, "would have done it." The police may be reached by dialing "O" for operator or SPring 7-3100.

The question of whether the witnesses can be held legally responsible in any way for failure to report the crime was put to the Police Department's legal bureau. There, a spokesman said:

"There is no legal responsibility, with few exceptions, for any citizen to report a crime."

Statutes Explained

Under the statutes of the city, he said, a witness to a suspicious or violent death must report it to the medical examiner. Under state law, a witness cannot withhold information in a kidnapping.

Today witnesses from the neighborhood, which is made up of one-family homes in the $35,000 to $60,000 range with the exception of the two apartment houses near the railroad station, find it difficult to explain why they didn't call the police. Lieut. Bernard Jacobs, who handled the investigation by the detectives, said:

"It is one of the better neighborhoods. There are few reports of crimes. You only get the usual complaints about boys playing or garbage cans being turned over."

The police said most persons had told them they had been afraid to call, but had given meaningless answers when asked what they had feared.

"We can understand the reticence of people to become involved in an area of violence," Lieutenant Jacobs said, "but where they are in their homes, near phones, why should they be afraid to call the police?"

He said his men were able to piece together what happened —and capture the suspect—because the residents furnished all the information when detectives rang doorbells during the days following the slaying.

"But why didn't someone call us that night?" he asked unbelievingly.

Witnesses—some of them unable to believe what they had allowed to happen—told a reporter why.

A housewife, knowingly if quite casual, said, "We thought it was a lover's quarrel." A husband and wife both said, "Frankly, we were afraid."

They seemed aware of the fact that events might have been different. A distraught woman, wiping her hands in her apron, said, "I didn't want my husband to get involved."

One couple, now willing to talk about that night, said they heard the first screams. The husband looked thoughtfully at the bookstore where the killer first grabbed Miss Genovese.

"We went to the window to see what was happening," he said, "but the light from our bedroom made it difficult to see the street." The wife, still apprehensive, added: "I put out the light and we were able to see better."

Asked why they hadn't called the police, she shrugged and replied: "I don't know."

A man peeked out from a slight opening in the doorway to his apartment and rattled off an account of the killer's second attack. Why hadn't he called the police at the time? "I was tired," he said without emotion. "I went back to bed."

It was 4:25 A.M. when the ambulance arrived for the body of Miss Genovese. It drove off. "Then," a solemn police detective said, "the people came out."

March 27, 1964

TV CALLED FACTOR IN SLAYING APATHY

Psychiatrist Gives Views on Witnesses in Queens

A confusion of fantasy with reality, fed by an endless stream of television violence, was in part responsible for the fact that 37 Queens residents could passively watch a murder taking place, a psychiatrist said yesterday.

The psychiatrist, Dr. Ralph S. Banay, addressed about 100 persons at a symposium on violence conducted at the Barbizon-Plaza Hotel by the Medical Correctional Association, of which he is president.

"We underestimate the damage that these accumulated images do to the brain," Dr. Banay said. "The immediate effect can be delusional, equivalent to a sort of post-hypnotic suggestion."

The killing took place in the early morning hours of March 13 on a well-lighted sidewalk in front of an apartment building in Kew Gardens. The victim was Miss Catherine Genovese, a night-club hostess who lived near by.

Screams Unanswered

Two weeks later the police announced that their investigation had disclosed that 38 persons saw the three knife attacks over more than 30 minutes that led to the woman's death. Despite Miss Genovese's repeated screams for help, the police said, no one went to her aid. A telephone call to the police was made by one woman only after the victim was dead.

The police disclosures of public apathy in the face of murder shocked the city, and led to many attempts to explain it.

Dr. Banay suggested yesterday that the murder vicariously gratified the sadistic impulses of those who witnessed it.

"They were deaf, paralyzed, hypnotized with excitation," he declared, "fascinated by the drama, by the action, and yet not entirely sure that what was taking place was actually happening."

Dr. Banay, who is professor of forensic psychiatry at Manhattan College, interpreted the readiness of the 37 persons to admit to the police that they had failed to act as an attempt through confession to purge the guilt that their enjoyment of the sight had aroused.

"Persons with mature and well-integrated personalities would not have acted in this way," he said.

Another speaker, Dr. Karl Menninger, the director of the Menninger Foundation in Topeka, Kan., touched on the same theme when he said that "public apathy [to crime] is itself a manifestation of aggressiveness."

Encouraged by Many

Noting that lawless behavior was tacitly encouraged in many ways, he added, "Crime has too much vicarious usefulness to society to be readily eliminated."

Dr. Walter Bromberg, a consultant in the defense of Jack Ruby, who was convicted of killing Lee Harvey Oswald, urged that a central registry be established for persons suffering from epilepsy and related diseases and that they be required to undergo treatment. Dr. Bromberg is clinical director of Pinewood Sanitarium in Katonah, N. Y.

Another psychiatrist, Dr. Maier I. Tuchler of Phoenix, said that parents often encourage delinquency in their children to gratify their own antisocial impulses. He said the problem was intensified in a rapidly changing, rootless society.

In a related paper on the family as "the breeding ground of violence," Dr. Lidia Koperni stated that a study of prisoners' families in Pennsylvania found that only one of 98 could be regarded as a well-adjusted unit.

April 12, 19

218

Hasidic Jews Use Patrols to Balk Attacks

Volunteers in Radio Cars Cruise After Dark in Brooklyn

By DOUGLAS ROBINSON

The Hasidic Jews of Brooklyn, turning to the tradition of the ancient Maccabees, have decided to fight their attackers.

The Maccabees of the Community, a group of about 120 volunteers, is patrolling the Crown Heights section in radio-equipped cars in an effort to protect members of the community.

Religious and community leaders decided to organize the patrols after a number of men and women were beaten and mugged. Recently, Jewish children at a yeshiva near Crown Heights were attacked by a group of Negroes.

The Hasidim, an ultra-Orthodox sect, are recognizable by their traditional Old World garb of long black coats and wide-brimmed black hats. The men wear beards and many have long sidecurls.

Although the Hasidic leaders are reluctant to identify their tormentors as Negroes, they say that most attacks are made by residents of the adjacent Bedford-Stuyvesant section, which is predominantly Negro.

Rabbi Samuel Schrage, administrator of the United Lubavitcher Yeshivoth, where the children were assaulted, said last night that the radio patrol cars were being used primarily to prevent trouble.

Each of four cars, he explained, is manned by six young men, all over 21 years old. They are not armed, but are "all strong," he said.

"In case of trouble," the Rabbi said, "our people try to overwhelm the attackers by sheer weight of numbers. If

The New York Times

As Moshe Pruzansky pinpoints location of complaint, Rabbi Schrage relays instructions to car. Call was false alarm.

The New York Times   May 27, 1964

Diagonal lines show area of Hasidic patrol activity.

it is beyond their capacity, they call us on the radio and we call the police."

The headquarters of the patrol force is a drab storefront at 459 Albany Avenue, between Montgomery Street and Empire Boulevard. Inside, it resembles a military command post, with a desk, a few chairs and a large map of Crown Heights on a wall. Volunteers answer the telephone while a reserve patrol car crew stands by.

The cars operate from 8 P.M. to 5 A.M. They make regular radio reports to headquarters on street conditions.

The number of volunteers in the patrol varies as the night progresses. Early in the morning, the number may shrink to four as men decide to call it a day. There is, however, a reserve force always at hand to take their places.

Non-Jewish volunteers — 12 whites and eight Negroes, at present — have volunteered to man the cars on Friday nights, the Jewish Sabbath.

The telephone number of the headquarters (SL 6-5100) is being circulated through the community so Jewish residents who plan to be out at night can call for protection.

Rabbi Schrage said the community had been virtually housebound by fear since it heard that a rabbi's wife had been dragged from her apartment at knifepoint. The attack occurred two weeks ago, the rabbi said.

The woman, he said, fought the man when he tried to rape her. She was slashed on the hand, but beat him off. She was in a hospital for a week for treatment of cuts and shock, he said.

Rabbi Schrage said there were 500,000 persons in the Crown Heights area, 75 per cent of them Jews

The radio patrol began operating on May 17 with two-way radios donated by the owner of a taxi business. Rabbi Schrage said it had been instrumental in three arrests: two suspicious men were observed breaking into a catering establishment and were held for the police, and a purse-snatcher was captured.

Appeals to the police about conditions in the area, the rabbi said, have led to conferences and the assignment of an extra police squad. However, the Hasidic leaders feel that the extra protection is not enough.

"The police know what we are doing," Rabbi Schrage said. "We didn't ask them if we could do it because we didn't expect them to sanction it."

Deputy Police Commissioner Walter Arm said that the set-up did not have the department's blessing but that there was nothing illegal about a group of citizens organizing for self-protection.

"We don't believe in the vigilante system in any society," he said. "That's what we have police for. We're aware of the situation and we're trying to do the best we can."

Last night, Capt. William Anderson and Sgt. Raymond Smith visited the headquarters to ask if they could help in any way. Rabbi Schrage assured the police officers he would call them if they were needed.

The community force takes its name from the Maccabees, a Jewish family that led a fight for religious freedom when the King of Syria attempted to force Hellenism upon Judea in the second century B.C.

NEGROES DEPLORE HASIDIC PATROLS

Decry 'Vigilante' Action by Brooklyn Sect — Police Also Condemn Move

By CHARLES GRUTZNER

The private radio car patrols of the Hasidic Jews in the Crown Heights section of Brooklyn were denounced yesterday by Negro leaders of the neighboring Bedford-Stuyvesant district as "vigilante" action.

Police officials in both neighborhoods took a disapproving view of the unofficial patrols but said they could not stop the operation so long as the volunteers remained unarmed, unless their actions led to a riot or other trouble.

The Bedford-Stuyvesant Business and Professional Men's Club, which is predominantly Negro, adopted unanimously a resolution condemning vigilante groups after several of its members voiced fear that any mistake by untrained members of the Hasidic patrols might lead to bloodshed.

Invited to Join Police

Police Capt. Eli Lazarus of the Empire Boulevard station, in Crown Heights, said he had told the Hasidic group two weeks ago that there was no need for "vigilantes." He invited its members to join the Police Department's civilian auxiliary, but gained only one recruit, he said.

The police auxiliary is composed of male civilians who, after a period of training, are attached to their home precincts for emergency duty. They carry nightsticks.

The precinct force has been augmented by the assignment since May 19 of 40 members of the tactical patrol unit, who have made several arrests and have had a deterrent effect by halting cars on suspicion and questioning occupants.

A police summons was put on one of the unofficial patrol cars of the Hasidim at 3:30 A.M. yesterday for double parking.

Capt. Edward Jenkins of the Gates Avenue station, in Bedford-Stuyvesant, said the police coöperated with all civic or taxpayer groups on specific problems, but added that "we are not by any means coöperating with this group or any other vigilantes."

"There is no redress for errors that untrained volunteers may make," Captain Jenkins said. "The Police Department trains a recruit for nine months, in techniques and in the rights of civilians — and even we make mistakes sometimes."

Rabbi Samuel Schrage, spokesman for the Hasidic enclave in Crown Heights, denied that the patrols were vigilantes or that they were directed against any racial group. He said they served chiefly as "crime spotters" for the police and as an escort service for members of the sect.

"Only when it is imperative to act promptly do our patrols take the legal action of making citizen arrests," he added.

A Bearded Sect

The Hasidim, an ultra-Orthodox sect, are conspicuous by their long black coats and wide-brimmed black hats. The men wear beards and many of the men and boys wear long sidecurls.

There have been several assaults on members of the sect, including the knifing and attempted rape of a rabbi's wife and attacks on children attending a yeshiva of which Rabbi Schrage is administrator, on Bedford Avenue near Dean Street.

The Crown Heights section, once almost solidly Jewish, has had an influx of Negroes in recent years from the teeming Bedford-Stuyvesant area. It now has about 25 per cent Negro population, including many professional and business people. The Hasidim have, for the most part, remained aloof from other Jews.

One of the criticisms yesterday was that it was difficult for leaders of other groups to seek joint solutions to sociological problems, including the increase in crime, because of this aloofness.

Impression of a 'Custer'

Dr. Oliver Harper, one of the Negro leaders, said that some meetings had been held with Rabbi Schrage, but that "he gave the impression he was General Custer surrounded by hostile Indians" or a Jew encircled by Arabs.

"Dr. Harper is not aware of the purposes of our patrols," said the rabbi. "We are fighting crime and criminals, without distinction as to color or creed. We are trying to protect ourselves because there is not adequate police protection."

There was agreement in both areas that more policemen were needed. The Negro leaders said that more policemen would not of themselves solve the problem, since the area also needed better recreational facilities, more employment opportunities and better education.

Police Commissioner Michael J. Murphy received a request yesterday from the Mayor's Committee of Religious Leaders for the assignment of additional police to the Crown Heights area.

The committee, after consulting with the Brooklyn Jewish Community Council and the Central Brooklyn Co-ordinating Council, reported "an unhealthy increase of attacks made daily upon Jewish members of the Crown Heights community [in which] adults as well as children have been attacked, threatened, robbed and molested."

The letter, sent by Rabbi Alfred L. Friedman of Union Temple of Brooklyn, declared that "fear is walking the streets." It said the three groups were also exploring ways "whereby we can ameliorate the situation with greater education, recreation and conciliation." The letter was made public by Emil N. Baar, head of the Brooklyn Jewish Community Council.

A state investigation into the need for better police protection in areas of this city was promised by Anthony P. Savarese Jr., chairman of the Assembly Committee on the Affairs of New York City.

Assemblyman Savarese, a Queens Republican, said he was aroused by the reports of the patrols organized by the Hasidic Jews. He said he feared that the Crown Heights action might be emulated in other neighborhoods and lead to dangerous situations.

"If it has reached the point where citizens need to take the law into their own hands," he said, "we must give them the protection we need and get these people off the roads."

The Crown Heights situation led the Bedford-Stuyvesant Business and Professional Men's Club to call a conference at the Bedford Y.M.C.A. before its regular luncheon meeting. Milton Mollen, chairman of the Housing and Development Board, the speaker outlined plans for the proposed Fulton Park Urban Redevelopment.

Edward C. Maxwell, club president, said the Negro leaders had been surprised by the formation of the unofficial patrols.

"We have been meeting with Rabbi Schrage for the past six weeks," he said. "We have formed a street block association around the yeshivah to bring better cooperation and goodwill between our groups. We are definitely opposed to any vigilante group."

Mr. Maxwell, who is superintendent of registry in the Brooklyn post office, said he had received calls from Assemblyman Stanley Steingut, Brooklyn Democratic leader, and other white leaders "who are standing by to discuss this matter."

Assemblyman Thomas R. Jones, Brooklyn Democrat, said he was disturbed because "wherever a vigilante group has been formed it has inspired terror" because vigilantes "take upon themselves the determination of who is a criminal and who is abroad for mischief."

Darwin Bolden, executive director of the Bedford-Stuyvesant Youth in Action Project, said the Crown Heights situation was "a series of incidents blown out of proportion as racial incidents." He echoed the call for more police protection.

May 28, 196—

TEACHER IS SLAIN IN CROWN HEIGHTS

Woman Raped in Elevator in Neighborhood Where Hasidim Set Up Patrol

By EMANUEL PERLMUTTER

A schoolteacher was raped and fatally stabbed early yesterday in the self-service elevator of her apartment house in the Crown Heights section of Brooklyn. The building is only three blocks from the headquarters of the citizen radio car patrol set up recently by Hasidic Jews.

The murder shocked residents of the quiet, tree-lined section. They said over and over that they had expected better protection as a result of the patrols, called the Maccabees, and the recently augmented official police squads.

Fifty new volunteers appeared at the Maccabees' headquarters last night.

The teacher, Miss Charlotte Lipsik was attacked shortly after midnight Friday on her return from Times Square, where she had attended the movie "Becket" with another woman teacher.

She was 38 years old and lived on the fifth floor of the six-story apartment house with her 70-year-old mother, Jean, an invalid. There are 53 apartments in the building.

Peter Baden, 26, a fourth-floor tenant, and an unidentified companion found Miss Lipsik at about 12:30 A.M. when they opened the door of the elevator at the ground floor. Her clothes were in disarray, the contents of her handbag were strewn about the elevator and her purse had been emptied.

Mr. Baden notified the police, and Miss Lipsik was taken to Kings County Hospital, where she died at 3:30 A.M. despite blood transfusions and other efforts to save her life. Chief of Detectives Philip Walsh took charge of 50 detectives who were sent to the area.

The murder threatened to impede official efforts to induce the Hasidic Jews to abandon their nightly patrols. Negro groups in the area and in adjoining Bedford-Stuyvesant have criticized the patrols as "vigilante" posses, and said they were aimed at Negroes.

A meeting of Crown Heights Jewish community leaders with Police Commissioner Michael J. Murphy is scheduled for tomorrow to discuss ways of merging the citizen patrols into the auxiliary police.

"I think this unfortunate incident will impress upon Commissioner Murphy and Mayor Wagner the need for more policemen in our area," Rabbi Benjamin Kreitman of the Brooklyn Jewish Center said yesterday. "I hope it will lead to a larger and more effective auxiliary police."

Early today, Rabbi Samuel Schrage, the leader of the Maccabees, said he would demand "at least three times more protection."

Because the Hasidim are Orthodox Jews whose religion limits their physical activity on Friday night and Saturday,

their Sabbath, the patrols were manned by Christian volunteers on Friday night.

The Rev. Bryan Griswold, rector of Crown Heights's predominantly Negro St. Mark's Protestant Episcopal Church, who served as the radio dispatcher for the patrols on Friday night, said:

"This incident obviously points up the need for something like the patrol force, and I would not think there would be any thought of disbanding now. I'm quite dismayed. I hope we can get some police action now."

Jesse Califano, a 24-year-old artist who was in charge of the headquarters at 459 Albany Avenue, issued a statement yesterday, which he said was made in behalf of Rabbi Samuel Schrage, leader of the patrols.

"Miss Lipsik would have been alive today had she called our office Friday night and asked for an escort," he said. "We would have seen her inside her door."

Attacks Lead to Patrols

Rabbi Schrage said last night that members of volunteer patrols had started a campaign to raise funds for Miss Lipsik's mother.

The patrols were organized May 17 as an outgrowth of attacks in the area. The specific incidents that led to the setup were the assault and robbery of a blind news dealer and the attempted rape of a rabbi's wife. Previously, children attending a yeshiva had been attacked by Negro youths.

The patrols operated with radio connections to their headquarters. They served as "spotters" of trouble for the police, and as escorts for residents who wanted such protection.

A long line of young men waited patiently to enlist for patrolling last night. An electrician who lives in the area offered his services, and said his

union would be willing to install lights in back yards for persons who wanted them.

An autopsy showed that Miss Lipsik had been raped, her nose and jaw fractured, and she had suffered seven stab wounds, four in the stomach, one on the forehead and two in the neck. In addition, there were finger marks on her throat indicating an attempt had been made to strangle her.

Assistant Chief Inspector James Knott, in charge of Brooklyn South Detectives, said that the physical layout of the lobby of the apartment house was such as to aid an assailant.

He explained that the elevator was at the right of the entrance to the house, directly across the hall from a door that led to a courtyard. He said a criminal could hide in the darkness of the yard until his victim was about to enter the elevator, and then rush into the lobby and seize her.

Chief Knott said that bits of flesh were found under Miss Lipsik's fingernails. He asked that anyone who saw a person bearing fresh scratches communicate with the police at a special telephone number, SLocum 6-1900, which will be available 24 hours a day.

Miss Lipsik was a sixth-grade teacher at Public School 284, Watkins Street and Sutter Avenue, in the neighboring Brownsville section. This semester she was teaching library work. She had been a member of the school system for 12 years.

Neighbors described her as an attractive, dark-haired woman who always had a smile for acquaintances.

She had gone to Manhattan Friday to spend the afternoon and evening with her friend, Miss Gail Mantell, a resident of Greenwich Village.

May 31, 1964

Philadelphia Police Using Dogs to Curb Violence in Subway

Special to The New York Times

PHILADELPHIA, March 13—The police here began using German shepherd dogs this week, in their efforts to stem mounting violence in subway and elevated stations.

The dogs and their uniformed masters are riding trains in the early morning and patrolling lonely concourses where danger for passengers, especially unescorted women, lurks around corners.

The plan was put into effect on Wednesday by Mayor James H. J. Tate and Police Commissioner Howard R. Leary.

Its adoption was spurred by an attack on a 15-year-old girl from Almonesson, N.J., in the Race-Vine Station of the Broad Street subway last Saturday night.

About a dozen teen-age boys dragged the girl along the station platform and beat her while a group of men stood nearby without going to her assistance. One Naval Reservist, not in the group, ran to help and was also beaten.

The assailants, who had

threatened to rape the girl, fled when someone finally called the police. Eight youths were subsequently arrested.

The dog patrols are being used on the Broad Street subway and on the Market-Frankford subway-elevated system. Eight teams, each composed of a man and a dog, are on duty, and an expansion of the patrol is planned.

On the first day the plan went into effect one such team broke up an impending gang fight at 56th and Market Streets.

In addition to riding the trains, some policemen with

dogs in jeeps are patrolling the streets along subway routes. They halt at stations and descend to make periodic surprise checks.

Since the dog patrols began, there have been no reports of violence in the subways.

Commissioner Leary also announced that other steps were being taken against subway crimes. These include the installation of police call boxes and public address systems in stations, and lights on poles outside stations that will blink in emergencies.

A "hot line" is being installed to link the police radio room in City Hall with subway patrol headquarters.

March 14, 1965

F.B.I. Crime Data Called Misleading By Sociologists

By MURRAY SCHUMACH

Prominent criminologists and sociologists, in a growing controversy with law enforcement agencies, are challenging official statistics and claims that show a sharp increase in the crime rate.

This dispute, developing beneath the turbulent surface of public emotion about national crime, could put the picture of crime in the United States into a new perspective.

Specifically at issue are contentions by the Federal Bureau of Investigation that the national crime rate rose 10 per cent over 1962 and that since 1958 it has soared five times as fast as the population. The 1963 crime rate figure was 1,198.3 crimes for every 100,000 persons.

No one doubts that the total number of crimes has increased and the F.B.I. does not say its crime rate figures measure the number of criminals. The figures reflect only serious crimes — murder, forcible rape, aggravated assault (obvious intent to kill), larceny and auto theft.

But scholars say that in computing its figures, the Federal agency has failed to give full value to factors that would have tended to show a reduction in the national rate. This is supported even by a sociologist used by the F.B.I.

Until these elements are considered, say the academicians, no one will really know what the crime picture is. However, they are certain it is not nearly so serious as the figures indicate.

What the bureau and other law enforcement agencies see as breakdown in public morality, the scholars regard as largely a reflection of traditional American behavior, such as violence in periods of great growth.

At the heart of the disagreement is this vital question: Is the nation in serious trouble or is it in process of normal change?

This controversy was examined in a New York Times survey that included interviews at the F.B.I. headquarters and with New York City police officials; conversations with noted academicians; examinations of statistics on crime and inspection of the New York City Police Department's method of collecting crime statistics.

Experts Skeptical

Typical of experts who are strongly skeptical of Federal crime statistics are Dr. Sophia Robison, professor of sociology at Columbia and one of the foremost consultants used by the Children's Bureau; Dr. Gilbert Geis, fellow at the Harvard Law School; and Dr. Clarence Senior, member of the New York City Board of Education and expert on migration and urbanization.

Says Dr. Robison: "Many of my colleagues will admit privately their doubts of the F.B.I. figures but they don't dare say so publicly."

Says Dr. Geis: "The F.B.I. figures are terribly in need of adjustment."

Says Dr. Senior: "I think most criminologists and sociologists are very skeptical of the significance of crime statistics." Confusing the entire subject in the public's mind, according to scholars, has been the tendency of mass media to concentrate on extreme aspects of crime. The F.B.I. itself has cautioned, repeatedly, in its reports against lurid interpretations of its figures.

Family Brawls Responsible

Nevertheless, amid the hullabaloo about violence, little has been said about the F.B.I.'s comment, in its 1963 report, that about a third of all murders ordinarily stem from family brawls and that there has been little change in the murder rate since 1958.

As for rape, the F.B.I. has pointed out that there has been little change in volume in six years and that the crime has increased in proportion to the population.

And amid the clamor about the rise of narcotics addiction — the Federal agency says it went up 10 per cent in 1963 — little attention was paid to the recent Senate report showing that during the years immediately preceding World War I — a period now regarded as serene — addiction was 10 times as high as it is today. The Senate report showed that in 1914 one person in 400 was a narcotics addict. The Bureau of Narcotics says that in 1963 the figure was one in 4,000.

Other Factors Cited

Scholars say that if a calmer view of crime were taken by mass media the situation would seem less alarming, particularly if more careful attention were paid to the following important factors:

¶There has been a disproportionate increase in the 15-to-24 age group — the "war babies" — responsible for about 70 per cent of serious crime.

¶Much of auto theft that is classified as a serious crime is really the much lesser offense of joyriding in borrowed property.

¶City police departments have been more diligent in reporting crime.

¶There have been changes in the meaning of some crimes, apart from differences in definition in various states.

Then there are two other points that are regarded as important in appraising crime but that are not measured in the F.B.I.'s statistics. They are:

¶Crime has been made easier and stimulated by the public's failure to take sensible precautions because it can count on insurance to cover losses.

¶There have been vast shifts in population back and forth across the country, a phenomenon traditionally accompanied by increased crime. This is therefore not peculiar to the present.

An extraordinary paradox is that while there has been a great deal of worry about juvenile delinquency it seems to have escaped notice that if the number of juveniles increases faster than the population the crime rate will automatically rise.

The Federal Bureau of Investigation says that as far back as it can recall the bulk of crimes of violence have been committed by those between 20 and 24 years of age and the serious property offenses by those between 15 and 19.

This would mean that even if the crime rate among youngsters remained stationary and there are scholars who think this may be so — an increase in the number of these youths would bring about an increase in the national rate of crime.

The need to adjust statistics for the disproportionate increase of the "war baby" generation is supported not only by outspoken critics of police crime statistics, but even by Dr. Peter P. Lejins, professor of sociology at the University of Maryland, who has assisted the F.B.I. in preparing its statistics and who is held in high regard by the agency.

Dr. Lejins says the bureau has been considering adjusting its figures to meet this criticism but has not done so yet.

Youth's Percentage Up

Population changes responsible for this discussion are clearly indicated by the Bureau of Census reports. In 1960 there were 11,155,000 persons between the ages of 14 and 17. This figure had increased to 14,201,000 by 1964. The percentage increase, despite the tendency of people to live longer, thus rose from 6.2 to 7.4 per cent of the population.

The age group from 18 to 24 showed a similar pattern. The population went from 15,604,000 in 1960 to 18,292,000 in 1964, a rise in percentage of the population from 8.7 to 9.6.

In calculating its rate of crime, the Federal Bureau of Investigation considers the over-all rise in population. Thus, when it speaks of its crime rate for 1963, it shows the figure of 1,198.3 for each 100,000 persons. But no special allowance is made for the disproportionate growth of any age group.

Another indication of the importance of this factor is that, according to the F.B.I., the crime rate did not rise appreciably during World War II.

An expert at the bureau's office in Washington said this was certainly a reflection of the fact that so many young men were out of circulation. The sweep of patriotism, the agency believes, is another reason.

Thus, any areas, such as suburban communities, where the growth of the "war babies" was greatest, were bound to have a sharper increase than elsewhere. This was shown in the recent preliminary report of the F.B.I. for 1964.

On the basis of this factor alone — even if all crime rates remain stationary — the United States is almost certain to have an ever-growing crime problem for the next 10 years. The forecast is in the census figures that show there are about 35 million persons now between the ages of 5 and 13.

In some areas, even where the official figures are not challenged, the crime rate can give a false picture because of failure to evaluate some elements. One such element is the casual public attitude about robbery because of insurance. On this point, the F.B.I., the New York City police and insurance companies are in agreement and there seems to be no dissent from academic circles.

An extreme, but illustrative, crime was reported from San Francisco. A woman discovered her home had been looted. But because she was going away for the weekend she did not bother to report it until she returned.

Representatives of insurance companies and of law enforcement agencies say that particularly in the field of jewelry and auto thefts there is evidence of gross carelessness on the part of the public that makes it easier for criminals to operate and thus stimulates the rise in crime.

The Federal Bureau of Investigation, the New York City Police Department and insurance representatives say that too often the public, instead of feeling victimized, seems almost pleased at the thought of being able to use the insurance payments to replace the stolen items.

By sheer numbers the crimes of burglary and auto theft greatly affect the over-all crime statistics. Burglary, for example, according to the F.B.I., was committed 975,900 times in 1963. The average for each of the three preceding years was 854,600.

Auto thefts were at 399,000 in the F.B.I.'s 1963 figures, compared with the average of 334,-400 for three previous years.

Thus auto theft and burglary made up 1,374,900 of the nation's 2,259,100 crimes reported to the F.B.I. in 1963.

Many auto thefts are likely to be auto thefts in name only. Insurance experts say that about 92 per cent of all cars are recovered and that most of the cars are taken for "joy rides." This compares with the recovery rate of only 13 per cent for jewelry, where the theft is clearly for profit.

Dr. Lejins has urged law enforcement groups to adjust their crime statistics to consider the noncriminal aspect of auto thefts, but has been turned down on the ground that if this were done it would only encourage auto thefts.

There is general agreement among law enforcement groups and scholars that when there are great shifts of population crime is likely to increase. Since the war, millions of families have been heading west in numbers never known even during the heaviest migration periods of this century. In addition, there have been large-scale population movements from South to North by Negroes and back and forth across the country by men and women seeking jobs.

The F.B.I. concedes that this restlessness, which is not measured in police statistics, has increased the crime rate.

To an extent that is difficult to measure the Federal overall crime statistics are dependent on the accuracy of local crime reports. If municipal reports are sloppy this will be reflected in national figures.

Until 1952, for instance, New York City statistics were considered so unreliable that the F.B.I. refused to accept them.

The demand for honest reports has forced police departments in the largest cities to break away from the custom of holding down crime figures for fear of adverse public reaction. Since about 85 per cent of serious crimes are committed in the nation's metropolitan areas, honest reporting alone can show up as an increase in the crime rate.

However, the Federal Bureau of Investigation guards against magnified deviations. If a report from a police department shows a marked increase or decrease from the preceding year, it checks to see if the reporting group has made important changes in its statistical technique.

When the F.B.I. began its program in 1930 it received reports from 400 police departments, representing about 16 per cent of the population. Now

its reports are from 8,300 to 8,500 agencies, representing about 94 per cent of the population.

Second only to burglary among serious offenses listed by the F.B.I. is larceny. Last year there were 611,400 such offenses, compared with an average of 505,000 for the three previous years. In this category are such crimes as pocket-picking, purse-snatching, shoplifting, thefts of bicycles and auto accessories and thefts from automobiles.

Bicycles More Costly

Since the Federal definition classifies as larceny the theft of anything worth more than $50, the mere increase in national prosperity is likely to stimulate the growth of this category. It is more probable that a bicycle will be worth $50 nowadays than three years ago.

The F.B.I. has been using the $50 figure since 1958. The New York City police distinction between petty and grand larceny is $100. Police experts here favor increasing the boundary to $250.

Social scientists say that until adjustments are made by police groups in statistical techniques and there are indications that the Federal Bureau of Investigation is looking into this possibility the dispute between the law enforcement agencies and the academic worlds of

criminology and sociology will become more heated and perhaps force an entirely new appraisal of crime in the United States.

The New York Times Studio

Dr. Clarence Senior of the Board of Education said he thought most sociologists were skeptical of significance of crime statistics.

March 22, 1965

STUDY CITES DROP IN NEGRO VIOLENCE

Sharp Fall in Crime During Rights Protests Is Noted

By NATALIE JAFFE

A sharp drop in crimes of violence among Negroes during periods of organized civil-rights protests has been found in a study of three Southern cities.

The study reviewed the records of police, hospitals and civil-rights workers during months when demonstrations, sit-ins and boycotts had mobilized most of the Negro communities involved

In one city of 500,000 persons, a research team from Howard University and The Johns Hopkins Hospital found a 31 per cent reduction in the rate of assault by Negroes upon other Negroes, coinciding with a two-year period of sit-ins and economic boycotts.

In a small town in a border state where Negroes normally account for about half the arrests for major crimes, the figures for three successive summers of mounting civil-rights activity showed a decline from 73 arrests during the five warm months of 1961 to 31 during the same period in 1963.

In the third city, for which crime statistics were not available, civil-rights workers reported a marked reduction in delinquency over a two-year period among about 200 teen-

age gang members who joined the protest movement.

The authors concede that the decrease in reported crime might have been because of police reluctance to enter Negro neighborhoods during periods of unrest. They also note that crime during such periods might have been hidden from white authorities.

But the study cites evidence to show that the police often pay close attention to Negro sections during times of racial violence. The correlation of police data with records kept by hospitals and physicians also supports the apparent decrease in personal violence.

In all three cities, the crime rates returned to previous levels after the peak periods of protest. However, the study found

that the rate did not increase along with population growth or the expectation that "frustrated hopes" might contribute to more violence.

Although the cities were not identified in the research, the chronology of events suggests that they were Atlanta, Ga., Cambridge, Md., and Albany, Ga.

The research, which was reported in the March issue of the Archives of General Psychiatry, was commented on in an unsigned editorial in the Journal of the American Medical Association.

"Regardless of the explanation," the editorial said, "such findings help to unsettle the popular stereotypes of the lower-class Negro, irretrievably predisposed to either a life of violence and 'antisocial' behavior or to servile compliance. Indeed, some of the nonviolent protest can be described as 'prosocial' activity in which participants seek not only to 'do society's work for it,' but simultaneously to undergo significant changes in their own lives."

The quoted phrases within the editorial are those of Dr. Frederic Solomon and Dr. Jacob R. Fishman, two psychiatrists at Howard University in Washington, who were members of the survey team.

In a telephone interview, Dr. Solomon defined "prosocial" activity as an outlet for pent-up anger that would otherwise be expressed in antisocial behavior or character disturbances.

"When there is a framework of community organization within which direct action protest occurs," he said, "there is an apparent transformation of the violence-prone segment of the population."

Dr. Solomon emphasized that the study's findings were suggestive rather than categorical. However, he noted that they appeared to confirm informal observations.

In the Negro communities of New York and Washington, for example, the police blotters were notably brief during the one-day March on Washington in 1963 and in the few days following. In Selma, Ala., in recent weeks, reporters have noted a virtual absence of crime in the neighborhood where protest activity has concentrated.

In the city thought to be Atlanta, the months of October, 1960, through January, 1961, were marked by mass arrests of demonstrators and a successful boycott of downtown stores. This period saw the lowest record of major crime in the Negro community in years.

In the small town presumed to be Albany, a civil-rights leader reported that youth gangs, which first came to his attention when they threw bricks at white policemen at Negro rallies, were eventually integrated into the nonviolent movement.

WAGNER ORDERS A NIGHT PATROL ON ALL SUBWAYS

Starting Tomorrow, Special Force Will Ride Trains From 8 P.M. to 4 A.M.

COST PUT AT $9 MILLION

But Mayor Stresses Safety Comes First—800 New Police to Be Recruited

---

By CLAYTON KNOWLES

Mayor Wagner opened a drive last night to free the subways of the terror spread by "the mugger, the hoodlum and the young punk."

Starting tomorrow, a policeman armed with a revolver and a nightstick will patrol every train between 8 P.M. and 4 A.M., the Mayor said in a radio and television address.

The Mayor, in ordering 1,200 men into the campaign against subway crime, also said that one or more policemen would patrol each of the 480 stations in the system after 8 P.M. He described the late evening and early morning hours as the key "trouble period."

While the Mayor was beginning his drive against terror in the subways, several bills aimed at cutting the crime rate in the city's system were filed in Albany by Assemblyman Thomas V. LaFauci, a Queens Democrat.

TV Surveillance Urged

The bills call for closed-circuit television to provide surveillance of each station, communications systems between cars in each train and between trains and stations, and a three-car limit on trains between 10 P.M. and 6 A.M.

Mayor Wagner also ordered the following steps to be taken immediately:

¶The closing and locking of doors of rear cars during non-rush hours as passengers thin out, to reduce the danger of crime in sparsely occupied cars.

¶The closing of auxiliary entrances and passageways into

The New York Times
ORDERS SUBWAY VIGIL: Mayor Wagner at taping for TV and radio broadcast on crime in the subways.

subway stations during night hours.

¶The granting of permission for members of Housing Authority police, correction officers and sanitation police to ride the subways free of charge to and from work or on assignment in uniform.

Firemen and city police already travel the subways free.

The cost of the program, which envisages the recruitment and training of 800 more full-time transit policemen by mid-July, will be more than $9 million a year for manpower alone. But the Mayor stressed that cost must be secondary to the safety of the public.

"The hoodlums and toughs who prey on innocent people are going to be taught a lesson—a lesson they need," he promised. "Police Commissioner Mike Murphy has his orders. He is going to have all the help and support he needs to carry these orders out."

Every major local television and radio station carried the Mayor's 15-minute broadcast, which was taped three

hours before it was broadcast at 6:15 P.M.

He sandwiched the taping of the program between a session with his labor advisers, who are working with him to avert a citywide newspaper strike, and a reception at City Hall for Maurice Yameogo, President of the Republic of Upper Volta.

Mr. Wagner, neatly dressed in a blue stripe suit and striped tie, appeared somewhat worn from the long hours he has been putting in on the newspaper dispute, but he was firm and serious as he taped the program at the WCBS-TV studios on West 57th Street.

The question of safety in the subways has become a major issue in the 1965 city election campaign, in which the Mayor is seeking a fourth term. Last week it was disclosed that serious crimes on subways rose 41.4 per cent in the first three months this year over a year ago.

Potential opponents, both Democrats and Republicans, have been pressing him on the matter. John J. Gilhooley, Republican member of the Transit Authority, I. D. Robbins, president of the City Club who plans to seek the Democratic nomination, and Representative William Fitts Ryan, Reform Democrat who is also contemplating a primary fight, have made subway crime a major campaign issue.

Michael J. Quill, head of the Transport Workers Union, added to the outcry last Wednesday with a call for more subway conductors as well as more policemen.

Mr. Gilhooley held a news conference immediately after the Mayor's broadcast last night at which he called Mr. Wagner's plan "a response to my urgent request of 12 to 15 days ago." Mr. Gilhooley added that the Mayor has given him "all that I asked him for."

Mr. Gilhooley, speaking at the Commodore Hotel, said this request had come in the form of a letter to Mr. Wagner asking for a two-way closed circuit television system, a buzzer warning system and "most important, men, bodies, out on the trains patroling."

In disclosing his plans, the Mayor said he has "now given the anticrime effort top priority among all our undertakings."

"The fight against crime must have the first call on our resources," he said. "I am going to be available for my part in it 24 hours a day. Crime is of nationwide concern today, but New York City can and will lead the way in the fight, as it has in so many others over the years."

Mr. Wagner made clear that the adding of 1,200 policemen to the drive represented emergency action. One thousand of them will be members of th regular city police force, working at overtime pay on their days off to police the subways. The other 200 will be transit police, doing extra duty on their days off.

Training to Be Speeded

In all, there will be 1,200 men on duty nightly— 800 of them in the subways—and they will be working on the overtime basis until the city can recruit and train 800 extra transit police, whom the city will begin hiring at once.

The city's overtime cost alone will be $1.8 million a month for the next three months, or until the new men are hired. The new recruits will be trained under "a speeded-up schedule of selection, examination and training at the Police Academy," the Mayor said.

He said this would make them available for duty "in approximately three months, or one-eighth the ordinary time."

The addition of the 800 men will bring the transit police force to 2,012 members. The

Mayor stressed that the recruits would meet tough departmental standards on health, education, intelligence and training.

"The selection and training of men—and women, too—who can be entrusted with badge, club and gun is a great responsibility," he said. "A transit policeman who lost his nerve or his temper in a crowded train could start a disastrous panic."

The Mayor said that four experimental programs had been agreed upon "and either are or will be in test operation promptly." These include television monitors on station platforms, a pushbutton alarm system connecting change booths directly with transit and city police headquarters, an alarm system in each car connected to the motorman's cab and a two-way radio communication system enabling the motorman on a train to summon police assistance

But the Mayor repeatedly stressed that police manpower was the key deterrent to crime.

"It is easy enough to talk

about safety and security in the subways in push-button terms," he said. "But there is no pushbutton formula for security against the kind of crime plaguing the subways. We had to adopt measures which would directly deter crime on the scene and catch criminals in the act. No electronic equipment can do this. Only policemen can."

And again he emphasized that "no price tag can be placed on safety."

Under a long-range program, the Mayor said he was conferring with Police Commissioner Michael J. Murphy and Transit Authority members with a view to merging the transit police, paid for entirely by the city, with the regular city police force.

"The war against crime is one war, whether it is in the subways or in the streets," he said. "I believe it can best be conducted under unified command—the command of Police Commissioner Murphy."

April 6, 1965

California to Aid Victims

SACRAMENTO, Calif., July 21 (AP)—California will soon be giving financial aid to victims of crimes of violence and to families of murder victims. Gov. Edmund G. Brown's office said he signed Monday a bill providing that the State Department of Social Welfare determine the need. Expenditures for the fiscal year 1965-66 are limited to $100,000.

July 22, 1965

TENANT SECURITY A PROBLEM IN CITY

Escort Service Among the Protective Measures for Self-Service Elevators

ARMED GUARDS IN USE

Big Apartment Developments Even Using Watchdogs to Discourage Prowlers

By THOMAS W. ENNIS

Protecting tenants from burglary and assault in self-service elevators has become a major concern to the owners of the city's new luxury apartment houses.

The latest of the security measures is an elevator "escort" service offered by three of Manhattan's new apartment houses. The escort, a uniformed lobby attendant, operates one of the building's self-service elevators during the late night hours. When requested, he sees timorous tenants to their door.

Security measures have grown more elaborate as the apartment houses have grown in size —quite a few new ones are 30 to 35 stories high. As is the custom nowadays, even the most expensive buildings have self-service elevators, thus requiring the utmost vigilance at the entrance to keep out intruders.

Armed Guards Stand By

The usual complement of 24-hour doormen are sometimes supplemented by armed guards. Some of the larger apartment developments employ armed guards accompanied by watchdogs to discourage prowlers.

One of the buildings offering an elevator escort service is the 35-story Dorchester Towers, which occupies the entire block between Broadway and Amsterdam Avenue and 68th and 69th Streets.

When Miss Rosemarie Paolinelli, an airline stewardess in her early 20's, or Mrs. Florette Nestler, a middle-aged widow, come home after 10 o'clock at night, an attended elevator is waiting for them. Among the regular users of the escort service are a number of elderly men who live alone and a woman who suffers from claustrophobia.

The other apartment houses that offer an escort service are the 35-story Regency Towers at 245 East 63d Street, at Second Avenue, and the 21-story Victoria, at 7 East 14th Street, off Fifth Avenue.

Like many other luxury apartment houses built here

since World War II, these buildings have self-service elevators, although 24-hour doorman service is generally provided. The buildings hope to attract tenants by offering the escort service as a safety feature.

Alarm Board Used

Both Regency Towers and the Victoria are owned by the Carlyle Construction Corporation, which finds that the escort service is especially appreciated by women. The escort is on service from 11 P.M. to 7 A.M. in both Carlyle buildings.

With 430 of its 685 apartments occupied since the building's opening last May, Dorchester Towers now has a total occupancy of 2,000 persons. They pass through a single entrance, attended day and night by a doorman.

Inside the huge glistening lobby are hall attendants, who help with packages and baggages and serve as elevator escorts. In addition there is a concierge, or clerk, behind a desk, who takes messages and packages when tenants are away. A uniformed guard is constantly on patrol.

As a further security precaution for tenants, Dorchester Towers has an alarm system similar to one installed in many new apartment buildings. This system connects each apartment entrance with a buzzer board in the lobby. If an apartment door is opened when the occupants are out or asleep, an alarm is set off.

The city's largest single apartment house, the 35-story

Pavilion at 550 East 77th Street, which has 852 apartments and 12 self-service elevators, does not include an elevator escort among its normal services. The building, opened last May, occupies the block between 76th and 77th Streets and York Avenue and Cherokee Place, a short block bordering John Jay Park. It has 3,900 tenants.

The building's lobby, a block long, is guarded around the clock by two doormen, two hallmen and an armed, uniformed security guard who patrols the structure. The security guards are especially wary of the service entrance, and they operate the service elevators. Deliverymen and workmen are given a pass on which is stamped the time they enter the building and the time they leave. The laundry room has a television monitor connected with the superintendent's office.

Visitors Are Announced

Ironically security precautions are quite a bit simpler in the older apartment houses on Park and Fifth Avenues, which contain the city's greatest concentration of personal wealth. Security measures can be less complex because the Park and Fifth Avenue buildings are generally smaller than the postwar structures, 15 to 20 stories high, and they contain fewer, though larger, apartments.

A cardinal rule on Park and Fifth Avenues is that all visitors must be announced from the lobby to the apartments above. In addition to 24-hour

225

doormen at least one elevator is constantly attended. As a further security precaution, service elevators at the back end of the house are connected by telephone to the building's switchboard.

Dogs Used on Patrols

Owing to the city's rising crime rate in the postwar years, a bill was introduced in the Legislature last year that would have required private owners of apartment developments having 2,000 or more residents to maintain a staff of uniformed armed guards. The Legislature approved the bill last March, but Governor Rockefeller failed to sign it.

The bill would have affected such large developments as Stuyvesant Town, the Corlears Hook co-op on the Lower East Side near Grand Street, and the Penn Station South co-op in Chelsea.

Nevertheless one of the city's largest privately owned apartment complexes for the last six years voluntarily employed guards who not only carry guns but are accompanied by dogs when making their rounds.

The development is Park West Village, an urban-renewal development of 2,500 apartments in seven buildings, each containing three to six self-service elevators. Park West Village is between Central Park West and Amsterdam Avenue, from 97th to 100th Street. It is owned by Alcoa Residences, an affiliate of the Aluminum Company of America.

Alcoa refuses to reveal the size of its security force, but it says that it is one of the largest in the city, exceeded perhaps only by the guards employed by the New York City Housing Authority. The development's crime rate, the management says, is "exceedingly low."

December 19, 1965

VICTIMS OF CRIMES TO GET STATE AID

Bill to Allow Compensation Is Signed by Rockefeller

By RICHARD L. MADDEN

Governor Rockefeller signed into law yesterday a program to allow the state to pay financial compensation to the victims of violent crimes.

The program, which was described by Mr. Rockefeller as "a revolutionary concept," sets up a three-member Crime Victims Compensation Board to investigate claims and to make awards.

"Under the bill, crime victims and their families would be eligible to receive, from the state, compensation both for out-of-pocket costs and for loss of earnings or support," the Governor said at a bill-signing ceremony in his office here, 22 West 55th Street.

The measure, which was proposed to the Legislature by the Governor, was an outgrowth of the death here last Oct. 9 of Arthur F. Collins. Mr. Collins, a 28-year-old father of a 15-month-old daughter, was stabbed to death in a subway when he went to the aid of two young women being molested by a young thug.

"The real significance is that the state is recognizing the tragic plight of the victims of crime in our state," Mr. Rockefeller said as he signed the bill.

Mr. Rockefeller said that California was the only other state to have a program to compensate crime victims, but he added that other states were studying the New York measure with a view toward adopting their own plans. Britain and New Zealand also have adopted recently some form of such compensation.

Maximum Award of $15,000

To be eligible for compensation under the New York plan, a crime victim or his spouse or dependent must prove a minimum out-of-pocket loss of $100, or the loss of at least two weeks' pay. The maximum award will be $15,000.

The compensation board, whose members will be appointed by the Governor, will have an initial appropriation of $500,000. The awards by the board will be subject to review by the Appellate Division. The new program will only apply to claims resulting from crimes committed after March 1, 1967.

In addition to the crime compensation measure, Mr. Rockefeller signed a number of other bills as groups of interested persons and legislators filed in and out of his office to watch the signing ritual and to pose for pictures with the Governor.

After the death of Mr. Collins, New York City enacted a Good Samaritan bill that provides payments by the city for persons injured or killed while trying to prevent crimes. Under the city program, the amount of compensation is determined by the Board of Estimate after a recommendation by the Controller.

Mr. Rockefeller said another bill that he signed "launches an all-out war on one of our most serious health problems—air pollution."

The measure seeks to encourage the construction of industrial air pollution control facilities by granting tax benefits under the state's tax laws and authorizing municipalities to exempt such facilities from local real property taxes. The bill also permits the state Air Pollution Control Board to require motor vehicle exhaust control devices on 1968-model automobiles.

A companion measure also signed by the Governor prohibits the discharge of sewage and litter from boats. The bill bars the operation of any boat containing a marine toilet unless the device is equipped with state-approved facilities that prevent pollution.

Mr. Rockefeller has until midnight Thursday to sign or veto all 332 bills left behind by the Legislature, which adjourned July 6.

The Governor also signed into law bills that do the following things:

◀¶Permit the Health Insurance Plan of Greater New York to own and operate its own hospitals to seek "broader protection and reduction in costs of medical care and services."

¶Allow employers in the electrical industry to adopt a plan for self-insurance as a group instead of buying workmen's compensation coverage from private insurance carriers or the State Insurance Fund.

¶Establish a Uniform Justice Court Act for procedures in town and village courts.

August 2, 1966

Interracial Assaults

Studies Show That Most Violent Crimes By Negroes Are Against Other Negroes

By SIDNEY E. ZION

There have been a number of unsolved murders in Brooklyn and Manhattan in recent weeks in which white people were slain by persons identified by witnesses as Negroes.

These killings included the stabbing of a postal worker in the Bedford-Stuyvesant section of Brooklyn, the shooting of a Marine Corps hero in Greenwich Village and the knifing of a college student on a Brooklyn street because he did not have any cigarettes.

News Analysis

The sensational nature of these murders, and the publicity surrounding them, has apparently served to confirm the view that Negroes are attacking whites.

But available evidence does not support this view and in fact indicates that violence against white people by Negroes is relatively infrequent both in New York City and nationally.

Prof. Marvin E. Wolfgang of the University of Pennsylvania, one of the nation's foremost sociologists, wrote in a 1964 pamphlet published by the American Jewish Committee and entitled "Crime and Race".

"It should be clear that if whites are afraid that Negroes are likely to attack and slay them, the fear is not supported by what we know about interracial crime."

Little Interracial Violence

The experience of the police, the research of sociologists and criminologists, and the few statistics available indicate that the victims of the vast majority of violent crimes are Negroes. And most violent crimes are committed by and against persons of the same race.

For example, almost 85 per cent of the 543 murders solved in New York City last year were within racial groups, a figure that has remained virtually stable since the police department began compiling these statistics in 1964.

Forty-three of the murders, or less than 8 per cent, were committed by Negroes against whites. On the other hand, 289 whites. On the other hand, 289

226

killings were Negro against Negro. Ninety-four whites who were not Puerto Ricans were killed by whites, also not Puerto Ricans. Sixty-four Puerto Ricans were murdered by Puerto Ricans. Seven Negroes were murdered by whites. The 46 other murders involved groups in which Negroes, Puerto Ricans and others took part.

While New York shows a far larger percentage of Negroes' killing whites than whites killing Negroes, this apparently has not been true around the country.

Professor Wolfgang said in his article:

"The amount of interracial homicide and the relative frequency of whites and Negroes in crossing the race line vary slightly in different parts of the country, but usually indicate that more whites slay Negroes than vice versa."

Professor Wolfgang particularly pointed to the South, where he noted a 1948 study showing that whites probably kill five times as many Negroes as Negroes kill whites.

Like nearly all police departments. New York's does not keep race statistics on the other violent crimes, such as forcible rape, felonious assault and robbery.

But neighborhood-by-neighborhood statistics indicate that a large majority of violent crimes are committed within ghetto areas such as Harlem, East New York and the precincts surrounding the Grand Concourse in the Bronx. Police officials agree that the great preponderance involve persons of the same race.

"The white people yell the loudest when somebody gets raped or killed in the neighborhood," a veteran police officer said last week. "But it's the Negroes that are getting hurt the most, and that's not because they're colored but just that they are living in the slums."

The New York police officer pointed to the recent clamor that arose in Peter Cooper Village on the East Side, a pre-dominantly white neighborhood, after a girl was raped in one of the buildings.

"I don't say they have no right to be upset, far from it," he said, "but that area happens to have a very low crime rate. The fact that a few murders and rapes happen doesn't say anything about a neighborhood or the character of a neighborhood. These guys can strike anywhere."

Contrary to popular belief, there are few crimes of violence in Central Park and Brooklyn's Prospect Park. There were no murders in either park last year and only two rapes in Central Park, three in Prospect Park.

There were 42 felonious assaults in Central Park and the police attribute most of these to youngsters fighting each other. There were eight felonious assaults in Prospect Park.

The most extensive studies into the incidence of violent crimes that cut across racial lines were conducted recently in Chicago and Washington, by the President's National Crime Commission and the President's District of Columbia Crime Commission.

In Chicago, 13,713 cases of assaultive crimes against the person other than homicide were studied.

Violence Within a Race

"The most striking fact," the national commission concluded in its report that appeared in February, "is the extent of the correlation in race between victim and offender."

"Thus," the report said, "while Negro males account for two-thirds of all assaults, the offender who victimizes a white person is most likely also to be white."

Moreover, a Negro man in Chicago runs the risk of being a victim nearly six times as often as a white man, a Negro woman nearly eight times as often as a white woman, according to the figures.

In Washington, the statistics were more detailed and perhaps even starker. Only 12 of 172 murders in 1966 were interracial. Eighty-eight per cent of rapes involved persons of the same race. Only 9 per cent of the aggravated assaults were committed outside racial boundaries. Robbery, the only violent crime in which whites were victimized more often than Negroes, is the one that was predominantly interracial, according to the Washington report.

These statistics would hardly surprise the nation's sociologists and criminologists, who have long pointed out that violence is usually inflicted on relatives, friends and acquaintances, often indoors and generally in the neighborhood. The primary exception is robbery, and while this is a violent crime in that it involves a personal confrontation, actual physical injury does not always result.

There are no national statistics on the likelihood of injury from robberies, but a survey by the District of Columbia Crime Commission of 297 robberies showed that some injury was inflicted in 25 per cent of them.

The scholars and the police attribute most of the apparent increase in the Negro crime rate to the fact that Negroes are now demanding and getting better police protection and are thus reporting more crime than in the past.

In any event, as Professor Wolfgang noted in his pamphlet:

"Enough research has been conducted to permit the definite statement that criminal homicide, like most other assaultive offenses, is predominantly an intragroup, intraracial act."

But as is sometimes the case, the facts are not as important as what people think the facts are.

And so sociologists say that the Negroes are being blamed, not for what they are doing to one another in the ghettos, but for what they are not doing to the whites in the nice neighborhoods.

Or, as the old Negro blues number has it: "If it wasn't for bad luck I wouldn't have no luck at all."

Nashville Jury Urges Arms

NASHVILLE, Dec. 27 (AP) —The Davidson County grand jury recommended today that citizens arm against an outbreak of crime that it implied the metropolitan police were unable to check.

The jury urged that 250 more policemen be hired immediately. The force totals 390.

The 14-page report urged the death penalty and maximum sentences to stem what it called an "avalanche of crime and arson that has come upon us." It mentioned "gangs of young criminals running rampant in the streets, shooting each other and other citizens."

The state's electric chair has not been used since 1961.

To protect themselves, the grand jury said, citizens should have at least one gun in every home.

April 18, 1967   December 28, 1967

CRIME STATISTICS: A NUMBERS GAME

Police Here Find 14% Rise in Major Violations, but Figures Are Deceptive

By MURRAY SCHUMACH

In his high-rent apartment on the East Side, a bachelor has rigged up a tape recording of a cocktail party. Whenever he plans to be out late, he sets a timing device that turns on the festive tape and apartment lights shortly after sundown. This synthetic merriment in an empty apartment behind locked doors is his antiburglary weapon.

In the slums, the poor dig into meager funds to buy iron fences for fire escape windows and reinforced locks and bars for the doors. From nearly every section of the city comes a clamor about streets unsafe at night and stores closing early; of sadistic muggings and brazen holdups. Though the police have set up an antimugging task force, worried citizens discuss plans for neighborhood vigilante patrols.

An attack on "rising crime and lawlessness" was the most strongly cheered point in President Johnson's State of the Union message to Congress. And Governor Rockefeller, Mayor Lindsay and Senator Robert F. Kennedy have made "crime in the streets" a prime theme in speeches to legislators, conventions, civic groups and seminars of experts.

While experts are in general agreement that crime has risen in the city—how much they do not know—they are just as convinced that the citywide fear of crime has become inflamed well beyond the actual conditions.

How accurate are the city's crime statistics? Are the figures being inflated by the greater diligence of the public and police in reporting crime? What elements in city life that did not figure importantly before World War II are now considered significant in the local crime picture?

These aspects were explored in a New York Times survey that included interviews with nearly all of the city's top police officials, some top state experts, sociologists and criminologists and civil libertarians.

"Crime statistics are almost worthless," says Prof. Lloyd Ohlin of the Harvard Law School, one of the experts on the Presidential Crime Commission. "But it is the only thing there is."

"Nobody knows a damned thing about crime," says Daniel P. Moynihan, Assistant Secretary of Labor under President Kennedy and now director of the Center of Urban Studies of Harvard and the Massachusetts Institute of Technology.

Nevertheless, to the public, crime statistics are beyond dispute. The latest figures for New York City, covering the last six months of 1967, showed reports of major crime—murder, forcible rape, robbery, assault, burglary, larceny of more than $50—had risen 14.4 per cent over the last six months of 1966.

More Reporting of Crime

But not considered in the statistical evaluation are some factors that would whittle down considerably the extent of the crime increase.

First is the decided change on the part of the public in reporting crimes. There is no doubt among the top police officials here that New Yorkers are now reporting a much larger percentage of crimes than they used to. This is of enormous significance since the statistics are based on crimes reported, not crimes committed.

"The percentage of crimes reported is greater than ever," says one of the city's most important police officers. "This alone could make the crime rate go up even if nothing else happened."

One reason the public is more likely to report crimes now is because it is alarmed and indignant. Civic groups know that the greater the number of crimes reported from their area, the better chances of getting increased police protection.

This is particularly true of the slums, where crime is at its worst. In these areas Negroes, deeply conscious of their civil rights, are no longer as reluctant as they used to be to report crimes, according to the police.

Public Encouraged

For one thing, the Police Department has been conducting an intensive campaign to encourage the public to report crimes. The establishment of a central number, 440-1234, and the installation of call boxes in the street that enable the public to call the police directly are part of this drive.

In addition, the Police Department has become increasingly conscientious in making certain that reports of crime are not buried or minimized as misdemeanors.

For example, when slum youths, strolling through a more prosperous neighborhood, force a youngster to surrender a bicycle or money—even just a few cents—this is no longer a misdemeanor. It is robbery because there is a threat of force, if not actual force. Purse thefts that used to be considered misdemeanors are also robberies now.

Precincts now make daily reports to headquarters on complaints received. The statistical compilation is done by the Crime Analysis Unit, not by precincts.

"We've reached the point," says Capt. James Meehan, in charge of the Crime Analysis Unit, "where if someone were to complain that a window was broken it could be listed as attempted burglary, not malicious mischief."

None of this considers the fact that many people exaggerate losses for the benefit of insurance claims or for tax deductions.

The crime statistics are also swollen by offenses that are not really the work of criminals. Chief of these is auto theft. In 1966, the total of felonies in the city was 304,156. Of this total, 40,943 were auto thefts. The police estimate that 60 per cent of violations listed as auto thefts are joyrides.

One of the by-products of rising crime statistics is that they create a cycle that distorts the actual situation. For as crime figures rise, the public becomes more alarmed and is more determined to report crimes.

The public pressure on the police makes them more efficient in processing reports. This creates higher crime statistics and further inflames the public fear.

There seems to be no end to how much the crime rate can be pushed upward merely by better crime reporting.

This was shown in a survey of some 10,000 families by the Presidential Crime Commission. It disclosed that unreported rapes and burglaries were about three times the number of those reported and that the number of larcenies and aggravated assault was about twice what was reported.

The survey noted that among the reasons people did not report a crime were that they considered it a private matter; they did not want to harm the offender; they were confused or they feared reprisal.

What of the Trends?

No one with sound knowledge of crime statistics tries to make a strong case for their accuracy. The Presidential Commission, said:

"If it is true, as the commission surveys tend to indicate, that society has not yet found fully reliable methods for measuring the volume of crime, it is even more true that it has failed to find such methods for measuring the trend of crime."

As for the city's figures, Captain Meehan says:

"The statistics may not be accurate, but we feel the trends are. The statistical summaries give us an indication of what the volume of crime is and what the trend is. It is probably as good as anything we can come up with."

Many theories are offered to explain the rise in the city's crime rate—apart from statistical distortion.

The easy explanation for today's outcry about "crime in the streets" is to blame the Negroes and Puerto Ricans in the slums, particularly the Negroes. There is little doubt among the police—though statistics are lacking — that the bulk of the crimes of street violence, apartment burglaries and store holdups are committed by Negroes and Puerto Ricans. But it has always been true, the police point out, that slum-dwellers commit most of the crimes in the city.

Police officials also note that the bulk of the victims of these crimes are the Negroes and Puerto Ricans in these slums.

More Mingling

One of the main reasons for the present furor, police officials say, is that the middle class and upper-income groups, largely white, are now being mugged and burglarized by slum-dwellers.

"There has been a general movement of people in the city," says one high police official. "Previously, people used to stay much more in their own communities. Now the haves and the have-nots are meeting. There will always be more attention paid when more affluent members of society are victims."

Dr. Kenneth B. Clark, a Negro psychiatrist and head of the Metropolitan Applied Research Center, points out, in support of this position:

"The crime of the Negro against the Negro storekeeper in the slum does not get the same attention in most of the mass media as the Negro against the white storekeeper. I sense there is a tendency to make crime in the streets synonymous with racial threats or the need to control the urban Negro problem."

But the public does not weigh the unseen forces behind statistics. Their ears and eyes are exposed daily to television and radio accounts of the most sensational aspects of crime. Newspapers tend to group isolated crimes into "waves." Dinner conversations and office chatter are filled with personal knowledge of crime.

Fear Helps Criminal

"I believe," says Professor Ohlin, "that the mass media have exacerbated the fear of crime in the public."

Jane Jacobs, author of "The Death and Life of Great American Cities," points out that this exaggerated fear keeps people off the streets and thus makes the operations of muggers easier. Police officials agree.

Still there is little doubt that the slums of the nineteen-twenties and -thirties, for all their poverty and congestion, were much safer for the public than they are today. Middle-aged New Yorkers can recall that before World War II they used to walk without fear on the city streets in any section at night.

Those who grew up in such slums as Brownsville or Harlem remember that during the day they left doors open for ventilation and at night they often slept on roofs, fire escapes, parks or beaches.

After concerts in Lewisohn Stadium, couples strolled down dimly lighted Riverside Drive without concern about muggers. Transit policemen were not needed on subway trains late at night and ice cream parlors did not worry about staying open until midnight to get the business of crowds leaving the last neighborhood movies.

Changes in Slums

Just before the nineteen-thirties ended, mugging began to become a problem, anti-mugging police patrols were tested and iron fences appeared on store windows in Harlem.

It is in the changes in the slums, more than in the statistics, that the nature of the city's crime is most discernible. Worse than the poverty is the frustration among the masses of Negroes. Racial discrimination has stifled the old city pattern that permitted the most intelligent, resourceful, energetic of slum residents to work themselves up into better neighborhoods. The frustration has created antisocial and criminal attitudes.

"I have a feeling," says Mrs. Jacobs, "that there is a sense of the American Dream being betrayed. This is very largely racial. But I think the same sort of thing is going on even among whites who do not turn to crime, but to anti-Establishment attitudes and demonstrations."

Then there is the enormous growth of narcotics addiction in the city, mostly in the slums. Estimates are that between 50,000 and 100,000 heroin addicts are in New York. Since there are no statistics to show how much of the city's crimes are committed by the addicts, there has been wild exaggeration.

The Desperate Addict

Nevertheless, there is no doubt among police experts that heroin addicts are responsible for a large share of the city's burglaries. In their desperation for the price of a "fix," they are daring and resourceful, invading good neighborhoods as well as slums.

It is largely because of the depredations of the addicts that the window fence and strong lock have become as much a trademark of the slums as the rats and - roaches. Ironically, one of the reasons the tenements are burglarized is that even among the poor these days the addicts can find something negotiable to steal.

But the addicts are rarely responsible for muggings. "Mugging is a violent crime."

says a key police official. "It is not their kind of crime. Addicts are human wrecks." Experts with the state's Narcotics Control Commission agree.

Looking back on the slums of the nineteen - twenties and thirties, the police point out that they had stronger community support than they have today. They have suffered a considerable loss in respect and authority in these areas. They are spat upon, abused and prisoners have been taken from them. In 1963, there were 2,621 assaults on policemen. Last year there were 4,409.

A Philosophical Problem

"There is a very real connection between racial tensions and crime in the city," says a prominent police official here. "Civil disobedience has been raised as a philosophical problem—the concept of whether laws considered unjust should be violated or not. Once you start to violate laws, then you raise serious issues. The spillover is into other laws. It affects crime very seriously and we're beginning to pay for it now."

At the same time, police officials admit, there had been years of rudeness and brutality by white policemen toward Negroes in the slums. This, too, is part of the reaction, they concede.

Another development that has pushed up crime in the slums in recent years, the police contend, is excessive leniency in probation, parole and setting of bail. They estimate that one of seven persons arrested for a serious crime in the city was out on bail, probation or parole at the time.

Recently, picking at random from a day's reports, a police official cited the case of a man arrested for the fourth time since 1956. He had just been released in $1,500 bail.

Civil libertarians tend to disagree with the theory that heavier punishment will deter crime. They cite studies on capital punishment.

Tied in with this is the heat-

Prof. Lloyd Ohlin of Harvard Law School says statistics on crime are "almost worthless," but adds that there isn't anything else.

ed controversy about whether the polices are being hampered by court decisions that limit their opportunities to question prisoners and search suspects, and by laws that make them reluctant to draw a gun.

In particular the police are concerned about limitations on their use of a gun. One high police officer says:

"I think the police are less disposed to use a gun now. It takes a Supreme Court justice to tell when you can use a gun. The criminals are aware of this."

That the police position is winning greater public favor as crime statistics rise is conceded glumly by Aryeh Neier, head of the local Civil Liberties Union. He says:

"I think the police have gotten their case across very well. There is a great change from public skepticism of the police position."

Fear of Muggers Looms Large In Public Concern Over Crime

By DAVID BURNHAM

Predatory, often senselessly savage, the mugger looms as the most menacing figure in the public concern over crime.

A mugging is a type of robbery that involves a physical attack. It is a crime that is reported to the police in Manhattan 16,200 times each year.

Although muggings represent only a fraction of all serious crimes reported to the police, the mugger exacts a high toll in terms of physical and mental anguish and personal property loss, and he diminishes the quality of life in a fearful city.

In an effort to learn more about the mugger, his habits and society's attempts to deal with him, The New York Times studied the court records of the 136 persons arrested in 100 cases in Manhattan during the first two months of 1967 on charges of assault and robbery, the legal charge placed against most muggers.

The broad conclusions suggested by this statistical study and by an examination of pertinent law enforcement records are:

¶The average mugger strikes many times before he is arrested.

¶Even when arrested and convicted, he will prowl the streets again in a relatively short time.

¶The time he spends behind bars is unlikely to furnish him with meaningful rehabilitation treatment.

Despite the enormous public concern over muggings, the mugger is a rare subject of statistical research. Neither the courts nor the police, for example, have compiled statistical information about the mugger because under state and Federal law mugging is classified as a kind of robbery and not singled out as a separate crime.

The Times's study examined the first 100 attacks in Manhattan in 1967 that resulted in arrests for assault and robbery. The period of the study was selected to permit the cases to work their way through the courts to final disposition. The specific findings of the study were:

¶Eighty-two per cent of the defendants had been arrested at least once before and 46 per cent had been arrested five or more times. Because details about a man's conviction record listed on the police arrest sheet is considered incomplete by lawyers and researchers, the exact percentage of those who had been convicted of previous crimes is not known. The arrest statistics suggest, however, that perhaps half of the defendants had at least one previous conviction.

¶Initial bail for 60 per cent of the suspected muggers was set at $2,000 or higher, high enough so that probably well over half the defendants were unable to make necessary premium payments and be released immediately. Although bail is sometimes lowered as subsequent hearings, the notations of such actions are erratic enough to make generalization difficult. However, the widely held belief that most muggers are immediately released on the streets by the courts is not supported by the evidence.

¶The cases against 31 per cent of the defendants were dismissed. Though the records often indicated that the cases were dismissed at the request of the assistant district attorney, the reason for the request usually was not given. Court officials say a major reason for the dismissals was the refusal of many victims to press charges. In this sense, police complaints that law enforcement is hampered by the public's unwillingness to cooperate have some substance.

¶The average sentence for guilty defendants was slightly more than a year. (Of the total, 62 per cent pleaded guilty and 7 per cent were tried, with half of them being convicted.) A one-year sentence usually means nine months in prison, because of time off for good behavior. At the time of the study, the mandatory sentence for first-degree robbery, one of the charges placed gainst many of the defendants, was 10 to 30 years. The difference between the actual sentences and the sentence required by law can be explained by the fact that not one of the 136 defendants was convicted of the crime for which he was arrested.

¶More than half of the incidents of assault and robbery— 54 per cent—occurred in hallways, elevators, stairs and apartments, and thus raised questions about whether police patrols that are legally restricted to the streets and parks can adequately protect the public from this kind of crime.

¶At least 20 per cent of the attacks studied were against chronic drunks or men seeking the company of prostitutes or homosexuals, victims who by their habits are unusually vulnerable to being mugged.

Linked to Narcotics

Much public discussion has attempted to link muggings with the serious narcotics problem in the city. The court records studied did not indicate how many of the 136 defendants were narcotics addicts. But a study published last week by the New York Police Department indicated that the number of addict attackers is far less than is generally believed.

According to the police, only 7.4 per cent of all those persons arrested for robbery in 1967 admitted they were narcotics users.

Although law enforcement experts believe some of the arrested persons would not tell the police about their narcotics habit, they believe that enough do to make the statistic roughly accurate.

The problems of the police in apprehending robbers is documented in the 1967 Statistical Report of the New York Police Department. According to this report, only one robber was arrested for every six robbery complaints.

And because many crimes are not reported at all, the statistics probably underestimate the total number of robberies and muggings that occur in the city. A survey by the National Opinion Research Corporation, for example, indicated that about 50 per cent of all robberies are never reported to the police.

Details of Attack

Perhaps one of the best ways of looking at the mugging problem, is to examine in detail one of the 100 cases selected for the study.

At 8:15 P.M. on Saturday, Feb. 4, 1967, Mrs. Virginia Haspel (that is not her real name) walked along 169th Street near Broadway in Washington Heights. It was a cold, cloudy evening.

Suddenly, a youth accosted her and tried to grab her purse. Mrs. Haspel fought back. In the struggle, her arm and leg were cut by a knife held by the assailant. The mugger yanked the purse from Mrs. Haspel's hand and started running.

Mrs. Haspel's screams attracted a patrolman, who chased and apprehended the youth, who was 20 years old. That night, he was fingerprint-ed, photographed and taken to Night Court, where he was held on $5,000 bail. The complaint typed out by the patrolman at the request of Mrs. Haspel charged the youth with assault and robbery, both felony charges.

Three days later, on Feb. 7, the youth pleaded guilty to assault in the third degree, a misdemeanor charge. On March 1 he was sentenced to six months in prison.

Typical and Untypical

In a number of ways, the attack on Mrs. Haspel and the way in which the court dealt with her assailant are typical of the manner in which New York City is now dealing with muggers. In other ways, it is not.

Most of the muggings examined, for example, were similar to the attack on Mrs. Haspel in that they were committed by an individual assailant. Seventy-two per cent of the attacks in the study involved a single assailant, the others by two or more persons. On the basis of the study, fears of roving gangs responsible for most of Manhattan's muggings are not supported by the evidence.

Can't Make Bail

The initial bail set for Mrs. Haspel's mugger, $5,000, is considerably higher than that set for most persons arrested for assault and robbery. Judges set the same or higher bail for only 25 per cent of the 136 defendants in the study. For 30 per cent of the defendants, the bail was set at $1,000 or lower. Bail for the rest of the defendants fell in between these two figures, with the largest concentration at $2,500. Judges are permitted wide discretion in the setting of bail.

According to a survey made by the Vera Institute of Justice, 25 per cent of all defendants here do not have enough money to pay the necessary premiums when bail is set at $500, about 45 per cent cannot make bail when it is set at $1,500 and 63 per cent cannot make bail when it is set at $2,500.

Thus the effect of initial bail is likely to keep mugging suspects in jail even though the legal purpose of bail is to assure the appearance of the defendant in court.

The fact that Mrs. Haspel's assailant had been arrested three times before (once for intoxication, once for auto theft and once for the possession of burglar tools) also was not unusual.

62% Plead Guilty

More than 80 per cent of the defendants in The Times's survey had been arrested at least once before and 40 per cent had previously been arrested five or more times. Though many of these arrests were for such minor charges as public intoxication, a majority of the defendants had previously been arrested for more serious offenses, such as burglary and robbery.

The number and seriousness of previous arrests appeared to influence the bail decisions. Those with no previous arrests or only a few minor arrests were granted the lowest bail while judges tended to require higher bail for those with more serious records.

The decision of the defendant in the Haspel case, on the advice of a Legal Aid lawyer, to plead guilty to assault (one of the lesser charges placed against him at the time of his arraignment) also was typical of most defendants in the study.

In 62 per cent of the cases the defendants were permitted to plead guilty to a less serious charge.

Studies done by the American Bar Association and the President's Commission on Law Enforcement and Administration of Justice indicate that judges, prosecutors and nearly every major city in the country encourage defendants to plead guilty to lesser charges by offering them the inducement of lighter sentences.

This is done, according to these studies, because the small number of available prosecutors, judges and lawyers would be unable to handle the workload if more than a handful of defendants demanded a time-consuming trial. A study by the President's Commission said that 95.5 per cent of all convictions in New York were obtained by pleas of guilty rather than at trials.

Donald J. Newman, a professor at the School of Criminal Justice of the State University of New York at Albany, and a leading authority on plea bargaining, said he believed that while plea bargaining was necessary, it had three major dangers.

"One is that the very dangerous recidivist [incorrigible criminal] escapes long control —he gets off too easily," Professor Newman said. "The other is that the person who may be innocent pleads guilty rather than face the chance of getting [jailed] for a long time."

Few Social Workers

Professor Newman said the third danger was that the plea-bargaining system often resulted in the defendant going to a short-term jail rather than to a prison "and that to the extent there is any rehabilitation and treatment, it is not in our jails."

Just how little rehabilitation is offered in the jails—the penal institutions that usually hold muggers imprisoned for a year or less—was suggested in a recent national survey of correctional agencies by the National Council on Crime and Delinquency. According to this survey, less than 3 per cent of all jail employes are social workers, psychologists, psychiatrists and teachers.

In The Times's survey, many of the 136 persons originally charged with assault and robbery were indicted on felony charges of first-degree robbery and assault and were later permitted to plead guilty to petit larceny and assault in the third degree, both misdemeanors.

In only 7 per cent of the cases was the matter of guilt or innocence decided by trial. Of these, slightly less than half the defendants were found not guilty. The remainder, after being arrested for assault and robbery, were indicted for petit larceny and third-degree assault, found guilty and given a variety of sentences ranging from a suspended sentence to four months.

The six-month jail sentence given to Mrs. Haspel's mugger was typical of the lower court that sentenced him. Those who were either found guilty or pleaded guilty in the Criminal Court received an average sentence of 5.6 months.

In the State Supreme Court, which in theory at least handles more serious incidents, such as a mugging in which the victim was slashed by a knife, the average minimum sentence was 18 months. The combined average sentence, using the minimum average of the upper court, was 12.4 months.

Most Get Time Off

This does not mean that those sentenced to a year will serve a year. Anyone sentenced to six months or more before September, 1967, was eligible for and usually received a third of his time off for good behavior.

Last Sept. 1 New York State's new penal law went into effect. The law, designed to simplify and improve the old statute, was drafted by the State Commission on Revision of the Penal Law and Criminal Code and approved by the State Legislature after several years of debate.

Under the new penal law, a person found guilty of first-degree robbery, typical charge placed against a mugger, could be sentenced to from 1 to 25 years in prison.

However, Richard Denzer, staff director of the commission, does not believe the penal law changes have meant any significant alteration in the length of sentences given to persons arrested for assault and robbery.

Police Commissioner Howard R. Leary has suggested the enormity of the over-all problem facing the agencies of criminal justice in dealing with criminals:

"Our problem as police officers is that we arrest the same person again and again for robbery, we arrest the same person again and again for burglary, we arrest the same person again and again for pushing narcotics.

"Until such a time that society generally, not the police alone, have a way of dealing with the problem of repeated offenders, we are constantly going to be faced with the problem of increased crime and assaults against the person."

Presiding Justice Bernard Botein of the Appellate Division's First Judicial Department said in an interview that because of the resources given the system of criminal justice are inadequate, "its accomplishments are minimal."

"We pay a lot more lip service to the idea of rehabilitation and deterrence and the safety of the individual citizenc than we actually seem to deliver." he said.

Justice Botein is supporting a bill now in Albany that would increase the number of Criminal Court judges in the city from 78 to 98 and increase the number of Supreme Court justices in the city from 89 to 122.

Because Democratic and Republican leaders have not been able to divide this rich source of patronage, the bill has been bottled up in the Legislature for a number of years, although last week a "general understanding" was reported to have been reached on the creation of new judgeships.

But Frank Remington, a professor of law at the University of Wisconsin and a leading legal researcher, believes that "increasing the number of judges isn't the only answer."

"With a few exceptions," he said, "there are no court systems in the country that have responded to the enormous challenge facing them. Much talk has been spent on the Supreme Court and crime. But talk is easy. Getting at the real problems of criminal courts' in the big cities, finding some way of dealing with individuals, is going to require an enormous amount of leadership, innovative research and money."

Gun Controls
Less Than Airtight, Say the Critics

WASHINGTON—"We can live with it," said Representative L. F. Sikes, Democrat of Florida, a member of the National Rifle Association.

"I suggest that tens of thousands of Americans can die with it," said Representative Charles S. Joelson, Democrat of New Jersey.

Those were the contrasting views last week when, after the shrillest debate of the year, the House passed a gun control bill and sent it to the Senate.

Stripped of registration, shorn of licensing, the bill is viewed by advocates of tough gun control as little more than a token response to the greatest outpouring of Congressional mail in years.

It would ban interstate mail order sales of rifles and shotguns and prohibit over-the-counter sales to persons not a resident of a dealer's state and to those under 18—the same restrictions placed on pistols and revolvers earlier this year.

It would forbid interstate mail order sales, too, of handgun ammunition; curb imports of surplus military weapons from foreign countries; and impose mandatory prison terms on those convicted of Federal felonies involving use of a gun.

Bill Weakened

Modest enough to begin with, the bill emerged from the house even slimmer. Pro-gun forces stripped away the proposed ban on rifle and shotgun ammunition. They pushed through special exemptions for gun collectors and for sportsmen who lose their guns while on hunting trips. And they turned back moves for Federal registration of guns and for state licensing of gun owners.

Much the same kind of bill—it, too, stripped of tough controls—was cleared by the Senate Judiciary Committee last week. Senate floor action is scheduled after Labor Day.

While efforts will be made in the Senate to strengthen the bill, it now seems likely that nothing more than the basic mail order ban will clear Congress this year, despite public demands for something stronger.

"How long are we to wait?" Representative Bertram L. Podell, Democrat of Brooklyn, cried out in despair last week. "Are we to wait until another President of the United States is assassinated or another U. S. Senator?"

Why did the House decide to wait, why did it ignore the polls showing a strong demand for tough gun controls?

Certainly, lobbying by the million-member National Rifle Association helped block moves for stronger controls. Too, many members of Congress are avid sportsmen themselves or represent districts where hunting is a favorite sport.

Discouraged advocates of stiff gun controls suggested privately —but not in floor debate—that the real reason for their defeat was the feeling on the part of many colleagues that guns are a symbol of manliness.

Even pro-gun forces conceded in debate that guns have become a major threat to the internal security of the nation. But they argued that strong gun controls would merely disarm or harass law-abiding citizens, while criminals would always find ways to get guns.

Crime Issue

Their feelings were perhaps best summed up by Representative Jamie L. Whitten, Democrat of Mississippi, when he said: "What we should be doing here is to stop this crime wave, and to do that we must take the Supreme Court shackles off our police."

Even the Cleveland outbreak, with its automatic rifle fire and 10 deaths, failed to sway House members. Representative Charles A. Vanik, Democrat of Ohio, in whose district the riot occurred, opened the debate the next day on a despairing note:

"I am just sick and tired of hearing some of my colleagues deplore violence and call for law and order when I have seen them go through teller (non-record) votes time and again and vote for amendments which would strike down adequate gun control laws."

While gun control supporters are unhappy at the prospect of getting nothing stronger than the mail order ban this year, talk of what might be accomplished in the next Congress is subdued. Much depends on the nature of that Congress—whether it will be even more conservative than the 90th—or whether another national trauma by gunshot will renew the public outcry that followed the Robert Kennedy assassination.

—MARJORIE HUNTER

July 28, 1968

WHERE THERE ARE MORE GUNS, THERE ARE MORE DEATHS

States with strong firearms laws tend to have lower overall murder rates than states with weak firearms laws.

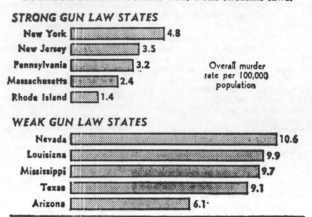

STRONG GUN LAW STATES

State	Rate
New York	4.8
New Jersey	3.5
Pennsylvania	3.2
Massachusetts	2.4
Rhode Island	1.4

Overall murder rate per 100,000 population

WEAK GUN LAW STATES

State	Rate
Nevada	10.6
Louisiana	9.9
Mississippi	9.7
Texas	9.1
Arizona	6.1

Deaths by firearms in foreign countries with strict controls are significantly lower than in the U.S.

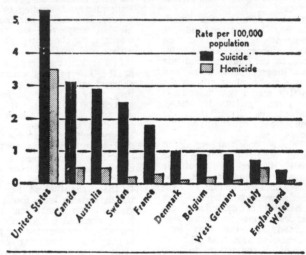

Rate per 100,000 population
■ Suicide
▨ Homicide

(United States, Canada, Australia, Sweden, France, Denmark, Belgium, West Germany, Italy, England and Wales)

Firearms sales in United States for individual use are up sharply.

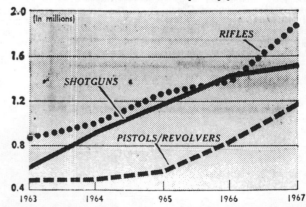

(in millions)

RIFLES
SHOTGUNS
PISTOLS/REVOLVERS

1963   1964   1965   1966   1967

MUCH CRIME HERE GOES UNREPORTED

Studies Find Thousands of Cases Kept From Police

By DAVID BURNHAM

On Saturday, Oct. 26, Robert Walters went into the vestibule of an apartment building on West 75th Street, leaned over the buzzer board and began searching for the name of a friend. Suddenly, two men appeared, placed a knife at his throat and demanded his money.

Mr. Walters, a visitor from Washington, did not report the armed robbery to the police. "It would have been a waste of my time and police time," Mr. Walters recalled recently. "They only took cash—which couldn't be traced — and the stickup was so fast and professional that I really didn't see their faces."

Several recent studies show that crimes such as this one are among hundreds of thousands of serious incidents that occur each year in New York, but are never reported to the police.

For example, on the same day that Mr. Walters was held up, Dr. Helen Mitchell, a sociologist and antipoverty official, was away from her apartment in the southern Bronx from 7 P.M. to 9 P.M. During this two-hour period someone broke into her apartment and took her television set and radio.

Dr. Mitchell did not report the burglary to the police. "I didn't bother calling them because there was nothing they could do," she said.

On Wednesday, Nov. 6, Allard K. Lowenstein, the recently elected congressman from Long Island, parked his car in midtown Manhattan. When he returned an hour later, his car had been broken into and a worn $60 suit and valuable papers stolen.

Mr. Lowenstein did not report the larceny to the police. "I didn't call the police because I was busy, because reporting takes so much time and because it is so hard to get the police interested," he said.

The fact that there are a vast number of unreported crimes — above and beyond the more than 500,000 murders, rapes, assaults, robberies, burglaries, larcenies and auto thefts reported in New York each year — raises a number of questions.

Because the crime statistics published by the New York Police Department and the Federal Bureau of Investigation count only those incidents reported to the police, are they an accurate index of crime? Do changes in reported crimes reflect changes in the total number of crimes?

¶Is the belief of many New Yorkers that the police are unable to do anything about a crime—once it has been committed — a fair assesment? What can the police do about crime?

Does the failure of many New Yorkers to tell the police when they have been victimized weaken law enforcement's ability to handle the problem of crime?

Official Comment Refused

Top New York police officials refused to comment on the record about the problem of unreported crime.

One such official, who asked not to be identified by name, agreed that there were many unreported crimes in New York and that the failure of the public to call the police weakened the department's ability to deal with crime.

The first concrete evidence of the huge number of unreported crimes in the United States came last year with the publication of a special survey by the National Opinion Research Corporation. In this survey, a representative sample of 10,000 American families were asked whether they had been the victims of a crime, what this crime was, whether they had reported the incident to police and if not, why not?

The answer found by this Federally financed study: During a recent year in the United States there were twice as many rapes, robberies, aggravated assaults, burglaries and larcenies $50 and over than were recorded in the crime statistics compiled by the nation's police departments and published by the Federal Bureau of Investigation.

Victims are not the only ones who fail to report crime. Sometimes, according to both the national and local surveys, it is the police.

Hughes Rudd, a correspondent for the Columbia Broadcasting System, told about one recent example of the New York police not reporting a serious crime.

"I was returning to my apartment about 1:30 A.M. on Election Day, Nov. 5," Mr. Rudd said. "On 79th Street near Broadway a group of men attacked me, knocking me unconscious and breaking a few ribs. They took my wallet and the few dollars I had in my pocket."

Mr. Rudd said he lay on the street with a concussion for four hours before any one approached him. About 6 A.M., he said, a young patrolman came up.

"He asked me what was wrong and I told him I had been mugged," Mr. Rudd continued. "Then he asked whether I wanted an ambulance. I said no, that I could make it to my apartment. He helped me to my feet and left. He didn't bother asking my name or who had attacked me or when I had been mugged—he just left."

Mr. Rudd said that when he got back to his apartment he did not call the police himself. "What was the use?" he asked. "All I did was call the credit card companies and tell them to cancel my cards."

Of the dozen victims of crime traced by The New York Times, most of them said they had not called the police because they felt such a call would result in neither the recovery of their property nor the arrest of the criminal.

The widespread belief among New Yorkers that the Police Department is unable to do anything about a crime—once it has been committed — was shared by 55 per cent of the national sample of crime victims who did not call the police.

The questioning of the ability of the police to solve a crime is a realistic assessment, even if the department's own statistics are used.

Only 20 per cent of the robberies and 13 per cent of the burglaries reported to the police in 1967, for example, resulted in an arrest. And if there were far more robberies and burglaries than were reported — as was suggested by the national and city surveys—then the police batting average was far lower than indicated by the official figures.

A recent precinct-by-precinct anaylsis of crimes reported to the New York Police Department by The New York Times, found a massive concentration of crimes of violence in the slums and a comparatively large number of crimes against property in the middle-class and commercial areas.

The national victimization survey confirmed that the poor were much more likely to be the victims of violent crimes. It also found, however, that the poor also were most likely to be the victims of crimes against property.

In a recent year, for example, a person from a family earning less than $6,000 a year was three and a half times more likely to be the victim of a robbery than a person from a family making more than $6,000. And a Negro was four times more likely to be robbed than a white. Roughly similar victim patterns were found for burglary.

To explain the contrast in crime patterns developed from reported crime statistics and the victim surveys, criminologists point out that because slum dwellers almost never have theft insurance or declare losses on their income tax returns, there is very little incentive for the poor to call the police about a stolen television set.

The serious inadequacies of the present crime statistics — both as a measurement of crime and as a planning tool for the police — prompted the United States Census Bureau this year to sponsor a series of four conferences to determine what statistics were needed to improve Government's ability to cope with crime.

As a result of these conferences, the Census Bureau several months ago published a 77-page "Report on National Needs for Criminal Justice Statistics."

A survey to measure the number and types of victims found in the nation, each state and the major cities was the first recommendation of this report.

Other new statistical programs recommended by the study included an annual census to determine the characteristics of all prisoners and all persons arrested in large cities; an annual census to determine county and city expenditures for law enforcement and an annual census to determine the workloads being handled by the police, courts and correctional agencies of the country.

N.A.A.C.P. DEPLORES HARLEM 'TERROR'

Asks for Harsher Penalties, on Mugging Especially, and More Patrolmen

By MAURICE CARROLL

An immediate halt to "the reign of criminal terror in Harlem," with remedial measures to include a mandatory five-year prison sentence for muggers, was demanded yesterday by the New York branch of the National Association for the Advancement of Colored People.

Vincent Baker, chairman of the branch's anticrime committee, said that no doubt crime was the product of "vast social evils" that demand solution, "but with people here being beaten, robbed and murdered, something should be done about crime right now."

A six-page report, prepared from studies initiated in February and approved a week ago by the branch's executive committee, was made public at a news briefing in the branch headquarters at 261 West 125th Street.

The report said that "the attitude toward crime and criminals must change" in Harlem.

"There are people known to cheer when some offender rushes from a store" with his loot, Mr. Baker told newsmen. "They seem to have the idea that these are some sort of 20th century Robin Hoods. With the hoods, we agree."

Among the report's demands were these:

¶Added protection, including more policemen on Harlem beats and "armed guards in every house in all public housing projects."

¶Harsher sentences, including a 10-year minimum for narcotics sellers and at least 30 years for those convicted of first-degree murder. The report also urged five years for muggers — even first offenders — "with no time off for good behavior and no eligibility for parole during that period."

¶Swifter court disposition of criminal cases.

¶Provision, to combat "the menace of vagrancy," of "tickets back home" for those who come in from other cities; "adequate temporary shelters" for the city's homeless and "vigorous" enforcement of antivagrancy laws.

The N.A.A.C.P. branch asked laws banning the use of binoculars to scrutinize bank customers, or the unauthorized use of cameras to photograph them.

There had been an instance, Mr. Baker said, in which youngsters who said they were from a high school newspaper snapped Polaroid pictures of people withdrawing money from a Harlem bank. There was no such newspaper, he said. The youths had given the pictures to criminals who used them to help spot victims, Mr. Baker asserted.

Mr. Baker said that while the N.A.A.C.P. would continue to combat police brutality, "it is not police brutality that makes people afraid to walk the streets at night."

Police brutality is declining, he said, and is being "superseded by criminal brutality."

Mugging—in which the criminal first assaults, then robs, his victim—is the crime "which induces more stark terror" than any other, he said, and that was why such harsh punishment was demanded.

Actually, there is no specific crime called "mugging." The offense is lumped in with other robbery statistics, making it nearly impossible to determine the extent of the crime, a Police Department spokesman said yesterday.

A New York Times survey earlier this year showed that most muggers repeated their crimes and, if convicted, were sentenced to little more than a year in jail for each crime.

The spokesman for the police echoed the N.A.A.C.P. call for swifter justice. A demonstration in England against the Vietnam war on a recent Sunday had produced some assaults against policemen, he said. By Monday, the accused had been convicted and were on their way to jail.

The N.A.A.C.P. report said the committee was "shocked to learn of the large number of persons charged with or convicted of crime who are permitted to roam the streets and hallways without hindrance."

It promised further inquiries into probation, bail and parole and said that a record would be kept of dispositions of all criminal cases in Manhattan courts.

"We shall publish it widely, be it good or bad, when such judges come up for re-election or reappointment," the report stated.

December 13, 1968

Pistol Production in U.S. Rising, Offsetting '68 Importation Ban

By NEIL SHEEHAN
Special to The New York Times

WASHINGTON, April 29 —. The effect of gun control legislation that barred the importation of cheap, concealable hand guns is being offset by domestic manufacture of the guns or by the importation of foreign parts for assembly here.

The purpose of the import restriction provisions in the Gun Control Act of 1968, passed on the wave of public outrage that followed the assassination of Senator Robert F. Kennedy, was to keep such cut-rate pistols out of the hands of criminals, delinquents and the mentally unstable by reducing the number available in this country.

But the domestic business in such guns, which retail from about $13 to $30, is burgeoning into an industry that will soon be producing 500,000 pistols a year, compared to 75,000 before the act.

As far as can be determined, the guns are being sold as fast as they are made.

The Gun Control Act allows foreign parts to be imported as long as the frame for the pistol is fabricated here.

A New York company, Imperial Metal Products, Inc., is preparing to produce about 200,000 cheap hand guns a year, while a Miami concern is gearing up to at least an equal level, according to sources knowledgeable about the gun industry. A second New York company, a Tennessee company and several smaller concerns elsewhere will be making 100,000 more annually.

Saul Eig, a slim, baldish man in his 40's, who Government records show was the leading importer of cheap foreign hand guns, is the owner of the Miami company. He is converting a former Pentecostal church and school compound next to his warehouse complex in Miami into a gun factory.

In a telephone conversation from the office of his concern, Eig Cutlery, Inc., Mr. Eig said, "we don't want publicity" and declined to disclose his contemplated production figures because "this information would be of value to our competitors."

Sources in the gun trade, however, said that since the import restrictions went into effect with the signing of the Gun Control Act last October, Mr. Eig had made arrangements to bring in enough parts from West Germany and Italy to make hundreds of thousands of revolvers and semi-automatic pistols a year.

One shipment of parts from the Tongfolio company of Brescia, Italy, for 10,000 semi-automatics recently cleared Miami Customs.

'Lightweight, Compact'

Mr. Eig acknowledged reports that last September, just before the law went into effect, he formed a new company called the Titan Manufacturing Corporation. For the last five months, he said, Titan, using machinery set up within his warehouse complex with the help of technicians from Tongfolio, has been producing .25-caliber semi-automatics from Italian and American parts.

In an advertisement mailed to gun dealers, Mr. Eig describes this pistol as a "vest pocket automatic" that is "lightweight, compact and yet sturdy enough to stand rough handling."

Mr. Eig refused to discuss the details of a cooperative arrangement that gun trade sources said he had entered into with a German company, Roehm Gesellschaft of Southeim Brenz, from which he was importing the parts for cheap .22-caliber revolvers.

Roehm, a machine tool company mass-produced such revolvers primarily for the American market and Mr. Eig was their principal importer. Sources said he made the cooperative arrangement with Roehm last October to produce the revolvers here from German and American parts.

The most common Roehm model was the BG-10, a small, snubnose .22-caliber, six-shot revolver with a 2⅛-inch barrel. Those still available in this country retail for $16.50. It is not known how many revolvers Roehm produced since beginning their manufacture in the late 1950's, but one gun expert said "they came off the assembly line like cookies."

A prominent gun dealer on the West Coast said the last RG-10 he received before the import restrictions went into effect carried a serial number higher than 1.4 million.

Familiar to U.S. Police

This revolver and similar Roehm guns, as well as copies made in smaller numbers by other German manufacturers, have become familiar to American police departments. Police officers also occasionally refer to them as Eig guns, because some were stamped with his name.

A detective on the Washington homicide squad, who asked not to be identified, estimated that 40 per cent of the guns seized in homicides here were Roehm guns. "Any rookie on the beat for two weeks learns to recognize a Roehm gun," another detective on the homicide squad said.

Lieut. Frank Connolly, supervisor of the New York City police ballistics section, said roughly 30 per cent of the 7,000 to 8,000 guns seized each year by the New York police for all reasons were German-manufactured revolvers, mainly Roehm-made.

"You rarely see a zip gun any more," he said. "it takes time to make a zip gun. The kids are lazy, so they buy one of these guns on a street corner from some guy who needs five bucks."

Mr. Eig said the revolver he intended to produce with Roehm and American parts would be an improvement over the RG-10 and would retail for

$23 or $28, depending on whether the finish was blued or chrome.

Until the import restrictions went into effect the American market was gradually being flooded with foreign-made hand guns. Commerce Department statistics show that hand gun imports tripled from 346,906 in 1965 to 1,155,368 in 1968. West Germany was the principal source, with 512,501 pistols in 1968. Italy, Brazil and Spain followed, in that order.

Rudolph Graf, owner of Precise Imports, Inc. in Suffern, N.Y., who does an eighth of his $4-million annual business in hand guns, says the import restrictions have "accomplished nothing" toward reducing the number of cheap hand guns in this country because the restrictions have simply left a brisk market open to Mr. Eig and purely domestic manufacturers who make all their own parts.

"This import law has been a blessing for these guys," Mr. Graf said. "Naturally they are doing a hell of a business."

Last fall Edward Kane, the vice president of Imperial Metal Products in New York, said his company intended to increase

production from 45,000 to 200,000 cheap .22-caliber revolvers a year. The IMP gun usually retals for $12.95.

Regrets Statement

In a telephone conversation last week, Mr. Kane said he now regrets his statement because "we don't like that kind of publicity." He would not say if his production had yet reached or was moving toward 200,000 pistols a year.

Other gun industry sources said the company had geared up production toward this level.

Martin Olivenstein, the treasurer of a second New York concern that makes cut-rate snubnose .22-caliber pistols, CDM Products, Inc., was also publicity shy and would not give his company's present or projected production figures.

A salesman for the Valor Import Corporation, a gun wholesaler in Hialeah, Fla., which advertises the CDM revolver for "immediate delivery" in lots of 50 and 100, said the six-shot revolver "takes up the slack" created by the import restrictions and that his company was selling about 2,000 a month.

Another Company Growing

Another purely domestic company that has recently begun to manufacture cheap .22-caliber pistols in quantity is the Arms Corporation of America, in Nashville. Its revolvers retail for slightly less than $20 and Harry Friedman, the president, said the company hoped to reach an annual production of 35,000 to 50,000 guns by the end of this year.

Several other companies have begun to fabricate cut-rate concealable hand guns in lots of 2,000 or so a month, with indications that the number of companies and their production will grow.

Steve Oznick, a salesman for the Buddie Arms Company of Fort Worth, said demand had "skyrocketed" since the import restriction and his company was now working "night and day" to manufacture .22-caliber Derringers that retail for between $25 and $30. He said the company hoped to produce 2,500 a month by the end of the year.

The $30 model has a thin 14-karat gold finish. "The women just buy the hell out of those gold-plated ones," he said.

April 30, 1969

Postmen in Some Areas Walk in Pairs

The United States Post Office is spending $360,000 a year in overtime pay to protect carriers delivering mail in high-crime areas of Brooklyn and the Bronx.

The money is being spent so that twice a month—when welfare checks are in the mail—two postmen can cover certain routes, rather than one. One postman, the regular carrier, puts the mail in boxes. The second postman sees to it that he does so without being attacked.

About 500 postmen in the two boroughs are volunteering for the protection duty. Postal officials call it "shotgun duty" or "riding shotgun." The second postman is not armed, however. Only huskier postal employes are urged to volunteer.

Frank Viola, postmaster of the Bronx, says he initiated the special service because 23 postmen were assaulted last year in Hunts Point, the South Bronx, Mott Haven and Morrisania — "some of them at knife-point."

Those areas contain heavy concentrations of narcotics

addicts who in recent years have come to regard welfare checks as potential sources of money with which to buy heroin.

Junkies either forge the checks or sell them at less than their face value to others who attempt to cash them.

In Brooklyn, Martin Shapiro, director of operations for the post office there under Postmaster Edward Quigley, said that 321 of Brooklyn's 1,700 postal routes required two postmen to deliver the mail when welfare checks were sent out. He said that volunteers were scarce.

In the first week in August, for example, only 239 volunteers were available, with the result that 82 routes were paired. Like the Bronx, the Brooklyn post office started shotgun duty late last year after postmen were attacked trying to make deliveries.

Postman Found Dead

Mr. Shapiro said that one postman was found dead in a hallway with his key in the mailbox. "The police called

it a homicide," he said, "but the man was buried right away and an autopsy was not done. I suppose it could have been natural."

Route doubling is extensively done in Brownsville and East New York, as well as in the Bushwick, Brevoort, Metropolitan and Adelphi postal zones.

There is no shotgun duty in Harlem, despite the fact that there are thousands of addicts there.

John J. Barbati, assistant inspector in charge of the postal inspection department for Manhattan, said the problem of thieving addicts "is an old one in Harlem and the people there are more adept in handling it."

He said there had been instances of Harlem residents going to the rescue of postmen who were being threatened.

At present the post office is not considering employing "shotgun duty" on the Lower East Side, although Mr. Barbati said that problems there were increasing for letter-carriers.

A postman in the Bronx, who asked that his name not be used, said that in the last 10 years of delivering mail in Hunts Point, "I have been knocked down and had my glasses broken three or four times." He added, "But I am not asking for a transfer because now I am used to it."

The postman said he always carried at least $10 "because if the junkies find less than that, they get mad."

A postal supervisor, who also asked that his name not be used, said that welfare recipients as well as junkies destroyed the mail boxes in apartment buildings.

He explained: "If the mailbox is broken, the postman will bring the check back to the post office and a clerk will issue the check there to each person who properly identifies himself. I guess a lot of them feel that if they pick up their checks in the post office, they have a better chance of spending the money before they get robbed."

September 23, 1969

A Reply to Rising Crime: Guard Dogs

LINCOLN, Neb., June 5 (AP)
—Nebraska's unicameral Legislature voted today to override
Gov. Norbert T. Tiemann's veto
of a so-called self-defense act.

The bill gives citizens the
right to use whatever means
are necessary to protect themselves and their property and
the lives and property of others.

Among other things, the Governor told the Legislature it
"had opened the door for the
criminal element to use the excuse of self-defense." He had
also complained that the bill
set no limits within which one
may protect himself and his
property.

By ROBERT D. McFADDEN

After enduring two armed holdups and five burglaries, Herbert P. Milanes, the owner of a South Boston dry cleaning shop, went out and bought himself a 210-pound, crossed German Shepherd-Great Dane.

"I haven't had any trouble since I got the dog 18 months ago," he said.

Like Mr. Milanes, businessmen and homeowners across the country are buying guard dogs in response to burglaries and robberies. Others, conscious of sharply rising crime rates, are not waiting to be victimized. They are buying dogs in the conviction that they are acquiring legal, economical and effective weapons.

The result has been that the demand for the dogs—mostly German Shepherds and Doberman Pinschers—is far outrunning the supply.

Interviews with dealers, trainers and guard dog owners in 15 cities showed:

¶The sale and rental of guard dogs and trained attack dogs has jumped 50 to 100 per cent in the last two years, and some concerns have doubled their business in the last year.

¶Among persons buying watchdogs for personal and home protection, a large proportion of sales—up to 90 per cent in some cases—are being made to Negroes and other residents of high crime, inner city areas.

¶A rapidly increasing number of small businesses and public institutions like churches and museums are renting trained guard dogs to patrol their premises, a practice followed for years by department stores, warehouses and other large concerns.

¶Guard and attack dogs have the generally enthusiastic approval of police departments, many of which have their own canine corps.

¶Owners report that the presence of guard and attack dogs has virtually eliminated burglaries.

The reports of rising dog use came from New York, Los Angeles, Chicago, Philadelphia, Detroit, San Francisco, Boston, St. Louis, Pittsburgh, Baltimore, Minneapolis, Miami, Dallas, Atlanta and New Orleans. Only St. Louis reported no increase in the demand for guard dogs.

In New York, 100 per cent business increases were reported this year by Captain Haggerty's School for Dogs, in the Bronx, and Mr. Lucky's Dog Training School and the Nova Kennels and Training Academy, both in Brooklyn. All three say their business is detrmined by the supply of dogs ,not the demand.

Thomas P. Nova, owner of the Nova Kennels, said his concern would soon be selling stock to the public. "We sold 250 dogs in 1967 and 400 last

The New York Times (by Lee Romero)

Lodi, a German shepherd, being held by Lieut. James Bennett of District Security Guard Service in Brooklyn. Trained guard dog accompanies Lieutenant Bennett on his rounds.

June 8, 1969

year. If we had the dogs, we could sell 700 or 800 this year with no problem," he said.

Here and in the other cities, one major reason for the demand was cited: The fear of crime, particularly burglaries, muggings, rapes and assaults. Such crimes rose 13 per cent in the nation this year, according to the Federal Bureau of Investigation.

Of some 41 million dogs in the country, about one million are used for security. These are of three basic types: untrained watchdogs for home protection, guard dogs trained to patrol alone, and attack dogs trained to work with a handler.

Most dealers will not sell trained attack dogs to persons seeking personal or home protection. It takes four to six months to train such a dog, and the result is a lethal weapon. "I equate a fully trained attack dog in the home with leaving a loaded, cocked pistol on the kitchen table," said Karl Prinz, a Boston guard dog dealer.

The spiraling demand has resulted in shortages and long waiting lists, mostly for German Shepherds and Dobermans, though Airedales, Great Danes, boxers and Giant Schnauzers are also sought.

The short supply has driven up prices. Depending on locale and dog type, untrained watchdogs for the home sell for $150 to $500, up $75 in the last few years; trained guard dogs sell for $800 to $2,800, up about $200 in the last year. The rental of trained dogs ranges from $35 to $100 a week.

Many businessmen say the price is cheap, noting that human guards would cost much more and no protection at all would be costliest.

In some cases, dealers said, burglars have learned to deal with guard dogs by using tranquilizers, chemical mace or poisoned food before making their entry. Most dogs, however, are trained not to eat on the job.

"A dog never sleeps and never drinks in the job," said Thomas McGinn, a Philadelphia trainer who sells 22 guard dogs a week. "A company can pay $2,100 for a dog and get many years' use out of it. To employ a man it would cost around $8,000 a year."

'Afraid to Sleep'

"It's amazing how many people are afraid to sleep in their own homes," said Mrs. William G. Paige, who with her husband runs K-9, Inc., Miami's biggest guard dog business.

"We have people come to us with stories of having been raped, beaten, tied up, locked in closets—everything imaginable. The main trouble in the past has been that they waited until after something happened. But now, people are beginning to come to us for protection before they have a break-in."

The Paiges' company represents one of many success stories in the guard dog business. It has grown from a husband-and-wife, one-dog operation in 1959 to a bustling concern with 30 employees, 300 dogs and 12 franchises in five Southern states and the Bahamas. It has set up canine corps for 32 police departments.

Some of K-9, Inc.'s dogs patrol avocado and mango groves; others patrol the stables at Tropical Park Racetrack, and, in a case of dogs guarding dogs, some watch greyhound kennels at Miami's dog racing tracks.

In Pittsburgh, Rick Wright is renting guard dogs to an increasing number of small businesses. Used car dealers, a beer distributor, two churches and the operator of a small fruit stand are among his customers.

Burglaries Thwarted

Thomas M. Stevenson, a Chicago leaser, rents to businesses seeking protection. "To my knowledge," he said, "no company with one of our dogs turned loose on its premises has experienced a burglary."

Gary Compton rents 75 dogs a night in San Francisco. Last year, he said, his clients found evidence of 100 unsuccessful burglaries. Ten burglars were caught after being held at bay by his dogs. One man, held by a dog for 14 hours, was found incoherent.

Robert Buesing, a Los Angeles leaser, said his dogs accounted for 12 arrests a month. One such burglar admitted he would rather face a policeman's gun than the bared fangs of an attack dog.

There have been instances of frightened burglars calling the police when faced with an attack dog. It happened at the Frito-Lay warehouse at 1261 Zerega Avenue, the Bronx, where a group of youths broke in recently and, after being held at bay by a dog, yelled to a passerby through a window and asked him to call the police.

Many dealers said heavy demands for dogs follow reports of sensational crimes or riots. The murder of Sharon Tate, the actress, produced more than 100 requests for dogs at one agency in Bel Air.

"People are afraid, scared to death," said the owner of K-9 College, Detroit's largest guard dog supplier, who asked that his name be withheld.

"Right after the [1967] riot, the demand for the German Shepherd and the Doberman was unbelievable. We couldn't get them fast enough. That was no coincidence."

The owner said about 90 per cent of his requests for watchdogs and guards come from the inner city. About one-third of the applicants are Negroes, he said.

Not all trained dogs are on the side of the law, according to Capt. Jack Auerback, commander of the Philadelphia Police Department's Canine Corps. Recently, he said, an otherwise unarmed robber with a German Shepherd entered a store, backed his victims up against a wall with the snarling animal and took their money at fang-point.

November 23, 1969

PANEL SEES CRIME TURNING THE CITIES INTO ARMED CAMPS

Warns of Violence Dividing Areas Into 'Fortresses' and 'Places of Terror'

By JOHN HERBERS

Special to The New York Times

WASHINGTON, Nov. 23—The National Commission on the Causes and Prevention of Violence warned today that American cities were on their way to becoming a mixture of "places of terror" and "fortresses."

Under present policies, the commission said in a report on violent crime, the central cities will be unsafe in varying degree, the well-to-do will live in privately guarded compounds, residents will travel in armored vehicles through "sanitized corridors" connecting safe areas, and radical groups will possess "tremendous armories of weapons that could be brought into play with or without provocation."

All this, the commission concluded, will lead to "intensifying hatred and deepening divisions" under which "violence will increase further and the defensive response of the affluent will become still more elaborate."

'Massive Action' Required

The commission said its gloomy prediction will come true "in a few more years" unless the nation alters its priorities and takes "the massive actions that seems to be needed" to build "the great, open, humane city-societies of which we are capable."

What is needed, the commission said, is a national urban policy of the kind recently suggested by Daniel Patrick Moynihan, President Nixon's Counselor on Urban Strategy, but which has not been adopted by the Administration or Congress. Such a policy would require a large expenditure of money.

"If the nation is not in a position to launch a full-scale war on domestic ills, especially urban ills, at this moment, because of the difficulty in freeing ourselves quickly from other obligations, we should now legally make the essential commitments and then carry them out as quickly as funds can be obtained," the commission said.

An important part of the 8,000-word report was a summary of the findings of the most detailed national study made of homicide, assault, rape and robbery. The study was based on reports by the Federal Bureau of Investigation and a commission survey of 17 major cities.

This type of crime, the study showed, is primarily centered in the large cities, is increasingly committed by males between 15 and 24 years of age and stems "disproportionately from the ghetto slums where most Negroes live."

The commission stressed that the causes are sociological, not racial.

"When poverty, dilapidated housing, high unemploy-

237

ment, poor education, overpopulation and broken homes are combined, an interrelated complex of powerful criminogenic forces is produced by the ghetto environment," the report said. "These social forces for crime are intensified by the inferiority-inducing attitudes of the larger American society—attitudes that today view ghetto blacks as being suspended between slavery and the full rights and dignity of free men."

'Most Important' Report

Milton S. Eisenhower, brother of the late President and chairman of the commission, said in a news conference on the report that he considered it "by all odds the most important" of several released by the 13-member commission since it was appointed in the summer of 1968 by President Johnson after the assassination of Senator Robert F. Kennedy.

Several other Presidential commissions and study groups have warned of increased hostilities, violence and deterioration unless a national commitment and new resources were made for the cities. Most of their recommendations have been rejected or ignored for various reasons.

In the commission's view, the nation has neglected not only the residents of the central cities but the entire system of criminal justice. As a result, it said, efforts of affluent citizens to provide for their own safety are "misshaping" the metropolitan area and providing only "precarious" security for themselves in the process.

The commission said that even though available statistics were inadequate to measure the extent of violent crimes, "it is still clear that significant and disturbing increases in the true rates of homicide and, especially, of assault and robbery, have occurred over the last decade."

To obtain a more accurate profile of violent crime, the commission studied 10,000 arrest records in 17 cities — Atlanta, Washington, Philadelphia, New York, Boston, Miami, Dallas, New Orleans, Detroit, Cleveland, Chicago, Minneapolis, St. Louis, Denver, Seattle, San Francisco and Los Angeles.

Among other things, the study showed "dramatic and disturbing increases" in the arrests of children between 10 and 14 years old for violent crimes — a 300 per cent increase for arrests for assault and 200 per cent for robbery between 1958 and 1967.

The commission said that, although crime had a direct connection with the condition of life in the slums, the incidence of crime had increased so rapidly that other explanations were needed.

The commission offered the following "informed judgments" about the reasons for the increase:

¶The rapid social change in the United States has "led to a breakdown of traditional social roles and institutional controls over the behavior of young and old alike, but particularly the young."

¶Law enforcement agencies have not been strengthened sufficiently to cope with the violence.

¶There has been a breakdown in the public belief, found especially in the slums, that rule-making institutions are entitled to rule.

The commission said that a 10 point urban policy recently outlined by Mr. Moynihan merits "careful consideration." This recommendation, which Mr. Moynihan made on his own, includes some of the policies being pursued by the Nixon Administration,

November 24, 1969

'You must be out of your mind to be out alone after dark in a neighborhood like this'

By JAMES K. BATTEN

WASHINGTON.

EVERY Sunday at Washington's big Metropolitan A.M.E. Church five blocks from the White House, when the ushers stride down the aisle with the offering, a blue-uniformed private policeman quietly slips out of a rear pew. A revolver tucked discreetly inside his jacket, he moves down a side aisle and takes a seat next to the collection plates, lest some pistol-packing visitor in the congregation be seized by a fit of covetousness.

This jarring liturgical innovation, which might strike many Americans as incredible, is the sort of thing that residents of the nation's capital are glumly coming to accept as routine. And the church's officials, who decided last year to hire the $35-a-Sunday collection-plate guard, are convinced that their precautions were justified. A few weeks ago at nearby Vermont Avenue Baptist Church, while eight ushers stood at the altar with the offering, a man stepped from a seat in the second row, pulled out a pistol and announced: "This is a stick-up!" An irate worshiper grabbed him before he could make off with the money.

Crime has been a serious problem in Washington for years. But now it is getting dramatically worse. One

The warning quoted was spoken by a passer-by to a woman in Washington. She looked up—and there was the White House.

238

grim assessment of what could lie ahead for Washington and other crime-ridden cities was suggested last December in the final report of the National Commission on the Causes and Prevention of Violence, chaired by Dr. Milton S. Eisenhower. The commission warned that American cities were well on their way toward becoming a mixture of "fortresses" and "places of terror."

Unless the rise in violent crime can be reversed, the commission predicted, tomorrow's big cities will look something like this: the black ghettos will be places of great danger, "perhaps entirely out of police control during the nighttime hours." Nearby downtown business districts will be reasonably safe in daylight but deserted at night except for police patrols. Middle-income and upper-income city dwellers will live in "fortified cells ...protected by private guards and security devices." In the suburbs, "ownership of guns will be almost universal [and] homes will be fortified by an array of devices from window grills to electronic surveillance equipment." High-speed expressways will be "sanitized corridors connecting safe areas, and private automobiles, taxicabs and commercial vehicles will be routinely equipped with unbreakable glass, light armor and other security features."

IF this nightmarish forecast is really more than headline-grabbing hyperbole, Washington is a promising place to sift the evidence and ponder its implications. Crime is Washington's obsession these days. In this center of Western power and politics, where most of mankind's awesome problems are grappled with on a daily basis, people worry more about being mugged than about being incinerated in a nuclear war.

From the elegant salons of the Watergate Apartments to the laundry rooms of the dreary public housing projects in Anacostia, everybody talks endlessly about crime. In his State of the Union speech in January, President Nixon felt moved to declare: "I doubt if there are many members of this Congress who live more than a few blocks from here who would dare leave their cars in the Capitol Garage and walk home tonight." He was undoubtedly right. Mark Russell, Washington's favorite in-group comedian, tells his audiences that the President sent a crime bill up to Capitol Hill, but somebody stole it.

Mr. Nixon might not find that very

funny. In his 1968 campaign for the White House, he made much of Washington's crime problem and promised to "sweep the streets clean of marauders and criminals." But a year after he took office, the marauders and criminals are busier than ever. It should be noted in Mr. Nixon's defense, however, that Congress has been slow to act on his anticrime proposals for Washington.

Meanwhile, crime statistics are soaring. In 1969, murders increased to 289, compared with 194 in 1968 and only 144 in 1966—a 100 per cent increase in three years. Rapes jumped from 260 in 1968 to 336 in 1969; robberies were up from 8,622 to 12,423. Over-all, serious crime in the District of Columbia rose 26.3 per cent last year, compared to the national urban average of 11 per cent.

This year-long orgy of blood and gunsmoke reached a sort of saturnalian climax on Christmas Eve, when in 24 hours there were 80 robberies, 42 of them with weapons, the highest daily total in Washington's history.

Despite these hair-raising figures, you can provoke a sharp argument from city officials by calling Washington the "crime capital of the world," as not a few politicians have

done. For the first nine months of 1969, Washington ranked first in selected serious crimes per 1,000 citizens among 15 U.S. cities with populations between 500,000 and one million. But because Washington's suburbs lie in Maryland and Virginia, most of Washington is, in effect, a "central city" where crime is normally higher. Thus, the argument goes, the District of Columbia is not statistically comparable to most other big cities. It is true that in 1968, in a ranking of the nation's 15 biggest metropolitan areas, the Washington area was seventh in serious crimes per 1,000 citizens—behind New York, Los Angeles, San Francisco, Baltimore, Detroit and Newark.

WHATEVER the precise ranking, Washington can be a dangerous place. Perhaps the most ironic case in point is furnished by the misfortunes that befell the staff of the violence commission itself during its work in Washington between August, 1968, and February, 1969.

"It was really terrible, to be honest with you," said William G. McDonald, who served as the commission's administrative officer. The toll goes this way: One key staff member, a law-

yer from Chicago, was mugged and badly beaten a few blocks from his downtown hotel in the middle of the evening. Another was jumped in an apartment lobby but fought off his attackers. The apartment of a third was cleaned out by thieves who took everything of value, including a $500 Government - owned tape recorder. One young woman was raped and brutally beaten by a man who broke into her apartment; another was a victim of an attempted rape and a successful robbery, also in her apartment. There were a number of less serious incidents.

Although the violence commission's offices were only a block from the White House, secretaries were reluctant to work later than 6 or 7 o'clock in the evening. Toward the end, when the staff was under intense pressure to wind up its work and secretaries were badly needed in the evening, precautions were taken to get them home safely. "We would take the girls down," McDonald recalled, "and put them in cabs in front of the building."

Washington's thugs show no reverence for the area around the White House; there is no safety in being a neighbor of Richard Nixon. Holdups within a few blocks of the White House are not infrequent, and when White House secretaries are late leaving for home, guards try to keep an eye on them until they are safely into their parked automobiles.

Jayne Brumley, a Newsweek correspondent, will never forget her experience just outside 1600 Pennsylvania Avenue at about 6:15 one winter evening. As she hurried along the sidewalk, a man approached and angrily lectured her: "Lady, you must be out of your mind to be out alone after dark in a neighborhood like this." Recalling the incident, Mrs. Brumley laughed sadly and said: "Isn't that awful? I looked over to my right, and there was the White House."

For many years, among the city's black-and-white liberal establishment and its image-conscious business leadership, it has been unfashionable to complain too loudly about crime in Washington "It's been crude and ugly to be against crime," explained the liberal white pastor of a downtown church. "We've had to be against racism."

TODAY the mood is changing. Fear of crime so grips large areas of the city that old ideological and commercial reflexes are giving way to a prag-

matic and frequently desperate search for ways to safeguard home, family and business.

The 1800 block of Wyoming Avenue, Northwest, provides a remarkable example. Lined with roomy, turn-of-the-century townhouses, the block was once in the middle of one of Washington's most fashionable neighborhoods. Now it stands nervously on the edge of the city's black ghetto. By last fall, it had become a "place of terror," to use the language of the violence commission.

In November, muggings and holdups had become so frequent that the residents — black and white, well-to-do and poor, professional people and Government clerks — finally banded together to fight back. Led by a 41-year - old lawyer named Tedson J. Meyers, a one-time speechwriter for Hubert Humphrey, they mounted 60 150-watt floodlights on their houses to illuminate the once-shadowy street from dark to dawn. Since the lights went up, crime has virtually disappeared from the block.

Because of the block's great diversity, Meyers believes that only the obvious common danger persuaded the residents to get together and install the lights. "People on this block," he said, "range from 19th-century, hidebound conservatives to people who think that putting up lights is vigilantism. The only thing we're agreed on is that you can't do your thing dead, and opinions don't matter from the grave."

Meyers was not being melodramatic. In the last two years, the block had seen two murders, two other serious shootings and more than 20 muggings and holdups. Meyers, simply by moving up and down the not unattractive street in front of his three-story townhouse, can provide one of the grisliest crime tours in Washington.

"Right here," he said, pointing to the steps of a building at the foot of the street, "a man was mugged and killed in the summer of 1968. Over there, a man was mugged and left lying in the dirt—an old taxi driver, as I recall. He was pretty bloodied up, lying with his head in the gutter when he was found."

A few houses up the street, Meyers pointed to the spot where the block's most infamous shrub cast its shadows until last fall. "We had three muggings out of that one bush in a single night." Now the plant has been pruned away, along with most of the other shrubbery on the block. Meyers stopped and gazed up and down the

street. "It's amazing, really. At every single house you can point to an encounter with crime—and in the last year it's been violent crime."

Finally, as we moved up the street, Meyers pointed to the sidewalk in front of a red-brick townhouse. That was the spot where, at about 7 one evening last March, he rushed from his home nearby to find James E. Nussman, a 29-year-old educator and Princeton graduate, dying from a shotgun blast in the chest. "I thought it was an explosion," Meyers recalled quietly. "That's what it sounded like."

An intense and articulate man, Meyers is deeply outraged by the violence he has seen. He recently called the Pentagon and was told that between 1961 and 1969, about 200 District of Columbia men died in combat in Vietnam. During the same nine-year period, he discovered, about 1,400 of the city's residents died by various kinds of homicide, including that stemming from domestic quarrels or arguments among friends as well as street violence. "That," he said, "is madness."

THE madness seems to be spreading. Veteran Washington police officers insist that the city is being terrorized these days by a new breed of criminals whose most distinctive trait is their viciousness.

"Robberies in which weapons were fired were unusual 20 years ago, or even 10 years ago," mused Inspector William D. Foran, a criminal investigator and 23 - year veteran of the Washington police force. "Today, it's quite common. You read these crime summaries—that's the first thing I do every morning—and you're always left wondering: Why did they shoot the weapon? Why did they kill the guy? In many cases, the only answer seems to be just pure malice."

Why is crime on the rampage in Washington? Part of the answer lies in the nature of Washington itself. Beyond the marble grandeur of official Washington, much of the city is a vast Negro slum. For tens of thousands of rural and small-town Negroes from the South, Washington has been the first — and often the final — stop in this century's historic migration to the urban North. But for many of the newcomers, Washington has proved to be not the promised land but a swamp of poverty and despair. And the city's black slums, in the all-too-familiar manner, have become breeding grounds for crime.

Crime in Washington has become, in the main, a Negro phenomenon.

The black slums are the most dangerous parts of town. The mostly white northwest is notably safer—though still far from unscathed by crime. In 1968, when the city was about 70 per cent black, 186 Negroes were arrested for homicide and only 15 whites. For robbery, there were 1,435 Negroes arrested and only 66 whites. For burglary, there were 3,437 Negroes and 221 whites. And so it went.

In most categories, predictably, blacks were also the principal victims. The significant exception was robbery and related offenses like purse-snatching. There, police records show, whites' complaints outnumbered those of blacks, 4,824 to 4,098, a fact that helps explain the racial overtones that permeate black and white Washingtonians' thinking about crime.

Some Negroes candidly admit what many whites nervously assume—that black rage against whites is a factor in some crimes. "Blacks are saying they want pay for all the years you didn't give them equal opportunity," said Hiawatha Burris, a black ex-convict now heading a private agency called Bonabond that helps rehabilitate drug addicts in trouble with the law. "And they say if you're not going to give it, then they got to take it. . . . If criminals could be selective in their victims, they would all be white."

Against this backdrop, at least two other key factors lie at the heart of Washington's crime crisis. One is the epidemic of drug addiction, which Washington shares with many other big cities; the other is the breakdown of the District of Columbia's criminal-justice system, which is made more serious by the Bail Reform Act of 1966.

Nobody knows how many heroin addicts live in Washington; the only certainty is that the number is in the thousands and growing. And most of them, by definition, are criminals. There is usually no other way to support habits that often cost more than $50 a day. In the past, Washington's addicts stuck mostly to nonviolent crime to raise the money they needed. Now that has changed.

Hiawatha Burris explained why: "Before, addicts got money by shoplifting and stealing off the backs of trucks. But now the downtown stores have gotten so sophisticated, it's getting harder to get money in petty crimes. So you have to turn to violent crimes. And so many guys don't know how to steal; they don't know how to get money with any degree of sophistication."

As crime has increased, Washington's machinery for bringing criminals to justice has sputtered and failed. Last December, an advisory panel of 13 prominent Washingtonians offered this grim conclusion to the Senate Committee on the District of Columbia: "Unfortunately, a fear of getting caught provides little deterrent to criminals in the national capital. Criminals committing armed robbery—the most prevalent armed crime—stand a much better chance of getting away than they do of getting caught." In the first 10 months of 1969, the police solved only about 18 per cent of the city's 5,500 armed robberies.

As for the unlucky criminals who are apprehended, the justice they face is "neither swift nor certain," in the words of the advisory panel. They are not likely to be tried for at least eight months, probably longer. The impact of this delay is sharply increased in Washington by the four-year-old Bail Reform Act. In most American courts, judges weigh the element of danger to the community in deciding whether to release a defendant on bail. But the Bail Reform Act forbids Federal judges—and in the District of Columbia there is no other kind—from considering anything except the likelihood that the defendant will flee.

The result is that dangerous men are loosed on the community for months before their trials, often to strike again. A police survey showed that 35 per cent of those released pending trial for armed robbery were rearrested on other felony charges, usually armed robbery. Bonabond's Burris explained: "A lot of guys want to have one last fling while they're on bail. They say, 'Well, I'll leave my family in good shape.' So they stick up a grocery store and leave $5,000 or $6,000 home for the wife."

AS things get worse, virtually all the city's institutions are feeling the pressures of crime—or at least, the fear of crime. This winter, for the first time in history, policemen were assigned to all 46 of Washington's junior and senior high schools. The city's library director has warned that some branches may be forced to close unless "disorder, theft and vandalism . . . can be brought under control."

Foreign diplomats have been clamoring for better police protection, citing repeated attacks against their staff members. In response, President Nixon has asked Congress to enlarge the White House police force to provide beefed-up protection to the embassies. Gallaudet College, whose deaf-mute students have proved peculiarly vulnerable to crime, has asked Congress for an extra $150,000 to triple its seven-man guard force and buy more lights and fencing for the campus.

Individual Washingtonians are ordering their personal lives in the same sort of dogged search for security. Sometimes the fear is well-founded, sometimes it obviously is not; but the effect is the same, and collectively, individual decisions in pursuit of safety are rapidly changing patterns of life in the nation's capital.

By day, the changes are substantial enough. Scores of merchants, even in the swanker sections of town, keep their doors locked, opening only to those thought to pose no threat. Bus drivers no longer carry change. Taxi drivers try to keep their cash to a minimum and avoid the rougher neighborhoods when they can.

But when night falls, the syndrome of fear becomes far more dramatic. Thousands of citizens hurry home from their jobs, lock their doors and refuse to venture out again until morning. The effect is to push more and more of the city's activities into the daylight hours.

Many of Washington's churches have given up on nighttime programs; their members simply refuse to show up. A Negro undertaker reports that increasing numbers of mourners want to view their departed friends in the afternoon instead of at night; he has changed his hours accordingly. The National Theater has found it necessary to move its curtain time up from 8:30 P.M. to 7:30. And theatergoers tend to make a beeline for the parking garages when the curtain falls; the idea is to get out of the downtown area as quickly as possible. Nearby restaurants, which once relied heavily on after-the-theater patronage, are feeling the squeeze.

By midevening, most of downtown Washington is virtually deserted. Except in such areas as Georgetown and the 14th Street nightclub strip, where after-dark activity persists, the few people still on the streets are not strolling to see the nation's capital at night; they are usually hurrying somewhere, as if uneasy about being out after dark. One of the nation's largest defense contractors, which has about 75 visiting executives in Washington during an average week, has issued pointed advice: "We suggest to our people that they travel in pairs where possible, take taxis wherever they go and stay in the hotel after dinner."

One of Washington's biggest growth industries is the security business, offering everything from iron window grills to fancy burglar alarms to the services of private guards. C.T. (Jimmie) James, who parlayed $200 borrowed in 1950 into a $2-million-a-year private-security agency, employs about 450 men. "I could put another 500 men to work tomorrow, with no trouble," he said, "if I could get them."

Virtually every store is equipped with security devices. Some are as simple as attack-trained German shepherds, which are in hot demand; others are as sophisticated as the camera that silently pans back and forth across the interior of a thrice-robbed dress shop a block from the White House. Another innovation winning popularity among businessmen is the "panic button"—a wireless device about the size of a cigarette pack that can be carried in a coat pocket or handbag. In the event of trouble, a tap on the button sets off an alarm blocks away, where the call is relayed to the police.

Locksmiths and burglar-alarm salesmen are also doing a brisk business with citizens eager to make their homes more secure. The latest sign of the times came a few weeks ago when a big downtown drugstore unveiled a window display of rod-like metal devices designed to keep doors securely shut. A then-and-now sketch depicted a lady of yesteryear jamming a chair under her doorknob to keep intruders out and her modern counterpart neatly achieving the same effect with the new $4.97 device.

In parts of the city, it seems clear that citizens' jitters have outrun any reasonable grounds for caution. In fact, a substantial number of Washingtonians, including some top police officials and criminologists, insist that hysteria about crime has gotten completely out of hand and, in a sense, become as damaging to the city as crime itself.

"The way people perceive crime is a lot of the problem," said the Washington police chief, Jerry V. Wilson. "The best example is that

for the white middle-class resident of the District of Columbia, traffic accidents cost a great deal more and involve greater risk of death than crime. Your chances of getting home without getting run over by an automobile are a hell of a lot worse than your chances of getting home without being raped or robbed."

Some ordinary citizens emphatically agree. One of them is Louise N. Ellis, a retired Government statistician who lives near Woodley Road in one of northwest Washington's handsomest residential areas. "I'm sick and tired of people being scared to death," she complained. "I can't even get up a table of bridge any more. My friends are scared to go out. Certainly there's a crime problem, but not enough to keep thousands of people behind a lot of doors. It's changed their whole way of life, which is ridiculous."

Crime is not the only problem that besets Washington, of course. There is the perennial difficulty caused by the absence of home rule, leaving ultimate control of the city's affairs in the hands of an often apathetic Congress. There are the bad schools, the heavy concentration of poor blacks and the pull of the suburbs. But without question, crime is a major reason why Washington, in the eyes of many worried observers, is sliding dangerously downhill as a viable community.

Middle-class whites have been fleeing for years. Today, the city's population of a little more than 800,000 is between 70 and 75 per cent black, and the Negro proportion—36 per cent 20 years ago—is still rising.

If present trends continue, Washington obviously could become a virtually all-black city in the nineteen-eighties, and some planners have predicted precisely that. But there is another distressing feature of this population shift: Washington is in danger of becoming not just a city of blacks, but a city of poor blacks.

In 1967 and '68, after years of steady Negro migration into Washington, an ominous and little-noticed switch occurred. Official city estimates showed a sudden net out-migration of 6,590 Negroes. There is good reason to believe that many of them were middle-class blacks fleeing to the suburbs from crime-ridden city neighborhoods. A favorite destination seems to be Prince Georges County, Md.

One black middle-class family that finally gave up on Washington is headed by William F. Proctor, a 49-year-old furniture salesman. Until last summer, Proctor, his wife and five children lived in the Brightwood section of Washington near Walter Reed Army Hospital. Unhappy with Washington's public schools but also apprehensive about rising crime in their neighborhood, they moved to Silver Spring, in Montgomery County, Md.

"I was afraid," sighed Mrs. Proctor, a management analyst at the U.S. Office of Education. "There had been so many purse-snatchings and muggings. You never knew when it might happen to you. When I came home at night from a meeting, I would sit in my car until I could see nothing moving on the street. Then I would run to the house."

The flight of Negro families like the Proctors could be a crippling blow for Washington. "I shudder to think about it, really," said Mrs. Proctor, discussing the future of Washington. "It perhaps is not fair to move and leave the burden on somebody else. But you do the best you can, and you feel you're not accomplishing very much. So you leave."

BUSINESSMEN are feeling the same pressures. A recent survey by the Mayor's Economic Development Committee showed that 17 per cent of the small-business owners interviewed in a limited sampling were ready to close or move to the suburbs. And 85 per cent said it would be foolhardy to expand, given Washington's plight.

Is Washington, then, to become a "fortified city" of the violence commission's nightmare? The depressing evidence suggests that it could. The city's 105,000 privately owned guns (the bulk of them in the hands of law-abiding but nervous citizens—though only about 30,000 are properly registered with the police), the prospering burglar-alarm salesmen, the elaborate security features of new luxury apartment buildings, the empty downtown streets after 9 P.M.—all this suggests that the **prologue to the nightmare may be at hand.**

President Nixon's anticrime program for the District of Columbia, now belatedly moving through Congress, offers a measure of hope— although some of its features deeply disturb civil libertarians. The Nixon package would reorganize the city's

floundering court system, authorize "no-knock" search warrants, expand wiretapping authority and permit the preventive detention of dangerous defendants. And with the President's support, the District of Columbia's 4,000-member police force is being expanded to 5,100.

Chief Wilson, a lanky North Carolinian who is regarded as one of the nation's most sensitive and progressive police chiefs, insists that Washington's crime problem is far from hopeless. "I am inclined to believe," he said, "that the District of Columbia has the best chance of improving of any of the big cities. There are lots of national resources and lots of national pressures here that don't apply to other cities."

Wilson can also point to certain hopeful straws in the wind. Robberies, for example, have been on the decline in the last few months—down from 1,348 in October to 1,097 in January. The police have been spectacularly successful in combating bank robbers, mainly by planting plainclothesmen in the banks. In January and February, 1969, just as Richard Nixon was settling in at the White House, there were 21 robberies or attempted robberies of financial institutions. During the same period this year, there were only four.

The most decisive question mark in Washington's fight against crime, however, may be the attitude of the city's black community. In the last few years, antipolice feelings have run high among many Washington Negroes. A black man cooperating with the police ran the risk of being labeled a traitor. Predictably, this hostility has often hamstrung the police. In the slums of Washington, as in the hamlets of South Vietnam, if the natives wish to protect fugitives from the authorities, they usually can succeed.

But now, black attitudes seem to be changing. For the sake of self-preservation, Washington's Negroes are beginning to rise up against the criminals in their midst. And the police—35 per cent of them black—are making it easier by paying more attention to good community relations.

Chief Wilson says he detects a "complete turnaround" in black attitudes toward crime and the police: "In 1965, 1966 and 1967, it was popular to oppose the police in various ways. There was a significant hue and cry in the ghetto that law enforcement was black oppression. But the black ghetto community affected by crime is coming to realize that crime is oppressive—much more so than law enforcement. . . . The complaints I get now of police misconduct are that they don't do enough to enforce the law."

William Raspberry, The Washington Post's respected black columnist, recently wrote: "Black Washingtonians feel better about the local police force than they did a year ago, perhaps better than at any time in the last decade. Don't ask me why this is, or even to prove that it's so. All I know is that when you talk to people—in the street, in bars, in barbershops, in their homes—you don't hear the antipolice talk that used to be so common . . . . Many people who used to feel intimidated by the police now feel still more intimidated by young thugs on the street—even to the point of finding themselves reluctant allies of the police in the fight against street crime."

The Rev. Walter Fauntroy, an associate of the late Dr. Martin Luther King and a former vice chairman of the District of Columbia City Council, agrees that Washington's black citizens are ready for tough action against crime. "If you ask the vast majority of people around here about the police," he said, "they say the police 'ought to knock those niggers [muggers and robbers] in the head.'"

But Fauntroy, like many other responsible black leaders, is still troubled by the legacy of animosity between the police and the black citizens of Washington. He thinks the best solution is more black policemen. "I'd feel much more comfortable saying to a black cop, 'Go get him, buddy, I'm with you,' than to say it to a white cop who shows up and says, 'That fellow didn't rape your daughter. Y'all rape one another all the time.'"

FOR those who doubt the depth of the Washington crime problem, there are sections of the city that may represent an ugly glimpse of the future—unless something is done.

Parts of Anacostia, in the city's southeast, for example, are so crime-ridden and bereft of essential services that thousands of people have moved away. Block after block of housing projects are boarded up, left to the vandals and the rats. In several public housing projects, where tenants remain but want to get above the easy reach of prowling thugs, nobody lives in the ground-floor units. All the windows of these units have been covered with plywood. It is an eerie sight. ■

Panel Asks Slum Reforms To Cut Black Crime Rate

By JACK ROSENTHAL
Special to The New York Times

WASHINGTON, Sept. 7—A Government study panel has concluded that the rate of violent crime by urban blacks appears to be markedly higher than that for whites—and that blacks also constitute a majority of the victims.

In a 2,436-page report, the panel says that urban blacks are arrested eight to twenty times more often than whites for homicide, rape, aggravated assault and robbery.

The report also concludes that, excepting robbery, 60 to 70 per cent of the victims are black. Despite widespread white racial fears, it said, "one of our most striking and relevant general conclusions" is that violent crime is predominantly intraracial.

'Total Effort' Urged

"The urgent need to reduce violent crimes among urban Negro youth is obvious," the report says, "requiring a total effort toward changing the demoralizing conditions and life patterns of Negroes, the unequal opportunity and discrimination they confront . . . and the overcrowding and decay of the urban ghettos."

The panel, on individual acts of violence, is the only one of seven that has not yet published its report to the parent National Commission on the Causes and Prevention of Violence, which completed its other work last December.

Lloyd N. Cutler, executive director of the commission, acknowledged today that "we have been concerned that some people would fail to recognize that crime is inherent among young slum residents, regardless of race, and see only 'black crime' merely because slums are now largely black."

Interference Denied

But, he said, there was no interference with the study panel. Publication has been delayed because of the complexity of the panel's work and by lack of funds, he said. The report now is to be released soon.

Among the panel's recommendations, which cover 110 pages, were the following:

¶Marijuana should be legalized. The panel did not endorse the use of marijuana. But it said present laws were archaic and ineffective and exacted great social cost. Perhaps the greatest cost, it said, "is that our youth has suffered a loss of respect for the law" and, prohibitions notwithstanding, are increasing marijuana use "at a staggering pace."

This recommendation was not endorsed by the full commission. It has called for medical studies of the effects of marijuana and, pending their outcome, for lowering penalties.

¶Urgent attention should be paid to the small fraction of youthful offenders who commit an exceptional proportion of violent crime. The report cited one study showing that a hard core of 6 per cent of youths in a sample committed 71 per cent of the robberies.

¶Prison sentencing practices should be revised, putting more emphasis on rehabilitation and reintegration into society, and less on simple restraint.

How long a term an offender serves appears to have no relationship to whether he will return to crime, the report said. "If anything, there may be a tendency for violent offenders who have served long sentences to recidivate more often than those who have served shorter sentences."

¶Greatly increased attention should be paid to suicides and auto accidents, which far exceed murder as causes of death.

Over-all white suicide rates are higher than black, the report said, but it suggested that the rate among young adult urban blacks exceeded that of whites. .

Federal and state governments should compensate victims of crime—as a matter of right. The cost, the panel estimated, would be far lower than might be imagined, citing estimates for a proposed compensation plan in Illinois of $2.5-million a year.

In discussing high rates of violent crime among blacks, the study panel said that conclusions based on arrest rates were inherently biased. Negroes, the report said, may be disproportionately arrested on suspicion compared with whites, suggesting more Negro crime than is valid.

"In spite of the numerous deficiencies in arrest data," the report said, "true rates of violent crime by Negroes appear to be considerably higher than rates for whites."

On the basis of computations made from data supplied by the Federal Bureau of IInvestigation and the Census Bureau, the panel estimated that blacks were arrested 18 times as often as whites for murder, 12 times as often for forcible rape, and 10 times as often for aggravated assault. For robbery, blacks of all ages are arrested 16 times as often as whites; the figure for blacks between 10 and 17 is 20 times that of whites of the same age.

The panel rejected any biological or genetic explanations for these differences, offering an extensive sociological analysis similar to that of previous major Presidential commissions on crime and violence.

A significant portion of increased crime is the inevitable result of the increased urbanization and increased youth of the population, the panel said.

For the population as a whole, the report said, persons 18 to 24 commit almost four times as many violent crimes as do persons over 25.

Beyond these factors, the report dealt at length with psychic and social conditions.

"To be young, poor, male, and Negro, to want what the open society claims is available, but mostly to others; to see illegitimate and often violent methods of obtaining material success; and to observe others using these means successfully and with impunity—is to be burdened with an enormous set of influences that pull many toward crime and delinquency," the report said.

Race and Crime

Special to The New York Times

WASHINGTON, Sept. 7 — Following is a table showing the intraracial nature of serious crimes:

Race of Offender and Victim	Criminal Homicide	Aggravated Assault	Forcible Rape	Armed Robbery
Both same race	90%	90%	90%	51%
Black vs. black	66	66	60	38
White vs. white	24	24	30	13
Black vs. white	6	8	10	47
White vs. black	4	2		2

SOURCE: Victim-offender survey made by Task Force on Individual Crimes of Violence, an agency of the National Commission on the Causes and Prevention of Violence, 1969-70.

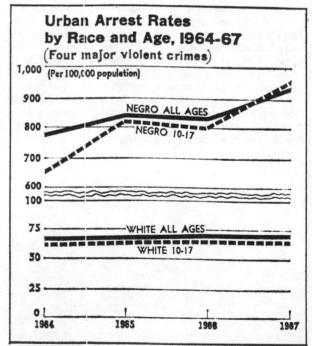

Urban Arrest Rates by Race and Age, 1964-67
(Four major violent crimes)

1,000 (Per 100,000 population)

NEGRO ALL AGES
NEGRO 10-17
WHITE ALL AGES
WHITE 10-17

The New York Times   Sept. 8, 1970

Arrest rates listed on chart cite urban arrests for crimes of homicide, forcible rape, robbery and aggravated assault. Information is based on uniform crime reports of Federal Bureau of Investigation and census data for years 1964-67.

September 8, 1970

Increasing Campus Crime Spurs Security Measures

By ANDREW H. MALCOLM

Until this fall, Libby Honeycutt, a 21-year-old senior at the University of South Carolina in Columbia, walked to the library in the evenings without a worry. Not any more.

There have been three rapes and several other assaults on campus since September. Now when Miss Honeycutt goes out at night, she telephones for an escort. An Alpha Phi Omega fraternity member, working in a new security program, drives her to her campus destination in a university car.

The University of South Carolina is not alone in its concern with crime. At many colleges and universities across the country there appears to be an increase in campus crime. Administrators are responding—often at student urging—with new security measures.

As a result of this concern, which is especially strong in holiday periods when campus crime is at a peak, many school security forces have rapidly grown into sizable, well equipped police departments.

There has always been some crime on the nation's 3,000 university and college campuses, ranging from indecent exposure and petty theft to armed robbery and isolated cases of murder.

Although no nationwide statistics are compiled, administrators and informed security officials believe campus crime is on the rise. They generally attribute the apparent increase to the growth of crime in adjacent communities, to larger student populations, to society's general permissiveness and to better statistical records.

These authorities can draw no clear picture of who is committing the crimes, but they believe nonstudents are involved in most cases on urban campuses.

In New York City, for example, arrest records show that the majority of serious crimes in city universities are committed by outsiders who find university buildings rich preserves on which to prey. Officials at the New York schools say theft has shown the sharpest rise amid a general increase in campus crime in recent years.

At the University of Arizona, Robert L. Houston, a vice president, said: "Twenty years ago our biggest problem on campus was a panty raid." But this year, he noted, there have been 18 assaults on students.

After several such assaults at Rutgers University, a group of students last month disrupted a Board of Governors meeting and staged a sit-in at a dean's office to demand additional security.

There were five rapes at the University of California at Santa Barbara in 1970 compared to none the year before. The crime rate of Colorado State University doubled in 1970, with $10,000 in property stolen in November alone.

Rutgers reported one armed robbery in 1969 and 13 in 1970. At Harvard, where officials began keeping figures this fall, more than $18,000 in property was stolen from the freshman dormitories between the opening of the school year in September and Nov. 9.

During the Stanford-Purdue football game Oct. 2, thieves took almost $3,000 in clothes, radios and stereo tape players from several rooms and cars on the Palo Alto campus. Reported theft losses there in 1969 totaled $117,757 — more than 10 times the 1965 figure.

Faced with political disruptions and the increased crime, many school, already hard-pressed financially, have had to create police departments complete with fleets of vehicles, radio networks, arsenals, student night patrols and even plainclothes detectives.

At South Carolina, security now costs almost $30 a year for each of the 15,000 students. Thirty-seven policemen (three times the 1968 force) patrol the 206-acre urban campus, each packing a .38-caliber Colt.

Even so, Miss Honeycutt said, "I just never go out alone at night anymore. The girls are just too scared."

Instead, as posters throughout the women's dormitories urge, she and perhaps 60 or 75 other women nightly use Alpha Phi Omega's free car service. In addition, members of Pi Kappa Alpha are on call to walk with women on campus after dark.

More Funds Sought

"In effect," said George A. Key, security director, "we're covering a small city of 20,000 people with all the attendant problems."

Mr. Key said it was difficult to solve such problems in the open atmosphere of an urban university campus. During the 12 months ending last June 30, he reported, $60,289 in property was stolen on campus. Only $8,641 worth was recovered.

The university recently spent $200,000 to illuminate some dark areas, to fence in others and to clear trees and shrubs that formed excellent hiding places for would-be attackers.

The trustees will seek $117,000 more from the Federal Government and $1-million from the state for further security measures.

Two university buses provide nightly transportation, and co-eds may park after dark in no-parking zones that are closer to their rooms than the lots. Many women take self-defense courses, while others carry sharpened nail files or small cans of irritant spray for protection.

On the night of Nov. 18, largely at the initiative of Howard Comen, an energetic junior, four casually dressed students began patrolling the campus from 8 P.M. to 2 A.M.

Equipped with flashlights and radios, they report anything suspicious to the campus police. In recent days they sighted a break-in at a gym, some unauthorized peddlers, a stolen auto and a leaking gasoline tank on a parked car.

"We're just another pair of security-conscious eyes on campus," said Rick Poznikc, a junior who joined the force after a friend was raped.

Although sexual assaults arouse the most fear and emotion, the major campus crime problem is theft. Students tell of thefts from their rooms even during brief walks to the drinking fountain down the hall.

"The smaller the item the faster it moves," said one policeman. Most popular these days are stereo tape players, radios, television sets, purses, wallets, clothing and office machinery.

The reasons for the rise in campus crime are varied.

There are more students and buildings to guard.

Full-time enrollment this fall was 5.8 million, or 2 million more than in 1960.

Students are generally more affluent than their parents' generation was, and they have more valuable property, such as record players and cars.

More students and outsiders need money to buy drugs, officials say. Many transients are attracted by campus life styles.

There are fewer restrictions on students—at many schools women's hours have been eliminated—and this has resulted in more time when dormitories, once locked throughout the night, are open to intruders.

John Marchant, president of the International Association of College and University Security Directors, said part of the increase was due to better reporting by an increasingly professional corps of campus policemen.

The long-term effects of the crime and new security steps are difficult to assess. They are diverting thousands of dollars from educational needs.

For instance, officials at Holy Cross, in the light of recent crimes, revised upward their estimates of the cost of admitting women. More guards and lights will be necessary, they decided.

Fear for Freedom

Others in the academic world are beginning seriously to fear that crime and the campus reaction to it will mean less openness and freedom in the universities.

A number of schools, including South Carolina and Rutgers, already check the identities of all persons entering and leaving certain buildings.

"I think campuses are on the verge of tightening up, said Audie Shuler, security chief at the University of Florida in Gainesville, who is regretfully considering several "very severe security measures" to help his 55 men guard the school's 3,600 acres.

One step would involve sealing off little-used portions of the campus at night. A group of buildings would be enclosed by a steel fence, and the perimeter would be regularly checked by armed patrols.

"Nobody would buy such a plan now," the chief said, "but in another year or so I think they would. It's the least expensive way."

U.S. Crime Insurance Found Failing

By JOHN HERBERS
Special to The New York Times

WASHINGTON, Nov. 12—The Federal Government's new crime insurance program, designed to arrest decay in the central cities. has proved so far to be unsuccessful, according to many involved with it.

A check of cities where the insurance is for sale and interviews with Federal administrators showed that many businessmen and residents in high-crime neighborhoods had never heard of the system, which covers losses from robbery, burglary and larceny. And those who have heard of the program, which went into effect Aug. 1, generally consider the rates too high and the regulations too restrictive to be worthwhile.

The number of policies sold at the end of October totaled less than 18,000, a figure far below that expected and hoped for by the Department of Housing and Urban Development, which administers the program.

Further, attempts to implement the program have demonstrated deep distrust of Federal efforts in crime-ridden areas. They have also disclosed the indifference of the insurance industry to the Government's endeavor to provide coverage in high crime districts that the industry had abandoned as too risky.

Under the program, policies are offered through private brokers and agents to commercial establishments and residents to cover losses from robbery, burglary and larceny at rates considerably below those of the private industry.

The plan was enacted by Congress in 1970 as one means of halting the flight of businesses and residents from the central cities. There were many reports that merchants could no longer stay in business because they could not buy crime insurance at any price or could not afford the high rates even when available.

Generally, the insurance companies had stopped selling policies in those areas because of the high incidence of losses from robberies and burglaries. It was decided that the Federal Government would provide the insurance at rates that small-business men and moderate-income people could afford.

What has happened is one more example of failure to shape Government programs in such a way that they will be effective in the slums. George K. Bernstein, a Federal insurance administrator, said he was deeply disappointed in the record so far but that "we are going to make whatever changes are necessary to make this work."

One indication of what is wrong came from Robert R. Lavelle, who described himself as a "black businessman in the heart of Pittsburgh's ghetto." He released a copy of a letter he wrote to Mr. Bernstein shortly after the program went into effect.

Mr. Lavelle operates a real estate agency and is executive vice president of the only black savings and loan company in western Pennsylvania.

He has chosen to keep his business in the poverty neighborhood, he said, "to provide hope, inspiration and aspiration to young black kids to stay in school and see a business that they can identify with and work for."

Mr. Lavelle said that in a two-and-a-half-year period he had had eight burglaries and three holdups. The first three burglaries were covered by insurance, but then the company canceled the policy. He heard about the Federal insurance plan being enacted and made a speech saying "how wonderful this is going to be."

But when the rate schedule came, he said, "I just couldn't believe it.

"Under this plan it would cost me over $200 a year to insure my business for $1,000, he said. "This, in addition to a $100 deductible provision. A merchant in Mount Lebanon, a close suburb, with an office like mine probably pays $25 for the same type [private] coverage for which I am required to pay $200.

Mr. Lavelle said that the day after he wrote the letter his business was held up again.

"A ghetto homeowner in our area will pay $40 for $1,000 crime insurance. This contrasts with a [private] $12,000 homeowner policy covering everything for $45" outside the high-crime districts.

"Even if I can afford this, it would destroy my integrity to have to pay it," Mr. Lavelle wrote.

In Washington, the situation is cast in a different light. The legislation calls for "affordable rates" to be set by the Department of Housing and Urban Development. The rates, based on crime statistics from the Federal Bureau of Investigation, vary from one metropolitan area to another but are uniform within an area. Mr. Lavelle is right, however, in that he would pay much more than his suburban counterpart insured by a private company.

The Federal rates are lower for small businesses. In Baltimore, for example, a business with $25,000 annual gross sales or less could buy the first $1,000 of coverage for $130 and a $100 deductible amount. But two agents say they advise prospective clients not to buy if they can do better through self-insurance, banking the money against possible loss.

It is not known how much the program will cost the Government, if anything. Apparently it will not be much under present rates, because there are no plans to ask for an appropriation to cover losses.

Insurance is available in nine states and the District of Columbia having cities where private or state insurance is not available: Connecticut, Illinois, Maryland, Massachusetts, Missouri, New York, Ohio, Pennsylvania and Rhode Island. California and Michigan have state insurance that fills the same purpose.

Policies are being placed through the private insurance industry. Contracts were awarded to the Aetna Casualty & Surety Company, the American Universal Insurance Company and the Insurance Company of North America on the basis of competitive bids. They service brokers and agents who sell the policies that are commissioned.

Mr. Bernstein said his office had publicized the insurance in a number of ways, including working through professional organizations. But nowhere does the insurance industry appear to be pushing the policy.

In New York State, where about 800 policies have been sold, mostly in New York City, agents and brokers indicated that the industry was not interested in pushing the insurance as it would have been had the industry initiated it.

Rural Crime Spreads Fear and Distrust

By B. DRUMMOND AYRES Jr.

Special to The New York Times

PERRY, Iowa, Jan. 15 — There was a time when the Durwood Scheibs left the front door of their farm home unlocked day and night and offered a steamy cup of coffee and a cheery "Hello, there!" to any stranger coming up their muddy lane to break their isolation.

No more.

Today, the big, windowless door stays solidly bolted shut round the clock and strangers are inspected cynically through a peephole, then greeted over an intercom with a cold, metallic: "Who are you and what do you want?"

The Scheibs have transformed their once-peaceful country home into a fortified camp because of a sharp increase in crime in rural America. It is not just an increase in such routine rural crime as cattle rustling and grain stealing but one in more fearful things like robbery, burglary and assault.

In fact, it is so serious that farm folk everywhere are abandoning traditionally trusting ways and adopting the fears, suspicions and protective measures most often associated with their city cousins.

When night closes in here, vapor lamps automatically flash on, pushing back the darkness with a brilliant ring of liminescence and adding a whiter-than-white patina to the Scheibs's home and the small collection of sheds and storage barns just beyond the kitchen door.

A shaggy mongrel dog is turned loose to sniff the cold prairie wind and to prowl about the soggy, stubble-strewn corn fields that stretch half a mile to the next farm and then on toward the granaries and high-rise office buildings of Des Moines, a 40-minute drive to the southeast.

Window locks and door latches are checked once more — along with a shotgun.

The Scheibs became victims of the crime rise about a year ago, just at the end of a decade in which the crime rate in farm areas more than doubled, from 4.2 incidents per 1,000 residents in 1960 to 9.3 incidents per 1,000 residents in 1970. (It was also a decade in which the crime rate in cities rose even more rapidly, from 13.3 incidents per 1,000 residents in 1960 to 34 incidents per 1,000 residents in 1970).

One chilly February evening, two men wearing ski masks and brandishing pistols burst through the Scheibs' front door — then unlatched—robbed the couple of $55, bound them with torn sheets, pushed them down, fired two shots into the floor nearby, ripped out the phone, then took the Scheibs' pickup and sped off into the darkness.

"It was awful, just awful," said Mrs. Scheib.

Since that night, about 20 other farm couples within a 75-mile radius of Perry have been robbed in a similar manner, possibly by the same masked bandits. Each time the two men have taken only cash, and each time they have gone through the same routine with their victims, from tying them up and pushing them about to cutting phone lines and escaping without leaving substantial clues.

As a result, there is an almost visible ring of apprehension—some would say terror —in the countryside surrounding Perry, a town of 6,500 people with the usual mid-America collection of neat frame houses radiating out toward flat fields from a tight nucleus of squat, brick stores.

"A lot of people are about ready to shoot first and ask questions later," says Deputy Sheriff Kim Sylvester of Dallas County, the county where the first of the robberies took place. He continues:

"It's gotten so serious that whenever I drive up to a farm home at night, I turn on my red roof flashers at the bottom of the lane, just so everybody will know who I am.

"Half a dozen years ago, when I first put on my badge, this was about the most friendly and open place I'd ever seen. Things sure have backed around."

Elsewhere in rural America these days, the story that Deputy Sheriff Sylvester tells is much the same, though the level of fear in other places is probably not as high since few farm areas have experienced as many robberies as Perry.

Nevertheless, most farmers in the United States now have their favorite tales of crime in the countryside — of a television set lifted from the house while they were out plowing, of half a dozen hogs that disappeared in the night, of a disk harrow hauled out of the middle of a field, of a bandit who held up a crossroads store.

Country criminals have even taken to stealing walnut trees, some of which are worth several thousand dollars if suitable for veneer.

There is no single explanation for the rapid rise in rural crime.

Law officers speak of the "permissiveness," the "weak laws" and the shortages in manpower and money so often mentioned by the city police.

They note, too, that the steady decrease in farm population — 2,000 farmers go out of business every week—has left fewer people around to keep an eye on things.

And they point out that superhighways and hardtop back roads that have made it easier for the farmer to get to the city with his products have also made it easier for the city thief to visit the farmer.

"We arrest a city boy out here three or four times a month," says Sheriff John Wright of Dallas County. "More and more of them figure there's a quick dollar to be made by knocking off a farmer."

How many dollars rural crime costs annually nationwide is almost impossible to compute. Some counties and states keep records and some do not.

The best estimate in Iowa, offered by the State Crime Commission, puts yearly losses in agricultural products alone at about $4-million. That estimate, of course, leaves a big question mark over the figure for losses in such items as cash, disk harrows and television sets.

There are also hidden costs in rural crime.

The automatic vapor lamps that now illuminate Durwood Scheib's barnyard and the barnyards of thousands of other American farmers burn up about $60 worth of current a year each. An extra set of window and door locks costs $10 to $20. And a good gun can cost anywhere from $25 to $125.

Currently, the Timberline Sports Shop here in Perry is doing a brisk business in pistols, rifles and shotguns. Ron Bronnenberg, the store's owner, says:

"Sales to farmers are up from a third to a half. Nobody makes any bones about why he's buying."

POLL FINDS A RISE IN FEAR OF CRIME

The number of people who express fear of walking alone in their own neighborhood at night has risen sharply, particularly in smaller cities, over the last four years, according to the latest Gallup Poll.

Nearly six out of every 10 women interviewed, 58 per cent, said they were afraid to go out alone at night, an increase of 14 per cent from the answers to a similar question asked in 1968. Nationally, 4 per cent of the men and women said they were afraid, an increase of 10 per cent from last time.

Those interviewed who live in cities with a population of from 2,500 to 50,000 showed the greatest percentage increase of those experiencing fear, up 19 per cent from 1968, as compared with increases of 11 per cent for cities with a population from 50,000 to 500,-000 and a rise of 9 per cent in cities with a population over 500,000.

The question asked nationwide by the Gallup survey of 1,478 persons over 18 years of age was as follows:

"Is there any area right around here—that is, within a mile — where you would be afraid to walk alone at night?"

The survey also showed that 35 per cent of those interviewed believe there is more crime in their communities than there was a year ago. Those believing there is "about the same" amount of crime number 42 per cent, while 11 per cent say they believe there is "less" crime now.

Following is a table released by the Gallup organization that summarizes the responses of all persons interviewed regarding what factors they believe are behind the high crime rate:

Laws are too lenient/
  penalties not stiff enough .25
Drugs/drug addiction 21
Lack of supervision
  by parents 13
Not enough jobs/poverty 13
Too much permissiveness
  in society 10
Lack of proper law
  enforcement 8
Ill feelings between groups/
  races 7
Lack of responsibility among
  younger people/disrespect
  for law 6
People have too much
  money/luxury 4
All other responses 23
No opinion 10

The total adds up to more than 100 per cent since some persons gave more than one reason.

April 23, 1972

Park Rangers to Get Guns

SAN FRANCISCO, June 25 (AP) — California's state park rangers will begin carrying guns this week for the first time. Jack Smyre, the park system's new police chief, said that side-arms were being issued starting July 1 as a "precautionary" measure against urban crimes of violence spreading to the outdoors.

June 26, 1972

After You're Mugged

By CAREY McWILLIAMS

The worst thing about a mugging is the shock of it—the sense of personal outrage. I was mugged recently in the elevator of a twelve-story loft building—now used for offices—at 5 P.M. on a weekday by four young blacks. Normal building traffic was still moving in and out at that hour and it simply did not occur to me that I should not step into the elevator with these rather clean-cut appearing young men. I was so surprised that I could not believe it when they slammed me against one wall of the elevator and demanded my wallet.

In fact I was so surprised that I foolishly blurted out: "What the hell goes on here?" which was interpreted as being hostile as well as uncooperative. So by the time the elevator—a slow-motion antique — had descended from the sixth to the first floor, my wallet had been ripped from my pants pocket and I had been worked over in a most professional manner. At the ground floor I was given a final clout which knocked me out for several seconds. I came to on the floor of the elevator with an empty wallet and miraculously undamaged glasses nearby.

Physically I did not fare too badly: a gorgeous black eye, some minor cuts and bruises, and a triangular fracture of the cheek bones. Not particularly painful injuries and no serious damage. But the shock was devastating. At nearby St. Vincent's, the delayed shock reaction provoked a spell of vomiting. By the time I was released, around 10 P.M., I could hardly keep my eyes open and yawned as though I had not slept for a week. I am told this is a fairly typical shock reaction. Several muggings have occurred in the Upper West Side apartment where we live—most of them in elevators. If I had been mugged in one of these elevators, I believe my reaction might have been different and the shock less severe. Certainly I would not have been so surprised.

Since the mugging, interviewers have inquired if the experience has caused me to modify in any way my thinking about racial issues. It has not nor will it. A fair share of the messages of sympathy that I have received have come from friends, neighbors and acquaintances who happen to be black. Some have been from individuals I don't know but who have identified themselves as being black.

One note reads: "I'm a black man and it happened to me and my date July 28th. Three 'brothers' held knives at my throat and took my vacation money, $100. My attitudes have not been affected but my friend has become very very bitter toward her 'black brothers.'"

248

Some messages have been of a different character. A few fall into the "this should teach you a lesson" category; others have taken me to task for being a "spokesman" for racial minorities. The truth is that I have never fancied myself as a spokesman for any group. One phone caller—a resident of the West Village—said that it served me right for being a supporter of Mayor John Lindsay!

On reflection, has the experience, I wonder, subtly changed my outlook or likely mode of behavior? I am not consciously aware of any mutations of this kind. But what would happen if the down elevator stopped at the sixth floor and a couple of husky young blacks were in it? Would I step in or would I suddenly remember that I had forgotten something in the office? The experience has not happened so I do not know how I would react. It might depend on circumstances—the hour, the appearance of the other occupants, how much of a hurry I was in, whether it was pay day or how I happened to feel at the moment.

But I think I would step in. I know that I do not want to live with the fear of blacks—any blacks—in or out of elevators.

September 29, 1972

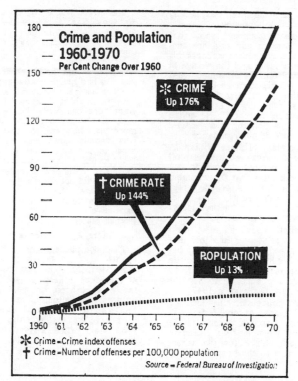

Crime and Population 1960-1970
Per Cent Change Over 1960

✳ **CRIME** Up 176%

✝ **CRIME RATE** Up 144%

POPULATION Up 13%

✳ Crime = Crime index offenses
✝ Crime = Number of offenses per 100,000 population

Source = Federal Bureau of Investigation

The New York Times/Jan. 15, 1973

January 15, 1973

Stennis Is Shot in Robbery In Front of Home in Capital

By JAMES T. WOOTEN

Special to The New York Times

WASHINGTON, Wednesday, Jan. 31—Senator John C. Stennis was shot here last night in an apparent robbery on the sidewalk in front of his home.

The 71-year-old Democrat from Mississippi underwent more than six hours of surgery at the Walter Reed Army Hospital. A hospital spokesman said the operation ended at 2:25 this morning but did not say what the Senator's condition was.

Mr. Stennis' press secretary said that he had been shot in the left side of the chest and left thigh and earlier described his condition as "stable."

Senator Lloyd M. Bentsen Jr., Democrat of Texas, said after leaving the office of Gen. William Moncrief, director of the hospital, "It's very serious, extremely serious, it really is."

A spokesman for the District of Columbia police said the Senator had told officers that he was wounded by two young men who took his wallet, 25 cents and his watch and had then said, "We're going to shoot you."

A hospital official said surgery was being performed by "the first team." Edd Jussely, the Senator's press secretary, told reporters that one bullet had entered his chest on the left side, just below the nipple, and had lodged in his back, while the other bullet had entered his left thigh and had fragmented.

Senator Stennis and his wife had attended a reception for the National Guard Association near the Capitol and were returning home when the shooting occurred.

The police said that Mrs. Coy Stennis had apparently preceded the Senator into their $70,000 home at 3609 Cumberland Street in Northwest Washington and did not see her husband wounded. The Senator, according to the police, made his way from the sidewalk up several steps and into the house after he was shot.

His briefcase and overcoat were still on a grassy strip an hour after he was shot as the police and agents of the Federal Bureau of Investigation swarmed through the neighborhood.

A 1971 law makes it a Federal crime to assault, kidnap or kill a member of Congress

and allows the F.B.I. to enter such a case immediately.

President Nixon spoke by telephone with Mrs. Stennis at the hospital. Senator James O. Eastland, the wounded legislator's colleague from Mississippi; Senator Henry M. Jackson, the Washington Democrat, and Representative Jamie L. Whitten, also of Mississippi, waited at the hospital while the surgery was performed.

All three, along with Mrs. Mildred Ward, the Senator's long-time personal secretary, met with General Moncrief.

A survey of his neighbors on the tree-lined street indicated that there were no eyewitnesses among them, but the police said that Mrs. Robert J. Best, who lives nearby, had seen two men running from the scene and getting into a parked car.

Notified at 7:40 P.M.

The shooting occurred sometime before 7:40 P.M., the time the police recorded their first notification, and officers arrived at the cream-colored, brick house shortly before the District of Columbia fire department ambulance that sped the wounded Senator to the hospital.

Inspector Charles Monroe of the District of Columbia police said that the first officers on the scene had been able to speak with Senator Stennis briefly before the ambulance arrived.

The assault took place on a grassy strip just behind the

Senator's new, white Buick sedan, the police said.

In addition to some 25 Washington police officers who were on the scene within 30 minutes after the first call from the Stennis home, at least four members of the Executive Protection Service, a special force assigned to the protection of foreign diplomats, and nine F.B.I. agents were at work on the investigation.

The surrounding neighborhood is home to many foreign diplomats, and the Federal agents, huddled together two houses from the Stennises' two-story home, appeared to be deferring to the Metropolitan police.

One police officer said that there might be a connection between the assault on the Senator and a traffic accident about a half-hour later. A police car reportedly was pursuing another car that struck a pedestrian and stopped. Three men left the car and fled, a spokesman for the police said.

Other officers at the Stennis home said that there had been a burglary at a house nearby.

Meanwhile, Senator Jackson, a member of the Senate Armed Services Committee of which Mr. Stennis is the chairman, talked with reporters at the hospital and said Mrs. Stennis had spoken with him about the shooting.

After he had been shot, Senator Stennis, according to Senator Jackson, came into the house and asked his wife to call the hospital, explaining what had happened.

Senator Jackson said that Mrs. Stennis had said her husband "gave" his assailants his watch, wallet and the change in his pocket. "The bullet went through his stomach twice," he continued. "It struck his pancreas, then his intestines and lodged in his back." He added that "the Senator told his wife he'd offered no resistance."

Secretary of State William P. Rogers arrived at the hospital shortly before 10 o'clock. He told reporters that the wounded Senator "is one of the great men in our country who is responsible in part for the success of our foreign policy."

Senator Jackson also said that Mrs. Stennis had told him she heard "two pops" just before her husband came into the house where they have lived since he succeeded Senator Theodore G. Bilbo in 1947.

The police said the Senator's vital signs, except for weakening blood pressure, were strong when he was placed in the ambulance for the three-mile ride to the hospital.

The street where the shooting took place is fairly dark. A street light illuminates the corner two houses away from the Senator's home.

Mrs. Gertrude V. Sullivan, who lives across the street, said that she had heard what sounded "like two firecrackers" and "the next thing I knew, the ambulance had come." A resident of the neighborhood for more than 35 years, she said it was usually quiet and could recall no previous violence.

Inspector Monroe theorized that the Senator's assailants probably did not realize that he was anyone other than a person of affluence driving an expensive car with inaugural license plates.

More Agents Arrive

The complement of F.B.I. agents quickly increased to more than 20, some remaining at the scene, others canvassing the neighborhood for possible witnesses. Eventually, John J. McDermott, the special agent in charge of the Washington F.B.I. field office, arrived and took charge of their inquiry.

The Senator and his wife

purchased the home, soon after he arrived in Washington, because of its proximity to what were then regarded as some of the better public schools in the city.

The Stennises celebrated their 43d wedding anniversary Dec. 24. They have a son, John Hampton Stennis, a state legislator in Jackson, Miss.; a daughter, Mrs. Margaret S. Syme of Winston-Salem, N. C., and three grandchildren.

Known for his courtly and judicial demeanor throughout his quarter-century tenure in the Senate, Senator Stennis is a gray-haired, drawling, former circuit judge and prosecuting attorney from De Kalb, Miss., a small town about 40 miles from Meridan.

Over his years on Capitol Hill, he has become a dominant figure in the Government, asserting enormous influence over military matters as chairman of the Armed Services Committee.

"If there is one thing I'm unyielding and unbending on," he once said, "it is that we must have the very best

weapons." Known as a stanch conservative segregationist, the Senator also took a firm stand against and voted against a gun-control bill in the Senate.

In Mississippi, Gov. William Waller said: "We are anxiously awaiting news about the condition of Senator Stennis as is the rest of the nation. Our prayers are with him in this tragic hour."

Associated Press
Senator John C. Stennis

January 31, 197

Crowd Chases and Beats Slayer Unconscious Here

100 Pursue Gunman

By MICHAEL T. KAUFMAN

A drunken gunman was beaten unconscious by a crowd of residents of West 134th Street yesterday morning after he shot and killed one man and wounded two of the dead man's brothers.

A few hours later, 30 cab drivers chased the suspects in the robbery of a gypsy cab, cornered them in the Bronx and beat them severely before the police arrived.

The two incidents appeared to lend support to the hopes expressed last month by high police officials who said they saw signs of a trend among New Yorkers toward involving themselves in the welfare of their neighbors.

The police officials had expressed that hope after three incidents in which civilians pursued and detained suspects in street crimes and turned them over to the police. The police officials had cited as the low point of New Yorkers' involvement with one another the Kitty

Genovese case of March, 1964, in which 38 neighbors in Kew Gardens, Queens, heard or watched but did nothing while a killer stalked a young woman in three attacks.

Last month and again yesterday, however, the police pointed out that there was a difference between public-spirited apprehension of a suspect and mob vengeance.

It was 2:45 A.M. when the lone gunman, identified by the police as 29-year-old Daniel Nenaya, weaved his way up 134th Street onto the block between Amsterdam and Columbus Avenues.

Suddenly, he stopped and reportedly shouted: "I'm going to kill everyone on 134th Street."

The police could not say how many shots were fired. However, the bullets went in the direction of the three brothers, who were standing in front of their house at No. 527.

Mario Morel, 23 years old, was hit in the chest and died on the way to Knickerbocker Hospital. Pio Morel, 22, was struck in the stomach. His condition at Knickerbocker was listed as serious. Candido Morel, 19, was wounded in the left wrist and was listed as in good condition.

In response to the shots and to the shouts that followed, the police said, the Morel's neighbor's raced into the street in pursuit of the gunman.

By the time the police arrived in response to an emergency phone call, the suspect was unconscious and the crowd was dispersing. Mr. Nenaya, who lives at 504 West 141st Street, had been kicked repeatedly and beaten.

The police said the gun used in the shooting had disappeared. One officer said a member of the crowd might have taken it.

Mr. Nenaya was also taken to Knickerbocker Hospital, where his condition was listed as satisfactory. He was booked at the hospital and charged with homicide, felonious assault and possession of a dangerous weapon.

The second chase began after Kenneth Dean, a gypsy-cab driver, reported by phone to the dispatcher at the L and M Car Service, for which he worked, that three men he had picked up as passengers had robbed him of $16 at gunpoint and had seized his cab.

This occurred at 4:40 A.M. at 135th Street and Amsterdam Avenue. Within a few minutes the police were notified, as were other cab drivers, who were told of the incident by the dispatcher using the radio.

Within half an hour of the robbery, a driver reported seeing the stolen cab at 170th Street and Amsterdam Avenue. The chase was on. Some 30 cabs from Harlem and the South

Bronx followed the stolen one onto the Cross Bronx Expressway, finally encircling it and forcing it to stop at Webster and Clay Avenues.

One of the three men inside jumped out firing a revolver and escaped. The two others, however, were set upon by the cabbies, who beat them severely before the police arrived to rescue them.

The two, identified as Eugene Chestung, 30 years old, of 451 East 140th Street, the Bronx; and James Lee, of 2641 Third Avenue, the Bronx, were taken to Fordham Hospital. Mr. Lee escaped from an X-ray room of the hospital, jumping 20 feet to the pavement. Mr. Chestung was admitted with head and chest injuries and was booked on charges of robbery, grand larceny and possession of stolen weapons.

A third incident of public involvement was reported by the police yesterday, but the object of the crowd's wrath in that case was the police, not the suspect.

At 10 P.M. Saturday, the police said, two officers attempted to arrest a man, identified as Eugene Green, 20, for allegedly swinging a three-foot metal pipe during the Mt. Carmel Feast, a celebration held at Pleasant Avenue at 116th Street.

The police said about 100 people began pushing the officers in defense of Mr. Greene.

Mr. Greene was charged with possession of a dangerous instrument, felonious assault, resisting arrest and riot.

July 23, 1

Homicide No. 700: An Ordinary Man (With a Gun) Cracks

On Dec. 9, a 44-year-old auto worker named Rendell McBride shot and killed his 42-year-old wife, Magnolia, in a quarrel in their home. It was homicide No. 700 of the year for Detroit, a new high for what has come to be called "Murder Capital, U.S.A." It was also a striking, almost classic, illustration of the way most American murders occur.

Last year there were 693 homicides in Detroit, or about one for every 2,500 people—the highest rate among the nation's 25 largest cities, and almost double the rate in New York.

But most such killings do not take place on the street or as a result of robberies or rapes or gang murders or kidnappings. They result from explosions of anger and frustration in people who are in many ways ordinary folk. Commonly, the killer has no prior criminal record.

Both in Detroit and in the nation at large, roughly three-quarters of all homicides in which the circumstances are known are committed as a result of quarrels between relatives or acquaintances, often at home. Usually, both the victim and the killer are black. Two times out of three, the weapon is a handgun.

The McBride case exhibits all of those characteristics. Here is the story behind Homicide No. 700. It is reconstructed from interviews with relatives and acquaintances of the McBrides, with law enforcement officers, and with the defendant himself.

By WILLIAM K. STEVENS
Special to The New York Times

DETROIT, Dec. 25—A few minutes after 7 o'clock that night, the phone rang in the office of the Controlled Atmosphere Processing Corporation, where an overtime shift was rushing to turn out tempered steel parts for 1974 automobiles.

"Is Vic there?" Rendell McBride asked.

"No, this is A. J.," said A. J. Martin, a foreman.

"I just called you, brother Jay, to tell you I shot my wife."

Long pause.

"Mac, you've got to be kidding," Mr. Martin said. When Mr. McBride said that he wasn't, Mr. Martin marveled to himself at how cool his fellow employe sounded. The very coolness scared him a little.

"Have you called the police?" Mr. Martin asked.

"Brother Jay, as soon as I get off the phone with you I'm going to call them."

And he did.

From then on it was what the police call a "platter case" — open and shut. Mr. McBride pleaded guilty to second-degree murder at his arraignment on Dec. 11. He was released from jail that day on his own recognizance to go back to the two-story, gray-shingled house at 15788 Idaho Street, where he and his wife had lived together; where a picture of John F. Kennedy greets a visitor inside the front door, and the walls are alive with pictures of butterflies and ballerinas and landscapes and the Rev. Dr. Martin Luther King Jr. and the Kennedys; where artificial flowers abound, and where clear plastic covers the furniture, and all is clean, comfortable and middle-class.

Mr. McBride himself is a taut, wiry man, perhaps 5 feet 7, weighing 128 pounds, with a thin neck and a sparse mustache, his hairline receding in front and a bald spot widening in back. Heavily lidded eyes give him a deceptively sad-sleepy look.

His story has its roots in the cotton country of northwestern Mississippi.

He was born there, the son of a farmer, went through the sixth grade, worked in a sawmill, then drove a truck for a living and farmed on the side. And for a time he owned a small cafe in the northwest Mississippi hamlet of Eupora.

Law enforcement officials in those parts say there is no criminal record on Mr. McBride (nor is there one in Detroit), even though he had a reputation for being highstrung and quick-tempered.

Other factors that seem to have led to this month's killing appear to have had their roots in those days in Mississippi.

There was Mr. McBride's belief in "hoodoo," the casting of voodoo-like spells or hexes, a belief that was to contribute to the killing of Dec. 9. Such beliefs are common among some Southerners, particularly blacks, and they have been transplanted to the North.

There was the gun. A .25-caliber automatic pistol of Italian make, a Galesi by brand name, small, easily concealed, with a blue-steel finish and a white plastic grip and an eight-shot magazine.

Mr. McBride said he bought it for about $45 seven or eight years ago at a general store in Eupora because he was afraid of getting held up while driving the truck.

Met a Girl

And it was down home that Mr. McBride met Magnolia Bell, a cheerful young girl, one of 14 children of a minister. The future man and wife met as teen-agers and began courting.

But the Bell family, believing the McBrides to be too volatile, too prone to combativeness, counseled against the relationship. "Mag," as she was called, stopped seeing Rendell.

In time Mr. McBride married another woman and had seven children. He later divorced his first wife. She died last May, and Mr. McBride's four youngest children came to live with him in Detroit.

By the early nineteen-fifties Magnolia Bell had grown to handsome womanhood, but with a recurrent weight problem. (She weighed 210 pounds when she was killed.)

In 1951 or 1952 Miss Bell left her parents' farm outside Eupora and headed to Detroit in search of a job, moving in at first with a sister, Elizabeth, who had preceded her.

Migration from South

Detroit today is largely a city of people much like that: proud, plucky blacks who, beginning in the forties, pulled up their roots in the South and came to Detroit by the thousands in search of prosperity, swelling in numbers until today they account for half the city's population.

At first glance, it might seem as if the massive influx of blacks from a sometimes violent rural society is responsible for Detroit's soaring homicide rate. Indeed, although many blacks have achieved middle-class affluence, there are still large numbers of poorer blacks, possibly more prone to violence. Detroit did have race riots in 1943 and 1967; and some observers believe that the murder rate here has jumped upward because of an upsurge in gun-buying after the 1967 riot. But the truth is that no one has really tied down the cause of the homicide surge.

Hurt Her Back

None of the violence in the city seemed to touch Magnolia McBride after she came North. She worked as a domestic for a time, and eventually landed a job packing chrome pieces for an automobile manufacturing supplier. Later still she went to work on the assembly line at Chrysler's big Hamtramck assembly plant.

After a while she was able to buy the two-family house at 15788 Idaho.

Things went well until she hurt her back lifting bucket seats on the assembly line and couldn't work anymore.

Soon after, in 1971, Rendell McBride, his first marriage heading for divorce, came North in search of better money. He boarded with Mrs. Alma Marshall, Magnolia's oldest sister.

He worked and prospered at Controlled Atmosphere Processing, where his job was to use a broom to push piles of small metal stampings onto a conveyor belt. Most recently, he was making nearly $150 a week, and, with overtime, $250 some weeks. He is described variously by fellow employes as the most meek, unassuming man," and "hyperactive; always had to be doing something."

Mr. McBride and Miss Bell started seeing each other again, and one day Mr. McBride said to her sister, "Miz Marshall, what would you think about it if I'd get to be your brother-in-law?"

Mrs. Marshall was against

it. She insisted that Mr. Mc-Bride did not have his divorce and was not free even to court, let alone marry.

And she so advised her sister, repeatedly.

Married on Christmas Eve

But Mr. McBride eventually prevailed, and he married Miss Bell on Christmas Eve, 1971.

Married life was tolerable for a time. In his leisure, Mr. McBride would visit his wife's brothers nearby, play his guitars, listen to blues records, work around the yard and make small improvements on the house.

But all along, bad feelings were building in Mr. McBride.

The root of the bad feelings appears to have been his growing conviction that the strong-willed Bell sisters were trying to run his life, to keep him from being a full man.

First, they had tried to discourage Miss Bell from marrying him. Later, he wanted Mrs. McBride to put the title to the house in his name.

Wanted to Move

"Mrs. Marshall," he pleaded with his wife's sister, "don't you think she ought to let me be the man of the house?" But his wife refused to sign the house over, and Mr. McBride was convinced that the sisters-in-law had a role in the refusal.

Mr. McBride tried, to no avail, to persuade his wife to move to another neighborhood, or back down South, away from his sisters-in-law.

And finally, he tried for months — and was still trying on Dec. 9 — to get Mrs. McBride to evict a downstairs tenant. The tenant was undesirable to him, and he wanted a friend, known as Early Boy, to move in. But Mrs. McBride saw nothing wrong with the tenant and would not evict him.

'That Society Stuff'

Mr. McBride felt, rightly or wrongly, that his sisters-in-law were influencing his wife's judgment, and thereby harming his own interest. And the way they exerted influence, he believed, was through a "society" that put "stuff" — that is, the hoodoo — on people. "You put stuff on her so she won't do what I say," he once told Mrs. Marshall.

For some weeks before Dec. 9, Mr. McBride had not worked because he was ill. Bronchitis and pulmonary emphysema, said the medical diagnosis. His employers say he was a man who wanted to

Mrs. Magnolia McBride and a photo of the type of gun with which she was shot. Below: Detectives' file card on the case, showing it was Detroit's 700th homicide in 1973.

work badly, that he once tried unsuccessfully to come back to work without the doctor's permission.

If all the evidence is accurate, it adds up to the picture of a tense, hyperactive man who, on Dec. 9, was nursing a long-time frustration of the ego, convinced that he was powerless against supernatural forces; who was reduced by illness to inactivity with no outlet for his nervous energy.

Sunday, Dec. 9, began peacefully enough.

The McBride family went out early to buy clothes for Mr. McBride's two sons, Billy Joe, 11, and Danny, 9.

But about 4 o'clock in the afternoon, Mr. and Mrs. McBride began quarreling about the downstairs tenant. There was some shoving, but no real violence.

About 5, Mr. McBride and his four children went over to Early Boy's to help him clean house. Mrs. McBride went upstairs to a small furnished attic to rest.

Mr. McBride returned at about 6:30 and made a telephone call to a brother-in-law asking him to come over. He sat down for five or 10 minutes to join his children in watching the Dallas-Washington football game on television. He got up to make another telephone call, but Mrs. McBride was on the upstairs phone. He slammed the phone down and went up to the attic.

There is only Mr. McBride's version of the argument that followed. According to him he told his wife to come down and prepare dinner. "Don't come up here and order me around," Mrs. McBride said, according to her husband.

'I Just Lost My Temper'

With that, the months of smoldering bad feeling exploded into flame. Mr. McBride says that his wife hit him, that he hit back, and that she threw a flower pot at him. The noise brought Billy Joe upstairs to see what was going on. According to Billy Joe's testimony in court, the 210-pound Mrs. McBride pushed the 128-pound Mr.

McBride down the stairs. He crashed onto a landing eight or 10 steps down.

That is when the .25-caliber Galesi came out of Mr. McBride's pocket. He fired one shot at his wife. Mrs. McBride grabbed Billy Joe and hid behind him. He broke loose and ran down the stairs. Mr. McBride emptied the gun into his wife.

"I just lost my temper there," Mr. McBride told this reporter as he showed where and how he shot his wife. "I'm sorry. I was sorry right after it happened. But it had to happen."

Almost everyone connected with the case, however, agrees that it didn't have to happen. To the law enforcement officials involved, the McBride case is powerful argument, once again, for strong national gun control laws.

"If he hadn't had that gun," said Sgt. Ralph Gajewski, one of those who investigated the case, "he probably would have punched her in the nose and that would have been it."

December 26, 197

GOLDWATER SAYS HE'D CURB COURT

Also Stresses States' Rights in Swing Through South

By CHARLES MOHR
Special to The New York Times

ST. PETERSBURG, Fla., Sept. 15—Senator Barry Goldwater pledged tonight to work to overturn a series of United States Supreme Court decisions on rights of defendants in criminal prosecutions.

The Republican Presidential candidate said in a speech here that criminals were being needlessly pampered and that law and order were being sacrificed "just to give criminals a sporting chance to go free."

To achieve his end, Mr. Goldwater said that, as President, he would first use his power of appointment to Federal courts to "redress constitutional interpretations in favor of the public."

Mr. Goldwater made this pledge at the end of his first day of campaigning in the South, a region on which his election hopes and strategy rest.

Some of his supporters have been telling Southerners for months that if Mr. Goldwater is elected President, the South's interests and sensibilities would be considered in making Supreme Court and Justice Department appointments. However, none of the crowd of about 10,000 that heard Mr. Goldwater speak tonight applauded his phrase about redressing constitutional interpretation.

He was repeatedly applauded at other times, however, especially in his reference to the "pampering" of criminals.

Leaving Washington this morning, Mr. Goldwater flew to and spoke at Winston-Salem, N. C., Atlanta, Ga., and Orlando, Tampa and St. Petersburg, Fla.

Sizable and enthusiastic crowds met Mr. Goldwater and warmly cheered his statements that "I happen to believe in states' rights" and his remark that he was not one of those who believed the "South is not part of the United States."

Of the three states he visited today, however, only Florida looks especially promising to Mr. Goldwater. Georgia has never gone Republican, and North Carolina only once, to vote against Al Smith in 1928. The Roman Catholic Governor of New York favored repeal of Prohibition.

Mr. Goldwater gave his major speech tonight at Al Lang baseball field, where a generation of New York Yankee teams held spring training.

It was the first time in the campaign that Mr. Goldwater had devoted virtually an entire speech to what he called the "law and order" issue, and what his critics call the "backlash" issue.

He said that he and the Republican Vice-Presidential candidate, William E. Miller, would "use our power and influence to see that law enforcement officers, on the state and local level, get back the power to carry out their job."

To accomplish this he suggested three steps, the first being the use of his appointment power to the Federal bench to alter the liberal character of recent court decisions.

"Secondly," he said, "if the Court's decision should remain unaltered, the President has the obligation to urge amendment of the Constitution to give back to the states those powers absolutely necessary for fair and efficient administration of criminal law."

Thirdly, he said, "The President should urge Congress to consider changing some of the rules of judicial procedure in the Federal court."

He explained he had specifically in mind such rules as that established in the Mallory case, in which a Federal court in the District of Columbia held that a confession was inadmissible because of an undue delay in arraignment of the defendant.

Mr. Goldwater advanced in argument that the power to punish crime has been taken from the states by Supreme Court decisions, which he asserted had "stretched" the 14th Amendment to the Constitution

He criticized decisions that state courts must follow Federal reules of evidence, which make illegally gathered evidence inadmissible. The evidence can come from anything from wire tapping to illegal search and seizure.

Mr. Goldwater said that an "obviously guilty defendant" could be freed under such a rules of evidence, which make called the Court's ruling that "a criminal conviction should be reversed, no matter how guilty the defendant, if it were shown that some technical violation of constitutional right occurred anywhere in the course of investigation and trial.

Of the Court's logic, the Senator said that it "seems to say that a criminal defendant must be given a sporting chance to go free even though nobody doubts in the slightest that he is guilty."

Mr. Goldwater began his speech by asking how a candidate for the Presidency could "brush aside" the issue of crime and lawlessness, which he said were increasing alarmingly.

For increases in national crime he blamed, in part, "a national spectacle in the incredible case of Bobby Baker — my opponent's protege — and of Matt McCloseky, his close associate."

Except for his formal speech this evening, Mr. Goldwater generally stuck to simpler, more emotional themes during his daytime appearances.

To about 5,000 persons at an Atlanta suburban shopping center he said the "central Government has even given you a

number to replace your name—now we went to give you freedom and your name back again."

He told the crowd at Hurt Park that one of the "most dangerous hopes" today was one that believed in the validity of the Sino-Soviet ideological dispute within world Communism.

"I don't care how you spell it," said Mr. Goldwater, "it's still Communism."

In both Winston-Salem and Atlanta he strongly attacked the Supreme Court decision ordering reapportionment of state legislatures. Applause was scanty, perhaps because such cities as Atlanta have long been among the most notable victims of rural-dominated apportionment.

At Orlando, Mr. Goldwater stood in a soaking rain and attacked programs for medical care for the aged, despite Florida's high proportion of retired citizens.

He also warned his Orlando audience that there was greater danger under the Democrats than under Republicans of military bases being closed. There are two Air Force bases near Orlando and a Martin Aircraft Company production plant there.

In the tobacco center of Winston-Salem he told a crowd of between 7,000 to 8,000 gathered under a hotel balcony that Americans had material wealth "but no freedom."

He said the Federal Government was "now going to tell you what to print on the front of your cigarette pack," a reference to proposals for a health warning on cigarettes.

Several registered Democrats were among the dignitaries who greeted Mr. Goldwater during the day, and at Tampa Airport he was introduced by Mallory Horne, the Democratic Speaker of the Florida House of Representatives, who has endorsed Mr. Goldwater.

Mr. Goldwater praised him for "a rare degee of political courage."

Phoenix Crime Rate Tops New York's

By WALLACE TURNER
Special to The New York Times

PHOENIX, Sept. 17 — When Senator Barry Goldwater opened his Presidential campaign two weeks ago on the Courthouse steps at Prescott, Ariz., he treated one of his favorite themes at the beginning and at the end of his speech.

Early in the talk he promised "to restore law and order, to make our streets safe, without losing liberty." Near the end of his speech he complained that "our wives, all women, feel unsafe on the streets."

He could have been talking about Phoenix, the city where he was born, grew up, directed a business, served on the City Council and from which he drew much of the top level talent that directs his campaign.

Phoenix has one of the higher crime rates of the nation.

As assessed by the Federal Bureau of Investigation's Uniform Crime Reports, this city in the desert has much more crime in proportion to population than New York does.

The F.B.I.'s statistical comparisons are based on the crimes for each 100,000 persons. The Phoenix metropolitan area measured in the 1963 reports had a population of 816,000, while the New York metropolitan area had 11,229,000.

Higher Murder Rate

The comparison showed 2,408 crimes in Phoenix per 100,000 residents, to 1,688 in New York. The murder rate was 6.4 in Phoenix to 5.2 in New York.

In Phoenix, the forcible rape rate was 18.6, while in New York it was 8.0. In Washington, D.C., where crime reports have tainted the backdrop against which Senator Goldwater delivers some of his most stinging "crime in the street" remarks, ers some of his most stinging "crime in the street" remarks, the rape rate was 10.4, far below that of Phoenix.

The rate in Miami, like Phoenix a large resort area, was 11.5. Only Bakersfield, Calif., Chicago, Denver, Houston, Kansas City and Los Angeles exceeded the Phoenix rape rate.

Comments on these figures were made in an interview by Capt. A. F. Fairbanks, an assistant to the Phoenix chief of police.

He said. "Our weather is highly condusive to outdoor life, and this causes more crome." He said that a man weighing the question of whether to commit an armed robbery might decide differently in a winter storm in New York than in the warm sun of the Phoenix winter.

The robbery rate in New York was 65.4 against 74.9 in Phoenix.

The Phoenix Police Department came off with good marks earlier this year from a local Citizens Task Force on Crime.

The police force is small for a city of this size. It has authorized strength of 774. The study noted especially that no question of police corruption had been raised.

The group was created by the Phoenix Chamber of Commerce. Its 28 members were appointed by the chambers of commerce here and in the 10 Phoenix suburbs in Maricopa County.

The study group was broken up into small units. These held hearings around the Phoenix area, soliciting comments from public officials. The Chamber of Commerce group had no official standing, and was not financed from public funds.

When the study was finished, the chief attack made in a report was against the conduct of the Juvenile Court and Probation Department. The accusation was that the judge and probation officers were too lenient.

Coupled with this was the suggestion that the crime rate was mostly built up to its considerable height by juvenile criminal activity. It was said that 60 per cent of the crime here was by persons under 18 years of age.

After a few days someone asked how this percentage could be established when the preponderance of crime was unsolved. The suggestion that Phoenix is made up of well-behaved adults and criminaly-inclined children then was abandoned.

However, some action did result from this citizens' inquiry. The judge of the juvenile court was "rotated" into another court room, and replaced by another judge. The chief probation officer was forced out of office.

With its report rendered, the citizens group last May became the Maricopa County Citizens Committee on respect for law.

Meanwhile, Judge Francis J. Donofrio, who had defended his record as juvenile judge by arguing that he was a stern judge, was assigned to other cases. He said he had remanded 31 boys to adult court in nine months.

John Walker, who had been chief probation officer for many years, was looking for another job.

One of the first serious problems to confront the new youth court regime is a traffic case.

Two cars collided. A boy was killed. Two Mexican-American boys were in a jalopy. The boy who was killed is what is here called an "Anglo." The two Mexican-American boys have been remanded to adult court for trial. This deprives them of the special protection afforded youthful offenders.

There are three big minority groups here. About 100,000 Indians live on reservations in the state, and their law enforcement is in the hands of tribal police for minor crime and the F.B.I. for major crime.

City, county and state officials have nothing to do with Indian reservation law enforcement in Arizona.

But the Mexican-American and Negro populations are subject to law enforcement machinery which has minimal representations from their population groups.

There is concern among Negroes and Mexican-Americans about this. One observer felt that social and economic pressures were responsible for much of the crime, and he also felt that the minority groups were being given less consideration in the courts than they have a right to expect.

A Mexican-American bitterly contrasted the handling of two criminal cases. In one, a 15-year old "Anglo" boy shot and killed two Mexican-American farm workers as they stood in an irrigation ditch, then explained that he just felt like killing them.

He was confined to the Arizona mental hospital, from which he escaped and now lives in another state.

In the other case, a Mexican-American workman killed a prostitute who was an "Anglo." He was speedily tried, sentenced to death and executed.

Violent crime is no stranger in Phoenix. Two murders were committed here, both of widely known criminals, within the last 10 years.

Willie Bioff, a notorious extortionist who preyed on the movie industry, was killed in 1955 when his pickup truck exploded from a charge of dynamite. Bioff had lived here for several years under the name of William Nelson.

Three years later, Mr. and Mrs. Gustave Greenbaum were found dead in their home here, their throats cut. Greenbaum had extensive underworld connections, once operated the illegal horse race book here, and had run both the Flamingo and Riviera hotels on the Las Vegas Strip.

Neither of these murders has been solved.

Not all the vicious murders that occur here are old, either.

Last February the bodies of a Sherill, N. Y., couple were found just off the main highway at Apache Junction, a desert intersection a few miles outside the Phoenix metropolitan area. Mr. and Mrs. John R. Bertella, both in their 60's, had been shot to death, then their bodies hacked to pieces.

This crime was committed by Herbert L. Shockey, 23, who wanted to take the couple's pickup truck and camping trailer. He was caught in Nevada and returned here for trial. It was found that he had last been arrested in Phoenix for writing spurious checks and had been in prison. Shockey was convicted by a jury that recommended leniency. He is serving consecutive life sentences.

Another vicious crime committed last year still is unsolved. In this one, a 21-year-old Texas girl came to Phoenix for a vacation, and within 24 hours of her arrival she had been raped, murdered, and her body thrown into a mine shaft.

Rights Take a Back Seat

By JOHN HERBERS

WASHINGTON — There were two developments in Washington last week which seemed unrelated but which taken together tell something of the decisive, almost sudden, shift that has taken place in two political issues—crime and civil rights.

President Johnson sent to Congress a broad and detailed message on crime. He urged enactment of legislation submitted last year to subsidize state and local construction, planning, research and action in all phases of law enforcement and to ban the sale of mail order firearms. He also called for a Federal anti-riot law, for a review and revamping of narcotics laws and agencies and for stiffer penalties for traffickers in LSD and other drugs, and for renewed efforts against organized crime, juvenile delinquency and alcoholism.

Essentially, it was a call for an all-out attack on what the President termed in his State of the Union Address last month the "rising crime and lawlessness."

The other development came in the Senate where debate groaned on for the third week on a House-passed civil rights bill that would broaden the criminal laws to protect persons exercising their civil rights, chiefly in the South. Liberals won the first round by killing a Southern-sponsored substitute, but indications were that if the bill is to be passed at all a compromise will have to be reached.

In 1966, the measure was one of the least controversial portions of an omnibus civil rights package that failed in the Senate after passing the House because it contained an open housing provision. That this mild portion of it is now in trouble is an indication of the rapid decline in support for civil rights since the Voting Rights Act was passed in 1965.

Support for Law

As crime has gone up as an issue civil rights has gone down, in almost direct proportion. In 1965, there was strong support for improving through law the barriers that prevented Negroes and other minorities from achieving equality of opportunity. Now, there is possibly even stronger support for using the law to stop civil disorders and crimes against individuals.

There are good reasons for the shift that have little relation between the two issues. Crime has mounted steadily in recent years. In the first nine months of 1967, for example, robberies were up 27 per cent over the same period of 1966, murders were 16 per cent higher, aggravated assault rose 9 per cent and rape increased by 7 per cent, according to F.B.I. statistics.

Also, each summer has brought more destructive riots in the slums. In Detroit alone last year, 43 persons were killed, hundreds were injured, 5,000 left homeless and there was millions of dollars in property damage.

While this was happening, the civil rights organizations that were in full bloom in 1965 declined and fragmented. With the rise of militancy among blacks, many whites who formerly pushed civil rights bills no longer do so. Many whites and Negroes feel that economic rather than legal remedies for the Negro are now the main need.

Anti-Negro Sentiment

But this is not the full explanation. Much of the rioting and crime involves Negroes. Many Negroes believe that anti Negro sentiment is behind many of the demands for stronger police action. Almost everyone agrees that there should be better and more effective law enforcement, but what causes concern among civil libertarians is that too much emphasis may be put on police action to stop crime and disorder rather than on curing the root causes.

Certainly it is more difficult because of the disorders to obtain white support for civil rights and economic legislation that will help the disadvantaged involved in the disorders, even though such legislation is intended to strike at the cause of crime and riots. Thus the two issues feed off one another in an area with high emotional content.

The prospect for this session of Congress, then, is that much legislation will be enacted to combat crime and riots; almost certainly the main bill proposed by the Administration—to improve local police departments and court systems through Federal grants and other assistance. And it is considered highly unlikely that any broad civil rights bill will be passed pending the return of a more conducive political climate.

81% IN A POLL SEE LAW BREAKDOWN

84% Feel Strong President Would Help, Harris Says

A Louis Harris poll reported yesterday that 81 per cent of voters questioned in a national sampling agreed with the statement "law and order has broken down in this country." The poll reported only 14 per cent disagreed and 5 per cent said they were not sure.

The poll, published in The New York Post, added that 84 per cent of those queried agreed with the statement that "a strong President can make a big difference in directly preserving law and order," with 10 per cent disagreeing and 6 per cent unsure.

Mr. Harris said the sampling consisted of a cross section of 1,481 voters who were asked on Aug. 24 whether they tended to agree or disagree with those two statements and six others.

In his report, Mr. Harris said that "next to ending the war in Vietnam, the most urgent demand of American voters in this election season is to bring back a sense of law and order.'"

Asked about their thinking on causes for a breakdown of law and order, the respondents listed "organized crime" in 61 per cent of the replies; "Negroes who start riots," 59 per cent; "Communists," 56 per cent, and "anti-Vietnam demonstrators," 38 per cent.

Only 13 per cent rated "police brutality" as a major cause Mr. Harris pointed out that the survey was made before police clashes with demonstrators during the Democratic National Convention in Chicago.

However, Mr. Harris said views of Negroes and the rest of the public contrasted sharply on this point—52 per cent of Negroes, he said, consider police provocation as a major cause of disorder.

By 63 to 27 per cent, he said, the public as a whole agreed that "until there is justice for minorities there will not be law and order."

"But he added that a 58 to 22 per cent majority rejected the statement that "demands for law and order are made by politicians who are against progress for Negroes."

Law and order is the battle cry

of the campaign but

There's Always A Crime Wave— How Bad Is This One?

By FRED J. COOK

ALL public pulse-taking these days shows that average Americans—and this applies to residents of ghetto areas as well as to the more affluent, living in the suburbs—want better guarantees for personal safety and protection of property. They are wrought up by the menace of "crime." But just what do they mean by the word? There are, of course, all kinds of crime. There is organized crime, a colossal, multi-billion-dollar-a-year conspiracy that has invaded almost every stratum of American life but seems virtually ignored in the present preoccupation with the kinds of everyday crime that most directly affect the average citizen.

The man in the street today seems most concerned with ghetto riots, the violence, the burning and looting, and with the robberies and muggings that threaten his personal safety on the streets, in the subways, in the hallways of apartment houses. To the public mind, it all seems connected; it's all "crime." The reality, of course, is not so simple.

The politicians of the day, responding to this mood sometimes in outright demagoguery, sometimes in genuine concern, are making law and order the battle cry of the 1968 Presidential campaign.

The Republican candidate, Richard M. Nixon, touched it all off in his acceptance speech at Miami, charging that "some of our courts in their decisions have gone too far in weakening the peace forces as against the criminal forces." He added that, "if we are to restore order and respect for law in this country, there's one place we're going to begin: we're going to have a new Attorney General of the United States of America...."

Vice President Hubert H. Humphrey, the Democratic nominee, responded by promising to halt "rioting, burning, sniping, mugging, traffic in narcotics and disregard for law." But he argued that law enforcement must proceed hand in hand with justice and held that "the answer lies in reasoned effective action by the authorities, not in attacks on our courts, our laws or our Attorney General."

Former Alabama Gov. George C. Wallace, the odd man out of this campaign, was the real rabble rouser on the law and order issue. The United States Supreme Court was his *bête noire*, and his solution was simple: free the police of all restraint. The pat Wallace speech, repeated everywhere he goes, contains a passage that usually brings down the house. It goes like this: "If you walk out of this hotel tonight and someone knocks you on the head, *he'll* be out of jail before *you're* out of the hospital, and on Monday morning they'll try the *police*man instead of the criminal.... That's right, we gonna have a *police* state for folks who burn the cities down. They aren't gonna burn any more cities."

Even to begin to understand what

the shouting is all about, one must come to grips first with the basic reality of the crime situation as it exists today. To the fundamental question (Just how bad is it?), the answer is paradoxical to a considerable degree. Experts agree that crime today is a major problem, that it is bad and is getting worse—and yet it is perhaps no worse than it has been in some unruly eras in our past, and much of the public agitation about it results from an exaggerated idea of the degree of menace.

The President's Commission on Law Enforcement and Administration of Justice, in its report "The Challenge of Crime in a Free Society," tried last year to put the problem and some of the irrational fears about it into clear perspective. Taking a broad historical view, it found little justification for the widespread popular belief that these are the worst of times. It wrote:

"A hundred years ago contemporary accounts of San Francisco told of extensive areas where 'no decent man was in safety to walk the street after dark; while at all hours, both night and day, his property was jeopardized by incendiarism and burglary.' Teen-age gangs gave rise to the word 'hoodlum'; while in one central New York City area, near Broadway, the police entered 'only in pairs, and never unarmed.' A noted chronicler of the period declared that 'municipal law is a failure . . . we must soon fall back on the law of self preservation.' 'Alarming' increases in robbery and violent crimes were reported throughout the country prior to the Revolution. And in 1910 one author declared that 'crime, especially in its more violent forms, and among the young is increasing steadily and is threatening to bankrupt the nation.'"

The commission emphasized that there is an ebb and flow in the tide of crime much like the ebb and flow of the sea. Its study of crime statistics showed that, in the number of offenses per 100,000 population, the year 1933 in some respects rivaled our own. "The willful homicide rate has *decreased* somewhat to about 70 per cent of its high in 1933, while robbery has fluctuated from a high in 1933 to a low during World War II to a point where it is now about 20 per cent above the beginning of the postwar era," the commission wrote. "The over-all rate for violent crimes, primarily due to the increased rate for aggravated as-

sault, now stands at its highest point, well above what it has been throughout most of the period."

Turning from the past to an analysis of the present, the commission cited Federal Bureau of Investigation statistics and other studies to show that "about 70 per cent of all willful killings, nearly two-thirds of all aggravated assaults and a high percentage of forcible rapes are committed by family members, friends, or other persons previously known to their victims." The chance that the average American will suffer from a crime of violence is still relatively minimal. Robert M. Cipes, a consultant to the commission, put it this way in his recent book, "The Crime War": "The risk of death by murder is one out of 20,000, about the same as the risk of drowning. The chances of being killed in an accidental fall are twice as great as those of being murdered, and the chances of being killed in a car accident more than four times greater!"

IN view of such facts, one may well wonder how the American people as a whole have become possessed by the idea that we are faced with a veritable crime crisis. Most experts agree that much of this mood stems from the riots in recent years; the violence, the burning and looting excited fears that we were verging on anarchy. These fears have been fed by the indisputable fact that many categories of crime have been increasing steadily from year to year—a rise that, on its face, seems shocking and sensational. It is only when one examines the basis for such statistics and tries to relate the circumstances of today to those of troubled eras of the past that one becomes aware of the built-in delusions in many alarming headlines.

The one accepted crime barometer for the nation is the Uniform Crime Report of the F.B.I. But the F.B.I. started to accumulate such data only in 1930, and it has steadily expanded the number of police departments reporting and the comprehensiveness of their reports. This means, as the President's crime commission found, that a lot more crime is being *reported* today, but it does not mean that more crime in the same proportion is being *committed*. The commission found that there has always been—and there is still today—a vast reservoir of unreported crime. The fact that much more of this previously hidden crime is being re-

ported today inflates crime statistics and distorts the comparative averages.

There are at least two major causes for such distortion. In the past, in many cities, the official attitude was that ghetto crimes did not matter much; either they were not reported at all, or only sketchily reported, unless all hell broke loose. Yet it is in precisely these areas, all studies show, that crime rates soar to their highest peaks, and so today, when ghetto crime is being much more fully recorded, it is inevitable that over-all statistics reflect much more crime.

A second major distortion has resulted from the practice of some police departments in the past of deliberately understating the volume of crime in their jurisdictions, so as to make themselves look good, to cultivate the public impression that they have crime under control.

In one city, the President's commission found a secret "file 13" containing a catalogue of citizens' complaints that were not included in the official crime record. At one time, in Philadelphia, a single precinct actually had 5,000 more complaints than it officially recorded.

The F.B.I., when it becomes aware of such practices, cracks down on offending departments by refusing to publish their statistics. When this happens, reporting techniques are usually changed — and the official crime index in the particular city rises in an almost perpendicular line.

In 1949, the F.B.I. refused to accept New York Police Department statistics because it no longer believed them. The department changed its procedures, and the next year it showed a jump of 400 per cent in the number of robberies reported, and an incredible 1,300 per cent rise in the number of burglaries. But then, in the late fifties, the department again adopted a "look good, don't rock the boat" policy and began watering down the number of officially reported crimes.

"The unwritten law was," one high department official says, "that you were supposed to make things look good. You weren't supposed to report all the crime that actually took place in your precinct—and, if you did, it could be your neck. I know captains who actually lost their commands because they turned in honest crime reports."

The Lindsay administration changed all this and insisted on truth, no matter how much it hurt. The result of this change in official policy was dramatic. Reported robberies leaped from between 7,000 and 8,000 a year to about 23,000; burglaries from 40,000 to 120,000. Anyone who was not aware of the figure juggling that had previously taken place, had to assume that the city was confronted with an unprecedented crime crisis.

THE high public fever over the crime issue may be traced, in part, to such distortions and exaggerations. This does not mean that crime is not a serious problem. It is. It is on the rise in this country—and also, as the President's commission found, in nearly every highly industrialized society of Western Europe. "Since 1955," the commission wrote, "property crime rates have increased more than 200 per cent in West Germany, the Netherlands, Sweden and Finland, and over 100 per cent in France, England and Wales, Italy and Norway."

What the commission found was that an industrialized, affluent society increases the incentives for crime. There is the urbanized life in which everyone is a stranger to everyone else—and so crime may be committed with less fear of detection, the unknown criminal melting into the anonymous crowd. There is the tempting spate of products that an affluent society produces, goods that clutter the shelves of the supermarkets and discount stores, a lure to the shoplifter—and shoplifting has become one of our fastest growing crimes. There is the ever-crying need for money and more money to enjoy the bounties of the affluent society—and so white-collar thefts, the looting of a store's inventoried stock or embezzlements from the till, have become another of our fastest growing crimes. Threaded through such misdeeds is a Robin Hood-like rationale—that it is not so great a sin for the little fellow to steal from the great, big, impersonal —and wealthy—corporation. Or, as the crime commission put it: "Restraints on conduct that were effective in a more personal and rural society do not seem as effective in an impersonal society of large organizations."

This urbanization, this affluence, this impersonalized bigness help push the crime rate upward, and they have another partner: youth. All crime studies show that most crime is committed by persons in the younger age groups; the United States is now a nation in which, by 1970, half the population will be 27 or younger. Adding this element of youth to all the other factors, the President's crime commission forecast that there would probably be a continuing rise in crime rates for some years to come.

The accuracy of this prediction has now been underlined by the latest F.B.I. and city police department reports. The annual F.B.I. Uniform Crime Report, issued Aug. 26, showed a 16 per cent rise in violent crimes in 1967 over 1966, and city police department figures, compiled now on a similar basis for both years, reflected a comparable increase. Another police department computation showed that murders in the city rose in the first six months of 1968 from 346 to 436, a jump of 26 per cent.

"IN recent years," says Vincent O'Leary, now a professor at the new Graduate School of Criminal Justice in Albany and until recently director of research and special services for the National Council on Crime and Delinquency, "there has been a real upsurge in ghetto crime. Now, the riots came out of the same whirlpool—out of the same poverty-stricken, ghetto areas—but, to me, the two are quite different things. The motivations, I feel sure, are not the same at all. There is this tendency today to lump all kinds of crime together—just to denounce 'crime,' as if it was all the same thing—and then to seek one certain, simple, quick solution. To me the most dangerous thing in the whole situation is this simplistic idea."

The individual mugger, burglar or sneak thief, O'Leary points out, takes to crime as the only means available to him to get his "piece of the system." Riots, on the other hand, he sees as a form of social protest. "Here, there is a suggestion of a desire to overthrow or change the whole system," he says. "This is the difference. And we've got to do something quick about this one, about this issue of collective behavior. We've got to get that one fast. We've got to wet down the fever."

The tragedy, as O'Leary and many other experts see it, is that the public's unrealistic vision of one monolithic "crime menace" leads most easily to cries for harsher law enforcement, for more sweeping and rigid anticrime measures, rather than to the broader and slower programs that might possibly get at some of the root causes—the kind of programs advocated in the much-praised but virtually ignored Kerner report.

O'Leary is an expert in the corrections-prison field, and after the wave of prison riots in the fifties, he was one of the major experts testifying before Congressional committees. From the work of years in trying to rehabilitate individual criminals, he has become convinced that, if you are to work a great reformation in the man, you must work equally great changes in the society of which he is a part.

"We used to have the idea in corrections," he says, "that you could deal with the individual; you sat down with him in prison, you tried to get his confidence, you tried to change him and then send him out. But we have learned that you don't get very far with that system. I have talked to these guys. I know. Oh, they'll play the game with you, they'll con you along—but change them? Not very often.

"What we have discovered is that there are definite subcultures in our society in which violence exists, in which violence is a way of life. You can talk to men who come out of such subcultures, and you can almost see them thinking, 'This is the way to go, man. This is the way it is. What you trying to do? Change me? What do you think I am—crazy?'

"If you are really going to change things, you are going to have to change, not just the man, but the whole of that violent subculture of which he is a part. You know Robert Kennedy talked about bringing business into the ghettos and rebuilding, remaking the ghettos; Gene McCarthy talked about moving the ghetto residents out into the countryside and establishing jobs and homes for them there. I don't know which is the better method, but I'm convinced that you are going to have to get at that subculture; you have to break it up and change it."

This brings us back to the imperatives set forth in the Kerner commission's report on urban riots— to the need for a massive attack on the intertwined problems of poverty and race, the ghetto and crime. Even if the nation moved in this direction, which it has shown little disposition to do, the struggle is one for the years, not for the days and months immediately ahead; and an American public, in typically impatient American mood when once aroused, seems to be demanding action now. What about the prospects for "action now"? Realistically, what can be done?

One high-ranking Federal law enforcement official argues that a vast increase in the army of policemen on city streets would help. "The best thing that has happened in Washington recently was the assignment of 1,000 extra policemen to street patrols," he says. Washington is also making use of a computerized crime-fighting system. All information about crimes, the time and place of their occurrence, is fed into a computer which sifts out the mass of data and pinpoints the major trouble spots and the times at which crimes are most likely to be committed. Police are then able to concentrate on these areas. This system, plus the presence of that extra 1,000 patrolmen on the streets, is having an effect in Washington, the official believes. "There is no deterrent like that of the cop in uniform visible on the street corner," he says. "This is such a simplistic idea that it is often overlooked."

OTHER experts are less optimistic. Prof. Henry S. Ruth Jr., of the University of Pennsylvania Law School, who served as deputy director of the President's crime commission, doubts that even a doubling of present police forces would produce the kind of quick solution Americans want. "Not enough research has been done on this to show its value," he says. "There have been a few experiments in specific areas of our cities, like more patrolmen on the New York subway system, for instance, and in some cases crime in those areas has dropped. But what has happened in the rest of the city? Have criminals just moved their activities somewhere else? [Professor Ruth was speaking *before* the latest release of Police Department crime figures, showing an over-all increase in crime.] The commission's crime report makes one important point in this regard, and that is that you can't make any correlation between the number of policemen per 100,000 population and the incidence of crime. Washington, D.C., for example, is one of the most heavily policed cities—and yet it has one of the highest crime rates.

"It is foolish to talk about doubling policemen and catching more criminals under the present system—that is, unless you think the situation is so bad that you are just going to stick people away behind bars for 30 years. And that is a thing we are not prepared to accept."

Professor Ruth, who probably has as comprehensive a view of the problem as anyone as a result of his crime commission role, says frankly: "I don't see anything anyone can do to reduce crime in a year or two." There are, as he sees it, two major roadblocks to really effective action.

"First," he says, "our criminal justice system has received too little attention in planning and resources, and so it is unable to cope realistically with the problem; and, second, the public refuses to take any responsibility to do anything about it." Expanding on the second point, Professor Ruth gives these illustrations:

"The businessman, if you ask him to hire a one-time offender, to give an ex-con a chance, refuses to have anything to do with him. I don't see how you can scream about crime and then say, 'I won't hire any man who has been in prison.' If a first-offender comes out of prison and can't get a job, he has only one alternative: to go back to crime. He has to live.

"Or, take another situation, try to get a small correctional institution established in a rural-suburban area maybe 10 or 15 miles away out in the country; at once, the public is up in arms, they don't want it. Yet, unless you can do something along these lines, you aren't going to make much progress. In the same way, try to hire more policemen and give them the kind of salaries that will attract high-caliber men — and the public howls about increased taxes."

UNREALISM haunts the whole issue, as Professor Ruth and many other experts see it. There is unrealism in the public frenzy about the crime menace—"The actual fear is exaggerated among people who have the least cause to worry about it," Professor Ruth says. "The most indignant letters come from people who live in the suburbs and rural areas, but all statistics show that people who live in the central cities are the ones who are most in danger." There is unrealism in the expectations now being aroused by campaign oratory that something

"Some police departments deliberately understate the volume of crime in their jurisdictions."

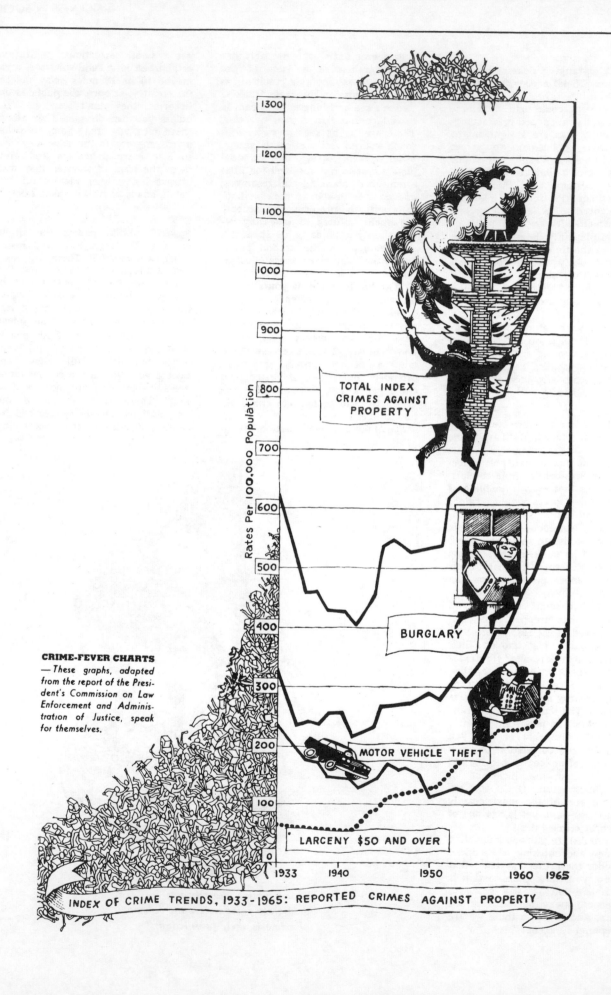

CRIME-FEVER CHARTS
— These graphs, adapted from the report of the President's Commission on Law Enforcement and Administration of Justice, speak for themselves.

TOTAL INDEX CRIMES AGAINST PROPERTY

BURGLARY

MOTOR VEHICLE THEFT

LARCENY $50 AND OVER

Rates Per 100,000 Population

1300
1200
1100
1000
900
800
700
600
500
400
300
200
100
0

1933   1940   1950   1960   1965

INDEX OF CRIME TRENDS, 1933-1965: REPORTED CRIMES AGAINST PROPERTY

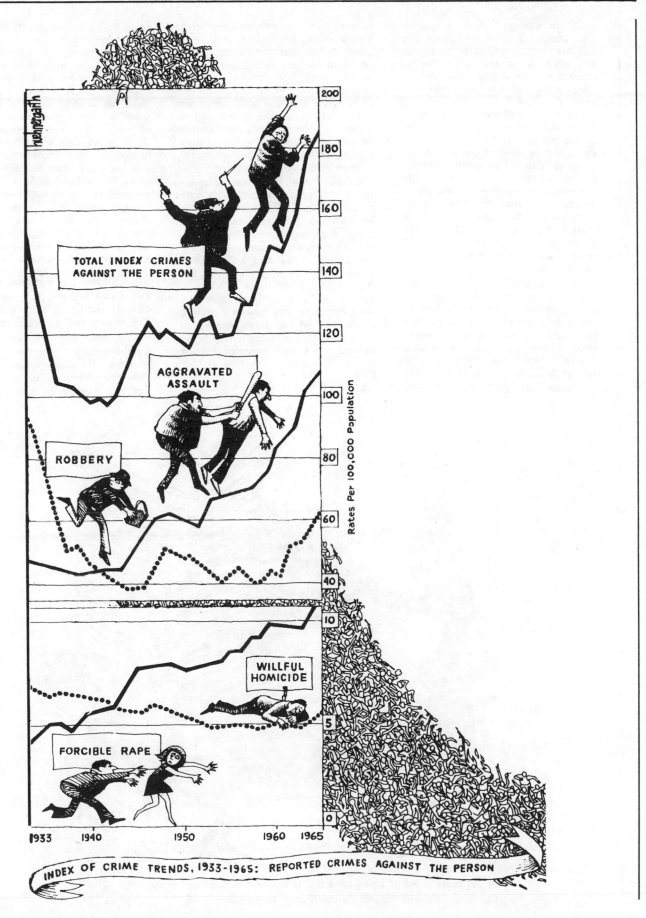

INDEX OF CRIME TRENDS, 1933-1965: REPORTED CRIMES AGAINST THE PERSON

swift and sure can be done; unrealism concerning the public's own role and the price it will have to pay to get what it wants, and, finally, unrealism concerning the whole complicated system of American criminal justice.

There is widespread agreement among the experts that the criminal justice system itself is archaic, inept and badly in need of top to bottom overhaul. The nation spends between $4- to $5-billion annually on its criminal justice system—an all-inclusive term that embraces police, corrections, courts and prisons. It is, most experts agree, a splintered and chaotic system that often serves to perpetuate the very evils it is supposed to correct.

Eliot Lumbard, who served this year as chief counsel to a New Jersey legislative committee investigating the state's criminal justice system, puts the issue in this perspective: "The structure of our criminal justice system dates back to the 17th and 18th centuries. Crime was then a neighborhood problem. Everybody

in small towns knew everybody else. People often prosecuted their own cases. Today that same system continues in an entirely different world —the world of modern, urban America where everyone is a stranger to everyone else. The basic American assumption is that the system, if not perfect, is at least pretty good simply because it is ours; but, in fact, it may be inefficient and inept and unable to cope with current problems."

Lumbard cites the fantastic splintering of police jurisdictions. He points out that Westchester County, for example, has some 46 separate police departments; in New Jersey, the state inquiry showed, there are 430 police chiefs and only 12,000 policemen. "Now, if you subtract the big-city forces like those in Newark, Jersey City and Camden from this total, you find you have a situation in the rest of the state where you have a lot of chiefs and virtually no Indians," Lumbard remarks. "It's a ridiculous situation."

THE evils that begin with splin-

tered police forces spread throughout the system. The lower courts—the night courts, the so-called "people's courts," those most intimately and directly involved with crime the instant an arrest is made—are inundated by a tidal wave of prisoners held for every imaginable kind of offense. Drunkards and derelicts are there in staggering numbers. So are narcotics users. Prostitutes. Bookies and numbers' runners. Mafia gangsters. Thugs and holdup men. All are dumped in an indiscriminate welter on the heads of the lower court magistrates. Some cases involve health and psychological problems, not crime, and never should come into court as criminal cases in the opinion of most experts; others involve all kinds and degrees of potential social menace. But how is one to sort these out from the welter? The answer is that one doesn't.

"To deal sensibly with crime," Lumbard says, "you have to break it down into manageable terms and deal with individual units. You can't use the same techniques in dealing

"A lot more crime is being reported today, but it does not mean that more crime in the same proportion is being committed."

with all of these problems. Specific programs must be addressed to specific problems. And one of our great problems today is that our present system of law enforcement doesn't reflect any such refinement."

The result is a hurried, haphazard processing of the always cluttered, always overflowing criminal calendar. Richard H. Kuh, who spent 12 years as an assistant district attorney in the office of District Attorney Frank S. Hogan, has made a special study of the manner in which potentially dangerous criminals are sped through the revolving doors of the lower courts, copping pleas to offenses far less serious than those they had committed, receiving slap-on-the-wrist penalties that are, in effect, licenses to go out and sin some more.

"The prosecutors and the courts are both to blame," Kuh says. "Basically, their obsession is that the only way to clear the calendar is to give away the courthouse."

In an article he wrote for the Bar Bulletin of the New York Bar Association, Kuh pointed out that, in New York County, "only about 3 per cent or less of the felony indictments go through to a jury verdict annually." The rest get off by copping a plea to a far less serious offense. Kuh argues that this "crime-plea gap" fosters crime by letting really dangerous criminals loose on society again and again. In his article, he cited several cases illustrative of the point. Here is one of them:

"William Townes, one April half-a-dozen years ago, at knife-point forced a woman he accosted in her building hallway to admit him to her apartment. Once there, he forced her to undress, speeding the process by cutting part of her clothing from her body. When, at the moment he ordered her into the bedroom, footsteps were heard, he snatched the watch from her wrist and fled. The victim went to phone from a neighbor's apartment—and Townes, during her absence, re-entered her apartment. She screamed on returning and he fled waving a knife—into the arms of waiting police.

"His prior record included 19 arrests over a 20-year period, showed an appreciable history of addiction, and embraced at least three prior reduced felonies. Charged with robbery in the first degree and cognate crimes (and so subject to imprisonment for a minimum of 10 years and a maximum of 30), he, too, was

"Experts agree that crime today is bad and getting worse...."

permitted to plead guilty to attempted grand larceny in the second degree, as a first felony offender; the maximum term under that plea was two and a half years in state's prison. His sentence, in fact, was one of 15 months to two and a half years, making him eligible for release in about 10 months, less credit for time served while awaiting disposition of the charges."

Cases like this, endlessly repeated, cause Vincent O'Leary to make this summation: "The most immediate and important problem is our system of criminal justice. We've got to get that under immediate control. The lower courts are where the action is, and they are the poorest financed and have, on the whole, the least competent judges. Some 40 per cent of the people who come before them are drunks who don't belong in the system in the first place; there are an incredible number of pot and kettle disputes. The first thing we

have to do is to unclog these courts; we must build up our other resources and get out of the system the people who don't belong there. Then we must have trials damn fast. If a man is held on a serious charge, try him quickly, give him the sentence he deserves—and then try to work with him. But all of this is what we are not doing today."

HOW far we are from doing it, ironically enough, is illustrated by a case involving one of O'Leary's own co-workers in the National Council on Crime and Delinquency. Miss Sally Niklas, who is employed in the council's public relations office, went home from work to her apartment at 162 West 85th Street one day last November. She had some packages in her arms, and she paused in the vestibule to pick up her mail. She sorted quickly through it, standing there, and as she did, she heard the hall door open behind her. Fumbling with her packages, she got out her key and was trying to unlock her apartment door when a man behind her said:

"Here, let me help you."

"Oh, thank you," Sally said.

Then she became aware that the man, instead of helping her, was trying to snatch her pocketbook.

"I forgot everything they tell us here," she says. "You know, don't fight; let him have your pocketbook and your money. Well, I fought. He slammed me up against the wall and wrenched the pocketbook from my hand. It fell open and the wallet dropped out. I made a last grab at him as he ran and tore out a piece of his coat."

Sally reported the incident to the police, and in just a few minutes two cops called at her door. They already had the suspect. They had been cruising in their prowl car when they saw him running down the street, a piece missing out of his flapping coat. "I have the missing piece," Sally told them—and a fit on the coat of the suspect showed she did.

IN the struggle with the robber, Sally had had her head bruised when she was banged against the wall, and a small bone in her right hand had been fractured, so that she had to wear a cast for six weeks. Her assailant was a young Puerto Rican. He had been arrested twice before on similar charges, but each time the complainants had been persuaded to drop the case and he had gone free. The youth's mother and sister were both working, and so they raised the money to hire a lawyer and get the youth out on bail. Let Sally tell the rest of the story.

"At first," she says, "they tried to get me to drop the charges as the other complainants had. His sister tried to talk to me, and then his lawyer tried to give me the argument that he was just a young boy, you know; he'd never been in trouble; he deserved a chance. I asked the lawyer what about the two previous charges, and that ended that; he didn't raise that issue again.

"But in all the months since this happened, the case has gotten nowhere. I have been in court 11 times —and it hasn't even come up yet. First, the lawyer needed time to prepare his case. Then, the boy was sick. Then, the lawyer was sick. Then, the lawyer still needed more

"Gene McCarthy talked about moving ghetto residents out into the countryside. . . ."

time, after six months, to prepare his case. The judges seem to take little interest; each time it's a different judge, each one just passes it along.

"In the meantime, the police tell me, the youth had been arrested on two other charges. The last time, it was for stealing a grand piano. He had repainted it, apparently figuring this would disguise it the way you would a stolen car, and the police spotted him, all alone, pushing his camouflaged piano down the middle of the sidewalk. They don't think he was a narcotics addict at the time he tried to rob me, but they think he is now; they've noticed needle

marks on his arms.

"Still the case hasn't come up. One time, I wasted a whole day in court, and the case wasn't even called; the calendar was too cluttered. If it wasn't that I work here and it's really almost a part of the job, I would have given up long ago and dropped the charges the way the other complainants did. I'm ready to do my patriotic duty, I want to, but how much are you supposed to take? You go to court, you waste a whole day, or most of it—and nothing happens. Over and over again. After a time, you begin to lose faith in the system." ■

Wallace Finding That the North Has as Much Appetite for Violence as South

By ROY REED

Special to The New York Times

WASHINGTON, Oct. 8 — Historians and social scientists have long held that Southerners are more violent than other Americans, and Southerners, with a touch of pride, have tended to agree.

However, George C. Wallace's visits to the North in pursuit of the Presidency have called the theory into serious question.

He visited seven Northern states last week and found in almost every city the same appetite for violence that has been accepted as commonplace in the South.

When the former Governor of Alabama addressed the residents of Buffalo, Newark and Indianapolis on the necessity of keeping anarchists in line, he was rewarded with the same wild cheers that he would have received in Tallahassee or Little Rock.

While he talked of freeing the police to do their job, the police of one city, Cleveland, were using clubs on protesters outside the building where Mr. Wallace was talking.

Fist Fights Frequent

Hardly a rally was concluded during last week's tour without at least one fist fight or shoving match between friends and enemies of Mr. Wallace.

A taste for violence is only the most obvious quality that Mr. Wallace elicits from his Northern supporters, a group that he joshingly refers to as fellow "rednecks."

Interviews in several Northern and Midwestern states with Wallace followers indicate that they understand his rhetoric in the same terms that Southerners do.

They are afraid of street disorders and crime, and he expresses the fear for them. They also hate provocative political demonstrators and they resent incursions of Negroes into predominantly white neighborhoods and schools.

Above all, they love and trust the police.

"If we have to have a police state for law and order, we'll have to have it," said Mrs. Raymond Forrest, a Clifton, N. J., grandmother who had driven to Jersey City to hear Mr. Wallace Saturday.

Others, while avoiding the scare words, "police state," expressed similar thoughts on increasing the power of the police to deal more harshly with disorderly persons.

Peter Damico of Clifton, a 31-year-old insurance adjuster, was asked what Mr. Wallace meant when he said: "You anarchists had better have your day now, because after November 5, you are through in this country."

Mr. Damico said he understood Mr. Wallace to mean that as President he would "give the police the authority to bang a few heads and break it up."

Many Wallace supporters in the North use the word "nigger" with the easy familiarity of a white Alabama segregationist, or, indeed, of Mr. Wallace himself in his unguarded moments.

Don Wasson, a reporter for The Montgomery Advertiser, traveling with Mr. Wallace last week, approached a woman at Jersey City and asked why she was working for Mr. Wallace.

She replied that she did not like having her children bused across town to go to school with "niggers."

Mr. Wasson, a little startled, asked: "Is it all that bad?"

"You don't know what bad is," she shot back. "You folks down South have got it soft. Up here, we've really got a nigger problem."

From comments like these, it appears that it would be a serious mistake to think that all of Mr. Wallace's supporters in the North are bloodthirsty rednecks who long for a season of authoritarianism.

As among Southerners, many of the Northerners who support Mr. Wallace are middle-class people who have become afraid. They would be appalled if anyone call them racist.

Yet, the element of race is almost always in their reasoning when they are asked why they like Mr. Wallace.

A gentle-faced man stood under a tree outside the courthouse at Kalamazoo, Mich., Oct. 1 and listened politely to Mr. Wallace. He was George Radig, 68 years old, a retired tool designer for General Motors.

He talked quietly for a few minutes about the need for order and then, summing up his feelings, he said: "The colored people are just trying to dictate too much. You shouldn't give them too much power, the colored people."

Beyond race-connected issues, Mr. Wallace's suporters tend to answer questions with slogans.

"Everybody should have equal rights," said one man. "If you want to rent your house to a person, rent it, and if you don't want to, don't."

They also appear to be misinformed.

A bartender from New Jersey, who declined to give his name, was asked what he thought Mr. Wallace meant when he talked of ending the Vietnam war.

"I think he would end it with the bomb," he said.

A nuclear bomb?

"Yes," he said.

Mr. Wallace has taken pains to say that he would not consider using nuclear weapons in Vietnam under any circumstances.

Poll Finds 83% of Negroes Plan to Vote for Humphrey

Eighty-three per cent of all Negroes in the United States intend to vote for Vice President Humphrey compared with only 26 per cent of the white majority, according to a poll by Louis Harris published yesterday in The New York Post.

The survey showed that 52 per cent of Negroes felt that police brutality was a major cause of the breakdown of law and order, while no more than 10 per cent of whites agreed.

Only 8 per cent of Negroes feel that "Negroes have gone too far in their demands" compared with 66 per cent of whites, the poll found, and 72 per cent of Negroes feel that "progress in civil rights should be speeded up" compared with 28 per cent of whites.

October 9, 1968   October 16, 1968

Law

Clark: Target on the Law and Order Issue

WASHINGTON — Ramsey Clark, the embattled Attorney General, likes to quote Thoreau's admonition that the man who hears a different drummer should "step to the music which he hears."

In his 20 months as the Federal Government's chief law enforcement officer, Clark has marched to a tune that has made him simultaneously one of the most admired and denounced men in Washington and a major issue in the Presidential campaign.

Like John Foster Dulles, Ezra Taft Benson, Dean Acheson and other Cabinet members who were attacked during campaign years, Clark's problems stem both from the fact that he is in a sensitive job and because his attitude toward it makes his opponents' flesh crawl.

At a time when "law and order" is on every candidate's lips, and Richard M. Nixon has promised to improve it by sacking him, Clark remains unflappably unimpressed with the importance of putting great numbers of people in jail.

When he listed the milestones of his tenure in a speech here last week, the emphasis was on "economic and legal justice."

Clark has engineered the first massive grant of Federal funds—$63-million—to improve local police, courts and jails. He helped push through the gun control bill, insisted on the fair housing law and stiffened enforcement of school and job desegregation.

His record on organized crime has been overshadowed by Robert F. Kennedy's earlier exertions in this field, but it is not bad. Compared to the 16 anti-Mafia indictments obtained by the Republicans in their last year, 1960, the Justice Department got 1,166 indictments last year.

Despite this record, he has not developed a "law enforcement" image. As Senator John Tower, Republican of Texas, sees it, he is "psychologically unsuited to the job of law enforcement."

Clark has refused to use the wiretapping power that Congress voted last June because he says wiretapping is inefficient and violates privacy. He has argued against capital punishment and the use of deadly force to stop looters.

On the one notable instance when Clark acted tough, his motive was to avoid violence. He succeeded so well that he got little credit for his efforts.

This happened last spring when he avoided confrontations with the Poor People's demonstrators in Washington for weeks, then lured them away from their "Resurrection City" base and bulldozed it to the ground without physical violence.

Congressional View

Nevertheless he still is called "cream puff" in some circles on Capitol Hill, where he has become a political liability for the Johnson Administration.

Last week President Johnson had to give recess appointments to the three officials he had selected to administer the new grant program for local justice. Senator John L. McClellan, Democrat of Arkansas, is so piqued at Clark that he blocked their confirmations.

Clark's unpopularity was also partly responsible for Congress' refusal to give the Justice Department a free hand in distributing the money. "I am not about to see Ramsey Clark handle $500-million," (the amount that may eventually be spent), Senator Everett McKinley Dirksen, Republican of Illinois, declared.

Although his critics are making the most noise these days, many liberals and moderates believe that his emphasis on equal justice and professionalism of police is the best way to get law and order in the long run. There is increasing talk here that a new Administration, with a tougher approach, may quickly find itself in hot water.

Last week Clark took the offensive himself when he delivered a tough speech in reply to Nixon's law-and-order theme. He accused Nixon of using "trigger words and misstatements on the crime issue," and warned that someday they must be squared with "a real world out there."

In fact, there is little that the Federal Government can do to achieve law and order, other than to help encourage and finance local community efforts. Wiretapping of gangsters probably will resume, and that should be popular — though not with nongangsters who may find little electric bugs in their homes.

Nixon urged Congress to pass the provision of the anticrime law that purports to countermand the Supreme Court's recent rulings limiting confessions and lineup identifications, and that may give any Nixon Attorney General a special problem.

The law is something of a Congressional put-on, and even its supporters admit it is unconstitutional. President Johnson has ordered his law enforcement agents to ignore it, and if the next President tries to enforce the law and embarrass the Supreme Court, it may bring nothing but grief to both.

Although the problems will be about the same, the style—and the identity—of the next Attorney General are almost certain to be different.

Last week Clark referred to Senator McClellan, one of the Senate's most powerful members, as "the man who cried the most about law enforcement," who later "prevented the disbursement of literally millions of dollars . . . . to protect the public."

"That," said one Senate staff member, "does not sound like a man who expects to stay long in his job."

—FRED P. GRAHAM

Nixon Scores 'Indulgence'
By E. W. KENWORTHY
Special to The New York Times

EL PASO, Tex., Nov. 2 — Richard M. Nixon, who has said at every stop this week that he would not indulge in "personal charges" against his opponents, wound up his formal speech-making today with a harsh attack on both Hubert H. Humphrey and Edmund S. Muskie.

In the last of a series of nationwide radio speeches, Mr. Nixon accused the Vice President of having "a personal attitude of indulgence and permissiveness toward the lawless."

1952 Speeches Recalled

And he charged Mr. Muskie with "giving aid and comfort to those who are tearing down respect for law across this country" when he said he had no quarrel with those who burn draft cards in his presence provided they were willing to pay the penalty for their illegal act.

Mr. Nixon has steadily criticized Mr. Humphrey on the issue of "law and order" and he has also criticized Mr. Muskie for the statement cited above. But he has rarely attacked them in such personal terms or in language that recalled the tone of his controversial speeches in 1952 and 1954.

Mr. Nixon attributed Mr. Humphrey's "attitude of indulgence and permissiveness" to what he called the Vice President's "near-exclusive emphasis upon poverty as the root of crime."

The Vice President, Mr. Nixon said, brought "these Depression-born notions" with him when he went to Washington 20 years ago. And, he added, Mr. Humphrey is apparently unaware that these notions "have little relevance to a crime wave afflicting the most affluent society in history."

"His diagnosis is simplistic and wrong," Mr. Nixon continued, "and, because it is wrong, the billion-dollar remedies this Administration prescribed have failed utterly in four years to make any visible progress against this national disease."

Mr. Nixon has repeatedly criticized decisions of the Supreme Court involving police powers and rights of defendants, asserting that these decisions—several of them by a 5-to-4 margin—had given the ad-

October 20, 1968

vantage to "the criminal forces over the peace forces."

But in his speech today he not only criticized the Court majority, suggesting they were unfamiliar with criminal justice, but also came close to saying that he would appoint to the Court only men who agreed with him.

"Among their qualifications I would consider would be experience or great knowledge in the field of criminal justice, and an understanding of the role some of the decisions of the high court have played in weakening the peace forces in our society in recent years," Mr. Nixon said.

One of the things that needs to be said in this campaign, Mr. Nixon went on, is "that the abused in our society deserve as much protection as the accused."

"The rights of the former have not been given sufficient consideration in recent decisions," he declared. "And any Justice I would name would carry to the bench a deep and abiding concern for these forgotten rights.

"There are other requirements I would make of nominees to the high court which the people have a right to know. They would be strict constructionists who saw their duty as interpreting law and not making law. They would see themselves as caretakers of

the Constitution and servants of the people, not super-legislators with a free hand to impose their social and political viewpoints upon the American people."

Mr. Nixon also pledged himself to appoint an Attorney General who would bring to the Federal campaign against crime the "kind of determined, aggressive leadership that Ulysses S. Grant brought to the flagging Northern cause in the Civil War.

Mr. Nixon also pledged that he would give to the problem of law and order "the kind of attention" that President Johnson "has given to the day-to-day operations of the war in Vietnam." He said further that he would "spare no measures and no resources to restore freedom from fear to the streets of our nation's capital."

This was Mr. Nixon's second successive day in Texas, as he drove hard to get the 25 electoral votes that were denied him in his narrow defeat in 1960.

Promises to Voters

As he campaigned in Austin and El Paso today—as in Fort Worth, Lubbock and San Antonio yesterday—he promised Texans the things they want promised. He promised to retain the 27½ per cent oil depletion allowance, to continue building the controversial F-111

fighter plane in Fort Worth, to keep America "first in space" and to stop the flow of 'cheap foreign beef to American markets."

He hinted — without exactly pledging—support for the Trinity River project, which would require several hundred miles of digging and dredging at a cost of hundreds of millions to make a waterway for ocean-going vessels from the Gulf of Mexico to Fort Worth.

Mr. Nixon continued to make no mention of the bombing halt in North Vietnam, which President Johnson put into effect yesterday morning. In his noon speech to about 4,500 in the Austin Municipal Auditorium, he did allude, however, to the conditional refusal of President Nguyen Van Thieu of South Vietnam to send representatives to the Paris talks.

"In view of the early reports that we've had this morning," Mr. Nixon said, "the prospects for peace are not as bright as we would have hoped a few days ago."

At the conclusion of his Austin speech Mr. Nixon said:

"This state is in the balance. It could go either way. If we win this state, we're in, no question about it."

When the applause died down and the crowd was beginning to file out, Mr. Nixon sat at a piano and played "The Eyes of Texas Are Upon You." The

crowd stopped and began singing.

According to his aides, Mr. Nixon was in a confident mood today as he crossed Texas and headed for his last campaign rally at Long Beach, Calif., airport.

Since Sept. 4, when he set out on his campaign, Mr. Nixon has flown 44,000 miles and spoken in 118 cities in 30 states. This is considerably short of his endeavors in 1960, when he flew 65,500 miles to keep his promise to campaign in every state in the union. In that year he spoke to 188 cities.

But the 1960 pace left him physically spent, emotionally drained and unable to summon the reserves of energy needed for the closing days of the campaign.

While Mr. Nixon has obviously been tired this week, he was not exhausted. He has concentrated on the seven largest states with 210 of the 270 electoral votes needed to win. These are, in order of electoral strength, New York, California, Pennsylvania, Illinois, Ohio, Texas and Michigan.

Tomorrow, Mr. Nixon will appear on the National Broadcasting Company's "Meet the Press" program. On Monday he will do no stump campaigning, but will conduct a four-hour telethon in N. B. C. studios in Burbank, Calif.

November 3, 1968

POLICEMAN WINS MINNEAPOLIS RACE

Stenvig Tops G.O.P. Rival —National Impact Seen

By E. W. KENNORTHY
Special to The New York Times

MINNEAPOLIS, June 10— Charles S. Stenvig, a detective on the police force who campaigned on a pledge "to take the handcuffs off the police," was elected Mayor of Minneapolis today by a margin of almost 2 to 1.

Dan Cohen, the Republican candidate conceded defeat an hour and 20 minutes after the polls closed.

In a statement, Mr. Cohen, who was 33 years old today, said: "I want to congratulate Mr. Stenvig and offer him my best wishes."

Forty-five minutes later, with all 195 precincts reported, the returns gave Mr. Stenvig 75,-748 votes to Mr. Cohen's 46,-739. Mr. Stenvig had received almost 62 per cent of the vote.

In a statement to his workers, Mr. Stenvig said:

"Maybe some people would say this isn't the time and place to do it, but I'm going to make my first appointment now. My chief adviser is going to be God, and don't you forget it."

Coming on top of Mayor Samuel W. Yorty's victory over his Negro opponent, Thomas Bradley, in the Los Angeles mayoral election two weeks ago, the victory of Mr. Stenvig is certain to have national im-

pact as confirmation of a conservative trend in protest against campus disorders and radical violence in the cities.

Size of Victory Shocking

Although politicians here in the Republican and Democratic-Farmer-Labor parties had been predicting victory for the 41-year-old Mr. Steinvig during the closing days of the campaign, the size of that victory when it came left this city stunned.

Among civic leaders of both parties, this sense of shock derived not simply because their city, so long regarded throughout the nation as a model of ordered and progressive municipal government, had turned to a policeman who had run on nothing more than a "law and order" platform.

The shock stemmed also from a belief that Mr. Stenvig,

however well-intentioned he might be, was without the knowledge and experience to deal effectively with the impacted problems of a great city.

Mr. Cohen, a Harvard-trained lawyer, has been an alderman for four years and a council presilent for two.

There was also concern because Minneapolis has a government that is built on the principle of "strong council, weak Mayor." The Mayor's influence rests largely on his ability to command public support through advocacy of programs. His only real statutory power comes from the fact that he has control of the police force.

What this will mean when the mayor is a policeman, committed to strengthening the power of the police, was a matter for some apprehension tonight among the members of "the establishment" of this city.

No D.F.L. Candidate

Pre-eminent in that establishment for a quarter of a century has been the Democratic-Farmer-Labor party. But for the first time, the D.F.L. did not have its endorsed candidate in the run-off. The D.F.L. candidate, a relatively unknown alderman named Gerard D. Hegstrom, had come in a humiliating third in the April 29 primary, behind Mr. Stenvig and Mr. Cohen.

Also at the top of the establishment have been many liberal Republican businessmen and leaders of finance—including Bruce, Kenneth and Donald Dayton, owners of department stores and shopping centers, and John Cowles Jr., head of the Cowles publications that include The Minneapolis Star and Tribune.

It seemed plain today that vast numbers of voters had turned against both establishments because in the labor-oriented northern wards, voters were not following the endorsement by labor organizations of Mr. Cohen, and Mr. Stenvig was running about even in some of the traditionally southern Republican wards.

The Principal Problem

Mr. Cohen's principal problem, it is agreed here, was that he had to run a campaign quite different from the one he had planned. In fact, he was forced to run out of character and out of phase.

Mr. Cohen is a conservative, not simply by D.-F.-L. standards but also by those of leading Minnesota Republicans. Last year he antagonized both the Negro community and many Republican civic leaders when he opposed Mayor Arthur Naftalin's nomination of Ronald Edwards, a 30-year-old, North Side black, to the Human Relations Commission.

Mr. Cohen's objection to Mr. Edwards was not that he was a fiery radical but that he had been once convicted of a misdemeanor. The Edwards nomination was eventually approved by the City Council, but in the process Mr. Cohen was attacked for appealing to the white racist vote.

Mr. Cohen was an early adherent to the cause of Richard M. Nixon, and he became the executive director of the Mayors for Nixon-Agnew Committee.

June 11, 1969

Democrats Shift to Right, in Line With G.O.P., on Crime Issue

By JOHN HERBERS
Special to The New York Times

WASHINGTON, Oct. 11 — Liberal Democrats, long accused of being soft on crime and disorder, have joined the Republicans in the current election campaigns in calling for tough law enforcement.

In recent years, Democratic candidates outside the South most often emphasized the need to attack the root causes of crime, such as poverty and social injustice, over the need for more stringent action by the police and the courts.

Now, the Democrats, both as a national party and as individual candidates, are putting the emphasis on cracking down on the lawbreakers. The Republicans, in turn, seem determined not to let them get away with the shift.

"How can the voters trust a party which spends 11 months of the year apologizing for violence and then pins on the sheriff's badge one month before election?" said Representative Rogers C. B. Morton of Maryland, Republican national chairman, in a speech in Hershey, Pa., last week.

The Democrats say they have not made any substantive shift in position but are seeking to neutralize a false charge against them—that they encourage permissiveness and coddle rioters, criminals and misfits.

Hubert H. Humphrey, 1968 Presidential nominee who is now a candidate for the Senate from Minnesota, explained the difficulty in a speech to the American Bar Association in St. Louis on Aug. 11:

"The so-called liberal is often and wealthy. He is pictured as concerned primarily about the welfare of the poor black man 'that he seldom sees'—but not about the poor or the lower-middle income white man. He is seen as a dove and he is identified with dissent and disruption. And most of all, he's perceived as soft on law and order, whatever that may mean."

Here is how the shift in emphasis by the Democrats has come about:

¶Richard M. Scammon, director of the elections research center, and Ben J. Wattenberg, former aide to President Johnson, published a book, "The Real Majority," in which they said the "social issue"—crime, race and violence—was of crucial importance, and they admonished Democrats to stress law enforcement over the root causes. A spokesman for the Democratic National Committee said the book had an important impact on Democratic candidates.

¶Mr. Humphrey, while not altering his stand for social justice, said in his speech to the Bar Association in St. Louis that liberals must "let the hard-hats, Mr. and Mrs. Middle America," know that they [liberals] too condemn crime and riots and violence and extreme social turbulence, and that they scorn extremists of the left as well as the extremists of the right." The national committee mailed copies to candidates across the country.

¶Senator Edward M. Kennedy of Massachusetts, assistant majority leader of the Senate and a candidate for re-election, said in a speech at Boston University Sept. 11: "Those who seek change by the threat of use of force must be identified and isolated, and subjected to the sanctions of the criminal law. They are the hijackers of the university . . . and like hijackers, they must be deterred and repudiated . . . any person who lends them aid and comfort, any person who grants them sympathy and support, must share the burden of guilt."

¶In September, the Democrats, who control Congress, began pushing to enactment a series of anticrime bills, most sponsored by President Nixon, which had been pending for months in committees. On Thursday in the Senate, the legislation was wrapped into one package, passed and sent to the House. The measures would increase penalties, give the Federal Government more authority and put more money into law enforcement activities of all kinds.

The Democratic moves were a response to both public opinion polls and to a well-financed, highly-organized campaign by the Republicans to make the Democrats vulnerable on the "social issue." The Republican Congressional campaign finance committee, conducting a poll among G.O.P. candidates for the House, says that eight of ten consider crime, disorder and drugs, grouped together, as "The No. 1 issue." Democrats consider the economy to be.

The Republican National Committee has been mailing to candidates statements by Democratic leaders intended to show they are soft on crime. A typical one quotes Senator Joseph D. Tydings, Democrat of Maryland, who is facing a tough re-election contest, as saying in March of 1969, "It cannot be shown, in most categories of crime, that stiffened sentences, mandatory minimums and the like have an appreciable effect on crime rates."

Senator Tydings is now advocating tough law enforcement, was one of the chief backers of President Nixon's District of Columbia Crime Act, which contains controversial no-knock and preventative detention provisions.

'Fear, Outrage, Reaction'

Both Senators Kennedy and Mr. Humphrey stressed the importance of public opinion on the "social issue." Mr. Kennedy said in his Boston University address that campus disturbances were producing "fear, outrage and reaction" that is leading the country away from a solution of social ills.

Mr. Humphrey said that in the past the nation has been indebted to "great liberals who stood firm when it was difficult, when it was unpopular. But what liberals must do now is an ironical imperative: They must show the courage to take on a popular position when the cause is right. And I happen to think the cause of justice and law and order is right."

The "social issue" was prominent in the campaigns of 1968, when President Nixon used it prominently against the Democrats. But political leaders of both parties say that spectrum of opinion in the political debates this year is further to the right, due to the shift of liberal Democrats.

Almost everyone is making some kind of "law and order" appeal. Even Senator Philip A. Hart, Democrat of Michigan, who has conspicuously continued to emphasize the need to attack the causes of crime, is showing a television advertisement in which a uniformed policeman looks on the Senator approvingly.

Some of the more crime-free places have spawned radical proposals for dealing with lawbreaking. In the Second Congressional District of South Da-

kota, the Republican candidate for the House, Fred Brady of Spearfish, proposed that youngsters between the ages of 15, and 26 be required to spend two 90-day sessions in special training camps to learn how to stay out of trouble.

The issue is said to be a factor in varying degrees in virtually all of the national and state races. Republicans, reminded by the literature of their national committee, are still using Mr. Humphrey's 1966 quote that if he had to live in a slum "I've got enough spark left in me to lead a mighty good revolt."

In Illinois, Adlai Stevenson 3d is on the defensive in his cam-

paign for the Senate for calling the Chicago Police "storm troopers in blue" because of their behavior at the Democratic National Convention in 1968. A television commercial for his opponent, Senator Ralph T. Smith, a Republican, said: "What's Adlai Stevenson got against the F.B.I. and the Chicago Police? Ask any Democratic precinct committeeman." The commercial is designed to drain organizational support from Mr. Stevenson.

In the New Mexico Governor's race, crime became the prime issue a few days ago following release of a Federal Bureau of Investigation report that showed Albuquerque as

having the second highest crime rate in the country in 1969. About the same time, an Albuquerque policeman was critically injured as he attempted to arrest five holdup men.

Peter V. Domenici, the Republican candidate, proposed an elaborate and extensive crime-fighting plan at a luncheon. His opponent, Bruce King, a rancher and a Democrat, had two agents at the luncheon, who hurried back to King headquarters with the news. Mr. King then came out with his own "battle on crime" plan.

The two candidates since have been battling for the anti-crime headlines.

October 12, 1970

Mitchell and Hoover:
Focus Differs on Crime Data

By FRED P. GRAHAM
Special to The New York Times

WASHINGTON, Sept. 7— For the last year, the office of Attorney General John N. Mitchell has been rewriting the Federal Bureau of Investigation's interpretations of the nation's crime statistics, which for four decades had been within the sole control of J. Edgar Hoover.

As a result of the interpretations placed on the crime situation by Mr. Mitchell's public relations staff, it has been made to appear that the F.B.I. believes the crime rise that began under a Democratic administration almost a decade ago is tapering off.

The figures, however, show that reported crime is rising at about the same velocity as before.

Mr. Mitchell's efforts with the crime figures are in line with the Nixon Administration's law-and-order political strategy. President Nixon won office in 1968 on a campaign of criticism of the high crime rates under the Democrats, coupled with promises to do better.

The Federal Bureau of Investigation has often been accused of presenting crime figures in a way that emphasizes the crime increases, supposedly because this will justify larger F.B.I. budgets. Attorneys General before Mr. Mitchell have tended to stress what good news could be found in the figures, as if to say that Justice Department programs were succeeding.

Uniform Crime Reports

Documents have come to light illustrating how the Attorney General began last June to change the interpretation placed on the crime figures without altering the figures themselves or omitting crucial statistics.

The F.B.I.'s Uniform Crime Reports are compilations of local police departments' statistics on crimes reported to them. Each year, the bureau issues the figures in four quarterly reports and an annual report.

The reports are presented in virtually impenetrable form, consisting of tables of figures plus some explanatory passages. So the public's impression of what the figures show is largely influenced by a press statement that is always issued on F.B.I. stationery with the reports.

Ever since the bureau began releasing crime figures in 1933, Mr. Hoover, the director, has drafted the statements to explain the figures. This changed last June 22, when Mr. Hoover's office prepared a statement, under his letterhead, that characterized the statistics to be released that day as follows:

"For release Monday P.M., June 22, 1970—according to figures made available through the F.B.I.'s Uniform Crime Reports and released by Attorney General John N. Mitchell, serious crime in the United States continued its upward trend, recording a 13 per cent rise nationally for the first three months in 1970 when compared to the same period in 1969."

Another Version

The statement, rewritten in Mr. Mitchell's office, and as it was actually issued under Mr. Mitchell's letterhead, began as follows:

"For release Monday P.M., June 22, 1970—Attorney General John N. Mitchell announced today that the F.B.I.'s Uniform Crime Reports show that the rate of increase of violent crimes in the first three months of 1970 slowed by 7 per cent in the major cities of the nation

—and by 3 per cent in the nation as a whole."

It was not until the third paragraph of Mr. Mitchell's release that it was disclosed crime had risen by 13 per cent.

Since then, each release of F.B.I. figures has revealed a difference in tone between the explanatory material written by the bureau and printed in the crime reports themselves, and the statement authorized by Mr. Mitchell and published under the F.B.I. letterhead.

The bureau's explanation invariably stated how much reported crime had risen. Mr. Mitchell's accompanying statement began with a passage that explained how the crime rise had slowed in certain respects.

The difference between Mr. Hoover's view and Mr. Mitchell's view of the crime figures came into sharp focus last week when the annual figures for 1970 were released. They showed that, in the two years since the Republicans took office, reports of major crimes have risen from 4.4 million in 1968 to 5.5 million last year—a rise of 25 per cent. The crime rate has also risen, but not as rapidly—from 2,235 reported major crimes per 100,000 United States residents in 1968 to 2,741 per 100,000 in 1970.

Explanatory Material

The explanatory material written by the F.B.I. in the report said that reported crime increased by 11 per cent in 1970 over 1969, and that it rose by 144 per cent since 1960. "The risk of becoming a victim of crime in this country is increasing," it concluded, and "population growth cannot alone account for the crime increases."

In issuing the report, Mr. Mitchell began his statement by saying: "Serious crime in the nation continued to increase in 1970. Attorney General John N. Mitchell announced today, but at a slower rate than in 1969. It marked the second year in a row that the crime statistics showed a tapering off of the sharp upward swing recorded during the mid-1960's"

When the figures were released on Tuesday, some news reports said that crime was rising, others said that it was "tapering off," and others quoted Mr. Hoover as having said that the risk of being a crime victim was rising, and then quoted Mr. Mitchell's statement that the crime rise was slowing down.

Commenting in response to questions about the revisions of the release, Jack W. Hushen, a Justice Department spokesman, said:

"Press releases come up to us from various divisions and we are continually changing things, putting emphasis on more newsworthy items and significant points that we find have been overlooked.

"What they send us is a proposed press release. We review them to see that they are set in the proper context. I can show you a lot that have been rewritten a lot more than that. After all, these are reports put out under the Attorney General's name."

A Matter of Stress

In no case has Mr. Mitchell's statements changed the figures or omitted crucial statistics. But he has stressed certain figures that tend to show that the crime picture has improved under the Nixon Administration, and the pattern seems clear enough by now to establish that the Republican candidates will probably stress certain points in discussing crime.

One is the "rate-of-increase" argument. It points out that, while the volume of reported crime was 11 per cent higher in 1970 than 1969, and 12 per cent higher in 1969 than 1968, this is a slower rate of increase than in 1968, when it rose 17 per cent over 1967, and 1967, when it rose 16 per cent over 1966.

Statisticians say that there is some validity to this argument, but that it also contains a built-in distortion because, as the volume grows, the rate of increase usually shrinks. They cite the following example:

If there were one million crimes in 1968, two million in 1969 and three million crimes in 1970, crime would have increased by 100 per cent in 1969, but by only 50 per cent in 1970. It could thus be said that the rate of crime increase had been cut in half in 1970.

September 8, 1971

RIZZO WINS RACE IN PHILADELPHIA

Defeats G.O.P. Opponent in Contest for Mayor

By DONALD JANSON
Special to The New York Times

PHILADELPHIA, Nov. 2— Frank L. Rizzo, who calls himself the "toughest cop in America," swept to a solid victory today over his Republican opponent, Thacher Longstreth, to become Mayor of the country's fourth largest city.

The triumph showed "law and order" sentiment to be strong here. Mr. Rizzo, a Democrat who resigned as Police Commissioner earlier this year to seek political office for the first time, overwhelmed Mr. Longstreth in white, blue-collar wards to become Philadelphia's first Mayor of Italian extraction.

With 1,749 of 1,755 precincts reporting, the tally was:

Rizzo 391,239
Longstreth 343,204

The election of Mr. Rizzo continued Democratic domination of City Hall. He was selected by Mayor James H. J. Tate, who was ineligible to run again after a decade in office, as the candidate of the entrenched party organization.

Mr. Rizzo won despite the defection of thousands of black Democratic voters who read his campaign slogan, "Rizzo means business," as a racist pledge to keep blacks "in their place."

Two hours after the polls closed, Mr. Longstreth conceded defeat. He said his opponent had won "a clear mandate from the people of Philadelphia" and urged all two million Philadelphians to support the Rizzo administration.

The Mayor-elect, alluding to racial polarization, said one of his first tasks would be to "bring this entire community back together again."

Mr. Rizzo, a 6-foot 2-inch 250-pound career policeman, became a national symbol of the "law-and-order" philosophy during his 28 years on the police force. His candidacy provided the principal test of this philosophy among voters this year. The main election issue was Mr. Rizzo, pro or con.

The New York Times/Bill Wingell
WINS PHILADELPHIA MAYORAL RACE: Frank L. Rizzo, the Democratic candidate, with his wife after victory.

With crime rates in Philadelphia lower than in other major cities, the Rizzo image as an administrator quick to use force to keep the lid on appealed to many and alarmed others.

Mr. Longstreth, an articulate Princeton graduate who resigned from the City Council to run for Mayor, equated Mr. Rizzo's methods with overkill and racism.

He won the endorsement of

liberal Democrats and blacks throughout the city and country, setting the stage for massive crossover voting that made party registration, nearly 2 to 1 Democratic, academic.

But ticket splitting by Democrats was offset by the votes of conservative Republicans for Mr. Rizzo, particularly in the large Italian section of South Philadelphia, where the 51-year-old Democratic candidate grew up.

"Us Italians brought culture to this country," Mr. Rizzo, a high school dropout, told the Order of the Italian Sons and Daughters of America Sunday night at Palumbo's Restaurant, his most frequent stop on the campaign trail, "That word 'Mafia' was thrown around for many years and I resented it."

Mr. Rizzo campaigned primarily in white, blue-collar neighborhoods, often receiving tumultuous receptions. All major unions endorsed him.

Mr. Rizzo pledged that he would hire 2,000 more policemen to insure law and order. Mr. Longstreth contended that four years of Mayor Rizzo would result in a police state.

Blacks voted overwhelmingly against Mr. Rizzo in the primary last May. It was their first defection in decades against the Democratic organization. Today, many went even further, voting Republican for the first time in their lives.

Major Issues Obscured

"You ain't much, baby," a black woman told Mr. Longstreth during a campaign stop, "but you're all we got."

The polarization was offset somewhat by a Democratic ticket that included nine blacks for lesser offices and the feeling of some blacks in high-crime areas that Mr. Rizzo could provide safer streets.

But crime and race and Mr. Rizzo's reputation were so prominent in this campaign that major issues often were obscured, including Longstreth charges that his opponent lacked experience and qualifications to deal with education, finances and other major city problems.

Mr. Longstreth cited a Rizzo pledge to ban tax increases in the next four years as "an insult to the intelligence of the voters" of a city already deep in fiscal deficits.

The two largest daily newspapers here, as well as the city's leading Negro and Jewish papers, endorsed Mr. Longstreth, a moderately liberal, 50-year-old Main Line Quaker. The newspapers contended that Mr. Rizzo was not the man to achieve needed racial harmony and offered no break with an administration marked by ineptitude and "political cronyism."

November 3, 1971

Nixon Says He Kept Vow To Check Rise in Crime

By ROBERT B. SEMPLE Jr.
Special to The New York Times

WASHINGTON, Oct. 15 — President Nixon said today that he had brought what he called a "frightening trend of crime and anarchy" to a standstill during his term in office. He pledged to do more to protect the "moral and legal values" of the nation in a second term.

In a paid political radio broadcast, Mr. Nixon quoted liberally from statistics that have been disputed to prove his assertion that he had done much to satisfy his 1968 campaign pledge to restore respect for "law, order and justice" in America.

The nationwide speech was the second in a series of radio broadcasts that Mr. Nixon intends to make to present his views on selected issues. Last week he addressed himself to economic issues.

Mistakes Termed Few

Mr. Nixon said that he had committed few if any mistakes in his four-year battle against "the criminal forces in America."

His appointments to Federal courts, he said, made the Constitution "more secure." At the same time, he said, the leaders of his Justice Department brought "backbone" to national law enforcement.

In addition, he asserted, his efforts to give more money to local law enforcement agencies slowed the rapid rise in domestic crime, while bureaucratic shake-ups and energetic diplomacy had stemmed "the raging heroin epidemic" of the last decade.

Mr. Nixon conceded that more remained to be done and, to build a "land free of fear," he promised to appoint more "strict constructionists" to the courts, overhaul the Federal criminal code and channel still more funds to the states and cities.

The President did not mention by name his Democratic opponent in the Presidential race, Senator George McGovern of South Dakota. But near the end of the 15-minute speech Mr. Nixon stressed some of his favorite themes of the campaign, associating himself with basic "values" that he suggested had been threatened by the forces of permissiveness.

"I will work unceasingly to halt the erosion of moral fiber in American life, and the denial of individual accountability for individual action," the President said.

"Government must never become so preoccupied with catering to the way-out wants of those who reject all respect for moral and legal values that it forgets the citizen's first civil right, the right to be free from domestic violence," he added.

Among the statistics cited by Mr. Nixon to prove the progress he had made in his war on crime at home were Federal Bureau of Investigation figures showing that serious crimes had risen by 122 per cent in the eight years before he took office.

Crime rose by 30 per cent in the first three years of the Nixon Administration. The President failed to mention this in his speech. But statistics from the F.B.I. show only a 1 per cent increase so far this year, and Mr. Nixon cited this figure.

Mr. Nixon also cited favorable figures reported earlier this year by the police department in the District of Columbia, which the President described in 1968 as the "crime capital of the world" and where he has greatly increased the number of policemen.

District of Columbia officials have contended that crime here has dropped by 50 per cent during Mr. Nixon's term in office and the President made this claim today. But some independent analysts—including a team from the Brookings Institution—have asserted that at least part of the reported decline in serious crime here stems from the fact that the police have downgraded the value of some stolen items, thus keeping a number of larcenies and, to a certain extent, burglaries out of the statistics.

Senator McGovern, using other statistics, charged that Mr. Nixon was making fraudulent claims and that crime had in fact increased at a more rapid rate during the Nixon Administration than ever before. Mr. McGovern said that drug addiction in the last two years reached new peaks.

Mr. Nixon spoke to the nation from his retreat at Camp David, Md. He later flew to the White House by helicopter.

October 16, 1972

271

Police in Philadelphia Called Corrupt; Panel Says Rizzo Tried to Bar Inquiry

By DAVID BURNHAM

The Pennsylvania Crime Commission has concluded that police corruption in Philadelphia is "ongoing, widespread, systematic and occurring at all levels of the police department."

The commission has also accused the police department and the city government of Mayor Frank L. Rizzo of actively attempting to block its year-and-a-half-long investigation by arresting state troopers serving as commission agents and failing to act when presented with concrete evidence of grafting.

In a 1,404-page report, the commission said that a former Philadelphia policeman had given sworn testimony that Mayor Rizzo, who was police commissioner from 1967 to 1971, had gone to a political fund-raising dinner with a gambler who had four arrests and one conviction and that Mr. Rizzo had used the occasion to make joking references about taking graft.

The commission said the incident, which occurred in October, 1971, was cited as an indication that the top leadership of the city was not seriously concerned about the problem of corruption.

The central recommendation of the commission report, based on a finding that the Office of the District Attorney was incapable of dealing with police corruption, was that a special prosecutor, somewhat like Maurice H. Nadjari, New York's special deputy attorney general, be appointed. Mr. Nadjari was appointed by former Gov. Nelson A. Rockefeller in the fall of 1972 to investigate and prosecute corruption in the criminal justice system of New York City.

The Pennsylvania Crime Commission, headed by Attorney General Israel Packer, was scheduled to issue its massively detailed report at a news conference today. But a newspaper, The Philadelphia Bulletin, broke the embargo agreement under which newsmen were permitted to read the report in advance and published accounts of the document yesterday.

The Associated Press reported from Philadelphia that Police Commissioner Joseph F. O'Neill had no comment on the report but Mayor Rizzo was quoted as saying that he deplored "any attempt to smear the entire police department with frivolous, unsubstantiated or undocumented allegations."

"I have discussed these charges with Police Commissioner Joseph O'Neill," the Mayor is quoted as saying, "and he has pledged to investigate them vigorously. If criminal action is warranted he will proceed quickly and without favor.

"The vast majority of the city's more than 8,000 police officers are hard-working and dedicated men and women who stand ready to sacrifice their lives for the protection and safety of all our citizens.

"To deliberately attempt to destroy police morale and to shake police confidence in our police department at this critical time is a tragedy we must avoid."

Meanwhile, the Fraternal Order of Police announced that it would seek an injunction to block the distribution of the report. Representatives of the group will appear today before Judge James S. Bowman in Commonwealth Court in Harrisburg.

The findings by the Pennsylvania commission about the nature and extent of police corruption in the nation's fourth-largest city were strikingly similar to those of the Knapp Commission, which in December, 1972, concluded that a "substantial majority" of New York policemen were corrupt.

The Philadelphia findings also parallel the corruption patterns suggested by the indictments during the last year of 60 Chicago policemen for extortion and bribery.

In summary, the commission report said "corrupt practices" had been found in each of Philadelphia's 22 police districts or precincts and that officers from the rank of patrolman to inspector had been involved.

"Specific acts of corruption involving improper cash payments to the police by gamblers, racketeers, bar owners, businessmen, nightclub owners, after-hours club owners, prostitutes and others" were uncovered, the commission said.

"More than 400 individual police officers are identified by first name, last initial and badge or payroll number as receiving improper payments in terms of cash merchandise, sexual service or meals," the commission continued.

Concerning the sale of liquor in Philadelphia, the commission said it had identified 70 officers who received illegal payments from bars and after-hours clubs. There are more than 2,000 such establishments in the Philadelphia area. Joseph D'Angelo, a bar owner and representative of the city's Tavern Association, testified during private hearings that "I could say that every tavern in the city of Philadelphia has given something to the police at one time or another."

Bar Owner Becomes Agent

One bar owner who worked as an undercover agent for the commission for a year was Irvin Goltzer. During this period Mr. Goltzer recorded conversations about payoffs with 12 officers and paid graft amounting to $800 a year.

Another bar owner said he paid bribes to more than 40 policemen between January, 1970, and September, 1972, the 40 including a lieutenant, two captains and two inspectors. The commission said these identifications had been verified "by direct observation of payoffs by commission agents, examination of a ledger maintained by the owner in which he recorded police payments and an examination of police assignment sheets."

The report said illegal gambling was flourishing in every part of the city and that commission agents had made bets themselves or observed bets being made at more than 200 locations. "Evidence was received by the commission of widespread and systematic payments to the police to protect illegal gambling operations," the report said.

Narcotics corruption was found by investigators to be less systematic than that discovered among gamblers and liquor violators. But at least eight officers were identified as being involved in narcotics-related corruption, and allegations about such corruption were made concerning 15 other police officers.

In addition, a former policeman testified that in more than half of the narcotics arrests, part of the contraband was

Mayor Frank L. Rizzo

kept by the arresting officer. The illegally seized drugs were retained for resale, the personal use of the officer, to buy information from informants or for "farming," the slang expression for planting false evidence, the former policeman said.

In addition to documenting the regular payment of what Philadelphia policemen call "dirty notes," the commission investigated the distribution to policemen of "clean notes" or "safe notes" by Philadelphia businessmen. The report said the businesses paying police included banks, insurance companies, automobile dealers, restaurants, supermarkets, jewelers, construction companies, street vendors, country clubs and moving companies.

"Although only a limited investigation of this matter was undertaken," the report said, "the commission uncovered identifying data on more than 200 police officers receiving cash payments from businesses."

These included one supervisor, one captain, 17 lieutenants, 26 sergeants, two detectives and one corporal, even though cash payments are specifically punishable under the Philadelphia City Charter by dismissal and up to 90 days in jail, the commission said.

One "fast food" chain, Gino's, Inc., was found to have paid various Philadelphia policemen $89,057 during 1972 and the first six months of 1973 in return for having a policeman stationed as a guard at 15 of the company's outlets eight hours a day, seven days a week.

The policemen involved also received a combined annual salary from the city of about $264,000. Discussing these and other payoffs by businesses, the commission charged that Philadelphia police services "are open for bidding, and the proceeds of the bidding go into the pockets of the individual police officers, not the City Treasury."

The commission said one of the city's major supermarket chains had paid Philadelphia policemen approximately $23,000 a year for extra guard and escort services. These illegal payments had become so institutionalized, the report said, that the company had a form called the "Weekly Cash and Sales Report," which had a place for recording money spent for "police protection."

Law enforcement sources said the supermarket chain in question was Food Fair Stores, Inc., the third-largest such chain in the United States.

During closed commission hearings, an executive from Gino's Michael Phillips, testified that, in the company's opinion, the police guards were "cheap at the price." But the commission undertook a complex analysis of the thefts that occurred at stores not covered by guards that suggested the illegal payments were considerably higher than any possible losses.

Based on conservative estimates, law enforcement officials believe that the corrupt members of Philadelphia's 8,303-man Police Department receive or extort bribes of at least $1-million a year.

Despite the reported openness of corruption found by the investigators, the commission said the District Attorney's Office had proved to be "ineffective at investigating the police" and that the "internal control mechanisms within the Police Department are vague, fractionalized and almost totally ineffective."

One example of the reputed failure of the Police Department and District Attorney's Office involved the reported payoffs by Gino's. The report said that more than six months ago it turned over to the police the names and badge numbers of 77 officers identified by sworn testimony and documentary evidence as having accepted illegal payments.

Aside from permitting one heavily involved officer to resign, however, the commission said no department action or criminal charges had yet been brought against any of the policemen.

The commission cited a political fund-raising dinner in October, 1971, which was attended by a former policeman, Felix Ruff, who became a commission undercover agent, and by Mayor Rizzo and an alleged gambler.

"There was a lot of drinking and joking," Mr. Ruff testified. During the conversation, Mr. Rizzo, the former police commissioner, warned the "policemen to be alert and constantly watch their back against any possible picture being taken," the witness testified.

The report said Mr. Ruff had also testified that there had been "joking remarks between the former police commissioner" and the reputed gambler "about note taking in the old days before the Federal authorities had jurisdiction over police corruption."

Associated Press

Joseph F. O'Neill, Philadelphia's Police Commissioner, said he would withhold comment on report on corruption.

At the Root Was Money

THE BUSINESS OF CRIME. By Robert Rice. 268 pp. New York: Farrar, Straus & Cudahy. $3.75.

By FRANK O'LEARY

LOUD cries of "Heresy!" are sure to fill the air when anyone suggests that too many business men share the ethics of the highwayman and that their broad knowledge of business techniques makes the more ruthless among them equal in social menace to the worst of our criminals. Undismayed by this prospect, Robert Rice says in a foreword that "he is venturesome enough to write on this extremely difficult subject because of his reportorial and, conceivably, literary conviction that all too often in our society the moral difference between a business man and criminal is imperceptible."

Mr. Rice spent seven years with the original staff of PM, and the past nine years writing for The New Yorker, where he originally published some of the material appearing in this, his first book. Here are not only fascinating case histories of business men-crooks but the story of "honest men" playing supporting and minor roles, men without whose covetousness and moral callousness the stellar performances of the sack-suited, manicured, genteel - mannered promoters must have been stillborn. The rogues' gallery that is assembled between these covers is a garish one—but the author makes the faces seem real enough. Most chilling of all, however, is the eternal climate of greed in which they flourished, as confidently as swamp-cabbages in the spring.

YOU will meet Sam Sapphile, the "torch" who ran an arson service patronized by at least 200 Brooklyn business men who found the collection of fire insurance preferable to bankruptcy. Elias Eliopoulos, a Greek merchant, walks on stage as a global "junk" distributor who pyramided millions spreading narcotics around the world in a generation-long career. These are followed by the members of the French Resistance movement who used their war-acquired skills to forge and distribute a fortune in American Express cheques; and, finally, Salvatore Sollazzo, a successful jewelry manufacturer and sucker for gamblers who dodged income taxes and sold gold on the black market to meet his gambling losses, ultimately corrupting college athletes so that he could win a few bets.

The veritable army of "legit-stiff's" (honest people) who played along with these leaders in "making a fast buck" do their part in supporting the author's thesis.

Executive Theft

American business stands to lose more than a billion dollars this year to internal thieves, according to Norman Jaspan, head of Investigations, Inc., a management engineering firm. Mr. Jaspan told a recent meeting of the Metropolitan Controllers' Association here that this figure excludes "such other losses as excessive overtime, deliberate damaging of stock and the like."

He urged management to look within itself to find the real source of these losses. "Reliance on accounting systems and automation to eliminate human error often blinds management to the losses it suffers," he said.

Mr. Jaspan reported that it was "not the rank-and-file worker who is mainly responsible for internal dishonesty * * * 60 per cent of the losses are directly traceable to employes on supervisory or executive levels."

BIG CONCERNS SAID TO HIRE CALL GIRLS

Murrow Broadcast Charges That Some Companies Keep Prostitutes on Payroll

By GEORGE BARRETT

Prostitution has become such a standard cost item for big business concerns in this country, a radio program contended last night, that some companies now keep call girls on their payrolls to please customers.

Statements were made by unidentified participants that prostitutes were hired, for example, to help persuade bank presidents to make loans and buyers to make purchases in large lots. It was said that the use of girls-for-hire had become so prevalent that some madams submitted monthly bills to companies instead of demanding separate payments for each date.

The descriptions of the alleged use of prostitutes by business concerns were presented on the Columbia Broadcasting System's radio network program "The Business of Sex." The fifty-five-minute program was a production of the Public Affairs Department of C.B.S. News. Edward R. Murrow, who was the narrator, told the radio audience that the program was "recommended for adult listening only."

Mr. Murrow said that call girls interviewed by reporters for the program had remarked that their assignments brought them "in contact with the highest levels of business."

Madam Is Described

The voice of an unidentified man, described by Mr. Murrow as a person who was "often approached to provide the services of top call girls," declared:

"There's a very famous madam in New York who takes care of your multi-millionaire only. She is a famous name in New York. She puts out a book every year, pictures of the girls she has working for her. And sends this book to her very, very exclusive clients. Now this woman is one who really works with big business; you know, when big corporations have a party, they'll contact this woman. She'll make a flat fee, $3,000, $5,000, all according to how many girls they want. And she'll send them a book, they'll pick out the girls. There's no guesswork here. And she deals with the largest corporations in the United States."

In some cases, according to the program, top executives were directly involved in the sex-entertainment arrangements, giving instructions on the type and the extent that the company would provide.

Make $25,000 a Year

Girls who were described as prostitutes said they made $25,000 a year and more through their deals with companies and did not have to pay income taxes. One girl said: "I don't feel as though the Government's entitled to anything, because these men are all legitimate business men. They deduct you at the end of the year."

Mr. Murrow introduced a man he described as the president of a large international company, who said there was "absolutely no doubt that prostitution per se does help business."

"This is the fastest way that I know of to have an intimate relationship established with a buyer," the executive declared. "It's an experience which has been shared, whether it's together or not makes no difference. The point is, that I know that the buyer has spent the night with a prostitute that I have provided. In the second place, in most cases the buyers are married, with families. It sort of gives me a slight edge; well, we will not call it exactly blackmail, but it is a subconscious edge over the buyer."

One girl described the technique of closing business deals. She said that business conferences were "usually conducted" at the end of the evening.

"After quite a bit of liquor has been consumed, and in this case the fee is $100, she said, "I will first be invited out to dinner. The man who is doing the entertainment will get tickets for whatever shows the buyer requests, and then I will go back to the hotel with the man and usually we'll spend till 2 o'clock in the morning with him. He will often give a verbal agreement, subject to confirmation the next morning."

January 20, 1959

Anatomy of Dishonesty

THE THIEF IN THE WHITE COLLAR. By Norman Jaspan with Hillel Black. 254 pp. Philadelphia and New York: J. B. Lippincott Company. $4.95.

By GERALD CARSON

SOMETIMES, when a secretary with a taste for mink puts a $15,000 dent in her boss' bank-account, the story moves on from the police blotter to the display pages of the tabloids. More often, the public never hears of the ingenious exploits of the white-collar defalcator who taps the till, forges checks, liberates merchandise, manipulates expense accounts, accepts bribes, alters time cards and inventory records to conceal shrinkages.

This book undertakes to throw new light into the dark corners of middle-class and upper-class dishonesty in money matters, revealing the swindlers, rascals, grafters, kickback artists and "honest crooks" who will, it is estimated, steal more than one billion dollars during 1960. The sum involved, incidentally, is more than twice that harvested in 1957, according to F. B. I. figures, by the nation's burglars, pickpockets, stick-up men and auto thieves.

Only one-thirtieth of the losses due to employe violation of trust are recovered; only 10 per cent of the defaulters are ever prosecuted.

The stated purpose of the authors, Norman Jaspan, a management consultant, and his collaborator, Hillel Black, a freelance writer, who presumably supplies the structure and pace of this expertly written tract, is "to try to explain the nature of white-collar crime," and to show why it exists. In story after clinical story, and episode after grisly episode, the authors appear almost as choreographers of a modern rogues' march. Men and women participate equally when the opportunity to sin is equal. Here pass in review the pillar of society who got caught, the ideal organization man who betrayed his trust. Here is Miss Minnie Clark Mangum, whose "only weapon was her fountain pen," yet who netted more than twice the haul made by an armed gang in the Boston Brink's robbery.

MOST of the author's examples come from the files of bonding and insurance companies and the records of Mr. Jaspan's own firm, with names and locations omitted. A few are well and publicly known occurrences sailing under their own black flag. The book attempts to go behind the headlines and interpret them; as with William Richard Rose, the kindly New York State banker who took nothing for himself but felt a compulsion "to play God."

There is the story of Mrs. Lydia Burton (one of twenty-two aliases) whose march upon Atlanta was almost as catastrophic as Gen. William T. Sherman's, and there is an extended report on the labor leaders whose financial chicaneries were exposed by Senator McClellan's Select Committee on Improper Activities in the Labor or Management Field. Climbing—or descending — the ladder of evil doing, we reach finally Serge Rubinstein, the wizard who enjoys a chapter all to himself as "The Complete Scoundrel."

Contributing factors in the general environment to this "moral collapse" are noted as war and post-war rootlessness, world tension, the great demand for workers, lax hiring standards, the increasing impersonality of business relationships. On the personal side, the immediate causes of thefts are alcoholism, the race track, cards and dice, high living, status seeking.

Domestic troubles, revenge for slow advancements, imaginary slights and, yes, even blackmail, have played an important part in the seduction of the hard-working and usually not-very-gay deceivers. With one it was loneliness. Another took medical books to read up on her son's illness. Yet another stole to buy Italian liras and a horse that came in ninth in the only race he ever ran. The motivation to steal may come from unusual family expenses, financial losses elsewhere or the climate of a business organization where "everybody's doing it."

The men at the top, the authors assert, too often do not know what is going on, and usually find out, if they do uncover evidence of wrong-doing, by sheer happenstance. The cost to corporate stockholders and the consuming public is astronomical. The book concludes with specific suggestions to business executives for dealing with the problem.

February 28, 1960

7 Electrical Officials Get Jail Terms in Trust Case

G. E. and Westinghouse Vice Presidents Must Serve 30 Days—$931,500 in Fines Imposed for Bid Rigging

By ANTHONY LEWIS
Special to The New York Times.

PHILADELPHIA, Feb. 6— Seven executives of the country's leading electrical manufacturing companies received jail sentences today for violating the antitrust laws. Federal District Judge J. Cullen Ganey sent each to jail for thirty days.

No appeals from the jail sentences are possible, because all the men had pleaded guilty or no defense.

In addition, Judge Ganey imposed fines totaling $931,500 on individuals and corporations in what the Government has called the largest of all criminal antitrust cases.

It was a long day in Judge Ganey's courtroom. It took from 10 A. M. to 4:30 P. M. to pass sentences in six of twenty pending indictments. The fourteen others are scheduled to be disposed of tomorrow.

Among those drawing prison terms were vice presidents of the General Electric Company and the Westinghouse Electric Corporation—the two largest companies in the industry. Aside from those going to jail, twenty men drew suspended prison sentences.

The charges to which all the defendants had pleaded guilty or no defense were fixing of prices and rigging of bids on heavy electrical equipment, such as power transformers. Sales of the products involved totaled $1,750,000,000 a year.

But the real drama in the courtroom today arose not from the money or the corporations involved. It lay with the men who stood before Judge Ganey to hear their fate.

They were typical business men in appearance, men who would never be taken for lawbreakers. Over and over their lawyers described them as pillars of their communities.

Several were deacons or vestrymen of their churches. One was president of his local Chamber of Commerce, another a hospital board member, another chief fund raiser for the Community Chest, another a bank director, another director of the taxpayer's association, another an organizer of the local Little League.

Judge Scores Companies

Lawyer after lawyer said his client was "an honorable man" —a victim of corporate morality, not its creator. To a degree Judge Ganey agreed.

"The real blame," the judge said in an opening statement, "is to be laid at the doorstep of the corporate defendants and those who guide and direct their policy."

Judge Ganey said the typical individual defendant was "the organization or the company man, the conformist, who goes along with his superiors and finds balm for his conscience in additional comforts and the security of his place in the corporate set-up."

Judge Ganey imposed jail sentences only on men he thought were high enough in their companies to make policy. Jail sentences of any kind are unusual, though not unprecedented, in antitrust cases.

Approximately fifty jail sentences have been imposed under the Sherman Antitrust Act since it was passed in 1890. A recent example was the sentencing of three defendants in a linen antitrust case to ninety days each by Federal District Judge Edmud L. Palmieri of New York. The cases are now on appeal.

Today's sentences were below the statutory maximums — a $50,000 fine on each count and a year in jail for the individual defendants. Most were also below Justice Department recommendations, which were for the most part short of the maximums.

Robert Kennedy Acts

The recommendations were sent to Judge Ganey Jan. 19, the day before the new Administration took office. But the acting chief of the department's antitrust division, W. Wallace Kirkpatrick, read the court a statement by the new Attorney General, Robert F. Kennedy.

Mr. Kennedy said he had reviewed the cases and considered the crimes "so willful and flagrant that even more severe sentences would have been appropriate." He suggested, "under the circumstances," that "sentences at least as severe as those recommended be imposed."

Forty-five individuals and twenty-nine corporations were named as defendants in the package of twenty indictments

Today sentence was imposed on thirty-six men and twenty-one companies. Some of the same defendants figure in the cases to be handled tomorrow.

The corporate defendants today drew a total of $822,500 in fines. The largest figures were $185,000 for General Electric, in five cases, and $180,000 for Westinghouse, in six.

All of the individual defendants also drew fines, ranging from $1,000 to $12,500. The total for them was $109,000.

These were the seven men who drew prison terms, listed in the order they were sentenced:

J. H. Chiles Jr., Westinghouse vice president and division manager.

W. S. Ginn, General Electric vice president and division manager.

Lewis J. Burger, General Electric division manager.

George E. Burens, General Electric vice president and division manager.

C. I. Mauntel, Westinghouse division sales manager.

J. M. Cook, vice president of Cutler-Hammer, Inc.

E. R. Jung, vice president, Clark Controller Company.

Judge Ganey said he had suspended the sentences of some other defendants "reluctantly," and only because of their age or bad health.

He repeatedly rejected pleas by counsel to the effect that their clients were not deeply involved. He would cut in crisply to remark that the defendant had been an "aggressive competitor" in a shocking case.

The formal charge in all the cases was violation of the Sherman Antitrust Act, which prohibits conspiracies in restraint of trade. That is a common charge, but the Government said these conspiracies were unusually elaborate and damaging.

The defendants were said to have held frequent secret meetings, and used codes. They allegedly parceled out Government contracts among each other, submitting low bids in rotation under a scheme called "the phase of the moon."

Some of the customers for this heavy electrical machinery are now expected to bring civil suits for treble damages. The Justice Department has prepared such suits for overcharges to the Federal Government, and states and municipalities and utilities may be next to sue.

The six indictments were handled in turn today, and the drama built slowly in the court room. Government lawyers read their recommendations aloud in each case, and then counsel for the defendants had a chance to plead for mercy, as some called it, or leniency.

Gerhard A. Gesell of Washington, counsel for G. E., took

George E. Burens

E. R. Jung

Lewis J. Burger

W. S. Ginn

J. H. Chiles Jr.

vigorous exception to Judge Ganey's comment about corporate responsibility for the violations.

He noted that G. E. had a company rule, known as Regulation 20.5, directing strict obedience to the antitrust laws. And he observed that the company had demoted all officials involved before any indictments were brought.

"It is simply not a fact that there was a way of life at General Electric that permitted, tolerated or winked at these violations," Mr. Gesell said. "The company abhors, sought to prevent and punished this ...nduct."

But Judge Ganey disagreed with Mr. Gesell. He said he thought General Electric's

Rule 20.5 "was honored in its breach rather than its observance."

Mr. Chiles was the first individual defendant called. A small man with gold-rimmed glasses, he stood with head slightly bowed as his attorney, Philip H. Strubing of Philadelphia, sought leniency.

"No further punishment is needed to keep these men from doing what they have done, again," Mr. Strubing said.

"These men are not grasping, greedy, cut-throat competitors. They devote much of their time and substance to ther communities."

Mr. Strubing listed Mr. Chiles' activities—senior warden of his church, benefactor of charities for crippled children and cancer victims, fellow of an engineering society.

Led Off by Marshal

When Judge Ganey imposed the jail sentence, Mr. Chiles turned to go back to his seat in the courtroom. Then, suddenly, a marshal appeared, grabbed him by the elbow and led him off.

Next was Mr. Ginn, tall and distinguished in appearance. His attorney, Henry T. Reath of Philadelphia, also made a general attack on the Government's demand for jail terms.

He said Government lawyers

were "cold-blooded" and did not understand what it would do to a man like Mr. Ginn to "put him behind bars" with "common criminals who have been convicted of embezzlement and other serious crimes."

In contrast to Mr. Gesell, Mr. Reath insisted that Mr. Ginn had had only followed long-established company policy by getting together with supposed competitors to arrange their business.

Mr. Reath said Mr. Ginn was chairman of the building fund for a new Jesuit novitiate in Lenox, Mass.; a director of the Schenectady, N. Y. boys' club and a member of Governor Rockefeller's Temporary State Committee on Economic Expansion.

"It would be a great personal tragedy for this fine man" to go to jail, Mr. Reath concluded. Judge Ganey took only a few seconds to mark Mr. Ginn down for thirty days in prison.

And so it went. Lawyers spoke of their clients' long years with one company, of their daughters in prominent colleges, of the shame that publicity had already caused.

Judge Ganey ordered the seven who were given jail sentences to begin their terms Monday at 10 A. M.

February 7, 1961

High Cost of Crime Adding To Retailers' Price Tags

By ISADORE BARMASH

Today's rising cost of living is being aggravated by today's rising curve of crime. Americans who are groaning about the ever-rising cost of food, clothing and furniture might groan all the more if they realized that part of the higher price tag they are paying comes from business's increasing losses from crime.

Retailers don't like to talk about it, but almost all of them figure into their costs of operation—which inevitably means the prices they charge—a compensating factor for the millions they lose through inventory shrinkage. That shrinkage includes employe fraud and dishonesty, shoplifting, pilferage and machine and human errors in the retailing process.

As their volume increases from year to year, the reserve which retailers put aside for theft losses must increase," said Lawrence Lief, a principal of Industrial Security Analysts, a New York security consultant.

Adds Thomas DeFeo, general sales manager of the Royal Audio-Visual Corporation, developer of security and surveillance equipment, here, "The merchant's price structure must inevitably rise to compensate for crime losses. But why should that be so surprising? When labor costs rise, this generally is passed on to the customer. Why shouldn't that follow for losses on crime, which is part of the rising costs of materials and overhead?"

"Without adding that cushion," Mr. DeFeo said, "many a small businessman would not be able to survive."

Within the last 10 days, Sears, Roebuck & Co., the country's largest merchandising company, felt compelled to deny a statement by H. Bruce Palmer, president of the National Industrial Conference Board, about Sears's reported losses from crime. Instead of the losses of 1½ per cent of its annual $8-billion sales, or $120-million, a Sears spokesman said that theft losses last year were only $12-million, or less than one-tenth of 1 per cent.

Skepticism Voiced

In addition, the spokesman

denied that Sears had raised its prices to cover theft losses but had a reserve to cover them, a reserve that has not been changed for years.

Several merchants, who insisted on remaining anonymous, expressed surprise and skepticism last week about Sears's statements. First, they pointed out, for many years, the shrinkage loss among department stores has wavered between 1 per cent and 1½ per cent of sales. However, in the last two or three years that figure has risen to 2 per cent on the average, with the spread ranging from 1 per cent to as high as 5 per cent.

Thus, they noted, if the Sears losses are less than one-tenth of 1 per cent, it is doing a miraculous job of keeping shrinkage to by far the lowest figure in the retail industry.

Second, these merchants observed, losses from theft must have risen at Sears along with its growth in sales over the last decade. If the reserve for theft losses has remained constant, as the company has insisted, earnings must have been adversely affected. Yet, Sears's earnings have shown a consistent rise over the same period.

Hence, the skepticism with which the Sears statements have been greeted by some of its business contemporaries.

The rise in crime incidence is unquestionably one of the most serious matters in retailing. Even for security service concerns, the big gain has become difficult to curb. As Joseph Bernstein, executive vice president of the Willmark Service System and director of its shortage control division put it, "The crime rise is so bad that we cannot supply enough people to handle it."

But even as the trend appears to spotlight a big increase in shoplifting, mainly on the part of young people from 17 to 25 years old, dishonesty among employes is by far the greater problem. According to Mr. Lief of Industrial Security Analysts, the incidence of crime by employes is four times greater in loss value than that from shoplifting.

A case in point is that of an Eastern department-store chain, which reported in a recent year catching 7,000 shoplifters and recovering $140,000 of goods. This meant an average shoplifting theft of $20. But the same concern reported in the same year that it had detected 500 dishonest employes, who confessed to having stolen $400,000.

"The reason for the much higher losses from employes compared to shoplifting," said Mr. Lief, "stems from the fact that employes have a greater chance of conducting their crimes over a period of time without apprehension, as compared to the outside pilferer."

New devices and systems are being developed by security-service companies to curb crime in the stores. Royal Addio-Visual, for example, is offering a combination of an eight-millimeter camera and closed circuit television. By setting the camera into a computerized system, photos of fraudulent and other activities can be taken at regular, brief intervals automatically, in tandem with use of the closed-circuit TV. The system, according to Mr. DeFeo, is available for both sales and rentals.

Morgenthau Tells Businessmen Of Rise in White-Collar Crimes

By ROBERT A. WRIGHT

"White-collar crime," which frequently goes undetected, is becoming more prevalent, United States Attorney Robert M. Morgenthau said here yesterday. Mr. Morgenthau declared that the rich man's crimes of stock fraud, tax evasion, embezzlement, and the like, were not only menaces to society in themselves, but also "fan the flames of violent crimes by the poor and are, to an ever increasing extent, responsible for them."

Speaking at a forum on business and crime of the National Industrial Conference Board, Mr. Morgenthau said there was a double relationship between the violent crimes of the poor and white-collar crimes. The poor, he said, are frequently the victims of these crimes, such as consumer fraud, and may react to them violently. Secondly, he said that "if the affluent flagrantly disregard the law, the poor and the deprived will follow that leadership."

VIP Crimes Cited

In the last few years, Mr. Morgenthau noted, his office had prosecuted three law professors, numerous lawyers, many prominent doctors, the executive vice president of a major bank, the treasurer of the New York State Committee of a political party, the executive vice president of a major publishing firm, the president of the Board of Trade, partners in one of the country's largest accounting firms, a New York Stock Exchange member firm and a number of its partners, and numerous corporate executives and businessmen.

Mr. Morgenthau deplored the fact that some people publicly denounce crimes of violence while privately committing more "socially acceptable" white-collar crimes.

"I recall, in this connection," Mr. Morgenthau said, "recent publicity concerning the president of a large association of businessmen who complained to the New York City Police Department about a recent wave of hijacking in the garment district at a time when he was under indictment for paying a kickback in connection with obtaining a loan from a union pension fund — a crime for which he subsequently was convicted."

The most vivid example of white-collar crime, Mr. Morgenthau said, was the illegal use by Americans of Swiss and other foreign secret bank accounts.

Other speakers at the N.I.C.B. forum at the Waldorf Astoria Hotel commented on the effects on business of the increasing crime rates.

Will Wilson, Assistant Attorney General of the Department of Justice's criminal division, warned the 300 businessmen in the audience that corporations were vulnerable to incursions from racketeers.

1 of 10 in a Report Called a Shoplifter

By DAVID BURNHAM

One out of 10 customers secretly followed into a large Manhattan department store in a recent study stole something before leaving.

The high rate of shoplifters was found by a consulting concern in a study during which customers were selected on a random basis as they entered the store and were kept under surveillance during their entire visit.

The study — in which 27 out of 263 customers were observed stealing—was conducted by Saul D. Astor, president of a 125-man company that specializes in helping factories and stores to reduce thefts by employes.

Because each store is different and each city is different, this study does not mean that one American in 10 is a thief," said Dr. Lloyd E. Ohlin, a former associate director of the President's Crime Commission and now a professor of sociology at Harvard University. "But the number of shoplifters is far higher than I would have anticipated."

Charles Binder, executive vice president of the National Retail Merchants Association, said that if further studies confirmed Mr. Astor's findings "retailers will have to direct even more attention to shoplifting prevention and control."

He said that the latest available reports indicated that about a half billion dollars of goods are taken each year by shoplifters and employes from department and specialty stores alone.

"There has been a general feeling among most of us that employe theft is much more important than shoplifting," a leading department store executive who did not want to be quoted by name said. "This study raises questions about that assumption."

The executive indicated that total losses have been moving steadily higher in recent years and that this loss, for some inexplicable reason, was especially serious in New York.

The official said he knew of one high volume self-service store in New York where stock shortages from internal and external theft had almost doubled, jumping from 1.1 per cent to 2 per cent of all retail sales between 1960 and 1968. He said losses in another store, which employed a large number of clerks, had increased from 1.2 to 1.8 per cent during the same period.

One large New York depart-ment store has reported that it loses as much as $50,000 a day to shoplifters, a figure that represents one-half of 1 per cent of a day's sales. Some stores in Greenwich Village have reported losses of as much as 5 per cent of a day's sales.

The Federal Bureau of Investigation has said that, across the country, shoplifting increased 93 per cent between 1960 and 1966.

In addition to the one-to-ten ratio of shoplifters, the study found:

¶Not one of the 27 shoplifters observed by Mr. Astor's staff was apprehended by the store's floor clerks and detectives.

¶Women were more than twice as likely to steal as men. Of the 195 women followed, 15.7 per cent stole. Of the 68 men followed, 6.3 per cent were observed stealing.

Negroes were somewhat more likely to shoplift than whites. Of the 72 Negroes followed, 12.5 per cent stole something. Of the 191 whites, 9.4 per cent stole.

Dr. Ohlin said that because Negroes on the average earned less than whites the higher incidence of shoplifting among Negroes was not surprising. "Another possible factor," he added, "is the feeling in the black community that they are being exploited by the white establishment. This feeling easily could lead to a weakening of the restraints against stealing from a white institution like a department store."

Most of the 27 shoplifters observed stole only one item such as a scarf, pair of stockings, a raincoat and the average retail value of the stolen goods was $8.37.

The age, sex and value of the stolen items suggest that a large number of shoplifters are middle- or lower-middle-class housewives, perhaps trying to stretch their budget by stealing something they need. The professional thief stealing to support himself or his addiction to heroin, on the other hand, does not appear to be a serious threat to the department stores.

The New York store that permitted Mr. Astor to make his study did so with the understanding that its identity would be kept secret.

The security consultant said he was amazed by his findings. He said he had undertaken the study to show that shoplifting was a much less serious problem than store managers thought and that they should concentrate their efforts on employe theft.

"It looks like I was wrong," Mr. Astor, a 45-year-old former college instructor, said in an interview in his New York office.

Mr. Astor explained that every effort was made to avoid pre-selecting the shoppers followed by his investigators. "My people were instructed to go to he front door of the store and stop," he said. "The third person who went in after the investigator stopped — regardless of whether he was a priest or an elderly Chinese gentleman—was our man."

November 8, 1969

Sees Corporate Mergers As Causing More Crime

By ROBERT J. COLE

The Harvard Business Review concluded not too long ago that mergers and acquisitions—when they are well conceived and well executed —remain one of the most expeditious means of corporate growth and equity enhancement.

But at least one specialist in white collar crime, Norman Jaspan, president of a management engineering firm bearing his name, feels that the wave of corporate mergers in the United States in the last two years has also set off a minor crime wave that extends heavily into the executive suite.

Consequently, he contends, many mergers are a drain on profits.

Some mergers, he believes, have created disloyalty, frustration insecurity and unfulfilled expectations, and, as a result, corporate loyalties soon disappear.

Consider This Case

Consider the case of Ed Johnson (that's not his real name, of course, executive vice president of a boat supply house in a southern state. Ed has spent 35 years with the company, considered it almost his own and had even been promised a share in the business.

But the boss suffered a heart attack and decided to sell out. After the merger, Ed lost his title — and his office —and a new executive crew moved in from the new owners.

A year later, when the new owners decided to evaluate their purchase, inventory discrepancies began to develop.

279

After a study of some 500 employes, the search narrowed down to about 25 supervisors and department heads.

The executive vice president, who had lost his title, his office and the prestige he had once enjoyed with dozens of prominent local businessmen, willingly admitted that he had stolen nearly $100,000 in the year since the merger.

A Rationalization

His rationalization: The money was "coming to me" —practically as a promise from the old boss.

Consider the case of Bill Simmons (also a fictitious name), a controller of a mail order house for 25 years. A year after the firm was sold to a major company, it began losing money instead of showing a profit, as had been expected. But the loss was attributed to new computers that had just been installed.

The following year, the loss doubled. So. Jaspan Associates was called in.

The controller willingly admitted that he had learned to "play around with" certain computer-records and with the help of other department heads, managed to get away with nearly $2-million.

The list goes on and on. Long-time employes quickly discover that their future, as

Mr. Jaspan put it, is "built on quicksand."

So they steal.

Exposure Is Feared

An executive for Mount Sinai Hospital, which had hired Mr. Jaspan a few years ago, told an interviewer for Harper's magazine that it was "shocking and painful" to him to see a "fine, well educated man come in, blurt out his misdeeds, and all but beat his breast before me."

Mr. Jaspan, himself, said in a recent interview that 90 per cent of those who embezzle on white-collar level will admit most of their wrong-doing "if psychologically handled with intelligent probing without lie detectors or threats of police action."

Obviously, he said, most white-collar criminals are afraid of exposure, but "once they belive you know of their wrongdoings—they don't consider these wrongdoings a crime at the moment—they want to unburden themselves."

Then, their first reaction is to ask, if they still have their job.

Pros and Cons

Generally, they don't because they're no longer bondable.

Prosecution, however, will depend on what the company's lawyers deem advis-

able. Mr. Jaspan feels that since most of the loss may be covered by insurance, some companies choose not to prosecute so as not to "air their dirty laundry."

There are advantages and disadvantages in prosecution, he says. One advantage is that it sets an example for others and may flush out more information or a desire to repay. Moreover, insurance is not recoverable unless the company can prove how the loss was incurred. One disadvantage to prosecution is that it's expensive, not always successful and can set off lawsuits.

According to one industry estimate, American business loses $1-billion a year as a result of internal theft from all sources, including from mergers. Theft of merchandise is seven times that of cash. Frauds drive more than 250 firms out of business each year.

Kickbacks and thefts of company secrets are widespread and inventory manipulations to show better performance cause some companies to pay income taxes on profits they have not earned.

Mr. Jaspan, whose list of clients includes more than 200 major companies, has his own recipe for control based on 40 years in the field.

¶Establish controls and procedures and an atmosphere of supervision to prevent recurrence of thefts.

¶Develop an ear-to-the-ground method of accounting. Do not use statistics alone. Get behind the figures and "humanize" them.

¶Never give a man responsibility beyond his capability. Bonuses and profit sharing and incentives only make him manipulate figures to give you the performance you expect of him.

Jail a Threat

Above all, Mr. Jaspan frowns on office executives not experienced in what he considers "a science," confronting dishonest employes.

Very often, he says, these people are threatened with jail, exposure and disgrace, and — on occasion — have been known to commit suicide to save their family further disgrace.

Often in such instances the dishonest executive rationalizes in his own mind that if he is insured, his wife collects, so this helps to ease the disgrace.

But as far as the firm is concerned, it is also generally covered by insurance and to collect, all it has to do is to reconstruct "beyond a reasonable doubt" how the loss was committed.

February 8, 19

Market Place: The Corporation And Embezzlers

By ROBERT METZ

Ask an embezzler why he didn't rob someone instead of taking money from his employer and he may react indignantly, "What do you think I am, a thief?"

This tendency to rationalize theft from an employer, whether that theft is a few envelopes or thousands of dollars, reflects both the unpopularity of impersonal corporations and large bureaucracies and a gap in our ethical standards.

At least those are the views of Prof. Erwin O. Smigel of New York University and Prof. H. Laurence Ross of the University of Denver in a new paperback book called "Crimes Against Bureaucracy." The book has been published by Van Nostrand Reinhold.

Their extensive studies of attitudes showed that crimes against large organizations were more acceptable to the public than other categories of crime, possibly because

our system of ethics lacks rules that apply specifically between individuals and large organizations.

"All major historical religions," Professors Smigel and Ross wrote, "originated in small communities, in which obligations concerned relatives, friends and neighbors.

"From these static and personal communities a set of personal ethical norms developed; responsibilities to great impersonal structures did exist. Today, when large-scale organizations dominate our lives, men may be ethically unprepared to cope with the problem of the relationship between the individual and the corporation."

•

People who steal from

the bureaucracy differ from "more stereotyped criminals in that they lack criminal records and criminal self conceptions," the authors say.

They add that in examining the most flagrant cases of wartime price-control and rationing violations, it was found that fewer than one in 10 had any kind of criminal record.

The study adds that shoplifters in a large Chicago department store, when arrested, would not admit that their behavior constituted theft.

The embezzlers, mentioned earlier, were accountants, bankers and business executives. The possibility of stealing or robbing to obtain needed funds never occurred to them, although "many objective opportunities for such crimes were present."

"The embezzlers were subsequently able to rationalize their acts on the basis that other people in business were doing similar things," the professors wrote.

"In fact . . . such rationalizations were a necessary step in the process of embezzlement. It is likely that other persons who commit crimes against bureaucracies also define the situation as noncriminal. At least, they are able to regard their conduct as not inappropriate, given their conceptions of the nature of the victim."

●

The authors comment that while the sums taken from the bureaucracies are "enormous" in comparison with the amounts stolen from personal victims, these criminal acts are rarely the subject of formal criminal process.

Partly because the bureaucratic officials are sensitive to the organization's unpopularity, "few of the perpetrators are prosecuted, and of those convicted, few are punished with imprisonment. . . . Often the theft is unobtrusive as when the thief occupies a position of responsibility."

The author of another selection in the book, Donald N. M. Horning, finds that in a factory the workers identify three classes of property: personal, corporate and property of uncertain ownership. Items which are small in size, plentiful, inexpensive and not subject to an established accounting procedure tend to fall into the last category. Pilfering of these items is not considered to be theft, providing that the intended use is personal and not commercial.

＊

The New York Stock Exchange, the American Stock Exchange and other securities markets will be open for business on Monday, Columbus Day, but some commodities exchanges will be closed.

Among those that will be closed are the New York Coffee and Sugar Exchanges, the New York Cocoa Exchange and the Commodity Exchange, Inc. Other commodity exchanges in New York and the Chicago Board of Trade will be open.

Banks will be closed in New York, Boston, Chicago, Newark and Philadelphia, but will be open in Atlanta, Cleveland, Dallas, Detroit, Los Angeles, Pittsburgh and San Francisco. The post office will make deliveries and most other Federal offices will be open.

In Canada, Monday is Thanksgiving Day and all exchanges, banks and Government offices will be closed.

October 10, 1970

SEYMOUR WARNS THOSE WHO BRIBE

Tells of New Policy to Press Prosecution of Persons Yielding to Shakedowns

By DAVID K. SHIPLER

In a hard-hitting attack on the business community here, United States Attorney Whitney North Seymour Jr. warned yesterday that his office was adopting a new policy of prosecuting the businessmen who pay bribes as well as the government officials and labor racketeers who receive them.

Deploring the private sector's failure to report white-collar crime, Mr. Seymour told a luncheon audience at the Rotary Club of New York that he was discarding the traditional view that businessmen were simply the "victims" of shakedowns.

"The man who pays the bribe," he said, "the man who buys labor peace, the man who makes a quick dollar on an illegal deal—all of these should expect to find themselves potential defendants unless they have promptly notified law enforcement officials about these unlawful transactions, preferably in time to prevent them from happening."

Mr. Seymour, who is the Federal attorney for the Southern District of New York, also assailed the counts for what he termed "light treatment" of white-collar criminals.

"Those who are arrested for stealing packages or automobiles worth hundreds of dollars know that they have a far greater chance of going to jail than those who steal thousands of dollars from investors or from the public," he said.

Of those convicted for stealing cars and driving them across state lines, 71 per cent are sent to prison, and the average sentence is three years, Mr. Seymour said.

About 50 per cent of those convicted of mail theft—usually of welfare checks—go to jail, with an average term of 2.6 years, he said.

By contrast, only 16.3 per cent of the securities fraud convictions result in jail terms, and those terms average less than a year, he said. The figures for income tax fraud are 35 per cent and 9.5 months, and for embezzlement, 22 per cent and 1.7 years, he said.

The news stories of such "favored treatment," Mr. Seymour said, "are read by those in the ghettos who have a brother or a son in Attica prison and wonder why there are two standards of justice in this country."

He chided businessmen for taking too little interest in the judicial process.

"For too many years, those of us in law enforcement have politely requested businessmen to come to us when they encounter problems of fraud or corruption," he said.

"We have offered our hands in friendship and promised to help business clean up its own house. Except in the rarest case, that invitation has been totally rejected.

"Businessmen seldom come

to us with information about stock manipulations, mail frauds, kickbacks, bid rigging, labor racketeering, bribe-taking by public officials or other crimes that frequently occur in the business world."

Mr. Seymour said that "virtually every single-one" of the scores of such cases now under prosecution by his office "was developed without any cooperation from the business community."

He condemned what he called a "look-the-other-way attitude" by businessmen who "run the other way, profess complete ignorance and generally adopt a code of silence" when investgators seek their help.

"Businessmen too often tend to smile understandingly at illegal conduct by their colleagues while loudly complaining about 'crime in the streets,'" Mr. Seymour said.

"We must set these things right."

"I serve notice on the business community that we will no longer wait hat-in-hand for businessmen to voluntarily bring forward information about possible crimes," he said.

"In the past we have tended to accept as made in good faith representations by businessmen who claim to have been the 'victims' of shakedowns by labor racketeers or corrupt public officials," he said.

"From now on, the primary evidence of that fact will come from the prompt reporting of such crimes and willingness to cooperate in bringing violators to justice."

Mr. Seymour was applauded politely by the 150 businessmen who had gathered in the Commodore Hotel for his address. The Rotary Club president, Rudolf P. Berle, thanked him for his "gloves-off" candor.

July 21, 197

Nixon Panel Says Official Corruption Impedes Nation's Effort to Curb Crime

By DAVID BURNHAM
Special to The New York Times

WASHINGTON, Aug. 18 — Government corruption "stands as a serious impediment to the task of reducing criminality in America," according to a commission established by the Nixon Administration to chart a national program against street crime.

The commission, formed by the suggestion of former Attorney General John N. Mitchell, concluded that, as long as official corruption flourished, "the war against crime will be perceived by many as a war of the powerful against the powerless, 'law and order' will be a hypocritical rallying cry, and 'equal justice under law' will be an empty phrase."

The National Advisory Commission of Criminal Justice did not mention the Watergate scandal. However, the commission decided to discuss the issue of integrity in government, it said, because the American public believes there is "widespread corruption" among public officials at all levels of gov-

ernment, because corruption results "in a staggering cost to the American taxpayer" and because corruption breeds further crime by providing a model of lawlessness "that undermines an acceptable rule of law."

2 Views on Demonstrations

The commission said that the public perception of government corruption and the power of large campaign contributors might have contributed to the belief that demonstrations were the only way to achieve change. President Nixon, in his Watergate statement last Wednesday, argued the opposing view, contending that the demonstrations created an atmosphere of lawlessness that may have infected some of his aides.

Although a summary report by the commission was made public on Aug. 9, the commission's 70-page section on "Integrity in Government" will not be published for several weeks.

The commission recommended hundreds of specific actions that state, county and local government should take to curb

corruption. Among the key recommendation were the following:

¶Every state should adopt laws requiring all state, county and local officials to publicly disclose each year—and at least two weeks before Election Day —all their financial and professional interests. If an official is a partner in a law firm, the disclosures should include all clients whose annual fees exceed $2,000 or 5 per cent of the firm's income.

¶Every state should add provisions to laws making certain specific conflict-of-interest situations a crime punishable by heavy penalties.

¶Every state should approve laws requiring the disclosure of campaign finances that are at least as stringent as those passed by Congress. These new reporting requirements would apply to all state, county and local officials.

¶Every state should add laws prohibiting campaign contributions by persons who transact more than $5,000 in business with the involved unit of gov-

ernment or who are directors or shareholders owning more than 10 per cent of a corporation engaged in such transactions.

¶All states having a history of organized crime should establish a continuing statewide ability to investigate and prosecute corruption both inside and outside of the criminal justice system. The office charged with this responsibility should have the power to compel testimony, obtain grants of immunity, hold private and public hearing and present evidence to a grand jury for indictment.

Outspoken Assessment

The comments and recommendations of the commission —contained in the final draf page proofs—are considered the most outspoken and detailed assessment of the corruption problem in the United States ever made by a Federal panel.

According to Thomas J. Madden, the commission's executive director, the commission members first onsidered the section on integrity in government las December and gave its fina approval to it in a meeting the following month.

The far-ranging report on corruption has emerged at a time when many officials in the Nixon Administration have been accused of being involved in a long series of illegal actions, conflicts of interest, corrupt acts and alleged attempts to cover then up.

The man who initiated the commission — former Attorney General Mitchell—has been indicted for the obstruction of justice on charges of attempting to block the investigation of a corporation whose president contributed $200,000 to Mr. Nixon's re-election campaign. Vice President Agnew has been informed that he is under investigation on charges involving extortion, bribery and tax evasion. The Justice Department's Watergate investigation has already resulted in the conviction of two men. Seven others have pleaded guilty and more indictments are expected.

The commission, headed by Russell W. Peterson, the former Republican Governor of Delaware, said it did not limit corruption to the simple cash purchase of a favor.

Corruption, the commission said, also includes subtle conflict-of-interest situations where the officeholder receives such a benefit as the promise of a job later on from a company that has come before him in his official capacity.

Electoral Process Criticized

"Finally, corruption, as defined here, may flow from the election process itself," the commission said. "Indeed, the commission recognizes the electoral process as a major source of corruption."

"The payment or promised payment of campaign contributions in return for official conduct constitutes a bribe," the commission continued. "Moreover, dependence on a source of campaign funding represents the most pervasive and constant pecuniary shackle on the judgment and action of elected officials."

August 19, 1973

Light Penalty for White-Collar Crime

By MICHAEL C. JENSEN

When Jack L. Clark, the former chairman of the scandal-ridden Four Seasons Nursing Centers of America, Inc., was sentenced earlier this week to one year in prison, with parole possible after only four months, the Federal prosecutors who had hoped to prove that there was no special privilege for people of "wealth and prestige" made it clear that they were chagrined. By their estimate, the Four Seasons scandal had cost unwary shareholders $200-million, and they had urged "substantial punishment" for Clark, a millionaire who could have received a maximum sentence of five years in prison and a fine of $10,000.

News Analysis

Problem of Privilege Underlined in Case of Four Seasons

The prosecutors had contended that Clark, who turned himself in on Thursday to begin serving his prison term, profited personally by $10-million from the massive securities fraud, and that he had "stashed" $4-million in a secret Delaware trust.

Yet the sentence was based on only a narrow set of facts, because Clark was allowed to plead guilty to a small part of what the Government had charged.

According to critics of the criminal justice system as it works on white-collar crime, Clark's case is more the rule than the exception.

Notwithstanding a few exceptions like the two-year jail sentence of convicted stock swindler Edward M. Gilbert, businessmen, stockbrokers and securities analysts who have violated securities laws all too often are disciplined with punishments that amount to little more than a slap on the wrist, the critics say.

For example, the following cases from the files of the Securities and Exchange Commission are representative of those in which Government investigations resulted in consent agreements between the commission and the individuals charged with violations:

¶Austen B. Colgate, the blue-blood managing partner of the small brokerage house of Middendorf, Colgate & Co., was charged by the S.E.C. earlier this year with "gross abuse of trust" and "personal misconduct" in his handling of an in-house mutual fund. His penalty was a 90-day suspension from engaging in the securities business.

¶James G. Joyce, a securities analyst with Weis, Voisin, Cannon, Inc., before it became Weis Securities, was found by the S.E.C. last year to have "willfully violated" securities laws by inducing customers to buy a company's stock through false and misleading statements about its prospects. His penalty was censure.

¶Howard J. Aibel, senior vice president and general counsel of the International Telephone and Telegraph Corporation, sold some of his I.T.T. stock on the basis of inside information, which when it became public caused the stock to decline, according to the S.E.C. Mr. Aibel did not contest the finding. His punishment? He was ordered not to repeat his performance.

September 22, 1973

283

CHAPTER **4**
The Police

A New York City policeman on the beat.
Courtesy The New York Times.

J. E. HOOVER HEADS NEW CRIME BUREAU

Division Created by Roosevelt Will War on Kidnappers and Racketeers.

IN THE WORK SINCE 1924

Special to THE NEW YORK TIMES.

WASHINGTON, July 29.—J. Edgar Hoover, chief of the Justice Department's Bureau of Investigation, was appointed by Attorney General Cummings today as director of the Division of Investigation created by the President's executive order of June 10.

This new division will include the present bureaus of investigation, identification and prohibition, effective Aug. 10. John S. Hurley, assistant prohibition director, was named assistant head of the division.

No reference was made in the official announcement to Major A. V. Dalrymple, chief of the Prohibition Bureau. Speculation immediately developed as to whether he would be retained in some capacity or dropped. The department refused to shed light on the subject other than to say other changes in connection with consolidations would be announced later.

Mr. Hoover succeeded the late William J. Burns. He was appointed a clerk in the Department of Justice in July, 1917. When Mr. Burns retired in May, 1924, former Attorney General Stone promoted Mr. Hoover to be acting director. He was appointed director in the following December.

Dalrymple Opposed Repeal.

Frequent reports have been circulated that Major Dalrymple will retire from the service, after a short but eventful service. His first conference with the newspaper correspondents developed an unpleasant situation and some of his actions were not approved by the Attorney General. Before a Congressional committee he opposed immediate repeal of the Eighteenth Amendment at a time when President Roosevelt and his advisers were urging prompt action.

The new division of the Justice Department will conduct the nation-wide warfare against racketeers, kidnappers and other criminals.

Organized World Criminal Bureau.

John Edgar Hoover was the youngest man to ever head the Bureau of Immigration, being only 30 when he was appointed director.

Mr. Hoover first served as an assistant to Attorney General Mitchell Palmer. In this capacity he handled the legal end of the deportation of radicals. He had charge of the government cases against Emma Goldman, Alexander Berkman and Ludwig Martens, Soviet Ambassador to the United States.

July 30, 1933

ON THE CRIME TRAIL WITH SILENT G-MEN

In the Weyerhaeuser Kidnapping Case The Federal Agents Reveal Their Technique and Their Mobility

By RUSSELL OWEN

WASHINGTON.

THE United States has come to have its romantic police force—the G-men—one which already ranks in attraction with Scotland Yard and the Canadian Mounties, and which far surpasses the French Sûreté as a dramatic weapon. But the full extent of its operations, the speed and mobility with which it moves, and its remarkable machinery were never so thoroughly illuminated as they were during the Weyerhaeuser kidnapping, when men in the field were directed from Washington, 2,500 miles away, by telephone.

The staff work of the Bureau of Investigation of the Department of Justice has been subordinated in the past by the rattle of machine guns and pistol shots, and the desperate man-hunts which have swept over the Eastern and Middle Western parts of the country. But in the Weyerhaeuser case there became evident the discipline and control which makes the G-men such an efficient organization against crime.

"National 7117, Washington."

That telephone call made anywhere in the country will start into action a smooth-working machine, so correlated and tied together that at all times any district office from Maine to California, and from the Mexican border to Canada, is put on its toes. What is more, the system of communications is so swift that every member of the bureau, no matter where he is stationed, is as familiar with the details of an important case as are the agents who are working on it near the scene of the crime.

• • •

THERE is a ring on National 7117, beside which sits a bureau employe day and night, or there may be a sudden clicking of a teletype in the Washington office, or perhaps the telephone on the desk of J. Edgar Hoover, director of the bureau, buzzes with a shrill insistence. It was Hoover's telephone in the Weyerhaeuser case, and that energetic person, who talks like a machine gun and has the intensity of a bloodhound, snapped up in his chair. This is an approximation of what happened.

"Take everybody in the Portland office over to Tacoma," snapped Hoover. "Go by airplane. Open an office and set up two teletypes. Tell the family to keep quiet and let us handle it. I'll send you help."

Desk phones buzzed in the bureau; in came an assistant director, supervisors, stenographers, who found Hoover running through a list of the men in his Western offices. He knows them all. Incidentally, every office is connected

Send Johnson from San Francisco, he's a good shot. Get two good men from the laboratory and have them hop a plane immediately. There may be some fingerprints or other things they can work on. Tell stenographers to get there from Chicago. They will need more cars. Send three from San Francisco, two from Los Angeles and one each from Salt Lake City and Denver. And be sure that machine guns, rifles and pistols are sent with the cars and from Chicago. They may need them."

Ten minutes after the first call came into the Washington bureau, men were starting for flying fields in half a dozen cities. Some of them carried odd-looking cases containing guns, others cameras and equipment with which to make chemical analyses and record fingerprints. But more than anything else, they carried intelligence, courage and the ability to work together.

• • •

HOOVER does not think there is much new to detective work, and no mystery about it. It requires speed, clear thinking, attention to details, and infinite patience. The paraphernalia of the modern detective is interesting and invaluable, but it is the system under which he works that solves crimes.

The bureau has developed a definite technique for use in major crimes of kidnapping, bank robbery and extortion, and methods vary only as circumstances require. Just as the staff of the army and navy fights imaginary battles at the war colleges, so do the agents of the bureau go through a period of training in which every crime with which they have to deal is outlined directly with the Washington bureau by teletype, so that communication can be made instantly.

"Take these messages," said Hoover. "Tell so and so in St. Paul, who worked on the Bremer case, to take a plane for Tacoma. Send Jones and Brown from New York, they know that country and they are good men on ransom notes, and a plan of attack devised to cope with it."

Hence within a few minutes of the time agents in Portland, Oregon, learned that the Weyerhaeuser boy had been abducted from Tacoma, the case stimulated activity in every branch in the country and each G-man knew what to do. The fact came over the teletypes, long before it could be distributed by the press associations. The Portland office was in action even before Hoover sent instructions. Local police authorities were notified, highways and railroad stations were placed under observation, every channel of escape was watched. If kidnappers could see the uproar they create throughout the country when they "snatch" somebody, it is doubtful if they would ever make the attempt.

The first effort was to do everything possible to bring about the safe return of the child. And this is where the bureau's policy of silence is so valuable. Agents do not talk; Hoover never denies or confirms any report. It was rumored that Alvin Karpis had something to do with the case. Hoover did not deny it, and it made an excellent red herring for the kidnappers. When the ransom note was delivered—although unfortunately it was handled by dozens of hands before the agents could get it—plans were made to meet the situation.

The money was obtained, $200,-000 in old bills, without consecutive numbers, 20,000 bills in all. The numbers were copied, and the list was sent to Washington. There every number was put on a card, and then the cards were sorted so that the numbers became as nearly consecutive as possible under the circumstances. That was a gruelling task, one of those patient efforts which get results, for through the bills Harmon M. Waley and his wife were caught.

For two days and nights men and women, working in shifts, copied the numbers, sorted them, and then printed them by a special process. There were 100,000 of these lists made, and they were sent by air express to the western offices for distribution through the mail to police departments, banks, garages, gas stations, and chain stores.

The cooperation that the bureau receives from the public because of its successful kidnapping hunts was shown by an almost unprecedented action on the part of Western newspapers. Many of them printed the entire list of numbers, giving up more than four pages of valuable space, so that the actual distribution of the lists after the boy had been released, was greater than had been obtained before in other cases. When the abandoned car of William Mahan, a confederate of the Waleys, was found, it contained a newspaper list against which he had checked off the numbers of the bills he had kept.

• • •

THE swift undercover work of the agents went on during the days the boy was missing, and while contact was being made with the kidnappers. More men were sent to Tacoma, as the teletypes in the Washington office sent in reports of what was going on, and with the aid of local police departments the entire area in which the kidnappers might be was subjected to a silent but careful examination. Then came the delivery of the ransom money and the release of the boy, and the entire organization snapped into action. There has probably never been a more complete watch kept for ransom money, for all the lessons learned in the other forty-one kidnapping cases which the bureau has solved—there have been forty-two altogether—were brought to bear on this situation.

For three days and nights neither Hoover in Washington nor his chief aides in Tacoma went to bed. They napped beside telephones, ate when they could. There are no time limits on the work of men chasing criminals. The excellent morale of the staff was revealed by the number of men on vacation who asked that their leave be cancelled so that they could work on the case. Hoover is proud of his men, and they like him because he backs them up. Infractions of discipline are punished severely—there is something ruthless about Hoover which shows in his eyes and the contour of his face—but he is jealous of his bureau and goes to the bat for it whenever it is challenged.

During this trying time there was sent to Washington and distributed every day by teletype to the other offices a summary of the case. This is the key to the way in which the bureau works. In the old days the usual procedure was to assign two or three agents to a case and let them stay with it. But as highways and automobiles improved, and airplanes came into use, the old method of sending one group of men chasing over the country after criminals became outmoded. Thus by means of the summaries every branch in the country knows what is going on; it has fingerprints, photographs, and descriptions of wanted criminals, and if a kidnapper or bank burglar jumps from Los Angeles to Chicago, or Salt Lake City, he has a grimly eager group of men waiting to receive him.

At any given time Hoover knows just where each one of his agents is working; he keeps track of them by means of an interesting map which hangs on the wall of his office. The map shows the resident agents and main offices in the country, and little tags attached to pins bear the name of each man. There are white tags for the special agents, blue for accountants, red for clerical workers and green for the agent in charge. The pins are shifted the moment a man is ordered to another spot.

When the Weyerhaeuser case cracked open pins and tags were massed thickly around Tacoma, the group at Salt Lake City and Butte was also enlarged. There were two green tags, for not only was an agent in the field put in charge of the case, but the assistant director in charge of investigations also went out from Washington. As Hoover lifts up the tags and reads the names he can tell not only where a man is ordinarily stationed, but also his special abilities.

• • •

THE bureau agents started on the Weyerhaeuser case without the slightest knowledge of who had committed the crime. That is a fact which illustrates the value of their methods. They did not know anything, but they thought it was probably the work of a local group. The Karpis angle they pooh-poohed; the suggestion that Volney Davis might have been mixed up in it made them laugh because they had Davis cooped up in a Chicago jail, and kept that fact to themselves for three days.

When a ransom bill turned up in Salt Lake City, having been passed by Mrs. Margaret Waley, the G-men were able to go to work in familiar ways. Her husband was caught soon after, and both of them were questioned. Waley told three stories, each more revealing than the other, and the reason for this progressive truthfulness lay in the fact that as soon as he made a statement it was put on the teletype for the home office where it could be checked. When it was found that he had lied, he was confronted with the lie—only a few minutes later—and he soon wilted. "When you catch any man in a lie, it does not matter what it is," says Hoover; "the chances of making him tell the truth become much greater. The detection of a few lies breaks him down. The old third degree is the bunk."

And this method of cooperation between the various districts shows again how the small bureau of 500 men, covering the entire United States and 126,000,000 people, works as the most efficient unit against gang crime which has yet been devised.

The statements made by the Waleys clinched the identification of Mahan. When the chase for him began, several of the men who took up the trail through the northwest woods and mountains were thoroughly familiar with that part of the country and used to the ways of Western folk. One of the Western agents wears a sombrero and when a tin can is tossed into the air he can put three bullets through it before it touches the ground. The bureau assigns men to districts and jobs which they know.

But there was another group of men who had a more inglorious and tiresome job, those who watched Mahan's former habitats. Detective work is not all melodramatic, much of it consists of watchful waiting.

"Can you imagine," said Hoover, "the patience required to sit in a room and watch a house across the street for days, weeks, and perhaps for months. But it has to be done because eventually our man will come to that house and we'll get him. No inspiration about that, just dogged patience and constant vigilance."

So when a criminal like Mahan gets loose the trail is not only in the neighborhood where he is known to have disappeared; it spreads to far-away regions. The agents learn the names of his friends, his relatives, his girls, and places where he has been known to drink and gamble, and they watch those places like hawks until he is found. It may be six months, but if the criminal is sufficiently important, like John Dillinger, there is no relaxation of vigilance.

"Sooner or later, we get him," says Hoover.

PATIENCE and cooperation—these two qualities have made the Bureau of Investigation. It was not by accident that agents got on the track of the Dillinger gang in every place to which it moved, that they chased the Karpis-Barker gang all over the Middle Western and Eastern States, from Cleveland to Detroit, to Chicago, to Florida, to Atlantic City. Each local group of agents was ready for these men when it was learned that they had come into a new territory. They knew their records, their faces, their mannerisms, and the way in which they used their guns.

And in time the gangsters began to learn the methods of the agents. It was Machine-gun Kelly, who named them G-men. When he was captured he walked out of a room, hands above his head, leaving two pistols behind him on a bed.

"Why didn't you use them?" asked one of the agents.

"I knew you G-men would kill me," said Kelly.

Kelly's case illustrates another instance of the mobility of the bureau. There were reports from many parts of the Middle West that Kelly had been seen, all of them false. Then came word from Memphis. There is no office of the bureau in Memphis, but the moment Hoover heard of the report he sent men in planes from Birmingham, St. Louis and Kansas City, knowing that the weather was bad and hoping that one plane would get through. The plane from Birmingham did, the other two were turned back. Regular transports are used when possible; if transports are not available, planes are chartered.

This prolific use of planes, the speed with which action is taken would indicate that the bureau has unlimited funds. That is not so. Last year the bureau had an appropriation of $2,500,000, and recovered $20,000,000 in fines and stolen property. This year, with an appropriation of $4,000,000 the bureau expects to double the amount of fines and recoveries, although only thirty-eight men have been added to the force.

The agents have no pension rights, because they are not under civil service, hence when a man is badly wounded, killed or retired because of age, his family must go along as best it can. Widows of men killed in the line of duty find jobs in the bureau; there were four of them last year.

Hoover's men are proud of their record. Aside from the kidnapping cases, all of which have been cleared up, extortion and bank robberies have decreased. The effect on bank robberies of having a mobile force of men who can be shifted over State lines and who cooperate perfectly has been one of the most revealing phases of the bureau's work. Chasing bank robbers is not so spectacular as trailing kidnappers, and it has not attracted as much attention, but bank robberies have decreased from fifteen a month a year ago to four or five a month at present.

The law making it a Federal offense to rob national banks, member banks of the Federal Reserve System and other institutions in which Federal funds are deposited was passed on May 18, 1934. The bureau then established a single fingerprint file of all known bank robbers in the United States, about 5,000 altogether. Descriptions of them were obtained, and their methods of work were studied by an examination of old bank robberies in which they had been involved.

The agents have become so efficient in running down this type of criminal that robbers are avoiding national banks. One of them, when caught by G-men after robbing a State bank, was highly indignant.

"What are you fellows in on this job for?" he demanded. "This wasn't a national bank."

"No, but it had national funds in it," replied the agent with a grin.

"I wish I'd known it," said the crestfallen robber.

• • •

When one gets behind the usual conception of the agents of the Bureau of Investigation, penetrates the smoke screen which popularly

hangs over their rifles and machine guns, one finds a group of men so intensely interested in their work, so fast moving and efficient, that they make detective stories rather tame reading. The only thing is that they won't talk much about themselves—Hoover does the talking for them, and when he wants to be silent on a subject he has the sphinx completely outmoded. But when he does talk he proves himself to be one of the best publicity men an anti-crime agency has ever had; perhaps that is one reason for the popularity of the G-men. As Gene Buck once said of him, "he's a good showman."

June 23, 1935

It Is 'F. B. I.,' Not 'G-Men.'
WASHINGTON, June 29 (AP).—The Department of Justice has no more "G-Men." They are agents of the "F. B. I." Henceforth the department will ignore the name made famous by "Machine Gun" Kelly. Just as England has its C. I. D., the United States will have its F. B. I., which stands for Federal Bureau of Investigation.

June 30, 1935

F. B. I. AND LOCAL CRIME

Special to The New York Times.

WASHINGTON, Sept. 1—While the Federal Bureau of Investigation often figures prominently and dramatically in the solution of what appear to be purely local crimes, in actuality its jurisdiction is limited by law to the investigation of offenses against Federal statutes only.

In the case of the acid blinding of labor columnist Victor Riesel, for example, G-men were called on immediately by the United States Attorney for the reason that Mr. Riesel was scheduled to give testimony before a Federal grand jury in a racketeering investigation. The assault on Mr. Riesel was construed as an attempt to intimidate him and to "influence" the testimony he would give.

The Federal authority relied on in this case was a statute aimed at conspiracies to obstruct the administration of justice.

F. B. I. jurisdiction in general covers all violations of Federal laws except those specifically assigned by statute to other agencies such as the Secret Service (counterfeiting, protection of the President, etc.) postal authorities, the Customs Service, and so on. There are 140 investigative matters exclusively in F. B. I. territory.

A number of special statutes

have been enacted over the last two decades, however, which greatly facilitate the F. B. I.'s participation with local police in the solution of non-Federal crimes.

One of the most frequently employed is known as the "unlawful flight" act. In a limited number of offenses such as murder, robbery, rape and aggravated assault, if local police are convinced the culprit has left the state, they can swear out a Federal warrant for his apprehension.

Kidnapping Law

The Federal kidnapping statute (enacted after the Lindbergh case twenty-four years ago) is predicated on the assumption that if the victim has not been recovered within twenty-four hours he has been taken across state lines, thus making it a "national" rather than a "local" offense.

The F. B. I. moves in immediately on all bank robberies on the ground that banks (with only a few exceptions) are subject to the authority of the Federal Reserve, the Federal Deposit Insurance Corporation, and other Federal laws relating to banking.

Roll of Dishonor

By CHARLES and BONNIE REMSBERG

AN Alcatraz alumnus named Carl Close stepped into a bank in Anderson, S.C., last fall and picked up $28,262 at gunpoint. As he backed out of the building and headed for his getaway car, however, he was seized by two detectives who happened to be cruising by. The swift apprehension of Close, a modern Dillinger who had embezzled a small fortune and robbed five banks, must have been particularly humiliating to him, for just the day before he had been elected to an exclusive fraternity that admits only a handful of the nation's top lawbreakers: the F.B.I.'s list of "Ten Most Wanted Fugitives."

Actually, Close need not have felt chagrined. To have made the "Top Ten" at all put him in a class with Willie Sutton, "One-Eye" Bobby Wilcoxson, Frederick Emerson Peters and other criminal kingpins.

Nor was Close's 24 hours on the list a record for short-lived infamy. Philip LaNor

mandin, who shot his way out of a police trap after a stick-up in Massachusetts, had been on the list only three hours when someone in New Jersey recognized him from his picture in the paper and called the F.B.I.

THE F.B.I. issued its first most-wanted list in 1950. Until then, the only list of the kind was the register of "public enemies" drafted by Municipal Judge John H. Lyle in the nineteen thirties in Chicago. The term "Public Enemy Number One" was coined by Henry Barrett Chamberlin, director of the Chicago Crime Commission, and was first applied to Al Capone; then, as newsmen picked it up, to such outlaws as Charles (Pretty Boy) Floyd, Lester (Baby Face Nelson) Gillis and Alvin (Old Creepy) Karpis.

In 1950, William K. Hutchinson, then Washington bureau chief of the old International News Service, decided it would be useful if public attention was focused on the country's top crooks and presented his idea to the F.B.I. At first there was some doubt among the law-enforcers about the list. But today the F.B.I. says it has proved of "exceptional value in combating one of our most perplexing problems—the fast - moving, far - ranging criminal fugitive."

The thinking behind the most-wanted list is that even the slickest criminal is likely to be seen by someone almost every day—eating, buying gas or looking for a place to hide. If his face, physical description and personal habits are widely known, the chances are good that he will be recognized.

The F.B.I. sends information on its listed men to 13,000 police agencies, all post offices, some 2,000 newspapers, nearly 40 radio and television stations and 50 magazines.

Sometimes it expands this coverage. Looking for Joseph Corbett Jr. a few years ago in the kidnap-killing of Colorado brewery baron Adolph Coors III, the Bureau increased its distribution by sending flyers to opticians (Corbett wore glasses), barbers, bus drivers in cities of more than 50,000 population, hospitals, gas stations, railroad stations and airlines. (Corbett was captured in Canada.)

NO rewards are offered by the F.B.I., but more than one-third of all captures over the years have resulted from tips from citizens—sometimes from as many as 20 who have spotted the same fugitive. In all, 169 of the 182 men named to the list since 1950 have been accounted for. In addition to those captured, some have committed suicide and some have been shot.

About 1,400 culprits are considered during a year for designation as "most wanted." ("The Ten" are not ranked, by the way; all are equally "most wanted.") There are at least a dozen criminals always on the waiting list. Often the fugitives' original crimes are of no official concern to the F.B.I.; the agency technically is after them for crossing state lines to avoid prosecution. To qualify for inclusion in the "Top Ten," a crook's trail must be cold and he must have been classified as "a menace to society." No woman has ever made the list.

TOP TENNERS have largely been loners, not members of gangs. Most of them—some 52 in all—have been wanted for murder. The number of kidnapers has declined since passage of the Lindbergh Law. Nor

do bank robbers make the list as often as they did. In the aggregate, robbery (not bank robbery) has placed second (51 fugitives); then bank robbery (25); then burglary (14).

Most Top Tenners surrender quietly when captured, despite their past histories of gunning down policeman and others and their almost universal boasts that they will "never be taken alive." On an average, they are captured 900 miles from the spot where their original crimes occurred and, according to F.B.I. officials, they usually show relief to be free at last of the constant fear that they are going to be recognized by everybody they see.

"Ever since I made the list, I've felt like I was walking down a glass sidewalk that might break at any minute," burglar Frank Sprenz said when he was picked up. "I'm glad it's over."

September 2, 1956

J. Edgar Hoover Made the F.B.I. Formidable With Politics, Publicity and Results

By CHRISTOPHER LYDON
Special to The New York Times

WASHINGTON, May 2 — When J. Edgar Hoover ambled through the Mayflower Hotel after one of his ritual fruit-salad-and-coffee lunches late last year, he passed almost unnoticed.

The once ruddy face was puffy and pale. The brushed-back, gray-brown hair was straight and thin—not the wiry dark curls of a few years ago. He walked stiffly, although his figure was trim and erect. Behind his glasses, his dark brown eyes looked fixed, and he seemed to be daydreaming.

At the age of 77, the legendary G-man—in his 48th year as director of the Federal Bureau of Investigation—the most enduring and perhaps, if there is such a thing as a cumulative total, the most powerful official in the long span of the American Government—looked deceptively like any other old gentleman in the hotel lobby.

In one of his rare reflections

on mortality a few years ago, Mr. Hoover told a reporter, "The greatest enemy is time." Time's advances against this seemingly indestructible official had become obvious. But then, Mr. Hoover was always more human than he or the myth admitted.

Mr. Hoover's power was a compound of performance and politics, publicity and personality. At the base of it all, however, was an extraordinary record of innovation and modernization in law enforcement — most of it in the first decade or so of his tenure.

The centralized fingerprint file (the print total passed the 200-million mark this year) at the Identification Division (1925) and the crime laboratory (1932) are landmarks in the gradual application of science to police work. The National Police Academy (1935) has trained the leadership élite of local forces throughout the

country. Mr. Hoover's recruitment of lawyers and accountants, although they now make up only 32 per cent of the special agent corps, set a world standard of professionalism.

The National Crime Information Center enables 4,000 local law enforcement agencies to enter records and get questions answered on a network of 35 computer systems, with its headquarters at the F.B.I. office here.

From the start, Mr. Hoover got results. His bureau rounded up the gangsters in the nineteen-thirties. It made the once epidemic crime of kidnapping a rarity ("virtually extinct," as the director's friends like to say). It arrested German saboteurs within days after their submarines landed them on the Atlantic Coast. And, in one of its most sensational coups, the F.B.I. seized the slayers of Mrs. Viola Gregg Liuzzo only hours after the civil rights worker's

shotgun death in Alabama in 1965.

The F.B.I. does not catch everybody, and it is sometimes many months before any of its "most wanted" suspects are arrested. But Mr. Hoover executed enough seemingly miraculous swoops to make any specific criticism perilous.

Mr. Hoover always understood the subtle currents of power among officials in Washington better than anyone know him. Not a New Dealer at heart, he had nonetheless dazzled President Franklin D. Roosevelt with his celebrated success against kidnappers.

He Got Results

Roosevelt liked him; he slapped the F.B.I. director's back and laughed when Mr. Hoover confessed that an agent had been caught in the act of illegal wiretapping, and he was amused at the bureau's temerity in putting a spy on Harry

289

Hopkins, Roosevelt's counselor, in London. Roosevelt's assignment of counter-espionage duties to the F.B.I. as war loomed in 1936 expanded the bureau's size and heightened Mr. Hoover's prestige.

But, when the Republicans won the White House again in 1952, Mr. Hoover's loyalty swung immediately to the new team.

The more awesome Mr. Hoover's power grew, the more plainly he would state, for the record, that there was nothing "political" about it, that the F.B.I. was simply a "fact-finding agency" that "never makes recommendations or draws conclusions." The most pointed such declaration, coming in the furor about Harry Dexter White in 1953, was, paradoxically, one of Mr. Hoover's most political acts.

In a speech in Chicago, Herbert Brownell, President Eisenhower's Attorney General, said that Mr. White, who had served as Assistant Secretary of the Treasury under Roosevelt, was named in 1946 as the United States executive director of the International Monetary Fund even though President Truman had been told that Mr. White was a Soviet spy. Mr. Truman, in retirement, replied that the F.B.I. had contributed to the judgment that it would be safer to keep Mr. White in office, under observation, than to dismiss him.

Rushing before Senate investigators, Mr. Hoover did not question the "conclusion" that Mr. White was a spy — although the F.B.I.'s evidence had not been enough to persuade a grand jury to indict Mr. White before he died in 1948. As for Mr. White's promotion to the International Monetary Fund, Mr. Hoover stated emphatically that, while he knew of Mr. Truman's reasoning, he had not been in on the decision nor had he approved it.

At a time when the Republican party chairman was promising to make Communism in government the central issue of the 1954 Congressional campaign, Mr. Hoover's eager testimony was taken by some to be a boldly partisan move.

House Speaker Sam Rayburn was one of many Democrats who never forgave Mr. Hoover and encouraged speculation that a Democratic President would find a new F.B.I. director.

But Mr. Hoover's reappointment was virtually the first decision John F. Kennedy announced on the day after his election to the Presidency in 1960.

Despite its acrimonious endings the Hoover-Kennedy relationship started out cordially, based apparently on Mr. Hoover's long acquaintance with the President's father, the late Joseph P. Kennedy.

Robert Kennedy had urged the President-elect to retain Mr. Hoover; and when John Kennedy weighed assignments for his brother, Mr. Hoover urged him to follow his instinct and make Robert the Attorney General.

Later Robert Kennedy and Mr. Hoover fought a long tug-of-war over the assignment of agents to civil rights and organized crime cases. Mr. Hoover was not used to having an immediate boss who could block his access to the White House. He was annoyed when the Attorney General installed a "hot line" between their Justice Department offices, and was even more annoyed when Robert Kennedy had the F.B.I. phone moved from the desk of Helen Gandy, Mr. Hoover's long-time secretary, to the director's desk.

Robert Kennedy never forgave Mr. Hoover for the cold telephone call that brought the first word of his brother's assassination. Mr. Hoover's voice, Robert Kennedy told William Manchester, the author, was "not quite as excited as if he were reporting the fact that he had found a Communist on the faculty of Howard University."

Later, according to William W. Turner, a former agent who wrote an unflattering book on "Hoover's F.B.I.," Robert Kennedy called back on the hot line. "Hoover was in his office with several aides," Mr. Turner wrote, "when it rang . . . and rang . . . and rang. When it stopped ringing, the director snapped to an aide, 'Now get that phone back on Miss Gandy's desk.'"

Although Robert Kennedy remained Attorney General until the summer of 1964, he and Mr. Hoover never spoke again after the President's assassination.

Until Representative Hale Boggs of Louisiana, the House majority leader, criticized Mr. Hoover in the House last spring as a "feudal baron" and a wiretapper, the F.B.I. director had been sacrosanct in Congress' deference. The case of former Senator Edward V. Long, a Missouri Democrat who denounced government wiretapping and was quickly undone by Life magazine's disclosure, leaked from the F.B.I., that he was splitting legal fees with a teamster lawyer in St. Louis, is often cited as an example of the director's tactics.

Mr. Hoover insisted that he did not tap the phones or "bug" the offices of Congressmen, and Mr. Boggs failed notably to prove the contrary. But Mr. Hoover always had other ways to keep critics in line anyway.

The late Senator Kenneth D. McKellar, a Tennessee Democrat and chairman of the Senate Appropriations Committee, harassed Mr. Hoover from time to time in the nineteen-thirties, and in the spring of 1936 drew the blushing testimony that the director of the F.B.I. had never made an arrest.

Less than a month later, as if by magic, Mr. Hoover led a raid in New Orleans that captured Alvin (Kreepy) Karpis, a star of the Ma Barker mob.

By his own account, Mr. Hoover rushed up to the unsuspecting Karpis as he sat in a car, threatened him with a gun, then snapped out the order to other agents: "Put the cuffs on him, boys." In his recently published memoirs, Karpis contends that Mr. Hoover "hid until I was safely covered by many guns. He waited until he was told the coast was clear. Then he came out to reap the glory."

Karpis's account is obviously suspect, and about 35 years too late to undo Senator McKellar's embarrassment. When Senator McKellar tried to cut $225,000 out of the F.B.I. budget that year, Senator Arthur H. Vandenberg of Michigan denounced him, according to one report of the Senate debate, "as a miser whose parsimony would cause the threat of kidnapping to hang once more over every cradle in America." Mr. Hoover's full budget request was then passed by a resounding voice vote. Since that time, the Senate has never questioned the F.B.I. budget as reported by the House.

And in the House, the veteran chairman of the Appropriations subcommittee that theoretically reviews the bureau's spending, Representative John J. Rooney, Democrat of Brooklyn, said that "I have never cut [Mr. Hoover's] budget and I never expect to."

As some of the men closest to him volunteer, Mr. Hoover's primary genius might well have been publicity. He had some famous fights with other police agencies — notably after the capture of Bruno Hauptmann, the Lindbergh kidnapper, in 1933 — to secure public credit for his bureau, but Mr. Hoover was no ordinary headline grabber.

The real foundations of his legend are built on more solid stuff than press relations; certainly his image was never dependent on the goodwill of newspapermen, to whom Mr. Hoover was normally inaccessible.

Mr. Hoover never held a news conference. The closest thing to a mouthpiece in the press was not a political pundit or a crime reporter but the late Walter Winchell, the Broadway gossip columnist, who traveled

Mr. Hoover aiming a submachine gun in an F.B.I. target range in 1935. He built skills not only of his men but also of many other officers of the law.

J. Edgar Hoover behind Franklin D. Roosevelt in 1934. The President liked and supported Mr. Hoover.

with an F.B.I. escotr and carried an item about "G-man Hoover" almost every day.

The making of the Hoover folk hero, in which Mr. Winchell played a large part, was undertaken purposefully in the early thirties — long atfer the director's quiet administrative mastery had established him securely.

Speakeasies were the fashion. Gangsterism ravaged the land, capturing headlines and, in a sense, the public fancy. For Mr. Hoover, the last straw was the Kansas City massacre of June 17, 1933, in which Charles (Pretty Boy) Floyd and his gang killed five men, including an F.B.I. agent and three local policemen. "If there is going to be publicity," the director raged, "let it be on the side of law and order."

Looking about for a symbol, Mr. Hoover found himself, and proceeded to orchestrate a dazzling range of movies, books, radio dramas and comic strips.

Mr. Hoover understood pop culture and its evolution. He promoted "junior G-man" clubs for boys, and sold two and a half million copies of "Masters of Deceit," a book on Communism. His "ten most wanted" list made a lot of seedy drifters into headline material. In the age of television, he shrewdly reserved the right to select the actor (Efrem Zimbalist Jr.) who would represent the F.B.I. in millions of living room in a popular television series.

The late Senator George Norris of Nebraska called Mr. Hoover "the greatest hound for publicity on the American continent." Even Chief Justice Harlan Fiske Stone, who had appointed the F.B.I. director in 1924, observed critically that "one of the great secrets of Scotland Yard has been that its movements are never advertised."

But Mr. Hoover, once committed to a public fight on crime, played the role with all his fierce energy. He unquestionably made a brilliant success of it. Even after political pot-shots at the director became fashionable in recent years, a Gallup Pol for Nelwsweek magazine last spring showed that 80 per cent of those who had any opinion about Mr. Hoover rated his performance "good" or "excellent."

Any general accounting of the F.B.I. director's power must also take note of the fact that

United Press International

Mr. Hoover with President Nixon, in whose Administration his tenure, begun under President Coolidge, ended.

his personality, as well as his office, has always inspired fear. Francis Biddle, President Roosevelt's Attorney General in the early nineteen-forties, sensed that, behind Mr. Hoover's "absolute self-control" was "a temper that might show great violence if he did not hold it on leash, subject to the domination of a will that is the master of his temperament."

There were hints of that temper in his passionate criticisms — favorite phrases such as "mental halitosis," and the "jellyfish" tag he put on former Attorney General Ramsey Clark. And Mr. Hoover had a hair-trigger sensitivity to criticism.

When the Warren commission was investigating President Kennedy's assassination and said that the F.B.I. had not shared its intelligence fully with the Secret Service, Mr. Hoover lashed out at what he called "a classic example of Monday morning quarterbacking," a charge that gravely displeased President Johnson.

And when the Rev. Dr. Martin Luther King Jr. said that Southern blacks could not turn to their local F.B.I. offices with any assurance of sympathy or zeal for civil rights, Mr. Hoover called Dr. King "the most notorious liar in the country." Later, Mr. Hoover had his staff invite newsmen to hear the taped record of F.B.I. bugs in Dr. King's hotel rooms as evidence that "moral degenerates," as Mr. Hoover put it, were leading the civil rights movement. This was a rare extension of Mr. Hoover's lifelong practice of entertaining Attorneys General and Presidents with spicy details about the secret lives of famous people.

Critics within the F.B.I. were crushed summarily, and men who were thought to have been good friends of the director reveal deeper levels of hostility in casual conversations. "I'm afraid of him," said a former aide who would seem to have been secure in a new and completely different public career. "I can't imagine what he'd do to me, but I'd rather not mess with him."

John Edgar Hoover was born in Washington on New Year's Day in 1895, the youngest of three children of Dickerson N. Hoover, an easy-going Federal official, and the former Annie M. Scheitlin, the granddaughter of Switzerland's first Consul General in America.

The Hoovers' stucco house on Seward Square has been torn down, but Mr. Hoover's birthplace is memorialized in a stained glass window of the Presbyterian church that stands on the site of the house.

Mrs. Hoover, who has been described as "old-world strict," instilled in her son an intense discipline and stern sensitivity to moral issues. By all accounts, she was the dominant influence on his character.

As a boy, he was known as "Speed"—a reference, apparently, to his agile mind, rattling speech and efficiency as a grocery delivery boy in the Capitol Hill section of Washington.

Admirers have compared his physique to Babe Ruth's—heavy torso, spindly legs — and indeed, his flattened nose was

The New York Times/George Tames

In February of 1961, soon after his inauguration, President John F. Kennedy conferred with Mr. Hoover and Robert F. Kennedy, left. After the assassination of his brother, Robert Kennedy never spoke to the F.B.I. chief.

291

the result of a hard-hit baseball. But Mr. Hoover was never an athlete. Remembering a day in 1909 when the football coach at Central High School rejected the puny volunteer brought twinges ever after.

In his disappointment, young Hoover turned all the more intensely to the school's military drill team, of which he became captain, and to public speaking. According to one biographer, he never had a regular girl friend in high school; friends teased him, wrote Mildred H. Comfort, "and accused him of being in love with Company A," an institutional attachment foreshadowing his marriage to the F.B.I.

As a debater, young Hoover argued "The Fallacies of Women Suffrage" with gusto and competitive success. He was valedictorian of his class and was described in the school yearbook as "a gentleman of dauntless courage and stainless honor." In his high school days, he also was a choir boy and Sunday school instructor.

Lessons on Indexing

Although the University of Virginia offered him a liberal arts scholarship, Mr. Hoover feared that his living expenses would be a burden on his father. Instead, he took a $30-a-month clerk's job at the Library of Congress (he would apply indexing lessons to law enforcement later), and enrolled at George Washington University, where he was able to win his law degree in three years.

With a master's degree in 1917, Mr. Hoover passed the bar and moved into a $1,200-a-year job at the Department of Justice — his only employer over a stretch that exceeded 55 years.

From the start, according to Jack Alexander's 1937 profile of Mr. Hoover in The New Yorker, he stood out from the other young lawyers around him.

"He dressed better than most, a bit on the dandyish side," Mr. Alexander wrote. "He had an exceptional capacity for detail work, and he handled small chores with enthusiasm and thoroughness. He constantly sought new responsibilities to shoulder, and welcomed chances to work overtime. When he was in conference with an official of his department, his manner was that of a young man who confidently expected to rise."

Mr. Hoover's first assignment in "counter-radical activities" left a profound mark. This was at the end of President Wilson's second term, the era of the "Red raids" under Attorney General A. Mitchell Palmer. Evidently caught up in the official agitation about bombs and Bolshevism, Mr. Hoover took charge of assembling a card file

on 450,000 "radicals," and built his first informer nework — a controversial tool of police work that he used with dramatic results later against the Communist party and the Ku Klux Klan.

Many years later, Mr. Hoover said he had always "deplored" the hysterical dragnet arrests of thousands of innocent aliens in 1919 and 1920, but the record is also clear that, as the head of the new General Intelligence Division at the Justice Department, he was responsible for planning the raids, if not their execution.

A still darker era followed under President Harding. Within the Justice Department, according to Alpheus T. Mason, the historian, the Bureau of Investigation "had become a private secret service for corrupt forces within the Government." Mr. Hoover nearly quit in disgust.

When Harlan Fiske Stone became Attorney General under President Coolidge in 1924, he determined to rebuild the bureau after the image of Scotland Yard and sought, as his director, a man experienced in police work but free of the "more usual police tradition that it takes a crook to catch a crook and that lawlessness and brutality are more to be relied upon than skill and special training."

Secretary of Commerce Herbert Hoover, an untainted holdover from the Harding Administration, recommended J. Edgar (no relation) as "a lawyer of uncommon ability and character."

Attorney General Stone, who held the appointive power, offered him the job. But Mr. Hoover, who was then only 29 years old, did not leap at what was unmistakably the chance of a lifetime.

With confidence and cunning that were very much in character, he said he would accept the assignment only if appointments to the bureau were divorced entirely from outside politics and if he would have sole control over merit promotions. Mr. Stone replied that he would not allow Mr. Hoover to take the job under any other conditions. And thus in 1924 the modern bureau — renamed the Federal Bureau of Investigation in 1935—was born.

Organizing Principle

From the start, Mr. Hoover's personal grip on all the important strings was the organizing principle at the bureau. It had everything to do with discipline and morale; Mr. Hoover made Siberia assignments and the compassionate transfers. It had a lot to do with the agency's efficiency and its incomparable record of probity. Under the Hoover inspection system, there

were no secrets and no independent power centers in the F.B.I. In recent years, the system also seemed to have inhibited the bureau from taking worthwhile risks. "The first rule," according to one former agent, was: "Do not embarrass the director."

The insulation from outside politics meant free play for Hoover politics. The 15,000 F.B.I. employes had neither the Civil Service nor a union to inhibit the director's whims. He shaped the bureau in his own Victorian image, and changed in the process himself.

Personal affairs were strictly regulated at the bureau. Women were not allowed to smoke on the job. No one got a coffee break. A clerk was once dismissed for playing with a yo-yo in the halls. In a case that went to court in 1967, a 26-year-old clerk was dismissed for keeping a girl friend in his apartment overnight. Agents have been reprimanded for reading Playboy magazine and transferred for being overweight.

Mr. Hoover wore custom-made, Brooks Brothers shirts and suits, and he ordered his agents to dress carefully, like young businessmen. The unofficial uniform for an agent includes a white shirt, dark suit, snap-brim hat and a handkerchief in the jacket pocket.

One-man rule also bred sycophancy. Flattery worked wonders around Mr. Hoover, according to an inside student of the director's office. "Let's say you're an agent," he said. "Go in there and tell him he looks better than ever, that you are inspired by his leadership, that he's saving America and you hope he lives forever. As soon as you leave there will be a memo from the director saying, 'This man has executive ability.' A lot of agents have caught on."

Agents admittedly quaked at the thought of the director's disapproval, expressed typically in the bright blue ink of Mr. Hoover's stub pen in the margins of their memorandums. His language was vehement ("This is asinine!"); the filling of all four borders around a typewritten sheet was known as a "four-bagger." Once, it is said, when an assistant's memorandum so filled the page that Mr. Hoover barely had room for a comment, he wrote, "Watch the borders," and his puzzled but obedient aides dispatched agents to patrol the Canadian and Mexican borders for a week.

Friends and detractors all agree that the system has mirrored and fed a colossal ego. In the office, for instance, Mr. Hoover never circulated; people came to him. He sat amid flags behind a raised, polished mahogany desk at the end of a

35-foot office. Visitors, if they sat, sank into deep leather chairs and inevitably looked up to the throned director.

A day in the life of J. Edgar Hoover testified to his unflagging energy and to the power of habit. The few changes in his routine were forced on him: His friend Clyde Tolson, the F.B.I.'s associate director, was not well enough to walk the last few blocks to the office in recent days, so their morning strolls along Constitution Avenue were abandoned. The old Harvey's Restaurant was razed, so Mr. Hoover and Mr. Tolson had lunch instead at the Mayflower Hotel next door on Connecticut Avenue.

Old patterns persisted. The chauffeur picked up Mr. Hoover and then Mr. Tolson, about 9 o'clock every morning, and delivered them to the offive about 9:30.

At the end the director was still the complete master of the bureau's huge flow of paper work. He did little sleuthing himself, but he kept abreast of the F.B.I.'s major cases. Certain categories of business were handled by Mr. Hoover alone, including high-level personnel decisions, liaison in other than routine matters with Congress, the Attorney General and the White House, and anything that brought unfavorable publicity on the bureau.

He left for lunch at 11:30 A.M., returned by 12:45 P.M. and usually took work home with him when he left for the day at 4:30.

There were things he did not do anymore. He outlived the Stork Club in New York where he long enjoyed café society's attention and the friendship of Sherman Billingsley, the owner. He no longer tended the azaleas around his house. He had to give up his favorite angel food cake and chocolate cream pie to keep his weight down. Once an avid walker, he said that "conditions in this city," presumably a reference to the crime rate, kept him out of Rock Creek Park, formerly a favorite stamping ground near his house.

Some Continuities

Still, the continuities in his life were as noticeable as the changes: the Jack Daniel's whiskey before dinner; the Miami vacation during the last two weeks of December and the July break and physical check-up in La Jolla, Calif., the passion for horse racing; and above all, the friendship with Mr. Tolson, a fellow bachelor with whom Mr. Hoover had lunch and dinner six days a week since the late nineteen-twenties.

Mr. Tolson, who always stayed a respectful step behind

Mr. Hoover in their famous walks together, lagged severely after two strokes and open-heart surgery. But the friendship was as fast as ever, and, through a special personnel device that Mr. Hoover engineered to get around Mr. Tolson's physical disability, Mr. Tolson remains the bureau's second-ranking officer.

Together they frequented the racetracks around Washington, as well as Gulfstream in Miami and Delmar in La Jolla. Mr. Hoover, who applied the same analytical imagination to the racing charts that he once used on kidnapping rings, was still bothered by touts who recognized him and wanted to tip him on a sure thing. But he bet only $2 on each race and would leave in disgust if his losses went over $10. Friends say it was Mr. Tolson, not Mr. Hoover, who sent junior F.B.I. agents around to the $50 and $100 windows with heavy side bets.

Mr. Hoover's humor usually ran to heavy-handed practical jokes. The late Julius Lulley, the restaurateur who always kept a special table set for Mr. Hoover and Mr. Tolson at Harvey's, once found his Maryland farm dotted with F.B.I. "wanted" posters bearing Mr. Lulley's picture.

Years ago, when Guy Hottel, a Hoover bodyguard and friend, got married, the F.B.I. director found out where Mr. Hottel was going on his honeymoon and conspired with the Virginia State Police to have the newly-weds picked up and held over-night on a fake charge.

Mr. Hoover was not always quick to appreciate other people's jokes. In his saloon-going days in New York, it was said that he avoided Toots Shor's restaurant because of the insults that were Mr. Shor's trademark.

However, there always was a droll undercurrent in many of Mr. Hoover's utterances—as in the W. C. Fields-like defense of racetracks as an outlet for people's emotions, "which, if they weren't at the track, they might use for less laudable escapades."

And Mr. Hoover recently took to public kidding about himself—the clearest sign of his rejuvenation under President Nixon and Attorney General John N. Mitchell.

Why Did He Stay?

At a party for Mr. Mitchell's wife Martha last summer, Mr. Hoover brought the house down with an impromptu speech. Referring to a recent Life magazine cover that featured a marble bust of his bulldog face and the headline, "Emperor of the F.B.I.," Mr. Hoover apologized to those who did not recognize him in a tuxedo.

"We emperors have our problems," he said. "My Roman toga was not returned from the cleaners."

Perhaps the most widely asked question about Mr. Hoover recently was why he stayed on the job, but that, too, had been around a while. Even in the nineteen-thirties his long tenure was considered remarkable. During the forties, a former aide recalls, "every year he'd ask for a computation of his retirement and there'd be a rumor that the old boy was stepping down." The inside gossip in the fifties was that Mr. Hoover had approved plans for the construction of his retirement villa at La Jolla.

After John Kennedy reappointed Mr. Hoover in 1960, it was thought he would bow out around the mandatory retirement age of 70, which would have come on New Year's Day, 1965. But as early as May, 1964, President Johnson waived the retirement law. The next obvious milestone was his 75th birthday in January, 1971, but that passed without incident, like all the rest.

Some people say that Mr. Hoover wanted to see the completion of the new $102-million F.B.I. building on Pennsylvania Avenue — sometime in 1974. Mr. Hoover says he will stay on the job as long as his physical condition permitted. But why? "I've always been against retiring a man by age," he said. "The longer a man is with us, the more valuable he becomes."

The men around Mr. Hoover pointed to his egotism—a sense of his own indispensability—and to the lack of family and interests that consoled other men in retirement. "For him the bureau is everything," said a friend.

May 3, 1972

BURGLARIES LAID TO AGENTS OF F.B.I. IN 30-YEAR PERIOD

National Security and Fight Against Crime Are Cited—Halt Reported in 1966

By JOHN M. CREWDSON
Special to The New York Times

WASHINGTON, Aug. 23 — Informed Justice Department sources disclosed today that what one of them called "illegal and unlawful" burglaries by agents of the Federal Bureau of Investigation had taken place in this country over a 30-year period that began under the Administration of President Franklin D. Roosevelt and ended in 1966.

One source, who like the others asked not to be named, said that the burglaries, "obviously" barred by the Fourth Amendment, had been conducted not only in connection with national security investigations, but also in criminal cases and against alleged crime figures.

The source said that the practice was "an old, established investigative technique," but that its use had never been known to any of the Attorneys General who served during the time it was employed, or to anyone else outside the F.B.I.

Disclosure Corroborated

The disclosure, which was corroborated by others familiar with the practice, followed a statement by President Nixon at a news conference in San Clemente, Calif., yesterday that such burglaries took place "on a very large scale" during the Administrations of Presidents Kennedy and Johnson.

Mr. Nixon made the remark, which brought rapid denials from two former Democratic Attorneys General, in response to a question about the constitutionality of the 1971 burglary of the office of a Los Angeles psychiatrist who had treated Dr. Daniel Ellsberg, the former Defense Department official who says he provided the Pentagon papers to the press.

Mr. Nixon said that such burglaries had been "authorized" in other Administrations, but did not say by whom. The sources said today, however, that approval of the technique had never come from any authority higher than J. Edgar Hoover, the late F.B.I. director, who ordered the practice ended in 1966.

Hunt for Codes Cited

The sources said that, in some instances, breaking and entering by specially trained F.B.I. men had been used against foreign embassies and missions in this country in hopes of finding "cryptographic materials," or code books.

Associated Press

Ramsey Clark, an Attorney General under President Lyndon B. Johnson, said he had refused permission for unlawful entry of a foreign mission in New York.

293

Whenever code books were found, one source said, they were turned over to the National Security Agency, an arm of the executive branch that specializes in code-breaking, among other top-secret functions.

According to one former Justice Department official, Mr. Hoover halted the practice in 1966 because he disliked lending his agents to such a risky enterprise, and because "the benefits we got out of it were for the N.S.A., not the F.B.I."

He recalled that Mr Hoover had said several times after that, when the security agency appealed for further burglaries, "if they need it [the information], let them get it themselves" But, he said, the security agency was not "equipped to do that—it takes some pretty sophisticated equipment and years of training. "

Memorandum by Huston

Tom Charles Huston, a former adviser to Mr. Nixon on internal security matters, wrote in a memorandum to the President in July, 1970, that the technique of burglarizing foreign embassies should be resurrected.

"We spend millions of dollars attempting to break these codes by machine," Mr. Huston noted. "One successful surreptitious entry can do the job successfully at no dollar cost."

Another source said that the technique had not been "limited to national security matters." He said: "It's been done on criminal cases, too. You can catch a fugitive much quicker [that way] than by looking for him for a year and a half."

The source said that one rule employed by F.B.I. agents on such cases was that "you never take anything except information." In the case of a criminal fugitive, he said, agents breaking into a house or apartment might find "any number of" clues pointing toward his whereabouts, or "to look for a sign that an individual was there."

He said that organized crime figures had been the object of such burglaries as well,

"They're not perfect — they leave documents behind them, too," he added.

All F.B.I. agents before 1966 "had the capability" to perform such burglaries, the source said, but those actually used were a more select group. "Just like a man has a special talent for playing the violin," he explained. "Well, it's the same with this business. For one thing, you need nerves of steel."

The source declined to name specific embassies or alleged criminals where the technique had been used, or to say how frequent it was, except that it was "done with prudence."

Asked whether the burglaries had in fact stopped in 1966, he said that "basically" they had, but that there had been a few "sporadic" approvals since then.

In a long statement on May 22 and again at his news conference yesterday, Mr. Nixon insisted that the practice had been halted in 1966.

The sources also said that periodic, illegal entries were made beginning in the early nineteen-sixties — at the time the Government began to intensify its fight against organized crime—to install concealed microphones, or bugs, in the homes or offices of suspected crime syndicate figures.

"They had to do it to put the bugs on the hoods," the man, a former Justice Department official, said. "They had to break and enter to put them in," he said, adding that such events were not strictly burglaries, since nothing was taken, and that on some occasions entry was gained through false pretenses, "by bribing the janitor or someone to let them in."

One source said that the use of such bugs was also unknown outside the F.B.I. until it came to light during the Kennedy Administration, when one was discovered in a Las Vegas, Nev., casino, and that Attorney General Robert F. Kennedy had "never" approved their use. But another source said he was certain that the late Mr. Kennedy had authorized the use of "one or

two" such devices, which, unlike telephone taps, cannot be installed without gaining physical entry to the room in question.

The planting of such bugs continues today, but since 1968, when the Omnibus Crime Control Act was passed, they cannot be installed without a court order.

Nicholas deB Katzenbach, who succeeded Robert Kennedy as Attorney General in 1964, declared today that if any "official" burglaries had taken place, he was unaware of them.

Ramsey Clark, Mr. Katzenbach's successor, recalled in a telephone interview today that he had been approached by Mr. Hoover on one occasion with a request to authorize the burglary of the New York City mission of what he believed was a "North African country," but that he had turned down the F.B.I. director.

Mr. Clark, who now practices law in Washington, said he believed that it was "most improbable" that Mr. Hoover might have continued the practice without his knowledge, something that apparently did take place.

Despite Mr. Nixon's assertion yesterday that the use of burglaries during previous Administrations was "quite well known," the practice appears to have been one of the best-kept secrets within the F.B.I.

Asked how the Nixon Administration might have learned of its prior existence, one source said he believed that the information had been included in a series of memorandums prepared over the last few months by William C. Sullivan, who recently retired from the Justice Department after having been a former assistant to the late Mr. Hoover. .

Although Mr. Nixon made a special point yesterday of the burglaries that had occurred during the two Administrations that preceded his, he was careful to point out that he believed that the September, 1971, break-in at the office of Dr. Ellsberg's psychiatrist had been "illegal, unauthorized," and "completely deplorable."

Gerald L. Warren, the deputy

White House press secretary, fended off questions today from reporters with the President in San Clemente dealing with the prior burglaries.

"The President said it because it was a fact," Mr. Warren stated, and he would add no details.

Yesterday, Mr. Nixon also noted that "the height of the wiretaps was when Robert Kennedy was Attorney General in 1963," and that the average number of taps installed each year in his own Administration and that of President Eisenhower, whom he served as Vice President, has been "about 110."

However, statistics released in June by Senator Hugh Scott of Pennsylvania, a Republican who is the minority leader, show that the greatest number of wiretaps, 519, were in place between 1945 and 1954, and that the average for each of the years of 1953 to 1960, when Mr. Eisenhower was President, was about 200.

Mr. Nixon also remarked yesterday that he had found a "rather complex situation set up" in the White House when he arrived there in 1969 that was designed to permit the tape recording of his conversations "in the President's office, the room outside of his office [and] also in the Cabinet Room and at Camp David."

He said that he had had "the entire system dismantled" then, but that it had been "put into place again in June of 1970" to provide a historical record of his Administration. It was this system that produced the tapes of conversations between Mr. Nixon and his former aides that have been subpoenaed by Archibald Cox, the special prosecutor in the Watergate case.

However, George Christian, a former press secretary to President Johnson, said in Austin, Tex., today that "what recording equipment there was at the White House was taken out before Mr. Nixon took office."

Mr. Christian added that he "never heard of any [equipment] at Camp David," the Presidential retreat in Maryland's Catoctin Mountains.

CRIME FIGHTING MECHANIZED

Detroit Police Now in Touch By Radio With Whole Country

DETROIT Mich. April 23.—Installation of a police wireless outfit, sufficiently powerful to afford communication with any point in the United States, was begun here today.

It is to be used to send broadcast descriptions of escaped criminals, license numbers of stolen automobiles and other police information.

TEN POLICE AUTOS BEGIN CRIME PATROL

Tours of City in Runabouts Started in Effort to Cope With Robbers.

Ten automobile runabouts, each containing a sergeant and a policeman, at 6 o'clock last night began to patrol the streets of the city in quest of hold-up men. The automobiles were assigned to four districts in which hold-ups have been numerous recently.

Two of the autos were sent to patrol the territory contiguous to the West Thirtieth Street station, two others to the Washington Heights section, with the West 152d Street station as a base, and two to the Arsenal in Central Park, with the middle east side as a field of operation. The remaining four were assigned to the Prospect Park station in Brooklyn, but will patrol wide areas in that borough.

The policemen detailed to the runabouts were instructed to arrest all suspected persons and to pursue automobiles when the occupants aroused their suspicions. The runabouts will be reinforced this morning by several high-powered automobiles, each of which will be manned by a sergeant and several policemen.

It was said at Police Headquarters that it was the intention of Commissioner Enright to keep the automobiles on a continuous patrol night and day with a view to apprehending thieves who have been evading arrest after hold-ups through the use of automobiles, usually stolen cars. It was understood that the motorcycle side cars which were installed for the purpose of coping with hold-up men some time ago had proved of little value.

SEVERAL METHODS DEVISED TO RADIO FINGERPRINTS

Transmission of Identification Marks Saves Time and Enables Instantaneous Recognition of Suspect Over Long Distance.

A NEW plan of tracking criminals by radio is soon to be tested on an elaborate scale between Scotland Yard and the Police Department of New York. Transmission of fingerprints and photographs gives the police a new weapon. Several tests have been tried in America and Europe, and it is predicted that the development of the system will enable the police to identify a suspect with absolute certainty without loss of time and at a long range.

Broadcasting of fingerprints has been found dependable. The methods employed are comparatively simple. One plan is to transmit the prints from all fingers of the criminal suspect. The fingerprints can be reproduced at any distance with accuracy exactly as a photograph is transmitted through the air. Every detail of the lines indicating the minute ridges of the skin is found in the picture reproduced by the apparatus.

The second plan is to transmit but one fingerprint, accompanying it with a short formula or cypher which enables the fingerprint experts at the other end of the line to reconstruct all ten fingerprints. This method is shorter and more economical, and has been found by actual tests to serve every purpose. The accompanying formulae mean absolutely nothing to the layman in such matters, but the fingerprint expert by referring to his collection can make sure of his man.

The great advantage of the new system lies in the saving of valuable time. In the test made between New York and Chicago all records for rapidity in identifying criminals at long range were broken. The fingerprints were sent out from the Police Department in New York and reproduced in Chicago, the suspect was identified by this evidence, and this information was sent back to New York all within one hour.

The police officials in English cities have furnished the police chiefs in large Continental cities with the key to their code, which makes it possible to identify suspects with an important economy of time. The print of a single finger of a suspect can thus be used for identification. In case the Police Department of a distant city has no fingerprints of the suspect, all ten fingerprints may be sent through the ether or a single print with the necessary code. A case is reported of a suspect being identified in this way in South Africa by fingerprints broadcast from London. Fingerprints have also been broadcast from the Eiffel Tower station in Paris.

The new method is expected to prove valuable in identifying criminals who seek to escape by crossing the Atlantic. If the New York police, for example, should learn that some criminal had sailed for Europe, it will be a simple matter to broadcast his fingerprints to the port of destination. When the steamer arrives the fingerprint experts will be on hand armed with a set of the suspect's fingermarks. It will not be necessary to hold the suspect until his fingerprints are sent by mail. The identification can thus be made in a few minutes.

In the American experiments in broadcasting fingerprints it was found that the cost of transmitting the data for identification was from $30 to $40. This is considered high by the police except for use in unusual cases. It is obviously cheaper to telegraph a general description of a suspect and have him arrested and held in jail awaiting the arrival of the absolute evidence of the fingerprints. Many cases may come up, however, where the saving of time made possible by broadcasting fingerprints will prove priceless. The method of broadcasting fingerprints is, of course, in its infancy, and the expense will be in time considerably reduced. The new method of instantaneous identification by means of radio has so many advantages that it is expected eventually to become a common practice.

SAYS 'LIE DETECTOR' FORCED CONFESSION

Seattle Prosecutor Declares It Led D. E. Mayer to Admit Killing J. E. Bassett of Annapolis.

VOLLMER'S MACHINE USED

Crime Commission Expert Had Studied Case—Officers Fail to Find Body at Spot Indicated.

Special to The New York Times.

SEATTLE, Wash., Nov. 22.—Decasto Earl Mayer has confessed that he murdered James Eugene Bassett of Annapolis in September, 1928, it was announced today by Prosecuting Attorney Ewing D. Colvin. The confession was due almost entirely to the use of a pneumo-cardio-sphygmometer, or "lie detector," Mr. Colvin said, and by the same means, the prosecutor asserted, he hopes to induce Mayer to lead officers to Bassett's body.

Mayer is in jail, facing a life term as a habitual criminal. He and his mother, Mrs. Mary Smith, were arrested in September, 1928, when they were found to have Bassett's car in Oakland, Cal. Bassett could not be found, but as the Washington authorities could not produce a corpus delicti they could not charge murder, and so extradited Mayer for the alleged theft of the automobile. Mayer said he had bought the car and Bassett's watch from him, but he was convicted for the car theft.

Vollmer Suggests Machine's Use.

Mr. Colvin's own story of an amazing seven-day session with the prisoner follows:

"On the recommendation of August Vollmer, consultant of President Hoover's crime commission, Professor of Criminology of the University of Chicago and former Chief of Police of Berkeley, Cal., I obtained the services of Leonard Keeler, Assistant State Criminologist for Illinois.

"Mr. Vollmer recently spent two days at the Bassett home in Annapolis. He has long been interested in this case.

"He recommended to me the use of his 'lie detector,' the machine which he invented. He recommended Mr. Keeler as the best technician on the machine.

"I obtained a leave for Mr. Keeler and arranged for his services. He arrived in Seattle Armistice Day. I took three days outlining to him every angle of the Bassett case and Mayer's supposed connection with it. We began using the lie detector on Mayer on Thursday, Nov. 14.

"Mayer treated the lie detector as a lark at first. Up to a certain point in our seven days of investigation he answered every question, but only with 'Yes, sir,' or 'No, sir.'

"The lie detector consists of two leather plates which go under the arms on either side of the breast and a chain which holds them in place from the back. There is a rubber tube wound around the arm to register blood pressure.

"A wire goes to a lamp socket and a wire to a needle touching a reel of ruled tape to make a graph of the reaction of respiration and blood pressure.

Maps Used to Find Body.

"The entire examination, for six or eight hours each day, has centred around the question: 'Where is Bassett's body?'

"We questioned him over and over, perhaps a hundred times. 'Is it in a lake?' 'Is it in the Sound?' 'Is it in a well?' On all these questions, if he answered, the answer was 'No,' and in any case a negative reaction was registered."

Mr. Colvin said that he and Mr. Keeler then used maps, finally, by "Yes" and "No" answers from Mayer, eliminating all sections except that in the town of Bothell, Wash.

The first positive reactions from the "lie detector" came, Mr. Colvin said, when he pointed to a spot on a map where Mayer once paid an instalment on a "little white house," and to the sites of two cemeteries.

"We found he would not answer any question relating to cemeteries," said the prosecutor. "When we worked along that line he struggled, threw his arms about, feigned fainting spells and convulsions.

"We had a plat made showing every grave in a Swedish cemetery, but Mayer positively refused to look at it.

"The most force that was used on him was last Sunday. When Mr. Keeler had just finished a series of questions on the graves and cemeteries about Bothell, Mayer suddenly roused from lethargy, sprang like a cat and smashed the machine.

Finally Agrees to Talk.

"Two deputies grabbed him and he was shackled and sent back to his cell. Since then his examinations have been made while he lay on a cot wearing an Oregon boot. Keeler repaired the lie detector and we began the questioning again Sunday evening.

"We gave him one day's rest in the last week. Every other day we reviewed all the maps briefly but thoroughly, and ended always where the big reaction showed, in the vicinity of Bothell.

"On Monday Mayer suddenly looked up at me and said, 'Colvin, I'll talk to you if you'll get these other fellows out.'

"The deputies handcuffed the prisoner, gave me a small pistol and left the room.

Mayer Defends His Mother.

"'Colvin,' Mayer said, 'will you give me a trial? I'd have a chance to beat circumstantial evidence.'

"I assured him I would.

"'I know what that machine is, Colvin,' he said then. 'I know it's recording the truth. I can't beat it. You know I killed Bassett. What will you do for me if I come clean?'

"'If you'll lead me to that body,' I told him, 'then I will not charge your mother with murder.'

"'I'll tell you,' he said, 'my mother has never done anything criminal except what I caused her to do.'

"'Lead me to that grave and will not charge your mother with murder,' I said.

"'All right, I'll go out there with you,' he said."

Mayer, however, has so far failed to look at the cemetery plot. Mr. Colvin said the deputies have searched in vain in the Swedish Cemetery for a clue except in a vault belonging to a family named Erickson. Permission to open the vault may be asked of the family.

Mayer late today denied that he had made a confession. He accused Mr. Colvin and other county officials of "torturing" him. A report that serum had been injected into him was denied by Mr. Colvin.

November 23, 1929

JUDGE DENOUNCES LIE DETECTOR USE

Seattle Court Likens Employment of Machine on Prisoner to Inquisition Methods.

FORBIDS FURTHER TESTS

Special to The New York Times.

SEATTLE, Wash., Nov. 23.—Use of a lie detector and truth serum on a prisoner in an effort to solve a crime smacks of the middle ages, declared Superior Judge Malcolm Douglas today. A restraining order prohibiting use of such methods on Decasto Earl Mayer or his mother, Mary Eleanor French, issued Thursday, was made permanent by the court this afternoon.

Mayer, who is suspected of the murder of James Eugene Bassett of Annapolis, is under life sentence as an habitual criminal, his mother is serving a five to ten year term for grand larceny in connection with the theft of Bassett's automobile.

Methods used by Prosecutor Ewing D. Colvin and Sheriff Claude G. Bannick in trying to learn what Mayer did with the body were denounced by Judge Douglas, who described treatments accorded to Mayer and his mother as "more in keeping with days of Gregory IX, and Conrad Marbough of the Middle Ages, and of the Spanish inquisition than of this present enlightened civilization.

"The Constitution gives every individual certain guarantees, and one of these is that he shall not be compelled to testify against himself.

"As a consideration of law this might be thought of as a rule of evidence, but in practice it will be a rule of conduct for officers who have custody of prisoners. And it is just as important that it be heeded in the case of one who has committed a dozen murders as it is in the case of a man who is entirely innocent."

"This is the twentieth century, not the thirteenth," the judge said. "The court does not countenance that method of handling business."

Both Mayer and his mother testified at the hearing. They declared that the truth serum had been administered by force and the woman declared her clothing had been torn in the struggle.

Mayer asserted that he was roughly handled, was chloroformed on one occasion and was not permitted to see his attorney. He charged that hypodermics were administered repeatedly by a man who was not a physician.

The examinations under the lie detector lasted eight to ten hours at a time, mostly throughout the night, and continued over a period of seven consecutive days, he said.

An attempt to demonstrate the lie detector in court was blocked by Henry Clay Agnew, counsel for Mayer.

When Agnew, in his closing remarks said that Colvin had "committed a worse crime against liberty and the rights of individuals than these people" (Mayer and his mother), the crowded court room rang with applause.

Several of the spectators who had applauded were ejected by bailiffs.

November 24, 1929

N. Y. U. WILL TRAIN MEDICAL OFFICERS

Dr. Charles Norris to Head New Branch Giving Instruction in Toxicology.

FEW SUCH COURSES HERE

Hailed as Step Toward System of Scientific Crime Detection Like Those in Europe.

New York University will train medical examiners and toxicologists in a newly formed department of Forensic Medicine at the university and Bellevue Hospital Medical College, Chancellor Elmer Ellsworth Brown announced yesterday.

Dean John Wyckoff of the Medical College, hailed the new department, one of the first of its kind in this country, as a step toward a system of scientific crime detection which might some day rank with the system of medico-legal institutes of Europe.

Dr. Charles Norris, chief medical examiner of New York, has been named Professor of Forensic Medicine and will head the new department. Dr. Harrison Martland, chief medical examiner of Essex County, N. J., has been appointed Associate Professor of Forensic Medicine.

Other members of the departmental faculty will be Dr. Alexander O. Gettler, city toxicologist, who will become Professor of Toxicology; Dr. Douglas Symmers, director of laboratories at Bellevue Hospital, who will be Professor of Gross Pathology; Dr. Armin V. St. George, Assistant Professor of Gross Pathology, and Dr. Thomas A. Gonzales, deputy chief medical examiner of the City of New York, Assistant Professor of Forensic Medicine.

The term "forensic medicine," the announcement explained, is a common one in Continental Europe, where institutes of legal medicine are an integral part of the Ministries of Justice and cooperate with police systems in the solution and prevention of crimes.

"Legal medicine is an important subject in most European universities, since the medico-legal institutes are usually a part of the university medical schools," said Dean Wyckoff.

"In most American universities the teaching of legal medicine is limited to a few lectures to undergraduate medical students on 'medical jurisprudence.'"

Dr. Norris explained that the courses planned by the new department will include a required short course to fourth year medical students covering salient points as to what constitutes medical examiners' cases, proper signing of death certificates, and testimony in court; an optional laboratory course to fourth year students consisting of a month's work in the medical examiner's office assisting at necropsies; a post-graduate course of three years in the office of the medical examiner leading to a degree, and a post-graduate course in toxicology leading to a degree.

The required course for seniors will consist of six lectures—two by Dr. Norris, two by Dr. Martland, one by Dr. Gettler, and one by a member of the faculty of law to be named later. The laboratory work for the fourth year students and the post-graduates will include attendance at autopsies, the taking of post-mortem notes, and laboratory work in connection with microscopic examination of sections and bacteriological examinations, Dr. Norris said.

June 11, 1933

LABORATORY FOR CRIME

New Section of Experts Helps Federal Agents Reach the Guilty

By OLIVER McKEE.

WASHINGTON.

A WELL-EQUIPPED laboratory, staffed by men expert in analyzing articles of evidence by scientific methods, has become an important aid to Department of Justice agents in their operations against crime involving Federal laws. Organized about a year ago, the laboratory plays an increasingly large part in the crime detection work of the division of investigation and its facilities are also extended to police departments throughout the country.

Extortion cases have taken up much of the laboratory's time. In such cases of course handwriting examinations are important. If guilty, a suspect will nearly always betray his guilt to the expert if compelled to supply a sufficient number of examples of his handwriting.

The typewriter, too, may tell a story to the initiated. The laboratory has on hand up-to-date specimens of the typing of the various machines in commercial use; its experts can easily tell the make of typewriter used in tapping out a given extortion note.

The paper used may provide the clue. Certain brands of paper are sold by certain stores. It may be of assistance to the investigator to have such knowledge in his possession. The laboratory has a complete collection of water-marks, useful in identifying paper. By means of the ultra violet ray, which brings out invisible ink, the laboratory is prepared to read secret messages.

Bullets and shells figure in many crimes. The laboratory maintains a full assortment of them; these have contributed to the identification of weapons used in hold-ups or murders. Under the comparison microscope, an expert can tell whether bullet or shell fragments belong to the same missile, and he can tell also whether two bullets were fired from the same pistol or rifle.

Identification of human hair may play a part in crime detection. Though not as trustworthy as fingerprint identification, often the microscope will show whether a given hair, on the apparel of a victim of crime, belongs to the person under suspicion. Other fibers may find a place in the crime picture, and under the powerful instruments developed for use in the Department of Justice laboratory in Washington identification of pieces of apparel can be made with a high degree of precision.

Through the application of chemistry, methods have been worked out whereby agents of the Department of Justice can quickly find out whether a stain was made by human or animal blood. It can be established that a given stain comes from the blood of persons with a certain blood grouping.

The development of latent fingerprints, that is, impressions on an article not visible to the naked eye, represents one of the most important modern advances in the science of crime detection. Not long ago a youngster was involved in an extortion case in New York. Latent prints on the extortion note were developed. The man in question was shot and wounded in a trap when he went to the appointed spot to receive the ransom money. He pleaded innocence, insisting he had been dispatched there as a messenger to get the money without knowing that a crime was in the making. The fingerprint developed from impressions on the extortion note convinced the jury that the man shot in the trap was the same person who penned the note, and a prison term of ten years was the result.

The crime laboratory expects to expand in personnel and scope as fast as new scientific methods prove effective or new instruments are developed. As Director J. Edgar Hoover says, "The detection of crime can no longer be carried forward by so-called strong-arm methods. There must be a scientific investigation at the scene of the crime, a search for fingerprints, for footprints, for dirt, for any article of evidence which may help to solve the crime. The scientific investigations have to be done by experts."

July 8, 1934

Mayor O'Dwyer will start at 10 A. M. tomorrow two-way police radio service between control points and mobile units in Manhattan, the last of the city's five boroughs to get that type of facility. The ceremony will take place in the Police Headquarters gymnasium.

With the addition of the new service the city's police radio network will outdistance that of any metropolis in the world, Police Commissioner William P. O'Brien declared. The system was begun in 1932. The first two-way radio system was installed in Richmond in 1946.

The Manhattan system will consist of two stations. Each station will have two transmitters, one for regular service and the other standby. Auxiliary power plants will insure operation of the network in the event the normal power supply fails. Mr. O'Brien said that the department also had added walkie-talkie sets for special work, particularly during disasters.

August 8, 1950

What the Lie Detector Really Detects

Last week the question came up in the Senate whether Charles E. Bohlen, chosen by President Eisenhower to be Ambassador to the Soviet Union, should be subjected to a lie-detector test. The proposal was made by Senator Joseph R. McCarthy of Wisconsin. Senator Robert A. Taft of Ohio squelched McCarthy's proposal.

We don't hear as much of the lie detector as we used to, though its use seems to be spreading. A few courts have admitted its records as evidence. Most judges will have none of it, but they accept as evidence fingerprints, analyses of blood, X-ray pictures. Though the lie detector is used by several hundred police departments to test suspects and by many banks to determine the honesty of employes, it is regarded by most intelligent people as a modern instrument of emotional torture that puts a man through a psychological third degree.

Records Emotions

A lie detector does not detect lies. It records emotional disturbances. Psychologists prefer to call the instrument a polygraph, a name which means "many-graph." W. M. Marston, John A. Larson and the late Prof. Leonarde E. Keeler were the pioneers of instrumental lie detection. Keeler's polygraph, one of the earliest, consisted of three units that respectively recorded respiratory changes, pulse waves and blood pressure and muscular reflex of the arm or leg. Dr. John A. Larson has been especially active in introducing the lie detector. He used a portable set in scores of criminal cases in California and Chicago.

A man accused of a crime may refuse to subject himself to a lie-detector test because the test would violate his Constitutional rights. But many criminals consent, thinking, probably, that the test is a legally authorized procedure. Lawyers for the defense usually object to the lie-detector test, and in most states the courts uphold them. The lie detector is by no means infallible. On the strength of its records a few indicted suspects have been found guilty and sentenced to long terms, only to be released later when the really guilty criminal confessed.

By Question and Answer

A preferable technique is followed by a skilled questioner. The questions are simple and direct, and they call for a "yes" or "no" answer. A typical examination would follow this course:

"Do you live in Brooklyn?"

"Yes."

"Did you rob the bank on the corner of Second and Third Street last Feb. 24?"

"No."

"Did you have anything to eat today?"

"Yes."

"Did you pass to the teller a note demanding all the money he had in the till?"

"No."

"Did you kill the teller?"

The polygraphers of police departments state that the lie detector makes 55.1 per cent of arrested crooks confess and that 74.4 per cent of those who refuse to tell the truth are convicted on the strength of the wavy lines that record their blood pressure, respiratory rate, reflexes and respiration.   W. K.

March 29, 1953

Palette-Packing Cop

By MURRAY SCHUMACH

PATROLMAN Richard F. Kenehan, the only New York City policeman who pursues criminals with drawing pencils and sketch pads, has noticed that gibes by other cops have mellowed since his portraits based on eyewitness descriptions led to the capture of two girls for the attack on the daughters of an Iranian diplomat in Bronx Park. "They still ride me a little about what a soft beat I got," says Patrolman Kenehan, "but there's no malice."

In three years as departmental artist—a few departments in other cities employ artists, but Kenehan is the first to hold such a position with the local force—the 35-year-old policeman has received a police commendation and may even get a filing cabinet one of these days for the 100-odd sketches that have proved important in numerous arrests, including two men for murder and a woman for kidnapping. Kenehan portraits have never been seen in museums or the galleries of Fifty-seventh Street. But his work can be found in any detective squad room in New York and they are pin-ups on scores of police locker doors. For Patrolman Kenehan's drawings, like rogues' gallery photos, are functional art with many admirers on the force.

It is fairly certain that no artist invites as much criticism as Patrolman Kenehan. Scores of times, while an eyewitness of a crime hesitantly describes the appearance of a criminal he may have seen fleetingly, he will erase the mouth, the nose,

ARTISTIC RESULTS—One of Kenehan's sketches (above, left) that led to the arrest of a suspected killer (above, right). The drawing (far left) worked, even though the suspect (left), was nearly six inches taller than witnesses remembered him.

reshape the face, even destroy the entire drawing and start again as the witness indicates doubt.

"I guess," he says, "my biggest talent is erasing. I depend entirely on the memory of the witness. You have to be very patient. You can't give up as long as the witness is willing to go on."

Much more than most artists, he has to be immune to flattery. "Some witnesses," he says, "want to be nice. They'll say the likeness of the criminal looks good even if they don't think so." Patrolman Kenehan's antidote for good-fellowship is to leave the witness alone with the drawing and a detective in one of the dim rooms at the Police Academy that he uses as a studio when he is not working in a police station or a victim's home. "While I'm out, the detective will draw out the witness about what he really thinks of the sketch. If there's any doubt, we start again."

KENEHAN'S general procedure is, first, to outline the face. Most people, he says, can remember the shape of a face. Then he takes one feature at a time, questioning the witness carefully enough to prod memory but not enough to plant suggestions. Finally, he inquires about scars and wrinkles. When there is more than one witness, he prefers to question them separately so they will not influence one another.

In most cases, it is difficult to know how much value a Kenehan sketch has. At the least, it is a clue that may be productive. Occasionally, it is an unquestionable triumph—as was his drawing of Dolores Byrd Phipps for a kidnapping in Harlem.

The child's mother was nearly hysterical as she tried to describe the woman who had snatched her baby. In addition, her English was so poor that a Spanish-speaking

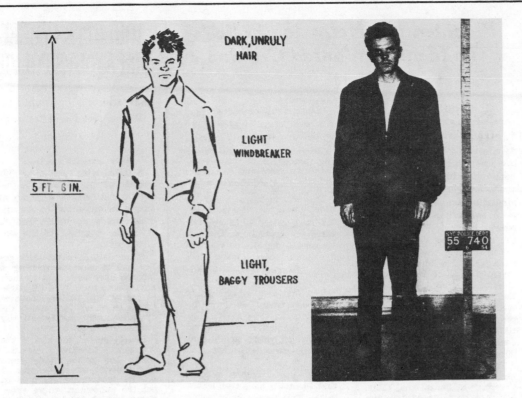

DARK, UNRULY HAIR

LIGHT WINDBREAKER

5 FT. 6 IN.

LIGHT, BAGGY TROUSERS

detective had to be called in to interpret. For three hours, Kenehan sketched and erased as the weeping mother talked. That day the picture was photostated and distributed throughout Manhattan. It was printed in newspapers, flashed on television and on screens of Spanish-language movies. The pictures brought telephone calls that led the police to the baby and kidnapper in less than a day.

A more grisly work of art was undertaken by Patrolman Kenehan when a woman was found murdered. To mask her identity, the murderer had scalped her, slashed most of the skin from her face and cut off her fingers to conceal prints. Working from the bone structure of the face, Kenehan drew what he considered a likely portrait. When the picture appeared in a newspaper, it was recognized and the

dead woman's husband was arrested for the murder.

Recently, the patrolman's art came in handy when the police realized that the only photograph they had of a notorious criminal had been taken twenty-five years ago. A detective who had seen the gangster within the year furnished information which enabled Kenehan to draw a picture that today is the most reliable likeness of the mobster the police department has.

Art and police work both attracted Kenehan in boyhood. He studied art in a Bronx high school. When he graduated, he worked as a magazine artist for several years and then, for a short time, with an advertising agency. "I found out there are better artists than I am," he says. When the ad agency collapsed he took, and passed, the police examination and was appointed to the force in 1951.

For more than two years he pounded a beat in the Bronx, where he still lives. His cartoons in the police magazine, SPring 3100, attracted the attention of superiors and he was assigned to do police posters and illustrations for study booklets. On his own time he submitted to superiors sketches of wanted criminals whose descriptions he knew only from printed accounts. Police officials then assigned him to his present work.

Patrolman Kenehan's taste in art is classical. Rembrandt is his favorite. He visits the Metropolitan Museum of Art whenever he can, dislikes the Museum of Modern Art—or any modern painting. In his spare time he paints landscapes in oils. "My mother likes the landscapes. But so far as being comparable to any good artists, I have no illusions."

Patented Kit Helps the Police To Identify Wanted Criminals

By STACY V. JONES
Special to The New York Times.

WASHINGTON, March 17—Equipment patented this week enables police to make up a composite picture of a wanted criminal's face by putting plastic features together.

As a robbery victim picks out the most likely looking eyes, nose, lips, brows, chin lines and other characteristics, the identification expert lays, one over the other, transparent sheets carrying drawings of the chosen features.

The method and paraphernalia (called the Identikit) were invented by Hugh C. McDonald, chief of the civil division of the Los Angeles Sheriff's Department, while he was assigned to the identification bureau. Identikit is already widely used in California and is being introduced in the Midwest and East.

The Identikit is manufactured by a division of the Townsend Company at Santa Ana, Calif., and has been leased thus far to 150 enforcement agencies after their operatives have attended a week-long instruction course.

E. B. Buster, vice president of the Townsend Company, recounted one example of many successful applications. After a California supermarket robbery, a composite picture was built from descriptions given by three men. The fourth victim, a woman, had not seen the robber's face but when shown the composite exclaimed, "Why, that's my brother-in-law!"

As the plastic overlays are numbered, the reporting bureau can telegraph all the numbers as a code and the picture can be reproduced in other offices. This procedure is followed by California state and city police and sheriff's departments, according to Mr. Buster.

The kit includes a catalog from which a witness makes his first choice of likely features and expressions. The plastic sheets include drawings of age lines, scars, glasses, hair lines, beards, mustaches and headgear.

The invention is said to be especially useful when no fingerprints have been left. The facial composite supplements evidence on height, weight, age, clothing, twitches, limps and speech.

The manufacturer reports that Identikits have been leased in the New York area to police departments in Paterson and Paramus, N. J., and Greenwich, Conn., as well as to the Connecticut State Police. Other clients are in Providence, Philadelphia and Pittsburgh.

Courtney Owens, manager of the Identikit division, is conducting an instruction course in Zurich, Switzerland, this week, and later will hold one in Germany.

The patent (2,974,426) is assigned to the Townsend Company, whose main plant is at Beaver Falls, Pa., and whose principal business is making industrial fasteners such as rivets, nuts, screws and bolts.

'ROULETTE WHEEL' DISPATCHES POLICE

Mathematical Formula Tells Where Need Is Likeliest

Special to The New York Times.

EDINA, Minn., Feb. 10—This suburb of Minneapolis is using the mathematical theory of games in an effort to tip the odds, which normally tend to favor the criminal, to the side of the police.

Since Jan. 1, night-shift police patrol cars completing a mission have been sent to their next patrol area by a dispatcher using a battery-operated "roulette wheel" that makes the assignment by mathematically sound random selection.

Simply stated, the aim of the "random selection device," which the police made from four roulette wheels bought at a local department store, is to put the policeman where experience has shown he might be needed, and where a wrongdoer might least expect to find him.

The system was installed by Edina's police chief, Wayne W. Bennett, after reading about a random theory as applied to police work. The operation was devised in consultation with two Indiana University mathematicians, Robert Shumate and Richard Crowther. They are keeping in close touch with its operation.

"They think we're on the right track," says Mr. Bennett, who has also received encouragement from the local high school mathematics instructor, University of Minnesota and local industrial mathematicians.

How System Works

The system is calculated to upset odds that favor a criminal, who can observe police patrolling, predict its pattern and strike where he believes policemen will not be. The Edina system works like this:

Using the previous twelve months' police calls as a basis and taking account of the special values of a well-to-do "bedroom" community of 32,000, the police assign mathematical weights to every kind of complaint received. This, Mr. Bennett concedes, is not simple, and

his system is far from perfected.

The suburb's sixteen square miles have been divided into four patrol zones—one for each one-man squad car—and these in turn into a total of fifty-one areas.

On a wall map, known as the "Random Patrol Game Matrix" each such area, or "strategy," is labeled with an index based on the volume of complaints originating there.

The map shows that, for instance, sub-area 201 was responsible for 14 per cent of the weighted total of one year's complaints. These values, in turn, are incorporated in the markings around the rims of the four assignment wheels (one for each zone). Of 100 notches around the wheel rim, for example, fourteen are allocated to "strategy 201," reflecting its hypothetical 14 per cent complaint incidence.

The patrolman with free time informs the dispatcher, who spins the wheel and assigns the car to whatever "strategy" the wheel dictates.

Tests Found Encouraging

In the first few weeks of operation, the police have noted several encouraging occurrences and "nothing detrimental," according to Chief Bennett. One night, for example, two cars that responded to a medical emergency in one "strategy" were able to cope quickly with a prowler complaint in the adjoining one. On three of nine calls during an early period of operation, a squad car was less than three blocks from the point where it was needed.

"Some of the men, when they go into these zones, almost expect something to happen and look for it," Mr. Bennett said. He believes the system has given dispatchers better control of patrol cars and is at least as good as any less scientific method of deployment.

Eventually the games theory operation will be extended to Edina's two other shifts: the night shift was considered the simplest for a first trial.

After a year's experience, the system will be judged against past years' law enforcement records. Meanwhile, data from the Edina experiment are being punched into computer cards at Indiana University, in the hope that some day a scientific police assignment system might be devised that could be applicable, with suitable local variations, to any city.

COMPUTER 'CLUES' MAY SOLVE CRIMES

City Police Explore Ways to Speed Detective Work With Electronic Aid

FINGERPRINTS ON TAPE

Officer Looks to Day When Network of Machines Will Help Trap Criminals

The time-honored—and time-consuming—practice of gathering detectives into a squad room to pool their knowledge and experience in solving a difficult case may one day be only a memory.

At present such "skull sessions," with one detective recalling a facet of an old case and another contributing another facet, sometimes suggest where to look for information on the baffling case.

But now high-speed electronic computers, supplied with vast stores of police information, are beginning to take the hit-and-miss out of the traditional method. The potential of electronic computers for almost every phase of police work has excited Police Commissioner Michael J. Murphy and Robert R. J. Gallati, his supervising assistant chief inspector.

Finger 'Taped'

Under Chief Gallati, an IBM 1401 computer, bought to process Police Department statistical data on crimes, personnel records and payrolls, has been adapted to help solve crimes.

For instance, the first 30,000 of the 5,000,000 sets of criminal fingerprints on record here are being filed on magnetic tape.

When the job is completed, it will be possible to find out in minutes if a suspect's prints match those on record. Now the job may take several days.

Deputy Inspector John O'Neill, head of the Bureau of Criminal Identification, hopes that not only fingerprints but all available information about criminals and past suspects can be "married" into one compact form on magnetic tape. This would make available almost instantaneously fingerprints, physical description, past criminal record and M. O. (the modus operandi, or characteristics of a crime).

Recently Chief Gallati met with police officials from the metropolitan region and suggested they all cooperate. He foresees the day when computers in many Police Departments will be linked by special telephone lines and the details of a crime, including the suspect's fingerprints and modus operandi, will be fed into one of the computers.

The files of each department would be "searched" in turn, and fingerprints on file in one department, a modus operandi on file somewhere else and other data possessed by a third police force might be combined to help identify one or several potential suspects.

The computer already is starting to provide precise data on the day of the week when a crime took place, the time of day on which it occurred—all in usable form. This information has been compiled for years, but making use of it was another matter.

Now the data are being punched into cards at the department's computer center at 400 Broome Street. Every precinct commander receives a concise monthly report showing his trouble spots—not only the obvious ones like street fights but also the sites of burglaries and other crimes.

A complete record of policemen's skills is also available. For instance, in an emergency the names of all policemen who can operate subway trains can be in the hands of a commanding officer within minutes.

September 20, 1963

F.B.I. Operating Computerized Criminal Data Bank

By FRED P. GRAHAM
Special to The New York Times

WASHINGTON, Nov. 29—The Federal Bureau of Investigation began operation today of a computerized criminal history data bank that will eventually give the police almost instantaneous access to an individual's criminal arrest record from any state and from Federal investigative agencies and courts.

The new system, which has created controversy among some law enforcement officials and civil libertarians, will by 1975 make available on a nationwide computer network most of the types of information that is now handled through the F.B.I.'s vast criminal record and fingerprint file.

It replaces a pilot project, called Project Search, in which only a computerized index was maintained. This was capable of telling the police only if a suspect had a criminal record. It did not put the details of the suspect's arrest and prison records on computers, an action that tends to make the information more readily available and potentially more widely distributable.

Delays in the States

The system went into operation today with only a handful of states providing information but with 104 state and local law enforcement agencies able to receive the data.

An F.B.I. spokesman said that as of today "less than 10" states had placed their arrest records on computers and linked them to the computerized criminal history. The spokesman refused to identify these states, but he said that a total of about 20 states would be fully linked to the system within the next few weeks.

Adam F. D'Allessandro, deputy director of the New York State Identification and Intelligence System, said in Albany today that New York's computerized arrest records were not yet plugged into the system because the Western Union Company had been late in providing a line from New York's computer to the F.B.I. computer here. New York is expected to be linked to the system in a few weeks.

By 1975, all 50 states are expected to have received grants from the Justice Department's Law Enforcement Assistance Administration, permitting them to place their arrest records on computers and plug them into the system.

Bureau officials say that concern over the system is unwarranted because it merely makes available by computers any long-distance lines information that qualified agencies can now obtain from the F.B.I. by mail.

Critics have asserted that errors will travel farther and faster now, that the system could lead to a data bank containing police intelligence on individuals, and that the new system should not be controlled by the F.B.I.

Bureau officials have consulted with local officials about their objections. F.B.I. spokesmen refused today to release a copy of the criminal data bank regulations, or to answer some questions regarding it.

Information Available

The announcement by J. Edgar Hoover, the bureau director, said: "In addition to personal identification information such as name, age, sex, physical description, and identifying numbers, the file will show, for each individual, arrest charges, the disposition of each case, sentencing details, and custody and supervision status."

Only "serious or significant violations" will be recorded. A spokesman said this would include some but not all felonies and a few types of misdemeanors. Examples of arrests that will not be recorded were said to be juvenile offenses, drunkenness and disturbing the peace.

This means that the basic philosophy of Project Search—that the computer will contain only an index of persons who have criminal records and that the states will retain control of details—has been expanded under the new system.

However, Thomas Bishop, spokesman for the F.B.I., said today that the regulations for the new system require states, subject to "reasonable administrative procedures," to give any person a copy of the F.B.I.'s computerized criminal record.

If a police agency enters an arrest on the computer and does not follow later with the disposition of the charge, the computer will automatically demand at intervals a record of the disposition.

The F.B.I. has also obtained written agreements with each participating police agency forbidding the unauthorized dissemination of the information to unauthorized persons. Bureau spokesmen say that access to the system will be restricted to law enforcement agencies.

The Federal agencies that will contribute and receive the data are the Secret Service, the Internal Revenue Service, the Alcohol and Tax Division of the Treasury Department, the Customs Service, the Immigration and Naturalization Service, the United States courts, the United States attorneys, the United States marshals and the Bureau of Prisons.

November 30, 1971

Men in Blue
Compiled by EDWARD F. MURPHY

❝The citizens will, as long as effective checks of democracy exist, pass upon whether the police meet proper standards, in terms of their understanding and value. To deny this competency to the citizen is to deny the efficacy of democratic control of policing."
—*Lewis J. Valentine, Police Commissioner of New York, 1934-1945.*

❝There is no question that the police are misunderstood, looked down upon, unfairly treated, ridiculed, criticized, overburdened, underestimated, and generally given a bad go of it in America."
—*Dr. Karl Menninger.*

❝A good policeman is just as necessary to the peace and happiness of the community as a good judge."
—*John F. Hylan, Mayor of New York, 1918-1925.*

❝It is difficult for civilians fully to grasp what it means to be on a post by oneself, armed with night stick and revolver, and to realize that single-handed one must cope with a group of criminals who would not stop at murder to carry out their purpose. The policeman is alone during most of his official life, and he could not begin to do his duty were it not that his profession compels courage and that the brand of comradeship between him and his brother officers is of such a high, helpful character."
—*Arthur Woods, Police Commissioner of New York, 1914-1918.*

❝In Moulmein, in Lower Burma, I was hated by large numbers of people—the only time in my life that I have been important enough for this to happen to me. I was sub-divisional police officer of the town, and in an aimless, petty kind of way anti-European feeling was very bitter . . . As a police officer I was an obvious target and was baited whenever it seemed safe to do so."
—*George Orwell.*

❝Has anyone ever seen a homely cop in New York?"
—*Harry Golden.*

❝The policeman, among all human beings, is singularly gregarious. His conversational qualities are unlimited. He dislikes to be by himself, and he loves to talk to someone or to something."
—*William McAdoo.*

❝Ah, take one consideration with another—A policeman's lot is not a happy one."
—*W. S. Gilbert.*

❝I am not fond of police anywhere. In Ireland or in France. In England, either. I have heard no good reports of the New York police, though most of them are of Irish descent." —*Brendan Behan.*

❝Every policeman knows that though governments may change, the police remain."
—*Leon Trotsky.*

❝Has it ever occurred to you that in the life of every policeman there is one day when he wears his majestic uniform in public for the first time? It must, of course, be so. No matter how many times he may have put it on at home privately, to get used to it, the day must at last come when he has to walk forth into the streets, and in the eyes of those who have known him ever since he was a boy, or even a baby, change from a man like themselves to an important and rather dreadful guardian of the peace."
—*E. V. Lucas.*

❝A policeman's gun is his cross, and he carries it always." —*Stephen Kennedy, Police Commissioner of New York, 1955-1961.*

❝One of the quickest ways for any law-enforcement officer to bring public disrepute upon himself, his organization and the entire profession is to be found guilty of a violation of civil rights. Our people may tolerate many mistakes of both intent and performance, but, with unerring instinct, they know that when any person is intentionally deprived of his constitutional rights, those responsible have committed no ordinary offense." —*J. Edgar Hoover.*

March 6, 1966

WICKERSHAM BOARD HITS 'THIRD DEGREE' AND BRUTAL POLICE

Traces Their "Lawless" Record of Enforcement, Discovering "Unprintable Barbarity."

STRESS ON NEW YORK CITY

Special to The New York Times.

WASHINGTON, Aug. 10.—A record of lawlessness in law enforcement in the representative larger cities of the United States, with methods degenerating at times from those of a dignified, civilized community into barbarities which were unprintable by their very nature, was laid bare to President Hoover by the Wickersham commission in its report, "Lawlessness in Law Enforcement," made public at the White House today.

The report, containing the most severe indictment yet lodged by the commission, pictured an almost nation-wide system of police brutality and "third-degree" methods which, it said, should bestir the people of the United States to a clamor for correction.

The report singled out New York City for the most attention, as one of the worst spots where brutal methods have been used relentlessly, it said, with almost the expressed sanction of the highest city authorities, and suggested that an apparent diminution of such practices had taken place in Chicago only because of the retaliation of gangs and gangsters against the police for brutal treatment of their companions.

In New York City "brutal" methods of practically every known kind were declared to have been employed. The report referred to speeches of Mayor Walker and former Police Commissioner Whalen as indicating their evident approval of some of the methods, adding that the record of the hearing being conducted by Judge Samuel Seabury into the magistrates' courts in New York City involved many instances of unfairness.

Favors Action by Congress.

The commission experts concluded that the "third degree" is "widely and brutally employed" in New York in the zeal of the police to wrest confessions from alleged criminals, being used particularly in cases where the police are under pressure to find the solution to some shocking crime.

So shocking was the sum of the evidence of illegal methods to the commission that it recommended consideration by Congress of a new code of favorable criminal procedure, to be used largely as a model for the States, for, it was stated, but little evidence of "third-degree" methods was found among Federal officials.

"But pending the adoption of legislation or constitutional amendment necessary to change, this commission deemed it to be its duty to lay the facts—the naked, ugly facts—of the existing abuses before the public," the report said, "in the hope that the pressure of public condemnation may be so aroused that the conduct so violative of the fundamental principles of constitutional liberty as that described, may be entirely abandoned."

Various cases of "proved" illegal methods in law enforcement were cited throughout the voluminous document.

The "rubber-hose" treatment, the "cold-storage" and "water cures," the "gold-fish" chamber and the "hard-and-soft" method entered the language of the report, particularly in the summary of facts gathered by the commission's experts.

The commission expressly refrained from discussing the Mooney-Billings case because of inability to examine original records and also because a pardon application for these men, convicted of the San Francisco Preparedness Day bombing in 1916, is pending before the Governor of California.

Report Makes 347 Pages.

The factual material in the 347-page report was printed by Zechariah Chafer Jr. of the Harvard Law School and Walter H. Pollak and Carl S. Stern of the New York Car. While the commission did not adopt all the recommendations of these experts, it accepted their facts in whole, and it was in these that the most severe indictment against the police of the country was made.

Studies were made by these experts in fifteen different cities, while "third-degree" methods were "proved" to have been employed during the last ten years in large or small degree in Albany, Birmingham, Buffalo, Camden, Chicago, Cincinnati, Cleveland, Columbus, Denver, Detroit, Kansas City, Kenosha, Wis.; Los Angeles, Miami, Newark, New Orleans, New York, Oakland, Cal.; Oklahoma City, Philadelphia, Richmond, Va.; St. Joseph, Mo.; St. Louis, San Francisco, Seattle, Waco and Wichita Falls, Texas; Washington and West Allis, Wis.

The report said that despite anti-"third-degrees" statutes in Illinois these brutal methods are "thoroughly at home" in Chicago.

"One of the best informed persons on Chicago practices tells us that it was an exception when a suspect was not subjected to personal violence," said the report.

"At the time of the Leopold-Loeb case, when an innocent school teacher was arrested and beaten until he falsely confessed, public attention was focused upon the 'third-degree.' An order was issued against it by Captain Stege, who was in charge of the Detective Bureau under Commissioner Russell. Well-informed persons, however, state that this order had little permanent effect."

Fear of Retaliation.

The report said that Chicago is much more interested now in reduction of crime than with official lawlessness. "Much crime in Chicago is committed by brutal ruffians; the public is less inclined to blame the police for beating such men than for letting them get away scot-free," said the report.

However, a reduction has been noted in brutal treatment of prisoners, but for another reason, the report pointed out:

"Some informants believe that this diminution is partly due to apprehension of retaliation; there are said to have been instances in the past where, after brutality was used, the victim's friends or gang have found out which policeman was responsible and taken revenge."

The report said that the heavy telephone book in Chicago was a frequently used weapon of torture. The "rubber hose" treatment in the pit of the stomach, beating the shins with a club or kicking them and visits to the "goldfish" room were listed as other widely used methods in Chicago.

The report stated that an exceptional number of confessions is obtained by the Buffalo police and there seems to be "little doubt" that the third degree is used there. The department itself, the report said, prides itself on ability to get confessions. In this connection the report quoted language alleged to have been used by the present Police Commissioner of Buffalo on the subject:

"If I have to violate the Constitution or my oath of office, I'll violate the Constitution. A policeman must be as fre as a fireman to protect his community. Nobody ever thinks of hedging a fireman about with a lot of laws that favor the fire. Shysters have turned the Constitution into a refuge for the criminal. * * * I'm going to protect the community. If in so doing I make a mistake and trespass on somebody's rights, let him sue."

No Organized Protest.

"It is noteworthy," the report continued, "that third-degree methods and illegal detentions in Buffalo are not the result of any lack of discipline, but are the practices of a department which has many modern traits and is under rigid control. There is no organized protest."

"Third-degree" methods were said by the report to be at a minimum in Boston, "though they are not quite non-existent. The Boston public would not stand for it, the report said, while the tradition of the Boston Police Department against lawlessness is "a most important factor." The press is "on the job" there, too, the report said, and no Boston newspaper "seems to be definitely 'tied up' with the Police Department."

The "third degree" exists in Newark, the report said, but "is subject to control." Pressure is used "but is kept within bounds, so that there have been no outstanding flagrant cases and public attention, therefore, has not been drawn to the so-called evil."

Philadelphia and Cincinnati were two other cities given relatively clean bills of health in the indictment of police brutality. In neither city has the practice disappeared, it was said. In Philadelphia, Inspector William Connelly has tried to stop physical brutality and has inaugurated the plan of putting a prisoner in "cold storage," or letting him remain in jail a few days, without mistreatment, so as to put him in a mood to confess. The whole policy of the Cincinnati police department is against brutal treatment, the report said.

In Cleveland, however, the condition is reversed and the "third degree" is prevalent, the report said. A former prosecutor told investigators, "You can't overstate it."

"Third degree" practices were reported to be "limited" in Detroit, although there were some instances. In Dallas and El Paso the prevailing practices were said to be long detention in jail and, in the case of the latter, actual physical brutality against loco-weel and heroin addicts. Long detention without proper charges was listed as the most prevalent practice in Dallas. The report showed that 40,106 prison hours were served by 1,823 persons booked merely "on suspicion."

Third Degree Conditions.

Sixty-nine printed pages of the report are devoted to studies of "third degree' conditions in fifteen cities—New York,, Buffalo, Boston, Newark, Philadelphia, Cincinnati, Cleveland, Detroit, Chicago, Dallas, El Paso, Denver, Los Angeles, San Francisco and Seattle.

The commission's comment on the use of "the third degree" in New York cities follows:

"New York has no third degree statute, but it is enacted that the defendant shall not be "subjected to any more restraint than is necessary his arrest and detention."

(New York Code of Criminal Proceedure, Sec. 172.)

"A confession is not admissible if made under the influence of fear produced by threats; and does not warrant a conviction without additional proof of guilt.

(Code Criminal Procedure, Sec. 395.) Section 165 of this code enacts:

"The defendant must in all cases be taken before the magistrate without unnecessary delay, and he may give bail at any hour of the day or night. This statute applies whether the arrest is made with or without a warrant. Willful or wrongful delay in taking a prisoner before a magistrate is a misdemeanor. The New York City Charter makes a more definite requirement: It is the duty of every policeman, immediately on making an arrest, to convey 'in person the offender' before the nearest sitting magistrate; and if he is not holding court, detention in the station house is permitted until the next regular sitting of the magistrate and no longer. The policeman who disobeys this provision is punishable by ten days' fine, or dismissal from the force.

Bars a Speedy Hearing.

"This provision of the charter seems to mean that a person arrested during the evening or night has no right to production before a magistrate until court opens next morning. Thus, it apparently takes away for many hours the statutory rights to a speedy hearing and the opportunity for immediate release on bail made mandatory by Section 165 of the code as quoted above. In practice this charter provision is said by a committee of the Bar Association of the city of New York, to be treated 'as authorizing' the police to detain arrested persons in station houses until the magistrates' courts are in regular session, and such detention gives to the police the opportunity, whether availed of or not, to perpetrate those acts of intimidation, and coercion, accusations of which have, as stated by Judge Andrews in the Doran case, become a standardized defense.

Association of the Bar of the City of New York, annual report of the committee on criminal courts, law and procedure for 1927 and 1928, p. 7. This says that the validity of the charter provision may be doubtful because of this conflict with the code.

"The same section of the city charter imposes upon the Police Commissioner the duty to make regulations 'to prevent the undue detention of arrested persons.' The police rules direct that all arrested persons shall be taken to the precinct station house for search, record and identification. Nothing appears to be said about prompt production in court. The Bar Association committee states that these rules, however necessary for efficiency of police administration, do by requiring prisoners to be taken to police stations on their way to court, further extend the opportunity for coercion.

"'The charter provision and the rules offer opportunity for physical violence to prisoners in police stations, with no witnesses present, and * * * accusations are prevalent that the police avail themselves of those opportunities for the purpose of extorting confessions from their prisoners by brutal and violent assaults upon them,'" the committee, which included three former United States Attorneys for the Southern District of New York and three former District Attorneys from New York County, also stated in this report in 1928.

Believe Charges Founded.

"From our aggregate experience and from such information as we have been able to acquire in our study of present conditions, we are of the opinion that these accusations (of brutal and violent assault to extort confessions) are well founded.

"The committee of the Bar Association, as we have seen, objected to the detention of prisoners overnight. Other reliable and well-informed persons have made the same objection, some declaring that longer periods of detention occur and that prisoners are at times held incommunicado.

"It is said on excellent authority that one device for extending the time of detention is to tell the counsel or friends of the prisoners that he will be arraigned in one court, when in fact he is brought to another court. Nevertheless, the period of detention or unauthorized detention is, as far as our information goes, much shorter in New York City than in most cities in which field work has been undertaken.

"The statement is made by a person well qualified by experience and observation, that the suspect is at times not booked at the station house until he has been questioned, but is merely held voluntarily for a period that is stated to be as long as a few days or a week. If he is ultimately released, he is considered by the police not to have been a defendant, so that in their opinion the statute did not apply and immediate production before a magistrate was not required.

"On the other hand, he may be 'arrested' and booked after he has been in the station house some time, and it is only after this that he is brought into court. During this period of unbooked investigation the beatings are said to be likely to occur.

Prizes For Violation.

"The criminals of New York present to the law-enforcing officials a very difficult problem. The prizes to be gained by violation of law are very large. This is true not only where the laws are faintly supported by public opinion, as in the case of prohibition, but also in the case of offenses like robbery and predatory murder. The apprehension of criminals is hampered, too, by the ease of escape into New Jersey or Connecticut, a few miles away on either side. Some of the criminals are organized into gangs. Fear of gang vengeance is widespread.

"The police often cannot learn facts in the usual manner by questioning disinterested witnesses. If one of the gang is arrested he will frequently keep silent from terror of what his associates would do to him if he told anything.

"Enemies of this nature can be decisively defeated only by a law-enforcing organization of very high quality. Judges and prosecutors, as well as police, would have to be men of high standards of honesty, intelligence, efficiency and faithfulness to duty. This is especially true if there is to be no resort to lawless methods against offenders. Whatever may be the advantages of independent searches for objective evidence, the collection of scientific data and the assembling of eye-witnesses of a crime as compared with confessions, there would seem to be little doubt that it is usually easier to get confessions.

"Policemen and detectives are not so likely to go after the other and better kinds of evidence unless they are well trained and energetic, and—what is very important—possess full confidence that their endeavors will be loyally and honestly supported by their superiors and by the prosecutors and the bench.

Courts Aware of Situation.

"The investigators were repeatedly told—not by sensation mongers but by observers of high position and ability, long experience and unquestioned disinterestedness—that the courts know that some of the prosecutors are crooked and the prosecutors know that some of the courts are crooked, and both know that some of the police are crooked, and the police are equally well informed as to them. If a policeman or a detective who has worked hard and effectively to land a bad criminal in jail sees him get off through improper influences, he will tend to be less zealous in the next prosecution. He will be inclined to take the easiest course and merely try to get a confession without a too nice regard for the means employed.

"Some of the prosecuting officials are reported to have condoned the free use of force, although it should be said that others have refused to use confessions when the defendant showed marks of injuries. Mayor Walker recently issued for publication a statement that for successful police work the old-fashioned night stick was far more effective than the new scientific ideas. Former Commissioner McLaughlin refused to take any action on complaints of brutality made by a committee of the New York County Lawyers' Association which included former district attorneys. Former Commissioner Whalen said in a public address that "these enemies of society were to be driven out of New York regardless of their constitutional rights." He described how a suspect was stripped of his clothing and put in a cold room until he gave the information the police wanted.

Partial Explanation Given.

"In partial explanation of this attitude the New York police are said to be influenced by what they say happened during the administration of Mayor Gaynor about twenty years ago. The Mayor had issued strict orders against the avoidable use of clubs in arrests. The result, it was said, was a substantial impairment of the zeal and efficiency of patrolmen. Many responsible persons interviewed expressed the fear that a let-up of harsh police methods today might result in an increase of criminal activity, such as they believe to have occurred at the time mentioned. It is important to observe that this argument does not point to any need for the third degree, but only to caution against restricting the police too severely in using force if they deem it necessary to effect an arrest.

"As to force at arrests, several informants urge the danger of slackening the impetus of the policeman by rendering him afraid of being brought up on charges if he makes an arrest in which he has to use force to overcome resistance. New York criminals are quick with their guns and always have the advantage over the policeman in that he does not know whether they are armed or not. He has no time to look up the law on doubtful points like a judge or a lawyer. He must decide on the spot in a few seconds what action to take. If he knows that the consequences of an honest mistake will be not only the risk of civil action by the prisoner but also the danger of being brought up on charges with the possibility of losing his job and his pension, then he may take the safe and easy course of doing nothing. These observers feel that a policeman who, in making arrests, beats men in the line of his duty and because he thinks he has to should be supported by the commissioner, even though he used unnecessary force.

The Habitual Mistake.

"Whatever the soundness of these arguments, there must be some limit to the use of force, and mistakes may occur so often as to become habitual practice. Although the Bar Association committee reported in 1928 that brutality during arrest was not a cause of general complaint, and this form of lawlessness is stated by a former commissioner to have greatly lessened in recent years, other informants declare that excessive force is common. Brutality during arrests raises a more difficult problem of prevention than brutality thereafter, for the policeman always has the possible argument that the prisoner resisted arrest or tried to escape.

"Statistics taken by voluntary defenders show 174 cases in three years where brutality was alleged at the time of the arrest (86 cases in 1930 alone), and their observation of visible injuries indicates that a large number of these claims are true.

"Statistics on police brutality taken from the files of the voluntary defenders' committee of the Legal Aid Society of New York for the year 1930 show that of a total of 1,235 cases, 289 defendants alleged they were beaten by the police (23.40 per cent). A descriptive summary of these cases is given in Appendix IV. Some statistics also appear in the published annual reports of the committee.

"Recent press clippings report many charges of this sort. More than forty instances of charges of violent arrests and other forms of brutality in New York City are covered by press clippings dated in 1930 and in the first three months of 1931.

"The fact that brutality is practiced at the time of arrest would make a policeman more likely to use it for other purposes, so that there is an obvious connection between this subject and the third degree.

New York City Conditions.

"The third degree is widely and brutally employed in New York City. Former prosecuting attorneys have declared this in print and in conversations with the investigators.

"A former prosecutor stated that the third degree was carried on consistently and persistently and more than people generally assumed. Six former United States and New York County District Attorneys (C. A. Perkins, E. R. Berker, C. F. Caffey, W. T. Jerome, S. S. Marshall and C. S. Whitman) joined in the Bar Association 1928 report already quoted, affirming the existence of the third degree, and another former district attorney, R. H. Elder, said in a published letter in 1929:

" 'The third degree has now become established and recognized practice in the Police Department of the city of New York. Every police station in the city is equipped with the instruments to administer the torture incident to that process.' "

"These statements of former officials as to the prevalence of the third degree are strongly corroborated by the persons interviewed. It is a widely used practice of the detective force in serious felony cases, especially where there is particular pressure on the police for a solution. It is said to be not often employed for misdemeanors. Most informants consider that the practice has not lessened of late years, although its form has somewhat altered. Instead, continuous questioning with accompanying mental strain is employed to break the suspect's nerve and make him talk. But the number of cases in which injuries are visible remains large. Arrested persons come to station houses or headquarters in good shape and are seen shortly afterward in the Tombs with swollen faces, all sorts of bruises and cuts and often with blood spots scattered over them. An observer with exceptional opportunities has seen many cases of face and body bruises and broken ribs. A distinguished magistrate reported to us that when several Italians were brought before him for alleged violence he looked at their backs and there was hardly a spot which was not raw from recent beating. Another magistrate recently sent back one badly bruised suspect so that photographs might be taken of the wounds. (This case, of W. F. Sutton, was reported in The World, Dec. 2, 1930; also in The Evening World, Evening Post, Sun, Telegram and Brooklyn Eagle on Dec. 8. See Telegram editorial, Jan. 19, 1931.)

Welts and Bruises.

"On May 23, 1931, two men charged with counterfeiting, brought before Federal Judge Woolsey, at his direction removed their clothes, displaying welts and bruises which they said they had received as a result of beating with a rubber hose at the hands of the city police and of the Federal Secret Service agents. Photographs were taken, and Mr. Medalie, the United States Attorney, declared he would order an investigation. (The case referred to is that of Giovanni Bertini and Luciano Barbaro, referred to in various newspapers, among others THE NEW YORK TIMES, Sunday, May 24, 1931. The correctness of the account in THE TIMES was confirmed to us by Judge Woolsey.)

"The police attempt to explain many of these cases of visible injuries by saying that the prisoners fell downstairs and occasionally the prisoners give the same stock explanation for fear of police reprisals. 'Prisoners frequently fall downstairs, but officers do not.' A former Federal prosecutor relates that when a New York policeman brought in a man whom he had arrested he asked him the cause of the prisoner's badly swollen eye, and received the reply: 'You must be a very young District Attorney.'

"Third-degree methods, authoritatively reported to us as recently employed, include punching in the face, especially a hard slap on the jaw; hitting with a billy, whipping with a rubber hose, kicking in the abdomen, tightening the necktie almost up to the choking point. * * * Methods are favored which do not leave visible marks, because these attract the attention of the courts and sometimes lead District Attorneys not to use the confession. There is said to be a practice that the arresting officer does not commonly do the beating; another man will do it, so that when the arresting officer takes the stand it cannot be charged that he used force.

"Lavine, in his book 'The Third Degree,' describes other extreme methods, but these have not been mentioned by other New York informants. Among the methods mentioned by Lavine are: A sharp, but not heavy, regular blow of a club on the skull, repeated at regular intervals, so that the regularity of the blows arouses anticipation which increases the torture; assuring suspects that they would not be hurt, then suddenly felling them unconscious by a blow from behind with a club or a slab of wood, followed by further sympathy and reassurance when the man revives, only to have the same thing suddenly happen again, the man never seeing who strikes him.

'They Came Through.'

"Fiaschetti, a former head of the Italian squad, says of one case: 'I went to the Tombs and got myself a sawed-off baseball bat and walked in on all those dogs. Yes, they came through with everything they knew.'

"A milder method, coming as we have been told, into increasing use, is to exhaust the prisoner by keeping him awake or constantly awakening him after a brief sleep. Or a man may be exhausted by long relays of questioning. Sometimes the questioning takes place in the presence of several burly officers, who rap the table sharply with their night sticks to terrorize the suspect. Deprivation of food is also practised. These methods are called the mental third degree.

"Keeping a prisoner in jail for long periods of time with nothing happening in his case is equivalent to the third degree—a mental suffering. A few instances have been mentioned of men who finally decide to plead guilty and pay a fine or serve a short sentence in order to return to their homes and work.

"Detentions may work a particular hardship for persons who are merely held as witnesses. Informants tell of such men having been kept for three or four months. An article by Mr. George Z. Medalie, now United States Attorney, mentions a sailor held eight months and a restaurant keeper held over a year, to the serious damage of his business.

"A symposium on the subject of material witnesses, the panel (February 1930). The practice is said by informants to be defended because of the difficulty of getting witnesses into court when they are in a neighboring State. This might be remedied by agreements with other States or reciprocal legislation among several States. Another difficulty is the rule against depositions in criminal cases, but this probably can not be overcome in view of constitutional sanction confrontation. Mr. Medalie recommends several other reforms, especially an immediate conditional examination of the witnesses before a magistrate who would take his deposition in the presence of the accused (thus overcoming the constitutional objection stated above) and an early trial of cases where witnesses are detained longer. He would also allow the defense to have the same privilege as the prosecution of requiring bail of material witnesses.

Murder of Wardens.

"Weiner, a man with a bad criminal record, was charged in 1926 with aiding and abetting the murder of two wardens of the city prison by some escaping prisoners. He himself was outside the prison and was alleged to have furnished the prisoners with pistols thrown over the prison wall, but the only evidence on this point was his confession, which was held on appeal to have been involuntary. Judge O'Brien said that the evidence was conclusive that Weiner was assaulted and threatened between his arrest and the time he was brought into the District Attorney's office. An Assistant District Attorney admitted that when Weiner was brought before him, he had a mark on his right cheek and red spots on his shirt and tie. Two jailkeepers testified that his nose was swollen and that he had an abrasion on his right cheek bone. The prison records contained a notation to the same effect. Weiner's conviction was reversed and a new trial ordered.

"The Barbato case grew out of the strangling of Julia Museo Quintieri in her apartment in September, 1929. Barbato, an Italian, was arrested within a few hours and questioned at midnight by the District Attorney, who, when he could obtain no information, departed, leaving him at the police station. Next morning he confessed. This detention until confession was obtained was declared by Judge Pound to be 'without legal warrant' and to have been previously condemned by the Court of Appeals as follows:

" 'The practice of detectives to take in custody and hold in durance persons merely suspected of crime in order to obtain statements from them before formal complaint and arraignment, and before they can see friends and counsel, is without legal sanction.'

"At the trial Barbato's defense was an alibi. The state relied on his fession of four words only: 'I kil Julia Museo.' He testified that these were obtained by threats and force, which the police officers denied. According to a press clipping, the detectives asserted that he had fallen out of an automobile in trying to escape. The confessions were admitted by the trial judge, and the jury was left to determine whether they were voluntary. His conviction was reversed and a new trial granted" on the ground that the confessions should have been excluded."

Judge Pound's Comment.

After describing the facts, Judge Pound commented as follows:

"'It has been said one is driven to the conclusion that the third degree is employed as a matter of course in most States and has become a recognized step in the process that begins with arrest and ends with acquittal or final affirmance. The practice in England seems otherwise. Statements made after arrest in answer to questions by police officers, if legal evidence (as to which the law is not settled), are cautiously received. Lawless methods of law enforcement should not be countenanced by our courts, even though they may seem expedient to the authorities in order to apprehend the guilty. Whether a guilty man goes free or not is a small matter compared with the maintenance of principles which still safeguard a person accused of crime. If torture is to be accepted as a means of securing confessions, let us have no pretense about it, but repeal Section 395 of the Code of Criminal Procedure (excluding involuntary confessions) and accept all evidence of all confessions however obtained, trusting to the jury to winnow the true from the false. As long as the section remains in the code, the courts are bound to give as full protection to an accused as the evidence warrants.'

"After a subsequent delay of five months, Barbato was released from the death house and prison, and it was doubted that he would be tried again.

"An earlier case in the Court of Appeals shows the possibility that false confessions may result from the protracted questioning. The defendant Joyce, a moron, was arrested in 1920 under a warrant against him for grand larceny, taken from police station to police station, and questioned for twelve hours about a murder, for which he was afterward tried and convicted. His disputed evidence of police brutality was left to the jury. No emphasis is laid on that matter by the Court of Appeals, but Judge Hogan, in granting a new trial, strongly doubted the truthfulness of the numerous oral confessions obtained with startling ease from a man with the mentality of a child of 10 or 12 years. One experienced police captain testified: 'The man confessed so easily I was rather impressed with the fact that he wasn't right, first off, to be honest with you.'

"Judge Hogan then described the methods used by the police and the Assistant District Attorney.

"'Examination of records in homicide cases justifies the assertion that the prevailing custom where statements are thus made is to proceed at once to the office of the public prosecutor, where the accused is advised of his rights, then examined by the District Attorney, the proceedings being taken by a stenographer or written out at length, read over to the accused, correction made if necessary, and his signature obtained to the statement if he is willing to sign the same. Such procedure was not adopted in the present case. For some reason it was deemed necessary to take defendant from one precinct station house to another, as heretofore referred to, covering a period of some twelve hours, that the statements of defendant might be made in the presence of various officers.

"'The first precinct station was reached about 2 o'clock in the afternoon, an hour when the public prosecutor or one of his assistants would doubtless be at the office, but defendant was not taken there until about half past nine the following morning. Up to that time no written statements had been prepared or made, neither had the various statements attributed to defendant been reduced to writing. Certain of the officers testified that they did not have defendant make a statement in writing because he confessed so easily. The detective who took defendant to the office of the District Attorney testified that defendant there made a statement, but the same was not put in writing; it is customary for a District Attorney to take a statement when a man goes through a case as he did, but the District Attorney didn't do it on account he never thought this man would deny that statement.'

"An unreported case is described by a former District Attorney: 'I know of one instance in which the punishment inflicted was so severe that a police surgeon was called in and stood by and at intervals took the pulse of the prisoner and gave advice as to whether he could stand more beating.'

"R. H. Elder, letter quoted in Bates's 'This Land of Liberty,' 205. This case is apparently the Mintz case, also described by Murphy, Third Degree, 151 Outlook 522 (1929), who says that forty bruises were counted by Dr. Lichtenstein on Mintz's body after he had been questioned at headquarters.

Other Cases Cited.

"Several other cases are narated by Murphy, OP, cit, supra, but these are not re-stated since they are not verified by officials. For the same reason we have omitted from the text many charges of the third degree in New York reported in recent press clippings.

"These include: Telegram, April 17, 1929 (attorney claims five clients beaten and kicked by detectives, one prisoner's teeth knocked out); ib, May 31, 1929 (Matts claims police broke ribs and beat him with rubber hose); ib, Oct. 14, 1929 (Lawson and Donald allege terrible beating by police, attorney seeks physical examination); ib, Nov. 11, 1929 (editorial); ib, March 28, 1930 (Goltz appears in court badly bruised, right arm possibly broken, claims this results from beatings); Times, Oct. 25, 1930 (Goltz charges denied by Tombs physician and police); Telegram, April 8, 1930 (editorial on advocacy of third degree; by Fiaschetti, former head of Italian squad); World, Sept. 21, 1930 (article by Fiaschetti, saying third degree common practice); Telegram, May 14, 1930 (Burlingham, head of New York City Bar Association, charges third degree still used); News, Sept. 28, 1930 (Mandala alleges beating with rubber hose, photograph of his back); World, Jan. 2, 1931 (detective steps on prisoner's injured foot, obtaining confession).

"Further trustworthy information has been obtained from material furnished by the Voluntary Defenders Committee of the Legal Aid Society. Each defendant is asked by an attorney of the committee at the time of his initial interview (almost always in prison) whether he has been assaulted by the police. This question is asked as a routine matter while a social history is being taken and the answer is recorded on the printed blank, together with an estimate of the probable truthfulness of the defendant's statement. This estimate is based on the attorney's personal judgment made of the defendant's veracity plus the consideration of physical marks, if there are any.

Rarely Admit Violence.

"The following is a statement of Mr. Leroy Campbell, attorney in charge of the Voluntary Defenders Committee, appended to a typewritten report of police brutalities:

"'In conclusion it may be said without exaggeration that it is exceptional for defendants to state voluntarily that they have been brutally treated by police officers or guards, for they seem to take it for granted that they will receive such treatment. It is almost always after questioning that they usually, rather reluctantly, go into the details. Their attitudes are usually such as to convince of the truthfulness of their statements.'"

These statistics on brutality cases are from the files of the Voluntary Public Defenders Committee:

	1928.	1929.	1930.
Total number of cases handled	957	785	1,235
Number of cases alleged brutality	127	167	289
Per cent of cases alleged brutality	17.9	21.2	23.40

Details of Alleged Brutality.

	1929.	P.C.	1930.	P.C.
Total number of cases of alleged brutality	167	100.0	289	100.0
At stationhouse	87	52.1	151	52.8
At time and place of arrest	37	22.1	86	29.6
At time and place of arrest and at stationhouse	10	5.9	13	3.88
En route to stationhouse	3	1.7	5	1.7
Police headquarters	2	1.1	...	...

"The statistics given in the following table were derived from the files of 1930 cases only, of the Voluntary Defenders Committee.

Prior Convictions.

Misdemeanor at least	500
Felony	40
No criminal record	133
Unascertained	16

Color.

Negro	101
Yellow	1
White	171
Unascertained	16
Foreign birth	41

Where age was given they fall into these groups:

Ages 15 to 24 inclusive	163
Ages 25 and over	107

Education.

In practically every case the defendant left school either on graduation from elementary school or before.

Crimes Charged.

Robbery (generally includes charges of assault and larceny)	80
Burglary	76
Larceny	44
Assault	27
Carrying revolver, burglar's tools	16
Rape	6
Homicide	5
Forgery	4
Sodomy	2
Arson	2
Blackmail	2
Drugs	2
Abduction	1
Perjury	1
Malicious mischief	1
Total	270
Unknown	19
Grand total	289

"In New York the voluntary defenders naturally would get no capital cases, since the code of criminal procedure provides for the payment of fees to counsel assigned in such cases.

"The Federal officials in New York City, with rare exceptions, do not employ the third degree. Rubber hose is reported to have been used on some arrested counterfeiters about four years ago, and a similar occurence has been reported within the last few weeks. The narcotic squad is stated by former Federal prosecutors to use some violence to elicit confessions.

Under prior Federal District Attorneys, instances have been related of the making of arrests late in the afternoon after the commissioner had gone, so that bail could not be procured until the next day, or else the bail demanded would be so high that it could not be furnished. The result would be the detention of a suspect with the opportunity for him to confess or disclose what he knows about other persons.

"Prohibition agents, Coast Guard officials and postoffice agents have in some cases detained men in order to get confessions. It is reported that customs men often keep persons, chiefly rum-runners, locked up in the Customs House to obtain information from them. What information we have is to the effect that no violence or ill-treatment is employed to the persons kept over night by Federal officials, but they are subjected to severe-long-continued questioning, and advised that it will be better for them if they 'come clean.' The postoffice agents pride themselves on seldom failing to get a confession from the criminals with whom they come in contact.

"The illegal practices which have been described in this study have not gone unchallenged. The Voluntary Defenders Committee keeps a unique record of police brutalities. The Bar Association of the City of New York made the vigorous report, already mentioned, in 1928. The New York County Lawyers Association has undertaken some study. These two associations are among the few bar associations in the country that are now making an effort to meet these problems.

"The bar association called upon the New York Crime Commission to make an investigation, as did the Prison Association of New York; but so far as our information goes, no such investigation has yet been undertaken. The newspapers have reported cases of police brutality very frequently and occasionally there have been editorial comments on the third degree."

RIGHTS UNIT ASKS CURBS ON POLICE

Finds Brutality Widespread —Urges New Legislation and Executive Action

By ANTHONY LEWIS
Special to The New York Times.

WASHINGTON, Nov. 16—The Civil Rights Commission reported today that police lawlessness and brutality remained "a serious problem throughout the United States." It recommended corrective action by both Congress and the Kennedy Administration.

A commission study of the administration of justice described beatings and even killings by the police in a number of states in recent years. It drew this conclusion, among others:

"Although whites are not immune, Negroes feel the brunt of official brutality, proportionately, more than any other group in American society."

Findings Unanimous

The six commissioners were unanimous in their findings and recommendations. They urged the Justice Department to be less "cautious" in prosecuting local policemen who violated the Constitution.

The commissioners also asked Congress to consider this new legislation:

¶A program of grants in aid to state and local governments to improve their police forces by better recruiting and training.

¶An amendment to the Federal criminal statute that now prohibits unconstitutional acts by local officers. The amendment would provide specific bans on police brutality, the coercing of confessions and inaction in the face of violence.

¶An amendment to the Federal Civil Rights Act to let citizens injured by official misconduct recover directly from local governments. Such victims may now sue policemen or other officials, but there is little chance of collecting from them.

¶A new statute to let the Justice Department bring civil suits to end racial discrimination in the selection of juries.

The commission noted that exclusion of Negroes from juries because of race has been a Federal crime since 1875. But it said discrimination continued. It pointed especially to eleven counties in the Deep South, heavily Negro in population, where it said no Negro had ever served on a grand jury or trial jury.

The usual method of challenging jury discrimination is to raise the issue in the criminal trial of a Negro. But the commission said it was often difficult or even dangerous for a lawyer to make that contention in a hostile atmosphere. It urged that the Justice Department share the burden of enforcement.

The commission found, overall, that "there is much to be proud of in the American system of criminal justice." It said most policemen acted fairly and lawfully. But it warned:

"Unfortunately, this is not the whole story. The commission is concerned about the number of unconstitutional and criminal acts committed by agents of American justice who are sworn to uphold the law and to apply it impartially."

Alabama Beatings Noted

In addition to police brutality, the report said there were some, though lessening, instances in which the police stood by while unpopular citizens were subjected to violence. It cited the assaults on the Freedom Riders in Alabama last spring in the presence of policemen.

The report also included a separate preliminary study of the status of American Indians. Most Indians, the commission found, are free to vote. But it said some children had been secluded from public schools because of race and suggested that the Justice or Interior Department take legal action against such discrimination.

"Employment opportunities appear to be as restricted for Indians as they are for Negroes," the commission said.

The entire report, entitled "Justice," was the fifth and last volume of the commission's studies of 1961. Others dealt with voting, schools, housing and jobs.

At the end of today's report the commission made some general observations on the five volumes and on the state of civil rights.

Among other things, it called on President Kennedy to exert his leadership by "explaining to the American people the legal and moral issues involved in critical situations when they arise," by reiterating his support for desegregation of schools and by urging citizens to exercise their voting rights.

Statement by Hesburgh

One member of the commission, the Rev. Theodore M. Hesburgh, president of the University of Notre Dame, issued a strongly worded separate statement.

"We are all excited about Communist subversion," he said, "while we perpetrate a much worse and studied subversion of our own Constitution that corrodes the nation at its core and central being—the ideal of equal opportunity for all."

The other members of the commission are Dr. John A. Hannah, president of Michigan State University, the chairman; Robert G. Storey of Dallas, vice chairman; Robert S. Rankin of North Carolina, Dean Spottswood W. Robinson 3d of Howard University Law School and Dean Erwin N. Griswold of Harvard Law School.

The report describes a number of incidents of police brutality. Some of the cases follow, as reported by the commission:

In 1958 James Brazier, a Negro of Dawson, Ga., died after a beating by the police. No reason was given for his arrest, but witnesses said the police had resented his prosperity and had told him:

"You is a nigger who is buying new cars and we can't hardly live."

Sheriff Is Quoted

A year after Mr. Brazier's death the county's sheriff allegedly told his widow, who survived with four children:

"I oughta slap your damn brains out. A nigger like you I feel like slapping them out. You niggers set around here and look at television and go up North and do to white folks here like the niggers up North do, but you ain't gonna do it."

The Justice Department impaneled a grand jury, presented evidence for five days and requested indictments against three of the Dawson police officers. The grand jury, made up of local citizens, refused to indict.

A retired Negro policeman in Detroit, Jesse Ray, told the commission what had happened to him when he waved at two white officers who were parked in a car as he drove by. They did not recognize him as a former policeman.

The white officers stopped him, apparently interpreting the wave as an insult. They pulled him out of the car, hit him on the head with a blackjack, choked him, knocked him to the ground and handcuffed his hands behind him. He was arrested and taken to a hospital, where he was shackled to a bed all night and not allowed to call a lawyer.

Mr. Ray was charged with reckless driving. A jury acquitted him. No action was taken against the officers.

November 17, 1961

The Case of the Public Eye

Operating without the glamorous trappings of the TV 'private eye,' the New York police detective nevertheless wars effectively against crime.

By ROBERT M. LIPSYTE

A MAN is murdered, three rapes are reported and 103 homes are burglarized on an average day in New York City. There are thirty-three assaults, 131 grand larcenies, and hundreds of wallets and pocketbooks stolen. There are also, in this city, 3,000 police detectives committed to lay open the tragic flesh of each of these bare statistics and run the perpetrators to ground.

The statistics, recently released by the Police Department, reflect an increase in city crime from 1960 to 1961 of 4.8 per cent. Arrests, however, increased 5.4 per cent—a tribute, in part, to the detectives, all but invisible in the day-to-day routine of keeping a deathwatch on the indices of violence. Most of them work out of the city's eighty-one police precincts. They are charged with the solution of all crimes, from malicious mischief to murder; with the location of missing persons and the recovery of lost and stolen property.

While the uniformed cop is charged with keeping the peace on his post and arresting offenders on the spot, the detective usually arrives at the scene of a crime long after the criminal is gone. From clues, witnesses, contacts, a knowledge of criminal habits and plain hunches, the detective must create the man to fit the crime, find him, and prove it.

AT any time of the day or night he may be found sitting in a grimy squad room interrogating an uncooperative prisoner; standing in a cramped doorway awaiting someone too shrewd to appear, or stalking through the rain without a hat. (He knows that if he wears a hat he will be immediately spotted for a detective.) In the jungle of city crime, the hunted is often as smart as the hunter.

Albert Giarnella is a detective second-grade assigned to the Eighteenth Squad on the West Side of midtown Manhattan. He is a large, serious, friendly man of 42. There are very few things in his life that he prefers to his work. On the rare occasions when he takes his wife to the movies, he looks for seat-tippers (criminals who push up theatre seats and catch the purses that drop through) and when he goes to a restaurant his eyes are continually scanning near-by tables for faces he has seen on "wanted" posters. Last Christmas he

took his three daughters to their first Broadway show, "My Fair Lady." They were entranced. He was bored. "I saw through the plot right away," he said. "I couldn't sit still."

Giarnella is known as a soft touch for a hungry felon and as a sympathetic ear. "I listen to what everyone tells me," he says "and I nod my head and I don't believe a word of it until I check it out myself." His squad commander says, with pride, that when the going gets rough Giarnella has a very fast and heavy pair of hands.

The going does not get rough very often. Unlike his various television counterparts, Giarnella has never killed or wounded a man (he always has aimed high or low to halt a fugitive). Still, although the violent moments are rare, he must be prepared to exert all of his training with very little warning.

ON a Sunday morning, three years ago, Giarnella was going home to the Bronx on the IND. The News was spread out on his lap, but the pages kept slipping through his fingers and his eyelids kept closing; he had been working for eighteen hours on a homicide. As his head drooped, a woman across the car pursed her lips in disapproval. Giarnella is 6 feet tall, he weighs 200 pounds, and his resemblance to the late Tyrone Power is startling. He was wearing a pin-striped suit under his raincoat and he looked like a character from "Guys and Dolls."

When his eyes opened again, it was because he thought he heard a scream. "They ought to oil these damn trains," he said and closed his eyes again. Then he was on his feet, and moving.

In the next car, a 6-foot 2-inch Negro, his eyes rolling wildly, was slashing with a butcher knife at a white woman and her baby. The other occupants of the car were rooted in horror.

Giarnella admits that he was still half asleep, but he reacted with conditioned reflex. He unbuttoned his coat and jacket as he stepped into the next car, and pulled his .38 Colt Detective's Special from its hip holster.

"Put the knife down," he said soothingly. "I'm a police officer. That's why I have this gun. No one will hurt you."

The man with the knife turned. He was four feet from Giarnella and he raised the knife higher.

"Its funny how quickly I woke up," says Giarnella. "I looked at that char-

acter and I wondered if I should shoot him, and if so, where. I was worried that the bullet would ricochet or go through him and hit somebody else. I thought about a sergeant I once knew who put three slugs into a guy's chest and the guy kept coming and stuck the knife in the sergeant's belly."

THE story is not a favorite of Giarnella's and he will stop in the telling to twist the ring on his little finger or squeeze his forehead. "I figured the guy wasn't too steady on his feet. I didn't shoot."

The man lunged. Giarnella sidestepped and wrapped one of his thick, square hands around the back of his neck. He carefully put his revolver away before he beat him into submission.

When the train pulled into the Tremont Avenue station, a parade of uniformed cops piled aboard. A subway employe had called ahead.

"I pleaded with those guys, I said, 'Look, fellas, I work nights, how about making the arrest?' Nothing doing. So I had to pinch the guy and fingerprint him and take him down to court and call my wife and tell her I wouldn't be able to make church."

LIKE all precinct detectives, however, a great deal of Giarnella's work is done on the typewriter. Every complaint (policemen call them "squeals") must be recorded, and every crime cross-indexed and filed according to type, location and date. The paper work is carried on in the Eighteenth's squad room on West Fifty-fourth Street, a disheveled, somber chamber whose only dash of color is a picture of a marijuana plant in bloom.

Detectives in the Eighteenth work in four-man teams, and unless the whole force "rolls out" on a catastrophe or a major crime, there are always at least two men in the office to "catch squeals." The five-day week (including day and night duty) that the detectives put in never works out that way. Victims often have to be interviewed at their own convenience and crimes frequently occur just before a team is slated to go off duty. There is no overtime pay on the force and days off can never be counted on.

Every two weeks Giarnella brings home $172.67. When he leaves for work he can never tell his wife when he will be back. Each time, though, he goes through the ritual of promising her that he will not be a hero, that he will never run down a dark alley after a man with a gun. He once confessed this lie to a priest, who told him it was permissible under the circumstances.

GIARNELLA'S most satisfying tour probably occurred on a summer night three years ago when he and Don Rolker, a detective first-grade, were sent out to investigate a gang fight in which a teen-age boy had been shot in the stomach. They figured on a tough night; youth-gang members rarely talk.

Giarnella usually walks softly, and as he approached the crowd around the body he was in no hurry to identify himself and allow the quick barrier of hostility to cut him off from a stray word.

"Gooch." Giarnella never found out who said it, but after questioning several youths it was still the only lead he had. So he turned to a clutch of boys on the outskirts of the crowd and pleasantly asked them where Gooch was. They shrugged. He asked them where Gooch lived. Around the corner, fourth floor rear, with his grandmother.

The trembling old woman who opened the door for the detectives was obviously pleased to find that her grandson had friends. Giarnella, genial and outgoing, told her that a pal of Gooch's had been hurt, and had asked for him. The old lady invited them in. The gun was in the bedroom.

For several hours, with Rolker leading the way, the two men toured luncheonettes and bars where the old lady thought her grandson might be. He was eating a hamburger when they told him that the boy he had shot had fingered him as his assailant. It was a lie. But Gooch broke down immediately and confessed. It turned out to be a very neat night's work.

BUT it was an atypical one. A detective is far more likely to run into frustration, unanswered questions and petty crime in a tour of duty.

A recent day-duty tour for Giarnella started at 9 A. M. with a telephone call from a film company in the West Fifties. It was a tired old story. The switchboard operator had received a call from an almost incoherent female voice warning against a bomb in the building. "We'll be there," said Giarnella.

Unlike television sleuths, detectives do not bolt out of the station house door after every squeal. There is always time to finish the coffee, light another cigarette, complete a report. "You wouldn't last very long on this job if you kept running." says John Ford, Giarnella's partner on the job, "but we move pretty

fast when we really have to."

The emergency squad and several uniformed men from the precinct had already rolled on the squeal. The information the detectives wanted would still be there when they arrived. Or the building would be gone.

The switchboard operator at the film company was a hawk-faced woman who began talking rapidly as soon as she saw Giarnella's blue and gold badge. "No grudges or animosity around here," she said. "No disgruntled former employes I can finger for a quick collar."

Giarnella and Ford exchanged a wan look and thanked the woman. They waited quietly while she rang the personnel director's office.

"These dames who watch television," said Ford, shaking his head.

The personnel director, after letting the detectives stand in the outer room like a clutch of unwanted salesmen, finally ushered them into his office. Giarnella carefully recorded the names of several former employes and promised he would call back when he had something. Meanwhile, the

emergency squad had completed a search of the floor and found no suspicious containers.

BACK in the squad room, Giarnella compared the complaint with several other recent bomb scares, found no common denominators, and filed the report.

At 11 A. M. he drove over to Pier 97 in the squad's unmarked, gray 1960 Plymouth sedan. (When it is unavailable he uses his own secondhand 1957 Mercury, at his own expense.)

A week before a cable had snapped in the hold of a freighter and a platform bearing twenty-seven 100-pound bags of coffee had plummeted down on a stevedore. The Homicide and Riverfront Squads had been called in, as well as the District Attorney's Office, but ultimate responsibility for the case rested with Al Giarnella, who had caught the original squeal.

Al spent an hour talking to one of the dock foremen. He came out of the pier shack squeezing his forehead and shaking his head. "You have to keep moving on these things, every day you have to plod a little further. It's like one of those fancy crossword puzzles in the papers. If you get the words going across, then you'll get the words going down, and sooner or later you'll know all the answers. Maybe."

HE headed the Plymouth downtown. Several pieces of cable were in the back seat, tagged and ready to be analyzed by the Police Laboratory on Poplar Street in Brooklyn. If the wires bore traces of tampering, Al would have a murder case.

"Sometimes we break our backs on a case and nothing happens, the whole thing just disappears in your hand. Or we know we got a guy cold, but not enough evidence." (A week later, the lab reported that the cable had parted naturally. No tampering, no murder case.)

Giarnella pulled the car under the wooden parapet of a construction project three blocks from the station house, and tip-toed lightly along the muddy planking until he found the man he was looking for. Several days before, one workman had split another's head open with a chisel. Al went over the story for the third

time with an eyewitness. He was still unsatisfied when he left. He said he would be back, as he pushed through a semicircle of glowering laborers who had formed up at the gleam of his badge.

"Nobody loves a cop unless they need him," he said, back in the car.

On his way back to the squad room Al bought a sandwich and a paper container of Sanka at a corner delicatessen. He ate his lunch at a desk, under a portrait of Donald Leroy Payne, No. 1 on the F. B. I.'s most-wanted list.

Unless a detective is immersed in a major case, his time is spent on a dozen other ones, picking up a clue here, a lead there, waiting for the puzzle to take shape. Most of his information is supplied by professional informers. Detectives pay these stool pigeons out of their own pockets and regard the money as an investment. A good tip can lead to a "good collar"—and promotion.

Stoolies have to be handled cautiously. The same greed that leads them to offer up a colleague for a sawbuck can lead them to foul an investigation or, if they are being depended upon as witnesses, to take a flyer before the case comes to court. Detectives despise informers ("Can you imagine making your living by ratting on your buddies?" asks Ford) but go to great lengths to protect them, even so far as arranging a short jail term to allay suspicion.

A RECENT Eighth Avenue tavern murder had detectives of the Eighteenth prowling round the clock. A man had been shot in full view of a packed bar but, because of gangland implications, no one "had seen nothing."

An old, reliable informer of Giarnella's called him up one night and made a date in a Brooklyn luncheonette. He had seen it all, he said, and would give the name of the killer if Giarnella would get him a job on the other side of town. Giarnella did. The killer was caught. (Giarnella refuses to give more details on the case or even swear that these facts are any more than "true to life." He says: "Killers read, too.")

At 4:45 P. M. another bomb complaint was called in. The Eighteenth rolled out again. Nothing. But Giarnella did not get back to the Bronx until 9 that night.

WITHIN the department. the detective's job is considered a glamorous one. Most uniformed patrolmen (who call detectives "brains") look forward to "making the Bureau" with a spectacular arrest and a sudden call from the Commissioner's office. A detective third-grade makes $7,611, almost $300 more than a patrolman first-grade. A detective first-grade starts at about $9,000, equivalent to a uniformed lieutenant. Detectives are free from the unpleasant chores of post duty—would-be suicides, water-logged bodies, unruly women drunks—wear their own clothes (called "working out of the bag"), and are allowed to drink on duty (bartenders are considered second only to stoolies as prime contacts).

Giarnella was appointed to the Detective Division on Jan. 23, 1952, after serving four years in a patrol car in the Bronx. He spent six weeks at the Police Academy's Detective School learning the proper methods of conducting an investigation; of "tossing" (searching) a suspect ("Don't forget to check his underwear for a sneak gun, his hatband for a razor and his hair for narcotics"); and of interrogating a prisoner ("Ask the same question over and over, only phrase it differently.")

He was impressed with the virtues of tenacity ("A case is never dead until the criminal is in the can") and of observation ("Always listen with your eyes"). In the years that

followed he developed some working propositions of his own, including: "Any guy that looks me straight in the eye is wrong. He's trying to con me because he's up to something."

HE is not completely sure how he turned out to be a hunter, instead of a quarry. Born in an Italian town on the Mediterranean, he was brought to this country when he was 5. His father, a Sanitation worker, settled the family in the Fordham section of the Bronx.

"It was a pretty rough neighborhood, and we were all scared of cops. We'd walk a block out of our way just to avoid the man on post, even if we were just minding our own business, strolling home from school," he recalls. "They were big, rough Irish cops and they straightened kids out with the back of their hands."

Giarnella shot pool with neighborhood kids who later attended some of the finest penitentiaries in the country, but he never got into trouble. "They used to say, 'Al, let's go for a ride,' and I'd say. 'Where?' and they'd say, 'Just come on, we'll have a good time.' I never went. After a while I'd just hide in the bedroom when they came around and my mother would say I was out."

A strong, agile kid, Al was on the varsity basketball team at Theodore Roosevelt High School and gained a reputation as a promising heavyweight club fighter. During his senior year, he shaped up every morning at the Borden's Milk factory, earning a dollar a day as a "dugan" or driver's helper. He spent 1940 with a

Civilian Conservation Corps work crew in Montana.

Drafted in 1941, Giarnella served in the Military Police and in the Allied Control Commission. A sergeant, he followed the advance through Italy (he was wounded at Cassino), helping to set up provisional governments in occupied Italian towns. He finally entered Scauro, his birthplace.

There he met the rest of his family and fell in love with a cousin.

IN 1946, he took the first ship to leave the United States for Italy after the war, carrying civilians. He married his cousin and brought her back. In 1947, he made the police force.

"It was a good job, steady, and I was interested in investigation after the M. P.'s. And if you don't think it's too corny," he said, "I wanted to be able to help people."

He twisted his ring at the show of emotion. "You know, cops are people, too. Sure, we get calloused after a while. I can't get as excited over the robbery of some insured mink coat as I do when somebody gets mugged, or a little girl gets molested. We all get excited then.

"And we forget about dinner, and our own kids at home, and we just keep going. And sooner or later, when the pieces start falling into place, we get what we're out for. And then there's one less wrong guy floating around the city."

LOS ANGELES AIRS POLICE BRUTALITY

Special to The New York Times.

LOS ANGELES, Sept. 15— Charges of racial discrimination and brutality against Los Angeles policemen were aired this week before the California Advisory Committee to the United States Commission of Civil Rights.

The accusations were denied or depreciated by William H. Parker, chief of police, and other officials.

Representatives of the Negro community testified that "malpractice" by the police was condoned by the present police system.

Morgan Moten, legislative chairman of the National Association for the Advancement of Colored People, said that the police bureau of internal affairs had failed to act on many citizen complaints.

Police Recruits Study Race Relations

By MURRAY ILLSON

As a result of the demonstrations against racial discrimination that have occurred here, the Police Department's recruit training program in human relations has taken on new significance.

A spokesman at the Police Academy outlined yesterday the department's program for training new members of the force in the critical art of getting along with a racially diverse and polyglot public while maintaining law and order.

Lieut. Robert E. Tuffy, a 44-year-old instructor at the academy, pointed out that the policeman's primary responsibility "is to preserve the public peace." The lieutenant, who has spent 21 years on the force, went on to say, however, that a vital part of that responsibility was the policeman's duty to act impartially and objectively.

Normally a police recruit gets 80 days of instruction covering 240 hours of classroom work, physical training, marksmanship, crowd control and related subjects. Three hours are spent in a lecture series dealing with racial prejudice.

The lesson plan for the first hour, titled "Racial Prejudice and Common Sense," gives as its objective: "To impress the recruit with the necessity for the development of a fair and impartial attitude in rendering every police service and the performance of every police duty irrespective of the race, religion or nationality of the person involved."

The lesson asserts that children are not born with prejudices, but rather, that they learn them at home, from classmates and even from teachers. It declares that "in a heterogeneous society such as ours" composed of Italians, Irish, Negroes, Jews, Germans, Puerto Ricans and others, prejudice "can lead to tragic conflict and civic shame."

The recruits are told that prejudice is based on "ignorance and superstition" and "scapegoating" among other things. The lesson adds:

"Remember, the great majority of every minority group are never found in the 'toils of the law.'"

The second an dthird hours of the instruction are devoted to "Racial Prejudice and the Law." The lesson plan says:

"Americans have believed from the earliest moments of our history that every human being has an essential dignity and integrity which must be respected and safeguarded. Notice the word 'essential.' It means that men have this dignity and integrity as a part of their very nature, implanted in them by God and not bestowed upon them by any benevolent governor or government. Men are free and equal by reason of the fact that they are human beings."

Several recruits at the academy, which is at 7 Hubert Street, on the lower West side, were asked yesterday about their reactions to the human relations program.

Lives Near Picketing Site

Charles E. Delaney, 26 years old, of 170-09 143d Street, Springfield Gardens, Queens, a Negro, noted that he lived near Rochdale Village, where racial demonstrations have been taking place. He said:

"I believe in the cause of the Negroes who are demonstrating, but not to the extent where there is violence and obstruction of justice. And I hope that in the future when things are straightened out we'll have more Negroes in the Police Department."

James T. Murphy, 23, of 160 St. Mary's Avenue, Staten Island, commented:

"No one can go against the principle of equal rights. And I think the force has made it clear and explicit that there is no room in the department for prejudice."

Salvatore Artusa, 28, of Lindenhurst, L. I., came here from Calabria, Italy, 15 years ago.

"Negroes," he said, "should have their rights, but the demonstrations should be peaceful."

Alfred C. Kennard, 26, of Bohemia, L. I., who emigrated from Newcastle, England, as a child, asserted: "People have the right to fight for their rights as long as they stay within the law."

Marvin Lapidus, 29, of 19 Jones Street, in Greenwich Village, who holds a bachelor's degree in economics from City College, said "the police lean backward" to avoid prejudicial actions. He added:

"I have found no prejudice in the force. When you work and play with guys you never think of their race or creed."

Rainer K. Korb, 25, who came here from Stuttgart, Germany, in 1959, said: "There shouldn't be any prejudice. Everyone should have equal opportunity and shouldn't be held back from a job. That is how this country started out—with everybody pitching in."

August 14, 1963

City Using Psychology

By JACK ROTH

The physical mishandling of prisoners by the police in New York County during interrogations is waning, according to a Legal Aid Society lawyer.

Instead of using physical violence to obtain information or confessions, it was learned from detectives, the police are relying on psychological pressures to a greater degree.

Anthony F. Marra, chief attorney for the criminal division of the Legal Aid Society, said yesterday that it had been three years since he had complained to the New York District Attorney about physical brutality by the police.

He attributed this to the "administration of the Police Department, its higher morality and tone of leadership," and to the fact that "the patrolmen and detectives of today are more intelligent and of a higher caliber than those of years ago."

"They use more psychology in questioning today and get as many admissions of guilt from criminals as through brutality," Mr. Marra said. "The days of the so-called third degree, where a man was beaten severely, appear to be gone—and it is a wonderful thing."

Police Commissioner Michael J. Murphy said that the beating of a confession out of a prisoner was as "passé as the nickel subway ride."

"For the last decade candidates for a detective's post undergo an intensive six-week course that stresses the interrogation of prisoners," he said. "Most detectives, and especially the detective commanders, have a built-in psychology based on instinct and experience in which a man's weak points are exploited. They can get prisoners to talk as a result of this.

"There have been tremendous improvements in the method of interrogation in the modern police department, and the police are certainly much better educated than they were years ago."

A lawyer interviewed yesterday, who resigned from the police force 14 years ago but who still retains friends on the force and has criminals for clients, agreed with Commissioner Murphy and Mr. Marra.

"When I was on the job," he said, "brass knuckles covered with leather strips were used more than once as well as blackjacks in newspapers.

"As a matter of fact I even knocked two women cold in my day and then told my commanding officer they had fainted. Both women scratched me, and I never hesitated to hit a woman as well as a man if I was annoyed.

"I recall one prisoner we arrested holding up a bar. We didn't bother questioring him much. There were seven of us in the squad room, and we took turns cracking him. They don't do that today."

Fear-Factor Employed

Other detectives interviewed explained that one carryover of the past was still used today, but to a much greater extent. It is called "good guy—bad guy."

Under this system, a 'tough' detective begins questioning an uncooperative prisoner. Should the prisoner continue to be uncooperative after a number of threats, he is either tied to a pipe with a light shining in his face or strapped to a chair.

The threats may include immediate electrocution (one detective put small light bulbs in a prisoner's ears) and the tossing of his body out a window.

As the tough, or 'bad guy,' appears about to strike the prisoner, the "good guy" comes into the picture. He remonstrates with the bad guy and says he will take over the case.

He offers the prisoner a shot of whisky, cigarettes, food and proceeds to "cuss out" the bad guy. Quite often he wins the confidence of the prisoner and gets the whole story of the crime on a friendly basis.

The variation on this is that the good guy starts the questioning first while the bad guy sits quietly staring at the prisoner from the other side of the room. If the prisoner refuses to cooperate with the good guy, he points to the man on the other side of the room and warns:

"If I turn you over to that guy, he'll kill you. He's just waiting to prove to me that the only way to get a man to talk is to half-beat him to death."

Fear Instilled

By this time so much fear has been instilled in the prisoner that he is on many occasions extremely anxious to tell the polite detective everything he knows.

In other cases, prisoners are tricked by being told that the victim he shot is still alive and he is lucky. The prisoner is delighted that he faces a felonious assault charge rather than a murder count, and he cooperates.

Other approaches include detectives telling prisoners that "it's only because I'm a cop or I might be in your shoes," and "your partner has already confessed [a lie] and why should you hold out."

Actually, when a felony suspect is brought into a precinct for questioning, it is his right under the law to stand mute, to tell the police nothing.

A deputy police commissioner who asked not to be identified had this to say yesterday:

"There is no requirement in law that we tell a prisoner what his rights are, and we don't.

If we did, we would be throwing an impediment into law enforcement that might well become insurmountable. If we did this, no one would tell us anything."

November 7, 1963

ARREST RESISTANCE UP IN PHILADELPHIA

Special to The New York Times

PHILADELPHIA, Aug. 28—In the first half of this year there was a sharp increase in the number of cases of resisting arrest and interfering with policemen making arrests here.

Police Department figures show that in the six-month period that ended June 30, citizens interfered with or resisted arrest 11,227 times, an average of 6.8 times daily. The number of cases for all of last year was 1,554.

Police Commissioner Howard R. Leary attributed the increase to lack of respect for authority.

"You can't have everybody critical of policemen, and in a sense tearing them down, and not feel the effects," he said.

In 72 of the cases, persons attacked policemen with clubs, bricks, guns or other weapons to stave off an arrest. They were charged with aggravated assault and battery.

In 523 cases, persons attacked, using hands or feet, and were charged with assault and battery. An additional 577 persons were charged with resisting arrest and 55 with interfering with an officer.

August 29, 1965

COURT'S DECISIONS FRUSTRATE POLICE

High and Low, They Believe Their Work Is Hampered

By The Associated Press

Directing traffic, shepherding school children across the street, walking his lonely nighttime beat, the American policeman is the street corner symbol of authority.

There are 300,000 full-time and part-time such symbols.

At times, it seems that they are convinced that as symbols of something sacred they are being sullied and despoiled.

Policemen in all parts of the country, individually and through their organizations, are preoccupied with several issues about which they are absolutely convinced. Some of them are these:

¶That the dice are loaded in favor of the criminal because of a series of court decisions involving constitutional rights.

¶That because of the civil rights movement, the Negro violates certain laws through protest demonstrations and this encourages widespread violation of all laws.

¶That civilian review boards, which would check charges against the police, are deliberate plots to undermine police authority.

Moving to a Crisis

Crime and law enforcement in the United States are moving rapidly to a crisis stage. The rise in crime in the last decade has been six times as great as the rise in population. And law enforcement people, ranging from J. Edgar Hoover, director of the Federal Bureau of Investigation, to Patrolman Frank Foucault of Detroit, express convictions that the police are being handcuffed in their attempts to combat crime.

"We mollycoddle young criminals and release unreformed hoodlums to prey anew on society." Mr. Hoover says in speeches on this theme. "The bleeding hearts, particularly among the judiciary, are so concerned for young criminals that they become indifferent to the rights of law-abiding citizens."

"I'm only a cop," says Patrolman Foucault, "but you look at me real close and you will see something that has more power than even the President of the United States. I don't mean me, Frank Foucault; I mean me, the cop.

"I have the power of life and death. In 10 seconds, I can kill someone or let him live, and I don't have a jury or a judge or anybody there to say yes or no.

"You give me this awesome responsibility but you don't want to pay to hire the very best. You cry 'police brutality' without knowing what is happening. You talk about crime in the streets but you tolerate courts giving criminals a slap on the wrist. You don't know what a cop is for or what he should do."

In terms of police work, three major Supreme Court decisions had direct impact on search and seizure, interrogation, and arrest and detention.

In once case, Andrew Mallory, a 19-year-old Washington Negro, was convicted of rape and sentenced to death. The police arrested him at 2:30 P.M. one day and detained him until he signed a confession at 12:30 A.M. the next day before arraigning him. The Supreme Court reversed the conviction saying that under the law the "delay between arrest and arraignment must not be of a nature to give opportunity for extraction of a confession."

In another, Danny Escobedo, a 22-year-old Mexican, was seized in connection with the slaying of his brother-in-law in Chicago. Attempts by a lawyer to see him were frustrated by the police, and Escobedo's plea to see his laywer were denied by the police. He made a full confession and he was subsequently convicted of murder.

In a 5 to 4 decision, the Supreme Court held "the refusal to honor the accused's request to consult with his attorney constituted a denial of his right to assistance of counsel under the Sixth and 14th Amendments, and that the statements should not have been admitted into evidence."

In a case involving Dollree Mapp, three Cleveland policemen went to her home seeking a person wanted for questioning in connection with a bombing and believed to be hiding out there. She called her lawyer and on his advice refused to let the police enter without a search warrant.

Three hours later, the police forced their way in. The police then searched the place and found some obscene and pornographic material. She was subsequently convicted of possession of obscene literature.

The Supreme Court reversed the decision, saying that "as a matter of due process, evidence obtained by search and seizure in violation of the Fourth Amendment is inadmissible in a state court as it is in a Federal court."

In some quarters these decisions were heralded as welcome and necessary, especially since they forced a review of arrest and search and seizure procedures.

But on the whole, the police felt they had been dealt a low blow.

Attorney General Nicholas deB. Katzenbach entered the debate between law enforcement and the judiciary, saying that recent court decisions had produced great confusion.

"As a result, policemen, district attorneys and trial court judges have become increasingly unsure of the law with respect to arrest and post-arrest procedures, often differing vigorously among themselves," he says.

He also comments that "it would be ridiculous to state that the overriding purpose of any criminal investigation is to insure equal treatment."

"Obviously, criminal investigation is designed to discover those guilty of crime," he adds.

September 5, 1965

Necessary Force—
Or Police Brutality?

By THOMAS R. BROOKS

IT was a summer evening and a Saturday night, last July 24, so Theodore (Teddy) Jones, a 20-year-old grocery clerk, and his date, 15-year-old Annie Lucas, decided to go to Coney Island with three friends. They arrived fairly late, rode the Himalaya Ride, and then joined some 150 teen-agers dancing to recorded music on the sidewalk outside.

Miss Lucas says they were encouraged to do so by a passing policeman. The patrolman in question, however, denies this. By then, it was already past midnight and he apparently told the crowd they could dance for another five minutes. Shortly after, a second policeman, Patrolman Arthur Crichlow, a 24-year-old Negro, came along and ordered the dancers to break it up.

"One cop tells you one thing, one cop tells you another," Teddy Jones remarked in a voice loud enough to be heard by Patrolman Crichlow. This led to an argument, and Patrolman Crichlow's saying: "O.K., I'm taking you in on a discon [disorderly conduct charge]."

HERE accounts begin to differ, agreeing only that Patrolman Crichlow asked for identification, which the youth gave him. "Then," continues Miss Lucas's account, "the cop just stands there looking at the wallet for about five minutes and Teddy gets tired of waiting, so he reaches for the wallet and the cop pulls the wallet back and grabs Teddy by the shirt.

"Teddy was talking pretty loud but he wasn't cursing or nothing, and the policeman says: 'Don't embarrass me in front of all these people.'

"And the next thing he does is to take the billy and hit Teddy right across the brow over his left eye."

Patrolman Crichlow later testified that he was holding Jones's wallet when the youth suddenly reached out to recover it. Crichlow, by his own account, reacted "instinctively" and struck Jones on the head with his nightstick.

Badly hurt, unable to stand, Jones was helped into a near-by bar before being driven to the 60th Precinct station house. There an ambulance was called and Jones arrived at Coney Island Hospital at 2 A.M. After six stitches in his forehead and three X-ray plates, Jones was taken back to the police station where he lay on a cell cot for five hours before his appearance in criminal court. A court officer noted that Jones "doesn't look good," and Patrolman Crichlow retorted, "He's drunk" — an exchange recorded by the court stenographer.

The judge postponed the hearing for a day. Jones was again examined by a physician, and sent to Kings County Hospital at 3 o'clock Sunday afternoon. The diagnosis was a fractured skull. A four-and-a-half-hour operation followed. But it was too late; Teddy Jones died Monday afternoon.

The Jones family is suing the City of New York for $1.5 million, a civil action for redress. A grand jury, however, has cleared Patrolman Crichlow of complicity in the death of Jones. He still may face a Police Department trial on a complaint filed by the Joneses' attorney, but no hearings have been held as yet under the department's Civilian Complaint Review Board procedures which must precede such a trial.

"The tragedy of Teddy Jones," Aryeh Neier, executive director of the New York Civil Liberties Union, told me, "underscores the need for a civilian review board to judge complaints of police brutality. So far, there has been no real response to the case from the police." Civil libertarians and civil-rights spokesmen fear that the Joneses' complaint will end in a department whitewash. "It's practically unheard of for a policeman involved in the killing of a citizen to be punished," Neier said. Recent police killings, like that of Jones, in New York, Philadelphia, Newark and St. Louis—all involving Negro victims—have raised serious questions about police behavior and practices.

Such questions have existed within the Negro community for a long time now. When the people of riot-torn Watts spoke of their grievances, they talked first about police brutality, then of price gouging, housing and job problems and the inadequacy of civic services in their community. Similar complaints about police practices are heard in other Negro communities. How substantial are such charges?

OFFICIALLY, the police tolerate only that amount of force necessary "to apprehend" the alleged criminal— the greater the resistance, the greater the force allowed. This may range from the twist of the arm used to subdue a panic-stricken drug addict to the shooting of a fleeing felon.

The latitude allowed the police officer involved is not fixed by the rule books. A well-trained officer should be able to judge exactly how much force is required. You cannot, after all, predict the exact reaction to every arrest.

Actually, the level of violence in police behavior tolerated at any given time is very much determined by society. Back in 1853, for example, Capt. George W. Walling organized the first "Strong Arm Squad," a half-dozen of his huskiest patrolmen dressed in civilian clothes and armed with locust clubs, and sent out against a local gang, the Honeymooners. This particular gang operated in midtown Manhattan, mugging well-dressed passersby. Walling's answer was simple: His men just walked up to any recognized member of the gang and slugged him silly. The Honeymooners soon moved south into Five Points and the Bowery.

The third degree for securing confessions outlasted Walling's wallopings as standard police practice. Nonetheless, it, too, appears to be on the way out, even in cities where the police are a good deal rougher than New York City's Finest. The third degree was much more routine in the past, as Emanuel H. Lavine's "Third Degree," published in 1930, and the 1931 report of the Federal Wickersham Commission amply detail. Lavine cites an instance in which a cooperative dentist ground down a murder suspect's molar to the roots "with an old dull burr." The man talked.

The courts are largely responsible for the demise of the third degree in its more brutal forms. The police, after all, want confessions to stand up in court; brutality now jeopardizes this. If the courts should decide that a suspect's lawyer ought to be on hand during interrogation by the police, the third degree may become altogether something of the past.

There are other changes,

too. One cannot conceive today of comparable public figures reacting as did Mayor Fiorello LaGuardia and Police Commissioner Lewis Valentine when visiting a police line-up in 1945. Irked at a prisoner, Commissioner Valentine said: "He's the best-dressed man in the room. Don't be afraid to muss 'im up. Blood should be smeared all over that velvet collar." LaGuardia chimed in: "That's the way I like to hear you talk, Lew. Muss 'em up if necessary."

And muss 'em up the police. In 1953, a spokesman for the Legal Aid Society reported that of 8,300 defendants represented in Felony Court by the society, one-third showed signs of physical injury, ranging from scratches to broken jaws. But a series of newspaper exposés in the early nineteen-fifties brought on a change. Under Police Commissioners Frank Adams, Steve Kennedy, Michael Murphy and Vincent L. Broderick new policies have resulted in a definite improvement. The N.Y.C.L.U., which has an active program of pushing civilian complaints against police malpractice, has only one real third-degree case on its dockets.

MUCH more typical of brutality cases is the experience of Kenneth Spencer, a Jamaican graduate student at the University of Washington. In sworn testimony before a Seattle City Council hearing on police practices, Spencer testified that he was stopped by two Seattle policemen while walking home late one night last fall. The officers insisted that he had to have an "I.D. card"; he insisted that he did not.

Finally, according to Spencer, one officer said "You smart, ——. I'm going to teach you a lesson." He then whacked Spencer across the chest and on the jaw.

The second officer, Spencer's testimony continued, "moved in behind me, grabbed hold of my neck and began to choke me violently." Spencer was thrown to the ground and handcuffed. "While still lying on the ground I was kicked." Later that night, after another beating with a flashlight in the police car, Spencer was booked for "being abroad."

As Seattle A.C.L.U. counsel Alvin Ziontz pointed out to the City Council, many brutality complaints arise out of minor offenses which usually do not involve exposure to juries, at-

torneys and prosecutors. "Apparently," Ziontz said, "any so-called back talk from a prisoner triggers violence. The most inflammatory statement a prisoner can make to a Seattle policeman is 'I know my constitutional rights.'"

Attorney Ziontz's observation tallies with that of sociologist William A. Westley, who in the July, 1953, issue of The American Journal of Sociology, reported on his survey of police in an industrial city of about 150,000 population. Westley asked about half the police in town (73 patrolmen): "When do you think a policeman is justified for roughing a man up?" More than one out of three—37 per cent—replied that violence was justified when the individual showed "disrespect for the police."

"In terms of the policeman's definition of the situation," wrote Dr. Westley, "the individual who lacks respect for the police, the 'wise guy' who talks back, or any individual who acts or talks in a disrespectful way deserves brutality."

THE victims of police brutality are often marginal people — pimp or prostitute, drifter, gambler or pot pusher. They rarely complain about the treatment they receive at the hands of the police. When they do, it is most revealing. This awakening among outcasts — that they, too have rights — is one of the fascinating asides of the civil-rights situation.

Betty Jay, a Detroit Negro prostitute (the name is fictitious; the incident is not), not long ago picked up a married white man. While they were sitting in the living room of a house waiting for a bed, a policeman knocked on the door. When the "John" saw the officer, he panicked and accused Betty of stealing $3. She was indignant, saying: "I wouldn't make the joint hot for three measly bucks."

On the way to the precinct house in the patrol car, she remained vociferous in asserting her innocence and cursing the cops. One officer in the car told her: "If you don't shut up, I'm going to put you in the hospital." Though handcuffed, Betty was still game and when they arrived at the station she kicked—and missed. She was thrown to the ground; one policeman picked her up and smashed

her face against a wall. Then, they took her upstairs to be booked, where she insisted on making a complaint. When she was taken to a hospital, the notation was made on her admission record: "Injured herself while falling out of patrol car."

Betty, however, did not let the matter rest there; she went to the N.A.A.C.P. The police picked her up again and tried to get her to say that it was her pimp who had beaten her. The owner of the bar where she "worked" was told: "She's hot, keep her out." The John, meanwhile, signed a statement that she had injured herself falling out of the police car. Still, Betty pressed her case, and corroborating witnesses were found. The Civil Rights Commission found for Betty; the police officers involved were transferred to another command. But if Betty had lacked gumption, the incident would have been no more than another disorderly conduct case, with possibly a suspended sentence ending.

WHAT happened to Betty Jay illustrates what may happen when those without voice give "lip" to the police. In essence, this is why police brutality today is so often a civil-rights matter rather than one of civil liberties. Lip often invokes harsh words, name-calling or a push from the policeman, exacerbating minority-group sensibilities. As the civil-rights leader Bayard Rustin told me: "There is a brutality of the spirit as well as that of the body."

Brutality, Rustin argues, goes with prejudice. "When men draw a line and put other people on the other side and say, 'Those people are different,' then it is possible to end up doing anything to them. Since prejudice is widespread in this country, then it follows that the basic attitude underlying police brutality is also widespread." Rustin added: "I don't know of a Negro family that has not had a member who has not met either physical or spiritual brutality on the part of the police."

The middle-class Negro carrying an attaché case to and from work is frequently stopped and his attaché case searched as a part of the police war on drugs. "It's brutalizing," a Negro professional man once told me, "and, frankly, I'd rather be clubbed."

Chester Washington, editor of The Los Angeles Sentinel,

a Negro weekly, tells of being stopped on his way to lunch with his publisher. "Both of us," he says, "were asked to put our hands against the wall and were searched after we had already identified ourselves. It's hard to imagine the same thing happening to the publisher of The Los Angeles Times."

THERE are no reliable statistics on police brutality, and police practices do vary widely from city to city. However, some figures from Detroit are revealing. In 1964, some 1,207 policemen (out of a force of 4,500) and 1,507 citizens (out of 3.9 million) were involved in "altercations." Of 1,048 citizens injured by policemen, 617 were Negro, 424 Caucasian, 4 Indian, 2 Mexican and 1 Japanese; 690 suffered face, scalp, eye, nose, head and jaw injuries. Of the 580 policemen injured by citizens, 303 suffered hand, knuckle and finger injuries.

I have no comparable figures for New York City. The department, however, reports 478 "lost-time injuries resulting from assaults on the police" for 1964. Broken down, these are: punch, 142; resisting arrest, 98; struck by object, 90; kick, 58; bite, 58; cut or stab, 19; gunshot, 13 (three officers killed).

Spokesmen point out that the department received only 231 complaints out of the 208,844 arrests made in 1964. Since the complaint department has moved to new and more pleasant headquarters at 201 Park Avenue South, the number of complaints has doubled. According to Inspector Arthur S. Savitt, who heads up the operation, his office now averages about eight complaints a week.

Of the 231 complaints made last year, five were referred to other agencies, 183 were "filed" as unsubstantiated, 19 are still pending. Of all these complainants, 53 claimed some injury and six had hospital records. The Civilian Complaint Review Board substantiated the remaining 24. In six of these, the policemen involved were "warned and admonished"; the rest were recommended for departmental trial. Of these 18 policemen one man was dismissed from the force, two were docked 30 days' pay (roughly $1,000 and the maximum penalty short of dismissal), three were fined 10 days' pay, one man was fined five days' and another two days'. Ten cases are still pending at the trial board level. In making its recommendations to the Police Commissioner for final action, the trial board takes into consideration the man's whole record. This explains why one case will lead to dismissal while a similar offense in another will not.

ODDLY enough, in most of the trial board cases where disciplinary action was taken, the policemen involved were off duty. The dismissed patrolman, for example, was off duty when he arrested a girl at the scene of a fire, accusing her of being an arsonist. He "manhandled" her and took her to a radio car which took them to precinct headquarters. The desk officer released the girl, and on her complaint charged the patrolman. The two men who were fined 10 days' pay had gone to a movie a little the worse for drinking and proceeded to roughhouse the manager and the porter.

A New York City policeman is supposedly "on duty" 24 hours a day; he must carry his gun with him at all times, except to bed. In Boston, contrariwise, policemen wear their uniforms and guns going to and from work. Once home, they check their guns in the closet—and then they may go and do as other men do, have a drink, go to the movies. Boston holds that no man, off-duty policeman or no, ought to enter a bar with a loaded revolver. Predictably, this cuts down on the number of incidents involving off-duty policemen; it also avoids tragedy.

Early this year, Patrolman Edward Ryan, 29, was in a Bronx bar with a friend, Thomas McCann, 25. An argument developed between McCann and another youth, Robert Owens, 20, and both stepped outside to continue the affair. Ryan sought to break it up; Owens punched him. Ryan identified himself as a policeman but Owens kept punching. Ryan then pulled his gun, which went off accidentally and killed Owens. There have been similar incidents over the last year or two in which the culpability of the policeman involved certainly was questionable. Just exactly how good is the judgment of any off-duty policeman relaxing in a bar? But, on the record, grand juries and the department have been reluctant to act against men caught in such tragedies.

And, in a less tragic vein,

what should be done about an off-duty policeman who, coming out of his apartment house, catches a couple of men urinating on a hedge, calls them "pigs," and wallops one on the chin? For this civic response, this particular patrolman was brought up on charges on a complaint filed by one of the two urinating citizens and fined five days' pay. Somehow, it seems unfair.

SIGNIFICANTLY, in the one complaint board case involving a policeman on duty, the complainant was not the victim. Actually, there were two complainants, Attorneys Seymour M. Waldman and Clayton Sinclair. The two lawyers had just left their office after a day's work one summer evening when they spotted a disturbance within Bryant Park, behind New York's Public Library on the 42d Street side. A patrolman chased and caught a young man. The two lawyers took him for a Puerto Rican; he turned out to be an American Indian. To force the youth to the fence for a search, the patrolman whacked him across the back of his legs with his nightstick. The youth fell and was roughly handled. The two lawyers spoke to the policeman and secured his badge number. The next day they filed a complaint.

Police Department investigators had some trouble locating the victim, whom they now knew to be a drifter "who lives off fags." When they found him in a West Side rooming house, he wanted no part of a complaint. He denied the beating, saying that he had dropped to the pavement because "I wanted to cop a plea on the cop's sympathy."

Nonetheless, the department proceeded with the complaint because, I was told, the complainants, Waldman and Sinclair, "were of upstanding character, being lawyers an' all." After a lengthy hearing, the trial board found that though the patrolman did not "use a degree of force considered brutal, he did use force unnecessary under the circumstances." He was fined 10 days' pay.

THE police, naturally enough, take the view that the complaint record is a vindication of current practices. Yet many complaints are never filed. When I visited the N.Y.C.L.U. office, for example,

I was shown photographs of a young man, white, in his early 20's, with his lip badly cut and swollen, eyes puffy, face badly bruised. He had come into the N.Y.C.L.U. office chiefly because his girl friend dragged him in. Reluctantly, he told his story:

He had been in a Lexington Avenue bar, drinking and showing off an unloaded gun. Someone tipped off the police. Two patrolmen came into the bar and insisted that he come along to the station.

"What the hell for?" he asked, belligerently. One officer replied: "Wise guy, eh?"

The two policemen dragged him out of the bar and gave him a good working over before taking him in and booking him for a Sullivan Law violation and disorderly conduct.

Why was no complaint lodged? First, as the N.Y. C.L.U. lawyer advised this young man, if he pressed a complaint, the police in all likelihood would make the Sullivan charge stick. If he did not press the complaint, he had a good chance of having the Sullivan violation dropped, with only a suspended sentence on the other charge, since his record was otherwise clean. What's more, the witnesses had all evaporated. But on the table were the photographs: the boy's bruised face staring up at us.

WHEN confronted with stories about police brutality, police officers often point out that if there is anything wrong they may be sued for false arrest. But suits for false arrest are notably difficult to win, and even after winning the victor may find it difficult to collect. Only in New York State and Florida can a citizen sue the civil authorities for redress. Of 13,000 personal-injury and property-damage claims filed against New York City from July 1, 1963 to July 1, 1964, a total of 326 were police-action suits. Over the same period, 72 claims were settled at a total cost of $232,424.60.

What can happen elsewhere is illustrated by a case in Boston. Back in 1958, a Negro named Ammons and a white bar owner had a minor car accident; a fight ensued. Ammons apparently had the best of it; in any event, the saloon keeper turned up at the Ammonses' home some hours later with six policemen in tow. Ammons was awakened

and beaten while Mrs. Ammons was forcibly restrained by one of the policemen. Mr. Ammons was charged with stealing some money from the bar owner; Mrs. Ammons, with assault and battery. The charges were dismissed in court, and the Ammonses brought suits of false arrest against the policemen and one of trespass against the bar owner. In June, 1959, a judgment of $7,000 was awarded the Ammonses. As of today, however, they have not collected one cent.

OBVIOUSLY, the New York law ought to be more widely emulated. Beyond this, however, what needs to be done about police brutality?

Clearly, there is a crisis. Police brutality—or rumors of it—was a catalyst in the riots of this summer and last; it could set off more rioting in the future. Moreover, as urban crime rises, the widespread Negro belief that the police are brutal hampers effective police work. Suspicious, honest Negroes, the overwhelming majority, just will not cooperate with the police in their difficult war on crime as long as they believe that involvement with the police invites brutality.

Negro and Puerto Rican leaders, and other civic spokesmen aware of this deep suspicion, have proposed the formation of civilian public-review boards to hear charges of police misbehavior. Unbiased and independent review of such charges, one might hope, could clear the air of untoward suspicions and ease tensions between minority groups and the police. Indeed, 37 police departments around the country now are trying out special community-relations programs.

But more, I think, is needed. Washington's police chief, John B. Layton, pointed up the problem at the recent annual conference of the International Association of Police Chiefs in Miami Beach. "The habitual drunkard, the housebreaker and the thief no longer constitute the sole threats to a community's peace," he said. "Burgeoning social problems which have developed in our swift sophisticated progress are demanding a greater share of our attention . . . and to cope with them calls for some change in the traditional police role in the community."

If this is so—and I think it is—we need another Wickersham Commission to examine the role of the police in our society, to discuss what it *ought* to be as well as what it is. Police power is an awesome thing; the determination as to how it is to be used ought not be a police matter. If changes are to be made, those changes are our responsibility.

Board's Defeat Elates Police, Saddens Negroes

By MICHAEL STERN

Bitter laughter, deep hurt, cynical shrugs, forebodings of violence, a feeling that once again the white man had turned his back on the black man—these were reactions of Harlem and Bedford-Stuyvesant residents last night when they learned that the Civilian Complaint Review Board had been abolished by the city's voters.

A sigh of relief, quiet satisfaction, a feeling that the man in the street still had confidence in the man in blue—these were the reactions of policemen when they heard the news.

"Don't expect a big reaction out of Harlem because of this," said Louise King, a 17-year-old high school senior who was strolling on Eighth Avenue near 126th Street when she learned about the board which had been established to investigate complaints of police brutality and discourtesy.

"Negroes have grown used to whites taking advantage of them," she said. "This is really something we should laugh about, to have ever thought that a review board would remain in force."

In Frank's restaurant on 125th Street, between Eighth and St. Nicholas Avenues, a gathering place for Harlem's middle class, half a dozen persons were watching the returns at the bar. When the first reports indicating that the review board would be defeated were flashed on the screen, George Cummings, a liquor salesman, said:

"I thought for once a bill backed by Negroes would pass."

A woman down the bar chuckled and said, "You should have known better."

Mr. Cummings joined in her laughter. "Yeah, baby," he said. "I should have known better."

At the 13th Precinct house on East 21st Street, a group of patrolmen carrying bundles of election materials were stopped

Cynical Reaction Is Shown in Harlem — Patrolmen Give a Sigh of Relief

by a reporter on the steps. Patrolman Frank Salvo of the 14th Precinct said he was surprised by the vote. At the polling place where he had worked through the day, he said, it had run heavily in favor of retaining the board.

He thought hard when he was asked for a reaction, then said: "It's the will of the people."

Another patrolman, who asked not to be identified, said: "I'm happy. Maybe I'll stay on the force another five years now."

In downtown Brooklyn, a patrolman sitting in his radio car in front of the 78th Precinct house at 65 Sixth Avenue, said "You're damned straight," when he was asked if he was pleased by the vote. Then he added: "We're all glad. Let me put it this way. Now the people have shown they have some faith in us."

Another patrolman, who was just reporting in after Election Day duty, said: "The way I figure, the people decided. I'd have been satisfied either way. That's the way I am. Some of the other guys undoubtedly were more concerned than I was."

In Bedford-Stuyvesant, at the corner of Nostrand Avenue and Fulton Street, three young men got the news as they were eating frankfurters in front of a snack bar. Sammy Lee Williams, 21, said:

"You mean we already blowed it? How can that be, when people were supposed to vote 'No.'"

His companion, Ronald Johnson, also 21, said sadly, "I thought maybe that by some miracle it would stay."

At the Club Baby Grand, a

bar at 1274 Fulton Street, a few doors from the corner, the bartender, James Anderson, said:

"I think it's an unfortunate thing, not just for the minorities, but for all the people. I don't think there will be any repercussions in the winter, but next summer there definitely will be. If there is an incident, there won't be a board to cool things down."

A customer, James Meekins, who lives nearby in Crown Heights, said he feared what might happen on the streets. "Any little incident that happens will lead to a lot of unnecessary bloodshed," he said. "As they say, who can I turn to if they, the board, is turned away?"

The uptown headquarters of the Federated Associations for Impartial Review at 243 West 125th Street in Harlem, was crowded with Negro civil servants who had campaigned to save the review board.

When the television returns showed the board was losing, Mrs. Richardine Randall, who works for the city's Corrections Department, got a big laugh when she called in mock seriousness:

"Let's all put on our 'yes' buttons and go down and celebrate with the P.B.A."

P.B.A. Was the Sponsor

The Patrolmen's Benevolent Association had sponsored the review board question on the ballot. A "Yes" vote was for abolishing the board.

Milton Mallory, free-lance photographer, was questioned in the Donut Fair, a snack bar on 125th Street, between Seventh and Eighth Avenues.

"We've got a police state," he said, then added: "A lot of whites are going to be sorry. Cops can now do whatever they want to do. Whites voted against Negroes because they were afraid of riots, but they will try to get a cop for bribery and find that they can't touch him."

December 5, 1965

November 9, 1966

Police Chiefs Feel Top Crime Problem Is Lack of Support

WASHINGTON, Nov. 30 (AP) —Police chiefs feel the nation's principal crime problem is not the criminal but the public and its lack of support for the police, a check by the Federal Bureau of Investigation showed today.

The F.B.I. quoted one of the chiefs, Daniel S. C. Liu of Honolulu, as saying:

"The declining respect for the rule of law and authority and the growing number of civil disobedience demonstrations reflect the apathy, indifference and moral regression of our society."

The bureau polled police chiefs in 10 cities. In addition to Mr. Liu, they were Harold A. Dill of Denver, Calvin F. Hawkinson of Minneapolis, James C. McDonald of Memphis, Frank C. Ramon of Seattle, Clarence M. Kelly of Kansas City, Mo., Edmund L. McNamara of Boston, Herman B. Short of Houston, John B. Layton of Washington, and Curtis Brostron of St. Louis.

Responses to the poll also blamed lenient courts, increasing urbanization, lack of parental control, baseless charges of police brutality, civil disobedience and criticism of the police rather than of criminals as contributing to the nation's growing crime problem.

They predicted chaos in 10 years "unless some material changes are forthcoming."

The results of the survey were published in the F.B.I.'s monthly Law Enforcement Bulletin.

About 58,000 copies of the bulletin, which the bureau considers a training publication, are distributed free to police departments, judges and prosecuting attorneys.

All but one of the chiefs predicted there would be no leveling-off or reduction in the crime rate in the near future. Mr. Dill of Denver said a reduction in crime might be imminent. "I think the public is aroused and demanding a reduction in crime," he said.

But most agreed with Mr. Hawkinson, who said, 'The American public should expect a continuing increase in crime for the future."

December 1, 196

U.S. CRIME STUDY FINDS POLICE BIAS

Charges Widespread Abuse —Calls Community Amity Law Enforcement Key

By FRED P. GRAHAM
Special to The New York Times

WASHINGTON, April 29— Deteriorating relations between the police and minority groups are thwarting efforts to improve the nation's law enforcement, the President's national crime commission reported today.

Widespread oral abuse and harassment of citizens by the police is largely responsible for the hostility, although police dishonesty and brutality also contribute to it, the report said.

The breakdown in relations affects not only Negroes but also Puerto Ricans, Mexicans and juveniles, the commission reported.

"No lasting improvement in law enforcement is likely in this country unless police-community relations are substantially improved," it concluded.

A Grim Prospect

The statements were published in a 228-page report by the commission's special force on the police. It is intended as a "how to do it" blueprint for police forces that wish to adopt the commission's recommendations for improving law enforcement.

A detailed study of attitudes of the police and toward the police presented a grim prospect for future police-minority group relations. It showed that:

¶Although most Americans, including a majority of Negroes, respect the police and look to them for protection, a large number of Negroes fear and distrust the police—especially white policemen. These Negroes think that the white policemen are often prejudiced against them.

¶Some white policemen admit prejudice against Negroes, and others demonstrate it. Commission observers said that in about 15 per cent of the street interviews they had seen policemen initiate had begun with a "brusque or nasty" command.

¶Negro policemen are often prone to use brutality and harsh treatment against Negroes because they are ashamed of the high rate of Negro crime.

¶Few police departments are creating community relations units to try to ease friction, and even high-ranking police officers frequently resist the efforts of the community relations units that do exist.

Although the commission concluded that physical brutality by the police is no longer a serious problem, except in parts of the South, its observers did see 20 instances of brutality in the 5,339 police-civilian encounters they observed.

One incident involved the arrest of a man who had brandished a musket made in 1905. "When they got him to the station garage, they kicked him all over," the commission's observer wrote.

The arresting officer "beat him as the others held him up," the observer reported; "the lieutenant arrived with everyone else and said there's going to be a beef on this one, so cover it up."

The identity of the commission's observer was known to the officers in every case, but the commission agreed that it would not identify the officers or their units in its report.

In a separate analysis of police corruption, the commission listed the most common forms as "improper political influence; acceptance of bribes for nonenforcement of laws, particularly those relating to gambling, prostitution and liquor offenses, which are often extensively interconnected with organized crime; the 'fixing' of traffic tickets; minor thefts and occasional burglaries."

In some cities, "corruption has been so highly organized within a precinct or department that there are regular fees for permitting various activities, collected at set intervals by a 'lieutenant's man,' " the report said.

The commission urged all medium-sized and large police departments to set up an internal investigation unit to combat such abuses. It strongly condemned, however, the use by Gov. Claude R. Kirk Jr. of Florida of a private police force to combat corruption. The commission said private forces lack the necessary controls to safeguard individuals' rights.

Referring to the proliferation of judicial restrictions on police activity, the commission urged police forces to employ lawyers to train and advise the men and, if necessary, work with them at the precinct level

The heart of the commission's police recommendations is a radical three-tiered organization plan that was advanced in the commission's formal report of last February.

It would establish three levels of entry into police departments instead of the present single level. Men could join the force as police agents — the elite crime-investigating corps; as police officers—those who do routine duties, or as community relations officers—cadets between 17 and 21 years of age who would work primarily with juveniles.

The police report was the first of nine studies that provided the background for the commission's report. The others are scheduled to be released at weekly intervals over the next two months. The formal name of the commission is the President's Commission on Law Enforcement and the Administration of Justice.

April 30, 19

316

Men in Uniform

BEHIND THE SHIELD: The Police in Urban Society. By Arthur Niederhoffer. 253 pp. New York: Doubleday & Co. $5.95.

By THEODORE CAPLOW

THIS is a book about policemen in big cities by a policeman turned sociologist. Its appearance is timely, just ahead of the books that will soon appear about this past summer's riots and that will try to show how they were provoked by police brutality or checked by police heroism, or both.

Mr. Niederhoffer does not touch directly on these matters, except for a brief account of the establishment and disestablishment of the Civilian Review Board. His subject is the individual policeman. He describes his career from high school to retirement, probes his personality with psychological tests, analyzes his self-image and explains his politics.

A very long Appendix reports a questionnaire study of police cynicism, based on a sample of New York policemen. According to the findings, it is in the Police Academy that recruits begin to acquire a stereotyped pattern of cynical attitudes that are reinforced in the course of their experience as patrolmen. In contrast to military officers, who have repeatedly been found less cynical than enlisted men, high-ranking police officials hold the same grievances as their subordinates. Detectives are a little more hopeful than the rest and some men brighten up as they approach retirement. But all in all, the policeman's view of his own organization is bleak.

In the cynicism study, a clear majority of the experienced patrolmen agreed with each of the following statements, among others: the average police superior is mostly concerned with his own problems; the average departmental complaint lodged against the policeman is a result of the pressure from higher authorities to give out complaints; Police Academy training of recruits cannot overcome the contradictions between theory and practice; when a patrolman appears at the Police Department trial room he will probably be found guilty even when he has a good defense; it is very difficult to perform an active tour of duty without violating some rules and regulations; summonses are issued because a patrolman knows he must meet his quota; the public usually has to be forced to cooperate with policemen; the newspapers in general seem to enjoy giving an unfavorable

YEARNING for professional status, the policeman claims to be a public servant, although he too secretly pictures himself as a leader. Unfortunately for the policeman, however, the public takes him at his word: he is only a servant. Until the police can convince the public that they deserve a position of leadership, their aspirations to professionalism will not be satisfied.—
"Behind the Shield."

slant to news concerning the police.

These beliefs illustrate the failure of a movement toward the professionalization of police work that began during the Depression and spent its force by the early 50's. For a while the recruitment of middle-class, college-educated candidates in considerable numbers threatened to change the whole character of the occupation, but the advantages they enjoyed in competitive examinations for promotion stiffened the resistance of the old-timers and soon brought the movement to a halt. Only one out of 20 police applicants accepted in New York during the past 15 years has had any college training at all.

Niederhoffer believes that the policeman's cynicism may lead him into anomie and alienation, but the evidence presented supports an opposite view. The suicide rate among New York City policemen is fairly stable around 22 per 100,000 per year, which is an extremely low rate for a male population with continuous access to firearms. And everything we are told about the Blue Curtain, and the Force's ability to protect itself against outside observation or interference suggests that policemen are, if anything, too secure and well adjusted to respond to the changing needs of the city. Their solidarity has become almost a religion. The author himself is so wary of offending his former colleagues on traditional issues that he draws most of the material in his brief discussion of graft from the works of Lincoln Steffens, the muckraker whose last work was published in the '30's!

He is less inhibited in analyzing personality traits and concludes that "the police system transforms a man into the special type of authoritarian personality required by the police role." To this transformation he attributes the attraction of the John Birch Society for policemen, their suspicion of nonconformists, their ambivalence toward women, their hatred of sex offenders, and perhaps their tendency to hypochondria. Moreover, he believes that the most authoritarian policemen, tough, uneducated and unsuited for promotion, are most likely to be assigned to slum neighborhoods where the hostility they meet matches their expectations.

The police in large cities have retained many of their customs and much of their organizational structure almost unchanged from the Gaslight Era, when the people in town houses viewed the patrolman literally as a public servant, and the people in tenements saw him as one of their own. Every political club had its ombudsman. The automobile had not yet made the average citizen into a petty criminal. He could generally be counted on to side with law-enforcement, but the policeman's personal power over him was checked by his ability to control the policeman or to reach those who could.

TODAY'S policemen are probably less brutal, more honest, and more devoted to duty than their occupational ancestors under the gas lights. But there is hardly any large segment of the public with whom they stand on really good terms. For instance, in the New York poverty districts where most of the trouble is, a force that Niederhoffer estimates as 42 per cent Irish, 25 per cent Italian, 11 per cent Jewish, 6 per cent Negro and less than 2 per cent Puerto Rican, faces a community it cannot dream of representing directly. Its stance is closer to that of an occupying army than an old-fashioned constabulary.

Policing may turn out to be another social responsibility too important to be left to professionals. The existing system is unable to maintain order in the streets, let alone cope with organized and unorganized crime. The need for innovation is unmistakable; the will to innovate, Niederhoffer tells us, is almost entirely lacking.

"Behind the Shield" raises more questions than it begins to answer. The problem of maintaining order while preserving freedom in American cities has barely begun to be discussed as seriously as present conditions require.

20th Precinct: Violence and Misery

By MAURICE CARROLL

Sometime earlier in the evening someone had cared enough to dress the little girl in a shiny costume, take her by the hand and lead her, a happy Halloween beggar, through the seedy side streets off Broadway.

Now, crying, she cowered in a tenement doorway on West 71st Street, watching while four adults, her mother among them, scuffled and shouted in a drunken fight.

Patrolman Charles Piccoli walked across the sidewalk and pushed the combatants apart. His partner, Patrolman Terence Gilroy, knelt next to the child. "Hi, how was Halloween?" he asked.

No More Treats

The little girl said nothing, but her sobs subsided. She clutched a paper bag against her colorful costume. Her mask had fallen into the gutter nearby.

Soon everybody was persuaded to go home, but for the little girl, trick-or-treat night was over. Slowly, the policemen got back into their car.

Patrolman Gilroy suddenly slammed his nightstick on the floor. "How can that kid grow up to be anything but a bum," he said to Patrolman Piccoli.

For the next few minutes, they drove along in unhappy silence.

The men in the police cars that cruise the streets of the 20th Precinct live that kind of life: long periods of watchful tedium broken now and then by violence and danger, but more often by confrontation with human misery.

The other night, Patrolmen Richard Selkowitz and Otto Mangels were just about to end their shift when they were summoned suddenly to help a woman who sobbed that her boy friend had threatened to stab her. The incident ended hours later, long past the policemen's scheduled quitting time, with the shaken woman seated at a desk in the shabby precinct while policemen comforted her as they filled out forms on the man's arrest.

A few years ago, the precinct, which runs from 66th to 86th Street between Central Park and the Hudson River, gained some attention as the site of Needle Park, a sliver of land where Broadway and Amsterdam Avenue cross at 71st Street. It was pictured as a hangout for drug users and pushers.

But even that small notoriety has left the site. Needle Park is usually deserted at night now. Some unpleasant looking people hang around on the nearby street corners, but the criminal activity maps shown by Detective Hugh Kelly on the second floor of the precinct at 150 West 68th Street have most of the pins clustered to the north, in the mid-80 blocks.

The detailed maps were one indication that the 20th has been, for the past year, an experimental precinct where innovations are tested for possible application elsewhere in the city.

Extra policemen have been put in, the area of responsibility for each patrol has been made smaller, and four roving patrols commanded by superior officers have been set up to provide extra help and to keep the sector patrols alert.

Over-all crime has shown a modest decrease and there are occasional nights of almost suburban quiet along some of the closely watched streets to the south.

When Patrolmen Gilroy and Piccoli patrolled the Needle Park sector the other night, they had to leave their car infrequently.

There were some drunks near Columbus Avenue who had pulled a shabby green easy chair out onto the sidewalk. One of them was sitting in it and the others leaning against it as they drank their wine.

Patrolman Piccoli asked them to move along. "We know them," he said. "They're regulars."

At another point, the crackle of their car radio alerted them. A prowler was reported in an apartment. They drove there and, briskly but watchfully, climbed to the third floor. "It was a man at the kitchen window," said the woman who answered the door. Patrolman Gilroy entered the apartment to talk to her.

Patrolman Piccoli continued on higher. Cautiously, he opened the door to the roof. Then he walked around, shining his flashlight here and there. "If there was somebody here, he is gone," he said.

In the northern sector of the precinct, which is tougher than the blocks to the south where the apartments of the well-to-do are beginning to spread out from Lincoln Center, Patrolman Selkowitz and Mangels were cruising one misty, drizzly night.

They pulled over to chat with a foot patrolman on 85th Street. "Rain," he said gratefully as he leaned in the passenger-side window. "That's the best policeman there is."

They drove along. "See that kid?" said Patrolman Selkowitz, gesturing toward a slim, dark-haired youth working behind the counter of a brightly lighted store. "My partner ran him in the other day. Assault. There was a complaint and the victim identified him. He's a good kid. It was just a fight. We know him."

They know all the regular faces along the two streets that are their responsibility. "Those kids hanging around in that hallway back there?" Patrolman Mangels said. "No, they're okay. They live there."

Then there are the girls, the street prostitutes who are a problem in this neighborhood. Groups of them break up with an insolent self-consciousness when the car cruises by.

The narcotics addicts pose another problem. The policemen on patrol attribute most of the precinct's most ubiquitous crime, breaking into parked cars, to them.

But the violence that is associated popularly with addiction is discounted by the policemen. "Junkies are too busy worrying about junk, for the most part," one patrolman said. Most of the violent crimes that the policemen deal with can be traced to alcohol or to fights among friends.

The evening was a quiet one for Patrolmen Selkowitz and Mangels. They remarked on it as their 11:30 P.M. quitting time drew near. They had investigated a burglary, checked out two tough-looking youths who were in a car with New Jersey license plates, issued four tickets for parking violations, and had driven again and again along wide and well lighted 86th Street, and dark and dismal 85th Street, and they had talked for a while about Patrolman Selkowitz's daughter, who was having some trouble in first grade.

They were almost ready to head south to check out for the night when the woman walked across the sidewalk to their car. "Could you help me?" she asked tensely. "My boy friend says he's going to kill me."

Patrolman Selkowitz sighed. They questioned the woman and then he walked with her to her rooming house. Patrolman Mangels drove the car around the block and met them there.

While they talked with the woman in the lobby, her boyfriend turned up suddenly on the steps outside. He ran, but came back when the policemen called him. Patrolman Selkowitz, searching the man, found a sharply honed piece of steel in an eyeglasses case in his pocket.

"I was peeling potatoes," the man said.

They arrested him a little later. Patrolman Selkowitz sat in the back seat of the squad car between the handcuffed man and the sobbing woman as Patrolman Mangels drove south toward the precinct. "You took me to the police. I'm gonna do you," the man yelled. The woman yelled back.

"Why don't you two shut up, for God's sake," said Patrolman Selkowitz. By now, the two policemen had been working an hour past their supposed quitting time.

It was shortly before 1 A.M., long after the patrolmen should have been on their way home, when they sat down at a desk in the grubby 76-year-old precinct building to start on their paperwork.

November 4, 1967

FEW POLICE FOUND TESTED ON EMOTIONS

Only one-quarter of the nation's police departments screen recruits for emotional fitness, but those that do report that "an amazing number of applicants are dropped," according to Look magazine.

Fletcher Knebel, in a report entitled "Police in Crisis" in the current issue, says that relatively few departments require psychiatric tests "to spot racial bias, sadism or panic response under stress."

In Portland, Ore., where applicants are given such psychiatric tests, 25 per cent of them fail, according to Mr. Knebel.

In a nationwide survey, he also found that 30 per cent of the country's police departments do not require applicants to have a high school diploma.

He described "the average American cop" as a 33-year-old white man earning about $130 a week in a job ranked rather low in public esteem; above average in height, stamina and eyesight, but not in education.

BIAS DISCOUNTED IN POLICE BEATING

Poor Whites More Affected Than Negroes, Study Finds

By JERRY M. FLINT
Special to The New York Times

DETROIT, July 3 — Race prejudice is not a major factor in any beatings of poor people by the police, a study directed by a sociologist has concluded.

Instead, the study indicates, whites are more likely to be handled roughly by the police than are Negroes.

It is the "officer culture" — a code or attitude prevailing in police departments — rather than prejudice that prompts the beatings, the study contends.

These points were made today by Prof. Albert J. Reiss, Jr., chairman of the department of sociology at the University of Michigan, who directed a study of police work that was sponsored by the President's National Crime Commission.

For the study, 36 observers trained in police work, law or sociology worked with the police two summers ago in Boston, Washington and Chicago.

Dr. Reiss concluded from their reports that one officer in 10 in high-crime areas uses force unnecessarily, at least occasionally. One-third of these incidents, covering the beating of suspects, occurred in the station house or patrol cars.

"On the street you can't beat them, but when you get to the station you can instill some respect in them." Dr. Reiss quoted a policeman as having said.

The study was described in the current issue of Transaction, a social science journal published by Washington University in St. Louis.

Dr. Reiss reported two cases from his observers involving the same two officers one night.

2 in Cemetery Searched

Early in the evening they were told to investigate two drunken men sleeping in a cemetery.

"Without questioning the men," the observer reported, "the older officer began a search of one, ripping his shirt from him. He also hit him in the groin with his nightstick."

"The younger officer, as he searched the second, ripped away the seat of his trousers, exposing fully his buttocks. The officers then prodded the men to the cemetery fence and forced them to climb it, laughing at their plight."

Later that night, the observer reported, according to Dr. Reiss, the policeman ran into a transit station where, they had been told a Negro was causing trouble. They grabbed the Negro, the observer reported, and without questioning him, "shoved him into a phone booth and began to beat him with their fists and a flashlight."

After the man had been dragged from the booth and kept on his knees, the observer went on, "he pleaded that he had just been released from a mental hospital that day and begged them not to hit him again, and to allow him to return to the hospital."

One of the patrolmen said, according to the observer, that "I like to beat niggers."

According to the report the policeman took the man outside and, telling him they were putting him on a bus for the hospital, "deliberately put him on a bus going in just the opposite direction."

"The man was crying and bleeding as he was put on the bus," the report concluded, "and one patrolman reported, 'he won't be back.'"

In a telephone interview from Ann Arbor Professor Reiss said that some police chiefs had been surprised not so much by the reports of beatings but by the fact that observers had been present at the beatings.

The observers recorded 3,826 nonriot encounters involving the police and 10,564 persons, of whom 1,394 were suspected of some crime. In 37 encounters involving 44 persons the observers said unnecessary force had been used.

There were 643 white suspects in the group and 27 were hit unnecessarily — a rate of 41.9 per 1,000—the study said. Of 751 Negro suspects, the study found that unnecessary force was used on 17, a rate of 22.6 per 1,000.

Negro suspects make up a larger proportion of the total Negro population than whites, Dr. Reiss noted, and thus the Negro's chances of improper treatment are closer to the white's chances, although the rate of beating of whites was higher.

"If the rates are comparable, then one might say that the application of force unnecessarily by police operates without respect to the race of the offender," he wrote in the article.

He said three-quarters of the police in predominantly Negro precincts expressed prejudice against Negroes but "prejudice does not necessarily carry over into discrimination."

Professor Reiss said in the interview that the general impression that police brutality was a race issue had been generated by reports from Negro organizations. White citizens who suffer at the hands of the police have no such organized voice, he said.

He attributed the beatings to what he called "officer culture" and noted that many officers had been present at some incidents but had done nothing to interfere and in some cases had promoted beatings.

MISCONDUCT LAID TO 27% OF POLICE IN 3 CITIES' SLUMS

A Study Made 2 Years Ago Reports Shakedowns and Payoffs Are Common

By DAVID BURNHAM

A Federally financed study of police operations in the slums of three Northern cities has found that 16.5 per cent of the policemen studied "were observed in some form of misconduct that could be classified as a felony or a misdemeanor."

In addition, 10.5 per cent more told observers that "they themselves engaged in this kind of behavior, and reported specific instances to the observer."

The report, which covered eight slum precincts in Washington, Boston and Chicago, said the police misconduct observed or reported included such things as shaking down traffic violators and accepting payoffs to alter sworn testimony.

"Altogether," the report concluded, "27 per cent of all the officers were either observed in misconduct situations or admitted to observers that they engaged in misconduct."

Part of Board Study

The seriousness of the problem of police misconduct was underscored Tuesday when District Attorney Frank S. Hogan obtained the indictment of 37 men — including 19 present and former New York police-

men — on charges involving "protection" payoffs to the police by gamblers and night-club owners.

The Federally financed report on misconduct was one part of a broad 11-month study of the police and crime patterns carried out in the three cities by the University of Michigan under a $144,535 grant from the Justice Department's Office of Law Enforcement Assistance.

The study of the three cities —selected because of the varying sizes of their police departments—was conducted in the summer of 1966 under the direction of Dr. Albert J. Reiss of the university's Bureau of Social Research.

Though other findings of the over-all project were published by the President's Commission on Law Enforcement and Administration of Justice, the separate report on police misconduct never was released. A copy of this report now has been obtained by The New York Times.

James Vorenberg, the former executive director of the commission, said the commission had always planned to publish the report, but that Dr. Reiss requested additional time to refine the statistics. Mr. Vorenberg, now a professor at Harvard Law School, said Dr. Reiss had promised to release the study by September, 1967.

Dr. Reiss said yesterday that he now planned to publish the report in a few months.

The actual study was made by teams of specially trained observers who were sent to each city. With the permission of the top police administrators, these observers accompanied policemen on a total of 850 eight-hour tours of duty taking notes on everything that happened. Because some were accompanied on more than one tour, the behavior of a total of 450 different policemen was observed.

The separate report on police misconduct prepared by the researchers said the major classes of such behavior were shakedowns of traffic violators, businessmen, drunks and deviants; theft from burglarized establishments and payoffs to the police to return stolen property, to alter testimony at trial and to protect illegal establishments.

Another class of misconduct cited by the report was the carrying of weapons by policemen to plant on citizens, for use as "evidence" in case a policeman injured or killed a citizen.

Excluded from the reported incidents of misconduct, according to the researchers, were shakedowns by the police for free meals, drinks and other small favors. They said such incidents were "extremely common in all districts studied."

The report did not break down the incidents by the actual names of the cities or the districts within these cities. It only said the eight districts or precincts in the three cities were "high crime rate, low income, Negro and white areas."

But supplementary reports of city "Z" and "Y" indicated that merchandise shakedowns by the police in exchange for favors, such as not enforcing various violations or giving extra protection, was the largest single category of misconduct.

The researchers said that because the worst policemen tended to be assigned to the slums that their findings should not be used as a gauge of misconduct for all the policemen in the three cities. But because some observers failed to report police misconduct and because their presence may have modified police behavior, the researchers said they thought their findings understated the amount of misconduct in the slums.

The report said the observers received detailed descriptions from four policemen about "accepting bribes to alter their testimony about a criminal incident."

"In three of the incidents,"

the report said, "the officer was willing to perjure himself because he received a substantial payoff. In the fourth incident, he was incensed by the behavior of the defendant toward him (a white officer and Negro defendant) and was willing to do so without substantial payoff."

The report gave no indication of the sources of the payoffs.

The report said the police practice of carrying a gun or knife to plant on persons for use as "evidence" of belligerence in instances where the police used violence during arrests was diffcult to measure.

"Our observers noticed that many officers, particularly in high crime rate areas in all of the cities, carried additional weapons," the report said.

It said that while the observers never saw policemen actually plant weapons, three policemen in one city and at least one policeman in the two other cities admitted the purpose of the extra weapons was to enable them "to argue self-defense if they injured a citizen and there was no weapon used by the citizen."

Discussing more systematic types of corruption, the researchers said that while the observers did not see "payoffs for protection from organized criminal groups, we have good reason to believe that some occurred in one of the police districts."

They said this belief was based on reports from several policemen "that one of the captains in the district was protecting gambling establishments."

Neither the Washington nor the Boston Police Departments had any comment on the study. Capt. Patrick Needham, the executive assistant to Chicago's Police Superintendent, James B. Conlisk Jr., said the department had welcomed the observers, had believed that it had received all portions of the results of the study and had no knowledge of any findings regarding misconduct of police officers.

WALLACE HAILED BY POLICE ON TOUR

Extra Guards Applaud Him and Toss Out Dissenters

By BEN A. FRANKLIN
Special to The New York Times

WASHINGTON, Sept. 7— The third-party Presidential campaign of George C. Wallace is adding a new term to the lexicon of political demography.

The new term is "the cop vote," and the Wallace campaign has it.

Over the years, political scientists and electoral statisticians have discerned, with more or less clarity, other blocs of voters. The allocation of "the Negro vote," "the Jewish vote," "the Southern vote," and "the labor vote," and so on, to one candidate or another, has become an accepted method of election analysis.

Serious poll-takers also try to estimate the loyalty of such groups to the candidates ahead of time by public opinion sampling.

The recent involvement of a large group of off-duty New York City policemen, many of them wearing Wallace campaign buttons, in a courthouse attack with blackjacks on militant Negroes attending a hearing, is only the latest indication of Mr. Wallace's impact in Police Departments across the country.

Mr. Wallace's grip on the loyalty of many policemen is readily observable.

Policemen in small towns and large cities have been turning out in what seems to be very large numbers to convoy Mr. Wallace's motorcades. In addition to a heavy complement of motorcycles and scout cars with flashing lights, foot patrolmen are usually posted at every intersection the caravan passes to block traffic as the candidate approaches.

Now that Mr. Wallace is receiving the same Secret Service protection extended to all Presidential candidates, much of the heavy local police turnout for his campaign tours undoubtedly is requested through official channels, as it is for the other candidates. But Mr. Wallace always seems to get a bonus.

Policemen, on and off duty, seek his hand and his autograph at airports and outside hotels. If they do not approach him, Mr. Wallace unfailingly detours toward waiting groups of uniformed men, with his hand extended and often with a congratulatory clap on the back.

In several cities in recent weeks, policemen on duty at Mr. Wallace's motel or at the halls where he holds his night rallies have been seen wearing gold "Wallace 68" tie clasps, distributed by the candidate's aides.

Reporters who have interviewed scores of policemen on such assignments in a number of cities have failed so far to find one who was not a committed Wallace supporter.

The special affection in which Mr. Wallace is held by the police also shows in their handling of dissenters and heckler's at the candidate's rallies.

At a rally in Hammond, Ind., two weeks ago, reporters noticed that a quiet, middle-aged couple sat high in an empty section of the gallery, rows away from any of Mr. Wallac's partisans, with a small hand-lettered sign reading: "Dick Gregory for President."

Minutes after the sign appeared supporting the Negro comedian and civil rights leader for President, and while it was still apparently unnoticed by the audience, uniformed policemen appeared in the gallery and led the dissenters briskly from the hall. The exit under police escort, not the sign, attracted attention and drew a roar of approval from the crowd.

At a packed rally in Louisville last weekend, Mr. Wallace's "commendation" of the conduct of the Chicago police department during the Democratic National Convention drew one, small-voted "boo."

Policemen sprinted from every direction to the gallery section from which the jarring sound had come but were not immediately able to pinpoint the troublemaker in the throng.

"Point him out to me," one policeman commanded. Fingers were pointed, and three cleanly dressed teen-agers, two boys and a girl, were paraded down the aisle and out of Louisville's Freedom Hall to a chorus of cheers and jeers.

The former Alabama Governor is the only national candidate this year who never fails to include in his speeches both an exhortatory "Let's hear it" for the local police — and his crowds always applaud on cue, sometimes with a standing ovation — but also a variety of stories about the Federal courts that are calculated to please the police by touching off a reaction of outrage among Mr. Wallace's listeners.

A standard item in the candidate's 50-minute rally speech is the complaint about crime that "you can't even walk in the streets, and if it were not for the police, you couldn't ride in them either." This line is followed by an attack on recent court decisions protecting the rights of accused persons.

September 8, 1968

POLICE IN U.S. SEEK TO EASE HOSTILITY

Survey Finds That a Rise in Efforts to Reduce Racial Tension Sometimes Fails

By JOHN HERBERS
Special to The New York Times

WASHINGTON, June 8 — In cities across the nation, white policemen and black militant leaders have been holding "confrontation sessions" in which they probe each other's motivations and prejudices in an effort to lower the level of hostility between the two groups.

Many police departments have opened storefront centers in the slums, at which residents can voice complaints against the police or other public employes to policemen who have a reasonably sympathetic ear.

Virtually every department has stepped up efforts to hire more Negro policemen, and there have been a number of new community relations efforts, such as Operation Handshake, in which a new patrolman must spend several days in the community making friends before he begins enforcing the law.

An Explosive Issue

Despite these efforts, however, the hostility between the police and the Negro communities has worsened in some cities and in others remains the most explosive issue in race relations.

This information is based on a New York Times survey of 13 cities and on interviews with national leaders familiar with the situation. The cities surveyed were Boston, New York, Philadelphia, Chicago, Detroit, Pittsburgh, St. Louis, Houston, Miami, Kansas City, Mo.; Los Angeles, San Francisco and Oakland, Calif.

In the last year, the police departments have made efforts to institute new community relations programs, many of them following the recommendations of the National Advisory Commission on Civil Disorders — the so-called Kerner Commission — and other national agencies.

Some of the programs have shown proven results but have not been sufficient, in most instances, to have much of an impact. In Houston, 1,500 policemen were required over a 15-month period to participate in confrontation sessions. While the sessions were in progress, minority complaints against the police declined 70 per cent, but once they ended the complaints started to rise again.

Lack of Funds Noted

The storefront complaint centers have helped ease hostilities in some cities but their numbers have been limited by the general lack of funds among city governments.

"I think the storefront centers have proven themselves," said Robert Barton, the 35-year-old director of the St. Louis Police Department's community relations program. "But there's a lot more we could do with them. Lack of money is a limitation, and the work isn't easy. Two of my men have gone to the hospital with bleeding ulcers in the past year. They face a lot of tensions."

There have been a multitude of other problems, including inability of officials at the top to enlist the cooperation of the police on the beat. In Detroit, Marvin Brown, a 34-year-old Negro who heads the Mayor's Committee for Human Resources Development, commended the efforts of the Police Commissioner Johannes Spreen in repeatedly admonishing his men to act with restraint and courtesy.

"But it hasn't filtered down," Mr. Brown said. "The man in the scout car is oblivious to the orders on the third floor (of police headquarters)."

Rebellion in Oakland

In Oakland, where the epithet "pig" is believed to have first been used against the police, policemen rebelled openly last year when Police Chief Charles R. Gain prohibited the use of guns in arresting burglary and car-theft suspects. The rule stands today, but Mr. Gain faces continued hostility within his ranks, and the department is reported to have a growing, clandestine group of John Birch Society members.

Officials in Washington who are familiar with the police problem say the general distrust of authority existing in the nation is found to some extent within police departments.

Recruitment of more Negro policemen has gone slowly even in cities where it has been given high priority. In Kansas City, where Police Chief Clarence M. Kelley said, "We want all we can get," the number of Negroes in a force of 940 has risen from 53 to 66 in the last year.

"There are many difficulties involved," Chief Kelley said. "The type of men we want have a lot of salable qualities and we are only bidding $532 a month as the opening salary. Many of them can get a better job elsewhere. There is also some stigma in the black community against working for the police department."

In many communities, it has been found that having Negro policemen patrolling Negro neighborhoods does little to ease the hostility. Frequently, Negroes display more hostility toward black officers than against whites, accusing them of working for the enemy.

"The key is image," said Houston's police chief, Herman Short, "and we quite obviously have a negative image."

In some areas, planning for the expenditure of funds under the Crime Control and Safe Streets Act of 1969 has increased the hostility of minority leaders. The Federal Government this summer will begin distributing grants, expected to total $300-million by 1970, to the states for improving local law enforcement.

Minority Representation

On Feb. 12, Deputy Attorney General Richard G. Kleindienst urged the states to include minority representatives in planning, saying, "If we forfeit the cooperation of citizens in

the high-crime areas, we will lose more ground than we gain."

"If your state law enforcement planning committee does not now include black people— and in some states, Spanish-speaking citizens — qualified persons from these groups should be sought out and induced to participate," he said.

In a number of states, however, minority groups have complained that the state committees are dominated by law enforcement professionals and have very little minority representation.

In some cities, the police say their community relations have improved while Negro leaders say they have worsened. There is a strong feeling among Negro leaders and outside observers that much of the community relations effort is public relations to improve the image of the police without making substantive changes in police methods.

There has been a proliferation of programs in which the police take youngsters from poor neighborhoods, on hikes, sight-seeing tours and other outings. In St. Louis there is a "Say Hi" program, in which grade school children are given identification cards and urged to "say hi" to any policeman they see.

"I think the people who run the programs are good men," said Clarence Hodges, chairman of the St. Louis Committee on Racial Equality. "But sometimes it looks as if they are trying to make the image of the police better, rather than make the police themselves better. I see this as basically a public relations program, designed to camouflage the real St. Louis Police Department."

In Philadelphia, several po-

lice officials said that the relationship between the Negro community and the police department had "improved tremendously" in the last two years. At the same time, a Federal grand jury is investigating the complaints of police brutality.

In Pittsburgh, a controversy is raging over a proposal for the police department to buy a $35,000 armored rescue vehicle, which officials say will not be used for riot duty.

"It's enough to start a riot," said City Councilman Louis Mason Jr., a Negro. "I can just see that thing clanking up Homewood Avenue (a Negro district)."

Nick Flournoy, a black militant leader, said: "If the police get that armored vehicle and use it as a show of strength— even in a minor situation—anything can happen."

The consensus of Federal and local officials is that if there is major violence in the cities this summer it will not be the massive kind of property destruction seen from 1965 through the spring of 1968, but conflicts involving militants and the police. The possibility of this seemed to have increased the tensions in several cities, particularly Detroit and San Francisco.

In other cities, there are reports of improved relations. But even there the comment of the Rev. C. Anderson Davis, Houston director of the National Association for the Advancement of Colored People, was typical.

"We feel the city administration will listen to our complaints," he said. "But police brutality is a real monster knawing at the roots of the Negro community."

Cop!

*A Closeup of Violence
and Tragedy.
By. L. H. Whittemore.
305 pp. New York: Holt,
Rinehart & Winston. $6.95.*

By STUDS TERKEL

It was but a few years ago: Lord Buckley, the gentle, hip comic, sang a love song, "His Majesty, the Policeman." Shortly thereafter, he was busted. The melody lingers on in most quarters: Law and Order, the fashion of the day.

L. H. Whittemore, working with a tape recorder, has made an attempt to capture "the human-ness" of the cop—the man in the middle. He visited three cities: New York, Chicago and San Francisco. With his police companions, he rode the squadrol, he walked the beat, he mounted project stairways; he was privy to raids and arrests; he was a listener to in-jokes, ambivalent philosophies, and, above all, their righteous hurts. "Cop!" is a remarkable piece of reportage. Subsequent events have made Lord Buckley's whimsical ditty a serious anthem and Whittemore's book frighteningly contemporary.

"I'm gonna pray now," murmured Ronald W. August, a Detroit policeman, on his acquittal of the Algiers Motel murder of a young black.

Scattered applause broke out in the courtroom as three Chicago policemen were acquitted of beating up a newspaperman during the Democratic Convention.

A policeman was elected Mayor of a city, once the heartland of Farmer-Labor and Wobbly sentiment.

Whittemore uses the tape-recorder beautifully; he gives it plenty of slack, but, a good editor, his eye is on the live rather than the dead sparrow.

One of Whittemore's case studies, Gary Cummings may have something, after all. He's a singular young cop who, with his uptight colleague, Colin Barker, patrols Haight-Ashbury. "I have a feeling that this country is, within five years, going to become a police state. . . . I have an emotional hang-up here, because I was raised from birth to believe in the free-enterprise system."

The casual beat and reflections of these two comprise the last and most revelatory sequence of this book. Two other case histories are involved: Joe Minelli, the car radio man whose beat is Harlem; and Ernie Cox, a black detective who works Chicago's South Side ghetto. They're familiar types, dangerously close to stereotype. Yet, at the moment of exasperation, Whittemore allows them to offer horrendous truths. About themselves, about us.

Minelli observes the clipping of Harlemites: "Seventy-eight weeks to pay, *grande venta*, big sale. A dollar deposit on any item, pay two bucks a week for the rest of your life. . . . Ha! That's a laugh. You couldn't save a nickel around here if you stood on your head. . . . That's why, when they have a riot around here, it doesn't hurt my heart."

He is touched, yet untouched. He comforts little black kids, while a black burglar is shot in the back—after the loot is dropped. The image of a young soldier in Vietnam comes to mind. In the ruins of a napalmed village, he tenderly dresses the wounds of a little brown child.

In Ernie Cox, we have a man on the make. In this instance, his skin color is irrelevant. As Minelli acts the zoo keeper to blacks, Cox makes animals of his own people. Not bru-tally; with a smile and ready cash. He buys informers. He's aware of injustice, too. "They were pulling down them raggedy hell houses like mine and putting up the high-risers, but the high-risers, to me, are one of the worst monstrosities ever perpetrated on this city. They're just *containing* the Negro in a specific area, building *up* instead of *out*." Detective Cox and Officer Minelli approach schizophrenia. This is what Whittemore's book is really about.

He points out in his introduction: "I found complex and sometimes confused individuals grappling first hand with the sickness of society, while the rest of us theorize about prevention and cure." That the cop has become surrogate for the Respectables is, by now, common knowledge. The juries that acquit and the voters that elect are overwhelmingly civilian.

Thus it is in young Colins Barker that we find the key to Gary Cummings's fears. Minelli and Cox, despite "just doing my job," are occasionally disturbed by flashes of humanity. Barker has no such problem. He had been a bank teller. Order is the sine qua non of his existence. Naturally, a law of sorts follows.

The disorderly joy of the hippies infuriates him. The orderly aberrations of the Respectables do not. He arrests a long-haired boy for wildly playing the banjo; he releases a well-dressed man who may have been guilty of indecent exposure. It is the law of the ledger: balance. One is a debit; the other, a credit. As an Appalachian lady of my acquaintance put it: one lives in a "Hey, you!" neighborhood; the other, in a "Sir" neighborhood.

Colin Barker is not schizophrenic. He is Orwellian. And he is our invention. In uncannily capturing the small truths of a cop at work, Mr. Whittemore may have revealed the big one. ∎

Color Line a Key Police Problem

By JOHN DARNTON

In the garage of a Chicago station house, a black patrolman removed his gunbelt, stared into the eyes of a white officer and said: "I'm going to beat your brains out."

According to three other black officers who moved in to break up the fight, it began when the white policeman hauled a black youth from a paddy wagon and clubbed him to the ground.

The white officer denied that he beat the prisoner. "But I'm not going to tell you what did happen," he said.

The recent incident is not an isolated one. In a number of major cities across the country —from New York to San Francisco—there is a rising hostility between black and white policemen.

In some cities, the conflict takes the form of a fistfight in the lockerroom; a racial slur scrawled on the precinct wall; a refusal to ride in the same patrol car with a colleague of a different color.

In other cities — San Francisco, Detroit, Chicago and Washington—there have been racial disputes in which officers are said to have drawn their service revolvers on each other.

"We've just been lucky that there hasn't been a real shootout," a black officer in San Francisco said.

"It's bad out here, man, real bad," said a black policeman walking his beat in Detroit's 10th Precinct. "And if something isn't done soon by somebody, you'll see a lot more black officers pulling their guns on white officers."

In many departments, undercurrents of racism have not grown into open animosity. But in others, the antagonism has come to the surface over the last two years, spreading and polarizing the men into two racial camps.

The reasons include the following:

¶The appearance of a new type of black officer, younger, more assertive and more outspoken than his Negro predecessor.

¶The increasing numbers of black policemen, many of them recruited from the slums.

¶The proliferation of new organizations of black policemen.

¶Charges of discrimination against the blacks within the departments.

¶In some areas, a trend among white policemen toward right-wing, antiblack conservatism.

¶The divisive effects of "outside" events such as civil disorders and "law and order" political campaigns.

The new breed of black policemen is a striking change from the old-time "colored cop," who became vilified by the black community as an "Uncle Tom."

"I don't know," said one older officer in Hartford recently. "These younger fellows are really talking out."

"We're black men first," said a 26-year-old San Francisco patrolman, Palmer Jackson. "We're black men first, and then we are police officers."

His statement is being supported from Watts to Harlem.

The new black policemen are usually in their early 20's. They are usually patrolmen, with fewer than three years on the force. Black pride is a magnet for many of them. They wear Afro haircuts under their police caps and Dashikis off duty. They greet one another as "brother."

Some of them live in the slum communities in which they are assigned to patrol. They identify with the communities and they talk—bitterly—about what they describe as the inequities of law enforcement there and the brutality of white officers toward blacks.

Badges the Same Size

"The black cop just isn't going to stand around and see that kind of stuff happen and do nothing," one policeman said.

"We were hired as the white man's assistant in dealing with blacks," remarked Renault Robinson, head of the Afro-American Patrolmen's League of Chicago. "Now we've measured our badges with his and found out they are the same size."

"I'm tired of hearing where black children are beaten by white cops; where black women are insulted by white cops. We're going to knock 'em up, knock 'em down, break 'em in, and treat them just as they treat us," said Patrolman Leonard Weir, president of New York's Society of Afro-American Policemen.

If a new black policeman is an enigma to many older Negro officers, he is an anathema to many white officers.

A white officer in Chicago explained his feelings this way: "I rode in the same car with one [a militant black policeman] once. He didn't say a word to me for four hours. Then all of a sudden he spout-ed off about 'racist institutions downtown.' I can't listen to that kind of talk."

"I wasn't prejudiced before," the officer continued. "Now I hate niggers."

A study in 1966 for the National Crime Commission, based on data from Boston, Chicago and Washington, found that 79 per cent of white policemen in black precincts were prejudiced. Forty-five per cent were classified as "extreme anti-Negro."

Negative Attitudes Cited

The same study found that 28 per cent of the black officers in these areas expressed negative attitudes toward blacks.

"In none of those three cities did we find the black militant officers. They have been emerging since then," said Dr. Albert J. Reiss Jr., a sociologist at the University of Michigan, who conducted the study.

Within the last two years, almost every major department in the country has seen at least one dispute that developed when a black officer objected to the treatment of prisoners at the hands of the whites.

In San Francisco, black policemen accused white policemen of using undue force in dealing with student demonstrators and threatened to arrest the white officers for brutality.

Also in San Francisco, a black officer rushed two whites, and, according to some versions, reached for his gun. He said the whites were beating a handcuffed black prisoner in a cell.

In York, Pa., one of the six blacks on the force resigned during recent disturbances. He objected to use of police dogs against blacks and a "senseless use of firepower."

And in Atlanta, a black patrolman held a news conference to state that he had witnessed three black prisoners being beaten by five white officers inside the station house.

Police officials in high echelons refused for the most part to acknowledge a racial division among the men under their command. But to many blacks—especially to those involved in organizing black policemen—there was no mistaking the seriousness of the situation.

Mr. Robinson, the president of the Chicago Afro-American Patrolmen's League, has more than 30 rules violations pending against him, including one for maligning a fellow officer after Mr. Robinson criticized an off-duty policeman for shooting a 16-year-old boy in the back.

Two weeks ago, Mr. Robinson was arrested on four driving charges and held briefly in jail. When he returned to his station house, he was told that a note was in his mailbox. "They had written 'nigger' all over it and stuffed it full of garbage," he said.

There have been other instances of name-calling. Racial slurs led to a fistfight on a police line in San Francisco and to the suspension of a black trainee who drew a revolver on an instructor in Washington.

In Boston, a policeman in a patrol car calling the communications center to report a fight between "two black men" was interrupted by an anonymous message from another car: "You mean two niggers, don't you?"

Often the feelings between blacks and whites come to a head over what has become in some places a delicate matter —riding in the same patrol car.

A San Francisco patrolman who angered whites by reading the Black Panther party newspaper in the station house, gave this as a reason: "When the sergeant tells one of those guys that he has to ride with one of us, you see them. They start yelling and complaining and everything. They do it right out loud and nobody says a damn thing."

In many cities, the gulf has widened as blacks have withdrawn from traditional police organizations to form their own. Virtually every major city now has a black policeman's organization.

"We don't meet as policemen. We meet as members of the black community," explained Mr. Weir of the Society of Afro-American Policemen. Mr. Weir's group, founded in 1965, now has chapters in Newark, Philadelphia, Chicago and Detroit. Its headquarters is in New York.

The society's younger, more militant officers are currently challenging the leadership of the Council of Police Societies which was formed in 1960 and now has 22 chapters.

But Mr. Weir still scoffs at black policemen in general, even those who join black organizations. "They're all mouth and no action," he said. "I don't want to hear the talk. I want to hear the thunder. I want to see the lightning."

Unlike previous ethnic organizations in police departments, the blacks are bound by strong complaints, which they tend to take outside regular channels in an attempt to gain support and establish rapport with the black community.

Two weeks ago in Chicago, the Afro-American Patrolmen's League held a news conference in Police Headquarters to announce that members would not be used as "strike-breakers" against black pickets at construction sites. Last week, the Coalition for United Community Action, a group seeking to put more blacks in the building trades, returned the gesture by holding a rally in support of the league, which says it is "under harassment" from the department.

The pledge of the Officers for Justice in San Francisco says in part: "We will no longer permit ourselves to be relegated to the role of brutal pawns in a chess game affecting the communities in which we serve. We are husbands, fathers, brothers, neighbors and members of the black community. Donning the blue uniform has not changed this."

The major concern of the black groups, and the one most responsible for stirring them to action, is their contention of almost continual brutality of the white policemen in the black slums.

"I have witnessed brutality and unnecessary roughness by white officers many times," said Capt. James Francis Jr. of the New York Police Department. "Every black cop has seen it."

A question that has divided many black groups is: Should black areas be patrolled only by black policemen?

In Hartford, 22 black policemen began a five-day sick-call protest because they felt they were being discriminated against by assignments to black areas. In Boston, during disturbances in Roxbury, black officers turned down a suggestion of the Police Commissioner that they all be assigned to the slums.

But in New York, the blacks and Puerto Ricans graduating from the Police Academy last week had only one complaint —they felt they were being assigned outside their communities.

In large part, the increasing membership in the black groups —and the increasing friction with the whites—is attributable to the increasing influx of black policemen.

The National Advisory Commission on Civil Disorders found that blacks were underrepresented, usually substantially, in every department for which statistics were available. Out of 80,621 sworn personnel in 28 major cities, only 7,046 were nonwhite.

Since the report was published in 1968, however, the numbers of blacks on the forces have significantly risen in several cities: In Washington, from 21 per cent to 30 per cent; in Detroit, from 5 per cent to 9 per cent, and in St. Louis, from 10 per cent to 15 per cent.

In New York, where black policemen remained at the level of 5 per cent for years, the figure has lately increased to 7 per cent. The department explains the disproportion in terms of the difficulty in recruiting blacks, but many Negroes on the force believe they are intentionally being kept at a minimum.

"With such a low ratio, the department never had blacks coming on in droves and therefore avoided the problems of other cities," one officer commented. "But as the ratio goes up, if it does, and younger black men join the force, they'll be different men altogether from what we were."

Many of the new black recruits are veterans who came in through two Defense Department programs that allow servicemen to be released from duty in the United States three months earlier for police training.

And many of them come from the slums. Why do they want to become policemen? "Where else can a young black without a college education find a job that pays $11,000 a year?" remarked the head of the Chicago Afro-American Patrolmen's League.

Because they come from the slums, a number of the black recruits have a poor formal education and a record that sometimes includes a brush with the law. This has given

rise to the theme of maintaining high standards in recruitment and performance, which is being sounded with increasing frequency by a number of established policemen's organizations.

Deeper Than Prejudice

Some observers see a rising conservatism among white officers that is more complex than simple racial prejudice. They argue that groups such as the Irish, who have a reverence for a kind of Puritanism on the force, are, in reality, reacting to an unarticulated fear that the police department is somehow losing its integrity.

"You should see the stuff they [Negroes] get away with," one white said. "Sleeping on the job. Being out of your district. Those are major violations. If it was a white guy, he'd be taken to a brick wall and be shot."

On the other side, a number of blacks see the recruiting program as inadequate. They feel that the hiring examinations are sometimes "white-oriented," that blacks are subjected to closer scrutiny during probation and that, in some areas, the whites use oral exams or rating systems to deny promotions to blacks who show sympathy to their own communities.

Black-white police relations are further strained during certain types of political campaigns. In Los Angeles, tension rose during the Mayoralty campaign between Samuel W. Yorty and Thomas Bradley. In Philadelphia, it happened when the head of the National Fraternal Order of Police, John J. Harrington, publicly endorsed George C. Wallace for President.

In San Francisco, passion is currently running high over a coming election on a city charter change that would elevate the Negro community relations head from a patrolman to the rank of director.

The animosity has been displayed to the greatest degree during a time of civil disorder.

A white officer in Newark

said: "I'm sorry, but after you've seen what I've seen— Negroes looting, burning, yelling—they just seem to be a bunch of animals."

A black in the same department said: "A lot of black officers I know stopped during the riots, stopped and asked: 'Could that be happening to me? Could I be over there?'"

"I was maybe what you'd call an Uncle Tom when I came on the force a few years ago," said a black policeman in Detroit. "But I saw things in that riot in '67 that caused me to see what a lot of these people [blacks] were feeling and saying.

"Then I understood a little more when they called me a 'traitor' and a 'white man's nigger.' It still hurts when I hear it—and I still do, believe me— but I can kinda see why they feel that way."

Sometimes the division between white and black officers seems as deep as the division between white and black cultures.

On a warm afternoon in San Francisco, a black policeman in civilian clothes stood in a doorway on Third Street in Hunters Point. He was engrossed in the scene before him. There were black faces all around.

One tall youth threw a dollar bill on the sidewalk. "Shoot it," he charged to the rhythmic snap of his fingers. "Shoot it." But he quickly pinned the bill down with a worn, pointy-toed shoe.

"Say brother, gimme some," he said. "Gimme some now, brother. What you say? You better turn me loose. Sister! Say there sister! Guess the sister's in a hurry."

The black policeman motioned toward the black youth. "That's what the white cop can never understand," he said. "The black cop sees that cat out there in yellow pants and he knows that's part of him. He sees beauty in blackness."

Graft Paid to Police Here Said to Run Into Millions

Survey Links Payoffs to Gambling and Narcotics—Some on Force Accuse Officials of Failure to Act

By DAVID BURNHAM

Narcotics dealers, gamblers and businessmen make illicit payments of millions of dollars a year to the policemen of New York, according to policemen, law-enforcement experts and New Yorkers who make such payments themselves.

Despite such widespread corruption, officials in both the Lindsay administration and the Police Department have failed to investigate a number of cases of corruption brought to their attention, sources within the department say.

This picture has emerged from a six-month survey of police corruption by The New York Times. The survey included an examination of police and court records and interviews with scores of police commanders, policemen, former policemen, law-enforcement experts and private citizens.

The picture also is drawn from interviews with a group of policemen — including several commanding officers — who decided to talk to The Times about the problem of corruption because, they charged, city officials had been remiss in investigating corruption.

The names of the policemen who discussed corruption with The Times are being withheld to protect them from possible reprisals.

On Thursday, Mayor Lindsay announced the formation of a special five-man committee to review the city procedures for investigating police corruption. Corporation Counsel J. Lee Rankin was named chairman and Police Commissioner Howard R. Leary is a member of the panel.

The announcement followed a series of meetings held at City Hall and Police Headquarters during the last few weeks after the Lindsay administration learned The Times was conducting a survey of police corruption.

The policemen and private citizens who talked to The Times describe a situation in which payoffs by gamblers to policemen are almost commonplace, in which some policemen accept bribes from narcotics dealers, in which businessmen throughout the city are subjected to extortion to cover up infractions of law and in which internal payoffs among policemen seem to have become institutionalized.

"Police officials always talk about the occasional rotten apple in the barrel when corruption comes up," said Ralph Salerno, a recently retired New York police sergeant and nationally respected expert on organized crime. "They'd be a lot more honest if they talked about the rotten barrel."

Only a relatively few cases of corruption are successfully investigated by the Police Department. In a recent letter to State Senator John Hughes, chairman of the Joint Legislative Committee on Crime, Commissioner Leary said that in the 137 cases of police misconduct referred to the department in the last three years, seven policemen were dismissed.

During a recently tape-recorded conversation with a policeman that was made available to The Times, the top uniformed police official responsible for stamping out corruption in his department — Supervising Assistant Chief Inspector Joseph McGovern — was asked what he had accomplished.

"What have we accomplished?" he replied. "I think I have done a damn good job protecting the Commissioner against the onslaughts of outside agencies."

Mayor's Order Cited

An example of the department's reluctance to openly acknowledge corruption as a problem is its response to an order issued by Mayor Lindsay to all city agencies last May 12.

The order required that "all allegations or indications of possible corruption or wrongdoing" be reported immediately to the Investigation Department before any action was taken by the agency involved.

According to a source in the Investigation Department, the Police Department has refused to comply with Mayor Lindsay's order.

One of the policemen who came to The Times discussed the effect of the department attitude toward corruption on the individual policeman.

"I believe that 90 per cent of the cops would prefer to be honest," he said. "But they see so much corruption around them that many feel it is pointless not to go along."

Public's Faith Affected

In addition to tarnishing the policeman's attitude toward himself and his job, students of law enforcement say, corruption also imposes a massive secret tax on the citizens of New York, dilutes the enforcement of many laws and undermines the public faith in justice.

Some of the assertions made by policemen in The Times survey follow:

¶Arnold G. Fraiman, now a State Supreme Court justice, and until January, 1969, head of the city's Investigation Department, refused to look into charges that Bronx gamblers were paying policemen between $800 and $1,000 a month.

Mr. Fraiman learned about the case during a three-hour conversation with two policemen in his Park Avenue apartment on May 30, 1968.

Just about a year later, with no known assistance from the Investigation Department, eight of the plainclothes men whom Mr. Fraiman had been told about were indicted as a result of an independent investigation by a Bronx grand jury.

Justice Fraiman said yesterday that there was a meeting with a plainclothes man who provided him with information, but he denied that he had ever discontinued an investigation of police corruption. He added that the information provided was extremely general and that "no specifics were ever given."

¶Jay Kriegel, Mayor Lindsay's staff assistant for law enforcement, told a policeman early in 1968 that the administration could not act on charges of police corruption because it did not want to upset the police during the possibly turbulent summer ahead.

About a year before making this statement, Mr. Kriegel arranged for Mayor Lindsay to meet a group of policemen so he could get a realistic understanding of the problem of corruption. The meeting was called off at the last moment with urgent instructions from Mr. Kriegel to the policeman assisting him to forget that it had ever been scheduled.

Mr. Kriegel had no comment yesterday.

¶A detective with many years of experience in the narcotics division said one of his colleagues had arranged payoffs to the police from major heroin dealers of up to $50,000, in return for such favors as the destruction of evidence gathered on secret wiretaps.

Because the detective arranging the payoffs was shot under mysterious circumstances a few months ago, he now is under investigation.

Some aspects of police corruption in New York and the related costs were discussed recently in a report by the Joint Legislative Committee on Crime. The committee charged that gambling in the slums of New York "could not function without official tolerance induced by corruption."

"Testimony before this committee clearly reveals," it said, "that the ghetto residents are perfectly aware of the corrupt relationship between police racketeers and certain elements in the Police Department, and, for this reason, have a deep cynicism concerning the integrity of the police in maintaining law and order in the community."

Another aspect emerged in the anger of a Brooklyn bookmaker who complained that the plainclothes men he regularly bribed continued to demand payments even after they had been transferred out of gambling enforcement into the narcotics division. He said his payment was $1,200 a month, divided by four levels of the department including one unit at headquarters.

The bookmaker said in an interview that some of his busier colleagues paid the police as much as $2,400 a month and that the police imposed an extra payment if a bookmaker took bets on both the flat races and the trotters.

Food Payoffs

Putting an exact price tag on corruption is impossible. The Joint Legislative Committee on Crime recently reported, however, that the city's 10,000 small Puerto Rican grocery stores were estimated to give the police $6.2-million a year in small weekly payments and free food to avoid summonses on minor charges.

Numbers operators, according to Federal and state agencies and private researchers' estimates, make payoffs between $7-million and $15-million a year. Builders in Manhattan report they sometimes pay local patrolmen between $40 and $400 a month for each building site or renovated building.

One West Side liquor dealer said he paid the police about $2,000 a year in cash tips and free and cut-rate liquor.

Beyond the financial cost of corruption is its corroding effect on the self-esteem of the policeman.

"One plainclothes man got a bit philosophical about taking it," a policeman recalled recently. "He stated he was a poor boy and one of the minority groups and he never had any money and now was his big chance. He said, 'I don't care what they offer me, a thousand, a hundred, two dollars, I'll take it.'

"And I said, 'Oh, my God, think about it.' And he said, 'If I did, I'd blow my brains out.'"

This sort of corruption, according to many on the force, is woven into the very fabric of the policemen's professional life. The men assigned to enforcing the gambling laws, for example, are expected to give the precinct desk officer a $5 tip for each gambler that the plainclothes man arrests and the desk officer must process.

"Of course a gambling arrest is a lot of extra work for the desk officer," a senior police, official explained. "But the real reason for the tip is that the desk officer knows the plainclothes man is making a lot of money—that the arrest usually is in some way phony—and he wants his share of the pie."

Some Don't Go Along

Some desk officers do not accept the tips to expedite the paperwork. "When I had a precinct," one unit commander said, "I had a desk officer that was not going along with this practice. I'd be in my office and I would hear him shouting: 'You put that back in your pocket! I get paid for this.'"

A plainclothes man agreed, in recalling an encounter with a desk officer, that the $5 tip was not mandatory. "I don't have a pad," he told the officer. "I'm not on the payoff. I'm not taking anything and there's nothing going out."

"And I was really surprised that this time I hit someone who was really impressed," the policeman added. "And he said, 'fine, that's O.K. with me.'"

In some precincts, policemen say, even to get a "good seat" in a radio car they must pay.

"I was recently a patrolman," a sergeant said. "In my precinct you were supposed to pay for getting a good sector on Sunday, for getting a good post. It's so systematized that the roll-call man actually would know in a dollar figure how many pickups were on your post, and you were supposed to kick in accordingly."

By "pickups," he said, he meant small weekly payments made by many businesses so they could operate on Sunday in violation of the state's sabbath law.

Policy the Main Source

According to the Joint Legislative Committee on Crime and most law-enforcement experts, the numbers racket, or policy game, is the single most regular source of police corruption in New York. The numbers racket — a six-day-a-week lottery in which players can put down small amounts of money —is an enormous business.

One estimate by United States Treasury agents several years ago figured that the five major number operations, or banks, in New York were receiving $1.5-billion a year in bets. If this estimate is correct, the numbers operation's annual gross is bigger than that reported by one of New York's major industries — dressmaking.

Some experts estimate that 1 per cent of the gross of the numbers operation, of $15-million a year, is spent on payoffs at all levels of government

Assigned to stamping out this popular, carefully organized and well-financed industry are 600 plainclothes men — patrolmen assigned to the uniformed force but who wear civilian clothes. The result, according to many knowledgeable sources, is corruption and the transformation of many of these units from law-enforcement agencies trying to suppress gambling to regulatory agencies licensing it.

Some policemen recalled that when they went to plainclothes school some of their classmates complained that going to the school was delaying them from getting out into the street and collecting graft.

Others asserted that the relationship between gamblers and policemen was so well organized that a special mark was put on the envelopes containing the number slips. The mark, they said, indicated to knowledgeable policemen that the "work" had been paid for and should be returned if possible.

'Controller's' Mark

"These markings are put on by the controller (a top man in the numbers racket)," one policeman said. "If there's an arrest made in the meantime, and the plainclothes men are on this work is supposed to go back because these people are paying for protection."

During the recent trial of a numbers operator who conducted his business in a hallway in the garment district, a policeman testified that he had stood in line and let 18 gamblers do business with the operator before he arrested him.

After the arrest, the special headquarters - level policeman testified, he told the gambler, "You act as if you have a license."

"I do," the gambler was quoted by the policeman as saying. "You don't think I'd operate in the open like this without a license." The policeman testified that the gambler then showed him two old lottery tickets that apparently had been given the gambler by a lower-level policeman as a sign that would guarantee freedom from arrest.

Harassment Charged

A plainclothes man working in Brooklyn said his Manhattan colleagues harassed him because he arrested every gambler he could, rather than the ones who failed to pay off.

"There were some who paid and seldom got arrested," he said. "It seemed like our real purpose was to beat down the competiton of the gamblers who paid, to help them maintain their monopoly."

Shortly after this policeman was assigned to a plainclothes squad, another policeman handed him an envelope with $300 in it. "This is from Jewish Max," the policeman was told.

The policeman, disturbed by the corruption, took his complaint to Capt. Philip J. Foran, then commander of the police unit assigned to Commissioner Fraiman's Investigation Department.

"Well, we do one of two things," the policeman and a colleague quoted Captain Foran as saying. "I'll take you into the Commissioner and he'll drag you in front of a grand jury and by the time this thing is through you'll be found floating in the East River, face down. Or you can just forget the whole thing."

After a discussion about what he should do with the money, the plainclothes man said, he "gave the envelope to my supervisor, who was a sergeant of plainclothes, and he was very grateful for it — he snapped it out of my hand like he was an elephant and I had a peanut.'"

Conversation in a Bar

In another instance, this time in the Bronx, a young plainclothes man was taken to a bar by another policeman and introduced to a gambler.

"This guy reached into his pocket and took out some bills and he peeled them off and he gave some to the other officer and peeled off some more and offered it to me," the policeman recalled.

"And I said to him, 'What's that for?' He says, 'Get yourself a hat.' And I said, 'Well, I have enough hats.' So he said, 'Go on, take it.' I said 'If you have anything for me, give it to him,' and turned around and walked out."

The policeman explained that to have taken any action against the gambler would have violated all the "rules" of plainclothes men and possibly put his life in danger. He went on:

"I know the payoff was around — it would fluctuate from $800 to $1.000 a month per man. I would go around with them and at times I've even helped them count it. They would put it into neat little bundles for everybody.

"They would have meeting places and some of the guys would maintain private apartments. And they would allot double or a share and a half for lieutenants."

'I'll Keep It for You'

The plainclothes man refused to keep any money for himself. "Well, it seemed that my partner told them that I was O.K. but he probably was keeping a double share for himself," he said.

He recalled one policeman who was "nice enough to say: 'I'll just keep it for you. Whenever you want it, I got it. And if you ever change your mind, I'll have it for you."

A lieutenant who did not know that the plainclothes man was not "on the pad" offered "to store my money — my share of the money — in his attic — he said he had a quite adequate amount of room in his attic."

The plainclothes man, appalled by what he saw, said he took the information about corruption in the Bronx to Cornelius J. Behan, now an inspector in charge of the Police Department's prestigious planning division, and to Mr. Kriegel, the mayoral assistant.

Both meetings took place in the fall of 1967 he said — one in a parked car and the other in Mr. Kriegel's basement office in City Hall.

Inspector Behan, according to the plainclothes man, said he would inform First Deputy Commissioner John F. Walsh. Mr. Kriegel said he would look into the matter, the plainclothes man said.

The plainclothes man said he went to Inspector Behan because he was a man of widely recognized integrity.

Six Months Later . . .

Six months later, with no sign of activity from Police headquarters or City Hall, the plainclothes man and a policeman friend who knew Mr. Fraiman said they met in the then Commissioner's apartment.

"That night, his reaction you know, really, he was sitting on the edge of his chair," the friend recalled. "Then we started discussing technical things of how we were really going to handle it. And the decision was made that I was going to get a bug and we were going to meet and I was going to bug the surveillance truck."

The surveillance truck was used by Bronx policemen to secretly observe gambling operations.

According to the policeman's account, two days after the meeting in the Fraiman apartment, Captain Foran, the commander of the unit assigned to the Investigation Department, called the policeman informant's friend. He said he was told to "bring the bug back to the office forthwith."

A few days later, according to the account, Commissioner Fraiman was asked by the plainclothes man's friend why the investigation was called off.

"He literally would not discuss it," the friend asserted. "He wouldn't discuss it for months. Ultimately, after months, the only answer Fraiman would make was that he [the plainclothes informant] was a psycho and that they couldn't get involved and that he wasn't willing to cooperate. And that just absolutely was not the case."

After many months of no visible action from Headquarters police investigators, the Police Department learned that the Investigation Department had also been informed about the regular payoffs to policemen in the Bronx. Information about the case then was sent to police officials in the Bronx and to District Attorney Burton B. Roberts.

In February, 1969, a Bronx grand jury indicted eight policemen on perjury charges and numerous gamblers for contempt charges, including one who was revealed to be an agent of Joseph (Bayonne Joe) Zicarelli. The case against one of the policemen now is being tried and the jury is expected to hand up its decision Monday. The cases against the seven other policemen are pending.

Police corruption in narcotics enforcement, according to all policemen interviewed, is nowhere near as carefully organized as corruption in gambling enforcement.

But because the potential profits are much larger, individual narcotics detectives are constantly tempted. In recent years, for example, three New York narcotics detectives, two Nassau County investigators and a Federal agent were arrested on charges of selling drugs.

Last year two detectives were arrested and accused of trying to bribe an assistant district attorney in the Bronx to go easy on a heroin wholesaler.

3 Charged With Extortion

Only last month three detectives were charged with extorting $1,200 in cash, 105 "decks" of heroin and a variety of personal possessions from five New Yorkers.

But there is some evidence that a more regular kind of corruption is not entirely unknown. One policeman, with six years of experience in the narcotics division and its elite special investigating unit, said one of his fellow detectives arranged payoffs to policemen from the largest heroin dealer.

These payoffs, he said, ranged from $5,000 for changing testimony just enough so a drug-seller would not be convicted to $50,000 for the sale of a "wire" — the recorded conversation made by a police wiretap or bug.

The detective who allegedly arranged the payoffs recently was shot and seriously wounded in a gun battle near a Bronx hangout of major heroin importers. The case now is under investigation.

The detective who described the alleged incident to The Times said that, in at least one case he knew, several of his colleagues collected a great deal of damaging evidence about a major heroin dealer, let the alleged payoff arranger know they had the evidence and then waited for a bid from the criminals. The bid came and the money was collected, he said.

Several high-ranking police officials said in interviews that many narcotic detectives — because they are encouraged to meet a quota of four felony arrests a month and because so little money is available to pay informers—resort to stealing drugs from one addict and giving it to another to buy information.

In addition to the graft potential in the narcotics traffic itself, corrupt policemen are in a position to exert considerable pressure on the owners of bars and restaurants. This is because a narcotics arrest in such an establishment means the owner can lose his liquor license.

A detective with several years of experience in narcotics enforcement said he heard a top commander in the narcotics division chastising another official for not demanding and receiving regular payoffs from the bars in his jurisdiction.

But the payments to policemen by an unknown number of New York's 4,434 licensed taverns is only one of a variety of payments made by legitimate businesses and institutions in New York.

Some of the 2,232 licensed liquor stores, for example, also make various kinds of payments to the police. One busy West Side liquor dealer said:

"At Christmas time, the eight men working in the patrol car get $5 apiece, the five sergeants get $10 each and the two lieutenants get $50 each. Then there are the Christmas bottles—they usually want the most expensive brand of Scotch—for the traffic policemen, the mounted policemen and eight or nine precinct patrolmen who come in with their hands out.

"Then over a year, the guys will come in and say, 'Well, I'm going on vacation, how about a bottle?' or give some other excuse why they should get something for nothing. Finally, I'm expected to sell at cost—no profit at all—to all the cops in the area. I estimate that all of this costs me between $2,000 and $3,000 a year."

The businessman knew he was acting in violation of state law, but said he got something for his money.

"First, I want my customers and suppliers to be able to double-park for a few minutes without getting a summons," he explained. "Second, I know that when I call for help the precinct will come pretty fast."

Construction companies are another vineyard for the police, although the amount paid seems to vary from borough to borough and even from precinct to precinct. A Manhattan architect said that it was his experience that the standard fee for the police was $400 a month and that the money usually was picked up by the sergeant.

A Greenwich Village contractor said in an interview that he recently paid the police $500 while he was renovating a brownstone.

"This guy came around and said, 'I've come to see you for the boys,'" the contractor declared. "I was amazed because he was so open. There were five laborers standing around watching. The job was pretty messy so I decided I better pay. I reached in my pocket and gave him $20. He said, 'That's not enough; it's $40 a month for the sergeant and $5 a month — $40 altogether — for the eight guys in the patrol car." What annoyed me was that this payment didn't even stop the parking tickets."

Another contractor new to the city and on his first job —a Lower East Side renovation —said a policeman came around and told him he wanted to make "some financial arrangements."

"The sergeant told me the fee for his services would be $40 a month," the contractor said. "I asked him what the $40 would give me and he said something about there being 13 sergeants in the precinct and they would leave me alone.

"After I gave him the money he was very congenial and kept asking me whether all the financial conditions were satisfactory. He was very pleasant. Prior to that he was sort of demanding."

According to another contractor, the extortion of money from construction companies is so regular that members of the force in one precinct did not even hesitate when the contractor started building a new precinct house for them. "I was amazed, they came around and put the arm on me for $40 a week," he said.

Another source of illegal money is said to be the "reward" some insurance companies and other concerns pay detectives for the return of stolen goods.

A few months ago a lieutenant and detective on the Lower West Side were indicted on charges of extorting $5,000 from Montgomery Ward with the promise that with the money they would be able to find two trucks filled with radio equipment that had been hijacked.

Because such arrangements usually remain secret, it is not easy to estimate how frequently they take place. But one knowledgable agent of the Federal Bureau of Investigation said he felt the payments of rewards was not unusual.

"It's a lot cheaper to pay a $5,000 bribe," he said," than to lose $100,000 worth of mink coats."

The $25 finder's fee normally given by car-rental agencies for the recovery of one of their stolen cars was described as another source of illegal income for policemen. "I don't see anything wrong with it — even though taking the dough is against regulations," a detective said.

Many policemen become lonely, despairing and frustrated because they feel there is nothing they can do about the continuing corruption they witness every working day.

"I remember one time we went on a call," a Brooklyn policeman said. "A girl had tried to commit suicide by taking an overdose of pills. Three patrol cars responded and there were six of us standing around this little one-room apartment, the girl lying there, just breathing.

"One of the guys walked over to her dresser and scooped up a large handful of subway tokens and dropped them in his pocket. No one said a word. It killed me, but there was nothing to do. There was no sense telling the sergeant because he was part of the club."

Police Use Own Words To Speak of Corruption

Slang, one theory holds, is sometimes created so that those who understand it can discuss subjects they want to keep secret. Whether this is true for the police is not known, but there are many police slang words that deal with corruption. For example:

Cousin—A gambler who is paying off. "Don't arrest him, he's a cousin."

Hook—High police official with power to help lower-ranked friends in the department get special assignments or rapid promotion in the detective division. Also known as rabbi.

Nut—The cash bribe. "How big is the nut?"

On the Arm—Obtaining merchandise without charge. "I got the TV on the arm."

Pad—A list of establishments—either legal or illegal —that provide policemen with regular payments, usually on a monthly basis. There also is a "Christmas pad."

April 25, 1970

Terrorism Against Policemen Makes Them Wary on the Beat

By AGIS SALPUKAS
Special to The New York Times

DETROIT, Aug. 26 — Sniper attacks, terrorist bombings, shootouts and rising assaults against big-city policemen are causing deep concern among the police about their personal safety and ability to do their job.

[Two New York City patrolmen were seriously wounded early Thursday in a gunfight in the Springfield Gardens section of Queens. One of the three assailants was killed.

"You think twice before answering a call," said Patrolman Dennis Wayne of Chicago, where four officers have been killed in ambushes in black areas since June. "The guys on patrol think that it might be their turn. When you do go in, you wait for another car to back you up."

The mounting level of attacks against the police in a number of the nation's major cities is promoting similar shifts in police practices, both official and unofficial.

Patrolman Wayne, whose right thumb was partly torn off by a .30-caliber bullet fired by a sniper July 27, said he still did not hesitate to go out on patrol on Chicago's South Side, the area where he was shot.

"But it's getting harder every day," he said. "There's no way you can protect yourself from a sniper. A lot of us are afraid."

Most of the attacks have occurred in black areas. Police officials believe that militants such as the Black Panthers and white radical groups have been involved, although it has been difficult to prove this even when arrests have been made.

So far this year, in less than eight months, 15 policemen have been killed throughout the nation in unprovoked attacks, primarily through bombings and snipers. This is already more than double the number for all of last year when, according to statistics from the Federal Bureau of Investigation, seven patrolmen died from unprovoked attacks, and triple the average of 4.3 such deaths in the last 10 years.

The total number of policemen killed in the line of duty this year is at least 56, according to unofficial reports gathered from 40 states. Ten states were unable to provide information. The 56 known deaths this year already exceed the full-year average of 53 a year in the period of 1960 to 1969 as reported by the F.B.I. Eighty-six policemen were killed in the line of duty in 1969, the highest recorded and 10 more than the previous record of 76 in 1967.

Reports from 14 major cities show that violence against the police has increased significantly in Chicago, Detroit, Los Angeles, San Francisco and New York and to a lesser degree in Pittsburgh, Cleveland and Houston.

In Washington, Philadelphia, and Kansas City officials said that there had been no significant increase in assaults against policemen, and in Atlanta and Wilmington, Del. they have decreased.

Two-thirds of the 15 deaths from terrorist attacks have occurred in two areas—five in or near the San Francisco Bay area and five in Chicago.

Patrolmen and police officials in cities where sniper attacks and bombings have often created an atmosphere resembling a small guerrilla war, said in interviews that the man on the beat has reacted by becoming more cautious — which has often meant being less effective.

In such cities as Chicago and Detroit, some patrolmen working in inner city precincts say they now often look the other way on such minor infractions as a car running a red light, so as to avoid a possibility that the driver might pull a gun or a crowd might gather and turn a routine ticket into a major confrontation.

Two California policemen, one in San Francisco and another in San Jose, have been killed by sniper fire this year while writing traffic tickets.

Many policemen also felt that they were bearing the brunt of anger from militant groups for such things as poor housing, unemployment and the Vietnam war—things for which they were not responsible. Some patrolmen said that local government officials did not want to respond with force against those who attacked them because they were afraid it would set off a major insurrection.

In precincts where policemen have been subjected to sniper attacks, some patrolmen said that many of the men now carry their own weapons in addition to their police revolvers.

In Chicago, one patrolman, in an interview patted his side where he keeps his .44-40, a big-bore gun with a 6-inch barrel. "That's my self-preservation," he said.

The heads of local patrolmen's benevolent and fraternal associations in Los Angeles, San Francisco and Detroit said that many of the older men felt the job had become so dangerous that they were retiring at the end of 20 years instead of re-enlisting, as in the past.

"Retirement parties used to be sad affairs," said Charles Withers, the vice president of the Detroit Police Officers Association. "Now it's a happy time. You've made it."

Carl Parsell, president of the International Conference of Police Associations, which was formed this year and says it represents 125,000 of the 430,000 policemen in the country, said that the new type of violence against the police, such as sniper attacks and bombings, has "accomplished the aim of intimidating and demoralizing the police officer. The irony is that the attacks are costing the people more than the policemen.

"Since the sniping, if a baby is sick and there's an emergency call in certain areas the men now take more time. They're suspicious it might be a trap. They drive around and look over a building and wait for a second car before they go in."

Such fears are not without grounds.

On May 22, a Minneapolis patrolman, James Sackett, and a partner answered a telephoned plea from a young woman who said, "My sister is having a baby. Get a squad car here right away."

At the address given, in a racially mixed neighborhood, the officers were unable to get a response and Patrolman Sackett's partner went to the rear of the building.

There he heard a shot. He returned to the front to find Patrolman Sackett dead from a high-powered rifle bullet fired from across the street.

Although the woman who lived at the address was pregnant, she had not called the police and was not expecting her child for several months.

In Plainfield, N.J., last month two policemen checking on a blaze at a vacant store in the city's black neighborhood were shot down by a sniper. One was killed, the other wounded. The police believe the fire was set to lure the men to the scene.

In Omaha, Neb., this month, policemen responding to an emergency call on the city's predominantly Negro Near

North Side found only a vacant house with a suitcase just inside the door. Seven men were injured and one was killed when the suitcase exploded as one started to inspect it.

Mr. Parsell, who is also the president of the Detroit Police Officers Association, said that the investigative role of the patrolman in the inner city precincts had also been affected because they were reluctant to approach people on the street.

He added that the fear on the part of the patrolmen increased the danger of a confrontation between the ghetto residents and the police.

In Detroit, he said, many policemen no longer talk to people in the neighborhoods they consider dangerous when making an arrest. "You used to explain things," he continued, "you tried to keep things calm. Now the guys want to get in and out as fast as possible."

Mr. Parsell blamed black militants and white radical groups for the attacks. Even though they may not actually be involved in many of the cases, he said, their rhetoric of "kill the pig" has made policemen the target.

"These groups," he said, "have found that an ideal way, to radicalize people and gain support is to bring about a confrontation with the police. It's hard to get at the politicians, judges and bureaucrats, but we're right there in the street."

He conceded that part of the reason policemen were targets was because in the past, mainly as a result of poor training, some overreacted in handling demonstrations and riots.

"We had one-sided training to fight crime," he explained. "We were taught to shoot our guns and use our clubs and then we were thrown in to cope with people that wanted to right social grievances. We are reaping some of the resentment in the ghetto and among the students."

In Chicago, there have been seven officers killed in eight months this year, compared to eight officers in all of 1969. Of the 15 killed, 12 were slain on the South Side of Chicago, the city's largest Negro area.

This year five patrolmen have been killed in ambushes attributed to street gangs. Firing at policemen has become almost a nightly occurrence.

Individual patrolmen said that men on the beat in the inner city have reacted to the ambushes by concentrating on protecting themselves, often at the expense of doing an effective job of patroling.

"As you go into the street," one said, "you walk straight ahead, watch all the buildings. You watch the front and your buddy watches your back and you just try to get through the day and hope to God you get home."

John Montgomery, who helped set up a special sniper unit for the Chicago department, said that many men now carry more powerful guns in addition to their regular .38-caliber pistols for protection against snipers and that some keep rifles beside them in their patrol cars.

The department issued rifles to the foot patrolmen in 1969 because of the increased attacks but they are supposed to be kept locked in the trunks of the patrol cars.

So far, there has been no effect on recruitment or men leaving the department, which has remained at an average of about 50 a month.

However, one patrolman with 14 years on the force who has won 104 citations and has eight children said that some of the older men are looking for jobs elsewhere.

Unless he is promoted to sergeant himself this year, he said that he would move to the Southwest and become a highway patrolman.

"Why should I risk getting my head blown off by some kid who can't read? For the policemen in the large cities, the risk is getting too great."

In Los Angeles, Robert Grogan, the vice president of the Fire and Police Protective League, said that numerous officers have asked for transfers out of dangerous precincts and that many candidates waiting to be appointed are now instead taking jobs in small towns, on the highway patrol and in private industry.

To get enough men, the department has relaxed standards and increased salaries.

During 1969, three patrolmen were killed in the line of duty, There were 80 instances of policemen being shot at and 69 cases of weapons being pointed at them. This year bomb threats have also become a daily occurrence and there have been two shoot outs with black militants.

"There are areas of this city," said Tom James, an inspector, "where residents feel they are at armed war with the police."

In New York, during the first five months of this year, three patrolmen have been killed in the line of duty while none were killed last year. There have been 21 gunshot incidents in the first five months of 1970 while there were only 23 in all of 1969.

Bombs have been found in patrol cars and police headquarters was heavily damaged last June 9 when 10 to 15 sticks of dynamite exploded, injuring seven people.

'Need to Get Even'

A police lieutenant said that "we know that the attacks have been increasing. The reason for this is that the policeman is the most visible symbol of the establishment and the justice that it represents. The people who shoot at policemen do it because they can't reach the Mayor, the President or even their wife to satisfy their pathological needs to get even."

In San Francisco, Oakland and Berkeley, police officials said that they have noticed a big increase in attacks of policemen although they have not compiled statistics recently.

Three weeks ago in Berkeley, two police cars were bombed and several local precincts in San Francisco have been under sniper fire. Last Feb. 4 a bomb exploded in a local precinct in Berkeley, killing one officer and injuring six.

The department in Oakland has had a problem keeping young officers. One young patrolman said that he had taken a bachecr's degree in sociology with the aim of working in a ghetto precinct.

Because of the attacks, however, he said, "No matter how I fight it I find my feelings hardening against Negroes. I'm scared most of the time. Sometimes I wonder whether it's worth it, stopping a car with two or three people in it at night even if I see a clear violation."

Similar reactions were also expressed in Detroit, where two policemen have died in the line of duty so far this year, compared to four in 1969. Last June 28, three policemen were shot but not seriously wounded by snipers in a mostly black area.

A bulletin has been issued to all policemen in Detroit warning that "a police officer who drops his guard, who approaches even the most innocent radio run as a routine incident, is inviting personal disaster. Be constantly alert, treat every radio run as a personal threat and live to enjoy a long and happy retirement."

Robert Milantoni, a 32-year-old patrolman who has worked for nine years in Detroit, said, "It's like being in a guerrilla war. The men on patrol are on edge.

"It's harder to keep a proper balance, especially in black areas. You know that every black man is not out to get you, but when you ask yourself the question 'Will he be a good citizen and back me up?' it's getting much harder to say yes."

Moses Baldwin, the head of the Guardians, an organization of 200 black patrolmen said that for the attacks to decrease it was crucial for the white officers not to harden their attitude but to admit that in the past there has been police harassment and mistreatment of people in the ghetto.

"Both sides have to stop generalizing. The white policeman has to stop saying it's a jungle and enforce the laws as if he were in his own community. The other side has to stop saying, they're all pigs."

In such cities as Cleveland and Houston, officials said that although attacks on police have increased, they have had little effect on the men.

In Cleveland, last February, a sniper shot 16 times at a police car which was pulling into a hospital emergency area and another police car was blasted with a shotgun near a park. There have been no serious injuries as a result of the attacks.

In Kansas City, there have been two bombings of a building formerly used to house the police academy and office building partly used by the police. But there have been no sniper attacks or an increase on the assaults on policemen.

Carlos Mix, a 31-year-old black patrolman who works in the inner city, said, however, that the stories about police being killed in other cities have bothered his wife.

"We've got six kids and I notice now that she doesn't go to sleep at night until I call and say I'm coming home. She'd like for me to get another job. The day after the killing in Chicago my mom called and wanted me to quit. But I told her and my wife that this was my life. I'll be here until I retire, get fired or somebody gets me."

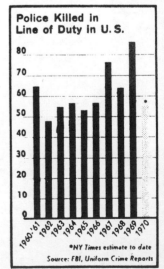

Police Killed in Line of Duty in U.S.

*NY Times estimate to date

Source: FBI, Uniform Crime Reports

The New York Times   Aug. 27, 1970

August 27, 1970

Recruiting of Negro Police Is a Failure in Most Cities

By PAUL DELANEY
Special to The New York Times

WASHINGTON, Jan. 24— The cry of the nineteen-sixties for more black policemen has lowered to a whisper today, with only the District of Columbia among the nation's major cities able to lay clair to any real success in significantly increasing the number of blacks on its force.

From New York to New Orleans to Seattle, most departments have at best been able to add only a few blacks and to increase only barely the percentage of blacks among the total.

"Our recruitment of blacks has never been highly successful," Clarence Giarusso, superintendent of the New Orleans Police Department, said in a typical summation.

Responding to the racial crisis of the last decade, many cities announced at least a desire to have more black policemen, while some conducted recruitment drives. Black leaders and policemen do not believe many of the recruitment efforts were serious, and, at any rate, few of the efforts were successful.

Washington was the most successful, and Chicago and Atlanta got fairly good results.

Other cities employed gimmicks that failed or merely stepped up their traditional recruitment programs that had not worked in the past. Among those cities were Milwaukee, Charlotte, N. C., Seattle, New Orleans, Charleston, W. Va., Dallas and Portland, Ore.

New York Up Slightly

New York City's major recruitment project is the state-financed cadet training program, which tutors minority group members in an effort to help them pass police exams. Sgt. William Perry, coordinator for this four-year-old program, said it had trained and placed on the force more than 400 members of minority groups. He termed the results "an upsurge," although the percentage of blacks on the force has risen only from 5 per cent to 7.5 per cent over the last decade.

A survey of recruitment efforts found the following:

¶Recruitment drives that achieved any measure of success occurred in cities with large and vocal black populations. Success was a result of very aggressive campaigns, and the drives usually followed serious racial disturbances.

¶Drives in most cities failed completely. The percentage of blacks on some forces is the same as it was a decade ago and in some cases has actually declined.

¶Police officials said they were desperately searching for Negroes for their departments, but in actuality little was being done in many places.

¶Discrimination on forces is still a problem that hurts recruitment. Many forces have token representation of blacks in the upper ranks, while some have none at all.

¶In the black community, the image of the police is still very negative. Black youngsters just do not want to be policemen. This attitude, combined with discrimination on the force, seems to be the major reason police recruiters meet with stiff resistance.

Demands of the 60's

The need for black policemen became apparent during the sixties with the steady increase in crime in black communities and rioting in the cities. Along with more policemen, some blacks, mostly militants, were demanding community control of the police. The latter issue faded even before the efforts to recruit.

In Berkeley, Calif., however, a fight is under way over a plan to reorganize the police force into three community-ruled zones—one "black," one "white" and one "campus," for the University of California area.

The most aggressive campaign to recruit blacks was conducted in Washington. However, the situation here is not typical: It has the biggest percentage of black residents of any city, 75.

Four years ago, blacks made up only 17 per cent of the capital's force of 3,100 men. In September, 1968, the percentage was up to 24.4 per cent, or 786 blacks of 3,207 men. By last August, 1,000 more blacks had been added, for a total of 1,797 of 4,994, or 35.9 per cent.

Washington did it by setting up recruit-mobiles in black sections, where written exams were given; recruiting on military bases; changing physical standards, such as lowering the height requirements and modifying the eye requirement, and changing the requirements on certain illnesses such as asthma and hay fever; conducing a "recruit-in-moviethon," where applicants and their dates attend free showings of Jim Brown and John Wayne movies, and a "radiothon" in which applicants were solicited over the radio and taxicabs were sent to pick them up and bring them to the station to take their tests.

Chicago has 2,100 black policemen on a force of 12,678, or 16.5 per cent. The city is one-third black. There were 1,842 Negroes on the force in 1967 and 2,037 last spring.

Atlanta's force of 942 has 260 blacks, or 28 per cent. The percentage is up five points from the annual total during the last decade, according to Superintendent Robert Lane, who is in charge of training.

Quota Charges Made

In New York, 2,400 of the 31,700 policemen are black, or 7.5 per cent. For years the percentage of blacks had remained at about 5 per cent, causing some blacks to charge the department with maintaining a quota system.

The Detroit force has 567 blacks out of nearly 5,100, about 12 per cent. Nearly 500 have been put on since 1966, with the bulk coming after the 1967 riots. The percentage of Negroes on the force in 1960 was 2.

Statistics in some other cities show Los Angeles with 350 blacks on a force of 6,705, or 5.2 per cent; Milwaukee, 50, of 2,098, or 2.3 per cent; Charleston, W. Va., 10 of 150, or 6.6 per cent; Charlotte, 22 of 459, or 4.5 per cent; San Francisco, 85 of 1,755, or 4.8 per cent; Dallas, 32 of 1,640, or 1.9 per cent; New Orleans, 83 of 1,359, or 6.1 per cent; Boston, 60 of 2,807, 2.1 per cent; Miami, 74 of 719, or 10 per cent; Hartford, 60 of 500, or 12 per cent, and Providence, R. I., 18 of 421, or 4.5 per cent.

In Philadelphia the number of blacks on the force has been declining the last few years. Philadelphia had 1,431 blacks on a force of 6,893, or 20.8 per cent, in 1967. This was down last year to 1,347 blacks out of 7,242, or 18.6 per cent.

"To get blacks, the only thing a police department has to do is to tell blacks they want black officers and mean it," commented Deputy Chief Tilman O'Bryant, one of the two top ranking blacks on the Washington force.

"You don't just go on the record in saying you want black officers," he said. "You've got to use just a little more effort to convince them you mean it. We've convinced the community here we mean it."

Many departments conduct recruitment drives by appointing a black to patrol the ghetto, sometimes with a small staff. Some use community organizations, such as the Urban League.

Other cities advertise in black papers and on radio stations aimed at the black community. Some departments have saturated the ghetto with posters, signs and billboards. The poster-billboard approach worked in Washington but apparently is failing in Philadelphia, where posters praise "the black in blue" and admonish residents to "cop in, don't cop out" and urge blacks to "join [Police Commissioner Frank] Rizzo's team." Philadelphia even hired a black advertising concern in an effort to stem the decline in blacks on the force.

Such efforts help most forces barely to maintain their current percentage of blacks.

A big problem is getting blacks who can pass the written tests. Larry Niles, recruitment officer with the Los Angeles police, said, "Negroes have more difficulty getting through the written tests. The tests give us people with over 100 I.Q. Whether it is a culturally fair test is another question." Detroit is attempting to eliminate the white middle-class "cultural bias" of its present tests.

Black policemen are convinced the tests are used to discriminate against them. White officials defend the exams as necessary to assure qualified officers. A black policeman in Indianapolis said the test issue was a "sham," that "if an applicant is wanted on the force, the tests wouldn't keep him off."

The testing problem has caused some cities to take steps, as New York has done, to help blacks to pass. Seattle has a training program to improve skills, while Boston intends to initiate one.

However, the major recruitment problem among blacks appears to be the negative image of the police in the black community, compounded by discrimination on the forces.

Regarding image, Deputy Chief Spurgeon Davenport of Indianapolis, highest ranking black on the force, said he had talked a black school teacher into joining the force, but a few days ago the teacher called.

"He told me to forget it, that he would not join the force because the image was too bad and his friends had already started kidding him about it," Chief Davenport said.

Many white officials are cognizant of the image problem.

The Public Safety Director in Louisville, Ky., George C. Burton, commented, "It is a problem and we're working on it."

Mr. Burton's black assistant director, A. Wilson Edwards, said the department had created the image problem. He cited 'the fact that the city had only 42 blacks on its force of 624. He feels, though, the image is changing.

Discrimination in promotion is also a problem. Mr. Edwards said that many departments had at least one black in the upper ranks. But some, including Milwaukee, Charlotte and Dayton, Ohio, do not. In several cities, San Francisco and Portland included, the ranking blacks are sergeants.

Mr. Edwards, a veteran of 30 years on the force, retired as lieutenant in 1966 after helping set up police units in several African and Asian countries. He recalled years of bitter frustration in trying to get a promotion himself.

"Every time they gave the captain's exam and I finished first or second, they held the promotion list for a year," he said. "They gave the exams again and the same thing happened. I took the test five times. When I finally finished out of the top three, from which the appointment was made, the job was filled. I stopped taking it."

INSPECTION UNIT FOR POLICE URGED

Yale Expert Favors National Anti-Corruption Body

By DAVID BURNHAM

Charging that the greatest failure of the police is to police themselves, a Yale sociologist recommended yesterday the formation of a national inspection service to prosecute corrupt and criminal policemen.

Dr. Albert A. Reiss made the recommendation after discussing the results of his government-financed survey which found that more than one of four of the policemen observed in Chicago, Boston and Washington committed a criminal violation in the presence of an observer.

Dr. Reiss, in response to a question, said interviews with various officials in New York led him to believe the level of criminality among policemen was higher here than in the three cities he studied.

The sociologist said his observers—in addition to measuring criminal violations — also examined how often policemen violated major department regulations. For the three cities, he said an average of about one of

three policemen were witnessed drinking on duty, sleeping on duty, neglect of duty or falsifying reports.

Major Failure Cited

The findings and recommendations were offered by Dr. Reiss at a seminar on behavioral sciences arranged by the Council for the Advancement of Science Writing at the Carnegie International Center, 345 East 46th Street.

"The greatest failure of the police is in handling their internal affairs and the main reason for this ineffectiveness is that most of the men assigned in these units eventually must return to the line," Dr. Reiss declared.

The sociologist cited the system in Britain where any police department that wishes to qualify for financial assistance from the central government must submit to rigorous national inspections.

Dr. Reiss said he was unable to understand how the Federal Government could give local agencies money "without requiring them to meet certain standards and investigations."

Appraises Murphy Move

Discussing recent moves by New York Police Commissioner Patrick V. Murphy to increase the number of supervisors in the Narcotics Division, Dr. Reiss said "such practices may well improve the quality of detec-

tive work and increase the probability of convictions."

"Whether they will reduce corruption and criminal violations within the detective division can be questioned," he said. "More effective external monitoring seems required for that to come about."

In his study, conducted in the summer of 1966, 36 trained observers rode with 597 patrolmen in the three cities.

In Chicago, 30.1 of 100 of the policemen were seen assaulting a citizen, stealing from an already burglarized establishment, accepting a bribe to alter testimony, shaking down deviants or traffic violators or accepting cash payoffs from businessmen. In Boston, 28.6 out of every 100 policemen were observed committing these crimes. In Washington, 20.8 out of 100.

Small Gratuities Ignored

Dr. Reiss said small gratuities such as free meals, drinks, small gifts and discounts were not counted in the study though "31 per cent of the officers made no payment for their meals and discounts for meals usually were obtained by all other officers."

The sociologist said that information from patrolmen and detectives suggested that "in high crime rate areas, particularly among the detectives in vice, supervisors and commanders, the rate of violation is higher than for patrolmen."

January 25, 1971

May 25, 1971

BLACK POLICEMEN DISSENT ON 'ORDER'

Leader Says Such a Policy Is for Benefit of Whites

By C. GERALD FRASER
Special to The New York Times

PHILADELPHIA, June 12— Black policemen and policewomen, emerging as an activist group in the black community, declared themselves today in opposition to the "law and order" wing of the traditional police establishment.

The all-black National Council of Police Societies, completing its four-day annual convention at the Hotel Sheraton, went on record

against "indiscriminate" use of stop-and-frisk laws and against "indiscriminate" use of preventive detention.

The council gave its support to the formation of civilian review boards to end police trial boards' "rubber stamp punishments" of police officers who deal out "negative treatment of the poor and the black community."

The group voted not to support a black police officer who "accepts assignment in the black community as an undercover officer dealing with investigation of politically oriented cases unless a violation of existing law occurs."

In other actions, the council went on record in favor of expunging, "free of charge," the police records of persons whose cases are dismissed after arraignment or at a preliminary hearing, and it promised to continue "to take direct action

against any law enforcement officer who abuses any citizen by the power of his office."

For Benefit of Whites

"The establishment enforces law and order in this country to the benefit of whites, not for the benefit of blacks," said Detective Henry Nelson, newly elected president of the council. "And we can't live with that.

"Law and order. It's a good term, a beautiful term, and we agree with it. We can live with and we can work with it and we can make it under law and order.

"But law and order as law and order clearly stands for, not law and .order as interpreted by those going out and talking about law and order. Because the people who are going out and talking about law and order are talking about law and order for black people and not for white people."

The council is a 10-year-old federation of black police organizations in New Jersey, New York, Michigan, Pennsylvania and Connecticut.

The delegates today elected Detective Nelson, a New York City Transit Authority policeman for 13 years. Other officers named were: Carl Spruill of Newark, first vice president; Rita Gross of Yonkers, second vice president; Al Best of Bridgeport, corresponding secretary; W. Reginald Randolph of New York City, financial secretary; Howard Steward of New York City, treasurer; and Robert Gill of New York City, sargeant-at-arms.

Attending College Urged

The council also adopted resolutions urging policemen to attend college, asking for improvements in police training, and supporting Earl Caldwell, a black reporter of The New York Times. Mr. Caldwell's refusal to appear at a closed-door grand jury hearing has resulted in a case that will be argued in the Supreme Court at its next session.

Attended by some 300 delegates representing thousands of blacks in law enforcement, the meeting is the only one of its kind held each year. It thus provided an opportunity for interested observers to take a reading on the black police officers' situation.

One observer was Booker Kent, a sergeant in the Washington police force, who retired after 27 years and now works for the Police Foundation in Washington.

The foundation is interested in, among other things, the relationship between black police groups and their respective governments, departments and white police organizations, Mr. Kent said.

James Russell, a member of the Pittsburgh Guardians, attributed "the growing responsiveness to the black community by black policemen to the changing of the times, the Martin Luther King movement, the riots in 1968 and the awakening of all black people."

"The day of the good tough cop is gone," he said. "It is now a job for a thinking man. I think the military aspect of the police departments throughout the nation should change, and I think the black officers are going to lead this.

"It gets down to a very simple thing that when they go home at night and take off that uniform they are black. They are not blue."

June 13, 1971

More College Men Seeking Police Jobs in Big Cities

By LINDA CHARLTON

Police departments in major cities are reporting a recent upsurge in job applicants, particularly applicants with more education than was usual in the past.

This is what is considered a significant shift from the pattern of only a few years ago, when jobs outnumbered seekers.

"We are getting an increasingly substantial number of men who have degrees, or who have some college," said Harold W. Barney, assistant director of public safety in Dade County (Miami), Fla.

This situation—and Mr. Barney's assessment was echoed in a number of other cities—is a relatively new one, according to a spokesman for the International Association of Chiefs of Police.

"A couple of years ago, we were getting calls for help from departments looking for somebody to hire," he said. "We just haven't got any calls like that in a year."

The spokesman also noted a "fairly clear correlation between the new applicants and industrial layoffs." And a sampling of big-city police departments showed fairly general agreement that alteration in the recruiting pattern had resulted largely from altered economic conditions—either the dwindling supply of jobs over all or improved police pay and benefits.

In Milwaukee, where a total of 487 persons applied for five vacancies on the force recently, there was a 25 per cent increase in the number of applicants with college degrees or at least some college training, compared with the preceding recruiting effort in November, 1969.

'Breaking Down the Doors'

"They're breaking down the doors," said a spokesman for Chicago's police academy. "We have far more applicants than we need."

No comparative educational statistics had been compiled, but the Chicago spokesman said that educational level of the most recently trained group of rookies was the highest ever: Of 120 trainees, 71 had some college training, and 11 of those 71 had degrees.

The country's largest police force, the 31,500-man New York City force, which has long had a backlog of applicants, recently announced plans to set more rigorous educational requirements. Within a few years, at least one year of college will be the minimum entrance requirement; within a decade, a college degree will be required for all new patrolmen and all policemen seeking promotion.

In Baltimore, where the number of applicants for the force had doubled in the last five years, "many men are coming in with a year or two of college," according to John Reintsell, of the police department's public-information office.

In Dallas, Tex., J. K. Bryant, director of personnel in the police department, said, "There has been a definite increase in better-educated applicants." And he attributed this to "the squeeze on jobs."

Inspector George Parker, in charge of recruitment for the Memphis department, also credited the tight job market for the fact that "we are getting more and better-qualified applicants."

In Pittsburgh, which has enjoyed a surplus of applicants for several years, according to Melanie Smith, the secretary and chief examiner of the city's Civil Service Commission, "a definite increase in education and training" is noticeable.

She attributed the easy recruiting situation to salary—$9,163 to start, rising automatically in three years to $10,000—and benefits.

Arthur C. Cadegan, deputy superintendent in charge of personnel and training for the Boston police force, also attributed the "substantial number of men" with college credits or degrees to economics.

"The reason is basically the pay," he said. "We increased the pay level to make it attractive." The patrolman's starting salary of $10,300 annually "makes police work more attractive," he said, to "many individuals in the teaching fields."

The Boston department, like many others, offers tangible encouragement to its members to continue their education. In Boston, this takes the form of a student-loan program that allows policemen to work a five-hour day at full pay, and have their college expenses paid. The loan will be "forgiven" or considered repaid at the rate of 25 per cent for each year the man stays on the force after graduation.

Another type of encouragement is offered by departments such as Los Angeles's, in which a novice policemen with a high school degree earns $799 a month; with two years of college, he earns $844, and with four years, $891.

"We are interested in the better-educated police officer because of the complicated problems he must face on his job," said Larry Niles, a Los Angeles police recruitment officer.

Policemen who take college

333

courses on their own time are rewarded with bonuses in Milwaukee. Albuquerque has an education-incentive pay program—$1 a month per hour of college credit added to the starting pay of $522 a month, with $100 for a bachelor's degree and $120 for a master's degree.

In Louisville, Ky., where most applicants for the force "still have only a high-school education," according to Jack B. Richmond, the city's Civil Service director, a 1970 regulation,

requested by the chief of police, requires police recruits under 21 to take at least one college course until they reach 21.

"By then," Mr. Richmond said, "we hope they will see the need to continue their education." Only 98 of the Louisville force's 668 members have any college experience, and only six have degrees.

While an increasing number of police departments are offering some form of program designed to upgrade the educational level of its members,

there are some that question the value of college education, and others that feel too much education will create particular problems.

"I think boredom is a real factor in questioning whether highly educated men are necessary for a patrolman's job," said a Chicago police lieutenant.

The one area where most departments report a lag in recruiting is in attracting minority-group members. Some departments cite difficulties with the standard tests, which

blacks and Spanish-Americans feel are loaded against them, but most concede that the root problem is one of attitude.

It is not easy to persuade blacks, who have traditionally viewed the police as oppressors, to join what they see as the enemy:

"Our major push is in minority recruiting," said Mr. Bryant. "We're sincere in our efforts to interest minority members to serve themselves as well as their minorities. But our major problem is convincing the minorities that we're serious."

November 6, 1971

Police Scandals Spreading;
Experts Believe Much Corruption Is Still Uncovered

By DAVID BURNHAM

Police corruption, including charges of selling heroin, accepting payoffs from gamblers and procuring prostitutes, has been uncovered recently in police departments and sheriffs' offices in at least 23 states and the District of Columbia.

But Dr. Albert J. Reiss, a Yale University sociologist who has been studying police matters for more than 10 years, says the number of official investigations seriously understates the extent of the police corruption problem.

"It is my conviction that there is extensive corruption in almost every major and many medium-sized police departments in the United States," he said in an interview.

"Because of the way our vice laws are enforced and because of the way most police departments are organized and led, I am convinced that investigations are a poor index of the size of the corruption problem," he continued.

Research Programs Started

Authorities indicated that it

was extremely difficult to say whether police corruption was on the rise. But the problem has become well enough recognized in the last two years for a variety of Federal and privately financed groups to begin research programs. They are aimed at answering such questions as what causes corruption, how can rookies be trained to avoid it and what techniques are best for investigating it.

One reason for believing that the number of known investigations by Federal, state and local authorities understates the ex-

tent of corruption is that many of the official inquiries, such as the Knapp Commission investigation in New York, appear to have been prompted by outside groups such as newspapers and television stations.

Several weeks ago, for example, the chairman of the House Select Committee on Crime said his staff had turned up concrete evidence among policemen of "relatively high rank" in Washington. The chairman, Representative Claude Pepper, Democrat of Florida, called for an independent citizens group like the

Knapp Commission to investigate.

After meeting with Mayor Walter E. Washington and Chief Jerry V. Wilson, Mr. Pepper said he had changed his mind and felt the investigation could be handled by the regular authorities. Sources in the United States Attorney's office, however, have said that grand juries in the District of Columbia are investigating allegations of kickbacks, shakedowns and perjury involving at least 16 policemen.

And last Friday, eight other policemen in Washington, including one lieutenant, were indicted for conspiracy and lodging false vice charges.

Because no single organization collects information about police corruption investigations going on throughout the country, many of them may not have been noted.

Even the Justice Department reports, for example, that it does not know how many policemen have been indicted in the last year by Federal prosecutors or how many police corruption cases have been investigated by the Federal Bureau of Investigation.

A check with correspondents around the country disclosed, however, that at least the United States Attorneys in the District of Columbia, Arkansas, Illinois, Kentucky, Louisiana, Michigan, New Jersey, New York, Ohio, Pennsylvania, Tennessee and Washington either have recently indicted policemen or are presently conducting official investigations of police corruption.

One recent Federal investigation of police corruption to become known was in Chicago, where nine policemen were suspended after refusing to answer the questions of a Federal grand jury that reportedly is investigating police involvement in the sale of narcotics, a "protection" racket for tavern

owners and receipt of stolen goods.

At the same time that the nine were suspended, Chicago Police Superintendent James B. Conlisk demoted two high police officials to their civil service rank of captain, including the commander of the department's anticorruption unit.

Response to Allegations

Many of the official investigations being conducted were initiated in response to newspaper and television allegations that local law enforcement agencies were corrupt.

In Arizona, for example, a sheriff, five of his deputies and a process server resigned on Sept. 24 rather than face prosecution on charges of bribery, job-selling and conspiracy, which grew out of an investigation by The Tucson Daily Citizen.

In Pennsylvania, The Philadelphia Inquirer on Nov. 16 published allegations of widespread corruption that so far have resulted in parallel investigations by the Philadelphia District Attorney, Arlen Specter, and the State Crime Commission. A half-dozen policemen have already been arrested.

In Albany, The Knickerbocker News-Union Star began Oct. 18 a series of articles alleging widespread corruption, including police involvement in the sale of narcotics. Three weeks later, Governor Rockefeller ordered the State Commission of Investigation to investigate.

Gambler Payoffs Charged

In Kentucky, WHAS-TV in Louisville broadcast last February a two-part documentary charging widespread payoffs to policemen and politicians by gamblers. Several county grand juries have investigated the charges—finding evidence to substantiate some of the allegations—and in March a special grand jury was sworn in to work with a Federal organized

crime strike force in an investigation officials said would take at least 18 months.

Some of the investigations have been initiated by groups other than news organizations. In Los Angeles, for example, Federal agents arrested a police intelligence officer, Hardy L. Fernimen, a former detective in the Hollywood division, on charges of possessing pure heroin with a retail value of $320,000.

This arrest prompted the Los Angeles Police Department to begin an intensive investigation, which two months ago led to the suspension of a detective on charges of cooperating with burglars and to a continuing review of the department's internal affairs procedures.

In Arkansas, a Little Rock grand jury on Nov. 16 indicted the North Little Rock Police Chief, Capt. James W. Gibbons, on charges of pandering and perjury. The indictment charged the captain and two women with procuring other women to work as prostitutes in North Little Rock. The Federal grand jury for the Eastern District of Arkansas, which also has been investigating police corruption, recenty returned three sealed indictments.

In Louisiana, Federal grand juries regularly indict county sheriffs for protecting local gambling and prostitution operations. Just recently, Federal charges were filed against Jim Garrison, the New Orleans District Attorney, and two New Orleans policemen for allegedly accepting bribes to protect pinball gambling operators.

Another Federal action came last May 6 when 151 persons, including a Detroit Police inspector and 15 other policemen, were indicted on Federal gambling charges.

Last June, Police Chief Elmer Briscoe of Reno and the head of the city's vice squad, Lieut. Jesse Williams, resigned

after a county grand jury investigation said the chief had accepted a large number of presents and the lieutenant a $5,000 loan from a local businessman who operated a string of bars.

The increasing efforts to combat police corruption are being financed by a variety of agencies. The Police Foundation, a national law enforcement group in Washington, decided several months ago to fund an extensive research program aimed at developing better training, screening and investigating techniques to control misconduct.

The National Institute of Law Enforcement and Criminal Justice, the research arm of the Justice Department, last year provided financial assistance to both the Knapp Commission in New York and a somewhat similar group in West Virginia.

Another branch of the Justice Department is supporting the development of statewide and regional organized crime intelligence groups. Among other functions, these new organizations were created to gain intelligence about police payoffs by gamblers and other organized crime figures.

The Justice Department has also contracted with William P. Brown, a former New York police inspector and professor of public administration at the State University of New York at Albany, to develop a brief book to show police chiefs around the country how to fight corruption better.

At least one local research group, the Fund for the City of New York, is attempting to work out the appropriate form for an experimental organization to run a legitimate numbers policy game. The aim is to point the way toward legalizing this kind of gambling and thus reduce the widespread corruption that almost inevitably seems to surround it.

More Women Join Ranks of Nation's Police Forces

By DAVID BURNHAM

A small but growing number of policewomen are patroling the streets of American cities and responding to emergency calls in exactly the same way as male police officers.

One reason for the movement of women into what has traditionally been the male world of flashing lights and screaming sirens appears to be the belief that women tend to be less threatening than men and thus prompt less hostile reaction from the public.

Increasingly, too, women are being assigned to gritty, dangerous undercover details, primarily in drug investigations, as well as to the more routine duties, such as traffic control.

Generally, male police officers are nonplussed when they are assigned a woman partner on street duty, but they seem to get used to it fairly quickly.

At the same time, police officials say they are wary of putting married women, particularly those with children, in dangerous jobs, apparently under the belief that mothers should be exposed to danger less readily than fathers.

The women's rights movement and salary discrimination in other occupations seem to be important factors.

"Nine thousand dollars for a starting salary is better than what most women can earn at first, even with a master's degree," observed Marcella Daniels, a married college graduate who patrols the streets of Peoria, Ill.

With 40 women performing regular patrol work in Washington, more than a score in Miami, seven in Peoria, 15 undergoing training for such work in New York and other cities testing or exploring the concept, the use of women to patrol the streets appears to be an important new development in urban enforcement.

In Miami, where there are now 35 policewomen, including two sergeants, Chief Bernard L. Garmire finds that women have proved effective in all types of police work and says that "in certain situations they are more effective than men."

Chief Garmire cited a recent memo from C. E. Daniel, a black policeman who had been training a black female partner.

"I was a little reluctant about riding with a female partner," Patrolman Daniel said, "but after a few hours I relaxed and realized that it had a great psychological effect on people in general. It was very beneficial in Liberty City [Miami's black area], especially in handling domestic disturbances. Women considered a policewoman as one of their own."

Less Violence Found

The extent of the growing trend toward a bigger role for women in police work and the merits of it are discussed in a report on "Women in Policing," to be published this week by the Police Foundation, a group established several years ago by the Ford Foundation to develop better approaches to police problems.

The report, written by the foundation's assistant director, Catherine Milton, says that the major reason for recommending a wider role for women is that it appears to reduce "the incidence of violence between police officers and citizens when women are assigned to patrol."

Mrs. Milton, previously on the staff of the International Association of Chiefs of Police, said that evidence from other fields and the experience of policewomen "suggest that women tend to defuse volatile situations and provoke less hostility than men."

Moreover, women undercover agents seem to have the same quieting effect on drug sellers and others they deal with.

The New York department utilizes several women — fewer than 10 — on its narcotics detail, primarily to buy from drug dealers.

One of them, a black woman whose name and age must remain confidential, regularly goes into the streets and into apartments where drugs are believed to be sold to make purchases. Normally, she will make more than one "buy" to establish that the suspect is in fact a dealer, not simply a one-time seller.

She holds the rating of a grade three detective and is paid $17,500 a year. "It's the easiest thing in the world to buy dope," she says. "The hardest thing is to stay alive."

Mrs. Milton, the author of the Police Foundation report, believes that a major reason for widening the opportunities for women in law enforcement is that the sex quotas maintained by many police departments and the separate promotion tests offered by some appeared to violate Federal and state laws outlawing discrimination against women.

She noted that the Law Enforcement Assistance Administration, the branch of the Justice Department that each year distributes millions of dollars in Federal grants, has already investigated and negotiated settlements of two complaints charging the departments in Wichita Falls, Tex., and Rochester with sex discrimination.

Despite the apparent benefits of using policewomen for a wider range of duties and the

Policewoman in Ann Arbor, Mich., frisking suspect before making arrest with partner

possible penalties of not doing so, Mrs. Milton found deep resistance to the concept in many police departments.

"Clearly," she wrote, "police departments are resisting a trend that is growing stronger. In effect, they are turning away female applicants by perpetuating arbitrary and discriminatory procedures which have evolved from the traditional assumption that policing is not a career for women, mostly because it is dangerous and may require 'unfeminine' behavior."

Chief Edward Davis of Los Angeles illustrated the deep feeling of some top police officials against the concept of using women on patrol during a recent recorded interview.

Asked whether he felt there was a place for women outside the normal clerical and other specialized jobs traditionally reserved for the country's 6,000 policewomen, he replied:

"Then are we going to let a 5-foot-2, 115-pound petit blonde girl go in there and wrestle with a couple of bank bandits? I personally don't think that's the role for women."

Mrs. Milton sees the situation differently. "By introducing women into jobs that have been held exclusively by men," she said in her report, "departments will be forced to rethink and re-evaluate traditional practices."

"For example, if a woman 5 feet 5 inches tall can perform the job of patrol, why can't a man who is the same height; if a woman needs better physical training, might not also a man; if a woman defuses a violent situation without having to make an arrest, shouldn't she or any man who does the same be given a high rating for effective law enforcement practice?"

Asked whether he felt the biological make-up of a woman might affect her performance, Chief Davis replied that "in the history of my wife and two daughters there were certain times during the month when they did not function as effectively as they did at other times of the month."

Another element blocking quick acceptance of women on patrol, according to Mrs. Milton, is the attitude of many policewomen themselves.

Discussing her research in New York, for example, Mrs. Milton said, "The most important obstacle to change is the resistance among the women themselves. Every woman interviewed agreed that the present situation is deplorable, but many find change acceptable in theory only."

This deep-seated feeling among many New York policewomen may be one reason that New York's first experiment is somewhat tentative.

Beginning June 23, according to Police Lieut. Victoria Renzulla, 15 volunteer policewomen now undergoing training will be assigned to work with the neighborhood police teams around the city. "Exactly how they will work will be within the discretion of the individual sergeant running each team," she explained.

The women training for neighborhood patrol work, now an experiment in New York, spend the mornings learning the art of self-defense: judo, jiu jitsui and aikido, firearms training, and baton (nightstick) work.

They spend the afternoons learning theory—laws and police and patrol techniques. They attend classes with visiting police and college teacher consultants for courses in human relations, community relations and awareness, the role of women as colleagues, citizens, victims and law-violators, and crisis intervention.

The women who have volunteered for the neighborhood patrol teams will not get any rise in pay. They now get from $12,500 to $14,500. One of them, Policewoman Ivy Forde, who has been doing clerical work in the first deputy commissioner's office and is the only black woman to volunteer for patrol, says she feels she has volunteered to be a pioneer.

CHAPTER **5**

Justice

The Warren Court. Standing, from left to right: Justices Byron R. White, William R. Brennan, Potter Stewart and Arthur J. Goldberg. Seated, from left to right: Justices Tom C. Clark, Hugo L. Black, Earl Warren, William O. Douglas and John M. Harlen.

ANDREWS UPHOLDS SEARCH FOR LIQUOR IN BOATS AND AUTOS

But Says There Must Be "Legal Probable Cause" for Stopping Suspects.

MUST HEED PUBLIC RIGHTS

Prohibition Chief Emphasizes the Need of Using Law to Full Justifiable Limit.

BUCKNER IS UNCHANGED

Says He Will Continue Policy of Prosecuting Chief Offenders Until He Gets More Judges.

Special to The New York Times.

WASHINGTON, Nov. 21.—Federal prohibition enforcement agents are admonished in instructions issued by the Treasury today that before making a search of vehicles and water craft for illicit liquor they must have "legal probable cause." Warning them that reckless and general search of vehicles "would do more harm than good and tend to bring the service into disrepute," Federal enforcement agents are told to perform their duty in this particular form "with equal regard to the interests of the Government and the rights of the public."

On the other hand, the statement is made that justifiable search is essential to the enforcement of the prohibition laws and when properly made is strictly within the law.

There have been many complaints of unwarranted stoppage of automobiles and motor boats by overzealous land agents and the Coast Guard, and in the case of the latter complaints have been made to Washington that the lives of those, on innocent pleasure craft have been endangered by reckless shots aimed at them by Government patrol boats. The subject has been one of heated debate in sessions of Congress.

Court Decisions Quoted.

The instructions sent out by Prohibition Director Jones and approved by General Andrews, Assistant Secretary of the Treasury, were in part as follows:

"Automobiles, wagons, boats and other vehicles used in the unlawful transportation of intoxicating liquors are subject to seizure and forfeiture. See Section 26, Title 2, of the National Prohibition act, and Section 3450 of the Revised Statutes. No search of any vehicle may be made unless the officer has reasonable grounds for believing that such vehicle is being used for the violation of the prohibition laws. There can be no search without legal probable cause for such search.

"Chief Justice Taft, in the case of Carroll vs. United States, 267 U. S. Reports, Page 132, holds that probable cause or sufficient grounds, in such cases, is derived from facts and circumstances within the knowledge of the searching officer, that is, the officer must have reasonably trustworthy information, sufficient in itself to warrant the belief in a man of reasonable caution that intoxicating liquor is being transported in the automobile or other vehicle which he proposes to search.

"In the case of Milam vs. United States, 296 Federal Reporter, Page 629, the Circuit Court of Appeals for the Fourth Circuit sustained the search of an automobile as founded on probable cause where the officers, having reliable information that liquor was to be transported over a certain road, stopped the car and searched it, although no liquor was found.

"In the case of Elrod vs. Moss, 278 Federal Reporter, Page 123, the same court held that probable cause existed where the transporter resisted search, struck the officer from the running board of his car and, in his flight, threw a package from the car.

"This court also held the search to be lawful in Ash vs. United States, 299 Federal Reporter, Page 277, where the officer, having information that Ash was transporting intoxicating liquor, jumped on the running board of his heavily loaded car, helped to back it and, upon search, found liquor in a locked compartment in the rear.

"In the case of Altshuler vs. United States, Third Federal Reporter, second series, Page 791, a search was sustained by the same court where the officers, believing that the defendant, who had previously pleaded guilty to a charge of transporting liquor, was continuing his unlawful practice, caused a representative to call his house on the telephone and order liquor delivered at a specific place, intercepted him, searched his car and found the liquor.

"Whether there are sufficient grounds, or probable cause, for stopping and searching a vehicle depends upon facts and circumstances of which the officer himself has knowledge or reliable information, and they must be such as to induce in him the belief that there is unlawful liquor in the car or other vehicle, and that an offense against the prohibition laws is being committed.

"There is no authority for hailing and searching vehicles generally, without reliable information or satisfactory grounds for belief that they are carrying unlawful liquor. Whether a search is proper and justifiable in a given case must be left to the prudent judgment and honest intentions of the officer. Experience teaches customs inspectors and prohibition agents how to recognize a loaded car which they are thus justified in stopping for search.

"The agent should leave no vehicle unsearched where he has satisfactory reason for believing that unlawful liquor is being conveyed therein, nor should he violate, hinder or delay innocent passengers by stopping and searching vehicles generally without sufficient grounds to warrant such action.

"Chief Justice Taft, in the Carroll case, said:

"'It would be intolerable and unreasonable if a prohibition agent were authorized to stop every automobile on the chance of finding liquor and thus subject all persons lawfully using the highways to the inconvenience and indignity of such a search.'

"Where an officer feels it his duty to search a vehicle he should hail it, give his name and official position, show his badge or pocket commission, and inform the driver that he has reasonable grounds for believing that he is transporting liquor and request the privilege of searching his vehicle. Harsh, insulting or offensive language should never be indulged and no more force should be applied than is actually needed to effect the search, except in a case of necessary self-defense."

Methodists Warn Republicans.

A warning that any proposition to modify the Volstead act will bring disaster upon the Administration which favors it, coupled with the insinuation that Republican councils have agreed to modification to make the law "enforceable and to satisfy the wet element," was contained in a notice of the Methodist Board of Temperance, Prohibition and Public Morals today.

"It is said that the Republicans have the 'drys' and that they can now afford to make a bid for the other crowd," the notice reads. "The proposition to modify the Volstead act will bring disaster upon the Administration which favors it, will wreck the party which approves it. Any change should be in the direction of making the act more drastic.

"More than anything else the nation needs for the 1928 campaign two strong parties which can command the respect of the people—and no 'wet' party can. There are just as many 'dry' Democrats as 'dry' Republicans, as was shown by the recorded vote passing the prohibition act. The 'dry' vote is not a fixed asset of any party. It is a reward for political virtue and efficiency."

In a statement issued today regarding the attitude of the next Congress on prohibition legislation Wayne B. Wheeler, general counsel of the Anti-Saloon League, said:

"It does not need prophetic power, but a mere knowledge of past events, joined to an understanding of the aroused conscience of the nation, to forecast that the wets will maintain their record of magnificent failures at the coming session of the Sixty-ninth Congress, with both houses, with majorities loyal to the Constitution, will adopt such additional legislation as they consider necessary to increase the effectiveness of prohibition enforcement.

"Each Congress since the ratification of the Eighteenth Amendment has been more friendly to prohibition enforcement than its predecessor. In the new Congress there will be at least twelve more members of the House and four more members of the Senate favorable to enforcement legislation."

Mr. Wheeler practically serves notice on District Attorney Buckner of New York that the "dry" organization will not support his plea for Federal police courts, by saying:

"It is believed that the best way to handle the situation is to provide an additonal number of judges without assignment to any district and have them assigned by the Justice Department or by the committee as provided in the former judicial reorganization bill."

WIRE TAPPING HELD LEGAL FOR EVIDENCE

Taft in 5-4 Decision Leaves It to Congress to Protect Privacy of Telephone.

DISSENTERS OUTSPOKEN

Brandeis Calls Method Used in Dry-Law Case Worse Than Tampering With Mail.

ASSAILS NEW "ESPIONAGE"

Holmes Holds It Better That Felons Escape Than That State "Play Ignoble Part."

Special to The New York Times.

WASHINGTON, June 4.—In a five to four decision the Supreme Court today held that evidence obtained by "wire tapping" is admissible in a criminal case arising under the Prohibition law and that a conviction obtained by such means is not in violation of the constitutional guarantees against "search and seizure."

Chief Justice Taft, who handed down the opinion, was supported by Associate Justices Sutherland, Vandevanter, McReynolds and Sanford. Dissent was expressed by Associate Justice Brandeis in one of the most sharply worded opinions from the bench in years, and by Associate Justices Holmes, Butler and Stone.

A large crowd was in attendance today as the court met for its final session this term. It will reassemble on Oct. 2.

Justice Brandeis, in his scathing rebuke to "wire tapping," described it as a resort to a crime "to detect a crime," and said:

"The evil incident to invasion of the privacy of the telephone is far greater than that involved in tampering with the mails"

Holds "Tapping" Is Not Searching.

The Taft opinion was rendered in two cases arising in the Western district of the State of Washington, where Roy Olmstead, Charles S. Green and others were convicted of conspiracy to violate the Federal dry law, largely by evidence obtained by wire tapping They had sold about $2,000,000 of liquor a year.

The accused urged that evidence by wire tapping was in violation of the constitutional provisions against "unreasonable search and seizure." The Circuit Court of Appeals affirmed the conviction of the trial court. These judgments were upheld in the Taft opinion today.

"We think that the wire tapping here disclosed," Chief Justice Taft ruled, "did not amount to a search and seizure within the meaning of the Fourth Amendment."

The Chief Justice held that while the Fourth Amendment might have a proper application to a sealed letter because of the constitutional provision for the Post Office Department and because such a paper is in the custody of the Government, it could not affect communications by wire. Then he added:

Says Congress May Ban Practice.

"The evidence was secured by the use of the sense of hearing and that only. There was no entry of the houses or offices of the defendants. The language of the amendment cannot be extended and expanded to include telephone wires reaching to the whole world from the defendant's house or office. The intervening wires are not part of his house or office any more than are the highways along which they are stretched."

At another point the Chief Justice said:

"Congress may of course protect the secrecy of telephone messages by making them, when intercepted, inadmissible in Federal criminal trials, by direct legislation, and thus depart from the common law of evidence. But the courts may not adopt such a policy by attributing an enlarged and unusual meaning to the Fourth Amendment."

Seeing Science Aiding Espionage.

Assailing the doctrine that such methods can properly be employed, Justice Brandeis said time works changes, and new conditions arise which did not obtain when the Constitution and the Fourth and Fifth Amendments were adopted. He went on:

"Subtler and more far-reaching means of invading privacy have become available to the Government. Discovery and invention have made it possible for the Government, by means more effective than stretching upon the rack, to obtain disclosure in court of what is whispered in the closed."

"The greatest dangers to liberty," he added, "lurk in insidious encroachment by men of zeal, wellmeaning, but without understanding."

Holmes Calls Method "Ignoble."

Justice Holmes, after saying that Justice Brandeis had exhaustively covered the case, added:

"It is desirable that criminals should be detected, and to that end all available evidence should be used. It also is desirable that the Government should not itself foster and pay for other crimes, when they are the means by which the evidence is to be obtained.

"If it pays the officers for having got evidence by crime I do not see why it may not as well pay them for getting it in the same way, and I can attach no importance to protestations of disapproval if it knowingly accepts and pays and announces that in future it will pay for the fruits. We have to choose, and for my part I think it a less evil that some criminals should escape than that the Government should play an ignoble part."

June 5, 1928

HIGH COURT BARS TESTIMONY BASED ON WIRE-TAPPING

Communications Act Forbids Evidence on intercepted Messages, Roberts Holds

TWO JUSTICES IN DISSENT

Special to The New York Times.

WASHINGTON, Dec. 20.—A powerful weapon for prosecution of the underworld was lost to the government today when the Supreme Court ruled, in a seven-to-two decision, that evidence obtained by tapping telephone wires cannot be used in criminal trials.

This was the first test of whether the Federal Communications Act forbids the government to employ evidence obtained by listening in on telephone conversations of gangsters, racketeers and other criminals. The court, in effect, reversed its attitude of nine years ago when it held, by a five-to-four decision, that a Washington State law insuring secrecy of telephone and telegraph messages did not bar convictions in a Puget Sound bootlegging case. The communications act was not passed until three years ago.

Justice Roberts handed down the majority opinion, in which Chief Justice Hughes and Justices Brandeis, Butler, Stone, Cardozo and Black joined. Justice Sutherland wrote a dissent, shared in only by Justice McReynolds.

For the majority, Justice Roberts held that the government, as well as any one else, was prohibited by the communications act from divulging the contents of intercepted messages. Alluding to the ethics of wire-tapping, he twice commented sharply on controversies over the morality of this practice.

Sees Court "Sentimentality"

In a short but sharp dissent, Justices Sutherland and McReynolds said that the majority finding would aid "depraved criminals," even murderers and kidnappers, and accused the majority of an "overflow of sentimentality" in not excepting government detectives from the inhibitions of the communications law.

Speaking of the communications law, Justice Roberts stated:

"The plain words of Section 605 forbid any one, unless authorized by the sender, to intercept a telephone message, and direct in equally clear language that 'no person' shall divulge or publish the message or its substance to 'any person.'

"To recite the contents of the message in testimony before a court is to divulge the message. The conclusion that the act forbids such testimony seems to us unshaken by the government's arguments."

Justice Sutherland, backed by Justice McReynolds, made this answer:

"The decision just made will necessarily have the effect of enabling the most depraved criminals to further their criminal plans over the telephone, in the secure knowledge that even if these plans involve kidnapping and murder, their telephone conversations can never be intercepted by officers of the law and revealed in court.

"My abhorrence of the odious practices of the town gossip, the Peeping Tom, and the private eavesdropper is quite as strong as that of any of my brethren. But to put the sworn officers of the law, engaged in the detection and apprehension of organized gangs of criminals, in the same category, is to lose all sense of proportion."

Department Weighs the Ruling

Even in the face of the absolute barrier against use of wire-tapping evidence in the courts, there was a question in the minds of some Department of Justice officials whether listening in on telephone conversations was not still permissible.

The case at point hinged around the admissibility of testimony, and careful reading of the Roberts opinion, according to some officials, seemed to bear out the department's theory that government detectives could still tap wires for the purpose of information as to the movements of criminals.

This question was being studied carefully at the department, as were others having relation to the decision's impact on men already imprisoned through wire-tapping evidence, or on the cases of those whom the government had intended to prosecute with such evidence.

Principals in the case decided by the Supreme Court today will receive a new trial in the New York Southern Federal District Court according to the majority's order and, in this trial, the wire-tapping evidence formerly used will, of course, be excluded.

The men who brought the case and who won out against the government in today's ruling are Frank Carmine Nardone, Austin L. Callahan, Hugh Brown and Robert Gottfried. The Second Circuit Court upheld their conviction on charges of smuggling 1,800 cases of alcohol into the Port of New York. Nardone had been sentenced to serve three years, with the others getting terms of a year and a day.

Wires Tapped for Months

Government detectives had tapped telephone wires for several months and listened to more than 500 conversations, of which the government attorney chose seventy-two for evidence. John Picarelli, agent of the Alcohol Tax Unit, was allowed to testify to these conversations over the protests of the defendants.

The four men challenged conviction on the ground that the Communications Act prevented the disclosure of the evidence. When they appealed, the Second Circuit Court sustained the admission of the messages, but said that "if they were erroneously admitted reversal must follow without question."

In upholding the District Court convictions and the use of the evidence, the Circuit Court cited the 1928 Olmstead decision as its authority and held that Congress had not specifically prohibited the use of such evidence. This was the position of the government. It insisted that, under the Olmstead ruling, Congress would have to prohibit use of such evidence specifically, and that the Communications Act did not do so.

Nardone's counsel answered that no Federal law existed at the time of the Olmstead decision, and, therefore, that when Congress came to frame the Communications Act it could have excepted Federal agents if it had so desired. But, the defense lawyers went on, Congress did not do this.

The opinion, delivered by Justice Roberts, repudiated the government's arguments.

Justices' Opinions Unchanged

In view of the fact that the Olmstead decision was referred to in the Roberts opinion, it is interesting to note that the five present justices who voted on that issue maintained today the same position toward wire-tapping evidence that they took then.

Justices Brandeis, Butler and Stone once more objected to wire-tapping evidence; Justices Sutherland and McReynolds supported wire-tapping in the Federal case as they did in the State case nine years ago.

Chief Justice Hughes and Justices Roberts, Cardozo and Black were not members of the bench in 1928.

There was some comment that Justice Black, who, as head of the Senate Lobby Committee, insisted that private telegraph messages should be copied, today voted that the provision against revelation of telephone messages extends even to Federal agents.

Since the Olmstead decision, several States have passed laws for or against testimony obtained through wire-tapping. Officials asserted that it would require study of these statutes to determine if State prosecutions were still feasible in view of the Roberts finding, even though the conversations were strictly within State borders and not in interstate commerce.

December 21, 1937

Abuses of Police Power Rebuked By Supreme Court in 3 Decisions

By LEWIS WOOD
Special to The New York Times.

WASHINGTON, Dec. 13—Protection of the individual from abuses by officers of the law was further strengthened by the Supreme Court in three decisions today.

By a vote of 6 to 3 the court upset the conviction of two Washington men for breaking gambling laws, making the ruling because the police obtained their evidence by pushing their way into a rooming house without a warrant and peeping over a transom.

By a vote of 5 to 4 it overturned the grand larceny conviction of another Washington man because the policed arrested him without a warrant and held him for thirty hours, during which an alleged confession was obtained.

By 6 to 3 it held that Pennsylvania courts must give a hearing to a prisoner serving 20 to 40 years for burglary who says that when he was convicted in 1938 at the age of 17, the right to have a lawyer was not offered him.

The divergent views of the high court were strongly expressed in seven documents in the three cases, and especially in the case of the man arrested for grand larceny. In this case the four dissenters accused the majority of "putting another weapon in the hands of the criminal world."

In the gambling case Justice William O. Douglas wrote the majority opinion, freeing Earl H. McDonald and Joseph F. Washington. The case involved a "numbers" lottery. Justice Harold H. Burton, Chief Justice Fred M. Vinson and Justice Stanley F. Reed dissented.

Washington police opened a window in the landlady's room at the boarding house, climbed through and then peeped over the transom of McDonald's door. They saw numbers slips, money and an adding machine, and arrested the two men. The court majority, commenting on the constitutional guarantee against unlawful search and seizure, said the police should have obtained a warrant.

"Power is a heady thing; and history shows that the police acting on their own cannot be trusted," wrote Justice Douglas, "and so the Constitution requires a magistrate to pass on the desires of the police before they violate the privacy of the home."

"Shocking Proposition"

In a concurrence Justice Robert H. Jackson saw a "shocking proposition when private homes, even quarters in a tenement, may be indiscriminately invaded at the direction of any suspicious police officer."

The dissenters, however, considered the arrest wholly lawful without the need for a warrant. They said the "crime, committed in the presence of the officers," was enough reason.

In the grand larceny case Justice Hugo L. Black wrote the majority opinion overturning the conviction of Andrew Upshaw. The four dissenters were Chief Justice Vinson and Justices Reed, Jackson and Burton.

Upshaw was charged with taking a $135 watch from a home where he was cleaning windows and subsequently, so police said, selling the watch for a $5 bottle of whisky. Sentenced to serve sixteen months to four years, he contested that he should have been taken before the nearest magistrate without needless delay instead of being held without warrant.

Justice Black based his majority opinion on this contention. He recited the Supreme Court ruling in the famous McNabb case of 1943. This held that confessions could not be used as evidence where they were "the plain result of holding and questioning persons without carrying them forthwith before a committing magistrate."

Illegality Held Admitted

The Black opinion said that the policeman arresting Upshaw admitted that the prisoner was "illegally detained for at least thirty hours for the very purpose of securing these challenged confessions."

Writing for the dissenters, Justice Reed held that the Upshaw ruling went beyond the McNabb finding. He declared that the majority had laid down "an extension of the scope of non-admissibility of confessions in the Federal courts."

He argued that the "judicial approach" to such situations "must be in a spirit of cooperation with the police officials in the administration of justice."

It was in the Upshaw case that the minority charged the majority with giving "another weapon" to criminals.

The third case concerned Elmer Uveges. The majority asserted that he should not have been permitted to plead guilty without an offer "of the advice of counsel." The prisoner said he had been held for two weeks without permission to communicate with anyone. Justice Reed wrote the majority ruling. Justices Felix Frankfurter, Jackson and Burton dissented.

Alleges "Dire" Threats

Uveges, now in the Western State Penitentiary, asserted that when tried in 1938 he was "not informed of his right to counsel nor was counsel offered to him at any time" between his arrest and conviction. He said that, "frightened by threats of dire consequences" if he dared to stand trial, he pleaded guilty under direction of an assistant district attorney, with the understanding that he would go to a reformatory.

In the dissent Justice Frankfurter declared that the court had dealt with the Uveges case on the wrong grounds. It had "granted a review of the action of the Pennsylvania Supreme Court (against Uveges) on the basis of allegations not before that court," he stated. He included an elaborate table to prove his claim and held that Uveges should proceed with his appeal on other grounds.

High Court Declares State Wiretap Illegal

By ANTHONY LEWIS
Special to The New York Times

WASHINGTON, Dec. 9—The Supreme Court held unanimously today that wiretapping by New York State law enforcement officers, although authorized by the State Constitution and statutes, violated Federal law.

The court found no exemption for state officials in Section 605 of the Federal Communications Act of 1934, which outlaws wiretapping in these words:

"No person not being authorized by the sender shall intercept any communication and divulge or publish the existence, contents, substance, purport, effect or meaning of such intercepted communication."

Broad Impact Likely

The court ruled that evidence obtained as a result of wiretapping by state officers was inadmissible in Federal prosecutions. This exclusionary rule had previously been applied only to evidence unearthed by Federal agents' wiretapping.

The restrictions are certain to have broad effects on Federal prosecutions, including two in the Southern District of New York. The impact will be felt immediately in a perjury case pending against James R. Hoffa, president-elect of the International Brotherhood of Teamsters, and in a motion by Frank Costello to set aside his income-tax conviction.

Just how today's decision will affect the use of wiretap evidence in state prosecutions cannot be predicted with assurance.

On the one hand, the court has said that state courts are legally and constitutionally free to adopt their own rules of evidence on illegally obtained matter. That is, the state courts may admit evidence that was concededly gathered illegally.

No departure from that rule was indicated today.

On the other hand, the court has now branded as a Federal crime any wiretapping by state

or local police or other officials, even though they may be acting pursuant to state law.

Violation of Section 605 is punishable by a maximum fine of $10,000 and jail sentences of a year.

It can be forecast that, as a matter of Federal-state comity, the Justice Department may well be reluctant to prosecute state officials for violating Section 605. Nevertheless, the threat will be there, as a deterrent to use of wiretap evidence in the state courts.

Today's opinion, written by Chief Justice Earl Warren, was the most important in the court's first big decision day of the 1957-58 term. The case stemmed from a Federal prosecution of Salvatore Benanti for possessing untaxed alcohol.

The New York police had found Benanti and the untaxed liquor after overhearing him fix a meeting place in a telephone conversation.

The Government, represented by John F. Davis at the oral argument before the Supreme Court, maintained that Congress had not intended to include state officials in the term "person" in Section 605, and that in any case the Federal courts should not exclude evidence obtained illegally by state officers.

Chief Justice Warren found that the statute's words permitted of no exception for state officials.

Benanti was represented by George J. Todaro.

In a companion case today the Supreme Court held that listening in on an extension telephone did not constitute wiretapping within the meaning of Section 605.

In the prosecution of Floyd L. Rathburn for threatening a man's life in an interstate telephone call, the police listened in on an extension at the invitation of the recipient of the call.

The court divided, 7 to 2. The Chief Justice, writing for the majority, said that such use of an extension was not an "interception."

Justice Felix Frankfurter, joined by Justice William O. Douglas, delivered a strongly worded dissent. He cited the language of Section 605 exempting only interceptions "authorized by the sender."

Mr. Davis also argued the Rathburn case for the Government. Rathburn was represented by Thomas K. Hudson.

INVASION OF HOME BARRED BY COURT

Narcotics Violator Is Freed Because Police Broke In Without Giving Notice

WASHINGTON, June 23 (AP)—The Supreme Court, citing the adage that every man's home is his castle, freed a man today described by a dissenting justice as a wholesale narcotics violator.

"Every householder, the good and the bad, the guilty and the innocent, is entitled to the protection designed to secure the common interest against unlawful invasion of the house," Justice William J. Brennan Jr. wrote for the majority.

Justice Brennan said that officers who had no warrant broke into the apartment here of William Miller without telling him they had come to arrest him.

Justice Brennan said that Miller could not be lawfully arrested in his home by officers breaking in without first giving him notice of their authority and purpose.

Because Miller did not receive such notice before the officers broke the door to invade his home, the justice said, the arrest was unlawful and the evidence seized, $100 in marked bills, must be suppressed.

Justice Tom C. Clark, joined by Justice Harold H. Burton, took vigorous exception in the 7-2 decision.

Justice Clark said the United States Court of Appeals here found that Miller had fully understood who the officers were and that they had sought to arrest him. He agreed with the Appellate court that Miller's arrest was valid under District of Columbia Law.

"This court now superimposes upon the local rule of the District an artificial and unrealistic requirement that, even under the circumstances found here, police must make 'an express announcement' in unmistakable words they are the police and have come to make an arrest."

Justice Clark said that Miller had a previous record in narcotics traffic. He said that Miller "carries on his abominable trade by using a juvenile as a dope peddler and co-conspirator."

The ruling has applicability on admission of seized evidence in Federal courts everywhere. It does not, however, affect what evidence is admissible in state court felony prosecutions.

HIGH COURT SHIFT SINCE 30'S NOTED

Rulings on States' Criminal Trials Now Routine— Confessions an Issue

By ANTHONY LEWIS
Special to The New York Times.

WASHINGTON, Jan. 17 — Without dissent and without a ripple of public attention, the Supreme Court last week set aside an Alabama robbery conviction because it was based on an "involuntary confession" by the defendant.

The case demonstrates how much the work of the Supreme Court can change in a generation. Today it is routine for the court to scrutinize state criminal cases for the use of coerced confessions. There are examples almost every term.

But this is a relatively recent pattern. In fact, the first time the Supreme Court ever reversed a state criminal conviction because of the use of a coerced confession was in 1936.

The court from the beginning has supervised the fairness of trials conducted by the Federal Government. But the Constitution as originally drafted gave the court no such general authority in state cases.

From Fourteenth Amendment

The court's power to deal with state cases comes from the Fourteenth Amendment, which became part of the Constitution in 1868. The crucial provision forbids any state to "deprive any person of life, liberty or property without due process of law."

The guarantee of "due process" would seem, at the least, to require fair procedure in criminal trials. But curiously the Supreme Court did not speak on the question for many decades. During that time, however, the due process clause was interpreted to bar "unreasonable" state economic regulations, such as minimum wage laws.

In 1915 there came the case of Leo M. Frank, a Georgian convicted of murder in a trial that he contended was dominated by mob hysteria. Historians now seem to agree that there was such hysteria, with overtones of anti-semitism.

The Supreme Court held that it could not look past the findings of the Georgia courts that there had been no mob atmosphere at the trial. Justices Oliver Wendell Holmes and Charles Evans Hughes dissented, arguing that the constitutional guarantee would be "a barren one" if the Federal courts could not make their own inferences from the facts.

Defendant Lynched

Frank's death sentence was commuted to life imprisonment, but he was then lynched.

Justice Holmes wrote the opinion of the court in the great 1923 case of Moore v. Dempsey. It involved five Arkansas Negroes convicted of murder and sentenced to death in a community so aroused against them that at one point they were saved from lynching only by Federal troops. Witnesses against them were said to have been beaten into testifying.

The court, though not setting aside the convictions, directed a lower Federal court to hold a habeas corpus hearing to find out whether the trial had been fair, or whether the whole proceeding had been "a mask—that counsel, jury and judge were swept to the fatal end by an irresistible wave of public passion."

After that decision Arkansas authorities, without contesting the case further, commuted the sentences and released the prisoners, who had been in jail four years.

The 1936 case in which the Supreme Court first actually upset a state conviction because of the confessions used involved three Mississippi Negroes sentenced to death for murder. There was evidence that they had been brutally whipped—and one hanged from a tree by a rope—until they confessed.

Defendant Mental Patient

Last week's case concerned Jesse Blackburn, convicted of robbery in Alabama. He had been in mental hospitals most of his adult life, and in fact was adjudged insane and held in an Alabama hospital for four years before being declared ready for trial.

Chief Justice Earl Warren, writing for the court, upset the conviction because it was based on a confession taken from Blackburn when, by all indications, he was mentally incompetent.

The Chief Justice mentioned a number of reasons for finding involuntary confessions unconstitutional—their unreliability, an abhorrence of brutality and the feeling that the police "must obey the law while enforcing the law."

There is unquestionably resentment on the part of some state judges and prosecutors at the Supreme Court's intervention in these matters.

Criticized in Report

This was a subject mentioned in the 1958 report of the Conference of State Chief Justices criticizing the high court.

The question arises why the court has so many cases on state criminal procedure now, while it had almost none a few decades ago. The reason is surely not that police were kinder and state trials fairer in the earlier period.

The court's willingness to protect the rights of state prisoners, beginning in the Nineteen Thirties, has undoubtedly led more prisoners to seek its protection. And constitutional standards for fair trials have slowly developed.

It is probably not surprising that in a world racked by totalitarian brutality, torture and official murder, the Supreme Court should place a high constitutional value upon fair criminal procedures.

January 18, 196

Tangled Issue of Wiretapping

It has defenders who consider it an essential tool of law enforcement, and critics who believe it an improper—possibly illegal—invasion of privacy.

By ANTHONY LEWIS

WASHINGTON.

FOR three decades, since the Supreme Court first dealt with the problem, wiretapping has been the subject of recurrent controversy in this country. Waves of public outrage at notorious uses of the dismal art have alternated with campaigns by law-enforcement officials to eliminate restraints on tapping.

At the moment the cycle seems to be in its second phase. Police and prosecutors, who consider wiretapping an essential weapon against crime, are concerned about what they believe is a movement in the courts to clamp down on tapping. "You can't hunt lions with a bean-shooter," Brooklyn's District Attorney Edward S. Silver explained to a group of Congressmen in urging them to support permissive wiretap legislation. Mr. Silver is president of the National District Attorneys Association, which shares his view.

Scientific developments have made wiretapping easy—and its detection extremely difficult. A cheap induction coil placed next to a telephone line will pick up a conversation without causing any tell-tale hum or interference. A device known as a pen register or dial recorder picks up the number dialed by the unsuspecting party and prints it in dots or dashes on ticker tape.

The legality of wiretapping is an intricate question that can be considered most simply if broken down into three parts—tapping by Federal agents, by

344

state and local officers, and by private persons.

The Federal constitutionality of wiretapping was upheld by the Supreme Court in 1928. Over the dissent of Justices Brandeis, Butler and Stone— and Holmes on non-constitutional grounds—the Court ruled that tapping was not an "unreasonable search and seizure" of the kind prohibited by the Fourth Amendment, and that use of wiretap evidence at a trial did not violate the Fifth Amendment's guarantee against compulsory self-incrimination.

Then, in Section 605 of the Communications Act of 1934, Congress provided: "No person not being authorized by the sender shall intercept any communication and divulge * * * the contents." This cryptic language was given content by the Supreme Court in 1937. It held that the statute applied to Federal agents as well as private persons and prohibited the use of wiretap evidence in Federal courts.

Despite Section 605, the Federal Bureau of Investigation and other Federal agents continue to wiretap. The F. B. I. asserts that its tapping is legal because Section 605 makes it a crime only to "intercept *and* divulge"—both acts, not just the first—and because only *public* disclosure, not merely reporting to an official superior, counts as "divulging" under the statute. These somewhat fragile legal theories have never been passed upon by the Supreme Court, but successive Attorneys General have supported them.

AT one time the director of the F. B. I., J. Edgar Hoover, opposed wiretapping on the ground that its benefits would be outweighed by the "discredit and suspicion" it would bring on law enforcement. But his views changed in the Nineteen Thirties, and in 1940 President Roosevelt officially authorized wiretapping by the F. B. I. provided that approval for each tap be obtained in advance from the Attorney General. That procedure is still followed. According to Mr. Hoover, the bureau uses taps only in internal security cases and where life is at stake, as in kidnapping and extortion. He testified last Feb. 8 that the F. B. I. then had seventy-eight wiretaps.

As for the states, only a few have restricted tapping. Illinois and Pennsylvania in 1957 enacted statutes flatly prohibiting all wiretapping, police taps included, and barring wiretap evidence. The courts of California and Florida have ruled out the use of wiretap evidence. In five states—New York, Massachusetts, Maryland, Oregon and Nevada—the police are permitted to tap if they first obtain a court order from a judge.

State and local officials are concerned now at the possible effects of the Federal law, Section 605, on their use of wiretap evidence. For in 1957 the Supreme Court said Section 605 applied to state officials and overrode any state laws purporting to authorize tapping. Since then a few judges in New York have refused to issue wiretap orders or have barred evidence obtained by tapping under other judges' orders. The Supreme Court said in 1952 that nothing in Section 605 compelled state courts to exclude wiretap evidence, but this principle is being challenged in a case which the Supreme Court will review next term.

PRIVATE wiretapping — by marital investigators, private eyes of all kinds and criminals—is illegal under Section 605 and under some state laws. Until recently there had been virtually no prosecutions, a fact sometimes said to result from government's embarrassment in punishing others for what its own agents do. But in the last half dozen years there has been significant action against private tappers. A tapping case in New York led to a legislative investigation and a general crackdown on tapping by private detectives. Other state prosecutions have been reported; and the Federal Government, which had obtained only one conviction in the first twenty years of Section 605, has chalked up six since 1954. (It lost the best-known case, against Teamster chief James Hoffa.)

In this legal wilderness, how much telephone tapping actually goes on? There are no reliable estimates, but undoubtedly there is a great deal. In 1955 a New York private detective, John Broady, was found in a room with access to 100,-000 telephone lines, some of which he was busily tapping. The New York City police, probably the most active official tappers, obtain perhaps 1,000 court orders a year authorizing taps. A recent study by the Pennsylvania Bar Association estimated that the police in New York actually tap as many as 20,000 lines a year without bothering to obtain court orders in advance, but officials ridicule this figure.

The foremost legal analyst of the problem, Alan F. Westin of Columbia University, wrote in 1952: "Despite the statutes and judicial decisions which purport to regulate wiretapping, today this practice flourishes as a wide-open operation at the Federal, state, municipal and private levels." This year Professor Westin has expressed the belief that the amount of tapping is down somewhat since "the high tide of the early Nineteen Fifties."

SINCE no one has a good word to say for private wiretappers, the question of what to do about wiretapping centers on official tapping by law-enforcement agencies. What, then, are the arguments pro and con?

The basic argument for police wiretapping is that it works. Taps are said to be an essential weapon against crime — especially against a criminal element that is becoming better and better organized. As distinguished a liberal as the late Robert P. Patterson, judge and Secretary of War, endorsed official wiretapping as a necessary device to fight ever more resourceful and sophisticated criminals who do not hesitate to use any contrivance against the law-abiding.

A second argument of those who favor official wiretapping is that, under modern conditions, respect for privacy is an insufficient basis for policy. Society and the individual himself have interests aside from privacy, and one of them is protection against crime. If wiretapping is "dirty business," as Justice Holmes said, so is crime. When the Supreme Court in 1937 construed Section 605 to bar wiretap evidence, Justice Sutherland wrote in dissent:

"My abhorrence of the odious practices of the town gossip, the Peeping Tom and the private eavesdropper is quite as strong as that of any of my brethren. But to put the sworn officers of the law, engaged in the detection and apprehension of organized gangs of criminals, in the same category is to lose all sense of proportion. * * * The necessity of public protection against crime is being submerged by an overflow of sentimentality."

Wiretapping proponents argue that under the control of court orders tapping is no more reprehensible than many traditional police practices — the use of informants, for example, or searches under warrant. They argue that regulated wiretapping will not touch the law-abiding.

Some who oppose wiretapping doubt that it is really necessary to law enforcement. Senator Thomas C. Hennings Jr., whose Constitutional Rights subcommittee has made an exhaustive study of the subject, says the verdict as to need is "not proven." Others concede that wiretapping helps the police, but say the price is not worth paying. Thomas McBride, former Attorney General of Pennsylvania, told the Hennings subcommittee that tapping does not catch enough criminals to outweigh the loss of "the feeling of freedom that people have that they are not being listened to."

THIS threatened loss of privacy is, of course, the basic

objection to wiretapping. The fear is that to put this weapon into the hands of Government agencies is to move toward totalitarian spying on individuals. The classic statement of the values at stake was that of Justice Brandeis, in his dissent from the 1928 decision upholding official wiretapping:

"The makers of our Constitution * * * recognized the significance of man's spiritual nature, of his feelings and his intellect. They knew that only a part of the pain, pleasure and satisfactions of life are to be found in material things. They sought to protect Americans in their beliefs, their thoughts, their emotions and their sensations. They conferred, as against the Government, the right to be let alone —the most comprehensive of rights and the right most valued by civilized men."

The right to be let alone— a phrase first used by Brandeis in an 1890 law-review article — sums up what lies behind the instinctive aversion to wiretapping. Opponents dispute the claim that tapping affects only the guilty or can be effectively regulated. A judicial order for a tap is not like a search warrant, limited to a particular time and place and object; it may go on indefinitely, without the notice that a search warrant gives the suspect. Conversations with innocent persons as well as conspirators are overheard.

MOREOVER, say the opponents, authorities may misuse supposedly limited wiretapping authority. A Brooklyn grand jury charged in 1950 that police were using taps to blackmail gamblers after attaching the taps without court approval, and that they were obtaining court orders wholesale on the basis of inadequate or false affidavits of need. The F. B. I. was said to have listened in on conversations between Judith Coplon, the alleged Soviet spy, and her lawyer.

In the present situation, one may conclude, there are elements that dissatisfy all sides. The police and others concerned with law enforcement see what they consider their necessary power to wiretap clouded by Section 605 of the Federal law. Opponents of official tapping think too much of it is going on. The citizen has no confidence that private tapping is effectively

controlled. Worst of all is the impression that law-enforcement officers themselves are violating the law. That was the situation in the 1928 Supreme Court case: Prohibition agents had wiretapped in violation of a District of Columbia statute. Justice Brandeis, in the greatest passage of his great dissent, foresaw the consequences:

"In a government of laws, existence of the Government will be imperiled if it fails to observe the law scrupulously. Our Government is the potent, the omnipresent teacher. For good or for ill, it teaches the whole people by its example. Crime is contagious. If the Government becomes a lawbreaker, it breeds contempt for law; it invites every man to become a law unto himself; it invites anarchy. To declare that in the administration of the criminal law the end justifies the means — to declare that the Government may commit crimes in order to secure the conviction of a private criminal—would bring terrible retribution."

The observer seeking a solution to the wiretapping dilemma may find the British example instructive. A country hardly insensitive to the claims of freedom and privacy, Great Britain nevertheless permits police wiretapping—under the strictest of controls. Each tap must be approved in advance by a high official of the Home Office. A 1957 report by a committee of Privy Councilors, approving the continuation of controlled wiretapping, said it was "an effective weapon" against crime and concluded:

"The interference with the privacy of the ordinary law-abiding citizen or with his individual liberty is infinitesimal, and only arises as an inevitable incident of intercepting the communications of some wrongdoer. It has produced no harmful consequences."

THAT conclusion of the Privy Councilors can be understood only against the background of the facts on wiretapping in Britain. Official taps in the entire United Kingdom have averaged fewer than 150 a year. The police invariably destroy all records of wiretaps, the Privy Councilors found; it was unthinkable that officials would use taps for private ends. Most astonish-

ing to an American, the councilors found no evidence of the existence of any private wiretapping whatsoever.

The secret behind the generally accepted and satisfactory wiretapping situation in Britain, then, is public confidence—confidence that power given officials will not be misused, confidence that the privacy of the honest citizen's conversation is unlikely to be invaded by either private eavesdroppers or overzealous police.

THE problem in this country is to create conditions giving rise to the same degree of confidence. Some argue that in a nation without Britain's tradition of official self-restraint, the only answer is absolute prohibition of all wiretapping. Others believe that there should be regulated wiretapping. Perhaps in part because complete prohibition is likely to be an unrealistic idea so long as crime remains as severe a problem as it is, the alternative of regulation seems to be gaining support among those concerned about wiretapping.

Professor Westin, who favors such limited tapping, notes that the vital element in any legislative plan to that end is control to insure against police excesses. The legislation must at the same time be sufficiently workable so that it will be obeyed and not avoided by law-enforcement officials. Because this is now overridingly a problem of Federal law, any meaningful resolution of the wiretapping conflict must come from Congress.

The legislation envisaged by Professor Westin and others would allow the states to wiretap—if they wished to at all —only under a court-order system rigorously defined by Congress. The state courts would be allowed to issue orders only upon a genuine, particularized showing of need. Orders would be good for a limited time, say a month. The wiretap authority might be limited to serious crimes and placed in the hands of District Attorneys rather than the police.

ON the Federal level— where the need for legislation is certainly less urgent—the ideal statute would provide a clear legal basis for the kind

of wiretapping now done by the F. B. I. Tapping authority might be limited to certain crimes, such as espionage and kidnapping, and certain Federal agencies, perhaps only the F. B. I. Some think a Federal court order should be required for each tap, while others think the Attorney General's personal approval, as at present, suffices.

Along with these permissive provisions, the legislation would include a flat and total prohibition on all other wiretapping—that is, on the tapping itself, without regard to fine points about "divulgence." There would be an assumption of strict enforcement by the Justice Department, including prosecution of officers who violate the law.

It would be foolhardy, in light of the record, to forecast early Congressional action. Dozens of bills have been introduced and dozens of hearings held in the last twenty years, and Congress has done nothing. But the pressures are rising now, and they come from several directions—from law-enforcement officials worried about their legal position, from libertarians concerned about wiretapping in general, from those who see a gradual breakdown of legal controls in this area. Perhaps the time is approaching when Congress will have to settle this particular conflict between liberty and order.

Wiretaps for State Trials Upheld by Supreme Court

Ruling in Pugach Case Says Evidence Is Admissible Even Though Obtained in a Manner Contrary to U. S. Law

Special to The New York Times.

WASHINGTON, Feb. 27—New York State's right to use wiretap evidence, even though it is obtained in a manner contrary to Federal law, was upheld today by the Supreme Court.

In a 7-to-2 ruling the court said that Federal courts could not issue injunctions against the introduction of wiretap evidence in state trials. It affirmed a decision of the Second Circuit Court of Appeals in New York.

Four other states besides New York allow wiretaps as evidence, provided a court order has been obtained. These states are Massachusetts, Maryland, Oregon and Nevada.

The New York case involved a Bronx lawyer, Burton N. Pugach. He was indicted on the charge of throwing lye at a young woman friend.

Before he could be brought to trial in the state courts he went to Federal court and contended that the state authorities were going to use wiretap evidence against him. He asked the Federal court to enjoin the Bronx District Attorney, Isidore Dollinger, from proceeding against him on that basis.

Even though Pugach lost in the lower Federal courts, he did succeed in getting temporary orders prohibiting the use of wiretap evidence until the issue was finally resolved. The state is now free of that restraint.

The issue is a complicated one arising from Section 605 of the Communications Act of 1934. That section prohibits the interception and divulgence of telephone communications.

The Supreme Court has construed the section as forbidding the use of wiretap material as evidence in the Federal courts.

But in 1952, in the case of Schwartz vs. Texas, it said that state courts were not bound by the same rule. In that case it was held that state courts were free to admit wiretap evidence even though it had been obtained in violation of Section 605.

At the time the Schwartz case was decided, it was not clear whether policemen acting under state law were covered by the section's ban on wiretapping. Then, in the Benanti case in 1957, the Supreme Court said they were.

In the Benanti case the tapping was done by New York policemen acting under a provision of the New York Constitution permitting wiretapping under court order. The court held that this New York provision was overridden by Section 605.

In the same decision, the court held that the Attorney General could prosecute police officers using wiretaps, because Section 605 made them illegal. However, the Attorney General later indicated that he did not intend to bring any such actions.

Thus, the Benanti case made plain that wiretapping, even with state approval, violated Federal law. But the Schwartz case indicated that, even so, the wiretaps could be admitted as evidence in state trials.

Pugach's lawyer sought to avoid the Schwartz case. Instead of waiting until the state trial and then objecting to the introduction of wiretaps—which the Schwartz case would allow—he moved before trial for a Federal injunction.

Today's decision rejecting that approach came in a one-sentence, unsigned opinion. It simply cited the Schwartz Case and a 1951 decision saying the Federal courts should not use injunctions to interfere with the use of illegally seized evidence in state trials.

A dissenting opinion by Justice William O. Douglas was joined by Chief Justice Earl Warren. They said the court should now overrule the Schwartz decision and construe Section 605 to bar the use of wiretap evidence in state trials.

Justice Douglas said it was illogical to say that wiretapping was illegal even though done by state officers, as the Benanti Case made clear, but still to let wiretap evidence be used.

He also criticized what he termed "an avid taste for violating the law" on the part of the New York policemen. He cited a book that charged that widespread police wiretapping went on in New York, some of it without even state court orders.

Justice William J. Brennan Jr. objected to the citation of the Schwartz Case by the majority. He indicated, therefore, that he did not approve the Pugach technique of pre-trial injunctions against wiretap evidence, but would vote to overrule the Schwartz Case and bar the actual introduction of the evidence at trial.

The decision settles a question that had brought cries of alarm from many prosecutors and police officials, especially in New York. They said wiretapping was essential to combat crime.

The case was argued by George J. Todaro of New York for Pugach and by Walter E. Dillon and Irving Anolik, assistant district attorneys for Bronx County.

February 28, 1961

High Court Bars Eavesdropping With Device Intruded Into Home

Special to The New York Times.

WASHINGTON, March 6—The Supreme Court held today that the Constitution bars the police from driving a spike wired for sound into the wall of a person's home and listening in on his conversation.

The decision was unanimous. It held that mechanical eavesdropping is a violation of the Fourth Amendment, which prohibits "unreasonable searches and seizures."

Justice Potter Stewart wrote the opinion of the court.

"The Fourth Amendment and the personal rights it secures have a long history," he said. "At the very core" stands the right of a man to retreat into his own home and there be free from unreasonable governmental intrusion."

The case is a significant one because it marks the first time that the Supreme Court has held a mechanical eavesdropping device unconstitutional. In 1928 the court refused to declare wiretapping unconstitutional and in 1942 it upheld a "detectaphone" held up against a wall.

Justice Stewart did not reexamine those cases. He said this one was different because it involved an actual physical intrusion of the eavesdropping device — the spike — into the home.

At issue in the case was a round, silver-colored metal device slightly thicker than a pencil and sharp at one end. It was about a foot long.

Attached to the blunt end were wires leading to an amplifier, power pack and earphones. The actual spike involved was demonstrated to the Supreme Court at the oral argument.

The spike was used by some District of Columbia policemen in the spring of 1958. They had an idea that a row house in a decaying neighborhood was being used as a gambling headquarters. They got permission to spend three days in the house next door, and from there they did their eavesdropping.

Stuck Into Party Wall

The police stuck the spike under a baseboard and on into the party wall between the houses. Several inches in—the exact measurement was in dispute—the spike hit something metallic that the police said "acted as a very good sounding board."

Justice Stewart said the record indicated that this was a heating duct in the alleged gamblers' house. He said the entire heating system thereupon became a "giant microphone," picking up conversations all over the house and transmitting them through the spike to the waiting police.

On the basis of what the police heard, three men were convicted as gamblers and sentenced to twenty months to five years in jail. They were Julius Silverman and Robert L. Martin of Washington and Meyer Schwartz of Pittsburgh.

They challenged the admission of evidence obtained by the eavesdropping. Since the Supreme Court has held that evidence obtained in violation of the Fourth Amendment is inadmissible, the question was whether the use of the spike violated the amendment.

The lawyer for the three men, Edward Bennett Williams of Washington, asked the Supreme Court to reconsider the whole question of the constitutionality of wiretapping and eavesdropping.

He said the old cases had been outdated by modern devices that made possible frightening techniques, such as listening to conversations hundreds of yards away without a wire. But Justice Stewart said those "large questions" need not be weighed now.

"We need not here contemplate the Fourth Amendment implications of these and other frightening paraphernalia which the vaunted marvels of an electronic age may visit upon human society," he said.

Justice Stewart said that in the old cases "eavesdropping had not been accomplished by means of an unauthorized physical encroachment." But here,

he said, it was undeniab'- that the police had listened ..i only by "usurping part of the petitioners' house—a heating system."

It did not matter, Justice Stewart said, whether insertion of the spike was technically a "trespass" under District of Columbia law. He said "inherent Fourth Amendment rights are not inevitably measured in terms of ancient niceties of tort and real property law."

"This court has never held," Justice Stewart said, "that a Federal officer may without warrant and without consent physically entrench into a man's office or home, there secretly observe or listen, and relate at the man's subsequent criminal trial what was seen or heard."

Justice Stewart said the lower courts had rejected as too fine any distinction between the use of a spike in a wall and the use

of a detectaphone held against the wall, as approved by the Supreme Court in 1942 in the Goldman case.

"We find no occasion to re-examine Goldman here," he said, "but we decline to go beyond it, by even a fraction of an inch."

Justice Stewart then quoted from a Supreme Court opinion of 1886 on the Fourth Amendment:

"It may be that it is the obnoxious thing in its mildest and least repulsive form; but illegitimate and unconstitutional practices get their first footing in that way, namely by silent approaches and slight deviations from legal modes of procedure."

The court reversed the convictions and ordered new trials without use of the overheard conversations.

John F. Davis argued the case for the Government.

March 7, 196

HIGH COURT GIVES VIEWS ON POLICE

Throws New Light on Use of Coercion to Obtain Criminal Confessions

By ANTHONY LEWIS
Special to The New York Times.

WASHINGTON, March 26— The Supreme Court threw new light last week on an old doctrine—the rule that confessions extracted from criminal defendants by police coercion may not be used in evidence against them.

For twenty-five years the court has held that the Constitution prohibits the use of involuntary confessions. It has defined "involuntary" broadly, to include both confessions produced by the third degree, or physical brutality, and those resulting from psychological pressure.

The reversal of state criminal convictions because of the use of coerced confessions has caused much resentment on the part of local policemen, prosecutors and even judges. They have complained that the court is interfering too much with "states' rights."

The state critics might agree that a coerced confession may be suspect because of the possibility that it was untrue. But, they have asked, why should the Constitution rule out such a confession if it leads to other evidence that proves it to be true?

Concerned With Means

That question was answered by the Supreme Court last Mon-

day more clearly than ever before.

The court said, in effect, that it was concerned with the means — police methods — for their own sake, and not with the end of the confession, true or false. In short, the constitutional doctrine was designed to discourage police brutality, no matter how effective its results.

The case came from New Haven. It concerned Harold D. Rogers, who was convicted and sentenced to death for murder during a liquor-store robbery in 1953.

After his arrest, Rogers was questioned by police officers for six hours but would say nothing. The police then pretended to issue an order that his wife be brought in for questioning. At that point Rogers agreed to confess. The next day, after being held incommunicado and without counsel, he repeated the confession to the coroner.

The Connecticut courts held the confessions voluntary and admissible as evidence. They rejected contentions that the fake order to arrest his wife, his detention incomunicado and the refusal to let his lawyer see him were improper coercive tactics.

Probable Truthfulness

In their reasoning the Connecticut courts relied in part on the probable truthfulness of Rogers' confession.

The trial judge said that the trick about his wife "had no tendency to produce a confession that was not in accord with the truth." He charged the jury that the confession need not be excluded "if the artifice or deception was not calculated to produce an untrue statement."

The State Supreme Court of Errors agreed. It said the question presented by the contention of incomunicado detention was whether it "induced the defendant to confess falsely that

he had committed the crime being investigated."

This reasoning was found constitutionally faulty by the Supreme Court last week. Seven justices—two went off on other grounds — spoke through an opinion by Justice Felix Frankfurter. They ordered a new trial for Rogers.

"Convictions following the admission into evidence of confessions which are involuntary," Justice Frankfurter said, "i.e., the product of coercion, either physical or psychological, cannot stand.

"This is so not because such confessions are unlikely to be true but because the methods used to extract them offend an underlying principle in the enforcement of our criminal law; that ours is an accusatorial and not an inquisitorial system—a system in which the state must establish guilt by evidence independently and freely secured and may not by coercion prove its charge against an accused out of his own mouth."

The philosophy of that explanation can be sensed in many earlier cases.

The first decision reversing a state conviction because of the use of coerced confessions came in 1936. Chief Justice Charles Evans Hughes, for a unanimous court, found a violation of the clause in the Fourteenth Amendment, which prohibits the states from depriving a person of life, liberty or property without due process of law.

The case involved three Mississippi Negroes who were whipped and beaten into confessing a murder. Chief Justice Hughes said that, under the due process clause, "the rack and torture chamber may not be substituted for the witness stand."

In 1952, Justice Frankfurter wrote that the use of involuntary confessions was "constitutionally obnoxious not only because of their unreliability" but because they "offend the community's sense of fair play and decency." And two years ago Chief Justice Earl Warren wrote for a unanimous court:

"The abhorrence of society to the use of involuntary confessions does not turn alone on their inherent untrustworthiness. It also turns on the deep-rooted feeling that the police must obey the law while enforcing the law; that in the end life and liberty can be as much endangered from illegal methods used to convict those thought to be criminals as from the actual criminals themselves."

PRESENTS OPINION: Justice Felix Frankfurter.

March 27, 19

HIGH COURT BARS EVIDENCE STATES SEIZE ILLEGALLY

Special to The New York Times.

WASHINGTON, June 19—The Supreme Court overruled today a landmark decision of 1949 and held that the Constitution forbids the use of illegally seized evidence in state criminal trials.

The vote was 5 to 4 for taking this historic step. Of the four justices in the minority, three disagreed on the constitutional issue. The fourth did not reach the issue.

This was the final day of the Supreme Court's term.

The search-and-seizure decision is expected to have sweeping effects on local law enforcement throughout the country. Some observers quickly described it as the most significant limitation ever imposed on state criminal procedure by the Supreme Court in a single decision.

The effect of the decision is to eliminate a long-standing difference in the rules for state and Federal courts.

24 States Involved

A 1914 case, Weeks v. United States, decided that Federal courts must exclude illegally seized evidence. But in 1949, in the case of Wolf v. Colorado, the Supreme Court said that state courts were not bound by the same rule.

At the time of the Wolf case, twenty-nine of the forty-eight states admitted illegally seized evidence. Today, twenty-four of the fifty do so, including New York, Connecticut and New Jersey.

The decision today effectively wipes out the local practice in the latter group of states. From now on in New York, for example, a defendant in a narcotics case will be able to move for exclusion of evidence of heroin found in his home on the ground that the police had no warrant or other legal basis for the search that produced the evidence.

Justice Tom C. Clark wrote the opinion of the court today. He was joined by Chief Justice Earl Warren and Justices Hugo L. Black, William O. Douglas and William J. Brennan Jr.

A dissent by Justice John Marshall Harlan was joined in by Justices Felix Frankfurter and Charles E. Whittaker. Justice Potter Stewart did not reach the search-and-seizure question but joined the majority for other reasons.

The decision does not directly affect the wiretapping problem.

In recent years the Supreme Court has held that the Communications Act of 1934 bars all tapping. But it has construed the same statute to let the state courts admit illegal wiretap evidence.

The court held in 1928 that tapping was not a search or seizure covered by the Constitution. That 5-to-4 decision has been much attacked. If it were ever overruled, the fruits of illegal tapping would be barred.

The case decided today arose from the prosecution of a Cleveland boarding house owner, Dollree Mapp, under an Ohio law making it a crime to possess obscene literature.

In 1957 three policemen went to Miss Mapp's house to look for gambling materials. They entered without a search warrant. When she resisted, they handcuffed her. They found no gambling material, but they did find some obscene books that she said belonged to a tenant.

The seized books were admitted at Miss Mapp's trial and she was convicted. She drew a sentence of from one to seven years.

It is always unusual for the Supreme Court to overrule one of its earlier decisions. But the result today was the more surprising because the search-and-seizure question had hardly been mentioned in the briefs and oral argument.

The major argument had been that the state law was unconstitutional. This law makes possession of obscene matter a crime even though it is not to be shown to anyone else. In fact, a majority of the Ohio Supreme Court thought the law unconstitutional but did not overturn it because of a peculiar Ohio

rule requiring a special majority to strike down a state statute.

One basis for Justice Harlan's dissent was a charge that the majority had "reached out" to decide a point not even argued before it. He observed that Miss Mapp's lawyer, in the oral argument, had said that he had never even heard of the Wolf case.

By deciding so important a question without real argument, Justice Harlan said, "our voice becomes only a voice of power, not of reason."

Justice Clark said simply that the Wolf case had been criticized ever since it was decided in 1949. He remarked that "no term of court ever passes that someone doesn't holler Wolf."

One reason given for overruling the Wolf decision was that some of its own arguments had weakened. Two of these arguments were that a majority of states preferred to admit illegal evidence and that there were other ways to deal with illegal searches besides excluding their fruits.

In fact, Justice Clark said, some states have found since 1949 that any remedies but exclusion of evidence are "worthless and futile, and they have decided despite strong police protest to rule out the fruits of illegal searches."

Justice Clark said that it was common sense and morality to require the same rule for Federal and state trials. He said that re-examination of the Wolf case had led the majority "to close the only courtroom door remaining open to evidence secured by official lawlessness."

'Ignoble Short Cut'

"The ignoble short cut to conviction left open to the state," he said, "tends to destroy the entire system of constitutional restraints on which the liberties of the people rest."

Justice Harlan, for the three dissenters, said that, quite the contrary, the nature of the American political system counseled against imposing rigid Federal restraints on local police practices. He called the decision "bewildering, unfortunate, ill-considered, far-reaching."

Justice Stewart agreed to the reversal of Miss Mapp's conviction, but without considering the search-and-seizure question. He found the Ohio obscenity law unconstitutional.

The case was argued for Miss Mapp by A. L. Kearns of Cleveland and, on behalf of the American Civil Liberties Union, Bernard A. Berkman of Cleveland. The state was represented by Mrs. Gertrude Bauer Mahon of Cleveland.

LIMIT ON SEARCHES SCORED BY POLICE

The Police Commissioners of Philadelphia and New York charged yesterday that a 1961 Supreme Court decision limiting the power of search and seizure was an obstacle to law enforcement.

A judge and a prosecutor supported the decision, however.

The decision in question was made last year in the case of Mapp v. Ohio. The high court held that evidence obtained illegally was not admissible in state courts. The ruling was the main topic yesterday at a seminar of the Academy of Police Science at the Fordham Law School, 140 West 62d Street.

Commissioner Albert N. Brown of Philadelphia, who received the academy's 1962 Honor Award said the decision had adversely affected his department's work. New York's Commissioner, Michael J. Murphy, said it had puzzled and frustrated many of his men.

But Justice Nathan R. Sobel of the State Supreme Court told the officials that laws could be properly enforced by obtaining search and arrest warrants. Assistant District Attorney H. Richard Uviller of New York County said he favored the ruling.

A Brooklyn lawyer, William W. Kleinman, said agents of the Federal Bureau of Investigation and Treasury Department "have been laboring under these restrictions for many years and are doing an excellent job."

SUPREME COURT EXTENDS RULING ON FREE COUNSEL

Holds States Must Provide Lawyers for All Poor in Serious Criminal Cases

REVERSES 1942 DECISION

Unanimous Opinion Could Permit Many Now Jailed to Ask New Trials

By ANTHONY J. LEWIS
Special to The New York Times.

WASHINGTON, March 18 The Supreme Court held today that the states must supply free lawyers to all poor persons facing serious criminal charges.

The court unanimously overruled its own 1942 decision in the landmark case of Betts v. Brady. There the ruling was that the Constitution required appointed counsel only in cases involving a death sentence or "special circumstances," such as an illiterate defendant.

Justice Hugo L. Black, who dissented in 1942, wrote the opinion for the majority today. He said Betts v. Brady was incorrectly decided.

"Reason and reflection," Justice Black said, "require us to recognize that in our adversary system of criminal justice any person haled into court who is too poor to hire a lawyer cannot be assured a fair trial unless counsel is provided for him.

This seems to us to be an obvious truth."

The decision, one of the most important ever made by the Supreme Court in the criminal law field, was provoked by Clarence Earl Gideon, a 52-year-old inmate of the Florida State Prison.

Gideon was convicted of breaking and entering the Bay Harbor Poolroom in Panama City, Fla., with intent to commit petty larceny. He asked for a lawyer at his trial but was turned down.

The Florida Supreme Court rejected a habeas corpus petition from Gideon. He then sent a hand-written petition to the United States Supreme Court, which agreed to hear the case and to reconsider the correctness of Betts v. Brady.

At present only five states have no regular provision for appointment of counsel except in capital cases—those with possible death sentences. These states are Florida, Alabama, Mississippi and North and South Carolina.

In a number of other states, however, appointing practices vary according to localities, with no regular provision in less populous areas for non-capital cases. And quite a few states do not provide counsel in misdemeanors or petty offenses.

Thus today's decision could have a great impact across the country. Among other things it could permit many thousands of persons now in prison to demand new trials.

Justice Black's opinion did not say whether the new constitutional doctrine was to be applied to those already jailed. But there was nothing to indicate that others in Gideon's position could not seek their release on habeas corpus as he did, because he had no lawyer at his trial.

Florida estimated, in this case, that perhaps 5,000 prisoners in her jails had had no lawyers at their trials and might ask for release. The state made this a strong ground for pleading with the court not to overturn Betts v. Brady.

One restriction on the effect of the decision may be the doctrine of waiver—the rule that a man may waive his right to a lawyer by not demanding one. Gideon specifically asked for a lawyer at this trial, but many prisoners may not have done so.

Justice Black's opinion did not settle, either, whether the new rule will apply to the most petty crimes, such as traffic offenses. That will presumably be worked out in later cases.

Justice John Marshall Harlan, in a concurring opinion, said he agreed that Betts v. Brady should be overruled but thought it deserved "a more respectful burial" than Justice Black's opinion saying it was wrong to start with.

Justice Harlan was persuaded by the fact that the Supreme Court in recent years had repeatedly found "special circumstances" requiring counsel. He said that "to continue a rule which is honored by this court only with lip service is not a healthy thing."

Justice Tom C. Clark also filed a separate concurrence, based on his conclusion that the Constitution made no distinction between capital and non-capital crimes.

In several other cases today the court took major steps to provide new protections for state criminal defendants.

It held, 6 to 3, that when a state provides a right to appeal criminal convictions, it must supply counsel on appeal for indigents. The dissenters were Justices Harlan, Clark and Potter Stewart.

The Justices divided 5 to 4 in deciding that Washington State had not given two prisoners an adequate record of their trial as a basis for appeal. Justice Byron White wrote the dissent, joined by Justices Harlan, Clark and Stewart.

A unanimous decision struck down an Indiana procedure under which the public defender might prevent a poor man from appealing by declaring the appeal frivolous.

By a vote of 6 to 3, with Justices Harlan, Clark and Stewart dissenting, the court held that Federal courts may release on habeas corpus a state prisoner who was turned down in the state courts because he failed to follow required procedure.

This case, which has great significance for the relations of state and Federal courts, involved Charles Noia of New York, serving a life sentence for murder.

Two co-defendants of Noia's were eventually released because confessions were found to have been coerced from all three. But Noia had never appealed — because, he said, he feared a death sentence in a new trial.

The New York courts said this failure to appeal barred any relief for him after his two co-defendants went free. The Supreme Court said today that, whatever restricted the New York judiciary, Federal courts could and should free Noia.

Finally, by a vote of 5 to 4, the court said an Indiana prisoner should have a full hearing before a Federal court on his assertion that he had confessed after he was given a "truth serum" drug.

The dissenters—Justices Stewart, Harlan, Clark and White —agreed that a confession obtained by drugs would be invalid. But they said the prisoner had had ample chance to prove his claim in the state criminal proceedings, failed and should not be given a new chance in the Federal courts.

This barrage of criminal law decisions, especially the Gideon case, should spur state efforts to set up new methods of providing counsel for indigents.

Attorney General Robert Kennedy has asked Congress for comprehensive legislation to provide counsel and other services for the poor in Federal courts.

March 19, 1963

States' Powers to Arrest Curbed by Supreme Court

Special to The New York Times

WASHINGTON, June 10—State law enforcement officers were told by the Supreme Court today that they are subject to the same constitutional limits as Federal officers

The Court's opinion, by Justice Tom C. Clark, was a follow-up to one he wrote two years ago. The Court held then that state courts must exclude evidence obtained by illegal searches and seizures, as the Federal courts have been required to do since 1914.

The question today was in making arrests, searches and seizures.

The 8-to-1 decision was significant for the police and prosecutors across the country. It means that thousands of local criminal cases will now be subject to the Supreme Court's scrutiny in potentially great detail.

whether state proceedings are subject to the same standards as Federal cases. In the past the Supreme Court has developed intricate standards of what is an "unreasonable" search or seizure prohibited by the Fourth Amendment.

Justice Clark said yes—that the states were now subject to "the same constitutional standard prohibiting unreasonable search and seizures."

This means that all the Supreme Court's past constitutional decisions on what is or is not permissible in arrests and searches are now applicable to the states.

Justice John Marshall Harlan, dissenting, said the decision threatened to put the states in a "constitutional straitjacket."

Instead, he said, the Court should apply only a general standard of fairness to state searches and seizures, letting the states work out their own detailed rules beyond that minimum constitutional requirement.

The dissenting opinion added that the states might now "be placed in an atmosphere of uncertainty since this Court's decisions in the realm of search and seizure are hardly notable for their predictability."

In the case decided today, Justice Harlan noted, the eight Justices in the majority could not agree on whether the particular state's search and seizure had violated the newly imposed constitutional standards.

While the Justices were 8 to 1 on the proposition that state enforcement officers are subject to the same constitutional limits as Federal officers, they did not agree on the disposition of the case involved.

The eight who voted as above were divided 4 to 4 on whether, in the case they were hearing, the challenged police practices had violated the standards imposed by their 8-to-1 vote.

Thus, with Justice Harlan voting to uphold the challenged practices the convictions of Mr. and Mrs. George Ker of California were confirmed.

Los Angeles police officers saw Ker meet a suspected marijuana peddler, found Ker's address by his automobile license and went to the apartment without either an arrest or a search warrant.

The police got a pass key from the building manager and walked in on Mr. and Mrs. Ker without warning. They found some marijuana, seized it and arrested the Kers. On the basis of the marijuana as evidence, they were convicted on narcotics charges.

Justice Clark noted the long-standing rule that arrests without a warrant are lawful if there is "probable cause" to believe a crime is being committed. Similarly, searches "incident to a lawful arrest" are constitutional.

The Clark opinion found that the arrest of Mr. and Mrs. Ker and the seizure of the marijuana met these tests. Joining in this view were Justices Hugo L. Black, Potter Stewart and Byron R. White.

Justice William J. Brennan Jr. wrote a dissent that was joined by Chief Justice Earl Warren and Justices William O. Douglas and Arthur J. Goldberg.

This opinion took the view that the arrest of the Kers had violated their constitutional rights because of the police officers' "unannounced intrusion into their apartment."

Since the arrest was illegal, the opinion said, the evidence was inadmissible.

Justice Clark conceded that in one recent Federal case the Court had condemned a surreptitious police entry into an apartment. But he said that decision had been based not on the Constitution but on the Court's general supervisory power over Federal law enforcement, not applicable to state proceedings.

In a portion of the opinion supported by eight Justices, Justice Clark said the Federal standards of constitutionality now applicable to the states were not so strict as to be "procrustean," a reference to the Greek myth about the host who trimmed or stretched his guests to fit their beds.

He said the findings of trial courts would be given weight. But he warned that the Supreme Court would re-examine the facts itself in search and seizure when necessary to protect individual rights.

Today's decision does not affect the legal status of wiretapping in the states. This is because the Supreme Court held in 1928, in a 5-4 decision still much criticized, that a wiretapping is not a "search" covered by the Fourth Amendment.

Apart from the Constitution, a Federal statute prohibits wiretapping and disclosure of messages. The Supreme Court has construed this as excluding wiretapping evidence in Federal but not in state courts.

The Department of Justice has always interpreted this to permit wiretapping by Federal agents in national security matters so long as messages are not disclosed in court or elsewhere. The taps are attached by the Federal Bureau of Investigation on authorization by the Attorney General.

The case was argued for the Kers by Robert W. Stanley or Los Angeles and for the state by Gordon Ringer, deputy Attorney General of California.

Supreme Court Ruling Steps Up Legal Aid for Poor Defendants

Legislatures, Tribunals and Bar Groups of Many States Are Meeting or Going Beyond Decision to Provide Lawyers

_By ANTHONY LEWIS
Special to The New York Times

WASHINGTON, June 28 — Last March 18 the Supreme Court laid down a new constitutional rule that the states must provide free lawyers for all poor persons facing serious criminal charges.

In the three months since, the decision has had widespread effects. A survey of the 50 states shows actions by legislatures, courts and bar groups that meet or go beyond the court's requirements. Here are some highlights:

¶Three states have moved, by legislation, toward the use of public defenders—lawyers employed by the state to represent indigent criminal defendants.

¶In four states that formerly did not guarantee counsel for the poor except in capital cases, varying steps are being taken to appoint lawyers in all felony trials.

¶In several states that had provided lawyers for the poor at felony trials, that provision is being extended to lesser crimes and to some pre-trial and post-conviction proceedings.

¶Reaction to the Supreme Court decision has been almost entirely favorable, even in states that have long resisted a counsel guarantee and among lawyers now carrying the burden of appointment to defend the poor.

1942 Ruling Overturned

The March decision overruled one in 1942 in which the Court refused to lay down an absolute requirement of counsel in state criminal cases. Instead the 1942 ruling required counsel only where there were "exceptional circumstances," such as an illiterate defendant.

Over the years the Court had found such circumstances more and more often in particular cases. It surprised almost nobody when it took the final step in March and laid down the general rule.

Many states had long expected the decision. In all but five, any poor felony defendant who had insisted on a lawyer at his trial was almost certain to have one provided.

Only 24 states, however, guaranteed the right to counsel in misdemeanor cases. There were widely varying practices as to counsel at pre-trial hearings and on appeals.

In all these areas the March decision is being felt. In addition, in a subtle way, the court's speaking out on the right to counsel seems to have focused attention on the issue and caused new thinking on ways to improve the defense of the indigent.

Perhaps the most dramatic reaction to the March decision was in the state from which the case had come, Florida.

Florida Finally Acts

For years the Florida Legislature, dominated by rural conservatives, had refused to do anything about counsel for the poor except in cases involving the death penalty. In recent years the Supreme Court had been getting more cases from Florida charging injustice in trials without lawyers than any other state.

Last month, under the impact of the Court decision, the Florida Legislature adopted a law creating a public defender in each of the state's 16 judicial circuits.

Although counsel for the state had vigorously defended its position in the Supreme Court, decrying an absolute counsel guarantee as "socialism," Gov. Farris Bryant spoke favorably of the decision.

"In this era of social consciousness," he told the Legislature, "it is unthinkable that an innocent man may be condemned to penal servitude because he is unfamiliar with the intricacies of criminal procedure and unable to provide counsel for his defense."

Governor Bryant, urging the Public Defender Law, said the Court decision had made its passage essential not only "to protect the innocent," but "in order that valid judgments of guilty may be entered and criminals kept confined for the protection of society."

Concern Arises

That comment reflected a concern that the March decision would be applied to men in prison, requiring that all those tried without counsel in the past be given new trials.

The Supreme Court has not said whether the decision will be given retroactive effect.

Florida estimates that 5,000 of its 8,000 prisoners had no lawyers at their trials. If all had to receive new trials, the impact on the legal system would be enormous.

The Florida prisoner whose case brought the Supreme Court decision has yet to benefit from it. He is Clarence E. Gideon, 52 years old, who was convicted of breaking into the Bay Harbor poolroom in Panama City. He received a five-year sentence. At his trial he had repeatedly asked for a lawyer, but was turned down.

From the state penitentiary in Raiford, Gideon filed a petition for habeas corpus with the State Supreme Court. When that was turned down, he filed a handwritten petition for review in the United States Supreme Court, which granted it.

Gideon is due to have a new trial next Friday. He will be represented by a lawyer from the American Civil Liberties Union.

The states that formerly provided no counsel in noncapital cases, in addition to Florida, were Alabama, Mississippi and North and South Carolina. In all, methods of assuring counsel have been or are being adopted.

The North Carolina Legislature has just approved an appropriation of $500,000 a year to pay lawyers assigned to represent the poor. Judges will make the assignments from lists, prepared by county bar associations, of lawyers with experience in criminal practice.

In Alabama, Mississippi and South Carolina, local bar associations are preparing rosters of lawyers available for appointment to represent the indigent.

Alabama Plan Drafted

A committee of the Alabama bar is drafting for early submission to the Legislature a plan for a system of appointments and compensation for those appointed.

Bar groups in Mississippi are working toward the Legislature's appropriation of funds for appointed counsel by next year.

The reaction in these Southern states has been surprisingly favorable to the Gideon decision.

In Mississippi, Howard McDonnell of Biloxi, chairman of the state bar's criminal law committee, told a meeting last week that the decision was "far sighted."

"Our penitentiary is loaded with inmates who are there because of no representation or improper representation," he said. He criticized the use of young, inexperienced lawyers to represent indigents, and said the Gideon case could be a catalyst to improve criminal law.

R. Mayne Albright of Raleigh, N. C., head of the Wake County Bar Association, said:

"I think few lawyers would disagree with the principle enunciated by the Supreme Court. It was time we recognized the need for the defendant who is indigent to have a lawyer."

James J. Carter, head of the Alabama Bar Association, said some lawyers had opposed the Gideon decision, but "it has been accepted even by those who disagree."

The day of the Gideon decision the Supreme Court held in a companion case that states must also provide a lawyer to handle an appeal by a convicted indigent.

Response by Oregon

In direct response to that ruling, the Oregon Legislature has just created the office of Public Defender to handle all indigent appeals and post-conviction proceedings, such as habeas corpus actions.

Poor defendants will continue to be represented at their trials in Oregon by court-appointed counsel, rather than a public defender.

In this year's session the Colorado Legislature passed a local-option public defender law. It authorized any county to use the system at its own expense. None has yet established a public defender office.

The Kansas Supreme Court adopted a rule April 16 requiring trial courts to appoint counsel to conduct the appeal of any poor man convicted of a crime.

In Nevada the State Supreme Court has asked the Legislature to authorize the appointment of counsel to carry on habeas corpus and similar post-conviction proceedings for poor prisoners, and to authorize funds to compensate the lawyers.

The Minnesota Legislature, for the first time, voted this session to provide funds for appointed counsel who represent the poor in appeals and post-conviction proceedings.

Justice Hugo L. Black, in giving the Court's opinion in the Gideon case, did not discuss whether the right to counsel applied in misdemeanor and more serious cases. But there is a wide impression in the states that the rule will, at some point, be applied to misdemeanors. Some states have begun to move on this assumption.

Chief Justice Charles L. Terry Jr. of the Delaware Supreme Court has called a conference of all lower-court judges to extend to misdemeanor cases the system of appointing counsel.

The New Hampshire Legislature is expected to pass a bill removing from the law a provision that counsel need be appointed only in cases involving possible sentences of three years or more.

When to Provide Lawyer?

The bill was drafted in response to the Gideon decision. New Hampshire judges, by practice, have often made appointments in lesser cases.

A bill before the Vermont Legislature would change a state law allowing compensation for attorneys appointed in felony cases to cover any criminal charge carrying a possible sentence of six months or more.

Another issue not reached by Justice Black in the Gideon opinion was at what stage in the criminal proceeding must a poor defendant be given a lawyer. Is the trial soon enough, or must there be a lawyer earlier?

In a decision later in its term the Court held that a Maryland prisoner should have had a lawyer at his first preliminary hearing after arrest. He had to plead then, and thus the hearing was a vital stage requiring counsel, the Court held.

In response to this decision the Baltimore Municipal Court, which holds preliminary hearings in cases later tried in the higher courts, held an emergency meeting with local bar leaders.

The Bar Association of Baltimore agreed to draw a list of lawyers to represent indigents in the lowest courts. Lawyers have even been provided in serious traffic cases, such as charges of driving while drunk.

The association intends to look over the situation after some time and recommend a permanent solution. But its president, Leon H. A. Pierson, is certain that representation

at the lowest court level will be required in the future.

"We are looking toward where the Supreme Court is pointing," he said, "or where if it isn't pointing, it should be."

In Iowa and Rhode Island, steps are also being taken to provide lawyers at pre-trial stages of criminal proceedings.

Burden on Lawyers Seen

Reports from many states indicate concern about the burden of unpaid representation on members of the bar. This characteristic comment came from Chief Justice Joseph Weintraub of New Jersey:

"Assigning lawyers to represent indigents does create an unfair burden on the bar, and I think we have reached the point where serious consideration must be given to a substitute program. The bar has been doing a fine job, but it, alone, should not be required to pick up the tab."

An Arizona lawyer made the point that those lawyers "best able financially to handle these

indigent cases are the last ones to be appointed."

In other states the use of young, inexperienced attorneys to represent the poor is being criticized as unfair to them and the defendants.

A majority of states provide compensation for appointed lawyers, but usually it is meager Payment ranges from as low as $10 a day in Kansas to $1,500 for a capital case in New York. The New York sum could amount to little on a daily basis, and there is no compensation in non-capital cases.

At least half a dozen states are considering the use of paid public defenders to reduce the burden on the bar. Public defenders are now used in Indiana, Connecticut, California, Illinois and about ten other states.

The alternative of compensating assigned counsel adequately and covering out-of-pocket expenses, is being pressed elsewhere. In Kansas, Attorney General William M. Ferguson

has urged assigned lawyers to keep track of their expenses and time spent, and to file claims with the Legislature.

All over the country complaints are heard about the failure of Federal courts to pay any compensation or expenses to assigned counsel. The problem is the more severe because Federal criminal cases tend to be longer and more difficult to try.

The Administration is strongly supporting legislation to let Federal District courts pay appointed counsel or have public defenders. The bill is before the House Judiciary Committee, with a decision expected shortly.

How to provide adequate representation for the poor is the subject of a nationwide study directed by the American Bar Foundation. State bar committees are cooperating.

In addition the Ford Foundation has granted $2,300,000 to the National Legal Aid and Defender Association to set up model programs.

June 30, 1963

USE OF CONFESSION IN TRIAL IS CURBED

Court Bars It as Evidence if Suspect Can't See Lawyer or Is Not Told of Rights

Special to The New York Times
WASHINGTON, June 22 — A 5-to-4 majority of the Supreme Court placed a sharp new restriction today on the use of confessions in criminal trials.

If the police focus on a principal suspect, the Court said, and question him without letting him see his lawyers or without warning him that his answers may be used against nim, any resulting confession must be barred from evidence.

Justice Arthur J. Goldberg wrote the decision, which is likely to have broad effects on law enforcement across the

country. The ruling was based on the integrity of the right to counsel—a right applied in full force just last year to state as well as to Federal trials.

A strong dissent by Justice Byron R. White was joined by Justices Tom C. Clark and Potter Stewart. Justice John Marshall Harlan dissented separately, and Justice Stewart also wrote his own dissenting opinion.

"I do not suggest for a moment that law enforcement will be destroyed by the rule announced today," Justice White said. "The need for peace and order is too insistent for that.

"But it will be crippled and its task made a great deal more difficult—all, in my opinion, for unsound, unstated reasons which can find no home in any of the provisions of the Constitution."

In a second case today, a different 5-to-4 majority struck down the New York procedure for determining whether a defendant's confession is voluntary. The same approach is used at least occasionally by 14 oth-

er states and by a number of Federal courts.

Under the New York rule, the issue of voluntariness is left to the jury. The jury considers the confession at the end of the case, along with other evidence, and is supposed to disregard the confession if it finds the circumstances involuntary.

Justice White, joined by Chief Justice Earl Warren and Justices Goldberg, William O. Douglas and William J. Brennan Jr., said this approach allowed other and possibly prejudicial matters to get into the jury's consideration of voluntariness.

The four justices in dissent approved the New York rule, which the Supreme Court had upheld as recently as 1953. They were Justices Clark, Stewart, Harlan and Hugo L. Black. Each, except Justice Stewart, wrote his own dissent.

Fears Release of Hundreds

Justice Black said in his that today's decision could lead to the release from prison of "hundreds" of persons who were convicted on confessions admitted under the New York rule.

Justice Harlan, in his dissent, criticized what he termed the majority's decision to apply its new doctrine retrospectively— to prior convictions.

The question of retrospective application figured in yet another matter decided by the Court today.

With dissent only from Justice Harlan, the Court left standing a decision of the Court of Appeals for the Second Circuit applying to past convictions the 1963 Supreme Court decision that the states must provide counsel for poor criminal defendants.

The Second Circuit made its ruling in a case involving prisoners held for long terms in New York as multiple offenders. Some of their earlier convictions had been in other states, where they had no counsel, and the Second Circuit said they were thus entitled to resentencing in New York.

The first confession case today came from Illinois. Danny Escobedo had been arrested on suspicion of the murder of his brother-in-law but released after his lawyer obtained a writ of habeas corpus

Ten days later Escobedo was arrested again, after an alleged accomplice had implicated him. He was questioned at police headquarters later at night until, finally, he confessed.

While he was being questioned, in handcuffs, his lawyer—told of the arrest by Escobedo's family—came to headquarters and tried to see him. The police would not allow a visit until after the questioning had been concluded.

It was also shown that no one had advised Escobedo, a 22-year-old man of Mexican extraction, of his constitutional right to remain silent.

Justice Goldberg found, on these facts, that Escobedo's right to counsel had been violated. His opinion also contained some general strictures against police dependence on confessions.

"We have learned the lesson of history, ancient and modern," he said, "that a system of criminal law enforcement which comes to depend on the "confession" will, in the long run, be less reliable and more subject to abuses than a system which depends on extrinsic evidence independently secured through skillful investigation."

"We hold only," he concluded, "that when the process shifts from investigatory to accusatory—when its focus is on the accused and its purpose is to elicit a confession—our adversary system begins to operate and, under the circumstances here, the accused must be permitted to consult with his lawyer."

Justice White said today's decision was "another major step in the direction of the goal which the Court seemingly has in mind—to bar from evidence all admissions obtained from an individual suspected of crime, whether involuntarily made or not."

The case on the New York rule for determining the voluntariness of confessions involved Nathan Jackson, convicted of killing a policeman in a gun duel in New York City.

Jackson, who was wounded, was questioned by the police while under the influence of drugs in a hospital. His confession was found voluntary by a jury and used against him.

The New York procedure cannot provide a "reliable" test of a confession's voluntary character, Justice White said, because the jury has so many other confusing matters before it.

Justice White said a trial judge must find a confession voluntary before letting the jury see it. Then, he said, the jury could still decline to rely on it if it chose.

The court did not grant Jackson an immediate new trial. It held that the New York courts could re-examine the voluntariness of his confession independently and then, only if they found the statement coerced, grant a new trial.

Barry L. Kroll of Chicago argued for Escobedo, and Seymour H. Bucholz of Chicago appeared on his side as a friend of the court, speaking for the American Civil Liberties Union. On the other side was James R. Thompson, assistant state's attorney.

Daniel G. Collins of New York represented Jackson, and William I. Siegel, assistant district attorney in Brooklyn, the state.

June 23, 1964

The Case Of 'Trial By Press'

By ANTHONY LEWIS

WASHINGTON.

A QUESTION that has long nagged at the conscience of Americans concerned about justice is posed most acutely by the report of the Warren Commission on the assassination of President Kennedy: Does this country's practice of unbridled liberty for the press, radio and television to report on pending criminal cases permit any man charged with a notorious crime to get a fair trial?

Chief Justice Earl Warren and his six colleagues on the commission were highly critical of what happened after the arrest of Lee Harvey Oswald. In the corridors of the Dallas Police Headquarters reporters and cameramen were so numerous and unruly that witnesses could hardly get through. Under the pressures of the press, officials repeatedly disclosed damaging evidence and said Oswald's guilt was certain. A desire to please the press was one reason for the ill-handled transfer that led to Oswald's murder. If he had lived, the commission said, his "opportunity for a trial by 12 jurors free of preconception as to his guilt or innocence would have been seriously jeopardized by the premature disclosure and weighing of the evidence against him."

What happened in Dallas last November was an extreme case. But the American Bar Association was stating the obvious when it observed, in a comment condemning conditions in Dallas, that "excessive and prejudicial publicity with respect to criminal cases is not unusual in America."

Everyone knows, as Justice Arthur J. Goldberg said recently, that the American press commonly uses "labels such as 'killer,' 'robber,' 'hoodlum' . . . to describe the accused weeks before and even on the eve of the trial." Thirteen years ago, a predecessor of his on the Court, Justice Robert H. Jackson, said that "trial by newspaper" was "one of the worst menaces to American justice."

Since Justice Jackson's day, television has emerged as a potentially even more searching intruder into the criminal process. The bar and most courts have steadfastly resisted demands for admission of TV cameras to trials because they believe such broadcasting would make the process of determining guilt still more a public spectacle and less the quiet inquiry the law intended it to be. Even without entry into the courtroom, television can outdo the newspaper in pretrial comment on criminal cases.

Even before the tragedy in Dallas, concern about the conflict between free press and fair trial had been growing. A number of newspapers were criticizing excesses on the part of their profession or by broadcasters. As for the bar, its prevailing sentiment was probably expressed by Federal District Judge Hubert L. Will of Illinois in this 1963 comment:

"The press, even when it reports crimes and criminal trials with reasonable thoroughness and accuracy—which is seldom—too often in the very process encroaches upon and subverts the constitutional right to a fair trial by an impartial jury."

The argument on the other side has also been vigorously pressed. A major contention is that the press helps to prevent official abuses by its close watch on criminal cases. J. Russell Wiggins, editor of The Washington Post, mentioning such police practices as the third degree, said: "These conditions much more menace the right of accused persons than pretrial disclosures in the press. . . . Newspaper publicity is the best way of treating these abuses."

AS for the performance in Dallas specifically, it has been defended by numerous editors, among them Mr. Wiggins's colleague on The Post, Alfred Friendly. He made the point that the press is fiercely competitive and that when some reporters moved in aggressively on the Dallas police, the others could hardly afford to be gentlemen. He seemed to be saying that there is a kind of Gresham's Law of the press, with the tawdry and sensational driving out the responsible.

Mr. Friendly argued also, as many others have, that it was basically up to the authorities in Dallas to lay down the rules—not up to the press. He said: "The press was not pretty in Dallas. But it may not

be fair to accuse it for failure to embrace a system that was not its to prescribe."

The Warren Commission was not insensitive to the point. It said that "primary responsibility for having failed to control the press and to check the flow of undigested evidence to the public must be borne by the [Dallas] Police Department."

BUT the commission also said that the disorder in Police Headquarters disclosed "a regrettable lack of self-discipline by the newsmen." Looking past the immediate incidents to a broader moral, the commission concluded:

"The experience in Dallas during Nov. 22-24 is a dramatic affirmation of the need for steps to bring about a proper balance between the right of the public to be kept informed and the right of the individual to a fair and impartial trial."

In considering how to balance these sometimes conflicting interests, it is well to put to one side first a slogan often shouted by press zealots: "The right to know." The phrase is used as if there were something in the Constitution, or in logic, that gave the press a right to demand the facts about anything.

There is no such abstract "right to know." The freedom of the press guaranteed in the Constitution, most students of the subject have agreed, is a freedom to publish — not a compulsion for everyone else to tell all to the press. Common sense supports that view. Surely reporters and television cameras have no "right" to be present at meetings of the National Security Council or conferences of the Supreme Court.

THERE is a *public* interest, as the Warren Commission phrased it, in being kept informed about criminal proceedings. This high interest is often cited by the press, but the desire to provide titillation and entertainment is usually the real motive for lofty demands to get the facts and admit the cameras. The honest argument for press entry in each case is that a useful social function will be served in the particular circumstances, not that the press has some "right."

The constitutional right that *is* involved here is the one guaranteed by the Sixth Amendment: "In all criminal prosecutions, the accused shall enjoy the right to a speedy and public trial, by an impartial jury. . . ."

The public trial, it should be noted, is for the benefit of "the accused," not of the press. Its purpose, in the minds of the Constitution's framers, was to prevent the former English practice — made infamous by the Star Chamber—of trying men *in camera,* without access to friends or public opinion.

"The public trial exists," Justice William O. Douglas explained a few years ago, "because of the aversion which liberty-loving people had toward secret trials and proceedings. That is the reason our courts are open to the public, not because the framers wanted to provide the public with recreation."

IT is the defendant who can demand a public trial, not the press. That was the holding of the New York courts in the case of Mickey Jelke, whose trial for sex offenses was held with the press excluded. Newspapers' demands to be admitted were rejected, but Jelke's own claim that he had a right to a trial in the open was sustained and his conviction reversed.

The Sixth Amendment's guarantee of "an impartial jury" is what gives concern about the performance of the American press. How can an impartial jury be found when the press and television and radio have been trumpeting for weeks ahead their certainty that a defendant is guilty?

The British deal with the problem in a clean-cut way. They punish for contempt of court virtually any publication about the defendant in a criminal case before trial except the bare fact of his arrest. And they punish severely. The editor of The Daily Mirror of London was sent to jail for

three months in 1949 for publishing details of alleged murders by a man just arrested. In 1961, The Daily Express was fined £5,000 ($14,000) for describing a suspect before his arrest.

The British are also severe on criticism of judges. Ronald Goldfarb, an American expert in this area, describes cases in which British publications were severely fined for having suggested that judges were less than wholly impartial — although their comments came after decision, when they could not possibly have affected the course of justice.

SUCH restrictions on the press cannot be squared with our written Constitution's broad assurance of the right to speak and write freely. Thus the Supreme Court, applying the First Amendment, has severely limited the power of courts to punish, as contempt, comments on pending criminal matters.

The leading case was decided in 1941. It involved public pressures applied to the courts from two contrasting sources —Harry Bridges, the cantankerous left-wing labor leader, and an editorial in The Los Angeles Times, a conservative newspaper.

Bridges had published a telegram denouncing a California court's decision in a labor case as "outrageous" and threatening a strike over it. The Times editorial dealt with the assault conviction of two union leaders — it called them "gorillas" — and demanded that they be sent to prison rather than put on probation. Both Bridges and The Times were held in contempt of court.

THE Supreme Court, by a vote of 5 to 4, set aside the contempt findings. Justice Hugo L. Black said the Constitution did not allow such punishment for comment on judicial proceedings unless the publication presented a "clear and present danger" of obstructing justice.

Under that difficult standard there is almost no chance of using contempt proceedings to discourage sensational pretrial publicity about criminal cases, no matter how severely the defendant's right to a fair trial may be hurt. Nor is there any sign that the Supreme Court may relax the standard, for Americans are wary of putting vaguely defined power in judges' hands to punish speech and writing.

Since the Bridges case, the damaging effects of publicity on criminal proceedings have become much more widely recognized. Justice Douglas, a strong believer in the Bridges rule, praised it in a 1960 speech, but then added:

"This is not to say that the influence of newspapers on trials should go unnoticed. At times the papers can arouse passions in a community so that no trial can be a fair one."

In the absence of direct control over press comment, the courts have been forced to other remedies. These are to delay a trial if a community has been saturated with adverse publicity about the defendant, or move the trial to another city.

Appellate courts are finding more and more often that convicted defendants could not have had a fair trial in the circumstances of publicity and that there should have been a change of venue. When this is decided at the appellate level, the result is to require a new trial, often long after the event.

The Supreme Court first reversed a conviction because of newspaper influence on a jury in 1959. That was a relatively narrow decision, involving a Federal trial in which jurors were shown to have read in the press material specifically excluded from evidence in the trial.

In 1961, the Supreme Court found an Indiana conviction unconstitutional because the jury had read numerous articles describing the defendant as a "mad-dog killer." This was followed in 1963 by a decision throwing out a Louisiana trial held after the defendant's alleged confession to the sheriff had been filmed and shown to the community on television three times. Justice Potter Stewart used the term "kangaroo-court proceedings" for that episode.

THE lower courts have got the message from the Supreme Court and are bearing down harder on trial by newspaper. Last summer, a Federal district judge in Ohio issued a writ of habeas corpus releasing Dr. Samuel Sheppard after 10 years in prison for the murder of his wife, on the ground —among others—that newspaper and broadcast intimations of his guilt before trial had fatally infected the proceedings with unfairness.

This technique — the setting aside of past convictions because of the influence of publicity—has obvious and serious deficiencies. If an innocent man really was railroaded to jail by public passion, it is not much cheer to him to have a new trial 10 years later. And the public may suffer as well as defendants. Years after a crime, at a new trial, it may be difficult or impossible for prosecutors to reassemble the evidence needed for conviction of even the guiltiest man.

For these reasons, there has been more and more thought about ways to stop the evil, not after it has had its effect, but before — to curtail indiscriminate, unfair publicity before criminal trials.

ONE course would be to move closer to the British system and curb irresponsible press or broadcast comments by contempt proceedings against those who make them. Retired Supreme Court Justice Felix Frankfurter, who dissented in the Bridges case, would have preferred this approach. He objected to the idea that, as he put it once, "while convictions must be reversed and miscarriages of justice result because the minds of jurors or potential jurors were poisoned, the prisoner is constitutionally protected in plying his trade."

But that does not seem a practical solution, for there is no discernible trend in the Supreme Court toward lessening the protections of freedom for the press. Some abuse goes along with freedom, the Court might say, but it must be handled in ways that do not lead to restriction and timidity.

The idea endorsed by the Warren Commission was "the promulgation of a code of professional conduct governing representatives of all news media" in reporting on pending criminal cases. This idea has had a good deal of attention in newspaper and broadcast circles, too.

With all deference, the proposal for a self-promulgated code is not very promising. It is likely to be ignored by those who sin most. H. L. Mencken disposed of the idea a generation ago when he wrote:

"Journalistic codes of ethics are all moonshine. . . . If American journalism is to be purged of its present swinishness and brought up to a decent level of repute—and God knows that such an improvement is needed—it must be accomplished by the devices of morals, not by those of honor. That is to say, it must be accomplished by external forces, and through the medium of penalties exteriorly afflicted."

ANOTHER course, which has attracted growing support, is for the courts to crack down on those more clearly within their disciplinary jurisdiction than the press — the prosecutors and defense lawyers and police who are the sources of the material printed or broadcast.

Senator Wayne Morse of Oregon and 10 other Senators introduced in the last Congress a bill along that line. It would punish as contempt, in Federal criminal cases, any disclosure by a Federal employe or defense attorney except of material already admitted as evidence. There would be a fine of $500 for violations.

A more sweeping proposal for legislation, state or Federal, has been put forward by Justice Bernard S. Meyer of the Supreme Court of Nassau County, N. Y. It would apply to newspapermen and broadcasters as well as lawyers and others involved in criminal trials. It would go into effect only when a defendant was to be tried by jury, the theory being that judges are less susceptible than laymen to influence by external forces.

THE Meyer proposal would flatly prohibit any disclosure of the existence of a confession, of the defendant's prior record and of similar damaging matters unless they were brought out at the trial. It would also ban any expression of opinion on the defendant's guilt or the credibility of evidence or witnesses.

Justice Meyer would go even further in a second section listing other practices which would not be automatically condemned but would be violations if a jury found that they threatened substantial prejudice to justice. Among these are interviews with victims of a crime, appeals to racial bias and publication of the names and addresses of jurors.

The theory is that such a statute would be constitutional because it would not put the press at the hazard of a judge's virtually undefined contempt power. Instead, there would be specific legislative findings that certain activities threaten the right to a fair trial, and all would be on notice to steer clear of these. The first, or mandatory, part of the statute would be more easily sustainable on this reasoning than the second section.

It can readily be seen that the Meyer proposal is a severe one. Yet it has attracted wide attention and support as worthy of consideration in light of the serious threat to fair trial in this country.

THE truth is that excessive pretrial publicity does flaw our generally civilized standards of criminal procedure. More of the press should recognize its responsibility and consider effective measures to prevent abuses instead of talking about "the right to know." Otherwise, there may come the external retribution of which Mencken spoke.

Judge Emory H. Niles—like Mencken a civilized Baltimorean—said recently:

"I believe that in the end there will be a popular revulsion as well as a judicial revulsion, a sharpening of the public conscience that will condemn the practice of entertainment and amusement through uncontrolled publication of gossip and scandal."

October 18, 1964

Bar Leader Finds High Court Too Lenient in Criminal Cases

Fears Recent Rulings Have Tipped Scales at Expense of the Public's Safety

By EDITH EVANS ASBURY

The president of the American Bar Association said yesterday that there was growing reason for the belief that recent Supreme Court decisions had tipped the scales of justice too far in favor of criminals at the expense of the public's safety.

As a result, Lewis F. Powell Jr., the A.B.A. president, said, "there are valid reasons for criminals to think that crime does pay, and that slow and fumbling justice can be evaded."

Mr. Powell, a Richmond attorney, addressed the annual meeting of the New York State Bar Association at the headquarters of the Association of the Bar of the City of New York, at 42 West 44th Street.

He cautioned that it was "unproductive and destructive to criticize the court itself" for performing its "historic function" of "protecting the constitutional rights of the individual against alleged unlawful acts of government."

However, the Supreme Court decisions that have, in recent years, strengthened the rights of accused persons have rendered the task of law enforcement more difficult at a time when crime is increasing at an alarming rate, he said.

"The right of society in general, and of each individual in particular, to be protected from crime must never be subordinated to other rights," Mr. Powell asserted.

"There is a growing body of opinion that the rights of law-abiding citizens are being subordinated. The pendulum may have swung too far in affording rights which are abused and misused by criminals."

Mr. Powell said there was a 10 per cent increase in crime in 1963 over the previous year and the trend continued in 1964 with a 13 per cent increase in the first nine months.

"The nature of the crimes committed is also disturbing," he continued, "with crimes of violence continuing to increase.

"The single most shocking statistic, documented in F.B.I. reports, is that since 1958 crime has been increasing five times faster than the population growth," he added.

Despite the annual cost in money and human misery, Mr. Powell said the American public seems apathetic about the crime situation.

"In a country which is said to stand on the threshold of the Great Society," Mr. Powell declared, it is incongruous that in some urban areas law-abiding citizens are unsafe in their homes and denied the privilege of using public streets and parks for fear of their personal safety.

'We Must Act Now'

This fear signifies a breakdown in the primary responsibility of government, which is "the duty to protect citizens in their persons and property from criminal conduct—whatever its source or cause," Mr. Powell said.

"Society cannot await the millennium when crime will lying causes have been removed," Mr. Powell said. "We must act now."

A major program to develop national standards for the administration of criminal justice was undertaken recently by the A.B.A. under the chairmanship of Chief Judge J. Edward Lumbard of the United States Court of Appeals for the Second Circuit.

The project, expected to require three years and cost $750,000 will consider "the entire spectrum of criminal justice," Mr. Powell said.

Another encouraging sign of attention to the problem of maintaining the proper balance between individual rights and the rights of the public, Mr. Powell said, is the new Office of Criminal Justice within the Department of Justice.

Also, he continued, Governor Rockefeller recently proposed "an imaginative anticrime program for New York," including a new penal code and a new school of criminal justice.

A number of other states are also re-examining their criminal codes, he said.

The State Bar Association elected Sidney B. Pfeifer of Buffalo, president, replacing Orison S. Marden of New York City. It also elected C. Everett Shults of Hornell as secretary and re-elected Robert C. Poskanzer of Albany treasurer.

The New York Times
Lewis F. Powell Jr.

January 30, 1965

JUSTICES EXPAND RIGHTS OF ACCUSED

By JOHN D. POMFRET
Special to The New York Times

WASHINGTON, April 5 — The Supreme Court held today that the Sixth Amendment's guarantee of the right of accused persons to be confronted with the witnesses against them applied to state criminal trials.

The Court said that the right was "fundamental" and was made obligatory on the states by the 14th Amendment.

The decision was another in a series of historic cases in which the Court gradually has been extending the protections of the Bill of Rights to state criminal proceedings.

Two years ago, the Court held that the Sixth Amendment's guarantee of the right to counsel was obligatory on the states. Last year it held that the Fifth Amendment's prohibition against self-incrimination also was made applicable to the states by the Fourteenth, which guarantees due process of law.

The Court announced the new doctrine in reversing a conviction in a Texas case, and then proceeded to apply it a second time in reversing a conviction in an Alabama case.

In both cases, under different circumstances, accused persons had been deprived of the right of cross-examination of witnesses against them.

The right of confrontation of witnesses has been held in past cases to include the right to cross-examine them. In the Texas case, Bob Granville Pointer was charged with having robbed Kenneth W. Phillips at gunpoint. Mr. Phillips gave testimony at a preliminary hearing at which Pointer was not represented by a lawyer. Mr. Phillips later moved from the state and was not present at Pointer's trial.

At the trial the prosecution introduced into evidence a transcript of Mr. Philip's testimony. The presiding state court judge overruled objections by Pointer's counsel to the procedure on the ground that Pointer was not being permitted to confront a witness against him.

The majority opinion in the Texas case, written by Justice Hugo L. Black, emphasized the importance of cross-examination. It also noted that in an earlier case the Court had held

that to deprive the accused of this right was a denial of the 14th Amendment's guarantee of due process of law.

The opinion went on to say that in light of the Court's decisions making the Sixth Amendment's guarantee of the right to counsel and the Fifth's against self-incrimination obligatory on the states, statements in other cases "generally declaring that the Sixth Amendment does not apply to the states can no longer be regarded as the law."

"We hold the petitioner," the Court further said, "was entitled to be tried in accordance with the protection of the confrontation guarantee of the Sixth Amendment, and that guarantee, like the right against compelled self-incrimination, is to be enforced against the states under the Fourteenth

Amendment according to the same standards that protect those personal rights against Federal encroachment."

In separate opinions, Justices John M. Harlan and Potter Stewart agreed with reversing the conviction, but said they would do so only on the basis that the procedure followed had deprived Pointer of due process of law guaranteed by the 14th Amendment.

Justice Arthur J. Goldberg wrote a separate opnion concurring with the six-member Court majority. He did so to explain his views on the issue of whether provisions of the Bill oof Rights were extended to the states by the 14th Amendment.

The Alabama case involved the conviction of Jesse Elliott Douglas on charges of assault with intent to murder. An alleged accomplice, whose appeal from a conviction in a separate

trial was pending, refused on the ground of possible self-incrimination to answer questions about a confession he had purportedly made.

The Supreme Court, in an opinion by Justice William J. Brennan Jr., said that Douglas had been deprived of his right of cross-examination.

Justices Harlan and Stewart concurred with the reversal of the conviction in this case, also, but objected to the reasoning of the seven-member majority on the same ground as in the Texas case.

Orville A. Harlan of Houston arued the Texas case for Pointer and Gilbert J. Pena, an assistant state attorney general, for the state. Charles Cleveland of Birmingham argued the Alabama case for Douglas and Paul T. Gish Jr., an assistant state attorney generl, for the state.

April 6, 1965

The Suspect Confesses— But Who Believes Him?

George Whitmore Jr. confessed to attempted rape and three murders. But one confession has been discredited and he recants the others. The case raises questions about how police obtain confessions — and prosecutors use them.

By SIDNEY E. ZION

AT 7:30 A.M. on April 24, 1964, George Whitmore Jr., a slow-witted 19-year-old Negro drift-er with no previous arrest record, was ushered into the back room of a Brooklyn police station. Within 22 hours, he had confessed to one attempted rape and three murders—that of Mrs. Minnie Edmonds, a Brooklyn charwoman, and the double killing of career girls Janice Wylie and Emily Hoffert, New York's most sensational crime in recent years.

Now, after two trials, a reversed conviction (in the attempted-rape case), a hung jury (in the Edmonds murder) and, most recently, a dismissed indictment (in the Wylie-Hoffert case), the Whitmore affair has become a *cause célèbre*.

Already it has seriously undermined the credibility of the New York Police Department and stained the reputations of the Manhattan and Brooklyn District Attorneys' offices. And for the future it promises to have an important impact on the revolution in criminal law now being forged by the Supreme Court of the United States.

That revolution reached its present high point last June—two months after Whitmore's arrest — when the Court issued a devastating, if limited, attack on the use of the confession, which has been the backbone of law enforcement in the United States. The Justices were concerned with a Chicagoan named Danny Escobedo, who had been convicted in 1960 of murdering his brother-in-law. They reversed the conviction on the grounds that his confession, while voluntary, had been made after he had been denied permission to see his lawyer.

The ruling sent shock waves through the nation's prosecutors. From public platforms and in private interviews, they charged that the Court was "coddling the criminal element" and "swinging the pendulum too far" in favor of defendants' rights as against the public's safety. And then George Whitmore Jr. came along and rained on their parade.

In a long harangue directed at a reporter, one of the top assistants of Manhattan District Attorney Frank S. Hogan explained the connection between the Escobedo and Whitmore cases. "Let me give you the perfect example of the importance of confessions in law enforcement," he said, leaning across his desk. "This, more than anything else, will prove how unrealistic and naive the Court is."

His finger punched the ... "Whitmore! The Whitmore case. Do you know that we had every top detective in town working on the Wylie-Hoffert murders and they couldn't find a clue. Not a clue!

"I tell you, if that kid hadn't confessed, we never would have caught the killer!"

Yet, last January, six months after this passionate statement, District Attorney Hogan dropped the charges against Whitmore for the Wylie-Hoffert murders (though the indictment was not quashed until May). In an affidavit filed in State Supreme Court he declared that Whitmore's confession had, upon investigation, been discredited. Shortly thereafter, another man, a drug addict named Richard Robles, was indicted for the murders. It will be a long time before the public can accept a confession without thinking of George Whitmore Jr.

• • •

THE Whitmore case began shortly after midnight on April 23, 1964. Frank Isola, a young patrol-

man, was walking his beat in the Brownsville section of Brooklyn, a neighborhood with a long history of criminal activity, when he heard a scream from an alleyway. The beam of his flashlight picked out a Negro who appeared to be molesting a heavy-set Spanish woman. He fired a shot, and the man ran.

After a fruitless four-block chase, Isola returned to interview the victim, Mrs. Elba Borrero. Isola has sworn that she gave him a detailed description of her assailant at that time.

Six hours later, Isola saw George Whitmore Jr. standing in the doorway of a laundromat. Whitmore asked what the shooting earlier had been about.

"Why?" asked Isola. "What do you know about it?"

"I heard the shots and then I saw a guy running down the street. He almost ran into me and he told me the cops were after him and could I hide him," Whitmore said.

Isola took Whitmore's name and walked away.

Twenty-four hours later, Patrolman Isola and Detective Richard Aidala found Whitmore in front of the same laundromat, where he was in the habit of meeting his brother before going to look for work. Whitmore was unemployed at the time. The officers asked him to accompany them to headquarters "to answer a few questions" as a possible witness in the case.

Whitmore agreed. "I figured I had to go if they asked me," he said. But when they got to the station house there were no questions. Instead, Whitmore was searched and placed behind a peep-hole door, and Mrs. Borrero was brought in to identify him, which she did.

Here the first note of mystery enters. Isola testified in court that by the time he first saw Whitmore, six hours after the attack, he had obtained from Mrs. Borrero a detailed description of the assailant: a 5-foot 9-inch, 165-pound Negro with pock-marked face, wearing a tan raincoat with the lapel button missing (Mrs. Borrero had pulled it off), black pants and a green hat.

Patrolman Isola said that when he talked to Whitmore that night he noticed that he had a pock-marked face, was wearing a tan raincoat with the lapel button missing and had on a green hat and black pants. Then why did he not arrest Whitmore at the time?

Because, he said, "I didn't think he was the man."

There are three possible explanations for this. First, Isola may have been put off because Whitmore is shorter (5 feet 5 inches) and thinner (140 pounds) than the description. But the officer did not offer this explanation, perhaps because the

prosecution was not anxious to stress the height and weight discrepancies.

Second, Isola may not have had the description he said he had. This seems most probable, since his own notes and the police reports do not reflect the details he testified to.

Finally, the patrolman may have been just incredibly negligent. This is the most logical explanation if we assume his testimony was truthful.

Regardless of which explanation one chooses to accept—with the possible exception of the last one—the fact that the arrest was not made the first night buttresses the defense contention that Whitmore was the victim of a frame-up.

IN any event, soon after Whitmore was identified by Mrs. Borrero—and it should be noted here that a peep-hole identification is notoriously suspect—he confessed, and in November, 1964, he was convicted of attempted rape. The evidence against him was powerful: his confession and the button that Mrs. Borrero had ripped from the coat of her attacker.

In his summation, Brooklyn Assistant District Attorney Sidney A. Lichtman thrust the button and Whitmore's coat before the jury and said: "We have nailed George Whitmore on the button, so to speak."

What Mr. Lichtman did not say was that he had an F.B.I. laboratory report which in no way connected the button to the coat Whitmore was wearing when arrested. While the report did not negate the possibility that the button could have come from the coat, it said that the remaining buttons were "different in size, design and construction" from the one Mrs. Borrero had pulled off the coat of her assailant. Moreover, Whitmore had maintained throughout that on the night Mrs. Borrero was attacked he was wearing his brother's raincoat, and not the one that he wore on the morning of his arrest.

Last February, the conviction was reversed with the consent of Brooklyn District Attorney Aaron E. Koota. In granting a new trial, the judge ruled that the prosecution had suppressed the F.B.I. report and that the jury was prejudiced. One juror testified that ugly racial slurs were made during deliberations and many jurors told the court that they had read about Whitmore's confessions to the three murders.

THE story of those confessions begins back at the Brooklyn police station on April 24, 1964, the day of Whitmore's arrest. By 10:30 that morning, he had confessed to the Borrero rape attempt. By noon, he had admitted the April 14 knife-slaying of Mrs. Edmonds. Then, at dusk, all the top brass of the New York City Police Department began to file into the 73rd Precinct in Brooklyn. The word had gone out: In this station house sat the perpetrator of one of the city's most sensational killings, the double murder of career-girls Janice Wylie and Emily Hoffert.

That brutal crime had stunned a town thought to be shockproof. On the morning of Aug. 28, 1963, Janice Wylie, the 23-year-old daughter of advertising executive Max Wylie and niece of author Philip Wylie, and her schoolteacher-roommate, Emily Hoffert, were found slashed to death in their East 88th Street apartment in Manhattan. Parents whose daughters were living on their own in the city were abruptly reminded that no neighborhood, however fashionable, was immune to violence, and the case touched off an unusual, if understandable, amount of hysteria.

Now, after eight months in which police had questioned 1,000 people, George Whitmore Jr. had confessed to the murders. At 4 A.M. on April 25, Chief of Detectives (now Chief Inspector) Lawrence J. McKearney announced to the press: "We've got the right guy; no question about it."

But Philip Wylie, far off in Honolulu, said skeptically: "It sounds to me like a guy who got scared into a confession. . . ."

And at his arraignment, Whitmore recanted all three confessions and charged that they had resulted from police brutality.

"That's ridiculous!" said a deputy inspector. But it is a story that Whitmore has clung to ever since.

ACCORDING to Whitmore's account, as soon as Mrs. Borrero identified him as her attacker, Detective Aidala and Patrolman Isola took him into a room and beat him "until I told 'em anything to get 'em off my back." He claims that everything he said after the beating—which he says was not repeated—resulted from the beating and from the fear of further beatings.

Aidala and Isola have denied the brutality charge. No one will ever know the truth. Policemen never admit to beating a man. To do so would mean instant expulsion from the department. Yet on many occasions appeals courts have thrown out confessions on the ground that they resulted from physical brutality. (For reasons they alone know, trial judges seldom rule out confessions.)

Whether or not Whitmore was beaten, the detectives who questioned him fit the tradition of interrogators to a fare-thee-well. The cliché calls for a "heavy" and a "buddy." The heavy fills the suspect with fear and the buddy puts him at ease—indeed, "saves" him from the heavy.

Detective Aidala is a big, burly man with hamlike hands and a tendency to lose his temper, as he occasionally did on the witness stand. Detective Joseph DiPrima, who entered the case at 8 A.M. on April 24, or, according to Whitmore, immediately after he was beaten, is calm, soft-spoken, fatherly. It was DiPrima who developed a 'rapport' with Whitmore—and took all three confessions.

"The boy told me," DiPrima said during a hearing into the voluntariness of Whitmore's confession to the Edmonds murder, "that I was nicer to him than his father ever was." Detective Aidala never made that claim.

FROM the point of view of district attorneys in general, the Whitmore case could not have come at a worse time—hard on the heels of the Escobedo decision. Although the Supreme Court was careful to limit its ruling to the particular circumstances—Escobedo's lawyer was actually at the police station, asking to see him, at the time of his confession — Justice Arthur J. Goldberg, writing for a five-man majority, went on to launch a blistering attack against confessions in general.

'A law-enforcement system that depends on the confession," he wrote, "is in the long run less reliable and more subject to abuses than a system which depends on extrinsic evidence independently secured through skillful investigation."

Does this mean that in the future the Court may rule that all suspects have a right to see a lawyer before the police can talk to them, whether they request counsel or not, and whether they can afford one or not? No one can be sure but the question itself is enough to turn district attorneys gray. If that should ever happen, most lawyers agree, confessions would disappear, because any lawyer worth his salt would advise his client to remain silent.

"No system worth preserving," answered Justice Goldberg, "should have to fear that if an accused is permitted to consult with a lawyer he will become aware of, and exercise, his constitutional rights."

But, contend the prosecutors, 75 to 80 per cent of all crimes are solved because of confessions. In murder cases the percentage is even higher, they claim, because there are seldom any witnesses to murder. One district attorney told a reporter recently that if the Escobedo case is extended to provide counsel for all suspects, "we may as well close up our homicide bureau." Others have echoed this view.

But prosecutors have cried wolf so often in the past few years that it is sometimes difficult to take them seriously. In 1961, for example, when the Supreme Court ruled that all evidence seized illegally would be inadmissible in state court trials, district attorneys, almost to a man, predicted they would have to shut down their narcotics and gambling bureaus. At last glance, they were still doing business—in some cases more than ever.

The fact is that district attorneys have no statistics to back up their claim that most murderers and rapists would walk out of the police stations, thumb to nose, if confessions were banned. And while it is true that a great many cases today are based on confessions, this does not prove that convictions could not be obtained without them.

Recently, a New York State Supreme Court justice, who was a prosecutor for many years before ascending the bench and is not known for being "soft" on defendants, told a reporter that cases in which the only evidence is a confession and a dead body are "extraordinarily rare." In most cases, he said (and New York Police Department statistics for 1964 bear him out), murder occurs after an altercation between people who know each other. Such cases can usually be put together through good police work even if there are no eyewitnesses.

Whatever the validity of the prosecutors' contentions, the fact is that they panicked over the implications of the Escobedo decision and launched a counterattack to swing public opinion against it. Then, in the midst of their campaign, at the height of the rhetoric, came the case of George Whitmore Jr.

"HOW could it happen to Frank?"
There were 300 prosecutors at the recent meeting of the National District Attorneys' Association in Houston. Most of them asked this question, in one form or another, when-

ever the Whitmore case was mentioned—and the Whitmore case was mentioned as often as the Escobedo case, which means every five minutes.

To other district attorneys, Frank Hogan is a little like Pope Paul to a parish priest. He runs the showcase office in the country, full of career people, many of whom have been there all their professional lives. They are very competent.

There are, to be sure, a few embarrassments, such as over-zealous aides (one former assistant apparently considered it his mission to save the city from Lenny Bruce; another top aide, still with Hogan, has been the scourge of local gypsies), but embarrassments can happen in any good family. The office is clearly above politics and is generally considered one of the best. As far as many district attorneys are concerned, the proof of Hogan's superiority lies in the fact that he has been in office since 1942. No one ever runs against him.

But now one of Frank Hogan's assistants had taken a 61-page confession—61 pages, which is really unheard-of—full of incredible details, intricate drawings and amazing nuances, and this confession, in one of the biggest cases to hit New York in years, had turned out to be a phony.

"Here we are, with Goldberg teeing off on us on Escobedo, saying that confessions are untrustworthy — here we are trying our best to fight what we know in our hearts is a rear-guard action," said one district attorney, "and then Hogan — of all people, Hogan, the best of all of us—has to come up with a stink bomb like this.

"Do you know what it's like? It's like you're defending Stalingrad and they take away the snow."

WELL then, how did it happen to Frank? How could one of his experienced assistants take a confession for more than two hours and not realize that it had been spoon-fed?

One of Mr. Hogan's former assistants cast some light on the mystery recently:

"You have to understand the way the system works," he said. "As far as I know, it works the same way in every borough in New York City. There's an assistant district attorney on duty 24 hours a day in the Homicide Bureau. When a murder suspect is picked up by the police, the assistant is notified. But he isn't asked to come into the station house until the police are 'ready' for him.

"Translated, this means he doesn't enter the picture until the accused has given a statement to the detectives — or worse, as in Whitmore's case, until the detectives have given a statement to *him*.

"In short, it's 'see no evil, hear no evil.' Which not only puts the suspect at the mercy of the police but inevitably puts the district attorney there with him. And so, on occasion, you must expect a Whitmore case.

"Now I don't know why the assistant who took Whitmore's Q. and A. didn't smell a rat. [A Q. and A. is the stenographic record of a suspect's answers to questions posed by the district attorney.] But look at it his way. The Wylie-Hoffert case is the hottest thing in years. All the police brass are involved. Everybody is looking for glory. Their ship is in. Under these conditions not many assistant district attorneys are going to look for trouble. They themselves want to believe it's true.

"And then again it is possible that the detectives had the kid so primed that you just couldn't know there was something wrong.

"But the point is that this policy of not moving in early lends itself to innuendo and heartache."

IT should be noted that many district attorneys do not move in at all during the interrogation stages. The first time they see a defendant is in court at the arraignment. At the other extreme, the Philadelphia District Attorney has a representative at the police station as soon as possible after a murder suspect is apprehended.

"It works very well," an assistant from that office said recently. "With us there, the cops don't dare mess a guy up. As a result, we have very few defendants attack a confession on the grounds of duress."

But if Mr. Hogan must share the blame with the police for the Wylie-Hoffert debacle, he deserves praise for running down and finally exposing the flaws in Whitmore's confession. It is rare for a prosecutor to investigate his own case once a confession has been obtained.

BUT this fine gesture was not without imperfections. When Mr. Hogan, last January, discredited the confession and charged another man with the Wylie-Hoffert murders, he did not at the same time move to dismiss the indictment against Whitmore. Instead, Whitmore was merely "discharged on his own recognizance."

This technicality was carefully exploited in Whitmore's trial in Brooklyn earlier this month for the Edmonds murder, when the prosecutor pointed out to the jury that Whitmore could still be tried for the Wylie-Hoffert slayings.

One result was to confuse the jurors. After 34 hours of deliberation, they reported themselves deadlocked and the judge ordered a mistrial.

Three days later, the Wylie-Hoffert indictment against Whitmore was dismissed with the consent of Mr. Hogan's office. Why had it not been dismissed before the Edmonds trial? The New York Civil Liberties Union charged that Mr. Hogan had delayed the dismissal in order to help his Brooklyn colleague win a conviction.

Mr. Hogan's office denied the charge and said Whitmore could have had the dismissal earlier if he had requested it. Whitmore's chief counsel, Stanley J. Reiben, in turn, implied that the Hogan office had told him it would oppose a dismissal motion before the Edmonds trial—and the publicity surrounding such opposition could only have damaged Whitmore's cause.

It is a mystery that will probably never be solved, but a minor one compared to some others: Did Whitmore commit *any* crime? Was he intentionally framed in the Wylie-Hoffert case?

Someday a jury will likely answer the first. Whitmore may be tried again for the Edmonds murder and will surely be retried on the Borrero charge. Whatever the verdict, doubts will remain in many minds. In fact, the police officers who took the Wylie-Hoffert confession still believe, almost to a man, that Whitmore is guilty, as do many people in the Brooklyn District Attorney's office.

In a way, this answers the second question. How can anyone say there was an intentional frame-up when those involved believe they have done no wrong? That, more than anything else in this strange case, is what puts a chill in the bones.

 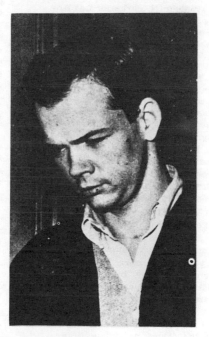

TWO MEN, ONE CRIME—Whitmore (far left) confessed to the Wylie-Hoffert double murder for which Richard Robles (left) later was indicted.

When the Cops Were Not 'Handcuffed'

By YALE KAMISAR

ARE we losing the war against crime? Is the public getting a fair break? Has the pendulum swung too far to the left? Do the victims of crime have some rights, too? Are the courts handcuffing the police?

If there were a hit parade for newspaper and magazine articles, speeches and panel discussions, these questions would rank high on the list. Not only are they being raised with increasing frequency, but they are being debated with growing fury.

Last year, probably the most famous police chief in the United States, William H. Parker of Los Angeles, protested that American police work has been "tragically weakened" through a progressive "judicial takeover." These are strong words, but Boston District Attorney Garrett Byrne, then president of the National Association of District Attorneys, easily topped the chief with the cry that the Supreme Court is "destroying the nation." (Despite this rant, Mr. Byrne has since been appointed to the President's newly established National Crime Commission, which has been assigned the task of making a systematic study of the entire spectrum of the problems of crime.)

This year, Michael J. Murphy, former Police Commissioner of New York, is the leading contender for anti-Supreme Court honors. Mr. Murphy's pet line is: "We [the police] are forced to fight by Marquis of Queensberry rules while the criminals are permitted to gouge and bite."

Not infrequently, one who dares to defend the Court, or simply to explain what the Court is doing and why, is asked which side he is on: the side of law and order—or the side of the robber, the dope peddler and the rapist. Any defense of the Court is an attack on the police. And any attack on the police (to quote Mayor Sam Yorty of Los Angeles, and he is not alone) is an "attack on our American system," perhaps even part of "a world-wide campaign by Communists, Communist dupes and sympathizers."

TODAY, the course of the Court is clear. Once concerned with property rights much more than with human liberty, it is now, as Anthony Lewis wrote several years ago, "the keeper, not of the nation's property, but of its conscience." If that role constitutes lending aid and comfort to the criminal element, then the Court is guilty.

As Judge Walter Schaefer of the Illinois Supreme Court pointed out in his famous Holmes Lecture of a decade ago, however, many of those safeguards of criminal procedure which we now take for granted came surprisingly late. Whether a state had to appoint counsel for an indigent defendant was a question which did not confront the Court until 1932, and it held then that counsel had to be provided only when the defendant was facing a possible death sentence. Whether the state could convict a defendant on the basis of a coerced confession was an issue first presented to the Court in 1936, and all the Court was asked to do then was ban confessions extracted by brutal beatings.

WHAT was it like in 1910 and 1920 and 1930 when the effectuation and implementation of criminal procedural safeguards were pretty much left to the states themselves? What was it like in the days when, as Dean Erwin Griswold of the Harvard Law School recently pointed out, "some things that were rather clearly there" (in the Constitution) had not yet "been given the attention and effect which they should have if our Constitution is to be a truly meaningful document"? Or, if you prefer, what was it like in the "good old days" before the Supreme Court began to mess up things?

In 1910, Curtis Lindley, president of the California Bar Association, declared the need for an "adjustment" in our criminal procedures "to meet the expanding social necessity." "Many of the difficulties," he continued, "are due to an exaggerated respect for the individual. . . ." He proposed (1) that a suspect be interrogated by a magistrate and, if he refused to answer the inquiries, that the state be permitted to comment on this fact at the trial; and (2) that the requirement of a unanimous verdict of guilty be reduced to three-fourths, "except possibly in cases where infliction of the death penalty is involved." This, he pointed out, would still "give the defendant three-fourths of the show."

The following year, 1911, in a hard-hitting Atlantic Monthly article entitled "Coddling the Criminal," New York prosecutor Charles Nott charged that "the appalling amount of crime in the United States compared with other civilized countries is due to the fact that it is generally known that the punishment for crime in America is uncertain and far from severe." Where lay the fault? According to Nott, the two law-enforcement obstacles which had to be cleared were the protection against double jeopardy and the privilege against self-incrimination.

Eight years later, Hugo Pam, president of the Institute of Criminal Law and Criminology, also addressed himself to the "crime problem," one which had been greatly aggravated by "the advent of the automobile." As he viewed the situation in 1919, "the boldness of the crimes and the apparent helplessness of the law have embittered the public to the extent that any advance in treatment of criminals save punishment is looked upon with disfavor." Law-enforcement officials, he noted, "have repeatedly charged that in the main these serious crimes have been committed by people on probation or parole." It followed, of course, that there was a strong movement afoot to curtail or completely repeal these provisions.

THE following year, 1920, and again in 1922, Edwin W. Sims, the first head of the newly established Chicago Crime Commission, added his voice to the insistent demands "for action" that would reduce crime. He had the figures: "During 1919 there were more murders in Chicago (with a population of three million) than in the entire British Isles (with a population of 40 million)." Moreover, the prosecution had obtained only 44 convictions as against 336 murders. The situation called for strong words and Mr. Sims was equal to the occasion:

"We have kept on providing criminals with flowers, libraries, athletics, hot and cold running water, and probation and parole. The tender solicitude for the welfare of criminals publicly expressed by social workers conveys to 10,000 criminals plying their vocation in Chicago the mistaken impression that the community is more interested in them than it is in their victims. . . .

"There has been too much mollycoddling of the criminal population. . . . It is time for plain speaking. Murderers are turned loose. They have no fear of the police. They sneer at the law. It is not a time for promises. It is a time for action. The turning point has come. Decency wins or anarchy triumphs. There is no middle course."

If Edwin Sims were still in fine voice today, he would be much in demand. At home and on the road, he would probably outdraw even Messrs. Byrne, Murphy and Parker. About all Sims would have to do would be to strike "social workers," insert "Supreme Court," and maybe add a paragraph or two about recent Supreme Court decisions. But his era, I repeat, was 1920.

The nineteen-twenties were troubled times. In speaking of the need for a National Crime Commission, The New Republic of Aug. 26, 1925, declared: "It is no exaggeration to assert that the administration of criminal justice has broken down in the United States and that in this respect American state governments are failing to perform the most primitive and most essential function which society imposes on government." At about the same time, the great criminologist Edwin H. Sutherland reported: "Capital punishment has been restored in four states since the war, and in many places there is a strenuous demand for the whipping post. . . . Crime commissions are recommending increased severity and certainty of punishment."

BY 1933, the public had become so alarmed at an apparent increase in professional criminality that a U.S. Senate investigating committee, headed by Royal S. Copeland of New York, scoured the country for information which could lead to a national legislative solution.

The Detroit hearings brought out that the murder rate in the United States was nine times higher than in England and in Wales, "where they have basically the same Anglo-Saxon institutions," and even twice as high as Italy's, "the home of the Mafia, the 'Black Hand.'" In New York, a witness solemnly declared that "the crime situation in this country is so serious that it approaches a major crisis in our history, a crisis which will determine whether the nation is to belong to normal citizens or whether it is to be surrendered completely to gangster rule."

In Chicago, drawing upon his 20 years of experience as a lawyer, prosecutor and municipal judge, a witness concluded that "there is entirely too much worry, consideration and too many safeguards about the criminal's constitutional rights." He recommended for the Senate committee's consideration Illinois's new 'reputation vagrancy law, which provides that all persons who are reputed to habitually violate the criminal laws and who are reputed to carry concealed weapons are vagrants." "Under this law," he reported, "we have harassed and convicted . . . numerous mad dogs of the West Side." (The following year, the Illinois Supreme Court struck down the law as unconstitutional.)

Senator Copeland told assembled witnesses of his desire for "a frank expression of opinion, no matter how critical you may be of existing institutions." Most of the witnesses were equal to the challenge.

A Maj. Homer Shockley urged that "constitutional and statutory guaranties, applicable to the average citizen, be suspended by special court procedure for the person who is known to be an habitual criminal . . . or who habitually consorts with criminals, to the end that the burden of proof of innocence of any fairly well substantiated charge be squarely placed on the accused; that he be tried without the benefit of a jury; and that, if convicted, all of his property and wealth be confiscated except such portion as the accused can prove were honestly gained by honest effort." The presumption of innocence is "fair enough" for the normal person, but not "for the dirty rat whom everybody knows to be an incurably habitual crook."

(Lest the major be peremptorily dismissed as a nonlegally trained commentator, it should be noted that two years earlier the dean of a Middle Western law school was reported to have advocated the establishment of a commission empowered to convict persons as "public enemies" and fix terms of their removal from society without convicting them for any specific offense, as historically required.)

CITING Toronto, where whippings were said to have broken a wave of jewelry-store stick-ups, another witness at the 1933 hearings, New York Police Commissioner Edward Mulrooney, came out for 30 or 40 lashes to be applied at the time a criminal entered prison, others every six months thereafter.

Lewis E. Lawes, the famous warden of Sing Sing prison, exclaimed: "Strip our hysterical reaction in the present emergency and what have you? A confession that our agencies are not keeping step with crime, are falling short of their mark. Yesterday it was robbery, today it is kidnapping, tomorrow it will be something else. With every new crime racket will come a new hysteria." After delivering these refreshingly sober remarks, Warden Lawes proceeded to disregard his own advice:

"I think I am a liberal, but at the same time, in case of war I would fight for the country, and this is war. I believe if they do not have some form of martial law against this particular group [racketeers and kidnappers] that there will come in . . . lynch law and from lynch law they will have the martial law. . . . It seems to me that this is a war to be stamped out quickly and could be stopped in 60 days if all the authorities get together honestly and let the public know exactly what they are doing. . . . If I were Mussolini I could do it in 30 days."

Even renowned defense attorney Sam Liebowitz, honored "to be called upon to speak from the viewpoint of the criminal lawyer," seemed to get into the swing of things. He proposed a "national vagrancy law," whereby if a well-dressed crook "cannot give a good account of himself" to a police officer who spots him on the street or in his Cadillac "you take him into the station house and question him, and then take him before a judge. The judge says, 'Prove you are earning an honest living.'

"No honest man need rebel against a thing like that," contended the great criminal lawyer. "If you are earning an honest dollar, you can show what you are doing. . . . It is the crook that sets up the cry of the Constitution, and the protection of the Constitution, when he is in trouble."

Detroit prosecutor Harry Toy agreed that "a national vagrancy act—we call it a public-enemy act—is a wonderful thing." Mr. Liebowitz had assumed that a national vagrancy act would require an amendment to the privilege against self-incrimination, but the Detroit prosecutor insisted that such an act "could be framed under the present Federal Constitution as it now stands." (His own state's "public-enemy" law was held unconstitutional by the Michigan Supreme Court a few months later. The following year New Jersey made it a felony, punishable by 20 years' imprisonment, to be a "gangster"; the U.S. Supreme Court struck the law down in 1939 on the grounds of vagueness and uncertainty.)

Chicago Municipal Court Judge Thomas Green plumped for an amendment to the Fourth Amendment permitting searches of persons "reputed" to be criminals and to be carrying firearms. The reason the framers of the Constitution stressed personal liberty, he explained, was that "there were no gangsters" then. "I think personal liberty is a wonderful thing," he hastened to add, "but today the man who takes advantage of personal liberty is the gangster, the gunman, the kidnapper."

VIRTUALLY every procedural safeguard caught heavy fire in the Senate hearings. One witness called "the right to the 'shield of silence'" (the privilege against self-incrimination) "the greatest stumbling block to justice and incentive to crime in all common-law countries." Another maintained that "the present provisions against self-incrimination were intended to protect the citizen against the medieval methods of torture, and they have become obsolete in modern life."

A report of the International Association of Chiefs of Police listed as "contributing factors to our serious crime problem . . . the resort to injunctions, writs of habeas corpus, changes of venue, etc., all with a view of embarrassing and retarding the administration of justice." The "founders of the Republic," it was argued, "never intended that habeas corpus and bail should be granted to a thug or serious thief."

Judge William Skillman of Detroit Criminal Court, known as "the one-man grand jury," maintained that permitting the state to appeal an acquittal "would do much to insure to society, represented by the state, a fair break in the trial of a lawsuit" because "the so-called 'former jeopardy clause' . . . has many times been used as a shield by a weak or timid or even a venal judge." Capt. A. B. Moore of the New York State Police proposed that an "expert adviser" or legally trained "technician" sit with and retire to the jury room with the jury "to advise them [on] those technicalities that had been implanted in their minds by a very clever attorney."

SO much for the teens

and twenties and thirties, the so-called golden era when the U.S. Supreme Court kept "hands off" local law enforcement.

When Chief Parker warns us in our time that "the police . . . are limited like the Yalu River boundary, and the result of it is that they are losing the war just like we lost the war in Korea," I wonder: When, if ever, weren't we supposedly losing the war against crime? When, if ever, weren't law enforcement personnel impatient with the checks and balances of our system? When, if ever, didn't they feel unduly "limited"? When, if ever, will they realize that our citizens are free *because* the police are "limited"?

When an official of the National District Attorneys Association insists in our time: "This country can no longer afford a 'civil-rights binge' that so restricts law-enforcement agencies that they become ineffective and organized crime flourishes," I wonder: When, if ever, in the opinion of law-enforcement personnel, could this country afford a "civil-rights binge"? When, if ever, wasn't there a "crime crisis"? When, if ever, weren't there proclamations of great emergencies and announcements of disbelief in the capacities of ordinary institutions and regular procedures to cope with them?

When Chicago's famous police chief, O. W. Wilson, stumps the country, pointing to the favorable crime picture in England, and other nations "unhampered" by restrictive court decisions, and exclaiming that "crime is overwhelming our society" (at the very time he is accepting credit in Chicago for a 20 per cent drop in crimes against the person). I am reminded of a story, apocryphal no doubt, about a certain aging promiscuous actress. When asked what she would do if she could live her life all over again she is said to have replied: "The same thing—with different people."

I venture to say that today too many law-enforcement spokesmen are doing "the same thing — with different people." They are using different crime statistics and they are concentrating on a different target—the Supreme Court rather than the state courts, parole boards, social workers and "shyster lawyers"—but they are reacting the same way they reacted in past generations.

They are reconciling the de-

lusion of our omnipotence with the experience of limited power to cope with the "crime crisis" by explaining failure in terms of betrayal. To borrow a phrase from Dean Acheson, they are letting a "mood of irritated frustration with complexity" find expression in "scapegoating."

Secretaries and ex-Secretaries of State know almost as much about scapegoating as Supreme Court justices. If the task of containing or controlling "change" in Africa or Asia is beyond our capabilities, to many people it means simply, or at least used to mean simply, that the State Department is full of incompetents or Communists or both. Here, as elsewhere, if things seem to be going wrong, but there is no simple and satisfactory reason why, it is tempting to think that "the way to stop the mischief is to root out the witches."

Crime is a baffling, complex, frustrating, defiant problem. And as James Reston once pointed out in explaining Barry Goldwater's appeal to millions of Americans: "The more complicated life becomes, the more people are attracted to simple solutions; the more irrational the world seems, the more they long for rational answers; and the more diverse everything is, the more they want it all reduced to identity."

As the Wickersham Report of 1931 disclosed, the prevailing "interrogation methods" of the nineteen-twenties and thirties included the application of the rubber hose to the back or the pit of the stomach, kicks in the shins and blows struck with a telephone book on the side of the victim's head.

These techniques did not stem the tide of crime. Nor did the use of illegally seized evidence, which most state courts permitted as late as the nineteen-forties and fifties. Nor, while they lasted, did the "public-enemy" laws, or the many criminal registration ordinances stimulated by the Copeland hearings.

IF history does anything, it supports David Acheson, who, when U. S. Attorney for the District of Columbia (the jurisdiction which has borne the brunt of "restrictive" court rules), dismissed the suggestion that "the crime rate will go away if we give back to law-enforcement agencies 'power taken from them by Federal court decisions'" with the as-

surance that "the war against crime does not lie on this front. Prosecution procedure has, at most, only the most remote casual connection with crime. Changes in court decisions and prosecution procedure would have about the same effect on the crime rate as an aspirin would have on a tumor of the brain."

Unfortunately this speech was not given the publicity it deserved. Nor were the refreshingly cool, thoughtful remarks of the new Deputy Attorney General, Ramsey Clark, who last August pointed out:

"Court rules do not cause crime. People do not commit crime because they know they cannot be questioned by police before presentment, or even because they feel they will not be convicted. We as a people commit crimes because we are capable of committing crimes. We choose to commit crimes. . . . In the long run, only the elimination of the causes of crime can make a significant and lasting difference in the incidence of crime.

"But the reduction of the causes of crime is a slow and arduous process and the need to protect persons and property is immediate. The present need for greater protection . . . can be filled not by . . . court rulings affirming convictions based on confessions secured after hours of questioning, or evidence seized in searches made without warrants. The immediate need can be filled by more and better police protection."

Chief Parker has expressed the hope that in searching for answers to our crime problem the new National Crime Commission "not overlook the influencing factor of the judicial revolution." The greater danger is that too much attention will be paid to this "revolution."

Critics of the courts are well represented, but not a single criminologist or sociologist or psychologist sits on the 19-man commission. These are conspicuous omissions for a group asked "to be daring and creative and revolutionary" in its recommendations. These are incredible omissions for those of us who share the views of the Deputy Attorney General that "the first, the most pervasive and the most difficult" front in the war on crime "is the battle against the causes of crime: poverty, ignorance, unequal opportunity, social tension, moral erosion."

BY a strange coincidence,

the very day the President announced the formation of the Crime Commission, the F.B.I. released new figures on the crime rate—soaring as usual —and J. Edgar Hoover took a sideswipe at "restrictive court decisions affecting police prevention and enforcement activity." And at their very first meeting, last September, the commission members were told by Mr. Hoover that recent court decisions had "too often severely and unfairly shackled the police officer."

Probably the most eminently qualified member of the President's Commission is Columbia Law School's Herbert Wechsler, the director of the American Law Institute and chief draftsman of the recently completed Model Penal Code. a monumental work which has already had a tremendous impact throughout the nation. The commission would have gotten off to a more auspicious start if, instead of listening to a criticism of recent court decisions, its members had read (or reread) what Mr. Wechsler, then a young, obscure assistant law professor, once said of other crime conferences in another era of "crisis" (those called by the U. S. Attorney General and a number of states, including New York, in 1934-36):

"The most satisfactory method of crime prevention is the solution of the basic problems of government—the production and distribution of external goods, education and recreation. . . . That the problems of social reform present dilemmas of their own. I do not pretend to deny. I argue only that one can say for social reform as a means to the end of improved crime control what can also be said for better personnel but cannot be said for drastic tightening of the processes of the criminal law— that even if the end should not be achieved, the means is desirable for its own sake."

November 7, 1965

HIGH COURT PUTS NEW CURB ON POWERS OF THE POLICE TO INTERROGATE SUSPECTS

DISSENTERS BITTER

Four View Limitation on Confessions as Aid to Criminals

By FRED P. GRAHAM
Special to The New York Times

WASHINGTON, June 13 — The Supreme Court announced today sweeping limitations on the power of the police to question suspects in their custody.

The justices split 5 to 4. In stinging dissents the minority denounced the decision as helping criminals go free to repeat their crimes.

The majority opinion, by Chief Justice Earl Warren, broke new constitutional ground by declaring that the Fifth Amendment's privilege against self-incrimination comes into play as soon as a person is within police custody.

Consequently, under the ruling, the prosecution cannot use in a trial any admissions or confessions made by the suspect while in custody unless it first proves that the police complied with a detailed list of safeguards to protect the right against self-incrimination.

The suspect, the Court said, must have been clearly warned that he may remain silent, that anything he says may be held against him and that he has a right to have a lawyer present during interrogation.

Court-Appointed Counsel

If the suspect desires a lawyer but cannot afford one, he cannot be questioned unless a court-appointed lawyer is present.

If the suspect confesses after receiving the required warnings but without having counsel, the burden is on the prosecution to prove a knowing waiver of rights. And any prolonged interrogation will be taken to show a lack of waiver.

Moreover, the majority opinion said, if the suspect makes a knowing waiver but later asks to see a lawyer, all questioning must stop until he sees one. If the suspect is alone and starts to talk, but then indicates "in any manner" that he wants to remain silent, the police must stop questioning him.

Ruling Called 'Dangerous'

Although Chief Justice Warren stressed that the ruling did not outlaw confessions, the majority's opinion drew bitter dissenting remarks from Justices Tom C. Clark, John M. Harlan, Potter Stewart and Byron R. White.

Justice Harlan, his face flushed and his voice occasionally faltering with emotion, denounced the decision as "dangerous experimentation" at a time of a "high crime rate that is a matter of growing concern."

He said it was a "new doctrine" without substantial precedent, reflecting a balance in favor of the accused.

Justice White said:

"In some unknown number of cases the Court's rule will return a killer, a rapist or other criminal to the streets and to the environment which produced him, to repeat his crime whenever it pleases him.

"As a consequence, there will not be a gain, but a loss, in human dignity."

Both the White and the Harlan dissents and one by Justice Clark insisted that the self-incrimination privilege did not apply at such an early stage in criminal proceedings. The self-incrimination clause of the Fifth Amendment says no person "shall be compelled in any criminal case to be a witness against himself."

Today's court action disposed of four appeals by prisoners who had confessed after having been interrogated by the police. They are Ernesto A. Miranda, convicted of rape in Phoenix, Ariz.; Michael Vignera, convicted of robbery in New York; Roy Allen Stewart, convicted of murder in Los Angeles, and Carl Calvin Westover, convicted of Federal charges of robbery in Sacramento, Calif.

All four convictions were reversed in today's action. The vote was 5 to 4 in each case except that of Stewart. Here it was 6 to 3; Justice Clark joined the majority because he thought the confession was involuntary, although he rejected in this case as in the others the Court's new limitations on interrogation.

Chief Justice Warren indicated that the Court would rule next Monday on a fifth confession case, which will determine whether the rules announced today will be applied retroactively to void old convictions.

In reading his 61-page opinion, Chief Justice Warren recounted a number of instances of the use of police brutality to obtain confessions. He also condemned psychological pressures.

At times the emotion in his voice equaled that of the dissenters and bespoke the deep division in the Court over the new doctrine.

The Chief Justice departed from his written opinion to praise the police "when their services are honorably performed." But he said that when they abandon fair methods "they can become as great a menace to society as any criminal we have."

He emphasized that the decision did not rule out questioning of witnesses at the scene of a crime or detention of a suspect while his story was being checked out. He made it clear that, despite some predictions by legal experts, the ruling did not require the presence of lawyers at police stations.

Spontaneous admissions of guilt also can be offered as evidence, he said, so long as they do not come after illegal interrogation without counsel.

By stating that police "custody" exists whenever a person is "deprived of his freedom of action in any significant way," the majority opinion makes clear that the police cannot avoid the new rules by conducting their interrogations during long rides in squad cars.

However, the opinion did seem to leave room for more litigation on the meaning of "custody" and on the circumstances under which a statement is truly spontaneous.

Also, it did not say specifically what proof would be necessary to show that a suspect had waived his rights—whether, ultimately, a suspect must have a lawyer to waive a lawyer.

The opinion also did not say whether other evidence than a confession, discovered as the fruits of an illegal interrogation, would be legally admissible.

Chief Justice Warren's reli-ance upon the Fifth Amendment surprised some legal authorities, because the famous parent case of today's decision, Escobedo v. Illinois, had ruled out a confession primarily because the defendant's Sixth Amendment right to see his lawyer had been violated.

The decision today tends to merge the two rights, to assure a person a right to counsel whenever he is in a situation that might cause him to incriminate himself. The doctrine applies to all felony and misdemeanor trials, in both Federal and state courts.

In support of his view that these rules would not cripple law enforcement, Chief Justice Warren pointed out that the Federal Bureau of Investigation has for years warned all suspects of their right to counsel and to remain silent. He said England, Scotland and India had not suffered from observing similar procedures.

Replying to the dissenters' complaint that the Court should have waited for the completion of pending confession studies by the American Bar Association, the American Law Institute and the President's Commission on Law Enforcement and Administration of Justice, Mr. Warren said:

"The issues presented are of constitutional dimensions and must be determined by the courts."

John J. Flynn of Phoenix argued for Miranda; Assistant Attorney General Gary K. Nelson argued for Arizona. Victor M. Earle 3d of New York argued for Vignera; William I. Siegel, Assistant District Attorney of Kings County, argued for New York State.

William A. Norris of Los Angeles argued for Stewart; Gordon Ringer, Deputy Attorney General of California, argued for the state. F. Conger Fawcett of San Francisco argued for Westover; Thurgood Marshall, Solicitor General of the United States, argued for the Government.

June 14, 1966

REPORT QUESTIONS CONFESSION ROLE

Coast Survey Challenges Importance to Prosecution

By SIDNEY E. ZION

The contention of many police officials and prosecutors that confessions are the backbone of law enforcement has been challenged by a survey of about 4,000 felony cases made by the district attorney of Los Angeles County. The office is reported to have the largest caseload in the nation.

The survey, the first made by a prosecutor, shows that confessions were needed for the successful prosecution in "only a small percentage of criminal cases," less than 10 per cent. Moreover, suspects are confessing despite advice by the police that they may remain silent and have free legal counsel if they are indigent.

"I'm amazed by our findings," Evelle J. Younger, the district attorney, said in a telephone interview yesterday.

"Like most prosecutors I had assumed that confessions were of the utmost necessity in the majority of cases."

Findings Are Similar

Although the findings closely paralleled smaller statistical studies made last year in Brooklyn and Detroit, prosecutors have generally said that confessions were necessary for conviction in 75 to 90 per cent of major cases. They have argued, along with most police officials, that suspects would not confess if advised of their rights.

Last June, many law enforcement officials predicted dire consequences after the Supreme Court ruled in Miranda v. Arizona that the police must advise suspects of their rights and offer them counsel before questioning.

Similar forebodings were made in California in 1964 when that state's highest court ruled in the People v. Durado, in a less sweeping manner, that the advice had to be given to suspects under certain circumstances.

"The most significant things about our findings," Mr. Younger said, "are that suspects will talk regardless of the warnings and that furthermore it isn't so all-fired important whether they talk or not."

The survey, published earlier this month, consists of two studies. The first involved 1,300 cases in December, 1965, conducted to test the impact of the Dorado ruling and thus called the Dorado Survey. The second covered 2,700 cases over a three-week period that ended July 15, 1966, and is called the Miranda Survey.

Mr. Younger said that the confession rate after the Miranda case remained the same as after the Durado ruling, about 50 per cent. There were no figures predating the Dorado case. The district attorney pointed out that "it might have been anticipated" that the rate would have dropped after the Miranda case "because of the increased scope of the admonitions required."

Why do people confess when they are told they do not have to say anything?

First, according to Mr. Younger, the fact that confessions are essential in such few cases "suggests strongly" that people talk because they are caught in situations where guilt is obvious.

'Best to Come Clean'

"If you're caught redhanded," he said, "you probably will figure that it's best to come clean and perhaps get some consideration from the prosecutor and judge.

"But also, in every human being, however noble or depraved, there is a thing called conscience. In some people the conscience is as small as a fly speck; in others it's as big as a grapefruit. Large or small, the conscience usually, or at least often, drives a guilty person to confess.

"If an individual wants to confess, a warning from a police officer, acting as required by recent decisions, is not likely to discourage him. Those who hope or fear these decisions will eliminate confessions as a legitimate law enforcement tool will be disappointed or relieved."

The Los Angeles findings appeared to support the controversial confession statistics produced last November by a Brooklyn Supreme Court Justice, Nathan R. Sobel. Justice Sobel, deriding the importance of confessions as "carelessly nurtured nonsense," said that of 1,000 Brooklyn indictments fewer than 10 per cent involved confessions.

The law enforcement establishment denounced the Sobel report in briefs to the Supreme Court on the confession cases decided in June. Justice Sobel has since said that later studies conducted by him showed that "confessions are even less important than I first found."

The statistics of Mr. Younger, a former agent for the Federal Bureau of Investigation who has been in law enforcement for 25 years, also support the findings of Detroit's chief of detectives, Vincent W. Piersante. He reported that confessions were essential in only 9.3 per cent of murder cases in that city during the first nine months of 1965. He said also that the police advice to suspects had little or no effect on the confession rate.

August 19, 1966

High Court Backs Police On Secrecy for Informers

By FRED P. GRAHAM
Special to The New York Times

WASHINGTON, March 20—The Supreme Court ruled today that the Constitution does not require that the police disclose in court the identities of informants who have tipped them off about crimes.

It held that the police can make an arrest based upon tips from unidentified informants, then search the arrested person without a warrant and use evidence obtained in the search to convict the arrested person—without disclosing the identity of the informant who initiated the process.

The majority, in an opinion written by Justice Potter Stewart, reasoned that a contrary ruling would "severely hamper the Government" in enforcing the narcotics laws, by forcing the police to reveal the name of an informer each time they justified an arrest in court.

The dissenters, speaking through an opinion by Justice William O. Douglas, declared that the ruling would "encourage arrests and searches without warrants" and would entrust constitutional rights "to the tender mercies of the police."

The other dissenters were Chief Justice Earl Warren and Justices William J. Brennan Jr. and Abe Fortas.

The decision reflected a recent conservative tone in the Supreme Court's rulings on criminal law.

Justice Stewart's opinion was joined by Justices Hugo L. Black, Tom C. Clark, John M. Harlan and Byron R. White. It refused to impose a Federal standard on the states on the use of informants to prove probable cause for arrests.

In a case in 1961 the Supreme Court declared state courts subject to the Fourth Amendment's rule against unreasonable searches.

The decision today gives the states flexibility in applying that provision by permitting each state to follow its own common law rule on the use of anonymous informants to establish whether there was "probable cause" to arrest the defendant. The Fourth Amendment permits searches without warrants as incident to most arrests made with "probable cause."

The appeal was brought by George McCray, who was arrested and searched by two policemen on a Chicago street in January, 1964. The search produced heroin, which led to his conviction.

At a pretrial hearing to determine whether the search was proper, the officers refused to identify their informer. They said only that the informer was reliable and had provided the information for many convictions.

McCray's lawyers pointed out that the officers knew that McCray had previously been convicted of narcotics violations, and may have arrested him on suspicion, without the benefit of an informant's evidence.

The trial judge and the Supreme Court of Illinois held that the anonymous tip was sufficient to establish probable cause, so that the search was legal and the heroin could be used against McCray.

Justice Stewart approved this on the ground that the Constitution does not require a state judge to "assume the arresting officers are committing perjury" when they say that an unnamed informant has provided the basis for an arrest.

Justice Stewart pointed out that Federal cases distinguish between the amount of proof needed to establish probable cause, and the greater amount needed to prove guilt at the trial.

He cited a Supreme Court decision in 1959 that held that Federal officers could use the hearsay testimony of informants to establish probable cause for an arrest, even though it would not be admissible at the subsequent trial.

The ruling today will do much to ease the widespread complaints by the police that the decision in 1961 had "handcuffed" them. It will permit an arrest and search to stand if the arresting officers testify that they were given sufficient evidence by a reliable witness to establish "probable cause."

If the search itself turned up enough evidence for a conviction, the tipster's name will not have to be told. The courts will not hear of the searches that did not produce such evidence, because no charges will be brought.

The result, Justice Douglas contended, is to "leave the Fourth Amendment exclusively in the custody of the police."

R. Eugene Pincham of Chicago argued for McCray. John J. O'Toole, assistant Attorney General of Illinois, argued for the state.

March 21, 1967

HIGH COURT RULES ADULT CODE HOLDS IN JUVENILE TRIALS

Finds Children Are Entitled to the Basic Protections Given in Bill of Rights

ONLY STEWART DISSENTS

Ruling Expected to Require Major Changes in Most of Nation's Youth Tribunals

WASHINGTON, May 15—The Supreme Court ruled today that juvenile courts must grant children many of the procedural protections required in adult trials by the Bill of Rights.

The landmark decision is expected to require that radical changes be made immediately in most of the nation's 3,000 juvenile courts.

In New York, judges said that the Supreme Court ruling would not affect juvenile cases, since "it already is the law" that minors have the same rights as adults. The change became effective in September, 1962, with the adoption of a new Family Court Act by the State Legislature.

In a detailed opinion by Justice Abe Fortas, the Supreme Court held that, in delinquency hearings before juvenile court judges, children must be accorded the following safeguards of the Bill of Rights:

¶Timely notice of the charges against them.

¶The right to have a lawyer, appointed by the court if necessary, in any case that might result in the incarceration of a child.

¶The right to confront and cross-examine complainants and other witnesses.

¶Adequate warning of the privilege against self-incrimination and the right to remain silent.

Rights Applied to All

"Neither the 14th Amendment nor the Bill of Rights is for adults only," Justice Fortas declared. He went on:

"Under our Constitution, the condition of being a boy does not justify a kangaroo court."

The decision was supported at least in part by eight of the justices, with only Justice Potter Stewart dissenting outright. He said the decision was "a long step backwards into the nineteenth century," because, he contended, it would abolish the flexibility and informality of juvenile courts, and would cause children once more to be treated as adults in courts.

Chief Justice Earl Warren and Justices William J. Brennan Jr., Tom C. Clark and William O. Douglas joined Mr. Fortas's opinion.

Justice Byron R. White and John M. Harlan both joined it in part and disagreed in part.

Justice Hugo L. Black wrote a separate concurring opinion, in which he disclosed that he had opposed reviewing the matter in the first instance because the case "strikes a well-nigh fatal blow to much that is unique about the juvenile courts in the nation."

Black Backs Finding

But Justice Black agreed with the outcome because of his belief that all of the guarantees of the Bill of Rights are applicable to all state criminal trials, including juvenile ones, by the 14th Amendment.

Justice Fortas took pains to state that the decision applied only to juvenile trials, and did not affect the handling of juvenile cases before or after trial. This means that the decision does not automatically apply the Supreme Court's limitations on police interrogation to the

367

investigation of juvenile suspects.

However, the Court's opinion mentioned several instances of improper questioning of young suspects, and Justice Fortas noted that "it would indeed be surprising if the privilege against self-incrimination were available to hardened criminals but not to children."

He found it unnecessary to deal with this issue, or with the rights of indigent children to free appellate transcripts and legal assistance, because the case before the Supreme Court could be decided solely on Constitutional deficiencies at the trial level.

The case before the Supreme Court was brought by Paul L. and Marjorie Gault, parents of Gerald Gault of Globe, Ariz., with the assistance of attorneys furnished by the American Civil Liberties Union. Gerald was adjudged to be a juvenile delinquent in June, 1964, when he was 15 years old, after a juvenile court judge found he had made lewd telephone calls to a female neighbor.

Young Gault served 6 months in the state industrial school. His parents challenged the constitutionality of the Arizona juvenile court law in a habeas corpus petition for his release.

They asserted, among other things, that they had been given inadequate notice of the charges, that the woman had not testified, that they had not been offered the assistance of counsel, that Gerald had not been warned that his testimony could be used against him, that no transcript had been made of the trial and that Arizona law does not permit an appeal of juvenile court decisions.

Old Doctrine Rejected

Justice Forta's opinion rejected a basic premise on which juvenile courts have operated since the first one was established in Chicago in 1899— that juvenile court trials are essentially civil in nature and that the children's rights are adequately protected by the judges, acting as parens patriae, or substitute parents.

He cited studies to show that about half of the nation's juvenile court judges have no undergraduate degree, a fifth have no college education and a fifth are not members of the bar.

He also cited data from the national crime commission showing that persons under 18 accounted for about one-fifth of all arrests for serious crimes and over one-half of all the arrests for serious property offenses, in 1965. About one out of nine children will eventually face charges of juvenile delinquency, the Justice further said.

While remarking that juvenile courts are failing to cope with this criminality, Mr. Fortas referred to a report by the District of Columbia Crime Commission showing that 66 per cent of the 16 and 17-year-old persons before the juvenile court there had been in court before. Fifty-six per cent of those in the juvenile receiving home were repeaters, the report said.

Lack of Protection Found

Justice Fortas noted that this was the first Supreme Court case involving the constitutional rights of children in juvenile court. He concluded that the parens patriae concept had not protected them, and held that they must be accorded the protection of the Bill of Rights.

The most far-reaching aspect of today's decision is expected to be the new requirement that counsel be provided in juvenile court.

According to the opinion, only New York, California, Minnesota and the District of Columbia now provide free counsel, and some of them do so only when the charge would be a felony in adult court. Today's decision requires counsel whenever the child might be incarcerated.

Initially, this could cause some paralysis in juvenile courts across the country, which could be followed by a scramble to make lawyers available. Few lawyers are familiar with the procedures of juvenile courts. With the annual number of juvenile cases in the country at 600,000 and rising, the burden

on the legal profession could be considerable.

In declaring that the Fifth Amendment's privilege against compulsory self-incrimination applied in juvenile cases, Justice Fortas acknowledged that in practice it might not operate as rigidly as in adult cases, since children are encouraged to talk things out informally with the judge.

But he said that the privilege had been violated in this case because young Gault had not first been told of his right to remain silent.

Justice White disagreed. He said the failure to give warnings did not prove that self-incriminating testimony had been compelled. He declared that the Court was repeating the same mistake in reasoning that led it last year to declare, in Miranda v. Arizona, that confessions are always coerced unless the suspects are first warned of their rights.

Justice Harlan agreed that the Gault decision should have been reversed, because the boy had been denied the "fundamental fairness" required of all criminal proceedings by the due process clause of the 14th Amendment.

In juvenile cases, this would require only timely notice, the right to be represented by retained counsel and an adequate transcript for appeal, Justice Harlan said.

Justice Black's concurring opinion was aimed primarily at this "fundamental fairness" approach.

"Due process of law," he said, means merely that persons must be tried under the law that existed when the offense was committed.

It should not be stretched by judges to "give courts power to fashion laws in order to meet new conditions, to fit the decencies of changed conditions, or to keep their consciences from being shocked by legislation, state or federal."

The dissent by Justice Stewart conceded that the record of juvenile courts did not measure up to their ideals, but he said that the solution "does not lie in the Court's opinion in this

case, which serves to convert a juvenile proceeding into a criminal prosecution."

To illustrate the possible abuses of this, he related the case of a 12-year-old New Jersey boy named James Guild, who was hanged for murder in the nineteenth century.

"It was all very constitutional," he said.

In a footnote, he repeated Blackstone's report of a 10-year-old boy who was sentenced to death for murder to squelch any "notion that children might commit such atrocious crimes with impunity."

In the Gault case, he found that despite the lack of formal procedures, Gerald's parents had known of the charges and their rights. He said he would dismiss the appeal.

Norman Dorsen of New York argued for the Gaults. Frank A. Parks, assistant Attorney General of Arizona argued for the state, and Merrit W. Green of Toledo, Ohio, argued as friend-of-the-court in support of the state, for the Ohio Association of Juvenile Court Judges.

The New York Times
Supreme Court Justice Abe Fortas wrote opinion on rights of young in court.

A SWEEPING BAN ON WIRETAPPING SET FOR U.S. AIDES

Attorney General's Rules Also Bar Most Bugging Except in Security Cases

OFFICIALS ARE CRITICAL

Federal Agents Decry Curb on Use of Devices Placed Without Actual Trespass

WASHINGTON, July 6—Attorney General Ramsey Clark has issued sweeping new regulations forbidding all wiretapping and virtually all eavesdropping by Federal agents except in national security cases.

The new regulations go beyond limitations placed on eavesdropping by President Johnson in 1965 in several respects, the most important of which is a ban on devices that can pick up conversations within a closed room without a physical trespass.

This action has generated widespread controversy among Federal agents and prosecutors, since conversations overheard by such devices are deemed constitutionally obtained and admissible in evidence under present Supreme Court decisions.

Reliance on Devices

Federal anticrime agents have relied increasingly on these devices in the last five years, since most other forms of eavesdropping have been declared unconstitutional by the courts, and several major organized - crime convictions have been obtained through their use.

The new regulations are the product of a two-year study by the Justice Department, ordered by President Johnson when he cracked down on Federal snooping in a memorandum to all agencies on June 30, 1965.

Mr. Clark's new rules were issued on June 16 but have not been made public. However, copies have begun to circulate on Capitol Hill and in the executive branch, where they have been criticized by some officials who insist that some police eavesdropping must be permitted if organized crime is to be controlled.

The rules, which apply to all agencies of the Federal Government but not to cases involving the national security, provide as follows:

¶Wiretapping—the interception of telephone conversations without the consent of either party—is absolutely forbidden. Although formerly the Justice Department said that the Federal law that outlaws wiretapping is not violated if the information is not divulged outside the Government, the new rules forbid wiretapping regardless of divulgence.

¶Bugging—the planting of hidden microphones by means of trespass—is also forbidden. Bugging is illegal under the laws of seven states but not under Federal statutes.

¶The use of other devices is forbidden if they pick up conversations, even without a trespass, in "constitutionally protected areas." Under present court decisions these are homes, private offices, hotel rooms and automobiles, but the memorandum points out that other areas may also be protected if under the circumstances they appear to be private places.

¶Electronic intrusions into constitutionally privileged relationships, such as attorney-client talks, are forbidden, whether or not the conversations take place in constitutionally protected places.

¶The use of electronic gear to monitor a conversation in which one party knows of the surveillance—such as a transmitter or recorder hidden on an agent's clothing—is permitted, but only with the written permission of the Attorney General. In emergencies, agency chiefs can authorize use of such devices without prior permission, but the Attorney General must be told of the incident within 24 hours.

Gear Must Be Locked Up

The new regulations also require agency heads to keep electronic eavesdropping gear locked up and require that detailed records be kept of any use of it.

President Johnson cracked down on Federal eavesdropping in the wake of a series of disclosures—many by a Senate investigating subcommittee headed by Senator Edward V. Long, Democrat of Missouri—that various forms of electronic snooping were being carried out by Federal agents often without the knowledge of their superiors.

The President's 1965 memorandum prohibited wiretapping in all but national security cases, but appeared to allow room for some other types of electronic surveillance. Mr. Johnson said merely that such eavesdropping should be "fully in accord with the law and with a decent regard for the rights of others."

However, the impression spread throughout the Government that President Johnson had ruled out all bugging that involved a physical trespass.

Devices Allowed

His memorandum did not appear to rule out the use of "detectaphones" (electronic stethoscopes that will pick up conversations within a closed room when pressed against the outside wall), "sill mikes" (tubular microphones that can be placed on the floor near a closed door and will overhear conversations inside the room), and parabolic microphones designed to pick up conversations across open distances.

Goldman v. United States, a 1942 Supreme Court decision, held that such devices do not violate the Fourth Amendment —and consequently that conversations picked up by them are admissible in evidence— because they do not involve a physical trespass.

However, many legal scholars have argued that the Supreme Court's emphasis on the element of trespass in eavesdropping cases is artificial, and have predicted that the Court eventually will prohibit all intrusions into private places, whether by trespass or not.

The Supreme Court has agreed to reconsider its Goldman decision in a case to be heard next fall. Mr. Clark, apparently expecting that the Court will change its mind, banned eavesdropping in areas protected by the Fourth Amendment, whether or not a trespass is involved.

On this point, the regulations say:

"Although the question has not been squarely decided, there is support for the view that any electronic eavesdropping on conversations in constitutionally protected areas is a violation of the Fourth Amendment even if such surveillance is accomplished without physical trespass or entry."

HIGH COURT EASES CURBS ON BUGGING; ADDS SAFEGUARD

Insists Police Must Obtain Warrant to Act—Doesn't Forbid Eavesdropping

BETTING CASE REVERSED

Justices Hold Phone Booth User Is Protected Against Unauthorized Snooping

WASHINGTON, Dec. 18—The Supreme Court made it clear today that the Constitution does not forbid electronic bugging by law enforcement officers if they first obtain warrants authorizing the eavesdropping.

At the same time, the Court extended the reach of the Fourth Amendment by holding that the warrant procedure must be followed by police officers, even when they planned to eavesdrop on persons in semi-public places, such as telephone booths.

Must Request Warrant

The Court also abandoned a precedent dating back to 1942. This precedent, maintained in a series of cases, held that the fruits of bugging by the police could be used in court so long as no physical trespass had been involved in installing the electronic listening device. Today, the Court said that such trespass was not the decisive point.

It also held that the police must first get a warrant approving surveillance if they are going to use a device that will let them overhear, without trespass, remarks that the subject of the eavesdropping "seeks to preserve as private, even in an area accessible to the public."

However, the wording of the decision erased an impression that had been created, in a decision of the Court last June, that the Supreme Court would insist on such elaborate procedures in connection with these warrants that bugging would become virtually useless as a police tool.

The Court took pains today to eliminate such an impression, using language that should buttress the constitutional arguments of those who are urging the adoption of state and Federal laws to permit court-approved bugging by the police in anticrime investigations.

In the few states that have such legislation now, it is customary, but not generally obligatory for the law enforcement officers to report back to the judges who authorized a bugging operation.

In other states, there are no procedures allowing the police to obtain eavesdropping warrants.

The effect of today's decision by the Supreme Court will be limited until the states generally adopt laws covering the grants of bugging warrants.

Both Sides Gain

Thus the decision today "gave" something to both sides in the current controversy over the constitutionality of electronic eavesdropping by police.

The decision was backed by all but one of the eight participating Justices. In a rare show of consensus on bugging, the only dissenter was Justice Hugo L. Black, who feels that the Fourth Amendment ban on "unreasonable searches and seizures" does not apply to eavesdroppings.

Justice Thurgood Marshall, who was Solicitor General during the early phases of the case, did not take part.

The case involved Charles Katz of Los Angeles, who was convicted of the Federal offense of transmitting wagering information by way of interstate telephone calls. He was fined $300.

Katz was convicted partly on evidence produced by a microphone that had been taped by agents of the Federal Bureau of Investigation to the top of a telephone booth that he customarily used. Since they could hear only his end of the conversations, the device was not a wiretap, which is illegal under a Federal statute.

The evidence was admitted against Katz under the authority of a series of Supreme Court rulings that have held eavesdropping evidence admissible if it was obtained without a physical penetration of a constitutionally protected area. These cases indicated that the Fourth Amendment bars police intrusion only into private premises, such as homes, offices and automobiles.

Privacy Right Upheld

But Justice Potter Stewart, writing today for the majority, said that "the Fourth Amendment protects people, not places."

"One who occupies [a telephone booth]," he added, "shuts the door behind him, and pays the toll that permits him to place a call, is surely entitled to assume that the words he utters into the mouthpiece will not be broadcast to the world."

He then overruled the cases that had held police eavesdropping to be permissible as long as there was no physical trespass.

Under these decisions, a "spike mike" driven a thumb tack's depth into the outer wall of a room, was unconstitutional. But an electronic stethoscope, which could pick up conversations within a room merely by being pressed against the outer wall could constitutionally be used.

Justice Stewart ruled out this distinction, stating that modern electronic technology had rendered the "penetration" distinction meaningless.

On these grounds, he held that Katz's conversations were protected by the Fourth Amendment. Since there was no "search" warrant for the "seizure" of his words, the conviction was reversed.

Early Impression Changed

He then went on to eliminate the impression created by the Court last June when it struck down New York's permissive bugging law in Berger v. New York, that the Court would impose impossible restrictions on police eavesdropping.

Speaking of the bugging used against Katz, he said:

"It is clear that this surveillance was so narrowly circumscribed that a duly authorized magistrate, properly notified of the need for such investigation, specifically informed of the basis on which it was to proceed, and clearly apprised of the precise intrusion it would entail, could constitutionally have authorized, with appropriate safeguards, the very limited search and seizure that the Government asserts in fact took place."

The decision said that the officers would not have to serve the warrant on the person to be bugged. The Berger decision had given the impression that an eavesdrop warrant would have to be served prior to any "search," as in the case of any search warrant. This struck many lawyers as an indirect way for the Supreme Court to make police eavesdropping a practical impossibility.

Today's decision also said that an eavesdropping warrant would not be invalid as a search for "mere evidence."

A footnote in the Stewart opinion noted that the warrant requirement, stipulated for this gambling conviction, would not necessarily apply in a national security case.

The opinion made it clear that Federal agents could eavesdrop in certain circumstances. However, the Federal rules of criminal procedure do not specifically authorize judges to issue warrants for eavesdropping, and legislation might be necessary before Federal agents could get such warrants.

DISSENTS: Justice Hugo L. Black held Fourth Amendment ban on unreasonable searches and seizures does not relate to eavesdropping.

GIVES COURT'S RULING: Justice Potter Stewart expressed the Supreme Court's opinion on police officers' legal use of eavesdropping.

December 19, 1967

President Risks Negroes' Anger, Signs Crime Bill for Washington

SAN ANTONIO, Tex., Dec. 27 —President Johnson signed tonight an anticrime bill for the District of Columbia.

In deciding to approve the measure rather than veto it, Mr. Johnson chose to accept whatever criticism might be forthcoming from the Negro community and civil rights supporters. At the same time, he might have been protecting himself in an election year against possible Republican charges that he was not doing enough to fight crime.

The bill has been attacked by prominent Congressional liberals, including Senator Robert F. Kennedy, Democrat of New York, as being unconstitutional and, in effect, discriminatory against the Negro community.

The Washington city government also made an unsuccessful last-minute appeal to the Senate earlier this month to delay passage of the bill until a key provision of doubtful constitutionality could be studied further.

Last year, Mr. Johnson vetoed on constitutional grounds a similar but more comprehensive Washington anticrime bill. This year's measure contained a number of softening amendments.

The current measure is still designed, however, to make judicial procedures and court sentences more favorable to the police and the prosecutor and thus to militate against Federal court decisions over the last decade in these two areas. In the view of a sizable portion of Congress, these decisions have produced lenient sentencing and hampered the police.

The bill upsets the so-called Mallory rule on police interrogation established by the Supreme Court in 1957. The rule states that a suspect must be arraigned before a magistrate "without unnecessary delay" after his arrest.

The rule has been variously interpreted, but one Federal appeals judge in Washington has ruled that prearraignment questioning of five minutes was enough to violate the rule and to invalidate a confession the suspect made.

The law authorizes the Washington police to question suspects for up to three hours before arraigning them, provided that the suspects are informed of their full constitutional rights. These consist of warnings that they may say nothing, that anything they say may be used against them, that they are entitled to legal counsel and that a lawyer will be obtained for them at no cost if they desire.

Confession Admissible

Any confessions or other statements the suspects made during these three-hour prearraignment interrogations would also be later admissible as evidence.

The Washington police have been operating under a three-hour prearraignment interrogation limit since last year, but the rule has not been tested in the courts.

The new law also establishes minimum prison sentences for serious crimes—the law now specifies only maximum sentences—and provides penalties of up to 10 years' imprisonment and a $10,000 fine for rioting or inciting to riot in the District.

The President said today that he had the support of the new chief executive of the District, Walter Washington, and the city administration in approving the measure.

But while signing the bill, Mr. Johnson dissented over the two most controversial provisions — the three-hour pre-arraignment interrogation limit for the police and minimum sentences for serious crimes.

On the first, the President noted that "in our system of Government, statements taken from an accused can never be a substitute for careful and painstaking work by law officers."

He criticized the minimum sentence provision as "a backward step in modern correctional policy."

The President cited as sound aspects of the law a tough anti-riot section, a provision for a comprehensive review of the District criminal code, and the grant of authority for policemen to issue simple citations to persons committing a misdemeanor rather than having to spend the time to take the arrested individuals to a station house.

The bill, most observers believe, will still leave criminal procedures in the District of Columbia more liberal than those in most of the states.

December 28, 1967

63% in Gallup Poll Think Courts Are Too Lenient on Criminals

PRINCETON, N. J., March 2 —Law courts in the United States are "too soft" on criminals in the opinion of large majorities of Americans interviewed by the Gallup Poll in each of the four major regions of the nation. Moreover, the proportion who hold this belief has grown appreciably over the last three years—from 48 per cent in April 1965, to 63 per cent today.

Only 2 per cent in the latest survey say that the courts in their area deal "too harshly" with criminals, while 19 per cent say the treatment is "about right."

The current attitude toward the treatment of criminals has important political implications for November. Crime is now considered by the people as the top domestic problem facing the nation and looms as one of the greatest issues in this year's Presidential race.

Of all candidates or potential candidates in the Presidential race, George C. Wallace has gone farthest in capitalizing on this issue. His criticism of the courts as being too lenient is likely to strike a responsive chord with a large segment of the United States public, the poll says.

Court Ruling Opposed

Consistent with current attitudes are results of an earlier survey showing opinion to be 2 to 1 against the United States Supreme Court ruling on confessions.

The Supreme Court has ruled that as soon as the police arrest a suspect, he must be warned of his right to remain silent and to have a lawyer. Only if he voluntarily waives these rights may the police question him.

Closely comparable proportions of Negroes and whites in the latest survey feel that the courts in their areas are too lenient. The issue also cuts across party lines.

This was the question asked of 1,503 adults across the nation:

"In general, do you think the courts in this area deal too harshly, or not harshly enough with criminals?"

The latest results and those from three years ago were:

	1968 %	1965 %
Not harshly enough	63	48
About right	19	34
Too harshly	2	2
No opinion	16	16

Although the mood of the public is for stiffer penalties, much support exists at the same time for attacking the root causes of crime in the community and in the home.

All persons in the latest survey were asked this question:

"In recent years there has been a sharp increase in the nation's crime rate. What steps do you think should be taken to reduce crime?"

Here are the top five proposals in order of frequency of mention:

1. Correct social and economic conditions (mentioned by 18 per cent).

2. More parental control—parents are too permissive; not interested in their children (also 18 per cent).

3. Changes are needed in the courts; give the police a freer hand (17 per cent).

4. Increase the size of the police force (15 per cent).

5. Make penalties more severe (13 per cent).

Question Asked of All

Other proposals offered by those interviewed included greater enforcement of existing laws; upgrading the quality of the police force; increasing the influence of religion and morality; involving the public to a greater extent; giving the police higher pay; encouraging juvenile rehabilitation programs; cracking down on drugs; stricter gun laws; controlling the "population explosion."

Law enforcement officials who believe the war on crime can be won only if citizens become involved to a greater extent can take encouragement from the latest survey, the poll says. Nearly 9 persons in 10 say they would be willing to help the local police in a community anticrime operation.

March 3, 1968

371

JUSTICES EXTEND FIVE LEGAL RIGHTS IN CRIMINAL CASES

Overturn Old Curbs on Jury Trials, Confessions and Appeals by Convicts

WASHINGTON, May 20—The Supreme Court broadened the rights of criminal defendants and convicted persons today in five decisions overturning its own more restrictive precedents.

The series of reversals came as the Senate approached a scheduled vote tomorrow on a bill to curb the Court's jurisdiction in criminal law.

In a two-and-one-half-hour session, the Court announced decisions in 15 cases, including the criminal law decisions that held:

¶That the Federal constitutional right to a jury trial in criminal cases is binding on the states.

¶That defendants charged with criminal contempt in state courts have a right to jury trials in all but petty cases.

¶That in joint Federal trials of several co-defendants, a confession by one defendant cannot be admitted in evidence if it also incriminates his co-defendants.

¶That a state prison inmate who is serving the first of two consecutive sentences may attack the second conviction in Federal habeas corpus proceedings, even though he is not in custody by virtue of that conviction.

¶That a state prison inmate using a Federal habeas corpus proceeding to attack his conviction can continue to a final decision in the appellate courts, even after the prisoner completes his sentence and is no longer in custody because of that conviction.

Jury Trials Mandated

The most far-reaching of the five rulings was Duncan v. Louisiana, in which the Court followed a line of recent cases that have made various provisions of the Bill of Rights binding on the states, even though only the Federal Government was originally covered by them. Today, the Court said that the states are also bound by the Sixth Amendment's requirement of jury trials in criminal cases.

Since 1900, when the Supreme Court ruled that a state jury of less than 12 members was permissible because the Sixth Amendment applied only to Federal trials, states have been constitutionally free to work out their own jury procedures.

All states guarantee jury trials in serious cases, but there are many variations that do not square with the Federal requirement of a unanimous 12-member panel.

But today, in an opinion by Justice Byron R. White, the Court ruled, 7 to 2, that jury trials are so fundamental to the American notion of justice that they are required in state cases by the provision of the 14th Amendment, that forbids states to deny individuals the right to life or liberty without due process of law.

Justice White pointed out that so-called "petty offenses" have traditionally been tried without a right of jury trial, and said that this would be true under the new ruling. He noted that in Federal cases a petty offense is one carrying a maximum penalty of six months' imprisonment and a 50-dollar fine.

Beyond that, he left for future decisions the delineation of the line between "serious" and "petty" state cases, because the case decided today was clearly a serious one in the Court's view.

It involved Gary Duncan, a young Negro from Plaquemines Parish, La., who was charged with simple battery after he pushed or touched a white youth while attempting to break up a threatened fight between white and Negro boys. The maximum penalty was two years

in jail and a fine of $300, but young Duncan was given a 60-day jail term and fined $150.

His request for a jury trial was refused and he was tried and found guilty by a judge.

The Court's decision could have a substantial impact on the system of justice in New York State. Louis J. Lefkowitz, the State's Attorney General, had noted in a friend-of-court brief that New York denies jury trials in misdemeanor cases carrying jail terms of up to one year.

In 1964, he said, 11,678 of these cases were tried before three-judge panels, resulting in 7,136 convictions. Mr. Lefkowitz said that there would be "a substantial impact on the present system of the administration of the criminal law" if these cases had to be tried before juries.

The ruling today did not say if jury trials could be denied in offenses carrying one-year penalties. Nor did it say if the ruling would be applied retroactively to free prisoners in jail.

Justice White was joined by Chief Justice Earl Warren and Justices Abe Fortas, Hugo L. Black, William O. Douglas, William J. Brennan Jr. and Thurgood Marshall.

Justice John M. Harlan dissented, joined by Justice Potter Stewart. They disputed the assertion that the federal jury trial standard is such a fundamental right that states should be bound to it.

Also by a 7-to-2 vote, the Court extended the Federal constitutional right to trial by jury to state criminal contempt cases. This finding overruled the decision in 1958 of Green v. United States and a series of earlier cases.

Justice White's opinion applied the new rule only to "serious" criminal contempt cases. It did not specify when a case would be considered serious enough to merit a jury trial.

However, the opinion left standing a two-year-old decision in which the Court rejected the contention that a six-month contempt sentence called for a jury trial.

In the case today, S. Edward Bloom, a lawyer from Chicago, had been given a two-year prison sentence on criminal contempt charges of having falsified and probated a will.

The Court threw out this conviction because Bloom had been denied a jury trial. Justice White's opinion said that

this matter was serious enough to require a jury, no matter where the line might later be drawn.

In a third decision today, the Court overruled its decision in Delli Paoli v. United States. That ruling, in 1957, held that a defendant's confession could be read to the jury even though it tended to incriminate a co-defendant who had not confessed and against whom it would not ordinarily be admissible.

Today the Court ruled the opposite in a 6-to-2 decision written by Justice Brennan. He held that "the risk that the jury will not, or cannot, follow instructions is so great" that the jury that decided the co-defendant's guilt should not be permitted to hear the confession.

The result will be that separate trials will be required in cases in which the prosecution plans to use confessions against some but not all defendants.

In an 8-to-0 decision, the Court also overturned its decision of 1934 in McNally N. Hill, which held that prisoners could not use Federal habeas corpus proceedings to challenge a conviction if they were serving another sentence and had not begun to serve the challenged sentence.

The Court held today that, although Federal law permits only persons who are "in custody" to challenge by habeus corpus proceedings the legality of their detention, a prisoner is "in custody" when he is serving a prior sentence, and should not be made to wait to bring his court challenge. Chief Justice Warren wrote this opinion.

The fifth criminal law decision today, a unanimous ruling written by Justice Abe Fortas, overruled the Court's decision of 1960 in Parker N. Ellis. The Court ruled then that the appeal of a habeas corpus case becomes moot when the prisoner completes his term and is released.

But today the Court ruled that a Long Island man, James P. Carafas, should be permitted to complete his appellate challenge to his burglary and larceny convictions in 1960.

Justice Fortas said that even though Carafas was paroled in 1964 he still suffers disabilities as a convicted felon, and his case is not moot.

Should the police be allowed to question
you just because you look suspicious?

The Cop's Right (?)
To Stop and Frisk

By FRED P. GRAHAM

WASHINGTON.

IT is not unusual for a Supreme
Court Justice to have had practical experience with a legal issue
that comes before the Court, but
Thurgood Marshall will bring a special expertise to the task of deciding
whether policemen can constitutionally stop and frisk suspicious-looking
people.

Justice Marshall recalls being
stopped and questioned twice by policemen in his younger days. The first
time was in Harlem many years ago.
He was just walking along—not, he
though acting suspiciously — so
when he was asked to identify himself he told the policeman to mind
his own business. There was a tense
moment as the policeman told Marshall that he could run him in, and
Marshall said, yes and he could take
the officer's badge number. Then
Marshall walked away and that was
that.

Several years later, Marshall, then
chief counsel for the National Association for the Advancement of
Colored People, was stopped again by
a policeman, this time in the affluent
surroundings of downtown Manhattan. He readily gave his name to the
officer and went his way, wondering
—as he does to this day—why he
reacted differently in the two situations.

In the next few months he will
have occasion to ponder those sidewalk scenes many times. For this fall,
in the 179th year of the Supreme
Court, the Justices are attempting for
the first time to lay down the constitutional rules for such confrontations between policemen and citizens
on the street.

The four appeals that raise the
issue are based on deceptively simple
incidents. But in deciding these cases,
the Supreme Court must come to
grips with two basic but unresolved
questions. The first concerns the right
to "stop": To what extent, if at all,
can the police detain and demand
answers of a person whom they suspect but have no legal reason to

arrest? There is one "stop" case before the Court:

¶Two policemen in New Orleans's
French Quarter are on the lookout
for a suspected killer with "Born to
Raise Hell" tattooed on his arm.
Does a young man on the street, who
answers the suspect's description but
claims to be a law student, have to
remove his jacket to prove his innocence?

The three other cases raise the
second question: If a policeman, having stopped a suspect but before
having legal reason to arrest him,
frisks him and finds incriminating
evidence, can that evidence be used
against the suspect in court? The
three "frisk" cases are these:

¶A New York policeman, at home
in his apartment house, collars a
suspicious-looking stranger tiptoeing
down the corridor and frisks him for
weapons. He finds burglar tools instead. Can they be used against the
prowler in court?

¶A suspected narcotics pusher in
Brooklyn, challenged by a policeman,
reaches for a gleaming object in his
pocket. The officer, thinking it might
be a knife, reaches into the pocket
too, and comes up with a container of
heroin. Can the heroin be used as
evidence to convict the man of possessing narcotics?

¶A detective in Cleveland frisks
two men who appear to be casing
a jewelry store in broad daylight.
Both have guns in their pockets. Can
the pistols be used as evidence in
prosecuting the men for carrying concealed weapons?

Like many other criminal law controversies that take constitutional
forms, these questions have deep
racial implications. Negroes, particularly young Negro males, are the ones
most likely to be stopped and frisked
in these casual, prearrest encounters
between police and passers-by—and
Negroes resent the fact. The President's National Crime Commission has
warned that "misuse of field interrogation . . . is causing serious friction
with minority groups in many loca-

tions. This is becoming particularly
true as . . . officers are encouraged
routinely to stop and question persons on the street who are unknown
to them, who are suspicious, or whose
purpose for being abroad is not readily
evident." And observers of the American Bar Foundation, who accompanied
Chicago police patrols, agreed that
"there is a de facto concentration on
Negroes and other minority groups
which results from the police decision
to concentrate field interrogation in
areas having high crime rates."

The number or frequency of stops
and frisks is almost impossible to
determine, but in San Diego, which is
one of the few cities where police
are supposed to submit written reports of each stop, 200,000 were reported in one recent year, and this
was estimated to be only one-half
the actual total.

IT is by design and not by accident
that the Court is confronting this
sidewalk issue more than a decade
after the Justices began their controversial overhaul of the nation's system of criminal justice. The Court
began with the rights of those already in the clutches of the law. It
poked its foot gingerly in the door in
1956 by demanding free trial transcripts for poor defendants who
wished to appeal. From this innocu-
ous toehold in state appellate procedure it moved backward through
the system of justice—requiring free
lawyers for the poor in state trials,
then guaranteeing counsel during station-house interrogation, and most
recently, last June, assuring legal
representation at police line-ups.

At each step, as the Supreme
Court's rules reached farther and
farther back toward the policeman's
first contact with the accused, cries
of "criminal coddling" became louder.
Some of the public concern stemmed
from the feeling—often unacknowl-
edged—that the new rules succeeded
too well in protecting Negroes and
the poor. But many responsible critics
feared that the Supreme Court's
method of upgrading local justice by
making state courts follow long-established Federal court rules would
prove impractical. The Federal rules
were developed primarily to deal with
"clean" crime—mail fraud, embezzlement, tax cheating—and there are
indications that the system cannot
be imposed on the pattern of big-city
crime without severe strain.

Now the stop-and-frisk issue carries the constitutional issue all the
way back to the initial "Hey, you!"
by the police, and public reaction to
any Supreme Court ruling that restricts the police can be expected to
be fierce.

So the Justices are faced with a choice betwen making a vastly unpopular and perhaps unenforceable decision and one that will compromise their previously ironclad prohibition against police searches that are not supported by "probable cause." This term appears only once in the Constitution (in the Fourth Amendment, where it is said that no search or arrest warrant can be issued except "upon probable cause"), but the Supreme Court has established it as the key to the policeman's power to exercise control over a citizen. "Probable cause" is defined as that quantum of evidence that would lead a prudent person to believe that a suspect has committed a crime.

Policemen can legally search an individual's person or premises only with a search warrant based upon proof of "probable cause," or in "hot pursuit" of a law violator, or as an incident to a legal arrest—which must also be based upon "probable cause." The catch is that the courts have applied the same high standard of "probable cause" for the issuance of a search warrant, where the officers have the leisure to marshal their evidence, to the situation when a policeman must make a snap decision to arrest or not arrest on the street. And in most stop-and-frisk situations there is no proof of "probable cause," even though the circumstances may be weird enough to arouse anyone's suspicions.

Lawyers have a game in which they try to outdo one another in dreaming up hypothetical situations where "probable cause" would not exist, but the appearance of wrongdoing clearly would. Some time ago, before he became a Justice, Thurgood Marshall sat in on one of these sessions and came up with this one:

"A man dressed as a longshoreman walks through the lobby of the Mayflower Hotel, carrying a new coat over his arm. It is a woman's coat.

"And get this—it's summertime!"

This hypothetical incident illustrates as well as any the dilemma posed by the stop-and-frisk issue: Under the established "probable cause" doctrine, a policeman could not legally arrest the longshoreman on the spot. Yet if the Court now says that police have a right to detain or search him on suspicion, it will be a breach in the system of immunity from arbitrary police control that has been built up over the years.

THE Supreme Court must first decide the "stop" issue—i.e., whether the police have any right to detain persons for questioning without "probable cause."

Under the common law of England, night watchmen had the authority to detain any stranger until daylight, when it could be determined if the suspect had committed a crime. This rule was not carried over automatically into American law, and although the power to stop and question is widely assumed by policemen, it has not been recognized as a legal right in many states. However, it is well-established in some states—a fact that the public does not always realize.

Several years ago William O. Douglas Jr., the actor-son of the Supreme Court Justice, stood on what he thought were his legal rights and refused to identify himself to officers who interrupted his early-hours hike through Beverly Hills. After spending the rest of the night in jail, Douglas learned that California is one of the few states where the law clearly requires citizens to identify themselves when questioned by police.

Both Douglas and the young Thurgood Marshall back in Harlem undoubtedly felt that they had done nothing to arouse legitimate suspicion and that the police were meddling rather than investigating. This points up the inherent dilemma of the stop issue: Suspicion in the mind of a policeman is such a highly subjective standard for justifying detention that the stop often seems capricious to the person involved. The law can hardly concede to the individual the prerogative to decide whether the officer's suspicions are genuine, yet to grant this power to the officer gives him more authority over passers-by than Americans like their policemen to have.

Charles A. Reich, a Yale law professor who likes to walk at night and who has been stopped and questioned some 9 or 10 times in recent years, retaliated last year with an article in The Yale Law Journal. In a persuasive and sometimes grumpy exposition of what he sees as a growing tendency of police to pry into the affairs of pedestrians and to make unnecessary "safety checks" of motorists. Professor Reich took the give-them-an-inch-and-they'll-take-a-mile position that police should not have the power to demand any information from apparently law-abiding citizens. He argued that, while police should have the right to stop people and ask questions, individuals should not be required to answer or produce identification. Unless the police have "probable cause" to make an arrest, he said, the citizen should have the right to clam up and just walk away.

Apparently this was also the belief of Stephen R. Wainwright, the law student who had the run-in with the New Orleans police in the first of the cases now before the Court. The officers thought he resembled an artist's drawing of the tattooed murder suspect, so they demanded to see his arm. Wainwright replied that he had no identification on his person, that he was wearing only a T shirt under his jacket, that he had an unsightly skin condition and that the law did not require him to remove his jacket on the street. He gave his name and address, and told the policemen: "That is all I am required to give you." Then he walked away. They promptly hustled him to the police station, where he was stripped of his jacket by six policemen. He was subsequently convicted of disturbing the peace.

When the case came up before the Supreme Court this fall, the lawyer for New Orleans put his argument in blunt terms: "If he can just walk away, then police power in this nation is gone." Yet in amicus curiae briefs the American Civil Liberties Union and the N.A.A.C.P. Legal Defense and Educational Fund insist with equal urgency that the police should not be permitted to detain anyone, for any period of time, without "probable cause."

A compromise has been offered by the American Law Institute, which has suggested in a draft model code that officers be empowered to detain a suspected law violator or a witness for up to 20 minutes, and to use nondeadly force, if necessary, to see that the subject stays put while his story is being verified.

When it rules on the police's constitutional power to stop, the Supreme Court will almost certainly have to bend to the practical realities mentioned by the New Orleans prosecutor—concessions that the civil-liberties groups will not like. Unless the Court is prepared to say that any person may walk away from an investigating officer with impunity, then it must either concede to the police the power to effect some degree of detention without "probable cause," or to recognize a watered-down form of "probable cause," based on suspicion, which would justify street detention.

And if the Court says the police do have the right to detain suspects for street questioning, the nation's defense lawyers will race to the courthouses to test a derivative question: Does this mean that the police on the street must first warn the suspect of his rights, as required for all "in-custody" interrogation by the Miranda v. Arizona decision? This conjures up an intriguing image of the cop on his beat, babbling his way along a crowded sidewalk: "You are warned that you may remain silent, that anything you say may be held against you. . . ."

WHATEVER the decision on the stop issue, the Court will be left with the further problem of the frisk.

Having stopped a dangerous-looking character for questioning, the prudent policeman first pats down the suspect's clothing to detect any lump that could be a gun or a knife. Then he asks questions. Otherwise, as the New York Court of Appeals has put it, "the answer to the question propounded by the policeman may be a bullet."

Very few courts have ever considered the legality of the frisk, but the President's National Crime Commission discovered that it is being increasingly used by police and is becoming a law enforcement stand-by in big-city ghettos. Observers for the Crime Commission found that in New York City, where a frisk is supposed to be permitted only when an officer believes he is in bodily danger, more than 8 out of 10 persons who were stopped were also frisked. Observers in another city noted that one out of five persons frisked were in fact carrying dangerous weapons—evenly divided between firearms and knives. Nevertheless, most lawyers believe that the usual frisk is unconstitutional under the Supreme Court's current interpretation of the Fourth Amendment.

The handwriting has been on the wall since 1961, when the Court ruled in *Mapp v. Ohio* that state courts cannot consider evidence obtained in violation of the Fourth Amendment. In later decisions the Court said the states must observe the same standards for determining reasonableness that had been developed in prior Federal cases. This meant that the fruits of a search could not be used as evidence unless the searching officer had "probable cause" for an arrest before he made the search. Since policemen often do not have "probable cause" until the frisk turns it up, it seemed obvious that the frisk had become worthless for gathering evidence, unless the Supreme Court could be persuaded to make an exception.

This prompted the New York State Legislature to pass its famous Stop and Frisk Law in 1964. The law says that "a police officer may stop any person abroad in a public place whom he reasonably suspects is committing, has committed or is about to commit a felony . . . and may demand of him his name, address and an explanation of his actions. When a police officer has stopped a person for questioning . . . and reasonably suspects that he is in danger of life or limb, he may search such person for a dangerous weapon."

Nebraska passed a similar law in 1965. Rhode Island, Delaware, Massachusetts and New Hampshire already had laws that authorized frisking without "probable cause," and New Jersey, Ohio, California and Pennsylvania accomplished the same result through court decisions. The Crime Commission gave frisk laws its strong endorsement, so other states will probably adopt them unless the Supreme Court slams the door.

SINCE state laws and court decisions are void if they conflict with the Supreme Court's interpretation of the Constitution, much thought has gone into explaining how these can be squared with *Mapp v. Ohio*.

State courts have taken two tacks in upholding their policemen's frisk powers: (1) that the Fourth Amendment does not apply at all, since a "stop" is not an "arrest" and a "frisk" is not a "search," and (2) that a frisk is a search but that officers frisk suspects anyway, to protect themselves, so no good purpose is served by refusing to use the fruits of the search as evidence.

The first rationale was invoked by the New York Court of Appeals when it upheld the state's Stop and Frisk Law in two of the cases now before the Supreme Court—that of the man in the apartment-house corridor with burglar tools in his pocket, and that of the Brooklyn man who was carrying heroin. The fact that in neither case did the frisk produce a weapon tends to reinforce the appellants' contention that the policemen were just fishing, and that frisk laws encourage the practice.

The New York court avoided this disturbing point by adopting a solution that rubbed many civil libertarians the wrong way. In a 5-to-2 decision, it reasoned that, since a "stop" constitutes a lesser limitation on an individual's freedom than an "arrest," police should be permitted to stop persons for "reasonable suspicion," without having to have "probable cause." Likewise, since a "frisk" is not a "full-blown search," it should be permitted on the basis of a "reasonable suspicion" of danger.

Critics of this semantic approach have complained that the term "frisk" can be extremely elastic: New York courts have upheld warrantless searches of a briefcase and of a car by calling them "frisks."

The second rationale was invoked by the Ohio Court of Appeals in the remaining case now before the Supreme Court—that of the Cleveland detective who frisked two men outside a jewelry store and found they were carrying guns. The judges reasoned that, although the officer did not have "probable cause," the search was necessary for his safety. Since the reason for excluding unconstitutionally obtained evidence is to discourage improper searches, the rule is irrelevant in situations where the search must be made anyway to protect the policeman, the court held.

These appeals confront the Supreme Court with three options: (1) to exclude all evidence produced by frisks conducted without "probable cause"; (2) to create an exception for frisks conducted by policemen acting under a reasonable apprehension of danger, and to admit as evidence weapons produced by such searches, or (3) to admit any evidence produced by a frisk, as long as the frisk seemed necessary to protect the policeman.

Logically, the same reasoning that permits the use of weapons as evidence would seem to justify the use of items other than weapons (such as the burglar tools and the heroin) so long as the frisk was really necessary. But the Ohio Court of Appeals as much as said this would be stretching the exception to the *Mapp v. Ohio* rule too far, and the dissenters in the New York case agreed.

THIS reluctance to give the police the slightest encouragement to stop and frisk underscores the growing concern over a shift in police strategy that may be in the process of undermining the power of the Supreme Court to determine how policemen shall treat citizens.

Ever since 1914, when the Supreme Court ruled in *Weeks v. United States* that evidence obtained by Federal officers in violation of the Fourth Amendment could not be used in Federal trials, there has been an assumption that the Supreme Court could effectively "police the police" if it was willing to exercise its power to rule out evidence obtained by unconstitutional methods. The assumption was that police overstep their bounds because they want convictions, and that rules invalidating illegally obtained evidence would therefore succeed in curbing the police.

This proved true of the ruling in

the *Mapp* case, in which the police had broken down the door of an apartment without a search warrant. Since police do not ordinarily bother to enter a home unless they want a conviction, the exclusionary rule effectively discourages warrantless searches of houses. The same reasoning held true when the Court ruled out many station-house confessions in its 1966 *Miranda* decision. Police usually do not question a suspect at the station house unless they want a conviction, so they must try to comply with the rules for interrogation contained in the *Miranda* case, or they are just wasting their time.

But the increasing use of the stop-and-frisk tactic is due to its proven success in reducing crime rates, rather than in producing convictions —and urban police are learning that reducing crime is not at all dependent on winning convictions. Several years ago, the Chicago police began to crack down on ghetto crime with a new technique called "aggressive patrol"—a euphemism for systematic stop-and-frisk forays through high-crime areas. The result was impressively lower crime rates in those neighborhoods, while crime was increasing almost everywhere else.

According to the American Bar Foundation observers who went along on some of these patrols, the purpose was to collect weapons and to throw potential criminals off balance, rather than to investigate crimes. "In most instances," they reported, "the officers have no ground for suspicion other than the facts that it is night, that the 'suspect' is male and that he is in an area with a high crime rate."

THIS shifting police emphasis from convicting criminals to preventing crimes suggests that the Supreme Court may be reaching the point of diminishing returns in its efforts to police the police by excluding illegally obtained evidence. According to the Bar Foundation's experts, big-city police officials are coming to the conclusion that prosecution is often so cumbersome and punishment so inadequate that their manpower is better spent in "aggressive patrol" than in trying to get convictions. "Since there is no particular police concern with prosecution, evidentiary standards enforced by the threat to exclude the evidence illegally obtained do not deter the police from engaging in these practices," they concluded.

This attitude on the part of the police seems to reflect a shift in public concern from "enforcing the law" to "reducing crime." Few people know what the conviction rate is in their community, but each year, as the percentages climb, more people worry about the crime rate. The discovery that "aggressive patrol" can actually reduce the crime rate has had a sharp impact on big-city police emphasis.

Thus, it seems likely that aggressive patrol will persist in the ghettos, despite what the Supreme Court says about stop and frisk. If so, a new and chilling element is entering the controversy over the "coddling of criminals" by judges. For if the Supreme Court is losing some of its power to "coddle criminals," then even those who have damned the Court for placing itself between the police and the accused must wonder who now remains with the strength and courage to do this when it should be done.

Opponents of the Supreme Court's activism are fond of quoting Chief Justice Harlan F. Stone's admonition to his brethren that "the only check upon our exercise of power is our own sense of self-restraint." Aggressive patrol could demonstrate in a disturbing way that there are practical limits to the Court's power, if not on its discretion to declare what conduct is unconstitutional.

In recent years the Supreme Court has tended to strike a balance, when ruling on Fourth Amendment questions, between the privacy rights of individuals and the law-enforcement needs of police. There is every reason to believe that the Court will find such an avenue of compromise between the horns of the stop-and-frisk dilemma, and that it will approve some police power to detain—and perhaps even search—persons whom they could not legally arrest.

If so, the decision will be a disappointment to those who see the Supreme Court as the best hope of policing the police. But the outcome could be a lesson well-learned: that while judges say what the Constitution means, enforcing the Constitution must be the responsibility of legislators, mayors, police chiefs and many others as well. ∎

HIGH COURT BACKS RIGHTS OF POLICE TO STOP AND FRISK

Approves Actions Deemed 'Reasonably' Necessary in Dangerous Situations

RULING IS FIRST OF KIND

Justices Also Say Articles Taken in Seizures May Be Used as Evidence

WASHINGTON, June 10—The Supreme Court upheld today the authority of policemen to stop suspicious-looking persons and frisk them for weapons when that is reasonably necessary for the safety of policemen and of others.

If such a frisk produces weapons or any other evidence of guilt, the Court said, the evidence may be used in court against the person searched.

The decision, contained in two opinions written by Chief Justice Earl Warren, stressed the need to protect policemen in their efforts to control street crime. This marked the first time, the Chief Justice noted, the Court had held that police can detain and search persons without the "probable cause" mentioned in the Constitution's Fourth Amendment.

The ruling gave the police virtually the full range of powers that law enforcement representatives had asked of the Court. It rejected appeals by civil rights and civil liberties groups to limit the "stop and frisk" power of the police.

Harassment Feared

The American Civil Liberties Union and the N.A.A.C.P. Legal Defense and Educational Fund, Inc., had argued that if the high court made such a ruling the power would be used to harass Negroes and other minority groups.

However, the Chief Justice laid down a rule of reasonableness that will permit policemen to search suspects when "a reasonably prudent man in the circumstances would be warranted in the belief that his safety or that of others was in danger."

The Court did not rule on the constitutionality of the New York "stop and frisk" law, which was the subject of one of the two opinions handed down today. Chief Justice Warren said this was unnecessary in view of the holding that police officers have constitutional power to stop and search suspects under proper circumstances without a statute.

The major elements of the new rule were announced in the case of John W. Terry, who was stopped and frisked on a downtown street in Cleveland on Oct. 31, 1963. The vote was 8 to 1, with Justice William O. Douglas dissenting.

The Court said that Terry and two other men appeared to be "casing" a store for a holdup, and that the officer who searched them had acted reasonably.

Terry was found to be carrying a loaded pistol and was convicted for carrying a concealed weapon. The Supreme Court affirmed the conviction.

The New York opinion concerned Nelson Sibron, who was convicted of possessing heroin after a policeman had frisked him outside a Brooklyn restaurant, and John Francis Peters, who was found guilty of possessing burglar tools. The tools were found when an off-duty policeman searched Peters after having caught him tiptoeing down an apartment house corridor in Mount Vernon.

The Court reversed Sibron's conviction on the ground that the policeman had been searching for narcotics, not necessarily constituting an immediate danger, when he made the search. It found that the officers who searched Peters reasonably thought he might be armed. It affirmed the conviction.

Fourth Amendment at Issue

Although the police in most communities have been stopping and frisking suspects for years, the question of whether the practice violated the Fourth Amendment to the Constitution was not meaningful until 1961. In that year the Supreme Court held that evidence obtained in violation of that amendment could not be used in state courts.

The Fourth Amendment declares in part that "the right of the people to be secure in their persons, houses, papers and effects, against unreasonable searches and seizures, shall not be violated, and no warrants shall issue, but upon probable cause . . ."

This has been construed by the Supreme Court to mean that the police cannot make an arrest or search unless they have objective evidence that a crime has been committed and the suspect did it.

In most frisk situations the police act on suspicious circumstances and do not have evidence of probable cause. Thus the Court would have ruled inadmissible the fruits of most frisks if it had insisted on the probable cause standard in stop and frisk situations.

Chief Justice Warren rejected the New York Court of Appeals' reasoning that the Fourth Amendment does not apply because a "stop" is not a "seizure" and a "frisk" is not a full-blown "search."

Amendment Applicable

He declared that the Fourth Amendment does apply, but that since the amendment rules out "unreasonable" searches the probable cause requirement can be ignored if a search for weapons is otherwise reasonable.

The reasonableness of each search will have to be decided according to its circumstances, he said. The officer cannot rely on "inarticulate hunches" but will have to show that there were objective grounds for his suspicions.

Also, the extent of the search must be limited to the exigencies of the situation. Usually, a patting-down of the suspect's clothing is all that will be upheld.

However, the Chief Justice said:

"We cannot blind ourselves to the need for law enforcement officers to protect themselves and other prospective victims of violence in situations where they may lack probable cause for an arrest.

"When an officer is justified in believing that the individual whose suspicious behavior he is investigating at close range is armed and presently dangerous to the officer or to others, it would appear to be clearly unreasonable to deny the officer the power to take necessary measures to determine whether the person is in fact carrying a weapon and to neutralize the threat of physical harm."

In his dissent, Justice Douglas said it was illogical to let policemen search without probable cause when they acted without a warrant, while they would have to show probable cause if they applied to a magistrate for a search warrant.

"To give the police greater power than a magistrate is to take a long step down the totalitarian path," he said. "Perhaps such a step is desirable to cope with modern forms of lawlessness. But if it is taken, it should be the deliberate choice of the people through a constitutional amendment."

Louis Stokes of Cleveland argued for Terry. Reuben M. Payne, assistant prosecuting attorney of Cuyahoga County, argued for the State of Ohio.

William I. Siegel, assistant district attorney of Kings County, and James J. Duggan, assistant district attorney of Westchester County, argued for the state. Michael Juviler, New York County, also argued for the state as friend of the court.

The New York Times

Chief Justice Earl Warren wrote opinions stressing need to protect policemen.

June 11, 1968

PRESIDENT SIGNS BROAD CRIME BILL, WITH OBJECTIONS

Asserts It Contains 'More Good Than Bad' and Will Lift 'Shadow of Fear'

ASSAILS WIDE WIRETAPS

But He Praises Massive Federal Help to Improve Local Law Enforcement

WASHINGTON, June 19—President Johnson signed the controversial omnibus crime bill tonight because he said it contained "more good than bad."

Expressing strong reservations, especially about the broad license it gives to state and local law enforcement agencies to tap telephones and engage in other forms of eavesdropping, the President said that despite its shortcomings the new law "will help to lift the stain of crime and the shadow of fear from the streets of our communities."

The heart of the measure, he noted, is the authorization for massive Federal grants to improve local law enforcement and methods, and this, the President indicated, is a great opportunity that should not be lost.

Repeal Is Urged

Mr. Johnson called for the repeal of the wiretapping provisions and indicated some reservation about elements of the law dealing with certain rules of evidence in Federal criminal trials.

But these provisions, which purport to overturn Supreme Court decisions on the rights of defendants, will not seriously affect the Federal practice, the President indicated, and can be so interpreted as to be constitutional.

The new law also contains controls on the sale of handguns, which the President previously called "a halfway measure" because it omitted rifles and shotguns.

Nonetheless, Mr. Johnson noted that the gun controls ended three decades of inaction by the Federal Government. He urged Congress to follow this up quickly by passing the controls over rifles and shotguns that he urged following the assassination June 5 of Senator Robert F. Kennedy, elements that the Senate had previously stricken from the bill.

Mr Johnson delayed action until less than five hours before the midnight deadline while 11 Government departments and many other aides considered the 110-page omnibus measure.

No department recommended a veto, the President noted, and it was after this advice and his own "searching examination" that he decided there was more to be gained than lost by his signing it.

"I sign the bill because it responds to one of the most urgent problems in America today—the problem of fighting crime in the local neighborhood and on the city street," the President said.

His aides, reviewing the recommendations that he sign it, said that their primary interest was in getting money out to the states and local communities so as to "professionalize" police forces, strengthen the courts and rehabilitation systems and pump Federal money into every aspect of law enforcement — "from police to prisons to parole," as the President put it.

Heart of the Law

This part of the law, which was the heart of what the President recommended early in 1967, is its Title I.

It authorizes up to $100-million in the fiscal year 1969 starting July 1 and $300-million the following year in planning research and direct action grants to improve enforcement methods. Greater sums are expected in the years thereafter.

The $400-million authorized for the first two years of the law's operation, officials said, amounted to almost 10 per cent of the approximately $4-billion now spent on all aspects of law enforcement in the United States.

The President had wanted the Attorney General to make these grants directly to local communities, but Congress insisted upon so-called block grants to the states for redistribution and allocation and stipulated that the grants be made by a three-member law enforcement administration under the general authority of the Justice Department.

The new law thus becomes the first major legislation embodying the concept of block grants, whose appeal has spread from the champions of states rights to others who think the local authorities know their needs better than Washington and can eliminate some of the Federal Government's cumbersome bureaucracy.

State Must Qualify

But the Administration was willing to settle for this system because the states will still have to qualify for the grants by getting approval for plans to spend the money.

Moreover if the states do not qualify for the sums set aside for them—on a formula patterned after the population of the states—the Federal Government will have the right to give that money directly to municipalities in those states.

Also contrary to the Administration's wishes, the new law requires that priority in the use of the Federal funds be given where possible to the fight against organized crime and for the prevention and control of riots.

But this expression of Congressional sentiment appears to be regarded as no major obstacle.

Title II of the law purports to overturn three Supreme Court decisions of the last decade dealing with the rights of suspects accused of Federal crimes.

A defendant's confession, it stipulates, is to be admissible in evidence if the court deems it "voluntary," even if the suspect had not been warned of his constitutional right to remain silent.

In addition, the law permits the police to hold a suspect for up to six hours—longer in some cases—before an arraignment and still obtain an admissible confession from him. It provides for the admissibility of eyewitness testimony even if the suspect has no lawyer when he is identified in a police line-up.

The President said he had been told by Attorney General Ramsey Clark that these provisions could be read as being "in harmony" with the Constitution and that in any case because they affected only Federal criminal procedures, the Federal Government would continue to make certain that they respect the Constitution.

'Full and Fair Warning'

Specifically, the President said he had asked the Attorney General and J. Edgar Hoover, the director of the Federal Bureau of Investigation, to assure that Federal agents and attorneys continued to give suspects "full and fair warning" of their constitutional rights. The state and local police will still have to abide by the Supreme Court decisions, officials said.

Title III of the law permits police wiretapping and eavesdropping in investigations of many types of crime.

Mr. Johnson had wanted such electronic surveillance limited to national security cases, but Congress authorized them on the issuance of a warrant—and without warrants for 48 hours in "emergencies" related to investigations of organized crime or national security cases.

Mr. Johnson called upon Congress to reconsider "immediately" what he called this "unwise and potentially dangerous" sanctioning of snooping by Federal, state and local law officials in "an almost unlimited variety of situations."

If the nation is not careful, he said, this provision "could result in producing a nation of snoopers bending through the keyholes of the homes and offices in America, spying on our neighbors."

Restraint Planned

Mr. Johnson indicated that he would not permit the Federal authorities to take advantage of this new law and would continue his policy of two and a half years to confine wiretapping and eavesdropping by Federal agents to national security cases—and then only with the explicit approval of the Attorney General.

Officials said that the Federal authorities had had their best year in fighting organized crime without any broader wiretapping or eavesdropping rights and that they would continue to practice this restraint.

Mr. Johnson called upon the state and local authorities to show similar "restraint and caution" if they took advantage of the broad powers of the new law.

Title IV of the law bans the mail order sale of handguns and ammunition to individuals, and prohibits the over-the-counter sales of handguns to residents of another state and to all persons under the age of 21.

It also provides for the licensing of gun dealers and makes it a Federal crime for felons, mental incompetents, illegal aliens, persons who have renounced citizenship and veterans without an honorable discharge to possess firearms.

Mr. Johnson reiterated his interest in broadening this to include shotguns and rifles and called upon Congress to act at once.

Other Steps Explored

In addition he said he was asking Attorney General Clark to explore what other gun control steps might be taken—apparently registration and licensing—so that Mr. Johnson could recommend them after the Congress acted on the proposals he submitted following the shooting of Senator Kennedy.

The indications in the Senate were that the Judiciary Committee would act favorably on the extension of controls to rifles and shotguns tomorrow and that a House committee would follow.

The Administration believes

that the resubmission of provisions stricken from the omnibus crime bill will pass because of the outpouring of supporting mail from all over the country.

Senator Mike Mansfield of Montana, the Democratic leader said he would support any move on the Senate floor to strengthen the measure still further by requiring the registration of all firearms and permits to own them.

The Administration has not wanted to sponsor such a measure because the new feature could force a lengthy

round of committee hearings, nullifying the psychological effect of an aroused public opinion at the moment.

Other provisions of the new law create a National Institute of Law Enforcement and Criminal Justice for research in the detection of crime, establishes college loans and grants for students specializing in law enforcement, expands training for state and local police officers at Federal institutions and requires the appointment of future directors of the F.B.I. to be confirmed by the Senate.

Another controversial provision states that a person convicted of a felony related to civil disorders must be disqualified from employment by the Federal Government for five years.

Mr. Johnson put his name to the new law at 7:14 P.M., less than five hours before the midnight deadline. The House passed the measure by a vote of 368 to 17 on June 6.

Mr. Johnson had the choice of signing the measure, vetoing it, or letting it automatically become law at midnight.

June 20, 1968

Flawed Anti-Crime Law

President Johnson's signature of the omnibus crime-control bill is more a surrender to public hysteria over crime in the streets than it is an expression of conviction that the bill represents a sound contribution to the defense of law and order.

"I have decided that this measure contains more good than bad," the President said, which seems to us no way to approve so fundamental a law. The Johnson statement asserted that he had consulted the "wisest counselors available to the President" and that no Federal department had advised a veto.

Yet a Department of Justice memorandum analyzing key titles in the bill found them deficient. And, on April 26, Attorney General Clark, the nation's chief law-enforcement officer, expressed "grave reservations" about the constitutionality of the title circumventing decisions of the Supreme Court. "It would be most unfortunate for law enforcement," he said, "and for the constitutional rights of citizens, if it is adopted as presently proposed."

Surely the 200 professors, including thirteen deans, from law schools across the United States might have

been taken into account on the constitutional and anti-Supreme Court aspects of the bill. In the Congressional Record of April 29 they are recorded against the measure, but, apparently, they did not qualify as wise counselors.

The bill is full of flaws. Its wiretapping authorization goes a long way toward encouraging low-level governmental invasion of privacy. Its title on the admissibility of evidence confuses police and courts —and is an attempt to overturn decisions and slap down the "Warren Court." Its harsh provision barring "rioters" from Federal employment is a simplistic solution that will not accomplish its aims. And the effort at gun control, discussed in an editorial below, is less than half a loaf.

The grants to improve anti-crime programs and police departments in the states and cities are the bill's best feature. The $100 million the first year and $300 million the second can go a long way toward attracting and educating better-qualified law officers. The Attorney General originally was supposed to make these grants directly to the cities, but the Congress interposed the states as distributive agencies. That could mean statehouse politics as a complicating element in local law enforcement.

June 21, 1968

MITCHELL TO USE WIRETAP POWERS IN FIGHT ON CRIME

Tells Senators He'll Widen Bugging Under '68 Law to Cover Major Cases

WASHINGTON, Jan. 14 — Wiretapping and other electronic surveillance will be used in the Nixon Administration's fight against crime, Attorney General - designate John N. Mitchell said today.

Testifying before a friendly Senate Judiciary Committee, Mr. Mitchell disclosed that the Justice Department would apply the eavesdrop power authorized by Congress last June "not only in national security cases but against organized crime and other major crimes."

He indicated that this and other efforts against organized crime would distinguish President-elect Richard M. Nixon's Justice Department from the present Administration's, which has refused on privacy grounds to use electronic surveillance in any but national security investigations.

Mr. Mitchell assured the Senators that the new power would be used "carefully and effectively." He said that the law contained ample safeguards to protect the privacy of individuals.

Impact on Controversy

After an hour-long hearing, the committee retired and informally approved Mr. Mitchell's nomination without a dissenting vote. The action was informal because, technically, no nomination may go before the Senate until Mr. Nixon's inauguration. Hearings are being held now in an effort to speed the transition.

Mr. Nixon has frequently mentioned his approval of the wiretap provisions of the new omnibus crime control law. But the Mitchell statement was the first time that a figure close to Mr. Nixon had declared that wiretapping would be used in criminal cases.

The development has deep symbolic implications in the controversy over how far Government should be permitted to expand its powers in the effort to cope with increasing crime.

Since the first Federal anti-wiretap law was passed in 1934, the Government's policy has been to use electronic devices only against suspected spies. Senator Hiram L. Fong of Hawaii warned Mr. Mitchell today that the new policy represented "a new road that we are taking."

Under the law, Federal officials may eavesdrop, if they obtain the prior approval of a Federal judge, in investigations of a wide range of Federal criminal offenses, including bribery, interstate gambling activities, labor racketeering and bankruptcy fraud. For the first time, the law permits the results of such surveillance to be admitted in Federal court.

Today's hearing was the first public performance here by the 55-year-old Wall Street lawyer since he was lifted from the relative obscurity of municipal bond practice by Mr. Nixon's appointment.

He answered the Senators' questions in short, soft-spoken sentences. On several occasions he admitted that he was uninformed on topics that were raised in questions.

The questions were gentle, with the exception of several posed by Senator Philip A. Hart, Michigan Democrat. He recalled Mr. Nixon's frequent campaign criticism of Attorney General Ramsey Clark and demanded to know how Mr. Mitchell's policies would differ.

Mr. Mitchell mentioned wiretapping and new stress on efforts to combat organized crime. Otherwise, he said, it would be "presumptuous" of him to anticipate how his regime might differ from Mr. Clark's.

"Did the President-elect have any deeper analysis than you when he made his speeches?" Senator Hart asked. "If his only quarrel with Ramsey Clark was wiretapping," he was most imprecise in his speeches."

Noting that Mr. Mitchell served as Mr. Nixon's Presidential campaign manager, Senator Sam J. Ervin Jr. questioned what he said was the recent tendency of Presidents to appoint their top political advisers Attorney General rather than Postmaster General.

The North Carolina Democrat complained that Attorneys General had been appearing before Congressional committees in the role of a Presidential "political adviser and agitator."

"I would hope that my activities of a political nature would have ended with the termination of the political campaign," Mr. Mitchell replied. He said he would "act as the legal and not the political adviser to the President."

A chunky, baldish man in a sober blue suit, Mr. Mitchell posed a striking physical contrast to his more youthful Democratic predecessors, Mr. Clark, Nicholas deB. Katzenbach and Robert F. Kennedy. They averaged 39 years of age when they assumed the office.

Mr. Mitchell was introduced by Senator Jacob K. Javits, New York Republican, who praised Mr. Mitchell's record in private life.

January 15, 1969

High Court Widens Curbs On Questioning by Police

WASHINGTON, March 25—The Supreme Court ruled today that its Miranda v. Arizona decision of 1966 requires the police to warn all suspects of their rights as soon as they are arrested, not just before interrogation at the police station.

The decision drew a heated dissent from Justice Byron R. White. He called it a "new and unwarranted" extension of the Miranda doctrine that "draws the straitjacket even tighter" on law enforcement.

However, Justice Hugo L. Black replied in the majority opinion that today's ruling did not extend the Miranda doctrine. He asserted that although the cases specifically decided in the Miranda decision all involved stationhouse questioning, the opinion itself said that warnings must be given to all persons "in custody" before questioning may commence.

The vote in today's case was 6 to 2, with Justice Potter Stewart joining Justice White's dissent. Justice John M. Harlan, who dissented in the Miranda case, said in a concurring opinion that he still considered the Miranda doctrine unsound but that since it was the law he felt bound to acquiesce in today's decision.

Justice Thurgood Marshall, who as Solicitor General represented the Government in the Miranda case and argued against the position that the Court eventually took, joined the majority today. The others in the majority were Chief Justice Earl Warren and Justices William J. Brennan Jr. and William O. Douglas. Justice Abe Fortas did not take part.

The case decided today involved Reyes Arias Orozco of Dallas, who was convicted of murder without malice after a jury found that he had gunned a man down after a fight outside a tavern shortly after midnight on Jan. 5, 1966.

Admitted Owning Pistol

The interrogation that was declared unconstitutional today took place about four hours later, when Orozco was in bed. Four policemen burst into his boarding house bedroom and stood about the bed, asking questions.

To a brief series of questions, Orozco admitted his name, that he had been at

380

the tavern and that he owned a pistol, which was hidden in a washing machine in another room.

The policemen stated at the trial that they had considered Orozco to be "in custody" as soon as he had admitted his identity, but they had not stopped then to recite the warnings required by the Miranda decision. The Texas courts held that Orozco's answers to the subsequent questions were admissible on the ground that the Miranda case does not preclude such cursory questioning.

In his dissent today, Justice White strongly agreed with the findings in Texas. He argued that the reasoning behind the Miranda decision was that pro-

longed questioning by the police in the intimidating surroundings of a stationhouse could result in coerced confessions, in violation of the Fifth Amendment's privilege against compulsory self-incrimination.

In the Miranda case the Court held that before asking any questions the police must warn suspects: (A) That anything they say may be used against them, (B) That they may remain silent, (C) That they have a right to counsel, and (D) That if they are poor a lawyer will be furnished by the state. All suspects must waive these rights before any questions may be asked.

Justice White argued that "the full panoply of Miranda

warnings" were not necessary to protect Orozco from compulsory self-incrimination. His bedroom admissions were "simply the terse remarks of a man who has been caught, almost in the act," Justice White said.

Shortly after the Miranda decision was announced some criminal law experts argued that it did not apply to questions asked before a prisoner arrived at the police station. Some defense lawyers have since complained that the police were plying suspects with questions at the scene of the crime and in patrol cars on the way to the stationhouse.

However, many police departments, anticipating today's

ruling, have given all policemen "Miranda cards" listing the required warnings that could be recited at the scene of arrest.

The opinion by Justice Black today did not make it clear whether in a second trial of Orozco the prosecution would be precluded from using as evidence the gun that was found as a result of the unconstitutional questioning, or the ballistics evidence that was developed as a result of finding the gun. The opinion did state that Orozco's admissions could not be used against him.

Charles W. Tessmer of Dallas argued for Orozco. Lonny F. Zwiener, assistant Attorney General of Texas, argued for the state.

March 26, 1969

Criminal Lawyers Are Put on the Defensive Today

Jack S. Hoffinger, a defense attorney, was on the telephone, talking to a lawyer he had never met about some minor civil litigation.

The lawyer, whose practice dealt only with civil matters, noted he had seen Mr. Hoffinger's name in a newspaper in connection with a murder case, and he asked:

"Do you get much criminal work?"

"Yes, I do," Mr. Hoffinger replied.

"You mean you frequently represent people accused of murder?"

"Yes."

"My God," the lawyer said. "And you sound like such a nice guy."

Mr. Hoffinger's experience was not unusual. Lawyers who defend clients accused of criminal acts said they believed that the average American finds their role less acceptable than it was, say, a half-dozen years ago. Lawyers expressing this sense of isolation include some of the best men in the business. They earn from $1,000 to $3,000 to handle a simple misdemeanor and $35,000 or more to try a felony for a well-heeled gambler.

Sensitivity to Criticism

The money is good, but not

enough to dull the lawyers' sensitivity to what they see as increased criticism from a society concerned about the breakdown of law and order, a society that frequently is heard to accuse defense lawyers (along with liberal judges) of making it possible for troublemakers to roam the streets.

Defenders say that even those who are normally quite sophisticated about courtroom procedure — such as prosecutors—now tend to see defense attorneys more as agents for the guilty and disreputable than participants in a system of jurisprudence that relies on advocacy.

"I could never become a defense lawyer," said a young assistant district attorney who asked that his name not be used. "I agree that everyone has the right to a fair trial, but because of my own personal feelings about what is happening to this country, I couldn't play a part in returning a criminal to the streets."

A Topic of Conversation

The defense lawyer's responsibilities to society as against his responsibilities to his profession have become a familiar topic of conversation among lawyers. In years past, it was not so. But now their

comments tend to reflect their commitment to their role in court as well as a sense of apprehension at a society they believe is becoming more concerned with jailing criminals than in rehabilitating people.

Mr. Hoffinger, an assistant district attorney-turned-defender, has represented some of New York's more unpopular citizens, including Richard Robles, who was convicted of the 1963 murder of two young career girls, Janice Wylie and Emily Hoffert.

"The way you measure the extent of freedom in society is the extent to which you protect the worst people, and I use the word 'worst' in quotes," Mr. Hoffinger said. "Our society is not supposed to be dedicated to the thesis that all the guilty should go to jail, but that all be treated equally under the law."

A similar attitude was expressed by Marvin B. Segal, a former special attorney for the Federal Government who helped try the Government's case against the men who attended the so-called gangland convention in Apalachin in 1957. Mr. Segal is now a lawyer who represents people accused of such "white-collar" crimes as embezzlement and fraud.

A Switch of Roles

"If you defend someone," he said, "you save him from the gaps in the law and at the same time show society where those gaps are. I am not society's enforcer. I have never felt any sorrow at an acquittal. If a man gets off, it is because the law process has failed. I have defended men I don't like, men who are despicable, men whose motives are alien to me. But they are entitled to a full and adequate defense."

Another prosecutor who has become an aggressive defense counsel is Jay Goldberg, whose clients now include people considered by the police to be among New York's most accomplished gamblers and con-men.

"I am a mercenary," he says. "A person who is accused of something comes into my office and he wants me to be his sword, he wants me to protect his rights. I must, if I accept his case, close my eyes to the needs of society and I do what I can to protect him within legal ethics, without any regard to society's needs or anyone else's needs.

"The fact is that society gains most of all by seeing to it that the rule of law applies to all. It is not tested with the law-abiding middle class, but with the people who need it most."

Many lawyers for the defense say that it is easier to be a prosecutor than it is to be a defender — especially these days.

Mr. Hoffinger sees society as armed to the teeth—with prosecutors, the police, elaborate crime-detection equipment and almost unlimited resources to pursue the criminal. He thinks of lawyers as the thin blue line between an avenging society and the defendant—a sort of countersentiment to the police who see themselves as a thin blue line between criminals and a largely unprotected society.

Some former prosecutors say they have had difficulty in making the transition to defender. Others are apprehensive about the prospect of someday defending confirmed criminals.

Michael H. Metzger, an assistant United States attorney in San Francisco, was asked if he could ever conceive of becoming a defense lawyer.

"I could," he said, "but there would be problems in representing the hardened criminal or the defendant who had committed a crime of great violence, like rape.

"No, I probably wouldn't take that kind of case if it meant going to trial," he said. "I might try to get him committed to an institution or something like that, but I wouldn't want him to get off scot free."

Nicholas Scoppetta, a former district attorney who dealt with labor racketeering and other aspects of organized crime, recently moved to the firm of Linden & Deutsch in Manhattan, which concentrates on literary properties and corporate matters.

Mr. Scoppetta says he could represent "any guilty person without doing anything unethical. But he noted that in the kind of work he was now doing, "it is not likely I will be forced to make those difficult choices that some cases would present."

Harold Rothwax, a lawyer who has handled many cases for the poor, recalled one in which he defended a young man accused of raping several girls who were only 10 to 14 years of age.

His defense was aided, he said, by shoddy police work: the accused didn't get a lawyer until after he was in cus-

tody for 10 hours; the police took no complete statement of his confession, chosing to scribble some notes on the back of an envelope rather than rely on the stenographer who was on duty in the police station; one of the witnesses was shown a picture of the accused by a policeman before making a positive identification.

Mr. Rothwax was further aided by the fact that at least six district attorneys handled the prosecution, as did the same number of judges over the period of a year. He was the only party to the case from beginning to end, a factor he feels was a great tactical advantage.

The defendant could have received sentences totaling 90 years; instead he was allowed to plead guilty to a Class E felony, which carried a penalty of only four years.

Mr. Rothwax said he was elated as a defense attorney and "shocked" as a private citizen. "It was frightening," he said, "from society's point of view."

The rapist is spending four years in jail where, Mr. Rothwax believes, the problems that led to the rapes will not

be solved. "With the prison sentence," he says, "we have neither protected society nor helped the man."

One of the best known criminal lawyers in New York is Maurice Edelbaum, who in his 38 years of diverse practice has represented assorted Mafiosi, a judge's son accused of drunken driving, a convicted abortionist, a judge who was involved in a bribery, a murderer, and an LSD-taker who was accused of doing away with his mother-in-law, among others.

Mr. Edelbaum thinks that the Supreme Court decisions of the last decade that provide more protection for the defendant is an indicaion that "the pendulum is finally swinging back because of all the injustices that have taken place over the years."

Mr. Edelbaum, who is normally has a client on trial every day from September to June, said he never felt ostracized because of the people he represented and that his friends understood what he was trying to do.

"If men like us die out," he said, speaking of the lawyers who try criminal cases, "then God help America."

May 24, 196

SENATE APPROVES STIFF CRIME BILL FOR WASHINGTON

Foes Say Measure, Passed by a Vote of 54 to 33, Is a Model for the Nation

NIXON'S ASSENT IS SEEN

'No-Knock' Searches by the Police as Well as Pretrial Detention Remain Intact

---

By WARREN WEAVER Jr.
Special to The New York Times

WASHINGTON, July 23 — The Senate decisively approved today the controversial District of Columbia crime bill. The vote, 54 to 33, was far from the close outcome that critics of the measure had hoped to achieve after a week of debate.

Passed in its final form by the House two weeks ago, the measure now goes to President Nixon for his signature, which is not in doubt. It is the first crime bill that Congress has sent the President since he took office 18 months ago.

Opponents of the measure had contended that it was not merely a local law enforcement bill but also represented the national crime policy of the Nixon Administration. Senator Sam J. Ervin Jr., the North Carolina Democrat who led the attack, said Attorney General John N. Mitchell had made this "very explicit."

"The Attorney General holds this bill up as a model for all the states of the nation," Senator Ervin declared. "All Senators should know he hopes to have it imposed on all their

constituents as well as the residents of the District."

'No-Knock' Included

Among the features of the stringent bill that were attacked by the critics as being unconstitutional or repressive were the following:

¶Authorization for "no-knock" searches, under which a policeman with a warrant could force his way into a building without announcing his presence or identifying himself if there was reason to believe evidence inside would otherwise be destroyed.

¶Preventive, or pretrial, detention, under which a defendant could be jailed without bail for up to 60 days if a hearing established that he might commit further crimes if he were released.

¶Establishment of a mandatory five-year sentence upon a second conviction for a crime of violence in which the defendant was carrying a gun.

¶Authorization for wiretaps by the police with court ap-

proval, but restricting their use when the communication involved was between physician and patient; attorney and client; clergyman and parishioner, or husband and wife.

During his 1968 Presidential campaign, Mr. Nixon had made crime in the District of Columbia a symbolic national issue, calling the city "the crime capital of the nation" and pledging to curb crime if elected.

Opponents of the crime bill fell far short of defeating it on the last available opportunity for at least two reasons. Senator Ervin, who had been able to attract a considerable bloc of Southern votes on similar occasions, won over only three Southerners today.

In addition, there was a distinct reluctance among Senators who are running for reelection this fall to vote against the bill. Of the 29 who are running for another term, eight opposed the measure on the final roll-call.

Senator Ervin had recognized this problem during the debate, saying: "I hear the siren voice of that old devil, political expediency, whisper in my ear, 'You better vote for the D.C. bill because it's a law-and-order bill. It's not politically sagacious, not politically wise, to vote against a law-and-order bill.' "

Supporters of the bill contended that, beyond its controversial features, it provides for a modernization and consolidation of the Washington court system; establishment of a new family court and new bail agency; creation of a public defender for poor defendants, and a revised code of criminal procedure.

Breakdown of Crimes

They stressed the need for more effective law enforcement in a city in which more than 56,000 felonies were reported last year, including 7,000 armed robberies, 287 murders and 336 cases of forcible rape.

Senator Mike Mansfield of Montana, the majority leader, said he was supporting the crime bill because the most controversial provisions "have been safeguarded to the extent that they are not, in fact, constitutionally impaired."

Mr. Mansfield also took pains to defend the Senate against repeated Republican charges that Congress had obstructed President Nixon's crime program. He listed 13 major crime proposals already passed by the Senate and said there was only one major exception—extending preventive detention to all Federal Courts.

The President has submitted a dozen crime bills to Congress, but the District of Columbia measure is the first to be approved in something resembling its original form. A number of

the Nixon requests have been passed by either the House or Senate in separate or omnibus bills but have not yet reached the President's desk

The measure approved by the Senate was a conference report, a compromise reached by representatives of the Senate and House after more than three months of efforts to reconcile the different bills that each house had earlier passed.

Senator Joseph D. Tydings, Democrat of Maryland, who was the chief Senate sponsor of the bill, argued for the last week that a large number of House provisions that would have made the measure even more objectionable to the Senate had been dropped by the conference committee.

But this did not prevent Senator Ervin from declaring today: "We are told it is necessary for us to throw provisions of the U.S. Constitution into the judical garbage pail in order to cope with crime in the District of Columbia."

Opponents contended that the pretrial detention provision of the bill violated the Eighth Amendment prohibition against excessive bail in noncapital cases. They also said that the "no-knock" search authorization ran counter to the Fourth Amendment's guarantees against unreasonable search and seizure.

Senator Tydings argued that the preventive detention plan was far less hypocritical than the current tacitly accepted system of keeping accused prisoners in jail by setting high bail. He said there were 1,400 such defendants currently in the District of Columbia jails awaiting trial, placed there without the hearing that pretrial detention would require.

July 24, 1970

MITCHELL REPORTS WIRETAPPING RISE

Says Government Steps Up Use in Criminal Cases— He Denies Repression

WASHINGTON, Oct. 5—Attorney General John N. Mitchell disclosed today that the Federal Government was rapidly expanding its use of wiretapping against suspected criminals.

"The only repression that has resulted is the repression of crime," Mr. Mitchell declared in a speech before the International Association of Chiefs of Police.

In reporting on the use of wiretapping against criminals, which was authorized by Congress in 1968, the Attorney General chided the Johnson Administration for refusing to use wiretapping on the ground that it might create fear of pervasive Government surveillance.

He termed such fears "bogeys" and said that one of his first acts had been to order the use of court-approved wiretapping, as authorized by the 1968 law.

133 in Seven Months

Mr. Mitchell said that a review of the first one and a half years' experience in using such wiretapping had convinced him that it was the most valuable tool available to his anticrime investigators, and that "we need not apologize to the ab-

solute civil libertarians" for using it.

Last year the Justice Department used 30 court-approved taps. During the first seven months of 1970 it used 133, Mr. Mitchell said. He said that about 80 per cent of the overheard telephone calls were incriminating — proof, he said, that the Government is not using wiretapping for "fishing expeditions."

So far this year, 419 arrests and 325 indictments have resulted from wiretapping, Mr. Mitchell said.

His speech was delivered at the police chiefs' annual meeting in Atlantic City. The text was released here. Mr. Mitchell urged the police chiefs to use wiretapping in those states where judges were permitted to authorize it, but he warned them that the Justice Department would prosecute police-

Associated Press

Attorney General John N. Mitchell addressing police chiefs in Atlantic City.

men who tapped without court authority.

Mr. Mitchell's speech was devoted entirely to court - approved wiretapping in criminal cases, and not the more controversial issue of Federal wiretapping and other electronic eavesdropping against radical domestic groups and suspected foreign spies.

He has asserted in court cases that he has legal authority to eavesdrop without court authority on both types of groups when he considers national security to be threatened. This type of surveillance has not been ruled upon by the Supreme Court, and the Government has not disclosed how much of it is going on.

Justice Department officials here said that of the 133 wiretaps used in criminal cases in the first seven months of this year, 82 were in gambling cases, 28 concerned narcotics investigations, and the rest involved loan sharking, interstate transportation of stolen property, counterfeiting, kidnapping and obstruction of justice. Document to disclose where the wiretaps were used were not available.

In informal statements after delivering his prepared remarks, Mr. Mitchell asked the organization of police chiefs to select representatives to attend a meeting with him and his top assistants at the Justice Department.

The meeting's purpose, he said, will be to discuss three major law enforcement problems: the series of attacks on police officers, the recent wave of bombings, and accusations of improper conduct by police officers.

Liberty and Safety

"If ever there was a worse Attorney General it was Ramsey Clark . . . like a jellyfish, a softie . . . You never knew which way he was going to flop on an issue. He was worse than Bobby [Kennedy]."

J. Edgar Hoover on Ramsey Clark

By RAMSEY CLARK

Our system of criminal justice fails to reduce crime. It is not working well. Police are not professional, courts are unable to process case loads, prisons make criminals of boys they could rehabilitate. We see the reforms that are desperately needed, yet we do not make them. But even if these public agencies were working at the most effective level possible, they could not substantially or permanently reduce crime while conditions exist that breed crime. Mere words of prohibition, with force and the threat of force their only sanction, cannot shape human conduct in mass society.

As turbulence, doubt and anxiety cause fear to increase, fear in turn seeks repressiveness as a source of safety. But experience tells us that the result of repressiveness is more turbulence and more crime. In frustration over the failure of law enforcement to control crime, new, quick and cheap methods by which police and courts and prisons might be made more effective are sought amid desperate hope and rising hatred. A public that believes the police alone are responsible for crime control, and therefore no other effort is needed, will vest any power in the police that seems to promise safety when fear of crime is great. But there is no such power.

Excessive reliance on the system of criminal justice is terribly dangerous. It separates the people from their government. It is the one clear chance for irreconcilable division in America. It puts institutions of government in which people must have confidence in direct confrontation with dynamics they cannot control. When the system is abusive, society itself is unfair and government demeans human dignity. Then there is a contest of cunning between the people and the state. The state can never win.

The dialogue over the proper limits of police action and barely relevant court rulings consumes most of the emotion and much of the energy that could be constructively used to strengthen the system of criminal justice. Instead of efforts to raise police standards, expand training, increase salaries, and improve judicial machinery, we debate in ignorance and anger whether police should be authorized to stop and frisk whenever they choose and whether the Miranda decision should be reversed. The resulting diversion of attention, emotionalization of concern and polarization of attitude damage the system of criminal justice. Those who stimulate prejudices in public opinion, who appeal to base instincts of fear, who protest their willingness—even desire—to sacrifice freedom on the altar of order add immeasurably to the burdens of achieving excellence in the performance of criminal justice agencies.

A narrow logic can even conclude that the use of deadly force—shooting looters, for instance—stops crime. After all, it does eliminate a criminal —if the right person is shot. Our total experience shows beyond question that the result of using such extreme repressiveness is always an increment to the dimension of violence and a new potential for more.

There are degrees of repression. Each demeans the dignity of the individual in its different way. Intimidation of speech or conduct by force or threat of force in essence says the state is supreme, the individual has no rights, he must do as he is told. We see this when police tell people to move along, when they stop and frisk without cause, arrest on suspicion, enter premises without a warrant or without knocking, deny permits to speak and assemble, break up meetings and raid places where unpopular people live or work, without legal justification.

Stealth and trickery as methods of repression mean that the state has no respect for the individual. It will deceive, lie, invade privacy, steal documents, do whatever it thinks necessary to catch people in crime. By wiretapping, the government says to its citizens: Do not trust us, for we do not trust you. We will hide, overhear, wait secretly for months for you to do wrong. If you do anything to displease us, we may choose to watch your every move.

Denial of bail and preventive detention are essentially premised on the belief that the individual must yield his liberty to the state if he is poor, ignorant, despised—and apparently dangerous. He can be tried later. Society will not presume him innocent.

No respecters of human dignity, these measures imply that judges can tell who the bad people—the dangerous ones—are and can say that they should be denied freedom and punished as guilty until proven innocent.

There is no conflict between liberty and safety. We will have both, or neither. You cannot purchase security at the price of freedom, because freedom is essential to human dignity and crime flows from acts that demean the individual. We can enlarge both liberty and safety if we turn from repressiveness, recognize the causes of crime and move constructively.

The major contribution the law can make is moral leadership. Only then can it hope to permanently influence the conduct of its citizens. The law cannot therefore impose immoral rules or act immorally. The government of a people who would be free of crime must always act fairly, with integrity and justice.

"The F.B.I. has so coveted personal credit that it will sacrifice even effective crime control ... This has been a petty and costly characteristic caused by the excessive domination of a single person, J. Edgar Hoover, and his self-centered concern for his reputation."

Ramsey Clark on J. Edgar Hoover

November 19, 1970

JUSTICES NARROW A CRIME DECISION BY WARREN COURT

Vote 5-4 to Limit Miranda Ruling, Which Restricted Interrogation by Police

BURGER WRITES OPINION

Brennan, for Minority, Sees a Blow to Progress Made on Rights of Suspects

By FRED P. GRAHAM
Special to The New York Times

WASHINGTON, Feb. 24—The Supreme Court split along conservative-liberal lines today in a 5-to-4 ruling that limited the effect of Miranda v. Arizona, the Warren Court's landmark decision that restricted police interrogation.

Chief Justice Warren E. Burger wrote the opinion for the majority, which held that a statement that was inadmissible as evidence because the suspect had not been warned of his rights might still be used in court to contradict the suspect's testimony.

He was joined by the four other members of the new majority that has coalesced in several recent decisions to narrow liberal criminal law rulings of the Warren Court. They were Harry A. Blackmun who, along with Mr. Burger, was appointed by President Nixon, and three Justices who dissented in the Miranda decision in 1966—John M. Harlan, Potter Stewart and Byron R. White.

Ruling Challenged

"This goes far toward undoing much of the progress made in conforming police methods to the Constitution," Justice William J. Brennan Jr. charged in the dissenting opinion.

"The Court today tells the police," he said, "that they may freely interrogate an accused incommunicado and without counsel and know that although any statement they obtain in violation of Miranda can't be used on the state's direct case, it may be introduced if the defendant has the temerity to testify in his own defense."

His dissent was joined by Justices William O. Douglas and Thurgood Marshall. Justice Hugo L. Black noted his dissent without giving reasons.

The Miranda case became the rallying point for critics and admirers of the libertarian Warren Court after the Court had used it to announce a broad ruling that statements could not be used in evidence unless the suspects had first been warned of their rights to silence and to free legal counsel.

Conviction Upheld

Today's decision upheld the narcotics conviction in 1966 of a New Rochelle, N. Y., man, Viven Harris. Shortly after his arrest, he gave a statement to the police, who had not told him of his rights.

At the trial, the prosecutor conceded that the statement was inadmissible as evidence, but after Harris told a different story from the witness stand, he was asked about the various conflicting remarks that he had made in his post-arrest statement.

Chief Justice Burger based his decision that this was proper on a 1954 Supreme Court decision that allowed a prosecutor to use inadmissible evidence obtained in an illegal search to contradict a defendant's testimony.

Likewise, he said, the Miranda doctrine "cannot be perverted into a license to use perjury" by shielding a defendant from exposure if he testifies falsely. He added that the benefits of exposing false testimony outweighed "the speculative possibility that impermissible police conduct will be encouraged" by today's holding.

The New York Times

Chief Justice Burger

The ruling today presented the strongest indication to date that President Nixon's appointment of Justice Blackmun has created the conservative majority on criminal law issues that Mr. Nixon has set as his goal.

So far during this Court term, Mr. Blackmun has joined with the other members of today's majority to issue narrowing interpretations of liberal Warren Court decisions on double jeopardy, plea bargaining and immunity of grand jury witnesses.

However, the decision today carries additional symbolic significance because it is the first ruling by the full Burger Court on the Miranda decision, and because the majority of the lower courts had taken the opposite position.

Yale Kamisar, a law professor at Michigan Law School, said in an interview today that while lower courts had generally given the Miranda decision restricted interpretations on other points, most of them had ruled that statements obtained in violation of the Miranda case could not be used to impeach the defendants' testimony.

He said that today's decision might "spur on a lot of lower courts to cut down on Miranda."

Joel Martin Aurnou argued for Harris. James J. Duggan, Administrative Assistant District Attorney of Westchester County, argued for the state, supported by Miss Sybil H. Landau of The New York County District Attorney's office, who appeared as friend of the court.

In a unanimous decision today, the Supreme Court held that servicemen could be court-martialed for offenses against civilians on military bases. The court had ruled in 1969 in a case involving an off-base crime by a soldier against a civilian that only the civilian courts could try such offenses that were not "service-connected."

Justice Blackmun said in the Court's opinion today that on-base offenses against civilians were service-connected. The decision upheld the 30-year sentence of Isiah Relford, who was convicted by military court of kidnapping and raping two women at Fort Dix, N. J., in 1961.

Court, 6-3, Says Jury Trial Is Not Required for Youths

Opinion by Blackmun Warns of an End to the 'Intimate, Protective Proceeding' Sought Under the Juvenile System

By JOHN HERBERS
Special to The New York Times

WASHINGTON, June 21— The Supreme Court ruled 6 to 3 today that juveniles do not have a constitutional right to a trial by jury.

Justice Harry A. Blackmun said in the majority opinion that although the juvenile system of justice may have fallen far short of perfection the requirement of a jury trial could "put an end to what has been the idealistic prospect of an intimate, informal protective proceeding."

The decision nevertheless went against a 23-year trend in which the Court in a succession of cases had extended Bill of Rights protections to juvenile proceedings.

Opinion by Douglas

Justice William O. Douglas said in the dissenting opinion that because many law enforcement officials had treated juveniles as criminals, and not as delinquents, they were entitled to the same procedural protections as adults.

Joining Justice Blackmun in the majority were Chief Justice Warren E. Burger and Justices John M. Harlan, Potter Stewart and Byron R. White and, to a partial extent William J. Brennen Jr. Voting with Mr. Douglas in dissent were Justices Hugo L. Black and Thurgood Marshall.

The ruling upholds laws existing in most states. Twenty-nine states and the District of Columbia have laws barring jury trials in youth courts, which provide for proceedings before a judge in closed hearings. In five other states there are no jury trials by virtue of court rulings. In the remaining states trials for youths are allowed under certain circumstances.

The judgment was based on cases from Pennsylvania and North Carolina in which teen-agers adjudged to be delinquent petitioned for jury trial.

In 1968, Joseph McKeiver of Philadelphia, then 15 years old, was charged with robbery, larceny and receiving stolen goods after he participated with 20 or 30 other boys in pursuing a teen-ager and taking 25 cents from him. He was adjudged a juvenile and placed on probation.

In 1969, Edward Terry, then 15, also of Philadelphia, was accused of assaulting a policeman with his fists. He was committed to a youth center after it was learned he also had assaulted a teacher.

In the North Carolina case, Barbara Burnrus and 45 other black minors, ranging from 11 to 15 years old, were charged with impeding traffic and found to be delinquent after a demonstration against a school consolidation in Hyde County.

In the majority decision, Justice Blackmun summarized the long list of rulings that had ex-

tended more and more constitutional guarantees to accused youths. He said that the "fond and idealistic hopes" of juvenile court proponents of three generations ago had not been realized.

"Too often the juvenile court judge falls far short of that stalwart protective and communicating figure the system envisaged," he wrote. "The community's unwillingness to provide people and facilities and to be concerned, the inefficiency of time devoted, the scarcity of professional help, the inadequacy of dispositional alternatives and our general lack of knowledge all contribute to dissatisfaction with the experiment."

But he said that despite these disappointments and failures "there is a possibility, at least, that the jury trial, if required as a matter of constitutional precept, will remake the juvenile proceeding into a fully adversary process and will put an effective end to what has been the idealistic prospect of an intimate, informal protective proceeding."

He said it would bring "the traditional delay, the formality and clamor of the adversary system and, possibly, the public trial."

"If the formalities of the criminal adjudicative process are to be superimposed upon the juvenile court system, there is little need for its separate existence," he said. "Perhaps that ultimate disillusionment will come one day, but for the moment we are disinclined to give impetus to it."

Justice Douglas wrote on the other hand that, "Where a state uses its juvenile court proceedings to prosecute a juvenile for a criminal act and to order 'confinement' until the child reaches 21 years of age or where the child at the threshold of the proceedings faces that prospect, then he is entitled to the same procedural protection as an adult."

Justice Brennan concurred in the Pennsylvania cases in the conclusions of the majority but joined the dissent in the North Carolina cases because the prosecutions in that case were carried out in secret.

Detention Power and No-Knock Warrants Used Little in Capital in First 7 Months

By ROBERT M. SMITH

Special to the New York Times

WASHINGTON, Sept. 26—In the nation's first experiment with preventive detention and no-knock police warrants, prosecutors, judges and police officials here are making scant use of either one of the controversial crime control measures.

But other less widely discussed changes—an increase in judges, an extension of felony jurisdiction, a shift of some juvenile cases to adult court, the "decriminalization" of some family offenses—are having a major impact.

It has been seven months since the comprehensive law providing for those changes went into effect, over strong constitutionalist objections but with the Nixon Administration's hope that it would serve as a model for the nation.

In that period three no-knock warrants have been issued and seven individuals have been held under preventive detention.

The police say they are intentionally limiting the use of no-knock warrants to necessary and important cases. But preventive detention has been found to involve so complex and time-consuming a process that it is being widely avoided.

In its place magistrates appear to be detaining defendants they consider dangerous by setting high money bail, an expedient that is not uncommon elsewhere but that here deprives the accused of precisely the due process hearing that preventive detention would call for.

Finding the 'Easy Way'

"We have between one and four cases a week that we consider are proper for preventive detention," John F. Rudy 2d, an assistant United States attorney, said in an interview. "But usually in those cases high money bond is set."

In setting bond, magistrates are not supposed to weigh a defendant's possible danger to the community, as they would do at a preventive detention hearing; their sole criterion should be whether they think he will flee.

But faced with a prosecutor reluctant to ask for detention and a three- to six-hour hearing if he does ask for it, high bond of $10,000 or more is, in the words of someone who is involved in the system every day, "the easy way."

The single most important element in the crime control package, it is generally agreed, is the reorganization of the district's courts.

Among other things, the law has extended the Superior Court's jurisdiction to include some felonies, increased the number of judges on the court by 10 to 37, and created the job of court administrator to handle the budget, hire non-judicial personnel, and schedule staff and supplies for court sessions.

Chief Judge Harold H. Greene is proud of the results. "Felony indictments are doubling this year," he said. "For the last 20 years, there have been about 2,000 cases. What happened was the District Court was not capable of trying more than 2,000 felonies, so the others were broken down to misdemeanors."

Backlog Cleared

Since taking over jurisdiction in some juvenile cases, Superior Court has succeeded in clearing up a backlog of 5,000 juvenile cases. Judge Greene says juveniles are now being tried within 45 days. Previously, there were delays of up to a year or more.

Under the act, the United States attorney may determine which juveniles he wants to try in adult court. In the past a hearing before a judge was required before a juvenile could be tried in adult court.

Now, in cases involving rape, homicide, armed felony and some burglaries, the decision is made by the prosecutor. That discretion is now under challenge in appeals court.

Lawrence H. Schwartz of the Public Defender Service estimates that "about 60 per cent of the juveniles are now tried in adult courts."

Under another provision of the act, juveniles' jury trials have been eliminated. This, Mr. Schwartz says, "means kids can't get fair trials. We were winning at least half or better of our cases with jury trial. With court trials, I can count on one hand the number we've won."

In a recent challenge, the Supreme Court ruled that juveniles need not be tried by a jury.

The crime control act also created a Commission on Judicial Disabilities, heartening those critics who think that judicial laziness and irresponsibility have reached scandalous proportions.

The commission, made up of a Federal judge, two lawyers and two laymen, investigates complaints of misconduct by judges and can impose a range of punishments up to removal,

subject to higher review. It has already taken a number of complaints under consideration.

The lawyer for the D.C. police department, Gerald M. Caplan, explained the value of the commission this way:

Shift on Family Offenses

"We have judges that feel like playing golf on Friday or come into court at 11 o'clock instead of 9:30. And sometimes a policeman avoids making an arrest to avoid getting into some crazy judge's court. This is important symbolically, and because it will temper intemperate judges."

Another important provision of the court reorganization allows intra-family offenses to be handled by social workers or through a civil relief order telling the husband to stay away from the wife.

There have been an average of 200 such cases a month since the law went into effect. Of those, more than 350 either have been or will be before full court hearings, with the rest handled by social workes.

Despite the wide impact of such court changes, by far the most attention was devoted to the new law's preventive detention and no-knock warrant provisions as it was progressing through Congress.

When the omnibus crime control bill was introduced, Attorney General John N. Mitchell said it would "point the way for the entire nation at a time when crime and fear of crime are forcing us to alter the pattern of our lives."

Senator Sam J. Ervin, a North Carolina Democrat and civil libertarian, said the bill was "as full of unconstitutional, unjust and unwise provisions as a mangy hound dog is full of fleas."

Despite Mr. Ervin's protests, the crime bill passed. The President signed the bill last July, and no knock and preventive detention have been available to the police and prosecutors since February.

Other Reasons Cited

Aside from the fact that preventive detention hearings sometimes take as long as the trial itself would, there are a number of other reasons why the Government has not sought preventive detention:

¶The bill provides for holding for five days anyone on parole or probation while the authorities decide if the new charge against him warrants revocation of his freedom. Mr. Rudy

explained that "generally when we get a person we would consider for preventive detention, he is on probation or parole and generally the probation officer or the parole board will move for revocation."

¶The Government must reveal a good part of its case to the defense to prove to the magistrate or judge that the man it wants detained is likely to be found guilty.

¶The Government attorneys do not feel they gain much from holding a man for only 60 days. As one of them said, "Offer me 120 days for all that effort, and we'll talk about it."

¶The Government has been waiting for strong cases.

One challenge to preventive detention is already before an appeals court. Citing the Eighth Amendment and the Due Process clause, as well as other parts of the Constitution, it asks that the preventive detention section of the law be struck down.

As an example of how preventive detention works, two of the seven defendants detained so far were alleged to have robbed a supermarket. According to the prosecutor, they were found about 20 minutes after the robbery in a car with the money, a gun and their accomplices. He said they were both narcotics addicts. The two were detained, and while they were in D.C. jail awaiting trial pleaded guilty.

Given the problems associated with preventive detention, why has the Administration already proposed a bill that would make it apply in Federal courts in all the states?

According to Donald E. Santarelli, an associate deputy attorney general and self-proclaimed "captain" of the Government's preventive detention team, "because we hadn't enough experience with it before we put it in again."

Mr. Santarelli blames the peculiarities of the district for the limited use of preventive detention. "In this jurisdiction," he said, "they want to take six days to do it. In other jurisdictions, it needs six hours. It's treated too complexly and it doesn't need to be. The United States Court of Appeals sets the tone and it's clearly a liberal court."

Use of No-Knock Clause

The no-knock statute, under

which the police may apply to a magistrate for a warrant that lets them enter a house without announcing their authority and purpose, has not been stymied by the courts, however. Mr. Caplan, the lawyer for the D.C. police department, explained why it has been so sparingly used this way:

"We've been reserving it for only the most important cases. Everything the police are given is subject to abuse. We never intended to use it routinely. It was always viewed as an extraordinary law enforcement need."

To try to make sure it stays extraordinary, Jerry V. Wilson the chief of the D.C. police, has issued an order requiring that he personally approve all requests for no-knock warrants.

Two of the warrants used so far have been for gambling raids. The third was issued in a narcotics case, but on the ground that the suspect was armed.

In the first gambling case, the police said they needed to burst into the apartment because it was on the third floor and if they announced themselves downstairs the suspect might have destroyed the gambling paraphernalia. They got their man—on his way to an adjoining room.

In the second case, the man had been arrested before, but had been able to throw all of his betting slips, which were water-soluble, into a bucket of water. He was still able to destroy some of them when the police burst in unannounced, apparently because it took them some time to knock down his well-buttressed door.

In the third case, the police were after an alleged narcotics distributor whose nickname was "yellow" but who reportedly carried a gun. They made the arrest, and he did have a pistol.

Mr. Caplan contends the no-knock issue was "a creature of the press."

"Every jurisdiction has no-knock," he said. "We've always had no-knock. The law never says how long a policeman has to wait after knocking—what, five seconds? ten seconds?"

Judge Greene calls the no-knock statute "the anti-perjury bill of 1970—it excuses the officers from saying they knocked."

In the end, Mr. Santarelli and his colleagues in the Justice Department argue that it is not any one of these specific provisions that really count.

"The biggest significance of the act," Mr. Santarelli said, "is that it has focused public attention on improving the system. Money is being broken off for every level."

"In the fall of 1968 there was almost a hysterical despair about crime here," he continued. "The climate now has not returned to the gay nineties.

but it's a lot better than it was."

Others agree, like the prosecutor who said, "Psychologically, at least, people are beginning to feel it's not all geared to protecting the defendant."

Some, like Senator Ervin, remain very worried about what they see as an impairment of constitutional rights. Others argue that the bill does nothing about the economic and social causes of crime. And others point out that the streets of downtown Washington are still empty at night.

When all the results are in, however, even Mr. Santarelli does not hope for too much.

"The bill," he pointed out, "was a comprehensive approach to the whole criminal justice system." But, he acknowledged, "There's so much cumbersomeness in the whole damn system that no matter how and where you tinker with it, the thing manages to elude you."

September 27, 1971

Indictment of Federal Grand Juries

By MICHAEL TIGAR
and MADELEINE LEVY

SANTA BARBARA, Calif. — The grand jury sits in secret, a practice begun to protect the innocent. But the modern-dress version makes the secrecy strikingly reminiscent of the oath *ex officio* procedure which for a time threatened to still the first stirrings of the adversary system, the presumption of innocence and the right of public trial. The evils which were disowned in the creation of the right to a fair trial are, in fact, quite at home in the grand jury room: there is no right to notice of the scope and nature of the crimes being investigated; there is no confrontation of the witnesses who have led the trail of the investigation to the witnesses' doorstep and, collaterally, there is no possibility, much less a right, to cross-examine those witnesses. In essence there is trial in secret, and by inquiry.

"The technology of privacy-invasion makes the grand jury on the loose doubly chilling."

There is the ordeal of examination without counsel, which even (Joseph McCarthy-type) Congressional committees never sought to impose. In the grand jury room, counsel is not permitted. True, the witness may ask the government lawyer to be excused and retire to the anteroom to consult counsel, but the atmosphere is heavily weighted in favor of the government. There is no judge or other supposedly impartial official present — only the grand jurors and government counsel.

There are limitations on the right to bail and to appeal. A defendant charged with crime, even a serious offense, can usually — in the Federal courts — secure prompt release on bail pending trial. A grand jury witness found summarily in contempt for refusal to answer can expect serious and often insurmountable difficulty in obtaining release pending appellate review. And the review available, under the 1970 crime bill, is truncated, providing in many cases no opportunity even to have the record of proceedings below transmitted to the appellate court.

The grand jury dispenses with the privilege against self-incrimination. By the consistent course of Federal decision, a witness may decline to provide any information which may form a link in a chain of evidence incriminatory of him or her. When government casts wide its conspiracy net, and the inquisition begins into friendships and

388

associations, almost any question is potentially productive of incriminatory testimony. To undermine the privilege against self-incrimination, the 1970 crime bill greatly expands the scope of the so-called "immunity" provision of the United States Code.

The bill provides not for complete immunity but for a partial, or "use" immunity. If A incriminates herself or himself, the government may not use the incriminatory testimony *itself* at a later trial of A, but there is no provision that having discovered the misdeed the government may not seek to prosecute it by gathering other evidence.

Let us consider this problem in the broader context of a sixth objection: the grand jury inquisition destroys associational freedom by an assault upon political privacy. To begin, the grand jury's organ grinder, the government lawyer, has access to wire-tap and other electronic surveillance material which can be used as a basis for questioning and intimidating witnesses.

The technology of privacy-invasion, and the public sense of its unbridled use, makes the grand jury on the loose doubly chilling. Another aspect of privacy-invasion arises from indiscriminate poking and prying into associational freedom. In an active political organization, meetings, friendships, discussions and interchange of ideas are the means by which business is done. Assume that one member is subpoenaed to testify. That member can invoke the privilege against self-incrimination as to his or her own activities, but not with respect to the activities, words or beliefs of others.

The grand jury is often convened to surveil a group or groups whom the Attorney General suspects, seeking some pretext for making a formal charge. Frequently, the indictments that do result are for offenses peripheral to the purported purpose of the grand jury, or are so ludicrously unsupported as to be *post hoc* apologies for having begun the investigation in the first place. The Federal grand jury is more and more utilized to probe, expose, and punish the exercise of political freedom by its immediate targets and chill dissent among all but the hardiest.

Michael Tigar and his legal colleague, Madeleine Levy, presented this paper at the Center for Democratic Institutions.

January 8, 1972

High Court Clarifies Rule on Confessions

By FRED P. GRAHAM
Special to The New York Times

WASHINGTON, Jan. 12—The Supreme Court ruled today, 4 to 3, that trial courts could admit into evidence the confessions of criminal defendants even if the courts were not convinced "beyond a reasonable doubt" that the confessions were voluntary.

Ruling on a question of criminal procedure that divided the Justices along liberal-conservative lines, the Court said that, although guilt must be proved beyond a reasonable doubt, confessions could go to the jury so long as it appeared by a preponderance of the evidence that the confessions had been voluntarily given.

The decision followed a recent trend, in which two Justices who frequently dissented from liberal rulings of the Warren Court, Byron R. White and Potter Stewart, lined up with President Nixon's first two nominees, Chief Justice Warren E. Burger and Harry A. Blackmun, in refusing to extend a ruling of the Warren Court that favored criminal defendants.

The dissenters were Justices William J. Brennan Jr., William O. Douglas and Thurgood Marshall, the three holdovers from the liberal majority under former Chief Justice Earl Warren.

In 1964, the Supreme Court ruled that before a confession may be presented in court, the judge must first hold a special hearing to determine if it had been voluntarily given. If so, it may then be read to the jury.

The court at that time left undecided what standard judges should follow in deciding if confessions are voluntary.

Some lower courts concluded that the judge must be persuaded of the confession's voluntariness beyond a reasonable doubt—the same level of proof that is required before a defendant can be found guilty. Others held that the law should not erect high barriers against the submission of evidence to a jury and that a judge could admit a confession if the weight of the evidence indicated that it was voluntary.

The issue was brought to the Supreme Court by Don Richard Lego, who is serving a 25-to-50-year prison term for armed robbery in Illinois, where courts follow the preponderance-of-evidence rule. He contended that detectives had beaten him with a pistol to make him confess, but the detectives denied it and the judge admitted the confession.

Today, in an opinion by Justice White, the Supreme Court adopted the "preponderance" test. Justice White said that test was sufficient to enforce the rule against admitting evidence obtained in violation of the Fifth Amendment's privilege against self-incrimination.

He added that a defendant could not demand that a jury reconsider whether his confession was involuntary but only whether, in view of all the circumstances, it was reliable.

The dissenters' opinion, written by Justice Brennan, said that, because the Supreme Court ruled in 1970 that guilt must be proved beyond a reasonable doubt, a confession should not be admitted unless the prosecution bore the same burden of proof in showing that it was voluntary.

In another opinion by Justice White, the Court upheld, 4 to 2, the Federal Power Commission's authority to regulate local public utilities if they join interstate power pools.

The Florida Power and Light Company, which otherwise would be subject only to regulation by the state power commission because it serves only Florida customers, was held subject to Federal regulation because some of the power it generates crosses the state line through its pooling or power with other companies.

Justice Douglas wrote the dissent, joined by Chief Justice Burger. They said it was only conjecture that the power generated by the local utility actually crossed state lines, and they protested "the fastening of the Federal bureaucracy on this local company" without express authority from Congress.

Justices Lewis F. Powell Jr. and William H. Rehnquist stayed out of both cases because they were not on the Court when the cases were argued. Justice Stewart took no part in the power case and, according to the custom, gave no reason.

January 13, 1972

WIRETAPS IN U.S. UP 37% IN YEAR; STATE HAS MOST

Congress Is Told in Report That Jersey Was Next in Eavesdropping Use

By FRED P. GRAHAM
Special to The New York Times

WASHINGTON, May 5 — A new report to Congress on court-approved wiretapping by the police has disclosed that the volume of police eavesdropping rose by 37 per cent last year across the country, with the heaviest activity concentrated in New York and New Jersey.

State prosecutors in New York and New Jersey together accounted for 83 per cent of the wiretapping done by state officials across the country.

Of 531 wiretap orders issued last year by state judges in the United States, 254 were granted to New York prosecutors, 187 to New Jersey officials, and 90 to officials in 11 other states.

Federal wiretaps were not so heavily concentrated in the New York and New Jersey area. Of 285 orders issued by Federal judges, 47 were in New York, 37 in New Jersey and the remainder were concentrated in major cities where Federal strike forces against organized crime have been active.

The report, which was compiled by the administrative office of the United States courts and filed with Congress last Monday, has not yet been officially released, but copies began to circulate on Capitol Hill today.

It disclosed that some New York judges were permitting devices to stay in operation for far longer periods than Federal or state laws appeared to anticipate.

While the statutes permit 30-day periods of surveillance, with 30-day extensions under certain circumstances, Supreme Court Justice John P. Cohalan Jr. let the District Attorney's office in Suffolk County wiretap two residences there for most of last year. In an investigation of widespread organized-crime activities, including gambling and extortion, one telephone was tapped for 300 days and another for 291 days.

Telephones were also tapped for longer than 100 days in Rockland, Queens, New York and Albany Counties. Elsewhere in the nation, a wiretap that stayed in effect for more than 20 days was rare, according to the report.

Experts on criminal justice attribute the extensive use of wiretapping by the New York police to the fact that court-approved eavesdropping has been authorized for decades by the state's laws and Constitution and, they say, some of the judges and the police have become casual about it. Many of these same authorities feel that whom the higher courts review convictions growing out of such lengthy surveillance, they may declare it illegal.

Few states allowed police wiretapping until 1968, when Congress declared, in the Omnibus Crime Control Act, that state legislatures could pass laws permitting the police to wiretap with court approval. Twenty states have now done so, but the new report showed that wiretap orders were obtained by the police in only 13 states—Arizona, Colorado, Florida, Georgia, Kansas, Maryland, Massachusetts, Minnesota, Nevada, New Jersey, New York, Rhode Island and Wisconsin.

The rapid rise in police wiretapping in New Jersey is due largely to the creation of a unit to fight organized crime. The anticrime unit, in the office of the State Attorney General, planted 86 listening devices in Mercer County last year and turned up evidence for 225 arrests.

The total of 816 court-authorized wiretaps last year compared with 597 in 1970. In that year, 215 were authorized in New York and 132 in New Jersey, accounting for more than 80 per cent of the 414 wiretaps permitted by state courts.

The report contained some evidence that police wiretapping was being used with increased care for individual privacy and with greater effectiveness. Last year, the average wiretap overheard 40 individuals making 643 calls, of which 60 per cent were described as incriminating. In the previous year, the average tap involved 44 persons and 656 calls, of which 45 per cent were incriminating.

One reason for the sharp increase in the percentage of incriminating calls overheard is the heavy use of wiretapping on illegal bookie's phones.

This is becoming a controversial feature of the wiretap program, as gambling is being legalized and taken over by state governments, and a growing number of persons are asking if the expense and invasions of privacy of police wiretapping are justified when so many of the targets are gamblers.

Last year, of the 816 taps authorized, 570 were aimed at gamblers. Narcotics was next, with 126 taps, followed by larceny, 31; homicide, 18; bribery, 16; robbery, 17; burglary, 7; loan sharking, 5, and miscellaneous offenses, 26.

All judges and prosecutors involved in court-approved eavesdropping must report the details annually to the administrative office of the United States courts. The new report is a compilation of those reports.

It does not include the wiretaps installed by the Federal Government without court authority in national security cases. These are believed to be fewer in number than the ones used by the Federal Government in ordinary criminal investigations, but the sketchy information available suggests that they are left in operation for much longer periods of time.

May 6, 197

Justices Back State Court Convictions Without Unanimous Verdicts by Juries

9-3 Decision Upheld in a Louisiana Case

By FRED P. GRAHAM
Special to The New York Times

WASHINGTON, May 22 — The Supreme Court held 5 to 4 today that unanimous jury verdicts are not required for convictions in state criminal courts.

The ruling, together with another decision today that broadened the power of prosecutors to compel witnesses to testify, demonstrated the conservative impact of President Nixon's four nominees.

The five-Justice majority in favor of upholding less-than-unanimous juries was composed of Byron R. White, a prosecution-minded holdover from the Warren Court, and Mr. Nixon's

4 Nixon Nominees Join White in Majority

four nominees — Chief Justice Warren E. Burger and Justices Harry A. Blackmun, Lewis F. Powell Jr. and William H. Rehnquist.

At issue were cases in which convictions were upheld on votes of 9 to 3 and 10 to 2. The dissenters protested that the majority's ruling "cuts the heart out" of the Constitution's jury trial guarantee and the due process requirement of proof of guilt beyond a reasonable doubt.

Studies conducted by law professors in Oregon and Louisiana, the two states that now permit less than unanimous jury verdicts in felony trials, have shown that such a system results in more convictions and fewer deadlocked juries.

A few other states do not require unanimity in misdemeanor trials. Today's ruling, which frees the states to change their laws, is expected to prompt other state legislatures to adopt the less than unanimous jury rule.

However, the Federal Government will apparently be precluded from adopting the same rule by the position taken by Justice Powell, who held the crucial fifth vote.

Justice Powell agreed that the due process clause of the 14th Amendment does not require unanimous verdicts in state trials. But he insisted that the framers of the Sixth Amendment, which requires a "speedy and public trial by an impartial jury," intended to require Federal courts to employ the unanimous 12-member jury of the English common law.

As written, the Sixth Amendment applied only to the Federal Government, but the Supreme Court has ruled that the due process clause of the 14th Amendment requires that the "fundamental" safeguards in it are also binding on the states.

The four dissenters, Justices William O. Douglas, William J. Brennan Jr., Potter Stewart and Thurgood Marshall, all insisted upon unanimity in all criminal trials. Thus, Justice Powell's position created a five-Justice majority against less than unanimous juries in Federal court.

The decision today arose out of convictions from Louisiana, where 9-to-3 votes can convict defendants, and Oregon, where 10-to-2 votes are valid.

Frank Johnson, a New Orleans man who had been given a 35-year sentence for armed robbery on a 9-to-3 vote, and three Oregon men who had been convicted of various offenses on votes of 10 to 2, asked the Supreme Court to hold that unanimous verdicts are required by the Constitution.

They argued that a defendant cannot be proved guilty beyond a reasonable doubt when three of nine jurors vote to acquit him. Also, they asserted that the essence of a trial by a jury of the defendant's peers is undercut when three jurors who may represent the race or class of the defendant may be ignored.

Smaller Juries Allowed

Writing for the majority, Justice White noted that under a 1970 Supreme Court decision, convictions by juries of less than 12 members are constitutional. He concluded that when a "heavy majority" of jurors votes for conviction, as in the cases today, it is similar to a unanimous vote by a smaller jury.

He also said that the framers of the Sixth Amendment de-

liberately left out a unanimity requirement and that the Constitution does not give minority groups "the right to block convictions" but only to be on the jury and to "be heard."

Justice Douglas charged in his dissent that the majority had succumbed to a "law and order judicial mood" to make a "radical departure from American traditions."

He and the other dissenters argued that the ruling would upset the dynamics of jury decision-making that require the panel to go slow, consider every juror's view and sometimes compromise on the severity of the conviction in order to reach a verdict.

Justice Stewart said that under today's ruling "nine jurors can simply ignore the views of their fellow panel members of a different race or class." This will weaken the jury as a bulwark between the citizen and the prosecutorial power of the state, the dissenters asserted.

Justice Blackmun, a member of the majority, said that he would have "great difficulty" in upholding a system employing a 7-to-5 standard.

Justice Douglas said that this leaves many prickly questions to be answered — such as the validity of an 8-to-4 vote, and whether juries of less than 12 members must be unanimous.

Also left unanswered was whether unanimous verdicts will be required in capital cases and how the Court will justify invalidating convictions if it is confronted, as Justice Douglas put it, with votes of "3 to 2 or even 2 to 1?"

Richard A. Buckley of New Orleans argued for Johnson. Richard B. Sobol of Washington argued for the Oregon defendants. Louis Korns, an assistant district attorney in New Orleans, represented Louisiana. Jacob B. Tanzer of Salem argued for Oregon.

Justice Byron R. White, wrote Court's decision.

May 23, 1972

COURT, 5-4, LIMITS RIGHTS IN LINE-UP

Says Suspect May Demand Presence of Counsel Only if He Has Been Indicted

By FRED P. GRAHAM
Special to The New York Times

WASHINGTON, June 7—The Supreme Court sharply limited a major liberal criminal ruling of the Warren Court today, holding 5 to 4 that suspects normally are not entitled to counsel at line-up identifications.

All four of President Nixon's appointees joined in the judgment as the Court limited the application of a 1967 ruling that suspects are entitled to lawyers at line-ups. President Nixon repeatedly criticized this doctrine during his campaign for the Presidency in 1968.

Justice Potter Stewart, who dissented in 1967 when the Warren Court declared that suspects were entitled to lawyers at line-ups, teamed up with the Nixon nominees and wrote the prevailing opinion today.

He said that the right to counsel at line-ups applies only after suspects have been indicted. The result is that as long as the police act before formal charges are brought,

they may place suspects in line-ups or confront them with witnesses in face-to-face "show-ups" without having defense lawyers present.

However, Justice Stewart stressed that if suspects could show that they were identified in line-ups or show-ups that were unfair or slanted against them the identifications would not be admissible in court.

Today was the first time since the addition of Mr. Nixon's four appointees that the Court has had an opportunity to rule on any of the three controversial doctrines of the liberal Warren Court era. These doctrines are that in line-ups, interrogations and searches, the police must follow certain procedures or the evidence obtained cannot be used in court.

A Limited Ruling

Of the three, the line-up doc-

trine requiring the presence of counsel had been most heavily criticized by lawyers beyond the ranks of prosecutors, primarily on the ground that lawyers could do little for clients at line-ups.

In the appeal decided today, the Court was asked by prosecutors from Illinois and California to overturn the Warren Court's 1967 decisions, United States v. Wade and Gilbert v. California.

The majority's decision just to limit the reach of those decisions, plus the refusal of Justice Byron R. White to go even that far, indicated that even with four Nixon nominees, the Court will be slow to throw out recent liberal rulings of the Warren Court.

Although Justice White dissented against the two 1967 decisions, he noted today in a one-sentence dissent that those decisions require the opposite result of today's majority judgment.

Justice William J. Brennan Jr., who wrote the two 1967 decisions, wrote another dissent today, joined by Justices William O. Douglas and Thurgood Marshall. He noted that those cases held that an individual's right to counsel under the Sixth Amendment applies at any "critical stage" of a case. He said that a line-up identification was such a critical stage.

Justice Brennan said that the Court today had seized upon the unimportant circumstance that the defendants in the Wade and Gilbert cases had been indicted before their line-ups.

The decision today upheld the robbery conviction of two Chicago men, Thomas Kirby and Ralph Bean, who had been identified in a police interrogation room by a victim of a mugging on the day after the robbery. There was no line-up and the victim was simply asked if they were the muggers.

A Concurring Opinion

Chief Justice Warren E. Burger and Justices Harry A. Blackmun and William H. Rehnquist joined Justice Stewart's opinion. Justice Lewis F. Powell Jr. said in a brief concurring opinion that he agreed with the judgment because he "would not extend" the 1967 ruling.

Justice Stewart's opinion said that it would amount to an extension of the 1967 ruling to grant the right of counsel to line-ups held before the commencement of "formal prosecutorial proceedings."

However, a number of state and Federal courts had construed the 1967 ruling to require counsel at all line-ups, and in most large cities the public defenders' offices have, until today, routinely sent lawyers to observe scheduled line-ups.

The Court handed down 11 decisions today in an unusual Wednesday decision session. This left 55 appeals that have been argued and are yet to be decided this term. The Court has scheduled sessions for the next three Mondays and has not announced if it will have to extend its term into July to dispose of all the cases.

June 8, 1972

HIGH COURT BARS ANY JAIL SENTENCE WITHOUT COUNSEL

Extends Its 6th Amendment Ruling on Felonies to Apply to Petty Cases

WIDE EFFECT FORESEEN

Justices Say the Poor Must Be Given a Free Lawyer Unless Right Is Waived

By FRED P. GRAHAM
Special to The New York Times

WASHINGTON, June 12—The Supreme Court ruled today that no poor person may be jailed for a petty offense unless he has been furnished free legal counsel or has waived his right to a lawyer.

The decision, which was the first Supreme Court ruling to extend the Sixth Amendment's guarantee of counsel to misdemeanor trials, is expected to create a vast new demand for lawyers' services across the nation.

In its decisions in recent weeks, the Court has taken a distinctly conservative turn in bolstering the authority of the police and grand juries to investigate crimes. But today's ruling was a historic extension of the constitutional right of defendants to counsel in court.

Action in 31 States

Before today, the Court had left open the question of the right to counsel in petty cases. It had held in its historic Gideon v. Wainwright decision in 1963 that poor defendants are entitled to free lawyers in felony trials—generally, those carrying punishments of more than a year in prison.

In the meantime, 31 states had extended the right to free counsel in certain misdemeanor cases. It had been widely assumed that the Supreme Court would eventually extend the Sixth Amendment's guarantee of counsel to some of these misdemeanor trials.

When the Supreme Court spoke today, it went well beyond what most of the states had done. In an opinion by Justice William O. Douglas, the Court held that after today judges will be precluded from imposing any sentence beyond money fines unless indigent defendants have been offered free counsel.

Advance Decision by Judge

This will require the judges to decide in advance if they might wish to impose a jail sentence and to appoint defense lawyers if they wish to hold that option open.

New York, California, Illinois, Massachusetts, Minnesota, New Hampshire and Texas have already provided a right to appointed lawyers in most cases in which imprisonment is a realistic possibility. Most other states do not furnish free lawyers to defendants facing less than six months in jail.

It is estimated that there are four to five million nontraffic misdemeanor arrests in the country each year—one third of them for drunkenness — compared with about 350,000 felony prosecutions.

Justice Douglas conceded that today's decision could place some strains on the legal profession and on state treasuries. However, he said that many misdemeanor cases would still be handled without counsel because the judges would have no intention of jailing the defendants.

The decision overturned the conviction of Jon Richard Argersinger, who had been convicted of carrying a concealed weapon and sentenced to pay a $500 fine or serve three months in jail in Leon County, Fla. The Supreme Court of Florida ruled that counsel was not required for offenses carrying less than six months' imprisonment.

The entire Supreme Court agreed that this ruling should not stand, but its two newest Justices, Lewis F. Powell Jr. and William H. Rehnquist, said in a concurring opinion that the states should not be bound to a rigid rule under the Sixth Amendment.

They said that judges should be free in each case to decide if the severity of the charges and the education of the defendant made a lawyer's assistance necessary.

Justice Powell, a former president of the American Bar Association, disputed in his opinion Justice Douglas's contention that the country's 335,200 lawyers, plus the current oversupply of students in law schools, would satisfy the needs created by today's decision.

Justice Powell said that many licensed lawyers were not in active practice, that many others were untrained or uninterested in criminal practice and that the cost of paying others to defend the poor might bear heavily on some communities.

'Stop and Frisk' Extended

In another criminal law ruling today the Court, 6 to 3, extended the reach of its 1968 "stop and frisk" decision, which granted the police the authority to search dangerous-looking persons "on suspicion" for weapons.

In the case today, Justice Rehnquist wrote the Court's opinion, which said that a policeman may "frisk" a suspect for a weapon, even if his suspicion is based upon the word of an anonymous tipster rather than his own observations.

The Court upheld the conviction of Robert Williams, who was arrested in Bridgeport, Conn., after a policeman, who did not have enough evidence to make an arrest, acted on a tip to stop Williams's car and snatch a pistol from his belt. A subsequent search of the car turned up heroin, and Williams was convicted on weapons and narcotics charges.

The dissenters were Justice Douglas, the lone dissenter in the 1968 "stop and frisk" decision, and Justices Brennan and Marshall. Justice Marshall expressed misgivings in a separate dissent that he had gone along with the Court when it granted the police "stop and frisk" authority in 1968.

"Today's decision invokes the specter of a society in which innocent citizens may be stopped, searched and arrested at the whim of police officers who have only the slightest suspicion of improper conduct," he said.

June 13, 1972

Press Loses Plea to Keep Data From Grand Juries

Special to The New York Times

WASHINGTON, June 29—. The Supreme Court held 5 to 4 today that journalists have no First Amendment right to refuse to tell grand juries the names of confidential sources and information given to them in confidence.

The decision overturned a lower Federal court ruling on behalf of Earl Caldwell, a reporter for The New York Times in San Francisco, who had refused to enter a Federal grand jury room to be questioned on information given him by the Black Panther party.

In two related cases, the Court held that Paul M. Branzburg, an investigative reporter for The Louisville Courier-Journal at the time his case arose, and Paul Pappas, a television newsman in New Bedford, Mass., must tell state grand juries names and other information given them in confidence or face imprisonment for contempt.

The sweeping decision by Justice Byron R. White, supported by President Nixon's four appointees, contained a firm rejection of the theory that the First Amendment shields newsmen under certain circumstances from having to testify when the result would be to cut off news sources and deprive the public of news.

This theory has never been considered before today by the Supreme Court. But in recent years, as a wave of subpoenas issued from grand juries for newsmen's notes, radio stations' tapes and television companies' films, some lower courts began to construe the First Amendment as giving journalists some protection against being compelled to disclose confidences.

The courts usually reasoned that if forcing a newsman to testify would cut off future information, he should be excused unless the Government could show a compelling need for his testimony.

"We cannot accept the argument," Justice White declared today, "that the public interest in possible future news about crime from undisclosed, unverified sources must take precedence over the public interest in pursuing and prosecuting those crimes reported to the press."

He concluded that "there is no First Amendment privilege to refuse to answer the relevant and material questions asked during a good-faith grand jury investigation." Thus newsmen, he said, have the same duty as any other citizens to obey grand jury subpoenas and give testimony.

No 'Newsman's Privilege'

To attempt to carve a "newsman's privilege" out of the First Amendment, he said, would embroil the courts in such decisions as whether pamphleteers and others are "journalists" and if lecturers, pollsters, and academic researchers are also protected.

Justice White said that the First Amendment would come into play only under such circumstances as a bad faith attempt by a prosecutor to harass a reporter and disrupt his relationship with his news sources.

The other members of the majority were Chief Justice Warren E. Burger and Justices Harry A. Blackmun, Lewis F. Powell Jr., and William H. Rehnquist.

Justice Powell added a concurring opinion that held out a faint prospect that some newsmen's claims of privilege could yet be honored, since his vote was vital to the narrow majority.

He declared that judges may still use the "balancing" technique of weighing the First Amendment considerations in each case against the citizens' obligation to give information to grand juries.

Vital Rehnquist Role

But his view of the proof a reporter must have to justify First Amendment protection was more demanding than the practice in lower courts. He said that a reporter would be excused from disclosing confidences if his testimony had only a "remote and tenuous relationship" to the investigation, or if law enforcement had no "legitimate need" for it.

Justice Rehnquist's crucial participation raised issues similar to those of last Monday when he cast the fifth vote to bar court suits challenging the Army's surveillance of civilians.

The American Civil Liberties Union announced in the army case that it would seek a rehearing on the grounds that Justice Rehnquist should have disqualified himself because he had taken the Army's side in Senate testimony when he was an Assistant Attorney General.

Some observers had thought Justice Rehnquist might disqualify himself from the press subpoena case because he represented the Justice Department in a debate on the issue in 1970 in Washington, where he argued against a First Amendment privilege for newsmen. He also helped prepare the Justice Department's guidelines for subpoenaing newsmen in 1970.

Justice Rehnquist also cast the deciding vote today as the Court ruled, 5 to 4, that an aide of Senator Mike Gravel of Alaska may be questioned by a Federal grand jury about the Senator's role in the publication of the secret Pentagon Papers in book form.

Some lawyers had expected Justice Rehnquist to disqualify himself from that case also because he helped prepare the Justice Department's suit that attempted to stop The New York Times from publishing the material.

Justice Potter Stewart argued in a dissent, joined by Justices William J. Brennan Jr. and Thurgood Marshall, that the right to publish must include the right to gather news and that this implies protection for confidential sources.

He said that when a reporter is subpoenaed to appear before a grand jury and reveal confidence he may first require the government to show that he probably has relevant information about a crime, that the government cannot obtain the information in another way, and that there is a compelling and overriding need for it.".

Justice William O. Douglas, the fourth dissenter, said that a reporter "has an absolute right not to appear before a grand jury" and predicted that the ruling today would tend to make journalists cautious about printing some sensitive news.

Arthur Ochs Sulzberger, president and publisher of The New York Times, said:

"The decision of the United States Supreme Court in the Caldwell case now makes it imperative that the Congress and those state legislatures that have not yet acted pass laws that would give to reporters the necessary protection of the confidentiality of their sources. This protection is vital to a free press and to the public it serves.

"The Court's decision," Mr. Sulzberger continued, "carries with it serious implications for a free press. However, Justice Powell's concurring opinion is significant because it indicates that in many circumstances, courts may still protect journalistic confidentiality.

"As Justice Stewart's dissent observes, that [Justice Powell's] opinion leaves room for hope that in some future case the Supreme Court may take a less absolute position."

The refusal of Mr. Caldwell, a black reporter, to testify before the San Francisco grand jury's inquiry into Black Panther affairs had produced the strongest lower court ruling to date on newsmen's First Amendment "privilege."

The United States Court of Appeals for the Ninth Circuit held that he not only did not have to give confidential information but that he also did not have to enter the secrecy of the grand jury room—and thus create fears that he had talked—unless the Government could show a strong need for his testimony.

Although theoretically he might now be recalled to testify and imprisoned for contempt if he refused, that prospect appeared unlikely today. James Browning, the United States attorney for San Francisco, said that the grand jury that had investigated the Black Panthers had lapsed and with it Mr. Caldwell's subpoena.

Also, the press subpoena guidelines adopted by the Justice Department since Mr. Caldwell was subpoenaed now require the Government to exhaust other sources and to observe other protective procedures before subpoenaing a reporter. This might rule out a subpoena for his testimony.

Mr. Branzburg had refused to identify individuals who let him observe them making hashish, and who told him about marijuana sales. He was held in contempt of court by the Kentucky courts. Justice White declared that the First Amendment does not protect "newsman's agreement to conceal the criminal conduct of his source" and affirmed the contempt ruling.

Mr. Pappas, a cameraman-reporter for WTEV-TV in New Bedford, had been allowed by Black Panthers to spend the night in their office on the night of an expected raid, after he promised to disclose nothing if there was no raid. No raid occurred, but a grand jury ordered him to testify.

Today the Supreme Court said he would have to testify before a proper grand jury investigation.

June 30, 1972

Failure of Preventive Detention

By SAM J. ERVIN Jr.

WASHINGTON — "Law and order" was a major political issue during the Presidential campaign of 1968 and the Congressional campaign of 1970. As one of his campaign promises, President Nixon vowed to make Washington, D. C., a model of safety for the rest of the nation.

In an effort to satisfy this promise, the Administration in late 1969 presented to the Congress its long-awaited plan to combat crime in the District of Columbia. The D. C. Crime Bill contained many valuable proposals for organizational reform of the District's criminal justice system. The bill's court reform proposals enjoyed bipartisan support and were not controversial because they were the product of the combined efforts of both the Johnson and Nixon Administrations and represented the best thinking on criminal-justice reform. They have proved to be a significant help in Washington's effort to improve criminal justice.

However, the Nixon Administration's major contribution to the D. C. Crime Bill was a grab bag of some of the most bizarre and repressive crime-control measures ever proposed to the Congress. These proposals included preventive detention, harsh changes in juvenile law, no-knock and overly broad wiretapping authority. Though loudly touted by the Administration at the time as the key to crime control, these repressive and unenlightened proposals have had little if any impact on crime in the District. In fact, the most notorious of these proposals—preventive detention—has now proved a complete failure. This failure is documented in a study recently conducted in Washington by the Georgetown Law School and the Vera Institute of Justice of New York City. The study contains a detailed analysis of what happened to each of the defendants for whom the Administration sought preventive detention during the first ten months of 1971.

The study discloses that despite extravagant claims by the Justice Department that preventive detention is indispensable to safety on the streets, the law was invoked against only twenty suspects out of a total of the more than 6,000 felony defendants who entered the District of Columbia courts during the first ten months of the law. Of the twenty, only ten were actually ordered detained and five of these detention orders were later reversed by the courts.

The study contains the best proof yet that preventive detention is unnecessary. For example, it shows that constitutional alternatives to the use of preventive detention, such as modification of bail conditions or revocation of parole or work release, or speedy trial, could have been used to far better advantage in all twenty cases and without any infringements of due process or other constitutional rights. This study reconfirms my conviction that pretrial crime could be virtually eliminated if the Constitution's speedy trial requirement were enforced. Of the twenty cases for which preventive detention was sought, fourteen had a prior charge pending for more than sixty days at the time of arrest. If trials had been held within sixty days of this prior charge, the subsequent criminal activity would have been prevented and preventive detention would have been unnecessary.

Rather than trying these defendants for the crimes with which they were charged, the Justice Department wasted time and energy in a fruitless effort at preventive detention. In one case the Justice Department tried for eight months to detain a defendant and after seven hearings had not only failed to detain the defendant under the statute but as of Dec. 31 had not even brought the defendant to trial. The "rights of society" would have been better protected if the Justice Department had expended some of this energy in trying the defendant for the crime of which he was accused.

This experience with preventive detention proves that we must be extremely skeptical of the other Administration "law and order" proposals which are also advertised as "indispensable" for crime control. We should not be surprised to find that many of the Administration's plans are no more practical or necessary than preventive detention, yet just as harmful to individual liberty.

The preventive detention fiasco may be a prelude to other disasters for both civil liberties and effective criminal justice. For example, the Administration proposes the expansion of preventive detention nationwide. It proposes that police be authorized to detain but not "arrest" citizens for the purpose of subjecting them to tests and experiments and other so-called "nontestimonial identification procedures."

Instead of clamoring after these bizarre and dangerous expedients which are offered in the name of law and order, the Administration should address itself to the admittedly slow, hard and expensive course of improvement and reform of our criminal justice system.

Senator Sam J. Ervin Jr., Democrat of North Carolina, is chairman of the Subcommittee on Constitutional Rights.

'No-Knock' Drug Raids Curbed Under New Federal Guidelines

By LINDA CHARLTON
Special to The New York Times

WASHINGTON, July 16 — The Drug Enforcement Administration issued today a new set of guidelines for Federal narcotics agents with the aim of preventing future abuses such as mistaken raids on the homes of innocent families.

The guidelines, described as a "shift in emphasis" combining existing regulations with new ones, were made public by John R. Bartels Jr., the acting administrator of the agency.

In a prepared statement Mr. Bartels said, "unhappily we are all too familiar with the incidents which made issuance of this policy necessary. Any recurrence of such incidents cannot and will not be tolerated."

The "incidents" to which Mr. Bartels referred were those in which Federal narcotics agents allegedly used verbal and physical violence and unauthorized forced entry into premises mistakenly believed to be harboring suspects.

Perhaps the most widely publicized of these incidents took place last April in Collinsville, Ill., when two families were terrorized by agents who burst into their homes and allegedly destroyed their possessions and used threats of violence and obscene language. In both cases, the raids were carried out at mistaken addresses.

The Collinsville episode is now under investigation by a grand jury, and the six agents and their supervisor involved have been suspended for 30 days without pay pending the grand jury's findings.

The new guidelines, which will be incorporated into the agents' manual, require agents to obtain approval from Mr. Bartels or his deputy for any "no-knock" raids. They prohibit forced entry without a warrant except when it is "not practical" to secure one, and add: "Before entering any premises, the agent will knock and announce his purpose and authority in an audible and distinctive manner."

Federal agents are required, under the new policy guidelines, to "wear distinctive markings, such as badges, caps or other devices in all cases involving forced entry."

They are forbidden, under these rules, to fire a weapon "except in self-defense or in defense of another person," and an officer must "give loud and clear notice of his authority and purpose and be refused admittance before he may forcibly enter a house."

Mr. Bartels said that some elements of the guidelines — the restriction on "no-knock" raids and the requirement that a warrant be secured if at all possible before an arrest, for instance—were being specified for the first time. Other parts of the policy statement, he said, are a matter of certain areas being "highlighted and emphasized."

In addition to the guidelines, Mr. Bartels announced that he had assigned John R. Enright, the former senior enforcement official of the Bureau of Narcotics and Dangerous Drugs, as a special assistant "to personally insure that all operations are conducted in a completely legal and professional manner." Mr. Enright, he said, will visit all of the agency's field offices "to make certain that every Federal narcotics agent fully understands" the policies.

Mr. Bartels also announced that the agency's chief medical officer was investigating the "potential value of a psychological screening program" for applicants. There is no such screening at present, he said.

The policy statement, he said, was directed "to those few agents who are tempted to violate" constitutional rights in the course of their duties. Its issuance, he said, did not indicate that these were new standards, merely "a re-emphasis of policy."

Associated Press

John R. Bartels Jr., acting head of the Drug Enforcement Administration, at news session in Washington on drug raids.

July 17, 1973

Supreme Court Widens Power of Police To Search Individual Without Warrant

By WARREN WEAVER Jr.
Special to The New York Times

WASHINGTON, Dec. 11— The Supreme Court broadened today the power of law enforcement officers to search persons without a warrant.

On a vote of 6 to 3, the Court held that persons taken into custody on minor charges may then be searched for evidence of more serious but unrelated crimes.

Thus, under the ruling, personal searches need not be confined to cases in which a policeman is frisking a suspect for dangerous weapons or looking for evidence of the crime for which the suspect has been arrested.

As long as the officer has made a valid custodial arrest— one to be followed by taking the suspect to the station—he needs "no additional justification" to search him thoroughly for any other sort of incriminating evidence, the majority ruled.

Specifically, the high court upheld the separate convictions of two men who had been arrested for motor vehicles infractions—driving without a license and with a revoked license—and then charged, after a search, with possession of narcotics. Both had contended that the search violated their constitutional rights.

'Departure From Tradition'

The three-Justice minority maintained that the decision represented "a clear and marked departure from our long tradition" of weighing each contested search to determine whether it violated the Fourth Amendment's guarantee against "unreasonable searches and seizures."

The dissenters were Justices William O. Douglas, William J. Brennan Jr. and Thurgood Marshall. Justice William H. Rehnquist wrote the majority opinion, joined by Chief Justice Warren E. Burger and Justices Potter Stewart, Byron R. White Harry A. Blackmun and Lewis F. Powell Jr.

The decision appeared to constitute another move by the Burger Court toward strengthening the hand of law enforcement officials at the expense of protecting the rights of accused criminals.

The effect of the ruling was to create another exception, of potential breadth, to the "exclusionary rule," the controversial principle first voiced by the Court in 1914 that illegally obtained evidence can be excluded in court at the request of the accused.

On its face, the decision appeared to empower any policeman to search any suspect he has taken into custody for any kind of completely unconnected incriminating evidence, even if the original offense was so insignificant that he could have given the accused a ticket instead.

Justice Marshall said in the dissent that the ruling raised "the possibility that a police officer, lacking probable cause to obtain a search warrant, will use a traffic arrest as a pretext to conduct a search."

Justice Rehnquist wrote: "The authority to search the person incident to a lawful custodial arrest, while based upon the need to disarm and to discover evidence, does not depend on what a court may later decide was the probability in a particular arrest situation that weapons or evidence would in fact be found upon the person of the suspect.

"A custodial arrest of a suspect based on probable cause is a reasonable intrusion under the Fourth Amendment; that intrusion being lawful, a search incident to the arrest requires no additional justification.

"It is the fact of the lawful arrest which established the authority to search, and we hold that in the case of lawful custodial arrest a full search of the person is not only an exception to the warrant requirement of the Fourth Amendment but is also a 'reasonable' search under that amendment."

The old rule, limiting a warrantless search to frisking for weapons or finding further evidence of the immediate crime, still applies to cases in which there is no probable cause for making the arrest, the majority said, but not to custodial arrests based on reasonable information.

During the last year, the Burger court has assisted the cause of law enforcement by rulings that a defendant who was lured into crime by the Government can be convicted if he was "predisposed" to the action, that a car abandoned by a drunken driver can be searched without a warrant and that the Government need not prove that a defendant who consented to a warrantless search knew he could have refused permission.

The principal case decided by the Court today involved a District of Columbia man, Willie Robinson Jr., who was arrested in 1968 for driving while his license was revoked. In searching him, a policeman found a crumpled cigarette package in his overcoat pocket and 14 capsules containing heroin inside the package.

Mr. Robinson was convicted in Federal District Court, over protests that the evidence had been illegally obtained and thus should not be admitted. The Court of Appeals for the District of Columbia reversed on the grounds that the warrantless search had been unconstitutional.

In the Robinson case, local police regulations authorized both taking the suspect into custody rather than giving him a ticket and a full body search following arrest.

In a second decision today, by the same 6-to-3 vote, the high court upheld a similar search by a policeman in Eau Gallie, Fla., in 1969, despite the fact that regulations there did not require a custodial arrest or set any standards for the use of a body search.

In that case, James Gustafson was arrested for driving without his license with him and was found, during an ensuing search, to be carrying marijuana cigarettes. Upon trial, he was convicted of unlawful possession of marijuana. The Florida District Court of Appeals reversed, but the State Supreme Court reversed in turn, reinstating his conviction.

In both cases, Justice Marshall wrote for the minority that there was no justification for the searches on the grounds of discovering evidence of the crime charged, since no further evidence of driving without a license was necessary

December 12, 1973

A Nixon Court Frees Still More Police Power

The "Nixon Court" left a clear imprint last week in still another case involving the power of police and prosecutors: The Court wrote a major exception into the exclusionary rule that bars the use of illegally obtained evidence in criminal proceedings.

The six-man majority, including four of the President's appointees, decided it was constitutional for grand juries to use illegally acquired evidence as a basis for questioning witnesses. Since the ruling does not apply to evidence before trial juries, the apparent effect is that a suspect can be indicted on the basis of evidence that would not be admissible to prove his guilt in court.

The so-called exclusionary rule prohibits the use against a criminal defendant of any evidence that the prosecution obtained by a search without a warrant, some types of wire tapping and other illegal means. The principle was adopted in Federal courts in 1914 and was extended by Supreme Court ruling to the state courts in 1961. Its purpose was to discourage unlawful police conduct by denying law enforcement machinery the fruits of that conduct.

Some critics argue that the principle puts too much emphasis on the rights of the accused and not enough on effective law enforcement. They contend that evidence is evidence, however obtained, and that criminals often go free on judicial technicalities.

Last week's ruling was in the case of a Cleveland businessman, John P. Calandra, whose machine tool plant was searched by Federal agents who had obtained a warrant in connnection with an investigation of illegal gambling. The agents found no gambling evidence but did uncover what appeared to be a record of loan-sharking activity.

The next year a new grand jury investigating loan-sharking called Mr. Calandra to question him about the records seized in the raid. He refused to testify and moved to suppress use of the records on grounds that there had been no probable cause to issue the warrant and the resulting search had exceeded the warrant's scope. His position was upheld by the lower courts.

Associate Justice Lewis F. Powell, writing for the majority, said the lower courts misconstrued the exclusionary rule. He maintained that exclusion of illegally obtained evidence was not "a personal constitutional right" but "a judicially created remedy" designed to discourage improper searches by law enforcement officers. He added that "the grand jury's investigative power must be broad if its public responsibility is to be adequately discharged."

Mr. Powell was joined in the majority by Chief Justice Warren E. Burger and Justices Potter Stewart, Byron R. White, Harry A. Blackmun and William H. Rehnquist. The six Justices have voted together several times in recent cases to toughen law enforcement. All but Justices White and Stewart are President Nixon's appointees.

The dissenters were Justices William O. Douglas, William J. Brennan Jr. and Thurgood Marshall. They argued that the ruling not only violated the Fourth Amendment prohibition of unreasonable searches and seizures, but also tended to ally the judiciary with illegality.

January 13, 1974

DUE PROCESS

Survey Indicates Public Skepticism On Juries' Ability

The public does not have a high regard for juries and believes that most intelligent people avoid jury service, according to a recent survey by the Missouri Bar Association.

The public also believes that juries decide cases hurriedly, place personal interest ahead of duty, are unduly swayed by emotion and are likely to be influenced unduly by the trial tactics of lawyers, the survey indicated.

In the course of the survey, 5,700 persons were interviewed. About 2,500 were lawyers. The study was sponsored by the Pren-Hall Foundation, an educational group set up by Prentice-Hall, Inc., publishers.

Three of four lawyers felt that money, social position and race affected standards of justice, largely because the poor could not afford adequate counsel.

The study indicated that persons who had had the least opportunity to observe courts in action had the most confidence in the courts and the highest regard for judges, juries and lawyers.

In an attempt to find out where legal business goes, laymen were asked whom they consulted when making their wills. Seventy-six per cent went to lawyers, 11 per cent made their own, 4 per cent went to bankers, 1 per cent to realty men and insurance men and 2 per cent to tax specialists or notaries public.

GOLDBERG ASSAILS U.S. BAIL PRACTICE

Calls It Unfair in Preface to Book Urging Abolition

By SIDNEY E. ZION

Arthur J. Goldberg has assailed the American bail system as "a highly commercialized racket" that "can no longer be tolerated."

The former Associate Justice of the Supreme Court charges that the bail system "operates to discriminate on account of poverty."

Mr. Goldberg, now United States Representative to the United Nations, made his attack while he was still on the Court, in a foreword to "Ransom," a critique of the bail system written by Ronald Goldfarb and published last week by Harper & Row.

Basis of Critique

Mr. Goldfarb, a former Justice Department attorney, advocates in his book the total abolition of bail.

Briefly, his argument is that bail is not a good deterrent where there is a real likelihood that a defendant will flee; and that where there is no substantial fear of flight, bail is unnecessary and illegal.

In cases when flight is a real risk or when the defendant is a probable danger to the community, Mr. Goldfarb proposes what he calls "preventive detention." This scheme, he admits, raises constitutional problems because of the presumption of innocence.

Mr. Goldberg, in his foreword, praises "Ransom" as a "timely and valuable study" that "demonstrates the inadequacies and unfairness of the American bail system and also makes valuable suggestions for overdue and much needed reform."

While he indicates that he does not necessarily agree with all of the author's specific suggestions, Mr. Goldberg says: "What is important is that the abuses of the present bail system be corrected, here and now."

Successful Use Here

Some of Mr. Goldfarb's proposals have been successfully employed in New York. Thus, the Manhattan Bail Project, under the auspices of the Vera Foundation, has had excellent experience with a system by which defendants are released on their own recognizance based on their roots in the community.

Likewise, Mr. Goldfarb's suggestion that the summons should supplant the arrest in a variety of crimes has worked well on a small scale here.

Mr. Goldfarb concedes that his proposal that a defendant be held before trial when the protection of society is at stake runs into serious constitutional problems. However, he contends that the same result is now reached surreptitiously through the setting of excessive bail. And he argues that his proposal provides more protection for the defendant.

Thus, Mr. Goldfarb would place the burden of demonstrating the need for holding a suspect, immediately on arraignment, upon the district attorney. Where this need could be shown, a defendant would be sent to a special detention building where medical treatment for sex perverts and narcotics addicts could be administered.

Mr. Goldfarb cites many examples of how the misuse of bail has frustrated civil rights demonstrators in a number of Southern cities.

According to the author, civil rights groups without a suitable "bail war chest" are effectively prevented from demonstrating in many Southern communities.

U.S. CRIME PANEL FINDS INEQUITIES IN LOWER COURTS

Presidential Study Asserts Overloading of Judges Is Hindering Justice Fight

RECOMMENDS OVERHAUL

Some Abuses Said to Result From Criminal Laws That Are Largely Unenforced

By FRED P. GRAHAM
Special to The New York Times

WASHINGTON, May 7—The President's National Crime Commission said today that inequities caused by the overloading of the nation's lower criminal courts were hindering crime-prevention efforts.

The commission reported widespread "inequity, indignity and ineffectiveness" in the country's misdemeanor courts, where about 90 per cent of the criminal cases are heard.

"No program of crime prevention will be effective without a massive overhaul of the lower criminal courts," the commission said.

"The many persons who encounter these courts each year can hardly fail to interpret that experience as an expression of indifference to their situations and to the ideals of fairness, equality and rehabilitation professed in theory, yet frequently denied in practice."

Special Report

The statements were made in a special report by the commission, officially named the President's Commission on Law Enforcement and Administration of Justice.

Some of the court abuses result from criminal laws that are on the books but largely unenforced, the report said.

It suggested that laws concerning gambling, prostitution, abortion, homosexuality and narcotics might well be modified "to bring the written law in closer conformity to the law as it in fact operates."

Among the suggested changes

were to legalize gambling sponsored by religious groups and among friends, to focus anti-prostitution laws on "commercial" and public activities as compared to more casual activities, and to discourage the use of nonsupport and bad check criminal laws to collect money.

The report was the second of nine by special study groups that will be released over the next two months to document recommendations by the commission. The commission's overall report based on the study group findings was published in February.

As examples of the overloading of lower court judges, the report cited the municipal courts of Atlanta, where three judges disposed of more than 70,000 cases in 1964, and of Detroit, where 20,000 minor cases must be handled each year by the single judge sitting in the early sessions division.

Clearing the dockets becomes a primary objective of such courts, the commission said. It said that judges rushed through trials in as little as five minutes, sometimes not advising defendants of their rights, and that the few lawyers who appeared often seemed more interested in extracting a fee from their clients than defending them.

The commission saw no reason for conducting separate courts for midemeanors, which are offenses involving prison terms of a year or less, and separate courts for felonies. It recommended the abolition of lower courts so that all cases would be heard in the courts that now handle more serious offenses.

The commission also charged unequal and overly harsh sentencing. It mentioned wide disparities in sentences in different areas for the same offense. One suggested remedy was a requirement that each judge confer with his fellows before imposing any sentence and to permit appellate courts to reduce harsh sentences.

The commission said that many statutes set sentences too high. In California, it said, a person who breaks into a car and pilfers the glove compartment can receive a 15-year sentence. If he stole the car, the maximum sentence would be 10 years.

The panel approved a proposal by the American Law Institute to incorporate two sentences for each offense, one for ordinary lawbreakers and a longer one for habitual or dangerous offenders.

The commission said that there was a serious shortage of criminal lawyers. It estimated that between 8,000 and 12,500 lawyers would be required to represent all adult defendants in all cases except traffic offenses each year, at a cost of between $84-million and $158-million.

There are about 900 public defenders in the country and between 2,500 and 5,000 lawyers who frequently handle criminal cases, the commission said.

May 8, 1967

Court System Is Blamed in Crime Rise

By DAVID BURNHAM

A study of professional crime in New York, Chicago, Atlanta and San Francisco has found that the operating procedures of the courts "tend to increase, rather than decrease, the over-all amount of crime that professional criminals commit."

The study said bail costs, lawyer's fees and other expenses assumed by the typical professional criminal to stay out of prison during the usually lengthy period between arrest and final disposition of his case "increases the pressures for him to engage in crime while free."

"Because the typical professional doesn't believe he can get a legitimate job," Dr. Leroy C. Gould said, "his only solution is to commit more crimes than he normally would."

The examination of professional criminals—independent entrepreneurs whose major source of income is crime—was undertaken for the President's Commission on Law Enforcement and Administration of Justice by a six-man team headed by Dr. Gould, an assistant professor of sociology at Yale University.

5 Recognized Categories
Professional crime is one of five categories of criminal behavior generally recognized. The four other categories are organized crime or that committed by criminals connected with corporation-like syndicates, white collar or business crime, youth crime and crimes of passion.

Financed by the Justice Department, the study is believed to be one of the most extensive ever undertaken in this particular field. It is based on interviews with 313 persons including 128 policemen, 30 prosecutors and 50 professional criminals, the last both in and out of prison. Of all of those questioned, 81 were from New York.

In addition to the central conclusion that some procedures of the criminal justice system work against the goal of controlling professional crime, the study also found:

¶While exact estimates are impossible, professional criminals today account for a "fairly large percentage" of crimes against property and a "significant amount" of crimes against persons.

¶Just as the general population responds to changes in the economy by abandoning absolete skills and turning to new opportunities, so do professional criminals. Because safes have become safer and most businesses have shifted from cash to credit transactions, for example, the highly skilled "box man" seems to be disappearing from the American scene. Professionals now appear to concentrate on such crimes as check passing, auto theft, auto stripping and home improvement frauds.

Again reflecting the general pattern of society, as Negroes have begun to assume a more important role in the economy, so are they beginning to move into the areas of professional crime in New York and Chicago. Some Chicago police officials predict Negroes will dominate professional crime in another generation.

Though the relationship between organized crime and professional crime is obscure, there is evidence that organized groups contract with professionals for special services much the way legitimate corporations hire subcontractors. One notorious "service" involves the hired killer, who murders on contract, but organized crime also uses the professional-for-hire to do jobs like driving get away cars and disposing of loot.

The reports finding that some court procedures increase the amount of crime committed by professional criminals was based on a detailed examination of a number of criminal careers.

"It's just like any other profession, the greater the pressure the harder you work," Dr. Gould said in an interview.

"A criminal has to keep working if he is going to make money," the sociologist said. "Because of the risks he takes, the typical professional looks on arrest as inevitable. But he must go on meeting his regular living expenses and he will use every legal strategem to stay out of jail as long as he can."

Dr. Gould pointed out that the money to pay the deposit on his bond, to pay the lawyer and, in many instances, to pay the interest rate on a loan from a loan shark needed to meet these expenses, sharply increases the professional criminal's usual need of money.

By the time the case of a professional criminal is finally disposed of, the report concluded, the bail bondsmen, the lawyer and the loan shark "have extracted a tremendous amount of money from the work that the criminal has been able to continue while his cases were pending in court."

The researchers were not able to develop statistics that would permit them to state the average income of professional criminals or to estimate how much they pay to delay going to prison. But from a variety of sources, rough estimates can be made. Though there are some professional criminals who make more, and many who make less, Dr. Gould believes a typical professional may make $400 a week.

If he is arrested for a nonviolent crime—such as burglary—the judge is likely to set bond at a level that will require a cash deposit of $300. The lawyer's fee—again in cash—may range from $300 to

$3,000. Many professional criminals are not eligible for assistance from the Legal Aid Society and many professionals don't want the services of the society.

With these demands above and beyond his normal living expenses, he often must make a loan from a "juice man," a loan which may involve an interest rate of 20 per cent a week.

In most cities, the period from arrest to final disposition will regularly be longer than six months.

The study suggested a number of ways to break the crime-producing cycle such as reducing bail, speeding the court process, and reducing the ease with which individuals who are

arrested while free on bail can be released again.

A second major conclusion of the study is that detectives spend too much of their time on activities that are "essentially irrelevant to crime control."

Dr. Gould said the traditional police procedure to control professional crime was to have detectives spend much of their time talking with individual complainants—developing evidence in the traditional Sherlock Holmes manner—while most professional criminals were arrested on the basis of tips from informers.

The report recommended that police give increased emphasis to information from tipsters by establishing departmentwide

professional crime intelligence centers like the one recently created by the Chicago Police Department.

The study said a second advantage of such a centralized intelligence center is that it would help break down the isolation of the specialized details such as the vice squad, the robbery squad, the auto theft squad. The study said that under present conditions the specialized squads often are frustrated by the professional criminal who knows "that when he burgles in one place he will be in the hands of one detective team; when he burgles in another place, a different team will be after him; and when he swindles, yet another team will be called into action."

August 20, 1967

City Courts Facing A Growing Crisis

By EDWARD C. BURKS

Every few minutes the assembly-line in the city's awesomely overloaded Criminal Court system lurches forward to produce a new defendant in an atmosphere of thinly masked impatience.

He is like a factory product—"like a can of peas being processed," says an important criminal lawyer—to be labelled, handled briefly, then moved on, and often forgotten.

The heavy volume forces such rapid handling—a dismissal, a guilty plea or an adjournment for a later hearing—that everyone is under pressure to get out of the way for the next case.

The courtroom is noisy and has an abrasive air of confusion.

Lawyers and defendants of one case stand around talking while the next one is being heard over their voices. In a seat in the spectators section a narcotics addict falls forward in a drugged stupor.

A Gallery of Outcasts

Pimps swagger in the hallways, waiting to put up bail for their prostitutes. A Bowery bum staggers out of a courtroom, newly freed, and pauses to pick up a half-smoked cigarette near a cuspidor. A self-styled minister, drunk, roams the corridors.

This is the scene in the towering Manhattan Criminal Court building at 100 Centre Street, where 235 defendants are arraigned every day. Each arraignment takes less than three minutes on the average. In Brooklyn and the Bronx the scene and situation are roughly parallel to Manhattan, except the buildings are older. Queens and Staten Island fare somewhat better.

Lester C. Goodchild, administrator of the system of 64 courtrooms, says that the pressure for quick decisions brings about a bargaining situation that is unfair to defendant and the people alike.

Although the defendant may get a circus-barker style announcement of his case and his legal rights, many judges and prosecutors believe that the process favors him.

There is pressure to dismiss cases where the guilt is not immediately obvious because there is not time to develop the evidence. Even an obviously guilty man, for the sake of time, may be permitted to plead guilty to a lesser charge under which he will receive a greatly reduced sentence.

Guilty Pleas Urged

On the other hand, there is pressure on the defendant to make a guilty plea to avoid a possible stay in jail before a trial can be held—usually a

delay of at least 8 to 14 days.

"The system causes judges to abdicate some of their responsibilities," according to Mr. Goodchild, "and the case is taken over by the defense lawyer and prosecutor who work out a disposition."

At arraignments, lawyers on either side have only a few minutes to prepare their cases. As for judges, there are 78 in the Criminal Court system to cope with a caseload that has doubled in a decade. No judges were added in that time. The great majority of them get their $25,000-a-year jobs on recommendation by district political leaders. The job, in short, is a political plum. The Mayor appoints them for 10 years.

In the last 10 years, felony cases (the most serious crimes, such as murder, robbery, and grand larceny) have more than doubled. Last year, there were 58,000 felony arraignments—more than 1,000 a week, a 10 per cent gain over 1966. That meant an average of 740 felonies for each of the judges, who rotate through the system.

Misdemeanor cases (not including traffic) rose by 14 per cent in the 10-year period, to 105,000, an average of 1,500 a judge last year. Traffic cases, which reached a total of more than four million in 1967, were up by 134 per cent in 10 years. And the traffic court system, part of the over-all Criminal Court apparatus, falls ever further behind because less than one half of the cases are settled each year. The average load of traffic cases a judge has now exceeded 50,000 a year.

The only category of cases to show a drop in the past decade—a modest 7 per cent—was "violations" or "summary offenses" other than traffic — offenses such as drunkenness, gambling and prostitution, which are less than misdemeanors. The reason was simple: The police were ordered to stop bringing in so many of the drunks and derelicts who used to jam the courts regularly.

Even so, there is a formidable workload. According to the most recent figures available, the system had a backlog of 33,000 cases, not including a four-month backup in traffic cases.

The Legislature, which has the power to create new judgeships, has failed to do so in recent years because of squabbles over how the judgeships should be divided politically. This session there is strong evidence of bipartisan support for more judgeships, and the citywide Association of the Bar is backing such efforts, but only if the judgeships are not to be allocated on the basis of political parties.

Meanwhile, the city system remains so crowded that the 10-minute trial is the general rule. But most of the time things do not reach a trial stage. If they did, there would be chaos, according to judges and court administrators.

Concerning the heavy percentage of guilty pleas, Jerome Kidder, a bureau chief in the Manhattan District Attorney's office, says: "A guilty plea is almost always a plea to something less than the original charge. Although he is not given a specific promise (of leniency) the defendant knows that if we let him plead to a lesser offense, he has a good chance of getting a reduced sentence on that charge, too."

A prominent criminal lawyer, surveying the carnival atmosphere of many Criminal Court rooms, declares: "The whole place looks like a block party on 110th Street."

"Maybe," says Mr. Goodchild, "somebody—the public, that is—ought to walk into court someday and shout, 'Stop! What are you doing here?' This thing is running on rather uncontrollably. Sure, they're moving the cases into and out of court. But because of the speed it's all sort of blurred. Nobody seems to be in control."

Harris B. Steinberg, a Broad Street lawyer specializing in "white collar" criminal cases, says: "The tremendous volume makes for a lack of feeling that there's any serious deliberative process going on."

"Instant justice" is the way Justice Bernard Botein, Presiding Judge of the Appellate Division for Manhattan and the Bronx, describes the Criminal Court process. "We're holding it together with Scotch tape and wire because of lack of manpower —lack of judges and court personnel," he explains.

At a time when the public is clamoring for greater police protection, Judge Botein explains why overloaded court personnel groan at the thought of more arrests. Most programs to combat "steadily rising crime rates" have a simple "cops and robbers" approach, he says— more policemen to catch more criminals with no thought of bolstering the sagging court system. He is urging 15 more Criminal Court judgeships.

Here is the present situation in the Criminal Court system:

¶One case in five (not counting traffic cases) is dismissed within a few seconds of a defendant's first-appearance before a judge, at the time of his arraignment. The reason: Not enough evidence or not enough time to develop the evidence.

¶Roughly another 10 per cent of all cases, except those dealing with traffic, end at arraignment because of a guilty plea.

¶More than one half of the defendants who move beyond the arraignment procedure to hearings or trials plead guilty later in the process, often to a reduced charge.

¶Only a quarter of all defendants arrested on felony charges are actually indicted and tried for felonies. Half of them have the charges reduced to misdemeanors. The remaining 25 per cent are dismissed at the outset.

The Criminal Court, with its many parts, is the court of original jurisdiction. It has no juries. Defendants charged with felonies cannot be tried in that court unless the charge is "knocked down" to a misdemeanor. Otherwise, a defendant is held for the grand jury; if indicted, he is arraigned in the Criminal Branch of Supreme Court. But only 5 per cent of those indicted actually go through a complete trial.

Mass of Paperwork

Justice Edward R. Dudley, Administrative Judge of Criminal Court, has been trying to keep pace with the massive caseload by keeping marginal cases out of court and by streamlining the mass of paperwork.

"This court will break a man," he says of the caseload on his judges, half of whom are more than 60 years old.

In Manhattan and in Brooklyn, the district attorney is now in charge of the "complaint rooms," where the actual charge is drawn up. Formerly the policeman and a court clerk drew up the complaint. Now, when the assistant district attorney in the complaint room feels that evidence is too flimsy he recommends immediate dismissal as soon as the defendant goes before the judge.

The "universal summons," a simplified, multicopy snap-out form, replacing several different forms, went into effect Jan. 1, saving policemen much paperwork and copying. This new form also permits traffic defendants for the first time to plead not guilty by mail. They fill in the proper space and get a trial date by return mail.

Microfilming Saves Space

An ambitious microfilming operation has been introduced to overcome a massive accumulation of paper traffic summonses. Because of the huge backlog in unsettled traffic cases, it takes 1,430 filing cases to hold just the Manhattan cases —and the filing cases side by side would extend the length of 13 football fields. In the future, the paper will not be kept for long. A total of 20 million summonses can be stored on microfilm in a filing case only two feet wide.

Another shortcut is a lock-box arrangement with the Chemical Bank, under which fine payments are mailed to the bank, and not the court, for processing.

Bewildered defendants and complainants still have to contend with an enigmatic nomenclature in the court system. Various sections of the system have such names as these in Manhattan: Part 1A1 (for daytime arraignments), 1A2 (night court), 2A2 (misdemeanor trials), 2B3 (misdemeanor cases before three judges), 3 (youth court), and 1D (felony hearings).

The busiest courtrooms have 150 felony hearings or 200 misdemeanor hearings on the calendar for a single judge in one day, an obviously impossible load. As a result, the court process in these parts becomes an exercise in clearing the calendar through quick dispositions or repeated adjournments to new dates.

Prisoners in the city's detention houses, where the census is 150 per cent of original capacity, are called first in these crowded parts. The detention homes have added to capacity by installing two bunks a cell.

"Give me a date," a judge often mutters with resignation, and a case is put off again, perhaps for the fifth or sixth time.

Repeated adjournments are a commonplace. "They are a great boon to the guilty man," especially under today's system of low bail or parole for many defendants, according to Justice Saul S. Streit, Administrative Judge of the First Judicial District (Manhattan and the Bronx).

The injured party in a mugging has to come back again and again, for example, before a hearing takes place, and if he loses patience, or cannot afford the time off from his job, the defendant goes free. Conversely, defendants, especially those who cannot make bail, are more likely to plead guilty to a lesser offense to put an end to the repeated postponements.

Many of the judges, such as Daniel S. Weiss and Reuben Levy, who must contend with the staggering workload, are admired by the lawyers who appear before them. But there is a widespread feeling among such lawyers that many other judges are at best mediocre.

"Maybe 50 per cent of the judges are qualified," says a prominent lawyer closely associated with the Criminal Court for a quarter of a century. "Half of them just don't belong. They slow things down by just trying to clear the calendar because that means adjourning cases to new dates and no disposition. They just compound the confusion. Many of them don't know the law."

Luck of the Draw

"The horrible fact," adds a prosecutor who used to be a defense lawyer, "is that a man's fate in these courts depends on the luck of the draw in judges. Many judges do not know the law, even though there are also some excellent ones. There are certain cases, for instance, that I could put before any of some 10 judges and be sure to get a conviction, and before one of 10 others there would surely be an acquittal."

Another lawyer notes that each judge is equipped with an array of rubber stamps bearing elaborate language on the disposition of cases. "If they took those stamps away," he says, "the judges would be helpless."

Paul DeWitt, executive secretary of the Association of the Bar, which has 8,500 members, says he doubts that crooked judges are a serious problem. "I don't think venality is the problem," he says. "The vice is mediocrity and that can be more serious, affecting more people."

Time Crisis Cited

The opposing lawyers in Criminal Court—an assistant district attorney and usually a young defense lawyer provided free of charge by the Legal Aid Society—may have 5 to 10 minutes to study a case before arraignment.

"Five minutes is more like it," says a Manhattan prosecutor.

"Fifteen minutes to prepare a case would be a luxury," according to to Bronx assistant district attorney.

Because of the pressures on both lawyers and the judge, there are usually some prehearing negotiations between the opposing counsel. The lawyers don't like to use the term "deal," but that is what these conferences amount to.

"A busy criminal lawyer is just like we are," says Assistant District Attorney Kidder. "He can't try all his cases either. Usually the initiative for a reduced charge comes from the defense and there's a little bargaining."

The outcome, in which the defendant pleads guilty to a reduced charge, is known as "an offer to walk him."

About 75 per cent of all Criminal Court defendants in Manhattan, and a large proportion in the other boroughs, are represented by lawyers provided by the Legal Aid Society, which helps defendants unable to pay for their own lawyers.

Assistant district attorneys who work closely with the Legal Aid lawyers say they are "frequently better than retained counsel." But some court administrators and lawyers see the Legal Aid Society as just another cog in the Criminal Court apparatus and they contend the Legal Aid lawyers join in the general effort to get through the calendar as quickly as possible, regardless of whether justice is being done.

"These Legal Aid people walk around with their clipboards, interview a client when he is practically before the judge and handle scores of arraignments on a single shift," says one high official of the Criminal Court system. "A whole new spirit is needed in their operations."

Such an appraisal is resented by Anthony F. Marra, a bustling veteran of courthouse battles who heads the criminal justice branch of the Legal Aid Society, which receives $1.2-million from the city and $800,000 from foundations and individuals to support a staff of 134 lawyers who get from $7,500 to about $10,000 a year.

Independent Agency

"We are an independent agency," he says, and we don't have to look to judges or politicians for our jobs. We don't have to submit to pressure from any agency."

Those cases that are not handled by Legal Aid lawyers are often taken by the "Baxter Street irregulars," whose names comes originally from the street behind Manhattan's Criminal Court building.

The philosophy of these lawyers, according to one of Manhattan's top prosecutors, is simple: "Whatever the defendant can scrape up, that's the fee, and from then on all the lawyer is interested in is disposition of the case as fast as possible."

Despite efforts to keep defendants moving in and out of the courtroom, the inmate population of the city's detention houses has risen sharply, from a daily average of 3,370 in 1957 to 4,975 in 1967.

Most do not spend long terms awaiting disposition of their cases. According to the best available figures, nearly two-thirds of all adult prisoners awaiting disposition of Criminal Court cases spent less than 10 days in dentention. Ninety-two per cent were incarcerated for fewer than 30 days.

In the case of indicted prisoners waiting for trial on more serious charges in Supreme Courts, a third were in detention fewer than 30 days, almost three-quarters were held fewer than four months and only about 1 in 200 were held more than a year.

These figures are for 1965, but officials say that the time in detention today is about the same.

After all of the sifting in Criminal Court, only a small percentage of cases—one quarter of the felony arraignments —reach the stage of a grand jury indictment reqiring disposition in the Criminal Branch of Supreme Court. There the overload problem is of a far different nature.

Only about 5 per cent of these Supreme Court cases go through a trial to completion. Justice Botein says: "If that percentage were ever increased much we'd have to close down completely."

About 80 per cent of the Supreme Court cases end with a plea of guilty, often to a reduced charge. Justice Streit says: "If such a big percentage didn't plead guilty justice would be at a standstill."

The judge gives the reason: Trials last two to three times as long as they did only a few years ago because of United States Supreme Court decisions protecting the defendant's rights. In addition, there are protracted pretrial and posttrial hearings having to do with motions to suppress evidence on the ground of illegal search or to nullify confessions on the ground of coercion or failure to notify the defendant of his rights.

Judge Streit fully indorses these extra protective devices, but notes that in the Bronx and Manhattan Supreme Courts there has been no increase in judgeships since 1923.

In summary, Judge Botein laments: "It is a pity that so many programs to combat crime are frustrated and so much public money dissipated by the inability of the courts, through sheer lack of manpower and facilities, to handle their workload adequately with justice to the prosecution and defense."

February 2, 1968

Random Selection Of U.S. Juries Voted

By FRED P. GRAHAM
Special to The New York Times

WASHINGTON, March 15 — The Senate approved last night and sent to President Johnson a far-reaching change in the Federal judicial system — a requirement that jurors be chosen by lot and not hand-picked.

In many communities, jury selection has changed little since the United States courts were created by Congress in 1789. President Thomas Jefferson agitated unsuccessfully for a law to require that jury panels be picked at random, and the method of selection has since been left largely to each of the 93 individual Federal district courts.

A majority of the districts still use the "key man" system of jury selection, which employs leading citizens to furnish the names of worthy individuals who are friends or friends of friends. The names are placed in the jury wheel and drawn when new jurors are needed.

This system has been criticized as producing juries that may be inclined to be too harsh. Last year the United States Court of Appeals for the Fifth Circuit in New Orleans declared it unconstitutional.

Under the bill passed yesterday, all districts will be required to obtain the names for the jury wheel by random selection from the lists of voters or registered voters. Other lists can be used to supplement this if the voter lists do not satisfy the law's requirement of "a fair cross-section of the community."

Members of grand juries and petit jury panels will be picked by lot from these lists. This will eliminate the "blue ribbon grand jury" and its trial jury counterpart.

The bill expressly rules out exclusion from jury service of any person because of race, color, religion, sex, national origin or economic status.

For years Federal judges and lawyers have argued against random selection of Federal jurors on the ground that persons of lower educational and economic status could not comprehend the complex issues posed by antitrust, tax fraud and other types of Federal litigation.

The new law qualifies for jury duty any adult who can speak English and write it well enough to fill out a simple form, and who is neither a felon nor mentally or physically infirm.

A jury selection bill was proposed by the Johnson Administration in 1966 as part of its omnibus civil rights bill. After this measure ran into trouble over fair housing, the jury portion was severed and advocated as a judicial reform measure by Senator Joseph D. Tydings, Maryland Democrat, who is chairman of the Judiciary subcommittee on improvements in judicial machinery.

Senator Tydings did not stress the fact that the law would put more Negroes on juries, and it was supported by a number of Southern Senators as well as by President Johnson.

Senator Tydings praised the law today as "a reform which makes a reality of what everybody has thought is our historic tradition—that a jury represents a cross-section of the community and not just the rich and well educated."

The particular bill that was passed was drafted initially by a committee of senior United States judges headed by Judge Irving R. Kaufman of the United States Court of Appeals for the Second Circuit. It gives the judiciary more flexibility in carrying out the random selection principle than the original Johnson Administration proposal did.

Federal jury selection in New York City and in about 40 other of the most populous districts will not be radically changed under the new law. Most of these are urban communities that abandoned the "key man" system because it was impractical in an impersonal, congested society.

Although names of Federal jurors have been obtained in New York from voter lists for a decade, for reasons of economy and convenience no communities north of White Plains have been included. Under the new law, names must be drawn from the entire Southern District, which extends almost to Albany.

Local United States judges will be given as much as 280 days to put the new plan into operation.

March 16, 1968

Criminal Cases Quashed as Police Fail to Show Up

By LESLEY OELSNER

Scores and sometimes hundreds of cases are dismissed each month in Manhattan's Criminal Court simply because policemen needed as witnesses fail to appear in court.

As a result, men charged with anything from attempted purse-snatching to armed robbery are freed, while other men charged with the same crimes, but blessed with less luck, are not. In felony cases, at least, the District Attorney may still go before a grand jury with whatever evidence he has to seek an indictment, but court officials say this does not happen very often.

On occasion it is the fault of policemen who do not want to spend a day sitting in the courtroom.

"They think it's a big joke," says Mrs. Laura Cook, who is in charge of notifying witnesses of the dates they are expected in court. "They tell me, 'I got your subpoena and I'm not going to show.' They just laugh."

But usually, according to court personnel, police officials and judges, it is the fault of what they all call "the system" —the combination of overloaded court calendars, of myriad court parts and clerks with no central calendar-control, of city funds too limited to pay for personal service of subpoenas, of the traditional defense tactic of asking for delays in hope of eventually winning a dismissal.

Because these problems of court congestion and delay have been increasing astronomically over the last few years, so also has the problem of such dismissals increased.

Many times the policeman does not receive the notice that he is to appear. Other times the policeman has several court appearances scheduled on the same day, and though he is in the courthouse there is no one to find him and tell him that the judge in one of his cases is ready to hear him. Sometimes he is sick; sometimes he is detained on another arrest.

Neither the police nor the district attorneys nor the judges like to lose cases. As one young assistant district attorney put it:

"If it's a good case and the defendant is the type of criminal that you'd like to see justice done to, well, it's annoying to have it dismissed because the cop doesn't show."

But in a court system where the average case is adjourned six or seven times before it is resolved, and where judges often spend hours each day doing nothing but setting new dates for cases already on the calendar, the judges tire of waiting for a policeman to appear.

So a judge, having already adjourned the case several times because either the police witness or some other witness did not appear or because either the District Attorney or the defense counsel wanted more time, sets a final, last-chance day on which the District Attorney must produce his policeman. If the policeman doesn't appear, the case is dismissed.

"The obligation of the People [the District Attorney] is to provide a speedy trial," explains Criminal Court Judge Irving Lang. "You can't wait forever."

The problem begins when the District Attorney notifies Mrs. Cook, supervisor of the court's complaint room, of the policemen who are to be summoned to testify.

For each policeman, she and her ten assistants fill out a short form telling him he is "commanded" to appear on a certain date in a certain room, to testify about a certain defendant. The form also states that if he fails to attend, he may be found guilty of contempt and either fined $250 or sentenced to 30 days in jail.

And here is the first flaw— for the law requires that subpoenas must be served personally before the recipient may be cited for contempt, and the court's so-called "subpoenas" are sent my mail.

The notices, moreover, are sent through the Police Department's internal mail system, and as one court officer said, "some of them get lost."

Most, though, are not, but still there are problems. If a policeman is unable to appear on the appointed day, he is supposed to call Lieutenant Dillon or his commanding officer. Sometimes these calls are made days before the scheduled date, but other times, they are not made until the morning of the expected appearance. Lieutenant Dillon says he gets about 50 such calls each day.

In each case, he notifies the assistant district attorney involved.

But not all the policemen to whom notices have been sent, and who cannot be in court, notify Lieutenant Dillon. And the lieutenant has no record of the men who have been notified, he learns of the absentees only if the district attorneys tell him.

"They are supposed to tell us," he says, but he concedes that often they do not.

But even if the District Attorney does call him, the problem is not always solved. By the time Lieutenant Dillon is able to locate the absent policeman—either by calling the man's commanding officer or by checking to see if he is in another part of the building —the case may be adjourned.

Then comes still another problem: Often the new date is a date on which the policeman will again be unavailable, either because it is his day off (and his appearance would cost the Police Department an extra day and a half's wages) or because he is scheduled to appear somewhere else. Or the new date may turn out to be unacceptable to the defendant, or even, if there is a heavy calendar, to the judge.

No one knows how many cases have been dismissed because of the failure of policemen to appear — as in many other facets of court administration, there are simply no statistics — but the estimate is high. Kenneth O. Conboy, the assistant district attorney who headed the Criminal Court Bureau of the Manhattan District Attorney's office in 1969, said that at least 1,000 cases were dismissed last year for this reason. Some judges have guessed that the figure is much higher.

All of the people involved in the program hope that it can be eased if not erased by establishing a master calendar-control program under which all parties are notified by telephone before a hearing or trial date is made definite. Thus no one would appear unless all the other relevant persons were also to appear.

An experimental telephone-appearance program has been under way in one of the courtrooms since the middle of January, established by District Attorney Frank S. Hogan and applauded by the police. Mr. Conboy assessed its progress so far as "moderately successful"

March 15, 1970

The Pretrial Hearing

Present Procedures Are Called Different From Those Court Used 10 Years Ago

By LESLEY OELSNER

Ten years ago, things were simpler for judges and lawyers and district attorneys: A man was arrested, arraigned, indicted if a felony was involved and sent to trial.

Occasionally, there was a pretrial hearing to see if the defendant was insane, or, perhaps a hearing to see if bail was too high. Mostly, though, either a guilty plea was entered quickly or a straight road was opened to a trial. But now it is different: a man is arrested, arraigned, indicted if a felony is involved and, almost always, sent to pretrial hearings. Some pretrial hearings take only a morning or a day, and require only a witness or two.

News Analysis

Other pretrial hearings—as in the Black Panther bomb plot case here in which hearings began in February and ended this week—take longer. The trials start after dozens of witnesses have been heard and thousands of pages of transcripts recorded.

And when the trial does begin, whether the pretrial hearings have lasted a day or a month or even a year, the process is far different than it would have been 10 years ago.

Rulings Set Ground Rules

The judge's rulings at the close of the hearings, in effect, tell the prosecutor what weapons he may and may not use in trying to convince the jury that the defendant is guilty.

Formerly, the prosecutor could wait until the middle of the trial and then, with a flourish, produce a confession or some other equally damaging bit of evidence. Now, though, the defendant can insist that the judge rule ahead of time whether the evidence can be shown to the jury at all.

And when the judge does rule, as one criminal lawyer put it, "you know whether the case against you is strong or weak."

Sometimes, too, the lawyer said, the hearings—which are held at the request of the defendant—disclose an additional piece of the prosecutor's case.

Formerly the issue of admissibility was argued before the jury—so that even if the evidence was later found not admissible, the jury would know it existed. Now, the issue can be resolved before the jury is selected—and as Charles McKinney, a lawyer in the New York Panther case, says, "Chances are better you'll get an impartial verdict."

As the law has developed in the last few years, the defendant is now required to raise these questions — such as whether guns or drugs were legally taken from his house, or whether a confession was voluntary—by means of a pretrial motion.

So almost always, lawyers say, a defendant who knows of potential evidence against him will make a pretrial motion to have this evidence suppressed.

Sometimes the contested evidence is crucial to the case; if the judge says it was unconstitutionally obtained, the prosecutor may drop the case. Sometimes, too, the evidence is overwhelming proof of the defendant's guilt; if the judge rules it admissible, the defendant may plead guilty and forgo a trial.

High Court Ruling Recalled

The widespread use of pretrial hearings began nine years ago — when the United States Supreme Court ruled for the first time, in a case called Mapp v. Ohio, that state prosecutors could not show juries any evidence that had been illegally obtained.

For 50 years before that only Federal prosecutors had been barred from using evidence obtained through illegal searches or seizures. State prosecutors had favored the view, once expressed by the late Justice Benjamin Cardozo, that "the criminal [should not go] free because the constable has blundered."

But the Supreme Court reasoned that unless illegally obtained evidence was declared useless, illegal searches and seizures would continue.

The aftermath of the case proved to some extent the court's point; for there were a plethora of pretrial hearings challenging the prosecutor's evidence, and many of them ended with the case being dismissed. More than one prosecutor acknowledged that the Fourth Amendment hadn't been taken very seriously.

Another Supreme Court ruling, this time three years later in a New York case involving confessions, also influenced pretrial hearings.

The procedure in New York for determining whether a confession was voluntary, had been to hold a hearing before the same jury that was deciding the case.

Even if the jurors decided the confession was obtained illegally, they would still remember the confession when they decided the defendant's guilt or innocence.

Because, as the court said, the jury "may find it difficult to understand the policy forbidding reliance upon a coerced, but true confession," the Supreme Court ruled that New York would have to change its procedure — that a separate hearing, out of view of the jury, would have to be held.

Then came other rulings establishing what was illegal search and seizure, and what was illegal coercion of confessions. These rulings gave defendants new issues to raise at the pretrial hearings the court had mandated.

Obviously, the pretrial hearings are vastly popular with defense counsel. As one New York lawyer put it: "It gives you a better chance of winning, that's all, even if sometimes the guy did what they accuse him of doing."

For precisely this reason, though, pretrial hearings are decidedly unpopular with prosecutors. A young Manhattan assistant district attorney explained the feeling this way:

"We have lost contact with the real issue: did the defendant commit the crime? The exclusionary rules are designed to hide the truth."

Another complaint, heard from prosecutors and judges too, is that pretrial hearings add to court delay — they require time, additional briefs by lawyers, additional opinions from judges. "I'm not quarreling with the underlying rationale of the hearings," says Chief Manhattan District Attorney Alfred J. Scotti. "But they do delay dispositions."

How valid are these objections? As the Supreme Court noted in the Mapp case, the Federal ban against using illegal evidence did not disrupt the Federal court structure or paralyze the Federal Bureau of Investigation. Why should it then disrupt the state authorities? And even when "the criminal goes free," the court said, he is freed by the law: if the police do not violate the law by contravening the Fourth Amendment, the criminal does not go free.

The criticism of hearings for their contribution to court congestion, however accurate, is not widely viewed as a reason for abolishing the hearings. In the case of the 13 Black Panthers here, Justice John M. Murtagh often accused the defense of delaying the trial.

Justice Murtagh did not, however, demand that the hearings be canceled—even though the Panthers here, like the New Haven Panther defendants whose lengthy pretrial hearings are still going on, consciously gave away at least part of the benefits of pretrial hearings.

The Panthers had the hearings opened to the press—a tactic that might have gained them the publicity they wanted for political purposes, but which exposed potential jurors to all the evidence that the defense wanted suppressed.

Yet as even Mr. Scotti said, he wouldn't challenge the rationale of the hearings. What he would do, he said, would be to seek some "intelligent way" of dealing with the delay.

At least one court administrator—Lester Goodchild of New York City Criminal Court—has long suggested an answer to court delay in general: "introducing modern management techniques" to the now poorly functioning courts.

Bargaining on Pleas Poses Court Problems

By CRAIG R. WHITNEY

A recent split decision by the United States Supreme Court has focused attention on a universal courtroom practice that is paradoxically regarded as both indispensable and undesirable by judges, prosecutors and even some defendants.

The practice is "plea bargaining" — the negotiating between prosecution and defense that often leads to guilty pleas in return for lenient sentences.

Bargaining for a plea to a lesser offense—by which a defendant may plead guilty to third-degree robbery instead of going to trial on a first-degree robbery charge, for example—occurs in about 90 per cent of all criminal cases in New York City.

The Supreme Court, while upholding the practice by a vote of 6 to 3 in an opinion handed down on Nov. 23, said that the states, "in their wisdom," might wish to eliminate the difficult moral problems plea bargaining creates by outlawing it. Then, the Court said, they would be in a position to insist that persons accused of crimes either plead guilty as charged or stand trial, but not be allowed to plead guilty to lesser offenses.

Basic Contradiction

The Supreme Court decision came in the case of a defendant accused of first-degree murder in North Carolina. He pleaded guilty to second-degree murder, only to avoid the possible death penalty for a conviction on the original charge, ain't shot no man."

Another case that illustrates both the advantages and shortcomings in the plea-bargaining process, involves two men who pleaded guilty to reduced theft charges in a Queens jewel robbery but say they did not get the early parole they bargained for.

In the seriously overloaded courts of New York City, District Attorneys say they must bargain with defendants charged with serious crimes and offer pleas to lesser offenses because the courts would collapse if they all insisted on jury trials.

As District Attorney Frank S. Hogan of Manhattan has written:

"It can readily be appreciated that if merely 50 per cent of the 7,000 defendants accused of crimes in Supreme Court, New York County, in 1969 had demanded trials, the situation would have been completely unmanageable. Plea bargaining thus becomes a necessity because prosecutors,

judges, courtrooms and defense counsel are too few to staff the number of possible trials."

Another Viewpoint

But some of his assistants, as well as others involved in the administration of criminal justice, believe that plea bargaining, if unchecked, can weaken the deterrent effect of the Penal Code.

Illustrating one extreme of the bargaining process is the current investigation of the Joint Legislative Committee on Crime, which is looking into an apparent pattern of light sentences handed out by certain state judges to organized-crime figures.

With few exceptions, official court records do not show any evidence of bargaining The American Bar Association's guidelines on the subject adjure judges not to participate in plea-bargaining discussions, but many lawyers say that judges in New York often do get involved in the bargaining. Some observers say that plea bargaining is the courts' greatest hypocrisy.

Plea bargaining, which started in the Middle Ages as a way of tempering justice with mercy, is sometimes justified today on humanitarian grounds. "If you get an 18-year-old kid for possession of an ounce of marijuana," an assistant district attorney said, "you don't want to see him get a felony record and ruin his life, you offer him the chance to plead to a misdemeanor."

Another reason for striking bargains is that a defendant charged with several crimes who gets lenient treatment in one case may be persuaded to give the prosecution more information. This is commonly known as "turning" a defendant, and without plea bargaining it would be much more difficult.

Getting Jewels Back

The reason for the state's offer of a plea bargain in the Queens case was to get back $4-million worth of jewels insured for only a fraction of their value. The jewels were stolen from the Provident Loan Society branch in Jamaica in February, 1969.

The defendants, Thomas Palermo and Sheldon Saltzman, are imprisoned in the Queens House of Detention. They contend that they returned the jewels in October, 1969, and pleaded guilty to reduced charges of stealing them in return for a promise by the Queens District Attorney that they would get early parole on their sentences for robbery in Staten Island. Palermo got 25

years and Saltzman 15 years.

But on June 3, the State Board of Parole decided that parole was six years off for Palermo, and five years away for Saltzman. The chairman of the board, Russell G. Oswald, commented later, "The board said, 'You don't have any arrangement with us.'"

Palermo has now asked Supreme Court Justice Peter T. Farrell of Queens for permission to withdraw his guilty plea. Both he and Saltzman have also brought suit in Manhattan to get "their" jewels back because they say the state failed to live up to its part of the "bargain" in their case.

In 1967, the President's Commission on Law Enforcement and Administration of Justice said in a report, which might have been written to describe that "bargain," that:

"There is ordinarily no formal recognition that the defendant has been offered an inducement to plead guilty.

"Although the participants and frequently the judge know that negotiation has taken place, the prosecutor and defendant must ordinarily go through a courtroom ritual in which they deny that the guilty plea is the result of any threat or promise.

"The judge, the public, and sometimes the defendant himself cannot know for certain who got what from whom in exchange for what."

Official Court Record

The official court record man and Palermo, who were represented at the time by Edward Bobick, reads like this:

The Court (Justice Farrell), to Palermo: This means that you admit that on February the 17th, 1969, acting in concert with Sheldon Saltzman, your co-defendant, you forcibly stole some property from people at the Provident Loan Society. Is that what you admit?

Palermo: Yes.

The Court: Now, where was this place that you stole the money, do you know?

Palermo: I don't remember, sir.

The Court: What time did you go in there and do this?

Mr. Bobick: Your Honor, I think this is a problem. May we approach the bench for a moment?

What happened then, Justice Farrell said at a hearing Friday on Palermo's motion to withdraw his guilty plea: "I was told that this question he could not answer properly because he was not in the premises — he was the lookout man outside."

The transcript resumes:

The Court: You knew that there was a robbery going to take place there, didn't you?

Palermo: Yes.

The Court: Did you share in the proceeds?

Palermo: I did.

The Court: Do you realize you are pleading guilty to robbery in the third degree, you understand that?

Palermo: Yes.

The Court: And I want the record to show that my understanding is that any sentence I give you within the limits prescribed by law is to be concurrent with the sentence already imposed on you from the County of Richmond. You understand that?

Palermo: Yes.

The Court: There is no other promise as to the number of years you are going to get in my sentence. Do you understand that?

Palermo: Yes.

On Friday, Palermo said his one-syllable answers were untruthful. "Mr. Bobick instructed me, should the judge ask me if any promises were made as to the term of a sentence, that I was to say, 'no'—but I shouldn't worry as Slatzman and myself would receive suspended sentences," he said.

"I was told that the end result was going to be my freedom," Palermo told the judge. "That was my only reason for pleading. I was home in my house when these jewels were stolen."

When Slatzman pleaded guilty, he, unlike Palermo, actually admitted stealing the jewels. But neither man has yet been sentenced because of Palermo's recantation, and both say in letters that they got the jewels from somebody else.

Heated Discussion

The hearing on Friday on Palermo's motion to withdraw his plea was heated. Justice Farrell was red-faced and angry and directed sharp questions at Palermo's present lawyer, Hyman Bravin; an assistant district attorney, Jerome M. Pines, and the chief assistant district attorney in Queens, Frederick J. Ludwig.

Mr. Bobick is on Mr. Bravin's list of witnesses to testify when the hearing resumes on Dec. 21. In an affidavit he has described part of the agreement he reached with Mr. Ludwing on behalf of Palermo this way:

"The pending charges in Queens Supreme Court would be disposed of by a plea and a suspended sentence or conditional discharge. Parole on the sentence from the Richmond

County charge would be obtained with a maximum time served of 18 months."

Mr. Ludwig took the stand Friday and said that all he had promised that "I would use my best efforts, all my efforts, to get him the most lenient treatment possible if he could return the proceeds of the robbery."

Justice Farrell asked: "Did you ever ask the Parole Board to give a promise of a definite time?"

"No definite time—no year or 18 months," Mr. Ludwig replied. And there was no mention of 18 months either in Queens District Attorney Thomas J. Mackell's affidavit of his understanding of the bargain, or in the letter he did in fact write to the Parole Board on April 24.

Meeting Authorized

But Mr. Ludwig did say that he had authorized a meeting between Detective James Caparell of his office and Howard A. Jones, a member of the Parole Board, before the letter was sent. "The purpose was to see whether they would accept any recommendation by the Queens District Attorney's office," he told Justice Farrell.

Another lawyer who briefly represented Palermo, Jacob R. Everoff, testified that "The Parole Commissioner had apparently indicated to Mr. Ludwig that he [Palermo] would be let out after a year." The point was not resolved on Friday, and Palermo and Saltzman may need a court inquiry to determine just what the terms of their bargain were. Their Federal Court suit is now before Judge Walter R. Mansfield in Manhattan. Even though Palermo apparently was misled by someone, he described himself in court paper as an "experienced and hardened bargainer."

A report the Joint Legislative Committee on Crime made two years ago noted that an inexperienced defendant accused of a felony, perhaps wrongfully, may feel under tremendous pressure to make a guilty plea to a lesser charge to avoid being erroneously convicted of the more serious crime.

Such pressure increases when judges intervene, and according to lawyers and district attorneys alike, they usually do try to advance plea bargaining in New York. Only a few state it for the record at the time the plea is taken.

But an experienced criminal knows that he can keep insisting on going to trial, the crime committee observed, until he gets the best possible bargain out of the prosecution. Thus he might be sentenced more lightly than a first offender, innocent in the ways of plea bargaining, who took the first offer he got.

A defendant named Robert Williams, now an inmate of Auburn State Prison, presented an unusual example of such tenacity in a case that was decided by the United States Court of Appeals for the Second Circuit on Monday.

Williams, indicted in 1963 for selling heroin, pleaded guilty to a lesser charge of attempted sale of narcotics in exchange for a sentence of three to seven years' imprisonment. Then, because of a mix-up, he withdrew his guilty plea, and was tried and convicted on the original charge, for which he was sentenced to five to 10 years' imprisonment.

In jail, he petitioned a Federal Court for release, saying that he should have been tried on the reduced charges he obtained by plea bargaining, not on the state's indictment, and that he should not have received a greater sentence. The Court of Appeals called this "heads-I-win - tails-you-lose"; Williams lost.

Williams's reduced charge was still a substantial one. By contrast, in any recent year, in Manhattan alone the police arrest about 30,000 people on felony charges, but only 5,000 to 8,000 felony indictments are ever returned.

With all its defects, plea bargaining has been more securely established by last month's Supreme Court decision, which erased doubts about the validity of the practice that some lawyers had read into earlier High Court decisions. Justice Byron R. White wrote the majority opinion, Justices William J. Brennan Jr., William O. Douglas and Thurgood Marshall dissented on the ground that a man who claimed innocence should not be allowed to plead guilty.

"The prohibitions against involuntary or unintelligent pleas should not be relaxed," Justice White wrote, "but neither should an exercise in arid logic render those constitutional guarantees [to a jury trial and to equal protection of the laws] counterproductive and put in jeopardy the very human values they were meant to preserve."

It was that same decision that said the states could make plea bargaining illegal if they wanted to stop it. In New York, where the courts depend on the practice to dispose of most cases, nobody seriously expects that to happen.

December 13, 1970

Maximum—15 Years, With Plea—3 Months

As an example of the way felony charges can be reduced, some officials point to the case of a reputed member of the Mafia, Nicholas Bianco. He was indicted with 15 other men for conspiracy to murder 22 men in the "Gallo war" in Brooklyn in the early nineteen-sixties.

Twelve men were killed in that underworld revolt by members of the Mafia "family" of the late Joseph Profaci; others were shot, but not fatally.

Most of the 16 men indicted for conspiracy to murder, which carries a maximum sentence of 15 years' imprisonment, pleaded guilty to lesser offenses in the end.

Bianco pleaded guilty to conspiracy to commit assault, a misdemeanor, and was sentenced to three months' imprisonment. The average sentence in New York City for a plea to a misdemeanor is four months.

December 13, 1970

Speed Crime Trials Or Quash Charges, U.S. Courts Told

By MORRIS KAPLAN

The United States Court of Appeals issued rules yesterday designed to give suspects in criminal cases a trial within six months in the Federal District Courts of New York, Connecticut and Vermont.

"If the Government is not ready for trial within such time, or within the periods extended by the District Court for good cause, then upon the application of the defendant or upon motion by the [judge of the] District Court, after opportunity for argument, the charge shall be dismissed," the court said.

The rules, scheduled to go into effect on July 5 and designed to speed trials in all District Courts of the Second Circuit, were drafted for the guidance of judges and the United States Attorneys of each district. If the rules were in effect now, about 2,700 defendants awaiting trial in Manhattan and Brooklyn would be affected.

Promulgated at a time when concern has been expressed locally and throughout the country about delays in the administration of justice, the rules provide also for releasing defendants from jail wherever practicable.

The six-month interim period before the rules go into effect is to give the Government lawyers time to decide which cases should be tried and which dropped.

Prison riots proliferated here last year at the Manhattan House of Detention for Men (the Tombs) and at other Correction Department jails in Queens and Brooklyn, with inmates expressing resentment against delays in the disposition of their cases.

There were similar outbreaks at the Federal House of Detention on West Street, where there were several escape attempts.

The Circuit Council of the Court of Appeals, which supervises court procedures, warned that when the law-enforcement process "is slowed down by repeated delays in the disposition of charges . . . public confidence is seriously eroded."

"The public interest is not properly served by taking up the time of the court with the trial of stale and ancient charges and thereby further delaying the disposition of more important current cases, absent special circumstances," wrote Chief Judge J. Edward Lumbard.

Long Trial Delays Noted

The council noted that in most districts in the three states an increasing percentage of criminal cases were awaiting trial for one year or longer, although the defendants in most cases were available for trial.

It found that pretrial sessions consumed a disproportionate amount of time in the courts, thus delaying the handling of thousands of civil cases.

It called for "firm control of criminal prosecutions by the District Courts" as the best way to protect both the public and defendants.

The rules emphasize the need to expedite not only the trial of jailed defendants but also those whose liberty before trial may present "unusual risks."

They call for reports every two weeks by the United States Attorneys in each district on persons in jail awaiting trial, the reason for their detention or for the delay in trying the case and for monthly reports on nonjail criminal cases when a trial has not begun six months after the arrest or filing of charges.

Excluded is "a reasonable period of delay" for specific proceedings, such as a defendant's competency to stand trial, pretrial motions, appeals and trials of other charges.

A defendant without counsel should not be deemed to have consented to a continuance, another rule states, "unless he has been advised by the court of his rights."

In addition the council considered delays resulting from the absence or unavailability of the defendant. It said the defendant should be considered absent whenever his whereabouts was unknown and he was trying to avoid apprehension or prosecution.

Another rule provides that if a United States Attorney knows that a person charged with a crime is serving time in prison for another offense, he must undertake to have the prisoner arraigned and tried. If this cannot be done, a detainer must be filed with the official having custody of the prisoner, who would be informed of his rights.

Whitney North Seymour Jr., United States Attorney for the Southern District of New York, praised the new rules and said he hoped to catch up with his backlog of 1,300 criminal indictments by next June. He reported that these involved about 2,000 defendants, one case dating to 1960. He said that 21 of the defendants were behind bars.

In the Eastern District of New York, United States Attorney Edward R. Neaher reported 386 cases pending, involving 717 defendants, with 83 in jail awaiting trail. His oldest criminal case dates to 1966.

January 6, 1971

Justice Is Slow and Unsure in Nation's Busy Courts

By WALTER RUGABER
Special to The New York Times

WASHINGTON, March 7— Congestion is strangling the courts in big cities throughout the country and is turning justice into a commodity that Americans regularly find elusive, capricious and uncertain.

Every day the court backlogs leave innocent men in the jails and guilty ones on the streets. Witnesses and victims wait hours for cases that are never called. The claims and causes of the injured remain unheard.

The delays are long and the effects are lasting, not only for the poor, the black and the young, but also for the rich, the white and the old, the businessman, the motorist and the consumer.

There is no count of untried cases, either for the country as a whole or for the majority of states and cities. But an examination of court dockets in a dozen major cities establishes beyond doubt that in almost every instance they are severely bloated and that the consequences are widely felt.

Beyond the routine, wholesale delays, gross overloading cripples the courts in dealing incisively with the broad problem of urban violence that has become a ranking priority at all levels of government.

Consider John McCullough and his wife, Nancy. They have operated a small grocery in Philadelphia for 34 years. They could be anyone in urban America.

They were at City Hall the month before last and last month, and they will be back this month and probably next month, because one night last September two men with a butcher knife robbed their store of $250.

Mrs. McCullough was not very surprised when, after a morning in the big and noisy courtroom, the case was postponed a second time. After all, she said, a previous case required eight appearances and one before that took 16.

The couple stood in the busy hallway and tried to recall how many times they had left their business to go downtown and wait, but finally they gave it up. They were asked why they do it.

"Well, they subpoena us, of course," Mrs. McCullough said, "but we want to show an interest too." Mr. McCullough added, "What else can you do in order to get any satisfaction? You can't take the law into your own hands."

The trouble stems from a great tangle of causes, both inside and outside the judicial process. Most broadly, the administration of justice, with its comfortable inefficiencies and its essential but slow procedures, becomes an easy victim of urban pressure.

The cases and people stack up. In New York, for example, the blame for the jail riots last fall was placed largely on notorious delays that had kept more than 40 per cent of the inmates waiting a year or more to be tried.

Concern over court congestion is extensive and of long standing. Calls for reform have come not only from radical elements but also from established authority—from two Presidents, scores of governmental officials, two Chief Justices and a long list of members of the bar, the bench and various civic organizations.

This week in Williamsburg Va., legal authorities from all 50 states will gather to discuss the problem. President Nixon is expected to appear there with plans for Federal help in trying to improve the court machinery.

There is no single representative system. But look within the courtrooms of almost any given big city, among the faces and numbers and voices and all the day-to-day reality, and the stress is rather vividly apparent. Philadelphia is an example.

Congestion shows up in numbers. In Philadelphia last year, the Court of Common Pleas faced 91,980 of the more substantial civil and criminal cases and managed to dispose of 67,402 of them by Dec. 31.

The number left over (24,578), is large, but the first and one of the most important things about a backlog is not its size but its quality. And on the criminal side, quality is at least implied by result.

6,828 of 15,845 Freed

A lot of the people flooding the system wind up looking like lambs. The Common Pleas judges in Philadelphia heard 15,845 criminal cases in 1970, but of that number 6,828 were acquitted outright.

More people were acquitted (the number includes 3,104 cases dismissed without trials) than were found guilty of the crimes with which they were charged (6,718). The rest (2,299) were convicted of lesser offenses.

Hardly anyone thinks this is very satisfactory. It is commonly attributed to the greatly increased protection extended to individual defendants over the last several years by the United States Supreme Court.

But whatever the merits or the significance of that trend, the record indicates that between a third and a half of the people pouring into Philadelphia's criminal court will not get convicted of anything.

An angry and frustrated judge, after a particularly questionable case, is said to have shouted at some policemen still in his courtroom: "There are wolves out there, and you keep sending me chipmunks and squirrels!"

There are in Philadelphia and in most other big cities several variations on this theme. There is some feeling, especially among defense lawyers, that the police make cases that are simply flimsy by any standard.

Dissatisfaction With 'Input'

The police consider this unfair, and they get what could be considered a strong if indirect defense from many observers whose dissatisfaction with the "input" is aimed mainly at the "system" itself.

Some of the more radical reformers argue that cases designed to uphold the community's moral standards have no business in the courts, no matter how carefully prepared and iron-clad the evidence seems.

These reformers say activities that are by themselves nonviolent, such as gambling or getting drunk or reading pornography, could be handled by social agencies, if necessary, and should in any case cease to be illegal.

The idea is discussed fairly widely and openly, but the suggested pruning is far too rigorous for many. No one wants to think of promoting, say, legalized smut in his state legislature. And the "social agencies" already are admittedly inadequate to the task.

A number of judges seem to be asking instead for law enforcement that is a little more discreet. The police could concentrate informally, for example, on the cases most important to the community—more wolves, fewer chipmunks and squirrels.

Robert N. C. Nix Jr, a young black, and aggressive Philadelphian considered one of the tougher judges on the Common Pleas bench, insists "the philosophy. behind arrests has to be re-evaluated."

"It's ridiculous to think you are going to be able to make an arrest for every crime that's committed," Judge Nix said. "If that was the case, we'd need hundreds and hundreds of more judges and courtrooms and everything else."

When officials talk about the basic quality of cases coming into the system and the various elements that contribute to overloading the courts, sooner or later most of them cite enforcement of the drug laws.

More people in Philadelphia came before the Court of Common Pleas for drug offenses than for any other cause last year. The judges handled 2,848 of these cases but only 2,613 burglaries, 1,330 robberies and 452 murders.

Neary half (1,419) of those accused of drug violation were acquitted. Only 1,220 were ruled guilty of the particular crime with which they had been charged, while 209 others were convicted of some lesser offense.

In Philadelphia, cases that once get into the system tend to stay there and, even in instances where the evidence is patently weak, survive all the various preliminary hearings and arraignments.

"Our system has been like a big square," one of the city's assistant district attorneys acknowledged recently. "Everything that comes in at the bottom goes out at the top."

Prosecutors ordinarily assigned to the preliminary stages are the least experienced, it is reported, and lack either the confidence or the authority to knock out the weakest cases early on.

A Probation Program

The district attorney, Arlen Specter, believes some of the difficulty will be relieved by a program of "pre-indictment probation" that he and a state Superior Court Judge, J. Sydney Hoffman, announced earlier this year.

It involves first offenders or people with "minimal" police records. The case against them

may be weak, Mr. Specter said, or it may be apparent "the guy's going to get probation anyhow."

If the prosecutor and the court agree that the defendants in such instances pose no risk to the community, they are taken out of the machinery and placed in a probationary status for six months or more.

Those who stay out of trouble during this time have the charges against them dropped. The authorities expect that between 12 per cent and 15 per cent of the city's criminal cases will be handled this way.

There is a similar plan aimed at the load of drug. cases. As outlined last month, first offenders caught with small amounts of drugs can receive probation promptly in a lower court if they plead guilty and agree to some form of rehabilitation.

The torrent of legal business is itself an active agent in a backlog. When it strikes the urban court, all the old weaknesses become monstrosities and long-accepted, even basic procedures may begin to seem intolerable.

Computer Use Urged

Creaking administrative machinery is often the first victim. Many observers propose putting the myriad records on computers. Among them is Milton B. Allen, the prosecutor in Baltimore, who says of the present arrangement there:

"By and large, it's handled the way it was a hundred years ago—hand-written dockets, for example. It apparently worked fairly well up to 20 years ago, then the onrush of cases proved too much for the system."

Presumably it was also too much for a 20-year-old youth who, it was reported recently, had been locked away in the Baltimore jail for nearly eight months after all the charges against him were dismissed.

There are widespread demands for more judges and backup personnel. But many authorities in the big city courts believe that expansion by itself is only a partial and short-term solution at best.

In Philadelphia, where the backlog reached a staggering 35,000 cases in 1968, the court turned to the extensive use of computers, an active administrative staff and a general tightening down on courtroom delays.

10,000 Cases Trimmed

More than 10,000 cases were promptly trimmed from the overload, but it was recently discovered that about half of all the charges that come up for trial on any given day in the city still are postponed.

The New York Times

In cell at Philadelphia's City Hall, men wait to be called to court. One defendant, arrested in August of 1969, has made 44 trips to City Hall and is still untried.

The authorities believe the record in a number of other big cities is worse. Many elements must come together perfectly to have a trial, they point out, and if just one of them is missing a postponement is mandatory.

A policeman or some other prosecuting witness may fail to appear, frequently because a subpoena has not been issued. Such defects in the prosecution are said to cause 39 per cent of the delays in Philadelphia.

A five-month survey of continuances that could be attributed to something (there was no explanation for many of them) showed that 20 per cent of the continuances occurred because the defense lawyer was unavailable.

"Delay is the essence of any defense," one prosecutor says, and obviously in many instances people facing a jail term hope that the cases against them will dry up or just that they can stay out of the cells a little longer.

There are still other reasons for postponements. The survey in Philadelphia showed that 3 per cent of the trials there are put off simply because the defendants were not produced from jail.

It now requires, according to the most recent figures available, 160 days to move the average criminal defendant in Philadelphia from arrest to disposition. This is down from a 240-day average in September, 1969.

But the pressures remain enormous. Many judges have been switched from the civil to the criminal bench, and it now takes an average of at least four or five years to get a lawsuit settled.

"Justice is being denied almost totally on the civil side of our court," an administrator said. All the smaller cases are being forced to arbitration by panels of lawyers in an attempt to relieve the jam.

It is the man waiting in prison who feels the pressure most acutely. There have been jail riots during the past year not only in New York but also in other cities. The one in Philadelphia occurred last July 4.

About 80 per cent of the 2,592 men and women in the four jails there are just waiting to be tried. That does not take as long as it does for the defendant who is out on bail, but the average still is said to be four months.

The prison superintendent, Edward J. Hendrick, points out that because most of the inmates have been convicted of nothing, they cannot be forced to work or to participate in training programs.

"If we knew their future we could do some planning," he says. "As it is, our efforts are concentrated on moving people back and forth to court every day. . . . I'm candid to admit we're running a human warehouse."

Each day about 150 people are awakened at 6 A.M. to get ready for the one-hour bus ride to City Hall. There they are packed into four extremely small cages on the seventh floor to await a summons to court.

The largest of these cells was estimated by a guard to measure six feet by 14 feet. Inside there are hard narrow benches and balky toilets. There is no drinking water. Roaches scurry over the debris.

The ventilation is so limited that on a single hot day late last summer seven men, including two of the guards, fainted. After a day of this, defendants often returned to jail without even glimpsing a courtroom.

Mr. Hendrick's records show that Ophus Lampkin has been hauled to court 24 times since March, 1970. John L. Sanders has made the trip 19 times since August, 1970. Robert Briscoe has gone to City Hall 44 times since August, 1969.

James Reynolds was arrested on robbery charges Dec. 27, 1969. He cannot post a recently set bond of $5,000. He has been bused to City Hall 19 times and has seen a courtroom once—for a hearing.

Still untried, the 21-year-old black man, who earned $125 a week as a roofer before his arrest, said he was not sure why he had never made it to trial. Like others in the jail, he is bitter.

"A couple of times," he said in a recent interview at Holmesburg prison, "I thought of just not going down there to City Hall. It ain't nothing down there. It ain't worth a dime. That place—it makes me sick."

"We are not giving justice by virtue of the fact that we're not bringing people to trial promptly," D. Donald Jamieson, the court's new president judge, observed. "The first element of due process is a speedy trial."

James Reynolds agreed. "It's very agitating," he added.

March 8, 1971

Wide Disparities Mark Sentences Here

By LESLEY OELSNER

Jack Greenberg took $15 from a post office; last May in Federal Court in Manhattan he drew six months in jail. Howard Lazeli "misapplied" $150,000 from a bank; in the same month in the same courthouse he drew probation.

Such are the contradictions in the sentencing system here, in both Federal and state courts. A study by The New York Times has found a host of such contradictions and a host of differences in sentencing. These reflect differences in the defendant's finances, in race, in geography and in the judges' personalities.

Defendants charged with the same crimes get widely disparate sentences. Crimes that tend to be committed by the poor get tougher sentences than those committed by the well-to-do. Sentences for serious offenses sometimes show no hint of the seriousness.

The problem of sentence disparities has increased as judges have been given more and more discretion. It has gotten to the point where many in the courts call sentencing "chaotic," and Federal Judge Marvin E. Frankel, an acknowledged expert on the subject, calls it "lawless."

The Times found that the sentencing system includes such elements as the following:

¶Stiffer sentences for defendants with assigned counsel than for defendants with private counsel. According to a report by the Administrative Office of the United States Courts for the fiscal year 1969, defendants who could not afford private counsel were sentenced nearly twice as severely as defendants with private or no counsel.

A new study by the Vera Institute of Justice of courts in the Bronx indicates a similar pattern in the state courts.

¶Longer prison terms for nonwhites than for whites. The Federal Bureau of Prisons' records of inmates sentenced to Federal prisons in fiscal 1970 show that the average sentence of whites was 42.9 months and for nonwhites, 57.5 months. Whites convicted of income tax evasion were committed for an average of 12.8 months and

nonwhites for 28.6 months. In drug cases, the average for whites was 61.1 months and for nonwhites, 81.1.

¶Stiffer sentences for those who are convicted after trial than for those who plead guilty ahead of time, thus saving the state the expense of trying them. In the state courts this difference is simply accepted and is a major consideration in plea negotiations between defense and prosecution. In the Federal system, with better record keeping, there are even statistics to prove it.

In fiscal 1969, the Administrative Office of the United States Courts reports, those who were convicted after trial were sentenced more than twice as severely as those who pleaded guilty ahead of time.

¶Differences in sentences between those convicted in New York City's local courts and those convicted for the same crimes upstate, with those upstate getting tougher sentences.

¶Differences in sentences between those convicted in Federal Court in Manhattan and those convicted in Federal Court in Brooklyn, with those in Brooklyn averaging longer terms.

¶Disagreement between judges as to whether the disparities are justified or not, with some, such as Chief Judge David N. Edelstein of Manhattan Federal Court, saying the problem is not serious, and others, such as Judge Frankel in the same court, taking the opposite stance.

The problem of sentence disparities surfaced decades ago and affects courts across the country. As District Attorney Frank S. Hogan of Manhattan says, "We've always been concerned with the disparate sentence."

It is a matter of increasing concern to lawyers, judges, penologists and legislators. Among other things, it is combined in the state's courts here with another sentencing problem: a general decline in sentencing that is caused in part by the courts' and the prosecutors' inability to handle their case loads.

A United States Senate subcommittee that is studying the proposed new Federal penal code has begun amassing figures on sentence disparities in the Federal district courts and the State Assembly Codes Committee will hold a hearing tomorrow on the sentencing system, covering disparities and eased-up sentences.

Beyond that, the system's critics are broadening their attack. Once they concentrated

on the fact that a man charged with murder could get 10 years from one judge and 40 from another. Now they also wonder how to justify or rationalize a system that provides a jail term for a man who took $15 from the post office but neither a jail term nor a fine to defendants in a $4-million stock fraud.

"There's a traditional difference in sentences for different types of crime, and it tends to discriminate against the uneducated, unloved social reject," says the United States Attorney, Whitney North Seymour Jr.

"The guy who steals packages from the back of the truck is going to get four years, and the guy who steals $45,000 is going to get three months."

The difference is more than the traditional distinction between violent and non-violent crime. The difference now, by Mr. Seymour's reckoning, is between "common crimes," which may or may not be violent, and white-collar crimes.

The "common crime" of auto theft is an example. Some 71 per cent of the people convicted of the offense in the last Federal fiscal year went to prison, Mr. Seymour noted, for an average term of three years. But with the white-collar crime of securities fraud, by his count, only 16.3 per cent went to prison—for an average term of less than a year.

Mr. Seymour has been making his point in speech after speech here and has started a study, headed by an aide named Poppy Quattlebaum, of recent dispositions of his office's cases. Some of those dispositions are graphic proof of his contention.

The case of U. S. v. Jerome Deutsch and Frank Mills, for example, involved a $530,000 kickback. Deutsch, executive vice president of one company gave the kickback to Mills's portfolio manager of a group of mutual funds, in return for Mills's purchase for the mutual funds of stock in Deutsch's company. Deutsch was fined $10,000 and Mills, $7,500. Neither received jail terms.

Or the Projansky case last fall, in which 13 defendants pleaded guilty or were convicted of a $4-million stock fraud — what Assistant United States Attorney Gary Naftalis, the prosecutor, called "the largest known manipulation of American Stock Exchange stock."

Of the 13, eight received no prison terms. While some of those eight were fined, others were not. The terms meted out to the remaining five defendants ranged from 30 days up to a year, for the mastermind of the scheme.

'Victim Is the Economy'

There were no victims in the sense of a man whose house was broken into or a woman who was raped. As Mr. Naftalis notes, though, "the victim is the economy."

Most judges justify the minimal sentences they give to businessmen-criminals — fines, probation or exceedingly short jail terms — on the ground that when such a man is convicted, he generally loses his job, his standing in the community and his family's respect.

"A conviction is still a conviction even if there is a suspended sentence," says Judge Edelstein. "He stands before the court and community for all his life as a convicted defendant . . . A suspended sentence is a sentence."

Yet such prosecutors as Mr. Seymour—and Mr. Hogan—reject such reasoning.

"Is it really hard to accept the fact that a poor black also can lose his job, also can lose his family's respect?" asks Mr. Seymour. "It's that argument, really, that shows dramatically the fact that the present system of criminal justice can identify with that kind of defendant [the businessman] but not with that poor black school dropout."

The penalties meted out for irregularities involving buildings also seem rather minimal. According to an audit last summer by Controller Arthur Levitt, the average fine imposed for elevator violations in Manhattan for 1970-1971 was $18.

Some of the violations may be minor, but the Controller's office lists two such violations involving elevators that went unrepaired after prosecution and subsequently caused fatal accidents.

One involved an electrical interlock in a passenger elevator at 22 East 29th Street. The interlock had not been approved. When the matter came to court, in December of 1970, the owner was fined a total of $15. The accident occurred eight months later.

In the other case, involving a loose operating cable in a freight elevator at 23 Park Place, there had been no fine at all.

"From the recalcitrant owners' point of view," said the Levitt audit, "we conclude that it is less expensive to defy the law than comply with it."

In addition to this, of course, is the traditional problem of defendants charged with the same crime who get different sentences.

The modern theory of sentencing is to fit the punishment to the criminal as well as the crime (as opposed to the old-fashioned rule of fitting it merely to the crime), thus necessitating at least some disparity. But The Times survey found that disparities crop up over and over in the city's courts that are not entirely explicable on the grounds of differences between either the crimes or the criminals. The explanation lies elsewhere.

In the judge, for instance. State Supreme Court Justice Paul A. Fino recently gave a small-time addict-pusher a 30-year sentence, explaining that drugs were ravaging the young and that pushers had to be kept off the streets. Many of his colleagues regularly hand out three-year sentences or even probation in such cases, explaining that the addict is sick and that prison will not do him any good.

Or, geography. "There's no question about it," says Paul J. Regan, chairman of New York State's Board of Parole, whose job entails seeing hundreds of sentences from all across the state. "In the city of New York a man may get four years, and for the same crime upstate he may get 10 years."

So too in the Federal system. Defendants sentenced to prison from Brooklyn Federal Court in 1970 for the crime of transportation of stolen motor vehicles, for example, received an average sentence of 51 months, according to the Federal Bureau of Prisons. Defendants sentenced in Manhattan Federal Court for the same offense received an average of 30.7 months. In the Federal District Courts for northern New York, the average was 20.9.

The laws contribute to sentence disparities: they set tougher penalties for bank robbery than for tax evasion, for example, and state laws are different from Federal laws.

Also, as some judges point out, the value of a crime may be different in one area from another. Burglary is almost an accepted risk of city life here, for example, while in a small town it may terrify a community.

Guidelines Are Lacking

To many observers the crucial factor is that sentences are determined by individual men with differing backgrounds and differing theories—and with no precise guidelines.

While the general purposes of sentencing are to rehabilitate the criminal, protect society, deter crime and create respect for the law, there are no rules spelling out how these purposes are to be achieved. Nor are their any rules saying, for instance, how much credit a man should get for pleading guilty rather than insisting on his right to a trial.

"The basic evil of sentencing is its lawlessness," says Judge Frankel, author of a forthcoming booklet on the subject. "There's too little law and too much discretion. There aren't enough rules of general application that tell everyone where he stands—the defendant, the judge."

Disparate sentences also stem from philosophical differences between judges about such things as society's right to punish.

Those who believe that punishment is a proper function of sentencing can logically be expected to be tougher than those who agree with District Attorney Burton B. Roberts of the Bronx, a candidate for the State Supreme Court. Mr. Roberts says that "the word 'punishment' shouldn't be used at all," and that the purposes of sentencing should be limited to protecting society, deterring crime and rehabilitating the criminal.

So too with the question of whether or not, or to what extent, sentences deter crime. Judges disagree, and sentence accordingly.

Beyond that there is, in the Federal courts, no right to appeal one's sentences—and thus no evening out of any disparity, however gross. In New York's state courts, sentences can be appealed to the Appellate Division. But since there are four Appellate Divisions, no real uniformity results.

Proposals for solving the problem of excessive disparities vary from interest group to interest group and from judge to judge. To an extent, the debate is between those who want to make it more common for a judge to send people to prison and those who want to make it less common.

Thus Mr. Seymour and Peter Preiser, director of the state's probation services, argue that there should be stiff criteria that would have to be met before anyone could be sent to prison—an argument that would undoubtedly mean an additional hearing in each case.

On the other extreme are those who want the state law changed back to the practice under which judges set minimum terms that a convict would have to serve before being released from prison.

Many judges favor an increase in appeals of sentences (though they disagree as to whether there should be a special appeals court, solely for sentence cases). Judge Edelstein says: "I think I would like to have the thought that in the event I went haywire, there would be somebody above me. ...I would sort of like that guardian angel."

United Press International

Federal Judge Marvin E. Frankel, an expert on sentencing, termed the problem here "lawless."

One Man in the Maze of Justice

By MICHAEL T. KAUFMAN

The complaint room on the fourth floor of the Criminal Court Building in Manhattan is a drab place with institutional yellow cinderblock walls and 88 green, molded-plastic chairs.

As on every morning of the week, the seats are all filled, mostly with drowsy policemen. In the second row is Patrolman Stanley Cagney. Like all the others, he is there because he arrested a suspect within the previous 12 hours.

It is 9 A.M., and Patrolman Cagney has already brought his prisoner to the massive court building at 100 Centre Street and turned him over to the Correction Department. The prisoner, a robbery suspect, is being fingerprinted, photographed and interviewed by probation officers. Ultimately, he will be put into a cell with 20 other men to wait for his arraignment.

Meanwhile, Patrolman Cagney is in the complaint room waiting to see an assistant district attorney to describe the arrest for him. The complaint room procedure is a preliminary step that accompanies practically every arrest in Manhattan. It is the prime intake valve for the system of criminal justice.

In the room, separated from the waiting area by a glass partition, are six cubicles, each with a typist. There are four young assistant district attorneys on duty, and they hop from one cubicle to another, listening to the accounts of policemen and of civilian complainants. Then the prosecutors dictate formal charges to the typist who fills out court papers.

One of the assistant district attorneys is William Purcell, who is two years out of law school. He joined Frank S. Hogan's office nine month ago after clerking for a Federal judge.

In the two hours before he got around to Patrolman Cagney, Mr. Purcell handled five other cases. They involved the theft of a $45 wristwatch; an alleged kidnapping and theft of $52; a robbery at gunpoint; a forged driver's license, and the illegal possession of a gun.

"We try to determine how strong a case we have," Mr. Purcell explained to a visitor. "In cases where there is a complainant, we try to determine whether he will cooperate and be available. In cases where there is physical evidence, like a gun or drugs, we have to determine whether these could withstand defense motions for suppresion on illegal search and seizure."

After listening to the accounts of the policeman and complainant in each case, Mr. Purcell weighed the factors and then dictated notes and a summary of the crime, both to be routed to Arraignment Court. Such notes form the basis of moves made at the arraignment by another assistant district attorney, who usually does not have a chance to speak to the arresting officer.

In the wristwatch case, for example, where the suspect had an arrest record and was caught red-handed, Mr. Purcell indicated in his notes a willingness to forgo felony charges and accept a plea of guilty to a lesser misdemeanor charge, with a maximum sentence of one year. The complainant, Mr. Purcell noted, lived out of town and there was little chance of getting him back to the city for hearings.

It took about 10 minutes to clear the paperwork on the wristwatch case before the typist summoned another policeman to the cubicle to tell his story.

In the case involving illegal possession of a gun, Mr. Purcell recommended dismissal of the charges. After the arresting officer left, the prosecutor and this was "a garbage charge" because the confiscation of the gun resulted from an obviously illegal search.

Then the typist again shouted "Next!" and it was Patrolman Cagney's turn. The red-haired officer, who works in northern Harlem, entered the cubicle with Ralph Carnillo, the complainant.

Patrolman Cagney outlined the case. At 10:50 the night before, he and his partner were cruising in a patrol car. As they turned the corner on 165th Street and Edgecombe Avenue, they saw Mr. Carnillo standing beside a car with two men who were holding knives to him. Mr. Carnillo, a gypsy cab driver, screamed, and the knife-wielders fled in opposite directions.

'Yellow Sheet' Checked

"I ran my guy down," said the patrolman, who bears a resemblance to his uncle, the actor James Cagney. "The other perpetrator escaped although my partner recovered a dropped knife. I was also able to recover a knife from the suspect's person."

The cab driver, who speaks no English, filled in the story with the aid of a bilingual friend. He said he had picked up the two men, taking them to the 165th Street address. They drew knives, took $50 and were about to take his car when the police arrived.

"Did the suspect say anything to you?" Mr. Purcell asked Patrolman Cagney.

"He just said he had been a junkie for 20 years and had 20-bag, $75-a-day habit. But I'll tell you, he didn't look like a junkie, and I've arrested a lot of them. He was well-mannered and well-dressed — even had Gucci shoes on. He told me he had never been arrested."

Mr. Purcell consulted the arrest record, known as the yellow sheet. The suspect's name was Larry Boyd; he was 34, and, indeed, the police had not been able to find any record of arrests. Mr. Purcell said that was unusual for someone who had been an addict as long as the suspect had claimed.

The lack of an arrest record, Mr. Purcell said, made it an unusual case. The offense was serious, and with both the complainant and the policeman as witnesses, the prosecution, he added, had a strong case.

Two-Court System

Furthermore, he went on, explaining his thoughts for a visitor, as an addict the man would make a very bad bail risk. After deliberating these variables, Mr. Purcell wrote up the case, recommended bail of $3,500 and observed, in writing, that notice should be served on the defense during arraignment that the prosecution intended to present the case to a grand jury.

This last point was perhaps the most important. From the complaint room, the cases move to Arraignment Court, which is part of the City Criminal Court. The Criminal Court deals with all cases until defendants are indicted by grand juries. At that point cases move into State Supreme Court.

In Manhattan, both courts are at 100 Centre Street, with the lower floors occupied by the Criminal Court and the upper ones by the Supreme Court.

Nominally, the distribution of labor calls for the Criminal Courts to deal with misdemeanors and the Supreme Court to deal with felonies, but until an indictment by a grand jury the case remains in Criminal Court and felony charges can be reduced to misdemeanors here.

Essentially, then, by filing notice of grand jury action, the prosecution is simply affirming for the defense that the case is being taken seriously and that this should be considered in any ensuing bargaining.

Arraignment Court Hectic

At any rate, by the time Mr. Purcell has completed his arraignment report, it is noon. Patrolman Cagney and Mr. Carnillo, the complainant, are asked to go to the Arraignment Court on the building's first floor to wait for Mr. Boyd to appear.

The courtroom is filled. The first two rows of benches are occupied by policemen waiting for their prisoners to be called before the bench where Judge Harold J. Rothwax is seated. The pace is very hectic.

Seven Legal Aid lawyers shuttle between the courtroom and the adjoining holding pens to interview their clients. The lawyer stands in the corridor and the defendant stands behind the bars of the pen in which as many as 20 men are sitting, sleeping or grumbling.

At about 2 P.M., while Patrolman Cagney waits impatiently for his case to come up, a black defendant in the back of the pen bursts out in vituperative rage, obscenely cursing the system, the courts, democracy, racism and "this Greek garbage."

The three women Legal Aid lawyers jump back at the verbal assault and just miss being hit by a book that comes flying through the bars. The book is the Modern Library edition of Plato's "Republic," presumably "the Greek garbage."

The correction officers at the end of the corridor smile at the outburst. They say it happens all the time, not just every day, almost every hour. "These are bad guys," says one of the guards.

"Bad guys" is a term that is heard a great deal in the courts. Policemen, district attorneys and correction guards use it. Legal Aid workers are upset when they hear it.

Another function of the arraignment is to determine whether defendants qualify for Legal Aid as indigents. In practice, this is done by assigning Legal Aid to everyone on the valid assumption that just about all the defendants are poor. Rarely will private counsel show up to represent a defendant.

There are seven Legal Aid lawyers in the arraignment part of the court, and they divide the work by picking up the court records of the men in the pens as they filter into the court. As a Legal Aid lawyer becomes available, he picks up a set of papers from the docket file and goes back to the pens to interview the man who belongs to them.

In Judge Rothwax's court, no one in the adjoining cells is aware of the outburst. A succession of men and women come before the bench. Judge Rothwax works efficiently, setting bail or releasing defendants in their own recognizance, or rarely taking a guilty plea and sentencing for minor violations.

A Prostitution Case

Judge Rothwax rides to work each day on a bicycle from his Upper West side home. He says he does this to work out physically the frustrations and pressures of his job.

A woman charged with prostitution appears before him. Since the charge is one punishable by less than three months in jail, he is empowered to hear a plea. She pleads guilty. He sets the sentence at 10 days in jail or a $250 fine, with a month to pay. The prostitute walks out of the courtroom with the patrolman who arrested her.

"Good-by, Barbara," the patrolman says.

"Good-by, John," says the girl, with no rancor.

The patrolman is approached by another policeman, a friend, and asked what happened. "The judge made a pimp of himself."

The arresting patrolman is asked what his friend meant. He explains: "Giving her a month to pay. She told me she'd be back on that corner tonight, only this time she'll be working for him. The whole thing is a merry-go-round." The officer shrugs and walks off.

It is 4:30, and Judge Rothwax is about four-fifths through the 80-odd cases on his calendar. The bridgeman, the court officer who keeps track of the case flow, calls the case of Larry Boyd, Docket No. 69,486. The dockets are numbered consecutively, dating from the first of the year.

Mr. Boyd is led from the pens. He is a tall and slender man with a reddish Afro. He stands before the bench on one side with a Legal Aid lawyer. On the other side, next to the assistant district attorney, stand Patrolman Cagney and Mr. Carnillo.

The prosecutor reads the charge: Robbery in the first degree. The Legal Aid lawyer makes a perfunctory application for reduced bail on the ground that the defendant has never been arrested before. No one speaks to either the patrolman or the complainant.

Judge Rothwax sets bail at $2,500 and orders a hearing for the next day in All-Purpose Part 7, on the second floor.

Mr. Boyd, who is mute throughout the two-minute process, is led back toward the pens, but now he is being taken to the Manhattan House of Detention, the Tombs, where, if he fails to make bail, he will stay until his case is disposed of.

Patrolman Cagney is now free to go. This has been his day off, and he will be paid overtime, for his day in court. He and Mr. Carnillo are told to return the next day for the hearing.

"Be there at 9:30," they are told.

December 3, 1972

Suspect Gets Day in Court And Says One Word: 'Yes'

By MICHAEL T. KAUFMAN

It was Patrolman Stanley Cagney's second consecutive day in court. The day before, he had spent eight hours at the Criminal Court Building while Larry Boyd, the 34-year-old suspect he had arrested on a robbery charge, was being funneled through the preliminary stages of the system of criminal justice.

During those eight hours, the red-haired, 36-year-old patrolman spent 10 minutes outlining the case to an assistant district attorney and two minutes standing speechless before a judge at the arraignment, where Mr. Boyd was ordered held for a hearing and bail set at $2,500. The rest of the time the patrolman sat.

Now he was sitting again, this time in the second-floor courtroom of All-Purpose Part 7 of the Criminal Court.

"I've been here for two hours, since 9:30, and God knows when I'll get out," said Patrolman Cagney as he sat among other arresting patrolmen in the first two rows of benches reserved for the police. "I don't know why they can't do it like they do in Los Angeles, where a cop makes an affidavit on the arrest at the stationhouse and that's it." He said some men spent half their time in court.

Action at the Bench

Periodically, the patrolman gestured and smiled at Ralph Carnillo, the gypsy cab driver whom Mr. Boyd was charged with robbing at knifepoint. "We should get out of here by sábado," the officer called to the non-English-speaking complainant sitting several rows behind him. The cab driver works nights, so he is not losing pay. Other complainants, of course, are less lucky.

Meanwhile, the bridgeman, a court attendant, called out cases by the names of the defendants. Frequently it was hard to tell what was going on.

Sometimes after a brief conference at the bench involving the assistant district attorney, the Legal Aid lawyer and Judge Mary Johnson Lowe, the clerk would announce that the matter was being postponed. Sometimes a defendant's name would be called and no one would respond.

In these instances, a bench warrant was ordered by the judge. These arrest orders are turned over to the police, who then try to pick up the defendants. When found, the defendants are returned to court, and a charge of bail-jumping, often later dismissed, is added to the other charges they face.

At other times the cases are very clear to the spectators: a young man whose lawyer pleads him guilty to endangerment of a minor, a man whose lawyer informs the court that her client is ready for a full hearing on drug charges, or a youth whose license is suspended and who is fined $75 for driving an unregistered car.

Most of the cases take only a few minutes, with the judge passing sentence or setting a new hearing date.

One Defendant's Reasoning

The real dramas are taking place away from the bench. A 35-year-old defendant, whose case has been postponed, is sitting in the spectator section in an emotional discussion with his Legal Aid lawyer.

"I think we can get probation if you go to Odyssey House," the lawyer tells him, referring to the drug rehabilitation center.

"You mean, I got to move in there?" asks the man, who is dressed in a green mock-leather jacket.

411

Larry Boyd
Defendant

The New York Times/Jack Manning
Judge Milton Samorodin
Heard Mr. Boyd's plea

"Yes," she says.

"Well. I'm not going to do it. There's no way I'm going to give up my apartment."

"Then they're going to give you time," she says. "Do you want time?"

"I'm not going to give up my apartment. I'll take six months, I'll even take eight months, but I'm not going to give up my apartment."

The lawyer urges him to reconsider, but he is adamant. He explains that his 12-year-old son spends the weekends with him at the apartment and that he had a hard time finding a place of his own. Then he attacks the drug program.

"I'm not a kid. You know what they do there? They shave your head if you do wrong. Nobody's going to shave my head. I can kick on my own and anyway,

since when is one bag of coke such a big deal? I'll take the time, and then we'll appeal on illegal search. You can subpoena a lot of people I know who'll tell you it was illegal."

The Legal Aid lawyer smiles dejectedly and walks off with the man's file. The man, who is free on bail, goes out of the courtroom to smoke.

The noon adjournment has come and gone and Patrolman Cagney still has no idea when Mr. Boyd's case will come up. The patrolman talks about the suspect.

"You know, he's not a bad dude. His partner, the one that got away, he was the bad guy. You know what must have happened? The other guy probably pulled a knife on the cab driver, and then what's my guy going to do? Sit there like some fruit? So he pulls a knife, too."

The policeman was asked how he expected the case to end. "Nothing would surprise me," he replied. "I've walked out of court with two guys I shot at the night before, burglars who had broken a window and were inside a store, and I've seen guys get three years for garbage."

The police in the front rows pass the time making wisecracks. They point out an obvious transvestite waiting for his case to be called. "Look at that aborigine disgrace," says one. Another says the court clerk reminds him of Carroll O'Connor, the actor who plays Archie Bunker. A third labels the judge. "Miss Postponement."

Suddenly, an impassioned voice breaks through the murmurings of the spectators. A young black man, short and slight, is addressing the bench in his own behalf.

"I would like to submit that I cannot see what crime I have committed other than being a black man found in a place where black men should not go. But I have been in jail for six days and I am tired and I want to go home. So I will plead guilty."

Judge Lowe, who is also black, responds by saying that she cannot accept a plea under these circumstances. The young man is crestfallen, but he brightens immediately when she says that she will order an immediate hearing on his case. "Hurray," he says to his Legal Aid lawyer.

On the spectator benches, the man who arrested the

youth is less exuberant. "The kid was in part of the Eighth Avenue subway station at 42d Street that has been sealed off because of a lot of incidents," he says.

"When he saw us, he started to run. It took seven of us to subdue him on the street. He kicked and screamed like crazy, but here they're all good guys."

The case is moved from the big courtroom to a small room just behind the tribunal. This is called a back-up part and, although the room measures only 20 feet square, there is a judge, a stenographer and a small spectators' gallery.

At 3:25, six hours after Patrolman Cagney's arrival in court, the Boyd case is called. The defendant enters the courtroom from adjoining pens to which he had been brought from the Tombs. He had not been able to raise the $2,500 bail. At 3:10, Linda Hupp, one of the Legal Aid lawyers assigned to the court, had interviewed Mr. Boyd.

She read the court papers showing that the defendant had never been arrested before, that he was a self-employed hosiery salesman and that he lived alone in an Upper West Side apartment. The interview, of course, was confidential.

At this point in the case, a number of factors could be discerned, all of which both defense and prosecution)knew. For one thing, there was a strong case against the man: Both the policeman and the complainant witnessed the crime.

Judge Samorodin orders Patrolman Cagney to leave the room during the complainant's testimony. Mr. Carnillo is about to be called when Miss Hupp approaches the judge along with the assistant district attorney.

Obviously, a bargain has been struck.

The defendant is asked if he would be willing to plead guilty to petit larceny, a misdemeanor, with a promise that if the probation report showed he, indeed, had no prior arrest record, he would receive eight months. (A probation report must be completed before anyone can be sentenced to more than three months.) There was also a promise that in no case would the sentence be more than a year.

The defendant nods and mumbles agreement.

Then the prosecutor asks a series of questions:

"Do you understand that a plea of guilty is the same as being found guilty in a

Judge Mary Johnson Lowe
Scheduled hearing

Linda Hupp
Legal Aid lawyer

trial? Are you pleading guilty of your own free will? The defendant replies "yes" in a firm voice. It is the first time his remarks have been entered on the court record.

Judge Samorodin sets sentencing for two weeks later, pending the completion of the probation report. Patrolman Cagney returns and is told what happened.

The defendant is led out of the room toward the Tombs, where he will continue to stay until sentencing and transfer to prison. He passes Patrolman Cagney.

The officer gives his pack of cigarettes to the prisoner.

"Thanks, man," says the prisoner. "Can you do me another favor? There's a hosiery shop in the basement on 155th near Audubon. If you're by there, could you tell the guy there that I'll be at Rikers Island?"

"Sure," says the policeman. "I'll do that."

December 4, 1972

Court Complexity:
Probation Check Delays the Sentencing

By MICHAEL T. KAUFMAN

Larry Boyd was ready to be sentenced. For 17 days, since his arrest in the knife-point robbery of a gypsy cab driver, he had been kept on the ninth floor of the Manhattan House of Detention, where he received methadone to help him overcome his heroin craving.

Now, on Nov. 9, he was about to make the last of four court appearances related to his case. The first had been on the day after his arrest when he was arraigned on a charge of armed robbery. The next day he appeared before another judge to apply for a hearing. The application was granted and a hearing was scheduled before another judge for later that day.

But just as testimony was about to be taken, a bargain was struck between Boyd's Legal Aid lawyer and an assistant district attorney.

Under the terms of this agreement Judge Milton Samorodin accepted Boyd's plea of guilty to the reduced charge of petit larceny. The defendant was given assurances that if it were to be found that he had no prior record of arrests, as had been indicated by a search of state records, he would receive an eight-month term; if, however, he had proir arrests, the term would be a year.

Inquiry Ordered

Judge Samorodin then set Nov. 9 as the sentencing day, and the court clerks sent the case records to the city Division of Probation for investigation and report.

Under a state law that went into effect on Sept. 30, 1971, no defendant who will receive a term of more than 90 days can be sentenced until a probation investigation has been completed.

The reports of these investigations are intended exclusively for use by judges and can be consulted or ignored entirely at the judges' discretion. The purpose of the investigations is to present to the judge a profile of the defendant with regard to his background and potential for rehabilitation.

As of the first week in November, there were 49 defendants who had already pleaded guilty who were being held in the Tombs awaiting the completion of such reports prior to sentencing. In addition, 101 more such defendants awaited investigation in the Supreme Court prior to sentencing. The Supreme Court has its own division of probation, and the backlog there is greater.

On Oct. 30, Allan Strauss, one of the 21 probation officers responsible for Manhattan Criminal Court investigations, received Boyd's dossier.

8 Inquiries a Week

Every week he and the other officers in his bureau are expected to complete eight investigations, providing as much information as they can for a three-page report. Mr. Strauss, who is 33 years old and has been a probation officer for seven years, earns a salary of $10,400, which, he says, is $4 a week more than that of the sanitation worker with one year's experience whom he once had to investigate. Mr. Strauss had to have a college degree and two years experience in social work to qualify for his job.

The report he must file includes such basic information as the description of the defendant's crime, his previous record and his family ties. There are also sections on military records, past employment and educational background.

"We are the social-work arm of the criminal justice system and the idea is for us to flesh out the judge's view of the defendant," Mr. Strauss explained.

The final section of these reports is an evaluation of the defendant that often contains recommendations for sentencing.

Mr. Strauss said that the probation officer often had no idea of what the court needed and so sought to provide as much information and do as much verification as possible. But in the Boyd case, the matter was simplified.

"Essentially, the judge has made it clear that what he wants to know is whether or not the defendant had ever been arrested before," Mr. Strauss said.

After reading the court papers, Mr. Strauss wrote immediately to the Federal Bureau of Investigation, sending a copy of Boyd's fingerprints and asking for a record of his arrests. Normally, this takes two weeks, and by the time of the sentencing the F.B.I. had not yet reported back.

Then Mr. Strauss went to the Tombs, which is in the same criminal courts building as his office, for an hour's interview with the defendant.

"I found him to be very cooperative, unusually honest and very personable," Mr. Strauss said of Boyd. "He told me he had come to New York a year and a half ago. He said he had used drugs for some time but had been addicted only for the last two years. He said he had a $30-a-day habit, which he supported by selling hosiery. He said he earned $35 a day.

"I asked him how he could support that kind of habit on that kind of income and he assured me that prior to his arrest he had done nothing illegal. I told him, 'O.K., I'll write that down, but if you see the judge laugh you'll know that's the part he's reading.'

"He told me he had been brought up in Kansas City, had a high-school education and served in the Air Force in Wyoming, getting an honorable discharge."

Record Is Disclosed

The defendant told the probation officer he had been married and divorced. As to the crime, he acknowledged he had attempted to rob the cab driver, but that the act had not been premeditated. He said his accomplice, who escaped, had pulled a knife on the driver and that he had then done the same thing.

Mr. Strauss said the defendant had talked openly about his life and about the crime. The only thing he said he would not discuss was his crime partner. At the time of his arrest, when he was first taken to the station house, he had also refused to talk of his accomplice.

Mr. Strauss asked Boyd about previous arrests, saying: "You know, I'm checking with the F.B.I."

"Sure, I know," Boyd is reported to have answered.

Then, according to the probation officer, the defendant acknowledged he had been arrested in many parts of the United States. He said the police had only asked him if he had ever been arrested in New York, and that he truthfully replied that he had not.

Boyd would not specify how many times he had been arrested, but said it was "between 5 and 15." He said his last arrest was two years ago in Chicago for a confidence scheme, and that he served 60 days. He told the probation officer most of the arrests were for confidence games, with one for breaking and entering.

Under guidelines for the filling out of reports, incriminating statements supplied by the defendant can be accepted without being verified. However, had Boyd contended he had never been arrested, his scheduled sentencing would have been postponed until the F.B.I. report arrived.

Actually, the document from Washington arrived five days after Boyd's sentencing. It showed he had been arrested 16 times in California, Illinois, Kansas and Maryland on charges ranging from auto theft to robbery. He had been convicted five times and the longest sentence he had previously served was three months in prison.

Mr. Strauss asked the defendant what plans he had made for when he was released from prison. Boyd told him that he loved traveling and had been all over the United States, and now he wanted to visit Europe. The two men, who were both in the Air Force at about the same time, then discussed various bases where they had served.

After the interview, Mr. Strauss placed a phone call

to the complainant, the cab driver, conversing with him in Spanish.

Victim Unhurt

"I always like to call the victim," Mr. Strauss said. "Often they see things about defendants that never get into court records. In this case, the call wasn't particularly significant, with the complainant just telling me he wasn't hurt."

Mr. Strauss then dictated his report for a typist. It went to his section chief, who reviewed it. On Nov. 8, the report was routed to the court where sentence would be passed. Mr. Strauss said that, as his investigations went, the inquiry had been relatively routine, taking a total of perhaps three or four hours to complete.

On Nov. 8, Judge George Roberts was told that he would be presiding at All Parts 8, a back-up court. Judge Samorodin, who had been in that court when Boyd had made his plea, had been shifted to other duties, and Judge Roberts, who had just ended a two-week stint in Night Court presiding at arraignments, was given All Parts 8 to work his way back into a daytime routine.

Before court convened on Nov. 9, Judge Roberts read Mr. Strauss's probation report. From the court records, he knew of the arrangement that had been made on the sentence, and he intended to give a year in light of Boyd's previous arrests.

Before Boyd was brought from adjoining cells at noon, five cases were heard in the former judges' chamber room that serves as the court.

"Are there any applications?" the judge asked.

"Yes," said Linda Hupp a 28-year-old Legal Aid attorney from West Virginia who had also counseled Boyd at his pleading. "My client would like to be sent to a drug-free program."

Judge Roberts was a bit startled by the request.

He explained to the defendant that he would not send him to any of therapeutic communities in lieu of a sentence, but that he could send him to the State's Narcotic Addiction Control Commission facility.

"But if I send you to NACC, the law says, I must do so for a term of 36 months," he pointed out. "Do you understand? That is longer than the sentence I had in mind."

"Yes," said the defendant, who was wearing the expensive leather jacket and knit shirt in which he had been arrested. "But unless I get medical treatment I will be back here in a year."

The judge explained that if the defendant insisted on going to the narcotic control facility he would have to be examined by physicians first to determine addiction and that another hearing would then be held, after which he would be sent to one of the institutions run by the commission.

"Then, should you be released prior to your 36 months, and should you flee parole, the state would have a three-year hold on you and be liable to charges of escape," Judge Robert continued. "Are you sure you want the 36 months instead of the year?"

"Yes," the defendant said.

The judge advised the man to talk it over with his lawyer before he came to a decision. He recessed the case, and Miss Hupp went to consult with Boyd in the pens.

During the pause, Judge Roberts explained what was on his mind:

"The defendant is a very smart guy. He must have been told in the Tombs that NACC really only holds you there for 90 days and that the rest of the sentence is outpatient care.

"After those 90 days he could split, go to Europe, do the grand tour. But then he'd be in big trouble. The state would have a big hold on him. If NACC got him back, they would make him serve at least his whole three years. He'd be much better off taking the year. I hope she can convince him to do that."

Ten minutes later, the defendant and his lawyer returned. Miss Hupp said Boyd had decided to take the year.

In point of fact, however, Boyd could serve less than that. Each city prisoner has five days cut from his sentence for each month of good behavior, meaning that in all probability Boyd will serve only 10 months. In addition, the 17 days he spent in detention counts as part of his sentence. He is also eligible for parole after six months.

After Judge Roberts formally imposed the sentence, he addressed the prisoner:

"You appear to be an intelligent man. I recommend that when you get to Rikers Island you contact a social worker."

"I want to get some kind of counseling," Boyd responded.

"Well, it's available. It's up to you to take the initiative and seek it."

"Thank you," the prisoner said before being led out. Later that day, he was sent to the reception center at Rikers Island.

Miss Hupp was asked how she had convinced her client to take the year.

"I didn't," she said. "I explained the alternatives and then he polled the other defendants in the pen. They all said he should take the year."

LOEB CASE INTRODUCES NEW PSYCHOLOGY

Judge Caverly's Rulings Mark Modern Era in Criminal Procedure

By GEORGE W. KIRCHWEY.

JUDGE CAVERLY'S procedure in the Leopold-Loeb cas: at Chicago is an expression of a marked tendency, daily becoming more manifest, to place at the service of our courts the new knowledge of human psychology they must have if they are to do justice to the community as well as to the offender.

The crucial moment of this momentous hearing came after Robert E. Crowe, the State's Attorney, had brought out evidence of premeditation in the crime—the painstaking preparation which the guilty parties made for it, as well as their later conduct under questioning. This was clearly relevant to show the aggravated character of the crime. Then Clarence S. Darrow, chief counsel for the defense, sought to introduce evidence as to the mental condition of the young men in an effort to show the existence of mitigating circumstances.

This raised a question for the Judge that—at least in its implications for the future of legal procedure in this country—was far more important than his final decision of life or death for the individual defendants at the bar. Should this evidence in mitigation be admitted? On the Judge's decision might rest not only the life or death of the two young men whose fate hung in the balance, but the capacity of our traditional system of criminal justice to absorb and apply new knowledge.

The State's Attorney objected to the admission of the testimony offered in mitigation. He argued that the evidence he had submitted to show aggravation had to do only with the circumstances attending the commission of the crime. He insisted that to admit evidence of the mental condition of the culprits could have no other effect than to revive the issue of insanity, which had been negatived by the plea of guilty. By admitting their guilt they admitted their responsibility, he contended. If the defendants were sane enough to commit such an atrocious crime with cool premeditation, they were sane enough to go to the gallows for it.

Judge Caverly met the issue presented to him like a man of the modern world. He may not have known much about the new psychology—few of us do—but he was not, like the State's Attorney, content to repose on the wisdom of the nineteenth century. He, at least, was willing to learn, so he admitted the evidence. He was untroubled by the fact, of which he cannot have been wholly unconscious, that in so doing he was opening the steel-barred doors of the criminal courts of this country and the world to a new concept of responsibility for crime. For that is what his decision amounted to.

New Science Fits Old Laws.

The rigidity of our legal procedure may still for many years to come maintain the trial procedure which makes the technical issue of guilt or innocence turn on the old legal definition of insanity; but the more vital issue of punishment or treatment for those found to be victims of a defective or of a dissociated or "split" personality will, in increasing measure, be determined on scientific principles.

Our present legal definition of responsibility rests upon the state of psychiatric knowledge which prevailed about the middle of the last century. The definition of insanity then adopted by the criminal courts of England has persisted in that country and in the United States with little or no change down to the present time. Insanity, as defined in the law reports, consists of such a delusional mental state as incapacitates a person from knowing the nature and consequences of the act which he is committing or which makes it impossible for him to distinguish between right and wrong.

It is small wonder that Dr. William A. White, testifying as to the psychopathic conditions that he had found in the defendants, when asked by the State's Attorney whether these conditions did not constitute a state of insanity, dryly remarked that psychiatrists no longer talked of insanity; they left that to the lawyers.

Conceding our ignorance as to some of the causative factors of mental abnormality, such as the possible influence of defective or excessive glandular secretions, it cannot be doubted that the mental science of the '50s of the last century was only a faint adumbration of the mental science of today. In no other department of human knowledge, not even in the prevention and cure of physical disease, has more progress been made. The human mind is not yet an open book, but it is rapidly yielding its secrets to the penetrating intelligence of the psychologists and psychiatrists of today.

What makes the Chicago hearing most momentous for criminal procedure is the fact that three or four of the best of these specialists—men who are in the forefront of this epoch-making enterprise of discovery—contributed their wisdom to the proceedings. These men were not of the ordinary run of "alienists," who make a business of testifying in capital cases on the legal issue of insanity. They are among the makers of the new science of human nature.

It is not for a layman to say whether they were right or wrong in their interpretation of the mental conditions of the two defendants. But if they were wrong, nobody could be right.

It might be well to emphasize at this point that Judge Caverly was well within the law, as well as far-sighted and courageous, in deciding to admit evidence in mitigation of the Leopold-Loeb crime. No informed and reasonable mind can doubt that the procedure he adopted was legally correct from a technical standpoint. The prevailing impression that, after a plea of guilty, no trial is necessary is sound. But what actually took place was not a trial but a judicial hearing. A reference to the Illinois law makes this clear—and incidentally discloses wherein the present machinery of criminal procedure can absorb much of the benefits of the new science of human nature.

Illinois is one of the many American States—thirty-two, to be exact—in which the imposition of the death penalty on conviction of a deliberate homicide, or on a plea of guilty, is not compulsory. If the fact is established by trial, the jury fixes the penalty. If a plea of guilty is entered, this duty devolves upon the Judge. The penalty may be death by hanging, in Illinois, or a sentence to imprisonment in the State penitentiary for life or for a fixed term of not less than fourteen years. Contrary to the general impression, Judge Caverly is not required by law to sentence Leopold and Loeb to more than a minimum of fourteen years.

In assuming that, even in a clear case of murder, there is a discretion to be exercised, the law in these thirty-two States recognizes the fact that not all murders are equally culpable. There may be mitigating circumstances or circumstances of aggravation. The plea of guilty admits only the bare fact of the crime. It reveals nothing of the circumstances under which it was committed, nothing of the state of mind of the guilty offender, nothing of the motives that governed him. If there were nothing else in such a case, murder would be murder—neither more nor less.

But every student of criminology knows that every crime, murder included, has a background, a history, a tangled web of circumstance, which differentiates it from every other crime of the same general description. To the man on the street all murders may look alike; but to the careful student—especially to the Judge upon whom the awful responsibility of life or death has been imposed—every murder is different from every other. Indeed, every murder remains a mystery long after the actual offender has been detected and convicted.

Every Murder a Mystery.

It is this mystery, latent in the personality of the murderer—the why and wherefore of the dreadful act—that the Judge must penetrate so far as he can before he can safely and conscientiously proceed to fix the appropriate penalty. It is this same mystery which has been one of the chief factors in exciting the phenomenal amount of interest in murders as a whole and especially in this particular case. If the expression may be pardoned, we have always been conscious of the unconscious. Freud and Jung and their followers have only made explicit what humanity has always dimly perceived. It is this, I venture to say, which constitutes the human appeal in the exclamation of the great English divine as he looked at a criminal passing by to execution: "There, but for the grace of God, goes Richard Baxter."

The progress of penological science has in recent years resulted in conferring on the courts a wide discretion in the matter of penalties to be imposed for crime. Formerly, in all cases of felony, the power of the Judge was restricted to "pronouncing" the sentence prescribed by law. Today, in all but a few cases in a few American States, he has a wide discretion.

In some cases he may suspend sentence and set the convicted offender free on probation. In most other cases he fixes the penalty of fine or imprisonment or both within wide limits prescribed by the penal law. Thus, in New York, the court may, upon conviction of first degree burglary, impose any term of imprisonment that it may deem wise and proper over the minimum of ten years. For second degree burglary the penalty may be anything under ten years; and for third degree anything under five years. Only the other day a Judge of the New York Court of General Sessions suspended sentence in the case of a young man who had pleaded guilty to burglary in breaking into a grocery store to get something to eat.

What the Judge does in these cases is to hear the statement of the convicted offender, to have his case-history looked up and reported on by a probation officer, to gather from any available source information that may enlighten him as to the motives for the criminal act and the aggravating or extenuating circumstances that characterized it. For these informal methods of getting at the root of the matter, adequate enough in the ordinary criminal case, the Illinois Legislature has, by State statute, substituted the regular procedure of a judicial hearing. It is out of this provision that the public confusion has grown of a trial that is not a trial in the Leopold-Loeb case.

Faulty Justice Needs Mercy.

In hearings of this sort the specific issue of fact which the jury decides upon in a regular trial is replaced by the more general issue of the degree of culpability of the confessed offender. The Illinois statute makes it the duty of the Court to take any testimony that may be offered relevant to this issue—that is to say, whatever may seem to the Court to have a material bearing on the question of the moral responsibility of the defendant.

There is a certain incongruity between this interpretation of the Loeb case as an application of scientific principles and the tone and temper of the arguments of counsel—particularly in the closing days of the hearing. Was not the State's Attorney's plea an appeal to the mob passions of the community, a demand for social vengeance on these perpetrators of a crime of singular atrocity? And was not the eloquence of Clarence Darrow aimed at the heart rather than the head of the presiding Judge, an impassioned appeal for mercy? It was even so. But the explanation lies in the fact that there is, under our present law and procedure, no other way in which to mitigate the hardness and cruelty of the penal law.

The discretion vested in the Court in such cases as this is, in effect, only a statutory authority to exercise mercy. We speak of the importance of tempering justice with mercy. But the truth is that mercy has no place in justice—only the justice must be a wise and discriminating exercise of the judicial power, unmoved by passion, dealing out to each one the treatment he needs and merits; not the indiscriminate justice which, like the rain from heaven, falls on all who have committed the same kind of offense.

Yet it is to this very sense of mercy—to what we call the humanitarian sentiment—that we owe all the progress which humanity has made in the process of eliminating the barbarous cruelties to offenders which make such a sorry chapter in human history. A hundred years ago there were still more than a hundred crimes punishable by death in the English law, from which we inherit our penal code. These have all but disappeared, not because our theories of crime and punishment or of criminal responsibility have changed but because juries have refused to convict. They would no longer condemn a poor girl to the gallows for the crime of stealing a pocket handkerchief. The same humane sentiment would long ago have transformed or abolished our present prison system if people knew it as it is.

This sentiment of mercy must still thrust itself upon the consciousness of our Judges and juries until the newer justice based on the new knowledge of human nature arises in place of the old.

Criminal Procedure Safe.

The sentimental view of justice as something so stern that it must be propitiated by an appeal to the merciful sentiments of the Judge finds its reflection in the French maxim: Tout comprendre, tout pardonner—to understand everything is to pardon everything. This is another concession to a justice which takes on the form of an offended deity. In my opinion pardon is as much out of place in justice as mercy. Justice—the justice based on understanding—will have no occasion for either mercy or pardon. Its one function will be to act in the public interest by so dealing with the offender as to protect society from his further depredations and, if possible, to convert him into an asset rather than a liability to the community. When our system of criminal justice once assumes this function, then, and not till then, will the cry for mercy be stilled.

The fear has been publicly expressed that if the procedure initiated by Judge Caverly should be employed in all criminal cases we should soon find ourselves facing a complete breakdown of criminal justice. An editorial writer in THE NEW YORK TIMES, commenting on Mr. Darrow's argument that the crime Leopold and Loeb committed was the result of unfortunate hereditary tendencies, molded by an unfortunate environment, called attention to the fact that heredity and environment were all that any of us had; every criminal is

what he is by virtue of what he brought into the world plus or minus what his experience of life has added to or subtracted from his original endowment.

This is, of course, true. But it seems to me beside the mark. It is like the question sometimes asked of me: "Are criminals only sick men, that is, morally sick?" All such questions are academic and there is little danger that the criminal law will ever run off into such abstractions.

Surely we may assume that, by the joint operation of heredity and environment, some of us are normal, with a substantial control over the operations which make up the business of living in a complex social order; and that some of us, relatively few only, are abnormal and obviously incapable of leading ordered lives in such a society. Even if, as Professor James suggested, there is no sharp line to be drawn between the mind of Dr. Charles W. Eliot and that of a hopeless lunatic, there is certainly no danger of confusing the two. We may all have our day-dreams, our delusions of power (especially in sleep), our propensities at war with our better nature—in all of us the "spirit warreth against the flesh." But that does not put us all in the class of the Leopolds and Loebs.

Psychiatrists Here to Stay.

I have known many criminals. Some of them were insane, some feeble-minded, some obviously psychopathic. But most of them have been so like our average humanity that I could not but marvel at the chance that had made criminals of them.

In spite of the implications of the Leopold-Loeb case the citadel of the criminal law still stands four-square on its old foundations. It will not be shaken by the discovery that there are more shades and degrees of criminal responsibility than are written in its ancient records. It can take the new wine of the new psychology into its old bottles without noticing the difference. This is the way of the law. The more it changes the more it is the same.

That does not mean, however, that the operation of the criminal law will not more closely approximate justice in response to developments such as Judge Caverly's hearing. The psychiatrist, with his revolutionary science of human

nature, has come to stay. He will help the court identify the psychopathic personalities among the criminals awaiting trial or final disposition of their cases, and will take them over for custodial care and treatment in institutions which the State will provide for that purpose. The commitment of such cases will not be for a definite term, but under an indeterminate sentence which will probably, in nearly all cases, be terminated only by death.

We are already witnessing the spread of this method of procedure in the more obvious cases. The criminally insane are disposed of in this way in many States. In New York and a few other progressive States a beginning has been made in the permanent segregation of the criminal feeble-minded. Eliminating these two classes and the identifiable cases of psychopathic personality there would remain perhaps 50 per cent. of our criminal population who, to all intents and purposes, are normal human beings. But these, too, we will study to find out the case of their criminality; to learn what they are good for, in order that we may make of their term of confinement an experience which will fit them for citizenship and enable them to make good in the world after their release. But in their case, too, the period of confinement should be wholly indeterminate and their fitness for parole should also be determined, not as is now too often the case, by their prison marks, but only after an expert study of the whole man.

New York is a leader in this development, so far, at least, as intention goes. The State has erected, in connection with the old prison at Sing Sing, a clearing house to which every person convicted of a State prison offense is to be committed for study and, thereafter, for such disposition as his case may demand. The law which authorized this new departure is defective in that it fails to provide for an indeterminate sentence for such offenders, and the installation of the actual machinery has been unwarrantably delayed; but it holds great promise for the future.

Massachusetts has, however, blazed a better trail to the goal of adequate justice in criminal cases. By a statute enacted in 1921 the Legislature of that State provided a regular procedure for the official examination of certain classes of offenders in advance of trial.

Whenever a person is indicted by a Grand Jury for a capital offense, or whenever a person is indicted who is known to have been indicted for any other offense more than once or to have been previously convicted of a felony, the State Department of Mental Diseases is required to make an examination of the accused. The report of this examination is filed with the Clerk of the Court having jurisdiction in the case and is available for the use of the Judge, the District Attorney and the counsel. If the case goes to trial this report is also admissible as evidence of the mental condition of the accused.

Whatever Judge Caverly's decision next Wednesday may be, the Leopold-Loeb case will go down in the annals of criminal procedure as a triumph for modern ideas of justice enlightened by the science of human psychology. That it should have received such unprecedented publicity will make its influence on criminal jurisprudence so much the more profound. Instances such as the Massachusetts case referred to by Dr. Glueck pass unnoticed even by the bench and the bar. But no one has failed to be impressed by the proceedings in Judge Caverly's courtroom.

DR. KIRCHWEY, formerly Dean of the Columbia Law School and later Warden of Sing Sing Prison, has been devoting his energies for many years to the cause of prison reform. He is head of the Department of Criminology of the New York School for Social Work, where he gives courses in penology and criminal psychology. His knowledge of both law and penology, illuminated and corrected by his first hand knowledge of prisoners in many penitentiaries, enables him to speak with authority on the implications of the Leopold-Loeb case, in which Judge Caverly will render a decision next Wednesday.

September 27, 192

The Issue: Vengeance v. Justice

THE URGE TO PUNISH: New Approaches to the Problem of Mental Irresponsibility for Crime. By Henry Weihofen. 213 pp. New York: Farrar, Straus & Cudahy. $4.

By WENZELL BROWN

THE urge to punish is a basic drive in human nature, wholly divorced from a desire for justice or a betterment of society. Overly severe punishment in childhood, with its at-

tendant sense of guilt, is generally recognized by psychiatrists as a primary cause of antisocial behavior. Repeated punishments exacerbate the disturbed personality and tend to increase crime.

Why then does a society insist on a system of justice which is both vengeful and destructive? According to Henry Weihofen, Professor of Law at

the University of New Mexico, "righteous indignation" against those who break our laws is the "unconscious expression of our strong but repressed aggressive impulses." Punishment of others gives a temporary satisfaction to a concealed desire for violence but at the same time strengthens the mass sadistic drives so that punishment becomes an end in itself.

Mr. Weihofen contends that this urge to punishment is "the main obstacle to the adoption of a rational penal code" and hammers his point home with facts and statistics. This book is a compilation of a series of lectures given before the law and medical schools of Temple University in Philadelphia under the auspices of the American Psychiatric Association.

Mr. WEIHOFEN is a lawyer, not a psychiatrist, but he points out the ever-widening gap between our tremendously increased knowledge of the mind of man and the use of that knowledge in the courts. Although psychiatry has broadened our horizons in other fields, the leaders of our bar associations still tend to emphasize "the antiquity and unchanging permanence" of legal procedures and rarely mention the dynamic and adaptive character of law. Only when the flexibility inherent in man is reflected in the courts can our judicial system help to advance the cause of mankind, he argues.

In his final chapter, the author summarizes the case against capital punishment. Execution by the state, he indicates, is actually a stimulus to crime. Sensational trials and the morbid details of executions tend to excite the emotionally unbalanced and to blunt the better instincts of the normal individual. By our failure to distinguish between vengeance and justice, by our emphasis on punishment instead of cure, our courts may become an instrument of corruption rather than a safeguard for society.

Whether one agrees with Mr. Weihofen or not, his book is worthy of painstaking examination by all who are genuinely interested in curbing delinquency, especially those who have the intellectual courage to sweep aside myths and approach the problems of crime from a scientific and humane angle.

November 18, 1956

U.S. Appeals Court Liberalizes Method For Defining Sanity

By EDWARD RANZAL

A century-old English common law, the M'Naghten Rule, until recently the rigid guideline for determining the mental competence of defendants in criminal cases, was discarded yesterday by the United States Court of Appeals, Second Circuit.

In a unanimous decision, the Appeals Court adopted a rule that it feels is far more liberal than competence tests set by many states and other Federal courts.

It provides: "A person is not responsible for criminal conduct if at the time of such conduct as a result of mental disease or defect he lacks substantial capacity either to appreciate the wrongfulness of his conduct or to conform his conduct to the requirements of law."

A key to the new test by the Appeals Court is that it recognizes that "in the past century, psychiatry has evolved from tentative, hesitant gropings in the dark of human ignorance to a recognized and important branch of modern medicine."

There have been a number of states across the country, including New York, that recently have adopted sections to penal codes setting up new rules to test a defendant's competence. The Appeals Court felt that these rules were either too vague or did not go far enough.

The common law that the Appeals Court discarded is known as the M'Naghten Rule. This permits acquittal on the ground of mental incompetence only when it can be proved that "at the time of the committing of the act, the party accused was laboring under such a defect of reason, from disease of the mind, as not to know the nature and quality of the act he was doing, or, if he did know it, that he did not know he was doing what was wrong."

Over the years, various courts in this country have added to M'Naghten what is called "the irresistible impulse rule." This takes into account that a defendant could not control his conduct in committing a crime even though he knew it to be wrong.

The Appeals Court, in its decision, adopted the definition of criminal responsibility laid down by the American Law Institute after a painstaking 10-year study.

The court's 45-page opinion was written by Judge Irving R. Kaufman. Judges Sterry R. Waterman and Paul R. Hays concurred. It will be binding on all Federal courts in New York, Connecticut and Vermont, which make up the Second Circuit.

In finding the McNaghten Rule too rigid and narrow, Judge Kaufman said:

"The gravaman of the objections to the M'Naghten Rule is that it is not in harmony with modern medical science which, as we have said, is opposed to any concept which divides the mind into separate compartments — the intellect, the emotions and the will.

"The Model Penal Code formulation (suggested by the American Law Institute) views the mind as a unified entity and recognizes that mental disease or defect may impair its functioning in numerous ways.

"The rule, moreover, reflects awareness that from the perspective of psychiatry absolutes are ephemeral and gradations inevitable. By employing the telling word 'substantial' to modify 'incapacity,' the rule emphasizes that 'any' incapacity is not sufficient to justify avoidance of criminal responsibility but that 'total' incapacity is also unnecessary.

"The choice of the word 'appreciate,' rather than 'know' in the first branch of the test also is significant; mere intellectual awareness that conduct is wrongful, when divorced from appreciation or understanding of the moral or legal import of behavior, can have little significance."

Last July 1, New York rejected M'Naghten and adopted a test based largely upon the American Law Institute formulation. This provides:

"A person is not criminally responsible for conduct if at the time of such conduct as a result of mental disease or defect he lacks substantial capacity to know or appreciate either:

"The nature and consequence of such conduct; or that such conduct was wrong."

Psychiatric scholars, according to sources knowledgeable in the field, consider New York's new test only a refinement of M'Naghten. Under this test, knowledge is paramount and—unlike the new Federal rule—it does not take into consideration the emotions and the will to resist.

The Federal rule will enable psychiatrists to go well beyond the old test of whether a defendant knew right from wrong.

Genesis of Old Rule

Daniel M'Naghten, for whom the rule was named, suffered from delusions of persecution. He considered Prime Minister Robert Peel his major persecutor and went to London to assassinate him. Peel, however, chose to ride in Queen Victoria's carriage because of her absence from the city, while his secretary, Drummond, rode in Peel's vehicle.

M'Naghten shot and killed Drummond.

After a lengthy trial, M'Naghten was found not guilty in 1843 by reason of insanity. The court was so impressed with medical evidence of M'Naghten's incompetency that Lord Chief Justice Tindal practically directed a verdict for the accused.

This was the start of a new approach to determining criminal responsibility.

The M'Naghten test long prevailed in most courts throughout the country. In recent years, New York, Illinois, Vermont, and Connecticut, among others, have abandoned this rule in favor of a modified version of the one suggested by the American Institute of Law.

Some courts follow the rule enunciated in Washington that simplified the test of competency to proving that the conduct of the accused was a product of mental disease.

"The genius of the common law," Judge Kaufman wrote, "has been its responsiveness to changing times, its ability to reflect developing moral and social values. Drawing upon the past, the law must serve—and traditionally has served — the needs of the present.

"In the past century, psychiatry has evolved from tentative, hesitant gropings in the dark of human ignorance to a recognized and important branch of modern medicine. The outrage of a frightened Queen has for too long caused us to forgo the expert guidance that modern psychiatry is able to provide."

Judge Kaufman suggested that those adjudged criminally irresponsible promptly be turned over to state officials for commitment. Pointing out that the court has not viewed the choice as one between imprisonment and immediate release, Judge Kaufman added:

"We believe the true choice to be between different forms of institutionalization — between the prison and the mental hospital. Underlying today's decision is our belief that treatment of the truly incompetent in mental institutions would better serve the interests of society as well as the defendants."

Case Involved Addict

The case before the Appeals Court involved Charles Freeman, 35 years old, who was convicted of selling heroin to

417

undercover agents. Freeman, an addict for 15 years, raised the issue of his competence at his trial.

After applying the M'Naghten Rule, Federal Judge Charles H. Tenney ruled that Freeman was competent to stand trial. Freeman was found guilty and sentenced to five years in prison.

The Appeals Court reversed the conviction, but only on the ground that Judge Tenney should apply the new rule of competency at a new trial. The Appeals Court did not say whether it believed Freeman might be declared incompetent under the new rule.

In respect to the case on appeal, Judge Kaufman wrote: "As legislation proliferates and judicial decisions multiply, our criminal law daily takes on increased complexity and sophistication. Subtle distinctions are constantly drawn; more perfect refinements continue to evolve.

"At the same time, however, there are a small number of more basic questions which cut across the whole of this evolutionary process, questions so fundamental to the very notion of criminal justice that they must continue to be asked—and, insofar as possible, answered—if the criminal law is truly to reflect the moral sense of the community. This appeal poses one of those questions."

In England, many attempts have been made to correct some of the weaknesses of the M'Naghten test, but it still prevails there.

The last attempt was in 1953, when the Royal Commission on Capital Punishment recommended abrogating M'Naghten and allowing the jury "to determine whether at the time of the act the accused was suffering from disease of the mind (or mental deficiency) to such a degree that he ought not to be held responsible."

March 1, 1966

Genetic Abnormality Is Linked to Crime

By RICHARD D. LYONS

The murder of a prostitute by a stable hand in a cheap Paris hotel has opened a twilight zone of criminology for unsuspecting jurists and scientists.

Confronting them are two profound questions whose implications transcend the case itself: Are some criminals—because of genetic abnormalities—born as well as made? If so, to what degree are they responsible for their actions?

An abnormality found in the chromosomes of the stable hand has also been found in a number of persons with a history of antisocial behavior.

The case, which some lawyers believe could set a legal precedent, dates to Sept. 4, 1965, when Marie-Louise Olivier, the prostitute, was found strangled in an apparently motiveless slaying.

The French police say that Daniel Hugon, now 31 years old, the central character in the grisly yet fascinating episode, fled Paris after the murder and went to Normandy where he worked on the farm of Jean Gabin, the actor.

Hugon eventually surrendered to the gendarmerie, who said he confessed, filled with remorse. The day before he was to stand trial in January, Hugon attempted suicide in Santé Prison. The court ordered extensive physical and mental examinations, tests that probably would never have been made but for Hugon's attempt on his own life.

One result, which may be the basis for Hugon's defense, amazed and confounded the jurists because it cast doubt on the defendant's responsibility for his actions.

An analysis, called a karyotyping, was made of Hugon's chromosomes, the thin strands of genetic material containing biochemical instructions for the growth of every living cell. These hereditary messages control physical traits such as eye, hair or skin color, and can cause conditions such as Mongolism.

Scientists on four continents have, in the last several years, also suggested that a person's genetic make-up may have an effect on behavior, perhaps a violent effect. Hugon was found to have a chromosomal abnormality, and studies have shown that such an abnormality is 60 times as prevalent in men convicted of violent crimes as in the general population.

Human body cells have 46 chromosomes arranged in two sets of 23, each parent donating one set. Two of these 46 chromosomes, labeled either "X" or "Y" because of their shape, determine sexual characteristics. Every cell in a woman's body contains two "X" chromosomes, while each cell in a man has one "X" and one "Y."

Contradiction by Nature

Yet once in every several hundred conceptions, nature contradicts itself for reasons that are incompletely understood and adds or subtracts a chromosome during the mating of sperm and ovum. The multiplying cells that eventually arrange themselves into the resulting human are not, strictly speaking, truly male or female.

Since the chromosomal content of the human cell was discovered only a dozen years ago, genetic studies are in their infancy, but many bizarre genetic aberrations have been found in persons who are either mentally retarded or physically deformed.

Daniel Hugon was found to be an XYY variant, a genetic deviation occurring in about one out of every 2,000 men. When the physicians reported the discovery of Hugon's extra Y chromosome to the court two months ago, they pointed out that five years ago a Scots scientist had found that some chromosomally abnormal men had a history of anti-social behavior.

Dr. W. H. Court Brown of Edinburgh, a Government geneticist, wrote a brief but important letter to the medical journal Lancet posing legal questions arising from recent chromosomal discoveries. First he questioned the legality of the marriages of "females" who were genetically male. Should such persons also be allowed to compete in sports events as women? he asked.

Dr. Court Brown then called attention to the abnormally high rate of chromosomally aberrant men who had been committed to mental institutions after crimes ranging from larceny to murder. An uncommon number of these men, he said, were XXY, XXYY and XYY.

Edinburgh colleagues, including Dr. Patricia Jacobs, then examined large numbers of inmates of maximum security prisons and hospitals for the criminally insane. She concluded that 3 per cent of these men had extra Y chromosomes.

Interested by the findings of Drs. Court Brown and Jacobs, geneticists took up the search for further evidence linking criminal behavior to chromosomal abnormalities. In Melbourne, Australia, two men who had been convicted of murder were found to have extra Y chromosomes.

One of the convicted killers, Robert Peter Tait, bludgeoned to death an 81-year-old woman in a vicarage where he had gone seeking a handout. He was due to be hanged in 1962, but his sentence was commuted to life imprisonment.

Dr. Saul Wiener, a Melbourne geneticist, later found that Tait and three other Pentridge Prison inmates who had been convicted of murder, attempted murder and larceny, were XYY.

"These results strongly support the concept that an extra Y chromosome is associated with antisocial or criminal behavior," Dr. Wiener reported in Lancet last January.

As other reports were made of XYY abnormalities, a pattern began to emerge: The XYY men tended not only to aggressive behavior but also, as Dr.

Wiener put it, "to be tall and dull."

Most aggressive XYY men were found to be six inches taller than men who are XY, and to have intelligence quotients between 80 and 95, although the range is wide.

Five Cases Found

Dr. Mary A. Telfer, a biologist at the Elwyn Institute in suburban Philadelphia, reported in Science magazine last month the finding of five XYY cases among 129 tall men who were studied at four Pennsylvania prisons and penal hospitals.

"There must be at least 100 XYY males who have already been found in prisons and hospitals for the criminally insane, although the phenomenon is little recognized in the United States," Dr. Telfer said in a telephone interview.

The aberration "may be far more common than is now thought," she said in urging an intensified chromosomal screening program. Little is known about the behavior of XYY people who are not institutionalized.

"The implications of gross chromosomal errors for the individual's legal status before the law and for the society that must provide either care or parole are fundamental," she said. "Is society, for example, morally justified in invoking the death penalty against a person with chromosomal abnormalities?" she asked.

Dr. Telfer offered other clues to the violent XYY male: He is almost always Caucasian, tends to have acne and usually has "a bizarre sexual history." A tendency toward homosexuality was noted of the six XYY men found among 200 tall inmates who were studied at the Atascadero (Calif.) State Hospital.

But the scientists who conducted the survey, Dr. Frank Vanasek, a research psychologist there, and Drs. John Melnyk and Havelock Thompson, Los Angeles pediatricians, rejected the idea that XYY people are "born to kill."

Instead they proposed in telephone interviews that the XYY boy matures sooner and becomes taller than other children. The failure of some of these boys to adjust emotionally to being different may cause antisocial behavior later in life, they said, pointing out that the vast majority of XYY people are not criminals.

These scientists also suggested that XYY persons may have abnormal sex hormone levels. One clue is the high incidence of acne, the cause of which has been linked to sex hormones.

Dr. Curt Stern, professor of genetics at the University of California, Berkeley, commented that "it could be that it is the interaction product of double Y aggressiveness and social environment which can get people more easily into trouble."

"It also is tempting to speculate that the female sex owes its gentleness to the absence of a Y chromosome and the normal male his moderate aggressiveness to the single Y," he said in a telephone interview.

"XYY people have a higher probability of getting into trouble and I think they are predisposed to social difficulties. But genetics never means absolute fate."

The XYY abnormality may never be an absolute defense to a criminal charge, according to some noted lawyers who were asked for comment.

Comment by Nizer

Louis Nizer, author of "My Life in Court," said "it isn't enough to have a genetic or chemical defense of this type because Anglo-Saxon law never considered aggressive tendencies as grounds for a defense."

"The central question is whether the defendant is able to tell the difference between right and wrong," Mr. Nizer said. "I think a genetic abnormality might only be used if it were the basis for a plea of insanity.

"The answer to all this might be that if a chromosomal 'imbalance' were found it might be considered in assessing the punishment, but not the guilt."

F. Lee Bailey, the Boston lawyer who has defended many accused murderers, said:

"I don't believe that a genetic defect would ever be a complete defense. It might be used as a partial defense, in the sense of limited mental capacity, but I doubt that it ever could be used as a complete defense for responsibility for a crime."

But, he added, "nothing is too wild to look into."

Belli Notes Testimony

Melvin Belli of San Francisco would not deprecate "the use of an XYY abnormality as a defense, but it still must be shown that the defendant is either insane or doesn't know the difference between right and wrong," he said.

Mr. Belli pointed out that the testimony of genetics experts had been used in the last few years to settle paternity suits scientifically, rather than emotionally.

"This shows that the law can adapt to scientific discoveries" he added.

It is these scientific discoveries that must be pondered by Dr. Leon Derobert, professor of legal medicine and former president of the French National Medical Association; Dr. Jean Lafon, a psychiatrist, and Prof. Jerome Lejeune, a geneticist.

Named by the court in Paris, this committee will offer advice as to whether Daniel Hugon's responsibility is in himself or in his genes.

Agence Scoop-France Soir

Daniel Hugon, facing a trial for murder, was subjected to analysis of chromosomes.

April 21, 1968

SCIENTISTS DOUBT 'CRIMINAL' GENES

Survey Finds XYY Pattern May Occur More Often

Surveys of several thousand newborn infants have indicated that the XYY chromosomal defect in men, which has been linked to criminal and antisocial behavior, may be more common than previously believed.

If this is so, the scientists involved suggest that there may be well-adjusted persons with an XYY make-up, casting doubt on its so-called predisposition to criminal tendencies.

However, the scientists believe that a much larger survey — perhaps of 10,000 or 15,000 consecutive newborns— may be needed to establish definitely the frequency of this genetic defect.

One survey, reported in yesterday's issue of the New England Journal of Medicine, indicated that the frequency may be as high as one in 250 males. The survey found four XYY boys among 2,159 consecutive births (1,066 of them male) at Victoria Hospital in London, Ontario.

Previously published estimates have placed the frequency of XYY at one in 2,000 male births.

However, one recent survey at Harvard Medical School turned up no xyy's in 3,000 consecutive births, whereas a similar survey at Yale found two XYY's in 1,800 consecutive births.

Dr. Fred Sergovich, leading author of the Ontario study, said that his finding of one in 250 males "May be a statistical artifact" resulting from the small size of the study. But in an interview yesterday, Dr. Sergovich expressed his belief that the true frequency of XYY "is not less than 1,000 and probably more like 1 to 500."

On the basis of their findings, Dr. Sergovich and his co-authors concluded that the association between the XYY genetic defect and "peculiar behavioral abnormalities and tall stature . . . may not be as strong as has previously been implied."

Authors Urge Caution

The authors urged caution "in accepting the interpretation that XYY is specifically associated with criminal behavior and particularly so with reference to the medico-legal validity of these arguments."

In a murder case now being heard in Supreme Court in Queens County, New York, the 6-foot 8-inch defendant, Sean Farley, has pleaded not guilty by reason of insanity resulting from his XYY chromosomal imbalance.

Normally, a male's cells contain 23 pairs of chromosomes, including one X and one Y chromosome. XYY males have the same 23 pairs plus an extra Y chromosome.

In Melbourne, Australia, last year, a man with the XYY abnormality was acquitted of a murder charge on the ground that he was legally insane when he killed his victim.

But in Paris a few days later, a jury failed to free a confessed murderer on the ground That he had the XYY abnormality.

Chromosomal studies of men institutionalized for criminal or antisocial behavior have indicated that about one per cent of them are XYY males, a finding that has led many people to assume that the XYY defect predisposes men to criminality or abnormal behavior patterns

Dr. Sergovich, who is genetiast, said he believed that the XYY abnormality "does influence behavior, but it probably isn't ann all-or-nothing phenomenon. There's too much diversity among the XYY's we have studied to say outright that an XYY man is inevitably going to have abnormal behavior.

He said that "if you look only at abnormal populations, you will find only abnormal XYY's. But unless you study the population at large, you can't say how many XYY men may be functioning reasonably normally."

The Ontario research team emphasized the urgent need for a long-term follow-up study of newborn XYY's to see how, in fact, they develop. The affected children would have to be followed at least through adolescence, Dr. Sergovich said.

April 18, 1969

Psychiatric Experiment on Violent Individuals Suggests That Crowding Is a Factor in Many Cases

By DAVID BURNHAM

Men imprisoned for crimes of violence appear to be far more sensitive to the physical closeness of others than prisoners convicted of property crimes, a study by a New York psychiatrist has found.

The study on the "body-buffer zone in violent prisoners" was conducted by Dr. Augustus F. Kinzel, now a teacher of psychiatry at Columbia University's College of Physicians and Surgeons. He made his findings at the United States Medical Center for Federal Prisoners in Springfield, Mo.

While Dr. Kinzel intends to repeat his study on a larger number of subjects before drawing any absolute conclusions, he feels it may lead to the development of a test to determine in advance which persons will explode in a violent outburst. Fifteen persons were studied in the first experiment.

The experiment also provides a possible explanation of why slums appear to have far more crimes of violence than less crowded areas.

A description of the experiment and its tentative conclusions were presented by Dr. Kinzel recently at the annual meeting of the American Psychiatric Association in Miami.

Dr. Kinzel reported that he had placed individual prisoners in the middle of a small bare room. He would then begin to walk slowly toward each subject.

The result after approaches from eight different directions: The "body buffer zones" among those prisoners with a history of violent behavior was almost four times larger than those without such a history.

"The behavior and comments of the subjects," Dr. Kinzel said in his paper, "supported the observations that violent individuals tend to perceive nonthreatening intrusion as attack."

"Misperceptions of the experimenter as 'looming' or 'rushing' at the subjects were reported frequently by the violent subjects," Dr. Kinzel continued. "By contrast, the nonviolent group let the experimenter approach closer than ordinary conversational distances and did not report 'looming' or 'rushing' sensations."

The psychiatrist, while emphasizing that more research was needed, said the findings suggested "that body buffer-zone measurements alone might be able to distinguish violent from nonviolent individuals."

He said a technique to identify violent persons quickly and reliably was urgently needed by judges, correctional officials and others working with offenders, because they "now have to make such distinctions on an impressionistic basis."

"It is probably," Dr. Kinzel continued, "that many [prisoners] could be freed or diverted from incarceration if a more definitive measure of violent potential could identify those who really needed it [prison]."

It is not known what triggers the strong sense of disquiet at the approach of others among some persons. However, Dr. Kurt Richter at the Johns Hopkins University in Baltimore, has shown that rats become seriously ill and develop aberrant behavior, such as homosexuality and destruction of their young, when they are forced to live under extremely crowded conditions."

And Dr. Edward T. Hall, an anthropologist now teaching at the Illinois Institute of Technology, has conducted research on the widely varying needs for physical separation shown by persons brought up in different cultures. On the basis of these studies, Dr. Hall has concluded that certain kinds of physical crowding may be a direct cause of crimes of violence.

Though Dr. Kinzel is reluctant to draw such broad conclusions at present, he is in the process of developing a far more extensive test of his initial findings.

May 18, 1969

Curbs on the Psychiatrist in Court

WASHINGTON — One of the remarkable legal developments of recent years, a growing estrangement between law and psychiatry, produced a new right for defendants last week — the right not to be examined by a psychiatrist.

Until the past five years or so it had been considered a mark of legal enlightenment that the professional judgments of psychiatrists played so crucial a part in the criminal process.

While most issues of fact in criminal trials have been entrusted only to juries, psychiatrists were permitted to give juries their conclusion as to two central questions: whether the defendant was too deranged to stand trial, and whether he was so insane at the time of the crime that he could not be held responsible for it.

All but a handful of the states had laws permitting prosecutors to subject defendants to mental examinations before trial. Furthermore, the Supreme Court ruled in a 1966 case, Pate vs. Robinson, that the Constitution requires judges to order mental examinations whenever a defendant's demeanor indicates he might be incompetent to stand trial.

The motives for these exceptions to criminal responsibility were humanitarian ones. It was felt that such individuals should be treated, not convicted.

In practice, this theory appears to have two flaws. First, some psychiatrists have been too quick to find people insane, since the "treatment" in asylums for the criminally insane has seldom been likely to make them rapidly well. Second, defendants have been known to bare their souls to the states' psychiatrists, only to have the doctors repeat their admissions in court.

The average ward patient in a public asylum sees a doctor for only about 15 minutes each month and defense lawyers have gradually come to realize that their clients may be locked up for much longer in a mental hospital, and under worse conditions, than if they were convicted. One case turned up recently where a defendant had been held 14 years before trial. Another defendant spent 34 years in an asylum before he was considered competent to stand trial.

Last December the Court of Appeals for the District of Columbia issued an order that psychiatrists would no longer be permitted merely to confront juries with their conclusion that defendants suffered from such conditions as "schizoid personality," "psychopathy" and "passive - aggressive personality." Instead, the doctors must relate in detail what the defendants are likely to think and do, and leave to the juries to decide if they are sufficiently deranged to escape conviction.

Last week the Supreme Court of New Jersey took another major step when it ruled that a defendant could not be forced to submit to psychiatric examination unless he wishes to plead insanity.

In the case of a man accused of murder, the lower court judge had followed the usual procedure and ordered a psychiatric examination when the prosecutor asked for one. The defendant, Daniel Obstein of Milburn, protested that he had no intention of pleading insanity. His objection was not that he might be locked up for years as a lunatic but that the psychiatrist would ask him questions about the alleged crime, and might well become the key witness against him in court. The Supreme Court of New Jersey unanimously agreed that a forced psychiatric examination might violate Obstein's privilege against self-incrimination.

Alan M. Dershowitz, a Harvard law professor who has warned that psychiatry has become "a knife that cuts both ways" in the law, applauded the ruling but said even more protection is needed. He asserted that courts must also consider how the privilege against self-incrimination protects defendants from being forced to give evidence that can be used to put them away for years under civil commitments.

Basically, he argued, a defendant should never be required to see a psychiatrist because the prosecutor considers the defendant incompetent to stand trial. No matter how odd the defendant's conduct appears to the prosecutor, the trial should begin, the defendant should not be turned over to the mental doctors unless the trial judge perceives that he is not able to participate in his own defense.

"I don't think prosecutors should act as if they have the best interests of the defendant in mind," Dershowitz said. "They should leave that to the defense attorney."

—FRED P. GRAHAM

October 27, 1968

11 Murderers in Texas Prisons Aid Research on Potential Killer

AUSTIN, Tex., March 1 — Studies of 11 convicted murderers in Texas prisons and mental hospitals show that potential murderers begin evolving in elementary school when they find they have no friends to play with and no fathers or other dominant male figures to look up to.

The studies also indicated that many murderers could be deterred by the availability of male counselors and teachers in elementary and junior high schools.

The studies were by Dr. Shervert H. Frazier, formerly the Texas Commissioner of Mental Health and Mental Retardation who is a professor of psychiatry at Columbia University; Dr.

Stuart L. Brown, formerly a professor at Baylor Medical School who is the director of the mental health unit of Mercy Hospital in San Diego, and James R. Lomax, a Baylor medical student.

Under a $4,100 grant from the Hogg Foundation for Mental Health, they interviewed 33 persons convicted of murder but narrowed their final report to 11—all white, male and under 20—to limit the sample.

None of the persons interviewed had been married, none had been convicted of a major crime previously, intelligence ranged from low to superior, three had suicidal impulses and three others were heavy users of alcohol or narcotics.

Leading the correlating characteristics of the 11, Dr. Frazier said, was "a deficiency of interpersonal relationships . . . they're loners, isolated."

"And there are a lot of anxiety factors built into their socialization. They never played with any peers as a child, or they received cruelty on the part of the parent."

Part of the interpersonal relationships deficiency was what the report calls inappropriate fathering. "Their families were deserted by the father, or somehow they came from broken homes. They are males with an absence of a father symbol."

Aside from—or perhaps deriving from—the big factor of interpersonal relationships, the research team found a common thread of a "deficiency in their capacity or ability to master circumstances" and of impulse-control problems.

"These deficiencies appeared fairly early in their lives, as they were able to recall it," Dr. Frazier said. "In elementary or junior-high school."

From their definition of the common factors among the convicted murderers, the researchers were able to come up with some general corrective or preventive suggestions.

"The lack of involvement in standard group activities in school and in the community should make them (potential murderers) identifiable," Dr. Brown said, adding quickly that "not all children who don't participate in games eventually murder."

March 2, 1969

Psychologist Says Pressures of Big-City Life Are Transforming Americans Into Potential Assassins

By DAVID BURNHAM

Americans are being transformed into potential assassins by the powerful social pressures of big-city living, according to a unified theory on violence and vandalism advanced by a Stanford University research psychologist.

The theory, and its pessimistic estimate of the harmful impact of the modern city on the human psyche, was developed by Dr. Philip G. Zimbardo, a 36-year-old New Yorker who was recently appointed a professor of psychology at the Palo Alto, Calif., institution.

The theory is based on a series of laboratory experiments about anonymity and aggression and field studies on vandalism among middle-class white citizens conducted during the last few years by Dr. Zimbardo. It was presented last month at the highly respected Nebraska Symposium on Motivation at the University of Nebraska.

To establish the boundaries of his violent world, Dr. Zimbardo pointed to the sharp increase

in murder during the last few years, the estimated total of 40,000 American youngsters who each year are beaten and tortured by their parents or their brothers and sisters, the 230 violent urban outbreaks of the last five years and the assassinations of Medgar Evers, Malcolm X., the Rev. Dr. Martin Luther King Jr., President John F. Kennedy and his brother, Senator Robert F. Kennedy.

He further noted that in 1967 vandals in New York City smashed 202,712 school windows and 360,000 pay telephones and did $750,000 worth of damage in the parks and $100,000 worth of damage to the transit system.

"What we are observing all around us, then, is a sudden change in the restraints which normally control the expression of our drives, impulses and emotions," Dr. Zimbardo wrote.

Recognizing the limitations of laboratory experiments, Dr. Zimbardo and a colleague conducted a field study on vandalism among middle-class whites in the Bronx and Palo Alto.

In both cities, cars were left across the street from a university campus with raised hood and without license plates. Hidden observers with cameras were placed nearby.

In the smaller city of Palo Alto, the car was left untouched for more than a week. Within three days in the Bronx, as a result of 23 separate attacks, the car was reduced to "a battered useless hulk of metal."

Discussing the vandalism in the Bronx, Dr. Zimbardo said the attacks were "almost always observed by one or more passerby, who occasionally stopped to chat with looters."

"Most of the destruction was done in daylight hours, not at night as we had anticipated," he continued. "The adults were all well dressed, clean-cut whites who would under other circumstances be mistaken for mature responsible citizens demanding more law and order."

On the basis of these experiments and a broad range of historical, psychological, anthropological and psychiatric observations of others, Dr. Zim-

bardo suggested that many of the old restraints in American life, imposed by such institutions as the large family, were being dissolved by a process he called "deindividuation."

During a recent interview, Dr. Zimbardo suggested that the sheer size of many American cities, the feeling of powerlessness in the face of big institutions, the widespread renting of apartments rather than the owning of houses and the immense mobility of Americans—whether a corporation executive or a Mississippi farmer—were among the factors that appeared to be leading toward a weakening of controls based on self-evaluation.

"Conditions which foster deindividuation," he said, "make each of us a potential assassin."

Discussing the experiment in the Bronx, he said the fact that the vandals did not feel they were committing a crime raised important questions about theories of deterring crime in a big city through the presence of large numbers of citizens, improved night lighting and aggressive police patrol.

April 20, 1969

Insanity in Criminal Behavior

By David Abrahamsen

Overcome by the complexity of insanity as a defense in crime, the Administration has decided, as a part

of a new criminal code, to solve it by abolishing insanity altogether. Instead of allowing the psychiatrist to examine the defendant in order to determine his mental condition at the time of his crime, it has suggested that he only shall determine whether the defendant had criminal intent. The reason for abolishing insanity is, in the words of President Nixon, to curb "unconscionable abuse" of the insanity defense by criminals.

Insanity, or to use the medical term, a psychosis, constitutes part of human behavior. It therefore cannot be eradicated by any law. There are, and we always will have, people who are in-

sane at the time they commit a crime, and hence not legally responsible.

The nagging increase of the insanity plea used by criminals to the point of exploitation is not unexpected. People in all walks of life try to get out of their troubles, particularly when faced with transgressions of the law. What is easier than to plead insanity in order to avoid their responsibility? It is "neat," and it preserves the dignity and self-esteem of the criminal.

In my work on the side of the state and the Federal Government, and on the side of the defense. I have observed that when serious crimes resulting in long prison sentences have been committed, the tendency to claim insanity is multiplied on an increasingly shaky basis.

Most illuminating of the exploitation of insanity as a defense in his crime was the skyjacker who since 1956 had apparently committed a number of serious crimes, among others bank robberies, and who after each crime had claimed insanity, resulting in his admission to mental hospitals, with a diagnosis of paranoid schizophrenia, instead of being sent to prison.

He had been for a short time in seventeen different mental hospitals and had escaped four times. With his I.Q. of 131, and having studied psychiatry and psychology, he had been able to fool during those many years forty psychiatrists, several psychologists, as well as lawyers and judges about the true nature of his mental status. The end of his criminal career and his deceptive insanity came in January 1972 when he skyjacked a plane while en route from Los Angeles to New York. After an eight-hour ordeal, he was shot, subdued and brought to Bellevue Hospital. Based upon my study of the transcript of what oc-

curred on the plane, and observed by radio - telephone, which revealed the skyjacker's coherent and controlled behavior, and through my own psychiatric examinations of him, I very quickly came to the conclusion that the skyjacker was not insane at the time of his air piracy, but that in fact he was malingering, feigning insanity. He was a fake, to my mind, and had been perpetrating one of the greatest hoaxes in the annals of psychiatry. He was found guilty.

During my five years of work as a member of Governor Rockefeller's State Commission to Study Legal Insanity, consisting of one judge, law professor, district attorney, two lawyers and three psychiatrists, no one ever thought of abolishing insanity. Instead, we proposed, and the state enacted (later followed by other states and Federal courts) the present law that a person is legally insane if at the time of criminal conduct he lacks substantial capacity to appreciate the wrongfulness of his act or is unable to conform his conduct to the requirements of law.

Abuses of the insanity plea can be curtailed if the defendant is examined very carefully by a well-trained psychiatrist, paying careful attention to the crime situation itself—how did the culprit behave before, during and after he had committed his deed? If this method had been followed, in all probability the skyjacker never would have been able to get away with his undaunted criminal behavior by feigning insanity.

Judge Cardozo said forty years ago: "If insanity is not to be a defense, let us say so, frankly and even brutally, but let us not mock ourselves with a definition that palters with reality. Such a method is neither good morals, nor good science, nor good law."

If psychiatry is difficult, so is life. Abolishing the concept of insanity from the law is the same as depriving the individual—even when psychotic—the God-given right to be a human being.

David Abrahamsen, a New York psychiatrist, is author of "The Murdering Mind."

July 8, 1973

PSYCHOSURGERY CURBED BY COURT

Michigan Decision Applies to Operations on Mentally Ill

By WILLIAM K. STEVENS
Special to The New York Times

DETROIT, July 10—Experimental psychosurgery may not be performed on persons confined against their will in state institutions, even when such a person's consent is formally obtained, a special three-judge panel ruled today in Wayne County Circuit Court.

The decision left the way open, however, for the performance of psychosurgery on such persons once the procedure has advanced to a level where its benefits clearly outweigh its risks. That is not now the case, the judges said, given the primitive state of current knowledge about how the brain works.

The unanimous, 41-page opinion by Judges Horace W. Gilmore, George E. Bowles and John D. O'Hair was regarded as setting a precedent, pending a possible appeal, in an area where basic issues of law and ethics have been murky.

Effect on Research Unclear

Psychosurgery is a procedure in which tiny portions of brain

tissue are destroyed in the hope of changing the behavior and emotional make-up of mentally ill persons who do not respond to conventional forms of treatment. It is performed on an estimated 400 to 600 Americans annually, sometimes as part of general research on brain functioning and sometimes as a last-ditch treatment for depression, uncontrollable violence or hyperactivity.

What effect today's decision would have on the conduct of brain research, should the precedent become generally applied, was unclear. Some authorities have maintained that the unavailability of hospital and prison inmates as research subjects would be a serious limitation.

But the judges, in their opinion, said that animal and "nonintrusive" human research on brain functioning "have not been exhausted," and asserted that "other avenues of research" apart from experimental psychosurgery must be pursued.

The case on which today's ruling was based involved a 36-year-old mental patient, known variously as Mr. L. and John Doe, who was committed involuntarily to Ionia State Hospital 18 years ago after he was charged with raping and murdering a nurse. He was classified as a "criminal sexual psychopath."

Mr. L. agreed last year to be the subject of psychosurgery

as part of an experiment at Detroit's Lafayette Clinic, a widely respected psychiatric research facility supported by the state. A portion of Mr. L.'s brain known as the amygdala, believed to be the seat of aggression in humans, was to have been examined for electrical abnormality; and if abnormality were shown, part of the amygdala was to have been excised in an attempt to eliminate violent tendencies.

Such psychosurgery "is clearly experimental, poses substantial danger to research subjects, and carries substantial unknown risks," the judges' opinion said. Among the risks listed were "the blunting of emotions," "the deadening of memory," "the reduction of affect [feeling]," and limitation of "the ability to generate new ideas."

Further, the judges continued, there is "no persuasive showing" that psychosurgery would have its intended beneficial effects.

'Risk-Benefit Ratio'

Given this unfavorable "risk-benefit ratio," the judges reasoned, and given the "dangerous, intrusive, irreversible" effects of a psychosurgical operation, the question of the patient's consent becomes much more important than, for example, "when they are going to remove an appendix."

Considering the question of patient consent, the judges con-

cluded that an involuntarily confined mental patient cannot really give his legitimate consent because he is living in "an inherently coercive atmosphere" that, through the pressures it imposes, deprives the patient of any real choice.

Today's decision applies to brain surgery in cases where there is abnormal behavior (murderous aggression, for example) and, at the same time, a "demonstrable physical abnormality in the brain" (for example, an unaccounted-for electrical discharge), but in which no connection between the abnormality and the behavior has yet been established.

Thus, the decision does not apply to widely accepted surgical treatments for such clearly defined physical-mental syndromes as epilepsy, Parkinson's disease or stroke.

When psychosurgery "becomes an accepted neurosurgical procedure and is no longer experimental," the judges' opinion said, it is possible that the decision could then be reviewed and changed.

The decision was based on the two-month-long trial of a suit brought on behalf of Mr. L. by Gabe Kaimowitz, a civil liberties lawyer. Early in the trial, the three judges declared that Mr. L. was being confined unconstitutionally under a law repealed in 1968. Mr. L. was released and is now free, undergoing conventional psychotherapy.

July 11, 1973

CHAPTER **6**

Punishment

Visiting day at New York's Ossining Correctional Facility (formerly Sing Sing Prison).

PRISONS CANNOT KEEP PACE WITH CRIMINALS

By EDWARD H. SMITH.

THE big gray house in the morning shadow of the little green mountain at Sing Sing is celebrating its completion of a century of service as a prison. Just what manner of festivity is appropriate for an occasion of this sort might be hard to say. Certainly, however, the most striking activity connected with the centennial has been the constructing of a new prison, now approaching readiness for use, on a site overlooking the old institution. When finished, the new Sing Sing will be the greatest and most elaborate penal structure in the world.

Time, the rise of population, the increase of criminality and the agitation for better prison conditions and more enlightened methods have all exerted their power in bringing about this fresh prison construction. The State must have a new and improved penal house. It must, as a matter of fact, have several of them. In spite of this necessity, however, the thoughtful student of penal and social problems can but ask himself disquieting questions.

Are the money and the effort well spent? Will they bring an adequate return? Have prisons done what has been expected of them? Or is the prison system bankrupt and in a state of collapse?

Are Prisons Successful?

While these misgivings are causing much uneasiness among understanding penologists, societies are forming in several parts of the country for the purpose of bringing about stricter enforcing of laws and more stringent applying of penal methods. Speaking generally, these new associations favor longer prison terms, the restricting of pardons and paroles, stiffer penalties generally, and speedier court trials. Their leaders believe that a wide application of these recommendations will greatly reduce crime and suppress criminals.

The revival of such popular ideas at this late day causes the student still further apprehension and abasement of the spirit. He questions whether such methods can ever succeed, knowing that they have always failed in the past. He wonders whether our concept of punishment as a cure for crime is not another of those human misconceptions belonging historically in the category with witchcraft, geocentricity, the Divine right of princes, magic, soul transmigration and the like—all of them credences stoutly held by our ancestors and still maintained by millions of men.

He cannot help wondering whether the whole legal-penal method of dealing with criminality is not rapidly proving valueless and writing its own doom.

Crime Goes Right On.

There are, according to those who have given the criminal and penal problem the most thought and the closest study, many affirmative indications, many facts and figures to be marshaled against our existing order in these fields. The most direct and telling fact is, however, a general one—namely that legal punishment has obviously and notoriously failed to stop the criminal.

On this point the evidence is conclusive, even overwhelming. Police hCiefs, Judges and Wardens may point out local and temporary shrinkages in the number of arrests or convictions or incarcerations, but close analysis always finds the flaws in the tabulations on which such reports are based. Worse still, even where the facts are as represented, they have little or no bearing on the whole situation, which not only does not improve, but seems to grow constantly worse—in so far, at least, as the United States is concerned.

There are many who affect to believe that the much bewritten present trouble is a more or less temporary or special condition due to the war, to immigration, to passing conditions of one kind or another. The only authentic and reliable figures available in this country, covering a period of time sufficiently long to offer a basis for competent conclusions, hold a severe disillusion for these optimists.

The United States census has taken a count of the average number of male and female convicts confined in the various Federal and State prisons and local jails since 1850. These figures are accurate, though not quite complete. They show that the increase in the ratio of convicts to the hundred thousand of population has been steady since the beginning of the tabulations, thus:

Year.	Prisoners.	Ratio.
1850	6,737	1 in 3,442
1860	19,086	1 in 1,647
1870	32,901	1 in 1,171
1880	58,609	1 in 855
1890	82,329	1 in 757

Since 1890 there has been a seeming fluctuation, but this has been due to fundamental changes in legal and penal administration. In thirty-five years many juvenile institutions have been erected, and these now house large numbers of younger offenders formerly sent to State prisons. Institutions for insane and feeble-minded convicts have also been put into operation in the last twenty-five years, which now contain others who formerly were numbered among the prison population. Finally, the parole and probation systems have been widely extended in recent years and the length of terms generally reduced, so that a great cut in prison totals has been made.

In spite of all this there were on Jan. 1, 1923 (the last census date completely available), 108,939 inmates in the reporting institutions, a ratio of about 1 to 1,000. As I have said, if this seems to show an improvement over 1890, the changes in method account for it, and a complete survey would undoubtedly show that we are worse off than ever. The need of larger prisons, which is not local to New York, but has been felt in three-fourths of the States in the present century, is sufficient index of the real state of affairs.

The Excuse for Prisons.

Whoever wishes to consider these facts in their proper perspective must first discover what prisons are, why they were built, what they were expected to do and what is their sole excuse for being. Euphemize and generalize as we like, the stopping of the criminal is the be-all and the end-all of any penal system or method. If our anti-criminal machinery fails to accomplish this end—if it does not reduce or hold stationary the amount of criminality—it is worthless, and something must be wrong. We may speak of the penal systems as aiming to protect society, to redress wrongs, to punish offenders, to prevent crimes, to deter fresh and old offenders or to reform convicts—all of the terms have had their vogue. But in the end it is all one thing: The legal-penal system either checks criminality or it does not. By this single test it must stand or fall. So much for the broad social aspect.

When we come to the prison as an instrument of punishment and crime reduction, we come upon a somewhat complicated matter which can be understood only by aid of a historical review. The ordinary citizen probably never thinks of prisons as an experiment. So far as he knows, prisons have always existed. Has he not seen references to them in the Bible, in the histories of ancient and medieval peoples? Has he not been told that they existed in the dawn lands of Mesopotamia and Egypt? Are they not a recognized permanent part of the life of the race?

Happily or otherwise, this is a serious misconception. The ancient kings and priests and the Middle-Age monarchs, hierarchs and barons undoubtedly had jails, dungeons, keeps and oubliettes in which men were confined, but they were restricted to the use of personal enemies, prisoners of war and political offenders. Criminals were punished in a more ready and sanguinary way.

State Prisons Are Recent.

We need not go into this unpleasant subject very far. Most of us know that there were about 250 offenses punishable by death in enlightened England at the end of the eighteenth century; that there were still 160 offenses so punishable in Britain after the time of the American Revolution, and that in the thirteen original American States the number of capital crimes varied from eleven to twenty-odd until the period beginning in 1790.

There were, of course, jails and lockups throughout Europe and America, in which men and women were held pending trial, in which debtors and vagrants were detained and where misdemeanors of the most venal kind were punished. But prisons as machinery for the punishment of major civil criminals belong exclusively to the last 150 years. They date from the lifetime of John Howard, the famous British reformer. The first real State prison in America was not erected until 1790—the old Walnut Street Prison in Philadelphia, built at the behest of the Quakers, who hated blood and cruelty.

Massachusetts, it is true, had something approaching a State prison as early as 1785, on Castle Island in Boston Harbor; and the notorious Newgate Prison in Connecticut—an abandoned copper mine—was used for housing war prisoners in the course of the Revolution, and was later converted into a civil prison. But the true beginnings of the State prison system were made in Pennsylvania and New York, with Walnut Street and with the Newgate or Greenwich Prison in this city, begun in 1796 at the foot of Greenwich Street, a block from the present Christopher Street Ferry slip.

These prisons were built because cruelty and blood-letting had failed to check crime—a solemn fact which the advocates of severity need to have brought before their eyes. Branding, whipping, ducking, pillorying, cutting off of ears, nose-tips, fingers and hands and public scourging through the streets at the tails of carts had all failed to bring results. Even the speedy and infallible hanging or decapitation of major offenders, for all its bloody conclusiveness, had not deterred men from stealing, robbing, maiming and killing.

In desperation the early American States turned toward a plan which William Penn had first advocated. If such men were detained inside of strong cells and walls—for life or for some years—they could not commit their wonted crimes and others would be deterred by the prospect of the loss of liberty under stringent confinement.

Chaos After 20 Years.

So Walnut Street and Greenwich were built and put to work. For a few years their effect was salutary. Criminality fell off in both these early big cities of America. Penal students came flocking from the ends of the earth to study our prison houses and disciplinary methods. Penal reformers were jubilant, and the advocates of severity, who existed then as now, were confused and in retreat.

But not for long. The American parent prisons were soon overcrowded. Their first idealistic officials were displaced by politicians and spoilsmen. Before twenty years were spun out the prisons were in chaos, and there was a loud and insistent outcry for the return to first principles—hanging and corporal inflictions, to be sure.

Yet no one must suppose that the inflictions for offenses in those first prisons were mild. In New York, for instance, only murder and treason remained on the capital list, but the twelve other offenses formerly punishable by death, which included robbery, grand larceny, mayhem, rape and arson, were to be punished by life imprisonment.

Fourteen years was the maximum and usual infliction for all crimes above the grade of petty larceny. For a second offense in this class of crimes the convict received a life sentence, often aggravated by the provision for hard labor or solitary confinement, or both.

Apparently, however, men were no more deterred from flagrant ways then than now. They soon so overcrowded Walnut Street and Greenwich that the States had to look about for ways of taking care of convicts. The reactionaries, as already said, wanted the foolish prison experiment abandoned and corporal punishments restored—and they came very near having their way. In the end, however, a somewhat scabby compromise was effected. It resulted in the building of new prisons—Auburn and Sing Sing in New York, and the Western and Eastern penitentiaries in Pennsylvania.

The Immorality Problem.

One of the chief troubles with the early prisons—a problem that still causes much embarrassment—had to do with the matter of segregation. Walnut Street and Greenwich had only a few single cells, where men were locked away in solitude as special punishment. Otherwise the convicts were herded into large rooms or cages containing from eight to thirty.

Naturally there was deep immorality, and the hardened old offenders contaminated the youngsters—some of them boys of 12 years and even younger. The States were seized with moral indignation. It was the general opinion that the new prisons should be so constructed as to give each convict private quarters. Auburn Prison was already partly built when this agitation came on, and operations were stopped while new plans were worked out. Thus the famous North Wing was begun in 1819 and finished in 1821.

The Auburn plan was to provide a very small solitary cell for each convict, to be occupied by one man only at night and during hours of leisure. By day all the Auburn convicts worked in common rooms or shops in association, but a discipline of perpetual silence was imposed on them. In the Pennsylvania prisons, on the other hand, the method of perpetual solitary confinement was adopted. Cells were built larger, so that men could work in them and turn out a certain amount of products, which the State might market and so partly defray the cost of prisons.

It needs to be said that the Auburn system, partly because it made prison construction much cheaper and prison labor much more profitable, was the one generally adopted in the United States and it is the modernized Auburn system which is now in use in nearly all parts of the country. The solitary confinement or Pennsylvania system found much favor in Europe, but in this country it was imitated only in New Jersey, and it has since been abandoned everywhere, even in Pennsylvania.

Both these systems were designed partly to prevent the contaminating of young or inexperienced convicts by hardened rascals. The main idea, however, was to effect reformation and deterrence by means of severe methods. At Auburn the most cruel beatings and other forms of punishment were inflicted for the slightest infraction of the rule of silence. In the Pennsylvania prisons similar punishments were not lacking, but the worst cruelty of all was the solitary confinement itself.

Meantime, in New York, the Auburn system was extended to Sing Sing, which was begun on May 14, 1825, by 100 convicts under Warden Lynds, brought to the village of Sing Sing by boat and set to work clearing the wilderness and quarrying the stone out of which they erected their own penal house. Sing Sing was thus the first convict-built prison in this country.

The horrors of the place soon achieved for this prison—then called Mount Pleasant—a worldwide notoriety. But, once more, for all the severity, for all the perpetual silence, for all the sinister reputation of the New York prisons, they failed to stop the criminal and the State was again looking about for new and better methods.

In one sense the New York prisons and the Auburn type of prisons in general (they were rapidly constructed in various other States) proved successful. They were self-sustaining and were soon turning in a considerable surplus to the State Treasury. Convict labor was let by contract or it was used in the manufacture of goods, which the State sold in the open market.

Auburn, Sing Sing, Maryland, Wethersfield (Conn.) Charlestown (Mass.), Maryland, Kentucky, Ohio and other prisons turned in tens of thousands of dollars annually. The penal gentlemen were delighted, even though the number of convicts increased constantly. But organized labor finally put an end to this happy system at the close of nearly a century of struggle, begun as early as 1800 by the free artisans in New York and other places.

Free labor insisted that the competition with convict labor let at a few cents a day was unfair and demoralizing. One State after another had to give up the profitable system, until it is now practiced only in minor institutions and backward States.

This change threw the cost of the prisons back on the taxpayer, and there it remains.

Prison Reforms.

In the years between about 1845 and 1850 and the present there has been in progress a slow and jerky, but none the less constant, softening of prison methods. The rule of silence has been gradually relaxed until it is no longer in use in any large prison known to this writer.

Solitary confinement has been abandoned except as a punishment for violation of the prison rules, and is usually not administered for more than a few days at a time. I do not mean to say, like a good many, that prisons are even now pleasant places, but there can be no doubt that the whole trend has been toward greater humanity.

Against this movement there has been a continued outcry. On literally hundreds of occasions in the various States the advocates of harsh and repressive methods have had their way and have passed bills for more severe prison treatment, for longer terms, for corporal punishment and the like. But in every instance these measures have to be repealed in a little time, and the drift toward leniency is allowed to go on.

The imposition of long terms, for instance, produces a swift effect that always has to be reckoned with. If the average term of convicts is increased, say from five years to ten, the number of discharges for the next ensuing ten years will be only half as many. Unless, then, the new commitments are also cut in half the prisons will soon be overloaded and new ones must be built.

This trouble has been encountered scores of times in the past. In some cases it has been met by new prison construction. Usually, however, the convicts have been doubled up in their cells for a time. Then, conditions having grown intolerable, the State Governors have been forced to issue pardons by the wholesale to obviate a great public scandal.

Recidivism is another subject that must be considered in judging the success or failure of prisons. Our first penal institutions were still glowing with new paint and fresh varnish when it became apparent that many men who had served one term came back for more. As time wore on and various methods were tried it was found that neither kindness nor cruelty seemed to reform the usual convict. Beating, closing in irons, straitjacketing, water cures, heavy labor, low rations, breaking, cowing and even the terrible solitary confinement failed signally to "reform" convicts.

Many came back for second, third, fourth and fifth terms, while some old prisoners are known to have served as high as twenty and even thirty separate and distinct sentences in jails and prisons in other countries as well as here.

One of the current beliefs dear to the heart of the more sentimental prison administrators is that convicts can be redeemed in large numbers by kindness, by individual personal attention on part of the Warden and his aids, by moral suasion and similar methods—the whole program which has caused the wild outcry against the coddling of criminals.

Experience at Sing Sing and elsewhere has shown that these newer methods do some good. They are successful in a very limited way. They make prison discipline easier to maintain. They induce a few of the higher type convicts to "go straight." But they certainly have not brought about any wholesale contrition or reformation. The reasons for this failure seem to be apprehended only by scientific men, and they will be set forth in a succeeding article, which will deal mainly with the medical aspects of criminal conduct.

Meanwhile, the original questions must be repeated and urged upon the intelligent reader:

Have not the prisons, after 150 years of experiment, proved themselves a failure?

Is not the legal-penal conception of crime on its last legs?

Has it not been shown, abundantly and without exception, that neither kindness nor severity, neither short terms nor long, neither quick trial nor slow, neither old methods nor new, neither incarceration nor corporal punishment, and not even the death penalty itself, have made any real progress against the criminal propensities of a large class of human beings, perhaps two men in every hundred?

To many progressive experts and students it seems that the true answer can be read in the statistics, incomplete and debatable as they may be; in the great new prison going up on the ironically named Mount Pleasant at Ossining, and in the scores of other new and huge prisons and jails being constructed throughout the country.

CONVICT 'CODDLING' IS DENIED BY LAWES

Warden of Sing Sing Says He Treats Inmates as Humans, and Not as Dogs.

Answering those who have criticized his policy as one of "coddling" law-breakers, and declaring that the trouble with our penal system was that punishment for crime was too slow and too uncertain, Lewis E. Lawes, warden of Sing Sing Prison, told a large audience in the meeting hall of the National Democratic Club, 233 Madison Avenue yesterday afternoon, that the criminal did not fear the severity of his sentence when he knew that much time would elapse before the law finally put him behind the bars. He also denounced the death penalty as a non-deterrent of crime, a punishment which failed to mete justice, and one which the rich could escape and the poor must face.

Justice Max S. Levine, introducing Warden Lawes, spoke briefly on the general problems facing a criminal judge, and paid a tribute to the New York Police Department as the finest in America.

"I have been criticized," Warden Lawes declared, "by individuals, organizations and the press, and some weak columnists who have to swing heavy columns, for 'coddling' prisoners. There is no such thing at Sing Sing. But I do believe that men should be treated like human beings. Treat them like dogs and they'll act like dogs after they come out, and remember that most of them do come out."

Combating the statement made recently that a life sentence to Sing Sing Prison meant not more than twelve years, Warden Lawes said that in the seven years he has been in charge only one "lifer" had received a commutation, that coming after eighteen years of confinement and being followed by deportation.

Discussing his stand for the abolition of the death penalty in New York, Warden Lawes said that he had made a thorough investigation of the problem in all the forty-eight states and in foreign countries, and had exchanged views with prison officials and others all over the world.

"The death penalty," he asserted, "is not a crime deterrent."

Federal Prison for Women
Is Nearing Completion

ANDERSON, W. Va., March 30 (AP).—The first Federal institution designed solely for women is taking form on the banks of the Greenbriar River here.

Final touches will not be taken before July, but already many women prisoners are installed in their quarters and are helping with the work necessary to easy functioning of the institution.

Until 500,000 club women all over the country, led by the General Federation of Women's Clubs, concentrated their efforts upon Congress for the passage of the bill making the appropriations, the Federal Government took care of women prisoners in overcrowded State prisons and jails.

PRISONS OF NATION DECLARED FAILURE; OUTWORN, INHUMAN

Wickersham Report Assails the Whole System as Worthless in Rebuilding Men.

BRUTAL DISCIPLINE DECRIED

Riots and Fires "Dramatic Evidence" of Futility—Auburn Type Forts "Needless."

NEW PENAL MODE URGED

Convict Wages, Segregation, Individual Education and Broad Use of Parole Advised.

Special to The New York Times.

WASHINGTON, July 26.—The prison system of the United States is branded as a failure so complete that a new type of penal system must be developed, in the report of the National Commission on Law Observance and Enforcement to President Hoover.

The report of the commission, which was headed by George Wickersham, is the ninth made by the body and was made public at the White House today. The commission officially went out of existence a month ago.

The commission's judgment that the present system has failed was based on its findings that it was valueless as an educational institution, since "no one claims that the men who are released are better equipped to accept an honest rôle in the world than before commitment"; on its costliness and business inefficiency, and on brutal conditions which it found almost incredible."

Inhuman punishments for trivial offenses in many prisons include shackling men to doors, tying them under streams of water, whipping them, confining them in constricted cages and keeping them for long periods in darkness, subsisting only on bread and water.

Dramatic evidence of the failure of prison discipline was cited in "the riots, the fires, the use of cruel and brutal measures of punishment, the persistent recurrence of murder within the prison, the presence of narcotics, the frequent atmosphere of hate and bitterness."

The commission did not simply content itself with attacking the present system and saying that a new one must be devised. It sketched the outlines of a new system, in which only the most desperate prisoners would be kept in confinement and in which prisoners would be segregated by groups. Prisoners would receive wages for their work, and intelligent efforts would be made to educate them for a useful life after their emergence from prison.

The strongest criticisms in the report are aimed at prisons of the type such as the one at Auburn, but there was little that escaped criticism in studies of the 3,000 Federal and State prisons and jails in the United States, which house about 400,000 inmates annually.

"It would not be far from the facts," the commission's report says, "to say that these 3,000 individual institutions represent 3,000 different examples of administrative arrangements, methods of control and of policy in dealing with the human material incarcerated in them. We have no uniform practices, except in a few places.

Inefficiency Is Stressed.

"The whole stands as an unwieldy, unorganized, hit-or-miss system which has grown up over hundreds of years of local policy making, local tradition and local objective. Certain broad influences have made themselves felt, especially in the last hundred years, in the development of prison buildings, in the use of labor, in the scheme of discipline. But, as a rule, even where general influences have appeared they have been so adapted, modified and absorbed into the older local pattern as to leave our national penal system nearly as complex, varied and unstandardized as it was before these 'reforms.'"

In keeping with this summation of "the magnitude of the problem" the commission dwelt at length on all its phases and evolved twenty-three conclusions and recommendations, the primary one being that the present system is antiquated and inefficient, fails to protect society, fails to reform criminals and possibly "contributes to the increase of crime by hardening the prisoner."

The general construction of such fortresses as that at Auburn was termed unwise, on the basis of a report of the Advisory Committee on Penal Institutions, Probation and Parole to the Wickersham Commission, to the effect that a study showed that not more than 41.8 per cent of all prisoners examined in this particular study appeared to require "maximum security."

The report of the Advisory Committee said: "In New York, Dr. V. C. Branham, deputy commissioner of the New York State Department of Correction, concluded, after examining more than 8,000 prisoners, that 41.8 per cent required maximum security, 34.7 per cent medium security and 24.5 per cent minimum security."

The commission recommended the segregation and classification of prisoners, so that the hardened types, the perverted, the vicious and the diseased, might be individually treated, and all set apart from the less abnormal types.

Individual Study Advised.

Individual study and treatment was especially recommended, particularly when this is combined with parole and probationary treatment of a type which the commission found still remains an ideal of the future.

It laid down the dogma that "no man should be sent to a penal institution until it is definitely determined that he is not a fit subject for probation," and, as for those sent to prison it urged the development of indeterminate sentences which would be conditioned on the reform and development of prisoners to resume places in normal life

The conclusions and recommendations were given as follows:

"1. We conclude that the present prison system is antiquated and inefficient. It does not reform the criminal. It fails to protect society. There is reason to believe that it contributes to the increase of crime by hardening the prisoner. We are convinced that a new type of penal institution must be developed, one that is new in spirit, in method and in objective. We have outlined such a new prison system and recommended its adaptation to the varying needs of the different States.

"2. We consider it both unwise and unnecessary for the States to spend large sums of money in the construction of maximum security, congregate prisons of the Auburn type. Experience has amply demonstrated that only a small proportion of the prison population requires fortress-like buildings.

Would Relieve Overcrowding.

"With proper classification of the prison population, the present overcrowded conditions can be relieved by housing a large number of the inmates in simple and inexpensive buildings of the minimum and medium security type. The millions of dollars now employed to construct elaborate maximum-security prisons could, with much better advantage, be used in the development and proper financing of adequate systems of probation and parole.

"3. We find the present sanitary and health conditions in our prisons inadequate and consider that no proper attack can be made on these essential problems without a classification and separation of the prison population into special problem groups.

"4. No proper penal system can be developed until means are found to remove the tubercular, the insane, the venereally diseased, the feeble-minded, the drug addict, the sex pervert, the aged and the feeble from the general prison population for such permanent or temporary treatment as may be required.

"5. The remaining penal population ought itself be separated into groups which may be housed in maximum, medium and minimum security buildings. Within each of the groups further differentiation is both possible and desirable. This can best be worked out in connection with a varied program of prison labor.

Cruelty Is Condemned.

"6. We find our present system of prison discipline to be traditional, antiquated, unintelligent and not infrequently cruel and inhuman. Brutal disciplinary measures have no justification. They neither reform the criminal nor give security to the prison. We recommend that they be forbidden by law. We wish to repeat that classification and segregation are prerequisite to the solution of the problem of discipline.

"7. The changes here suggested cannot be carried through without an improved official personnel. This involves the more careful seelction, better compensation and training of prison officers. The prison officers' training school now maintained by the Federal Government is a step in the right direction. Greater security of tenure is also needed. It will be difficult, if not impossible, to reorganize our penal system if prison officers are subject to change with every change in political administration.

"8. Though we recognize the difficulties of transition to a new system of prison industry we commend the Congress of the United States for the passage of the Hawes-Cooper bill and consider the agitation for its repeal as ill advised and contrary to the public interest. The contract system is essentially iniquitous and its disappearance from our prisons is most earnestly to be desired. The prison will serve the State best if it surrenders the idea of profit-making and turns its attention and energy to the less arduous task of discovering means of becoming economically self-sufficient.

"In so far as the prison has to employ labor for other than local consumption we recommend the 'State use' system and the employment of prison labor on public works as most advantageous to the State and least injurious to outside capital and labor.

Prisoner Wage Recommended.

"9. We recommend that some wage be paid to the prisoner, not merely as an incentive to good work but as a means of maintaining his dependents and promoting his self-respect.

"10. Education in the broadest sense is the profoundest responsibility and opportunity of the prison. Unless the prison succeeds in educating—educating in character, in industry, in habits, in new attitudes and interests, capacities and abilities—it fails. It is therefore urged that every possible agency that may be utilized for the educational progress of the prison inmates be employed and developed.

"11. Individualization is the root of adequate penal treatment and the proper basis of parole. For proper individualization it is necessary that a comprehensive personal study covering every important detail of his career should come to the prison with the prisoner. It should be amplified by the prison record, kept up to date by periodic revision, and ultimately used as the basis for parole.

"12. An indeterminate sentence is necessary for the development of a proper institutional program and essential to the establishment of an adequate system of parole. It is not possible to require the prison to rehabilitate the offender if its hands are tied by an obligation to release him at a time when it feels that such release is contrary to the public interest.

"It must, however, be held to view that an absolutely indeterminate sentence is a powerful instrument in the hands of prison administration and ought not to be extended to any group of men without the greatest safeguards for the protection of the individual, and not until the prison system is so built up as to make the prospect of character reconstruction within the prison much more nearly a certainty than it is today.

"To give the typical penal administrator the right to say whom he will release and when, would not be consistent with the best public policy. We therefore suggest the granting of the broad powers implied in an absolutely indeterminate sentence only with the greatest caution and only after the prison system itself has been sharply reconstructed along modern lines.

Value of Parole Emphasized.

"13. Parole must be considered the best means yet devised for releasing prisoners from confinement. It affords the safest method of accomplishing the ex-prisoner's readjustment to the community. No prison system, no matter how well organized, can be expected to achieve its best results without the cooperation of a well-staffed, well-financed and properly organized system of parole.

"14. A number of State have already established full-time, well-paid, central boards of parole, with full power to decide on applications for parole release. We believe that many other States might profitably follow their example. Every effort should be made to guarantee these bodies an expert personnel and freedom from political interference.

"15. Of even more importance is the skillful and sympathetic supervision of the prisoner who is on parole. It is not enough to write a parole provision into the statutes. Persons of technical competence must be employed and trained to supervise paroles in the field. Such agents must be provided in numbers sufficient to guarantee the adequate and effective oversight of every prisoner who is released on parole. Without this, parole amounts to little more than an automatic reduction of the sentence. With it parole may become a positive force for social security.

"16. Probation must be considered as the most important step we have taken in the individualization of treatment of the offender.

"17. The success of probation is dependent upon the care with which cases are originally chosen and upon the sufficiency of later supervision.

Central Supervision Favored

"18. No man should be sent to a penal institution until it is definitely determined that he is not a fit subject for probation. To this end it is urged that every effort be made to broaden probation and provide more and better probation supervision. With adequate probation staffs the number of persons who might be placed on probation with success can be materially increased. It is clear that probation, where it is applicable, is much less expensive and, from the social point of view, much more satisfactory than imprisonment.

"19. Those States that have not as yet made provision for probation should do so.

"20. Central supervision of probation should be provided for and measures looking to some sort of State-wide standards should be encouraged.

"21. Only persons possessing adequate technical training and experience should be selected to serve as probation officers. They should be freed from other duties and allowed to give all of their time to their duties as agents of the court in the supervision of probationers. The 'case load' of many probation officers is at present too high to permit effective oversight. Sufficient officers should be provided to keep the number down.

"22. There are now seven States, where no legal limit is set upon the discretion of the court in the use of probation. Experience shows that such discretionary powers have proved ample protection against the release of the anti-social and degenerate criminal while at the same time they make it possible to 'temper justice with mercy' where mercy is justified. The extension of this prerogative of the court is recommended.

"23. We call attention to the recommendations made by the Advisory Committee on Penal Institutions, Probation and Parole, in its report, which is appended hereto. We endorse these specific recommendations with the single exception of that which calls for an absolutely indeterminate sentence. We consider this proposal ideally desirable, but are not ready to recommend its adoption, as a practical matter, until such a time as the community has so completely reorganized its penal system as to warrant the transfer to an administrative agency of the great powers of sentence now exercised by the court."

General Overcrowding Found.

In a study of prisons themselves the commission found that about 100 Federal and State institutions contain about 100,000 long-term prisoners. Of these eight, including Auburn, are more than 100 years old and seventeen were built from seventy to 100 years ago. Naturally, these prisons not only lack plumbing and modern sanitary conveniences but were found to reflect antiquated ideas of handling prisoners as well. In addition, the old cell blocks were found to be without proper ventilation and 58 per cent of them contain less than the 364 cubic feet of air space now required for each cell by the New York State Department of Correction.

The commission found that overcrowding in prisons is a common thing, Federal prisons in 1930 being represented as being overcrowded 65.9 more than the capacity of the institutions. The following quotation from a report on Auburn in 1930 by the New York State Commission of Correction also was included in the report, as a typical example:

"Prisoners are sleeping in double-deck cots in the corridors in front of the cells in the north hall and in a small dormitory over a portion of the cells in the same building. These men also occupy double-deck beds. The situation is intolerable."

The commission also repeated criticisms frequently heard from other sources of the idleness enforced on prisoners by these conditions.

Data on Discipline Given.

Prison discipline, as shown in a study of sixty-eight prisons and nineteen reformatories, was shown in a tabulation which follows:

	Sixty-eight Prisons.		Nineteen Reformatories.	
	No.	P. C.	No.	P.C.
Loss of privileges...	56	82	15	79
Loss of good time...	37	54	12	63
Punishment or isolation cells	60	88	18	95
Screen cells	9	13	5	26
Locked in own cell..	10	15	4	21
Dark cells	10	15	1	5
Semi-dark cells (as given)	10	15	2	11
Restricted diet (bread and water)	*36	53	10	53
In punishment cells under two weeks...	26	39	8	42
In punishment cells over two weeks....	6	9	..	..
Handcuffed to door of cell	8	12	2	11
Strap used	8	12	..	..
Miscellaneous punishments	9	13	6	32
Well ventilated cells (as given).........	11	16	1	5

*This is an understatement, as few, if any, prisons in the country fail to use this method.

In an extended study of parole and probation, the commission reached the conclusion that "parole is not leniency; on the contrary, parole really increases the Satte's period of control." It found that parole systems already are used widely, as in 1927 only 42 per cent of prisoners released had served their full sentences, but it found many faults in extant parole practice.

"Methods of supervision are inadequate," the commission found. "Eighteen States attempt to keep in touch with paroled persons by correspondence alone. Printed rules are announced but are not enforced. Written reports are required, but there is no body to check on the accuracy of the replies. The parole officer becomes a mere clerk of record.

"Men who are on parole find it easy to beat the game. They are not watched and they know it. Paroles are seldom recommitted unless they are caught in a new crime. The whole paper system becomes a huge joke and parole comes to nothing more than a speedy method of emptying prison cells. This is unfortunately the case in the majority of the American States today."

New York Parole Plan a Model.

The New York State parole system, with a full-time board of well-paid members, field agents and laws setting up strict requirements for these parole officials was described as a model of modern practice.

Probation was differentiated from parole in the studies in that it begins before prisoners are committed to institutions, while paroles are granted only to men who have served portions of their sentences. Probation was recommended in practice as a means of reform which begins before law-breakers have experienced the deteriorating effects of prison life.

"It falls back upon those interests, contacts and habits which the individual has in his own little world," the commission stated, "and utilizes them for the submergence of the act which has brought the individual into contact with the law and gradually readjusts him to the continuance of the normal life which went on before the act took place and which, it is hoped, will continue after the period of training has passed."

The probation practice, the commission found, was originated as recently as 1878, when Massachusetts adopted such a statute. New York State did not follow suit until 1901, even so being the sixth State to adopt such a law, and the Federal Government inaugurated probation work in the Federal courts only in 1925. Probation also was strongly recommended for its economy.

"It has been estimated," the report stated, "that in New York imprisonment costs about nineteen times as much as does probation. The institutional cost of confinement was estimated in 1926 at $555.72 per inmate, as against $29.34 for probation supervision per case. In Ohio for the same year probation cost $32 as against $236 for imprisonment.

Points to Savings.

"In Massachusetts the cost is $35 for probation and $350 for incarceration. In Indiana the cost comparison

between these two methods of treatment has been estimated at $18 for probation and $300 for imprisonment. This cost comparison, though striking, is only partial.

"It does not include the investment by the State of millions of dollars in the land, building and equipment of the original prisons. An example of the possible initial cost of housing per inmate is indicated by the following:

"If the plans for the Attica prison in New York State are carried out to provide adequately for 2,000 inmates, the cost per inmate would be undoubtedly $5,000."

Pointing to other savings engendered by paroles such as the fact that the subject is kept employed and supporting his family, the commission added:

"In any account, therefore, in terms of cost, the expenditure for probation as against imprisonment per individual is so much lower as to make imprisonment, when it can possibly be avoided without injury to society, an unwarranted waste of public funds.

"It must be clear that only when we have taken the means and the effort to spend as much money upon probation supervision in our most difficult cases as we spend on an average on all prison cases, and have had an equal number of failures, as it is generally admitted must be credited to the prison, may we admit that with equal expense and effort both methods are equally ineffective in those specific instances which are known to be most

refractory. Not until we have done that can we assume, and much less assert, that probation is as ineffective in the recalcitrant cases as we know institutional treatment has proved to be."

Criticism was directed at the reformatory at Concord, Mass., as an example of the failure of the reformatory system, which, the commission said, started "with a great flourish" but fell short of the rehabilitation of younger men that was its goal.

"The reformatory does not reform," the report declared. "If there was doubt of this before the recent study by (Bernard) Gluecks of the reformatory at Concord is conclusive."

Fault was found also with the State prison at Charlestown, Mass.

With reference to the prison at Trenton, N. J., the commission quoted from a report by the Prison Inquiry Commission of New Jersey in 1917 which stated that "many of the men who have passed years of their lives in controlling prisoners under the repressive methods which have existed at Trenton, constantly conscious of the necessity for self-defense under the conditions which they were themselves helping to create, have by their very training become temperamentally unfitted to serve in the important capacity of prison keeper."

Experts Who Made Study.

The report is a volume of 344 pages. Of this 174 are devoted to the report proper. The remainder is occupied by a report by an advisory

committee of penal authorities, including Warden Lewis E. Lawes of Sing Sing. The other members of this advisory committee were:
Dr. HASTINGS H. HART, consultant in penology of the Russell Sage Foundation, chairman.
WINTHROP D. LANE, secretary.
Dr. HERMAN J. ADLER, former State criminologist for the State of Illinois.
SANFORD BATES, director of the Bureau of Prisons in the Department of Justice.
Dr. AMOS W. BUTLER, former secretary of the Indiana State Board of Charities and Corrections.
EDWARD R. CASS, general secretary of the American Prison Association.
CHARLES L. CHUTE, general secretary of the National Probation Association.
O. H. CLOSE, superintendent of the Preston School of Industry at Waterman, Cal.
EDWIN J. COOLEY, former chief probation officer of the New York City Court of General Sessions.
CALVIN DERRICK, superintendent of the New Jersey State Home for Boys.
WILLIAM J. ELLIS, Commissioner of Institutions and Agencies in New Jersey.
Dr. BERNARD GLUECK, psychiatrist.
IRVING W. HALPERN, chief probation officer of the New York City Court of General Sessions.
JESSIE D. HODDER, superintendent of the Massachusetts State Reformatory for Women.
C. W. HOFFMAN, judge of the Cincinnati Juvenile Court.
JAMES A. JOHNSTON, director of the California Department of Penology.
Dr. RUFUS B. VON KLEINSMID, president of the University of Southern California.
OSCAR LEE, warden of the Wisconsin State Prison.
HERBERT C. PARSONS, Commissioner of Probation for the State of Massachusetts.
Dr. ELLEN C. POTTER of the New Jersey Department of Institutions and Agencies.
JOSEPH M. PROSKAUER, formerly Justice of the Appellate Division of the Supreme Court of New York.
Dr. LOUIS N. ROBINSON of the National Crime Commission.
WALTER N. THAYER, Commissioner of the Department of Correction of New York.

August 2, 1931

ATTICA PRISON TO BE CONVICTS' PARADISE

Each Prisoner Will Have Spring Bed and Radio With a Cell to Himself.

CAFETERIA TO SUPPLY FOOD

But Despite Luxuries New York's $7,000,000 Penal Unit Designed to Be Escape-Proof.

By WILBUR G. LEWIS.

Editorial Correspondence, THE NEW YORK TIMES
ROCHESTER, N. Y., July 29.—Condemned by the Wickersham Commission for its maintenance of Auburn and Clinton Prisons, New York State will have an answer to charges of inhuman penal conditions when the new Wyoming State Prison opens at Attica within the next few months with its full quota of 2,000 convicts.

Said to be the last word in modern prison construction, the new unit in the State's penal system will do away

with such traditions as convict bunks, mess hall lock step, bull pens and even locks and keys. In their places will be beds with springs and mattresses, a cafeteria with food under glass, recreation rooms and an automatic signal system by which convicts will notify guards of their presence in their cells. Doors will be operated by compressed air. Sunlight will stream into cells and every prisoner will have an individual radio.

Architecturally handsome, the prison will be strong. It will be surrounded by a 30-foot wall. Armed guards will patrol it like a fortress. Machine guns will peep from behind turrets, and the most modern searchlights will stand ready to flood the prison yard with light at the slightest sign of trouble. Within, the prison will be as comfortable as the State can make it, but it will nevertheless be a prison.

Whole Town Interested.

Despite the fact it will be owned and operated by the State, Wyoming prison is essentially a community enterprise. The village of Attica takes as much pride in it as Niagara Falls does in its cataract, and Gettysburg its battlefield. Committees of citizens sought the prison before the State Department of Corrections when a Western New York site was about to be chosen, and later formed a home guard to aid prison authori-

ties in the event of riots and to track down escaping convicts.

Although fear replaced enthusiasm for a few weeks after riots at Dannemora, Auburn and Canon City gave the village a hint of what may be expected in any prison town, prison boosters succeeded in accomplishing a so-called "hand of fellowship" program for the first time in the history of the East. The first convict arrivals at the temporary camp on the prison site were accepted as fellow-citizens. The entire community contributed books and magazines for their library, an amateur projectionist brought free-motion pictures to the mess hall and others contributed delicacies. Wyoming prison almost overnight became a major part of the Attica community.

And Atticans take as much pride in the fact that Wyoming is the latest in so-called "humane" prisons as in the fact their village has been selected for its site. Almost any citizen can tell the transient that in the new unit, costing $7,000,000 when completed, nothing has been spared to assure decent living conditions for its inmates. The athletic field near the edge of the 1,000-acre site, flower beds and landscaping enterprises laid out by the convicts, the prison walls of yellow brick, long-stained glass windows and ornamental iron grill work are pointed out. Even though the prison walls will extend twelve feet below ground to thwart convicts ambitious enough to try to tunnel to freedom, every citizen knows that overcrowding, lack of segregational facilities and other things that worry practical sociologists do not prevail at Wyoming.

Four cell blocks, equipped with bars which will shatter hacksaw or file, but admitting far more light than the century-old gratings at Auburn, will house the prison population. Two cell blocks, each of which will accommodate 500 convicts, are nearly complete. Shops, an administration building, hospital, laundry, bath building, chapel, warden's residence, library and school are under construction. Only one man will be housed in each cell. He will have individual toilet facilities. Arms of a huge ventilating system will penetrate every cell.

Although imprisonment at Wyoming will be regarded by convicts more or less as a privilege, the State has taken the precaution of providing facilities for segregation of hardened felons from those whom it still hopes to reform. No prisoner, unless he is undergoing special punishment for misdeeds committed within the prison, will be deprived of the library, recreational facilities or his radio. As in older prisons, trusties will be permitted outside the walls to attend flower beds and work the 600-acre farm adjoining.

The State, however, is taking no chances. The walls, constructed of steel and concrete, are smooth and slippery and cannot be penetrated even by a fair-sized blast. The architect, William J. Beardsley of Poughkeepsie, has designed it to be escape-proof.

Attica citizens themselves will take a hand in the conduct of the prison, and are expected to provide free motion-picture shows, books and other entertainment.

August 22, 1931

A NEW FEDERAL PRISON.

The Federal penitentiary at Lewisburg, Pa., now open to receive its first involuntary guests, embodies the latest principles of prison architecture. Over one of the portals are graved BACON'S words: "That "which is past and gone is irrev- "ocable; wise men have enough to do "with things present and to come." Protection of society through reformation of the criminal is the goal. Mr. BATES, director of the Federal Prison Bureau, is not discouraged by previous failures to make men over before they are turned back to the community whence they came; he believes that with adequate facilities and proper surroundings the miracle can be performed, at least for a large number of prisoners. To this end the buildings are of pleasant aspect, far different from the familiar fortress type; modern shops have been provided and full opportunity will be afforded for classification and segregation, while the facilities for educational work are said to be the most complete to be found in any American prison.

Nor has the immediate protection of the community been neglected. A twenty-one foot wall, with the usual watch-towers, surrounds the prison, which has been erected in the middle of a 1,000-acre lot. While the old Sing Sing type of cell block has been abandoned, plenty of steel cells remain for caging desperate criminals, as well as strong rooms for the untrustworthy. For those found trustworthy and tractable, however, less forbidding surroundings have been furnished. One result of careful planning and segregation is reduced cost. The institution has been built and equipped at a cost of $2,000 per inmate, about a third of the price New York State is paying for its new institution at Attica. Lewisburg will house 1,200 men normally, 1,500 in an emergency, and will afford immediate relief for the overcrowding which has recently reached menacing proportions at Atlanta and Leavenworth.

JERSEY BOY, 14, TELLS OF CHAIN GANG TERM

Runaway, Seized as Vagrant, Says He Wore Shackles and Was Lashed in South.

Special to The New York Times.

NEWARK, N. J., Jan. 12.—David Kraft, 14-year-old student at the Central High School here, was back at the home of his parents, Mr. and Mrs. Julius Kraft, at 556 South Thirteenth Street, this city, today telling a story of ten days in a Greenville (S. C.) chain gang. The boy arrived here yesterday from Washington, where his father had met him after arranging for his release from the Southern prison camp. The parents said they would try to have the record of their son's conviction as a vagrant and his fingerprints removed from the South Carolina files.

Dissatisfied with school, David left home during the Christmas holidays for a hitch-hiking trip to the South. He ate and slept at charity lodging houses on the way, writing his parents four days later from Virginia. He was arrested in Greenville on New Year's Eve on a charge of vagrancy. Advised to plead guilty, David was sentenced to pay a $10 fine or pass thirty days in jail. The boy said he was sent to one of the county prison camps, where he was clothed in stripes and where shackles were forged about his ankles.

He said he had worked on roads with pick and shovel from 5 A. M. to sundown, every day. He was lashed across the back several times by a guard, he declared, when the keeper accused him of feigning illness. He smuggled a letter to his father out of the camp by a trusty late last week. Julius Kraft, a truckman, went to the capital, where he arranged by telegraph to pay his son's fine and costs. David was freed Tuesday and sent by bus to Washington to meet his father.

From Greenville. The Associated Press reported that Magistrate C. L. Cooley, by whom young Kraft was sentenced, said the boy had been convicted under another name and that his age had not been told the court. County Supervisor J. Ed. Means, in charge of chain gangs, said:

"If any prisoner in Greenville County has been beaten I don't know anything about it. Besides, we don't whip prisoners. I installed the sweat-box more than a year ago and unruly prisoners are put in there."

LONE ISLAND PICKED TO IMPRISON WORST OF OUR CRIMINALS

Alcatraz, at San Francisco, Is Acquired by Cummings From the War Department.

FOR BAILEY AND KELLY

Trouble-Makers, Jail-Breakers to Spend Days Where Only One Has Ever Escaped.

Special to The New York Times.

WASHINGTON, Oct. 12.—Acquisition of the military prison on rocky, inaccessible Alcatraz Island in San Francisco Bay for confinement of defiant and dangerous criminals was announced tonight by Attorney General Cummings.

Speaking before the National Anti-Crime Conference of the United States Flag Association, and also over the National Broadcasting System, he made known that George (Machine-Gun) Kelly, kidnapper, and Harvey Bailey, jailbreaker, would probably be transferred to the island, but refused to commit himself as to the possible inclusion with them of Al Capone, now in Atlanta.

Others, both men and women, who were regarded as presenting a menace to society and the good conduct of penal institutions on the mainland would spend their days there.

For a long time Attorney General Cummings had cherished the plan of isolating in a prison, so remote and inaccessible as to present insurance against escape, recidivists and other prisoners "who when at large prey upon society, and when confined plan and encourage prison outbreaks."

It was not his purpose to find a prison in which the inmates would be subjected to any "unusual or unreasonable environment," but a place "apart from large centres of population, preferably on an island which would not be easy of access."

Escapes Almost Impossible.

"You can appreciate, therefore, with what pleasure I make public the fact that such a place has been found," he said. "By negotiation with the War Department we have obtained the use of Alcatraz prison, located on a precipitous island in San Francisco Bay more than a mile from shore.

"The current is swift and escapes are practically impossible. It has secure cells for 600 persons. It is in excellent condition and admirably fitted for the purposes I had in mind. Here may be isolated the criminals of the vicious and irredeemable type so that their evil influences may not be extended to other prisoners who are disposed to rehabilitate themselves."

The Attorney General said he had in mind the transfer to Alcatraz of four types of prisoners—first, jailbreakers, especially those for whom escape is planned and aided by relatives, friends and fellow-gangsters who congregate near prisons to await opportunity; after these, the "dangerous" criminals, the "irredeemables" and the "trouble-makers."

"There are, roughly, 12,000 prisoners in Federal institutions, and 6,000 Federal prisoners boarded out in State prisons," the Attorney General said. "But not more than 600 or 700 of them all constitute real problems in penology.

"If we could transfer about 75 or 100 prisoners of the types I have described away from Leavenworth and Atlanta, for instance, there would be no more trouble at those penitentiaries for any one.

"The majority of the inmates of our prisons are comparatively well-behaved, but a few desperate criminals among them present a menace to any penal institution."

Island Entirely of Rock.

Alcatraz, he declared, was "sanitary and healthful," and imprisonment there could not be called cruel or inhumane. Its outstanding attraction was the difficulty of escape, which outweighed in Mr. Cummings's judgment the consideration of increased expense of maintenance there of Federal prisoners transferred from other penal institutions.

Military prisoners confined there now will be transferred to the disciplinary barracks at Fort Jay on Governors Island.

There have never been any "lifers" on Alcatraz and comparatively few military prisoners have gone there for long sentences.

The island is entirely of rock, vocational shops providing the only employment on it, although many prisoners are now used in port and dock work on military reservations in the vicinity. These latter activities are not contemplated for the prisoners described by the Attorney General.

Speaking of the more general problems of crime reduction, Mr. Cummings urged "whole-hearted cooperation between the proper Federal and State authorities," as more to be desired than creation of "a great Federal police force in the nature of Scotland Yard."

"The structure and functions of this famous and efficient organization are hardly adaptable to our complex problems," he added.

"There are many curious misconceptions about Scotland Yard, which, contrary to popular belief, is not a detective force and does not have jurisdiction throughout England or the British Isles, but is simply the metropolitan police department of greater London and one of the 187 police forces in England and Wales."

Comparison Made With "Yard."

The criminal office of the "yard," he said, acted as a clearing house of identification data as did the identification unit of the Department of Justice, which, according to the Attorney General, had more than 3,925,000 finger-print records as against Scotland Yard's collection of 500,000.

"Even if it were assumed that Scotland Yard operated over the total area of Great Britain, its problem could not be compared to the conditions which exist in the United States," he declared.

Among the "constructive suggestions" approved by the Attorney General were establishment of a national institute of criminology, providing for scientific research and training of officials in specialized fields of law enforcement; formation of State constabularies in every State in the Union, and cooperation between these bodies and the municipal authorities.

The agreement made by American manufacturers of machine guns not to dispose of machine guns to other than law enforcement officials "is gratifying," the Attorney General said, but "the smuggling of machine guns from abroad still presents aspects of difficulty." Congressional action on this subject might well be considered.

Assails Lawyers as to Crime.

"Unscrupulous lawyers who aid and abet criminals in their unlawful undertakings and employ every unworthy artifice in their defense" were denounced by the Attorney General as "scavengers of the bar, unworthy of the profession they disgrace."

"There is reason to believe," he declared, "that in many localities certain members of the bar are in touch with and regularly employed by the criminal element. Their elimination is part of the problem of crime."

In discussing the Urschel case, the Attorney General departed from his prepared address to pay a tribute to the Justice Department investigators who ran down the kidnappers and to the judge who presided at their trial.

"I am proud of these men of the Crime Investigation Bureau of the department," he declared, "and I send my salutations and thanks to Judge Vaught, who today sentenced Machine Gun Kelly and his wife to life imprisonment."

The Attorney General was presented by Patrick J. Hurley, former Secretary of War, who presided at the meeting and made a speech on the organization and plans of the "Council of '76," the crime-combating division of the Flag Association, of which he is chairman.

Colonel James A. Moss, retired, founder and president general of the association, reviewed figures on number and types of crimes, and told of "astounding" growth of the crime problem in the last fifteen years.

Five business sessions, opening tomorrow and closing at noon on Saturday, will be held.

GEORGIANS BLOCK A RETURN OF LASH

They Also Doom Chain Gangs and Force Move to Revise the Whole Prison System

By EDWIN CAMP

ATLANTA, Ga., Sept. 17.—The people of Georgia will not tolerate return of the lash in the State prison system. When, to their amazement, they heard the proposal last week, they spoke with such emphasis that they did more than put an end to the suggestion. They also sealed the doom of the "Georgia chain gang," and they insured thorough reform of prison methods before the end of this year.

The proposal to reinstate flogging as a disciplinary measure came from a meeting of the county convict wardens who met here on the call of Governor E. D. Rivers to discuss the escape of more than 100, many of them hardened felons, within the previous thirty days.

The wardens proposed the lash; the Governor listened to the suggestion and started an inquiry as to how it might be made legal. Governor Hardwick had abolished the lash seventeen years ago. Leaders of committees from both sides of the Legislature said they would recommend it as part of a new program of prison administration on which they had been working for several months.

But the news brought a storm of protests from press and public, who not only denounced the lash but added a demand for reformation of the entire penal system of the State.

Mandate for Governor

They gave to Governor Rivers a mandate which perhaps he expected; certainly he lost no time in acting upon it.

The system will be reorganized inside and out and the chain gang will be abolished. The reform will not come without some opposition, the system being involved in the maze of politics and patronage natural in county government.

But Governor Rivers and the legislative joint committee have determined and announced the general changes to be made. The program hinges on the new prison in Tattnall County, built as a Federal works project and taken over by the State.

All prisoners will be sent to Tattnall, which is called the Georgia Alcatraz because of its modernity of sanitation and security. A penologist grounded in modern methods will be engaged to administer the new revised program.

To Be Try-Out Prison

Tattnall will be maintained as a try-out for the convicts, who will be employed at such tasks as manufacturing automobile license plates and covers for school books provided by the State.

Those whose conduct wins approval will be graduated to honor camps, in which there will be no shackles, no chains and all members will have the status of trusties.

"We expect to put Georgia's prison system on a par with the best in the nation," Governor Rivers announced. "In preparing the program the legislative committee is consulting the set-up in other States and will take into consideration the report soon to be presented to the Federal Government by a committee of penologists."

The program will be presented to the special session of the Legislature to be summoned in November. The proposal to restore the lash has been dropped.

TO BAN CHAIN GANGS

Times Wide World
New prison methods will be tried in Georgia by Governor Rivers.

56% OF EX-CONVICTS GO BACK TO PRISON

So Reports J. V. Bennett, Head of U. S. Penal Institutions, in Urging Reforms

SAYS REHABILITATION PAYS

Holds Failure to Apply It to Thousands of Prisoners Is a 'Serious Indictment'

Fifty-six per cent of the 70,000 to 80,000 men and women leaving prison gates this year will be back within five years if past experience holds true, James V. Bennett, director of the Federal Bureau of Prisons, said last night at the sixty-ninth annual convention of the American Prison Congress, in session this week at the Hotel New Yorker.

Conceding that this "is surely no record of which we may be proud," Mr. Bennett said that classification —which he defined as the thorough study of each prisoner as an individual and the working out of a program for fitting him to return to freedom at some future time— offered the best method yet devised for the rehabilitation of prisoners.

"Classification presupposes a thorough study of the individual from the standpoint of the prison administrator, the physician, the psychologist, the psychiatrist, the educational director, the social worker, the parole officer, the chaplain and the vocational director," Mr. Bennett said.

"One individual, though he be as wise and understanding as Solomon, cannot possess all the techniques and the experience necessary to analyze a prisoner's problems, to determine what factors have made him a criminal and to guide and direct him toward an acceptable way of life. Classification focuses on the individual case all of the knowledge and experience of the prison personnel, both administrative and professional, and through the conference method assures the coordination and application of that knowledge and experience."

Mr. Bennett said that a recent survey of the problem showed that out of 162,000 penitentiary prisoners at least 100,000 were not, during their entire period of imprisonment, subjected to any "conscious, organized rehabilitative efforts of any kind." He said that this was "a serious indictment" of our prison system that ought to be remedied.

The Federal prison head deplored the understaffing that he said was to be found in many State prisons.

Frederick A. Moran, a member of the New York State Parole Board, said that within the last two years a number of States, profiting by justifiable criticisms that had been leveled against them, have "completely revolutionized their parole systems."

Sanford Bates, who was Mr. Bennett's predecessor as Federal Director of Prisons and is now executive director of the Boys' Clubs of America, told the convention that prison management should be a professional career, but he strongly denied that it was one now. He said that a recent questionnaire he circulated showed that out of thirty-eight States answering, twenty-eight "have no civil service applicable to the penal institutions."

Extension of well-administered parole and probation systems and further development of opportunities for self-supporting prison labor activities were urged by Sam A. Lewisohn, president of the Miami Copper Company and a member of the New York State Commission of Correction.

Felons Soon to Be Freed Get Rights in 'Honor' Unit

By The Associated Press.

SAN FRANCISCO, Nov. 25—To his long list of penal innovations Warden Clinton Duffy of California's San Quentin Prison added today the "honor block," where men awaiting parole can get an idea once more of life on the outside.

Two hundred cells have been set aside for convicts soon to be released, the principal feature of the new Duffy plan being to permit a three-hour nightly release of prospective parolees from their cells.

During that time the men will be permitted to mingle in the corridor, to read, write, play games such as ping pong, attend basketball games or even go to the movies.

Mr. Duffy, trying out the idea as a readjustment measure, explained that the usual practice of suddenly sending convicts from rigid discipline to freedom left them bewildered and all the more likely to offend society again. There are penalties for those who take advantage of the system.

Talk With Warden Duffy

By HARVEY BREIT

THERE is no experience that this writer knows of (except maybe reading the recently published "The San Quentin Story") that prepares one adequately for a meeting with Clinton T. Duffy. Warden Duffy, of course, heads up San Quentin prison, and he (together with Dean Jennings) has written his "story." But even that modest account falls short of the modesty (as well as the gentleness and simplicity) in the man.

A far cry from the tough, bitten, sadistic jailer is Warden Duffy. And he has the most uncomplicated feelings about the place. "It is home for me," he says. "I am at home, I am more at home living there than in a civilian community." This sentiment is a natural one considering Warden Duffy's history, but, it must be pointed out, it takes a natural man like Warden Duffy not to distort it.

Warden Duffy was born on the San Quentin reservation in 1898, four years after his father came to work there. He was raised in San Quentin, went to school in San Quentin, as did Mrs. Duffy (she was a Johnny-come-lately though, having been brought to the reservation by her father when she was ten months old). There were a couple of Duffy prison breaks: the warden was in the Marine Corps during World War I, and worked a short time after that for the Northwestern Pacific. For the rest it has all been time at San Quentin.

What about the good citizens, or inmates, of the jail? How did Warden Duffy feel about them? "I now have seven men working in the twenty-two-room house Mrs. Duffy and I live in," he said, replying practically rather than theoretically. We have to take care of the many official guests." (Warden Duffy was explaining the size of his home and staff.) "Well, four of these fellows are in for murder, two for narcotics, one for robbery. Six are Orientals and one is a Negro. They don't go inside the prison at all. They live with us. They stay in a little house next door twenty-four hours around the clock. When I'm away Mrs. Duffy is alone and isn't the least concerned."

He thought. "As a matter of fact," he said after a bit, "Mrs. Duffy is most carefully protected by them. They take especially good care of the jewelry and money that are usually lying around." Would it be difficult for them to escape? "Not for them. They're on the reservation, but outside the prison walls. They could go right over the hill at night, sometime between the head-counts. But I've never lost a man from our home during the ten years as warden."

Why didn't they walk over the hill? "Well," Warden Duffy said amiably and realistically, "they're carefully selected men, semi-trusties. We're friendly to them and we help solve their problems and they know they get a good report for the parole authority. Usually men of that type want to do their time and get it behind them. Even the murderers, who have killed because of jealousy or rage. They are not interested in killing."

Here Warden Duffy paused, philosophically as it were. "A first-degree murderer," he said, "unless he has committed his crime in the course of robbery, is our best prisoner. . . . Why? Because his incident is behind him and he has not committed other types of crimes."

WHEN Warden Duffy took over at San Quentin one of his first acts was the abolishment of the dungeon, the spot, the lash. He came in with corporal punishment and moved on to a concept of training and treatment. Did the warden have a fairly crystallized set of notions about the penal problem?

The warden nodded encouragingly at what he knew in advance was being asked him. "Having grown with the thing," he said, "I had noticed that every man, every young man, needs a particular training. The problem for me was to find out why he had behaved as he had and then to have a training program for him. Most often it has been a failure of the home background. Most often he has not had the love, the understanding, the discipline. So we have to give it to him. It's pretty late in the day, but he doesn't come to prison just for punishment. Anyway, confinement in itself is the punishment."

There must be rare gratification in seeing a prisoner who had been trained at the prison do well in civilian life? "Tremendously gratifying," Warden Duffy replied. "Otherwise," he said, "you couldn't live."

What about the movies, the Jimmy Cagney sort of thing? "The prisoner is not that kind of a man," Warden Duffy said. "He doesn't slouch around. The only way I can express it is: a prisoner's head is up. And another thing: you can take the best-looking girl through here and she'd not get a whistle."

Wasn't that going a bit far? "They don't have to whistle," Warden Duffy said. "They learn to talk at San Quentin. Our debating teams go against the colleges and usually win. Why do they? Well, I always say, they have more time for research."

CHRONOLOGY OF MAJOR PRISON RIOTS IN THE PAST YEAR

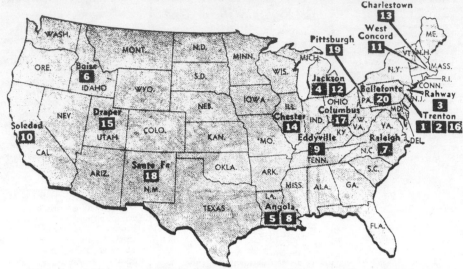

Last week's disturbances in two prisons in Pennsylvania brought to twenty the number of major uprisings in state institutions since last March. These incidents involved some 8,000 convicts, about 5 per cent of the 147,000 inmates of state prisons. Federal and local prisons have been relatively unaffected by the disturbances. Following is a chronology (numbers refer to map above):

(1) MARCH 30, 1952—At a New Jersey prison twenty-three convicts seize guards, riot two days.

(2) APRIL 15—Sixty-nine New Jersey prisoners renew riots for three days with heavy damage.

(3) APRIL 17—At a second New Jersey institution 231 take part in revolt lasting five days.

(4) APRIL 20—At a Michigan penitentiary five-day riots and fires involve 2,000 prisoners.

(5) MAY 11—At a Louisiana penitentiary 120 inmates engage in a hunger strike for four days.

(6) MAY 24—At an Idaho reformatory 300 convicts join in a riot lasting for several hours.

(7) JUNE 4—At a North Carolina reformatory 150 of the 800 inmates take part in brief uprising.

(8) JUNE 6—Louisiana penitentiary again the scene of a strike, involving more than 200 men.

(9) JUNE 27—At a Kentucky prison about 300 of the 1,100 inmates riot for eight hours.

(10) JUNE 30—At a California prison fifty of 1,400 convicts take part in noisy demonstration.

(11) JULY 1—At a Massachusetts reformatory thirty-four of the 680 prisoners stage uprising.

(12) JULY 6—New protests at Michigan prison erupt in a rebellion lasting for about two hours.

(13) JULY 22—At a second Massachusetts institution forty-three convicts stage an uprising.

(14) SEPT. 23—At an Illinois prison 800 inmates start a 27-hour demonstration of protest.

(15) OCT. 1 — At a Utah penitentiary some 500 convicts stage a sixty-six hour uprising.

(16) OCT. 13 — Rebellion, this time involving 350 prisoners, erupts in New Jersey prison.

(17) OCT. 31 — At an Ohio prison 1,600 riot for five days and set fire to prison buildings.

(18) DEC. 7—At a New Mexico reformatory fourteen prisoners take part in a 24-hour escape try.

(19) JAN. 18, 1953 — At a Pennsylvania penitentiary inmates seize six guards and fire prison.

(20) JAN. 19—At a second Pennsylvania prison convicts grab guns and hold out for four days.

UNREST SEETHING IN MANY PRISONS

Despite Changes After Recent Riots, Tensions Are High, National Survey Shows

By MURRAY ILLSON

After coming through the most explosive year in American prison history, many penal institutions in various parts of the United States, are still racked by unrest.

Among some of the twenty-three prisons and reformatories where major riots and disorders erupted in the last eleven months there has been extensive stock-taking of physical plant and personnel. Several institutions have had changes in administration and in certain instances there has been a severe tightening of security controls.

In some overcrowded or obsolete plants the tension is so high that new rebellions could be sparked by small groups of disgruntled "long-termers" who have most of their sentences ahead of them and therefore feel they have little to lose. Other dangers arise from power-seeking prisoners who compete for leadership of various cliques, or from psychopaths who have not been recognized as such or who have not been segregated from the rest of the inmates because of a lack of facilities.

The twenty-three institutions—and a number of them report improved conditions since last year's outbreaks—are in every section of the country. Three uprisings last March and April in New Jersey state prisons touched off disorders in plants from Massachusetts to California and from Michigan to Louisiana.

Disorders Continuing

The disturbances continued into this year with two riots in western Pennsylvania last month and three outbreaks at Arizona State Prison last week. On Monday two officials of Washington State Penitentiary at Walla Walla were injured critically and five others less seriously by the explosion of a convict-made bomb. A second bomb did not go off.

On the same day a five-hour rebellion took place at Oregon State Penitentiary in Salem with the seizing of five guards as hostages, who were finally released unharmed. The following day across the country, in Montpelier, Vt., ten prisoners of Washington County jail staged a sit-down strike,

demanding immediate pay for work outside the jail.

In Canada, too, there have been disorders—three serious riots involving as many as 700 prisoners at a time occurred at Montreal City Prison from last May 4 to Aug. 1.

For years penologists, criminologists, educators and social workers have argued and expounded on the causes and possible cures of prison uprisings, and investigation committees and reform organizations have grappled with the problem. Innumerable reports and recommendations have been issued from time to time and improvements in prison conditions and administration have been made. Today, while there may be conflict among some authorities on the emphasis given various details, there are on the whole wide areas of agreement.

Problem Called Complex

One point on which there is unanimity is this: the problem is enormously complex and there are no easy solutions or magic formulas for dealing with the uncertanties of human behavior, especially when they involve the extremes of anti-social and criminal activities.

Among the most frequently mentioned causes of prison troubles, though not necessarily in the order of their importance, are these:

¶Obsolete plants—About one-third of the prisons now in use are more than seventy years old. Twenty-four are more than 100 years old. One still in use was built 148 years ago!

¶Overcrowding—Often two men must occupy a cell built for one. In some plants, even those that are relatively new, inmates have had to sleep in corridors.

¶Idleness—Overcrowding or poor administration in many instances keep prisoners idle, which in turn leads to boredom. Estimates of the number of idle inmates range from one-third to one-half the prison population.

¶Politics—In many states, wardens are political appointees who are unqualified for their jobs. Their attitude sometimes may be summed up in the statement: "Give the men what they want as long as they are quiet."

¶Food—Poorly prepared or inadequate food is one of the biggest sources of discontent.

¶The Incompetent Personnel— Trained guards are hard to get for the low salaries that are paid in many places. In at least one Southern state some guards have been paid $100 a month and have worked a sixty-hour week.

¶Brutality—The lash and other extreme forms of punishment are still used in a number of places.

¶Lack of Segregation—Hardened criminals, mental cases, diseased convicts and perverts are often permitted to mingle with other prisoners.

Cells Were 'Modernized'

An official report after the New Jersey disorders disclosed that the 117-year-old state prison at Tren-

ton still had in use a wing in which no basic construction changes had been made since it was built, although each cell had been "modernized" with the installation of an electric light, radiator, toilet and washbowl.

The investigating committee consisted of New Jersey Supreme Court Justice Harry Heher; Austin H. MacCormick, former New York City Commissioner of Correction and now Professor of Criminology at the University of California, and Stanley P. Ashe, former president of the American Prison Association.

Although constructed to hold 1,190 men, the Trenton prison had 1,312 shortly before the second outbreak last April. The committee said that the prison was so badly overcrowded that many idle men were "compelled to spend approximately twenty hours a day in their cells, even more during the winter months or when the weather was bad during the summer months."

Sanford Bates, Commissioner of New Jersey's Department of Institutions and Agencies and one of the country's leading authorities on prison administration, said last week that improvements had been made in the Trenton prison since the investigation committee's report was submitted to Gov. Alfred E. Driscoll two months ago. Prison morale was now "normal," he said.

Mr. Bates, who was director of the Federal Bureau of Prisons under Presidents Herbert Hoover and Franklin D. Roosevelt from 1930 to 1937, indicated that New Jersey's penal problems could be made much lighter if the Legislature in its current session voted $4,800,000 for the construction of a new prison.

Last April 20, three days after the third uprising in New Jersey, which involved 231 men of the state prison farm at Rahway, rioting exploded at the State Prison of Southern Michigan near Jackson, the largest walled prison in the country and one of the most crowded.

With a current population of about 5,950 inmates, the prison is considered by its warden and many penologists to be an administrative monstrosity. Since the April disorders, which lasted five days and involved 2,000 prisoners, the Jackson institution had briefer sequels in July and November. It is now reported to be a "powder keg" and will remain one until the various inmate groups are segregated and the prisoner population reduced to no more than 2,000.

Tear gas barrages were used to break up sit-down strikes last May and June at Louisiana State Penitentiary at Angola, a system of farm camps seventy miles northwest of Baton Rouge. The penitentiary, with 2,700 inmates, has a long history of brutality and violence, which was climaxed in mid-1951 when thirty-seven convicts slashed their heel tendons in protest against whippings.

Following a change of state administration last year, the Angola institution also got new leadership. Conditions there now are said to be vastly improved with a policy

that permits neither coddling nor brutalizing of prisoners.

The original building of Massachusetts State Prison at Charlestown is the oldest in the country. It was opened 148 years ago and its most modern annex is more than sixty years old. The forty-three convicts who staged an uprising there last July were apparently not appeased by the fact that a modern state prison is under construction at Norfolk, Mass.

The Charlestown unit, which is to be abandoned and its 600 inmates transferred to Norfolk eventually, has neither toilet nor dining hall facilities. Prisoners eat their meals from trays they carry from the kitchen and each cell is supplied with a slop bucket that is emptied in the morning. The new prison is not expected to be ready for occupancy for about two years. Until then the situation at Charlestown is expected to remain tense.

Massachusetts Reformatory at West Concord is almost a model institution compared with the Charlestown unit. The reformatory's original buildings are seventy-five years old but have toilet facilities and a dining hall as a result of modern additions. A riot there early last July was blamed partly on brutality by guards. Investigators found that inmates could have liquor and dope smuggled in to them.

At Ohio Penitentiary where 1,600 inmates rioted for five days last October, setting fire to prison buildings, there is said to be more idleness than before the disorders because of prevailing unrest. However, a new $8,500,000 appropriation for prison expansion is expected to improve the morale of inmates and guards.

State troopers armed with rifles were needed to reinforce the regular guards of Western State Penitentiary at Pittsburgh and Rockview Penitentiary, its branch at Bellefonte, about 160 miles to the east. On Jan. 18, rioting inmates at Pittsburgh seized six guards and fired the building, while the next day at Bellefonte convicts grabbed guns and held out for four days of siege.

$150 a Month for Guards

Morale is reported to be low at New Mexico State Penitentiary at Santa Fe both among prisoners and guards—pay among the latter averaging about $150 a month. There have been several disorders there including the killing of a guard by two convicts last June and the fatal stabbing of a prisoner by another inmate last month.

At Utah's two-year-old $2,-000,000 prison near Draper, eighteen miles south of Salt Lake City, most of the institution's 570 inmates are reported to be idle. Plans for equipping a new industrial structure there are said to be stalled by the Legislature's reluctance to appropriate sufficient funds. Last October, the convicts rioted in protest against the food served them.

Reports on these conditions were supplied by correspondents of THE NEW YORK TIMES. Variations of them can be found in correctional institutions throughout the country. While it would seem that in some places the physical plant and treatment of prisoners have advanced hardly beyond the Dark Ages, some officials take the stand that although there may be room for improvement, prisons are not "country clubs" or were they ever intended to be.

CITY JAILS CALLED SCHOOLS OF CRIME; CROWDING BLAMED

Built for 4,200 Inmates, They Average 6,685 This Year— Greater Jam Is Feared

By RUSSELL PORTER

Overcrowding in the city's prisons has become a dangerous and worsening problem.

They were built with cells for about 4,200 inmates, according to the city's Commissioner of Correction, Mrs. Anna M. Kross. By one makeshift or another their capacity has been expanded to accommodate — inadequately— 6,825. But on last Sept. 7 they were jammed with 7,921 men and women.

This total was a record high. It constituted more than 80 per cent overcrowding compared with original cell capacity, and nearly 20 per cent in relation to present emergency accommodations.

The average daily number of inmates this year to Dec. 1 was 6,685. Last year it was 5,704. In 1945, before the post-war rise in prison population, it was 3,537. New admissions have increased from 48,243 in 1945 to 89,610 in 1953 and 102,038 in the first eleven months of 1954. Thus in ten years, while no new prisons have been built, the number of inmates has doubled.

Of the 7,921 peak daily total, adolescents numbered 1,268 and women inmates 474. Latest available figures on recidivism, the after-punishment relapse of former inmates into criminal or antisocial habits, show that in 1952 about 40 per cent of persons sentenced to penitentiary and workhouse terms were first offenders, while about 60 per cent were repeaters.

Seriousness Emphasized

The seriousness of the overcrowding cannot be exaggerated, according to Commissioner Kross. A former city magistrate and long an advocate of preventing crime and juvenile delinquency by a sociological approach, she was put in charge of the city's prison system by Mayor Wagner last Jan. 1.

"This overcrowding is a chronic disease, not merely an acute attack that will subside," she says. "In every likelihood it will continue, if not worsen. Right now there is a seasonal pre-Christmas decline in the prison population, but after the first of the year the increase can be expected to resume.

"Our estimates, based on crime-rate indices, forecast an increase of 17 to 22 per cent during the next five years. We will continue to have overcrowding until we build prisons to take care of the predictable peak load, like power-houses, and adopt a modern inmate rehabilitation program to reduce recidivism."

Visiting some of the major city prisons recently, a reporter and a photographer found unwholesome and explosive conditions, confirming the Commissioner's estimate of the situation. Housing conditions for inmates are generally inadequate, and in some places dangerous to the individual and to the community.

Prisoners Are Doubled Up

Many prisoners are being doubled up in small cells that were built to house one person, but have been equipped with double-decker beds or two cots separated by a narrow space. Other inmates are stacked in double-decker bunks in dormitories.

Sanitary and health conditions are inadequate. Moral deterioration is invited by sometimes promiscuous association of young and old, innocent and guilty, teen-age unfortunate and teen-age hoodlum, first offender and hardened "repeater," casual petty offender and professional criminal. Efforts are made to separate different types of inmates but they are often inadequate because of the overcrowding. Education in crime flourishes during close contact under unnatural conditions amidst demoralizing idleness.

The situation has been aggravated by the postwar increase in serious crime among adolescents. A growing proportion of youthful offenders have had to be housed in the same buildings with adults.

Prison officials and staff appear to be working hard and doing their best to keep the lid on despite tensions and pressures that sometimes threaten to blow it off. There are not enough facilities and officers to separate, supervise and guard the prisoners properly. There is no adequate rehabilitation program to combat idleness. There are not enough opportunities for work, recreation or education. There are not enough physicians, nurses, psychiatrists, psychologists, social workers, educational or recreational directors.

The worst conditions are to be seen in the detention prisons. In the city's penal system prisoners 16 years of age or older are kept in two kinds of institutions—detention prisons and sentence prisons. While awaiting court action, persons charged with all kinds of offenses from vagrancy to murder, unless freed on bail, are held in detention prisons until the courts dispose of their cases.

Parole violators, material witnesses, short-term sentenced prisoners employed as inmate help, sentenced prisoners awaiting transfer to city and state penitentiaries, Federal prisoners and miscellaneous prisoners also are held temporarily in the detention prisons.

Those detained include innocent, as well as guilty. Not all are convicted when their cases come to trial. Some are acquitted after being detained for varying lengths of time.

Many of those awaiting court action are the small fry of crime and vice who do not have the means to put up bail. Professional criminals and racketeers often are able to get bail through underworld connections.

Bail Denied to Some

Some are held on charges for which city magistrates are not permitted by law to fix bail. These include persons charged with homicide or against whom warrant has been lodged for a previous offense.

Some are detained for six months or more awaiting court action—some as long as two years, according to Commissioner Kross. She recently found a boy under 16 who had been detained eleven months. Though most inmates are 16 or older, a few 15-year-olds charged with homicide are sent to detention prisons.

At one time or another in 1953 the city had 10,000 adolescents (16 to 21 years of age) in its detention prisons, of whom 1,100 were later sentenced to city institutions.

There are four detention prisons for males: in Manhattan, where Staten Island as well as Manhattan prisoners are sent; and in Brooklyn, Queens and the Bronx. All female prisoners in the city go to the House of Detention for Women in Manhattan, which is both a detention prison and a sentence prison.

To facilitate transfer of inmates between prison and court at time of examination, arraignment, indictment, trial and sentence, and to minimize transportation costs, detention prisons are located near the criminal courts. Urban land costs limit prison space, and overcrowding is aggravated by enforced idleness. A prisoner cannot legally be compelled to work until he has been convicted and sentenced.

3 Institutions Visited

The reporter and photographer visited three detention institutions: the City Prison, Manhattan; the City Prison, Brooklyn;

February 12, 1953

and the House of Detention for Women.

The City Prison, Manhattan, is at 125 White Street, at the north end of the Criminal Courts Building at 100 Centre Street. This most modern of the city's prisons is known as the Tombs. It was opened in 1941, replacing the long-obsolete old Tombs, which stood across the way on Centre Street.

In only thirteen years the new Tombs has itself become inadequate to house Manhattan's current prison population. Its record peak was reached with 1,622 inmates on Oct. 3. This was 673 or about 70 per cent more than its normal capacity of 949 (824 in cells and 125 in dormitory bunks).

"Capacity" has been stretched by doubling up inmates on most of the ten floors where inmates are housed. Cell blocks built for 124 now house 248.

An inspector for the State Commission of Correction who visited the Tombs on Oct. 20, when it contained 1,396 inmates, reported overcrowding was "rapidly reaching the point of complete saturation."

"On most floors prisoners were milling about like cattle in congested corrals, in corridors designed to accommodate about half their number," he added. "The air was foul and many showed the effect of the extreme heat and poor ventilation. Conditions are a menace to the health of the prisoners and apparently are steadily getting worse.

"It is often necessary to place three in one cell and at such times blankets are spread on the cell floor's only available space. The homosexuals were housed two in a cell regardless of age, and the officer in charge said it is often necessary to place three of this type in one cell."

Turnover Is 800 a Day

The inspector found the overcrowding aggravated by a turnover that sometimes reaches more than 800 inmates a day, as they are taken to or from court and other prisons.

On a smaller scale similar conditions prevail in other detention prisons. In the century-old labyrinth officially called the City Prison, Brooklyn, at 149 Ashland Place, better known as the Raymond Street Jail, there is doubling up in 70 per cent of the cells. Some prisoners have to sleep on cots in a corridor outside their cell block. At times 400 to 500 men mill around in the small exercise yard, guarded by eight officers.

The normal capacity of the Raymond Street Jail is 465, but on Sept. 7, its peak day, it was jammed with 818 prisoners.

At the House of Detention for Women, 10 Greenwich Avenue, in Greenwich Village, Manhattan, with a normal capacity of 401, the peak of 482 was reached in September. Conditions are so wretched here that Commissioner Kross calls it a "shocking penological anachronism." It was built in 1930 as a house of detention only. Lack of any other place to house prostitutes and other women sentenced to penitentiary and workhouse terms has dictated its use as both a detention and sentence prison.

Thus, women who have been arrested but some of whom have never been found guilty of any misdeed, are held in the same prison as women who have been convicted and sentenced, sometimes for repeated and serious offenses. While both types are housed under the same roof, the Commissioner says, it is humanly impossible to carry out any substantial degree of rehabilitation.

It is inhumane, she adds, to imprison some of these women as long as three years in such an unwholesome atmosphere, with such insufficient clothing, insufficient space, insufficient supervision, and insufficient care and treatment as are provided for them.

In 1953 more than 8,000 women were sent to the House of Detention, 80 per cent of them to await court action and 20 per cent to serve terms ranging from one day to three years. The State Commission of Correction has severely criticized conditions at the House of Detention, and Mrs. Kross agrees the criticism is just.

The City Prison, Bronx, at 653 River Avenue, with a normal capacity of 239, housed a peak of 423 inmates in September. The City Prison, Queens, at 1 Court House Square, Long Island City, capacity 199, had 316 last April.

The sentence prisons for males are the penitentiary and workhouse at Rikers Island in the East River, off La Guardia Airport, the workhouse on Hart Island in Long Island Sound off City Island and Pelham Bay Park, and the reformatory at New Hampton in upstate Orange County, seventy-five miles from New York City.

The penitentiary is basically for men sentenced for crime, the workhouse chiefly for vagrants, alcoholics, disorderly persons and other casual petty offenders, a motley group of social misfits and rejected humans, and the reformatory for petty first offenders between 16 and 30 years of age.

Rikers Island has a capacity of 2,887—1,887 in penitentiary cells and 1,000 in workhouse dormitories. Last August it reached its peak of 3,718. Since then the load at Rikers Island has been eased by the transfer of about 800 workhouse prisoners to Hart Island, where an old workhouse has been reopened.

The reporter and photographer visited Rikers Island and Hart Island. In both places inmates for whom there was work to do appeared more contented and better adjusted, less sullen and less embittered looking, than the idle ones milling about the corridors and sitting or lying on their bunks there and in the detention prisons. The chief problem in the sentence prisons now appears to be lack of facilities and personnel to keep the inmates busy in order to reduce the demoralizing idleness.

The reformatory, capacity 261, contained 258 inmates on Sept. 7. For lack of facilities at the reformatory, at times many adolescents have to be thrown in among the heterogeneous mass of offenders at Rikers Island.

Various prisoners are kept from time to time in Bellevue Hospital and King's County Hospital prison wards and in the hospital at Rikers Island.

The overcrowding in the prisons has been attributed to various causes. Among them are the post-war rise in population, in crime and in juvenile delinquency; increased police activity in recent years against drug addiction; and this year's police raids on street hoodlums.

Police figures show that every day about 320 persons are arrested in New York. There was a 10 per cent increase in major crimes reported in the first six months of 1954 compared with the same period last year.

Closing of certain district prisons in recent years for economy and other reasons also is cited. Likewise failure to plan existing prisons to allow for an increase in population and in crime.

Some believe that over the years too much stress has been put on building escape-proof prisons. These critics say less expensive minimum-security measures would suffice for the majority of petty, short-term prisoners so that larger prisons could be built at equal or smaller cost. They likewise say that too little emphasis has been placed on providing prison space and personnel for inmate rehabilitation programs designed to reduce the number of repeaters.

Edward R. Cass, member of the State Commission of Correction, general secretary of the Prison Association of New York, and a nationally recognized authority on prisons, agrees with Commissioner Kross on the seriousness of the overcrowding problem.

"It has continued year after year and is worse than ever this year," says Mr. Cass. "Serious efforts to solve it are essential."

Mrs. Kross has been struggling energetically to solve it during her first year as head of the city's Department of Correction. She has relieved the situation in various ways. But with crime still rampant she has been waging a losing battle.

Summary of Prison Riots So Far in 1955

Jan. 19—Massachusetts State Prison, Boston. Four convicts of an overcrowded population of 577 seized five guards as hostages. They surrendered Jan. 21 to seven unofficial peacemakers they had named. They complained of long solitary confinement for punishment and lack of hope of ever reaching time off for good behavior. Political appointments have hampered prison reform. Parole system is termed inefficient. New prison at Norfolk designed to cope with riots. No deaths or injuries.

March 27—Nebraska State Penitentiary, Lincoln. Twelve convicts revolted and held two guards as hostages. Attributed to guards' carelessness and poor segregation building. Revolt ended March 30, the felons yielding to Gov. Victor Anderson's stern terms. No deaths or injuries.

April 14—Texas State Prison, Huntsville. Fifty-two convicts staged a two-day sitdown strike, demanding three meals a day, instead of two. Officials ignored the protest, saying the men were nonworking and refused to work. No deaths or injuries.

April 16—Rusk State Hospital, Rusk, Tex. Eighty inmates rioted and held superintendent and four others as hostages. Dr. Charles Castner, superintendent, said riot had been planned after inmates heard of the Texas State Prison disturbance. Negro patients complained that their recreational facilities were not equal to white patients. Hospital built for 1,700 patients, now has 2,300. No deaths, thirteen persons injured.

May 11—Nassau County Jail, Mineola, L. I. Twenty young inmates staged thirty-five-minute demonstration. Peace restored by tear-gas shells. Warden E. J. O'Hara attributed it to general disrespect for authority and boredom. No deaths or injuries.

May 13—State Prison Camp, Greenville, N. C. Superintendent Paul Crawford shot and wounded two inmates after five convicts had taken over a cell block and held sway for fourteen hours. Mr. Crawford called it a "spur-of-the-moment affair." No deaths.

June 6—Ionia State Reformatory, Ionia, Mich. Four armed prisoners ran amok and wounded two guards with homemade knives. General restlessness and "pressures" given as cause by Guy Harrison, Michigan director of Department of Correction. He noted that ringleaders had low intelligent quotients. No deaths.

July 5—Walla Walla State Penitentiary, Walla Walla, Wash. Rioters seized nine hostages and beat one badly. Two-day revolt ended with major concessions to convicts. Idleness, obsolete cell blocks, primitive sanitary facilities, overcrowding called causes. Politics plays big role in guards' appointment. Guards' viewpoint that prisoner is there for one purpose—to be punished.

July 11—Rhode Island State Prison, Howard, R. I. Three hundred and forty convicts staged an hour sitdown strike in dining room. Officials said program deficiencies and lack of recreational facilities was cause. No deaths or injuries.

July 16—Wyoming State Penitentiary, Rawlins, Wyo. Seventy-five armed prisoners rioted in protest against two guards they accused of harsh and unfair treatment. Fifteen-hour rebellion ended only after officials agreed to discharge the two guards. Convicts gained promises of better conditions on food, solitary confinement and recreation. One guard wounded, no deaths.

July 18—Nevada State Prison, Carson City. Two-hundred and twenty-two inmates, led by thirty, staged fifty-hour strike. Ringleaders placed in solitary. Serious overcrowding, with "hardened criminals" placed with first offenders, juveniles. Not enough jobs, only one for every three men. Convicts sought personal appearances before parole board, instead of relying on their records and/or attorneys. No deaths or injuries.

July 26—Bexar County Jail, San Antonio, Tex. A small disturbance began night of July 2, culminating in more serious riot. Firehoses used to quell uprisings. Sheriff Owen Kilday said poor food was to blame. No injuries or deaths.

Aug. 2—Bexar County Jail. Sheriff Kilday shot and killed a prisoner to halt a riot. Four others were wounded. Guards are actually deputy sheriffs hired by the sheriff, who does not expect more trouble. If they ever take one of his guards as hostage, he said, "they'll just have to kill the hostage. I'll call their hand and go in there shooting. I don't believe in giving in to them and the guards knew what they were getting into when they got their jobs."

Aug. 14—Walla Walla Penitentiary. Fourteen guards seized as hostages in six-hour uprising broken up by tear gas and telephone persuasion. No deaths or injuries.

Aug. 17—Nebraska Penitentiary. Three hundred inmates rioted and burned half the buildings, protesting segregation of two of their friends, according to Warden Joseph Bovey. Two inmates injured, no deaths in thirteen-hour disturbance.

Aug. 17—Great Meadow Correctional Institution, Comstock, N. Y. Ten-hour sitdown strike was broken in thirty-minute pitched battle that left fourteen inmates, eight guards and three state troopers injured. One State Commissioner of Correction, Thomas J. McHugh, in report to Governor Harriman said uprising was "in large part spontaneous, with little prior organization or planning." Investigation of 174 rioters continuing. Reported friction between young and older prisoners. No deaths.

Aug. 21 and 22—Nebraska State Penitentiary. Thirteen of the sixteen convicts were involved in these rebellions were involved in the Aug. 17 riot. Called "psychotics who don't learn from past experience," by warden. They set fire to prison segregation building Aug. 21. Armed guards forced their surrender. Warden Bovey reported everything under control, but on next night 100 inmates shouted and started fires to cover up an escape attempt. Governor Anderson has National Guardsmen standing watch until unrest subsides. George Morris, head of State Reformatory, criticized the Governor, the Board of Control, Warden Bovey and the State Penal Director, B. B. Albert. Mr. Morris said there were "too many cooks in the broth."

The Second Chance

CRIME, COURTS, AND PROBATION. By Charles Lionel Chute and Marjorie Bell. Introduction by Roscoe Pound. 268 pp. New York: The Macmillan Company. $4.75.

By CROSWELL BOWEN

PROBATION, a peculiarly American institution, involves the study and supervision of a person convicted of an illegal act and given a suspended sentence. The social study of a convicted person, prepared for a judge as a guide in helping him to sentence the person, is commonly known as a probation report. The word probation is sometimes misused interchangeably with parole, which is the study and supervision of a released prisoner who has been permitted to go out into the world before the expiration of his sentence.

The man most responsible for the introduction of probation in our legal system was Charles Lionel Chute. Son of a Congregational minister, he saw in probation and parole, a practical means of implementing the ethic of earthly redemption.

In 1907 Chute met with a handful of probation officers to form what is today the powerful National Probation and Parole Association. From 1915 to 1925, he worked tirelessly for passage of the Federal Probation Act. When he retired as director of the association in 1948, he set about writing the history of the movement in which he had worked so long and so hard. Midway in the project, on Sept. 25, 1953, he died. His sister-in-law, Marjorie Bell, also worked in the field, and she has completed this important narrative of the development of probation as a social policy.

"Crime, Courts and Probation" is destined to be an authoritative work in its field not because it is well-done and scholarly. Except for a few fragmentary works, there is no comprehensive volume on the subject available. No self-respecting criminal court judge in the country will risk having to admit he hasn't read this book. The general reader will learn much here that will enlighten and clarify his thinking about crime and punishment.

WE learn, for example, that "there is no evidence that severe laws and cruel punishment deter the potential criminal or protect society." Yet today society frequently operates on "the proposition that punishment is not an end in itself but a means of preventing crime by instilling terror in the mind of the poten-

August 29, 1955

438

tial lawbreaker as to the consequences."

"The trail and pursuit of the lawbreaker is almost as bloody as the trail of crimes committed," the authors write. Stealing a shilling was once punishable by death in England. At public hangings in England "pickpockets plied their trade in the very shadow of the gallows." During the middle of the last century, a prison chaplain in England interrogated 167 persons under sentence of death as to whether they had ever witnessed a hanging. All but three had been witnesses.

The United States did not import many of the oppressive measures for treating criminals that prevailed in Europe. Yet, probation was not introduced into our Federal Courts until 1925, forty-seven years after the

Sculpture by Ruth Nickerson. Courtesy National Sculpture Society.

first state (Massachusetts) had

adopted it and not until thirty other states had followed suit.

Chute failed, he wrote, to get Woodrow Wilson to support the Federal Probation Act. Eventually, it passed the House 170 to 49. The opposition was from drys who thought probation would be used to get bootleggers out of jail. Calvin Coolidge signed the bill on March 4, 1925.

THE battle for enlightened treatment and therapy of criminals is not yet fully won. Salaries of probation workers are pitifully low in some states. There are many courts who do not even have probation facilities. The whipping post is still legal in Delaware and Maryland. It would seem that society continually vacillates in its attitude toward the handling of criminals. The distinguished

Roscoe Pound states in the introduction to the book that "the retributive impulse, the deep-seated human tendency to hurt someone or something when anything goes wrong [is like] Huck Finn's father who, when he stumbled over a barrel, got up and kicked the barrel."

For specific human cases, the authors print the stories of six probationers as told by New York City's own Judge Louis Goldstein. Reading this chapter is a heartening experience. In summing up, the authors point out that a judge's placing a man on probation is popularly believed to be a matter of "giving a man another chance." "Society, too," the authors tell us, "has a second chance—a chance to understand, to steady, to sustain, to encourage, to prevent."

March 4, 1955

Parole—The Issue and the Promise

It is generally accepted as the most effective means of rehabilitating prisoners, but even its advocates admit that the system has weaknesses in practice.

By GERTRUDE SAMUELS

RECENT events involving crime and punishment have focused attention on the problem of parole. Notably, there was the case of Frederick C. Wood, who had served more than seventeen years of a term for murder, and had been on parole less than a month from Clinton (N. Y.) State Prison when he was charged with a new double killing.

These questions began to be asked: Just what is parole? What are the procedures? Is the system right? If it is not, what can be done about it?

* * *

PAROLE (from the French word for "promise") is a relatively new concept. It dates from shortly before the turn of the century and is part of all state correctional systems today. It is, in essence, a selective process that is intended to screen the better risks among convicted offenders from the rest of the prison population, and give them early releases, under supervision, after they have served part of their sentences behind bars.

Ninety-five per cent of all prisoners return to society (the other 5 per cent either die in prison or are executed). The issue is: What happens to them after they leave prison?

If a man were forced to finish his maximum sentence behind bars, he would be entitled under the law to go free at the prison gates without any restraints. He might then turn back to crime. On the other hand, it is argued, if the better risks are screened out, given an earlier release and supplied with guidance during the difficult period of adjustment to freedom, the chances of redemption are greater and society is better protected.

In New York State, all prison sentences since 1936 have been "indeterminate" with minimum and maximum sentences fixed by the court. In general, when an offender has served his minimum term minus time for good behavior—so-called "good time"—he may apply for parole consideration.

For example, if a man receives a five-to-ten-year sentence, he is eligible for parole at the end of five years minus "good time" (usually one-third off his minimum).

Parole does not "forgive" or reduce

a sentence. The inmate is still considered to be "serving" his sentence, but in his community, under restrictions and the supervision of an assigned parole officer. If he violates his parole rules, he can be returned to prison to serve the rest of his term, plus whatever additional sentence is imposed by the court for a new offense.

If, however, he lives up to the rules of his release, he can finish out his sentence in the community and eventually be discharged from parole.

There are at present about 15,000 serious offenders in New York State prisons. There are some 10,000 convicted persons released on parole, about 7,000 of them in New York City. The number released on parole has been increasing during the past ten years (from 3,359 in 1950 to 5,291 in 1959).

A study of New York's 1959 parolees shows that 85.2 per cent have stayed out of trouble, and that 14.8 per cent have violated parole. Eight per cent of the backsliders have been convicted of new crimes.

However, long-term studies indicate that while the great majority succeeds at first on parole, many tend to slip into old ways again. For example, a study of 27,180 New York parolees between 1946-55 shows that 43 per cent returned to prison—20 per cent for new crimes and 23 per cent for lesser parole violations. The causes for this backsliding, or recidivism, are complex, and no one puts all the blame on parole.

The data on paroled murderers is exact: in New York State during the ten-year period 1950-59, 357 convicted murderers were paroled. None of them has committed another homicide. Wood, who was paroled this year, is an exception. A recent National Conference On Parole concluded that "those who commit robbery, burglary and larceny tend to have poorer parole records than those convicted of sex offenses, assault or homicide."

* * *

PAROLE consideration begins, of course, in the prison. A two-day visit to Clinton Prison at Dannemora, from which Wood was released, reveals a fascinating drama.

Clinton, in the Adirondacks, is the "Siberia" of the state's prisons because of its distance from New York and its long, cold winters. A twenty-foot-high wall, topped by twelve glass-enclosed guard towers dams in the 2,000 prisoners.

Inside the wall, all seems silent and static. The stillness is broken occasionally by the noise of prisoners during their free period in the yard or coming back from work in the laundry or fabric factory. The unnatural landscape is softened by a Gothic-style church, built by the inmates and called, with seeming irony and hope, the Church of the Good Thief, after the thief on the cross who pleaded with Jesus to "remember me."

THERE are few first offenders in Clinton. The inmates for the most part are hardened criminals who have been in conflict with the law all their lives. Among them are thieves, forgers, drug sellers and users, rapists and murderers. Under New York law (as in most states), "lifers" are not barred from parole consideration eventually (though, in many cases, not before forty years minus "good time").

In a small, green-painted room in the Administration Building, three members of the five-man Parole Board, appointed by the Governor, sit as a panel at the conference table, silently and swiftly studying thick dossiers on the prisoners, who wait under guard outside the door. The most common offenses are armed burglary and robbery, use of drugs and sex abuses.

Each large file, with its closely typed, intimate details of a man's social, psychological and institutional history, of all his inadequacies and offenses against society, most of it reaching back into his youth, reads like a piling up of inevitable tragedy.

Except for the bars at the windows, the atmosphere is purposely informal—to give inmates a chance to ventilate their feelings; to give the commission-

ers a relaxed atmosphere in which to gain insights into the prisoners, to judge whether a man will be a safe risk on the outside under supervision.

Before the three commissioners, empty and waiting, is a straight wooden chair. At 8:15 A. M., the first inmate, wearing the prison gray uniform, is admitted.

"Good morning," a commissioner begins. "Your name is ———?"

ALL day, at ten- and fifteen-minute intervals, there unfolds a panorama of lost humanity.

Some come in clean white shirts, hopefully brought by their families, desperate to make a good impression. Some are old, white-haired and listless, their whole lives spent going from prison to prison. Some are hostile and arrogant.

A sampling of the prisoners affords a glimpse of the board's problems:

The preparole summary of one married man shows a long history of crime, including drugs. He is serving a two-to-five-year term after pleading guilty to attempted robbery and rape while armed with a knife; his maximum sentence is to expire in 1963.

"What does parole mean to you?" a commissioner asks.

"I used to eat, sleep, live drugs," the prisoner replies nervously. "Parole would mean a new, decent life to me. I feel that I love my wife and children and I would like to be a husband and a father to them."

"There's a history of rape and dope here," another commissioner puts in. "A lot of this is locked up in your head. When we look at the record, we don't see your interest in your wife and family. We want to believe you, but it's hard to. The record does contain some good things—you've learned to work here, you're capable," reading from the record. "But," he adds, flagging down the man's hope, "it's a difficult case. We'll think it over."

The man rises unsteadily and remembers to thank the commissioners before leaving the room.

The commissioners, after talking it over, decide that he is not ready for release, that he be held for another year before reconsideration, and "that we get a psychiatric report on him." (There is one full-time psychiatrist in Clinton, and two visiting psychiatrists.) The inmate will get a note on the decision from one of the three parole officers who serve the prison.

The drug addicts all seem to resemble one another—passive and confused, with hands clenching and unclenching, as though desperately seeking answers in the faces before them. One addict who was "driven to steal to buy drugs" begs not to be sent back to his old associations in New York.

"At any time we release you," a commissioner says, "it's going to be a gamble."

"It will be," the man agrees dully.

The board decides to hold him. Under the law, it is powerless to treat him as anything but a criminal, al-

though, the commissioners say, he clearly needs hospital care.

THE most dramatic cases are two homicides—the first to come up since the Wood case.

One, a tall, graying man who was once an artist, beat his girl friend to death while he was in a drunken rage. It was the only offense of his life. Sentenced to thirty-five years to life, he has waited twenty-three years for this day.

His family writes, the dossier shows, that they want him home. They have a job waiting for him. His institutional and medical record is uniformly good. After a half-hour interview, the board puts a six-month "hold" on him, and decides to consider parole then, "if we receive a favorable report from the new psychiatric panel." (Under a new executive order by the Governor, all prospective parolees convicted of murder or serious sex crimes are now transferred to Sing Sing or Attica Prison for examination by at least two psychiatrists working independently; the final decision on whether to parole, however, still resides with the Parole Board.)

The other homicide case is also a first-felony offender for manslaughter. He has served six years of a ten-to-twenty-year term for strangling his wife. His record is long and vicious, showing criminal assaults since his early youth.

On the basis of his record and the interview, the board unhesitatingly decides to hold him for two years before considering him again for parole. At that time, he may be held again.

THE board members vary in their approach to the prisoners.

Chairman Russell G. Oswald, sociologist, lawyer and former Director of Corrections of Wisconsin, looks like a rumpled professor, outwardly mild, but his questions are edged with steel.

Commissioner Paul Regan, a parole officer for eighteen years, is a gray-haired, stolid man, with a no-nonsense manner, to whom churchgoing is meaningful.

Frank L. Caldwell, a slender Negro, a criminal lawyer who has also taught law, has the courtroom approach—suave, keen, quick, sometimes booming questions as his brows knit with anger, or softening his voice to probe an antagonist's mind.

THOSE they recommend for parole do not instantly leave prison. Most must show that they have jobs waiting—and many are held back for months while they write hundreds of letters to no avail. However, many prisoners are now released if they can show "reasonable assurance" of getting jobs on the outside. This is one reason for the rise in the number of parolees.

On leaving prison, the parolee gets a suit of clothes, $20 plus his prison earnings and his fare home, where he must promptly report to the local parole office (in Manhattan, at 320 Broadway). Before leaving, he signs an agreement which binds him to sixteen restrictions, among them:

He must always be home at certain hours. He may not change jobs, or leave the community, without permission of his parole officer. He may not get married without permission. He is forbidden to drive a car. He is forbidden to use liquor or drugs. He may not vote. He may not take up with old friends.

In the area parole office, he is assigned to a parole officer, who has studied his dossier. The initial interview may take from a few minutes to an hour—but, from the first moment, the parole officer undertakes to help to rehabilitate the man while protecting society.

The parolee is required at first to report in person once or twice a week—later, once or twice a month—depending on how much surveillance he appears to need. The officer also checks regularly on him, by phone or in person, at his home and on the job, unannounced, at any time of day or night, and checks with local detective squads on his doings.

LIFE on parole is not easy. A parolee knows that he may be taken into custody and returned to prison not only if he violates the rules but if he even appears to be slipping into his old ways. He is returning, however, to the same community that started him on his criminal career, and he may come to depend on his parole officer, trained in social work, as the first decent element in his life.

But the parole officer must spread himself thin. In New York City there are 137 parole officers for 7,000 parolees. A small number can do intensive work—in specialized units for the mentally retarded, youthful offenders and narcotic addicts. But most parole officers carry heavy case loads, an average of seventy-five per man. Some parolees, whose residence, job and community

THE WALL—A view from within Clinton Prison at Dannemora, N. Y. An inmate is first considered for parole after serving his minimum sentence minus time off for good behavior.

adjustments are quickly achieved, need little help. Others stand in great need of counseling and guidance.

Parole officers often work around the clock in their offices or visiting their cases on the job, or in their homes or neighborhoods, but they can accomplish very little supervision in the few minutes that they can spend on each man. As one parole officer put it: "The active element is the man himself—he is his own greatest resource—but he needs skilled help and strengths. Obviously, little can be done for many of them because of the heavy case loads."

* * *

TO the questions of whether the system is right, and of what, if anything, needs to be done about it there are two main answers.

One small group doubts the value of any system that suggests leniency for criminals. Its adherents regard the grant-

ing of parole as "maudlin sentiment" and "coddling" of prisoners that undermines justice and respect for the law. All too often, they say, a man is released on parole and the police are soon hunting him again for another crime. They believe that, since the Parole Board is quasi-judicial, its first obligation should be to the public —and that any element of doubt is too often resolved in favor of the inmate, "without giving the public a break." As evidence they cite the high percentage of repeaters.

A larger group, throughout the state and country, accepts the parole system as the most practical and humane way of bringing convicted persons back into society. We dare not lose sight of the fact, this group says, that we are dealing with human beings, not inferior animals. Behavior patterns are not immutable, but can be altered for the better.

Whether we like it or not, 95 per cent of all inmates return to society. Most defenders of parole concur in Chief Justice Earl Warren's comment that, too often, "an appraisal of work done is made on the basis of the failures of a few parolees instead of on the basis of the rehabilitation of the vast majority."

BUT among experts and laymen who accept parole as progress, there is genuine concern about the system in practice. This stems from (1) weaknesses inside the prison at the time of release; (2) rigidity in the sentencing system; (3) a lack of tools in and out of the prison system to do an adequate job of rehabilitation.

As to the first point, many who believe strongly in parole are worried, along with critics of the system, that when there is an element of doubt about a prisoner it is resolved in his favor. They believe that a separate panel of disinterested experts should periodically re-evaluate parole procedures.

Since protection of society is paramount, the all-important question, they say, is not whether an offender will be released, but *how* he will be released. The easiest thing would be to hold all prisoners to their "max" terms, then set them free without supervision, as the New York law allows. Many convicts would like that; also, there could be no reflection on the parole system if they committed more crimes.

Studies show that New York is behind several states which believe that society is best protected when all inmates, after serving part of their sentences, come out under correctional treatment. Wisconsin, for example, usually cited as having the most advanced system, has, in addition to its parole system, a "conditional release law"—so that even an ex-prisoner who

has served his maximum time behind bars remains under supervision for at least the length of the "good time" he earned in prison.

SECOND, the courts of New York State sentence defendants to longer terms than do most state courts, and parole is delayed longer than in most states. For example, the average time served before a prisoner is released on parole in New York is thirty-three months, compared with fifteen months in Wisconsin. The National Council on Crime and Delinquency believes that society is less, not better, protected by punitive sentencing, and points to California's experiments. These show that many inmates can be released at least three months earlier than usual without any increased threat to public safety.

Finally, there is a lack of tools. A prisoner improperly diagnosed in prison, or poorly supervised on parole, can weaken the entire system.

A large body of evidence shows that the greatest single need is for diagnostic and research studies, both in and outside the prisons, to find what therapies are most effective for the inmates. It is a fact that in no state or Federal prison system are the psychiatric and related services adequate to do the job.

Many also believe that a 'midway" institution is needed—probably part prison, part hospital—for the offenders who are in need of long-term psychiatric care—the sex offenders, the drug addicts, those who are mentally ill without being criminally insane.

It is in the area of personnel that the system, here and in most states, falls most short of the ideal. The heavy case

loads taxing parole officers mean that parolees cannot possibly get the close supervision that many need. The low salaries, averaging $6,000 a year before taxes, discourage many college graduates and trained workers from coming into this highly specialized field.

Perhaps the toughest hurdle is the public itself. There is great need for the community to consider parolees as it does any other "handicapped" group seeking rehabilitation. If parolees are to prove themselves, they need understanding that they want to—must—make good on parole.

ONE estimate of the worth of the system comes from those who have been helping.

In the blighted Bedford-Stuyvesant area of Brooklyn, which breeds a large proportion of the city's crime, you accompany a parole officer checking parolees on their jobs. A service-station owner tells you warmly: "My parolee served two years in Sing Sing for robbery. I get more loyalty from him than from my other employes because he feels that I've given him something to work for."

In Manhattan, the owner of a skirt factory, who has been hiring parolees for seventeen years—about 150 men— as pleaters, pressers, cutters and machine operators, currently has ten parolees among his 250 workers. Why?

"Because I feel that a man who is recommended by the Parole Board is worth a helping hand. Only one ever backfired—he went over to my competitor. Sure, I don't have to do it. But don't you think I feel good about it?"

September 18, 196

From 7 A.M. to 10 P.M. at Sing Sing

By FRED J. COOK

OSSINING, N. Y.

AT 7 o'clock on these gray winter mornings a bell sounds in the cell blocks of the red brick buildings perched on the steep east bank of the Hudson and, at its ring, an entire, separate town of some 2,300 persons comes to life. It is the prison town of Sing Sing, walled off from the outside world, dominated by fourteen turreted guard posts, a world of men in confinement, but a world of men living, working, playing — and hoping. Sing Sing is a town that lives on hope.

The 7 o'clock bell is the signal for Sing Sing's 1,748 inmates and 514-man staff to begin another round of duties. Even before it goes off, some of the

men are stirring in their narrow cells. They rise, wash and dress. They make up their narrow beds, army-style, and they make certain that the objects on their narrow dressers, only an arm's length from the bed, are regulation neat. They perhaps take a look at a favorite photograph — mother, girl friend or wife — and by 7:15, when guards come along the runways to unlock the individual cells, they are ready to come out.

They file slowly from cell block to mess hall, falling into step along the way with friends and acquaintances. Each man grabs a tray and gets a breakfast of oatmeal with milk and sugar, bread and coffee; he takes his seat at one of the long rows of eating benches, places the tray before him and begins his breakfast.

So starts a day in Sing Sing. It can be any day, every day. There has been only one time in recent memory when it was different.

Last Nov. 15 the prison's morning bell echoed on an unnatural stillness. Instead of the usual bustle, there was the ominous silence of inactivity. The men sat stubbornly in their cells and refused to come out. It was the beginning of a sit-in strike that lasted for two days and made newspaper headlines.

Today the memory of the Sing Sing sit-in lingers only in the background. It was an event that is almost certain to prod the State Legislature this year into a discussion of its causes and a consideration of possible remedies, but it seems to have had little lasting effect on the routine at Sing Sing.

"When trouble is brewing in a prison, you can smell it like gas fumes in the air," veteran keepers will tell you.

No such reek of imminent trouble lurks about Sing Sing today. The inmates go about their chores with the air of men living a rigid, but not unbearable, routine. Breakfast over, they file from the mess hall and, under the watchful eyes of guards, drop their knives and forks and spoons into boxes provided at the doors. At five minutes to 8, they pass out into the open and flow in a long, chattering line down the steep pitch of the Hudson's banks to the cluster of prison workshops.

Sing Sing is built on two levels and is set on a tract of real estate that would seem more appropriate for a millionaire's castle than for a prison. Just a few miles to the south the new Tappan Zee Bridge winds across the Hudson; below and beyond the prison to the west the waters of the river sparkle in the sunlight.

Rimmed in by brick walls and barbed wire fences, the prison's twenty buildings are located on a fifty-five-acre waterfront plot. The new buildings contain the cell blocks, the mess hall, auditorium and chapels, and stand on the high ground of the Hudson cliffs. Two hundred feet below, on a flat stretch of land by the river, lie the buildings of the old prison, constructed in 1826. These are now used as warehouses and workshops.

Life at Sing Sing also flows on many levels. The prison itself serves a dual function. It has its own permanent population, but it also serves as a receiving station for the great flow of prisoners from New York City. Here they come to be examined, screened, and eventually transferred to upstate institutions.

For the first two weeks, the day of the new arrival bears some resemblance to that of a freshman in college. He is put through a series of mental, physical and psychological examinations. He is given indoctrination courses to prepare him for prison life. In each batch there are hardened incorrigibles for whom prison can serve just one function—to pack them away from society and keep them from doing further harm; but in each batch, too, there are those who can be helped and encouraged and turned into law-abiding citizens. It is to these that the major portion of effort at the prison is directed.

"We run the prison like a city of 1,800 people, only of course with a lot more police," says Warden Wilfred L. Denno. "Anything you couldn't do on the outside, you can't do on the inside. You can't fight, you can't abuse an officer, you can't steal. If you do, you'll be punished. We hold court twice a week and try to make the punishment fit the crime."

THIS code is impressed on the prisoner from the start. It underlies his every move on every day he spends in Sing Sing. He is faced with clear alternatives: if he misbehaves, punishment in the form of restricted privileges, possibly strict confinement, the loss of "good time" that can win him earlier parole; if he behaves—hope. The one hope that stirs all Sing Sing, the hope of freedom.

Sing Sing is a school, hospital, factory as well as a prison. If initial tests show that a man is illiterate and hopelessly handicapped, he goes to the prison school to acquire the equivalent of an eighth grade education. If he needs medical treatment, he will be sent to the prison hospital, occupying four floors in one wing of the prison buildings.

If he shows some special aptitude, or if he appears capable of working at a trade and learning it, he is assigned to a regular job in one of the shops down by the river. In the end, on an average, some 300 of Sing Sing's inmates go to daily school; some 700 labor in the shops.

The shops cover a wide range of activities. A man may be assigned to the print shop, equipped with its old flat-bed press, there to learn the printer's trade, or he may be assigned to the neighboring machine shop supervised by Jess Collyer Jr., long-time Mayor of Ossining. Collyer has mapped out a twelve-month course to turn raw trainees into good auto mechanics.

For the first six months his men are put to tearing down and rebuilding motors. Then they are graduated to work on the prison's vehicles and instructed in the mysteries of front-end and rear-end assemblies. It is Collyer's proud boast that many of his "graduates," incapable of earning an honest living before, now support themselves on the good wages they make as auto mechanics.

"One of my men wrote me that he had given his mother the first $10 he had ever earned honestly and she has it framed on the wall," Collyer reports with a grin.

OTHER men with other skills, or potential skills, work in the industrial shops under the supervision of Fred Christ. These Sing Sing shops, though they refrain from competing with private industry and make articles for use only by the states, annually chalk up sales in excess of $1 million.

In the sheet metal shop the air resounds with the bong of mallets clanging on metal as prisoners shape garbage cans or hammer out dog tags. The shop turns out some 40,000 units a year. In the brush shop, inmates fashion everything from fingernail brushes to the brooms used by street sweepers. The leather shop produces 100,000 pairs of shoes a year; the textile shop, some 35,000 dozen pieces of underwear.

This is good-sized industry. Some of its problems are unique. The telephone rings in Fred Christ's office, for example, and he listens to a baffled clerk at the shipping dock.

"I've got twelve shoes that just came in from Dannemora," the clerk says. "They're all different. What do I do? Throw them away?"

Christ laughs.

"No, that's all right," he says. "Send them up."

It seems that Clinton Prison at Dannemora suddenly discovered it had twelve odd shoes in stock and had shipped them down to Sing Sing so that prison leather-factory workers could fashion appropriate mates.

WITH such activities, the shops of Sing Sing are busy until 11:40 A. M. Then the men leave their various tasks and straggle up the slope to the mess hall. Friends walk together, and the hum of many voices fills the air. Inside the hall, the hubbub is not unlike that in a college cafeteria. Early arrivals may squat in a corridor and pull out a pack of cards to pass the time; two buddies sit on the steps and talk low-voiced about what they will do when they get out. When the food is ready, they troop in to eat.

A TYPICAL dinner consists of liver, turnips, string beans, as much bread as a man can eat, and coffee. In the mess hall there is no rush, no bell-ringing. Some loners sit and eat, staring straight before them; others join friends at the long eating benches and continue their conversations. Over all is the generally cheerful hum of talk and the rattling of utensils, and one wonders at a scene that contrasts so sharply with the silence and the tension during the two-day, mid-November sit-in strike. What could have caused that novel demonstration?

The genesis of the disturbance, officials tell you, lay in a particularly shocking crime and its aftermath. On June 30, 1960, Frederick Charles Wood, 50, a drifter with violent crimes in his past and a recent parolee, struck up an acquaintance with two men in Astoria,

L. I. They took him home with them to their basement apartment and there Wood, as he later confessed, bludgeoned them to death. The savage nature of the crime and the fact that Wood had only recently been paroled led to a public outcry over the parole system. Governor Rockefeller ordered more stringent psychiatric tests for prisoners about to be released.

THE effect of the Wood case was far-reaching. In prisons throughout the state, inmates began to notice, so they contend, that the State Parole Board was adopting a harsher attitude. The board denies this but some independent prison experts believe, as the prisoners believe, that there was a natural tendency to tighten up on parole. To inmates in the state prisons it appeared that a man's "good time" was doing him no good at all.

"Good time" for most prisoners nourishes the wellsprings of hope. It is the time by which, through his own good conduct, a prisoner may reduce his minimum sentence. Good behavior earns a man ten days "good time" a month, a reduction of one-third of his minimum sentence. So a prisoner facing a three-to-six-year term would be able to appear before the parole board for possible release at the end of two years.

Release then is not, of course, automatic. The parole board must consider many other factors affecting the prisoner's future—the environment to which he is returning, for example, and his prospects for an honest job. Technically, all that "good time" does is to guarantee prisoners the right to appear before the parole board earlier than they otherwise could; it has never been a guarantee of release.

BUT prisoners turned down by the board in the aftermath of the Wood case felt that they were being deprived of the "good time" they had "earned." Their "good time" was no longer winning them earlier parole and, once it fails to do this, it becomes, to the prisoner, virtually worthless. It has no effect on his maximum sentence, but prisoners felt that it should have. They began to agitate for a change in parole regulations (not altered in twenty years) so that

the "good time" a man earns in prison can be used to reduce his maximum sentence. This was the point that the prisoners of Sing Sing sought to make by their sit-in protest. This is the issue that the State Legislature is expected to study this year.

It is an issue that is submerged now, part of the prison's routine. In the afternoons of this routine some men go back to the shops. Others may meet and talk with relatives in the prison's visiting room. Athletes go to the gymnasium and spend hours running and drilling on the basketball court; they work themselves into such good shape that the Sing Sing five usually runs its opponents ragged by the end of the first half.

The day's work ends at 3:30. This gives the men more than an hour of relative freedom before the supper whistle sounds at 4:40. During that time a prisoner can play shuffleboard or cards, visit the commissary and buy a pie or write a letter to his family.

WITH the evening meal, the day ends. After supper, the men file from the mess hall directly to their cell blocks and are locked in for the night. Each cell is equipped with a set of radio headphones tuned into programs sent over the prison circuit from the radio shack. A prisoner may read one of the well-thumbed volumes from the prison library, which circulates about 35,000 volumes a year. Or he may work, as many inmates do, on a correspondence course to improve his chances of making a livelihood when he gets out. On special nights he can join the crowd in the gymnasium to cheer on the basketball team and every Saturday night he can see a first-run movie in the prison auditorium. Lights go out at 10 o'clock.

This routine does not vary greatly for any of Sing Sing's inmates. The prison has two minimum security and two maximum security cell blocks, plus a segregation wing. The five-tiered maximum security cell blocks rise from the center of the floor, like a building built inside a building, so that even should a prisoner break out of his cell he would still be confined.

The minimum security cells are built against the outside

walls and have windows, so are much more airy, bright and pleasant.

IN the segregation wing the cells are the same and the food is the same (there are no dark holes and bread-and-water routines at Sing Sing) but a man's movements are restricted. He is kept locked in his cubicle, isolated from his fellows. He cannot go to the movies or to the commissary and he gets only brief periods of exercise in special, fenced-in pens.

By all visible evidence, the segregation wing at Sing Sing is one of the least populated areas of the prison. Many cells stand empty. "Usually, we have no more than a dozen or so here," a guard says. "Once we got down to three. If we had any less, we'd have to do the cleaning work ourselves."

The weekly disciplinary reports bear out the impression one gets from visiting the prison—that the sit-in strike of last November has left no major morale problems at Sing Sing. In one typical week there were only five infractions of prison rules; in the previous week, only nine. Most were minor offenses and were punished by mere reprimands. One man was reprimanded for failing properly to clean the washroom; another for not reporting promptly to his work location; a third for having a contraband article in his cell.

AMONG the more serious offenses, a man who had been in a fist fight was penalized fifteen days "good time" and lost in addition fifteen more days of a suspended sentence for a previous offense. Another who had left work early to go to the movies received ten days suspended. So did a prisoner who had created a disturbance by trying to shove his way into the mess-hall line ahead of those already waiting.

But in three weeks of reports there was only one case of serious, outright rebellion against prison discipline. This involved an inmate who had been compelled to serve out his maximum time and was scheduled for release within a month. He suddenly rebelled at an officer's order and, in the words of the prison report, "refused to perform

duties in the presence of other men who obeyed." He ignored the officer and stalked off the work gang.

Warden Denno promptly revoked all his privileges and placed him in segregation for the remainder of his brief stay at the prison. "What else could you do?" he asks. "There was no other way to punish him."

But the warden feels that this case of sudden, bitter rebellion is typical of what happens when prisoners are deprived of the benefits of "good time" and are compelled to serve out their maximum sentences to the last day. In such cases, they become increasingly resentful. It is a situation, Warden Denno believes, that means trouble inside a prison while such men are confined there, and trouble outside when they are released.

"Once you take away a man's hope, you make a bitter man," Warden Denno says. "This is not mollycoddling, but there must be fairness. The incentive must be there."

What happens then, one inevitably asks, in the case of lifers? What hope have they? Are they bad actors?

"Definitely not," says Louis J. Kelley, Warden Denno's righthand man. "Lifers are usually the best-behaved men in the prison. They know they have to be if they are ever to have any hope of getting out."

EVEN a lifer, Kelley points out, hopes. He hopes for executive clemency; he hopes to discover some legal flaw that may enable him to reopen his case and reduce his sentence. These things sometimes happen, but they can happen only to a lifer who hasn't a blemish on his record. Sing Sing's most perfect prisoner, Kelley says, is a lifer who has been there nearly thirty years and hasn't received a single demerit. He still hopes.

A prisoner has to hope. And that is the crux of the problem the Legislature will be asked to study—the problem of using "good time" as incentive time, the problem of punishing and yet of avoiding the deprivation of hope that can only serve to make an imprisoned man more desperate, more vengeful and a greater menace to society.

March 4, 196

BLACK MUSLIM GIVES TESTIMONY IN COURT

BUFFALO, Oct. 23 (AP)—An inmate of Attica State Prison testified in United States District Court today he had been put in solitary confinement for telling another prisoner Christ "did not die upon the cross."

The prisoner, Thomas R. Bratcher, 30 years old, a member of the Black Muslim movement, said he also had been put in solitary when he tried to file a formal complaint charging segregation in the prison sports program and in the prison barbershop.

Bratcher is one of five Attica inmates who have charged in a civil-rights suit that the state ban on Black Muslim religious services at its prisons is unconstitutional. The trial began its second week today.

The prisoner told Judge John O. Henderson he was ordered into solitary confinement in November, 1961, for making "blasphemous remarks" to another prisoner within hearing of a guard.

He said he had told the prisoner "that Jesus Christ was a prophet of Allah and did not die upon the cross."

The state has said the movement is based on hate and is not a religion. State attorneys contend that Black Muslim religious services at state prisons could lead to rioting.

Alcatraz, Which Held Tough Ones, Closes as Prison

By WALLACE TURNER
Special to The New York Times.

SAN FRANCISCO, March 21 — The Federal prison on Alcatraz Island became a hollow, echoing shell today with the removal of the last 27 prisoners. After nearly 29 years in the Federal prison system and 54 years of exposure, Alcatraz has almost succumbed to the salt air that blows through the Golden Gate. The main building was built as an Army prison in 1909, then converted to a Federal prison on June 19, 1934. Great flakes of rust fell away from steel reinforcements in the basement today as Fred T. Wilkinson, associate director of the Federal Bureau of Prisons, brushed his hand across them to show their condition. Wide cracks have appeared in the concrete tiers that pass through the brick walls beneath the prison. The walls are from a fort built on the island in the 18th century. The concrete itself is badly decomposed. Since the renovation would cost more than $5,000,000, Federal officials decided last year to close Alcatraz.

The prison was the most expensive of any operated by the Federal Government. It cost $13 a day to keep a prisoner there, compared with about $5.40 a day average through the other prisons.

Further, the prison had survived by many years the immense public relations value it had during the Federal Government's expansion of its law enforcement activities in the Nineteen Thirties when the bank robbery gangs were broken up and such criminals as Al Capone were held in Alcatraz.

Today's removal of the last prisoners was not announced until midway through a mass tour for newsmen. About 60 photographers, reporters and cameramen were shown around the place, and the remaining prisoners were held during those few remaining hours in a room in the basement of the cell house.

After the tour was ended, the prisoners were led to a launch, taken to the Alcatraz dock in a slip at Fort Nathan at the tip of the San Francisco peninsular. They were taken by air today to prisons at Atlanta, Leavenworth, Kan., McNeil's Island Wash., and Lewisburg, Pa.

When the launch had cleared the slip on the island, the guard whose station was in a tower overlooking the slip came down. Alcatraz was no longer a prison. Families of the guards stood on the balconies of an old apartment building and watched. Some of the women appeared to be wiping tears from their eyes.

Tomorrow the cell house will be open to the inspection of wives and children of guards. There are wives of guards who have lived 28 years on the island, seeing their husbands off to work every day but yet never able to see the inside of the prison.

There have been only about 1,550 different men imprisoned on Alcatraz, although the individual prison numbers run up to 1,576. The difference is that some men have been there twice and have received new numbers. One man, Blakie Audette, who robbed banks, was the holder of three Alcatraz numbers. He wrote a book called "Rap Sheet."

In addition to Capone, the island has held many other notorious criminals such as Alvin Karpis, a kidnapper and bank robber; George R. (Machine Gun) Kelly, a bootlegger and kidnapper; Basil (The Owl) Banghart, an escape expert; and more recently, Mickey Cohen, a Los Angeles underworld figure, and Frankie Carbo, a shadowy figure in the sports world.

For the last two decades the prison has been used as a place to tuck away those Federal convicts who were too difficult to keep in other prisons. Almost all the Alcatraz prisoners are known personally to the top officials of the Federal prison system since a man was sent there only after a thorough review of his case.

Frequently various of the states have asked the Federal Government to lodge state prisoners at Alcatraz for the state penitentiaries have been unable to cope with them.

The last prisoner off the Rock today was one of these. He is Frank G. Weatherman, 29 years old, who was serving 10 years for armed robbery in Anchorage, Alaska, when he was caught trying to smuggle guns into the prison. The state of Alaska paid the Federal Government $13 a day to keep him since he arrived last Dec. 14. The payment will go down now that he is in a more economical prison elsewhere in the Federal system.

Although there were no echoes of it today except in minds and memory, Alcatraz has upon occasion been a place of great violence. It has always been called escape proof, and Federal officials still insist that death by drowning overtook those prisoners who broke out and were never heard from again.

But last December John Paul Scott, 35 years old, reached the shore alive, having floated on an improvised life jacket made of inflated plastic bags. He came ashore weak and exhausted, unable to move, on rocks beneath the southern end of the Golden Gate Bridge. But he made it. He has seen the last of Alcatraz for he now is in the San Francisco jail awaiting trial on a charge of escaping custody.

PRISON IS BUILT WITH FREE LOOK

New Federal Penitentiary Has No Bars or Walls

MARION, Ill., Nov. 16 (AP) —When the newest federal prison opens in April, its 600 inmates will not look out through bars at massive stone walls. There are none.

But the inmates, some of them problem prisoners, will be closely supervised.

The penitentiary, first major construction by the Federal Bureau of Prisons in 24 years, is about 10 miles from this one-time southern Illinois mining town.

Federal officials dislike the name of "Midwest Alcatraz" that some people have given the prison.

"This is not going to be anything like Alcatraz," says Warden John T. Willingham. "The concept of locking up a problem prisoner and forgetting about him is not a policy of the Bureau of Prisons."

When the Government closed Alcatraz, the somber stone institution in San Francisco Bay, last July, its inmates were transferred to other maximum security penitentiaries, such as Leavenworth and Atlanta. Some may come to Marion.

"But it won't be because they once were held at Alcatraz." Mr. Willingham says. "It will be because they proved to be a problem elsewhere."

Why would they be transferred to such an unlikely looking prison as this? Mainly because of a new Government outlook on prisons.

The Marion penitentiary has no walls, just a 30-foot double-chain fence enclosure with barbed wire at the top. Six 60-foot gun towers add to security.

Cell windows do not have the usual barred appearance, but they will not be easy to get through. With the appearance of simple louvered windows, they contain carbon steel believed to be saw-proof.

"There won't be guards, as such, on the premises, or off," the warden says. "Our staff will have to be able to do more than manhandle convicts. Some will work in the vocational training units and some will be classroom teachers."

The prison is more secure than a first glance would indicate.

Between each of the two fences, spaced 12 feet apart, are several inches of white crushed limestone. It will be used as a reflector for powerful floodlights at night and, should anyone get over the fences, for tracking purposes. Concrete, 48 inches deep, anchors both fences.

Mercury vapor lights will illuminate the huge yard at night, making it bright as day.

Mr. Willingham endorsed the fence, against the traditional wall, for economic and security reasons.

"A wall would have cost $1.2 million," he says. "The fence cost $200,000. You can pull down a fence for expansion purposes much easier and cheaper than you can a wall.

"But aside from that, a fence system has two major security advantages: It doesn't permit a false sense of security to officers that a wall might, and no one can hide in its shadows. Besides, we'll probably be getting the kind of prisoner here that we call 'management problems,' rather than escape artists."

The prison, a $12-million project, occupies a 50-acre section on a 1,000-acre Government tract.

"The purpose of this institution," Warden Willingham says, "is to take men from other institutions, expose them to our system and treatment, and then return them to their original prisons. We will try to see if a man can be more able to cope with his problems when he is released to the outside, than when he came here."

November 17, 1963

The Prison 'Culture' —From the Inside

By M. ARC

FOR 23 months I was a prisoner in a Federal Correctional Institution. Along with 650 other men. I wore a blue uniform, worked at a prison job (in the kitchen office), dreamed of freedom. I shared the prisoners' myths and rituals, learned their language and found my place in an intricate social maze.

But, unlike the others, I took part in prison life with some objectivity. I am an anthropologist (convicted in a security matter), and as far as I know the first member of my profession to study a prison culture from the inside. My scientific colleagues would call me a "participant-observer." The United States Bureau of Prisons called me an inmate. I served in both capacities, of course, on an involuntary field trip among an isolated tribe of fellow human beings.

My habitat was one of the more progressive institutions in our prison system, located a few miles from a small town in the East. This was no Hollywood Big House with towering gray walls and searchlights that pierced the night. Trees and flower beds brightened the yard. The windows were not barred, but had unobtrusive steel frames. Instead of numbered cell blocks, we lived in "houses" named after a city or state in the East. Individual cells were "private rooms," and as residents in a minimum security prison our doors were usually unlocked except during a routine head count or at night. There was a reasonably well-stocked library, a school that offered courses leading to a high school diploma, and a cafeteria with piped-in music.

The adequate living conditions reflected more than the humane approach of the Prison Bureau. Our institution was "correctional," not "penal," a distinction that emphasized the goal of rehabilitating the criminal offender, not merely punishing him. The physical setting was intended to nurture self-respect, social responsibility and hope. Guided by a psychologically skilled and tolerant prison administration, the inmate would be prepared for his ultimate return to society as a "respectable citizen."

An excellent theory, but it did not work. Most of the prison personnel go through the motions of accepting the concept of rehabilitation because it is the professed policy of Federal experts, but in daily practice they act on the stereotype of the cunning, lying, thieving "habitual criminal." On the whole, they think of prison jobs as a means of punishment and a source of cheap labor, not as a way to develop vocational skills and good work habits.

For example, a key element in the rehabilitation process is the Classification Committee, which is supposed to assign living quarters and jobs according to the prisoner's social and economic needs, his talents and interests. In reality, the committee considers simply the current manpower shortage in a particular department, and how much hardship the prisoner deserves in view of his attitudes toward authority. Accordingly, aged Dr. S., in the terminal stage of a chronic disease, was assigned to sorting dirty socks in the laundry. Little Joe, an expert in passing checks and a drug addict, was given a job in the hospital. The Professor applied his educational experience in the kitchen while former bookmakers worked in the library and the Department of Education.

By scarcely concealing their distrust and contempt for inmates, prison guards and administrators soon erase any reforms that the system might produce. The officials are expected to develop a relationship with inmates based on trust and respect, without endangering discipline and order, but since the staff does not really believe in rehabilitation the inmates react with understandable cynicism. Thus do the enemy camps coexist in an atmosphere of mutual fear and hostility.

The climate spawns two characteristics of prison culture that often confuse an outsider: the appearance of conformity within the official system, and an underground pattern of nonconformity by which the individual inmate tries to live by his own code, preserving as best he can his personal preferences and habits. This response to rules and regulations is another example of human ability to adapt to a new environment and transform oppressive circumstances into a tolerable existence.

The newcomer's introduction to prison life goes on for several weeks during an orientation period. He lives in isolation from the prison population and hears lectures by various members of the administration, from the warden to the kitchen steward. He learns the rules of prison conduct and the penalties for transgressing them (such as being deprived of watching television or reduction in time off from his sentence). He learns that anything except food and shelter is a privilege which can be taken away for misconduct or lack of cooperation. Finally, he learns the Golden Rule of prison—"doing your own time"—complete dissociation from other inmates' problems, needs and interests.

Thus prepared, the initiate is released among the inmates; slowly and cautiously he discovers the fact and fiction of what he has been told.

THE myth of equality is among the first to be shattered. Just as in the outside world, the society of prisoners is composed of rich and poor, leaders and followers, "better men" and "bums," black and white, Jews, Italians, Irish and other ethnic groups —all participants in a complex web of prejudices and hostilities, friendships and alliances.

Though we were all identically dressed in blue uniforms, some of us had well-fitted coats, clean shirts and pressed pants, while others wore discolored and baggy garb, coats with missing buttons and torn pockets, footwear which had seen better days. In the dormitories some beds had thicker mattresses, ironed sheets and cleaner blankets. Although newspapers, books and magazines were available to everyone, some inmates managed to have the most recent best sellers and the latest periodicals.

What makes some prisoners more equal than others? How do some inmates acquire "luxuries," while others receive only the scant necessities? The key to the puzzle is the "connection," a magic substance that can be as intangible as having status, or as real as a package of cigarettes.

Among the ways to be a "somebody," recognized occasionally even by the prison staff, is reputation. Big Joe has prestige simply because he has a venerable career as a lawbreaker. Murph the Bookie is a millionaire. Max is a "real lawyer who got into trouble." Fat Leo has status by association; he knows "the right people," including Big Joe, Murph and Max. Many reputations were established by the news media. To have made the newspapers or television is a mark of distinction that convicts share with politicians and performing artists.

Occasionally, a reputation can be a nuisance. When a guard discovered a crudely jimmied lock on the warehouse door, the obvious suspect was Franks and Beans, a former safecracker. The fellow was indignant. "It's a sloppy, non-professional job," he said. "I could open any lock in the joint without a trace just by using a nail clipper." Thereupon Franks and Beans demonstrated his skill and—he thought—his innocence, by effortlessly opening several locks in the presence of the lieutenant and captain of the guards and the embarrassed prison locksmith. Nevertheless, he suffered the usual consequences of being a suspect. He was sentenced to two weeks in "segregation," a locked, completely isolated cell with minimum physical comforts.

But the troubles of Franks and Beans were not over. A few weeks later, after all the locks had been replaced with an improved design, the kitchen steward called upon his expert talent to open the lock on the bakery door, which the new key did not fit. Against his better judgment, Franks and Beans helped out the steward and used his nail clipper to open the door. Word of the "crime" filtered back to the guards, and the good Samaritan got another stretch in segregation.

ANOTHER avenue to status is a prison job that offers access to things ordinarily beyond the reach of the average inmate. The Old Greek works in the hospital and can provide his friends with extra vitamins, aspirin or sleeping pills. Johnny, the kitchen clerk, knows the cafeteria menus 10 days in advance, an eagerly sought piece of news because, in the monotony of prison, food assumes a vital importance. The library clerk can save the latest novel or magazine, and a mailroom worker knows whether your letter was withheld by the prison censor.

Such favors are exchanged as simple expressions of friendship or as signs of respect toward men with status. In either case it is considered poor taste to expect compensation for a favor; feelings of gratitude and obligation are sufficient. The same services, however, if they are not offered as favors, have a specific market value in the unique "cigarette economy" of prison life.

Prisoners are allowed to spend up to $15 a month, which some of them may earn by their work. But the money is credited to a commissary account and actual cash never changes hands. The unit of underground currency is the cigarette, the most desirable commodity in prison, which determines poverty and wealth. Everyone is entitled to buy two cartons a week, but there are enough nonsmokers or light smokers who use their weekly ration for various transactions with heavy smokers. Two packs of cigarettes will buy a shoe shine or a pressing for a pair of pants; for four or five packages a week the bed will be made every morning. A carton is the price of a new peajacket from the clothing room.

447

Doing favors for free or for cigarettes is strictly prohibited and the penalties are severe. I never heard of a guard being bribed. When the offender is caught the prison code dictates that he take his punishment "like a man" and keep his mouth shut, even when wrongly accused.

Albie, the prison butcher, had an almost neurotic compulsion for storing food and feeding people, a weakness he attributed to his hungry childhood during the Depression. One day Albie decided to feed the inmates chicken salad sandwiches instead of the usual leftovers of luncheon meat. He hid a package of boiled chicken in a filing cabinet, assuming that during the routine "shakedown" search the custodial officer would not examine the cabinet. Unfortunately, the package was discovered by a department head who happened to be looking for a file of papers.

Albie was not suspected. Instead, officials accused the office clerk, a young man with a history of getting into trouble, and brought him to trial before the "captain's court."

One of the peculiar characteristics of this court (euphemistically called "the adjustment council" in official language) is that the accused inmate hardly has a chance of winning his case. If he denies the charge, he is automatically punished for implying that the accusing officer is not telling the truth ("officers never lie, inmates always do"); if he admits guilt he is punished for breaking the prison laws.

The "court" found the clerk guilty and placed him in segregation. Albie was disturbed by the miscarriage of justice and confessed. But the guard lieutenant at first refused to accept the confession, suspecting some "dirty deal." Finally, the officer acted with Solomon's wisdom: Albie was clapped in segregation but the clerk was not released. Since the lieutenant was not certain who actually stole the chicken, it was better to punish both men rather than free the guilty one. It was a bitter lesson in the old prison principle: "Truth does not pay."

INMATES select their friends from among equals and associate very little with their social inferiors or betters. They wait for each other at mealtimes, stand in line together, and choose their own table. It is poor manners to join a table without an explicit invitation. Everybody knows that the "jail house lawyer" eats with the librarian, the "professor," and the "real lawyer." Two income tax dodgers have their meals with an ex-stockbroker. The cliques are not surprising. As in any society, common interests, intellectual affinity and mutual sympathy form the basis for social ties and friendships.

When inmates discuss the "better people" they usually describe them as "men" and "gentlemen" — connoting the highest praise. Giovanni is a real "gentleman." He is reputed to be a wealthy man. He is friendly but distant, ready to do a favor, never gets into trouble, has two or three friends among the "better people." Giovanni is heard attentively when he expresses an opinion on the latest prison rumors, decisions of the United States Supreme Court or a current trial in the Southern District.

"Don't waste your time in jail by talking with your friends only about sex and broads. Listen to men who can teach you something useful." This was the advice an old-timer gave a young offender. In many ways the influence of people like Giovanni upon the younger crowd is rather constructive. I saw several youngsters whom he taught good manners and advised to get a legitimate job when they were released from jail.

At the opposite end of the social scale from "gentlemen" are the lowest of the low—the homosexuals. The traditional American intolerance toward sex deviation is increased to fantastic proportions in this atmosphere of tension and sexual deprivation. Inmates with a homosexual record are segregated from the rest of the prison population in a special house within single, barred cells like cages where they can be observed day and night by the officer on duty. Other inmates treat them like lepers. Newcomers are often labeled as homosexuals by other prisoners even though they are not so identified by the administration or lodged in special quarters.

Speech mannerisms, posture, facial expressions are considered sufficient clues for identifying a new man as a "fag." Henceforth, he will be referred to as "she" and will be ostracized and victimized. Homosexuals are routinely accused of crimes against the prison code, such as stealing cigarettes, getting others into trouble and committing the contemptible crime of being a "rat," an administration informer.

There are, of course, a number of inmates who sexually use the homosexuals for "free" or for payment in cigarettes, but that does not change their attitude in public. Prison breeds homosexuality just as the outside society breeds prostitution; in both places the respectable citizen hides his guilt and shame by loudly condemning the practice, though sometimes indulging in it.

More conspicuous than the social distance between somebodies and nobodies is the chasm between races. Although the prison is officially integrated, the conflict between whites and Negroes seethes with prejudice, hatred, sexual stereotypes, and as much segregation as the prison will permit.

The rows of chairs in the auditorium are divided by a center aisle; on days when movies are shown Negroes voluntarily sit on the right side and whites on the left side of the aisle. In the "honor house" there is a "black" side and a "white" side. If either side is temporarily filled up the newcomer might be forced to take a bed in a hostile camp. But as soon as a vacancy occurs he will tend to move in with his own kind, which may be not only whites or Negroes but Jews, Italians or Puerto Ricans who also usually cluster together with their beds side by side.

LOYALTIES become increasingly intense and follow clear patterns. They begin with the general loyalty of inmates against the administration, then narrow to the prisoner's own race, to his ethnic group, to his friends, and finally, most intensely, to himself. Life in prison frequently requires the sacrifice of some loyalties to others, but the sacrifices must be made to survive in the highly rigid maze of conflicts, emotions, and unsatisfied needs.

No culture is complete without its myths and legends. Prison culture rejects the myths supplied by the administration — myths of justice, equality and rehabilitation. Inmates dream of the day when they will be back on the "street" and have a woman, a car, a soft bed or a "real steak with French fries."

There is the myth of a bill in Congress which will allow each prisoner additional "good time" deductible from his sentence, and many men spend their time calculating to the hour when they will be out if the bill is passed. There is the myth of a Parole Board reform that will inform the inmate of the reason for being denied parole; moreover, he will be able to appeal the adverse opinion. There is the myth that inmates will be allowed to spend a night with their wives "like in some places abroad." There are legends of heroic escapes, never recovered "loot," people who "beat the law." Finally, there is the dream of the "last big job" and a trip abroad, beyond the reach of the law where one will live without fear or worry.

In many ways, these hopes seem to contradict each other; they echo a desire for justice and respectability while wishing for more criminal success. The contradictions only reflect the average prisoner's state of mind. He is tired of the endless cops and robbers game. He is tired of fear and anxiety, of eventually being caught and incarcerated.

HOW to break this vicious cycle of crime and punishment? The question is as acute for the prisoner as for the penologist. Many times I heard the words, "It's the last time. I don't come back again." But neither the speaker, his friends, nor the administration believe it. "He'll be back," says the guard opening the gate. "He'll be back," repeat friends after shaking his hand and wishing him good luck. And, of course, sooner or later he *will* be back, another statistical unit in the tables of criminal repeaters despite the progress in penology, despite the theory of rehabilitation, despite the learned seminars on "What's Wrong With Our Prison System?"

And why shouldn't he be back? Prison offered only a system of punitive rules, a staff composed mostly of indifferent guards, and values formed by fear, anger and frustration. The inmate leaves prison totally unprepared to face a life of "respectability" in an inhospitable society.

Stigmatized by imprisonment, unable to cope with his social and economic problems, frequently without family and friends, he will sooner or later fall back on the old "connections" and "skills." Then, again behind bars, his experience enriched by the prison culture, he can dream anew of a time when his human dignity will be respected, and when the time spent in prison will lead to a meaningful change in life.

Working Their Way Through Jail

By GERTRUDE SAMUELS

SAN JOSE, Calif.

JAMIE JOHNSON, a 29-year-old Sioux Indian, rises at 6 o'clock, showers, dresses in a rough work shirt, blue jeans, work boots He makes his bed, breakfasts, clears away the dishes, dons a yellow construction helmet and, by 7:30, stands waiting in the road. A friend picks him up in his old Buick and they drive together to work, where they start promptly at 8 as $125-a-week machine operators for United Concrete Pipe Corporation.

Johnson works all over the yard, stacking, patching and repairing pipes. He operates a forklift. A tall, placid man with watchful eyes, he lunches on salami and ham sandwiches, milk and cake. The one indication that Johnson's status is different from his co-workers' comes when he smiles tolerantly at a friend's joke to "come out for a beer" after work. Johnson will not and cannot, and his co-workers know it. For Johnson is a prisoner of Santa Clara County's jail system, serving 60 days with a $200 fine for petty theft and driving without a license. At 4:30, he must reverse his schedule: ride back to jail, check in at the sheriff's office, return to barracks, shower and dress in prison blues.

Johnson is one of 94 prisoners (their real names are withheld) currently enrolled in a rehabilitation program known here as Work Furlough. Furlough is simple in theory and simple in practice. It allows selected groups of sentenced prisoners to leave jail daily to work at jobs in the community at standard wages and return to confinement after working hours.

Instead of serving "dead time" behind bars while his family goes on relief, Johnson is supporting his wife and four children, paying the county for room and board, meeting his union dues and paying off his fine. There is even something left over, after his personal expenses, which is being held in trust until his discharge. And when he comes out, he will have a job.

ONE of the oldest such programs in the country, Work Furlough in Santa Clara County is in its eighth year. Nearly 2,500 prisoners have taken part since its inception and this year there have been close to 450. Los Angeles County now has a similar scheme, as do agencies in at least 24 other states and many European countries, but the idea has made little headway in New York State. (Governor Rockefeller recently signed a bill to allow Family Court judges to send delinquent fathers in nonsupport cases to jail for parts of days and on weekends, thus permitting them to work, but its scope is limited to this particular class of offenders.)

The basic objective is to build a bridge, of self-respect and responsibility, between abnormal prison life and normal community living. As Louis Bergna, Santa Clara County's forceful young District Attorney, told me: "For years, the theory has been to stick the offender in jail and forget him—in short, to throw away all his responsibility to family and society. I think this program, by taking away only some of his rights, still gives the offender the chance to behave like a good citizen."

The brain behind Work Furlough is George K. Williams, the County Rehabilitation Officer, a civilian. But he could not have handled his job without the militant support of the sheriff's department, and notably of Capt. James Geary (who has a degree in sociology) and many judges. The County Board of Supervisors created his post back in 1954 to coordinate a program of rehabilitation among prisoners in the county jail and farm. A Navy lieutenant commander with degrees from Oregon, Stanford and Pennsylvania Universities, Williams, then 34, had worked with German prisoners of war, trying to de-Nazify them and change their attitudes. Now the sheriff virtually told him, "Go out and rehabilitate my prisoners."

AT first, Williams devised a traditional program of counseling, education and recreation, but was dissatisfied with the results. He was working with able-bodied men who remained idle while their families went on relief. He read about Wisconsin's so-called Huber Plan where, as far back as 1914, legislation had given local judges the power to sentence selected offenders to jail, but to "furlough" them during the day to jobs in local businesses. Williams studied that program with growing enthusiasm.

This, he felt, was something that had a concrete value: money saved, for taxpayers and offenders; families supported; individuals on their way to self-respect.

Williams launched his experiment with 26 prisoners. There was uneasiness in some courts and in the community. Yet six months later, in June, 1957, under the impetus of the experiment, the California State Legislature enacted the Work Furlough Rehabilitation Law (Section 1208 of the Penal Code). An enabling act gave the county the option of appointing as its administrator either the sheriff or the Adult Probation Officer. The sheriff was appointed, but he assigned Williams to administer the program. In the next seven years, Williams expanded and refined it, until by February, 1965, 2,373 prisoners had been furloughees.

SANTA CLARA COUNTY, with a population of 850,000, lies some 30 miles south of San Francisco in a valley of rich orchards and big industry. And although visitors are reminded that Work Furlough is strictly an extension of jail, the atmosphere at Elmwood Rehabilitation Center, where furloughees are in custody, is anything but that of a jail.

Situated on 200 acres, a few miles from the county seat of San Jose, with spectacular views of the Santa Cruz and the Sierra Madre Mountains, the jail is a compound of sparkling white, Spanish style buildings and low, modern structures with walks shaded by palms and pines. Prisoners on their way to the library and dormitories pass by peacocks who live on the grounds. Throughout the nation, jails are demoralizing and negative institutions; this ranch — as the inmates call it — is certainly designed to encourage their aspirations.

Elmwood Rehabilitation Center is a special kind of open prison—an honor camp. There are no cells. There are guards, but they are not armed; there are no guns and no watchtower. There are security precautions — head count, bed check — but they are not designed to prevent escapes. The gates are wide open. There is a cyclone fence around the compound, but, officials say, only to keep the curious out and not the prisoners in. The prisoners can, in effect, walk out any time they choose, but few have escaped (under 1 per cent).

Men selected for the center are carefully screened on the basis of their past arrest record and performance in custody. The total prison population varies from 500 to 600 men, and all must work at something on or off the grounds — flood-control projects, maintenance of public parks and buildings, raising vegetables for county institutions, etc.

The élite of the population are the furloughees. They live apart from the other prisoners, in their own two dormitories. Of the 94 men currently in the furlough plan, all but a handful are white, about a third of them Mexican-Indians. The rest are Negroes and Indians. Their offenses include armed robbery, burglary, grand theft, forgery, assaults, drunk-driving and non-support. Those convicted of narcotics offenses are not usually acceptable as they are considered too unreliable.

Most prisoners are anxious to go out on a paying job, although with budget limitations, only 18 to 20 per cent are accepted. The selection process is flexible and realistic. The prime goal is to rule out prisoners of "dubious stability" or poor security risks.

The majority of furloughees are misdemeanants serving short terms (30 to 90 days). But felons, including several sentenced for manslaughter, have also been placed by county courts in the program. Each case is judged on its merits.

The screening process by rehabilitation officials includes personal interviews, an evaluation of the whole "criminal profile," including the offender's past arrest record, evaluation of family and job status, psychological tests.

If approved by the rehabilitation staff, the case goes to the sentencing court, with a request for modification of sentence to admit the prisoner for Work Furlough. Often at this stage, the judge wants the prospective furloughee back in court; he feels it is more meaningful if the man in black robes actually sentences the offender to the program.

Over the years, the furlough office has developed lists of firms and farms which take furloughees. Williams has found that for the employed man who lands in jail and is qualified for furlough it is desirable, monetarily and psychologically, to get him back on the job, earning the same salary, as soon as possible. Thus, when Jamie Johnson's employer was told how Work Furlough operates, he said he would hold Johnson's job for him. Within 10 days of his sentence, Johnson drew his first week's pay as a furloughee.

Men who are jobless can, through family, friends or attorneys, secure job interviews and a rehabilitation officer will transport them to prospective employers or otherwise help in securing them jobs. If a furloughee is a member in good standing of a union, he is allowed to go unescorted to the union hiring hall in San Jose to seek or be placed in a job—another radical advance in penology.

No training is done at the ranch. Williams and his staff help the unskilled find "stoop labor" jobs — gathering harvests, pruning, weeding on farms. To help a furloughee begin work, a loan of up to $20 may be made to him by the ranch to pay for work clothes, tools and transportation to work. The loan is repaid out of his first pay check.

The wages he earns must go (by weekly check) to the furloughee administrator who keeps account sheets for each worker. The administrator makes disbursements—to the wife or parents; to satisfy debts or fines or restitution; to defray personal expenses. The furloughee is charged $3.50 a working day for room and board at the ranch. (Since it costs $3.56 daily for the ordinary prisoner, a furloughee in custody thus costs the county only 6 cents a day.)

For his part, the furloughee always carries with him a copy of his agreement with the furlough office, which contains the rules of conduct. Failure to obey them results in disciplinary action and removal from the program. He must wear civilian clothes on the job and is forbidden to go to taverns or to drink; to make unauthorized telephone calls or visits to his family. He must "go to and return directly from" work, and not return with purchases (to avoid contraband).

THE psychology behind the furlough system is to induce prisoners to accept the responsibility for their decisions—something quite different from the position of the man doing straight time, who is told when to get up, when to eat, when to work. But it is not too pleasant to put in a full day's work and then have to return to jail every evening.

In fact, about 15 per cent of furloughees are "busted" each year for infractions. One got drunk and visited his girl friend—and landed back in Santa Clara's maximum security jail. His employer said sadly: "It sure throws you off. He was one good worker, and I couldn't see how he could miss."

If a man is missing for only a few hours, it is considered an "escape" and, therefore, a felony. Since the program began, there have been 23 escapees — under 1 per cent. Most were found. Some went to state prison; others got extra time at the county jail.

But the average furloughee knows he is on his honor and is anxious to do his job and keep his job. Williams is always on the go between the courts, the district attorney and the places of employment, for one of his main concerns is his responsibility to the community. Spot checks are made on furloughees at work —and to interest employers in more jobs for candidates.

AT 45, George Williams is a husky (5 feet 11 inches, 170 pounds), hard-driving man, with graying hair, penetrating eyes and an incisive manner. A mutual respect between Williams and the furloughees is evident—as he mingles with them on the grounds or goes over their problems in his office—and this is rare in a prison setting. His three assistants, all college graduates, are also specialists.

"People are actually anxious to get our men," Williams says wryly, "because there's no absenteeism, and the men come to work well rested, well fed and without a hangover."

At United Concrete, Johnson comes off the forklift to tell Williams: "It's a real good program. If I were just in jail, I would have lost my job here. All my bills would have piled up and I would be ruined."

Out of the weekly $125 that he grosses, Johnson pays the county $17.50 room and board for five working days; sends $35 to his wife; satisfies his fine at $25 a week; pays the union $6.50 a month dues; retains $10 for personal expenses. The remainder, about

$20 after taxes, goes in his trust fund. When the fine is paid off, an extra $25 will go to his wife.

Johnson is the second furloughee placed by Williams in United Concrete. Bob Empey, the manager, tells Williams enthusiastically: "You're sure as heck saving money for the taxpayers with this program of yours. These men are good and willing workers. And actually"—he laughs—"we're safer with them than the average guy. We know where they are at night."

Williams says warmly: "Without employers like you, we obviously couldn't succeed with this program. We appreciate your cooperation."

ANOTHER furloughee is 18-year-old Harry Simms, an eager, gray-eyed youth with braces on his teeth. After committing a burglary, he had been thrown out by his father. The boy stole from a store where he was formerly employed: $75 in cash, a radio and a television set and a pickup truck valued at $1,200. All but $35 was recovered. The court sentenced him to 6 months but consented to his placement in Work Furlough because of his youth.

Bob Miller, a wholesale drapery manufacturer who was recently elected to the San Jose City Council, gave Simms a job of trust involving access to money. Simms earns $1.60 an hour. He says earnestly: "All these people went to a lot of trouble to get me in this program, and I owe something to them—to myself, too."

Out of his long experience with youths in trouble, Bob Miller told Williams: "A person will be very hesitant to violate a trust, not because he fears you but because he doesn't want to."

Not all sheriffs would agree. In fact, there is a good deal of antipathy to the idea in certain sheriffs' departments. When, for example, that remark was quoted to one deputy sheriff, he retorted, "That's garbage!"

"As a policeman, I think there should be punishment for a crime," he went on bitterly, "and I can't see putting felons, especially habitual felons, on a furlough program.

Punishment is the deterrent. A criminal belongs behind bars."

THE worth of the program is reflected partly in the statistics. Since February, 1957, the 2,373 furloughees (to February, 1965) achieved these earnings and savings to taxpayers:

Wages earned:	$1,212,780.35
Disbursements:	
Family support	$554,314.03
Fines paid	9,663.64
Room & Board	298,011.39
Personal Expenses	182,126.94
Misc. including trust funds	168,664.35
	$1,212,780.35

But the program must be measured in more than dollars. Captain Geary says: "If we can send them back holding up their heads, we can hope that there will be less possibility of their returning. Given the staff and facilities, I feel we could handle three or four times the number of men in this program."

Judge Robert Beresford, the senior judge of Municipal Court, who has sent many prisoners into Work Furlough, says: "I feel that this modern approach to penology should be more broadly used in the land. Policies should be designed so that on his release the offender should not be a threat to society or prepared to repeat his offenses."

SOME critics argue, however, that the offender who is given jail with a "work furlough" proviso would have been as good a candidate for straight probation and should not be in jail at all.

In reply, Williams says: "Many have already failed on probation. This is a compromise. It's less harsh than actual confinement, and yet a great deal more confining than simple probation. The courts are in a quandary sometimes. When you punish a man by putting him in jail, whom are you punishing? Him? Or his wife, his parents, his children?"

What deeply concerns Williams, Geary and many judges is the lack of scientific research on the rehabilitative effects of Work Furlough. Williams has applied to the National Institute of Mental Health in Washington for funds for this crucial research. He would enlist the aid of sociology professors in San

Jose State College to get the answers—"it may take years to find out"—to such questions as: What does Work Furlough do for the individual offender when he returns to society? Is the recidivist rate lower in this program than it is in conventional jails? Does it have a lasting effect on the individual's attitude toward society?

It is generally accepted that many thousands of prisoners do not need the expensive, close custody of prison cells and walled-in yards. Yet there persists the historic, punitive attitude toward social outcasts: judges, D.A.'s, custodial officials still fear the risks of new penological techniques. Then, too, the public must be educated to the advantages of the program. Many taxpayers believe in strict incarceration of lawbreakers (at least until it touches their own families) and employers hesitate to become involved in radical rehabilitation programs.

There are also practical problems: Furloughees mean casework, minimum custody away from the prison population (to ease security safeguards), and extensive bookkeeping facilities for their accounts — calling for additional staff and higher budgets.

MANY California counties now use Work Furlough, yet even Los Angeles, which leads the country in such penological reforms as work-and-education camps for delinquents, hesitated until last year to try the experiment. Now, after several months' trial with 70 prisoners, the program is so "operationally feasible and economically advantageous to Los Angeles County" that the chief probation officer has recommended a broader program for the coming year.

But New York still lags miserably behind. Our jails remain overcrowded with prisoners doing dead time. One official at Women's Prison in Manhattan told me, not long ago: "We teach our prisoners merely to be good inmates. By not giving them responsibilities and jobs in the community—to which they have to return—we defeat our own purposes."

That is what society forgets, or doesn't want to remember: that virtually all

prisoners return to the outside world. The real question is, should they be encouraged to come back with some degree of respect for themselves or with bitterness toward society?

San Jose's venerated poet, Edwin Markham ("The Man With the Hoe"), gives one answer in his famous quatrain:

He drew a circle that shut me out—
Heretic, rebel, a thing to flout.
But love and I had the wit to win:
We drew a circle that took him in!

Women Furloughees

About 100 women prisoners have entered the Work Furlough plan since it began. Mrs. Anne Morris, for example, a former cocktail waitress, is now an office worker. She is serving three months in jail and 2 years on probation for participating in "attempted abortion"—a felony. Married twice, with two small sons now living with her mother, she is, at 25, divorced, and supporting them while in custody.

When she leaves Women's Prison each day, she gives the turnkey her handbag, taking along only her makeup, a few dollars (for cigarettes, gas, coffee) and her car key (she drives her 1957 Mercury to work). Just before 9 o'clock, she opens the building-supplies office where she earns $50 a week. She handles the phones and files, carries deposits to the bank and says that she is "thrilled" with her first office job.

"If more employers would help people like me," she says feelingly, "instead of turning their backs on us, it would give us a better outlook on society. When you have a felony on your record, it makes a person go down altogether—unless someone shows that he has faith in you."—G.S.

U.S. JUDGE SCORES ISOLATION CELLS

Says Coast Prison Violated 'Concepts of Decency'

SAN FRANCISCO, Sept. 6 (UPI)—A Federal judge ruled today that so-called "strip cells" at a model California prison violated the United States Constitution and "elemental concepts of decency."

District Judge George B. Harris ordered the state to provide prisoners in the small concrete cells with a basin, water pitcher, towel, toothbrush, toothpaste, toilet tissue and an automatic toilet flusher.

"Strip cells" are solitary units in which prisoners are kept for terms of up to 29 days as a punishment.

The target of the judge's ruling was Soledad Prison near Monterey. His action stemmed from a petition filed by an inmate, Robert Jordan Jr., 27 years old of Los Angeles.

Jordan and 10 other prisoners had filed affidavits saying that they had been kept naked and without light, heat or ventilation in the 6-by-9-foot cells, which are sometimes called "black holes." The prison has six such cells.

Some of the prisoners also said they were not allowed to shower, given only two cups of water daily and confined in cells made filthy by the smearing of human waste on walls and floors by previous occupants.

The prisoners detailed the conditions in a two-week hearing called by Judge Harris on Jordan's petition. The judge also spent one day at the prison to listen to the inmates and to inspect the cells.

In his 20-page opinion, Judge Harris described Jordan's testimony as "clear and convincing" in spite of vigorous cross-examination. He said testimony by other prisoners also "contained the essentials of truth and are credible and convincing."

"When, as it appears in the case at bar, the responsible prison authorities in the use of the strip cells have abandoned elemental concepts of decency by permitting conditions to prevail of a shocking and debased nature," the judge wrote, "then the courts must intervene—and intervene promptly—to restore the primal rules of a civilized community in accord with the mandate of the Constitution of the United States.

"In the opinion of the court, [this] type of confinement . . .

San Quentin Guards Thwart a Race Riot By 2,000 Convicts

SAN QUENTIN, Calif., Jan. 18 (AP)—Quick action by prison guards averted today a threatened race riot by 2,000 whites and Negroes in the walled yard of San Quentin Prison.

Warden Lawrence Wilson said that a group of about 1,000 whites and Mexican-Americans had got to within about 50 feet of a slightly smaller group of Negroes but "we fired a lot of rounds of ammunition describing limits for people."

Mr. Wilson said that the convicts had been armed with pieces of pipe, wooden clubs, rocks and some used mess trays for shields.

"A racial clash has been averted," the associate warden, James W. L. Park, said after the guards fired 40 warning shots and then began herding prisoners into cells.

Fourteen prisoners were hurt, eight by gunfire, as guards fired more warning shots to control the restive inmates being moved back to the cells.

Prison officials said one inmate was wounded in the head and seven were hit around the legs, apparently by ricocheting bullets.

The threatened racial clash had been averted when close to 1,000 Negro prisoners were returned to cells, but sporadic gunfire continued as guards sought to control the white and Mexican-American inmates remaining in the yard.

The inmates burned benches in the compound as prison authorities made plans to move the men out of the 40-degree cold and back to cells 25 at a time.

Mr. Park attributed the crisis to "the activists' hoodlum element and maybe some Black Muslims."

White inmates were apparently angry about the fatal stabbing of a white prisoner Monday in a Black Muslim attempt to stop work, Mr. Park said.

Shortly before prison officials decided the racial crisis was past, at least for the night, Gov. Ronald Reagan in Sacramento ordered 260 highway patrol members rushed to the prison to stand outside the walls. He directed 200 more to stand by.

CONJUGAL VISITS IN PRISON HAILED

Mississippi System Credited With Saving of Marriages

Conjugal visits for married inmates of the Mississippi State Penitentiary have probably kept marriages intact and have probably bolstered morale, and reduced recidivism and homosexuality, according to an article in the June issue of the Criminal Law Bulletin.

The article, written by Columbus B. Hopper, associate professor of sociology at the University of Mississippi, reported that one unmarried prisoner had said that because of the conjugal visits "I have seen less rioting, less homosexuality, and an altogether different attitude in the inmates in general."

The penitentiary is the only one in the United States that officially allows such visiting.

On the visiting days, on the first and third Sundays in each month, a trustee, like the manager of a motel, gives keys and checkout times for each of the institution's 8 by 10 feet rooms set up for the purpose. The rooms furnished with beds, tables and mirrors, are situated in half a dozen small buildings scattered throughout the prison's 21,000 acres in Parchman, Miss.

Formerly the prison allowed inmates to bring girl friends and wives into the prisoners' regular sleeping qarters. The prisoners were allowed to hang blankets around their beds for privacy. Later the institution allowed inmates to build separate units—and girl friends were barred.

Parchman has about 1,7000 inmates, about one-quarter of whom are allowed to use the little rooms. Women inmates are not allowed conjugal visits from husbands—in order to avoid pregnancies.

---

70 Deaths in Arkansas Prison Since 1936 Linked to Violence

By WALTER RUGABER
Special to The New York Times

GRADY Ark., Feb. 6—At least 70 of the 254 deaths reported at the Arkansas State Penitentiary since 1936 resulted from violence, an inspection of the prison records showed today.

Inmates were murdered, shot "accidentally" and during what were described as escape attempts, burned to death, poisoned, drowned, run over by farm wagons, and "accidentally" electrocuted. On separate occasions, two men were killed by a "falling tree."

Other deaths were attributed to "natural causes." A substantial number of prisoners, some of them teen-agers, died from "organic heart disease." Thirteen died of sunstroke, including four on a single day.

The prison records and penitentiary officials indicated that few of the deaths had been investigated by independent authorities from outside the penitentiary. Moreover, several officials have suggested that a number of deaths went unreported.

Thomas O. Murton, a new prison superintendent who began a reform effort early last month, said in an interview today it was a "reasonable assumption" that the available death records disguised some criminal activity.

Mr. Murton had earlier voiced concern that some inmates might have been slain and secretly buried on the grounds at Cummins Prison Farm near here. He discovered three skeletons in unmarked graves last week.

The state police began an investigation, apparently designed primarily to determine the nature of the burial ground. A police official asserted that it was merely a cemetery for paupers.

Some observers considered this a side issue, however. The main question, they believe, is not so much the nature of the graves but rather how the inmates buried there and elsewhere died.

The penitentiary's records are

---

sketchy in the extreme. An examination that covered records of about 25,000 inmates, conducted over several days by a reporter for The New York Times, generally found only the most cryptic death notices.

For example, the record of a 25-year-old Negro inmate who died in 1965 bore only the notation that he had been "shot four times with a 38-caliber revolver" in the barracks at Cummins.

Mr. Murton described the records that do exist as "cruddy," saying that he could think of only two plausible explanations for their condition. He listed the reasons as follows:

"One, a total lack of administrative skill. No one would keep records like they've been kept around here. The other thing, obviously, is that no one would record anything that would reflect negatively on the administration."

Despite the many mysteries involved, the prison death records suggest the pattern of ill-treatment and brutality reported by many inmates and sustained by the findings of several official investigations.

The records of inmates who entered the state's prison system after March 26, 1936, show that 254 have died either at Cummins or at Tucker Prison Farm, a smaller unit about 55 miles away.

The reporter examined 13 ledgers containing legal and personal data on inmates entering the state's penal system. When a death was noted in the ledgers the entire file was obtained for closer examination.

Calls Death Rate High.

Dr. Edwin N. Barron Jr., who now serves as the penitentiary physician, made the general assessment today that the death rate was "considerably higher than would be expected for a population of that size and age."

The prisons now hold about 1,500 men. The number has fluctuated somewhat, but it has remained about that number for several years. The median age is thought to be about 29.

The deaths of 23 inmates were attributed to escape attempts. A number of convicts have charged that guards and prison officials often killed men who had been returning to the farm and had raised their hands upon capture.

Seven deaths were reported as homicides. In several cases it was apparent that another convict had been charged with the crime, but in other instances it was not clear whether the murderers had been apprehended.

Killed by Horse Medicine

Three men were poisoned. One died when, for no specified reason, he drank a mixture called "Dr. Sylvester's antispasmodic medicine for flatulent and spasmodic colic in horses and mules."

Among the violent deaths of the 70 reported were twelve by drowning, five by suicide, two when "struck by lightning," and three by burning to death in unexplained accidents.

Vaguely described heart ailments were the leading cause

of nonviolent death at the prison. Two men died of "heart failure" and four others of a "heart attack." The most frequent listing was "organic heart disease."

The deaths of some 41 inmates were attributed to this cause, which Dr. Barron said was "a real, real broad classification" that would be "meaningless on a death certificate" without further explanation.

He noted that heart ailments had killed a number of inmates, some in their thirties and twenties, who had no record of such a problem. Also, he said, it seems that some medical "histories" were compiled after death.

Several Avenues Open

The prison records show that one dead youth had suffered from a "leaking heart." Dr. Barron said this notation seemed to have been made after the youth had died from "organic heart disease." He said no physician would have considered "leaking heart" a proper medical description.

These cursory but official notations of the 254 deaths would be one avenue of investigation, prison officials believed, but there are other ways in which additional deaths might have been covered up.

Mr. Murton said that slain inmates might have been listed as having "escaped." Or, he went on, they may have been killed and recorded as on "probation" or "indefinite furlough" to disguise their actual fate.

The records showed hundreds in these categories. In previous years, Mr. Murton said, peni-

tentiary superintendents were permitted to grant furloughs without consultation with the state penitentiary board or anyone else.

4 Dead of Sunstroke

Even the nonviolent deaths on record occasionaly revealed glimpses of the harsh life that has prevailed at the two prison farms. For example, four men died at Cummins on a single day, July 8, 1939.

Records of the United States Weather Bureau at Little Rock indicate that it was a broiling day with the temperature reaching 100 degrees in the afternoon. The four men were working in the fields.

One by one, they collapsed. The men, three Negroes and a white man, all died a few hours later of sunstroke, it was reported. Inmates have often described how they were forced to work in the sun from dawn to dusk. The white prisoner, a 23-year-old inmate named Jay V. Partin, had entered the penitentiary only a few weeks before his death. The sheriff in his home town had written a letter in his behalf.

"We had a young man sent down there about a week ago by the name of Jay V. Partin," the sheriff informed prison officials. "It will be very much appreciated for any favors that you may extend to this young man."

About six weeks before the inmate died in the fields, Superintendent Al Reed assured the sheriff that "at the first opportunity I shall look him [Partin] up and do what I think is best for him."

Revengers' Tragedy

By ROGER JELLINEK

THE CRIME OF PUNISHMENT. By Karl Menninger, M.D. 305 pages. Viking. $8.95.

LAW AND ORDER was an issue that Richard M. Nixon stressed in his campaign for the Presidency, and Nelson A. Rockefeller used a TV series on crime in his last campaign for the Governorship. The suppression of violence appears to be the touchstone of political success.

Strengthening the police, and so the number of convictions, will simply result in more crime, argues Dr. Karl Menninger in this thunderous plain-speaking indictment of traditional law enforcement. It is an angry book, for the famous psychiatrist, a founder of the pathbreaking Menninger Clinic and Foundation in Topeka, Kan., has been arguing what seems an obvious case for 40 years, to little effect. In one terrible example after another

Dr. Karl Menninger

he shows how the present system of arrest, prosecution and punishment of criminals is fantastic in its expense and its waste. The system is commonly justified on three counts: it penalizes the criminal, reforms him, and deters others like him. In practice, this is absurd. Perhaps only one in 10 crimes are even reported, recidivism is unconscionably high, and the crime rate is booming.

Why do we tolerate this obvious failure? Because, Dr. Menninger asserts, our penal system is fantastic in intention as well as in effect. Its purpose is not deterrence but primitive retaliation. We enjoy violence. We are fascinated by crime and punishment. Criminals are the scapegoats of our violent fantasies. A trial is a revenger's ritual, and with the criminal's conviction and sentence our guilt is resolved. He is sent to a *penitentiary*. At that point we lose interest.

Crimes Against Criminals

That point is Dr. Menninger's focus: the crimes against criminals. There are a few congenital criminals, and they must be isolated. But in most cases, he states, crime is a stage in mental illness, a regression into childish fantasy of destruction or self-destruction. Prison only reinforces childish regression by demanding total dependence and blind obedience, and by encouraging humiliation, brutality and sexual perversion. On release a prisoner is not fit for society; recidivism may be an escape from its responsibilities.

Fantasy is the self-defeating basis of both crime and criminal prosecution—but this is not irredeemable. The social sciences, says Dr. Menninger, offer laws of behavior by which we can understand "the vital balance" in the struggle between the individual and his environment. If there is an upset in the balance, it can be analyzed and compensated.

The obstacle to scientific solution to what Dr. Menninger calls "the social safety problem" is the legal system used to regulate it. For lawyers reason deductively, adapting solutions from precedents. Scientists reason inductively, acting on pragmatic experience. The law assumes that all men are either reasonable or insane; unconscious motives of mental illness are unacceptable in court without specific labels. So psychiatrists have testified against each other about unscientific labels such as "psychosis," "schizophrenia," and "responsibility," if not simple lunacy. Psychiatrists have themselves undermined their credibility by answering legalese with their own incomprehensible jargon.

Psychiatric Care Emphasized

The book proposes that criminal prosecution be limited to proving antisocial acts and demanding prompt penalties. Psychiatric opinion should be heard, not in the argument, but by the judge after the jury's verdict, to help him assess the circumstances of the crime before passing sentence. After sentence intense psychiatric care should be available to the prisoner-patient. Initially expensive, this would prove cheaper in the long run.

Dr. Menninger assumes that today's crimes and social disorders are a "psychological epidemic," the result of intolerable environmental pressure. "We have to find ways . . . to treat not hundreds but millions of patients." This solution seems as questionable as his confidence in the behavioral sciences—both are retrospective. Specific future acts cannot be predicted from behavioral "laws." As Dr. Menninger proves so searingly, criminals are surely ill and not evil. But in the "vital balance" between individuals and their environment, psychological adjustment sounds about as effective in establishing a healthy society as a rigorous application of law and order..

Role Playing: A Judge Is a Con, A Con Is a Judge

By RICHARD HAMMER

ANNAPOLIS, Md.

FOR nine days this summer, the grassy, groomed and venerable campus of St. John's College in Annapolis was the scene of a remarkable confrontation. The college kids and their professors were off on vacation, and the "great books"—the core of the St. John's curriculum—had been laid on the shelf. In place of the faculty and students were 21 convicts from three state prisons and about 100 lawyers and judges, prosecutors, policemen, prison officials and state legislators and some "interested citizens." Before the nine days ended, the participants had been enlightened and, in some cases, emotionally scarred by their experiment, a "Workshop in Crime and Correction."

This was anything but a gathering of dreamers and bleeding hearts concerned over the failures of the prison system. Those failures, of course, are beyond argument. The "correctional institutions," as they call themselves these days, neither correct nor rehabilitate; more than half, some say more than 70 per cent, of those released from the nation's prisons end up behind bars again, and what they usually learn behind those bars is how to make better "hits," how to be better burglars or bank robbers the next time they walk free. The nonprisoners at the workshop were not ignorant of these facts, but they lacked an appreciation of the personal and emotional realities behind the statistics. That appreciation was provided in psychodramas, seminars, all-night bull sessions and in hours spent as "inmates" themselves in three Maryland prisons.

The workshop had the best "establishment" credentials: It was financed with $67,000 from the Social and Rehabilitation Service of the Department of Health, Education and Welfare and was sponsored jointly by the Maryland Governor's Commission on Law Enforcement and the Administration of Justice and the National College of State Trial Judges, which claims the membership of more than 4,000 jurists in all 50 states.

Directing the conference were the Berkeley Associates, a consulting organization formed by three Californians whose experience in the prison system has left them disillusioned. They are: Dr. David Fogel of the University of California at Berkeley, a heavy-set, bearded, emotional sociologist who worked seven years in the Marin County jail system; Dr. Richard Korn, a U. of C. criminologist who resigned after three years as a psychologist at a New Jersey prison farm "when I found one night that I could lock up my assistant, a prisoner, in his cell and walk away without feeling anything," and Douglas Rigg, a public defender in Berkeley, a former associate warden at San Quentin who once resigned as the warden of a Minnesota state prison after his reform efforts led to charges that he was "coddling convicts."

GIVEN the workshop's credentials, the conference organizers found it easy enough to round up participants among the professionals. Finding the right convicts, however, was another matter. Berkeley Associates did not want a group hand-picked by prison administrators, but a representative sampling of both men and offenses. Above all, they sought the right to select the 21 convict participants themselves. Ultimately, they settled for a compromise: Prison officials chose a group of more than 100 inmates from which Berkeley Associates picked the 21 they wanted.

The convicts came from three institutions in Jessups, Md.—the Maryland House of Correction, a medium-security prison with a reputation as little more than a warehouse for men convicted of anything from nonsupport to murder and rape; the Maryland Correctional Camp Center, a minimum-security institution where some inmates are on a work-release program, and the Patuxent Institution, a maximum-security prison for "defective delinquents," all of them serving indeterminate sentences.

Some of the 21 men chosen for the workshop were serving terms as short as two years, others had been sentenced to "life plus"; some had been behind bars for only a year, others for 20 years or more. Their crimes ranged from possession of narcotics to burglary to rape and murder. One participant was even an alumnus of death row; his sentence had been commuted to life shortly before his date in the gas chamber.

As a group, the participants were not entirely representative of Maryland's 6,000 convicts. They were articulate and intelligent, with considerable insight into themselves and others. Most of them seemed to retain some hope for a future life beyond the walls. As the workshop progressed, however, it became evident that most of the participants from the outside world looked upon the con-sultants (as they called themselves) not as a select group but as a random sampling of the prison population. The effect of their words and actions during the conference was thus generalized—and magnified.

A TYPICAL day began at 8 A.M. as the convicts, dressed in casual sports clothes, arrived at St. John's by bus. More than one prisoner was amused at the thought of breakfasting with the judge who had sentenced him—a judge dressed in Bermuda shorts and a flowered shirt.

The business session usually opened with a speaker after breakfast, then a psychodrama, a brief play in which the magistrates and the miscreants were the cast, sometimes playing their real-life roles and sometimes trading roles. The scene was always one having to do with the judicial process: a disciplinary hearing for a policeman accused of having used abusive language; a grand jury session; a parole hearing; the arrival in prison of a new con. Fogel or Korn set the scene and the actors improvised as the plot developed. Members of the audience were allowed to interrupt if they thought the portrayals lacked realism.

Later in the day, the workshop broke up into seven groups for discussion and more psychodrama. After the prisoners had returned to their cells for the evening, the "outside" participants heard another speaker, then attended informal bull sessions that typically lasted until 4 or 5 A.M.

In the first days of the workshop, there was a tentative feeling, a sparring for openings, an evident wariness. The cops sat in a back row, isolated; the judges sat together; the cons sat in a group. A psychodrama about a policeman's being reprimanded for the use of a racial epithet produced only yawns and bored rustling.

What broke the conference open was a psychodrama on prison life. Fogel set the stage: The action was to be the arrival in prison of a new con, a first offender sentenced to four years for assault. To play the new con Fogel selected a young, blond correctional officer who looked indeed as though he could be in that position. The inmates who processed him into the prison were played by real cons. The only other roles in the play were two prison officials, a guard and a counselor, played by men whose real-life roles these were.

The drama began as "Scag," a black inmate who supposedly worked as a runner in the prison storeroom, led the new con, "Frank," from the storeroom, where he'd been issued prison clothes and other gear, to the tier where he would be locked into a cell.

SCAG: You know anybody here, anybody can help you?

FRANK (shaking his head): No, I don't know anybody.

SCAG: Not nobody at all?

FRANK: Nobody. I don't think I belong here.

SCAG (laughs): That's what everybody says. You know, you gonna need some protection.

FRANK: Protection? From what?

SCAG: Man, you is gonna be approached.

FRANK: What for?

SCAG: Man, I ain't got to tell you.

FRANK: Well, I don't want any part of it.

SCAG: You ain't got no choice.

FRANK: If they come to me, I'll fight.

SCAG (laughs): You can't fight three-four men at a time.

FRANK: What can I do?

SCAG: Man, you can avoid it.

FRANK: How?

FUZZ—A policeman gives his reaction to a prison visit. Said a legislator who was processed like a convict: "I can't tell you what this did to me spiritually. . . . What if I had known that I was to be locked in there for years?"

FELON—An inmate-participant in the workshop. "If you don't trust us at all inside," one con told a prison official, "you ain't going to trust us outside, and we know it, and you're going to have us right back with you."

SCAG: You can pick somebody to protect you. . . . You got any money?

FRANK: No. But I've got a ring and a watch.

Reaching the tier that contains Frank's cell, Scag holds a mumbled conference with Slim, a black inmate assigned as a runner in the tier.

SCAG: We got a new chicken here.

SLIM: Yeah, what we gonna do with him?

SCAG: I'll tell you. I'm gonna play his friend. You make

him think he's got to turn to me to protect him from you.

SLIM: Yeah, that's right, I'll scare him right to you and we'll split what he's got. Only don't do like you did the last time and hit me when you're protecting him.

SCAG: Don't worry, we'll play this cool.

As Scag leaves, Slim explains prison life to Frank, telling him that he can order once a week from the commissary and that he must come out of his cell immediately when the bell rings for a meal or an exercise period in the yard or he will be locked in again. Slim offers to give Frank a pack of cigarettes in exchange for two packs after Frank has received his order from the commissary. Then a bell rings and Slim patrols the tier, chanting, "Yard time. Yard time."

The scene shifts to the crowded prison yard, and when Frank appears there are whistles. "Say, man," says one con, "that's a real sweetie." Another yells: "Hey, baby, I think you need a protector." The action then moves back to the cell tier.

SLIM: Where you been?

FRANK: In the yard.

SLIM: How come you didn't tell me you was going?

FRANK: I did.

SLIM: Man, I says you didn't! You callin' me a liar?

FRANK: No. I thought. . . .

SLIM: Man, you want to go someplace, you tell me. Whenever you go someplace, you don't go without you let me know, dig?

FRANK: Why are you jumping all over me?

SLIM: Man, you is askin' for it. I gonna come in that cell with you and lock the door you don't watch out.

Scag suddenly appears, telling Slim to leave the new inmate alone. After Slim wanders off, Scag offers to take Frank into the yard during the next exercise period and walk around with him, explaining: "That'll let everybody know I'm protecting you." He says it will cost a carton of cigarettes a week.

Frank says he will think about it and stays in his cell during the next few exercise periods. A few days later, against Slim's urgent advice, he insists upon seeing an officer.

FRANK: It seems there are all these guys who want to be my buddies. They want to protect me. But they want cigarettes and they seem to want my watch and ring and shoes, too. And they seem to be able to do anything they want and nobody stops them.

GUARD: When did all this start? When did they approach you?

FRANK: As soon as I got in here.

GUARD: Can you identify them?

FRANK: I'm afraid. I don't want it to get back to them.

GUARD: Well, anytime you want to tell me anything, you just ask. I'll come. You just ask. We'll protect you.

FRANK: I'm scared to tell.

The realization that the guards cannot effectively protect him sends Frank back to Scag. At the next yard call, they go out together and Scag introduces Frank to other cons, among whom blacks outnumber whites by more than two to one.

FOGEL interrupted the action to ask several of the convicts what they were feeling as Frank was being introduced. Among the answers were these:

"I'm feeling that colored guys have all the goodies. I feel like they must feel out in the streets. I'm a minority in here, and I'd like a crack at that goody."

"I don't care what Scag or the rest of the black guys do as long as they don't touch my man."

"I've got a feeling of fear. I know what happens to young cons like him; it happened to me."

"He's a white boy, and I don't care what happens to him."

The action resumes in the office of a counselor with whom Frank has requested an interview.

FRANK: I've had some weird things happen since I came in here. There's a lot of

homosexuals running around loose and they all seem to be looking at me.

COUNSELOR: Well, what would you like us to do?

FRANK: I don't know. I think I'm more afraid of the inmates here than I am of the institution itself, and I thought it would be the other way.

COUNSELOR: What do they want?

FRANK: Everything I've got. My watch, my ring, my shoes, all my personal possessions. Can I send them home?

COUNSELOR: Yes. If you give them to me I can have them sent home for you.

FRANK: They want my tail, too.

COUNSELOR: I'm afraid I can't send that home. You want to tell me who these guys are who are doing these things to you?

FRANK: If I tell you, what will happen to me?

COUNSELOR: We'll try to protect you.

FRANK: How?

COUNSELOR (bursts out): I'll adopt you!. . . . Seriously, the only assurance I can give you is close supervision.

The psychodrama ended there, amid shouts and cries from the convicts in the audience. "Man, you can't give him no protection. He'll have boiling coffee thrown at him even if you lock him up in solitary," said one. "He ain't got no assurance. You think his only salvation is in protection and custody, but that won't work. Somebody'd get to him."

"Maybe you'd put him in B-3, where they keep all the sissies," said another con, "and then he'd be branded one, and he'd be branded a rat, too, and that wouldn't be no protection."

"There's a million ways to get to him," a third convict warned. "We'd be in contact with him and that would be that." Another added:

"Nothing anybody can do will make any difference because it's a jungle we live in. The only ones who can do anything for him or against him are the other inmates."

One of the prison administrators asked the actor who had played Slim, "Would you protect him for a guaranteed parole?"

Slim stared at him. "For a guaranteed parole? Man, I guess so."

Another con leaped up: "And who would protect Slim? Then who would protect the next guy and the next? You gonna let us all out on parole to protect this one guy?"

As more members of the workshop joined the discussion on prison life and its purposes, one inmate rose and asked: "What's rehabilitation? I've never seen it. We come in laborers and go out laborers. All we learn in here is how to make [license] tags, and there ain't no place outside where you can make tags. We're the same guy when we go out, and that's where it's at, baby."

THE psychodrama had shaken the workshop. For many in the audience—judges, policemen, lawyers and even some prison officials—it was the first good look at what goes on behind the walls and at criminals as real people. Save for the criminal himself, almost everyone's contact with the problems of crime, correction and justice is severely limited. The average citizen's only glimpse of crime occurs when he is a victim, and even then the contact is usually just the discovery that something is missing from his home or car; the policeman's contact with the criminal begins with the arrest, often a dangerous and charged confrontation, and ends at the station house or in the courtroom; the judge and attorneys see the criminal only when his behavior is circumscribed, when he is wearing a face that is often not his real one; prison officials see him only as a number, and parole officers only when he has finished his term and is again a free man.

The disclosures made in the psychodrama—of homosexuality, rackets, brutality and fear—therefore came as something of a shock to many. In the smaller sessions later in the day, emotions ran high and every suggestion brought sharp probing and searching questions.

A discussion of prison apprenticeship programs, for instance, remained optimistic until the convict participants gave their point of view. The training program in printing, they said, was limited to those serving sentences of at least 15 years; it was a five-year program, and—since parole is often granted when one-third of a man's term is served (though it is possible after one-fourth of the sentence)—men serving shorter terms might leave before their training was complete. Convicts sentenced to less than 15 years could enter the program only if they agreed to forgo parole until the training was over. Further, since the apprenticeship program was given only at the House of Correction, an inmate had to agree to remain there and not accept transfer to a minimum-security prison farm where he might be eligible for an occasional weekend home leave.

When prison officials complained that they did not have the money to buy some necessary equipment for a course, the cons said that most of what was needed could be bought through Army surplus for less than $100.

And, of course, there was always the problem of food. "How can we feed these guys decent meals," one official asked, "when all the state allows us is 61 cents a day per con for meals?" You can't feed them very much or very well on that, it was agreed, just as you can't "rehabilitate" them totally when the state budget comes out to less than $2,000 a year for each con. But, one judge wanted to know, isn't at least something good possible—say, ice cream on occasion? "How can we give them ice cream," the official asked, "when it costs about 8 cents a brick wholesale? That's more than 10 per cent of the daily food budget. It's just impossible." The prisoners replied that Army-surplus ice-cream makers could be bought for less than

$75—and that one of them could produce ice cream for an entire prison at less than a penny a serving.

Even if all the equipment were available, the prison officials declared, it would still be difficult to do anything about training the inmates to use it. There was a major problem in getting outside instructors to teach because of low salaries. How about using the expertise of the cons? "We don't trust the prisoners to run the programs," said an administrator. "Whenever we've tried it, we've had a bad experience. Rackets have developed—you know, prisoner-teachers selling grades, things like that. So we don't feel we can use them."

"Man," one inmate said, "you'd better realize that the only way you're going to help prepare us to make it on the outside so that we don't come back in is by beginning to show you trust us a little. That's the name of the game. If you don't trust us at all inside, you ain't going to trust us outside, and we know it, and you're going to have us right back with you."

"Why the hell should we trust you?" asked one official. "Look what happens whenever we start trusting you guys. Look at the jungle you guys live in."

"You know you ain't never trusted us one little bit," the con replied, "and maybe that's why we do what we do in there, because there ain't no trust. And you're right, prison's a jungle. But who's really responsible for it, us? Or all you people who dump us in there and want to forget about us until it's time to let us back into society, until we've served out our time?"

The cons challenged one another as well as the prison system. When one of them complained that the state was charging him $2.50 room and board plus his transportation costs from what he earned on the outside in a work-release program, another snapped: "Man, when you get out, who the hell is going to give you free room and board? Are you a ward of the state or are you

a man? You better learn to pay your own way; you're going to have to if you ever get out."

Behind all the criticism was the evident desire to transform prisons from schools for crime into institutions that would produce men able to adapt to society. The cons quickly dispelled the idea that they sought to turn prisons into pleasant resort hotels. They had committed crimes, they agreed, and society had a right to punish them. The point was that if the system was to be successful it had to be more than just institutionalized punishment.

THE emotions released by the psychodrama were heightened the next day when the conference adjourned behind prison walls. A third of the delegates went to each of the three prisons, where most of them were led on tours by the inmate conferees, unhampered by guards and officials. And at each of the prisons, three or four of the outside workshop members, including a couple of judges, were processed as though they were new inmates. The convicts and guards who processed them were—officially, at least—unaware that they were not real prisoners, though it was evident that word had leaked out.

While the rest of the outside visitors entered the prisons through the main gates, the men chosen to be pretend-convicts were handcuffed and shackled together, put on prison vans and driven into the processing areas. There they were checked in, stripped and made to sit naked on wooden benches while being interviewed. Then they were forced to undergo a flashlight examination under the arms, between the legs, in all the hairy parts of the body—"we're looking for crabs, narcotics, you know, things like that," said the inmate-clerk conducting the examination at one of the prisons. The new "convicts" were showered, given prison clothes, mugged, fingerprinted and asked other detailed questions about their lives. Then they were led to cells and locked in.

When the doors closed, one "convict," an elderly white-haired state representative, sank onto his cot, put his elbows on his knees and buried his head in his hands. "I can't tell you what this did to me spiritually," he said later. "I knew that any time I wanted to get out, all I had to do was yell and they would come and let me loose. What if I had known that I couldn't get out, that I was to be locked in there for years?"

A judge who had sentenced scores of men to the prison through which he was processed suddenly pretended to be a mute. Later, he was to say that he had enjoyed the experience, but those who saw him doubted it. He was certain, he said, that he had been spotted, "and I didn't know whether I was going to get a knife or just be pointed out to everyone else." Within a couple of hours, he asked to be released from his cell.

When another judge left his cell for lunch, a knife was planted in it by one of the few guards who was in on the pretense. The judge was pulled out of the lunch line and thrown into solitary confinement in the "hole" next to a black convict who was lying on his cell floor, his legs in the air, screaming, "White mother-f----s, white mother-f-----s. . . ." (The judge later said he had not heard a word.)

After a half hour in the hole, the judge was brought before a five-man disciplinary board, none of whose members knew that this was all a pretense. The judge was dressed in prison slacks and shirt, white socks without shoes; his hair was tousled, his face distraught.

The board chairman asked, "Do you know why you're here?"

"They told me you found a knife in my cell."

"That's right. Can you tell us how it got there?"

"No. I can't think how."

"Did you bring it in with you?"

"No. Somebody must have put it there."

"When did you get here?"

"This morning."

"Do you know anybody in here?"

"No."

"Does anybody in here have anything against you?"

"No."

"Then why would somebody have planted a knife in your cell?"

The judge, knowing that he was innocent, was sentenced to 30 days in the hole.

ONE of the civilians who went to the House of Correction was later to describe the place as being "like a decayed military school." There was no morale, he said, and there were no screens on the windows; there were razor blades in his cell, splinters of steel in the food, a total lack of communication between the cons and the staff, and everywhere he looked "there were flaming fagots making assignations."

Perhaps one of the most concerned men of all, however, was a high-ranking police officer who was visiting a prison for the first time in his 18 years on the force. He met a prisoner who seemed familiar, talked with him and discovered that he had first met the man many years before, when the convict was 11 years old. "He was a truant and I happened to be at school that day and I talked with him. And then the next day, I got a call and went to a house and there was this little boy. He had had an argument with his mother and stabbed her in the side with a paring knife. He hadn't done much damage, but it was pretty serious. Anyway, he kept getting in trouble, but I never had much time for him, there were always other things. Now he is in for life, for murder, for cutting up someone into eight pieces." The policeman paused and looked around. "I wondered if maybe I couldn't have done something, back then, to have prevented all this. But I'll tell you one

thing: I'm going to be a better cop because of this. And I'll tell you something else: Nobody's going to work for me for 18 years without going into an institution this way again. Every man under me is going to spend a day in prison."

"This is a jungle," said one of the judges. "And if all the guys inside come out as they have to live in there, pretty soon we're all going to be living in that jungle. We'd better do something and we'd better do it damn fast."

How did the cons react to the tour through their homes? "I'll tell you," one inmate said the next day, "the guys inside all look at us as traitors for revealing what's been going on. They're telling us, and some of the guards are telling us, 'This thing will cool off and then we'll see about the guys who've opened up on us.'"

And how did the prison administrators react? "We have lousy prisons and no one in the administration will disagree with you," said one. "But where are all of you when we need help? I don't think anybody gives a damn." Another official commented: "Nobody around here understands us; nobody appreciates what we're doing. We're sitting on the lid of a garbage can keeping the garbage off the streets."

Korn tried to pull the reactions together and get at some of the basic truths behind the conferees' experiences of the previous few days. "We do know," he said, "how to deal with the people we love and the people we hate and the people we don't give a damn about, despite all the myths. We protect and defend the people we love. And the people we hate we turn over to the people we don't give a damn about, to people who hate them. We turn animals over to animals to cage them."

What we ask of people we

put in prison, Korn said, is conformity, something we do not want for ourselves or anyone we love. In prison we want men to conform to rules that have no meaning. "We call it correction," he said, "but it is not correction."

KORN laid out some of his ideas for a solution, which he called a new-careers program. Under it, the massive institutions would be gradually dispensed with, giving way to community-based and neighborhood correction centers. The inmates would be given responsible, meaningful jobs, often working with youthful offenders in an attempt to stop the young men from becoming professional criminals.

During the last days of the conference there were hundreds of resolutions for action — supporting conjugal visits in prisons, urging improvements in the food, backing the idea of neighborhood correction centers, even making the St. John's Council on Crime and Correction a continuing organization that would meet again to try to reform the Maryland prison system.

There was a graduation ceremony, including diplomas for all those who had attended, and a commencement address. The speaker was Petey Green, a former long-term convict who is working in a new-careers program in Washington. Society has to make use of the talents of the prisoners, Green said over and over again. "And how can you say these guys ain't got no skills when they can reach over and lift your wallet without you feeling it? Who's going to be a better store detective than an ex-booster? Maybe the stores ought to think about hiring somebody like that."

It's not hard to motivate the cons, Green said, if you do it the right way. "Why, when I began to change and got to working in the prison school, there was this one

guy, a bank robber, who kept telling me he'd rather play basketball than come to school. So I told him, 'Man, when you went into that bank, they had a big sign sayin' this bank is guarded by cameras. But you couldn't read, and that's how come you got busted.' That guy became one of the best students in the school."

And then, when Green had finished, the cons went back to prison and the free people went their separate ways.

THE end of the conference, though, did not mean the end of the campaign for better prisons. The St. John's Council continues, with task forces meeting weekly to work out reform recommendations requested by a joint Legislative committee on corrections.

The convict who played Scag in the psychodrama was paroled on July 28, has a factory job and is applying for a scholarship to study penology at Catonsville Community College. The inmate who played Slim is scheduled to face a parole board soon and, if he is released, may get an $8,000-a-year job—about which he has not yet been told—working with fellow ex-cons. Several other inmate-participants in the conference have won paroles since June and still others have been transferred to minimum-security prisons.

So far, the resolutions of the workshop have not been abandoned. One convict from each of the three prisons attends a weekly meeting, and interest among the inmate-participants remains high. Some of the judges, policemen and legislators are more concerned than they were before the workshop. They seem to agree that what is at stake is not the coddling of criminals but the very fate of society. This is, however, a short-range reaction. Whether the St. John's workshop will lead to anything permanent remains a question. ■

PRISON REFORMS URGED BY PANEL TO REDUCE CRIME

Coordinating and Improving Federal, State and Local Systems Found Vital

STUDY TOOK 3 YEARS

Congressional Commission Asks $25-Million a Year to Implement New Act

By PAUL DELANEY
Special to The New York Times

WASHINGTON, Nov. 9 — A special study commission warned today that the nation's increasing crime rate would not be checked until sweeping reforms were made in the prison systems.

After a three-year study of prisons, the Joint Commission on Correctional Manpower and Training, which was authorized by Congress in 1965, said the problem of repeat offenders would not be solved as long as "harsh laws, huge, isolated prisons, token program resources and discriminatory practices" were tolerated.

The report was also highly critical of what it described as the generally poor training of correctional workers.

Legislation Proposed

To handle the number of prison inmates, projected to rise from 1.1 million to 1.6 million by 1975, the study said much more money would be needed to educate, train and equip correctional personnel.

It recommended enactment of legislation aimed at coordinating and improving the Federal, state and local prison systems and proposed $25-million annually to finance the improvements. The recommendations were sent to President Nixon and Congress.

When Congress created the commission, it specified that 95 public and private organizations would conduct the study. The commission was headed by James V. Bennett, retired director of the Federal Bureau of Prisons.

Reforms Urged Here

In New York, the State Senate Committee on Penal Institutions made public a report charging that city and county jails were "more fertile breeding grounds for crime than the streets." The report called for reforms to overcome "intense overcrowding, inadequate personnel and poorly designed facilities."

The Federal panel aimed its report at all Americans, "because only with their help can we bring about a more effective correctional system in this country and reduce the incidence of crime and delinquency by restoring thousands of persons each year to productive lives."

"Money is essential, much more money," the report said. "But it will not be forthcoming — or wisely spent — without strong leadership. To put into effect almost all of the recommendations of this report, correctional leadership must be strengthened at national, regional, state and local levels.

"This commission believes legislation is necessary to the orderly development of educational and training programs for corrections," the report said. "At present, education, training and manpower utilization remain near the bottom of the priorities established by the Federal agencies that do support programs for corrections.

"This will continue to be the case until correctional manpower matters are elevated to a level at which adequate funding, technical assistance and administrative support can be made possible."

According to the commission, the act should provide funds for incorporation of all its recommendations; coordinate all Federal prison programs involving education, training and personnel, and provide technical assistance to correctional agencies, nonprofit organizations and institutions of higher education.

The proposed funding of $25-million a year would be a minimum, the commission's report said, since "there is no appropriate formula by which to draw up detailed cost figures to meet such a diverse accumulation of occupations as that required by correctional agencies.

"More important than total cost, however, is the necessity of continued Federal commitment," the report continued.

While calling for an expanded Federal role in corrections, the report supported a theme of the Nixon Administration by calling for strengthened roles of state and local governments in prison systems.

In support of that recommendation were statistics showing that the states and localities had 464, or 93 per cent, of the institutions, compared with 33, or 7 per cent, for the Federal Government. The figures also showed that the states employed 73 per cent of correctional personnel, while local governments employed 20 per cent, and the Federal Government employed 7 per cent.

Regarding personnel, the report expressed concern over the number of poorly trained and unqualified correctional workers, as well as low pay. It said:

"There are far too many employes in institutions, probation departments and parole agencies who are there not because they were educated and trained for particular jobs, but because their appointments satisfied political needs.

"There are still far too many correctional workers who look for other kinds of jobs to satisfy economic and personal needs because they cannot earn a decent living in corrections.

"There are still too few educational resources devoted specifically to teaching and training persons working in or desiring to enter the field of corrections. There is still insufficient Federal financial support available to state and local correctional agencies, despite enactment in 1968 of two major crime and delinquency laws aimed at strengthening state and local criminal justice."

The commission made several recommendations aimed at solving these problems, including career and management development programs, staff promotional policy changes, increased Federal and state funding, and more programs in conjunction with colleges and universities.

The commission also suggested more aggressive recruiting of minorities, noting:

"Minority group members are being aggressively recruited and trained for responsible jobs in other sectors of the American economy. But if there are such efforts in corrections, they have had little impact on the over-all situation.

"While Negroes make up 12 per cent of the total population, only 8 per cent of correctional employes are black. Negroes are conspicuously absent from administrative and supervisory ranks, and they form only 3 per cent of all top and middle-level administrators."

U.S. Tightens Up Giving of Paroles

By FRED P. GRAHAM
Special to The New York Times

WASHINGTON, Dec. 23—The Justice Department disclosed today that it was reorganizing its parole procedures, in part to combat urban crime by making paroles more difficult to obtain.

George J. Reed, chairman of the United States Board of Parole, said today that paroles and parole violations had "skyrocketed" in recent years and that the new approaches were expected to reduce recidivism by cutting back on the number of paroles granted.

Mr. Reed, who was appointed by President Nixon in May, said in an interview that casual parole procedures in recent years had given paroles to far more convicts than were granted a decade before. This resulted in the freeing of a "higher risk group," he said, which contributed to the rise in parole violations.

The Justice Department said in a statement today that one reason for the new procedures was "to help control the urban crime problem." The statement said that in 1957, 33.7 per cent of the inmates who applied for paroles got them. Fifteen per cent of these were later cited for parole violations.

Last year, however, 45.2 per cent of all parole applications were granted and the violation rate was 40 per cent, the statement said. Mr. Reed said past studies showed that about one-third of those who violated parole broke some parole rule and the rest were charged with a new law violation.

He said that since he became chairman of the board in May, the rate of paroles granted had dropped to 39 per cent, because a "more thorough study" of each application is now being made.

J. Edgar Hoover, Director of the Federal Bureau of Investigation, has denounced "leniency" in the granting of parole and probation on several occasions. Today, the Justice Department's statement cited the F.B.I.'s statistical report that 48 per cent of persons imprisoned are subsequently arrested again.

The statement explained that the parole board will be converted into an appellate body that will hear appeals from recommendations of parole hearing examiners. The full board will conduct formal appellate hearings in cases of serious offenders and will review hearing examiners' recommendations on other applications.

Transcripts of trial examiners' hearings will be taken, and the board will place more reliance on psychologists' reports, Mr. Reed said. He said the board would also use the uniform parole report system, a computerized technique that attempts to isolate and tabulate the attributes of the good and bad risks.

He added that there would be increased emphasis on the use of halfway houses—a step between prison and complete freedom—and outpatient psychological counseling rather than outright release.

Under the present system, the eight parole board members—five in the adult division and three in the youth division—hear parole applications individually and then the individual board member votes with the full unit on the appeal. Under the new rules, which will go into effect early next year, the person who conducts the hearing will not take part in the review.

The system covers 20,500 persons now in Federal prisons and an additional 10,300 on parole or mandatory release. The three largest categories of offenders are those convicted of car theft, narcotics violations and Selective Service violations.

Attorney General John N. Mitchell announced the new procedures today. He said they are "aimed at making parole more meaningful and effective for both the public and the ex-convict."

The Tombs Called 'Dungeon of Fear'

By DAVID BURNHAM

A world of fear, violence, filth and degradation has been described by many of the prisoners who answered an uncensored questionnaire about their living conditions while awaiting trial in the Tombs, the Manhattan House of Detention for Men.

Half the number of persons held in the city's various detention facilities have been awaiting trial for at least two months, according to a previous study by the Corrections Department, and 20 per cent have been behind bars for at least six months.

According to the questionnaire:

¶More than four out of ten prisoners said they had seen a guard assault an inmate.

¶Fewer than one out of ten said they had a mattress and blanket during their first few days in the Tombs. About half said they obtained a mattress and blanket a week or more after entering, often from another prisoner who was leaving the jail.

¶Nine out of ten prisoners who had blankets said they were filthy. A large proportion of the respondents complained about the presence of rats, roaches and body lice and a severe shortage of soap.

¶About half the inmates said a total of three men were assigned to their cells. The standard cell—six feet wide, seven feet nine inches long and seven feet ten inches high — originally was designed for one man.

When a second bunk has been placed in the cell, the third inmate sleeps on the cement floor. The Tombs is now 209 per cent beyond capacity.

The survey was undertaken by Representative Edward I. Koch, Democrat of Manhattan who said that he planned to prepare a report to the House Judiciary Committee. The report would recommend a number of possible remedies for jail conditions, including the passage of a Federal law establishing minimum standards of treatment and facilities.

A total of 907 prisoners—about half the number housed in the Tombs—responded to Mr. Koch's questionnaire. It was conducted in early February with the permission of Corrections Commissioner George A. McGrath, and is believed to be the first attempt to draw a statistical portrait of how prisoners perceive their surroundings.

Possible Exaggeration

Commissioner McGrath, while acknowledging that living conditions in the Tombs were "very unpleasant," said the survey's findings included "some extremely serious exaggerations."

He added that because of the severe overcrowding, the total lack of training and work programs and the high level of boredom, the men living in the Tombs were "under unbelievable kinds of pressures, pressures that make them feel their very rough world is even rougher than it actually is."

One penal authority, Dr. Daniel Glaser, a former assistant commissioner of the New York State Narcotics Addiction Control Commission and now a professor of sociology at the University of California, said the descriptions seemed "generally credible" though he felt some prisoners probably exaggerated.

Although most of the prisoners signed their names, Mr. Koch asked that the names be withheld because most of the signers had not been convicted of the crimes for which they were being held.

Among the prisoners who said they had seen a guard assault an inmate, one wrote: "Beatings not only happen in situations where they could be avoided—in all fairness they sometimes cannot— they also are a threat you must constantly live under in this house of detention where you supposedly are innocent until proven guilty."

'Dungeons of Fear'

"The name of the 'Tombs' is a misnomer," another wrote. "This place should be called the 'Dungeon of Fear.' It is operated under one rule alone, physical abuse and the threat of it."

Commissioner McGrath said that sometimes situations demanded that a guard use lawful force and such instances easily could be considered unfair by the prisoners watching them.

Over and over again, the men awaiting trial complained about the sanitary conditions. "Rats come in my

461

cell every night and day," wrote one prisoner.

"Rats and roaches running rampant all over us while we try to sleep," said another.

"Lice and bugs. Exterminator sprayed only one half of those cells needing to be sprayed and asking to be sprayed. Said he did not have any more spray," a third prisoner reported.

Lack of Soap Decried

Nine out of ten of the prisoners said they were not given enough soap. Commissioner McGrath said he was investigating this problem, but that it was standard prison procedure to issue only small amounts of soap because prisoners put it in a sock and use it as a club.

Nine out of ten of the inmates answered "No" to the question, "Do you receive adequate medical care?"

One prisoner, who said he had been in the Tombs for seven months, wrote: "I had a bullet wound in the back at the time of my incarceration and have not been able to be committed to the hospital for removal of the bullet. This should give you some idea of the quality of the medical facilities here and the consideration afforded an inmate in this institution."

Commissioner McGrath defended the quality of the medical staff and medical service. He also said that because there is no training or schooling for the men awaiting trial in jail that time hangs heavy. "Going on sick call is one of the few available diversions," he said.

In response to the question, "Do you have the services of a social worker?" nine out of ten of the prisoners said no.

Commissioner McGrath said that because of a tight budget the Tombs only had the service of one part-time psychiatrist and one psychiatic social worker.

ALL HOSTAGES OUT; HOLDOUT INMATES IN QUEENS YIELD

Last 41, Barricaded on Top Floor at Long Island City, Taken Out at Midnight

GUARDS CLUB PRISONERS

Lindsay Talks With Leaders During Visit to Queens After Dawn Surrender

By ROBERT D. McFADDEN

The five-day revolt of city prisoners demanding judicial and penal reforms ended early today where it began—at the Queens House of Detention in Long Island City—with the negotiated surrender of the last 41 inmates barricaded on the top floor.

The end came 18 hours after 300 prisoners at the same jail had released their last three hostages unharmed and had surrendered in the face of a mayoral ultimatum and a show of overpowering force by policemen and guards.

At 12:34 A.M. today the last holdouts, insisting that they feared beatings similar to those administered to some surrendering inmates by guards early yesterday, started coming down in groups of three in the bucket of the Fire Department's 75-foot "cherry picker" tower ladder in full view of 200 cheering supporters and scores of newsmen.

Lawyers Pick Observers

The prisoners were accompanied throughout the operation by 10 observers picked by the inmates' lawyers. Well over 400 policemen were in and around the jail.

The theatrical, but peaceful, removal of the last rebels, who were sent in vans to Rikers Island lockups, marked the apparent close of one of the worst prison crises in the city's history. It had swung from rioting in five jails by thousands of inmates and the seizure of 28 hostages, to violent battles with Correction Department guards and tactical threats by the Lindsay administration.

In the light of other events during the crisis, the final surrender was anticlimactic.

The collapse of the final strongpoint in the inmate uprising came at dawn yesterday as a force of 300 guards and 300 policemen massed outside the walls of the 95-year-old jail on Courthouse Square. It was the guards alone, however, who cleared the jail.

Lindsay Inside Jail

According to reporters who watched the incident, at least eight inmates were clubbed and kicked and three guards were hurt, none seriously, as the prisoners emerged from the jail into a courtyard.

The beatings, which led to the admission of the eight inmates to Bellevue Hospital, oc-

United Press International

INMATE BEATEN: A prisoner at Queens House of Detention in Long Island City being pushed from prison yesterday morning as correction guards began wielding their clubs.

curred as Mayor Lindsay was inside the jail, keeping his pledge to talk with prisoner representatives about the grievances that had led to the uprising: long trial delays, high bail and living conditions in the prisons.

The Mayor, apprised of the violence when he emerged from the jail at 10 A.M., later instructed Correction Commissioner George F. McGrath to provide a full report on the incidents, which were witnessed by newsmen looking down on the courtyard from a warehouse across the street.

Among the top-floor holdouts were nine of the 13 Black Panthers currently on trial on charges of conspiring to blow up public places. Upon learning of this yesterday Justice John M. Murtagh recessed the trial in State Supreme Court, pending the recapture of the defendants.

The last group of inmates agreed to surrender after a three-hour meeting with three attorneys for the Black Panthers—Gerald Lefcourt, Sanford Katz and William Crain. Mr. Lefcourt acting as spokesman for the group, said the inmates had primarily been "afraid for their safety—they don't want to be beaten."

The pattern that led to the release of the hostages in Long Island City—a radio-broadcast ultimatum by the Mayor and a show of force by policemen and guards—was the same sequence that had persuaded 200 mutinous inmates at the Manhattan House of Detention to free 17 hostages and surrender themselves late Sunday night.

The price of securing two other jails—the Brooklyn House of Detention and the Queens House of Detention in Kew Gardens—was higher. In both instances guards had used clubs and tear gas early Sunday in hand-to-hand combat with inmates, more than 200 of whom were injured. There were no injuries reported in the crushing of a brief rebellion by young prisoners at the Adolescent Remand Shelter on Rikers Island Sunday afternoon.

The inmate uprising had wrought a heavy toll over the last five days: injuries to guards and inmates, mostly minor, numbered in the hundreds and damage to prison facilities may run into millions of dollars. The emotional strain on the 28 hostages held for varying periods of time, and on their families, is incalculable.

Nevertheless, there were mitigations. The hostages were all freed unharmed. Shortcomings in the judicial and penal systems attracted wide attention. And pledges of efforts toward reform have been made in several official quarters.

The beginning of the end of the rebellion actually started not with the invasions of the Brooklyn and Kew Gardens jails by guards Sunday morning, but later in the afternoon with a strategy meeting at Gracie Mansion.

Attending the meeting with the Mayor were Commissioner McGrath, Acting Police Commissioner John F. Walsh, Deputy Mayors Aurelio and Timothy W. Costello and several other mayoral aides.

According to Thomas Morgan, the Mayor's press secretary, the general view expressed at the meeting was that force had worked in Brooklyn and Kew Gardens, and that the same methods should be used at the Tombs and in Long Island City.

This view prevailed and at 6 P.M., Commissioner Walsh left to assemble the necessary force of men and equipment at the Tombs, which was selected as the first target because there appeared to be less unity among the prisoners there.

WINS Used for Ultimatum

After Mr. Walsh had left, however, the remaining officials had second thoughts. Commissioner McGrath reportedly recalled that many of the inmates at the Tombs had transistor radios, and he had heard that, as a result of the extensive news coverage, most were tuning in to WINS, an all-news radio station.

The decision was then made to give the inmates a last chance by issuing an ultimatum and using force only if it was rejected. Live time on WINS was requested and granted.

When the force of hundreds of policemen and guards had been assembled at the Tombs, ready for action, the Mayor went on the air to lay down a 30-minute deadline for release of the hostages, warning that "other courses of action" would be taken if the inmates refused.

The deadline passed, but no immediate action was taken because the warden of the Tombs, Milton Batterman, who had met briefly with the rebel inmates, reported that there appeared to be movement on the prisoners' part.

The Mayor also received reports of factionalism, intense debate and even some fist-fighting among the inmates, who included adherents of the Black Panthers, the Young Lords and the Muslims.

The first sign that agreement was close came at 11:30 P.M. Shortly thereafter, 14 of the 17 hostages were released. A few minutes later the other three hostages were freed.

When the Mayor learned that all the Tombs hostages had been released, he immediately went in his limousine to the jail, arriving shortly before midnight.

At the Tombs he met for nearly three hours with a committee of 11 inmate representa-

tives, as he had promised in his broadcast ultimatum. All 11 were described by Mr. Morgan as "articulate." They spelled out the prisoners' grievances and "did most of the talking," Mr. Morgan said. The Mayor, for his part, told the inmates that he felt the holding of innocent persons as hostages had been "heinous."

Emerging from the meeting at 3 A.M., the Mayor told newsmen he believed the inmates' grievances were real, but he blamed them on the judicial system.

Returning to Gracie Mansion, the Mayor again met with Commissioners Walsh and McGrath, who recommended that the two-pronged action that had been successful at the Tombs—the ultimatum and the show of force—be applied to the situation at Long Island City.

Following similar procedures, the Commissioners moved more than 300 policemen and 300 correction guards into place outside the Long Island City jail.

Newsmen who had been moved back from the jail entrance noted that many of the correction guards wore civilian clothes, and no badges. The guards did not have guns, but in addition to nightsticks many carried iron pipes, pickax handles, baseball bats and even a few table legs. Guards have guns but are not ordinarily permitted to carry them inside the city jails.

Floodlights Turned On

Tear gas and acetylene torches were unloaded from police vans and by 5 A.M. all appeared in readiness for an invasion of the jail.

At that time, loudspeakers and floodlights were used to awaken any inmates in the jail who might be asleep. They were told over a bullhorn to turn on their radios to hear the Mayor's statement to them.

The Mayor went on the air shortly after 5 A.M., giving the same message to the men in Long Island City as had been given to the men in the Tombs—30 minutes to release the hostages or face "other courses of action."

According to Mr. Morgan talks with the hostages later revealed that the prisoners took a vote on whether to accept. The vote was to stand and fight.

But the presence of the force of policemen and guards outside prompted continued debate and another vote. The second vote was in favor of releasing the hostages and, for those who wanted to, surrendering voluntarily.

The decision was relayed to Gracie Mansion at 5:50 A.M. The Mayor first talked to the freed hostages by telephone, in what Mr. Morgan called "the most emotional moments" of the prison rebellion.

The Mayor then went to the jail, arriving a few minutes after 6 and went inside to engage in a discussion of grievance with inmate representatives that lasted two hours 10 minutes. He also met inside with prison officials.

While he was inside the inmates who had declined to surrender barricaded themselves in the top floor. Most of them were described by mayoral aides as Panthers or Panther followers.

At the same time, backed up by policemen who remained outside the prison walls, the force of correction guards entered and began handcuffing and removing the prisoners.

Despite the Mayor's pledge that there would be no violence or reprisals against the inmates, at least eight of them were beaten as they were taken out of the jail into a courtyard.

Newsmen, who had been kept back a full block from the courtyard, had climbed to a vantage point on the ninth floor of a warehouse on Courthouse Square, from which they saw guards club and kick the inmates as they were dragged from the jail.

Correction Captain Anthony Peraino said some of the prisoners had either been carrying weapons or refused to be handcuffed. "If they refused to be handcuffed, I guess that the men would use some kind of force," he said.

Another correction officer who declined to identify himself said, "As the prisoners came out, some began fighting us and we fought back." He said the inmates had about 150 weapons, including sharpened spoons and clubs made of broken furniture.

Inmates Sent to Other Jails

Most of the prisoners were not harmed, however. They were made to kneel or sit in the courtyard until about 9 A.M., when 11 buses arrived to take them to other jails in the city. Most went to Rikers Island.

The inside of the Long Island City jail was a scene of heavy destruction. "It's a total wreck," said one prison official. "Everything that could be broken was broken."

Mayor Lindsay left the jail at 10 A.M. Told that guards had dragged and beaten a few inmates, Mr. Lindsay said: "I understand there were some injuries on both sides, but I don't know their extent." He then said he would order a full report from Commissioner McGrath.

The Mayor, who flew to Buffalo later in the day to put in a campaign appearance on behalf of Senator Charles E. Goodell, was back at Gracie Mansion late in the afternoon, discussing strategy for the recapture of the holdouts on the top floor of the Long Island City jail.

Last night Judge Jack B. Weinstein of the United States District Court In Brooklyn rejected an application from the Legal Aid Society for a temporary restraining order that would have barred the city from committing any acts of brutality against the inmates who were then holding out in the Long Island City jail. He did so after being assured by lawyers for the city that such acts were "neither the policy nor practice" of the city.

He did, however, sign an order directing the city to show cause next Tuesday why it should not be enjoined then from committing any acts of brutality against the inmates.

October 6, 1970

Rising Protests and Lawsuits Shake Routine in State Prisons

By MICHAEL T. KAUFMAN

Within the last few months, tremors of discontent and protest and a heavy file of lawsuits have shaken the bureaucracy, the routine and the discipline of the state prison system.

At prisons in Attica, Napanoch and Auburn inmates have demonstrated, refusing to report to their work details. At the same time the courts have been flooded with writs seeking to extend prisoner rights and curb the traditional prerogatives of prison administrations.

"There is no doubt that the prisons are under attack," said Paul D. McGinnis, the Commissioner of Correction, who announced last week that he would retire next Jan. 1 after 46 years of state service.

Russell G. Oswald, who is rumored as the man who will take over the new state super-agency governing prisons, parole and the state police when it becomes operative on Jan. 1, concurs. Mr. Oswald, who is now chairman of the Parole Board, feels that the prison turmoil is part of a larger social upheaval.

"What's happening in the prisons," he said, "is a reflection of what has happened outside. Most of the country's institutions have come under attack—the colleges, the schools, the courts — now, it's the prisons."

But unlike these other institutions, prisons are sealed off from public view and are usually in remote regions. Still, disquiet has been seeping through the stone-walled fortresses where some 12,500 felons are under sentence.

The first major signs came with the waves of troubles that struck the city's detention houses last summer. There, the grievances were generally universal: overcrowded conditions and inept and dilatory court and bail procedures.

At the state institutions the issues are far different and much more diffuse. Yet, the morphology of prison disorders is such that when trouble breaks out in one place, it is likely to erupt elsewhere.

Or, as John R. Cain, who has just retired as Deputy Commissioner of Correction, said: "Our prisoners read the newspapers."

The specific gripes to emerge from the state prison protests range from demands for galoshes to calls for the hiring of more black and Puerto Rican guards and for more counselors and psychiatrists.

But underlying the wide variety of complaints is a challenge that goes to the very nature of what a prison is and what its functions should be.

Conscious of Rights

"What you've got now," said Commissioner McGinnis, "are prisoners who are much more conscious of their civil rights than they ever were before. Some of them, and I'm talking about groups like the Black Panthers, the Young Lords and the Five Percenters, have a consciousness of themselves as victims or political prisoners. They preach this and through coercion or force they pick up a following."

He contrasted this growing consciousness with an earlier time when, generally, both inmates and administrators tacitly agreed on certain ground rules. Essentially these stemmed from a mutual understanding that if a person was caught and convicted of a crime, he had to submit to the authority of the prison administration.

"Take Willie Sutton," said the Commissioner, referring to the bank robber who made several escapes. "We never had any trouble with Willie. He stayed by himself. He was never a militant. Now you have these groups that first of all want to overthrow the prison administration."

Security vs. Rehabilitation

Mr. McGinnis said that these activists represented only a small part of the prison population but that their presence had created enormous problems.

In a sense, the current turmoil is just a newer version of one of the oldest arguments in penology: Should primary emphasis be placed on security or on rehabilitation?

The state system has always had a reputation for tight security. In fact one long-standing complaint has been that most of its institutions have physical plants built for maximum security and impose programs that might suit the most hardened criminals but not lesser offenders whose rehabilita-

tion might be more effective under less stringent security.

Opposing View Reinforced

For the men who have run the state prison system, the general view has been that security comes first, that they have been charged by the state with keeping felons apart from society.

Charles McKendrick, the late warden of Wallkill — the state's most open institution— wrote in a textbook called "Contemporary Correction":

"The prison is a totalitarian community in which the most significant values of the governed, the values of freedom, are limited in the interest of the state."

In the past, there has been some opposition to the heavy emphasis on security. Most of it has come from the psychiatrists, counselors and chaplains, whose professional roles were often subordinated to the custodial chores involved in keeping men behind locked walls.

Now, however, challenges to this view are being made with greater force by civil rights organizations and by the prisoners themselves.

The New York Civil Liberties Union, the N.A.A.C.P. Legal Defense and Educational Fund, Inc., the National Council on Crime and Delinquency and the Criminal Appeals Division of the Legal Aid Society have banded together in an informal conference and are making a full legal assault on the authority of prison administrators.

To date the most significant effort has dealt with the issue of prison discipline. There was, for example, the case of Martin Sostre, who had been placed in solitary confinement at Green Haven prison for 372 days.

Last May, Federal Judge Constance Baker Motley ruled here that Sostre's punishment had resulted from his "legal and Black Muslim activities." She ordered payments of $13,020 in damages to the convict and further ruled that the Department of Correction draw up formal rules governing the imposition on solitary confinement.

'Burden' Argued

In its argument before Judge Motley, the state insisted that a codification of such procedures "would be unduly burdensome in their application." The state's appeal in this case is now pending before a higher court.

In another recent decision, Federal Judge James T. Foley of the Northern District also ordered the state to develop specific standards to be used in sending men into isolation. This case involved two in-

464

mates at Clinton Prison — William Wright and Robert Mosher. Wright, who had complained that he had been thrown into a strip cell — the harshest form of confinement in which a prisoner is forced to remain naked in an empty cell — was awarded a cash judgment of $1,500. Mosher' complaint was that he was placed in solitary when he refused to sign an agreement to work in a particular prison shop.

When the case was heard last August, the state had already reported that it had abandoned the use of strip cells.

In his ruling, Judge Foley noted this but cited the "awesome" power to impose sanctions within prisons, and declared that there should be written procedures providing fo for what he called "practically judicial hearings" before harsh forms of punishment could be imposed.

The cancellation of "good time," another tool for enforcing prison discipline, has also been attacked in several recent suits.

"Good time" is the 10 days that is credited to each prisoner for every month he serves without getting into trouble. It is cumulative and comes off the prisoner's sentence. It has been the practice that portions of "good time" could be taken away at the discretion of the prison superintendent.

Eugene Rodriguez, the former State Senator from the Bronx who was sentenced to prison for perjury and attempted grand larceny, brought suit against the state charging that he had arbitrarily been denied "good time." He said he had lost 120 days because a photograph of his family that he had in his possession had been ruled contraband. He won the suit and was ordered released by a Federal judge.

Another prisoner, Michael Katzoff, won a suit in which he charged that he had lost "good time" because of things he had written in a diary.

There are now many similar cases in various stages of argument or appeal. Some concern the limitations on the censorship of mail and reading matters. There are others dealing with the right to counsel at parole hearings.

McGinnis Fears Chaos

Taken together, the rulings have frustrated the prison authorities. "These judges just don't know what a prison is all about," Mr. McGinniss said in a recent interview. "If you do not maintain a degree of discipline, you're going to have nothing but chaos and you can't run any kind of programs in chaos."

But the same decisions have cheered the various civil rights groups involved in the suits. They have also pleased the Fortune Society, a group of former inmates who seek prison reforms.

"What you have to understand about discipline in prison," said Kenneth Jackson, an officer of the society, "is that breathing is a privilege that can be taken away by the hacks [guards]."

"One time, when I was at Coxsackie [the State Vocational Institution at West Coxsackie], a guard stepped on my mirror and cracked it during a shakedown inspection. I told him he had feet like an elephant. He turned to me and said. 'You just lost your mirror privileges.' So I served my last two years without a mirror in my cell."

Daniel Keane said he had received two days of keep-lock — the least restrictive form of punitive confinement, in which men are just kept in their cells — for "fishing." Someone had thrown him a cigarette that landed outside his cell. He pulled it to him with a towel.

Maurice Kessler, who served time at Clinton and Auburn, was sent to isolation on what he insists was a frame-up.

"The hacks were mad at me because I had a good kitchen job that usually went to white guys," he said. "They said I had stolen a jar of tomato paste that they said was found in my cubby. I never saw it and I never stole. They sent me to the box for three weeks."

While he was in the isolation block, where except for an hour's exercise a day, men are confined to cells and kept on short rations, eight Black Muslims were placed in neighboring cells. He said they told him they had been charged with "spitting on the grass."

All of the former inmates interviewed admitted that they had also been punished for far more serious offenses, such as fighting and the rape of a fellow prisoner. But they pointed out these lesser examples show the absolute authority wielded by the administration.

Prentiss Williams came out of Green Haven last Christmas after serving 12 years for armed robbery. What upsets him about prison structure is the inconsistency of its regulations. For example, he said, the commissary sells jars of instant coffee and boxes of rice, but cooking is an offense that can be punished.

"Now the guards come by and smell the coffee and they know you've been cooking," he said. "They can pinch you if they want or not. There's a rule against sleeping with the covers over your head. A man can pull his blanket up in his sleep, and the guard keeps him in keep lock in the morning."

Sometimes, the former prisoner said, the arbitrary procedures benefitted the inmates who could strike up personal relationships with individual guards.

One former inmate at Green Haven admitted that with the knowledge and protection of the guards, he was able to make and sell wine, rent out "shortheist" books (pornography), run a numbers bank that paid off 22 to 1 on cigarettes and sell nutmeg purchased for him by guards. Prisoners used the nutmeg with hot water believing they could get a marijuana-like high.

Many of the former convicts, both black and white, said that frequently what determined how an individual prisoner was treated was his race. Jackson said that as late as 1961 there were separate black and white drinking buckets for field workers at Coxsackie. Certain good jobs, such as clerks and inmate nurse, were generally reserved for whites, said Keane.

In his suit, Sostre contended that the racism of the state prison system could be seen by the fact that there were no black wardens, deputy wardens or commissioners and that while 70 per cent of the prisoner population was black or Puerto Rican, there were very few black or Spanish-speaking guards.

After the riot at Auburn, which was touched off by a black solidarity day sitdown, prisoners issued 13 demands. The first of these were for the hiring of more Spanish-speaking guards. They contended that there were great delays in both the receipt and sending of letters by Puerto Ricans, since there were not enough prison censors who could read Spanish.

Commissioner McGinnis believes this is a legitimate request and said he would hire 100 Spanish-speaking guards immediately if he could find them. He said he had the height requirement for the job reduced by an inch and has held emergency examinations hoping to attract black and Puerto Ricans as correctional officers.

"Last year after an exam I could have hired a hundred," the Commissioner said. "You know how many I got? Three. Those three, he said, went to Sing Sing and Coxsackie.

"They just don't want to go upstate," the Commissioner said "Maybe they feel they won't get housing or they think the social situation will be difficult."

JAIL CENSUS FINDS 52% NOT CONVICTED

First National Study of City and County Facilities Is Critical of Conditions

By JACK ROSENTHAL

WASHINGTON, Jan. 6 — A pioneering Federal census of city and county jails showed today that 52 per cent of their inmates had not been convicted of a crime and that many inmates, whether convicted or not, endured "less than human conditions."

Four jails still in daily use, including one in Fulton County, N.Y., were built before George Washington's inauguration, the study showed. A quarter of the 97,500 local jail cells in the country are more than 50 years old.

The $140,000 study was made by the Census Bureau for the Law Enforcement Assistance Administration, an arm of the Department of Justice estab-lished to aid the local police, courts and corrections systems.

Judges Pick Jurors

To speed up criminal trials in New York State, judges were taking over from lawyers the job of selecting jurors. [Page 18.]

While state prisons have been receiving increased public attention, the jail census is the first comprehensive study ever of American county and city lockups.

Generally, jails are used for people detained before trial and for those convicted of less se-rious crimes. Jail sentences, un-like prison sentences, usually do not exceed one year. But there are jails where prisoners have been held for five years or longer.

"Many more wrongdoers pass through our jails than our pris-ons and yet until this study we didn't even know how many jails there are," Richard W. Velde, associate administrator of the law agency, said.

The jail census, which achieved a 100 per cent response, showed that there were 4,037 jails operated by municipal or country govern-ments in which people were held for more than 48 hours.

As of March 15, 1970, the day of the jail census, 160,863 persons were incarcerated, 7,800 of them juveniles.

The state and Federal prison population is estimated at 350,000.

A full report on the jail cen-sus will not be released until spring, but a number of findings are already available. These in-clude the following:

¶Of the 160,863 prisoners, 83,000, or 52 per cent, had not been convicted of a crime. A to-tal of 35 per cent had been ar-raigned but were awaiting trial. The remaining 17 per cent were still awaiting arraignment.

¶Jails in urban areas are, for the most part, "terribly over-crowded," Mr. Velde said, while rural jails are operating far be-low capacity.

¶Some 500 jails now in serv-ice were built in the nineteenth century and six in the eighteenth century. The oldest are those in Albemarle County, Va., built in 1705, and Cumberland County, Pa., in 1754. The jails in Fulton County, N.Y., and Hagerstown, Md., were erected in 1776.

¶Although 65,000 people are serving sentences in local jails, 10,000 for a year or more, many jails are ill-equipped to do more than keep them locked up. "Most prisons have at least some correction and education programs," Mr. Velde said. "It is clear that many jails don't have even. that."

¶Of the 3,300 jails in large communities, 85 per cent have no recreational or educational facilities of any kind. About half lack medical facilities. About one-fourth have no fa-cilities for visitors.

¶Texas has more jails than any other state, with 325, fol-lowed by Georgia with 240. The largest jail population is in California, with about 28,000 in 166 jails. New York has the second-largest jail population, 17,399 in 75 jails.

$500-Million Slated

Discussing overcrowding of jails, Mr. Velde said, "There are many cases where inmates — children, mental incompetents and hardened felons — are all lumped together in less than human conditions of over-crowding and filth."

He said that the jail census would provide the basis for en-larged assistance from the law agency for corrections pro-grams. The agency this year will distribute about $500-mil-lion to various parts of the criminal justice system.

The agency now expects to devote about $100-million in the next six months to both jails and prisons and "signifi-cantly more" in the fiscal year 1972, which begins next July 1, Mr. Velde said.

Total state and local spend-ing on correctional facilities around the country is estimated at $1.5-billion a year.

January 7, 1971

COURT EXTENDS CONVICTS' RIGHTS

U.S. Appeals Bench Limits Punishment and Censorship

By ARNOLD H. LUBASCH

A decision that substantially advances the rights of prison inmates was issued yesterday by the United States Court of Appeals here.

In a 52-page opinion written by Judge Irving R. Kaufman, the court declared that the time was long past when a prisoner could be treated "as temporarily a slave of the state."

The far-reaching decision cited safeguards against arbi-trary punishment of prisoners, said they could not be punished for merely expressing their views, restricted the censor-ship of their mail and upheld their right to sue prison of-ficials for violations of consti-tutional rights.

However, the court reversed several additional rights and re-quirements that Federal Dis-trict Judge Constance Baker Motley had ordered last year in the case of Martin Sostre, a convict who was held in soli-tary confinement for over a year.

Judge Motley ruled that Sostre could not be subjected to solitary confinement without written notice of the charges against him, the right to coun-sel, a recorded hearing with a right to question witnesses and a written decision specifying the legal basis for the punish-ment.

She also ordered prison of-ficials to submit rules for her approval regarding the dissem-ination of political literature in prison as well as for the impo-sition of all disciplinary charges involving solitary confinement.

Judge Motley's decision awarded Sostre $13,000 in da-mages from State Correction Commissioner Paul D. McGinnis and Warden Harold W. Follette of Green Haven Prison, in Stormville, where Sostre was serving a sentence of 30 to 40 years for selling narcotics.

The appeals court reversed the award of damages against the Correction Commissioner, but it affirmed the compen-satory damages from the prison warden, although it noted that he had died and it left open whether the money could be collected from his estate.

Sued for $1.2-Million

The action was initiated from prison in a handwritten complaint by Sostre, a 47-year old former operator of a black militant bookstore in Buffalo. He had sued the two officials for $1.2-million on the ground they had subjected him to "cruel and unusual punish-ment" in violation of the Con-stitution.

Warden Follette insisted that he held Sostre in solitary con-finement because the prisoner remained defiant, refused to answer questions, assisted other convicts with legal papers and violated other regu-lations.

Unfairness Cited

Judge Motley ruled that the warden had punished Sostre because he was a black militant who persisted in expressing his radical views in prison.

Yesterday's decision by the Court of Appeals for the Sec-ond Circuit, which consists of New York, Connecticut and Vermont, rejected Judge Mot-ley's ruling that solitary con-finement for longer than 15 days represented "cruel and un-usual punishment" that violated constitutional rights.

In upholding the compensa-tory damages against the war-den, however, the court accepted Judge Motley's ruling that the reasons for punishing the prisoner were unfair.

It decided that Judge Motley was in error when she ordered prison officials to adhere to numerous "trial-type procedures" in punishing prisoners, but it warned the officials against any "arbitrary and capricious" punishment.

"We would not lightly condone the absence of such basic safeguards against arbitrariness as adequate notice, an opportunity for the prisoner to reply to charges lodged against him and a reasonable investigation into the relevant facts, at least in cases of substantial discipline," Judge Kaufman wrote.

"However, as consideration of Sostre's case does not properly raise any question whether New York prisons regularly or systematically ignore due process requirements, we must reverse the order of the district court that defendants submit for its approval proposed rules and regulations governing future disciplinary actions."

Censorship Issue

The decision affirmed Judge Motley's ruling that prison officials should not censor mail between Sostre and any court, public agency or lawyer concerning his conviction or complaint.

In a modification of a ruling by Judge Motley, the appeals court enjoined the prison officials "from punishing Sostre for having literature in his possession and for setting forth his views, orally or in writing, except for violation of reasonable regulations."

The court also affirmed the crediting of 124 days of "good time" towards Sostre's eventual release from prison because his solitary confinement would have deprived him of this benefit.

"Our constitutional scheme does not contemplate that society may commit lawbreakers to the capricious and arbitrary actions of prison officials," Judge Kaufman asserted.

Most of the rulings in the Kaufman opinion were supported by six other judges on the nine-member appeals court. All of them participated in the case because of its significance.

Judge Kaufman declared that the decision raised "important questions concerning the Federal constitutional rights of state prisoners which neither Supreme Court precedent nor our past decisions have answered."

Prisons Curb Brutal Discipline; Find Relaxed Control Effective

By WALTER RUGABER

WASHINGTON, May 14 — The nation's prisons are moving away from the most severe and physically punishing forms of discipline, and the sternest measures remaining are often imposed with increasing restraint.

Bread-and-water diets and long stints in tiny cages without clothing, lights, adequate ventilation, bedding, water or toilet facilities are disappearing from penal routines across the country.

Practically every institution retains some kind of jail-within-a-jail for the most disobedient inmates. Generally, however, there are not as many special restrictions as in the past and confinements are much less extended.

The authorities are turning toward more sophisticated controls, including discharges from preferred jobs, suspensions of visiting, recreational and other privileges, and forfeitures of earned "good behavior time."

"The penalties today do not compare with those of five or 10 years ago," said one official, voicing an assessment of the general relaxation common among observers inside and outside correctional facilities.

Substantial problems and abuses still abound in the prisons. There are regular reports of brutality by guards, homosexual attacks, random fights and stabbings, drug abuse and other difficulties.

And the disciplinary process as a whole still includes a number of unsettled issues, such as prison regulations themselves, their enforcement and the administrative hearings that rule on alleged infractions.

Many critics find major injustices in these areas. But official dissatisfaction with the automatic imposition of extremely discomforting punishments at the end of the process is relieving the most lurid and durable sore spots.

Inquiries in many of the states suggest a number of reasons for this trend. Many administrators have simply accepted the view that the most crushing penalties are unnecessary and counterproductive as well.

The American Correctional Association held in its official guidelines, published five years ago, that "the routine use of severe disciplinary measures usually served to embitter inmates rather than deter them."

In addition, the milder alternatives are being found more meaningful and effective on their own. Ellis C. MacDougall, a prominent penologist who became the corrections director in Georgia this year, is experimenting with ordinary fines.

Measures Described

He recently recalled an incident in which an inmate, participating in a work-release program that allowed him to leave prison and hold a job in the community during the day, returned drunk one evening.

"Right away they wanted to take him off the program," said Mr. MacDougall, referring to some prison officials. "I said, 'fine him $25 and put him back to work. He'll feel that $25 a lot more than anything else.'"

Judicial orders, particularly in the Federal District courts, have outlawed some of the more trying punishments. A Federal judge has assumed close watch over disciplinary practices in Rhode Island prisons.

Among the more brutal measures employed in some of the prisons in the past were the following:

¶In North Carolina a decade or so ago, men were thrown naked into solitary confinement cells where guards used high-pressure water hoses from time to time to "knock them up against the wall."

¶In Maryland, inmates were disciplined until recently by receiving a meal only once every 72 hours.

¶In Pennsylvania, before a reform movement in 1953, prisoners were placed for days in dark, damp underground holes.

¶In Arkansas five years ago, men were whipped on the bare buttocks with rawhide straps (flogging was practiced in 26 prisons as recently as 1963) and had needles pushed under their fingernails.

Public pressure is sometimes a factor in ending severe punishment. One warden who practically eliminated his punishment cells said that he had done so with a feeling that "there's so much hullabaloo raised over them that it's just not worth it."

The national trend is subject to local variations, but it can be examined in fuller detail at a single prison. Many places display some evidence of the change; among them is the grim and hulking Ohio facility on the edge of downtown Columbus.

The Ohio penitentiary, opened in 1834, now holds more than 1,800 men. Its history is marked here and there by spectacular disasters, such as a fire in 1930 that killed 320 inmates.

It is a maximum-security institution with the usual stone wall (this one is 30 feet high) behind which the inmates march around in close formation as guards question, search, count and watch them.

In 1968, discontent and tension erupted in two major riots that seared morale, caused a million dollars worth of destruction and added to the penitentiary's already unsavory reputation.

The facility appears doomed. The state intends to transfer all its inmates to a new prison late this summer and there is talk in Columbus of tearing the old structure down.

One morning earlier this month, Richard Simpson (that is not his real name) failed to get out of bed when a guard summoned him, first at 3:30 A.M. and again at 3:45 A.M., to help get breakfast for his fellow inmates.

Simpson took the first step in the disciplinary process when a captain on the correctional force arrived at 3:55 A.M. to find him still asleep. The inmate was charged with refusing to work or, in the prison jargon, "freezing up."

Many of the regulations were dropped last year in a liberalization effort of uncertain effect, but refusing to work is still prohibited by one of the 22 "cardinal rules" published in the inmate manual.

These prohibit serious misconduct, such as stealing, lying, gambling, fighting and possessing any weapon. Some, such as "agitating talk," seem vague to critics and especially subject to uneven enforcement.

If Simpson's conduct had been covered only by one of the more than 200 detailed rules pruned from the manual, he would have apparently got off at least the first time with merely a warning.

A year ago, according to Warden Harold J. Cardwell, guards immediately and routinely brought formal charges for conduct such as whistling (except during the Sunday "music hour") or sitting on another man's bunk.

Now, he said during an interview, no complaint is filed unless the warning is ignored, and then the case must come under one of the "cardinal rules."

The distinction escapes some of the penitentiary's critics, but the disciplinary records suggest that the number of citations issued by the guards has undergone a striking decline in the last 30 months.

From 569 to 173

From 569 cases in October, 1968, an analysis cited by Mr. Cardwell shows, the number fell to 173 last February. Other figures suggest that the guards are increasingly concentrating on the more serious infractions.

Simpson's failure to arise and go to work brought him, later the same morning, to a small, barren room where he would tell his story, part complaint and part apology, to a "rules infraction board" made up of three officials.

"I can't get any rest up there in the dormitory," said Simpson, who is among the inmates who do not live in cells. "They play pool and the TV is yelling and screaming all over," he is quoted in the board's minutes as having said.

Simpson went on to promise that he would try to get excused from what is known as the "early get-up." Except for that, he added, he liked working in the dining room and hoped to keep the job.

Among the things that have not changed much anywhere are these rules-infraction-board kind of hearings. The inmates are seldom if ever allowed to question the accusing officials or to summon witnesses in their behalf.

These bodies may still impose very heavy penalties. Their right to do so without the fundamental due process is under widespread attack.

The Ohio penitentiary's board quickly and unanimously found Simpson guilty of "freezing up." While it did not take away his job in the dining room, it did send him to what is known as a "correction cell" for two days.

Two or three years ago, these cells were little boxes where men are said to have lived as long as 90 or 100 days on one meal every 72 hours and nothing but bread and thin soup in between. Ten-day stretches with the doors unopened are said to have driven a number of men insane.

Those in the regular correction cells nowadays must still do without reading material, radios, tobacco and exercise, but there are bunks, toilets, doors that are merely barred and outside lights.

Eight months ago, the inmates are said to have begun to receive three full meals a day, like those served everyone else except for the elimination of some condiments. Independent reports and inspections confirmed this.

More important, the inmates seem to be sent to the correction cells less often and for much shorter periods. An examination of more than 200 recent cases found only three sentences for 10 days, two for eight and one for seven. The median was below three days.

Penitentiary figures show that inmates spent a total of 1,626 days in the correction cells during November, 1968, and only 330 days in them during last February.

In Ohio and elsewhere, there is some resistance to disciplinary changes. Warden Cardwell, a former state policeman, said:

"I'd like to do away with the correction cells completely. But I've had to do everything gradually."

May 15, 1971

Jackson Called Blacks' Symbol Of Anger With Judicial System

By EARL CALDWELL

George Jackson was often described as a symbol, and he was. For many blacks, he was a clear reflection of the rising tide of discontent that they now hold with the judicial system as a whole.

It is a dissatisfaction that is deep-rooted and mixed now with anger and distrust. It showed as word of Jackson's death flashed across the country.

"I don't know what happened," black people were saying, "but I don't believe he was just out trying to escape. There's more to it than that."

Once the black concern for Negro prisoners was limited chiefly to the Nation of Islam —the Black Muslims. And later it was the Black Panther party. But today, blacks at all levels often express the feeling that the judicial system has two standards—one for whites and another for blacks.

They assert that prisons are filled with blacks and that guards and administrators and parole authorities are white.

White Judges and Juries

They mention, too, that often the juries that convict Negro defendants are white, that the judges are white, that the prosecutors are white and that the arresting officers are most often white.

In the late nineteen-sixties when the Panthers were saying that all blacks serving time in jail were political prisoners, the Panthers had little visible support. But there has been a remarkable change in that attitude.

Now, prominent Negro lawyers and even Negro judges are saying openly that the judicial process is being used to contain blacks and the poor. And often, when they cite examples, they use George Jackson.

"Something is wrong," they would say, "when a man pleads guilty to stealing $70 and spends 10 years in jail and still has no hope of getting out."

When he was 18 years old, George Jackson was sentenced to from one year to life imprisonment for stealing $70 from a gas station. On the advice of his lawyer, he pleaded guilty.

On Saturday, he was shot and killed at San Quentin Prison in California. He was killed, the authorities said, while trying to escape. Three prison guards and two white prisoners also were left dead.

Perhaps the most significant aspect is that Negroes in their comments did not focus on the killing of the guards or the other prisoners but on Jackson.

"At least," as one of them put it, "he wasn't the only victim."

Jackson became a symbol when he was charged along with two other Negro prisoners with the killing of a white guard at Soledad Prison in California in January, 1970. The guard was killed just after three black inmates were shot and killed by a tower guard.

Among Negroes, the right or wrong of the killings was not the issue. Rather, it was the conditions of the prison, the conditions that blacks saw behind the atmosphere of the killings.

Increasingly, Negroes saw the prisoners treated as subhumans. And more and more, they accepted the argument that too many blacks were held not as criminals but as political prisoners.

George Jackson was not simply a symbol. He was also perhaps the most prominent politicizer of the plight of black prisoners and a powerful writer.

He revealed much of his feeling and philosophy in his recently published book, "The Soledad Brother." The book is a collection of his letters from prison.

In a letter to one of his lawyers during which he discussed prison life, he wrote:

"How can the sick administer to the sick?

Equipment and Programs

"In the well ordered society prisons would not exist as such. If a man is ill he should be placed in a hospital, staffed by the very best of technicians. Men would never be separated from women. These places would be surfeited with equipment and meaningful programs, even if it meant diverting funds from another or even from all other sectors of the economy. It's socially self-destructive to create a monster and loose him upon the world."

Jackson often wrote Angela Davis, the black activist who is facing trial in California on charges of murder, kidnapping and criminal conspiracy. In one of those letters, he wrote:

"This is the last treadmill I'll run. They created this situation. All that flows from it is their responsibility. They have created in me one irate, resentful nigger—and it's building — to what climax?"

There had been speculation that the climax for George Jackson would be violent.

But the opinion was widely expressed yesterday that the incident at San Quentin was only a beginning of what was yet to come.

"The prisons in California are seething," a white writer who visited Jackson before his death said. "They are on the verge of overt, open rebellion."

The writer said that he came away with a great feeling of sadness.

"I couldn't help but think," he said, "how pathetic it was that a man like this had to be an outlaw, a person on the outside looking in—that the American system is such that it could not reconcile a man of such high intelligence and dedication."

He, too, saw Jackson as a symbol—a symbol of failure.

August 23, 1971

Convicts Revolt at Attica, Hold 32 Guards Hostage

By FRED FERRETTI
Special to The New York Times

ATTICA, N. Y., Friday, Sept. 10—More than 1,000 prisoners seized 32 guards as hostages and took over part of the Attica State Correctional Facility yesterday. As the outbreak began, the prisoners broke windows, set fires and shredded fire hoses. Negotiations to end the rebellion were still going on early today between inmates and correction officials.

In statements read aloud through a makeshift megaphone in the prisoner-held yard of Cellblock D, the inmates issued a list of demands that included coverage by state minimum-wage laws, freedom to be active politically, "true" religious freedom, an end to censorship of reading materials, the right to communicate with anyone at their own expense, "realistic rehabilitation" and "understanding," "not so much pork" and "more fresh fruit," "competent" doctors, more recreation and less cell time, and no reprisals for their uprising.

Commissioner Negotiates

Often during the reading of the statements, the words "racist" and "pigs" were shouted out.

Twice yesterday, in efforts to obtain the release of the guards, State Correction Commissioner Russell C. Oswald met with groups of inmates who had barricaded themselves behind piled-up furniture, lengths of hose and coils of wire mesh in the cellblock in the southeast corner of the maximum security prison's 55-acre compound.

Shortly after 11 P.M., Gerald Houlihan, a spokesman for Commissioner Oswald, came out of the prison's main gate to report that in addition to the 32 prison's civilian work force were also in the rear of the prison. He said that it could not be determined whether they were also being held by the rebellious inmates or had simply locked themselves away from the day's violence.

Mr. Houlihan said that the prisoners had "plenty of food and water" because they had managed to capture the prison's supplies, which prison authorities said would last "many days."

At least one of the day's fires, in a metal works shop, was still burning, Mr. Houlihan said.

Earlier Mr. Oswald had waded through pools of filthy water, ankle-deep mud and shards of glass, followed by five newsmen who were asked by the inmates to accompany the Commissioner as witnesses at a three-quarter-hour negotiating session.

The session, which took place within the captured courtyard across a battered gray bench, was in vain, despite two written assurances that the prisoners would suffer neither administrative reprisals nor be put in solitary confinement.

The captured guards could not be seen, but it was known that they were ringed by groups of prisoners armed with baseball bats, tools and pieces of pipe and hose. The convicts were wearing football helmets and masks made up of towels and various kinds of cloth.

Last night Mr. Oswald and the prison's superintendent, Vincent R. Mancusi, mulled over the demands of the prisoners, most of whom are black.

The convicts said they wanted specific visitors to see the conditions at the prison. Among those they listed were William M. Kunstler, the militant civil rights lawyer; Assemblyman Arthur Eve of Buffalo, a prison reformer; representatives of the Young Lords, the Black Muslims, the Fortune Society and the Solidarity Prison Committee of New York; Huey P. Newton of the Black Panthers, and Federal Judge Constance Baker Motley.

Attica, in addition to being a maximum-security prison, is one of the state's three "receiving" prisons, for processing and orientating new inmates. The two others are at Ossining and Clinton.

The determination of where a prisoner is to be ultimately incarcerated is made by the State Correction Department's classification and movement division. Joseph M. Ryan, director of the division, said the factors considered were the inmates' criminal history—including escape attempts he length of sentence, his mental and physical state, and his potential for rehabilitation.

The rioting at Attica began at 8:30 A.M., when, right after

breakfast, one group of prisoners refused to form into ranks to go on a work detail. The slight rebellion spread like wildfire, and soon about half of the prison population of 2,254—about 85 per cent of which is black—were running about the corridors, breaking windows, burning sheds and outbuildings, bedding and office furniture.

Smoke from fires in buildings and in the courtyard, and from the prison chapel and school, could be seen rising above the 30-foot concrete walls.

The prison employs 533 people, about half of Attica's work force. Of these, 378 are correction officers, 18 are correction supervisors and the remainder are civilians who work in the prison's hospital, farm, power plant and in educational, clerical and industrial jobs.

At any one time, from 50 to 100 guards patrol the prison's 28 buildings.

Word of the disturbances within the prison walls spread quickly through this town of 2,800 people, and sightseers from as far away as Buffalo, 40 miles to the west, and from Erie, Monroe, Wyoming, Genesee and Livingstone Counties came by bus, taxi, private automobiles and air to stand in front of the prison.

They would exclaim as smoke puffs rose above the walls. A local Lions Club set up a hamburger grill right outside the prison wall. Parents took children, who spent the afternoon either dashing about on the grass in front of the main gate or playing in fields directly across the road, State Route 238.

Approximately 500 law-enforcement officers, including state troopers from 14 counties, as well as deputy sheriffs and their staffs from surrounding counties and towns, began filing into the prison's main gate yesterday morning.

The state troopers were under the command of Superintendent William E. Kirwan, and his chief of the bureau of criminal investigation, Capt. Henry Williams.

Captain Williams, a tall, heavy man, assumed tactical control of the combined law-enforcement groups, which de-

ployed themselves around the inner perimeter of the prison, inside the four cellblocks, atop the prison walls and within the administration building.

Marksmen with .270-caliber rifles and sniperscopes were posted atop the highest building within the prison compound. They kept their rifles at the ready while Commissioner Oswald negotiated with the rebels.

At least six guards who had been seized were injured, and the prisoners allowed them to go free. They were hospitalized with injuries of varying degrees.

One inmate and one guard suffered heart attacks and were taken by separate entrances from the prison to the town of Batavia, 12 miles to the north.

No shots were fired during the day of rioting, although a great deal of tear gas was propelled into the captured cellblock.

State correctional officers do not carry guns; their only protection is a three-foot-long oak billy club. The state troopers carried 12-gauge shotguns, with special loads of heavy slugs.

The first state official to arrive today was Commissioner Oswald, who flew here from Albany in a state plane. He arrived at 2 P.M.

Shortly after his arrival, Assemblyman Eve arrived. He is a member of the Assembly Codes Committee and of the penal institutions subcommittee of the Assembly.

After conferring on the grassy lawn between the main entrance and the administration building, the two men went inside shortly after 3 P.M.

Assemblyman Eve said he had heard that there was an incident Wednesday at the prison in which an inmate threw a piece of glass at a guard and was sent to what is called "special housing" — the new prison terminology for solitary confinement.

He said there had been another report that, earlier this week, three prisoners had been beaten by guards and thrown into this "special housing."

As the state troopers continued to arrive during the day, they were followed by trucks carrying gas masks, riot helmets and clubs. Helicopters also began circling over the prison. A deputy in the Wyoming County sheriff's office said:

"This town has never seen such an accumulation of police power."

The helicopters were grounded shortly after 4 o'clock when the prisoners threatened to kill the hostages if the copters were not removed. To emphasize their demands, several hostages were paraded in the prison yard with pillowcases over their heads.

Negotiations Opened

The first negotiating took place shortly before 4 P.M. when Herman Schwartz, a professor of law at the State University of Buffalo, and Mr. Oswald went into the captured cellblock to talk with the inmates.

Before going in, Mr. Oswald said he was going to insist that the hostages be released and that the men return to their cells, and then grievances would be discussed. He said he would also insist that hostages and inmates in need of medical attention receive it immediately.

The negotiating team returned shortly after 4:30. Two newspaper reporters, Robert Buyer of The Buffalo Evening News and this reporter—who were acting as pool reporters for the scores of newsmen and television teams outside of the main gate—were approached by Mr. Oswald's deputy commissioner, Walter Dunbar, and asked if they would agree to accompany Mr. Oswald to a second negotiating session. He said the prisoners had demanded the presence of the media at the session.

In addition, he said, the prisoners had asked for one representative from television and one from radio. Two reporters, Myron Yancey of Radio Station WUFO in Buffalo, and Stewart Dan of WGR-TV in Buffalo, and Mr. Dan's cameraman, Terry Johnson, along with the two newspaper reporters, were ushered through the main gate.

Some Felons Sealed Off

The party moved through cellblock A—where two prison work details who had not joined in the rioting were sealed off—and into cellblock D. As they went in, Captain Williams was instructing the state troopers:

"Here's the word. The sheriffs' guys will back us up. We're going right in the front door. Nobody better lose a weapon or a pack. Defend yourself; use whatever force you have to. Be ready if negotiations break down."

That was at 4:55 P. M.

A minute later Captain Williams ordered all the troopers to load their guns, and at 4:57 he asked for a detail of 20 men to go in through the administration building gate.

The sheriffs' deputies carried Thompson submachine guns and new AR-15 Army rifles, currently being used in Vietnam.

At 5:07 P.M. the five newsmen, Commissioner Oswald and Mr. Schwartz went through a locked gate, down a destroyed corridor, where they were met by a cordon of prisoners armed with bats and pipes and escorted through the mud to the courtyard.

One inmate, a tall black man, read the first group of demands. He was followed by another black inmate, who called himself L.D. and who read a statement asserting that "the entire incident that has erupted here at Attica is a result . . . of the unmitigated oppression wrought by the racist administration network of this prison."

"We are men," the statement went on. "We are not beasts, and we do not intend to be beaten or driven as such. . . . What has happened here is but the sound before the fury of those who are oppressed. We will not compromise on any terms except those that are agreeable to us.

"We call upon all the conscientious citizens of America to assist us in putting an end to this situation that threatens the life of not only us but of each and every person in the United States as well."

September 10, 1971

ROCKEFELLER BARS A VISIT TO ATTICA

Cites Lack of Authority to Grant Total Amnesty

Signaling a harder line toward rebellious inmates at the Attica Correctional Facility, Governor Rockefeller yesterday rejected a prisoner demand and a citizen committee's recommendation that he go to the prison.

The Governor declared in a statement issued from his Pocantico Hills estate that he could not legally grant total amnesty to the rebellious inmates and would not even if he could.

"In view of the fact that the key issue is total amnesty . . . I do not feel that my physical presence on the site can contribute to a settlement," Mr Rockefeller said.

Sources close to the Governor indicated that the use of force to break the rebellion would be the next step if the prisoners rejected the 28 concessions offered by State Correction Commissioner Russell G. Oswald with the approval of the Governor. The concessions do not include total amnesty against possible criminal charges.

The citizen group that has been asked by the prisoners to serve as mediators and observers at the embattled prison had suggested the Governor go to Attica but stopped short of endorsing a prisoner demand that he negotiate in the prison yard with the inmates.

Time Seen Running Out

Rejecting any direct intervention, Mr. Rockefeller said the prisoners must now be given the opportunity to respond to the concessions offered by Mr. Oswald. One state aide described the Governor's reply as a veiled warning that time was running out for negotiations.

Mr. Rockefeller made it plain that he would not back down on his refusal to offer total amnesty.

"I do not have the constitutional authority to grant such a demand and I would not even if I had the authority because to do so would undermine the very essence of our free society —the fair and impartial application of the law," the Governor said.

Mr. Rockefeller, faced with the most serious prison rebellion during his administration, remained at his Westchester estate over the weekend but was in constant telephone contact with state and other public officials at the scene.

Officials at the scene included, according to Rockefeller aides, State Senator John R. Dunne, Republican of Garden City, L.I., who has been serving as chairman of the unofficial citizen committee at the prison; Representative Herman Badillo, Democrat of the Bronx, and Tom Wicker, a columnist of The New York Times.

Also at the scene are the Governor's two top aides, Robert R. Douglass, his secretary or chief of staff, and T. Norman Hurd, Director of State Operations, as well as Mr. Oswald. A Rockefeller aide said that no major moves had been made by the state officials without the approval of Mr. Rockefeller.

The Governor himself was described as "deeply distressed" by the rebellion and the threat to the hostages particularly.

He had been scheduled to appear at a Nassau County Republican dinner Saturday evening but canceled the engagement in order to keep in touch with the Attica rebellion.

meeting in San Juan, P. R., today but these plans could also be changed if the rebellion continues.

September 13, 1971

9 HOSTAGES AND 28 PRISONERS DIE AS 1,000 STORM PRISON IN ATTICA; 28 RESCUED, SCORES ARE INJURED

'LIKE A WAR ZONE'

Air and Ground Attack Follows Refusal of Convicts to Yield

By FRED FERRETTI
Special to the New York Times

ATTICA, N. Y., Sept. 13— The rebellion at the Attica Correctional Facility ended this morning in a bloody clash and mass deaths that four days of taut negotiations had sought to avert.

Thirty-seven men — 9 hostages and 28 prisoners — were killed as 1,000 state troopers, sheriff's deputies and prison guards stormed the prison under a low-flying pall of tear gas dropped by helicopters. They retook from inmates the cellblocks they had captured last Thursday.

In this worst of recent American prison revolts, several of the hostages — prison guards and civilian workers — died when convicts slashed their throats with knives. Others were stabbed and beaten with clubs and lengths of pipe.

Most of the prisoners killed in the assault fell under the thick hail of rifle and shotgun fire laid down by the invading troopers.

Doctor Fears More Deaths

A volunteer doctor who worked among the wounded after the assault said the prison's interior was "like a war zone." Standing in front of the prison in a blood-stained white coat, he said that many more of the wounded "are likely to die."

Late today a deputy director of correction, Walter Dunbar, said that two of the hostages had been killed "before today" and that one had been stabbed and emasculated.

Of the remaining seven, five were killed instantly by the inmates and two died in the prison hospital.

Mr. Dunbar said that in addition to the 28 dead inmates, eight other convicts of the total of 2,237 were missing. Two of the dead prisoners, he said, were killed "by their own colleagues and lay in a large pool of blood in a fourth-tier cellblock."

Oswald Orders Attack

He said he considered the state's recapture of the prison an "efficient, affirmative police action."

The action was ordered with "extreme reluctance" by State Correction Commissioner Russell G. Oswald after consultation with Governor Rockefeller. It followed an ultimatum to the more than 1,000 rebellious prisoners that they release the hostages they held and return to their cells.

Most of the 28 hostages rescued by the invaders and scores of prisoners were treated for wounds and the effects of tear gas dropped into the prison before the assault.

The recapture of the maximum-security prison was hampered by trenches dug by the convicts, filled with burning gasoline and ignited in cellblock corridors; by electrically wired prison bars separating detention areas; by homemade bombs and booby traps hidden in underground tunnels and conduits; by barricades and by salvos of molotov cocktails and bursts from captured tear-gas guns.

The attack began before 10 o'clock and ended four hours later as troopers fought hand to hand with stubborn knots of prisoners in the second tier of cellblock D, the portion of the prison that the prisoners had completely controlled since the riots on Thursday.

It came three hours after Mr. Oswald's ultimatum had been delivered.

The ultimatum was answered, Mr. Oswald said, when the prisoners "callously herded eight hostages within our view with weapons at their throats."

"The armed rebellion of the type we have faced threatens the destruction of our free society," Mr. Oswald declared. "Further delay and negotiations would have jeopardized more lives."

Members of a citizens' observers committee, which had been called to Attica by the state at the request of the inmates, were locked in an Administration Building office inside the prison walls during the assault. Those who cared to speak expressed deep regret that no way had been found to avert the killings.

Kunstler Is Bitter

William M. Kunstler, civil rights lawyer and one of a group of 10 persons who negotiated with the prisoners and acted as agents for Commissioner Oswald, was most bitter.

"A bloody mistake," he said, "this will go down in history as a bloody mistake. They sold the lives far too cheaply. I guess they always do."

The prison uprising began last Thursday when the convicts seized 32 guards and then, through a makeshift megaphone in the yard of cellblock D, issued a list of demands.

The prisoners set fires, broke windows and shredded fire hoses. Twice on that first day, Commissioner Oswald met with the inmates and attempted to negotiate the demands.

The demands included "complete amnesty" and freedom from "physical, mental and legal reprisals," "speedy and safe transportation out of confinement to a nonimperialistic country" and "true" religious freedom.

The uprising was viewed as the result of tension that had been building up in Attica for some time. In addition to the customary complaints about services, there were the added ingredients of a predominantly black body of prisoners being controlled by an armed white force and of the increasing political and radical awareness of the black prisoners that often infuriated the guards.

The assault on the prison followed four days of negotiations in which the convicts won agreement to 28 demands for social, administrative and legal reforms but held out for complete amnesty from criminal prosecution and the ouster of the prison superintendent, Vincent R. Mancusi.

The latter two issues were turned down by Mr. Oswald as nonnegotiable, and the amnesty demand was rejected Sunday by Governor Rockefeller as being beyond his constitutional authority.

This rejection came a day after the death of a guard, William Quinn, who was reported injured by the prisoners early in the revolt. He was one of 12 guards who had been hospitalized from injuries during the early rioting.

The action today began at 9:46 A. M. with two National Guard CH-34 helicopters dropping cannisters of tear gas into cellblock D, in the northeast corner of the 55-acre prison compound.

The 500-man contingent of state troopers had received orders to form up outside the prison walls by 6 A.M. Two hundred more troopers were transported into Attica, and 50 National Guard vans with about 600 troops drove through the night and arrived here before dawn. A dense rain began falling as day broke.

Sheriff's deputies from this Wyoming County and 14 other surrounding counties poured in in their own automobiles, carrying 30-30 deer rifles, pistols, surplus Army carbines and shotguns. All received riot helmets, yellow and orange rain slickers and gas masks and were sent through the main gate of the prison to a vast grassy lawn that lies between the gate and the compound proper.

There they were formed into makeshift companies under the direction of Capt. Henry Williams, chief of the local office of the State Bureau of Criminal Investigation.

Tear-gas cannisters were loaded into the two helicopters. Troopers armed with high-powered rifles equipped with sniperscopes were sent up to the guard towers atop the walls of the prison. Squads of troopers, deputies and guards, armed with tear-gas guns, were driven to points around the prison's perimeter.

By 8 o'clock the assault force was virtually in position. Even then members of the committee of observers began to filter into the prison. State Senator Robert Garcia, Democrat of the Bronx; Tom Wicker, columnist for The New York Times, and Louis Steel of the National Lawyers Guild were permitted in.

By the time Mr. Kunstler arrived, the assault force was at the ready, and he was barred from the gate. Fifteen more of the observers had spent the night inside Attica Prison.

At 8:30 an aide to Mr. Oswald, Gerald Houilihan, stepped outside into the rain and announced that the Commissioner had sent a memo to one of the leaders of the rebellious inmates, Richard Clark. Clark told him, Mr. Houilihan said, that the memorandum would be referred to the "people's central committee" in the yard of cellblock D.

The memo recounted the concessions made to the convicts and called on them to release the hostages and end the rebellion. .

The deadline for answering was set for 8:46 A.M. At that time the prisoners asked for more time to consider. Mr. Oswald gave them until 9 o'clock.

Clark walked back down a corridor that separated the Commissioner from the barricaded prisoners. Several minutes later the eight hostages with knives at their throats were paraded before Commissioner Oswald. But even as this final strain of negotiating took place, the last preparations for the assault were made.

At 8:37 A.M. grappling hooks had been brought in. The two National Guard helicopters and two state police choppers equipped with public-address sound systems warmed up.

At 8:55 a van loaded with riot helmets was backed up to the main gate, and at 9 o'clock the state police helicopters took off. The observer helicopter circled the prison yard in ever tightening circles.

8 Hostages Threatened

Troopers and deputies atop the prison walls and on the roofs of buildings that surrounded four cellblocks began relaying information by walkie-talkie back to the command post set up in the superintendent's office.

As the observer helicopter circled above the yard of D block, the eight hostages who had been shown to Mr. Oswald were dropped into a pit filled with gasoline. Then they were taken out and dragged to a trench full of gasoline, where their feet were thrown in and their bodies were bent backwards, so that their throats were exposed to the sky. Prisoners stood over them with knives.

At 9:30 A.M. the helicopter pilots spoke to one another. "There's a 200-foot ceiling," one said. "The low stuff is coming in from the west. It'll be about 100 feet."

At 9:42 Captain Williams's voice came over the short-wave radio: "All forces in position."

At 9:43 he ordered all power in the prison cut off. Only lights powered by portable generators remained on.

At 9:44 he ordered high-powered water hoses connected. At the same time an order was sent out for all available county ambulances to come to the truck gate of the prison, opposite the captured cellblocks.

At 9:45 Captain Williams ordered: "Zero in on targets. Do not take action until the drop."

A voice answered: "The drop has been made. Jackpot One has made the drop." This indicated that CS gas was flooding the yard of cellblock D.

At 9:46 Captain Williams shouted: "Move in. Move in. The drop has been made."

Gas seeping over the 30-foot-high walls caused those standing outside to weep. Also standing by, silently huddled in the rain, were the relatives of the hostages, most of whom had stood vigil since Thursday night. Some sobbed openly in parked cars.

Troopers were deployed in front of the gate, and nobody was allowed even to walk across a street.

At 9:52 a voice came over the radio: "Cease fire. Cease fire. Easy. Do not overextend your positions."

A call came at 9:45: "A rescue unit in the center of the yard. Expedite. Expedite. I've got an officer down."

"What yard?"

"D yard. Expedite the medical assistance, will you."

At 9:55: "The cease-fire only applies to the helicopter."

The observer helicopter circled the yard. Coming from its sound system continually was this message: "Place your hands on top of your heads and move to the outside of B and D blocks. Do not harm the hostages. Surrender peacefully. Sit or lie down. You will not be harmed. Repeat, you will not be harmed."

But by this time the hostages were dead.

At 9:57 a call came: "I need a stretcher, for God's sake a stretcher."

A minute later: "Clear the door in D yard. They're trying to get out. Jam that door up. Jam it up."

At 10 o'clock: "Force them into B yard".

One minute later, Captain Williams's voice came on: "Any thing that's interfering with the herding of the prisoners, clear it

away. You need more assistance in the yard?"

"Yeah, in D, where the negotiations were going on."

"Should I commit the reserve to join you in the yard?"

"Send in help, I need help to clean up that tent-city area."

At 10:16 the helicopters were ordered down: Ground your birds. Just be ready. Stand by for evacuations."

Commissioner Oswald came out of the front gate at 10:25. He was trembling but in control of himself. As he spoke the pops of tear-gas guns and the sharper cracks of rifle shots could be heard over the wall.

'Everything Humanly Possible'

"For the past four days," he said, "I have been doing everything humanly possible to bring this tragic situation to a peaceful conclusion."

He repeated the chronology of negotiations and the concessions he had made and said: "In spite of all these efforts, the inmates have steadfastly refused to release the hostages."

An observer reported that last night Mr. Kunstler had told the inmates that "third-world nations" were across the street from the prison "ready to help you—are you ready to go?" There were shouts of "yeah," the observer said.

"They continued to make weapons," Mr. Oswald said, "spread gasoline, make booby traps and electrical traps. I extended the deadline. They asked for more time. This was only a delaying tactic."

He then described the prisoners with knives at the throats of hostages.

"We hope to protect the lives of hostages if possible," the Commissioner said. "I pray to God that this works out to the best interests of all of us."

'We Got 30 Out'

Even as he talked, Captain Williams's voice continued to bark over the radio: "There's 30 out. We got 30 out."

At 10:35 the order was given: "Get as many pictures of these homicides as possible. Take them to the morgue in the Maintenance Building."

But some of the hostages were alive. A raincoated guard at the main entrance began shouting names to the relatives huddled in the rain.

"They're out," he yelled. He shouted nine names. Several women cried. Two of them embraced each other.

"Steve Wright," the guard yelled. "Miller. Walker's out."

One released hostage ran out of the door shouting, "White power!"

Standing behind the relatives was another observer, Clarence Jones, publisher of The Amsterdam News. "Time was all we

Associated Press
GAVE ORDER: Russell G. Oswald, State Correction Commissioner, after action.

asked for," he said quietly. "Time." His head was bowed.

At 10:40 a voice came over the radio: "How much of D block is secure to us if any?"

"The first floor south side is secured. Get us another radio."

"Get in there in D block and clean it out. Are National Guardsmen needed as replacements?"

"No."

"Don't overextend yourselves. We're doing beautifully. Let's not anyone get hurt now."

At 10:45 Captain Williams asked: "Is D block secured?" But another voice interrupted: "There is a possible explosive device in C block. Get me a demolition detail."

And from Captain Williams: "No shooting unless it's absolutely necessary. No more forward progress until everybody's accounted for. Let's get D block mopped up."

Outside of the gate Mr. Kunstler looked at a guard. "You murdering bastards," he said. "They're shooting them. They're murdering them."

At 10:55 Captain Williams urged: "Use extreme caution. No gunfire unless absolutely necessary. Utilize gas. We're coming in both ways through D block. . . . I need two men with shotguns at the south end of the Administration Building. Forthwith."

At 11:02: "There is one explosive device in cellblock C— in the tunnel to C block. Get everybody the hell out of there."

At 11:10 a voice on the radio said: "Thirty came out alive. Eight are dead."

A minute later Captain Williams said: "A block. Assistant bring prisoners back to their cells. Get them past Times Square [the junction of the corridors which separte the prison yard into four parts]."

At 11:15 all power was ordered out, so electrically wired bars could be deactivated, and Captain Williams ordered: "M3 backpack gas dispensers needed in the rear of D cellblock."

For a long while there was no communication as the troopers gradually gained the upper hand. The words "mop up" kept coming over the radio.

Then explosive "gas devices" were found in the prison chapel and in the metal machine shop. Demolition crews were ordered to these buildings.

At 12:30 P.M. Mr. Houlihan came out to announce the first death toll. "There are 37 dead," he said. "Nine of them hostages."

He said that it had been hoped by Commissioner Oswald that the gas dropped by the helicopters "would immobilize them quickly—the plan worked well."

Asked to weigh the success of the plan against the lives lost, Mr. Houlihan said: "No one ever had to make a tougher decision than this." He said Commissioner Oswald had consulted with Governor Rockefeller before ordering the assault on Attica.

As for the demands that had been agreed to by Mr. Oswald on Sunday, Mr. Houlihan said: "We'll have to take a look at

that. You must understand that an agreement was never reached, because they refused to talk with us."

Governor Rockefeller's decision not to come to Attica was harshly criticized by two members of the observer committee.

Representative Herman Badillo, New York City Democrat, came out of the prison late today looking haggard. "We wanted time," he said. "More time."

He was asked if he had wanted Governor Rockefeller to join in negotiations. He said: "No. We wanted the Governor to come to talk with us and get the benefit of our experience before he made a final and irrevocable decision. As far as

I'm concerned, there's always time to die."

And Assemblyman Arthur Eve, Buffalo Democrat, said: "We all felt the seriousness of the situation. Everyone felt that the situation was at a point that the Governor's presence was needed here."

Yet another member of the observer committee, State Senator John Dunne, Republican of Garden City, L. I., and chairman of the Senate Committee on Crime and Correction, said he would order public hearings into the causes of the Attica tragedy.

Late today State Department Correction officials said they would move 160 prisoners to other institutions and that several hundred others would soon follow.

September 14, 1971

AUTOPSIES SHOW SHOTS KILLED 9 ATTICA HOSTAGES, NOT KNIVES; STATE OFFICIAL ADMITS MISTAKE

INQUIRIES SLATED

Oswald Cites Factors That Could Have Led to False Reports

By FRED FERRETTI
Special to The New York Times

ATTICA, N. Y., Sept. 14—The nine hostages killed in the uprising in the Attica Correctional Facility died of bullet wounds, it was reported today after official autopsies.

Yesterday state correction officials asserted that the hostages had been killed by convicts in knife attacks and beatings. Some of the victims had

their throats slashed, the officials said.

Late tonight, State Correction Commissioner Russell G. Oswald confirmed that the nine hostages had died of gunshot wounds and not from slashed throats.

Report on Autopsies

The Monroe County Medical Examiner, Dr. John F. Edland, who performed eight of the autopsies, said earlier today in Rochester:

"All eight cases died of gunshot wounds. There was no evidence of slashed throats."

He added, however, that some of the guards and inmates on whom he performed post-mortems had clotted blood on their faces and necks.

The ninth wounded hostage, who was taken to nearby Batavia because of inadequate

medical facilities at Attica, was declared dead of gunshot wounds at the Genesee Memorial Hospital by Dr. Muhtesem Veznedaroglu.

A 10th hostage died at a Rochester hospital on Saturday night of injuries suffered when he was thrown from a cellblock window during last Thursday's riot, according to prison officials.

4 Studies Ordered

Word of the autopsy findings came as four separate investigations were ordered into the prison tragedy.

Commissioner Oswald made his explanation in a long, rambling statement that contradicted reports by several of his deputies on what happened inside Attica during yesterday's assault, when 1,000 state troopers, sheriff's deputies and

prison guards armed with rifles and shotguns stormed rebellious inmates.

He said: "They all died of gunshot wounds—none of them from slashed throats."

Gerald Houlihan, an aide to the Commissioner, said twice today that the inmates who rioted had no guns.

Mr. Oswald stood inside a grassy area directly inside the main gate, his back against the prison wall, illuminated by dozens of television lights. Off to his left was a grove of lilies, and right next to it was a small hand-lettered sign, which noted that the Lions Club of Attica intended to erect a monument for guards living and dead.

About 60 reporters were grouped in a 30 - by - 30 - foot square created by looping cord through gasoline cans. The perimeter was surrounded by correctional guards.

473

Mr. Oswald came out of the Main Administration Building at 10:45 P.M. He began by saying that he would like to explain a misstatement of fact—"that all hostages died as a result of cut throats."

He said a physical inspection recently completed on the bodies of all the dead hostages had revealed slash marks on throats and backs of necks, broken arms, broken faces, abrasions and lacerations.

He said the two questions that had to be answered were, first, why the exact cause of death was not known until this late hour, and, secondly, how the hostages died of gunshots.

He said: "A number of factors could have contributed to this," including the fact that for four days inmates had threatened to kill all hostages. "This was told to me personally on many occasions," he said.

Secondly, he said correction officers had seen hostages drop down as their throats were apparently being cut during the assault.

Third, he said that during the evacuation of the dead and wounded "a number of those evacuated had slashed throats; it has been verified that there are at least two with lacerated throats."

Men at Knifepoint

Next, several eyewitnesses saw men being held at knifepoint at the juncture of the corridors separating the four courtyards.

"It is possible. . . . given all of these factors that unauthorized reports" were circulated of hostages dying of slashed throats, Mr. Oswald said.

He paused, looked up from the paper from which he was reading, and said emphatically: "I never told you this."

He addressed himself to the second point: how the hostages could have died of gunshot wounds.

He said the contributing factors were that the hostages were dressed in prison garb and that "additionally, they could have been used as shields."

Mr. Oswald said 400 homemade weapons were recovered after the "action." Today, he added, additional hundreds of weapons were recovered.

These included, he said, "dozens and dozens of molotov cocktails," highly sharpened shears, table knives, spears, steel and metal pipes, tear-gas guns and projectiles, wire bolos, a half-dozen razors, swords, and bats with extended spikes.

The Commissioner said that a press report in a newspaper reported that a hostage had said that the throats of eight hostages had been slit. He said this illustrated the strain that the hostages were under.

'Not a Hostage'

He added: "I was not a hostage. What is clearly known and verified is that . . . 38 hostages stood with knives at their throats and crowbars at their heads, and that each hostage had been assigned an executioner. The rescue operation saved 29 of these fine men."

Walter Dunbar, deputy to State Correction Commissioner Russell G. Oswald, arrived in the prison early in the evening. He was asked about the report of the guards being shot, about the Medical Examiner's report that no throats had been slashed and no bodies mutilated.

"I have no knowledge of that," Mr. Dunbar said.

He was reminded that he had been a member of a team that briefed reporters on Monday and told them of the stabbing and castration of one hostage. Mr. Dunbar shook visibly and said, "It deserves to be investigated."

Yesterday, in the wake of the assault on Attica Prison, Gerald Houlihan, an aide to Commissioner Oswald, said that the dead hostages had had their throats slashed and had been beaten. He said then that the inmates had not had guns.

He had no comment on the report that the hostages had died of gunshot wounds and not because their throats had been slashed.

Today, Mr. Houlihan twice repeated that more than 1,000 inmates who rioted had not had guns.

"I don't know of any guns found," he said, standing in front of the main gate of the prison. And when he was asked if he was certain that there were no guns, he said: "Not to my knowledge."

Throughout the four days of negotiations Mr. Houlihan and other observers had maintained that the inmates had no guns—only bats, clubs, makeshift knives, swords and captured tear-gas canisters. When Mr. Houlihan was informed of Dr. Edland's disclosures, he acknowledged that he and Commissioner Oswald were aware of them.

Later Mr. Houlihan came out once again from the prison to announce that the state police and guards, searching the debris-strewn cellblocks, had turned up a quantity of homemade zip guns.

Dr. Edland was asked if any of the wounds could have come from zip guns. He said, "No."

The disparity between Mr. Houlihan's and the medical accounts of the death of the hostage guards was only one of several contradictions and highlights of a day that saw groups of lawyers armed with a court order barred from the prison; that saw a group of volunteer doctors told they were not

needed to help treat wounded inmates still in the prison, although "medical teams were on the way from western New York."

It was a day when the first of several hundred prisoners were bused out of Attica for other prisons; when guards threatened to resign and retire; when the official death toll in the worst prison riot in recent history rose to 41—31 inmates and 10 guards; when the District Attorney of Wyoming County, Louis James, who has criminal juristdiction over the prison, was described as "confused" as to how his prosecutions for murder and other criminal acts would proceed.

Dr. Edland said that 27 bodies of prisoners and guards have been delivered to him at the County Medical Examiner's Building in Rochester early today. The prisoners' bodies had tags on their toes marked P-1, P-2 and so on, up to P-18. The guards' bodies had their names on tags tied to toes.

Assisted by Dr. Kenneth Marten and Assistant Medical Examiner Richard Abbott, two of the few forensic pathologists in western New York State, and observed by the state police, who had requested him to do the autopsies, Dr. Edland examined all of the bodies and concluded that all of the guards had died from gunshot wounds.

"Some were shot once, some as many as five, 10, 12 times," he said, with "two types of missiles, buckshot and large-caliber missiles; many were shot at, I believe a fair distance." He said the bullets came either from rifles or handguns.

Dr. Edland was asked if the bullets could have come from state troopers' rifles. He said, "I'm not familiar with the weapons carried by the state police." He refused to speculate further, saying: "I'm not interested in prosecution or defense in any case."

Nevertheless he carefully addressed himself to points that contradicted official versions of how the guards had died.

Mr. Houlihan had said that one guard was emasculated. Dr. Edland said: "None of the bodies were mutilated except by gunshot and stab wounds."

Mr. Houlihan had said that two of the guards had been killed before the assault on the prison took place and that rigor mortis had set in. Dr. Edland said: "All died yesterday morning."

The Medical Examiner said that one of the hostages had "a single cut in the back of the neck" but that the cause of death for all of the hostages was gunshot wounds. He said that all of the slain hostages had their hands tied behind their back, "that many were beaten severely about the head"

and that "one had his back beaten and his buttocks."

Dr. Edland was asked if there was any difference in the character of the wounds in the bodies of the guards and those of the inmates. He said "no difference," and he answered similarly when asked if the men were dressed alike.

He discounted a report that he had received a phone call from Governor Rockefeller, urging him to cancel his press conference at which his disclosures were made.

He said a "Mr. Johnson" from the Governor's office had called simply to get the results of the autopsy and had "absolutely not" put any pressure on him. He pointed out that post-mortems were matters of public record and added:

"I am my own man and, I call things as I see them. All I know is I have 27 bodies in my office, which is more than I ever want to see again in one day."

A spokesman for the Governor said in New York City tonight said that "there is no Mr. Johnson on the Governor's staff."

Dr. Edland said that state trooper observers watched as he performed the autopsies. "I think they kept waiting for the next case to show up. Finally we ran out of hostages. I'm used to not finding what people tell me I will find," he said.

Some details of circumstances surrounding the initial examination of the bodies at the prison were disclosed today. The coroner's physician in Attica, Dr. Merlin Bissell, did not make the examinations.

Coroner Paul Slusarzcyk of nearby Perry said he had been informed by prison officials yesterday that Dr. Bissell was not available and that, as a result, the prison's physician, Dr. Paul Sternberg, had been appointed acting coroner to make the initial check of the causes of death.

The inmate's list of grievances expressed during the uprising had included complaints about Dr. Sternberg's care.

Dr. Bissell indicated he had been available for the job.

Besides the investigation announced by Governor Rockefeller, there were also inquiries by the District Attorney of Wyoming County, a legislative committee headed by State Senator John R. Dunne, Republican of Garden City, and one by a team of observers that had participated in the fruitless negotiations to win release of the hostages.

A reported total of 42 inmates, some seriously injured, are in the prison hospital ward.

Before dawn today a caravan

of six cars brought nine doctors and three nurses to Attica. They said they were from the Medical Committee for Human Rights—from Lincoln Hospital, St. Luke's Hospital, Harlem Hospital and the Albert Einstein Medical Center in New York City—and that they wanted to assist the prison doctors. They were refused entry to the prison.

They were joined by 35 lawyers, led by Walter Hellerstein of the Buffalo Legal Aid Society, who said that the group was disturbed about reports of prisoners being interrogated without legal counsel. He pointed out that Commissioner Oswald had granted that demand of the prisoners.

They, too, were denied entry although earlier they had obtained a preliminary Federal court order in Buffalo requiring that the prison officials permit them to enter. But guards refused to let them in, physically barring them with guns over their chests.

Likewise, barred was Robert Alexander, director of the Cleveland Court Offender Rehabilitation Program, who said he had spoken to Commissioner Oswald over the phone and had told him he was coming.

In Buffalo this afternoon, Federal Judge John T. Curtin vacated the preliminary order and turned down a request for a preliminary injunction that would have permitted lawyers and nurses to enter the prison.

Mr. Dunbar, the deputy commissioner had told the judge that the prisoners would be advised of their constitutional rights and that it was not practical or necessary to admit the lawyers for that purpose.

Six buses carrying prisoners to other correctional institutions left in three separate caravans escorted by state troopers. The first left shortly after 5:30 this morning and the last five hours later.

Sheriff Dalton G. Carney of Wyoming County was an early visitor at the prison. He came out saying that the inside was "a mess." He said some cleaning up was being done by crews of guards; that National Guard teams were searching for explosive devices believed still hidden in the underground conduits beneath the prison cellblocks; that six convicts were still unaccounted for.

The sheriff said that Governor Rockefeller had called him last night to congratulate him on an excellent job of police work. He quoted the Governor as saying "I've been thinking of you" and of adding that "the Commissioner [Oswald] has been sitting on a powder keg."

Sheriff Carney said he would be assisting the Wyoming County District Attorney in his criminal investigation of the events at Attica. He said the prosecutor, Mr. James, was "confused like all of us—when you have something like this where do you go?"

The sheriff said the Governor had also telephoned Mr. James to congratulate him on the amnesty stand he had taken. The District Attorney said last week that he would prosecute the prisoners for their criminal acts during the riots. Complete amnesty from criminal prosecution was one of the prisoners' main demands.

Bitterness directed at Governor Rockefeller came from Assemblyman Arthur Eve of Buffalo, a member of the citizen observers' committee that had attempted to negotiate a settlement with the rebellious convicts. "I think the Governor ought to be indicted," he said.

He was asked if the decision was Commissioner Oswald's. He answered: "No. Absolutely, unadulteratedly, positively, no."

Assemblyman Eve said that he had attempted to have the Governor go to the prison. He had tried, the Assemblyman continued, to see Robert R. Douglass, secretary of the Governor, who for three days was in an office next to that assigned to the observers.

"He refused to see me," Mr. Eve reported. "I went to the office. I was stopped by guards. He did not want to see me."

September 15, 1971

Prisons Feel a Mood of Protest

By STEVEN V. ROBERTS

A "movement" paralleling those that have arisen in recent years among blacks, students and women has now begun to emerge in the nation's prisons.

In states like California and New York, the traditional seedbeds for new causes and ideas, this movement is often highly political and radical. It tends to identify with such groups as the Black Panthers and has spawned a network of supporting organizations outside the prison walls.

The recent outbreaks at San Quentin and Attica, which killed a total of 46 inmates and prison employes, are only the most visible and most violent results of this movement.

In many other states prisoners are neither so radical nor so organized, but they are causing considerable concern among corrections officers. Instead of taking hostages, they are making speeches, demanding meetings, and occasionally calling strikes.

"There's a feeling of constant crisis," said Sheriff William Lucas, who is responsible for the Wayne County jail in Detroit. "You have to handle each day as it comes in hope that you have the right thread of strength going in the right direction."

'Attica Was No Surprise'

"We're heading for a civil rights revolution inside prisons like we had on the outside," explained Ronald L. Goldfarb, a Washington lawyer who has frequently advocated prison reforms. "No one realizes how many riots there have been in prisons in the last few years. Attica was no surprise; it's just one of many. There was nothing unique about Attica, and no one has any reason to think this is the end."

The prison movement is a confusing and controversial development that has caused great polarization among those involved. Many rebellious inmates feel they are fighting for justice against a racist and repressive system. Many prison officials view them as dedicated revolutionaries intent on manipulating and murdering others for their own destructive ends.

In dozens of interviews in the last week with prisoners, guards, administrators, lawyers and academicians, an attempt was made to sort out these views and produce a picture of what is happening among the more than 200,000 Americans who spent today in prison.

One basic fact about the prison movement is that it is led largely by blacks and other minority groups. Members of these groups get arrested and incarcerated far more often than whites. In California the non-white prison population is 45 per cent. In Attica it was 85 per cent. In the Lorton Correctional Complex, serving Washington, it is 98 per cent black.

"Look at the people in prison," added Mr. Goldfarb. "The whites are the dregs of their society. The black guys in prison—not to over-romanticize them—are often the most attractive people. They're in prison because they've demonstrated qualities that in other groups have often meant advancement — acquisitiveness, high mobility. That's what made the frontiersmen great, but for a black kid in the ghetto those are bad things to be."

Most experts agree that prisons reflect what is happening outside, and that the prison movement is closely tied to the general climate of the country.

"They saw the welfare groups organize, the students, the blacks organize for their rights," explained Gus Harrison, director of corrections in Michigan for 19 years. Prisons are like a microcosm of outside society. There's much more awareness that to organize is the way to go."

John O. Boone, who once worked for the Southern Regional Council in Atlanta and is now warden of Lorton, added: "They're just like the black kids I saw in Gulfport, Miss., and Sandersville, Ga. They're not going to tolerate the oppression their parents tolerated. They aren't taking it any more in any community, the prison community or the free community."

This determination not to "take it" any more shows itself

475

in the recurring demand of prisoners for "dignity" and "respect." The rebel at Attica who shouted: "We want to be human beings, we will be treated as human beings," spoke for thousands of inmates in dozens of prisons.

The new prison mood emerges in many ways. In Colorado State Penitentiary, blacks and Chicanos have organized their own exclusive groups to bring in outside speakers and discuss racial and political issues.

In Jackson State Prison in Michigan, prisoners staged a three-day strike demanding a minimum wage of $1 an hour.

In Sing Sing near Ossining, N. Y., prisoners objected to lock-step discipline, and "rehabilitation" programs, such as the bake shop. "Baking is no longer considered rehabilitation — just a way for the state to make money," said Warden J. Leland Casscles.

In Texas and Maryland, prison administrators meet regularly with inmates, hoping to avoid the problems that plagued college administrators who ignored student demands for more participation in decision-making.

In California, attempts have been made to form a "prisoner's union" to negotiate with officials. But in some cases, the growing tension has led to violence and death.

Last Thursday in Folsom prison, two hours after a New York Times reporter had interviewed the warden, a white civilian employe was stabbed to death in the prison laundry. A black convict, a known associate of the prison's most militant inmates, was held as a suspect.

The roots of these feelings are varied and interrelated. Probably the single most important cause, as Mr. Harrison said, is the general concern throughout the society for more

individual rights and "self-determination."

Moreover, more people who were active in the movements outside prison are now becoming inmates. Henry di Suvero, a New York lawyer with many inmate clients, said:

"The guys coming off the street, the guys who have been in the Black Panthers, in heavy actions outside, will not all of a sudden junk what they've learned and thought about, what to organize around."

A second major factor is prison conditions themselves: the outmoded buildings, the poor food, the make-work programs, the whole experience of looking at the world through a set of bars.

Recruitment by Muslims

"The young people on the street who belong to one of the black radical groups are talking about repression, but in most instances, their talk is theoretical," explained George Bohlinger, director of the Institute for Correctional Administration at American University. "They have no real evidence or experience of repression. But when these people are declared social deviants, they are faced with a repression that is not theoretical but tangible."

In addition, a tremendous process of education or, some would say, indoctrination, is taking place in many prisons. One aspect of this is the continuing recruitment by the Black Muslims, although the Muslims in most places are now concentrating on religious issues and sometimes even oppose such political groups as the Panthers.

One lawyer called prisons a "university' for political education. The "sacred texts" of black revolution — Eldridge Cleaver's "Soul on Ice," "The Autobiography of Malcolm X," George Jackson's "Soledad

Brother"—are treasured like gold.

In Auburn prison in New York, such books rent for a pack of cigarettes a night. In Jackson, inmates circulate typed manuscripts of those that are banned.

Many of these works put forth two similar themes. One is that blacks are "political prisoners" who are jailed because of their skin color and their poverty. The other is that poor blacks and whites must join in a class revolution against "Establishment" figures of any race.

Particularly in California, these themes have crystalized in the concept of a "convicted class," an idea with great appeal to prisoners. The quasi-Marxist concept gives prisoners a new status—that of "victim" —and a new role in the "historical class struggle."

"Prisoners no longer think of themselves as pathetic or evil or sick," explained Fay Stender, the founder of the Prison Law Project in Oakland.

Mrs. Stender represents another element in the movement, the rising interest of young lawyers and free-lance radicals in the prison problem.

"It was a real iceberg a couple of years ago, none of us were aware of it," said Peter Franck, a Berkeley lawyer. "Once we got into it, we saw the way in which prisons were a microcosm of the total society."

Prisoners are one of the few causes left in which the aid of middle-class whites is still welcome, and many radicals in a place like California are surprised and grateful to find themselves needed.

Half the prisoners confined in the maximum security wing of San Quentin when George Jackson was killed there are represented by radical attorneys.

Moreover, prison law is virtually virgin territory, since the Federal courts have only recently begun to look into the whole question of prisoners' rights. Already, for example, the lawyers have forced California to improve procedures used at parole revocation hearings.

There is also plenty of work for nonlawyers, either as investigators for the attorneys, money-raisers for defense committees, helping hands to transport prisoners' families, or as foot soldiers in the periodic demonstrations over prison conditions.

All this activity has left many prison officials worried and confused. Some accuse "outside agitators" of stirring up trouble. As Warden Walter Craven of Folsom put it:

"Our prisoners are consumed with bitterness and resentment and are ideal recruits for the more sophisticated radicals on the outside who cloak their real intentions with talk of humanitarian reforms."

Others are caught between their desire to meet prisoner complaints and yet to keep control. To some, the delemma is almost overwhelming. Warden Casscles of Sing Sing said:

"First psychiatry had the answer, then education was the answer, now it's environment— what made the prisoner the way he is? We're no longer trying to force a prisoner into a particular mold, so we have no criteria any more for running a prison. The only criterion is to keep it trouble free.

"But maybe it's trouble free because the lid is on tight, who knows? You don't know when to join them or what side to take—and the nature of everything today is taking sides. The same thing that happened in Attica could happen to me. . . . "

The Other Prisoners

By TOM WICKER

Like the policeman, the prison guard is a much-maligned man. To prisoners, they are all "pigs"; to many others they represent everything brutal and insensitive in American society. No doubt that view is warranted, in many cases; but as a general indictment it is grossly unfair.

As a result of the uprising at Attica, and the bloody crushing of it, the prison guard is at the moment more in the public eye than ever before. In fact, school children in the once placid town of Attica—where the prison is the primary employer—have been complaining to reporters that it is untrue that their fathers and brothers are cruel and brutal to prisoners.

Actually, the worst faults of the Attica prison can hardly be laid to its guards; at worst, they are the instruments of an inhuman system, and at best—as many showed in the aftermath of the uprising—they may understand more of the prisoner's grim plight than do high state officials.

In the first place, neither at Attica nor elsewhere are guards well-trained for their demanding, difficult and dangerous jobs. To refer to these men as "corrections officers" is an exercise in euphemism. Most qualify for their positions by passing a civil service examination and a physical, not by going through even as much training as most city policemen receive.

Statistics show that most guards have a low level of general education, with 16 per cent of them not having completed high school. They are paid commensurately, with 79 per cent earning less than $8,000 a year. Thus, it is too much to expect that many of these men will have a sophisticated understanding of social issues, or that their handling of prisoners will reflect sensitive psychological approaches; society just doesn't seek out men of those qualities to guard its prisoners.

Moreover, the prison guard's job is highly dangerous and many of these men—particularly in a time like the present, when there is widespread unrest among prisoners—spend their working days and nights in something near terror. They know that prisoners most anywhere, if led by determined men, can stage the kind of revolt that erupted at Attica; so guards are constantly subject to being held hostage, as well as to the hourly dangers of working among desperate and hostile men.

At the same time, of course, prisoners are substantially in the power of guards at most times, and since many guards are insensitive and brutal, the prisoners, too, live in fear. Men who fear other men usually come to hate them, so in these vast and

"Men who fear other men usually come to hate them, so in these vast and gloomy fortresses, where everything is largely hidden from the public, fear and hatred mount in an ever-tightening circle. This hideous atmosphere can almost be touched and felt...."

gloomy fortresses, where everything is largely hidden from the public, fear and hatred mount in an ever-tightening circle. This hideous atmosphere can almost be touched and felt, as if it were tangible, in many prisons.

So, as a Utah state prison guard told Wallace Turner of The New York Times, the guards are in jail with the prisoners. It is a situation that is always ripe for violence; and when, as at Attica, there is also present in its most virulent form the racial animosity that so divides American society today, these prisons are little more than explosives waiting to be set off.

Moreover, ample history from the earliest times shows that a master-slave relationship is more corrupting for the master than for the slave. To have absolute power over another human being can bring out the worst in a man—just as, in some cases, abject slaves have been known to rise to heights of character and nobility. When guards have nagging fear for their own safety, when they are irritated and frustrated by the conditions in which they work, when they find prisoners in their power, with no one to see—in such cases, even good family men and churchgoers can be corrupted into physical brutality.

None of this is meant to suggest that guards have no personal moral responsibility for their own conduct; nor is it meant as a justification for the excesses that some observers and prisoners allege New York state prison guards even now are visiting upon the recaptured Attica rebels.

But if American society is going to tolerate a prison system designed primarily to cage animals, and if the men who operate it are going to be recruited from the lowest educational levels, paid the minimum and pitted physically against the inmates in Darwinian struggle for survival, then nobody should expect much in the way of "corrections" or "rehabilitation."

We get from our guards, that is, just about what we ask and just about what we pay for.

September 28, 1971

Agnew Blames Convicts
Special to The New York Times

BUFFALO, Oct. 7 — Vice President Agnew said this afternoon that in his opinion the violence at Attica had been "caused by the convicts, without question."

"These situations do not evolve because society in general failed these people," the Vice President told a group of reporters at the airport here. "It evolved because they [the prisoners] attempted to politicize their plight, caused by their antisocial conduct, and to utilize the conscience of society in an improper fashion, in my mind, to bring about public sentiment in their favor."

Mr. Agnew said he read a detailed report of the Attica riot this week in The New York Times, which he described as a newspaper for which he has "great respect in the reporting sense."

From reading The Times article, Mr. Agnew continued, "it was completely evident to me that the acts of violence and outrage which triggered the Attica situation were initiated by the convicts."

Mr. Agnew was in Buffalo to speak at a fund-raising dinner for the Erie County Republican Committee.

October 8, 1971

477

U.S. Judge Bids Virginia Halt Abuse of Prisoners

By BEN A. FRANKLIN
Special to The New York Times

WASHINGTON, Oct. 31 — A Federal judge in Virginia has issued a sweeping injunction against that state's prison system, barring as cruel and unusual punishment of inmates the regular use of bread and water, chains, physical punishment, enforced nudity and the censorship of mail.

The order of Federal District Judge Robert H. Merhige Jr., accompanied by a 78-page opinion, was filed yesterday without public notice at his court in Richmond. It was released here today by Philip J. Hirschkop of suburban Alexandria, Va., the lawyer who argued the case for the plaintiffs.

The prohibitions were effective immediately.

Mr. Hirschkop, who was engaged by the American Civil Liberties Union, called the court's action "a bill of rights for inmates."

"I think you have to expect the state to appeal this decision," he said, "unless Governor Holton can prevail upon his Attorney General and others to accept it. I really expect an appeal, but I do not think that any important part of Judge Merhige's order will be stayed pending the appeal. This is going to be affirmed."

Key state officials received advance notice of Judge Merhige's findings several days ago so that his ruling could be put immediately into effect.

Judge Merhige declared in his opinion that the evidence presented during a two-week trial last November disclosed "a disregard of constitutional guaranties of so grave a nature as to violate the most common notion of due process and humane treatment."

He specifically enjoined the State Department of Welfare and its Division of Corrections from doing the following:

¶Imposing bread and water punishment on any inmate for any infraction of prison rules.

¶Using chains, handcuffs, hand-restraining tape or tear gas "except when necessary or required to protect a person from imminent physical harm or to prevent escape or serious injury to property." Testimony at the trial disclosed that such restraints were used commonly on "obstreperous" inmates, often without disciplinary hearings.

¶Using physical force "against any inmate for purposes of punishment."

¶Forcing nudity or bodily restraint of any kind as a means of punishment or otherwise "for any period longer than it shall be reasonably necessary to secure the services of a doctor" to determine whether an inmate must be restrained to protect himself from self-inflicted injury.

¶Placing more than one inmate in the same solitary confinement—Virginia's solitary cells are 6½ by 10 feet— "except in an emergency."

¶Interfering with or imposing punishment for efforts by inmates to file court documents, to have confidential communication with lawyers, even when confined to solitary, and to write legislative or other government officials.

The judge also ordered the restoration of "good time," or credit toward early release for good behavior, to all prisoners who had been docked such time without hearing or "without compliance with minimum standards of due process," such as written charges and written findings by disciplinary boards.

Judge Merhige gave the defendants, who are the top correctional officials and the directors of many of the 36 state prison facilities, 60 days to institute uniform due-process hearing procedure for cases involving the docking of good time.

All prisoners now in solitary or "padlocked cells" as a result of discipline that cost them good time were ordered freed from such confinement pending a rehearing.

In most Virginia prisons, particularly the maximum-security penitentiary in Richmond and the medium-security state prison farm at Goochland, Judge Merhige said, a prisoner who is docked good time and placed in solitary is effectively denied any reaccumulation of good time as long as he remains in solitary. Such punishment, he said, has been meted out for "indeterminate" periods.

In a specific reference to the so-called C-cell, the solitary confinement cell block at the Virginia State Penitentiary in Richmond, where a week of the trial was held, Judge Merhige directed that prisoners being held there be afforded full due-process hearings within 30 days or be released to the general prison population.

The judge ordered the State Division of Corrections to prepare and distribute to the court, as well as to Virginia's 6,000 state prisoners, a complete list of rules and regulations setting forth "standards of behavior expected of each inmate" and the minimum and maximum punishments for each rule violation.

"In many instances," the judge found, "punishment has been of such a nature as to be abusive and violative of the most generic elements of due process and humane treatment."

Judge Merhige ruled that Virginia's prison system had consistently violated the Eighth Amendment to the Constitution, which prohibits cruel and unusual punishment.

He said that inmates could be sentenced to punishment for such undefined offenses as insolence, sarcasm or agitation and that there was no appeal.

He noted that prisoners committed to solitary confinement were sometimes placed on bread and water, were in every case given a diet of no more than two meals a day, were allowed to shave and take showers only once a week and were denied exercise, sometimes for months.

In cases of misconduct, "obstreperousness," "agitation" or "bad attitude," Judge Merhige said, the trial record disclosed that inmates were denied mattresses and forced to sleep on a concrete floor.

Mr. Hirschkop said that two different United States Courts of Appeals overturned within the last three years district court findings less sweeping than Judge Merhige's, but he described the Virginia case as "the first one of these suits with such a massive trial record."

The case is known as Landman v. Royster. The plaintiffs included Robert J. Landman, who is now free after serving a sentence for armed robbery. M. L. Royster, the former superintendent of the state prison farm, is dead.

Guards View Life From Inside Cells

By PHILIP WECHSLER
Special to The New York Times

BORDENTOWN — The cell doors clanked open, and the 20 young men slowly entered the sparsely furnished cells. Then the heavy bars slammed shut and the men were locked in for the night.

"I can't go nowwhere, I can't even get a pack of cigarettes," Herbert Schiff remembered saying to himself that first night as he lay on his cot in the isolation cellblock of the state reformatory here.

But he consoled himself with the knowledge that his confinement was only temporary, that in fact it was part of his training as a new prison guard.

Mr. Schiff, 32 years old, who was a retail manager for the Woolworth Stores before deciding to become a guard, said:

"It was eerie laying there, looking through the bars. But I think I got to know how a real prisoner must feel."

And that is the goal of an experimental training program run by the New Jersey Division of Correction and Parole — to give new guards an understanding of how it is to be a "real" prisoner.

It starts the first day of the three-week course here, when Mr. Schiff and the other 19 new officers were processed like the inmates they would soon guard.

Naked and Searched

They were stripped naked, had their whole body searched for contraband and weapons ("It's easy to hide a small razor inside your lip," Mr. Schiff explained.), fingerprinted, given an impersonal number and issued khaki prison garb.

"It really bothered me, you feel completely defenseless," said Van Moses, 30, recalling the search of his body.

Mr. Moses, a former clerk in the Mercer County Court, said the body search "really strips away all your dignity; it's difficult to think of yourself as a human being in that situation."

Capt. William Anderson, a 15-year veteran of the state prisons system and an instructor in the new program, said: "We want the officers to relate to the inmates, to have an understanding of their problems. In essence, what we are trying to do with this program is to give the officer the ability to detect an inmate's problem before it gets out of hand.

"These men have to supervise the inmates by their intelligence and ability to lead, and not by a billy club. We believe that can only be done if the officers experience, at least to some degree, what the inmates experience."

The experimental program began in January with a Federal grant of $350,000.

Captain Anderson and other officials pointed out that they had devised the program and received tentative approval before the prisoner outbreaks in Attica and Rahway last year.

During the three-week program, the guards-in-training put in five 15-hour days a week and receive close to 200 hours of instruction, ranging from psychology of the inmate, self-defense, to criminal justice. Some of the course titles are "Dehumanization," "Inmate Culture," and "Psychopathology of Inmates."

A Realistic Feeling

The men also receive lectures on narcotics, race relations and homosexuality, three critical problem areas within prison walls. They also take a course on the use of keys, because the officers are armed only with keys and whistles. Thus, knowing how to use the keys to a complicated lock system can save a life in an emergency.

An important part of the training is the locking up of the new guards. During the three weeks the officers are put in the 7-by-9-foot cells on Mondays, Tuesdays and Thursdays. Although the cells are not locked after the first night, the men are prohibited from leaving the cellblock area, one used strictly for the program.

The cells are furnished only with beds, chairs, sinks, toilets and footlockers.

"You cannot really understand what it means to be an inmate until you are locked behind the bars in a cell," Mr. Moses, said.

Mr. Moses and the other guards-in-training, who spend one week in the institution where they will work regularly before undertaking the program, all agreed it was a great help to their understanding of the inmates.

"Unfortunately, the public image of the prison guard is that of a brute," Captain Anderson said. "But we don't run prisons today with fists and nightsticks. Times have changed and so have our correction officers. And we know it is changing for the better."

June 18, 1972

Attica a Year Later: Calmer, but Grievances Persist

By MURRAY SCHUMACH
Special to The New York Times

ATTICA, N. Y., Sept. 10— "I don't want to be a puppet just to prevent a riot," said Edwin Temple, one of 28 prisoners elected by fellow inmates to speak for them to administrators of the state prison here.

This outburst came almost a year after 32 prisoners and 11 hostages died here in the bloodiest prison riot in the nation's history. Temple's comment, during a heated discussion with Edward Young, another committee member, reflected the complex situation that has developed in the cells, corridors, halls and offices behind the high walls since the five-day riot that began Sept. 9, 1971.

Many grievances still smolder, but the general tension, inmates and officers agree, is far less than before the riot. Improvements— many in response to demands by the rioters—have been made, but prisoners insist that far more should be done.

"The whole system," said Young during the verbal free-for-all in the exercise yard, "is still geared for recidivism, instead of getting you to walk out like a man."

Aggravating life at this prison are the many visible signs—as well as memories— of the riot. The prisoners, moving two abreast, and the officers with clubs cannot help seeing the closed-down sections, gates lying on floors, cracked windows.

Grass is nonexistent or discolored where once there were trenches dug by convicts. Piles of donated books are being removed from cartons by inmates to restock the library. School classes are reborn. The chapel, which is also the movie house, has new draperies.

Ernest L. Montanye, who became prison superintendent here four months after the state police crushed the riot with guns, says that despite the setback of a brief sit-in, "rapport between prisoners and officers has been making progress, so that we are at least able to talk and get along while the place is being rebuilt."

Major changes, besides the formation of the liaison committee, include these:

¶The prison population has been reduced from 2,200 to 1,158, with the black percentage down from 80 per cent to less than 50 per cent.

¶The number of officers has been increased from 380 to 415, with 19 of them black and two Spanish-speaking. There were no black or Spanish-speaking officers when the riot started.

¶Regulations on visitors have been relaxed. Friends, acquaintances and potential employers may visit prisoners, whereas only close relative used to be allowed. In addition the screen between visitors and inmates has been removed.

¶Censorship restrictions on mail and publications have been greatly eased.

¶New clothing has been issued, the commissary and mess hall operations have been improved and a law library has been established for inmates.

One change was welcomed over the weekend by the inmates. They may now make collect telephone calls to family or close friends. An officer places the call from newly installed booths and when it is accepted, the prisoner takes over the phone.

Among the important grievances that continue to rile inmates are the following:

¶The Parole Board does not tell an inmate why he has been turned down. To correct this would require a change in state policy.

¶Vocational programs enable those with skills to continue to use them but do not help those without skills to acquire them.

¶There is no indoor gymnasium, and the exercise yard is not pleasant during the bitter upstate winter. Deputy Superintendent Harold J. Smith says bids have been let for a gym; he was surprised the inmates did not know this.

¶Inmates get from 20 cents to a dollar a day for work at the prison, mostly less than 50 cents a day.

On one point all inmates and officers interviewed here seemed agreed: Racial tensions among inmates are not important and are certainly much less bitter than in the world outside the prison.

That blacks and whites seem to be mostly in separate clusters is not the result of racial hostilities but because they feel more at ease that way.

"That's no conflict between white and black," said a black inmate as inmates played basketball, handball, lifed weights, jogged or just talked in the yard. "We are together because we got something to rap about. We don't hate each other."

The disagreements about the inmate liaison committee are of particular concern because the committee was born of the riot, and the disagreements explore basic attitudes of inmate and officer and touch the nerve endings of both groups.

In failing to achieve more, the inmates say, the committee creates frustration among some prisoners. This either makes them more bitter or induces them to be contemptuous of the committee.

"We were established to stop trouble before it starts," says Young. "But the way things are we can't talk about any officer. And yet the most important relationship is between officer and inmate, so far as stopping trouble is concerned."

Of the original 28 elected to the committee—the inmates select roughly one for every 40 inmates—only six remain, according to prisoners. The administration says 10 are still there. Prisoners say that most of the originals were forced out by punishment or transfer or a sense of futility.

The administration says that while some committee members gave up in disgust, most finished their prison terms or were paroled or transferred elsewhere at their own request. Some, the administration says, were transferred for disciplinary reasons.

Guards have mixed feelings about the liaison committee. They agree with the idea, but some think it will undermine discipline.

"Some of these committee members," one officer said, "found power and became very aggressive. They wanted to run the place."

Young contends that the committee should represent all views of the inmate population. "Otherwise," he says, "some elements will go underground, and this is what we do not want to see happen."

There seems to be general agreement among inmates that the introduction of black and Spanish-speaking guards has tended to reduce tensions. Some, however, think this is not so much because they are black and Spanish-speaking but because they are young, with less resistance to new ideas than the older officers whose friends died in the riot.

One of the black officers, Ulysses Westbrook, said that white as well as black inmates had told him they were pleased that black officers had been assigned to the prison.

Inmates seem to think that Superintendent Montanye is better than his predecessor, Vincent R. Mancusi. They say that he is prevented from doing the things he thinks are necessary by a lack of funds or his superiors in Albany.

Mr. Montanye is convinced that the inmates and most prison officials want to see huge prisons replaced by smaller ones closer to populated areas.

"Inmate reaction would be very favorable," he said. "They would like to be near home."

September 11, 1972

A model, clockwork-orange prison

By Phil Stanford

JESSUP, Md.: The Patuxent Institution for Defective Delinquents is widely considered a "model rehabilitative prison" and a showplace of enlightened penology. At Patuxent (named for a nearby river), inmates are called patients, which means that they are here not to be punished but to be cured. Patuxent's director, Dr. Harold M. Boslow, a properly benign gentleman with a soft pink face, swept-back white hair and glasses that slide down his nose, is a psychiatrist. Two of the three associate directors are behavioral scientists, and for a prison population of about 400, there are more than 40 psychiatrists, psychologists and social workers on the staff. To use a phrase I heard there frequently in interviews, Patuxent is more a "therapeutic community" than a prison.

In one of Patuxent's many brochures, Dr. Boslow describes the institution this way: "Dealing with nonpsychotic patients, it combines the functions of a mental hospital and a penal institution." To a visitor, the second function is immediately apparent. Patuxent is surrounded by a 30-foot chain-link fence fronted with a sheet of slick plastic "climb-proofing" and with barbed wire along the top. The guards in the towers carry high-powered rifles, and all the windows on the two main buildings in the compound come equipped with steel bars. (The buildings themselves—sprawling, three-story renditions of fifties institutional architecture—look as much like high schools as prisons, but that probably says more about high school, than anything else.) The mental hospital for nonpsychotics is, of course, not so obvious from the outside.

Under Maryland's Defective Delinquency Law, convicted lawbreakers who appear by their records to have a compulsive criminal nature can be referred to Patuxent for a psychiatric evaluation. The trial judge, the prosecuting attorney, or even the defense lawyer may request the diagnosis after sentencing. (The men referred, it might be emphasized, are all legally sane, or as Dr. Boslow puts it, "nonpsychotic." If they were judged insane, they would go to the state hospital.) Once a person has been diagnosed as a "defective delinquent," he may be formally committed to Patuxent by a civil court —or, if not, returned to the penitentiary to complete his sentence. If he is committed to Patuxent, which happens 85 per cent of the time, he will receive treatment for his condition. When he is well, he can leave.

From the first, Patuxent has had the enthusiastic support of America's liberal psychiatric establishment, which has long seen crime as a social and emotional problem. One member of the panel of psychiatrists that recommended Patuxent to the Maryland Legislature was Dr. Robert Lindner, author of "The Fifty-Minute Hour" and "Rebel Without a Cause." Another member, well-known in the profession as an expert on the burgeoning field of forensic psychology, was Dr. Mannfred Guttmacher. Guttmacher, who was chief medical officer of the Maryland courts when Patuxent was established in 1955, is considered something of a patron saint by the administrators.

Dr. Karl Menninger, perhaps the country's most honored psychiatrist, thinks Patuxent is a "great idea." He says, "It's the only one of its kind." In fact, as Menninger later qualified himself, prison systems in other states, particularly California, have attempted treatment programs like Patuxent's, "but none of them have done anything in nearly as much detail." (The U.S. Bureau of Prisons is now building a Behavioral Research Center at Butner, N.C., where it will develop behavior-modification programs for

Federal prisons, but that won't be in operation until 1974.) "Patuxent is a progressive step forward," says Dr. Menninger.

Dr. Thomas Szasz, professor of psychiatry at New York's Upstate Medical Center, sees it somewhat differently. Szasz, an author who is critical of nearly everything about institutional psychiatry today, says Patuxent is a "concentration camp." "Patuxent," he told me, "is worse than the way they use mental institutions in Russia, except that when they haul someone off over there everyone here gets upset. It reminds me of the Biblical proverb of the mote in the eye." In Patuxent Szasz sees merely a further extension of psychiatry's already abused power to "define and rule."

When I asked Menninger if he had any response to Szasz's charges, he sounded grumpy over the phone and refused to say anything at all. Szasz, for his part, says people like Patuxent's director, Dr. Boslow—and therefore, presumably, Menninger himself—ought to be hanged. Some days it is particularly difficult to find a nice, reasonable discussion.

On the third Thursday of every month, the Patuxent Institution Board of Review meets in a basement room of the administration building. It is a very ordinary, utilitarian room, and in the middle of it there is a long conference table. The seven members of

the board sit around three sides of the table. The patient, when he is summoned, sits at the other end. Over a year, every one of the 400 or so patients at Patuxent will get a hearing, and depending on his progress toward responsible citizenship, as indicated by his disciplinary record, achievements in a vocational program and in psychotherapy, the board may vote to release him or to bind him over for another year.

The members of the board besides Dr. Boslow are: Dr. Arthur Kandel, Dr. Giovanni Croce and Forrest Calhoun, Patuxent's three associate directors; Dr. Olive Quinn of the Goucher College sociology department; Leonard Briscoe, a lawyer from Baltimore; and Edward Tomlinson, a young law professor from the University of Maryland. The representation of various professions on the board is determined by Maryland law.

Board of Review meetings are closed to the public, even to lawyers of the patients. I was allowed to attend one session (July 20-21) only on the condition that I would not embarrass any of the patients by printing their names. Except in the case of one patient who expressly asked me to use his name, I have observed this ground rule.

PATIENT I

The man before the board is a large Negro with heavy scar tissue above his eyes and what appears to be a knife mark on his right cheek. The mimeographed sheet that each of the seven board members holds says he is 35 years old. Under "Antisocial/Criminal Activity" is the entry "Armed Robbery." There is another notation that reads "Murder (2nd), charge dropped." The patient takes his place at the end of the table.

"You know why you're here," says Dr. Boslow, who is sitting at the other end of the table. "What would you like to tell us?"

"At this time I would like

to ask for work release. I feel at this time that I understand myself where I didn't understand myself before. Before I felt I wasn't really loved or understood. I even took a man's life."

"Did you really do it?" someone asks.

"Yes," says the patient. He says the charge was dropped for lack of evidence.

"Tell us about it."

The patient explains that he killed the man in a barroom brawl because of his mother's teachings. "She always told me to defend my younger brother," he says. "But now I see that I was wrong. I feel I was very immature in my thinking."

"What do you mean by that?" Dr. Croce asks.

"I mean I would never find fault in myself. I always found fault in the other person."

The board asks about his fighting.

"I know my place isn't out in the street fighting," he says. "I know now that fighting doesn't solve anything. It doesn't bring any understanding."

"How are you going to handle your alcohol problem?"

"I realize now that I used alcohol as a crutch. I don't need it any more."

After about 10 minutes the board runs out of questions.

"Is there anything else you want to say?" Dr. Boslow asks. This is a standard courtesy of the interviews.

"Yes," says the patient earnestly, "I do. I'd like to say that all these things I've done, I can see now that my ways and concepts were all wrong. I can see now that they caused a great deal of pain and sorrow to other people. I'm truly sorry for that." He develops this theme with a few additional variations before moving on: "I used to think it was a weakness to show weakness."

BOSLOW (showing some excitement): Wait a minute. What do you mean?

PATIENT: To cry, to be sorry.

BOSLOW: *You mean to show love.*

PATIENT: *Yes.*

BOSLOW (*after a pause*): *Thank you.*

The patient departs and the board votes on his request for work release. The count is 5 to 2 against. The majority, although pleased with the patient's evident progress, feels on the basis of the interview and the report before the board that more therapy is required in this particular case.

Dr. Boslow explains that Patuxent "is designed to identify dangerous offenders, retain and treat them." Of the 425 patients currently at Patuxent, 305 have been committed and the other 120 are waiting to be diagnosed. A recent breakdown of patients' crimes shows murder (4), second-degree murder (18), assault with intent to murder (43), robbery (35), robbery with a deadly weapon (87). There are a number of convictions for sex offenses, including rape (45), attempted rape (14), statutory rape (2), perverted practices (29), indecent exposure (4), and attempted perversion (1). The list also includes breaking and entering (9), housebreaking (14), rogue and vagabond (2), petty larceny (3), car theft (10), forgery (2) and writing bad checks (2).

Dr. Arthur Kandel, who was my guide for most of my visits, anticipates the question. Dr. Kandel, who grew up in the Bronx and retains the accent and the brashness, is an excellent host, affable and loquacious. During a recent case against Patuxent, the prosecution chose to question Kandel rather than Dr. Croce because Kandel was such a good witness. Kandel explains that 78 per cent of the patients are in for crimes involving violence. The others were examined and found to be "potentially violent." A patient's criminal record is of course important to the psychiatrist making a diagnosis,

but it is only one consideration. "Our focus here is on behavior," says Kandel, "and we are not that concerned with the concept of guilt or innocence." What all patients committed to Patuxent have in common is that all of them have been diagnosed as "defective delinquents."

Under Maryland's unique statute, a defective delinquent is "an individual who, by the demonstration of persistent, aggravated, antisocial or criminal behavior, evidences a propensity toward criminal activity, and who is found to have either such intellectual or emotional unbalance, or both, as to clearly demonstrate an actual danger to society so as to require such confinement and treatment, when appropriate, as to make it reasonably safe for society to terminate the confinement and treatment."

As the Patuxent staff interprets the law, this means a very particular type of criminal. The brochures stress that certain lawbreakers, such as a professional gunman, wouldn't qualify. Dr. Kandel explained why. "The professional gunman," he said, "ordinarily has chosen this as a way of earning a living, and in most other respects you won't tell him apart from any other human being. He may very well have a wife and kids that he's devoted to. He'll probably pay his taxes reasonably well. He'll probably live in a decent neighborhood, in a decent home. You know, it's just that he picks this peculiar way of earning a living. Now a professional gunman, for example, doesn't act on impulse or he wouldn't be a professional. Whereas our people, by and large, one of of their characteristics is they're very impulsive. The professional gunman can delay frustration, he can tolerate delay, he can plan. And if he plans a hit at this time and this place and it doesn't pan out, so he retracts and makes new plans and goes ahead again."

A defective delinquent, to

use psychiatric language, is someone afflicted with a behavioral problem called an antisocial disorder. Until recently the official term was sociopath, and before that it was psychopath, but both terms have been dropped from the official nomenclature of the American Psychiatric Association. Perhaps the best description of a defective delinquent comes from Dr. Guttmacher, who played such an important role in getting Patuxent started. In a 1965 court case (when it was still fashionable to refer to a defective delinquent as a sociopath), Guttmacher was asked to describe the symptoms, which he did at some length:

"My own feeling is that probably the most basic thing is their inability to make any strong identifications with other people, and by that I mean they don't become a real member of the group. They are not team players; they don't have strong loyalties toward their country, toward their family, toward anyone. Their affectionate relationships are very shallow. They become involved in numerous affairs with women, frequently with multiple marriages. . . .

"Then there is this underlying hostility which manifests itself in many ways. As I said before, there is, in a sense, a war with society, and they get great satisfaction in seeing what they can get away with in their acting out against society. They are an extremely restless group of people. . . . They normally have not the success in school which their intelligence would indicate they might have. . . . They very frequently become dropouts. They frequently have conflict with teachers because part of their pattern is to be in conflict with authority figures. . . . They can't take criticism with any degree of equanimity, so that their work records are almost universally very fugitive. They rarely stick to anything for any great length of time. They are basically hedonistic, and

they must satisfy their needs as rapidly as they possibly can and at the expense of others."

Interestingly enough, elsewhere in his testimony Guttmacher referred to a defective delinquent as "a rebel without a cause." Robert Lindner, who was another of the founding fathers of Patuxent, must have been very surprised when the character James Dean played in the movie version of his book became the antihero of a generation. Lindner wanted to cure him.

PATIENT II

An 18-year-old black takes his seat and folds his hands quietly before him on the table. The record says he was convicted of rape.

"At this time I would like to ask the board for leave," *he says.*

"All right," *says Dr. Boslow.* "Tell us why you think you are ready for leave."

"When I first came to this institution I was a very confused and mixed-up 15-year-old boy. I had a low opinion of myself," *he says.*

He says he hated his father and mother. He tells how, when he was a small boy, his father would come home and beat him, then lock him in his room. He had come to have a low opinion of his mother because she hadn't done anything to stop it.

BOSLOW: *Do you like yourself now?*

PATIENT: *Yes. I've come to accept myself. I accept my mother for what she is.*

BOSLOW: *How about your father.*

PATIENT: *He's dead.*

BOSLOW: *But that doesn't help. You know that you still carry your father with you in your mind. Until you come to accept your father too, you won't be able to solve anything.*

PATIENT: *Oh yes, I accept my father too.*

The board votes unanimously to grant the leave.

"Frankly," says Dr. Boslow, "I think the most important thing in the development of the character is the early family relationship. That's the one thing that stands out in our case histories. Well over 95 per cent of our patients have easily detected pathological home situations. You know, overprotective, domineering mother, brutal, alcoholic father, sadistic father, bad relationships between the parents. That sort of thing.

"That's the type of therapy that we've attempted to incorporate in the institution——a stable, structured environment with therapists who have some concept of themselves as human beings and who are able to impart this to our patients. Our people come to us, they're all school dropouts—I think we've had only one or maybe two college guys here. They've never really learned to live in society, and essentially they have no skills. We've got to treat them in all these areas."

Dr. Giovanni Croce is the associate director in charge of treatment programs. He wears gold wire-rimmed glasses and speaks in a charming mamma mia accent. When Dr. Croce finished medical school in 1946, he left Rome and spent the next 10 years as a psychiatrist for the Venezuelan Justice Department. From Venezuela he came to the United States.

"What is very important to me," he says, "is the relationship you develop with these people. Therefore, at the beginning when they go out, they're going to be dependent on you. You make yourself available. I make myself available at any time. Most of my best friends now are people who were here and were released, black and white. They still call, they still let me know when a child is born or how they're doing. This is the relationship of which they were deprived. Whether I take the role of the father, the mother or the big brother doesn't matter. They know there is a somebody who will be there ready to listen."

Would he say, then, that the institution was acting in the role of a parent?

"I think to a certain extent we are acting in the role of a superego, which means we act as the parent, yes."

"What we do," Dr. Boslow told me, "is socialize them."

At Patuxent a patient enters what the professional staff calls a "therapeutic milieu." That means it is a total environment, every part of which —including group psychotherapy, vocational therapy and a programed system of incentives—is intended to work toward the patient's rehabilitation and prepare him to return to society.

Patients are expected to attend weekly group-therapy sessions, where (to quote from another of Patuxent's brochures) "they are made aware of their distorted perceptions, feelings and attitudes, and the part these distortions play in developing their antisocial behavior pattern." Therapy groups are generally composed of 5 to 10 patients and a therapist. Therapists "use their own methods," Dr. Kandel told me. He, for example, is more "directive" in his approach. "Other therapists like to let patients talk it out themselves."

The core of the program is the "graded-tier" system, which "provides rewards for socially acceptable behavior." There are four levels to the system, and a new patient must start on the lowest and work his way up. "As he moves upward in the tier system, a patient gains more privileges, but also more obligations and responsibilities. . . . The rewards reinforce the positive aspects of his behavior." Fourth-level patients, for example, can stay up as late as they want, third-level patients must be in bed by 11:30 and second-level patients by 11. Only fourth-level men get to have Sunday afternoon picnics on the prison lawn with members of their families or other approved guests. Fourth-level day rooms have

pool tables, but third-level day rooms have only Ping-Pong tables. Most important, to be eligible for parole a patient must have reached the third or fourth level. "It works," Dr. Croce told me, "because that's the way life itself is set up."

Dr. Kandel, helpful and talkative as usual, says the institution has also tried a number of drug programs with Johns Hopkins, the University of Maryland and the National Institute of Mental Health. "We have ongoing research with all of these agencies in terms of drugs that are coming out that may be effective as behavioral controls in terms of impulsivity," he said. "They use all the usual psychotropic drugs." Johns Hopkins, he said, was currently doing a great deal of research with Dilantin, on the theory that in some of the patients "the electrical transmissions of the brain are messed up." He says, "It's no sweat getting volunteers because all of these programs pay volunteers." Kandel recalls that once Patuxent started an aversive therapy program using electroshock. "But we caught so much flak we had to drop it before we could even get going."

"Our experience," says Dr. Boslow, who has been Patuxent's director since it began, "has confirmed the fact that all human beings are essentially alike, that all people can be treated and helped, provided they want to be. I don't believe in punishment. I don't think in those terms. I think that people who commit crimes should be treated until they are capable of going out into society again."

That, in outline, is Patuxent's treatment program. The only thing that remains is perhaps to underscore what Dr. Boslow has already stated—that once a patient is committed to Patuxent, he must stay until he is cured. One of Patuxent's unique features as a prison—another one borrowed from practice at mental

institutions—is the indeterminate sentence. To get out, a patient must meet the approval of the institution's Board of Review, which is responsible only to itself. Failing that, he can try a recommitment hearing, to which he is entitled every three years.

PATIENT III

"This is an interesting case," whispers Dr. Boslow in an aside as the next patient enters the room. He is an extremely tall and muscular young white man. The record says he is 21. It quickly develops that he is an XYY chromosome mutant* and under study by Johns Hopkins. The first thing he does when he sits down is to object about the Johns Hopkins students who have been showing up at the Patuxent gate, "tossing [my] name around." He has a plaintive, boyish voice. Dr. Kandel assures him that he is quite right in being annoyed and that the practice will be halted immediately.

The patient requests a leave to visit his family at Christmas time. "If I may have a few minutes I'd like to speak of what I have planned for the future," he says.

"Of course," says Dr. Boslow.

For the future he wants to see his family for Christmas, earn money for an apartment, get a learner's permit and marry a 20-year-old girl who began writing to him after he came to Patuxent.

When XYY came to Patuxent three years ago he had been both violent and suicidal.

"Do you ever think of cutting yourself now?" Dr. Boslow asks him.

"No," he says, "I have not only myself to live for anymore. I have someone I love."

*Humans normally carry a pair of sex-determining chromosomes, XX in the female and XY in the male (with Y being the male chromosome). While the evidence is so far unconvincing, some studies suggest that males born with an extra Y chromosome may be more inclined to aggressive behavior than XY males.

Dr. Boslow thanks him and he leaves.

While the board is voting, Edward Tomlinson, the young law professor, asks about the research program that Johns Hopkins is conducting with the patient. Someone explains that XYY is getting dosages of a female hormone, presumably to counteract his "supermasculinity."

TOMLINSON: Does he understand the effects of the drug?

BOSLOW: Yes, we explained the whole thing to him. We don't want any misunderstandings.

TOMLINSON: Well, what are the effects?

KANDEL: We don't know. That's what they're trying to find out.

The board votes unanimously to grant the patient's request for Christmas leave.

According to figures released by the institution, 38 per cent of all patients are now serving beyond their original sentences. Of those who were sentenced to terms of five years or less, 75 per cent are, as they might see it, overdue. Dr. Boslow acknowledges that Patuxent has been under fire lately, particularly for its indeterminate sentence. "What they don't understand," he says, "is that it is necessary for therapeutic reasons." In one of his pamphlets, Dr. Boslow writes that "there is a long history of disbelief in the efficacy of psychotherapy with persons having strong antisocial tendencies." At first, many defective delinquents won't even admit that they're sick. The indeterminate sentence is simply "a mechanism for making them realize that they need help," he explains. "That's why the indeterminate sentence is so important. It's a means of attracting their attention to the fact that they need to make some changes to get out."

Dr. Kandel develops the point. "No one likes to admit

he's not normal," he says. "Everybody who's in here, their primary drive is toward getting back in society. This is part of their problem—the inability to delay gratification. From a treatment point of view, the indeterminate sentence is very helpful."

The patients, who have staged four publicized disturbances this year, including a 60-man sit-in in August, may have another viewpoint. But they are not the only nonpsychiatrists who have failed to appreciate Patuxent's therapeutic approach to criminal behavior. Lawyers are a source of constant complaints. Patients' lawyers are not allowed to be present during psychiatric examinations, although they argue that the information gathered there, including facts about crimes for which the patient was never charged, is used against the patient at his commitment trial. Lawyers are also excluded from the Board of Review because they would "interfere with the therapeutic program."

One of the most irritating of these lawyers to the staff (Dr. Kandel calls him "a kooky young lawyer trying to make a name for himself") is Julian Tepper, head of the National Law Office of the Legal Aid and Defender Service in Washington, D.C. On behalf of 13 patients, Tepper in 1971 brought suit in Maryland court (*McCray et al. v. Patuxent*) on a lengthy list of complaints.

During the trial several patients complained of being locked up for long periods of time in totally dark cells. Besides the regular four tiers of cells that are part of Patuxent's "graded-tier system," there are two separate rows where patients who misbehave are frequently sent. Some of these cells are smaller and can be closed with a heavy steel door. Critics of Patuxent often refer to them as "punishment" or "solitary confinement."

When Dr. Kandel was called

to the witness stand, he explained this misunderstanding to the court. There are some people who respond favorably to positive reinforcement, as for example, the graded-tier system, he said. "There are also people who don't respond and need [to devote] a certain period of time to what is known as negative reinforcers." Patuxent's negative-reinforcement program included "deprivation schedules" and perhaps a certain amount of "sensory deprivation," which is probably what the patients referred to when they said there wasn't any light in their cells.

To judge from comments by the Patuxent administrators, the McCray case was an even more traumatic episode than the U.S. Supreme Court decision (*McNeil v. Patuxent*) this summer.

In *McCray*, Patuxent was ordered to establish a written disciplinary code, to limit the time patients could be put in "negative-reinforcement' cells and to allow access to the press. In June the Supreme Court told Patuxent to release noncommitted patients whose terms had expired. These "noncooperatives," as they are called, had refused to let a psychiatrist interview them for their precommitment diagnosis. Patuxent has released about 10 of these patients since the decision. There are at present about 60 to 70 "noncooperatives" at Patuxent. The ruling, of course, does not affect the more than 305 patients already committed.

Dr. Boslow and his staff are used to misguided criticism by now. I asked Dr. Boslow why Patuxent wouldn't let patients facing commitment read books about psychology or psychiatry. "We don't allow them for a good reason," Boslow replied a little wearily. "We want to get the story just as it is and not a profusion of jargon which would serve to hide the basic pathologies present. Later in treatment, if they want to read books on psychol-

ogy or psychiatry, yes. When it's deemed appropriate by the patient's treatment team." Boslow suggests that "The Crime of Punishment" by Menninger might be suitable. "Even something by Bettelheim." Dr. Boslow, a gentle and cultivated man (University of Virginia Medical School, class of 1939), says one of his favorite books on psychiatry is Bruno Bettelheim's "The Understanding Heart."

PATIENT IV

The next patient to enter the board room is a 26-year-old fellow with long wavy hair, drooping mustache and quizzical, diffident eyes. His name, one judges from the mimeographed fact sheet, is Jewish. This is notable only because almost all the patients at Patuxent are either from the black Baltimore slums or the dirt-poor Anglo-Saxon hinterlands. The record shows that the patient is in for assault. When he was 17, in jail awaiting trial for burglary, he hit a guard over the head with a rock in a sock. He received a two-year sentence. That was in 1964.

The patient is before the board because he has violated the terms of his "school-out-live-in" program. He had been studying music at one of the local colleges. One night when he returned to Patuxent he was caught with a marijuana cigarette in his jacket pocket.

The board members ask him why. The best answer he can come up with is that some people he knew were smoking and he joined them because he was "feeling empty at the time." He explains himself in spiritless abstractions, attempting to assess his sickness, but obviously not quite sure what it is.

"I know what's right here," he says, tapping his temple with his forefinger. "But when it's between me and society, I'm, ah, undeft. I guess that's right. I can't think of another word."

"That's a good word," says Dr. Kandel approvingly.

"I guess I just have to keep trying to understand," the patient says. He gets up to go.

After he leaves, Dr. Kandel says that he is very fond of the patient. Dr. Boslow agrees that he is "a very engaging fellow." Dr. Olive Quinn, the sociology professor from Goucher, apparently doesn't. "He's not my style," she says. Dr. Quinn, a squarely built, middle-aged woman smiles a lot when she talks.

There is some discussion about whether it is legal for the board to revoke parole programs, such as "school-out-live-in," without observing due process. This had come up in an earlier case as well, with the law professor Tomlinson making the objection.

TOMLINSON: I wish we could get a ruling from the Attorney General on this. I don't think it's legal to revoke work release without a full hearing.

QUINN: No, I don't think so. I think all we need is new terminology. We're working here in a therapeutic situation.

The board decides to revoke the patient's school privileges, but to reconsider him in a few months.

This summer Patuxent received a couple days of publicity in the Baltimore and Washington papers when the courts ordered the release of a 29-year-old patient, Grover Miller, who had already served more than eight years for breaking a window. The exact charge was "malicious destruction of property." Miller's disciplinary record, which the institution let me see, showed page after page of entries saying, "refused medication" and "refused meals," but nothing that indicated violent or even unruly behavior.

To get the complete story I talked to Miller's therapist, a bearded young man with an M.S. in psychology from Wisconsin, Lee Runkle. (Patuxent is proud of the fact that all its psychologists have at least their master's. Runkle, it turns out, is even working on his doctorate.) Runkle told me he

had found that Miller was an "extremely unstable individual." He often had "insupportable fantasies" of what he would do on the outside. Runkle couldn't give me any examples without violating his professional ethics as a therapist. "But I'll tell you one thing that won't appear on the records," Runkle confided, "Grover Miller had a habit of throwing beer bottles at people when he got drunk."

When I approached Dr. Kandel, he took a look at the record and said that Miller was "probably one of those marginal cases." Running an institution such as Patuxent is no simple matter, he acknowledged. Administering the indeterminate sentence was perhaps the most difficult problem of all. "They say to you, 'How do you know I'm going to foul up if you don't give me the chance to get out there and foul up?' It's not an easy thing to handle," said Kandel.

Well, what do you say to a man who was sent up for two years and after four years is still inside?

"I tell him that based on my best professional judgment, this is my opinion," said Kandel. "You've got to consider the probabilities. You have to think that if you release a patient and he fouls up, he's the one who's going to pay for it, not you."

The responsibility weighs heavily on Kandel and the rest of the staff. In nearly 18 years of operation, out of a total of 985 patients committed to Patuxent, only 115 have been released as cured. Another 332 have left through recommitment hearings — those whose sentences have expired go free; the others serve out their terms in the penitentiary.)

PATIENT V

When Roosevelt Murray came to Patuxent in 1958, a skinny 17-year-old kid from the black part of Baltimore, it became apparent to the pro-

fessional staff that he was a defective delinquent. Tests showed a decided potential for violence. A psychiatrist who interviewed him diagnosed the problem as a "Sociopathic Disorder—Antisocial (with affinity for auto theft)," and on Oct. 11, 1961, Murray was committed to Patuxent, just as his four-year sentence for unauthorized use of a motor vehicle was about to expire. He has never really gotten used to the idea.

Murray, 31, a starchy 5-foot-8 or so, sits glaring across the conference table, at everyone in general, but particularly at Dr. Boslow. He is in handcuffs and a guard waits by the door. Clearly no one is taking any chances. Not long ago Murray slugged his social worker. He is also charged with stabbing another social worker, whom, as Dr. Boslow explained later, "he didn't even know."

"You know why you're here," says Dr. Boslow. "Tell us what you want to tell us."

"I want to tell you that you have no right to be holding me," begins Murray at somewhere near a shout. "I want to say, for all the damn good it will do me, that I want to get out of here, man. That's what I want to tell you."

The board listens to approximately two minutes of this tirade before it decides to ask Murray about his behavior. "Mr. Murray," asks the sociologist Olive Quinn in a conciliatory voice, "why don't you behave some way so we feel we can let you out?"

In truth, as the file shows, Murray has always been a problem at Patuxent. In 1962 he made his first appearance before the Board of Review. The record says he appeared hostile and spoke belligerently to the board. "I don't like the idea of my time being up and me still being here," he had said. In 1963 Dr. Boslow interviewed Murray at length for a psychiatric evaluation. Toward the end of the session, Murray apparently lost control of his emotions. "Murray

launched into a hostile attack on the United States and said he wanted to go to Russia," Dr. Boslow wrote in his report. "At this point he seemed very angry, paranoid and disturbed." In 1965 at his recommitment hearing, Murray lashed out again. After the judge finished reading a list of Murray's disciplinary infractions at Patuxent, Murray was said to have turned over the table he was sitting at and shouted, "This is the unfairest court I've ever seen." The newspaper account says he threatened Dr. Boslow.

Murray's ample disciplinary record, which begins with entries for smoking, throwing a bag out the window and fighting with another inmate, shows a similar progression toward violence. The board asks about the recent incidents which are mentioned on the mimeographed sheet. Someone asks Murray why he stabbed a social worker. "Because I wanted to get out of this place any way possible," he shouts.

QUINN (sweetly): And did you think the proper way to get out of here was to kill a social worker?

MURRAY (loudly, pleadingly): You're killing me, aren't you? You people don't realize what you did to me in my 14 years here. You know that Roosevelt Murray never stabbed anyone before he came here.

I don't like what you're doing to me here. If you had any decency you'd let me go free. Why don't you send me to the pen? Does it make any sense to hold me here when you can see it isn't doing me any good?

BOSLOW (after a pause): Is there anything else?

MURRAY: Yes. I'd like to know why you postponed my hearing three times. I think it was a deliberate attempt to harass me and provoke me into actions you could use to keep me here. I'd like to know why.

(No answer.)

MURRAY: Don't you have

the decency to do things right?

BOSLOW: Don't you have the decency to do things right?

Murray is led out shouting: "You're not a man, you're an animal. Let me out. If you just take these handcuffs off me, I'll show you man to man."

After the meeting I ask Dr. Kandel about Murray. "Well, you saw for yourself," he says. "He's a very violent man."

Isn't it possible, I suggest, that Murray is really angry at the institution for keeping him beyond his sentence, just as he said?

"It's a matter of projection," Kandel says. "Many of these people like to blame anything instead of what really bothers them. That's part of their problem."

I ask why Murray was put in Patuxent in the first place, since Patuxent is for dangerous and violent criminals.

"It's true," Kandel says. "that Murray came here for something relatively minor, like stealing a car or something. But when he came here we examined him and judged him to be potentially violent. Events have proved us right."

The question that remains, then, is how do you know when a patient is cured, or, to use Dr. Boslow's word, "socialized"? When is he ready to move out into society?

"It's a matter of experience and judgment," says Dr. Boslow. "There's no problem in saying who will commit a crime when he's released. If you just say yes all the time you'll be right 70 or 80 per cent of the time. The art is in saying who won't."

Dr. Boslow says Patuxent is "the most successful penal institution in the country, in fact in the Western world." For proof he cites a study showing that Patuxent's recidivism rate over the years has been 37 per cent, compared with a national average of almost 80. (When the study was presented at a meeting of the American Psychiatric Association, it was immediately attacked for "methodological deficiencies," but Boslow discounts the criticism.)

"You become convinced," says Dr. Boslow, "when a patient begins relating to you as a human being, when he no longer has to be defensive and hostile, when he develops a sense of self-regard. One of the greatest things is the increase in self-esteem and the capacity to relate to other people as a warm, meaningful

human being. It's the guy who can come to you and ask you to help him. He's admitting he's a human being and that he has problems."

"What do you think holds society together?" Boslow asks, suddenly intense. Before I can say I don't know he answers himself. "Love," he says. "It's love."

I'm not sure, I tell him.

"Yes," says Dr. Boslow, "it is. Love in its broadest sense, which includes the need for the regard and esteem of one's fellow men. Without this mutual need our society would fall apart. For example, what do you think causes a man to walk into a machine-gun nest?"

I don't know. I really don't.

"It's love," Dr. Boslow says, wondering perhaps what it is that makes me so slow to see this very basic equation of our civilization. ■

September 17, 1972

Prison Reform Program Pushed Under Bay State Reform Law

By BILL KOVACH
Special to The New York Times

BOSTON, Nov. 17 — In the wake of nearly a year of agitation and rebellion behind prison walls, the Massachusetts Department of Corrections is pushing ahead with a major program of penal reform.

Using the flexibility offered by a prison reform law that went into effect last month, officials here are easing inmates back into free society at a rate that could cut the number of prisoners by half within a few months.

The major thrust of the program is to move prisoners back into the community as rapidly as possible under such systems as:

¶Work-release programs that allow selected inmates outside the prison during working hours to continue outside jobs.

¶Vocational and educational programs that allow inmates to pursue study or training outside the prison on a regular basis.

¶Contracts with privately operated halfway houses that pro-

vide supervision and counseling to newly paroled prisoners.

¶Development of prerelease centers that will function as "decompression" units for prisoners nearing release.

¶A system of furloughs that, with proper approval and supervision, will allow any prisoner the opportunity to spend limited time on visits outside the prison.

As noted by Kenneth Bishop, the Deputy Commissioner of Corrections, none of these reforms is particularly new and many are now in effect in other states. Few states, however, have developed programs that cover the range represented by the Massachusetts plan, he said.

According to Mr. Bishop, officials here hope to use each program to "the maximum extent possible" almost immediately and to cut the prison population of 3,300 in half in the next few months.

The concept is an old one in Massachusetts. The first work-release program in the

nation was designed here by a legislative act of 1879 to allow women inmates of the Framingham House of Corrections to pursue outside jobs. That program, while it has continued in operation, was not broadened to include male prisoners until this year.

The reform program has followed closely an overhaul of the state's youth correction program. Nearly all juvenile detention centers have been replaced by 60 community-based juvenile residential centers. A similar program of de-emphasizing large, custodial institutions is under way in the State Department of Mental Health, which announced yesterday that it hoped to move all patients from Grafton State Hospital to community-based facilities by December, 1973.

As one official of the State Department of Human Resources described the accelerated trend here: "Within the next two years we should see an end to the whole network of large, custodial institutions in Massachusetts, both in corrections and mental health, that serve neither the public nor the inmate very well."

Search for Incentives

Prison disturbances in Massachusetts began after the Attica rebellion in New York last

year and have continued sporadically for months. Commissioner of Corrections John O. Boone spoke of the need for new approaches shortly after he took office here last January.

"The officers," Mr. Boone pointed out, "have nothing to offer as far as rehabilitation goes, just the threat of a lockup. We have no incentives."

The authorities hope that the new opportunities for supervised temporary or long-term release will also serve as an incentive for controlled behavior on the part of all inmates. Under most programs, inmates can participate only with the approval of screening committees that include members of each prison's security and administrative staff.

Implementation of the programs has moved quickly. Work release, vocational educational programs and the furlough program are already in effect. Contracts have been awarded to three privately operated halfway houses and will soon receive their first released inmates. Selected inmates at the Concord Reformatory are now completing work on the first prerelease center on the grounds of Boston State Hospital. It is expected to be open by the end of the month.

November 18, 197

Suicides in Prison: A Cry for Help

To the Editor:

I have read with interest the press' recent attempts to understand the increasing number of suicides in the New York City prison system. There can be no simple answer to this problem, for each suicide seems to point to a different problem within the prisons, the courts, the hospital prison wards or at times the very structure of our society.

As 1973's suicides are reviewed, the trends which are revealed seem very similar to those of previous years.

One trend is that individuals with long histories of mental illness and suicidal behavior are placed under the most stressful physical and psychological conditions imaginable in tiny, dark prison cells. Another trend is that very self-destructive individuals are shuttled back and forth from prison to overcrowded hospital to overcrowded prison mental observation units.

A sad frequent occurrence is the impaired communication about mental symptoms among relatives, lawyers, courts, mental health staff and the correction officers ultimately responsible for care. Still sadder is when this lack of understanding breaks down into overt hostility between the in-volved parties in which the inmate is the ultimate sufferer.

It is of interest that suicide is non-existent at the Women's House of Detention and quite rare at several other houses. Invariably, those prisons with low suicide rates are the best-organized and most therapeutic prisons in the system. The high suicide rates in other institutions are almost directly proportional to such conditions as disorganization, overcrowding, noise, filth, quality of medical and psychiatric care and cooperation between mental health and correctional staff.

Just as the individual's suicidal behavior must be considered a cry for help for that individual, so must the rising suicide rate in the entire system be considered a cry for help for that ailing system. This cry must not be dealt with solely by enhanced observation of suicidal inmates. It must be met by the desperately needed changes which are being screamed out for and focused on by these suicides.

EDWARD KAUFMAN, M.D.
New York, Aug. 21, 1973
The writer is former director of psychiatry of the Prison Health Services of New York City.

Siema

August 27, 1973

Women in Prison

By Kathryn Watterson Burkhart. Illustrated. 465 pp. New York: Doubleday & Co. $10.

By LESLEY OELSNER

The inmates are robbers, addicts, forgers, murderers. They are considered threats to society, and sometimes, threats to one another. They are locked behind bars, regimented, disciplined for the slightest infraction of prison rules. And how do they know the prison rules? On the wall of the dining room, in best summer-camp style, a neatly-lettered sign spells one thus:

*Words were made to be spoken
Voices were made to be used
If you speak lightly, and also politely,
This privilege will not be abused.*

It is, of course, a prison for women, the Women's House of Correction in Chicago—at a prison for men, even the looniest warden would hesitate before giving his inmates summer-camp ditties. Kathryn Burkhart, a freelance journalist, has written a long and heavily documented study of women behind bars, and as her account makes clear, women's prisons have a logic of their own — or as Burkhart would have it, a non-logic.

On the one hand, Burkhart tells us, many wardens flinch if someone calls their inmates "criminals"—most of the pris-oners at the Ohio Reformatory for Women were sent there for "acting out of their inadequacies as individuals," not for being criminals, according to the superintendent there.

But on the other hand, the wardens handily dispatch the "girls" off to solitary confinement; they permit all the horrors of Attica, the dehumanizing cellblocks, the brutality, the forced labor in the prison industry or laundry, the excruciating boredom.

"Women in Prison" is too flawed to be a definitive study—it is repetitive, somewhat disorganized, often biased in favor of the inmates. But it is valuable nonetheless and, in fact, long overdue, for though we know a great deal about men in prison—or should, at least, after hundreds of books and studies and well-publicized

487

prison riots—we have had little information about female prisoners.

Burkhart gives us the statistics — on any single day, there are more than 7,730 women in local and county jails, more than 15,000 in state and Federal prisons. They are incarcerated for the same crimes that put men behind bars, from fraud to murder. The usual charges, though are theft, prostitution, drugs, drunkenness and disorderly conduct.

She notes that women are less likely than men, proportionately, to be arrested or prosecuted or imprisoned; one reason, she suggests, may be that men are simply *considered* more dangerous than women. "People are more afraid of being hurt by a man than of hurting him," she says. "This is not so true with women." At the same time, she says, women are sometimes treated relatively worse than men— some states have laws permitting indeterminate sentences for women, and according to Burkhardt, the practical effect of these sentences is often a longer prison term than a man would get for the same crime.

Where information is simply unavailable—or seems unreliable — Burkhart tells us that, too. She quotes totally contradictory opinions by prison administrators on such questions as whether women inmates are more violent now than they used to be. She relays the 1971 F.B.I. report that the arrests of females for major crimes rose 156.2 per cent from 1960 to 1969—and questions whether this really means an increase in crime, or, instead, the result of a new system of reporting crime.

The best part of the book though, is its pictures of individual prisoners and their life on cellblocks and prison "cottages" across the country. Burkhart tells her story with case histories and interviews, with fat chunks of verbatim quotes, and gore enough to shame the toughest warden.

Much of the life she describes is familiar, for it matches what we know of men's prisons. But much is new, the special horrors that prison means to a woman.

Was she pregnant when arrested? Then she'll likely lose the baby by miscarriage, due to shock, inadequate medical care or overwork in her mandatory prison job. One prisoner was pregnant when arrested in Connecticut on a murder charge; in jail, pending trial, she began to hemorrhage. She asked for the doctor but he didn't come; instead, he recommended—via telephone, apparently—that an ice pack be placed on her stomach. Ten days later she miscarried, and that day, even the nurse refused to come.

If the prisoner does manage to bear her child, she'll probably go through childbirth shackled to the delivery table —and then be forbidden to hold the child. A California inmate was unconscious during delivery; when she woke up, she asked to see her baby.

"If you wanted to see your baby you wouldn't have been arrested," the guard replied. "What kind of mother are you?"

Is the prisoner already a mother, with two or three youngsters? Then, Burkhart tells us, the children will be scattered about in foster homes and the mother won't be consulted about their care, notified if they are sick, or even, for months at a time, told where they are.

Women prisoners are subjected to repeated vaginal examinations — they might be hiding contraband, drugs even, the authorities explain. Is the woman frail? No matter, she will still have to lift 75 or 100 pound soap bags in the prison laundry.

Burkhart clearly is on the prisoners' side, and to a great extent she seems justified. But something seems wrong—she seems to have left something out.

The inmates she describes are all pleasant—except for one who is unpleasant but pathetic—and all the inmates she quotes at any length are quite likable. It is probable that many of the women in prison are likeable—but all of them?

At one point she mentions an incident in which some inmates beat up another inmate, but it is only a mention. When she describes the terrors that the women face, she describes only those terrors inflicted on the inmates by the prison staff or the system. Yet even her brief mention of the beating indicates that sometimes, at least, inmates are terrorized by each other as well.

There are other problems with the book: it quotes over and over from "Alice in Wonderland," it provides few ideas for reform (other than doing away with prisons altogether) and it is sometimes saccharine. Burkhart herself, in her introduction, calls the book "only a beginning" in the study of women in prison. And as a beginning, it is valuable, compelling and worth reading. ∎

THE CHESSMAN CASE: A COURT PERENNIAL

Years of Appeals From 'Death Row' Have Stirred Worldwide Interest

By LAWRENCE E. DAVIES
Special to The New York Times.

SAN FRANCISCO, Dec. 12—Before the United States Supreme Court once more is the perennial case of Caryl Chessman, California convict-author, who is in the twelfth year of his residence in San Quentin's "death row."

Seven dates have been set for his appearance in the prison's green-walled gas chamber. Seven times the courts have given him a stay of execution.

He is the 38-year-old son of a Hollywood movie studio worker—"a producer who went broke," Chessman says. He had seen the inside of a string of California penal institutions for armed robberies and automobile thefts dating from the age of sixteen before he was arrested in 1948 as "the red light bandit" who terrorized couples in parked cars in lonely spots around Los Angeles.

Chessman, after conducting his own defense at his 1948 trial, was convicted in the Los Angeles Superior Court of seventeen felonies. These embraced eight counts of robbery, four of kidnapping, two of sex perversion, one of attempted robbery, one of attempted rape and one of auto theft. They drew him two death sentences, under the California "Little Lindbergh" kidnaping statute, a life term and, for good measure, sixty additional years in prison.

He wasted no time in plunging into a legal campaign from "death row" to save himself from the gas chamber. Although he had not completed high school, he already had assiduously studied law. Petitions and briefs began rolling from a typewriter he was permitted to have in an "office" cell.

Three Books

Since his incarceration, while pounding out briefs with his right hand, as it were, he has written three published books with his left: "Cell 2245, Death Row," an autobiography; "Trial by Ordeal" and "The Face of Justice."

The key issue in many of the appeals has revolved about the court reporter's notes of the Chessman trial of 1948. The reporter died with about two-thirds of the notes not yet transcribed. An outside reporter was hired to complete the transcript.

Chessman and his cooperating lawyers have hammered on the theme that the transcript as finally certified was "prejudicially incomplete and inaccurate" and represented "fraudulent collaboration" between the substitute reporter and the prosecutor, who were relatives by marriage.

In his new appeal, carried to Washington by his San Francisco attorney, George T. Davis, he is asking for outright discharge if the court finds there has been sufficient denial of "due process."

Where is the backing for Chessman coming from? Who cares what happens to him?

As in the "free Sacco-Vanzetti," "free Tom Mooney" and other campaigns in American penal history in this century, the support for Chessman has become international in scope.

Appeals for clemency have come from individuals and groups in Uruguay, Brazil, Portugal and other countries.

Distinguished persons in this country have come forward too in the condemned man's behalf. During a single day in October Governor Brown received appeals from more than 230 persons, including Mrs. Eleanor Roosevelt, Aldous Huxley, the writer-philosopher and Steve Allen, the entertainer.

Mr. Huxley is in a group of twenty-three professional persons, including Dr. Carl Menninger, the psychiatrist, who have submitted a brief to the Supreme Court in Chessman's behalf.

Broad Support

What is the reasoning of those who have sprung to the defense of a man convicted of seventeen felonies?

There are several facets. One is an apparently growing antipathy to capital punishment. This is compounded in the Chessman case because the prisoner himself is not accused of taking a life.

Papers like L'Osservatore Romano and The Guardian of Manchester contend that eleven years under sentence of death is psychological punishment enough.

Creeping into the case also has been the contention that as the author of books on his prison experience Chessman should be recognized as having contributed to the science of penology.

There are others who seem fervently to believe that Chessman is correct in his contention that he did not have a fair trial in 1948 and that the least he has coming to him, after his years on "death row," is a new opportunity to face a jury.

There is notable reluctance everywhere to say that the Supreme Court's next act will be the final judicial step in the case of Caryl Whittier Chessman. Too many persons recall newspaper stories of as long as five years ago beginning: "The final legal recourse open to Caryl Chessman in his fight to avoid the gas chamber was taken today."

December 13, 1959

Caryl Chessman Executed; Denies His Guilt to the End

Kidnapper Goes Calmly to Death After Appeals in Last Hours to California High Court and Justice Douglas

By LAWRENCE E. DAVIES
Special to The New York Times.

SAN FRANCISCO, Calif., May 2—Caryl Chessman was executed today.

After a series of last-hour legal maneuvers in state and Federal courts on opposite sides of the country, the convict-author kept his ninth scheduled appointment in the gas chamber at San Quentin Prison. He had lived nearly twelve years in the prison's death row.

[The execution of Caryl Chessman set off a wave of revulsion in many parts of the world, according to United Press International. Several anti-American demonstrations were reported.]

Chessman was escorted into the little octagonal steel room, with its dark green walls, and strapped into the right hand one of two chairs just after 10 A. M., Pacific Coast time (1 P. M. New York time).

At 10:03:15, cyanide pellets were dropped from a container under the chair into a basin of sulphuric acid solution. At 10:12, prison doctors said Chessman was dead of the resulting acid fumes.

Warden Fred Dickson said Chessman's last request to him had been "to specifically state that he was not the red-light bandit" for whose crimes he was paying the penalty.

Chessman, 38 years old, was convicted in 1948 on numerous felony counts growing out of depredations against parked couples in lonely places around Los Angeles. The counts invoking the death penalty included kidnapping, "with bodily harm."

An hour and fifty-five minutes ahead of the scheduled execution hour the seven-justice State Supreme Court began discussion in near-by San Francisco of a petition filed on Saturday afternoon. The petition had sought a writ of habeas corpus.

At 9:10 A. M. the court ruled, 4 to 3, against the first request. Fifteen minutes later George T. Davis of Chessman counsel asked for a stay so that

489

the decision might be appealed to the United States Supreme Court.

This was denied at 9:50 by the same vote.

Five minutes later Mr. Davis and Miss Rosalie Asher, co-counsel, were in the chamber of Federal District Judge Louis E. Goodman. They wanted a brief stay, time enough to argue on a request to petition the United States Supreme Court for a writ of review.

At almost the same time Associate Justice William O. Douglas of the Supreme Court had sent word of his denial of a plea for a stay of execution. The papers had been airmailed to him in Washington.

Judge Goodman listened to Mr. Davis and Miss Asher, then sent his clerk, Edward Evansen, to ask Miss Celeste Hickey, his secretary, to put a phone call through to the warden at San Quentin at 10:03

The prison number was passed along to Miss Hickey orally through several persons and somehow, in the noise and tension, a digit was dropped. She had to dial again after having verified the number. Associate Warden Louis Nelson told her that the cyanide pellets had just been dropped.

Miss Asher emerged, weeping, from the judge's chambers.

Wanted an Hour's Stay

Judge Goodman told reporters he had planned to ask the warden to stay the execution one hour.

At Sacramento, Gov. Edmund G. Brown received the news of the execution as he sat in his private study in his Capitol office. Outside the Capitol, a group of pickets was marching. It leader, Dr. Isadore Ziferstein, a Los Angeles psychiatrist, called the Governor "the hangman of California."

Other pickets had marched outside the prison all night.

As Chessman was led into the gas chamber, sixty witnesses, about two-thirds of them news-paper, radio and television reporters, were crowded into a first-floor room in the death house. Set into one side of this room was the gas chamber.

Five guards sat on a bench outside, one for every window through which the witnesses watched.

Chessman, in white shirt, new blue jeans and stockings, walked into the chamber without show of emotion, accompanied by four guards. Two of them strapped him into the chair. All walked out.

At that moment Chessman looked to his right and saw two reporters with whom he had often talked. He moved his lips carefully to shape the words:

"Tell Rosalie [his attorney and executrix] I said good-by. It's all right."

A woman reporter made a circle with her thumb and fore-finger to show she understood. The other reporter nodded. Chessman half smiled.

A moment later the cyanide pellets were released. Later, the physicians estimated he had been conscious for thirty-two seconds.

Warden Dickson told a news conference after the execution that Chessman had been "hopeful until ten minutes to ten," when the warden informed him of the State Supreme Court's refusal to grant a stay.

He said that Chessman had stayed awake all night writing letters and had left seven with him for delivery. Prison chaplains had stopped by but Chessman, an agnostic, had requested no last rites.

Mr. Davis, reflective and solemn, said afterward in his San Francisco office that perhaps his client's "greatest flaw, his greatest lack of character, was his unrelenting unwillingness to believe in something greater and bigger than himself."

"He almost prided himself on the fact that he remained an agnostic to the end," the attorney said. "

Some Doubts On Death Row

88 MEN AND 2 WOMEN. By Clinton T. Duffy with Al Hirshberg. 288 pp. New York: Doubleday & Co. $4.50.

By WENZELL BROWN

IN 1961 there was a total of forty-two executions in the United States. Of this number, eight took place in the octagonal gas chamber of California's San Quentin Prison. During the twelve-year tenure of Clinton Duffy as warden of the prison, which ended in 1952, he supervised the asphyxiation of ninety persons, the "88 Men and 2 Women" of his title. This book is a seemingly endless parade of the unfortunates who passed through Death Row on their way to the execution chamber.

Why has Mr. Duffy written such a harrowing chronicle? He states as his reason an all-consuming conviction that the death penalty must be abolished and "it must be publicized if it is to be eliminated." He would like to force every advocate of capital punishment to witness an execution; but, as this is not feasible, he has tried to give an account that will shock the public from their apathy.

Actually many of the thumb-nail sketches of convicted criminals that Mr. Duffy presents pre-date his appointment as warden for, quite literally, he has spent his life within the grounds of San Quentin. His father was a guard there, and as a boy Duffy attended the prison school. Since his retirement, he has worked with California's Adult Authority in the rehabilitation of released convicts.

MR. DUFFY finds only one common denominator among those executed, which is that, with one exception, they were without funds. He insists that "the punishment for murder depends more upon the resources of the killer than his crime." The single man of substance to be executed was Leslie B. Gireth, who was determined to die. Gireth, who killed his paramour in a suicide pact, lacked the courage to turn the gun upon himself. Instead, he successfully pleaded with the court that the state should be his executioner.

In each of the ninety who died Mr. Duffy finds some human value. In conclusion he lists the reasons for his opposition to capital punishment. His arguments are familiar, but they assume a compelling force when written by a man who, despite his intimacy with the gas chamber, was sickened anew each time that he was a reluctant participant in a killing sanctioned by laws he believes to be unjust.

U.S. Executions Down to 7 in 65; Death Penalty Gone in 13 States

WASHINGTON, Feb. 17 (AP) — Only seven Americans were put to death by legal authorities in 1965, the Justice Department said today.

It was the first time on record the number of executions fell below 10 and reflected a consistent decline in executions in recent years.

All seven men who died were convicted murderers. Four died on the gallows at Kansas State penitentiary at Lansing. Two of these—Perry Smith and Richard Hickock—were hanged last April, ending a five-year drama that is the subject of Truman Capote's best seller, "In Cold Blood," published by Random House.

Missouri and Wyoming killed a man each in the gas chamber. In Alabama, a man died in the electric chair. Except for Utah, where the condemned may choose between shooting and hanging, these are the only methods of capital punishment employed in the United States.

Four states—New York, Vermont, Iowa and West Virginia—abolished the death penalty except for special crimes. The death penalty has now been wiped out in 13 states.

Thirty-seven states, the District of Columbia and the Federal Government continue to carry the death penalty. Attorney General Nicholas deB. Katzenbach says, however, that the Administration would support legislation to abolish the penalty for Federal crimes.

Since 1954, when 81 persons were put to death, the number of executions has regularly declined except for 1960 and 1962. In 1964, the total was 15. The previous year it was 21, and in 1962 it was 47.

Last year was the first in which the penalty was administered for murder only. In 1964, six of the 15 condemned had been convicted of rape. In previous years, the death penalty was administered for such crimes as armed robbery, kidnaping, burglary, espionage and aggravated assault.

The highest number of executions in one year since 1930, when the Federal Bureau of Prisons began compiling statistics, was 199, in 1935.

February 18, 1966

High Court Opens Juries To Foes of Death Penalty

By FRED P. GRAHAM
Special to The New York Times

WASHINGTON, June 3—The Supreme Court struck a blow at capital punishment today by ruling that persons expressing general conscientious scruples against the death penalty could not automatically be kept off juries in capital cases.

The Court ruled that no death sentence could stand if it had been handed down by a jury that had been purged of all persons who said they opposed the death penalty or had conscientious or religious scruples against it.

The Court said that the convictions themselves could stand in all such cases. But the decision, because it applies retroactively, opened the way for new appeals by most of the 435 persons now under death sentences.

A 'Narrow' Ruling

The result of the Court's stand, as stated in Justice Potter Stewart's opinions in two cases, was a "narrow" ruling that expressed the Court's distaste for the death penalty. It hinted at the possibility of more drastic action in the future, but stopped far short of ruling out the death sentence for the present.

Justice Stewart declared, however, that "a state may not entrust the determination of whether a man should live or die to a tribunal organized to return a verdict of death."

Justice Hugo L. Black delivered long, passionate dissents from the bench in both cases, charging that the ruling would produce juries biased against capital punishment.

He also repeated a charge that he has made frequently in recent months—that the Court is "making law," overturning convictions of obviously guilty persons on narrow technicalities, and weakening law enforcement "at a time of serious crime in our nation."

In the two appeals, the Court had been asked to declare unconstitutional the long-established practice In capital cases of excusing all prospective jurors who say they have scruples against imposing a sentence of death. The Federal courts and all states that have capital punishment, except Iowa and South Dakota, now follow such procedures.

According to the two convicts who brought the cases to the Court, this procedure produces "prosecution prone" juries that are more likely than the average jury to find the accused guilty, and also more disposed to impose the death sentence.

Justice Stewart's opinion said that the sociological and psychological data offered in these cases were "too tentative and fragmentary" to prove that such juries were more likely to find defendants guilty. However, the opinion left the Court room to reach this conclusion in some future case.

Scope of Ruling Defined

For the present, the Court held, jurors may not be excluded merely because they state under further questioning, that have scruples against capital punishment.

However, it said they might be excluded if they made such a statement and then said, under further questioning, that they could not make an impartial finding of guilt and could not vote for a death penalty because of their opposition to it.

Justice Black noted in his dissent that the future impact of the ruling might be scant, since the jurors who now rule themselves out on the ground of scruples might also do so under the new test.

But the Court specifically stated that its decision would apply retroactively to death sentences already handed down but not yet carried out. According to the Federal Bureau of Prisons, there are 435 persons now on death rows in prisons across the country.

No estimates are now available of how many of the men on Death Row were convicted by juries selected under the procedure that was struck down today.

In a few states juries either have no say in imposing the death penalty or their recommendation of death is not binding on judges. Today's ruling presumably will not affect them, since their juries decide only guilt.

Thus today's ruling will apparently block for the present the executions of many of the residents of death row, but it was silent as to their futures.

491

It did not say whether its decision amounts to a commutation of these sentences to life imprisonment, or if states could bring the men before new juries, selected under the procedures announced today, and obtain new and valid death penalties.

In one decision today, the Supreme Court threw out the death penalty, but not the conviction, of William C. Witherspoon, who was convicted of killing a Chicago policeman in 1960.

The Court divided, 6 to 3, with Justice Stewart being joined by Chief Justice Earl Warren and Justices William J. Brennan Jr., Abe Fortas and Thurgood Marshall. Justice William O. Douglas said in a separate opinion that he would not exclude from juries those who say they could never vote for death.

Justices Byron R. White and John M. Harlan joined in Justice Black's dissent.

The second case involved Wayne D. Bumper, a Negro from North Carolina who was found guilty of the capital offense of rape but was given a life sentence. The Court ruled against him on the jury issue, since it declined to find that such a jury cannot constitutionally find a defendant guilty.

Search Held Illegal

But it threw out the conviction on the ground that Bumper's grandmother had admitted the police to her house to make a search after they had said they had a search warrant that was not produced at the trial. That search produced the rifle used in the crime. The Court held today that the grandmother's "consent" was not valid and the search was unconstitutional.

This prompted Justice Black's charge that the Supreme Court had gone too far in announcing a "per se" rule that voids all convictions in which evidence obtained through illegal searches was introduced.

Albert E. Jenner Jr. of Chicago argued for Witherspoon. Donald J. Veverka, assistant Attorney General of Illinois, argued for the state.

In the Bumper case, Norman B. Smith of Greensboro argued for the appellant and Harry W. McGalliard, deputy Attorney General of North Carolina, argued for the state.

June 4, 1968

SUPREME COURT, 5-4, BARS DEATH PENALTY AS IT IS IMPOSED UNDER PRESENT STATUTES

COURT SPARES 600

4 Justices Named by Nixon All Dissent in Historic Decision

By FRED P. GRAHAM
Special to The New York Times

WASHINGTON, June 29—The Supreme Court ruled today that capital punishment, as now administered in the United States, is unconstitutional "cruel and unusual" punishment.

The historic decision, came on a vote of 5 to 4.

Although the five Justices in the majority issued separate opinions and did not agree on a single reason for their action, the effect of the decision appeared to be to rule out executions under any capital punishment laws now in effect in this country.

The decision will also save from execution 600 condemned men and women now on death rows in the United States, although it did not overturn their convictions. Most will be held in prison for the rest of their lives, but under some states' procedures some of the prisoners may eventually gain their freedom.

Eighth Amendment Cited

The decision pitted the five holdovers of the more liberal Warren Court against the four appointees of President Nixon, who dissented. The ruling came as the Supreme Court handed down its final decisions of the year and recessed until Oct. 2.

Three Justices in the majority, William O. Douglas, William J. Brennan Jr. and Thurgood Marshall, concluded that executions in modern-day America necessarily violate the Eighth Amendment's prohibition against "cruel and unusual punishments."

The other two in the majority, the two "swing men" of the Court, Justices Potter Stewart and Byron R. White, reasoned that the present legal system operates in a cruel and unusual way, because it gives judges and juries the discretion to decree life or death and they impose it erratically.

As Justice Stewart put it, the death penalty is "so wantonly and so freakishly imposed" that those who are sentenced to death receive excessively harsh treatment.

View of Chief Justice

"These death sentences are cruel and unusual in the same way that being struck by lightning is cruel and unusual," he said.

As the dissenters pointed out, this alignment means that no death sentence can pass muster before the present Supreme Court unless it satisfies the objections voiced by Justices Stewart and White.

Chief Justice Warren E. Burger suggested that legislatures could attempt to do this in two ways. One is to state in statute books in detail the conditions under which a judge or jury can impose the death penalty—such as rape accompanied by a vicious assault, or a convict's murder of a prison guard.

The second would be to revert to the practice of more than a century ago, and impose mandatory death sentences for those convicted of certain crimes.

In any event, Chief Justice Burger said, Congress and the state legislatures will be required to "make a thorough reevaluation of the entire subject of capital punishment," including a serious inquiry into whether it serves as a deterrent.

All four dissenters also filed separate opinions, in a judicial outpouring that required 243 pages to express the view of all nine Justices.

The gist of the dissenters' position was that the Eighth Amendment has been in effect for 191 years and has not, until today, been held to rule out executions. They charged that the majority had usurped the prerogative of the legislatures in the decision today.

Justice Lewis F. Powell Jr. said the action would have a "shattering effect" upon the rule that prior decisions should be followed, as well as on the principles of "Federalism, judicial restraint, and — most importantly — separation of powers."

Justice Harry A. Blackmun implied strongly that the majority had been "propelled toward its result" to stroke down capital punishment by the recent decision of the Supreme Court of California, which outlawed executions under the state constitution's prohibition against "cruel or unusual" punishments.

Justice Blackmun added an unusually personal insight by saying that while he had an "abhorrence" of capital punishment he felt only the legislatures could abolish it.

Justice William H. Rehnquist's dissent said the decision had underscored a fundamental question about the Supreme

492

Court's role in reviewing the nation's laws. While overreaching legislatures may encroach upon individual rights, he said, an overreaching Supreme Court can "sacrifice the equally important right of the people to govern themselves."

The decision today culminated a campaign initiated by the N.A.A.C.P. Legal Defense and Educational Fund, Inc., five years ago, when the liberal coloration of the Warren Court made success appear much more likely than it had been presumed to be before the present Court.

Although the Supreme Court had never directly ruled that the death penalty was not cruel and unusual punishment, this was because it had been assumed throughout most of the country's history that it was not. The Court had said so, in passing, without actually making a ruling to that effect.

In his 50-page concurring opinion today, Justice William J. Brennan Jr. traced the evolu-

tion of the "cruel and unusual" punishment concept, and pointed out that the Supreme Court has traditionally considered it a growing concept, which develops with the changing mores of the times.

Therefore, even though the framers of the Bill of Rights did not intend to outlaw executions when they adopted the Eighth Amendment, Justice Brennan asserted that present conditions bring the death penalty within the prohibition.

His reasoning was that the penalty was unusually severe and degrading, it appeared to be arbitrarily imposed. It was widely condemned by contemporary society, and it might be no better a deterrent than prison.

Justice Thurgood Marshall expressed similar arguments, adding that the penalty was "morally unacceptable," if for no other reason than that it most frequently fell upon blacks, "the poor, the ignorant, and the underprivileged members of society."

Justice Douglas asserted that it is "implicit" in the ban on cruel and unusual punishment that executions cannot be imposed indiscriminately. Because it is the poor and minority groups that most ofen are executed, he concluded, capital punishment violates the 14th Amendment's guarantee of equal protection of the laws, as well as the Eighth Amendment.

Prior to today's decision, 11 state legislatures had abolished capital punishment completely, or with such narrow exceptions as the murder of a prison guard by a life convict. Thirty-nine states, the District of Columbia and the Federal Government had laws that authorized executions for various crimes.

The defendants before the Court today were William Henry Furman, sentenced to death for a robbery-murder in Georgia and Lucius Jackson Jr. of Georgia, and Elmer Branch of Texas, both condemned to death for rape.

Anthony G. Amsterdam, a professor of law at Stanford

University, and Jack Greenberg of New York argued the cases for the legal defense fund. Melvyn C. Bruder of Dallas also argued against the death penalty.

The prosecutors who argued the other side were Mrs. Dorothy T. Beasley, Assistant Attorney General of Georgia, and Prof. Charles Alan Wright of the University of Texas.

In another decision the Court held, 8 to 1, that a parolee who has been returned to prison for violation of parole must be given a prompt hearing, with notice of the reasons for the revocation and an opportunity to cross-examine witnesses against him.

Justice Douglas dissented, saying that a parolee should not be returned to prison until after his hearing. He also gave his answer to a point that the Court left open, saying he believes a parolee should have counsel furnished by the state, if necessary, at such a hearing.

June 30, 1972

57% IN POLL BACK A DEATH PENALTY

Gallup Finds Support Is at Highest Point Since '53

Despite the United States Supreme Court's ruling striking down the death penalty, public support for capital punishment is currently at its highest point in nearly two decades, according to the Gallup Poll.

In the latest survey, completed last week, 57 per cent of adults 18 years old and older said they favored the death penalty for persons convicted of murder. This percentage represents a sharp increase in support since March of this year when the figure was 50 per cent in favor.

The previous high was recorded in 1953 when 68 per cent of all adults interviewed voted in favor of capital punishment.

The following table shows the latest results and trend since 1953, when the current question wording was first used.

	Yes	No	No Opin.
	%	%	%
November, '72	57	32	11
March, '72	50	41	9
1971	49	40	11

1969	51	40	9
1966	42	47	11
1965	45	43	12
1960	51	36	13
1953	68	25	7

The increase in support for the death penalty since March may be due in considerable measure to widespread fear concerning personal and family safety—the "hidden issue" in this year's Presidential election, according to Gallup Poll analysts.

The latest survey results are based on in-person interviews with 1,207 persons interviewed in more than 250 scientifically selected localities from Nov. 10 to 13. This question was asked:

"Are you in favor of the death penalty for persons convicted of murder?"

Following are the latest results by key population groups:

	Yes	No	No Opin.
	%	%	%
National	57	32	11
Men	64	26	10
Women	50	37	13
Whites	60	29	11
Non-whites	29	53	18
College	58	36	6
High school	60	28	12
Grade school	50	34	16
Under 30 yrs.	50	39	11
30-49 yrs.	60	30	10
50 & over	60	27	13
Community size.			
1,000,000 & over	58	31	11
500,000-999,999	54	35	11
50,000-499,999	53	38	9
2,500-49,999	57	35	8
Under 2,500, Rural	58	32	10

November 23, 1972

Capital Punishment Revived in 19 States Since Court Ruling

WASHINGTON, Aug. 24 (UPI)—Nineteen states have revived the death penalty since it was struck down by the Supreme Court, saving 600 persons from execution.

Generally speaking, the new laws confine capital punishment to such crimes as mass murder, murder of a policeman, fireman or prison guard, and murder while perpetrating rape, kidnapping, arson or hijacking of a commercial vehicle.

Two young men held in Houston in the homosexual

slaying of more than 25 boys could draw the death penalty if convicted under a recently enacted Texas law.

Florida was the first state to re-establish capital punishment after the Supreme Court ruled existing statutes unconstitutional June 29, 1972. Florida's action came in a special legislative session last December.

Additional United States Supreme Court rulings on capital punishment are certain, and the Florida law could be the first one considered.

Besides Texas and Florida, other states that have re-established capital punishment are Rhode Island, Georgia, Oklahoma, Idaho, Louisiana, Wyoming, Ohio, Connecticut, Indiana, Arkansas, Arizona, Nevada, Nebraska, Montana and Utah, where the condemned have a choice of death by hanging or firing squad.

August 25, 1973

Suggested Reading

Criminology

Abrahamson, David. *The Psychology of Crime.* New York: Columbia University Press, 1960.

Caldwell, Robert G. *Criminology.* New York: Ronald Press, 1965.

Conrad, John P. *Crime and Its Correction: An International Survey of Attitudes.* Berkeley, Calif.: University of California Press, 1965. Pb*

Johnson, Elmer H. *Crime, Correction, and Society.* Homewood, Ill.: Dorsey Press, 1965.

Roebuck, Julian B. *Criminal Typology: The Legalistic, Physical-Constitutional-Hereditary, Psychological-Psychiatric, and Sociological Approaches,* Springfield, Ill.: C. C. Thomas, 1967.

Sutherland, Edwin H., and Donald R. Cressey, *Principles of Criminology.* Chicago: Lippincott, 1960.

The Problem of Crime Today

Campbell, James S., et al. *Law and Order Reconsidered: Report of the Task Force on Law and Law Enforcement to the National Commission on the Causes and Prevention of Violence.* New York: Bantam Books, 1970.

Clark, Ramsey. *Crime in America: Observations on its Nature, Causes, Prevention, and Control.* New York: Simon and Schuster, 1970. Pb

Harris, Richard. *The Fear of Crime.* New York: Praeger, 1969. Pb

Mulvihill, Donald J., and Melvin M. Tumin, *Crimes of Violence: A Staff Report Submitted to the National Commission on the Causes and Prevention of Violence.* Washington: U.S. Government Printing Office, 1969.

President's Commission on Law Enforcement and Administration of Justice. *The Challenge of Crime in a Free Society.* Washington: U.S. Government Printing Office, 1967. Pb

Wolfgang, Marvin E., and Bernard Cohen. *Crime and Race: Conceptions and Misconceptions.* New York: Institute of Human Relations, 1970.

Schur, Edwin M. *Our Criminal Society: The Social and Legal Sources of Crime in America.* Englewood Cliffs, N.J.: Prentice Hall, 1969. Pb

The Twenties and Thirties

Allsop, Kenneth. *The Bootleggers and Their Era.* New York: Doubleday, 1961.

Karpis, Alvin, with Bill Trent. *The Alvin Karpis Story.* New York: Coward, McCann & Geoghegan, 1971. Pb

Katcher, Leo. *The Big Bankroll: The Life and Times of Arnold Rothstein.* New York: Harper & Row, 1959. Pb

Kobler, John. *Capone: The Life and World of Al Capone.* New York: Putnam, 1971. Pb

Lyle, John H. *The Dry and Lawless Years.* Englewood Cliffs, N.J.: Prentice Hall, 1960.

Peterson, Virgil W. *Barbarians in Our Midst: A History of Chicago Crime and Politics.* Boston: Little, Brown, 1952.

Tolland, John. *The Dillinger Days.* New York: Random House, 1963.

Turkus, Burton B., and Sid Feder. *Murder Inc.: The Story of "The Syndicate."* New York: Farrar, Straus and Young, 1951. Pb

Organized Crime

Albini, Joseph L. *The American Mafia: Genesis of a Legend.* New York: Appleton-Century-Crofts, 1971. Pb

Cooke, Fred J. *The Secret Rulers: Criminal Syndicates and How They Control the U. S. Underworld.* New York: Duell, Sloan and Pearce, 1966.

Cressey, Donald R. *Theft of the Nation: The Structure and Operations of Organized Crime in America.* New York: Harper & Row, 1969. Pb

Gage, Nicholas. *The Mafia Is Not an Equal Opportunity Employer.* New York: McGraw-Hill, 1971. Pb

Gardiner, John A. *The Politics of Corruption: Organized Crime in an American City.* New York: Russell Sage Foundation, 1970.

Kefauver, Estes. *Crime in America.* Garden City, N.Y.: Doubleday, 1951.

Maas, Peter. *The Valachi Papers.* New York: Putnam, 1968. Pb

Messick, Hank. *Lansky.* New York: Putnam, 1971. Pb
Syndicate in the Sun. New York: Macmillan, 1968.

Salerno, Ralph, and John S. Tompkins. *The Crime Confederation: Cosa Nostra and Allied Operations in Organized Crime.* New York: Doubleday, 1969.

Talese, Gay. *Honor Thy Father.* New York: World Publishing Co., 1971. Pb

Law Enforcement

Chevigny, Paul. *Police Power: Police Abuses in New York City.* New York: Pantheon Books, 1969. Pb

Daley, Robert. *Target Blue: An Insider's View of the N.Y.P.D.* New York: Delacorte Press, 1973.

Knapp Commission. *The Knapp Commission Report on Police Corruption.* New York: G. Braziller, 1973. Pb

Niederhoffer, Arthur. *Behind the Shield: The Police in Urban Scoiety.* New York: Doubleday, 1967. Pb

Skolnick, Jerome H. *Justice without Trial: Law Enforcement in Democratic Society.* New York: Wiley, 1966. Pb

Westley, William A. *Violence and the Police: A Sociological Study of Law, Custom, and Morality.* Cambridge, Mass.: MIT Press, 1970. Pb

Whittemore, L. H. *Cop!: A Closeup of Violence and Tragedy.* New York: Holt, Rinehart and Winston, 1969. Pb

The Courts

Blumberg, Abraham S. *Criminal Justice.* Chicago: Quadrangle Books, 1967. Pb

Cressey, Donald, ed. *Crime and Criminal Justice.* Chicago: Quadrangle Books, 1971. Pb

Friendly, Alfred. *Crime and Publicity: The Impact of News on the Administration of Justice.* New York: Twentieth Century Fund, 1967. Pb

Lewis, Anthony. *Gideon's Trumpet.* New York: Random House, 1964. Pb

U.S. Task Force on the Administration of Justice. *Task Force Report: The Courts.* Washington: U.S. Government Printing Office, 1967.

Penology

Bedau, Hugo A., ed. *The Death Penalty in America.* Garden City, N.Y.: Anchor Books, 1967. Pb

Meltsner, Michael. *Cruel and Unusual: The Supreme Court and Capital Punishment.* New York: Random House, 1973.

Menninger, Karl A. *The Crime of Punishment.* New York: Viking Press, 1968. Pb

Mitford, Jessica. *Kind and Unusual Punishment: The Prison Business.* New York: Alfred A. Knopf, 1973.

Minton, Robert J. *Inside: Prison American Style.* New York: Random House, 1971. Pb

New York State Commission on Attica. *Attica.* New York: Bantam Books, 1972. Pb

Pritchard, John L. *A History of Capital Punishment.* New York: Citadel Press, 1960.

Wright, Erik. *The Politics of Punishment: A Critical Analysis of Prisons in America.* New York: Harper & Row, 1973. Pb

*Pb Indicates available in paperback.

Index

Mitchell, John N.: and FBI crime statistics, 269-70; Mafia and, 160; on wiretapping, 383-84
Mitchell, William D., 22-23
Moonshining, 6, 7
Moore v. *Dempsey*, 344
Moran, George ("Bugs"), 20-21
Morgenthau, Robert M., 156-58, 278
Motion pictures, 41, 45-49, 109, 171-77
Motley, Judge Constance B., 466-67
Mugging, 210-11, 230-31, 248-49
Murder, Inc., 85-86, 95; *see also* Buchalter, Louis (Lepke); Reles, Abe
Murrow, Edward R., 274-75
Murton, Thomas O., 452-53

NAACP, 464-65: on penalties for mugging, 234; on probable cause, 374
Narcotics: and addicts, 197, 206-8; international traffic in, 101-2, 109; and Mafia, 101-2, 105, 106; and organized crime, 81; and property losses, 205; national traffic in, 195, 200-2; raids curbed, 395; war on, 195, 199
National Commission on the Causes and Prevention of Violence, Report of, 237-38, 239, 244
National Rifle Association, 232
Negroes. *See* Black people
Nelson, George ("Baby Face"; born Lester Gillis), 37-38, 288
Ness, Eliot, 24-25
New Jersey, 144-55
New York: city jails, 436-37, 461-62; Civilian Complaint Review Board, 315, 317; criminal justice in, 410-14; drug distribution area, 200-2, 206-8, 209; police corruption in, 326-28; State war on crime, 58, 68,69; subway patrols in, 224-25, 357-58; tenant security in, 225-26
New York Civil Liberties Union, 312-15 *passim*, 361, 464-65
Niederhoffer, Arthur, 187, 317
Nitti, Frank, 23-24
Nixon, Pres. Richard M., 266-67, 271, 293-94, 382-83
Nizer, Louis, 419
Norris, Dr. Charles, 297
Numbers Racket (policy gambling). *See* Racketeering

O'Banion, Dion, 13, 14-15, 20-21, 27
O'Donnell gang, 15, 17
O'Dwyer, William, 72-73, 75-77, 83-87, 150
O'Leary, Prof. Vincent, 258,263
Organized crime. *See* Mafia
Oswald, Russell G., 464, 469-74

Parker, Bonnie, 33, 34, 39
Parole system, 439-42, 461

Patriarca, Raymond L., 117
Patuxent Institution for Defective Delinquents, 480-86
Peterson, Henry, 125-26
Phoenix, Ariz., 254
Plea bargaining, 263, 399-401, 404-5
Police: Blacks and 321-22, 324-25, 331-33; brutality, 234, 255, 302-6, 309, 310-15, 319; characterization of patrolmen, 323, 324-25; civilian review board, 315, 317; failure of, 3, 317-18, 402; hampered by courts, 311; interrogation powers, 365-66, 380-81, 385-86; in political office, 267-68, 270-71; public opinions on, 302, 316; rebuked by U. S. Supreme Court, 342-43; recruits, 310, 319; rise in education of, 333-34; romanticized by FBI, 286, 291; search powers, 373-76, 377, 395-96; technology and, 289, 295, 298, 300; unprovoked attacks on, 329-30; view of drug addicts, 206-9; as Wallace supporters, 320; women in ranks of, 336-37
Pornography, 168-70
Powell, Rep. Adam Clayton, 105-6, 210
Powell, Justice Lewis F., 357
President's Commission on Law Enforcement and Administration of Justice, 127, 231: Report of, 257-64, 320, 397-98, 398-99, 404
Press, 354-56, 393
Pretrial hearings, 403
Pretrial publicity, 354-56; *see also* Rights
Preventive detention, 394
Prisons: disturbances in, 434 (table), 435-36, 438, 462-64, 475-76; deaths in, 452-53; failures of system examined, 455-59; guards in, 477, 479; history of, 426-27; life in described, 446-49, 455-59; rehabilitation programs in, 449-51, 467-68; reforms urged, 460, 462-64, 486; relaxation of discipline in, 467-68; suicides in, 487; women in, 428, 487-88; Wickersham Report on, 428-30; *see also* Criminal justice; names of specific prisons
Probation reports, 438-39
Profaci, Joseph, 102, 103, 120, 122, 130-31, 139-40
Prohibition: chronology of, 6; cost of, 10-11; probable cause and, 340; repeal, 11-12; wiretapping and, 341-42; *see also* Bootlegging; Corruption; Mafia; Organized crime; Racketeering; "Scofflaw"; Smuggling
Property loss, 11 (table)
Prostitution, 274-75
Psychiatrists, 421
Psychology: in criminal procedure, 415-16
Psychosurgery. *See* Insanity
Public defenders, 160
Public Enemy, The, 41
Pugach, Burton N., 347
Punishment: as crime preventive, 438-39; inequality of, 281-82, 283; as vengeance, 354; *see also* Criminal